collection

CO

NANCY S. MESSNER
San Jose State College

GERALD MESSNER
Cañada College

Assisted by DENNIS ROBY
Ohlone College

ection

Literature for the Seventies

D. C. HEATH AND COMPANY
Lexington, Massachusetts   Toronto   London

To Adelaide and Harris,
Bertha and Lewis,
Clarence and Katherine

preface

Collection: *Literature for the Seventies* brings together the beauty, harmony, and message of the most creative and imaginative minds in the western literary tradition. This book is designed to introduce today's college student to those works most fundamental in defining man's unique place in the universe. The text will not be successful if it does not provoke discussion about the expression of human ideas, ideals, and problems; and the 1970's seems to be the ideal time to pause and review carefully what we should all do with the multiple messages we have received over several thousand years.

The text is designed to encourage almost any emphasis the instructor may choose; we have not forced material into prefabricated themes, but instead have assembled the materials in more-or-less historical order. The short story section opens with the first American master of literature's youngest form in Nathaniel Hawthorne's "The Minister's Black Veil," and closes with the late Diane Oliver's important Afro-American story, "Neighbors." The extensive selection of poetry—including lengthy sections devoted to both the "classic" and the "romantic" styles—ranges from Chaucer to the best-known balladeers of the early 1970's—John Lennon and Paul McCartney. The drama section begins with a new translation of Aristophanes' war-domestic comedy, *Lysistrata,* and, after including an example of each important dramatic form, ends with the first reprinting of the screenplay of Michael Roemer and Robert Young's film *Nothing But a Man.*

Each section begins with a brief paragraph of introduction, focusing the reader's attention on the most important aspects of technique. More elaborate discussion of each author and his works will be found in the teacher's guide.

Our students have been of the greatest help over the past several years by showing us what the keen minds of this generation continue to find worthwhile in "classic" literature. To them we owe a great debt. More specifically, we must thank one of those former students, Dennis Roby, who not only assisted editorially, but also whose questions continually provoked us to sharpen our minds. To him we further owe special thanks for providing us with a fresh and literate translation of Aristophanes' *Lysistrata.*

contents

SHORT STORIES

POETRY

DRAMA

collection

short stories

Short story is the newest of the major literary forms. It is wise to make a good deal of its name—"story" implies that there is something to be told, and "short" most usually indicates that the work can be read in one sitting. Short stories are brothers to jokes, in which any attempt at making the story plausible is left out in order to hurry on to the punch line, and novels, in which the writer may make use of great detail, an enormous number of characters, and several years of aging and conflict. The short fiction author must use enough detail to persuade the reader that what he reads could have happened; he must invent characters who have only a few pages to show who they are, what their conflicts amount to, and what solutions they will choose. The writer may elect to emphasize action, setting, mystery, history—or any other aspect of the character's life or his dilemma.

The short stories in this *Collection* ask you to define short fiction. What is the author emphasizing in his work? How does he go about telling you the story, and what has dictated his choice of these devices? Is there a story beyond the obvious one—a theme which the author has chosen to illustrate for us? How does the story achieve plausibility for you?

1

NATHANIEL HAWTHORNE

The Minister's Black Veil

The sexton stood in the porch of Milford meeting-house, pulling busily at the bell-rope. The old people of the village came stooping along the street. Children, with bright faces, tripped merrily beside their parents, or mimicked a graver gait, in the conscious dignity of their Sunday clothes. Spruce bachelors looked sidelong at the pretty maidens, and fancied that the Sabbath sunshine made them prettier than on week days. When the throng had mostly streamed into the porch, the sexton began to toll the bell, keeping his eye on the Reverend Mr. Hooper's door. The first glimpse of the clergyman's figure was the signal for the bell to cease its summons.

"But what has good Parson Hooper got upon his face?" cried the sexton in astonishment.

All within hearing immediately turned about, and beheld the semblance of Mr. Hooper, pacing slowly his meditative way towards the meeting-house. With one accord they started, expressing more wonder than if some strange minister were coming to dust the cushions of Mr. Hooper's pulpit.

"Are you sure it is our parson?" inquired Goodman Gray of the sexton.

"Of a certainty it is good Mr. Hooper," replied the sexton. "He was to have exchanged pulpits with Parson Shute, of Westbury; but Parson Shute sent to excuse himself yesterday, being to preach a funeral sermon."

The cause of so much amazement may appear sufficiently slight. Mr. Hooper, a gentlemanly person, of about thirty, though still a bachelor, was dressed with due clerical neatness, as if a careful wife had starched his band, and brushed the weekly dust from his Sunday's garb. There was but one thing remarkable in his appearance. Swathed about his forehead, and hanging down over his face, so low as to be shaken by his breath, Mr. Hooper had on a black veil. On a nearer view it seemed to consist of two folds of crape, which entirely concealed his features, except the mouth and chin, but probably did not intercept his sight, further than to give a darkened aspect to all living and inanimate things. With this gloomy shade before him, good Mr. Hooper walked onward, at a slow and quiet pace, stooping somewhat, and looking on the ground, as is customary with abstracted men, yet nodding kindly to those of his parishioners who still waited on the meeting-house steps. But so wonder-struck were they that his greeting hardly met with a return.

"I can't really feel as if good Mr. Hooper's face was behind that piece of crape," said the sexton.

"I don't like it," muttered an old woman, as she hobbled into the meeting-house. "He has changed himself into something awful, only by hiding his face."

"Our parson has gone mad!" cried Goodman Gray, following him across the threshold.

A rumor of some unaccountable phenomenon had preceded Mr. Hooper into the meeting-house, and set all the congregation astir. Few could refrain from twisting their heads towards the door; many stood upright, and turned directly about; while several little boys clambered upon the seats, and came down again with a terrible racket. There was a general bustle, a rustling of the women's gowns and shuffling of the men's feet, greatly at variance with that hushed repose which should attend the entrance of the minister. But Mr. Hooper appeared not to notice the perturbation of his people. He entered with an almost noiseless step, bent his head mildly to the pews on each side, and bowed as he passed his oldest parishioner, a white-haired great-grandsire, who occupied an arm-chair in the centre of the aisle. It was strange to observe how slowly this venerable man became conscious of something singular in the appearance of his pastor. He seemed not fully to partake of the prevailing wonder, till Mr. Hooper had ascended the stairs, and showed himself in the pulpit, face to face with his congregation, except for the black veil. That mysterious emblem was never once withdrawn. It shook with his measured breath, as he gave out the psalm; it threw its obscurity between him and the holy page, as he read the Scriptures; and while he prayed, the veil lay heavily on his uplifted countenance. Did he seek to hide it from the dread Being whom he was addressing?

Such was the effect of this simple piece of crape, that more than one woman of delicate nerves was forced to leave the meeting-house. Yet perhaps the pale-faced congregation was almost as fearful a sight to the minister, as his black veil to them.

Mr. Hooper had the reputation of a good preacher, but not an energetic one: he strove to win his people heavenward by mild, persuasive influences, rather than to drive them thither by the thunders of the Word. The sermon which he now delivered was marked by the same characteristics of style and manner as the general series of his pulpit oratory. But there was something, either in the sentiment of the discourse itself, or in the imagination of the auditors, which made it greatly the most powerful effort that they had ever heard from their pastor's lips. It was tinged, rather more darkly than usual, with the gentle gloom of Mr. Hooper's temperament. The subject had reference to secret sin, and those sad mysteries which we hide from our nearest and dearest, and would fain conceal from our own consciousness, even forgetting that the Omniscient can detect them. A subtle power was breathed into his words. Each member of the congregation, the most innocent girl, and the man of hardened breast, felt as if the preacher had crept upon them, behind his awful veil, and discovered their hoarded iniquity of deed or thought. Many spread their clasped hands on their bosoms. There was nothing terrible in what Mr. Hooper said, at least, no violence; and yet, with every tremor of his melancholy voice, the hearers quaked. An unsought pathos came hand in hand with awe. So sensible were the audience of some unwonted attribute in their minister, that they longed for a breath of wind to blow aside the veil, almost believing that a stranger's visage would be discovered, though the form, gesture, and voice were those of Mr. Hooper.

At the close of the services, the people hurried out with indecorous confusion, eager to communicate their pent-up amazement, and conscious of lighter spirits the moment they lost sight of the black veil. Some gathered in little circles, huddled closely together, with their mouths all whispering in the centre; some went homeward alone, wrapt in silent meditation; some talked loudly, and profaned the Sabbath day with ostentatious laughter. A few shook their sagacious heads, intimating that they could penetrate the mystery; while one or two affirmed that there was no mystery at all, but only that Mr. Hooper's eyes were so weakened by the midnight lamp, as to require a shade. After a brief interval, forth came good Mr. Hooper also, in the rear of his flock. Turning his veiled face from one group to another, he paid due reverence to the hoary heads, saluted the middle aged with kind dignity as their friend and spiritual guide, greeted the young with mingled authority and love, and laid his hands on the little children's heads to bless them. Such was always his custom on the Sabbath day. Strange and bewildered looks repaid him for his courtesy. None, as on former occasions, aspired to the honor of walking by their pastor's side. Old Squire Saunders, doubtless by an accidental lapse of memory, neglected to invite Mr. Hooper to his table, where the good clergyman had been wont to bless the food, almost every Sunday since his settlement. He returned, therefore, to the parsonage, and, at the moment of closing the door, was observed to look back upon the people, all of whom had their eyes fixed upon the minister. A sad smile gleamed faintly from beneath the black veil, and flickered about his mouth, glimmering as he disappeared.

"How strange," said a lady, "that a simple black veil, such as any woman might wear on her bonnet, should become such a terrible thing on Mr. Hooper's face!"

"Something must surely be amiss with Mr. Hooper's intellects," observed her husband, the physician of the village. "But the strangest part of the affair is the effect of this vagary, even on a sober-minded man like myself. The black veil, though it covers only our pastor's face, throws its influence over his whole person, and makes him ghostlike from head to foot. Do you not feel it so?"

"Truly do I," replied the lady; "and I would not be alone with him for the world. I wonder he is not afraid to be alone with himself!"

"Men sometimes are so," said her husband.

The afternoon service was attended with similar circumstances. At its conclusion, the bell tolled for the funeral of a young lady. The relatives and friends were assembled in the house, and the more distant acquaintances stood about the door, speaking of the good qualities of the deceased, when their talk was interrupted by the appearance of Mr. Hooper, still covered with his black veil. It was now an appropriate emblem. The clergyman stepped into the room where the corpse was laid, and bent over the coffin, to take a last farewell of his deceased parishioner. As he stooped, the veil hung straight down from his forehead, so that, if her eyelids had not been closed forever, the dead maiden might have seen his face. Could Mr. Hooper be fearful of her glance, that he so hastily caught back the black veil? A person who watched the interview between the dead and living, scrupled not to affirm, that, at the instant when the clergyman's features were disclosed, the corpse had slightly shuddered, rustling the shroud and muslin cap, though the countenance retained the composure of death. A superstitious old woman was the only witness of this prodigy. From the coffin Mr. Hooper passed into the chamber of the mourners, and thence to the head of the staircase, to make the funeral prayer. It was a tender and heart-dissolving prayer, full of sorrow, yet so imbued with celestial hopes, that the music of a heavenly harp, swept by the fingers of the dead, seemed faintly to be heard among the saddest accents of the minister. The people trembled, though they but darkly understood him when he prayed that they, and himself, and all of mortal race, might be ready, as he trusted this young maiden had been, for the dreadful hour that should snatch the veil from their faces. The bearers went heavily forth, and the mourners followed, saddening all the street, with the dead before them, and Mr. Hooper in his black veil behind.

"Why do you look back?" said one in the procession to his partner.

"I had a fancy," replied she, "that the minister and the maiden's spirit were walking hand in hand."

"And so had I, at the same moment," said the other.

That night, the handsomest couple in Milford village were to be joined in wedlock. Though reckoned a melancholy man, Mr. Hooper had a placid cheerfulness for such occasions, which often excited a sympathetic smile where livelier merriment would have been thrown away. There was no quality of his disposition which made him more beloved than this. The company at the wedding awaited his arrival with impatience, trusting that the strange awe, which had gathered over him throughout the day, would now be dispelled. But such was not the result. When Mr. Hooper came, the first thing that their eyes rested on was the same horrible black veil, which had added deeper gloom to the funeral, and could portend nothing but evil to the wedding. Such was its immediate effect on the guests that a cloud seemed to have rolled duskily from beneath the black crape, and dimmed the light of the candles. The bridal pair stood up before the minister. But the bride's cold fingers quivered in the tremulous hand of the bridegroom, and her deathlike paleness caused a whisper that the maiden who had been buried a few hours before was come from her grave to be married. If ever another wedding were so dismal, it was that famous one where they tolled the wedding knell. After performing the ceremony, Mr. Hooper raised a glass of wine to his lips, wishing happiness to the new-married couple in a strain of mild pleasantry that ought to have brightened the features of the guests, like a cheerful gleam from the hearth. At that instant, catching a glimpse of his figure in the looking-glass, the black veil involved his own spirit in the horror with which it overwhelmed all others. His frame shuddered, his lips grew white, he spilt the untasted wine upon the carpet, and rushed forth into the darkness. For the Earth, too, had on her Black Veil.

The next day, the whole village of Milford talked of little else than

Parson Hooper's black veil. That, and the mystery concealed behind it, supplied a topic for discussion between acquaintances meeting in the street, and good women gossiping at their open windows. It was the first item of news that the tavern-keeper told to his guests. The children babbled of it on their way to school. One imitative little imp covered his face with an old black handkerchief, thereby so affrighting his playmates that the panic seized himself, and he well-nigh lost his wits by his own waggery.

It was remarkable that of all the busybodies and impertinent people in the parish, not one ventured to put the plain question to Mr. Hooper, wherefore he did this thing. Hitherto, whenever there appeared the slightest call for such interference, he had never lacked advisers, nor shown himself averse to be guided by their judgment. If he erred at all, it was by so painful a degree of self-distrust, that even the mildest censure would lead him to consider an indifferent action as a crime. Yet, though so well acquainted with this amiable weakness, no individual among his parishioners chose to make the black veil a subject of friendly remonstrance. There was a feeling of dread, neither plainly confessed nor carefully concealed, which caused each to shift the responsibility upon another, till at length it was found expedient to send a deputation of the church, in order to deal with Mr. Hooper about the mystery, before it should grow into a scandal. Never did an embassy so ill discharge its duties. The minister received them with friendly courtesy, but became silent, after they were seated, leaving to his visitors the whole burden of introducing their important business. The topic, it might be supposed, was obvious enough. There was the black veil swathed round Mr. Hooper's forehead, and concealing every feature above his placid mouth, on which, at times, they could perceive the glimmering of a melancholy smile. But that piece of crape, to their imagination, seemed to hang down before his heart, the symbol of a fearful secret between him and them. Were the veil but cast aside, they might speak freely of it, but not till then. Thus they sat a considerable time, speechless, confused, and shrinking uneasily from Mr. Hooper's eye, which they felt to be fixed upon them with an invisible glance. Finally, the deputies returned abashed to their constituents, pronouncing the matter too weighty to be handled, except by a council of the churches, if, indeed, it might not require a general synod.

But there was one person in the village unappalled by the awe with which the black veil had impressed all beside herself. When the deputies returned without an explanation, or even venturing to demand one, she, with the calm energy of her character, determined to chase away the strange cloud that appeared to be settling round Mr. Hooper, every moment more darkly than before. As his plighted wife, it should be her privilege to know what the black veil concealed. At the minister's first visit, therefore, she entered upon the subject with a direct simplicity, which made the task easier both for him and her. After he had seated himself, she fixed her eyes steadfastly upon the veil, but could discern nothing of the dreadful gloom that had so overawed the multitude: it was but a double fold of crape, hanging down from his forehead to his mouth, and slightly stirring with his breath.

"No," said she aloud, and smiling, "there is nothing terrible in this piece of crape, except that it hides a face which I am always glad to look upon. Come, good sir, let the sun shine from behind the cloud. First lay aside your black veil: then tell me why you put it on."

Mr. Hooper's smile glimmered faintly.

"There is an hour to come," said he, "when all of us shall cast aside our veils. Take it not amiss, beloved friend, if I wear this piece of crape till then."

"Your words are a mystery, too," returned the young lady. "Take away the veil from them, at least."

"Elizabeth, I will," said he, "so far as my vow may suffer me. Know, then, this veil is a type and a symbol, and I am bound to wear it ever, both in light and darkness, in solitude and before the gaze of multitudes, and as with strangers, so with my familiar friends. No mortal eye will see it withdrawn. This dismal shade must separate me from the world: even you, Elizabeth, can never come behind it!"

"What grievous affliction hath befallen you," she earnestly inquired, "that you should thus darken your eyes forever?"

"If it be a sign of mourning," replied Mr. Hooper, "I, perhaps, like most other mortals, have sorrows dark enough to be typified by a black veil."

"But what if the world will not believe that it is the type of an innocent sorrow?" urged Elizabeth. "Beloved and respected as you are, there may be whispers that you hide your face under the consciousness of secret sin. For the sake of your holy office, do away this scandal!"

The color rose into her cheeks as she intimated the nature of the rumors that were already abroad in the village. But Mr. Hooper's mildness did not forsake him. He even smiled again—that same sad smile, which always appeared like a faint glimmering of light, proceeding from the obscurity beneath the veil.

"If I hide my face for sorrow, there is cause enough," he merely replied; "and if I cover it for secret sin, what mortal might not do the same?"

And with this gentle, but unconquerable obstinacy did he resist all her entreaties. At length Elizabeth sat silent. For a few moments she appeared lost in thought, considering, probably, what new methods might be tried to withdraw her lover from so dark a fantasy, which, if it had no other meaning, was perhaps a symptom of mental disease. Though of a firmer character than his own, the tears rolled down her cheeks. But, in an instant, as it were, a new feeling took the place of sorrow: her eyes were fixed insensibly on the black veil, when, like a sudden twilight in the air, its terrors fell around her. She arose, and stood trembling before him.

"And do you feel it then, at last?" said he mournfully.

She made no reply, but covered her eyes with her hand, and turned to leave the room. He rushed forward and caught her arm.

"Have patience with me, Elizabeth!" cried he, passionately. "Do not desert me, though this veil must be between us here on earth. Be mine, and hereafter there shall be no veil over my face, no darkness between our souls! It is but a mortal veil—it is not for eternity! O! you know not how lonely I am, and how frightened, to be alone behind my black veil. Do not leave me in this miserable obscurity forever!"

"Lift the veil but once, and look me in the face," said she.

"Never! It cannot be!" replied Mr. Hooper.

"Then farewell!" said Elizabeth.

She withdrew her arm from his grasp, and slowly departed, pausing at the door, to give one long shuddering gaze, that seemed almost to penetrate the mystery of the black veil. But, even amid his grief, Mr. Hooper smiled to think that only a material emblem had separated him from happiness, though the horrors, which it shadowed forth, must be drawn darkly between the fondest of lovers.

From that time no attempts were made to remove Mr. Hooper's black veil, or, by a direct appeal, to discover the secret which it was supposed to hide. By persons who claimed a superiority to popular prejudice, it was reckoned merely an eccentric whim, such as often mingles with the sober actions of men otherwise rational, and tinges them all with its own semblance of insanity. But with the multitude, good Mr. Hooper was irreparably a bugbear. He could not walk the street with any piece of mind, so conscious was he that the gentle and timid would turn aside to avoid him, and that others would make it a point of hardihood to throw themselves in his way. The impertinence of the latter class compelled him to give up his customary walk at sunset to the burial ground; for when he leaned pensively over the gate, there would always be faces behind the gravestones, peeping at his black veil. A fable went the rounds that the stare of the dead people drove him thence. It grieved him, to the very depth of his kind heart, to observe how the children fled from his approach, breaking up their merriest sports, while his melancholy figure was yet afar off. Their instinctive dread caused him to feel more strongly than aught else, that a preternatural horror was interwoven with the threads of the black crape. In truth, his own antipathy to the veil was known to be so great, that he never willingly passed before a mirror, nor stooped to drink at a still fountain, lest, in its peaceful bosom, he should be affrighted by himself. This was what gave plausibility to the whispers, that Mr. Hooper's conscience tortured him for some great crime too horrible to be entirely concealed, or otherwise than so obscurely intimated. Thus, from beneath the black veil, there rolled a cloud into the sunshine, an ambiguity of sin or sorrow, which enveloped the poor minister, so that love or sympathy could never reach him. It was said that ghost and fiend consorted with him there. With self-shudderings and outward terrors, he walked continually in its shadow, groping darkly within his own soul, or gazing through a medium that saddened the whole world. Even the lawless wind, it was believed, respected his dreadful secret, and never blew aside the veil. But still good Mr. Hooper sadly smiled at the pale visages of the worldly throng as he passed by.

Among all its bad influences, the black veil had the one desirable effect, of making its wearer a very efficient clergyman. By the aid of his mysterious emblem—for there was no other apparent cause—he became a man of awful power over souls that were in agony for sin. His converts always regarded him with a dread peculiar to themselves, affirming, though but figuratively, that, before he brought them to celestial light, they had been with him behind the black veil. Its gloom, indeed, enabled him to sympathize with all dark affections. Dying sinners cried aloud for Mr. Hooper, and would not yield their breath till he appeared; though ever, as he stopped to whisper consolation, they shuddered at the veiled face so near their own. Such were the terrors of the back veil, even when Death had bared his visage! Strangers came long distances to attend service at his church, with the mere idle purpose of gazing at his figure, because it was forbidden them to behold his face. But many were made to quake ere they departed! Once, during Governor Belcher's administration, Mr. Hooper was appointed to preach the election sermon. Covered with his black veil, he stood before the chief magistrate, the council, and the representatives, and wrought so deep an impression, that the legislative measures of that year were characterized by all the gloom and piety of our earliest ancestral sway.

In this manner Mr. Hooper spent a long life, irreproachable in outward act, yet shrouded in dismal suspicions; kind and loving, though unloved, and dimly feared; a man apart from men, shunned in their health and joy, but ever summoned to their aid in mortal anguish. As years wore on, shedding their snows above his sable veil, he acquired a name throughout the New England churches, and they called him Father Hooper. Nearly all his parishioners, who were of mature age when he was settled, had been borne away by many a funeral: he had one congregation in the church, and a more crowded one in the churchyard; and having wrought so late into the evening, and done his work so well, it was now good Father Hooper's turn to rest.

Several persons were visible by the shaded candle-light, in the death chamber of the old clergyman. Natural connections he had none. But there was the decorously grave, though unmoved physician, seeking only to mitigate the last pangs of the patient whom he could not save. There were the deacons, and other eminently pious members of his church. There, also, was the Reverend Mr. Clark, of Westbury, a young and zealous divine, who had ridden in haste to pray by the bedside of the expiring minister. There was the nurse, no hired handmaiden of death, but one whose calm affection had endured thus long in secrecy, in solitude, amid the chill of age, and would not perish, even at the dying hour. Who, but Elizabeth! And there lay the hoary head of good Father Hooper upon the death pillow, with the black veil still swathed about his brow, and reaching down over his face, so that each more difficult gasp of his faint breath caused it to stir. All through life that piece of crape had hung between him and the world: it had separated him from cheerful brotherhood and woman's love, and kept him in that saddest of all prisons, his own heart; and still it lay upon his face, as if to deepen the gloom of his darksome chamber, and shade him from the sunshine of eternity.

For some time previous, his mind had been confused, wavering doubtfully between the past and the present, and hovering forward, as it were, at intervals, into the indistinctness of the world to come. There had been feverish turns, which tossed him from side to side, and wore away what little strength he had. But in his most convulsive struggles, and in the wildest vagaries of his intellect, when no other thought retained its sober influence, he still showed an awful solicitude lest the black veil should slip aside. Even if his bewildered soul could have forgotten, there was a faithful woman at his pillow, who, with averted eyes, would have covered that aged face, which she had last beheld in the comeliness of manhood. At length the death-stricken old man lay quietly in the torpor of mental and bodily exhaustion, with an imperceptible pulse, and breath that grew fainter and fainter, except when a long, deep, and irregular inspiration seemed to prelude the flight of his spirit.

The minister of Westbury approached the bedside.

"Venerable Father Hooper," said he, "the moment of your release is at hand. Are you ready for the lifting of the veil that shuts in time from eternity?"

Father Hooper at first replied merely by a feeble motion of his head; then, apprehensive, perhaps, that his meaning might be doubtful, he exerted himself to speak.

"Yea," said he, in faint accents, "my soul hath a patient weariness until that veil be lifted."

"And is it fitting," resumed the Reverend Mr. Clark, "that a man so given to prayer, of such a blameless example, holy in deed and thought, so far as mortal judgment may pronounce; is it fitting that a father in the church should leave a shadow on his memory, that may seem to blacken a life so pure? I pray you, my venerable brother, let not this thing be! Suffer us to be gladdened by your triumphant aspect as you go to your reward. Before the veil of eternity be lifted, let me cast aside this black veil from your face!"

And thus speaking, the Reverend Mr. Clark bent forward to reveal the mystery of so many years. But, exerting a sudden energy, that made all the beholders stand aghast, Father Hooper snatched both his hands from beneath the bedclothes, and pressed them strongly on the black veil, resolute to struggle, if the minister of Westbury would contend with a dying man.

"Never!" cried the veiled clergyman. "On earth, never!"

"Dark old man!" exclaimed the affrighted minister, "with what horrible crime upon your soul are you now passing to the judgment?"

Father Hooper's breath heaved; it rattled in his throat; but, with a mighty effort, grasping forward with his hands, he caught hold of life, and held it back till he should speak. He even raised himself in bed; and there he sat, shivering with the arms of death around him, while the black veil hung down, awful, at that last moment, in the gathered terrors of a lifetime. And yet the faint, sad smile, so often there, now seemed to glimmer from its obscurity, and linger on Father Hooper's lips.

"Why do you tremble at me alone?" cried he, turning his veiled face round the circle of pale spectators. "Tremble also at each other! Have men avoided me, and women shown no pity, and children screamed and fled, only for my black veil? What, but the mystery which it obscurely typifies, has made this piece of crape so awful? When the friend shows his inmost heart to his friend; the lover to his best beloved; when man does not vainly shrink from the eye of his Creator, loathsomely treasuring up the secret of his sin; then deem me a monster, for the symbol beneath which I have lived, and die! I look around me, and lo! on every visage a Black Veil!"

While his auditors shrank from one another, in mutual affright, Father Hooper fell back upon his pillow, a veiled corpse, with a faint smile lingering on the lips. Still veiled, they laid him in his coffin, and a veiled corpse they bore him to the grave. The grass of many years has sprung up and withered on that grave, the burial stone is moss-grown, and good Mr. Hooper's face is dust; but awful is still the thought that it mouldered beneath the Black Veil!

HERMAN MELVILLE

Bartleby the Scrivener

A Story of Wall Street

I am a rather elderly man. The nature of my avocations, for the last thirty years, has brought me into more than ordinary contact with what would seem an interesting and somewhat singular set of men, of whom, as yet, nothing, that I know of, has ever been written—I mean, the law-copyists, or scriveners. I have known very many of them, professionally and privately, and, if I pleased, could relate divers histories, at which good-natured gentlemen might smile, and sentimental souls might weep. But I waive the biographies of all other scriveners, for a few passages in the life of Bartleby, who was a scrivener, the strangest I ever saw, or heard of. While, of other law-copyists, I might write the complete life, of Bartleby nothing of that sort can be done. I believe that no materials exist, for a full and satisfactory biography of this man. It is an irreparable loss to literature. Bartleby was one of those beings of whom nothing is ascertainable, except from the original sources, and, in his case, those are very small. What my own astonished eyes saw of Bartleby, *that* is all I know of him, except, indeed, one vague report, which will appear in the sequel.

Ere introducing the scrivener, as he first appeared to me, it is fit I make some mention of myself, my *employés*, my business, my chambers, and general surroundings; because some such description is indispensable to an adequate understanding of the chief character about to be presented. Imprimis: I am a man who, from his youth upwards, has been filled with a profound conviction that the easiest way of life is the best. Hence, though I belong to a profession proverbially energetic and nervous, even to turbulence, at times, yet nothing of that sort have I ever suffered to invade my peace. I am one of those unambitious lawyers who never address a jury, or in any way draw down public applause; but, in the cool tranquillity of a snug retreat, do a snug business among rich men's bonds, and mortgages, and title-deeds. All who know me, consider me an eminently *safe* man. The late John Jacob Astor, a personage little given to poetic enthusiasm, had no hesitation in pronouncing my first grand point to be prudence; my next, method. I do not speak it in vanity, but simply record the fact, that I was not unemployed in my profession by the late John Jacob Astor; a name which, I admit, I love to repeat; for it hath a rounded and orbicular sound to it, and rings like unto bullion. I will freely add, that I was not insensible to the late John Jacob Astor's good opinion.

Some time prior to the period at which this little history begins, my avocations had been largely increased. The good old office, now extinct in the State of New York, of a Master in Chancery, had been conferred upon me.

It was not a very arduous office, but very pleasantly remunerative. I seldom lose my temper; much more seldom indulge in dangerous indignation at wrongs and outrages; but I must be permitted to be rash here and declare, that I consider the sudden and violent abrogation of the office of Master in Chancery, by the new Constitution, as a —— premature act; inasmuch as I had counted upon at life-lease of the profits, whereas I only received those of a few short years. But this is by the way.

My chambers were up stairs, at No. —— Wall Street. At one end, they looked upon the white wall of the interior of a spacious skylight shaft, penetrating the building from top to bottom.

This view might have been considered rather tame than otherwise, deficient in what landscape painters call "life." But, if so, the view from the other end of my chambers offered, at least, a contrast, if nothing more. In that direction, my windows commanded an unobstructed view of a lofty brick wall, black by age and everlasting shade; which wall required no spy-glass to bring out its lurking beauties, but, for the benefit of all near-sighted spectators, was pushed up to within ten feet of my window-panes. Owing to the great height of the surrounding buildings, and my chambers being on the second floor, the interval between this wall and mine not a little resembled a huge square cistern.

At the period just preceding the advent of Bartleby, I had two persons as copyists in my employment, and a promising lad as an office-boy. First, Turkey; second, Nippers; third, Ginger Nut. These may seem names, the like of which are not usually found in the Directory. In truth, they were nicknames, mutually conferred upon each other by my three clerks, and were deemed expressive of their respective persons or characters. Turkey was a short, pursy Englishman, of about my own age—that is, somewhere not far from sixty. In the morning, one might say, his face was of a fine florid hue, but after twelve o'clock, meridian—his dinner hour—it blazed like a grate full of Christmas coals; and continued blazing—but, as it were, with a gradual wane—till six o'clock, P.M., or thereabouts; after which, I saw no more of the proprietor of the face, which, gaining its meridian with the sun, seemed to set with it, to rise, culminate, and decline the following day, with the like regularity and undiminished glory. There are many singular coincidences I have known in the course of my life, not the least among which was the fact, that, exactly when Turkey displayed his fullest beams from his red and radiant countenance, just then, too, at that critical moment, began the daily period when I considered his business capacities as seriously disturbed for the remainder of the twenty-four hours. Not that he was absolutely idle, or averse to business then; far from it. The difficulty was, he was apt to be altogether too energetic. There was a strange, inflamed, flurried, flighty recklessness of activity about him. He would be incautious in dipping his pen into his inkstand. All his blots upon my documents were dropped there after twelve o'clock, meridian. Indeed, not only would he be reckless, and sadly given to making blots in the afternoon, but, some days, he went further, and was rather noisy. At such times, too, his face flamed with augmented blazonry, as if cannel coal had been heaped on anthracite. He made an unpleasant racket with his chair; spilled his sand-box; in mending his pens, impatiently split them all to pieces, and threw them on the floor in a sudden passion; stood up, and leaned over his table, boxing his papers about in a most indecorous manner, very sad to behold in an elderly man like him. Nevertheless, as he was in many ways a most valuable person to me, and all the time before twelve o'clock meridian, was the quickest, steadiest creature, too, accomplishing a great deal of work in a style not easily to be matched—for these reasons, I was willing to overlook his eccentricities, though, indeed, occasionally, I remonstrated with him. I did this very gently, however, because, though the civilest, nay, the blandest and most reverential of men in the morning, yet, in the afternoon, he was disposed, upon provocation, to be slightly rash with his tongue—in fact, insolent. Now, valuing his morning services as I did, and resolved not to lose them—yet, at the same time, made uncomfortable by his inflamed ways after twelve o'clock—and being a man of peace, unwilling by my admonitions to call forth unseemly retorts from him, I took upon me, one Saturday noon (he was always worse on Saturdays) to hint to him, very kindly, that, perhaps, now that he was growing old, it might be well to abridge his labors; in short, he need not come to my chambers after twelve o'clock, but, dinner over, had best go home to his lodgings, and rest himself till tea-time. But no; he insisted upon his afternoon devotions. His countenance became intolerably fervid, as he oratorically assured me—gesticulating with a long ruler at the other end of the room—that if his services in the morning were useful, how indispensable, then, in the afternoon?

"With submission, sir," said Turkey, on this occasion, "I consider myself your right-hand man. In the morning I but marshal and deploy my columns; but in the afternoon I put myself at their head, and gallantly charge the foe, thus"—and he made a violent thrust with the ruler.

"But the blots, Turkey," intimated I.

"True; but, with submission, sir, behold these hairs! I am getting old. Surely, sir, a blot or two of a warm afternoon is not to be severely urged against gray hairs. Old age—even if it blot the page—is honorable. With submission, sir, we *both* are getting old."

This appeal to my fellow-feeling was hardly to be resisted. At all events, I saw that go he would not. So, I made up my mind to let him stay, resolving, nevertheless, to see to it that, during the afternoon, he had to do with my less important papers.

Nippers, the second on my list, was a whiskered, sallow, and, upon the whole, rather piratical-looking young man, of about five-and-twenty. I always deemed him the victim of two evil powers—ambition and indigestion. The ambition was evinced by a certain impatience of the duties of a mere copyist, an unwarrantable usurpation of strictly professional affairs such as the original drawing up of legal documents. The indigestion seemed betokened in an occasional nervous testiness and grinning irritability, causing the teeth to audibly grind together over mistakes committed in copying; unnecessary maledictions, hissed, rather than spoken, in the heat of business; and especially by a continual discontent with the height of the table where he worked. Though of a very ingenious mechanical turn, Nippers could never get this table to suit him. He put chips under it, blocks of various sorts, bits of pasteboard, and at last went so far as to attempt an exquisite adjustment, by final pieces of folded blotting-paper. But no invention would answer. If, for the sake of easing his back, he brought the table-lid at a sharp angle well up towards his chin, and wrote there like a man using the steep roof of a Dutch house for his desk, then he declared that it stopped the circulation in his arms. If now he lowered the table to his waistbands, and stooped over it in writing, then there was a sore aching in his back. In short, the truth of the matter was, Nippers knew not what he wanted. Or, if he wanted anything, it was to be rid of a scrivener's table altogether. Among the manifestations of his diseased ambition was a fondness he had for receiving visits from certain ambiguous-looking fellows in seedy coats, whom he called his clients. Indeed, I was aware that not only was he, at times, considerable of a ward-politician, but he occasionally did a little business at the justices' courts, and was not unknown on the steps of the Tombs. I have good reason to believe, however, that one individual who called upon him at my chambers, and who, with a grand air, he insisted was his client, was no other than a dun, and the alleged title-deed, a bill. But, with all his failings, and the annoyances he caused me, Nippers, like his compatriot Turkey, was a very useful man to me; wrote a neat, swift hand; and, when he chose, was not deficient in a gentlemanly sort of deportment. Added to this, he always dressed in a gentlemanly sort of way; and so, incidentally, reflected credit upon my chambers. Whereas, with respect to Turkey, I had much ado to keep him from being a reproach to me. His clothes were apt to look oily, and smell of eating-houses. He wore his pantaloons very loose and baggy in summer. His coats were execrable; his hat not to be handled. But while the hat was a thing of indifference to me, inasmuch as his natural civility and deference, as a dependent Englishman, always led him to doff it the moment he entered the room, yet his coat was another matter. Concerning his coats, I reasoned with him; but with no effect. The truth was, I suppose, that a man with so small an income could not afford to sport such a lustrous face and a lustrous coat at one and the same time. As Nippers once observed, Turkey's money went chiefly for red ink. One winter day, I presented Turkey with a highly respectable-looking coat of my own—a padded gray coat, of a most comfortable warmth, and which buttoned straight up from the knee to the neck. I thought Turkey would appreciate the favor, and abate his rashness and obstreperousness of afternoons. But no; I verily believe that buttoning himself up in so downy and blanket-like a coat had a pernicious effect upon him— upon the same principle that too much oats are bad for horses. In fact, precisely as a rash, restive horse is said to feel his oats, so Turkey felt his coat. It made him insolent. He was a man whom prosperity harmed.

Though, concerning the self-indulgent habits of Turkey, I had my own private surmises, yet, touching Nippers, I was well persuaded that, whatever might be his faults in other respects, he was, at least, a temperate young man. But, indeed, nature herself seemed to have been his vintner, and, at his birth, charged him so thoroughly with an irritable, brandy-like disposition, that all subsequent potations were needless. When I consider how, amid the stillness of my chambers, Nippers would sometimes impatiently rise from his seat, and stooping over his table, spread his arms wide apart, seize the whole desk, and move it, and jerk it, with a grim, grinding motion on the floor, as if the table were a perverse voluntary agent, intent on thwarting and vexing him, I plainly perceive that, for Nippers, brandy-and-water were altogether superfluous.

It was fortunate for me that, owing to its peculiar cause—indigestion—the irritability and consequent nervousness of Nippers were mainly observable in the morning, while in the afternoon he was comparatively mild. So that, Turkey's paroxysms only coming on about twelve o'clock, I never had to do with their eccentricities at one time. Their fits relieved each other, like guards. When Nippers' was on, Turkey's was off; and *vice versa*. This was a good natural arrangement, under the circumstances.

Ginger Nut, the third on my list, was a lad, some twelve years old. His father was a carman, ambitious of seeing his son on the bench instead of a cart, before he died. So he sent him to my office, as student at law, errand-boy, cleaner and sweeper, at the rate of one dollar a week. He had a little desk to himself, but he did not use it much. Upon inspection, the drawer exhibited a great array of the shells of various sorts of nuts. Indeed, to this quick-witted youth, the whole noble science of the law was contained in a nutshell. Not the least among the employments of Ginger Nut, as well as one which he discharged with the most alacrity, was his duty as cake and apple purveyor for Turkey and Nippers. Copying lawpapers being proverbially a dry, husky sort of business, my two scriveners were fain to moisten their mouths very often with Spitzenbergs, to be had at the numerous stalls nigh the Custom House and Post Office. Also, they sent Ginger Nut very frequently for that peculiar cake—small, flat, round, and very spicy—after which he had been named by them. Of a cold morning, when business was but dull, Turkey would gobble up scores of these cakes, as if they were mere wafers—indeed, they sell them at the rate of six or eight for a penny—the scrape of his pen blending with the crunching of the crisp particles in his mouth. Of all the fiery afternoon blunders and flurried rashness of Turkey, was his once moistening a ginger-cake between his lips, and clapping it on to a mortgage, for a seal. I came within an ace of dismissing him then. But he mollified me by making an oriental bow, and saying—

"With submission, sir, it was generous of me to find you in stationery on my own account."

Now my original business—that of a conveyancer and title hunter, and drawer-up of recondite documents of all sorts—was considerably increased by receiving the Master's office. There was now great work for scriveners. Not only must I push the clerks already with me, but I must have additional help.

In answer to my advertisement, a motionless young man one morning stood upon my office threshold, the door being open, for it was summer. I can see that figure now—pallidly neat, pitiably respectable, incurably forlorn! It was Bartleby.

After a few words touching his qualifications, I engaged him, glad to have among my corps of copyists a man of so singularly sedate an aspect, which I thought might operate beneficially upon the flighty temper of Turkey, and the fiery one of Nippers.

I should have stated before that ground-glass folding-doors divided my premises into two parts, one of which was occupied by my scriveners, the other by myself. According to my humor, I threw open these doors, or closed them. I resolved to assign Bartleby a corner by the folding-doors, but on my side of them, so as to have this quiet man within easy call, in case any trifling thing was to be done. I placed his desk close up to a small side-window in that part of the room, a window which originally had afforded a lateral view of certain grimy brickyards and bricks, but which, owing to subsequent erections, commanded at present no view at all, though it gave some light. Within three feet of the panes was a wall, and the light came down from far above, between two lofty buildings, as from a very small opening in a dome. Still further to a satisfactory arrangement, I procured a high green folding screen, which might entirely isolate Bartleby from my sight, though not remove him from my voice. And thus, in a manner, privacy and society were conjoined.

At first, Bartleby did an extraordinary quantity of writing. As if long famishing for something to copy, he seemed to gorge himself on my documents. There was no pause for digestion. He ran a day and night line, copying by sunlight and by candle-light. I should have been quite delighted with his application, had he been cheerfully industrious. But he wrote on silently, palely, mechanically.

It is, of course, an indispensable part of a scrivener's business to verify the accuracy of his copy, word by word. Where there are two or more scriveners in an office, they assist each other in this examination, one reading from the copy, the other holding the original. It is a very dull, wearisome, and lethargic affair. I can readily imagine that, to some sanguine temperaments, it would be altogether intolerable. For example, I cannot credit that the mettlesome poet, Byron, would have contentedly sat down with Bartleby to examine a law document of, say five hundred pages, closely written in a crimpy hand.

Now and then, in the haste of business, it had been my habit to assist in comparing some brief document myself, calling Turkey or Nippers for this purpose. One object I had, in placing Bartleby so handy to me behind the screen, was, to avail myself of his services on such trivial occasions. It was on the third day, I think, of his being with me, and before any necessity had arisen for having his own writing examined, that, being much hurried to complete a small affair I had in hand, I abruptly called to Bartleby. In my haste and natural expectancy of instant compliance, I sat with my head bent over the original on my desk, and my right hand sideways, and somewhat nervously extended with the copy, so that, immediately upon emerging from his retreat, Bartleby might snatch it and proceed to business without the least delay.

In this very attitude did I sit when I called to him, rapidly stating what it was I wanted him to do—namely, to examine a small paper with me. Imagine my surprise, nay, my consternation, when, without moving from his privacy, Bartleby, in a singularly mild, firm voice, replied, "I would prefer not to."

I sat awhile in perfect silence, rallying my stunned faculties. Immediately it occurred to me that my ears had deceived me, or Bartleby had entirely misunderstood my meaning. I repeated my request in the clearest tone I could assume; but in quite as clear a one came the previous reply, "I would prefer not to."

"Prefer not to," echoed I, rising in high excitement, and crossing the room with a stride. "What do you mean? Are you moonstruck? I want you to help me compare this sheet here—take it," and I thrust it towards him.

"I would prefer not to," said he.

I looked at him steadfastly. His face was leanly composed; his gray eye dimly calm. Not a wrinkle of agitation rippled him. Had there been the least uneasiness, anger, impatience or impertinence in his manner; in other words, had there been anything ordinarily human about him, doubtless I should have violently dismissed him from the premises. But as it was, I should have as soon thought of turning my pale plaster-of-paris bust of Cicero out of doors. I stood gazing at him awhile, as he went on with his own writing, and then reseated myself at my desk. This is very strange, thought I. What had one best do? But my business hurried me. I concluded to forget the matter for the present, reserving it for my future leisure. So, calling Nippers from the other room, the paper was speedily examined.

A few days after this, Bartleby concluded four lengthy documents, being quadruplicates of a week's testimony taken before me in my High Court of Chancery. It became necessary to examine them. It was an important suit, and great accuracy was imperative. Having all things arranged, I called Turkey, Nippers, and Ginger Nut, from the next room, meaning to place the four copies in the hands of my four clerks, while I should read from the original. Accordingly, Turkey, Nippers, and Ginger Nut had taken their seats in a row, each with his document in his hand, when I called to Bartleby to join this interesting group.

"Bartleby! quick, I am waiting."

I heard a slow scrape of his chair legs on the uncarpeted floor, and soon he appeared standing at the entrance of his hermitage.

"What is wanted?" said he, mildly.

"The copies, the copies," said I, hurriedly. "We are going to examine them. There"—and I held towards him the fourth quadruplicate.

"I would prefer not to," he said, and gently disappeared behind the screen.

For a few moments I was turned into a pillar of salt, standing at the head of my seated column of clerks. Recovering myself, I advanced towards the screen, and demanded the reason for such extraordinary conduct.

"Why do you refuse?"

"I would prefer not to."

With any other man I should have flown outright into a dreadful passion, scorned all further words, and thrust him ignominiously from my presence. But there was something about Bartleby that not only strangely disarmed me, but, in a wonderful manner, touched and disconcerted me. I began to reason with him.

"These are your own copies we are about to examine. It is labor saving to you, because one examination will answer for your four papers. It is common usage. Every copyist is bound to help examine his copy. Is it not so? Will you not speak? Answer!"

"I prefer not to," he replied in a flute-like tone. It seemed to me that, while I had been addressing him, he carefully revolved every statement that I made; fully comprehended the meaning; could not gainsay the irresistible conclusion; but, at the same time, some paramount consideration prevailed with him to reply as he did.

"You are decided, then, not to comply with my request—a request made according to common usage and common sense?"

He briefly gave me to understand, that on that point my judgment was sound. Yes: his decision was irreversible.

It is not seldom the case that, when a man is browbeaten in some unprecedented and violently unreasonable way, he begins to stagger in his own plainest faith. He begins, as it were, vaguely to surmise that, wonderful as it may be, all the justice and all the reason is on the other side. Accordingly, if any disinterested persons are present, he turns to them for some reinforcement for his own faltering mind.

"Turkey," said I, "what do you think of this? Am I not right?"

"With submission, sir," said Turkey, in his blandest tone, "I think that you are."

"Nippers," said I, "what do _you_ think of it?"

"I think I should kick him out of the office."

(The reader of nice perceptions will have perceived that, it being morning, Turkey's answer is couched in polite and tranquil terms, but Nippers replies in ill-tempered ones. Or, to repeat a previous sentence, Nippers' ugly mood was on duty, and Turkey's off.)

"Ginger Nut," said I, willing to enlist the smallest suffrage in my behalf, "what do _you_ think of it?"

"I think, sir, he's a little _luny_," replied Ginger Nut, with a grin.

"You hear what they say," said I, turning towards the screen, "come forth and do your duty."

But he vouchsafed no reply. I pondered a moment in sore perplexity. But once more business hurried me. I determined again to postpone the consideration of this dilemma to my future leisure. With a little trouble we made out to examine the papers without Bartleby, though at every page or two Turkey deferentially dropped his opinion, that this proceeding was quite out of the common; while Nippers, twitching in his chair with a dyspeptic nervousness, ground out, between his set teeth, occasional hissing maledictions against the stubborn oaf behind the screen. And for his (Nippers') part, this was the first and the last time he would do another man's business without pay.

Meanwhile Bartleby sat in his hermitage, oblivious to everything but his own peculiar business there.

Some days passed, the scrivener being employed upon another lengthy work. His late remarkable conduct led me to regard his ways narrowly. I observed that he never went to dinner; indeed, that he never went anywhere. As yet I had never, of my personal knowledge, known him to be outside of my office. He was a perpetual sentry in the corner. At about eleven o'clock though, in the morning, I noticed that Ginger Nut would advance toward the opening in Bartleby's screen, as if silently beckoned thither by a gesture invisible to me where I sat. The boy would then leave the office, jingling a few pence, and reappear with a handful of ginger-nuts, which he delivered in the hermitage, receiving two of the cakes for his trouble.

He lives, then, on ginger-nuts, thought I; never eats a dinner, properly speaking; he must be a vegetarian, then, but no; he never eats even vegetables, he eats nothing but ginger-nuts. My mind then ran on in reveries concerning the probable effects upon the human constitution of living entirely on ginger-nuts. Ginger-nuts are so called, because they contain ginger as one of their peculiar constituents, and the final flavoring one. Now, what was ginger? A hot, spicy thing. Was Bartleby hot and spicy? Not at all. Ginger, then, had no effect upon Bartleby. Probably he preferred it should have none.

Nothing so aggravates an earnest person as a passive resistance. If the individual so resisted be of a not inhumane temper, and the resisting one perfectly harmless in his passivity, then, in the better moods of the former, he will endeavor charitably to construe to his imagination what proves impossible to be solved by his judgment. Even so, for the most part, I regarded Bartleby and his ways. Poor fellow! thought I, he means no mischief; it is plain he intends no insolence; his aspect sufficiently evinces that his eccentricities are involuntary. He is useful to me. I can get along with him. If I turn him away, the chances are he will fall in with some less indulgent employer, and then he will be rudely treated, and perhaps driven forth miserably to starve. Yes. Here I can cheaply purchase a delicious self-approval. To befriend Bartleby; to humor him in his strange wilfulness, will cost me little or nothing, while I lay up in my soul what will eventually prove a sweet morsel for my conscience. But this mood was not invariable with me. The passiveness of Bartleby sometimes irritated me. I felt strangely goaded on to encounter him in new opposition—to elicit some angry spark from him answerable to my own. But, indeed, I might as well have essayed to strike fire with my knuckles against a bit of Windsor soap. But one afternoon the evil impulse in me mastered me, and the following little scene ensued:

"Bartleby," said I, "when those papers are all copied, I will compare them with you."

"I would prefer not to."

"How? Surely you do not mean to persist in that mulish vagary?"

No answer.

I threw open the folding-doors nearby, and turning upon Turkey and Nippers, exclaimed:

"Bartleby a second time says, he won't examine his papers. What do you think of it, Turkey?"

It was afternoon, be it remembered. Turkey sat glowing like a brass boiler; his bald head steaming; his hands reeling among his blotted papers.

"Think of it?" roared Turkey. "I think I'll just step behind his screen, and black his eyes for him!"

So saying, Turkey rose to his feet and threw his arms into a pugilistic position. He was hurrying away to make good his promise, when I detained him, alarmed at the effect of incautiously rousing Turkey's combativeness after dinner.

"Sit down, Turkey," said I, "and hear what Nippers has to say. What do you think of it, Nippers? Would I not be justified in immediately dismissing Bartleby?"

"Excuse me, that is for you to decide, sir. I think his conduct quite unusual, and, indeed, unjust, as regards Turkey and myself. But it may only be a passing whim."

"Ah," exclaimed I, "you have strangely changed your mind, then—you speak very gently of him now."

"All beer," cried Turkey; "gentleness is effects of beer—Nippers and I dined together to-day. You see how gentle *I* am, sir. Shall I go and black his eyes?"

"You refer to Bartleby, I suppose. No, not to-day, Turkey," I replied; "pray, put up your fists."

I closed the doors, and again advanced towards Bartleby. I felt additional incentives tempting me to my fate. I burned to be rebelled against again. I remembered that Bartleby never left the office.

"Bartleby," said I, "Ginger Nut is away; just step around to the Post Office, won't you?" (it was but a three minutes' walk) "and see if there is anything for me."

"I would prefer not to."

"You *will* not?"

"I *prefer* not."

I staggered to my desk, and sat there in a deep study. My blind inveteracy returned. Was there any other thing in which I could procure myself to be ignominiously repulsed by this lean, penniless wight?—my hired clerk? What added thing is there, perfectly reasonable, that he will be sure to refuse to do?

"Bartleby!"

No answer.

"Bartleby," in a louder tone.

No answer.

"Bartleby," I roared.

Like a very ghost, agreeably to the laws of magical invocation, at the third summons, he appeared at the entrance of his hermitage.

"Go to the next room, and tell Nippers to come to me."

"I prefer not to," he respectfully and slowly said, and mildly disappeared.

"Very good, Bartleby," said I, in a quiet sort of serenely-severe self-possessed tone, intimating the unalterable purpose of some terrible retribution very close at hand. At the moment I half intended something of the kind. But upon the whole, as it was drawing towards my dinner-hour, I thought it best to put on my hat and walk home for the day, suffering much from perplexity and distress of mind.

Shall I acknowledge it? The conclusion of this whole business was, that it soon became a fixed fact of my chambers, that a pale young scrivener, by the name of Bartleby, had a desk there; that he copied for me at the usual rate of four cents a folio (one hundred words); but he was permanently exempt from examining the work done by him, that duty being transferred to Turkey and Nippers, out of compliment, doubtless, to their superior acuteness; moreover, said Bartleby was never, on any account, to be dispatched on the most trivial errand of any sort; and that even if entreated to take upon him such a matter, it was generally understood that he would "prefer not to"—in other words, that he would refuse pointbank.

As days passed on, I became considerably reconciled to Bartleby. His steadiness, his freedom from all dissipation, his incessant industry (except when he chose to throw himself into a standing revery behind his screen), his great stillness, his unalterableness of demeanor under all circumstances, made him a valuable acquisition. One prime thing was this—*he was always there*—first in the morning, continually through the day, and the last at night. I had a singular confidence in his honesty. I felt my most precious papers perfectly safe in his hands. Sometimes, to be sure, I could not, for the very soul of me, avoid falling into sudden spasmodic passions with him. For it was exceeding difficult to bear in mind all the time those strange peculiarities, privileges, and unheard-of exemptions, forming the tacit stipulations on Bartleby's part under which he remained in my office. Now and then, in the eagerness of dispatching pressing business, I would inadvertently summon Bartleby, in a short, rapid tone, to put his finger, say, on the incipient tie of a bit of red tape with which I was about compressing some papers. Of course, from behind the screen the usual answer, "I prefer not to," was sure to come; and then, how could a human creature, with the common infirmities of our nature, refrain from bitterly exclaiming upon such perverseness—such unreasonableness? However, every added repulse of this sort which I received only tended to lessen the probability of my repeating the inadvertence.

23

Here it must be said, that, according to the custom of most legal gentlemen occupying chambers in densely-populated law buildings, there were several keys to my door. One was kept by a woman residing in the attic, which person weekly scrubbed and daily swept and dusted my apartments. Another was kept by Turkey for convenience sake. The third I sometimes carried in my own pocket. The fourth I knew not who had.

Now, one Sunday morning I happened to go to Trinity Church, to hear a celebrated preacher, and finding myself rather early on the ground I thought I would walk round to my chambers for a while. Luckily I had my key with me; but upon applying it to the lock, I found it resisted by something inserted from the inside. Quite surprised, I called out; when to my consternation a key was turned from within; and thrusting his lean visage at me, and holding the door ajar, the apparition of Bartleby appeared, in his shirtsleeves, and otherwise in a strangely tattered deshabille, saying quietly that he was sorry, but he was deeply engaged just then, and—preferred not admitting me at present. In a brief word or two, he moreover added, that perhaps I had better walk round the block two or three times, and by that time he would probably have concluded his affairs.

Now, the utterly unsurmised appearance of Bartleby, tenanting my lawchambers of a Sunday morning, with his cadaverously gentlemanly *nonchalance*, yet withal firm and self-possessed, had such a strange effect upon me, that incontinently I slunk away from my own door, and did as desired. But not without sundry twinges of impotent rebellion against the mild effrontery of this unaccountable scrivener. Indeed, it was his wonderful mildness chiefly, which not only disarmed me, but unmanned me, as it were. For I consider that one, for the time, is a sort of unmanned when he tranquilly permits his hired clerk to dictate to him, and order him away from his own premises. Furthermore, I was full of uneasiness as to what Bartleby could possibly be doing in my office in his shirt-sleeves, and in an otherwise dismantled condition of a Sunday morning. Was anything amiss going on? Nay, that was out of the question. It was not to be thought of for a moment that Bartleby was an immoral person. But what could he be doing there?—copying? Nay again, whatever might be his eccentricities, Bartleby was an eminently decorous person. He would be the last man to sit down to his desk in any state approaching to nudity. Besides, it was Sunday; and there was something about Bartleby that forbade the supposition that he would by any secular occupation violate the proprieties of the day.

Nevertheless, my mind was not pacified; and full of a restless curiosity, at last I returned to the door. Without hindrance I inserted my key, opened it, and entered. Bartleby was not to be seen. I looked round anxiously, peeped behind his screen; but it was very plain that he was gone. Upon more closely examining the place, I surmised that for an indefinite period Bartleby must have ate, dressed, and slept in my office, and that too without plate, mirror, or bed. The cushioned seat of a rickety old sofa in one corner bore the faint impress of a lean, reclining form. Rolled away under his desk, I found a blanket; under the empty grate, a blacking box and brush; on a chair, a tin basin, with soap and a ragged towel; in a newspaper a few crumbs of ginger-nuts and a morsel of cheese. Yes, thought I, it is evident enough that Bartleby has been making his home here, keeping bachelor's hall all by himself. Immediately then the thought came sweeping across me, what miserable friend-lessness and loneliness are here revealed! His poverty is great; but his solitude, how horrible! Think of it. Of a Sunday, Wall Street is deserted as Petra; and every night of every day it is an emptiness. This building, too, which of week-days hums with industry and life, at nightfall echoes with sheer vacancy, and all through Sunday is forlorn. And here Bartleby makes his home; sole specta-tor of a solitude which he has seen all populous—a sort of innocent and trans-formed Marius brooding among the ruins of Carthage!

For the first time in my life a feeling of overpowering stinging melan-choly seized me. Before, I had never experienced aught but a not unpleasing sadness. The bond of a common humanity now drew me irresistibly to gloom. A fraternal melancholy! For both I and Bartleby were sons of Adam. I remem-bered the bright silks and sparkling faces I had seen that day, in gala trim, swan-like sailing down the Mississippi of Broadway; and I contrasted them with the pallid copyist, and thought to myself, Ah, happiness courts the light, so we deem the world is gay; but misery hides aloof, so we deem that misery there is none. These sad fancyings—chimeras, doubtless, of a sick and silly brain—led on to other and more special thoughts, concerning the eccentricities of Bartleby. Presentiments of strange discoveries hovered around me. The scrivener's pale form appeared to me laid out, among uncaring strangers, in its shivering winding-sheet.

Suddenly I was attracted by Bartleby's closed desk, the key in open sight left in the lock.

I mean no mischief, seek the gratification of no heartless curiosity, thought I; besides, the desk is mine, and its contents, too, so I will make bold to look within. Everything was methodically arranged, the papers smoothly placed. The pigeon-holes were deep, and removing the files of documents, I groped into their recesses. Presently I felt something there, and dragged it out. It was an old bandanna handkerchief, heavy and knotted. I opened it, and saw it was a saving's bank.

I now recalled all the quiet mysteries which I had noted in the man. I remembered that he never spoke but to answer; that, though at intervals he had considerable time to himself, yet I had never seen him reading—no, not even a newspaper; that for long periods he would stand looking out, at his pale window behind the screen, upon the dead brick wall; I was quite sure he never visited any refectory or eating-house; while his pale face clearly indi-cated that he never drank beer like Turkey, or tea and coffee even, like other men; that he never went anywhere in particular that I could learn; never went out for a walk, unless, indeed, that was the case at present; that he had de-clined telling who he was, or whence he came, or whether he had any relatives in the world; that though so thin and pale, he never complained of ill-health.

25

And more than all, I remembered a certain unconscious air of pallid—how shall I call it?—of pallid haughtiness, say, or rather an austere reserve about him, which had positively awed me into my tame compliance with his eccentricities, when I had feared to ask him to do the slightest incidental thing for me, even though I might know, from his long-continued motionless, that behind his screen he must be standing in one of those dead-wall reveries of his.

Revolving all these things, and coupling them with the recently discovered fact, that he made my office his constant abiding place and home, and not forgetful of his morbid moodiness; revolving all these things, a prudential feeling began to steal over me. My first emotions had been those of pure melancholy and sincerest pity; but just in proportion as the forlornness of Bartleby grew and grew to my imagination, did that same melancholy merge into fear, that pity into repulsion. So true it is, and so terrible, too, that up to a certain point the thought or sight of misery enlists our best affections; but, in certain special cases, beyond that point it does not. They err who would assert that invariably this is owing to the inherent selfishness of the human heart. It rather proceeds from a certain hopelessness of remedying excessive and organic ill. To a sensitive being, pity is not seldom pain. And when at last it is perceived that such pity cannot lead to effectual succor, common sense bids the soul be rid of it. What I saw that morning persuaded me that the scrivener was the victim of innate and incurable disorder. I might give alms to his body; but his body did not pain him; it was his soul that suffered, and his soul I could not reach.

I did not accomplish the purpose of going to Trinity Church that morning. Somehow, the things I had seen disqualified me for the time from church-going. I walked homeward, thinking what I would do with Bartleby. Finally, I resolved upon this—I would put certain calm questions to him the next morning, touching his history, etc., and if he declined to answer them openly and unreservedly (and I supposed he would prefer not), then to give him a twenty dollar bill over and above whatever I might owe him, and tell him his services were no longer required; but that if in any other way I could assist him, I would be happy to do so, especially if he desired to return to his native place, wherever that might be, I would willingly help to defray the expenses. Moreover, if, after reaching home, he found himself at any time in want of aid, a letter from him would be sure of a reply.

The next morning came.

"Bartleby," said I, gently calling to him behind his screen.

No reply.

"Bartleby," said I, in a still gentler tone, "come here; I am not going to ask you to do anything you would prefer not to do—I simply wish to speak to you."

Upon this he noiselessly slid into view.

"Will you tell me, Bartleby, where you were born?"

"I would prefer not to."

"Will you tell me *anything* about yourself?"

"I would prefer not to."

"But what reasonable objection can you have to speak to me? I feel friendly towards you."

He did not look at me while I spoke, but kept his glance fixed upon my bust of Cicero, which, as I then sat, was directly behind me, some six inches above my head.

"What is your answer, Bartleby?" said I, after waiting a considerable time for a reply, during which his countenance remained immovable, only there was the faintest conceivable tremor of the white attenuated mouth.

"At present I prefer to give no answer," he said, and retired into his hermitage.

It was rather weak in me I confess, but his manner, on this occasion, nettled me. Not only did there seem to lurk in it a certain calm disdain, but his perverseness seemed ungrateful, considering the undeniable good usage and indulgence he had received from me.

Again I sat ruminating what I should do. Mortified as I was at his behavior, and resolved as I had been to dismiss him when I entered my office, nevertheless I strangely felt something superstitious knocking at my heart, and forbidding me to carry out my purpose, and denouncing me for a villain if I dared to breathe one bitter word against this forlornest of mankind. At last, familiarly drawing my chair behind his screen, I sat down and said: "Bartleby, never mind, then, about revealing your history; but let me entreat you, as a friend, to comply as far as may be with the usages of this office. Say now, you will help to examine papers tomorrow or next day: in short, say now, that in a day or two you will begin to be a little reasonable:—say so, Bartleby."

"At present I would prefer not to be a little reasonable," was his mildly cadaverous reply.

Just then the folding-doors opened, and Nippers approached. He seemed suffering from an unusually bad night's rest, induced by severer indigestion than common. He overheard those final words of Bartleby.

"*Prefer* not, eh?" gritted Nippers—"I'd *prefer* him, if I were you, sir," addressing me—"I'd *prefer* him; I'd give him preferences, the stubborn mule! What is it, sir, pray, that he *prefers* not to do now?

Bartleby moved not a limb.

"Mr. Nippers," said I, "I'd prefer that you would withdraw for the present."

Somehow, of late, I had got into the way of involuntarily using this word "prefer" upon all sorts of not exactly suitable occasions. And I trembled to think that my contact with the scrivener had already and seriously affected me in a mental way. And what further and deeper aberration might it not yet produce? This apprehension had not been without efficacy in determining me to summary measures.

As Nippers, looking very sour and sulky, was departing, Turkey blandly and deferentially approached.

"With submission, sir," said he, "yesterday I was thinking about Bartleby here, and I think that if he would but prefer to take a quart of good ale every day, it would do much towards mending him, and enabling him to assist in examining his papers."

"So you have got the word, too," said I, slightly excited.

"With submission, what word, sir?" asked Turkey, respectfully crowding himself into the contracted space behind the screen, and by so doing, making me jostle the scrivener, "What word, sir?"

"I would prefer to be left alone here," said Bartleby, as if offended at being mobbed in his privacy.

"*That's* the word, Turkey," said I—"*that's* it."

"Oh, *prefer?* oh yes—queer word. I never use it myself. But, sir, as I was saying, if he would but prefer—"

"Turkey," interrupted I, "you will please withdraw."

"Oh certainly, sir, if you prefer that I should."

As he opened the folding-door to retire, Nippers at his desk caught a glimpse of me, and asked whether I would prefer to have a certain paper copied on blue paper or white. He did not in the least roguishly accent the word "prefer." It was plain that it involuntarily rolled from his tongue. I thought to myself, surely I must get rid of a demented man, who already has in some degree turned the tongues, if not the heads of myself and clerks. But I thought it prudent not to break the dismission at once.

The next day I noticed that Bartleby did nothing but stand at his window in his dead-wall revery. Upon asking him why he did not write, he said that he had decided upon doing no more writing.

"Why, how now? what next?" exclaimed I, "do no more writing?"

"No more."

"And what is the reason?"

"Do you not see the reason for yourself?" he indifferently replied.

I looked steadfastly at him, and perceived that his eyes looked dull and glazed. Instantly it occurred to me, that his unexampled diligence in copying by his dim window for the first few weeks of his stay with me might have temporarily impaired his vision.

I was touched. I said something in condolence with him. I hinted that of course he did wisely in abstaining from writing for a while; and urged him to embrace that opportunity of taking wholesome exercise in the open air. This, however, he did not do. A few days after this, my other clerks being absent, and being in a great hurry to dispatch certain letters by the mail, I thought that, having nothing else earthly to do, Bartleby would surely be less inflexible than usual, and carry these letters to the post-office. But he blankly declined. So, much to my inconvenience, I went myself.

Still added days went by. Whether Bartleby's eyes improved or not, I could not say. To all appearance, I thought they did. But when I asked him if they did, he vouchsafed no answer. At all events, he would do no copying. At last, in reply to my urgings, he informed me that he had permanently given up copying.

"What!" exclaimed I; "suppose your eyes should get entirely well—better than ever before—would you not copy then?"

"I have given up copying," he answered, and slid aside.

He remained as ever, a fixture in my chamber. Nay—if that were possible—he became still more of a fixture than before. What was to be done? He would do nothing in the office; why should he stay there? In plain fact, he had now become a millstone to me, not only useless as a necklace, but afflictive to bear. Yet I was sorry for him. I speak less than truth when I say that, on his own account, he occasioned me uneasiness. If he would but have named a single relative or friend, I would instantly have written, and urged their taking the poor fellow away to some convenient retreat. But he seemed alone, absolutely alone in the universe. A bit of wreck in the mid-Atlantic. At length, necessities connected with my business tyrannized over all other considerations. Decently as I could, I told Bartleby that in six days' time he must unconditionally leave the office. I warned him to take measures, in the interval, for procuring some other abode. I offered to assist him in this endeavor, if he himself would but take the first step towards a removal. "And when you finally quit me, Bartleby," added I, "I shall see that you go not away entirely unprovided. Six days from this hour, remember."

At the expiration of that period, I peeped behind the screen, and lo! Bartleby was there.

I buttoned up my coat, balanced myself; advanced slowly towards him, touched his shoulder, and said, "The time has come; you must quit this place; I am sorry for you; here is money; but you must go."

"I would prefer not," he replied, with his back still towards me.

"You *must.*"

He remained silent.

Now I had an unbounded confidence in this man's common honesty. He had frequently restored to me sixpences and shillings carelessly dropped upon the floor, for I am apt to be very reckless in such shirt-button affairs. The proceeding, then, which followed will not be deemed extraordinary.

"Bartleby," said I, "I owe you twelve dollars on account; here are thirty-two; the odd twenty are yours—Will you take it?" and I handed the bills towards him.

But he made no motion.

"I will leave them here, then," putting them under a weight on the table. Then taking my hat and cane and going to the door, I tranquilly turned and added—"After you have removed your things from these offices, Bartleby, you will of course lock the door—since every one is now gone for the day but you—and if you please, slip your key underneath the mat, so that I may have it in the morning. I shall not see you again; so good-bye to you. If, hereafter, in your new place of abode, I can be of any service to you, do not fail to advise me by letter. Good-bye, Bartleby, and fare you well."

But he answered not a word; like the last column of some ruined temple, he remained standing mute and solitary in the middle of the otherwise deserted room.

As I walked home in a pensive mood, my vanity got the better of my pity. I could not but highly plume myself on my masterly management in getting rid of Bartleby. Masterly I call it, and such it must appear to any dispassionate thinker. The beauty of my procedure seemed to consist in its perfect quietness. There was no vulgar bullying, no bravado of any sort, no choleric hectoring, and striding to and fro across the apartment, jerking out vehement commands for Bartleby to bundle himself off with his beggarly traps. Nothing of the kind. Without loudly bidding Bartleby depart—as an inferior genius might have done—I *assumed* the ground that depart he must; and upon that assumption built all I had to say. The more I thought over my procedure, the more I was charmed with it. Nevertheless, next morning, upon awakening, I had my doubts—I had somehow slept off the fumes of vanity. One of the coolest and wisest hours a man has, is just after he awakes in the morning. My procedure seemed as sagacious as ever—but only in theory. How it would prove in practice—there was the rub. It was truly a beautiful thought to have assumed Bartleby's departure; but, after all, that assumption was simply my own, and none of Bartleby's. The great point was, not whether I had assumed that he would quit me, but whether he would prefer to do so. He was more a man of preferences than assumptions.

After breakfast, I walked down town, arguing the probabilities *pro* and *con*. One moment I thought it would prove a miserable failure, and Bartleby would be found all alive at my office as usual; the next moment it seemed certain that I should find his chair empty. And so I kept veering about. At the corner of Broadway and Canal Street, I saw quite an excited group of people standing in earnest conversation.

"I'll take odds he doesn't," said a voice as I passed.

"Doesn't go?—done!" said I, "put up your money."

I was instinctively putting my hand in my pocket to produce my own, when I remembered that this was an election day. The words I had overheard bore no reference to Bartleby, but to the success or non-success of some candidate for the mayoralty. In my intent frame of mind, I had, as it were, imagined that all Broadway shared in my excitement, and were debating the same question with me. I passed on, very thankful that the uproar of the street screened my momentary absent-mindedness.

As I had intended, I was earlier than usual at my office door. I stood listening for a moment. All was still. He must be gone. I tried the knob. The door was locked. Yes, my procedure had worked to a charm; he indeed must be vanished. Yet a certain melancholy mixed with this: I was almost sorry for my brilliant success. I was fumbling under the door mat for the key, which Bartleby was to have left there for me, when accidentally my knee knocked against a panel, producing a summoning sound, and in response a voice came to me from within—"Not yet; I am occupied."

It was Bartleby.

I was thunderstruck. For an instant I stood like the man who, pipe in mouth, was killed one cloudless afternoon long ago in Virginia, by summer lightning; at his own warm open window he was killed, and remained leaning out there upon the dreamy afternoon, till some one touched him, when he fell.

"Not gone!" I murmured at last. But again obeying that wondrous ascendancy which the inscrutable scrivener had over me, and from which ascendancy, for all my chafing, I could not completely escape, I slowly went down stairs and out into the street, and while walking round the block, considered what I should next do in this unheard-of perplexity. Turn the man out by an actual thrusting I could not; to drive him away by calling him hard names would not do; calling in the police was an unpleasant idea; and yet, permit him to enjoy his cadaverous triumph over me—this, too, I could not think of. What was to be done? or, if nothing could be done, was there anything further that I could *assume* in the matter? Yes, as before I had prospectively assumed that Bartleby would depart, so now I might retrospectively assume that departed he was. In the legitimate carrying out of this assumption, I might enter my office in a great hurry, and pretending not to see Bartleby at all, walk straight against him as if he were air. Such a proceeding would in a singular degree have the appearance of a home thrust. It was hardly possible that Bartleby could withstand such an application of the doctrine of assumption. But upon second thoughts the success of the plan seemed rather dubious. I resolved to argue the matter over with him again.

"Bartleby," said I, entering the office, with a quietly severe expression, "I am seriously displeased. I am pained, Bartleby. I had thought better of you. I had imagined you of such a gentlemanly organization, that in any delicate dilemma a slight hint would suffice—in short, an assumption. But it appears I am deceived. Why," I added, unaffectedly starting, "you have not even touched that money yet," pointing to it, just where I had left it the evening previous.

He answered nothing.

"Will you, or will you not, quit me?" I now demanded in a sudden passion, advancing close to him.

"I would prefer *not* to quit you," he replied, gently emphasizing the *not*.

"What earthly right have you to stay here? Do you pay my rent? Do you pay my taxes? Or is this property yours?"

He answered nothing.

"Are you ready to go on and write now? Are your eyes recovered? Could you copy a small paper for me this morning? or help examine a few lines? or step round to the post-office? In a word, will you do anything at all, to give a coloring to your refusal to depart the premises?"

He silently retired into his hermitage.

I was now in such a state of nervous resentment that I thought it but prudent to check myself at present from further demonstrations. Bartleby and I were alone. I remembered the tragedy of the unfortunate Adams and the still more unfortunate Colt in the solitary office of the latter; and how poor Colt, being dreadfully incensed by Adams, and imprudently permitting himself to get wildly excited, was at unawares hurried into his fatal act—an act which certainly no man could possibly deplore more than the actor himself. Often it had occurred to me in my ponderings upon the subject that had that altercation taken place in the public street, or at a private residence, it would not have terminated as it did. It was the circumstance of being alone in a solitary office, up stairs, of a building entirely unhallowed by humanizing domestic associations—an uncarpeted office, doubtless, of a dusty, haggard sort of appearance—this it must have been, which greatly helped to enhance the irritable desperation of the hapless Colt.

But when this old Adam of resentment rose in me and tempted me concerning Bartleby, I grappled him and threw him. How? Why, simply by recalling the divine injunction: "A new commandment give I unto you, that ye love one another." Yes, this it was that saved me. Aside from higher considerations, charity often operates as a vastly wise and prudent principle—a great safeguard to its possessor. Men have committed murder for jealousy's sake, and anger's sake, and hatred's sake, and selfishness' sake, and spiritual pride's sake; but no man, that ever I heard of, ever committed a diabolical murder for sweet charity's sake. Mere self-interest, then, if no better motive can be enlisted, should, especially with high-tempered men, prompt all beings to charity and philanthropy. At any rate, upon the occasion in question, I strove to drown my exasperated feelings towards the scrivener by benevolently construing his conduct. Poor fellow, poor fellow! thought I, he don't mean anything; and besides, he has seen hard times, and ought to be indulged.

I endeavored, also, immediately to occupy myself, and at the same time to comfort my despondency. I tried to fancy, that in the course of the morning, at such time as might prove agreeable to him, Bartleby, of his own free accord, would emerge from his hermitage and take up some decided line of march in the direction of the door. But no. Half-past twelve o'clock came; Turkey began to glow in the face, overturn his inkstand, and become generally obstreperous; Nippers abated down into quietude and courtesy; Ginger Nut munched his noon apple; and Bartleby remained standing at his window in one of his profoundest dead-wall reveries. Will it be credited? Ought I to acknowledge it? That afternoon I left the office without saying one further word to him.

Some days now passed, during which, at leisure intervals I looked a little into "Edwards on the Will," and "Priestley on Necessity." Under the circumstances, those books induced a salutary feeling. Gradually I slid into the persuasion that these troubles of mine, touching the scrivener, had been all predestinated from eternity, and Bartleby was billeted upon me for some mysterious purpose of an all-wise Providence, which it was not for a mere mortal like me to fathom. Yes, Bartleby, stay there behind your screen, thought I; I shall persecute you no more; you are harmless and noiseless as any of these old chairs; in short, I never feel so private as when I know you are here. At last I see it, feel it; I penetrate to the predestinated purpose of my life. I am content. Others may have loftier parts to enact; but my mission in this world, Bartleby, is to furnish you with office-room for such period as you may see fit to remain.

I believe that this wise and blessed frame of mind would have continued with me, had it not been for the unsolicited and uncharitable remarks obtruded upon me by my professional friends who visited the rooms. But thus it often is, that the constant friction of illiberal minds wears out at last the best resolves of the more generous. Though to be sure, when I reflected upon it, it was not strange that people entering my office should be struck by the peculiar aspect of the unaccountable Bartleby, and so be tempted to throw out some sinister observations concerning him. Sometimes an attorney, having business with me, and calling at my office, and finding no one but the scrivener there, would undertake to obtain some sort of precise information from him touching my whereabouts; but without heeding his idle talk, Bartleby would remain standing immovable in the middle of the room. So after contemplating him in that position for a time, the attorney would depart, no wiser than he came.

Also, when a reference was going on, and the room full of lawyers and witnesses, and business driving fast, some deeply-occupied legal gentleman present, seeing Bartleby wholly unemployed, would request him to run round to his (the legal gentleman's) office and fetch some papers for him. Thereupon, Bartleby would tranquilly decline, and yet remain idle as before. Then the lawyer would give a great stare, and turn to me. And what could I say? At last I was made aware that all through the circle of my professional acquaintance, a whisper of wonder was running round, having reference to the strange creature I kept at my office. This worried me very much. And as the idea came upon me of his possibly turning out a long-lived man, and keeping occupying my chambers, and denying my authority; and perplexing my visitors; and scandalizing my professional reputation; and casting a general gloom over the premises; keeping soul and body together to the last upon his savings (for doubtless he spent but half a dime a day), and in the end perhaps outlive me, and claim possession of my office by right of his perpetual occupancy: as all these dark anticipations crowded upon me more and more, and my friends continually intruded their relentless remarks upon the apparition in my room; a great change was wrought in me. I resolved to gather all my faculties together, and forever rid me of this intolerable incubus.

Ere revolving any complicated project, however, adapted to this end, I first simply suggested to Bartleby the propriety of his permanent departure. In a calm and serious tone, I commended the idea to his careful and mature consideration. But, having taken three days to meditate upon it, he apprised me, that his original determination remained the same; in short, that he still preferred to abide with me.

What shall I do? I now said to myself, buttoning up my coat to the last button. What shall I do? what ought I to do? what does conscience say I *should* do with this man, or, rather, ghost. Rid myself of him, I must; go, he shall. But how? You will not thrust him, the poor, pale, passive mortal—you will not thrust such a helpless creature out of your door? you will not dishonor yourself by such cruelty? No, I will not, I cannot do that. Rather would I let him live and die here, and then mason up his remains in the wall. What, then, will you do? For all your coaxing, he will not budge. Bribes he leaves under your own paper-weight on your table; in short, it is quite plain that he prefers to cling to you.

Then something severe, something unusual must be done. What! surely you will not have him collared by a constable, and commit his innocent pallor to the common jail? And upon what ground could you procure such a thing to be done?—a vagrant, is he? What! he a vagrant, a wanderer, who refuses to budge? It is because he will *not* be a vagrant, then, that you seek to count him *as* a vagrant. That is too absurd. No visible means of support: there I have him. Wrong again: for indubitably he *does* support himself, and that is the only unanswerable proof that any man can show of his possessing the means so to do. No more, then. Since he will not quit me, I must quit him. I will change my offices; I will move elsewhere, and give him fair notice, that if I find him on my new premises I will then proceed against him as a common trespasser.

Acting accordingly, next day I thus addressed him: "I find these chambers too far from the City Hall; the air is unwholesome. In a word, I propose to remove my offices next week, and shall no longer require your services. I tell you this now, in order that you may seek another place."

He made no reply, and nothing more was said.

On the appointed day I engaged carts and men, proceeded to my chambers, and, having but little furniture, everything was removed in a few hours. Throughout, the scrivener remained standing behind the screen, which I directed to be removed the last thing. It was withdrawn; and, being folded up like a huge folio, left him the motionless occupant of a naked room. I stood in the entry watching him a moment, while something from within me upbraided me.

I re-entered, with my hand in my pocket—and—and my heart in my mouth.

"Good-bye, Bartleby; I am going—good-bye, and God some way bless you; and take that," slipping something in his hand. But it dropped upon the floor, and then—strange to say—I tore myself from him whom I had so longed to be rid of.

Established in my new quarters, for a day or two I kept the door locked, and started at every footfall in the passages. When I returned to my rooms, after any little absence, I would pause at the threshold for an instant, and attentively listen, ere applying my key. But these fears were needless. Bartleby never came nigh me.

I thought all was going well, when a perturbed-looking stranger visited me, inquiring whether I was the person who had recently occupied rooms at No. —— Wall Street.

34

Full of forebodings, I replied that I was.

"Then, sir," said the stranger, who proved a lawyer, "you are responsible for the man you left there. He refuses to do any copying; he refuses to do anything; he says he prefers not to; and he refuses to quit the premises."

"I am very sorry, sir," said I, with assumed tranquillity, but an inward tremor, "but, really, the man you allude to is nothing to me—he is no relation or apprentice of mine, that you should hold me responsible for him."

"In mercy's name, who is he?"

"I certainly cannot inform you. I know nothing about him. Formerly I employed him as a copyist; but he has done nothing for me now for some time past."

"I shall settle him, then—good morning, sir."

Several days passed, and I heard nothing more; and, though I often felt a charitable prompting to call at the place and see poor Bartleby, yet a certain squeamishness, of I know not what, withheld me.

All is over with him, by this time, thought I, at last, when, through another week, no further intelligence reached me. But, coming to my room the day after, I found several persons waiting at my door in a high state of nervous excitement.

"That's the man—here he comes," cried the foremost one, whom I recognized as the lawyer who had previously called upon me alone.

"You must take him away, sir, at once," cried a portly person among them, advancing upon me, and whom I knew to be the landlord of No. —— Wall Street. "These gentlemen, my tenants, cannot stand it any longer: Mr. B——," pointing to the lawyer, "has turned him out of his room, and he now persists in haunting the building generally, sitting upon the banisters of the stairs by day, and sleeping in the entry by night. Everybody is concerned; clients are leaving the offices; some fears are entertained of a mob; something you must do, and that without delay."

Aghast at this torrent, I fell back before it, and would fain have locked myself in my new quarters. In vain I persisted that Bartleby was nothing to me —no more than to any one else. In vain—I was the last person known to have anything to do with him, and they held me to the terrible account. Fearful, then, of being exposed in the papers (as one person present obscurely threatened), I considered the matter, and, at length, said, that if the lawyer would give me a confidential interview with the scrivener, in his (the lawyer's) own room, I would, that afternoon, strive my best to rid them of the nuisance they complained of.

Going up stairs to my old haunt, there was Bartleby silently sitting upon the banister at the landing.

"What are you doing here, Bartleby?" said I.

"Sitting upon the banister," he mildly replied.

I motioned him into the lawyer's room, who then left us.

"Bartleby," said I, "are you aware that you are the cause of great tribulation to me, by persisting in occupying the entry after being dismissed from the office?"

No answer.

"Now one of two things must take place. Either you must do something, or something must be done to you. Now what sort of business would you like to engage in? Would you like to re-engage in copying for some one?"

"No; I would prefer not to make any change."

"Would you like a clerkship in a dry-goods store?"

"There is too much confinement about that. No, I would not like a clerkship; but I am not particular."

"Too much confinement," I cried, "why, you keep yourself confined all the time!"

"I would prefer not to take a clerkship," he rejoined, as if to settle that little item at once.

"How would a bar-tender's business suit you? There is no trying of the eye-sight in that."

"I would not like it at all; though, as I said before, I am not particular."

His unwonted wordiness inspirited me. I returned to the charge.

"Well, then, would you like to travel through the country collecting bills for the merchants? That would improve your health."

"No, I would prefer to be doing something else."

"How, then, would going as a companion to Europe, to entertain some young gentleman with your conversation—how would that suit you?"

"Not at all. It does not strike me that there is anything definite about that. I like to be stationary. But I am not particular."

"Stationary you shall be, then," I cried, now losing all patience, and, for the first time in all my exasperating connection with him, fairly flying into a passion. "If you do not go away from these premises before night, I shall feel bound—indeed, I *am* bound—to—to—to quit the premises myself!" I rather absurdly concluded, knowing not with what possible threat to try to frighten his immobility into compliance. Despairing of all further efforts, I was precipitatively leaving him, when a final thought occurred to me—one which had not been wholly unindulged before.

"Bartleby," said I, in the kindest tone I could assume under such exciting circumstances, "will you go home with me now—not to my office, but my dwelling—and remain there till we can conclude upon some convenient arrangement for you at our leisure? Come, let us start now, right away."

"No: at present I would prefer not to make any change at all."

I answered nothing; but, effectually dodging every one by the suddenness and rapidity of my flight, rushed from the building, ran up Wall Street towards Broadway, and, jumping into the first omnibus, was soon removed from pursuit. As soon as tranquillity returned, I distinctly perceived that I had now done all that I possibly could, both in respect to the demands of the landlord and his tenants, and with regard to my own desire and sense of duty, to benefit

Bartleby, and shield him from rude persecution. I now strove to be entirely care-free and quiescent; and my conscience justified me in the attempt; though, indeed, it was not so successful as I could have wished. So fearful was I of being again hunted out by the incensed landlord and his exasperated tenants, that, surrendering my business to Nippers, for a few days, I drove about the upper part of the town and through the suburbs, in my rockaway; crossed over to Jersey City and Hoboken, and paid fugitive visits to Manhattanville and Astoria. In fact, I almost lived in my rockaway for the time.

When again I entered my office, lo, a note from the landlord lay upon the desk. I opened it with trembling hands. It informed me that the writer had sent to the police, and had Bartleby removed to the Tombs as a vagrant. Moreover, since I knew more about him than any one else, he wished me to appear at that place, and make a suitable statement of the facts. These tidings had a conflicting effect upon me. At first I was indignant; but, at last, almost approved. The landlord's energetic, summary disposition, had led him to adopt a procedure which I do not think I would have decided upon myself; and yet, as a last resort, under such peculiar circumstances, it seemed the only plan.

As I afterwards learned, the poor scrivener, when told that he must be conducted to the Tombs, offered not the slightest obstacle, but, in his pale, unmoving way, silently acquiesced.

Some of the compassionate and curious by-standers joined the party; and headed by one of the constables arm-in-arm with Bartleby, the silent procession filed its way through all the noise, and heat, and joy of the roaring thoroughfares at noon.

The same day I received the note, I went to the Tombs, or, to speak more properly, the Halls of Justice. Seeking the right officer, I stated the purpose of my call, and was informed that the individual I described was, indeed, within. I then assured the functionary that Bartleby was a perfectly honest man, and greatly to be compassionated, however unaccountably eccentric. I narrated all I knew, and closed by suggesting the idea of letting him remain in as indulgent confinement as possible, till something less harsh might be done—though, indeed, I hardly knew what. At all events, if nothing else could be decided upon, the alms-house must receive him. I then begged to have an interview.

Being under no disgraceful charge, and quite serene and harmless in all his ways, they had permitted him freely to wander about the prison, and, especially, in the inclosed grass-platted yards thereof. And so I found him there, standing all alone in the quietest of the yards, his face towards a high wall, while all around, from the narrow slits of the jail windows, I thought I saw peering out upon him the eyes of murderers and thieves.

"Bartleby!"

"I know you," he said, without looking round—"and I want nothing to say to you."

"It was not I that brought you here, Bartleby," said I, keenly pained at his implied suspicion. "And to you, this should not be so vile a place. Nothing reproachful attaches to you by being here. And see, it is not so sad a place as one might think. Look, there is the sky, and here is the grass."

"I know where I am," he replied, but would say nothing more, and so I left him.

As I entered the corridor again, a broad meat-like man, in an apron, accosted me, and, jerking his thumb over his shoulder, said—"Is that your friend?"

"Yes."

"Does he want to starve? If he does, let him live on the prison fare, that's all."

"Who are you?" asked I, not knowing what to make of such an unofficially speaking person in such a place.

"I am the grub-man. Such gentlemen as have friends here, hire me to provide them with something good to eat."

"Is this so?" said I, turning to the turnkey.

He said it was.

"Well, then," said I, slipping some silver into the grub-man's hands (for so they called him), "I want you to give particular attention to my friend there; let him have the best dinner you can get. And you must be as polite to him as possible."

"Introduce me, will you?" said the grub-man, looking at me with an expression which seemed to say he was all impatience for an opportunity to give a specimen of his breeding.

Thinking it would prove of benefit to the scrivener, I acquiesced; and, asking the grub-man his name, went up with him to Bartleby.

"Bartleby, this is a friend; you will find him very useful to you."

"Your sarvant, sir, your sarvant," said the grub-man, making a low salutation behind his apron. "Hope you find it pleasant here, sir; nice grounds—cool apartments—hope you'll stay with us some time—try to make it agreeable. What will you have for dinner to-day?"

"I prefer not to dine to-day," said Bartleby, turning away. "It would disagree with me; I am unused to dinners." So saying, he slowly moved to the other side of the inclosure, and took up a position fronting the dead-wall.

"How's this?" said the grub-man, addressing me with a stare of astonishment. "He's odd, ain't he?"

"I think he is a little deranged," said I, sadly.

"Deranged? deranged is it? Well, now, upon my word, I thought that friend of yourn was a gentleman forger; they are always pale and genteel-like, them forgers. I can't help pity 'em—can't help it, sir. Did you know Monroe Edwards?" he added, touchingly, and paused. Then, laying his hand pietously on my shoulder, sighed, "he died of consumption at Sing-Sing. So you weren't acquainted with Monroe?"

"No, I was never socially acquainted with any forgers. But I cannot stop longer. Look to my friend yonder. You will not lose by it. I will see you again."

Some few days after this, I again obtained admission to the Tombs, and went through the corridors in quest of Bartleby; but without finding him.

"I saw him coming from his cell not long ago," said a turnkey, "may be he's gone to loiter in the yards."

So I went in that direction.

"Are you looking for the silent man?" said another turnkey, passing me. "Yonder he lies—sleeping in the yard there. 'Tis not twenty minutes since I saw him lie down."

The yard was entirely quiet. It was not accessible to the common prisoners. The surrounding walls, of amazing thickness, kept off all sounds behind them. The Egyptian character of the masonry weighed upon me with its gloom. But a soft imprisoned turf grew under foot. The heart of the eternal pyramids, it seemed, wherein, by some strange magic, through the clefts, grass-seed, dropped by birds, had sprung.

Strangely huddled at the base of the wall, his knees drawn up, and lying on his side, his head touching the cold stones, I saw the wasted Bartleby. But nothing stirred. I paused; then went close up to him; stooped over, and saw that his dim eyes were open; otherwise he seemed profoundly sleeping. Something prompted me to touch him. I felt his hand, when a tingling shiver ran up my arm and down my spine to my feet.

The round face of the grub-man peered upon me now. "His dinner is ready. Won't he dine to-day, either? Or does he live without dining?"

"Lives without dining," said I, and closed the eyes.

"Eh!—He's asleep, ain't he?"

"With kings and counselors," murmured I.

There would seem little need for proceeding further in this history. Imagination will readily supply the meagre recital of poor Bartleby's interment. But, ere parting with the reader, let me say, that if this little narrative has sufficiently interested him, to awaken curiosity as to who Bartleby was, and what manner of life he led prior to the present narrator's making his acquaintance, I can only reply, that in such curiosity I fully share, but am wholly unable to gratify it. Yet here I hardly know whether I should divulge one little item of rumor, which came to my ear a few months after the scrivener's decease. Upon what basis it rested, I could never ascertain; and hence, how true it is I cannot now tell. But, inasmuch as this vague report has not been without a certain suggestive interest to me, however sad, it may prove the same with some others; and so I will briefly mention it. The report was this: that Bartleby had been a subordinate clerk in the Dead Letter Office at Washington, from which he had been suddenly removed by a change in the administration. When I think over this rumor, hardly can I express the emotions which seize me. Dead letters! does it not sound like dead men? Conceive a man by nature and mis-fortune prone to a pallid hopelessness, can any business seem more fitted to heighten it than that of continually handling these dead letters, and assorting them for the flames? For by the cart-load they are annually burned. Sometimes from out the folded paper the pale clerk takes a ring—the finger it was meant for, perhaps, moulders in the grave; a bank-note sent in swiftest charity—he whom it would relieve, nor eats nor hungers any more; pardon for those who died despairing; hope for those who died unhoping; good tidings for those who died stifled by unrelieved calamities. On errands of life, these letters speed to death.

Ah, Bartleby! Ah, humanity!

MARK TWAIN

The Mysterious Stranger

1

It was in 1590—winter. Austria was far away from the world, and asleep; it was still the Middle Ages in Austria, and promised to remain so forever. Some even set it away back centuries upon centuries and said that by the mental and spiritual clock it was still the Age of Belief in Austria. But they meant it as a compliment, not a slur, and it was so taken, and we were all proud of it. I remember it well, although I was only a boy; and I remember, too, the pleasure it gave me.

Yes, Austria was far from the world, and asleep, and our village was in the middle of that sleep, being in the middle of Austria. It drowsed in peace in the deep privacy of a hilly and woodsy solitude where news from the world hardly ever came to disturb its dreams, and was infinitely content. At its front flowed the tranquil river, its surface painted with cloud-forms and the reflections of drifting arks and stone-boats; behind it rose the woody steeps to the base of the lofty precipice; from the top of the precipice frowned a vast castle, its long stretch of towers and bastions mailed in vines; beyond the river, a league to the left, was a tumbled expanse of forest-clothed hills cloven by winding gorges where the sun never penetrated; and to the right a precipice overlooked the river, and between it and the hills just spoken of lay a far-reaching plain dotted with little homesteads nested among orchards and shade trees.

The whole region for leagues around was the hereditary property of a prince, whose servants kept the castle always in perfect condition for occupancy, but neither he nor his family came there oftener than once in five years. When they came it was as if the lord of the world had arrived, and had brought all the glories of its kingdoms along; and when they went they left a calm behind which was like the deep sleep which follows an orgy.

Eseldorf was a paradise for us boys. We were not overmuch pestered with schooling. Mainly we were trained to be good Christians; to revere the Virgin, the Church, and the saints above everything. Beyond these matters we were not required to know much; and, in fact, not allowed to. Knowledge was not good for the common people, and could make them discontented with the lot which God had appointed for them, and God would not endure discontentment with His plans. We had two priests. One of them, Father Adolf, was a very zealous and strenuous priest, much considered.

There may have been better priests, in some ways, than Father Adolf, but there was never one in our commune who was held in more solemn and awful respect. This was because he had absolutely no fear of the Devil. He was the only Christian I have ever known of whom that could be truly said. People stood in deep dread of him on that account; for they thought that there must be something supernatural about him, else he could not be so bold and so confident. All men speak in bitter disapproval of the Devil but they do it reverently, not flippantly; but Father Adolf's way was very different; he called him by every name he could lay his tongue to, and it made every one shudder that heard him; and often he would even speak of him scornfully and scoffingly; then the people crossed themselves and went quickly out of his presence, fearing that something fearful might happen.

Father Adolf had actually met Satan face to face more than once, and defied him. This was known to be so. Father Adolf said it himself. He never made any secret of it, but spoke it right out. And that he was speaking true there was proof in at least one instance, for on that occasion he quarreled with the enemy, and intrepidly threw his bottle at him; and there, upon the wall of his study, was the ruddy splotch where it struck and broke.

But it was Father Peter, the other priest, that we all loved best and were sorriest for. Some people charged him with talking around in conversation that God was all goodness and would find a way to save all his poor human children. It was a horrible thing to say, but there was never any absolute proof that Father Peter said it; and it was out of character for him to say it, too, for he was always good and gentle and truthful. He wasn't charged with saying it in the pulpit, where all the congregation could hear and testify, but only outside, in talk; and it is easy for enemies to manufacture *that*. Father Peter had an enemy and a very powerful one, the astrologer who lived in a tumbled old tower up the valley, and put in his nights studying the stars. Every one knew he could foretell wars and famines, though that was not so hard, for there was always a war and generally a famine somewhere. But he could also read any man's life through the stars in a big book he had, and find lost property, and every one in the village except Father Peter stood in awe of him. Even Father Adolf, who had defied the Devil, had a wholesome respect for the astrologer when he came through our village wearing his tall, pointed hat and his long, flowing robe with stars on it, carrying his big book and a staff which was known to have magic power. The bishop himself sometimes listened to the astrologer, it was said, for, besides studying the stars and prophesying, the astrologer made a great show of piety, which would impress the bishop, of course.

But Father Peter took no stock in the astrologer. He denounced him openly as a charlatan—a fraud with no valuable knowledge of any kind, or powers beyond those of an ordinary and rather inferior human being, which naturally made the astrologer hate Father Peter and wish to ruin him. It was the astrologer, as we all believed, who originated the story about Father Peter's shocking remark and carried it to the bishop. It was said that Father Peter had made the remark to his niece, Marget, though Marget denied it and implored the bishop to believe her and spare her old uncle from poverty and disgrace. But the bishop wouldn't listen. He suspended Father Peter indefinitely, though he wouldn't go so far as to excommunicate him on the evidence of only one witness; and now Father Peter had been out a couple of years, and our other priest, Father Adolf, had his flock.

Those had been hard years for the old priest and Marget. They had been favorites, but of course that changed when they came under the shadow of the bishop's frown. Many of their friends fell away entirely, and the rest became cool and distant. Marget was a lovely girl of eighteen when the trouble came, and she had the best head in the village, and the most in it. She taught the harp, and earned all her clothes and pocket money by her own industry. But her scholars fell off one by one now; she was forgotten when there were dances and parties among the youth of the village; the young fellows stopped coming to the house, all except Wilhelm Meidling—and he could have been spared; she and her uncle were sad and forlorn in their neglect and disgrace, and the sunshine was gone out of their lives. Matters went worse and worse, all through the two years. Clothes were wearing out, bread was harder and harder to get. And now, at last, the very end was come. Solomon Isaacs had lent all the money he was willing to put on the house, and gave notice that to-morrow he would foreclose.

2

Three of us boys were always together, and had been so from the cradle, being fond of one another from the beginning, and this affection deepened as the years went on—Nikolaus Bauman, son of the principal judge of the local court; Seppi Wohlmeyer, son of the keeper of the principal inn, the "Golden Stag," which had a nice garden, with shade trees reaching down to the riverside, and pleasure boats for hire; and I was the third—Theodor Fischer, son of the church organist, who was also leader of the village musicians, teacher of the violin, composer, taxcollector of the commune, sexton, and in other ways a useful citizen, and respected by all. We knew the hills and the woods as well as the birds knew them; for we were always roaming them when we had leisure—at least, when we were not swimming or boating or fishing, or playing on the ice or sliding down hill.

And we had the run of the castle park, and very few had that. It was because we were pets of the oldest servingman in the castle—Felix Brandt; and often we went there, nights, to hear him talk about old times and strange things, and to smoke with him (he taught us that) and to drink coffee; for he had served in the wars, and was at the siege of Vienna; and there, when the Turks were defeated and driven away, among the captured things were bags of coffee, and the Turkish prisoners explained the character of it and how to make a pleasant drink out of it, and now he always kept coffee by him, to drink himself and also to astonish the ignorant with. When it stormed he kept us all night; and while it thundered and lightened outside he told us about ghosts and horrors of every kind, and of battles and murders and mutilations, and such things, and made it pleasant and cozy inside; and he told these things from his own experience largely. He had seen many ghosts in his time, and witches and enchanters, and once he was lost in a fierce storm at midnight in the mountains, and by the glare of the lightning had seen the Wild Huntsman rage on the blast with his specter dogs chasing after him through the driving cloud-rack. Also he had seen an incubus once, and several times he had seen the great bat that sucks the blood from the necks of people while they are asleep, fanning them softly with its wings and so keeping them drowsy till they die.

He encouraged us not to fear supernatural things, such as ghosts, and said they did no harm, but only wandered about because they were lonely and distressed and wanted kindly notice and compassion; and in time we learned not to be afraid, and even went down with him in the night to the haunted chamber in the dungeons of the castle. The ghost appeared only once, and it went by very dim to the sight and floated noiseless through the air, and then disappeared; and we scarcely trembled, he had taught us so well. He said it came up sometimes in the night and woke him by passing its clammy hand over his face, but it did him no hurt; it only wanted sympathy and notice. But the strangest thing was that he had seen angels—actual angels out of heaven—and had talked with them. They had no wings, and wore clothes, and talked and looked and acted just like any natural person, and you would never know them for angels except for the wonderful things they did which a mortal could not do, and the way they suddenly disappeared while you were talking with them, which was also a thing which no mortal could do. And he said they were pleasant and cheerful, not gloomy and melancholy, like ghosts.

It was after that kind of talk one May night that we got up next morning and had a good breakfast with him and then went down and crossed the bridge and went away up into the hills on the left to a woody hill-top which was a favorite place of ours, and there we stretched out on the grass in the shade to rest and smoke and talk over these strange things, for they were in our minds yet, and impressing us. But we couldn't smoke, because we had been heedless and left our flint and steel behind.

Soon there came a youth strolling toward us through the trees, and he sat down and began to talk in a friendly way, just as if he knew us. But we did not answer him, for he was a stranger and we were not used to strangers and were shy of them. He had new and good clothes on, and was handsome and had a winning face and a pleasant voice, and was easy and graceful and unembarrassed, not slouchy and awkward and diffident, like other boys. We wanted to be friendly with him, but didn't know how to begin. Then I thought of the pipe, and wondered if it would be taken as kindly meant if I offered it to him. But I remembered that we had no fire, so I was sorry and disappointed. But he looked up bright and pleased, and said:

"Fire? Oh, that is easy; I will furnish it."

I was so astonished I couldn't speak, for I had not said anything. He took the pipe and blew his breath on it, and the tobacco glowed red, and spirals of blue smoke rose up. We jumped up and were going to run, for that was natural; and we did run a few steps, although he was yearningly pleading for us to stay, and giving us his word that he would not do us any harm, but only wanted to be friends with us and have company. So we stopped and stood, and wanted to go back, being full of curiosity and wonder, but afraid to venture. He went on coaxing, in his soft, persuasive way; and when we saw that the pipe did not blow up and nothing happened, our confidence returned by little and little, and presently our curiosity got to be stronger than our fear, and we ventured back—but slowly, and ready to fly at any alarm.

He was bent on putting us at ease, and he had the right art; one could not remain doubtful and timorous where a person was so earnest and simple and gentle, and talked so alluringly as he did; no, he won us over, and it was not long before we were content and comfortable and chatty, and glad we had found this new friend. When the feeling of constraint was all gone we asked him how he had learned to do that strange thing, and he said he hadn't learned it at all; it came natural to him—like other things—other curious things.

"What ones?"

"Oh, a number; I don't know how many."

"Will you let us see you do them?"

"Do—please!" the others said.

"You won't run away again?"

"No—indeed we won't. Please do. Won't you?"

"Yes, with pleasure; but you mustn't forget your promise, you know."

We said we wouldn't, and he went to a puddle and came back with water in a cup which he had made out of a leaf, and blew upon it and threw it out, and it was a lump of ice the shape of the cup. We were astonished and charmed, but not afraid any more; we were very glad to be there, and asked him to go on and do some more things. And he did. He said he would give us any kind of fruit we liked, whether it was in season or not. We all spoke at once:

"Orange!"

"Apple!"

"Grapes!"

"They are in your pockets," he said, and it was true. And they were of the best, too, and we ate them and wished we had more, though none of us said so.

"You will find them where those came from," he said, "and everything else your appetites call for; and you need not name the thing you wish; as long as I am with you, you have only to wish and find."

And he said true. There was never anything so wonderful and so interesting. Bread, cakes, sweets, nuts—whatever one wanted, it was there. He ate nothing himself, but sat and chatted, and did one curious thing after another to amuse us. He made a tiny toy squirrel out of clay, and it ran up a tree and sat on a limb overhead and barked down at us. Then he made a dog that was not much larger than a mouse, and it treed the squirrel and danced about the tree, excited and barking, and was as alive as any dog could be. It frightened the squirrel from tree to tree and followed it up until both were out of sight in the forest. He made birds out of clay and set them free, and they flew away, singing.

At last I made bold to ask him to tell us who he was.

"An angel," he said quite simply, and set another bird free and clapped his hands and made it fly away.

A kind of awe fell upon us when we heard him say that, and we were afraid again; but he said we need not be troubled, there was no occasion for us to be afraid of an angel, and he liked us, anyway. He went on chatting as simply and unaffectedly as ever; and while he talked he made a crowd of little men and women the size of your finger, and they went diligently to work and cleared and leveled off a space a couple of yards square in the grass and began to build a cunning little castle in it, the women mixing the mortar and carrying it up the scaffoldings in pails on their heads, just as our work-women have always done, and the men laying the courses of masonry—five hundred of these toy people swarming briskly about and working diligently and wiping the sweat off their faces as natural as life. In the absorbing interest of watching those five hundred little people make the castle grow step by step and course by course, and take shape and symmetry, that feeling and awe soon passed away and we were quite comfortable and at home again. We asked if we might make some people, and he said yes, and told Seppi to make some cannon for the walls, and told Nikolaus to make some halberdiers with breast-plates and greaves and helmets, and I was to make some cavalry, with horses, and in allotting these tasks he called us by our names, but did not say how he knew them. Then Seppi asked him what his own name was, and he said, tranquilly, "Satan," and held out a chip and caught a little woman on it who was falling from the scaffolding and put her back where she belonged, and said, "She is an idiot to step backward like that and not notice what she is about."

It caught us suddenly, that name did, and our work dropped out of our hands and broke to pieces—a cannon, a halberdier, and a horse. Satan laughed, and asked what was the matter. I said, "Nothing, only it seemed a strange name for an angel." He asked why.

"Because it's—it's—well, it's his name, you know."

"Yes—he is my uncle."

He said it placidly, but it took our breath for a moment and made our hearts beat. He did not seem to notice that, but mended our halberdiers and things with a touch, handing them to us finished, and said, "Don't you remember?—he was an angel himself, once."

"Yes—it's true," said Seppi; "I didn't think of that."

"Before the Fall he was blameless."

"Yes," said Nikolaus, "he was without sin."

"It is a good family—ours," said Satan; "there is not a better. He is the only member of it that has ever sinned."

I should not be able to make any one understand how exciting it all was. You know that kind of quiver that trembles around through you when you are seeing something so strange and enchanting and wonderful that it is just a fearful joy to be alive and look at it; and you know how you gaze, and your lips turn dry and your breath comes short, but you wouldn't be anywhere but there, not for the world. I was bursting to ask one question—I had it on my tongue's end and could hardly hold it back—but I was ashamed to ask it; it might be a rudeness. Satan set an ox down that he had been making and smiled up at me and said:

"It wouldn't be a rudeness, and I should forgive it if it was. Have I seen him? Millions of times. From the time that I was a little child a thousand years old I was his second favorite among the nursery angels of our blood and lineage—to use a human phrase—yes, from that time until the Fall, eight thousands years, measured as you count time."

"Eight—thousand!"

"Yes." He turned to Seppi, and went on as if answering something that was in Seppi's mind, "Why, naturally I look like a boy, for that is what I am. With us what you call time is a spacious thing; it takes a long stretch of it to grow an angel to full age." There was a question in my mind, and he turned to me and answered it, "I am sixteen thousand years old—counting as you count." Then he turned to Nikolaus and said: "No, the Fall did not affect me nor the rest of the relationship. It was only he that I was named for who ate of the fruit of the tree and then beguiled the man and the woman with it. We others are still ignorant of sin; we are not able to commit it; we are without blemish, and shall abide in that estate always. We—" Two of the little workmen were quarreling, and in buzzing little bumblebee voices they were cursing and swearing at each other; now came blows and blood; then they locked themselves together in a life-and-death struggle. Satan reached out his hand and crushed the life out of them with his fingers, threw them away, wiped the red from his fingers on his handkerchief, and went on talking where he had left off: "We cannot do wrong; neither have we any disposition to do it, for we do not know what it is."

It seemed a strange speech, in the circumstances, but we barely noticed that, we were so shocked and grieved at the wanton murder he had committed —for murder it was, that was its true name, and it was without palliation or excuse, for the men had not wronged him in any way. It made us miserable, for we loved him, and had thought him so noble and so beautiful and gracious, and had honestly believed he was an angel; and to have him do this cruel thing—ah, it lowered him so, and we had had such pride in him. He went right on talking, just as if nothing had happened, telling about his travels and the interesting things he had seen in the big worlds of our solar system and of other solar systems far away in the remoteness of space, and about the customs of the immortals that inhabit them, somehow fascinating us, enchanting us, charming us in spite of the pitiful scene that was now under our eyes, for the wives of the little dead men had found the crushed and shapeless bodies and were crying over them, and sobbing and lamenting, and a priest was kneeling there with his hands crossed upon his breast, praying; and crowds and crowds of pitying friends were massed about them, reverently uncovered, with their bare heads bowed, and many with the tears running down—a scene which Satan paid no attention to until the small noise of the weeping and praying began to annoy [him], then he reached out and took the heavy board seat out of our swing and brought it down and mashed all those people into the earth just as if they had been flies, and went on talking just the same.

An angel, and kill a priest! An angel who did not know how to do wrong, and yet destroys in cold blood hundreds of helpless poor men and women who had never done him any harm! It made us sick to see that awful deed, and to think that none of those poor creatures was prepared except the priest, for none of them had ever heard a mass or seen a church. And we were witnesses; we had seen these murders done and it was our duty to tell, and let the law take its course.

But he went on talking right along, and worked his enchantments upon us again with that fatal music of his voice. He made us forget everything; we could only listen to him, and love him, and be his slaves, to do with us as he would. He made us drunk with the joy of being with him, and of looking into the heaven of his eyes, and of feeling the ecstasy that thrilled along our veins from the touch of his hand.

3

The Stranger had seen everything, he had been everywhere, he knew everything and he forgot nothing. What another must study, he learned at a glance; there were no difficulties for him. And he made things live before you when he told about them. He saw the world made; he saw Adam created; he saw Samson surge against the pillars and bring the temple down in ruins about him; he saw Caesar's death; he told of the daily life in heaven; he had seen the damned writhing in the red waves of hell; and he made us see all these things, and it was as if we were on the spot and looking at them with our own eyes. And we felt them, too, but there was no sign that they were anything to him beyond mere entertainments. Those visions of hell, those poor babes and women and girls and lads and men shrieking and supplicating in anguish —why, we could hardly bear it, but he was as bland about it as if it had been so many imitation rats in an artificial fire.

And always when he was talking about men and women here on the earth and their doings—even their grandest and sublimest—we were secretly ashamed, for his manner showed that to him they and their doings were of paltry poor consequence; often you would think he was talking about flies, if you didn't know. Once he even said, in so many words, that our people down here were quite interesting to him, notwithstanding they were so dull and ignorant and trivial and conceited, and so diseased and rickety and such a shabby, poor, worthless lot all around. He said it in a quite matter-of-course way and without bitterness, just as a person might talk about bricks or manure or any other thing that was of no consequence and hadn't feelings. I could see he meant no offense, but in my thoughts I set it down as not very good manners.

"Manners!" he said. "Why, it is merely the truth, and truth is good manners; manners are a fiction. The castle is done. Do you like it?"

Any one would have been obliged to like it. It was lovely to look at, it was so shapely and fine, and so cunningly perfect in all its particulars, even to the little flags waving from the turrets. Satan said we must put the artillery in place now, and station the halberdiers and display the cavalry. Our men and horses were a spectacle to see, they were so little like what they were intended for; for, of course, we had no art in making such things. Satan said they were the worst he had seen; and when he touched them and made them alive, it was just ridiculous the way they acted, on account of their legs not being of uniform lengths. They reeled and sprawled around as if they were drunk, and endangered everybody's lives around them, and finally fell over and lay helpless and kicking. It made us all laugh, though it was a shameful thing to see. The guns were charged with dirt, to fire a salute, but they were so crooked and so badly made that they all burst when they went off, and killed some of the gunners and crippled the others. Satan said we would have a storm now, and an earthquake, if we liked, but we must stand off a piece, out of danger. We wanted to call the people away, too, but he said never mind them; they were of no consequence, and we could make more, some time or other, if we needed them.

A small storm-cloud began to settle down black over the castle, and the miniature lightning and thunder began to play, and the ground to quiver, and the wind to pipe and wheeze, and the rain to fall, and all the people flocked into the castle for shelter. The cloud settled down blacker and blacker, and one could see the castle only dimly through it; the lightning blazed out flash upon flash and pierced the castle and set it on fire, and the flames shone out red and fierce through the cloud, and the people came flying out, shrieking, but Satan brushed them back, paying no attention to our begging and crying and imploring; and in the midst of the howling of the wind and volleying of the thunder the magazine blew up, the earthquake rent the ground wide, and the castle's wreck and ruin tumbled into the chasm, which swallowed it from sight, and closed upon it, with all that innocent life, not one of the five hundred poor creatures escaping. Our hearts were broken; we could not keep from crying.

"Don't cry," Satan said: "they were of no value."

"But they are gone to hell!"

"Oh, it is no matter; we can make plenty more."

It was of no use to try to move him; evidently he was wholly without feelings and could not understand. He was full of bubbling spirits, and as gay as if this were a wedding instead of a fiendish massacre. And he was bent on making us feel as he did, and of course his magic accomplished his desire. It was no trouble to him; he did whatever he pleased with us. In a little while we were dancing on that grave, and he was playing to us on a strange, sweet instrument which he took out of his pocket; and the music—but there is no music like that, unless perhaps in heaven, and that was where he brought it from, he said. It made one mad, for pleasure; and we could not take our eyes from him, and the looks that went out of our eyes came from our hearts, and their dumb speech was worship. He brought the dance from heaven, too, and the bliss of paradise was in it.

Presently he said he must go away on an errand. But we could not bear the thought of it, and clung to him, and pleaded with him to stay; and that pleased him, and he said so, and said he would not go yet, but would wait a little while and we would sit down and talk a few minutes longer; and he told us Satan was only his real name, and he was to be known by it to us alone, but he had chosen another one to be called by in the presence of others; just a common one, such as people have—Philip Traum.

It sounded so odd and mean for such a being! But it was his decision, and we said nothing; his decision was sufficient.

We had seen wonders this day; and my thoughts began to run on the pleasure it would be to tell them when I got home, but he noticed those thoughts, and said:

"No, all these matters are a secret among us four. I do not mind your trying to tell them, if you like, but I will protect your tongues and nothing of the secret will escape from them."

It was a disappointment, but it couldn't be helped, and it cost us a sigh or two. We talked pleasantly along, and he was always reading our thoughts and responding to them, and it seemed to me that this was the most wonderful of all the things he did, but he interrupted my musings, and said:

"No, it would be wonderful for you, but it is not wonderful for me. I am not limited like you. I am not subject to human conditions. I can measure and understand your human weaknesses, for I have studied them; but I have none of them. My flesh is not real, although it would seem firm to your touch; my clothes are not real; I am a spirit. Father Peter is coming.["] We looked around, but did not see any one. "He is not in sight yet, but you will see him presently."

"Do you know him, Satan?"

"No."

"Won't you talk with him when he comes? He is not ignorant and dull, like us, and he would so like to talk with you. Will you?"

"Another time, yes, but not now. I must go on my errand after a little. There he is now; you can see him. Sit still, and don't say anything."

We looked up and saw Father Peter approaching through the chestnuts. We three were sitting together in the grass, and Satan sat in front of us in the path. Father Peter came slowly along with his head down, thinking, and stopped within a couple of yards of us and took off his hat and got out his silk handkerchief, and stood there mopping his face and looking as if he were going to speak to us, but he didn't. Presently he muttered, "I can't think what brought me here; it seems as if I were in my study a minute ago—but I suppose I have been dreaming along for an hour and have come all this stretch without noticing; for I am not myself in these troubled days." Then he went mumbling along to himself and walked straight through Satan, just as if nothing were there. It made us catch our breath to see it. We had the impulse to cry out, the way you nearly always do when a startling thing happens, but something mysteriously restrained us and we remained quiet, only breathing fast. Then the trees hid Father Peter after a little, and Satan said:

"It is as I told you—I am only a spirit."

"Yes, one perceives it now," said Nikolaus, "but we are not spirits. It is plain he did not see you, but were we invisible, too? He looked at us, but he didn't seem to see us."

"No, none of us was visible to him, for I wished it so."

It seemed almost too good to be true, that we were actually seeing these romantic and wonderful things, and that it was not a dream. And there he sat, looking just like anybody—so natural and simple and charming, and chatting along again the same as ever, and—well, words cannot make you understand what we felt. It was an ecstasy; and an ecstasy is a thing that will not go into words; it feels like music, and one cannot tell about music so that another person can get the feeling of it. He was back in the old ages once more now, and making them live before us. He had seen so much! It was just a wonder to look at him and try to think how it must seem to have such experience behind one.

But it made you seem sorrowfully trivial, and the creature of a day, and such a short and paltry day, too. And he didn't say anything to raise up your drooping pride—no, not a word. He always spoke of men in the same old indifferent way—just as one speaks of bricks and manure-piles and such things; you could see that they were of no consequence to him, one way or the other. He didn't mean to hurt us, you could see that; just as we don't mean to insult a brick when we disparage it; a brick's emotions are nothing to us; it never occurs to us to think whether it has any or not.

Once when he was bunching the most illustrious kings and conquerors and poets and prophets and pirates and beggars together—just a brick-pile—I was shamed into putting in a word for man, and asked him why he made so much difference between men and himself. He had to struggle with that a moment; he didn't seem to understand how I could ask such a strange question. Then he said:

"The difference between man and me? The difference between a mortal and an immortal? between a cloud and a spirit?" He picked up a woodlouse that was creeping along a piece of bark: "What is the difference between Caesar and this?"

I said, "One cannot compare things which by their nature and by the interval between them are not comparable."

"You have answered your own question," he said. "I will expand it. Man is made of dirt—I saw him made. I am not made of dirt. Man is a museum of diseases, a home of impurities; he comes to-day and is gone to-morrow; he begins as dirt and departs as stench; I am of the aristocracy of the Imperishables. And man has the *Moral Sense*. You understand? He has the *Moral Sense*. That would seem to be difference enough between us, all by itself."

He stopped there, as if that settled the matter. I was sorry, for at that time I had but a dim idea of what the Moral Sense was. I merely knew that we were proud of having it, and when he talked like that about it, it wounded me, and I felt as a girl feels who thinks her dearest finery is being admired and then overhears strangers making fun of it. For a while we were all silent, and I, for one, was depressed. Then Satan began to chat again, and soon he was sparkling along in such a cheerful and vivacious vein that my spirits rose once more. He told some very cunning things that put us in a gale of laughter; and when he was telling about the time that Samson tied the torches to the foxes' tails and set them loose in the Philistines' corn, and Samson sitting on the fence slapping his thighs and laughing, with the tears running down his cheeks, and lost his balance and fell off the fence, the memory of that picture got him to laughing, too, and we did have a most lovely and jolly time. By and by he said:

"I am going on my errand now."

"Don't!" we all said. "Don't go; stay with us. You won't come back."

"Yes, I will; I give you my word."

"When? To-night? Say when."

"It won't be long. You will see."

"We like you."

"And I you. And as a proof of it I will show you something fine to see. Usually when I go I merely vanish; but now I will dissolve myself and let you see me do it."

He stood up and it was quickly finished. He thinned away and thinned away until he was a soap-bubble, except that he kept his shape. You could see the bushes through him as clearly as you see things through a soap-bubble, and all over him played and flashed the delicate iridescent colors of the bubble, and along with them was that thing shaped like a windowsash which you always see on the globe of the bubble. You have seen a bubble strike the carpet and lightly bound along two or three times before it bursts. He did that. He sprang—touched the grass—bounded—floated along—touched again—and so on, and presently exploded—puff! and in his place was vacancy.

It was a strange and beautiful thing to see. We did not say anything, but sat wondering and dreaming and blinking; and finally Seppi roused up and said, mournfully sighing:

"I suppose none of it has happened."

Nikolaus sighed and said about the same.

I was miserable to hear them say it, for it was the same cold fear that was in my own mind. Then we saw poor old Father Peter wandering along back, with his head bent down, searching the ground. When he was pretty close to us he looked up and saw us, and said, "How long have you been here, boys?"

"A little while, Father."

"Then it is since I came by, and maybe you can help me. Did you come up by the path?"

"Yes, Father."

"That is good. I came the same way. I have lost my wallet. There wasn't much in it, but a very little is much to me, for it was all I had. I suppose you haven't seen anything of it?"

"No, Father, but we will help you hunt."

"It is what I was going to ask you. Why, here it is!"

We hadn't noticed it; yet there it lay, right where Satan stood when he began to melt—if he did melt and it wasn't a delusion. Father Peter picked it up and looked very much surprised.

"It is mine," he said, "but not the contents. This is fat; mine was flat; mine was light; this is heavy." He opened it; it was stuffed as full as it could hold with gold coins. He let us gaze our fill; and of course we did gaze, for we had never seen so much money at one time before. All our mouths came open to say "Satan did it!" but nothing came out. There it was, you see—we couldn't tell what Satan didn't want told; he had said so himself.

"Boys, did you do this?"

It made us laugh. And it made him laugh, too, as soon as he thought what a foolish question it was.

"Who has been here?"

Our mouths came open to answer, but stood so for a moment, because we couldn't say "Nobody," for it wouldn't be true, and the right word didn't seem to come; then I thought of the right one, and said it:

"Not a human being."

"That is so," said the others, and let their mouths go shut.

"It is not so," said Father Peter, and looked at us very severely. "I came by here a while ago, and there was no one here, but that is nothing; some one has been here since. I don't mean to say that the person didn't pass here before you came, and I don't mean to say that you saw him, but some one did pass, that I know. On your honor—you saw no one?"

"Not a human being."

"That is sufficient; I know you are telling me the truth."

He began to count the money on the path, we on our knees eagerly helping to stack it in little piles.

"It's eleven hundred ducats odd!" he said. "Oh dear! if it were only mine—and I need it so!" and his voice broke and his lips quivered.

"It is yours, sir!" we all cried out at once, "every heller!"

"No—it isn't mine. Only four ducats are mine; the rest . . . !" He fell to dreaming, poor old soul, and caressing some of the coins in his hands, and forgot where he was, sitting there on his heels with his old gray head bare; it was pitiful to see. "No," he said, waking up, "it isn't mine. I can't account for it. I think some enemy . . . it must be a trap."

Nikolaus said: "Father Peter, with the exception of the astrologer you haven't a real enemy in the village—nor Marget, either. And not even a half-enemy that's rich enough to chance eleven hundred ducats to do you a mean turn. I'll ask you if that's so or not?"

He couldn't get around that argument, and it cheered him up. "But it isn't mine, you see—it isn't mine, in any case."

He said it in a wistful way, like a person that wouldn't be sorry, but glad, if anybody would contradict him.

"It is yours, Father Peter, and we are witness to it. Aren't we, boys?"

"Yes, we are—and we'll stand by it, too."

"Bless your hearts, you do almost persuade me; you do, indeed. If I had only a hundred-odd ducats of it! The house is mortgaged for it, and we've no home for our heads if we don't pay to-morrow. And that four ducats is all we've got in the—"

"It's yours, every bit of it, and you've got to take it—we are bail that it's all right. Aren't we, Theodor? Aren't we, Seppi?"

We two said yes, and Nikolaus stuffed the money back into the shabby old wallet and made the owner take it. So he said he would use two hundred of it, for his house was good enough security for that, and would put the rest at interest till the rightful owner came for it; and on our side we must sign a paper showing how he got the money—a paper to show to the villagers as proof that he had not got out of his troubles dishonestly.

4

It made immense talk next day, when Father Peter paid Solomon Isaacs in gold and left the rest of the money with him at interest. Also, there was a pleasant change; many people called at the house to congratulate him, and a number of cool old friends became kind and friendly again; and to top all, Marget was invited to a party.

And there was no mystery; Father Peter told the whole circumstance just as it happened, and said he could not account for it, only it was the plain hand of Providence, so far as he could see.

One or two shook their heads and said privately it looked more like the hand of Satan; and really that seemed a surprisingly good guess for ignorant people like that. Some came slyly buzzing around and tried to coax us boys to come out and "tell the truth"; and promised they wouldn't ever tell but only wanted to know for their own satisfaction, because the whole thing was so curious. They even wanted to buy the secret, and pay money for it; and if we could have invented something that would answer—but we couldn't; we hadn't the ingenuity, so we had to let the chance go by, and it was a pity.

We carried that secret around without any trouble, but the other one, the big one, the splendid one, burned the very vitals of us, it was so hot to get out and we so hot to let it out and astonish people with it. But we had to keep it in; in fact, it kept itself in. Satan said it would, and it did. We went off every day and got to ourselves in the woods so that we could talk about Satan, and really that was the only subject we thought of or cared anything about; and day and night we watched for him and hoped he would come, and we got more and more impatient all the time. We hadn't any interest in the other boys any more, and wouldn't take part in their games and enterprises. They seemed so tame, after Satan; and their doings so trifling and commonplace after his adventures in antiquity and the constellations, and his miracles and meltings and explosions, and all that.

During the first day we were in a state of anxiety on account of one thing, and we kept going to Father Peter's house on one pretext or another to keep track of it. That was the gold coin; we were afraid it would crumble and turn to dust, like fairy money. If it did—But it didn't. At the end of the day no complaint had been made about it, so after that we were satisfied that it was real gold, and dropped the anxiety out of our minds.

There was a question which we wanted to ask Father Peter, and finally we went there the second evening, a little diffidently, after drawing straws, and I asked it as casually as I could, though it did not sound as casual as I wanted, because I didn't know how:

"What is the Moral Sense, sir?"

He looked down, surprised, over his great spectacles, and said, "Why, it is the faculty which enables us to distinguish good from evil."

It threw some light, but not a glare, and I was a little disappointed, also to some degree embarrassed. He was waiting for me to go on, so, in default of anything else to say, I asked, "Is it valuable?"

"Valuable? Heavens! lad, it is the one thing that lifts man above the beasts that perish and makes him heir to immortality!"

This did not remind me of anything further to say, so I got out, with the other boys, and we went away with that indefinite sense you have often had of being filled but not fatted. They wanted me to explain but I was tired.

We passed out through the parlor, and there was Marget at the spinnet teaching Marie Lueger. So one of the deserting pupils was back; and an influential one too; the others would follow. Marget jumped up and ran and thanked us again with tears in her eyes—this was the third time—for saving her and her uncle from being turned into the street, and we told her again we hadn't done it; but that was her way, she never could be grateful enough for anything a person did for her; so we let her have her say. And as we passed through the garden, there was Wilhelm Meidling sitting there waiting, for it was getting toward the edge of the evening, and he would be asking Marget to take a walk along the river with him when she was done with the lesson. He was a young lawyer, and succeeding fairly well and working his way along, little by little. He was very fond of Marget, and she of him. He had not deserted along with the others, but had stood his ground all through. His faithfulness was not lost on Marget and her uncle. He hadn't so very much talent but he was handsome and good, and these are a kind of talents themselves and help along. He asked us how the lesson was getting along, and we told him it was about done. And maybe it was so; we didn't know anything about it, but we judged it would please him, and it did, and it didn't cost us anything.

5

On the fourth day comes the astrologer from his crumbling old tower up the valley, where he had heard the news, I reckon. He had a private talk with us, and we told him what we could, for we were mightily in dread of him. He sat there studying and studying awhile to himself; then he asked:

"How many ducats did you say?"

"Eleven hundred and seven, sir."

Then he said, as if he were talking to himself: "It is ver-y singular. Yes . . . very strange. A curious coincidence." Then he began to ask questions, and went over the whole ground from the beginning, we answering. By and by he said: "Eleven hundred and six ducats. It is a large sum."

"Seven," said Seppi, correcting him.

"Oh, seven, was it? Of course a ducat more or less isn't of consequence, but you said eleven hundred and six before."

It would not have been safe for us to say he was mistaken, but we knew he was. Nikolaus said, "We ask pardon for the mistake, but we meant to say seven."

"Oh, it is no matter lad; it was merely that I noticed the discrepancy. It is several days, and you cannot be expected to remember precisely. One is apt to be inexact when there is no particular circumstance to impress the count upon the memory."

"But there was one, sir," said Seppi, eagerly.

"What was it, my son?" asked the astrologer, indifferently.

"First, we all counted the piles of coin, each in turn, and all made it the same—eleven hundred and six. But I had slipped one out, for fun, when the count began, and now I slipped it back and said, 'I think there is a mistake— there are eleven hundred and seven; let us count again.' We did, and of course I was right. They were astonished; then I told how it came about."

The astrologer asked us if this was so, and we said it was.

"That settles it," he said. "I know the thief now. Lads, the money was stolen."

Then he went away, leaving us very much troubled, and wondering what he could mean. In about an hour we found out; for by that time it was all over the village that Father Peter had been arrested for stealing a great sum of money from the astrologer. Everybody's tongue was loose and going. Many said it was not in Father Peter's character and must be a mistake; but the others shook their heads and said misery and want could drive a suffering man to almost anything. About one detail there were no differences; all agreed that Father Peter's account of how the money came into his hands was just about unbelievable—it had such an impossible look. They said it might have come into the astrologer's hands in some such way, but into Father Peter's, never! Our characters began to suffer now. We were Father Peter's only witnesses; how much did he probably pay us to back up his fantastic tale? People talked that kind of talk to us pretty freely and frankly, and were full of scoffings when we begged them to believe really we had told only the truth. Our parents were harder on us than any one else. Our fathers said we were disgracing our families, and they commanded us to purge ourselves of our lie, and there was no limit to their anger when we continued to say we had spoken true. Our mothers cried over us and begged us to give back our bribe and get back our honest names and save our families from shame, and come out and honorably confess. And at last we were so worried and harassed that we tried to tell the whole thing, Satan and all—but no, it wouldn't come out. We were hoping and longing all the time that Satan would come and help us out of our trouble, but there was no sign of him.

Within an hour after the astrologer's talk with us, Father Peter was in prison and the money sealed up and in the hands of the officers of the law. The money was in a bag, and Solomon Isaacs said he had not touched it since he had counted it; his oath was taken that it was the same money, and that the amount was eleven hundred and seven ducats. Father Peter claimed trial by the ecclesiastical court, but our other priest, Father Adolf, said an ecclesiastical court hadn't jurisdiction over a suspended priest. The bishop upheld him. That settled it; the case would go to trial in the civil court. The court would not sit for some time to come. Wilhelm Meidling would be Father Peter's lawyer and do the best he could, of course, but he told us privately that a weak case on his side and all the power and prejudice on the other made the outlook bad.

So Marget's new happiness died a quick death. No friends came to condole with her, and none were expected; an unsigned note withdrew her invitation to the party. There would be no scholars to take lessons. How could she support herself? She could remain in the house, for the mortgage was paid off, though the government and not poor Solomon Isaacs had the mortgage-money in its grip for the present. Old Ursula, who was cook, chambermaid, housekeeper, laundress, and everything else for Father Peter, and had been Marget's nurse in earlier years, said God would provide. But she said that from habit, for she was a good Christian. She meant to help in the providing, to make sure, if she could find a way.

We boys wanted to go and see Marget and show friendliness for her, but our parents were afraid of offending the community and wouldn't let us. The astrologer was going around inflaming everybody against Father Peter, and saying he was an abandoned thief and had stolen eleven hundred and seven gold ducats from him. He said he knew he was a thief from that fact, for it was exactly the sum he had lost and which Father Peter pretended he had "found."

In the afternoon of the fourth day after the catastrophe old Ursula appeared at our house and asked for some washing to do, and begged my mother to keep this secret, to save Marget's pride, who would stop this project if she found it out, yet Marget had not enough to eat and was growing weak. Ursula was growing weak herself, and showed it; and she ate of the food that was offered her like a starving person, but could not be persuaded to carry any home, for Marget would not eat charity food. She took some clothes down to the stream to wash them, but we saw from the window that handling the bat was too much for her strength; so she was called back and a trifle of money offered her, which she was afraid to take lest Marget should suspect; then she took it, saying she would explain that she found it in the road. To keep it from being a lie and damning her soul, she got me to drop it while she watched; then she went along by there and found it, and exclaimed with surprise and joy, and picked it up and went her way. Like the rest of the village, she could tell every-day lies fast enough and without taking any precautions against fire and brimstone on their account; but this was a new kind of lie, and it had a dangerous look because she hadn't had any practice in it. After a week's practice it wouldn't have given her any trouble. It is the way we are made.

I was in trouble, for how would Marget live? Ursula could not find a coin in the road every day—perhaps not even a second one. And I was ashamed, too, for not having been near Marget, and she so in need of friends; but that was my parents' fault, not mine, and I couldn't help it.

I was walking along the path, feeling very downhearted, when a most cheery and tingling freshening-up sensation went rippling through me, and I was too glad for any words, for I knew by that sign that Satan was by. I had noticed it before. Next moment he was alongside of me and I was telling him all my trouble and what had been happening to Marget and her uncle. While we were talking we turned a curve and saw old Ursula resting in the shade of a tree, and she had a lean stray kitten in her lap and was petting it. I asked her where she got it, and she said it came out of the woods and followed her; and she said it probably hadn't any mother or any friends and she was going to take it home and take care of it. Satan said:

"I understand you are very poor. Why do you want to add another mouth to feed? Why don't you give it to some rich person?"

Ursula bridled at this and said: "Perhaps you would like to have it. You must be rich, with your fine clothes and quality airs." Then she sniffed and said: "Give it to the rich—the idea! The rich don't care for anybody but themselves; it's only the poor that have feeling for the poor, and help them. The poor and God. God will provide for this kitten."

"What makes you think so?"

Ursula's eyes snapped with anger. "Because I know it!" she said. "Not a sparrow falls to the ground without His seeing it."

"But it falls, just the same. What good is seeing it fall?"

Old Ursula's jaws worked, but she could not get any word out for the moment, she was so horrified. When she got her tongue she stormed out, "Go about your business, you puppy, or I will take a stick to you!"

I could not speak, I was so scared. I knew that with his notions about the human race Satan would consider it a matter of no consequence to strike her dead, there being "plenty more"; but my tongue stood still, I could give her no warning. But nothing happened; Satan remained tranquil—tranquil and indifferent. I suppose he could not be insulted by Ursula any more than the king could be insulted by a tumble-bug. The old woman jumped to her feet when she made her remark, and did it as briskly as a young girl. It had been many years since she had done the like of that. That was Satan's influence; he was a fresh breeze to the weak and the sick, wherever he came. His presence affected even the lean kitten, and it skipped to the ground and began to chase a leaf. This surprised Ursula, and she stood looking at the creature and nodding her head wonderingly, her anger quite forgotten.

"What's come over it?" she said. "Awhile ago it could hardly walk."

"You have not seen a kitten of that breed before," said Satan.

Ursula was not proposing to be friendly with the mocking stranger, and she gave him an ungentle look and retorted: "Who asked you to come here and pester me, I'd like to know? And what do you know about what I've seen and what I haven't seen?"

"You haven't seen a kitten with the hair-spines on its tongue pointing to the front, have you?"

"No—nor you, either."

"Well, examine this one and see."

Ursula was become pretty spry, but the kitten was spryer, and she could not catch it, and had to give it up. Then Satan said:

"Give it a name, and maybe it will come."

Ursula tried several names, but the kitten was not interested.

"Call it Agnes. Try that."

The creature answered to the name and came. Ursula examined its tongue. "Upon my word, it's true!" she said. "I have not seen this kind of a cat before. Is it yours?"

"No."

"Then how did you know its name so pat?"

"Because all cats of that breed are named Agnes; they will not answer to any other."

Ursula was impressed. "It is the most wonderful thing!" Then a shadow of trouble came into her face, for her superstitions were aroused, and she reluctantly put the creature down, saying: "I suppose I must let it go; I am not afraid—no, not exactly that, though the priest—well, I've heard people—indeed, many people . . . And, besides, it is quite well now and can take care of itself." She sighed, and turned to go, murmuring: "It is such a pretty one, too, and would be such company—and the house is so sad and lonesome these troubled days . . . Miss Marget so mournful and just a shadow, and the old master shut up in jail."

"It seems a pity not to keep it," said Satan.

Ursula turned quickly—just as if she were hoping some one would encourage her.

"Why?" she asked, wistfully.

"Because this breed brings luck."

"Does it? Is it true? Young man, do you know it to be true? How does it bring luck?"

"Well, it brings money, anyway."

Ursula looked disappointed. "Money? A cat bring money? The idea! You could never sell it here; people do not buy cats here; one can't even give them away." She turned to go.

"I don't mean sell it. I mean have an income from it. This kind is called the Lucky Cat. Its owner finds four silver groschen in his pocket every morning."

I saw the indignation rising in the old woman's face. She was insulted. This boy was making fun of her. That was her thought. She thrust her hands into her pockets and straightened up to give him a piece of her mind. Her temper was all up, and hot. Her mouth came open and let out three words of a bitter sentence, . . . then it fell silent, and the anger in her face turned to surprise or wonder or fear, or something, and she slowly brought out her hands from her pockets and opened them and held them so. In one was my piece of money, in the other lay four silver groschen. She gazed a little while, perhaps to see if the groschen would vanish away; then she said, fervently:

"It's true—it's true—and I'm ashamed and beg forgiveness, O dear master and benefactor!" And she ran to Satan and kissed his hand, over and over again, according to the Austrian custom.

In her heart she probably believed it was a witch-cat and an agent of the Devil; but no matter, it was all the more certain to be able to keep its contract and furnish a daily good living for the family, for in matters of finance even the piousest of our peasants would have more confidence in an arrangement with the Devil than with an archangel. Ursula started homeward with Agnes in her arms, and I said I wished I had her privilege of seeing Marget.

Then I caught my breath, for we were there. There in the parlor, and Marget standing looking at us, astonished. She was feeble and pale, but I knew that those conditions would not last in Satan's atmosphere, and it turned out so. I introduced Satan—that is, Philip Traum—and we sat down and talked. There was no constraint. We were simple folk, in our village, and when a stranger was a pleasant person we were soon friends. Marget wondered how we got in without her hearing us. Traum said the door was open, and we walked in and waited until she should turn around and greet us. This was not true; no door was open; we entered through the walls or the roof or down the chimney, or somehow; but no matter, what Satan wished a person to believe, the person was sure to believe, and so Marget was quite satisfied with that explanation. And then the main part of her mind was on Traum, anyway; she couldn't keep her eyes off him, he was so beautiful. That gratified me, and made me proud. I hoped he would show off some, but he didn't. He seemed only interested in being friendly and telling lies. He said he was an orphan. That made Marget pity him. The water came into her eyes. He said he had never known his mamma; she passed away while he was a young thing; and said his papa was in shattered health, and had no property to speak of—in fact, none of any earthly value—but he had an uncle in business down in the tropics, and he was very well off and had a monopoly, and it was from this uncle that he drew his support. The very mention of a kind uncle was enough to remind Marget of her own, and her eyes filled again. She said she hoped their two uncles would meet, some day. It made me shudder. Philip said he hoped so, too; and that made me shudder again.

"Maybe they will," said Marget. "Does your uncle travel much?"

"Oh yes, he goes all about; he has business everywhere."

And so they went on chatting, and poor Marget forgot her sorrow for one little while, anyway. It was probably the only really bright and cheery hour she had known lately. I saw she liked Philip, and I knew she would. And when he told her he was studying for the ministry I could see that she liked him better than ever. And then, when he promised to get her admitted to the jail so that she could see her uncle, that was the capstone. He said he would give the guards a little present, and she must always go in the evening after dark, and say nothing "but just show this paper and pass in, and show it again when you come out"—and he scribbled some queer marks on the paper and gave it to her, and she was ever so thankful, and right away was in a fever for the sun to go down; for in that old, cruel time prisoners were not allowed to see their friends, and sometimes they spent years in the jails without ever seeing a friendly face. I judged that the marks on the paper were an enchantment, and that the guards would not know what they were doing, nor have any memory of it afterward; and that was indeed the way of it. Ursula put her head in at the door now and said:

"Supper's ready, miss." Then she saw us and looked frightened, and motioned me to come to her, which I did, and she asked if we had told about the cat. I said no, and she was relieved and said please don't, for if Miss Marget knew, she would think it was an unholy cat and would send for a priest and have its gifts all purified out of it, and then there wouldn't be any more dividends. So I said we wouldn't tell, and she was satisfied. Then I was beginning to say good-by to Marget, but Satan interrupted and said, ever so politely—well, I don't remember just the words, but anyway he as good as invited himself to supper, and me, too. Of course Marget was miserably embarrassed, for she had no reason to suppose there would be half enough for a sick bird. Ursula heard him, and she came straight into the room, not a bit pleased. At first she was astonished to see Marget looking so fresh and rosy, and said so; then she spoke up in her native tongue, which was Bohemian, and said—as I learned afterward—"Send him away, Miss Marget; there's not victuals enough."

Before Marget could speak, Satan had the word, and was talking back to Ursula in her own language—which was a surprise to her, and for her mistress, too. He said, "Didn't I see you down the road awhile ago?"

"Yes, sir."

"Ah, that pleases me; I see you remember me." He stepped to her and whispered: "I told you it is a Lucky Cat. Don't be troubled; it will provide."

That sponged the slate of Ursula's feelings clean of its anxieties, and a deep, financial joy shone in her eyes. The cat's value was augmenting. It was getting full time for Marget to take some sort of notice of Satan's invitation, and she did it in the best way, the honest way that was natural to her. She said she had little to offer, but that we were welcome if he would share it with her.

We had supper in the kitchen, and Ursula waited at table. A small fish was in the frying-pan, crisp and brown and tempting, and one could see that Marget was not expecting such respectable food as this. Ursula brought it, and Marget divided it between Satan and me, declining to take any of it herself; and was beginning to say she did not care for fish to-day, but she did not finish the remark. It was because she noticed that another fish had appeared in the pan. She looked surprised, but did not say anything. She probably meant to inquire of Ursula about this later. There were other surprises: flesh and game and wines and fruits—things which had been strangers in that house lately; but Marget made no exclamations, and now even looked unsurprised, which was Satan's influence, of course. Satan talked right along, and was entertaining, and made the time pass pleasantly and cheerfully; and although he told a good many lies, it was no harm in him, for he was only an angel and did not know any better. They do not know right from wrong; I knew this, because I remembered what he had said about it. He got on the good side of Ursula. He praised her to Marget, confidentially, but speaking just loud enough for Ursula to hear. He said she was a fine woman, and he hoped some day to bring her and his uncle together. Very soon Ursula was mincing and simpering around in a ridiculous, girly way, and smoothing out her gown and prinking at herself like a foolish old hen, and all the time pretending she was not hearing what Satan was saying. I was ashamed, for it showed us to be what Satan considered us, a silly race and trivial. Satan said his uncle entertained a great deal, and to have a clever woman presiding over the festivities would double the attractions of the place.

"But your uncle is a gentleman, isn't he?" asked Marget.

"Yes," said Satan indifferently; "some even call him a Prince, out of compliment, but he is not bigoted; to him personal merit is everything, rank nothing."

My hand was hanging down by my chair; Agnes came along and licked it; by this act a secret was revealed. I started to say, "It is all a mistake; this is just a common, ordinary cat; the hair-needles on her tongue point inward, not outward." But the words did not come, because they couldn't. Satan smiled upon me, and I understood.

When it was dark Marget took food and wine and fruit, in a basket, and hurried away to the jail, and Satan and I walked toward my home. I was thinking to myself that I should like to see what the inside of the jail was like; Satan overheard the thought, and the next moment we were in the jail. We were in the torture-chamber, Satan said. The rack was there, and the other instruments, and there was a smoky lantern or two hanging on the walls and helping to make the place look dim and dreadful. There were people there —and executioners—but as they took no notice of us, it meant that we were invisible. A young man lay bound, and Satan said he was suspected of being a heretic, and the executioners were about to inquire into it. They asked the man to confess to the charge, and he said he could not, for it was not true. Then they drove splinter after splinter under his nails, and he shrieked with the pain. Satan was not disturbed, but I could not endure it, and had to be whisked out of there. I was faint and sick, but the fresh air revived me, and we walked toward my home. I said it was a brutal thing.

"No, it was a human thing. You should not insult the brutes by such a misuse of that word; they have not deserved it," and he went on talking like that. "It is like your paltry race—always lying, always claiming virtues which it hasn't got, always denying them to the higher animals, which alone possess them. No brute ever does a cruel thing—that is the monopoly of those with the Moral Sense. When a brute inflicts pain he does it innocently; it is not wrong; for him there is no such thing as wrong. And he does not inflict pain for the pleasure of inflicting it—only man does that. Inspired by that mongrel Moral Sense of his! A sense whose function is to distinguish between right and wrong, with liberty to choose which of them he will do. Now what advantage can he get out of that? He is always choosing, and in nine cases out of ten he prefers the wrong. There shouldn't be any wrong; and without the Moral Sense there couldn't be any. And yet he is such an unreasoning creature that he is not able to perceive that the Moral Sense degrades him to the bottom layer of animated beings and is a shameful possession. Are you feeling better? Let me show you something."

6

In a moment we were in a French village. We walked through a great factory of some sort, where men and women and little children were toiling in heat and dirt and a fog of dust; and they were clothed in rags, and drooped at their work, for they were worn and half starved, and weak and drowsy. Satan said:

"It is some more Moral Sense. The proprietors are rich, and very holy; but the wage they pay to these poor brothers and sisters of theirs is only enough to keep them from dropping dead with hunger. The work-hours are fourteen per day, winter and summer—from six in the morning till eight at night—little children and all. And they walk to and from the pig-sties which they inhabit—four miles each way, through mud and slush, rain, snow, sleet, and storm, daily, year in and year out. They get four hours of sleep. They kennel together, three families in a room, in unimaginable filth and stench; and disease comes, and they die off like flies. Have they committed a crime, these mangy things? No. What have they done, that they are punished so? Nothing at all, except getting themselves born into your foolish race. You have seen how they treat a misdoer there in the jail; now you see how they treat the innocent and the worthy. Is your race logical? Are these ill-smelling innocents better off than that heretic? Indeed, no; his punishment is trivial compared with theirs. They broke him on the wheel and smashed him to rags and pulp after we left, and he is dead now, and free of your precious race; but these poor slaves here—why, they have been dying for years, and some of them will not escape from life for years to come. It is the Moral Sense which teaches the factory proprietors the difference between right and wrong—you perceive the result. They think themselves better than dogs. Ah, you are such an illogical, unreasoning race! And paltry—oh, unspeakably!"

Then he dropped all seriousness and just overstrained himself making fun of us, and deriding our pride in our warlike deeds, our great heroes, our imperishable fames, our mighty kings, our ancient aristocracies, our venerable history—and laughed and laughed till it was enough to make a person sick to hear him; and finally he sobered a little and said, "But, after all, it is not all ridiculous; there is a sort of pathos about it when one remembers how few are your days, how childish your pomps, and what shadows you are!"

Presently all things vanished suddenly from my sight, and I knew what it meant. The next moment we were walking along in our village; and down toward the river I saw the twinkling lights of the Golden Stag. Then in the dark I heard a joyful cry:

"He's come again!"

It was Seppi Wohlmeyer. He had felt his blood leap and his spirits rise in a way that could mean only one thing, and he knew Satan was near, although it was too dark to see him. He came to us, and we walked along together, and Seppi poured out his gladness like water. It was as if he were a lover and had found his sweetheart who had been lost. Seppi was a smart and animated boy, and had enthusiasm and expression, and was a contrast to Nikolaus and me. He was full of the last new mystery, now—the disappearance of Hans Oppert, the village loafer. People were beginning to be curious about it, he said. He did not say anxious—curious was the right word, and strong enough. No one had seen Hans for a couple of days.

"Not since he did that brutal thing, you know," he said.

"What brutal thing?" It was Satan that asked.

"Well, he is always clubbing his dog, which is a good dog and his only friend, and is faithful, and loves him, and does no one any harm; and two days ago he was at it again, just for nothing—just for pleasure—and the dog was howling and begging, and Theodor and I begged, too, but he threatened us, and struck the dog again with all his might and knocked one of his eyes out, and he said to us, 'There, I hope you are satisfied now; that's what you have got for him by your damned meddling'—and he laughed, the heartless brute." Seppi's voice trembled with pity and anger. I guessed what Satan would say, and he said it.

"There is that misused word again—that shabby slander. Brutes do not act like that, but only men."

"Well, it was inhuman, anyway."

"No, it wasn't, Seppi; it was human—quite distinctly human. It is not pleasant to hear you libel the higher animals by attributing to them dispositions which they are free from, and which are found nowhere but in the human heart. None of the higher animals is tainted with the disease called the Moral Sense. Purify your language, Seppi; drop those lying phrases out of it."

He spoke pretty sternly—for him—and I was sorry I hadn't warned Seppi to be more particular about the word he used. I knew how he was feeling. He would not want to offend Satan; he would rather offend all his kin. There was an uncomfortable silence, but relief soon came, for that poor dog came along now, with his eye hanging down, and went straight to Satan, and began to moan and mutter brokenly, and Satan began to answer in the same way, and it was plain that they were talking together in the dog language. We all sat down in the grass, in the moonlight, for the clouds were breaking away now, and Satan took the dog's head in his lap and put the eye back in its place, and the dog was comfortable, and he wagged his tail and licked Satan's hand, and looked thankful and said the same; I knew he was saying it, though I did not understand the words. Then the two talked together a bit, and Satan said:

"He says his master was drunk."

"Yes, he was," said we.

"And an hour later he fell over the precipice there beyond the Cliff Pasture."

"We know the place; it is three miles from here."

"And the dog has been often to the village, begging people to go there, but he was only driven away and not listened to."

We remembered it, but hadn't understood what he wanted.

"He only wanted help for the man who had misused him, and he thought only of that, and has had no food nor sought any. He has watched by his master two nights. What do you think of your race? Is heaven reserved for it, and this dog ruled out, as your teachers tell you? Can your race add anything to this dog's stock of morals and magnanimities?" He spoke to the creature, who jumped up, eager and happy, and apparently ready for orders and impatient to execute them. "Get some men; go with the dog—he will show you that carrion; and take a priest along to arrange about insurance, for death is near."

With the last word he vanished, to our sorrow and disappointment. We got the men and Father Adolf, and we saw the man die. Nobody cared but the dog; he mourned and grieved, and licked the dead face, and could not be comforted. We buried him where he was, and without a coffin, for he had no money, and no friend but the dog. If we had been an hour earlier the priest would have been in time to send that poor creature to heaven, but now he was gone down into the awful fires, to burn forever. It seemed such a pity that in a world where so many people have difficulty to put in their time, one little hour could have been spared for this poor creature who needed it so much, and to whom it would have made the difference between eternal joy and eternal pain. It gave an appalling idea of the value of an hour, and I thought I could never waste one again without remorse and terror. Seppi was depressed and grieved, and said it must be so much better to be a dog and not run such awful risks. We took this one home with us and kept him for our own. Seppi had a very good thought as we were walking along, and it cheered us up and made us feel much better. He said the dog had forgiven the man that had wronged him so, and maybe God would accept that absolution.

There was a very dull week, now, for Satan did not come, nothing much was going on, and we boys could not venture to go and see Marget, because the nights were moonlit and our parents might find us out if we tried. But we came across Ursula a couple of times taking a walk in the meadows beyond the river to air the cat, and we learned from her that things were going well. She had natty new clothes on and bore a prosperous look. The four groschen a day were arriving without a break, but were not being spent for food and wine and such things—the cat attended to all that.

Marget was enduring her forsakenness and isolation fairly well, all things considered, and was cheerful, by help of Wilhelm Meidling. She spent an hour or two every night in the jail with her uncle, and had fattened him up with the cat's contributions. But she was curious to know more about Philip Traum, and hoped I would bring him again. Ursula was curious about him herself, and asked a good many questions about his uncle. It made the boys laugh, for I had told them the nonsense Satan had been stuffing her with. She got no satisfaction out of us, our tongues being tied.

Ursula gave us a small item of information: money being plenty now, she had taken on a servant to help about the house and run errands. She tried to tell it in a commonplace, matter-of-course way, but she was so set up by it and so vain of it that her pride in it leaked out pretty plainly. It was beautiful to see her veiled delight in this grandeur, poor old thing, but when we heard the name of the servant we wondered if she had been altogether wise; for although we were young, and often thoughtless, we had fairly good perception on some matters. This boy was Gottfried Narr, a dull, good creature, with no harm in him and nothing against him personally; still, he was under a cloud, and properly so, for it had not been six months since a social blight had mildewed the family—his grandmother had been burned as a witch. When that kind of a malady is in the blood it does not always come out with just one burning. Just now was not a good time for Ursula and Marget to be having dealings with a member of such a family, for the witch-terror had risen higher during the past year than it had ever reached in the memory of the oldest villagers. The mere mention of a witch was almost enough to frighten us out of our wits. This was natural enough, because of late years there were more kinds of witches than there used to be; in old times it had been only old women, but of late years they were of all ages—even children of eight and nine; it was getting so that anybody might turn out to be a familiar of the Devil—age and sex hadn't anything to do with it. In our little region we had tried to extirpate the witches, but the more of them we burned the more of the breed rose up in their places.

Once, in a school for girls only ten miles away, the teachers found that the back of one of the girls was all red and inflamed, and they were greatly frightened, believing it to be the Devil's marks. The girl was scared, and begged them not to denounce her, and said it was only fleas; but of course it would not do to let the matter rest there. All the girls were examined, and eleven out of the fifty were badly marked, the rest less so. A commission was appointed, but the eleven only cried for their mothers and would not confess. Then they were shut up, each by herself, in the dark, and put on black bread and water for ten days and nights; and by that time they were haggard and wild, and their eyes were dry and they did not cry any more, but only sat and mumbled, and would not take the food. Then one of them confessed, and said they had often ridden through the air on broomsticks to the witches' Sabbath, and in a bleak place high up in the mountains had danced and drunk and caroused with several hundred other witches and the Evil One, and all had conducted themselves in a scandalous way and had reviled the priests and blasphemed God. That is what she said—not in narrative form, for she was not able to remember any of the details without having them called to her mind one after the other; but the commission did that, for they knew just what questions to ask, they being all written down for the use of witch-commissioners two centuries before. They asked, "Did you do so and so?" and she always said yes, and looked weary and tired, and took no interest in it. And so when the other ten heard that this one confessed, they confessed, too, and answered yes to the questions. Then they were burned at the stake all together, which was just and right; and everybody went from all the country-side to see it. I went, too; but when I saw that one of them was a bonny, sweet girl I used to play with, and looked so pitiful there chained to the stake, and her mother crying over her and devouring her with kisses and clinging around her neck, and saying, "Oh, my God! oh, my God!" it was too dreadful, and I went away.

It was bitter cold weather when Gottfried's grandmother was burned. It was charged that she had cured bad headaches by kneading the person's head and neck with her fingers—as she said—but really by the Devil's help, as everybody knew. They were going to examine her, but she stopped them, and confessed straight off that her power was from the Devil. So they appointed to burn her next morning, early, in our market-square. The officer who was to prepare the fire was there first, and prepared it. She was there next —brought by the constables, who left her and went to fetch another witch. Her family did not come with her. They might be reviled, maybe stoned, if the people were excited. I came, and gave her an apple. She was squatting at the fire, warming herself and waiting; and her old lips and hands were blue with the cold. A stranger came next. He was a traveler, passing through; and he spoke to her gently, and, seeing nobody but me there to hear, said he was sorry for her. And he asked if what she confessed was true, and she said no. He looked surprised and still more sorry then, and asked her:

"Then why did you confess?"

"I am old and very poor," she said, "and I work for my living. There was no way but to confess. If I hadn't they might have set me free. That would ruin me, for no one would forget that I had been suspected of being a witch, and so I would get no more work, and wherever I went they would set the dogs on me. In a little while I would starve. The fire is best; it is soon over. You have been good to me, you two, and I thank you."

She snuggled closer to the fire, and put out her hands to warm them, the snow-flakes descending soft and still on her old gray beard and making it white and whiter. The crowd was gathering now, and an egg came flying and struck her in the eye, and broke and ran down her face. There was a laugh at that.

I told Satan all about the eleven girls and the old woman, once, but it did not affect him. He only said it was the human race, and what the human race did was of no consequence. And he said he had seen it made; and it was not made of clay; it was made of mud—part of it was, anyway. I knew what he meant by that—the Moral Sense. He saw the thought in my head, and it tickled him and made him laugh. Then he called a bullock out of a pasture and petted it and talked with it, and said:

"There—he wouldn't drive children mad with hunger and fright and loneliness, and then burn them for confessing to things invented for them which had never happened. And neither would he break the hearts of innocent, poor old women and make them afraid to trust themselves among their own race; and he would not insult them in their death-agony. For he is not besmirched with the Moral Sense, but is as the angels are, and knows no wrong, and never does it."

Lovely as he was, Satan could be cruelly offensive when he chose; and he always chose when the human race was brought to his attention. He always turned up his nose at it, and never had a kind word for it.

Well, as I was saying, we boys doubted if it was a good time for Ursula to be hiring a member of the Narr family. We were right. When the people found it out they were naturally indignant. And, moreover, since

Marget and Ursula hadn't enough to eat themselves, where was the money coming from to feed another mouth? That is what they wanted to know; and in order to find out they stopped avoiding Gottfried and began to seek his society and have sociable conversations with him. He was pleased—not thinking any harm and not seeing the trap—and so he talked innocently along, and was no discreeter than a cow.

"Money!" he said; "they've got plenty of it. They pay me two groschen a week, besides my keep. And they live on the fat of the land, I can tell you; the prince himself can't beat their table."

This astonishing statement was conveyed by the astrologer to Father Adolf on a Sunday morning when he was returning from mass. He was deeply moved, and said:

"This must be looked into."

He said there must be witchcraft at the bottom of it, and told the villagers to resume relations with Marget and Ursula in a private and unostentatious way, and keep both eyes open. They were told to keep their own counsel and not rouse the suspicions of the household. The villagers were at first a bit reluctant to enter such a dreadful place, but the priest said they would be under his protection while there, and no harm could come to them, particularly if they carried a trifle of holy water along and kept their beads and crosses handy. This satisfied them and made them willing to go; envy and malice made the baser sort even eager to go.

And so poor Marget began to have company again, and was as pleased as a cat. She was like 'most anybody else—just human, and happy in her prosperities and not averse from showing them off a little; and she was humanly grateful to have the warm shoulder turned to her and be smiled upon by her friends and the village again; for of all the hard things to bear, to be cut by your neighbors and left in contemptuous solitude is maybe the hardest.

The bars were down, and we could all go there now, and we did—our parents and all—day after day. The cat began to strain herself. She provided the top of everything for those companies, and in abundance—among them many a dish and many a wine which they had not tasted before and which they had not even heard of except at second-hand from the prince's servants. And the tableware was much above ordinary, too.

Marget was troubled at times, and pursued Ursula with questions to an uncomfortable degree; but Ursula stood her ground and stuck to it that it was Providence, and said no word about the cat. Marget knew that nothing was impossible to Providence, but she could not help having doubts that this effort was from there, though she was afraid to say so, lest disaster come of it. Witchcraft occurred to her, but she put the thought aside, for this was before Gottfried joined the household, and she knew Ursula was pious and a bitter hater of witches. By the time Gottfried arrived Providence was established, unshakably intrenched, and getting all the gratitude. The cat made no murmur, but went on composedly improving in style and prodigality by experience.

In any community, big or little, there is always a fair proportion of people who are not malicious or unkind by nature, and who never do unkind things except when they are overmastered by fear, or when their self-interest is greatly in danger, or some such matter as that. Eseldorf had its proportion of such people, and ordinarily their good and gentle influence was felt, but these were not ordinary times—on account of the witch-dread—and so we did not seem to have any gentle and compassionate hearts left, to speak of. Every person was frightened at the unaccountable state of things at Marget's house, not doubting that witchcraft was at the bottom of it, and fright frenzied their reason. Naturally there were some who pitied Marget and Ursula for the danger that was gathering about them, but naturally they did not say so; it would not have been safe. So the others had it all their own way, and there was none to advise the ignorant girl and the foolish woman and warn them to modify their doings. We boys wanted to warn them, but we backed down when it came to the pinch, being afraid. We found that we were not manly enough nor brave enough to do a generous action when there was a chance that it could get us into trouble. Neither of us confessed this poor spirit to the others, but did as other people would have done—dropped the subject and talked about something else. And I knew we all felt mean, eating and drinking Marget's fine things along with those companies of spies, and petting her and complimenting her with the rest, and seeing with self-reproach how foolishly happy she was, and never saying a word to put her on her guard. And, indeed, she was happy, and as proud as a princess, and so grateful to have friends again. And all the time these people were watching with all their eyes and reporting all they saw to Father Adolf.

But he couldn't make head or tail of the situation. There must be an enchanter somewhere on the premises, but who was it? Marget was not seen to do any jugglery, nor was Ursula, nor yet Gottfried; and still the wines and dainties never ran short, and a guest could not call for a thing and not get it. To produce these effects was usual enough with witches and enchanters—that part of it was not new; but to do it without any incantations, or even any rumblings or earthquakes or lightnings or apparitions—that was new, novel, wholly irregular. There was nothing in the books like this. Enchanted things were always unreal. Gold turned to dirt in an unenchanted atmosphere, food withered away and vanished. But this test failed in the present case. The spies brought samples: Father Adolf prayed over them, exorcised them, but it did no good; they remained sound and real, they yielded to natural decay only, and took the usual time to do it.

Father Adolf was not merely puzzled, he was also exasperated; for these evidences very nearly convinced him—privately—that there was no witchcraft in the matter. It did not wholly convince him, for this could be a new kind of witchcraft. There was a way to find out as to this: if this prodigal abundance of provender was not brought in from the outside, but produced on the premises, there was witchcraft, sure.

7

Marget announced a party and invited forty people; the date of it was seven days away. This was a fine opportunity. Marget's house stood by itself, and it could be easily watched. All the week it was watched night and day. Marget's household went out and in as usual, but they carried nothing in their hands, and neither they nor others brought anything to the house. This was ascertained. Evidently rations for forty people were not being fetched. If they were furnished any sustenance it would have to be made on the premises. It was true that Marget went out with a basket every evening, but the spies ascertained that she always brought it back empty.

The guests arrived at noon and filled the place. Father Adolf followed; also, after a little, the astrologer, without invitation. The spies had informed him that neither at the back nor the front had any parcels been brought in. He entered and found the eating and drinking going on finely, and everything progressing in a lively and festive way. He glanced around and perceived that many of the cooked delicacies and all of the native and foreign fruits were of a perishable character, and he also recognized that these were fresh and perfect. No apparitions, no incantations, no thunder. That settled it. This was witchcraft. And not only that, but of a new kind—a kind never dreamed of before. It was a prodigious power, an illustrious power; he resolved to discover its secret. The announcement of it would resound throughout the world, penetrate to the remotest lands, paralyze all the nations with amazement— and carry his name with it, and make him renowned forever. It was a wonderful piece of luck, a splendid piece of luck; the glory of it made him dizzy.

All the house made room for him; Marget politely seated him; Ursula ordered Gottfried to bring a special table for him. Then she decked it and furnished it, and asked for his orders.

"Bring me what you will," he said.

The two servants brought supplies from the pantry, together with white wine and red—a bottle of each. The astrologer, who very likely had never seen such delicacies before, poured out a beaker of red wine, drank it off, poured another, then began to eat with a grand appetite.

I was not expecting Satan, for it was more than a week since I had seen or heard of him but now he came in—I knew it by the feel, though people were in the way and I could not see him. I heard him apologizing for intruding; and he was going away, but Marget urged him to stay, and he thanked her and stayed. She brought him along, introducing him to the girls, and to Meidling, and to some of the elders; and there was quite a rustle of whispers: "It's the young stranger we hear so much about and can't get sight of, he is away so much." "Dear, dear, but he is beautiful—what is his name?" "Philip Traum." "Ah, it fits him!" (You see, "Traum" is German for "Dream.")

"What does he do?" "Studying for the ministry, they say." "His face is his fortune—he'll be a cardinal some day." "Where is his home?" "Away down somewhere in the tropics, they say—has a rich uncle down there." And so on. He made his way at once; everybody was anxious to know him and talk with him. Everybody noticed how cool and fresh it was all of a sudden, and wondered at it, for they could see that the sun was beating down the same as before, outside, and the sky was clear of clouds, but no one guessed the reason, of course.

The astrologer had drunk his second beaker; he poured out a third. He set the bottle down, and by accident overturned it. He seized it before much was spilled, and held it up to the light, saying, "What a pity—it is royal wine." Then his face lighted with joy or triumph, or something, and he said, "Quick! Bring a bowl."

It was brought—a four-quart one. He took up that two-pint bottle and began to pour; went on pouring, the red liquor gurgling and gushing into the white bowl and rising higher and higher up its sides, everybody staring and holding their breath—and presently the bowl was full to the brim.

"Look at the bottle," he said, holding it up, "it is full yet!" I glanced at Satan, and in that moment he vanished. Then Father Adolf rose up, flushed and excited, crossed himself, and began to thunder in his great voice, "This house is bewitched and accursed!" People began to cry and shriek and crowd toward the door. "I summon this detected household to—"

His words were cut off short. His face became red, then purple, but he could not utter another sound. Then I saw Satan, a transparent film, melt into the astrologer's body; then the astrologer put up his hand, and apparently in his own voice said, "Wait—remain where you are." All stopped where they stood. "Bring a funnel!" Ursula brought it, trembling and scared, and he stuck it in the bottle and took up the great bowl and began to pour the wine back, the people gazing and dazed with astonishment, for they knew the bottle was already full before he began. He emptied the whole of the bowl into the bottle, then smiled out over the room, chuckled, and said, indifferently, "It is nothing—anybody can do it! With my powers I can even do much more."

A frightened cry burst out everywhere. "Oh, my God, he is possessed!" and there was a tumultuous rush for the door which swiftly emptied the house of all who did not belong in it except us boys and Meidling. We boys knew the secret, and would have told it if we could, but we couldn't. We were very thankful to Satan for furnishing that good help at the needful time.

Marget was pale, and crying; Meidling looked kind of petrified; Ursula the same; but Gottfried was the worst—he couldn't stand, he was so weak and scared. For he was of a witch family, you know, and it would be bad for him to be suspected. Agnes came loafing in, looking pious and unaware, and wanted to rub up against Ursula and be petted, but Ursula was afraid of her and shrank away from her, but pretending she was not meaning any incivility, for she knew very well it wouldn't answer to have strained relations with that kind of a cat. But we boys took Agnes and petted her, for Satan would not have befriended her if he had not had a good opinion of her, and that was indorsement enough for us. He seemed to trust anything that hadn't the Moral Sense.

Outside, the guests, panic-stricken, scattered in every direction and fled in a pitiable state of terror; and such a tumult as they made with their running and sobbing and shrieking and shouting that soon all the village came flocking from their houses to see what had happened, and they thronged the street and shouldered and jostled one another in exictement and fright; and then Father Adolf appeared, and they fell apart in two walls like the cloven Red Sea, and presently down this lane the astrologer came striding and mumbling, and where he passed the lanes surged back in packed masses, and fell silent with awe, and their eyes stared and their breasts heaved, and several women fainted; and when he was gone by the crowd swarmed together and followed him at a distance, talking excitedly and asking questions and finding out the facts. Finding out the facts and passing them on to others, with improvements—improvements which soon enlarged the bowl of wine to a barrel, and made the one bottle hold it all and yet remain empty to the last.

When the astrologer reached the market-square he went straight to a juggler, fantastically dressed, who was keeping three brass balls in the air, and took them from him and faced around upon the approaching crowd and said: "This poor clown is ignorant of his art. Come forward and see an expert perform."

So saying, he tossed the balls up one after another and set them whirling in a slender bright oval in the air, and added another, then another and another, and soon—no one seeing whence he got them—adding, adding, adding, the oval lengthening all the time, his hands moving so swiftly that they were just a web or a blur and not distinguishable as hands; and such as counted said there were now a hundred balls in the air. The spinning great oval reached up twenty feet in the air and was a shining and glinting and wonderful sight. Then he folded his arms and told the balls to go on spinning without his help—and they did it. After a couple of minutes he said, "There, that will do," and the oval broke and came crashing down, and the balls scattered abroad and rolled every whither. And wherever one of them came the people fell back in dread, and no one would touch it. It made him laugh, and he scoffed at the people and called them cowards and old women. Then he turned and saw the tight-rope, and said foolish people were daily wasting their money to see a clumsy and ignorant varlet degrade that beautiful art; now they should see the work of a master. With that he made a spring into the air and lit firm on his feet on the rope. Then he hopped the whole length of it back and forth on one foot, with his hands clasped over his eyes; and next he began to throw somersaults, both backwards and forward, and threw twenty-seven.

The people murmured, for the astrologer was old, and always before had been halting of movement and at times even lame, but he was nimble enough now and went on with his antics in the liveliest manner. Finally he sprang lightly down and walked away, and passed up the road and around the corner and disappeared. Then that great, pale, silent, solid crowd drew a deep breath and looked into one another's faces as if they said: "Was it real? Did you see it, or was it only I—and I was dreaming?" Then they broke into a low murmur of talking, and fell apart in couples, and moved toward their homes, still talking in that awed way, with faces close together and laying a hand on an arm and making other such gestures as people make when they have been deeply impressed by something.

We boys followed behind our father, and listened, catching all we could of what they said; and when they sat down in our house and continued their talk they still had us for company. They were in a sad mood, for it was certain, they said, that disaster for the village must follow this awful visitation of witches and devils. Then my father remembered that Father Adolf had been struck dumb at the moment of his denunciation.

"They have not ventured to lay their hands upon an anointed servant of God before," he said; "and how they could have dared it this time I cannot make out, for he wore his crucifix. Isn't it so?"

"Yes," said the others, "we saw it."

"It is serious, friends, it is very serious. Always before, we had a protection. It has failed."

The others shook, as with a sort of chill, and muttered those words over—"It has failed." "God has forsaken us."

"It is true," said Seppi Wohlmeyer's father; "there is nowhere to look for help."

"The people will realize this," said Nikolaus' father, the judge, "and despair will take away their courage and their energies. We have indeed fallen upon evil times."

He sighed, and Wohlmeyer said, in a troubled voice, "The report of it all will go about the country, and our village will be shunned as being under the displeasure of God. The Golden Stag will know hard times."

"True, neighbor," said my father, "all of us will suffer—all in repute, many in estate. And, good God!—"

"What is it?"

"That can come—to finish us!"

"Name it—um Gottes Willen!"

"The Interdict!"

It smote like a thunderclap, and they were like to swoon with the terror of it. Then the dread of this calamity roused their energies, and they stopped brooding and began to consider ways to avert it. They discussed this, that, and the other way, and talked till the afternoon was far spent, then confessed that at present they could arrive at no decision. So they parted sorrowfully, with oppressed hearts which were filled with bodings.

While they were saying their parting words I slipped out and set my course for Marget's house to see what was happening there. I met many people, but none of them greeted me. It ought to have been surprising, but it was not, for they were so distraught with fear and dread that they were not in their right minds, I think; they were white and haggard, and walked like persons in a dream, their eyes open but seeing nothing, their lips moving but uttering nothing, and worriedly clasping and unclasping their hands without knowing it.

At Marget's it was like a funeral. She and Wilhelm sat together on the sofa, but said nothing, and not even holding hands. Both were steeped in gloom, and Marget's eyes were red from the crying she had been doing. She said:

"I have been begging him to go, and come no more, and so save himself alive. I cannot bear to be his murderer. This house is bewitched, and no inmate will escape the fire. But he will not go, and he will be lost with the rest."

Wilhelm said he would not go; if there was danger for her, his place was by her, and there he would remain. Then she began to cry again, and it was all so mournful that I wished I had stayed away. There was a knock, now, and Satan came in, fresh and cheery and beautiful, and brought that winy atmosphere of his and changed the whole thing. He never said a word about what had been happening, nor about the awful tears which were freezing the blood in the hearts of the community, but began to talk and rattle on about all manner of gay and pleasant things: and next about music—an artful stroke which cleared away the remnant of Marget's depression and brought her spirits and her interests broad awake. She had not heard any one talk so well and so knowingly on that subject before, and she was so uplifted by it and so charmed that what she was feeling lit up her face and came out in her words; and Wilhelm noticed it and did not look as pleased as he ought to have done. And next Satan branched off into poetry, and recited some, and did it well, and Marget was charmed again; and again Wilhelm was not as pleased as he ought to have been, and this time Marget noticed it and was remorseful.

I fell asleep to pleasant music that night—the patter of rain upon the panes and the dull growling of distant thunder. Away in the night Satan came and roused me and said: "Come with me. Where shall we go?"

"Anywhere—so it is with you."

Then there was a fierce glare of sunlight, and he said, "This is China."

That was a grand surprise, and made me sort of drunk with vanity and gladness to think I had come so far—so much, much farther than anybody else in our village, including Bartel Sperling, who had such a great opinion of his travels. We buzzed around over that empire for more than half an hour, and saw the whole of it. It was wonderful, the spectacles we saw; and some were beautiful, others too horrible to think. For instance—However, I may go into that by and by, and also why Satan chose China for this excursion instead of another place; it would interrupt my tale to do it now. Finally we stopped flitting and lit.

We sat upon a mountain commanding a vast landscape of mountain-range and gorge and valley and plain and river, with cities and villages slumbering in the sunlight, and a glimpse of blue sea on the farther verge. It was a tranquil and dreamy picture, beautiful to the eye and restful to the spirit. If we could only make a change like that whenever we wanted to, the world would be easier to live in than it is, for change of scene shifts the mind's burdens to the other shoulder and banishes old, shop-worn weariness from mind and body both.

We talked together, and I had the idea of trying to reform Satan and persuade him to lead a better life. I told him about all those things he had been doing, and begged him to be more considerate and stop making people unhappy. I said I knew he did not mean any harm, but that he ought to stop and consider the possible consequences of a thing before launching it in that impulsive and random way of his; then he would not make so much trouble. He was not hurt by this plain speech; he only looked amused and surprised, and said:

"What? I do random things? Indeed, I never do. I stop and consider possible consequences? Where is the need? I know what the consequences are going to be—always."

"Oh, Satan, then how could you do these things?"

"Well, I will tell you, and you must understand if you can. You belong to a singular race. Every man is a suffering-machine and a happiness-machine combined. The two functions work together harmoniously, with a fine and delicate precision, on the give-and-take principle. For every happiness turned out in the one department the other stands ready to modify it with a sorrow or a pain—maybe a dozen. In most cases the man's life is about equally divided between happiness and unhappiness. When this is not the case the unhappiness predominates—always; never the other. Sometimes a man's make and disposition are such that his misery-machine is able to do nearly all the business. Such a man goes through life almost ignorant of what happiness is. Everything he touches, everything he does, brings a misfortune upon him. You have seen such people? To that kind of a person life is not an advantage, is it? It is only a disaster. Sometimes for an hour's happiness a man's machinery makes him pay years of misery. Don't you know that? It happens every now and then. I will give you a case or two presently. Now the people of your village are nothing to me—you know that, don't you?"

I did not like to speak out too flatly, so I said I had suspected it.

"Well, it is true that they are nothing to me. It is not possible that they should be. The difference between them and me is abysmal, immeasurable. They have no intellect."

"No intellect?"

"Nothing that resembles it. At a future time I will examine what man calls his mind and give you the details of that chaos, then you will see and understand. Men have nothing in common with me—there is no point of contact; they have foolish little feelings and foolish little vanities and impertinences and ambitions; their foolish little life is but a laugh, a sigh, and extinction; and they have no sense. Only the Moral Sense. I will show you what I mean. Here is a red spider, not so big as a pin's head. Can you imagine an elephant being interested in him—caring whether he is happy or isn't, or whether he is wealthy or poor, or whether his sweetheart returns his love or not, or whether his mother is sick or well, or whether he is looked up to in society or not, or whether his enemies will smite him or his friends desert him, or whether his hopes will suffer blight or his political ambitions fail, or whether he shall die in the bosom of his family or neglected and despised in a foreign land? These things can never be important to the elephant; they are nothing to him; he cannot shrink his sympathies to the microscopic size of them. Man is to me as the red spider is to the elephant. The elephant has nothing against the spider—he cannot get down to that remote level; I have nothing against man. The elephant is indifferent; I am indifferent. The elephant would not take the trouble to do the spider an ill turn; if he took the notion he might do him a good turn, if it came in his way and cost nothing. I have done men good service, but no ill turns.

"The elephant lives a century, the red spider a day; in power, intellect, and dignity the one creature is separated from the other by a distance which is simply astronomical. Yet in these, as in all qualities, man is immeasurably further below me than is the wee spider below the elephant.

"Man's mind clumsily and tediously and laboriously patches little trivialities together and gets a result—such as it is. My mind creates! Do you get the force of that? Creates anything it desires—and in a moment. Creates without material. Creates fluids, solids, colors—anything, everything—out of the airy nothing which is called Thought. A man imagines a silk thread, imagines a machine to make it, imagines a picture, then by weeks of labor embroiders it on canvas with the thread. I think the whole thing, and in a moment it is before you—created.

"I think a poem, music, the record of a game of chess—anything—and it is there. This is the immortal mind—nothing is beyond its reach. Nothing can obstruct my vision; the rocks are transparent to me, and darkness is daylight. I do not need to open a book; I take the whole of its contents into my mind at a single glance, through the cover; and in a million years I could not forget a single word of it, or its place in the volume. Nothing goes on in the skull of man, bird, fish, insect, or other creature which can be hidden from me. I pierce the learned man's brain with a single glance, and the treasures which cost him threescore years to accumulate are mine; he can forget and he does forget, but I retain.

"Now, then, I perceive by your thoughts that you are understanding me fairly well. Let us proceed. Circumstances might so fall out that the elephant could like the spider—supposing he can see it—but he could not love it. His love is for his own kind—for his equals. An angel's love is sublime, adorable, divine, beyond the imagination of man—infinitely beyond it! But it is limited to his own august order. If it fell upon one of your race for only an instant, it would consume its object to ashes. No, we cannot love men, but we can be harmlessly indifferent to them; we can also like them, sometimes. I like you and the boys, I like Father Peter, and for your sakes I am doing all these things for the villagers."

He saw that I was thinking a sarcasm and he explained his position.

"I have wrought well for the villagers, though it does not look like it on the surface. Your race never know good fortune from ill. They are always mistaking the one for the other. It is because they cannot see into the future. What I am doing for the villagers will bear good fruit some day; in some cases to themselves; in others, to unborn generations of men. No one will ever know that I was the cause, but it will be none the less true, for all that. Among you boys you have a game: you stand a row of bricks on end a few inches apart; you push a brick, it knocks its neighbor over, the neighbor knocks over the next brick—and so on till all the row is prostrate. That is human life. A child's first act knocks over the initial brick, and the rest will follow inexorably. If you could see into the future, as I can, you would see everything that was going to happen to that creature; for nothing can change the order of its life after the first event has determined it. That is, nothing will change it, because each act unfailingly begets an act, that act begets another, and so on to the end, and the seer can look forward down the line and see just when each act is to have birth, from cradle to grave."

"Does God order the career?"

"Foreordain it? No. The man's circumstances and environment order it. His first act determines the second and all that follow after. But suppose, for argument's sake, that the man should skip one of these acts; an apparently trifling one, for instance; suppose that it had been appointed that on a certain day, at a certain hour and minute and second and fraction of a second he should go to the well, and he didn't go. That man's career would change utterly, from that moment; thence to the grave it would be wholly different from the career which his first act as a child had arranged for him. Indeed, it might be that if he had gone to the well he would have ended his career on a throne, and that omitting to do it would set him upon a career that would lead to beggary and a pauper's grave. For instance: if at any time—say in boyhood—Columbus had skipped the triflingest little link in the chain of acts projected and made inevitable by his first childish act, it would have changed his whole subsequent life, and he would have become a priest and died obscure in an Italian village, and America would not have been discovered for two centuries afterward. I know this. To skip any one of the billion acts in Columbus's chain would have wholly changed his life. I have examined his billion of possible careers, and in only one of them occurs the discovery of America. You people do not suspect that all of your acts are of one size and importance, but it is true; to snatch at an appointed fly is as big with fate for you as is any other appointed act—"

"As the conquering of a continent, for instance?"

"Yes. Now, then, no man ever does drop a link—the thing has never happened! Even when he is trying to make up his mind as to whether he will do a thing or not, that itself is a link, an act, and has its proper place in his chain; and when he finally decides an act, that also was the thing which he was absolutely certain to do. You see, now, that a man will never drop a link in his chain. He cannot. If he made up his mind to try, that project would itself be an unavoidable link—a thought bound to occur to him at that precise moment, and made certain by the first act of his babyhood."

It seemed so dismal!

"He is a prisoner for life," I said sorrowfully, "and cannot get free."

"No, of himself he cannot get away from the consequences of his first childish act. But I can free him."

I looked up wistfully.

"I have changed the careers of a number of your villagers."

I tried to thank him but found it difficult, and let it drop.

"I shall make some other changes. You know that little Lisa Brandt?"

"Oh yes, everybody does. My mother says she is so sweet and so lovely that she is not like any other child. She says she will be the pride of the village when she grows up; and its idol, too, just as she is now."

"I shall change her future."

"Make it better?" I asked.

"Yes. And I will change the future of Nikolaus."

I was glad, this time, and said, "I don't need to ask about his case; you will be sure to do generously by him."

"It is my intention."

Straight off I was building that great future of Nicky's in my imagination, and had already made a renowned general of him and hofmeister at the court, when I noticed that Satan was waiting for me to get ready to listen again. I was ashamed of having exposed my cheap imaginings to him and was expecting some sarcasms, but it did not happen. He proceeded with his subject:

"Nicky's appointed life is sixty-two years."

"That's grand!" I said.

"Lisa's, thirty-six. But, as I told you, I shall change their lives and those ages. Two minutes and a quarter from now Nikolaus will wake out of his sleep and find the rain blowing in. It was appointed that he should turn over and go to sleep again. But I have appointed that he shall get up and close the window first. That trifle will change his career entirely. He will rise in the morning two minutes later than the chain of his life had appointed him to rise. By consequence, thenceforth nothing will ever happen to him in accordance with the details of the old chain." He took out his watch and sat looking it at a few moments, then said: "Nikolaus has risen to close the window. His life is changed, his new career has begun. There will be consequences."

It made me feel creepy; it was uncanny.

"But for this change certain things would happen twelve days from now. For instance, Nikolaus would save Lisa from drowning. He would arrive on the scene at exactly the right moment—four minutes past ten, the long-ago appointed instant of time—and the water would be shoal, the achievement easy and certain. But he will arrive some seconds too late, now; Lisa will have struggled into deeper water. He will do his best but both will drown."

"Oh, Satan! oh, dear Satan!" I cried, with the tears rising in my eyes, "save them! Don't let it happen. I can't bear to lose Nikolaus, he is my loving playmate and friend; and think of Lisa's poor mother!"

I clung to him and begged and pleaded, but he was not moved. He made me sit down again, and told me I must hear him out.

"I have changed Nikolaus's life, and this has changed Lisa's. If I had not done this, Nikolaus would save Lisa, then he would catch cold from his drenching; one of your race's fantastic and desolating scarlet fevers would follow, with pathetic after-effects; for forty-six years he would lie in his bed a paralytic log, deaf, dumb, blind, and praying night and day for the blessed relief of death. Shall I change his life back?"

"Oh no! Oh, not for the world! In charity and pity leave it as it is."

"It is best so. I could not have changed any other link in his life and done him so good a service. He had a billion possible careers, but not one of them was worth living; they were charged full with miseries and disasters. But for my intervention he would do his brave deed twelve days from now—a deed begun and ended in six minutes—and get for all reward those forty-six years of sorrow and suffering I told you of. It is one of the cases I was thinking of awhile ago when I said that sometimes an act which brings the actor an hour's happiness and self-satisfaction is paid for—or punished—by years of suffering."

I wondered what poor little Lisa's early death would save her from. He answered the thought:

"From ten years of pain and slow recovery from an accident, and then from nineteen years' pollution, shame, depravity, crime, ending with death at the hands of the executioner. Twelve days hence she will die; her mother would save her life if she could. Am I not kinder than her mother?"

"Yes—oh, indeed yes; and wiser."

"Father Peter's case is coming on presently. He will be acquitted, through unassailable proofs of his innocence."

"Why, Satan, how can that be? Do you really think it?"

"Indeed, I know it. His good name will be restored, and the rest of his life will be happy."

"I can believe it. To restore his good name will have that effect."

"His happiness will not proceed from that cause. I shall change his life that day, for his good. He will never know his good name has been restored."

In my mind—and modestly—I asked for particulars but Satan paid no attention to my thought. Next, my mind wandered to the astrologer, and I wondered where he might be.

"In the moon," said Satan, with a fleeting sound which I believed was a chuckle. "I've got him on the cold side of it, too. He doesn't know where he is, and is not having a pleasant time; still, it is good enough for him, a good place for his star studies. I shall need him presently; then I shall bring him back and possess him again. He has a long and cruel and odious life before him, but I will change that, for I have no feeling against him and am quite willing to do him a kindness. I think I shall get him burned."

He had such strange notions of kindness! But angels are made so, and do not know any better. Their ways are not like our ways; and, besides, human beings are nothing to them; they think they are only freaks. It seems to me odd that he should put the astrologer so far away; he could have dumped him in Germany just as well, where he would be handy.

"Far away?" said Satan. "To me no place is far away; distance does not exist for me. The sun is less than a hundred million miles from here, and the light that is falling upon us has taken eight minutes to come; but I can make that flight, or any other, in a fraction of time so minute that it cannot be measured by a watch. I have but to think the journey, and it is accomplished."

I held out my hand and said, "The light lies upon it; think it into a glass of wine, Satan."

He did it. I drank the wine.

"Break the glass," he said.

I broke it.

"There—you see it is real. The villagers thought the brass balls were magic stuff and as perishable as smoke. They were afraid to touch them. You are a curious lot—your race. But come along; I have business. I will put you to bed." Said and done. Then he was gone; but his voice came back to me through the rain and darkness saying, "Yes, tell Seppi, but no other."

It was the answer to my thought.

8

Sleep would not come. It was not because I was proud of my travels and excited about having been around the big world to China, and feeling contemptuous of Bartel Sperling, "the traveler," as he called himself, and looked down upon us others because he had been to Vienna once and was the only Eseldorf boy who had made such a journey and seen the world's wonders. At another time that would have kept me awake, but it did not affect me now. No, my mind was filled with Nikolaus, my thoughts ran upon him only, and the good days we had seen together at romps and frolics in the woods and the fields and the river in the long summer days, and skating and sliding in the winter when our parents thought we were in school. And now he was going out of this young life, and the summers and winters would come and go, and we others would rove and play as before, but his place would be vacant; we should see him no more. Tomorrow he would not suspect, but would be as he had always been, and it would shock me to hear him laugh, and see him do lightsome and frivolous things, for to me he would be a corpse, with waxen hands and dull eyes, and I should see the shroud around his face; and next day he would not suspect, nor the next, and all the time his handful of days would be wasting swiftly away and that awful thing coming nearer and nearer, his fate closing steadily around him and no one knowing it but Seppi and me. Twelve days—only twelve days. It was awful to think of. I noticed that in my thoughts I was not calling him by his familiar names, Nick and Nicky, but was speaking of him by his full name, and reverently, as one speaks of the dead. Also, as incident after incident of our comradeship came thronging into my mind out of the past, I noticed that they were mainly cases where I had wronged him or hurt him, and they rebuked me and reproached me, and my heart was wrung with remorse, just as it is when we remember our unkindnesses to friends who have passed beyond the veil, and we wish we could have them back again, if only for a moment, so that we could go on our knees to them and say, "Have pity and forgive."

Once when we were nine years old he went a long errand of nearly two miles for the fruiterer, who gave him a splendid big apple for reward, and he was flying home with it, almost beside himself with astonishment and delight, and I met him, and he let me look at the apple, not thinking of treachery, and I ran off with it, eating it as I ran, he following me and begging; and when he overtook me I offered him the core, which was all that was left; and I laughed. Then he turned away, crying, and said he had meant to give it to his little sister. That smote me, for she was slowly getting well of a sickness, and it would have been a proud moment for him, to see her joy and surprise and have her caresses. But I was ashamed to say I was ashamed, and only said something rude and mean, to pretend I did not care, and he made no reply in words, but there was a wounded look in his face as he turned away toward his home which rose before me many times in after years, in the night, and reproached me and made me ashamed again. It had grown dim in my mind, by and by, then it disappeared; but it was back now, and not dim.

Once at school, when we were eleven, I upset my ink and spoiled four copy-books, and was in danger of severe punishment; but I put it upon him, and he got the whipping.

And only last year I had cheated him in a trade, giving him a large fish-hook which was partly broken through for three small sound ones. The first fish he caught broke the hook, but he did not know I was blamable, and he refused to take back one of the small hooks which my conscience forced me to offer him, but said, "A trade is a trade; the hook was bad, but that was not your fault."

No, I could not sleep. These little, shabby wrongs upbraided me and tortured me, and with a pain much sharper than one feels when the wrongs have been done to the living. Nikolaus was living but no matter; he was to me as one already dead. The wind was still moaning about the eaves, the rain still pattering upon the panes.

In the morning I sought out Seppi and told him. It was down by the river. His lips moved, but he did not say anything, he only looked dazed and stunned, and his face turned very white. He stood like that a few moments, the tears welling into his eyes, then he turned away and I locked my arm in his and we walked along thinking, but not speaking. We crossed the bridge and wandered through the meadows and up among the hills and the woods, and at last the talk came and flowed freely, and it was all about Nikolaus and was a recalling of the life we had lived with him. And every now and then Seppi said, as if to himself:

"Twelve days!—less than twelve."

We said we must be with him all the time; we must have all of him we could; the days were precious now. Yet we did not go to seek him. It would be like meeting the dead, and we were afraid. We did not say it, but that was what we were feeling. And so it gave us a shock when we turned a curve and came upon Nikolaus face to face. He shouted gaily:

"Hi-hi! What is the matter? Have you seen a ghost?"

We couldn't speak, but there was no occasion; he was willing to talk for us all, for he had just seen Satan and was in high spirits about it. Satan had told him about our trip to China, and he had begged Satan to take him on a journey, and Satan had promised. It was to be a far journey, and wonderful and beautiful; and Nikolaus had begged him to take us, too, but he said no, he would take us some day, maybe, but not now. Satan would come for him on the 13th and Nikolaus was already counting the hours, he was so impatient.

That was the fatal day. We were already counting the hours, too.

We wandered many a mile, always following paths which had been our favorites from the days when we were little, and always we talked about the old times. All the blitheness was with Nikolaus; we others could not shake off our depression. Our tone toward Nikolaus was so strangely gentle and tender and yearning that he noticed it, and was pleased, and we were constantly doing him deferential little offices of courtesy, and saying, "Wait, let me do that for you," and that pleased him, too. I gave him seven fish-hooks —all I had—and made him take them, and Seppi gave him his new knife and a humming-top painted red and yellow—atonements for swindles practised upon him formerly, as I learned later, and probably no longer remembered by Nikolaus now. These things touched him, and he said he could not have believed that we loved him so; and his pride in it and gratefulness for it cut us to the heart, we were so undeserving of them. When we parted at last, he was radiant, and said he had never had such a happy day.

As we walked along homeward, Seppi said, "We always prized him but never so much as now, when we are going to lose him."

Next day and every day we spent all of our spare time with Nikolaus, and also added to it time which we (and he) stole from work and other duties, and this cost the three of us some sharp scoldings, and some threats of punishment. Every morning two of us woke with a start and a shudder, saying, as the days flew along, "Only ten days left"; "only nine days left"; "only eight"; "only seven." Always it was narrowing. Always Nikolaus was gay and happy, and always puzzled because we were not. He wore his invention to the bone trying to invent ways to cheer us up, but it was only a hollow success; he could see that our jollity had no heart in it, and that the laughs we broke into came up against some obstruction or other and suffered damage and decayed into a sigh. He tried to find out what the matter was, so that he could help us out of our trouble or make it lighter by sharing it with us; so we had to tell him many lies to deceive him and appease him.

But the most distressing thing of all was that he was always making plans, and often they went beyond the 13th! Whenever that happened it made us groan in spirit. All his mind was fixed upon finding some way to conquer our depression and cheer us up; and at last, when he had but three days to live he fell upon the right idea and was jubilant over it—a boys-and-girls frolic and dance in the woods, up there where we first met Satan, and this was to occur on the 14th. It was ghastly, for that was his funeral day. We couldn't venture to protest; it would only have brought a "Why?" which we could not answer. He wanted us to help him invite his guests, and we did it —one can refuse nothing to a dying friend. But it was dreadful, for really we were inviting them to his funeral.

It was an awful eleven days; and yet, with a lifetime stretching back between to-day and then, they are still a grateful memory to me, and beautiful. In effect they were days of companionship with one's sacred dead, and I have known no comradeship that was so close or so precious. We clung to the hours and the minutes, counting them as they wasted away, and parting with them with that pain and bereavement which a miser feels who sees his hoard filched from him coin by coin by robbers and is helpless to prevent it.

When the evening of the last day came we stayed out too long; Seppi and I were in fault for that; we could not bear to part with Nikolaus; so it was very late when we left him at his door. We lingered near awhile, listening; and that happened which we were fearing. His father gave him the promised punishment, and we heard his shrieks. But we listened only a moment, then hurried away, remorseful for this thing which we had caused. And sorry for the father, too; our thought being, "If he only knew—if he only knew!"

In the morning Nikolaus did not meet us at the appointed place, so we went to his home to see what the matter was. His mother said:

"His father is out of all patience with these goings-on, and will not have any more of it. Half the time when Nick is needed he is not to be found; then it turns out that he has been gadding around with you two. His father gave him a flogging last night. It always grieved me before, and many's the time I have begged him off and saved him, but this time he appealed to me in vain, for I was out of patience myself."

"I wish you had saved him just this one time," I said, my voice trembling a little; "it would ease a pain in your heart to remember it some day."

She was ironing at the time, and her back was partly toward me. She turned about with a startled or wondering look in her face and said, "What do you mean by that?"

I was not prepared, and didn't know anything to say; so it was awkward, for she kept looking at me; but Seppi was alert and spoke up:

"Why, of course it would be pleasant to remember, for the very reason we were out so late was that Nikolaus got to telling how good you are to him, and how he never got whipped when you were by to save him; and he was so full of it, and we were so full of the interest of it, that none of us noticed how late it was getting."

"Did he say that? Did he?" and she put her apron to her eyes.

"You can ask Theodor—he will tell you the same."

"It is a dear, good lad, my Nick," she said. "I am sorry I let him get whipped; I will never do it again. To think—all the time I was sitting here last night, fretting and angry at him, he was loving me and praising me! Dear, dear, if we could only know! Then we shouldn't ever go wrong; but we are only poor, dumb beasts groping around and making mistakes. I sha'n't ever think of last night without a pang."

She was like all the rest; it seemed as if nobody could open a mouth, in these wretched days, without saying something that made us shiver. They were "groping around," and did not know what true, sorrowfully true things they were saying by accident.

Seppi asked if Nikolaus might go out with us.

"I am sorry," she answered, "but he can't. To punish him further, his father doesn't allow him to go out of the house to-day."

We had a great hope! I saw it in Seppi's eyes. We thought, "If he cannot leave the house, he cannot be drowned." Seppi asked, to make sure:

"Must he stay in all day, or only the morning?"

"All day. It's such a pity, too; it's a beautiful day, and he is so unused to being shut up. But he is busy planning his party, and maybe that is company for him. I do hope he isn't too lonesome."

Seppi saw that in her eye which emboldened him to ask if we might go up and help him pass his time.

"And welcome!" she said, right heartily. "Now I call that real friendship, when you might be abroad in the fields and the woods, having a happy time. You are good boys, I'll allow that, though you don't always find satisfactory ways of proving it. Take these cakes—for yourselves—and give him this one, from his mother."

The first thing we noticed when we entered Nikolaus's room was the time—a quarter to 10. Could that be correct? Only such a few minutes to live! I felt a contraction at my heart. Nikolaus jumped up and gave us a glad welcome. He was in good spirits over his plannings for his party and had not been lonesome.

"Sit down," he said, "and look at what I've been doing. And I've finished a kite that you will say is a beauty. It's drying in the kitchen; I'll fetch it."

He had been spending his penny savings in fanciful trifles of various kinds, to go as prizes in the games, and they were marshaled with fine and showy effect upon the table. He said:

"Examine them at your leisure while I get mother to touch up the kite with her iron if it isn't dry enough yet."

Then he tripped out and went clattering down-stairs, whistling.

We did not look at the things; we couldn't take any interest in anything but the clock. We sat staring at it in silence, listening to the ticking, and every time the minute-hand jumped we nodded recognition—one minute fewer to cover in the race for life or death. Finally Seppi drew a deep breath and said:

"Two minutes to ten. Seven minutes more and he will pass the death-point. Theodor, he is going to be saved! He's going to—"

"Hush! I'm on needles. Watch the clock and keep still."

Five minutes more. We were panting with the strain and the excitement. Another three minutes, and there was a footstep on the stair.

"Saved!" And we jumped up and faced the door.

The old mother entered, bringing the kite. "Isn't it a beauty?" she said. "And, dear me, how he has slaved over it—ever since daylight, I think, and only finished it awhile before you came." She stood it against the wall and stepped back to take a view of it. "He drew the pictures his own self, and I think they are very good. The church isn't so very good, I'll have to admit, but look at the bridge—any one can recognize the bridge in a minute. He asked me to bring it up. . . . Dear me! it's seven minutes past ten, and I—"

"But where is he?"

"He? Oh, he'll be here soon; he's gone out a minute."

"Gone out?"

"Yes. Just as he came down-stairs little Lisa's mother came in and said the child had wandered off somewhere, and as she was a little uneasy I told Nikolaus to never mind about his father's orders—go and look her up. . . . Why, how white you two do look! I do believe you are sick. Sit down; I'll fetch something. That cake has disagreed with you. It is a little heavy, but I thought—"

She disappeared without finishing her sentence, and we hurried at once to the back window and looked toward the river. There was a great crowd at the other end of the bridge, and people were flying toward that point from every direction.

"Oh, it is all over—poor Nikolaus! Why, oh, why did she let him get out of the house!"

"Come away," said Seppi, half sobbing, "come quick—we can't bear to meet her; in five minutes she will know."

But we were not to escape. She came upon us at the foot of the stairs, with her cordials in her hands, and made us come in and sit down and take the medicine. Then she watched the effect, and it did not satisfy her; so she made us wait longer, and kept upbraiding herself for giving us the unwholesome cake.

Presently the thing happened which we were dreading. There was a sound of tramping and scraping outside, and a crowd came solemnly in, with heads uncovered, and laid the two drowned bodies on the bed.

"Oh, my God!" that poor mother cried out, and fell on her knees, and put her arms about her dead boy and began to cover the wet face with kisses. "Oh, it was I that sent him, and I have been his death. If I had obeyed, and kept him in the house, this would not have happened. And I am rightly punished; I was cruel to him last night, and him begging me, his own mother, to be his friend."

And so she went on and on, and all the women cried and pitied her, and tried to comfort her, but she could not forgive herself and could not be comforted, and kept on saying if she had not sent him out he would be alive and well now, and she was the cause of his death.

It shows how foolish people are when they blame themselves for anything they have done. Satan knows, and he said nothing happens that your first act hasn't arranged to happen and made inevitable, and so, of your own motion you can't ever alter the scheme or do a thing that will break a link. Next we heard screams, and Frau Brandt came wildly plowing and plunging through the crowd with her dress in disorder and hair flying loose, and flung herself upon her dead child with moans and kisses and pleadings and endearments; and by and by she rose up almost exhausted with her outpourings of passionate emotion, and clenched her fist and lifted it toward the sky, and her tear-drenched face grew hard and resentful, and she said:

"For nearly two weeks I have had dreams and presentiments and warnings that death was going to strike what was most precious to me, and day and night and night and day I have groveled in the dirt before Him praying Him to have pity on my innocent child and save it from harm—and here is His answer!"

Why, He had saved it from harm—but she did not know.

She wiped the tears from her eyes and cheeks, and stood awhile gazing down at the child and caressing its face and its hair with her hand; then she spoke again in that bitter tone, "But in His hard heart is no compassion. I will never pray again."

She gathered her dead child to her bosom and strode away, the crowd falling back to let her pass, and smitten dumb by the awful words they had heard. Ah, that poor woman! It is as Satan said, we do not know good fortune from bad, and are always mistaking the one for the other. Many a time since I have heard people pray to God to spare the life of sick persons, but I have never done it.

Both funerals took place at the same time in our little church next day. Everybody was there, including the party guests. Satan was there, too; which was proper, for it was on account of his efforts that the funerals had happened. Nikolaus had departed this life without absolution, and a collection was taken up for masses, to get him out of purgatory. Only two-thirds of the required money was gathered, and the parents were going to try to borrow the rest, but Satan furnished it. He told us privately that there was no purgatory, but he had contributed in order that Nikolaus's parents and their friends might be saved from worry and distress. We thought it very good of him, but he said money did not cost him anything.

At the graveyard the body of little Lisa was seized for debt by a carpenter to whom the mother owed fifty groschen for work done the year before. She had never been able to pay this, and was not able now. The carpenter took the corpse home and kept it four days in his cellar, the mother weeping and imploring about his house all the time; then he buried it in his brother's cattle-yard, without religious ceremonies. It drove the mother wild with grief and shame, and she forsook her work and went daily about the town, cursing the carpenter and blaspheming the laws of the emperor and the church, and it was pitiful to see. Seppi asked Satan to interfere, but he said the carpenter and the rest were members of the human race and were acting quite neatly for that species of animal. He would interfere if he found a horse acting in such a way, and we must inform him when we came across that kind of horse doing that kind of a human thing, so that he could stop it. We believed this was sarcasm, for of course there wasn't any such horse.

But after a few days we found that we could not abide that poor woman's distress, so we begged Satan to examine her several possible careers, and see if he could not change her, to her profit, to a new one. He said the longest of her careers as they now stood gave her forty-two years to live and her shortest one twenty-nine, and that both were charged with grief and hunger and cold and pain. The only improvement he could make would be to enable her to skip a certain three minutes from now, and he asked us if he should do it. This was such a short time to decide in that we went to pieces with nervous excitement, and before we could pull ourselves together and ask for particulars he said the time would be up in a few seconds; so then we gasped out, "Do it!"

"It is done," he said, "she was going around a corner; I have turned her back; it has changed her career."

"Then what will happen, Satan?"

"It is happening now. She is having words with Fischer, the weaver. In his anger Fischer will straightway do what he would not have done but for this accident. He was present when she stood over her child's body and uttered those blasphemies."

"What will he do?"

"He is doing it now—betraying her. In three days she will go to the stake."

We could not speak; we were frozen with horror, for if we had not meddled with her career she would have been spared this awful fate. Satan noticed these thoughts, and said:

"What you are thinking is strictly human-like—that is to say, foolish. The woman is advantaged. Die when she might, she would go to heaven. By this prompt death she gets twenty-nine years more of heaven than she is entitled to, and escapes twenty-nine years of misery here."

A moment before we were bitterly making up our minds that we would ask no more favors of Satan for friends of ours, for he did not seem to know any way to do a person a kindness but by killing him; but the whole aspect of the case was changed now, and we were glad of what we had done and full of happiness in the thought of it.

After a little I began to feel troubled about Fischer, and asked, timidly, "Does this episode change Fischer's life-scheme, Satan?"

"Change it? Why, certainly. And radically. If he had not met Frau Brandt awhile ago he would die next year, thirty-four years of age. Now he will live to be ninety, and have a pretty prosperous and comfortable life of it, as human lives go."

We felt a great joy and pride in what we had done for Fischer, and were expecting Satan to sympathize with this feeling; but he showed no sign and this made us uneasy. We waited for him to speak, but he didn't; so, to assuage our solicitude we had to ask him if there was any defect in Fischer's good luck. Satan considered the question a moment, then said, with some hesitation:

"Well, the fact is, it is a delicate point. Under his several former possible life-careers he was going to heaven."

We were aghast. "Oh, Satan! and under this one—"

"There, don't be so distressed. You were sincerely trying to do him a kindness: let that comfort you."

"Oh, dear, dear, that cannot comfort us. You ought to have told us what we were doing, then we wouldn't have acted so."

But it made no impression on him. He had never felt a pain or a sorrow, and did not know what they were, in any really informing way. He had no knowledge of them except theoretically—that is to say, intellectually. And of course that is no good. One can never get any but a loose and ignorant notion of such things except by experience. We tried our best to make him comprehend the awful thing that had been done and how we were compromised by it, but he couldn't seem to get hold of it. He said he did not think it important where Fischer went to; in heaven he would not be missed, there were "plenty there." We tried to make him see that he was missing the point entirely, that Fischer, and not other people, was the proper one to decide about the importance of it; but it all went for nothing; he said he did not care for Fischer—there were plenty more Fischers.

The next minute Fischer went by on the other side of the way and it made us sick and faint to see him, remembering the doom that was upon him, and we the cause of it. And how unconscious he was that anything had happened to him! You could see by his elastic step and his alert manner that he was well satisfied with himself for doing that hard turn for poor Frau Brandt. He kept glancing back over his shoulder expectantly. And, sure enough, pretty soon Frau Brandt followed after, in charge of the officers and wearing jingling chains. A mob was in her wake, jeering and shouting, "Blasphemer and heretic!" and some among them were neighbors and friends of her happier days. Some were trying to strike her, and the officers were not taking as much trouble as they might to keep them from it.

"Oh, stop them, Satan!" It was out before we remembered that he could not interrupt them for a moment without changing their whole after-lives. He puffed a little puff toward them with his lips and they began to reel and stagger and grab at the empty air; then they broke apart and fled in every direction, shrieking, as if in intolerable pain. He had crushed a rib of each of them with that little puff. We could not help asking if their life-chart was changed.

"Yes, entirely. Some have gained years, some have lost them. Some few will profit in various ways by the change, but only that few."

We did not ask if we had brought poor Fischer's luck to any of them. We did not wish to know. We fully believed in Satan's desire to do us kind-nesses, but we were losing confidence in his judgment. It was at this time that our growing anxiety to have him look over our life-charts and suggest improvements began to fade out and give place to other interests.

For a day or two the whole village was a chattering turmoil over Frau Brandt's case and over the mysterious calamity that had overtaken the mob, and at her trial the place was crowded. She was easily convicted of her blasphemies, for she uttered those terrible words again and said she would not take them back. When warned that she was imperiling her life, she said they could take it in welcome, she did not want it, she would rather live with the professional devils in perdition than with these imitators in the village. They accused her of breaking all those ribs by witchcraft, and asked her if she was not a witch? She answered scornfully:

"No. If I had that power would any of you holy hypocrites be alive five minutes? No; I would strike you all dead. Pronounce your sentence and let me go; I am tired of your society."

So they found her guilty, and she was excommunicated and cut off from the joys of heaven and doomed to the fires of hell; then she was clothed in a coarse robe and delivered to the secular arm, and conducted to the market-place, the bell solemnly tolling the while. We saw her chained to the stake, and saw the first film of blue smoke rise on the still air. Then her hard face softened, and she looked upon the packed crowd in front of her and said, with gentleness:

"We played together once, in long-agone days when we were innocent little creatures. For the sake of that, I forgive you."

We went away then and did not see the fires consume her, but we heard the shrieks, although we put our fingers in our ears. When they ceased we knew she was in heaven, notwithstanding the excommunication, and we were glad of her death and not sorry that we had brought it about.

One day, a little while after this, Satan appeared again. We were always watching out for him, for life was never very stagnant when he was by. He came upon us at that place in the woods where we had first met him. Being boys, we wanted to be entertained; we asked him to do a show for us.

"Very well," he said, "would you like to see a history of the progress of the human race?—its development of that product which it calls civilization?"

We said we should.

So, with a thought, he turned the place into the Garden of Eden, and we saw Able praying by his alter; then Cain came walking toward him with his club, and did not seem to see us, and would have stepped on my foot if I had not drawn it in. He spoke to his brother in a language which we did not understand; then he grew violent and threatening, and we knew what was going to happen and turned away our heads for the moment; but we heard the crash of the blows and heard the shrieks and the groans; then there was silence, and we saw Abel lying in his blood and gasping out his life, and Cain standing over him and looking down at him, vengeful and unrepentant.

Then the vision vanished, and was followed by a long series of unknown wars, murders, and massacres. Next we had the Flood, and the Ark tossing around in the stormy waters, with lofty mountains in the distance showing veiled and dim through the rain. Satan said:

"The progress of your race was not satisfactory. It is to have another chance now."

The scene changed, and we saw Noah overcome with wine.

Next, we had Sodom and Gomorrah, and "the attempt to discover two or three respectable persons there," as Satan described it. Next, Lot and his daughters in the cave.

Next came the Hebraic wars, and we saw the [victors] massacre the survivors and their cattle, and save the young girls alive and distribute them around.

Next we had Jael; and saw her slip into the tent and drive the nail into the temple of her sleeping guest; and we were so close that when the blood gushed out it trickled in a little, red stream to our feet, and we could have stained our hands in it if we had wanted to.

Next we had Egyptian wars, Greek wars, Roman wars, hideous drenchings of the earth with blood; and we saw the treacheries of the Romans toward the Carthaginians, and the sickening spectacle of the massacre of those brave people. Also we saw Caesar invade Britain—"not that those barbarians had done any harm, but because he wanted their land, and desired to confer the blessings of civilization upon their widows and orphans," as Satan explained.

Next, Christianity was born. Then ages of Europe passed in review before us, and we saw Christianity and Civilization march hand in hand through those ages, "leaving famine and death and desolation in their wake, and other signs of the progress of the human race," as Satan observed.

And always we had wars, and more wars, and still other wars—all over

Europe, all over the world. "Sometimes in the private interest of royal families," Satan said, "sometimes to crush a weak nation; but never a war started by the aggressor for any clean purpose—there is no such war in the history of the race."

"Now," said Satan, "you have seen your progress down to the present, and you must confess that it is wonderful—in its way. We must now exhibit the future."

He showed us slaughters more terrible in their destruction of life, more devastating in their engines of war, than any we had seen.

"You perceive," he said, "that you have made continual progress. Cain did his murder with a club; the Hebrews did their murders with javelins and swords; the Greeks and Romans added protective armour and the fine arts of military organization and generalship; the Christian has added guns and gun-powder; a few centuries from now he will have so greatly improved the deadly effectiveness of his weapons of slaughter that all men will confess that without Christian civilization war must have remained a poor and trifling thing to the end of time."

Then he began to laugh in the most unfeeling way, and make fun of the human race, although he knew that what he had been saying shamed us and wounded us. No one but an angel could have acted so; but suffering is nothing to them, they do not know what it is, except by hearsay.

More than once Seppi and I had tried in a humble and difficult way to convert him, and as he had remained silent we had taken his silence as a sort of encouragement; necessarily, then, this talk of his was a disappointment to us, for it showed that we had made no deep impression upon him. The thought made us sad, and we knew then how the missionary must feel when he has been cherishing a glad hope and has seen it blighted. We kept our grief to ourselves, knowing that this was not the time to continue our work.

Satan laughed his unkind laugh to a finish; then he said: "It is a remarkable progress. In five or six thousand years five or six high civilizations have risen, flourished, commanded the wonder of the world, then faded out and disappeared; and not one of them except the latest ever invented any sweeping and adequate way to kill people. They all did their best—to kill being the chiefest ambition of the human race and the earliest incident in its history—but only the Christian civilization has scored a triumph to be proud of. Two or three centuries from now it will be recognized that all the competent killers are Christians; then the pagan world will go to school to the Christian—not to acquire his religion, but his guns. The Turk and the Chinaman will buy those to kill missionaries and converts with."

By this time his theater was at work again, and before our eyes nation after nation drifted by, during two or three centuries, a mighty procession, an endless procession, raging, struggling, wallowing through seas of blood, smothered in battle-smoke through which the flags glinted and the red jets from the cannon darted; and always we heard the thunder of the guns and the cries of the dying.

"And what does it amount to?" said Satan, with his evil chuckle. "Nothing at all. You gain nothing; you always come out where you went in. For a million years the race has gone on monotonously propagating itself and monotonously reperforming this dull nonsense—to what end? No wisdom can guess! Who gets a profit out of it? Nobody but a parcel of usurping little monarchs and nobilities who despise you; would feel defiled if you touched them; would shut the door in your face if you proposed to call; whom you slave for, fight for, die for, and are not ashamed of it but proud; whose existence is a perpetual insult to you and you are afraid to resent it; who are mendicants supported by your alms, yet assume toward you the airs of benefactor toward beggar; who address you in the language of master to slave, and are answered in the language of slave to master; who are worshiped by you with your mouth, while in your heart—if you have one—you despise yourselves for it. The first man was a hypocrite and a coward, qualities which have not yet failed in his line; it is the foundation upon which all civilizations have been built. Drink to their perpetuation! Drink to their augmentation! Drink to—" Then he saw by our faces how much we were hurt, and he cut his sentence short and stopped chuckling, and his manner changed. He said, gently: "No, we will drink one another's health, and let civilization go. The wine which has flown to our hands out of space by desire is earthly, and good enough for that other toast; but throw away the glasses, we will drink this one in wine which has not visited this world before."

We obeyed, and reached up and received the new cups as they descended. They were shapely and beautiful goblets, but they were not made of any material that we were acquainted with. They seemed to be in motion, they seemed to be alive; and certainly the colors in them were in motion. They were very brilliant and sparkling, and of every tint, and they were never still, but flowed to and fro in rich tides which met and broke and flashed out dainty explosions of enchanting color. I think it was most like opals washing about in waves and flashing out their splendid fires. But there is nothing to compare the wine with. We drank it, and felt a strange and witching ecstasy as of heaven go stealing through us, and Seppi's eyes filled and he said worshipingly:

"We shall be there some day, and then—"

He glanced furtively at Satan, and I think he hoped Satan would say, "Yes, you will be there some day," but Satan seemed to be thinking about something else, and said nothing. This made me feel ghastly, for I knew he had heard; nothing, spoken or unspoken, ever escaped him. Poor Seppi looked distressed, and did not finish his remark. The goblets rose and clove their way into the sky, a triplet of radiant sundogs, and disappeared. Why didn't they stay? It seemed a bad sign, and depressed me. Should I ever see mine again? Would Seppi ever see his?

It was wonderful, the mastery Satan had over time and distance. For him they did not exist. He called them human inventions and said they were artificialities. We often went to the most distant parts of the globe with him and stayed weeks and months, and yet were gone only a fraction of a second, as a rule. You could prove it by the clock. One day when our people were in such awful distress because the witch commission were afraid to proceed against the astrologer and Father Peter's household, or against any, indeed, but the poor and the friendless, they lost patience and took to witch-hunting on their own score, and began to chase a born lady who was known to have the habit of curing people by devilish arts, such as bathing them, washing them, and nourishing them instead of bleeding them and purging them through the ministrations of a barber-surgeon in the proper way. She came flying down, with the howling and cursing mob after her, and tried to take refuge in houses, but the doors were shut in her face. They chased her more than half an hour, we following to see it, and at last she was exhausted and fell, and they caught her. They dragged her to a tree and threw a rope over the limb, and began to make a noose in it, some holding her, meantime, and she was crying and begging and her young daughter looking on and weeping, but afraid to say or do anything.

They hanged the lady, and I threw a stone at her, although in my heart I was sorry for her; but all were throwing stones and each was watching his neighbor, and if I had not done as the others did it would have been noticed and spoken of. Satan burst out laughing.

All that were near by turned upon him, astonished and not pleased. It was an ill time to laugh, for his free and scoffing ways and his supernatural music had brought him under suspicion all over the town and turned many privately against him. The big blacksmith called attention to him now, raising his voice so that all should hear, and said:

"What are you laughing at? Answer! Moreover, please explain to the company why you threw no stone."

"Are you sure I did not throw a stone?"

"Yes. You needn't try to get out of it; I had my eye on you."

"And I—I noticed you!" shouted two others.

"Three witnesses," said Satan: "Mueller, the blacksmith; Klein, the butcher's man; Pfeiffer, the weaver's journeyman. Three very ordinary liars. Are there any more?"

"Never mind whether there are others or not, and never mind about what you consider us—three's enough to settle your matter for you. You'll prove that you threw a stone or it shall go hard with you."

"That's so!" shouted the crowd, and surged up as closely as they could to the center of interest.

"And first you will answer that other question," cried the blacksmith, pleased with himself for being mouthpiece to the public and hero of the occasion. "What are you laughing at?"

Satan smiled and answered, pleasantly: "To see three cowards stoning a dying lady when they were so near death themselves."

You could see the superstitious crowd shrink and catch their breath, under the sudden shock. The blacksmith, with a show of bravado, said:

"Pooh! What do you know about it?"

"I? Everything. By profession I am a fortune-teller and I read the hands of you three—and some others—when you lifted them to stone the woman. One of you will die to-morrow week; another of you will die to-night; the third has but five minutes to live—and yonder is the clock!"

It made a sensation. The faces of the crowd blanched, and turned mechanically toward the clock. The butcher and the weaver seemed smitten with an illness, but the blacksmith braced up and said, with spirit:

"It is not long to wait for prediction number one. If it fails, young master, you will not live a whole minute after, I promise you that."

No one said anything; all watched the clock in a deep stillness which was impressive. When four and a half minutes were gone the blacksmith gave a sudden gasp and clapped his hands upon his heart, saying, "Give me breath! Give me room!" and began to sink down. The crowd surged back, no one offering to support him, and he fell lumbering to the ground and was dead. The people stared at him, then at Satan, then at one another; and their lips moved but no words came. Then Satan said:

"Three saw that I threw no stone. Perhaps there are others; let them speak."

It struck a kind of panic into them, and, although no one answered him, many began to violently accuse one another, saying, "You said he didn't throw," and getting for reply, "It is a lie, and I will make you eat it!" And so in a moment they were in a raging and noisy turmoil, and beating and banging one another; and in the midst was the only indifferent one—the dead lady hanging from her rope, her troubles forgotten, her spirit at peace.

So we walked away, and I was not at ease, but was saying to myself, "He told them he was laughing at them, but it was a lie—he was laughing at me."

That made him laugh again, and he said, "Yes, I was laughing at you, because, in fear of what others might report about you, you stoned the woman when your heart revolted at the act—but I was laughing at the others, too."

"Why?"

"Because their case was yours."

"How is that?"

"Well, there were sixty-eight people there, and sixty-two of them had no more desire to throw a stone than you had."

"Satan!"

"Oh, it's true. I know your race. It is made up of sheep. It is governed by minorities, seldom or never by majorities. It suppresses its feelings and its beliefs and follows the handful that make the most noise. Sometimes the noisy handful is right, sometimes wrong; but no matter, the crowd follows it. The vast majority of the race, whether savage or civilized, are secretly kind-hearted and shrink from inflicting pain, but in the presence of the aggressive and pitiless minority they don't dare to assert themselves. Think of it! One kind-hearted creature spies upon another, and sees to it that he loyally helps in iniquities which revolt both of them. Speaking as an expert, know that ninety-nine out of a hundred of your race were strongly against the killing of witches when that foolishness was first agitated by a handful of pious lunatics in the long ago. And I know that even to-day, after ages of transmitted prejudice and silly teaching, only one person in twenty puts any real heart into the harrying of a witch. And yet apparently everybody hates witches and wants them killed. Some day a handful will rise up on the other side and make the most noise—perhaps even a single daring man with a big voice and a determined front will do it—and in a week all the sheep will wheel and follow him, and witch-hunting will come to a sudden end.

"Monarchies, aristocracies, and religions are all based upon that large defect in your race—the individual's distrust of his neighbor, and his desire, for safety's or comfort's sake, to stand well in his neighbor's eye. These institutions will always remain, and always flourish, and always oppress you, affront you, and degrade you, because you will always be and remain slaves of minorities. There was never a country where the majority of the people were in their secret hearts loyal to any of these institutions."

I did not like to hear our race called sheep, and said I did not think they were.

"Still, it is true, lamb," said Satan. "Look at you in war—what mutton you are, and how ridiculous!"

"In war? How?"

"There has never been a just one, never an honorable one—on the part of the instigator of the war. I can see a million years ahead, and this rule will never change in so many as half a dozen instances. The loud little handful—as usual—will shout for the war. The pulpit will—warily and cautiously—object—at first; the great, big, dull bulk of the nation will rub its sleepy eyes and try to make out why there should be a war, and will say, earnestly and indignantly, 'It is unjust and dishonorable, and there is no necessity for it.' Then the handful will shout louder. A few fair men on the other side will argue and reason against the war with speech and pen, and at first will have a hearing and be applauded; but it will not last long; those others will outshout them, and presently the anti-war audiences will thin out and lose popularity. Before long you will see this curious thing; the speakers stoned from the platform, and free speech strangled by hordes of furious men who in their secret hearts are still at one with those stoned speakers—as earlier—but do not dare to say so. And now the whole nation—pulpit and all

—will take up the war-cry, and shout itself hoarse, and mob any honest man who ventures to open his mouth, and presently such mouths will cease to open. Next the statesmen will invent cheap lies, putting the blame upon the nation that is attacked, and every man will be glad of those conscience-soothing falsities, and will diligently study them, and refuse to examine any refutations of them; and thus he will by and by convince himself that the war is just, and will thank God for the better sleep he enjoys after this process of grotesque self-deception."

10

Days and days went by now, and no Satan. It was dull without him. But the astrologer, who had returned from his excursion to the moon, went about the village, braving public opinion, and getting a stone in the middle of his back now and then when some witch-hater got a safe chance to throw it and dodge out of sight. Meantime two influences had been working well for Marget. That Satan, who was quite indifferent to her, had stopped going to her house after a visit or two had hurt her pride, and she had set herself the task of banishing him from her heart. Reports of Wilhelm Meidling's dissipation brought to her from time to time by old Ursula had touched her with remorse, jealousy of Satan being the cause of it; and so now, these two matters working upon her together, she was getting a good profit out of the combination—her interest in Satan was steadily cooling, her interest in Wilhelm as steadily warming. All that was needed to complete her conversion was that Wilhelm should brace up and do something that should cause favorable talk and incline the public toward him again.

The opportunity came now. Marget sent and asked him to defend her uncle in the approaching trial, and he was greatly pleased, and stopped drinking and began his preparations with diligence. With more diligence than hope, in fact, for it was not a promising case. He had many interviews in his office with Seppi and me, and threshed out our testimony pretty thoroughly, thinking to find some valuable grains among the chaff, but the harvest was poor, of course.

If Satan would only come! That was my constant thought. He could invent some way to win the case, for he had said it would be won, so he necessarily knew how it could be done. But the days dragged on, and still he did not come. Of course I did not doubt that it would win, and that Father Peter would be happy for the rest of his life, since Satan had said so; yet I knew I should be much more comfortable if he would come and tell us how to manage it. It was getting high time for Father Peter to have a saving change toward happiness, for by general report he was worn out with his imprisonment and the ignominy that was burdening him, and was like to die of his miseries unless he got relief soon.

At last the trial came on, and the people gathered from all around to witness it; among them many strangers from considerable distances. Yes, everybody was there except the accused. He was too feeble in body for the strain. But Marget was present, and keeping up her hope and her spirit the best she could. The money was present, too. It was emptied on the table, and was handled and caressed and examined by such as were privileged.

The astrologer was put in the witness-box. He had on his best hat and robe for the occasion.

Question. You claim that this money is yours?

Answer. I do.

Q. How did you come by it?

A. I found the bag in the road when I was returning from a journey.

Q. When?

A. More than two years ago.

Q. What did you do with it?

A. I brought it home and hid it in a secret place in my observatory, intending to find the owner if I could.

Q. You endeavored to find him?

A. I made diligent inquiry during several months, but nothing came of it.

Q. And then?

A. I thought it not worth while to look further, and was minded to use the money in finishing the wing of the foundling-asylum connected with the priory and nunnery. So I took it out of its hiding-place and counted it to see if any of it was missing. And then—

Q. Why do you stop? Proceed.

A. I am sorry to have to say this, but just as I had finished and was restoring the bag to its place, I looked up and there stood Father Peter behind me.

Several murmured. "That looks bad," but others answered, "Ah, but he is such a liar!"

Q. That made you uneasy?

A. No; I thought nothing of it at the time, for Father Peter often came to me unannounced to ask for a little help in his need.

Marget blushed crimson at hearing her uncle falsely and impudently charged with begging, especially from one he had always denounced as a fraud, and was going to speak, but remembered herself in time and held her peace.

Q. Proceed.

A. In the end I was afraid to contribute the money to the foundling-asylum, but elected to wait yet another year and continue my inquiries. When I heard of Father Peter's find I was glad, and no suspicion entered my mind; when I came home a day or two later and discovered that my own money was gone I still did not suspect until three circumstances connected with Father Peter's good fortune struck me as being singular coincidences.

Q. Pray name them.

A. Father Peter had found his money in a path—I had found mine in a road. Father Peter's find consisted exclusively of gold ducats—mine also. Father Peter found eleven hundred and seven ducats—I exactly the same.

This closed his evidence, and certainly it made a strong impression on the house; one could see that.

Wilhelm Meidling asked him some questions, then called us boys, and we told our tale. It made the people laugh, and we were ashamed. We were feeling pretty badly, anyhow, because Wilhelm was hopeless, and showed it. He was doing as well as he could, poor young fellow, but nothing was in his favor, and such sympathy as there was was now plainly not with his client. It might be difficult for court and people to believe the astrologer's story, considering his character, but it was almost impossible to believe Father Peter's. We were already feeling badly enough, but when the astrologer's lawyer said he believed he would not ask us any questions—for our story was a little delicate and it would be cruel for him to put any strain upon it—everybody tittered, and it was almost more than we could bear. Then he made a sarcastic little speech, and got so much fun out of our tale, and it seemed so ridiculous and childish and every way impossible and foolish, that it made everybody laugh till the tears came; and at last Marget could not keep up her courage any longer, but broke down and cried, and I was so sorry for her.

Now I noticed something that braced me up. It was Satan standing alongside of Wilhelm! And there was such a contrast!—Satan looked so confident, had such a spirit in his eyes and face, and Wilhelm looked so depressed and despondent. We two were comfortable now, and judged that he would testify and persuade the bench and the people that black was white and white black, or any other color he wanted it. We glanced around to see what the strangers in the house thought of him, for he was beautiful, you know—stunning, in fact—but no one was noticing him; so we knew by that that he was invisible.

The lawyer was saying his last words; and while he was saying them Satan began to melt into Wilhelm. He melted into him and disappeared; and then there was a change, when his spirit began to look out of Wilhelm's eyes.

That lawyer finished quite seriously, and with dignity. He pointed to the money and said:

"The love of it is the root of all evil. There it lies, the ancient tempter, newly red with the shame of its latest victory—the dishonor of a priest of God and his two poor juvenile helpers in crime. If it could but speak, let us hope that it would be constrained to confess that of all its conquests this was the basest and the most pathetic."

He sat down. Wilhelm rose and said:

"From the testimony of the accuser I gather that he found this money in a road more than two years ago. Correct me, sir, if I misunderstood you."

The astrologer said his understanding of it was correct.

"And the money so found was never out of his hands thenceforth up to a certain definite date—the last day of last year. Correct me, sir, if I am wrong."

The astrologer nodded his head. Wilhelm turned to the bench and said:

"If I prove that this money here was not that money, then it is not his?"

"Certainly not; but this is irregular. If you had such a witness it was your duty to give proper notice of it and have him here to—" He broke off and began to consult with the other judges. Meantime that other lawyer got up excited and began to protest against allowing new witnesses to be brought into the case at this late stage.

The judges decided that his contention was just and must be allowed.

"But this is not a new witness," said Wilhelm. "It has already been partly examined. I speak of the coin."

"The coin? What can the coin say?"

"It can say it is not the coin that the astrologer once possessed. It can say it was not in existence last December. By its date it can say this."

And it was so! There was the greatest excitement in the court while that lawyer and the judges were reaching for coins and examining them and exclaiming. And everybody was full of admiration of Wilhelm's brightness in happening to think of that neat idea. At last order was called and the court said:

"All of the coins but four are of the date of the present year. The court tenders its sincere sympathy to the accused, and its deep regret that he, an innocent man, through an unfortunate mistake, has suffered the undeserved humiliation of imprisonment and trial. The case is dismissed."

So the money could speak, after all, though that lawyer thought it couldn't. The court rose and almost everybody came forward to shake hands with Marget and congratulate her, and then to shake with Wilhelm and praise him; and Satan had stepped out of Wilhelm and was standing around looking on full of interest, and people walking through him every which way, not knowing he was there. And Wilhelm could not explain why he only thought of the date on the coins at the last moment, instead of earlier; he said it just occurred to him all of a sudden, like an inspiration, and he brought it right out without any hesitation, for, although he didn't examine the coins, he seemed, somehow, to know it was true. That was honest of him, and like him; another would have pretended he had thought of it earlier, and was keeping it back for a surprise.

He had dulled down a little now; not much, but still you could notice that he hadn't that luminous look in his eyes that he had while Satan was in him. He nearly got it back, though, for a moment when Marget came and praised him and thanked him and couldn't keep him from seeing how proud she was of him. The astrologer went off dissatisfied and cursing, and Solomon Isaacs gathered up the money and carried it away. It was Father Peter's for good and all, now.

Satan was gone. I judged that he had spirited himself away to the jail to tell the prisoner the news; and in this I was right. Marget and the rest of us hurried thither at our best speed, in a great state of rejoicing.

Well, what Satan had done was this: he had appeared before that poor prisoner, exclaiming, "The trial is over, and you stand forever disgraced as a thief—by verdict of the court!"

The shock unseated the old man's reason. When we arrived, ten minutes later, he was parading pompously up and down and delivering commands to this and that and the other constable or jailer, and calling them Grand Chamberlain, and Prince This and Prince That, and Admiral of the Fleet, Field Marshal in Command, and all such fustian, and was as happy as a bird. He thought he was Emperor!

Marget flung herself on his breast and cried, and indeed everybody was moved almost to heartbreak. He recognized Marget, but could not understand why she should cry. He patted her on the shoulder and said:

"Don't do it, dear; remember, there are witnesses, and it is not becoming in the Crown Princess. Tell me your trouble—it shall be mended; there is nothing the Emperor cannot do." Then he looked around and saw old Ursula with her apron to her eyes. He was puzzled at that, and said, "And what is the matter with you?"

Through her sobs she got out words explaining that she was distressed to see him—"so." He reflected over that a moment, then muttered, as if to himself, "A singular old thing, the Dowager Duchess—means well, but is always snuffling and never able to tell what it is about. It is because she doesn't know." His eyes fell on Wilhelm. "Prince of India," he said, "I divine that it is you that the Crown Princess is concerned about. Her tears shall be dried; I will no longer stand between you; she shall share your throne; and between you you shall inherit mine. There, little lady, have I done well? You can smile now—isn't it so?"

He petted Marget and kissed her, and was so contented with himself and with everybody that he could not do enough for us all, but began to give away kingdoms and such things right and left, and the least that any of us got was a principality. And so at last being persuaded to go home, he marched in imposing state; and when the crowds along the way saw how it gratified him to be hurrahed at, they humored him to the top of his desire, and he responded with condescending bows and gracious smiles and often stretched out a hand and said, "Bless you, my people!"

As pitiful a sight as ever I saw. And Marget, and old Ursula crying all the way.

On my road home I came upon Satan, and reproached him with deceiving me with that lie. He was not embarrassed, but said, quite simply and composedly:

"Ah, you mistake, it was the truth. I said he would be happy the rest of his days, and he will, for he will always think he is the Emperor, and his pride in it and his joys in it will endure to the end. He is now, and will remain, the one utterly happy person in this empire."

"But the method of it, Satan, the method! Couldn't you have done it without depriving him of his reason?"

It was difficult to irritate Satan, but that accomplished it.

"What an ass you are!" he said. "Are you so unobservant as not to have found out that sanity and happiness are an impossible combination? No sane man can be happy, for to him life is real, and he sees what a fearful thing it is. Only the mad can be happy, and not many of those. The few that imagine themselves kings or gods are happy, the rest are no happier than the sane. Of course, no man is entirely in his right mind at any time, but I have been referring to the extreme cases. I have taken from this man that trumpery thing which the race regards as a Mind; I have replaced his tin life with a silver-gilt fiction; you see the result—and you criticize! I said I would make him permanently happy, and I have done it. I have made him happy by the only means possible to his race—and you are not satisfied!" He heaved a discouraged sigh, and said, "It seems to me that this race is hard to please."

There it was, you see. He didn't seem to know any way to do a person a favor except by killing him or making a lunatic out of him. I apologized, as well as I could; but privately I did not think much of his processes—at that time.

Satan was accustomed to say that our race lived a life of continuous and uninterrupted self-deception. It duped itself from cradle to grave with shams and delusions which it mistook for realities, and this made its entire life a sham. Of the score of fine qualities which it imagined it had and was vain of, it really possessed hardly one. It regarded itself as gold, and was only brass. One day when he was in this vein he mentioned a detail—the sense of humor. I cheered up then, and took issue. I said we possessed it.

"There spoke the race!" he said, "always ready to claim what it hasn't got and mistake its ounce of brass filings for a ton of gold-dust. You have a mongrel perception of humor, nothing more; a multitude of you possess that. This multitude see the comic side of a thousand low-grade and trivial things— broad incongruities, mainly; grotesqueries, absurdities, evokers of the horse-laugh. The ten thousand high-grade comicalities which exist in the world are sealed from their dull vision. Will a day come when the race will detect the funniness of these juvenilities and laugh at them—and by laughing at them destroy them? For your race, in its poverty, has unquestionably one really effective weapon—laughter. Power, money, persuasion, supplication, persecu-tion—these can lift at a colossal humbug—push it a little—weaken it a little, century by century; but only laughter can blow it to rags and atoms at a blast. Against the assault of laughter nothing can stand. You are always fussing and fighting with your other weapons. Do you ever use that one? No, you leave it lying rusting. As a race, do you ever use it at all? No, you lack sense and the courage."

We were traveling at the time and stopped at a little city in India and looked on while a juggler did his tricks before a group of natives. They were wonderful, but I knew Satan could beat that game, and I begged him to show off a little, and he said he would. He changed himself into a native in turban and breech-cloth, and very considerately conferred on me a temporary knowledge of the language.

The juggler exhibited a seed, covered it with earth in a small flower-pot, then put a rag over the pot; after a minute the rag began to rise; in ten minutes it had risen a foot; then the rag was removed and a little tree was exposed, with leaves upon it and ripe fruit. We ate the fruit, and it was good. But Satan said:

"Why do you cover the pot? Can't you grow the tree in the sunlight?"

"No," said the juggler, "no one can do that."

"You are only an apprentice; you don't know your trade. Give me the seed. I will show you." He took the seed and said, "What shall I raise from it?"

"It is a cherry seed; of course you will raise a cherry."

"Oh no; that is a trifle; any novice can do that. Shall I raise an orange-tree from it?"

"Oh yes!" and the juggler laughed.

"And shall I make it bear other fruits as well as oranges?"

"If God wills!" and they all laughed.

Satan put the seed in the ground, put a handful of dust on it, and said, "Rise!"

A tiny stem shot up and began to grow, and grew so fast that in five minutes it was a great tree, and we were sitting in the shade of it. There was a murmur of wonder, then all looked up and saw a strange and pretty sight, for the branches were heavy with fruits of many kinds and colors— oranges, grapes, bananas, peaches, cherries, apricots, and so on. Baskets were brought and the unlading of the tree began; and the people crowded around Satan and kissed his hand, and praised him, calling him the prince of jugglers. The news went about the town, and everybody came running to see the wonder—and they remembered to bring baskets, too. But the tree was equal to the occasion; it put out new fruits as fast as any were removed; baskets were filled by the score and by the hundred, but always the supply remained undiminished. At last a foreigner in white linen and sun-helmet arrived and exclaimed angrily:

"Away from here! Clear out, you dogs; the tree is on my lands and is my property."

The natives put down their baskets and made humble obeisance. Satan made humble obeisance, too, with his fingers to his forehead, in the native way, and said:

"Please let them have their pleasure for an hour, sir—only that, and no longer. Afterward you may forbid them, and you will still have more fruit than you and the state together can consume in a year."

This made the foreigner very angry, and he cried out, "Who are you, you vagabond, to tell your betters what they may do and what they mayn't!" and he struck Satan with his cane and followed this error with a kick.

The fruits rotted on the branches, and the leaves withered and fell. The foreigner gazed at the bare limbs with the look of one who is surprised, and not gratified. Satan said:

"Take good care of the tree, for its health and yours are bound together. It will never bear again, but if you tend it well it will live long. Water its roots once in each hour every night—and do it yourself; it must not be done by proxy, and to do it in daylight will not answer. If you fail only once in any night, the tree will die, and you likewise. Do not go home to your own country any more—you would not reach there; make no business or pleasure engagements which require you to go outside your gate at night—you cannot afford the risk; do not rent or sell this place—it would be injudicious."

The foreigner was proud and wouldn't beg but I thought he looked as if he would like to. While he stood gazing at Satan we vanished away and landed in Ceylon.

I was sorry for that man; sorry Satan hadn't been his customary self and killed him or made him a lunatic. It would have been a mercy. Satan overheard the thought, and said:

"I would have done it but for his wife, who has not offended me. She is coming to him presently from their native land, Portugal. She is well, but has not long to live and has been yearning to see him and persuade him to go back with her next year. She will die without knowing he can't leave that place."

"He won't tell her?"

"He? He will not trust that secret with any one; he will reflect that it could be revealed in sleep, in the hearing of some Portuguese guest's servant some time or other."

"Did none of those natives understand what you said to him?"

"None of them understood, but he will always be afraid that some of them did. That fear will be torture to him, for he has been a harsh master to them. In his dreams he will imagine them chopping his tree down. That will make his days uncomfortable—I have already arranged for his nights."

It grieved me, though not sharply, to see him take such a malicious satisfaction in his plans for this foreigner.

"Does he believe what you told him, Satan?"

"He thought he didn't, but our vanishing helped. The tree, where there had been no tree before—that helped. The insane and uncanny variety of fruits—the sudden withering—all these things are helps. Let him think as he may, reason as he may, one thing is certain, he will water the tree. But between this and night he will begin his changed career with a very natural precaution—for him."

"What is that?"

"He will fetch a priest to cast out the tree's devil. You are such a humorous race—and don't suspect it."

"Will he tell the priest?"

"No. He will say a juggler from Bombay created it, and that he wants the juggler's devil driven out of it, so that it will thrive and be fruitful again.

The priest's incantations will fail; then the Portuguese will give up that scheme and get his watering-pot ready."

"But the priest will burn the tree. I know it; he will not allow it to remain."

"Yes, and anywhere in Europe he would burn the man, too. But in India the people are civilized, and these things will not happen. The man will drive the priest away and take care of the tree."

I reflected a little, then said, "Satan, you have given him a hard life, I think."

"Comparatively. It must not be mistaken for a holiday."

We flitted from place to place around the world as we had done before, Satan showing me a hundred wonders, most of them reflecting in some way the weakness and triviality of our race. He did this now every few days—not out of malice—I am sure of that—it only seemed to amuse and interest him, just as a naturalist might be amused and interested by a collection of ants.

11

For as much as a year Satan continued these visits, but at last he came less often, and then for a long time he did not come at all. This always made me lonely and melancholy. I felt that he was losing interest in our tiny world and might at any time abandon his visits entirely. When one day he finally came to me I was overjoyed, but only for a little while. He had come to say good-by, he told me, and for the last time. He had investigations and undertakings in other corners of the universe, he said, that would keep him busy for a longer period than I could wait for his return.

"And you are going away, and will not come back any more?"

"Yes," he said. "We have comraded long together, and it has been pleasant—pleasant for both; but I must go now, and we shall not see each other any more."

"In this life, Satan, but in another? We shall meet in another, surely?"

Then, all tranquilly and soberly, he made the strange answer, "*There is no other.*"

A subtle influence blew upon my spirit from his, bringing with it a vague, dim, but blessed and hopeful feeling that the incredible words might be true—even *must* be true.

"Have you never suspected this, Theodor?"

"No. How could I? But if it can only be true—"

"It is true."

A gust of thankfulness rose in my breast, but a doubt checked it before it could issue in words, and I said, "But—but—we have seen that future life—seen it in its actuality, and so—"

"It was a vision—it had no existence."

I could hardly breathe for the great hope that was struggling in me. "A vision?—a vi—"

"Life itself is only a vision, a dream."

It was electrical. By God! I had had that very thought a thousand times in my musings!

"Nothing exists; all is a dream. God—man—the world—the sun, the moon, the wilderness of stars—a dream, all a dream; they have no existence. *Nothing exists save empty space—and you!"*

"I!"

"And you are not you—you have no body, no blood, no bones, you are but a *thought.* I myself have no existence; I am but a dream—your dream, creature of your imagination. In a moment you will have realized this, then you will banish me from your visions and I shall dissolve into the nothingness out of which you made me. . . .

"I am perishing already—I am failing—I am passing away. In a little while you will be alone in shoreless space, to wander its limitless solitudes without friend or comrade forever—for you will remain a *thought,* the only existent thought, and by your nature inextinguishable, indestructible. But I, your poor servant, have revealed you to yourself and set you free. Dream other dreams, and better!

"Strange! that you should not have suspected years ago—centuries, ages, eons, ago!—for you have existed, companionless, through all the eternities. Strange, indeed, that you should not have suspected that your universe and its contents were only dreams, visions, fiction! Strange, because they are so frankly and hysterically insane—like all dreams: a God who could make good children as easily as bad, yet preferred to make bad ones; who could have made every one of them happy, yet never made a single happy one; who made them prize their bitter life, yet stingily cut it short; who gave his angels eternal happiness unearned, yet required his other children to earn it; who gave his angels painless lives, yet cursed his other children with biting miseries and maladies of mind and body; who mouths justice and invented hell—mouths mercy and invented hell—mouths Golden Rules, and forgiveness multiplied by seventy times seven, and invented hell; who mouths morals to other people and has none himself; who frowns upon crimes, yet commits them all; who created man without invitation, then tries to shuffle the responsibility for man's acts upon man, instead of honorably placing it where it belongs, upon himself; and finally, with altogether divine obtuseness, invites this poor, abused slave to worship him! . . .

"You perceive, *now,* that these things are all impossible except in a dream. You perceive that they are pure and puerile insanities, the silly creations of an imagination that is not conscious of its freaks—in a word, that they are a dream, and you the maker of it. The dream-marks are all present; you should have recognized them earlier.

"It is true, that which I have revealed to you; there is no God, no universe, no human race, no earthly life, no heaven, no hell. It is all a dream—a grotesque and foolish dream. Nothing exists but you. And you are but *a thought*—a vagrant thought, a useless thought, a homeless thought, wandering forlorn among the empty eternities!"

He vanished and left me appalled, for I knew, and realized, that all he had said was true.

HENRY JAMES

The Beast in the Jungle

I

What determined the speech that startled him in the course of their encounter scarcely matters, being probably but some words spoken by himself quite without intention—spoken as they lingered and slowly moved together after their renewal of acquaintance. He had been conveyed by friends an hour or two before to the house at which she was staying; the party of visitors at the other house, of whom he was one, and thanks to whom it was his theory, as always, that he was lost in the crowd, had been invited over to luncheon. There had been after luncheon much dispersal, all in the interest of the original motive, a view of Weatherend itself and the fine things, intrinsic features, pictures, heirlooms, treasures of all the arts, that made the place almost famous; and the great rooms were so numerous that guests could wander at their will, hang back from the principal group and in cases where they took such matters with the last seriousness give themselves up to mysterious appreciations and measurements. There were persons to be observed, singly or in couples, bending toward objects in out-of-the-way corners with their hands on their knees and their heads nodding quite as with the emphasis of an excited sense of smell. When they were two they either mingled their sounds of ecstasy or melted into silences of even deeper import, so that there were aspects of the occasion that gave it for Marcher much the air of the "look round," previous to a sale highly advertised, that excites or quenches, as may be, the dream of acquisition. The dream of acquisition at Weatherend would have had to be wild indeed, and John Marcher found himself, among such suggestions, disconcerted almost equally by the presence of those who knew too much and by that of those who knew nothing. The great rooms caused so much poetry and history to press upon him that he needed some straying apart to feel in a proper relation with them, though this impulse was not, as happened, like the gloating of some of his companions, to be compared to the movements of a dog sniffing a cupboard. It had an issue promptly enough in a direction that was not to have been calculated.

It led, briefly, in the course of the October afternoon, to his closer meeting with May Bartram, whose face, a reminder, yet not quite a remembrance, as they sat much separated at a very long table, had begun merely by troubling him rather pleasantly. It affected him as the sequel of something of which he had lost the beginning. He knew it, and for the time quite welcomed it, as a continuation, but didn't know what it continued, which was an interest or an amusement the greater as he was also somehow aware—yet without a direct sign from her—that the young woman herself hadn't lost the thread. She hadn't lost it, but she wouldn't give it back to him, he saw, without some putting forth of his hand for it; and he not only saw that, but saw several things more, things odd enough in the light of the fact that at the moment some accident of grouping brought them face to face he was still merely fumbling with the idea that any contact between them in the past would have had no importance. If it had had no importance he scarcely knew why his actual impression of her should so seem to have so much; the answer to which, however, was that in such a life as they all appeared to be leading for the moment one could but take things as they came. He was satisfied, without in the least being able to say why, that this young lady might roughly have ranked in the house as a poor relation; satisfied also that she was not there on a brief visit, but was more or less a part of the establishment—almost a working, a remunerated part. Didn't she enjoy at periods a protection that she paid for by helping, among other services, to show the place and explain it, deal with the tiresome people, answer questions about the dates of the building, the styles of the furniture, the authorship of the pictures, the favourite haunts of the ghost? It wasn't that she looked as if you could have given her shillings—it was impossible to look less so. Yet when she finally drifted toward him, distinctly handsome, though ever so much older—older than when he had seen her before—it might have been as an effect of her guessing that he had, within the couple of hours, devoted more imagination to her than to all the others put together, and had thereby penetrated to a kind of truth that the others were too stupid for. She was there on harder terms than any one; she was there as a consequence of things suffered, one way and another, in the interval of years; and she remembered him very much as she was remembered—only a good deal better.

By the time they at last thus came to speech they were alone in one of the rooms—remarkable for a fine portrait over the chimney-place—out of which their friends had passed, and the charm of it was that even before they had spoken they had practically arranged with each other to stay behind for talk. The charm, happily, was in other things too—partly in there being scarce a spot at Weatherend without something to stay behind for. It was in the way the autumn day looked into the high windows as it waned; the way the red light, breaking at the close from under a low sombre sky, reached out in a long shaft and played over old wainscots, old tapestry, old gold, old colour. It was most of all perhaps in the way she came to him as if, since she had been turned on to deal with the simpler sort, he might, should he choose to keep the whole thing down, just take her mild attention for a part of her general business. As soon as he heard her voice, however, the gap was filled up and the missing link supplied; the slight irony he divined in her attitude lost its advantage. He almost jumped at it to get there before her. "I met you years and years ago in Rome. I remember all about it." She confessed to disappointment—she had been so sure he didn't; and to prove how well he did he began to pour forth the particular recollections that popped up as he called for them. Her face and her voice, all at his service now, worked the miracle—the impression operating like the torch of a lamplighter who touches into flame, one by one, a long row of gas-jets. Marcher flattered himself the illumination was brilliant, yet he was really still more pleased on her showing him, with amusement, that in his haste to make everything right he had got most things rather wrong. It hadn't been at Rome—it had been at Naples; and it hadn't been eight years before—it had been more nearly ten. She hadn't been, either, with her uncle and aunt, but with her mother and her brother; in addition to which it was not with the Pembles *he* had been, but with the Boyers, coming down in their company from Rome—a point on which she insisted, a little to his confusion, and as to which she had her evidence in hand. The Boyers she had known, but didn't know the Pembles, though she had heard of them, and it was the people he was with who had made them acquainted. The incident of the thunderstorm that had raged round them with such violence as to drive them for refuge into an excavation—this incident had not occurred at the Palace of the Caesars, but at Pompeii, on an occasion when they had been present there at an important find.

He accepted her amendments, he enjoyed her corrections, though the moral of them was, she pointed out, that he *really* didn't remember the least thing about her; and he only felt it as a drawback that when all was made strictly historic there didn't appear much of anything left. They lingered together still, she neglecting her office—for from the moment he was so clever she had no proper right to him—and both neglecting the house, just waiting as to see if a memory or two more wouldn't again breathe on them. It hadn't taken them many minutes, after all, to put down on the table, like the cards of a pack, those that constituted their respective hands; only what came out was that the pack was unfortunately not perfect—that the past, invoked, invited, encouraged, could give them, naturally, no more than it had. It had made them anciently meet—her at twenty, him at twenty-five; but nothing was so strange, they seemed to say to each other, as that, while so occupied, it hadn't done a little more for them. They looked at each other as with the feeling of an occasion missed; the present would have been so much better if the other, in the far distance, in the foreign land, hadn't been so stupidly meagre. There weren't apparently, all counted, more than a dozen little old things that had succeeded in coming to pass between them; trivialities of youth, simplicities of freshness, stupidities of ignorance, small possible germs, but too deeply buried—too deeply (didn't it seem?) to sprout after so many years. Marcher could only feel he ought to have rendered her some service—saved her from a capsized boat in the Bay or at least recovered her dressing-bag, filched from her cab in the streets of Naples by a lazzarone with a stiletto. Or it would have been nice if he could have been taken with fever all alone at his hotel, and she could have come to look after him, to write to his people, to drive him out in convalescence. *Then* they would be in possession of the something or other that their actual show seemed to lack. It yet somehow presented itself, this show, as too good to be spoiled: so that they were reduced for a few minutes more to wondering a little helplessly why—since they seemed to know a certain number of the same people—their reunion had been so long averted. They didn't use that name for it, but their delay from minute to minute to join the others was a kind of confession that they didn't quite want it to be a failure. Their attempted supposition of reasons for their not having met but showed how little they knew of each other. There came in fact a moment when Marcher felt a positive pang. It was vain to pretend she was an old friend, for all the communities were wanting, in spite of which it was as an old friend that he saw she would have suited him. He had new ones enough—was surrounded with them for instance on the stage of the other house; as a new one he probably wouldn't have so much as noticed her. He would have liked to invent something, get her to make-believe with him that some passage of a romantic or critical kind *had* originally occurred. He was really almost reaching out in imagination—as against time—for something that would do, and saying to himself that if it didn't come this sketch of a fresh start would show for quite awkwardly bungled. They would separate, and now for no second or no third chance. They would have tried and not succeeded. Then it was, just at the turn, as he afterwards made it out to himself, that, everything else failing, she herself decided to take up the case and, as it were, save the situation. He felt as soon as she spoke that she had been consciously keeping back what she said and hoping to get on without it; a scruple in her that immensely touched him when, by the end of three or four minutes more, he was able to measure it. What she brought out, at any rate, quite cleared the air and supplied the link—the link it was so odd he should frivolously have managed to lose.

"You know you told me something I've never forgotten and that again and again has made me think of you since; it was that tremendously hot day when we went to Sorrento, across the bay, for the breeze. What I allude to was what you said to me, on the way back, as we sat under the awning of the boat enjoying the cool. Have you forgotten?"

He had forgotten and was even more surprised than ashamed. But the great thing was that he saw in this no vulgar reminder of any "sweet" speech. The vanity of women had long memories, but she was making no claim on him of a compliment or a mistake. With another woman, a totally different one, he might have feared the recall possibly even of some imbecile "offer." So, in having to say that he had indeed forgotten, he was conscious rather of a loss than of a gain; he already saw an interest in the matter of her mention. "I try to think—but I give it up. Yet I remember the Sorrento day."

"I'm not very sure you do," May Bartram after a moment said; "and I'm not very sure I ought to want you to. It's dreadful to bring a person back at any time to what he was ten years before. If you've lived away from it," she smiled, "so much the better."

"Ah if *you* haven't why should I?" he asked.

"Lived away, you mean, from what I myself was?"

"From what *I* was. I was of course an ass," Marcher went on; "but I would rather know from you just the sort of ass I was than—from the moment you have something in your mind—not know anything."

Still, however, she hesitated. "But if you've completely ceased to be that sort—?"

"Why I can then all the more bear to know. Besides, perhaps I haven't."

"Perhaps. Yet if you haven't," she added, "I should suppose you'd remember. Not indeed that *I* in the least connect with my impression the invidious name you use. If I had only thought you foolish," she explained, "the thing I speak of wouldn't so have remained with me. It was about yourself." She waited as if it might come to him; but as, only meeting her eyes in wonder, he gave no sign, she burnt her ships. "Has it ever happened?"

Then it was that, while he continued to stare, a light broke for him and the blood slowly came to his face, which began to burn with recognition. "Do you mean I told you—?" But he faltered, lest what came to him shouldn't be right, lest he should only give himself away.

"It was something about yourself that it was natural one shouldn't forget—that is if one remembered you at all. That's why I ask you," she smiled, "if the thing you then spoke of has ever come to pass?"

Oh then he saw, but he was lost in wonder and found himself embarrassed. This, he also saw, made her sorry for him, as if her allusion had been a mistake. It took him but a moment, however, to feel it hadn't been, much as it had been a surprise. After the first little shock of it her knowledge on the contrary began, even if rather strangely, to taste sweet to him. She was the only other person in the world then who would have it, and she had had it all these years, while the fact of his having so breathed his secret had unaccountably faded from him. No wonder they couldn't have met as if nothing had happened. "I judge," he finally said, "that I know what you mean. Only I had strangely enough lost any sense of having taken you so far into my confidence."

"Is it because you've taken so many others as well?"

"I've taken nobody. Not a creature since then."

"So that I'm the only person who knows?"

"The only person in the world."

"Well," she quickly replied, "I myself have never spoken. I've never, never repeated of you what you told me." She looked at him so that he perfectly believed her. Their eyes met over it in such a way that he was without a doubt. "And I never will."

She spoke with an earnestness that, as if almost excessive, put him at ease about her possible derision. Somehow the whole question was a new luxury to him—that is from the moment she was in possession. If she didn't take the sarcastic view she clearly took the sympathetic, and that was what he had had, in all the long time, from no one whomsoever. What he felt was that he couldn't at present have begun to tell her, and yet could profit perhaps exquisitely by the accident of having done so of old. "Please don't then. We're just right as it is."

"Oh I am," she laughed, "if you are!" To which she added: "Then you do still feel in the same way?"

It was impossible he shouldn't take to himself that she was really interested, though it all kept coming as perfect surprise. He had thought of himself so long as abominably alone, and lo he wasn't alone a bit. He hadn't been, it appeared, for an hour—since those moments on the Sorrento boat. It was *she* who had been, he seemed to see as he looked at her—she who had been made so by the graceless fact of his lapse of fidelity. To tell her what he had told her—what had it been but to ask something of her? something that she had given, in her charity, without his having, by a remembrance, by a return of the spirit, failing another encounter, so much as thanked her. What he had asked of her had been simply at first not to laugh at him. She had beautifully not done so for ten years, and she was not doing so now. So he had endless gratitude to make up. Only for that he must see just how he had figured to her. "What, exactly, was the account I gave—?"

"Of the way you did feel? Well, it was very simple. You said you had had from your earliest time, as the deepest thing within you, the sense of being kept for something rare and strange, possibly prodigious and terrible, that was sooner or later to happen to you, that you had in your bones the fore-boding and the conviction of, and that would perhaps overwhelm you."

"Do you call that very simple?" John Marcher asked.

She thought a moment. "It was perhaps because I seemed, as you spoke, to understand it."

"You do understand it?" he eagerly asked.

Again she kept her kind eyes on him. "You still have the belief?"

"Oh!" he exclaimed helplessly. There was too much to say.

"Whatever it's to be," she clearly made out, "it hasn't yet come."

He shook his head in complete surrender now. "It hasn't yet come. Only, you know, it isn't anything I'm to *do*, to achieve in the world, to be distinguished or admired for. I'm not such an ass as *that*. It would be much better, no doubt, if I were."

"It's to be something you're merely to suffer?"

"Well, say to wait for—to have to meet, to face, to see suddenly break out in my life; possibly destroying all further consciousness, possibly annihilating me; possibly, on the other hand, only altering everything, striking at the root of all my world and leaving me to the consequences, however they shape themselves."

She took this in, but the light in her eyes continued for him not to be that of mockery. "Isn't what you describe perhaps but the expectation—or at any rate the sense of danger, familiar to so many people—of falling in love?"

John Marcher wondered. "Did you ask me that before?"

"No—I wasn't so free-and-easy then. But it's what strikes me now."

"Of course," he said after a moment, "it strikes you. Of course it strikes *me*. Of course what's in store for me may be no more than that. The only thing is," he went on, "that I think if it had been that I should by this time know."

"Do you mean because you've *been* in love?" And then as he but looked at her in silence: "You've been in love, and it hasn't meant such a cataclysm, hasn't proved the great affair?"

"Here I am, you see. It hasn't been overwhelming."

"Then it hasn't been love," said May Bartram.

"Well, I at least thought it was. I took it for that—I've taken it till now. It was agreeable, it was delightful, it was miserable," he explained. "But it wasn't strange. It wasn't what *my* affair's to be."

"You want something all to yourself—something that nobody else knows or *has* known?"

"It isn't a question of what I 'want'—God knows I don't want anything. It's only a question of the apprehension that haunts me—that I live with day by day."

He said this so lucidly and consistently that he could see it further impose itself. If she hadn't been interested before she'd have been interested now. "Is it a sense of coming violence?"

Evidently now too again he liked to talk of it. "I don't think of it as—when it does come—necessarily violent. I only think of it as natural and as of course above all unmistakable. I think of it simply as *the* thing. *The* thing will of itself appear natural."

"Then how will it appear strange?"

Marcher bethought himself. "It won't—to *me*."

"To whom then?"

"Well," he replied, smiling at last, "say to you."

"Oh then I'm to be present?"

"Why you *are* present—since you know."

"I see." She turned it over. "But I mean at the catastrophe."

At this, for a minute, their lightness gave way to their gravity; it was as if the long look they exchanged held them together. "It will only depend on yourself—if you'll watch with me."

"Are you afraid?" she asked.

"Don't leave me *now*," he went on.

"Are you afraid?" she repeated.

"Do you think me simply out of my mind?" he pursued instead of answering. "Do I merely strike you as a harmless lunatic?"

"No," said May Bartram. "I understand you. I believe you."

"You mean you feel how my obsession—poor old thing!—may correspond to some possible reality?"

"To some possible reality."

"Then you *will* watch with me?"

She hesitated, then for the third time put her question. "Are you afraid?"

"Did I tell you I was—at Naples?"

"No, you said nothing about it."

"Then I don't know. And I should *like* to know," said John Marcher. "You'll tell me yourself whether you think so. If you'll watch with me you'll see."

"Very good then." They had been moving by this time across the room, and at the door, before passing out, they paused as for the full wind-up of their understanding. "I'll watch with you," said May Bartram.

II

The fact that she "knew"—knew and yet neither chaffed him nor betrayed him—had in a short time begun to constitute between them a goodly bond, which became more marked when, within the year that followed their afternoon at Weatherend, the opportunities for meeting multiplied. The event that thus promoted these occasions was the death of the ancient lady her great-aunt, under whose wing since losing her mother, she had to such an extent found shelter, and who, though but the widowed mother of the new successor to the property, had succeeded—thanks to a high tone and a high temper—in not forfeiting the supreme position at the great house. The deposition of this personage arrived but with her death, which, followed by many changes, made in particular a difference for the young woman in whom Marcher's expert attention had recognised from the first a dependent with a pride that might ache though it didn't bristle. Nothing for a long time had made him easier than the thought that the aching must have been much soothed by Miss Bartram's now finding herself able to set up a small home in London. She had acquired property, to an amount that made that luxury just possible, under her aunt's extremely complicated will, and when the whole matter began to be straightened out, which indeed took time, she let him know that the happy issue was at last in view. He had seen her again before that day, both because she had more than once accompanied the ancient lady to town and because he had paid another visit to the friends who so conveniently made of Weatherend one of the charms of their own hospitality. These friends had taken him back there; he had achieved there again with Miss Bartram some quiet detachment; and he had in London succeeded in persuading her to more than one brief absence from her aunt. They went together, on these latter occasions, to the National Gallery and the South Kensington Museum, where, among vivid reminders, they talked of Italy at large—not now attempting to recover, as at first, the taste of their youth and their ignorance. That recovery, the first day of Weatherend, had served its purpose well, had given them quite enough; so that they were, to Marcher's sense, no longer hovering about the headwaters of their stream, but had felt their boat pushed sharply off and down the current.

They were literally afloat together; for our gentleman this was marked, quite as marked as that the fortunate cause of it was just the buried treasure of her knowledge. He had with his own hands dug up this little hoard, brought to light—that is to within reach of the dim day constituted by their discretions and privacies—the object of value the hiding-place of which he had, after putting it into the ground himself, so strangely, so long forgotten. The rare luck of his having again just stumbled on the spot made him indifferent to any other question; he would doubtless have devoted more time to the odd accident of his lapse of memory if he hadn't been moved to devote so much to the sweetness, the comfort, as he felt, for the future, that this accident itself had helped to keep fresh. It had never entered into his plan that any one should "know," and mainly for the reason that it wasn't in him to tell any one. That would have been impossible, for nothing but the amusement of a cold world would have waited on it. Since, however, a mysterious fate had opened his mouth betimes, in spite of him, he would count that a compensation and profit by it to the utmost. That the right person *should* know tempered the asperity of his secret more than his shyness had permitted him to imagine; and May Bartram was clearly right, because—well, because there she was. Her knowledge simply settled it; he would have been sure enough by this time had she been wrong. There was that in his situation, no doubt, that disposed him too much to see her as a mere confidant, taking all her light for him from the fact —the fact only—of her interest in his predicament; from her mercy, sympathy, seriousness, her consent not to regard him as the funniest of the funny. Aware, in fine, that her price for him was just in her giving him this constant sense of his being admirably spared, he was careful to remember that she had also a life of her own, with things that might happen to *her*, things that in friendship one should likewise take account of. Something fairly remarkable came to pass with him, for that matter, in this connexion—something represented by a certain passage of his consciousness, in the suddenest way, from one extreme to the other.

He had thought himself, so long as nobody knew, the most disinterested person in the world, carrying his concentrated burden, his perpetual suspense, ever so quietly, holding his tongue about it, giving others no glimpse of it nor of its effect upon his life, asking of them no allowance and only making on his side all those that were asked. He hadn't disturbed people with the queerness of their having to know a haunted man, though he had had moments of rather special temptation on hearing them say they were forsooth "unsettled." If they were as unsettled as he was—he who had never been settled for an hour in his life—they would know what it meant. Yet it wasn't, all the same, for him to make them, and he listened to them civilly enough. This was why he had such good—though possibly such rather colourless— manners; this was why, above all, he could regard himself, in a greedy world, as decently—as in fact perhaps even a little sublimely—unselfish. Our point is accordingly that he valued this character quite sufficiently to measure his present danger of letting it lapse, against which he promised himself to be much on his guard. He was quite ready, none the less, to be selfish just a little, since surely no more charming occasion for it had come to him. "Just a little," in a word, was just as much as Miss Bartram, taking one day with another, would let him. He never would be in the least coercive, and would keep well before him the lines on which consideration for her—the very highest—ought to proceed. He would thoroughly establish the heads under which her affairs, her requirements, her peculiarities—he went so far as to give them the latitude of that name—would come into their intercourse. All this naturally was a sign of how much he took the intercourse itself for granted. There was nothing more to be done about *that*. It simply existed; had sprung into being with her first penetrating question to him in the autumn light there at Weatherend. The real form it should have taken on the basis that stood out large was the form of their marrying. But the devil in this was that the very basis itself put marrying out of the question. His conviction, his apprehension, his obsession, in short, wasn't a privilege he could invite a woman to share; and that consequence of it was precisely what was the matter with him. Something or other lay in wait for him, amid the twists and the turns of the months and the years, like a crouching beast in the jungle. It signified little whether the crouching beast were destined to slay him or to be slain. The definite point was the inevitable spring of the creature; and the definite lesson from that was that a man of feeling didn't cause himself to be accompanied by a lady on a tiger-hunt. Such was the image under which he had ended by figuring his life.

They had at first, none the less, in the scattered hours spent together, made no allusion to that view of it; which was a sign he was handsomely alert to give that he didn't expect, that he in fact didn't care, always to be talking about it. Such a feature in one's outlook was really like a hump on one's back. The difference it made every minute of the day existed quite independently of discussion. One discussed of course *like* a hunchback, for there was always, if nothing else, the hunchback face. That remained, and she was watching him; but people watched best, as a general thing, in silence, so that such would be predominantly the manner of their vigil. Yet he didn't want, at the same time, to be tense and solemn; tense and solemn was what he imagined he too much showed for with other people. The thing to be, with the one person who knew, was easy and natural—to make the reference rather than be seeming to avoid it, to avoid it rather than be seeming to make it, and to keep it, in any case, familiar, facetious even, rather than pedantic and portentous. Some such consideration as the latter was doubtless in his mind for instance when he wrote pleasantly to Miss Bartram that perhaps the great thing he had so long felt as in the lap of the gods was no more than this circumstance, which touched him so nearly, of her acquiring a house in London. It was the first allusion they had yet again made, needing any other hitherto so little; but when she replied, after having given him the news, that she was by no means satisfied with such a trifle as the climax to so special a suspense, she almost set him wondering if she hadn't even a larger conception of singularity for him than he had for himself. He was at all events destined to become aware little by little, as time went by, that she was all the while looking at his life, judging it, measuring it, in the light of the thing she knew, which grew to be at last, with the consecration of the years, never mentioned between them save as "the real truth" about him. That had always been his own form of reference to it, but she adopted the form so quietly that, looking back at the end of a period, he knew there was no moment at which it was traceable that she had, as he might say, got inside his idea, or exchanged the attitude of beautifully indulging for that of still more beautifully believing him.

It was always open to him to accuse her of seeing him but as the most harmless of maniacs, and this, in the long run—since it covered so much ground—was his easiest description of their friendship. He had a screw loose for her, but she liked him in spite of it and was practically, against the rest of the world, his kind wise keeper, unremunerated but fairly amused and, in the absence of other near ties, not disreputably occupied. The rest of the world of course thought him queer, but she, she only, knew how, and above all why, queer; which was precisely what enabled her to dispose the concealing veil in the right folds. She took his gaiety from him—since it had to pass with them for gaiety—as she took everything else; but she certainly so far justified by her unerring touch his finer sense of the degree to which he had ended by convincing her. *She* at least never spoke of the secret of his life except as "the real truth about you," and she had in fact a wonderful way of making it seem, as such, the secret of her own life too. That was in fine how he so constantly felt her as allowing for him; he couldn't on the whole call it anything else. He allowed for himself, but she, exactly, allowed still more; partly because, better placed for a sight of the matter, she traced his unhappy perversion through reaches of its course into which he could scarce follow it. He knew how he felt, but, besides knowing that, she knew how he *looked* as well; he knew each of the things of importance he was insidiously kept from doing, but she could add up the amount they made, understand how much, with a lighter weight on his spirit, he might have done, and thereby establish how, clever as he was, he fell short. Above all she was in the secret of the difference between the forms he went through—those of his little office under Government, those of caring for his modest patrimony, for his library, for his garden in the country, for the people in London whose invitations he accepted and repaid—and the detachment that reigned beneath them and that made of all behaviour, all that could in the least be called behaviour, a long act of dissimulation. What it had come to was that he wore a mask painted with the social simper, out of the eye-holes of which there looked eyes of an expression not in the least matching the other features. This the stupid world, even after years, had never more than half-discovered. It was only May Bartram who had, and she achieved, by an art indescribable, the feat of at once—or perhaps it was only alternately—meeting the eyes from in front and mingling her own vision, as from over his shoulder, with their peep through the apertures.

So while they grew older together she did watch with him, and so she let this association give shape and colour to her own existence. Beneath *her* forms as well detachment had learned to sit, and behaviour had become for her, in the social sense, a false account of herself. There was but one account of her that would have been true all the while and that she could give straight to nobody, least of all to John Marcher. Her whole attitude was a virtual statement, but the perception of that only seemed called to take its place for him as one of the many things necessarily crowded out of his consciousness. If she had moreover, like himself, to make sacrifices to their real truth, it was to be granted that her compensation might have affected her as more prompt and more natural. They had long periods, in this London time, during which, when they were together, a stranger might have listened to them without in the least pricking up his ears; on the other hand the real truth was equally liable at any moment to rise to the surface, and the auditor would then have wondered indeed what they were talking about. They had from an early hour made up their mind that society was, luckily, unintelligent, and the margin allowed them by this had fairly become one of their commonplaces. Yet there were still moments when the situation turned almost fresh—usually under the effect of some expression drawn from herself. Her expressions doubtless repeated themselves, but her intervals were generous. "What saves us, you know, is that we answer so completely to so usual an appearance: that of the man and woman whose friendship has become such a daily habit—or almost—as to be at last indispensable." That for instance was a remark she had frequently enough had occasion to make, though she had given it at different times different developments. What we are especially concerned with is the turn it happened to take from her one afternoon when he had come to see her in honour of her birthday. This anniversary had fallen on a Sunday, at a season of thick fog and general outward gloom; but he had brought her his customary offering, having known her now long enough to have established a hundred small traditions. It was one of his proofs to himself, the present he made her on her birthday, that he hadn't sunk into real selfishness. It was mostly nothing more than a small trinket, but it was always fine of its kind, and he was regularly careful to pay for it more than he thought he could afford. "Our habit saves you at least, don't you see? because it makes you, after all, for the vulgar, indistinguishable from other men. What's the most inveterate mark of men in general? Why the capacity to spend endless time with dull women—to spend it I won't say without being bored, but without minding that they are, without being driven off at a tangent by it; which comes to the same thing. I'm your dull woman, a part of the daily bread for which you pray at church. That covers your tracks more than anything."

"And what covers yours?" asked Marcher, whom his dull woman could mostly to this extent amuse. "I see of course what you mean by your saving me, in this way and that, so far as other people are concerned—I've seen it all along. Only what is it that saves you? I often think, you know, of that."

She looked as if she sometimes thought of that too, but rather in a different way. "Where other people, you mean, are concerned?"

"Well, you're really so in with me, you know—as a sort of result of my being so in with yourself. I mean of my having such an immense regard for you, being so tremendously mindful of all you've done for me. I sometimes ask myself if it's quite fair. Fair I mean to have so involved and—since one may say it—interested you. I almost feel as if you hadn't really had time to do anything else."

"Anything else but be interested?" she asked. "Ah what else does one ever want to be? If I've been 'watching' with you, as we long ago agreed I was to do, watching's always in itself an absorption."

"Oh certainly," John Marcher said, "if you hadn't had your curiosity—! Only doesn't it sometimes come to you as time goes on that your curiosity isn't being particularly repaid?"

May Bartram had a pause. "Do you ask that, by any chance, because you feel at all that yours isn't? I mean because you have to wait so long?"

Oh he understood what she meant! "For the thing to happen that never does happen? For the beast to jump out? No, I'm just where I was about it. It isn't a matter as to which I can *choose*, I can decide for a change. It isn't one as to which there *can* be a change. It's in the lap of the gods. One's in the hands of one's law—there one is. As to the form the law will take, the way it will operate, that's its own affair."

"Yes," Miss Bartram replied; "of course one's fate's coming, of course it *has* come in its own form and its own way, all the while. Only, you know, the form and the way in your case were to have been—well, something so exceptional and, as one may say, so particularly *your* own."

Something in this made him look at her with suspicion. "You say 'were to *have* been,' as if in your heart you had begun to doubt."

"Oh!" she vaguely protested.

"As if you believe," he went on, "that nothing will now take place."

She shook her head slowly but rather inscrutably. "You're far from my thought."

He continued to look at her. "What then is the matter with you?"

"Well," she said after another wait, "the matter with me is simply that I'm more sure than ever my curiosity, as you call it, will be but too well repaid."

They were frankly grave now; he had got up from his seat, had turned once more about the little drawing-room to which, year after year, he brought his inevitable topic; in which he had, as he might have said, tasted their intimate community with every sauce, where every object was as familiar to him as the things of his own house and the very carpets were worn with his fitful walk very much as the desks in old counting-houses are worn by the elbows of generations of clerks. The generations of his nervous moods had been at work there, and the place was the written history of his whole middle life. Under the impression of what his friend had just said he knew himself, for some reason, more aware of these things; which made him, after a moment, stop again before her. "Is it possibly that you've grown afraid?"

"Afraid?" He thought, as she repeated the word, that his question had made her, a little, change colour; so that, lest he should have touched on a truth, he explained very kindly: "You remember that that was what you asked *me* long ago—the first day at Weatherend."

"Oh yes, and you told me you didn't know—that I was to see for myself. We've said little about it since, even in so long a time."

"Precisely," Marcher interposed—"quite as if it were too delicate a matter for us to make free with. Quite as if we might find, on pressure, that I *am* afraid. For then," he said, "we shouldn't, should we? quite know what to do."

She had for the time no answer to his question. "There have been days when I thought you were. Only, of course," she added, "there have been days when we have thought almost anything."

"Everything. Oh!" Marcher softly groaned as with a gasp, half-spent, at the face, more uncovered just then than it had been for a long while, of the imagination always with them. It had always had its incalculable moments of glaring out, quite as with the very eyes of the very Beast, and, used as he was to them, they could still draw from him the tribute of a sigh that rose from the depths of his being. All they had thought, first and last, rolled over him; the past seemed to have been reduced to mere barren speculation. This in fact was what the place had just struck him as so full of—the simplification of everything but the state of suspense. That remained only by seeming to hang in the void surrounding it. Even his original fear, if fear it had been, had lost itself in the desert. "I judge, however," he continued, "that you see I'm not afraid now."

"What I see, as I make it out, is that you've achieved something almost unprecedented in the way of getting used to danger. Living with it so long and so closely you've lost your sense of it; you know it's there, but you're indifferent, and you cease even, as of old, to have to whistle in the dark. Considering what the danger is," May Bartram wound up, "I'm bound to say I don't think your attitude could well be surpassed."

John Marcher faintly smiled. "It's heroic?"

"Certainly—call it that."

It was what he would have liked indeed to call it. "I *am* then a man of courage?"

"That's what you were to show me."

He still, however, wondered. "But doesn't the man of courage know what he's afraid of—or *not* afraid of? I don't know *that*, you see. I don't focus it. I can't name it. I only know I'm exposed."

"Yes, but exposed—how shall I say?—so directly. So intimately. That's surely enough."

"Enough to make you feel then—as what we may call the end and the upshot of our watch—that I'm not afraid?"

"You're not afraid. But it isn't," she said, "the end of our watch. That is it isn't the end of yours. You've everything still to see."

"Then why haven't *you*?" he asked. He had had, all along, today, the sense of her keeping something back, and he still had it. As this was his first impression of that it quite made a date. The case was the more marked as she didn't at first answer: which in turn made him go on. "You know something I don't." Then his voice, for that of a man of courage, trembled a little. "You know what's to happen." Her silence, with the face she showed, was almost a confession—it made him sure. "You know, and you're afraid to tell me. It's so bad that you're afraid I'll find out."

All this might be true, for she did look as if, unexpectedly to her, he had crossed some mystic line that she had secretly drawn round her. Yet she might, after all, not have worried; and the real climax was that he himself, at all events, needn't. "You'll never find out."

III

It was all to have made, none the less, as I have said, a date; which came out in the fact that again and again, even after long intervals, other things that passed between them wore in relation to this hour but the character of recalls and results. Its immediate effect had been indeed rather to lighten insistence—almost to provoke a reaction; as if their topic had dropped by its own weight and as if moreover, for that matter, Marcher had been visited by one of his occasional warnings against egotism. He had kept up, he felt, and very decently on the whole, his consciousness of the importance of not being selfish, and it was true that he had never sinned in that direction without promptly enough trying to press the scales the other way. He often repaired his fault, the season permitting, by inviting his friend to accompany him to the opera; and it not infrequently thus happened that, to show he didn't wish her to have but one sort of food for her mind, he was the cause of her appearing there with him a dozen nights in the month. It even happened that, seeing her home at such times, he occasionally went in with her to finish, as he called it, the evening, and, the better to make his point, sat down to the frugal but always careful little supper that awaited his pleasure. His point was made, he thought, by his not eternally insisting with her on himself; made for instance, at such hours, when it befell that, her piano at hand and each of them familiar with it, they went over passages of the opera together. It chanced to be on one of these occasions, however, that he reminded her of her not having answered a certain question he had put to her during the talk that had taken place between them on her last birthday. "What is it that saves you?"—saved her, he meant, from that appearance of variation from the usual human type. If he had practically escaped remark, as she pretended, by doing, in the most important particular, what most men do—find the answer to life in patching up an alliance of a sort with a woman no better than himself—how had she escaped it, and how could the alliance, such as it was, since they must suppose it had been more or less noticed, have failed to make her rather positively talked about?

"I never said," May Bartram replied, "that it hadn't made me a good deal talked about."

"Ah well then you're not 'saved.' "

"It hasn't been a question for me. If you've had your woman I've had," she said, "my man."

"And you mean that makes you all right?"

Oh it was always as if there were so much to say! "I don't know why it shouldn't make me—humanly, which is what we're speaking of—as right as it makes you."

"I see," Marcher returned. " 'Humanly,' no doubt, as showing that you're living for something. Not, that is, just for me and my secret."

May Bartram smiled. "I don't pretend it exactly shows that I'm not living for you. It's my intimacy with you that's in question."

He laughed as he saw what she meant. "Yes, but since, as you say, I'm only, so far as people make out, ordinary, you're—aren't you?—no more than ordinary either. You help me to pass for a man like another. So if I *am*, as I understand you, you're not compromised. Is that it?"

She had another of her waits, but she spoke clearly enough. "That's it. It's all that concerns me—to help you to pass for a man like another."

He was careful to acknowledge the remark handsomely. "How kind, how beautiful, you are to me! How shall I ever repay you?"

She had her last grave pause, as if there might be a choice of ways. But she chose. "By going on as you are."

It was into this going on as he was that they relapsed, and really for so long a time that the day inevitably came for a further sounding of their depths. These depths, constantly bridged over by a structure firm enough in spite of its lightness and of its occasional oscillation in the somewhat vertiginous air, invited on occasion, in the interest of their nerves, a dropping of the plummet and a measurement of the abyss. A difference had been made moreover, once for all, by the fact that she had all the while not appeared to feel the need of rebutting his charge of an idea within her that she didn't dare to express—a charge uttered just before one of the fullest of their later discusions ended. It had come up for him then that she "knew" something and that what she knew was bad—too bad to tell him. When he had spoken of it as visibly so bad that she was afraid he might find it out, her reply had left the matter too equivocal to be let alone and yet, for Marcher's special sensibility, almost too formidable again to touch. He circled about it at a distance that alternately narrowed and widened and that still wasn't much affected by the consciousness in him that there was nothing she could "know," after all, any better than he did. She had no source of knowledge he hadn't equally— except of course that she might have finer nerves. That was what women had where they were interested; they made out things, where people were concerned, that the people often couldn't have made out for themselves. Their nerves, their sensibility, their imagination, were conductors and revealers, and the beauty of May Bartram was in particular that she had given herself to his case. He felt in these days what, oddly enough, he had never felt before, the growth of a dread of losing her by some catastrophe—some catastrophe that yet wouldn't at all be *the* catastrophe: partly because she had almost of a sudden begun to strike him as more useful to him than ever yet, and partly by reason of an appearance of uncertainty in her health, coincident and equally new. It was characteristic of the inner detachment he had hitherto so successfully cultivated and to which our whole account of him is a reference, it was characteristic that his complications, such as they were, had never yet seemed so as at this crisis to thicken about him, even to the point of making him ask himself if he were, by any chance, of a truth, within sight or sound, within touch or reach, within the immediate jurisdiction, of the thing that waited.

When the day came, as come it had to, that his friend confessed to him her fear of a deep disorder in her blood, he felt somehow the shadow of a change and the chill of a shock. He immediately began to imagine aggravations and disasters, and above all to think of her peril as the direct menace for himself of personal privation. This indeed gave him one of those partial recoveries of equanimity that were agreeable to him—it showed him that what was still first in his mind was the loss she herself might suffer. "What if she should have to die before knowing, before seeing—?" It would have been brutal, in the early stages of her trouble, to put that question to her; but it had immediately sounded for him to his own concern, and the possibility was what most made him sorry for her. If she did "know," moreover, in the sense of her having had some—what should he think?—mystical irresistible light, this would make the matter not better, but worse, inasmuch as her original adoption of his own curiosity had quite become the basis of her life. She had been living to see what would *be* to be seen, and it would quite lacerate her to have to give up before the accomplishment of the vision. These reflexions, as I say, quickened his generosity; yet, make them as he might, he saw himself, with the lapse of the period, more and more disconcerted. It lapsed for him with a strange steady sweep, and the oddest oddity was that it gave him, independently of the threat of much inconvenience, almost the only positive surprise his career, if career it could be called, had yet offered him. She kept the house as she had never done; he had to go to her to see her—she could meet him nowhere now, though there was scarce a corner of their loved old London in which she hadn't in the past, at one time or another, done so; and he found her always seated by her fire in the deep old-fashioned chair she was less and less able to leave. He had been struck one day, after an absence exceeding his usual measure, with her suddenly looking much older to him than he had ever thought of her being; then he recognised that the suddenness was all on his side—he had just simply and suddenly noticed. She looked older because inevitably, after so many years, she *was* old, or almost; which was of course true in still greater measure of her companion. If she was old, or almost, John Marcher assuredly was, and yet it was her showing of the lesson, not his own, that brought the truth home to him. His surprises began here; when once they had begun they multiplied; they came rather with a rush: it was as if, in the oldest way in the world, they had all been kept back, sown in a thick cluster, for the late afternoon of life, the time at which for people in general the unexpected has died out.

One of them was that he should have caught himself—for he *had* so done—*really* wondering if the great accident would take form now as nothing more than his being condemned to see this charming woman, this admirable friend, pass away from him. He had never so unreservedly qualified her as while confronted in thought with such a possibility; in spite of which there was small doubt for him that as an answer to his long riddle the mere effacement of even so fine a feature of his situation would be an abject anti-climax. It would represent, as connected with his past attitude, a drop of dignity under the shadow of which his existence could only become the most grotesque of failures. He had been far from holding it a failure—long as he had waited for the appearance that was to make it a success. He had waited for quite another thing, not for such a thing as that. The breath of his good faith came short, however, as he recognised how long he had waited, or how long at least his companion had. That she, at all events, might be recorded as having waited in vain—this affected him sharply, and all the more because of his at first having done little more than amuse himself with the idea. It grew more grave as the gravity of her condition grew, and the state of mind it produced in him, which he himself ended by watching as if it had been some definite disfigurement of his outer person, may pass for another of his surprises. This conjoined itself still with another, the really stupefying consciousness of a question that he would have allowed to shape itself had he dared. What did everything mean—what, that is, did *she* mean, she and her vain waiting and her probable death and the soundless admonition of it all—unless that, at this time of day, it was simply, it was overwhelmingly too late? He had never at any stage of his queer consciousness admitted the whisper of such a correction; he had never till within these last few months been so false to his conviction as not to hold that what was to come to him had time, whether *he* struck himself as having it or not. That at last, at last, he certainly hadn't it, to speak of, or had it but in the scantiest measure—such, soon enough, as things went with him, became the inference with which his old obsession had to reckon: and this it was not helped to do by the more and more confirmed appearance that the great vagueness casting the long shadow in which he had lived had, to attest itself, almost no margin left. Since it was in Time that he was to have met his fate, so it was in Time that his fate was to have acted; and as he waked up to the sense of no longer being young, which was exactly the sense of being stale, just as that, in turn, was the sense of being weak, he waked up to another matter beside. It all hung together; they were subject, he and the great vagueness, to an equal and indivisible law. When the possibilities themselves had accordingly turned stale, when the secret of the gods had grown faint, had perhaps even quite evaporated, that, and that only, was failure. It wouldn't have been failure to be bankrupt, dishonoured, pilloried, hanged; it was failure not to be anything. And so, in the dark valley into which his path had taken its unlooked-for twist, he wondered not a little as he groped. He didn't care what awful crash might overtake him, with what ignominy or what monstrosity he might yet be associated—since he wasn't after all too utterly old to suffer—if it would only be decently proportionate to the posture he had kept, all his life, in the threatened presence of it. He had but one desire left—that he shouldn't have been "sold."

IV

Then it was that, one afternoon, while the spring of the year was young and new she met all in her own way his frankest betrayal of these alarms. He had gone in late to see her, but evening hadn't settled and she was presented to him in that long fresh light of waning April days which affects us often with a sadness sharper than the greyest hours of autumn. The week had been warm, the spring was supposed to have begun early, and May Bartram sat, for the first time in the year, without a fire; a fact that, to Marcher's sense, gave the scene of which she formed part a smooth and ultimate look, an air of knowing in its immaculate order and cold meaningless cheer, that it would never see a fire again. Her own aspect—he could scarce have said why—intensified this note. Almost as white as wax, with the marks and signs in her face as numerous and as fine as if they had been etched by a needle, with soft white draperies relieved by a faded green scarf on the delicate tone of which the years had further refined, she was the picture of a serene and exquisite but impenetrable sphinx, whose head, or indeed all whose person, might have been powdered with silver. She was a sphinx, yet with her white petals and green fronds she might have been a lily too—only an artificial lily, wonderfully imitated and constantly kept, without dust or stain, though not exempt from a slight droop and a complexity of faint creases, under some clear glass bell. The perfection of household care, of high polish and finish, always reigned in her rooms, but they now looked most as if everything had been wound up, tucked in, put away, so that she might sit with folded hands and with nothing more to do. She was "out of it," to Marcher's vision; her work was over; she communicated with him as across some gulf or from some island of rest that she had already reached, and it made him feel strangely abandoned. Was it—or rather wasn't it—that if for so long she had been watching with him the answer to their question must have swum into her ken and taken on its name, so that her occupation was verily gone? He had as much as charged her with this in saying to her, many months before, that she even knew something she was keeping from him. It was a point he had never since ventured to press, vaguely fearing as he did that it might become a difference, perhaps a disagreement, between them. He had in this later time turned nervous, which was what he in all the other years had never been; and the oddity was that his nervousness should have waited till he had begun to doubt, should have held off so long as he was sure. There was something, it seemed to him, that the wrong word would bring down on his head, something that would so at least ease off his tension. But he wanted not to speak the wrong word; that would make everything ugly. He wanted the knowledge he lacked to drop on him, if drop it could, by its own august weight. If she was to forsake him it was surely for her to take leave. This was why he didn't directly ask her again what she knew; but it was also why, approaching the matter from another side, he said to her in the course of his visit: "What do you regard as the very worst that at this time of day *can* happen to me?"

He had asked her that in the past often enough; they had, with the odd irregular rhythm of their intensities and avoidances, exchanged ideas about it and then had seen the ideas washed away by cool intervals, washed like figures traced in sea-sand. It had ever been the mark of their talk that the oldest allusions in it required but a little dismissal and reaction to come out again, sounding for the hour as new. She could thus at present meet his enquiry quite freshly and patiently. "Oh yes, I've repeatedly thought, only it always seemed to me of old that I couldn't quite make up my mind. I thought of dreadful things, between which it was difficult to choose; and so must you have done."

"Rather! I feel now as if I had scarce done anything else. I appear to myself to have spent my life in thinking of nothing *but* dreadful things. A great many of them I've at different times named to you, but there were others I couldn't name."

"They were too, too dreadful?"

"Too, too dreadful—some of them."

She looked at him a minute, and there came to him as he met it an inconsequent sense that her eyes, when one got their full clearness, were still as beautiful as they had been in youth, only beautiful with a strange cold light—a light that somehow was a part of the effect, if it wasn't rather a part of the cause, of the pale hard sweetness of the season and the hour. "And yet,' she said at last, "there are horrors we've mentioned."

It deepened the strangeness to see her, as such a figure in such a picture, talk of "horrors," but she was to do in a few minutes something stranger yet—though even of this he was to take the full measure but afterwards—and the note of it already trembled. It was, for the matter of that, one of the signs that her eyes were having again the high flicker of their prime. He had to admit, however, what she said. "Oh yes, there were times when we did go far." He caught himself in the act of speaking as if it all were over. Well, he wished it were; and the consummation depended for him clearly more and more on his friend.

But she had now a soft smile. "Oh far—!"

It was oddly ironic. "Do you mean you're prepared to go further?"

She was frail and ancient and charming as she continued to look at him, yet it was rather as if she had lost the thread. "Do you consider that we went far?"

"Why I thought it the point you were just making—that we *had* looked most things in the face."

"Including each other?" She still smiled. "But you're quite right. We've had together great imaginations, often great fears; but some of them have been unspoken."

"Then the worst—we haven't faced that. I *could* face it, I believe, if I knew what you think it. I feel," he explained, "as if I had lost my power to conceive such things." And he wondered if he looked as blank as he sounded. "It's spent."

"Then why do you assume," she asked, "that mine isn't?"

"Because you've given me signs to the contrary. It isn't a question for you of conceiving, imagining, comparing. It isn't a question now of choosing." At last he came out with it. "You know something I don't. You've shown me that before."

These last words had affected her, he made out in a moment, exceedingly, and she spoke with firmness. "I've shown you, my dear, nothing."

He shook his head. "You can't hide it."

"Oh, oh!" May Bartram sounded over what she couldn't hide. It was almost a smothered groan.

"You admitted it months ago, when I spoke of it to you as of something you were afraid I should find out. Your answer was that I couldn't, that I wouldn't, and I don't pretend I have. But you had something therefore in mind, and I now see how it must have been, how it still is, the possibility that, of all possibilities, has settled itself for you as the worst. This," he went on, "is why I appeal to you. I'm only afraid of ignorance to-day—I'm not afraid of knowledge." And then as for a while she said nothing: "What makes me sure is that I see in your face and feel here, in this air and amid these appearances, that you're out of it. You've done. You've had your experience. You leave me to my fate."

Well, she listened, motionless and white in her chair, as on a decision to be made, so that her manner was fairly an avowal, though still, with a small fine inner stiffness, an imperfect surrender. "It would be the worst," she finally let herself say. "I mean the thing I've never said."

It hushed him a moment. "More monstrous than all the monstrosities we've named?"

"More monstrous. Isn't that what you sufficiently express," she asked, "in calling it the worst?"

Marcher thought. "Assuredly—if you mean, as I do, something that includes all the loss and all the shame that are thinkable."

"It would if it should happen," said May Bartram. "What we're speaking of, remember, is only my idea."

"It's your belief," Marcher returned. "That's enough for me. I feel your beliefs are right. Therefore if, having this one, you give me no more light on it, you abandon me."

"No, no!" she repeated. "I'm with you—don't you see?—still." And as to make it more vivid to him she rose from her chair—a movement she seldom risked in these days—and showed herself, all draped and all soft, in her fairness and slimness. "I haven't forsaken you."

It was really, in its effort against weakness, a generous assurance, and had the success of the impulse not, happily, been great, it would have touched him to pain more than to pleasure. But the cold charm in her eyes had spread, as she hovered before him, to all the rest of her person, so that it was for the minute almost a recovery of youth. He couldn't pity her for that; he could only take her as she showed—as capable even yet of helping him. It was as if, at the same time, her light might at any instant go out; wherefore he must make the most of it. There passed before him with intensity the three or four things he wanted most to know; but the question that came of itself to his lips really covered the others. "Then tell me if I shall consciously suffer."

She promptly shook her head. "Never!"

It confirmed the authority he imputed to her, and it produced on him an extraordinary effect. "Well, what's better than that? Do you call that the worst?"

"You think nothing is better?" she asked.

She seemed to mean something so special that he again sharply wondered, though still with the dawn of a prospect of relief. "Why not, if one doesn't *know*?" After which, as their eyes, over his question, met in silence, the dawn deepened and something to his purpose came prodigiously out of her very face. His own, as he took it in, suddenly flushed to the forehead, and he gasped with the force of a perception to which, on the instant, everything fitted. The sound of his gasp filled the air; then he became articulate. "I see—if I don't suffer!"

In her own look, however, was doubt. "You see what?"

"Why what you mean—what you've always meant."

She again shook her head. "What I mean isn't what I've always meant. It's different."

"It's something new?"

She hung back from it a little. "Something new. It's not what you think. I see what you think."

His divination drew breath then; only her correction might be wrong. "It isn't that I *am* a blockhead?" he asked between faintness and grimness. "It isn't that it's all a mistake?"

"A mistake?" she pityingly echoed. *That* possibility, for her, he saw, would be monstrous; and if she guaranteed him the immunity from the pain it would accordingly not be what she had in mind. "Oh no," she declared; "It's nothing of that sort. You've been right."

Yet he couldn't help asking himself if she weren't, thus pressed, speaking but to save him. It seemed to him she should be most in a hole if his history should prove all a platitude. "Are you telling me the truth, so that I shan't have been a bigger idiot than I can bear to know? I *haven't* lived with a vain imagination, in the most besotted illusion? I haven't waited but to see the door shut in my face?"

She shook her head again. "However the case stands *that* isn't the truth. Whatever the reality, it *is* a reality. The door isn't shut. The door's open," said May Bartram.

"Then something's to come?"

She waited once again, always with her cold sweet eyes on him. "It's never too late." She had, with her gliding step, diminished the distance between them, and she stood nearer to him, close to him, a minute, as if still charged with the unspoken. Her movement might have been for some finer emphasis of what she was at once hesitating and deciding to say. He had been standing by the chimneypiece, fireless and sparely adorned, a small perfect old French clock and two morsels of rosy Dresden constituting all its furniture; and her hand grasped the shelf while she kept him waiting, grasped it a little as for support and encouragement. She only kept him waiting, however; that is he only waited. It had become suddenly, from her movement and attitude, beautiful and vivid to him that she had something more to give him; her wasted face delicately shone with it—it glittered almost as with the white lustre of silver in her expression. She was right, incontestably, for what he saw in her face was the truth, and strangely, without consequence, while their talk of it as dreadful was still in the air, she appeared to present it as inordinately soft. This, prompting bewilderment, made him but gape the more gratefully for her revelation, so that they continued for some minutes silent, her face shining at him, her contact imponderably pressing, and his stare all kind but all expectant. The end, none the less, was that what he had expected failed to come to him. Something else took place instead, which seemed to consist at first in the mere closing of her eyes. She gave way at the same instant to a slow fine shudder, and though he remained staring—though he stared in fact but the harder—turned off and regained her chair. It was the end of what she had been intending, but it left him thinking only of that.

"Well, you don't say—?"

She had touched in her passage a bell near a chimney and had sunk back strangely pale. "I'm afraid I'm too ill."

"Too ill to tell me?" It sprang up sharp to him, and almost to his lips, the fear she might die without giving him light. He checked himself in time from so expressing his question, but she answered as if she had heard the words.

"Don't you know—now?"

" 'Now'—?" She had spoken as if some difference had been made within the moment. But her maid, quickly obedient to her bell, was already with them. "I know nothing." And he was afterwards to say to himself that he must have spoken with odious impatience, such an impatience as to show that, supremely disconcerted, he washed his hands of the whole question.

"Oh!" said May Bartram.

"Are you in pain?" he asked as the woman went to her.

"No," said May Bartram.

Her maid, who had put an arm round her as if to take her to her room, fixed on him eyes that appealingly contradicted her; in spite of which, however, he showed once more his mystification. "What then has happened?"

She was once more, with her companion's help, on her feet, and, feeling withdrawal imposed on him, he had blankly found his hat and gloves and had reached the door. Yet he waited for her answer. "What was to," she said.

V

He came back the next day, but she was then unable to see him, and as it was literally the first time this had occurred in the long stretch of their acquaintance he turned away, defeated and sore, almost angry—or feeling at least that such a break in their custom was really the beginning of the end—and wandered alone with his thoughts, especially with the one he was least able to keep down. She was dying and he would lose her; she was dying and his life would end. He stopped in the Park, into which he had passed, and stared before him at his recurrent doubt. Away from her the doubt pressed again; in her presence he had believed her, but as he felt his forlornless he threw himself into the explanation that, nearest at hand, had most of a miserable warmth for him and least of a cold torment. She had deceived him to save him—to put him off with something in which he should be able to rest. What could the thing that was to happen to him be, after all, but just this thing that had begun to happen? Her dying, her death, his consequent solitude—*that* was what he had figured as the Beast in the Jungle, that was what had been in the lap of the gods. He had had her word for it as he left her—what else on earth could she have meant? It wasn't a thing of a monstrous order; not a fate rare and distinguished; not a stroke of fortune that overwhelmed and immortalised; it had only the stamp of the common doom. But poor Marcher at this hour judged the common doom sufficient. It would serve his turn, and even as the consummation of infinite waiting he would bend his pride to accept it. He sat down on a bench in the twilight. He hadn't been a fool. Something had *been*, as she had said, to come. Before he rose indeed it had quite struck him that the final fact matched with the long avenue through which he had had to reach it. As sharing his suspense and as giving herself all, giving her life, to bring it to an end, she had come with him every step of the way. He had lived by her aid, and to leave her behind would be cruelly, damnably to miss her. What could be more overwhelming than that?

Well, he was to know within the week, for though she kept him a while at bay, left him restless and wretched during a series of days on each of which he asked about her only again to have to turn away, she ended his trial by receiving him where she had always received him. Yet she had been brought out at some hazard into the presence of so many of the things that were, consciously, vainly, half their past, and there was scant service left in the gentleness of her mere desire, all too visible, to check his obsession and wind up his long trouble. That was clearly what she wanted, the one thing more for her own peace while she could still put out her hand. He was so affected by her state that, once seated by her chair, he was moved to let everything go; it was she herself therefore who brought him back, took up again, before she dismissed him, her last word of the other time. She showed how she wished to leave their business in order. "I'm not sure you understood. You've nothing to wait for more. It *has* come."

Oh how he looked at her! "Really?"

"Really."

"The thing that, as you said, *was* to?"

"The thing that we began in our youth to watch for."

Face to face with her once more he believed her; it was a claim to which he had so abjectly little to oppose. "You mean that it has come as a positive definite occurrence, with a name and a date?"

"Positive. Definite. I don't know about the 'name,' but oh what a date!"

He found himself again too helplessly at sea. "But come in the night—come and passed me by?"

May Bartram had her strange faint smile. "Oh no, it hasn't passed you by!"

"But if I haven't been aware of it and it hasn't touched me—?"

"Ah your not being aware of it"—and she seemed to hesitate an instant to deal with this—"your not being aware of it is the strangeness *in* the strangeness. It's the wonder *of* the wonder." She spoke as with the softness almost of a sick child, yet now at last, at the end of all, with the perfect straightness of a sibyl. She visibly knew that she knew, and the effect on him was of something to co-ordinate, in its high character, with the law that had ruled him. It was the true voice of the law; so on her lips would the law itself have sounded. "It *has* touched you," she went on. "It has done its office. It has made you all its own."

"So utterly without my knowing it?"

"So utterly without your knowing it." His hand, as he leaned to her, was on the arm of her chair, and, dimly smiling always now, she placed her own on it. "It's enough if *I* know it."

"Oh!" he confusedly breathed, as she herself of late so often had done.

"What I long ago said is true. You'll never know now, and I think you ought to be content. You've *had* it," said May Bartram.

"But had what?"

"Why what was to have marked you out. The proof of your law. It has acted. I'm too glad," she then bravely added, "to have been able to see what it's *not*."

He continued to attach his eyes to her, and with the sense that it was all beyond him, and that *she* was too, he would still have sharply challenged her hadn't he so felt it an abuse of her weakness to do more than take devoutly what she gave him, take it hushed as to a revelation. If he did speak, it was out of the fore-knowledge of his loneliness to come. "If you're glad of what it's 'not' it might then have been worse?"

She turned her eyes away, she looked straight before her; with which after a moment: "Well, you know our fears."

He wondered. "It's something then we never feared?"

On this slowly she turned to him. "Did we ever dream, with all our dreams, that we should sit and talk of it thus?"

He tried for a little to make out that they had; but it was as if their dreams, numberless enough, were in solution in some thick cold mist through which thought lost itself. "It might have been that we couldn't talk?"

"Well"—she did her best for him—"not from this side. This, you see," she said, "is the *other* side."

"I think," poor Marcher returned, "that all sides are the same to me." Then, however, as she gently shook her head in correction: "We mightn't, as it were, have got across—?"

"To where we are—no. We're *here*"—she made her weak emphasis.

"And much good does it do us!" was her friend's frank comment.

"It does us the good it can. It does us the good that *it* isn't here. It's past. It's behind," said May Bartram. "Before—" but her voice dropped.

He had got up, not to tire her, but it was hard to combat his yearning. She after all told him nothing but that his light had failed—which he knew well enough without her. "Before—?" he blankly echoed.

"Before, you see, it was always to *come*. That kept it present."

"Oh I don't care what comes now! Besides," Marcher added, "it seems to me I liked it better present, as you say, than I can like it absent with *your* absence."

"Oh mine!"—and her pale hands made light of it.

"With the absence of everything." He had a dreadful sense of standing there before her for—so far as anything but this proved, this bottomless drop was concerned—the last time of their life. It rested on him with a weight he felt he could scarce bear, and this weight it apparently was that still pressed out what remained in him of speakable protest. "I believe you; but I can't begin to pretend I understand. *Nothing,* for me, is past; nothing *will* pass till I pass myself, which I pray my stars may be as soon as possible. Say, however," he added, "that I've eaten my cake, as you contend, to the last crumb —how can the thing I've never felt at all be the thing I was marked out to feel?"

She met him perhaps less directly, but she met him unperturbed. "You take your 'feelings' for granted. You were to suffer your fate. That was not necessarily to know it."

"How in the world—when what is such knowledge but suffering?"

She looked up at him a while in silence. "No—you don't understand."

"I suffer," said John Marcher.

"Don't, don't!"

"How can I help at least *that?*"

"*Don't!*" May Bartram repeated.

She spoke it in a tone so special, in spite of her weakness, that he stared an instant—stared as if some light, hitherto hidden, had shimmered across his vision. Darkness again closed over it, but the gleam had already become for him an idea. "Because I haven't the right—?"

"Don't *know*—when you needn't," she mercifully urged. "You needn't —for we shouldn't."

"Shouldn't?" If he could but know what she meant!

"No—it's too much,"

"Too much?" he still asked but, with a mystification that was the next moment of a sudden to give way. Her words, if they meant something, affected him in this light—the light also of her wasted face—as meaning *all,* and the sense of what knowledge had been for herself came over him with a rush which broke through into a question. "Is it of that then you're dying?"

But she watched him, gravely at first, as to see, with this, where he was, and she might have seen something or feared something that moved her sympathy. "I would live for you still—if I could." Her eyes closed for a little, as if, withdrawn into herself, she were for a last time trying. "But I can't!" she said as she raised them again to take leave of him.

She couldn't indeed, as but too promptly and sharply appeared, and he had no vision of her after this that was anything but darkness and doom. They had parted for ever in that strange talk; access to her chamber of pain, rigidly guarded, was almost wholly forbidden him; he was feeling now moreover, in the face of doctors, nurses, the two or three relatives attracted doubtless by the presumption of whatever she had to "leave," how few were the rights, as they were called in such cases, that he had to put forward, and how odd it might even seem that their intimacy shouldn't have given him more of them. The stupidest fourth cousin had more, even though she had been nothing in such a person's life. She had been a feature of features in *his,* for what else was it to have been so indispensable? Strange beyond saying were the ways of existence, baffling for him the anomaly of his lack, as he felt it to be, of producible claim. A woman might have been, as it were, everything to him, and it might yet present him in no connexion that any one seemed held to recognise. If this was the case in these closing weeks it was the case more sharply on the occasion of the last offices rendered, in the great grey London cemetery, to what had been mortal, to what had been precious, in his friend. The concourse at her grave was not numerous, but he saw himself treated as scarce more nearly concerned with it than if there had been a thousand others. He was in short from this moment face to face with the fact that he was to profit extraordinarily little by the interest May Bartram had taken in him. He couldn't quite have said what he expected, but he hadn't surely expected this approach to a double privation. Not only had her interest failed him, but he seemed to feel himself unattended—and for a reason he couldn't seize—by the distinction, the dignity, the propriety, if nothing else, of the man markedly bereaved. It was as if in the view of society he had not *been* markedly bereaved, as if there still failed some sign or proof of it, and as if none the less his character could never be affirmed nor the deficiency ever made up. There were moments as the weeks went by when he would have liked, by some almost aggressive act, to take his stand on the intimacy of his loss, in order that it *might* be questioned and his retort, to the relief of his spirit, so recorded; but the moments of an irritation more helpless followed fast on these, the moments during which, turning things over with a good conscience but with a bare horizon, he found himself wondering if he oughtn't to have begun, so to speak, further back.

He found himself wondering indeed at many things, and this last speculation had others to keep it company. What could he have done, after all, in her lifetime, without giving them both, as it were, away? He couldn't have made known she was watching him, for that would have published the superstition of the Beast. This was what closed his mouth now—now that the Jungle had been threshed to vacancy and that the Beast had stolen away. It sounded too foolish and too flat; the difference for him in this particular, the extinction in his life of the element of suspense, was such as in fact to surprise him. He could scarce have said what the effect resembled; the abrupt cessation, the positive prohibition, of music perhaps, more than anything else, in some place all adjusted and all accustomed to sonority and to attention. If he could at any rate have conceived lifting the veil from his image at some moment of the past (what had he done, after all, if not lift it to *her*?) so to do this today, to talk to people at large of the Jungle cleared and confide to them that he now felt it as safe, would have been not only to see them listen as to a goodwife's tale, but really to hear himself tell one. What it presently came to in truth was that poor Marcher waded through his beaten grass, where no life stirred, where no breath sounded, where no evil eye seemed to gleam from a possible lair, very much as if vaguely looking for the Beast, and still more as if acutely missing it. He walked about in an existence that had grown strangely more spacious, and, stopping fitfully in places where the undergrowth of life struck him as closer, asked himself yearningly, wondered secretly and sorely, if it would have lurked here or there. It would have at all events *sprung*; what was at least complete was his belief in the truth itself of the assurance given him. The change from his old sense to his new was absolute and final: what was to happen *had* so absolutely and finally happened that he was as little able to know a fear for his future as to know a hope; so absent in short was any question of anything still to come. He was to live entirely with the other question, that of his unidentified past, that of his having to see his fortune impenetrably muffled and masked.

The torment of his vision became then his occupation; he couldn't perhaps have consented to live but for the possibility of guessing. She had told him, his friend, not to guess; she had forbidden him, so far as he might, to know, and she had even in a sort denied the power in him to learn: which were so many things, precisely, to deprive him of rest. It wasn't that he wanted, he argued for fairness, that anything past and done should repeat itself; it was only that he shouldn't, an as anticlimax, have been taken sleeping so sound as not to be able to win back by an effort of thought the lost stuff of consciousness. He declared to himself at moments that he would either win it back or have done with consciousness for ever; he made this idea his one motive in fine, made it so much his passion that none other, to compare with it, seemed ever to have touched him. The lost stuff of consciousness became thus for him as a strayed or stolen child to an unappeasable father; he hunted it up and down very much as if he were knocking at doors and enquiring of the police. This was the spirit in which, inevitably, he set himself to travel; he started on a journey that was to be as long as he could make it; it danced before him that, as the other side of the globe couldn't possibly have less to say to him, it might, by a possibility of suggestion, have more. Before he quitted London, however, he made a pilgrimage to May Bartram's grave, took his way to it through the endless avenues of the grim suburban metropolis, sought it out in the wilderness of tombs, and, though he had come but for the renewal of the act of farewell, found himself, when he had at last stood by it, beguiled into long intensities. He stood for an hour, powerless to turn away and yet powerless to penetrate the darkness of death; fixing with his eyes her inscribed name and date, beating his forehead against the fact of the secret they kept, drawing his breath, while he waited, as if some sense would in pity of him rise from the stones. He kneeled on the stones, however, in vain; they kept what they concealed; and if the face of the tomb did become a face for him it was because her two names became a pair of eyes that didn't know him. He gave them a last long look, but no palest light broke.

VI

He stayed away, after this, for a year; he visited the depths of Asia, spending himself on scenes of romantic interest, of superlative sanctity; but what was present to him everywhere was that for a man who had known what *he* had known the world was vulgar and vain. The state of mind in which he had lived for so many years shone out to him, in reflexion, as a light that coloured and refined, a light beside the glow of the East was garish, cheap and thin. The terrible truth was that he had lost—with everything else— a distinction as well; the things he saw couldn't help being common when he had become common to look at them. He was simply now one of them himself— he was in the dust, without a peg for the sense of difference; and there were hours when, before the temples of gods and the sepulchres of kings, his spirit turned for nobleness of association to the barely discriminated slab in the London suburb. That had become for him, and more intensely with time and distance, his one witness of a past glory. It was all that was left to him for proof or pride, yet the past glories of Pharaohs were nothing to him as he thought of it. Small wonder then that he came back to it on the morrow of his return. He was drawn there this time as irresistibly as the other, yet with a confidence, almost, that was doubtless the effect of the many months that had elapsed. He had lived, in spite of himself, into his change of feeling, and in wandering over the earth had wandered, as might be said, from the circumference to the centre of his desert. He had settled to his safety and accepted perforce his extinction; figuring to himself, with some colour, in the likeness of certain little old men he remembered to have seen, of whom, all meagre and wizened as they might look, it was related that they had in their time fought twenty duels or been loved by ten princesses. They indeed had been wondrous for others while he was but wondrous for himself; which, however, was exactly the cause of his haste to renew the wonder by getting back, as he might put it, into his own presence. That had quickened his steps and checked his delay. If his visit was prompt it was because he had been separated so long from the part of himself that alone he now valued.

It's accordingly not false to say that he reached his goal with a certain elation and stood there again with a certain assurance. The creature beneath the sod *knew* of his rare experience, so that, strangely now, the place had lost for him its mere blankness of expression. It met him in mildness—not, as before, in mockery; it wore for him the air of conscious greeting that we find, after absence, in things that have closely belonged to us and which seem to confess of themselves to the connexion. The plot of ground, the graven tablet, the tended flowers affected him so as belonging to him that he resembled for the hour a contended landlord reviewing a piece of property. Whatever had happened—well, had happened. He had not come back this time with the vanity of that question, his former worrying "what, *what?*" now practically so spent. Yet he would none the less never again so cut himself off from the spot; he would come back to it every month, for if he did nothing else by its aid he at least held up his head. It thus grew for him, in the oddest way, a positive resource; he carried out his idea of periodical returns, which took their place at last among the most inveterate of his habits. What it all amounted to, oddly enough, was that in his finally so simplified world this garden of death gave him the few square feet of earth on which he could still most live. It was as if, being nothing anywhere else for any one, nothing even for himself, he were just everything here, and if not for a crowd of witnesses or indeed for any witness but John Marcher, then by clear right of the register that he could scan like an open page. The open page was the tomb of his friend, and *there* were the facts of the past, there the truth of his life, there the backward reaches in which he could lose himself. He did this from time to time with such effect that he seemed to wander through the old years with his hand in the arm of a companion who was, in the most extraordinary manner, his other, his younger self; and to wander, which was more extraordinary yet, round and round a third presence—not wandering she, but stationary, still, whose eyes, turning with his revolution, never ceased to follow him, and whose seat was his point, so to speak, of orientation. Thus in short he settled to live—feeding all on the sense that he once *had* lived, and dependent on it not alone for a support but for an identity.

It sufficed him in its way for months and the year elapsed; it would doubtless even have carried him further but for an accident, superficially slight, which moved him, quite in another direction, with a force beyond any of his impressions of Egypt or of India. It was a thing of the merest chance—the turn, as he afterwards felt, of a hair, though he was indeed to live to believe that if light hadn't come to him in this particular fashion it would still have come in another. He was to live to believe this, I say, though he was not to live, I may not less definitely mention, to do much else. We allow him at any rate the benefit of the conviction, struggling up for him at the end, that, whatever might have happened or not happened, he would have come round of himself to the light. The incident of an autumn day had put the match to the train laid from of old by his misery. With the light before him he knew that even of late his ache had only been smothered. It was strangely drugged, but it throbbed; at the touch it began to bleed. And the touch, in the event, was the face of a fellow mortal. This face, one grey afternoon when the leaves were thick in the alleys, looked into Marcher's own, at the cemetery, with an expression like the cut of a blade. He felt it, that is, so deep down that he winced at the steady thrust. The person who so mutely assaulted him was a figure he had noticed on reaching his own goal, absorbed by a grave a short distance away, a grave apparently fresh, so that the emotion of the visitor would probably match it for frankness. This fact alone forbade further attention, though during the time he stayed he remained vaguely conscious of his neighbour, a middle-aged man apparently, in mourning, whose bowed back, among the clustered monuments and mortuary yews, was constantly presented. Marcher's theory that these were elements in contact with which he himself revived, had suffered, on this occasion, it may be granted, a marked, an excessive check. The autumn day was dire for him as none had recently been, and he rested with a heaviness he had not yet known on the low stone table that bore May Bartram's name. He rested without power to move, as if some spring in him, some spell vouchsafed, had suddenly been broken for ever. If he could have done that moment as he wanted he would simply have stretched himself on the slab that was ready to take him, treating it as a place prepared to receive his last sleep. What in all the wide world had he now to keep awake for? He stared before him with the question, and it was then that, as one of the cemetery walks passed near him, he caught the shock of the face.

His neighbour at the other grave had withdrawn, as he himself, with force enough in him, would have done by now, and was advancing along the path on his way to one of the gates. This brought him close, and his pace was slow, so that—and all the more as there was a kind of hunger in his look—the two men were for a minute directly confronted. Marcher knew him at once for one of the deeply stricken—a perception so sharp that nothing else in the picture comparatively lived, neither his dress, his age, nor his presumable character and class; nothing lived but the deep ravage of the features he showed. He *showed* them—that was the point; he was moved, as he passed, by some impulse that was either a signal for sympathy or, more possibly, a challenge to an opposed sorrow. He might already have been aware of our friend, might at some previous hour have noticed in him the smooth habit of the scene, with which the state of his own senses so scantly consorted, and might thereby have been stirred as by an overt discord. What Marcher was at all events conscious of was in the first place that the image of scarred passion presented to him was conscious too—of something that profaned the air; and in the second that, roused, startled, shocked, he was yet the next moment looking after it, as it went, with envy. The most extraordinary thing that had happened to him —though he had given that name to other matters as well—took place, after his immediate vague stare, as a consequence of this impression. The stranger passed, but the raw glare of his grief remained, making our friend wonder in pity what wrong, what wound it expressed, what injury not to be healed. What had the man *had*, to make him by the loss of it so bleed and yet live?

Something—and this reached him with a pang—that *he*, John Marcher, hadn't; the proof of which was precisely John Marcher's arid end. No passion had ever touched him, for this was what passion meant; he had survived and maundered and pined, but where had been *his* deep ravage? The extraordinary thing we speak of was the sudden rush of the result of this question. The sight that had just met his eyes named to him, as in letters of quick flame, something he had utterly, insanely missed, and what he had missed made these things a train of fire, made them mark themselves in an anguish of inward throbs. He had seen *outside* of his life, not learned it within, the way a woman was mourned when she had been loved for herself: such was the force of his conviction of the meaning of the stranger's face, which still flared for him as a smoky torch. It hadn't come to him, the knowledge, on the wings of experience; it had brushed him, jostled him, upset him, with the disrespect of chance, the insolence of accident. Now that the illumination had begun, however, it blazed to the zenith, and what he presently stood there gazing at was the sounded void of his life. He gazed, he drew breath, in pain; he turned in his dismay, and, turning, he had before him in sharper incision than ever the open page of his story. The name on the table smote him as the passage of his neighbour had done, and what it said to him, full in the face, was that *she* was what he had missed. This was the awful thought, the answer to all the past, the vision at the dread clearness of which he grew as cold as the stone beneath him. Everything fell together, confessed, explained, overwhelmed; leaving him most of all stupefied at the blindness he had cherished. The fate he had been marked for he had met with a vengeance—he had emptied the cup to the lees; he had been the man of his time, *the* man, to whom nothing on earth was to have happened. That was the rare stroke—that was his visitation. So he saw it, as we say, in pale horror, while the pieces fitted and fitted. So *she* had seen it while he didn't, and so she served at this hour to drive the truth home. It was the truth, vivid and monstrous, that all the while he had waited the wait was itself his portion. This was the companion of his vigil and at a given moment made out, and she had then offered him the chance to baffle his doom. One's doom, however, was never baffled, and on the day she told him his own had come down she had seen him but stupidly stare at the escape she offered him.

The escape would have been to love her; then, *then* he would have lived. *She* had lived—who could say now with what passion?—since she had loved him for himself whereas he had never thought of her (ah how it hugely glared at him!) but in the chill of his egotism and the light of her use. Her spoken words came back to him—the chain stretched and stretched. The Beast had lurked indeed, and the Beast at its hour, had sprung; it had sprung in that twilight of the cold April when, pale, ill, wasted, but all beautiful, and perhaps even then recoverable, she had risen from her chair to stand before him and let him imaginably guess. It had sprung as he didn't guess; it had sprung as she hopelessly turned from him, and the mark, by the time he left her, had fallen where it *was* to fall. He had justified his fear and achieved his fate; he had failed, with the last exactitude, of all he was to fail of; and a moan now rose to his lips as he remembered she had prayed he mightn't know. This horror of waking—*this* was knowledge, knowledge under the breath of which the very tears in his eyes seemed to freeze. Through them, none the less, he tried to fix it and hold it; he kept it there before him so that he might feel the pain. That at least, belated and bitter, had something of the taste of life. But the bitterness suddenly sickened him, and it was as if, horribly, he saw, in the truth, in the cruelty of his image, what had been appointed and done. He saw the Jungle of his life and saw the lurking Beast; then, while he looked, perceived it, as by a stir of the air, rise, huge and hideous, for the leap that was to settle him. His eyes darkened—it was close; and, instinctively turning, in his hallucination, to avoid it, he flung himself, face down, on the tomb.

JOSEPH CONRAD

The Secret Sharer

I

On my right hand there were lines of fishing-stakes resembling a mysterious system of half-submerged bamboo fences, incomprehensible in its division of the domain of tropical fishes, and crazy of aspect as if abandoned for ever by some nomad tribe of fishermen now gone to the other end of the ocean; for there was no sign of human habitation as far as the eye could reach. To the left a group of barren islets, suggesting ruins of stone walls, towers, and blockhouses, had its foundations set in a blue sea that itself looked solid, so still and stable did it lie below my feet; even the track of light from the westering sun shone smoothly, without that animated glitter which tells of an imperceptible ripple. And when I turned my head to take a parting glance at the tug which had just left us anchored outside the bar, I saw the straight line of the flat shore joined to the stable sea, edge to edge, with a perfect and unmarked closeness, in one levelled floor half brown, half blue under the enormous dome of the sky. Corresponding in their insignificance to the islets of the sea, two small clumps of trees, one on each side of the only fault in the impeccable joint, marked the mouth of the river Meinam we had just left on the first preparatory stage of our homeward journey; and, far back on the inland level, a larger and loftier mass, the grove surrounding the great Paknam pagoda, was the only thing on which the eye could rest from the vain task of exploring the monotonous sweep of the horizon. Here and there gleams as of a few scattered pieces of silver marked the windings of the great river; and on the nearest of them, just within the bar, the tug steaming right into the land became lost to my sight, hull and funnel and masts, as though the impassive earth had swallowed her up without an effort, without a tremor. My eye followed the light cloud of her smoke, now here, now there, above the plain, according to the devious curves of the stream, but always fainter and farther away, till I lost it at last behind the mitre-shaped hill of the great pagoda. And then I was left alone with my ship, anchored at the head of the Gulf of Siam.

She floated at the starting-point of a long journey, very still in an immense stillness, the shadows of her spars flung far to the eastward by the setting sun. At that moment I was alone on her decks. There was not a sound in her—and around us nothing moved, nothing lived, not a canoe on the water, not a bird in the air, not a cloud in the sky. In this breathless pause at the threshold of a long passage we seemed to be measuring our fitness for a long and arduous enterprise, the appointed task of both our existences to be car-

From *Twixt Land and Sea* by Joseph Conrad. Reprinted by permission of J. M. Dent & Sons, Ltd. and the Trustees of the Joseph Conrad estate.

ried out, far from all human eyes, with only sky and sea for spectators and for judges.

There must have been some glare in the air to interfere with one's sight, because it was only just before the sun left us that my roaming eyes made out beyond the highest ridge of the principal islet of the group something which did away with the solemnity of perfect solitude. The tide of darkness flowed on swiftly; and with tropical suddenness a swarm of stars came out above the shadowy earth, while I lingered yet, my hand resting lightly on my ship's rail as if on the shoulder of a trusted friend. But, with all that multitude of celestial bodies staring down at one, the comfort of quiet communion with her was gone for good. And there were also disturbing sounds by this time—voices, footsteps forward; the steward flitted along the maindeck, a busily ministering spirit; a hand-bell tinkled urgently under the poop-deck. . . .

I found my two officers waiting for me near the supper table, in the lighted cuddy. We sat down at once, and as I helped the chief mate, I said:

"Are you aware that there is a ship anchored inside the islands? I saw her mastheads above the ridge as the sun went down."

He raised sharply his simple face, overcharged by a terrible growth of whisker, and emitted his usual ejaculations: "Bless my soul, sir! You don't say so!"

My second mate was a round-cheeked, silent young man, grave beyond his years, I thought; but as our eyes happened to meet I detected a slight quiver on his lips. I looked down at once. It was not my part to encourage sneering on board my ship. It must be said, too, that I knew very little of my officers. In consequence of certain events of no particular significance, except to myself, I had been appointed to the command only a fortnight before. Neither did I know much of the hands forward. All these people had been together for eighteen months or so, and my position was that of the only stranger on board. I mention this because it has some bearing on what is to follow. But what I felt most was my being a stranger to the ship; and if all the truth must be told, I was somewhat of a stranger to myself. The youngest man on board (barring the second mate), and untried as yet by a position of the fullest responsibility, I was willing to take the adequacy of the others for granted. They had simply to be equal to their tasks; but I wondered how far I should turn out faithful to that ideal conception of one's own personality every man sets up for himself secretly.

Meantime the chief mate, with an almost visible effect of collaboration on the part of his round eyes and frightful whiskers, was trying to evolve a theory of the anchored ship. His dominant trait was to take all things into earnest consideration. He was of a painstaking turn of mind. As he used to say, he "liked to account to himself" for practically everything that came in his way, down to a miserable scorpion he had found in his cabin a week before. The why and the wherefore of that scorpion—how it got on board and came to select his room rather than the pantry (which was a dark place and more what a scorpion would be partial to), and how on earth it managed to drown itself in the inkwell of his writing-desk—had exercised him infinitely. The ship within the islands was much more easily accounted for; and just as we were about to rise from table he made his pronouncement. She was, he doubted not, a ship from home lately arrived. Probably she drew too much water to cross the bar except at the top of spring tides. Therefore she went into that natural harbour to wait for a few days in preference to remaining in an open road-stead.

"That's so," confirmed the second mate, suddenly, in his slightly hoarse voice. "She draws over twenty feet. She's the Liverpool ship *Sephora* with a cargo of coal. Hundred and twenty-three days from Cardiff."

We looked at him in surprise.

"The tugboat skipper told me when he came on board for your letters, sir," explained the young man. "He expects to take her up the river the day after tomorrow."

After thus overwhelming us with the extent of his information he slipped out of the cabin. The mate observed regretfully that he "could not account for that young fellow's whims." What prevented him telling us all about it at once, he wanted to know.

I detained him as he was making a move. For the last two days the crew had had plenty of hard work, and the night before they had very little sleep. I felt painfully that I—a stranger—was doing something unusual when I directed him to let all hands turn in without setting an anchor-watch. I pro-posed to keep on deck myself till one o'clock or thereabouts. I would get the second mate to relieve me at that hour.

"He will turn out the cook and the steward at four," I concluded, "and then give you a call. Of course at the slightest sign of any sort of wind we'll have the hands up and make a start at once."

He concealed his astonishment. "Very well, sir." Outside the cuddy he put his head in the second mate's door to inform him of my unheard-of caprice to take a five hours' anchor-watch on myself. I heard the other raise his voice incredulously—"What? The Captain himself?" Then a few more murmurs, a door closed, then another. A few moments later I went on deck.

My strangeness, which had made me sleepless, had prompted that un-conventional arrangement, as if I had expected in those solitary hours of the night to get on terms with the ship of which I knew nothing, manned by men of whom I knew very little more. Fast alongside a wharf, littered like any ship in port with a tangle of unrelated things, invaded by unrelated shore people, I had hardly seen her yet properly. Now, as she lay cleared for sea, the stretch of her main-deck seemed to me very fine under the stars. Very fine, very roomy for her size, and very inviting. I descended the poop and paced the waist, my mind picturing to myself the coming passage through the Malay Archipelago, down the Indian Ocean, and up the Atlantic. All its phases were familiar enough to me, every characteristic, all the alternatives which were likely to face me on the high seas—everything! . . . except the novel responsibility of command. But I took heart from the reasonable thought that the ship was like other ships, the men like other men, and that the sea was not likely to keep any special surprises expressly for my discomfiture.

Arrived at that comforting conclusion, I bethought myself of a cigar and went below to get it. All was still down there. Everybody at the after end of the ship was sleeping profoundly. I came out again on the quarter-deck, agreeably at ease in my sleeping-suit on that warm breathless night, barefooted, a glowing cigar in my teeth, and, going forward, I was met by the profound silence of the fore end of the ship. Only as I passed the door of the forecastle I heard a deep, quiet, trustful sigh of some sleeper inside. And suddenly I rejoiced in the great security of the sea as compared with the unrest of the land, in my choice of that untempted life presenting no disquieting problems, invested with an elementary moral beauty by the absolute straightforwardness of its appeal and by the singleness of its purpose.

The riding-light in the fore-rigging burned with a clear, untroubled, as if symbolic, flame, confident and bright in the mysterious shades of the night. Passing on my way aft along the other side of the ship, I observed that the rope side-ladder, put over, no doubt, for the master of the tug when he came to fetch away our letters, had not been hauled in as it should have been. I became annoyed at this, for exactitude in small matters is the very soul of discipline. Then I reflected that I had myself peremptorily dismissed my officers from duty, and by my own act had prevented the anchor-watch being formally set and things properly attended to. I asked myself whether it was wise ever to interfere with the established routine of duties even from the kindest of motives. My action might have made me appear eccentric. Goodness only knew how that absurdly whiskered mate would "account" for my conduct, and what the whole ship thought of that informality of their new captain. I was vexed with myself.

Not from compunction certainly, but, as it were mechanically, I proceeded to get the ladder in myself. Now a side-ladder of that sort is a light affair and comes in easily, yet my vigorous tug, which should have brought it flying on board, merely recoiled upon my body in a totally unexpected jerk. What the devil! . . . I was so astounded by the immovableness of that ladder that I remained stock-still, trying to account for it to myself like that imbecile mate of mine. In the end, of course, I put my head over the rail.

The side of the ship made an opaque belt of shadow on the darkling glassy shimmer of the sea. But I saw at once something elongated and pale floating very close to the ladder. Before I could form a guess a faint flash of phosphorescent light, which seemed to issue suddenly from the naked body of a man, flickered in the sleeping water with the elusive, silent play of summer lightning in a night sky. With a gasp I saw revealed to my stare a pair of feet, the long legs, a broad livid back immersed right up to the neck in a greenish cadaverous glow. One hand, awash, clutched the bottom rung of the ladder. He was complete but for the head. A headless corpse! The cigar dropped out of my gaping mouth with a tiny plop and a short hiss quite audible in the absolute stillness of all things under heaven. At that I suppose he raised up his face, a dimly pale oval in the shadow of the ship's side. But even then I could only barely make out down there the shape of his black-haired head. However, it was enough for the horrid, frost-bound sensation which had gripped me about the chest to pass off. The moment of vain exclamations was past, too. I only climbed on the spare spar and leaned over the rail as far as I could, to bring my eyes nearer to that mystery floating alongside.

As he hung by the ladder, like a resting swimmer, the sea-lightning played about his limbs at every stir; and he appeared in it ghastly, silvery, fish-like. He remained as mute as a fish, too. He made no motion to get out of the water, either. It was inconceivable that he should not attempt to come on board, and strangely troubling to suspect that perhaps he did not want to. And my first words were prompted by just that troubled incertitude.

"What's the matter?" I asked in my ordinary tone, speaking down to the face upturned exactly under mine.

"Cramp," it answered, no louder. Then slightly anxious, "I say, no need to call any one."

"I was not going to," I said.

"Are you alone on deck?"

"Yes."

I had somehow the impression that he was on the point of letting go the ladder to swim away beyond my ken—mysterious as he came. But, for the moment, this being appearing as if he had risen from the bottom of the sea (it was certainly the nearest land to the ship) wanted only to know the time. I told him. And he, down there, tentatively:

"I suppose your captain's turned in?"

"I am sure he isn't," I said.

He seemed to struggle with himself, for I heard something like the low, bitter murmur of doubt. "What's the good?" His next words came out with a hesitating effort.

"Look here, my man. Could you call him out quietly?"

I thought the time had come to declare myself.

"I am the captain."

I heard a "By Jove!" whispered at the level of the water. The phosphorescence flashed in the swirl of the water all about his limbs, his other hand seized the ladder.

"My name's Leggatt."

The voice was calm and resolute. A good voice. The self-possession of that man had somehow induced a corresponding state in myself. It was very quietly that I remarked:

"You must be a good swimmer."

"Yes. I've been in the water practically since nine o'clock. The question for me now is whether I am to let go this ladder and go on swimming till I sink from exhaustion, or—to come on board here."

I felt this was no mere formula of desperate speech, but a real alternative in the view of a strong soul. I should have gathered from this that he was young; indeed, it is only the young who are ever confronted by such clear issues. But at the time it was pure intuition on my part. A mysterious communication was established already between us two—in the face of that silent, darkened tropical sea. I was young, too; young enough to make no comment. The man in the water began suddenly to climb up the ladder, and I hastened away from the rail to fetch some clothes.

Before entering the cabin I stood still, listening in the lobby at the foot of the stairs. A faint snore came through the closed door of the chief mate's room. The second mate's door was on the hook, but the darkness in there was absolutely soundless. He, too, was young and could sleep like a stone. Remained the steward, but he was not likely to wake up before he was called. I got a sleeping-suit out of my room and, coming back on deck, saw the naked man from the sea sitting on the main-hatch, glimmering white in the darkness his elbows on his knees and his head in his hands. In a moment he had concealed his damp body in a sleeping-suit of the same grey-stripe pattern as the one I was wearing and followed me like my double on the poop. Together we moved right aft, barefooted, silent.

"What is it?" I asked in a deadened voice, taking the lighted lamp out of the binnacle, and raising it to his face.

"An ugly business."

He had regular features; a good mouth; light eyes under somewhat heavy, dark eyebrows; a smooth, square forehead; no growth on his cheeks; a small, brown moustache, and a well-shaped, round chin. His expression was concentrated, meditative, under the inspecting light of the lamp I held up to his face; such as a man thinking hard in solitude might wear. My sleeping-suit was just right for his size. A well-knit young fellow of twenty-five at most. He caught his lower lip with the edge of white, even teeth.

"Yes," I said, replacing the lamp in the binnacle. The warm, heavy tropical night closed upon his head again.

"There's a ship over there," he murmured.

"Yes, I know. The *Sephora*. Did you know of us?"

"Hadn't the slightest idea. I am the mate of her——" He paused and corrected himself. "I should say I *was*."

"Aha! Something wrong?"

"Yes. Very wrong indeed. I've killed a man."

"What do you mean? Just now?"

"No, on the passage. Weeks ago. Thirty-nine south. When I say a man——"

"Fit of temper," I suggested, confidently.

The shadowy, dark head, like mine, seemed to nod imperceptibly above the ghostly grey of my sleeping-suit. It was, in the night, as though I had been faced by my own reflection in the depths of a sombre and immense mirror.

"A pretty thing to have to own up to for a Conway boy," murmured my double, distinctly.

"You're a Conway boy?"

"I am," he said, as if startled. Then, slowly . . . "Perhaps you too——"

It was so; but being a couple of years older I had left before he joined. After a quick interchange of dates a silence fell; and I thought suddenly of my absurd mate with his terrific whiskers and the "Bless my soul—you don't say so" type of intellect. My double gave me an inkling of his thoughts by saying: "My father's a parson in Norfolk. Do you see me before a judge and jury on that charge? For myself I can't see the necessity. There are fellows that an angel from heaven——And I am not that. He was one of those creatures that are just simmering all the time with a silly sort of wickedness. Miserable devils that have no business to live at all. He wouldn't do his duty and wouldn't let anybody else do theirs. But what's the good of talking! You know well enough the sort of ill-conditioned snarling cur——"

He appealed to me as if our experiences had been as identical as our clothes. And I knew well enough the pestiferous danger of such a character where there are no means of legal repression. And I knew well enough also that my double there was no homicidal ruffian. I did not think of asking him for details, and he told me the story roughly in brusque, disconnected sentences. I needed no more. I saw it all going on as though I were myself inside that other sleeping-suit.

"It happened while we were setting a reefed foresail, at dusk. Reefed foresail! You understand the sort of weather. The only sail we had left to keep the ship running; so you may guess what it had been like for days. Anxious sort of job, that. He gave me some of his cursed insolence at the sheet. I tell you I was overdone with this terrific weather that seemed to have no end to it. Terrific, I tell you—and a deep ship. I believe the fellow himself was half crazed with funk. It was no time for gentlemanly reproof, so I turned round and felled him like an ox. He up and at me. We closed just as an awful sea made for the ship. All hands saw it coming and took to the rigging, but I had him by the throat, and went on shaking him like a rat, the men above us yelling, 'Look out! look out!' " Then a crash as if the sky had fallen on my head. They say that for over ten minutes hardly anything was to be seen of the ship—just the three masts and a bit of the forecastle head and of the poop all awash driving along in a smother of foam. It was a miracle that they found us, jammed together behind the forebits. It's clear that I meant business, because I was holding him by the throat still when they picked us up. He was black in the face. It was too much for them. It seems they rushed us aft together, gripped as we were, screaming 'Murder!' like a lot of lunatics, and broke into the cuddy. And the ship running for her life, touch and go all the time, any minute her last in a sea fit to turn your hair grey only a-looking at it. I understand that the skipper, too, started raving like the rest of them. The man had been deprived of sleep for more than a week, and to have this sprung on him at the height of a furious gale nearly drove him out of his mind. I wonder they didn't fling me overboard after getting the carcass of their precious ship-mate out of my fingers. They had rather a job to separate us, I've been told. A sufficiently fierce story to make an old judge and a respectable jury sit up a bit. The first thing I heard when I came to myself was the maddening howling of that endless gale, and on that the voice of the old man. He was hanging on to my bunk, staring into my face out of his sou'wester.

" 'Mr. Leggatt, you have killed a man. You can act no longer as chief mate of this ship.' "

His care to subdue his voice made it sound monotonous. He rested a hand on the end of the skylight to steady himself with, and all that time did not stir a limb, so far as I could see. "Nice little tale for a quiet tea-party," he concluded in the same tone.

One of my hands, too, rested on the end of the skylight; neither did I stir a limb, so far as I knew. We stood less than a foot from each other. It occurred to me that if old "Bless my soul—you don't say so" were to put his head up the companion and catch sight of us, he would think he was seeing double, or imagine himself come upon a scene of weird witchcraft; the strange captain having a quiet confabulation by the wheel with his own grey ghost. I became very much concerned to prevent anything of the sort. I heard the other's soothing undertone.

"My father's a parson in Norfolk," it said. Evidently he had forgotten he had told me this important fact before. Truly a nice little tale.

"You had better slip down into my stateroom now," I said, moving off stealthily. My double followed my movements; our bare feet made no sound; I let him in, closed the door with care, and, after giving a call to the second mate, returned on deck for my relief.

"Not much sign of any wind yet," I remarked when he approached.

"No, sir. Not much," he assented, sleepily, in his hoarse voice, with just enough deference, no more, and barely suppressing a yawn.

"Well, that's all you have to look out for. You have got your orders."

"Yes, sir."

I paced a turn or two on the poop and saw him take up his position face forward with his elbow in the ratlines of the mizzen-rigging before I went below. The mate's faint snoring was still going on peacefully. The cuddy lamp was burning over the table on which stood a vase with flowers, a polite attention from the ship's provision merchant—the last flowers we should see for the next three months at the very least. Two bunches of bananas hung from the beam symmetrically, one on each side of the rudder-casing. Everything was as before in the ship—except that two of her captain's sleeping-suits were simultaneously in use, one motionless in the cuddy, the other keeping very still in the captain's stateroom.

It must be explained here that my cabin had the form of the capital letter L the door being within the angle and opening into the short part of the letter. A couch was to the left, the bed-place to the right; my writing-desk and the chronometers' table faced the door. But any one opening it, unless he stepped right inside, had no view of what I call the long (or vertical) part of the letter. It contained some lockers surmounted by a bookcase; and a few clothes, a thick jacket or two, caps, oilskin coat, and such like, hung on hooks. There was at the bottom of that part a door opening into my bathroom, which could be entered also directly from the saloon. But that way was never used.

The mysterious arrival had discovered the advantage of this particular shape. Entering my room, lighted strongly by a big bulkhead lamp swung on gimbals above my writing-desk, I did not see him anywhere till he stepped out quietly from behind the coats hung in the recessed part.

"I heard somebody moving about, and went in there at once," he whispered.

I, too, spoke under my breath.

"Nobody is likely to come in here without knocking and getting permission."

He nodded. His face was thin and the sunburn faded, as though he had been ill. And no wonder. He had been, I heard presently, kept under arrest in his cabin for nearly seven weeks. But there was nothing sickly in his eyes or in his expression. He was not a bit like me, really; yet, as we stood leaning over my bed-place, whispering side by side, with our dark heads together and our backs to the door, anybody bold enough to open it stealthily would have been treated to the uncanny sight of a double captain busy talking in whispers with his other self.

"But all this doesn't tell me how you came to hang on to our side-ladder," I inquired, in the hardly audible murmurs we used, after he had told me something more of the proceedings on board the *Sephora* once the bad weather was over.

"When we sighted Java Head I had had time to think all those matters out several times over. I had six weeks of doing nothing else, and with only an hour or so every evening for a tramp on the quarter-deck."

He whispered, his arms folded on the side of my bed-place, staring through the open port. And I could imagine perfectly the manner of this thinking out—a stubborn if not a steadfast operation; something of which I should have been perfectly incapable.

"I reckoned it would be dark before we closed with the land," he continued, so low that I had to strain my hearing, near as we were to each other, shoulder touching shoulder almost. "So I asked to speak to the old man. He always seemed very sick when he came to see me—as if he could not look me in the face. You know, that foresail saved the ship. She was too deep to have run long under bare poles. And it was I that managed to set it for him. Anyway, he came. When I had him in my cabin—he stood by the door looking at me as if I had the halter round my neck already—I asked him right away to leave my cabin door unlocked at night while the ship was going through Sunda

Straits. There would be the Java coast within two or three miles, off Angier Point. I wanted nothing more. I've had a prize for swimming my second year in the Conway."

"I can believe it," I breathed out.

"God only knows why they locked me in every night. To see some of their faces you'd have thought they were afraid I'd go about at night strangling people. Am I a murdering brute? Do I look it? By Jove! if I had been he wouldn't have trusted himself like that into my room. You'll say I might have chucked him aside and bolted out, there and then—it was dark already. Well, no. And for the same reason I wouldn't think of trying to smash the door. There would have been a rush to stop me at the noise, and I did not mean to get into a confounded scrimmage. Somebody else might have got killed—for I would not have broken out only to get chucked back, and I did not want any more of that work. He refused, looking more sick than ever. He was afraid of the men, and also of that old second mate of his who had been sailing with him for years—a grey-headed old humbug; and his steward, too, had been with him devil knows how long—seventeen years or more—a dogmatic sort of loafer who hated me like poison, just because I was the chief mate. No chief mate ever made more than one voyage in the *Sephora*, you know. Those two old chaps ran the ship. Devil only knows what the skipper wasn't afraid of (all his nerve went to pieces altogether in that hellish spell of bad weather we had)—of what the law would do to him—of his wife, perhaps. Oh, yes! she's on board. Though I don't think she would have meddled. She would have been only too glad to have me out of the ship in any way. The 'brand of Cain' business, don't you see. That's all right. I was ready enough to go off wandering on the face of the earth—and that was price enough to pay for an Abel of that sort. Anyhow, he wouldn't listen to me. 'This thing must take its course. I represent the law here.' He was shaking like a leaf. 'So you won't?' 'No!' 'Then I hope you will be able to sleep on that,' I said, and turned my back on him. 'I wonder that *you* can,' cries he, and locks the door.

"Well, after that, I couldn't. Not very well. That was three weeks ago. We have had a slow passage through the Java Sea; drifted about Carimata for ten days. When we anchored here they thought, I suppose, it was all right. The nearest land (and that's five miles) is the ship's destination; the consul would soon set about catching me; and there would have been no object in bolting to these islets there. I don't suppose there's a drop of water on them. I don't know how it was, but to-night that steward, after bringing me my supper, went out to let me eat it, and left the door unlocked. And I ate it—all there was, too. After I had finished I strolled out on the quarter-deck. I don't know that I meant to do anything. A breath of fresh air was all I wanted, I believe. Then a sudden temptation came over me. I kicked off my slippers and was in the water before I had made up my mind fairly. Somebody heard the splash and they raised an awful hullabaloo. 'He's gone! Lower the boats! He's committed suicide! No, he's swimming.' Certainly I was swimming. It's not so easy for a swimmer like me to commit suicide by drowning. I landed on the nearest islet before the boat left the ship's side. I heard them pulling about in the dark, hailing, and so on, but after a bit they gave up. Everything quieted down and the anchorage became as still as death. I sat down on a stone and began to think. I felt certain they would start searching for me at daylight. There was no place to hide on those stony things—and if there had been, what would have been the good? But now I was clear of that ship, I was not going back. So after a while I took off all my clothes, tied them up in a bundle with a stone inside, and dropped them in the deep water on the outer side of that islet. That was suicide enough for me. Let them think what they liked, but I didn't mean to drown myself. I meant to swim till I sank—but that's not the same thing. I struck out for another of these little islands, and it was from that one that I first saw your riding-light. Something to swim for. I went on easily, and on the way I came upon a flat rock a foot or two above water. In the daytime, I dare say, you might make it out with a glass from your poop. I scrambled up on it and rested myself for a bit. Then I made another start. That last spell must have been over a mile."

His whisper was getting fainter and fainter, and all the time he stared straight out through the port-hole, in which there was not even a star to be seen. I had not interrupted him. There was something that made comment impossible in his narrative, or perhaps in himself; a sort of feeling, a quality, which I can't find a name for. And when he ceased, all I found was a futile whisper: "So you swam for our light?"

"Yes—straight for it. It was something to swim for. I couldn't see any stars low down because the coast was in the way, and I couldn't see the land, either. The water was like glass. One might have been swimming in a con-founded thousand-feet deep cistern with no place for scrambling out any-where; but what I didn't like was the notion of swimming round and round like a crazed bullock before I gave out; and as I didn't mean to go back . . . No. Do you see me being hauled back, stark naked, off one of these little islands by the scruff of the neck and fighting like a wild beast? Somebody would have got killed for certain, and I did not want any of that. So I went on. Then your ladder——"

"Why didn't you hail the ship?" I asked, a little louder.

He touched my shoulder lightly. Lazy footsteps came right over our heads and stopped. The second mate had crossed from the other side of the poop and might have been hanging over the rail, for all we know.

"He couldn't hear us talking—could he?" My double breathed into my very ear, anxiously.

His anxiety was an answer, a sufficient answer, to the question I had put to him. An answer containing all the difficulty of that situation. I closed the porthole quietly, to make sure. A louder word might have been overheard.

"Who's that?" he whispered then.

"My second mate. But I don't know much more of the fellow than you do."

And I told him a little about myself. I had been appointed to take charge while I least expected anything of the sort, not quite a fortnight ago. I didn't know either the ship or the people. Hadn't had the time in port to look about me or size anybody up. And as to the crew, all they knew was that I was appointed to take the ship home. For the rest, I was almost as much of a stranger on board as himself, I said. And at the moment I felt it most acutely. I felt that it would take very little to make me a suspect person in the eyes of the ship's company.

He had turned about meantime; and we, the two strangers in the ship, faced each other in identical attitudes.

"Your ladder——" he murmured, after a silence. "Who'd have thought of finding a ladder hanging over at night in a ship anchored out here! I felt just then a very unpleasant faintness. After the life I've been leading for nine weeks, anybody would have got out of condition. I wasn't capable of swimming round as far as your rudder-chains. And, lo and behold! there was a ladder to get hold of. After I gripped it I said to myself, 'What's the good?' When I saw a man's head looking over I thought I would swim away presently and leave him shouting—in whatever language it was. I didn't mind being looked at. I—I liked it. And then you speaking to me so quietly—as if you had expected me—made me hold on a little longer. It had been a confounded lonely time—I don't mean while swimming. I was glad to talk a little to somebody that didn't belong to the *Sephora*. As to asking for the captain, that was a mere impulse. It could have been no use, with all the ship knowing about me and the other people pretty certain to be round here in the morning. I don't know—I wanted to be seen, to talk with somebody, before I went on. I don't know what I would have said. . . . 'Fine night, isn't it?' or something of the sort."

"Do you think they will be round here presently?" I asked with some incredulity.

"Quite likely," he said, faintly.

He looked extremely haggard all of a sudden. His head rolled on his shoulders.

"H'm. We shall see then. Meantime get into that bed," I whispered. "Want help? There."

It was a rather high bed-place with a set of drawers underneath. This amazing swimmer really needed the lift I gave him by seizing his leg. He tumbled in, rolled over on his back, and flung one arm across his eyes. And then, with his face nearly hidden, he must have looked exactly as I used to look in that bed. I gazed upon my other self for a while before drawing across carefully the two green serge curtains which ran on a brass rod. I thought for a moment of pinning them together for greater safety, but I sat down on the couch, and once there I felt unwilling to rise and hunt for a pin. I would do it in a moment. I was extremely tired, in a peculiarly intimate way, by the strain of stealthiness, by the effort of whispering and the general secrecy of this excitement. It was three o'clock by now and I had been on my feet since nine, but I was not sleepy; I could not have gone to sleep. I sat there, fagged out, looking at the curtains, trying to clear my mind of the confused sensation of being in two places at once, and greatly bothered by an exasperating knocking in my head. It was a relief to discover suddenly that it was not in my head at all, but on the outside of the door. Before I could collect myself the words "Come in" were out of my mouth, and the steward entered with a tray, bringing in my morning coffee. I had slept, after all, and I was so frightened that I shouted, "This way! I am here, steward," as though he had been miles away. He put down the tray on the table next the couch and only then said, very quietly, "I can see you are here, sir." I felt him give me a keen look, but I dared not meet his eyes just then. He must have wondered why I had drawn the curtains of my bed before going to sleep on the couch. He went out, hooking the door open as usual.

I heard the crew washing decks above me. I knew I would have been told at once if there had been any wind. Calm, I thought, and I was doubly vexed. Indeed, I felt dual more than ever. The steward reappeared suddenly in the doorway. I jumped up from the couch so quickly that he gave a start.

"What do you want here?"

"Close your port, sir—they are washing decks."

"It is closed," I said, reddening.

"Very well, sir." But he did not move from the doorway and returned my stare in an extraordinary, equivocal manner for a time. Then his eyes wavered, all his expression changed, and in a voice unusually gentle, almost coaxingly:

"May I come in to take the empty cup away, sir?"

"Of course!" I turned my back on him while he popped in and out. Then I unhooked and closed the door and even pushed the bolt. This sort of thing could not go on very long. The cabin was as hot as an oven, too. I took a peep at my double, and discovered that he had not moved, his arm was still over his eyes; but his chest heaved; his hair was wet; his chin glistened with perspiration. I reached over him and opened the port.

"I must show myself on deck," I reflected.

Of course, theoretically, I could do what I liked, with no one to say nay to me within the whole circle of the horizon; but to lock my cabin door and take the key away I did not dare. Directly I put my head out of the companion I saw the group of my two officers, the second mate barefooted, the chief mate in long india-rubber boots, near the break of the poop, and the steward half-way down the poop-ladder talking to them eagerly. He happened to catch sight of me and dived, the second ran down on the main-deck shouting some order or other, and the chief mate came to meet me, touching his cap.

There was a sort of curiosity in his eye that I did not like. I don't know whether the steward had told them that I was "queer" only, or downright drunk, but I know the man meant to have a good look at me. I watched him coming with a smile which, as he got into point-blank range, took effect and froze his very whiskers. I did not give him time to open his lips.

"Square the yards by lifts and braces before the hands go to breakfast."

It was the first particular order I had given on board that ship; and I stayed on deck to see it executed, too. I had felt the need of asserting myself without loss of time. That sneering young cub got taken down a peg or two on that occasion, and I also seized the opportunity of having a good look at the face of every foremast man as they filed past me to go to the after braces. At breakfast time, eating nothing myself, I presided with such frigid dignity that the two mates were only too glad to escape from the cabin as soon as decency permitted; and all the time the dual working of my mind distracted me almost to the point of insanity. I was constantly watching myself, my secret self, as dependent on my actions as my own personality, sleeping in that bed, behind that door which faced me as I sat at the head of the table. It was very much like being mad, only it was worse because one was aware of it.

I had to shake him for a solid minute, but when at last he opened his eyes it was in the full possession of his senses, with an inquiring look.

"All's well so far," I whispered. "Now you must vanish into the bathroom."

He did so, as noiseless as a ghost, and then I rang for the steward, and facing him boldly, directed him to tidy up my state-room while I was having my bath—"and be quick about it." As my tone admitted of no excuses, he said, "Yes, sir," and ran off to fetch his dust-pan and brushes. I took a bath and did most of my dressing, splashing, and whistling softly for the steward's edification, while the secret sharer of my life stood drawn up bolt upright in that little space, his face looking very sunken in daylight, his eyelids lowered under the stern, dark line of his eyebrows drawn together by a slight frown.

When I left him there to go back to my room the steward was finishing dusting. I sent for the mate and engaged him in some insignificant conversation. It was, as it were, trifling with the terrific character of his whiskers; but my object was to give him an opportunity for a good look at my cabin. And then I could at last shut, with a clear conscience, the door of my stateroom and get my double back into the recessed part. There was nothing else for it. He had to sit still on a small folding stool, half smothered by the heavy coats hanging there. We listened to the steward going into the bath-room out of the saloon, filling the water-bottles there, scrubbing the bath, setting things to rights, whisk, bang, clatter—out again into the saloon—turn the key—click. Such was my scheme for keeping my second self invisible. Nothing better could be contrived under the circumstances. And there we sat; I at my writing-desk ready to appear busy with some papers, he behind me out of sight of the door. It would not have been prudent to talk in daytime; and I could not have stood the excitement of that queer sense of whispering to myself. Now and then, glancing over my shoulder, I saw him far back there, sitting rigidly on the low stool, his bare feet close together, his arms folded, his head hanging on his breast—and perfectly still. Anybody would have taken him for me.

I was fascinated by it myself. Every moment I had to glance over my shoulder. I was looking at him when a voice outside the door said:

"Beg pardon, sir."

"Well!" . . . I kept my eyes on him, and so when the voice outside the door announced, "There's ship's boat coming our way, sir," I saw him give a start—the first movement he had made for hours. But he did not raise his bowed head.

"All right. Get the ladder over."

I hesitated. Should I whisper something to him? But what? His immobility seemed to have been never disturbed. What could I tell him he did not know already? . . . Finally I went on deck.

II

The skipper of the *Sephora* had a thin red whisker all round his face, and the sort of complexion that goes with hair of that colour; also the particular, rather smeary shade of blue in the eyes. He was not exactly a showy figure; his shoulders were high, his stature but middling—one leg slightly more bandy than the other. He shook hands, looking vaguely around. A spiritless tenacity was his main characteristic, I judged. I behaved with a politeness which seemed to disconcert him. Perhaps he was shy. He mumbled to me as if he were ashamed of what he was saying; gave his name (it was something like Archbold—but at this distance of years I hardly am sure), his ship's name, and a few other particulars of that sort, in the manner of a criminal making a reluctant and doleful confession. He had had terrible weather on the passage out—terrible—terrible—wife aboard, too.

By this time we were seated in the cabin and the steward brought in a tray with a bottle and glasses. "Thanks! No." Never took liquor. Would have some water, though. He drank two tumblerfuls. Terrible thirsty work. Ever since daylight had been exploring the islands round his ship.

"What was that for—fun?" I asked, with an appearance of polite interest.

"No!" He sighed. "Painful duty."

As he persisted in his mumbling and I wanted my double to hear every word, I hit upon the notion of informing him that I regretted to say I was hard of hearing.

"Such a young man, too!" he nodded, keeping his smeary blue, unintelligent eyes fastened upon me. "What was the cause of it—some disease?" he inquired, without the least sympathy and as if he thought that, if so, I'd got no more than I deserved.

"Yes; disease," I admitted in a cheerful tone which seemed to shock him. But my point was gained, because he had to raise his voice to give me his tale. It is not worth while to record that version. It was just over two months since all this had happened, and he had thought so much about it that he seemed completely muddled as to its bearings, but still immensely impressed.

"What would you think of such a thing happening on board your own ship? I've had the *Sephora* for these fifteen years. I am a well-known ship-master."

He was densely distressed—and perhaps I should have sympathised with him if I had been able to detach my mental vision from the unsuspected sharer of my cabin as though he were my second self. There he was on the other side of the bulkhead, four or five feet from us, no more, as we sat in the saloon. I looked politely at Captain Archbold (if that was his name), but it was the other I saw, in a grey sleeping-suit, seated on a low stool, his bare feet close together, his arms folded, and every word said between us falling into the ears of his dark head bowed on his chest.

"I have been at sea now, man and boy, for seven-and-thirty years, and I've never heard of such a thing happening in an English ship. And that it should be my ship. Wife on board, too."

I was hardly listening to him.

"Don't you think," I said, "that the heavy sea which, you told me, came aboard just then might have killed the man? I have seen the sheer weight of a sea kill a man very neatly, by simply breaking his neck."

"Good God!" he uttered, impressively, fixing his smeary blue eyes on me. "The sea! No man killed by the sea ever looked like that." He seemed positively scandalised at my suggestion. And as I gazed at him, certainly not prepared for anything original on his part, he advanced his head close to mine and thrust his tongue out at me so suddenly that I couldn't help starting back.

After scoring over my calmness in this graphic way he nodded wisely. If I had seen the sight, he assured me, I would never forget it as long as I lived. The weather was too bad to give the corpse a proper sea burial. So next day at dawn they took it up on the poop, covering its face with a bit of bunting; he read a short prayer, and then, just as it was, in its oilskins and long boots, they launched it amongst those mountainous seas that seemed ready every moment to swallow up the ship herself and the terrified lives on board of her.

"That reefed foresail saved you," I threw in.

"Under God—it did," he exclaimed fervently. "It was by a special mercy, I firmly believe, that it stood some of those hurricane squalls."

"It was the setting of that sail which——" I began.

"God's own hand in it," he interrupted me. "Nothing less could have done it. I don't mind telling you that I hardly dared give the order. It seemed impossible that we could touch anything without losing it, and then our last hope would have been gone."

The terror of that gale was on him yet. I let him go on for a bit, then said, casually—as if returning to a minor subject:

"You were very anxious to give up your mate to the shore people, I believe?"

He was. To the law. His obscure tenacity on that point had in it something incomprehensible and a little awful; something, as it were, mystical, quite apart from his anxiety that he should not be suspected of "countenancing any doings of that sort." Seven-and-thirty virtuous years at sea, of which over twenty of immaculate command, and the last fifteen in the *Sephora,* seemed to have laid him under some pitiless obligation.

"And you know," he went on, groping shamefacedly amongst his feelings, "I did not engage that young fellow. His people had some interest with my owners. I was in a way forced to take him on. He looked very smart, very gentlemanly, and all that. But do you know—I never liked him, somehow. I am a plain man. You see, he wasn't exactly the sort for the chief mate of a ship like the *Sephora.*"

I had become so connected in thoughts and impressions with the secret sharer of my cabin that I felt as if I, personally, were being given to understand that I, too, was not the sort that would have done for the chief mate of a ship like the *Sephora.* I had no doubt of it in my mind.

"Not at all the style of man. You understand," he insisted, superfluously, looking hard at me.

I smiled urbanely. He seemed at a loss for a while.

"I suppose I must report a suicide."

"Beg pardon?"

"Sui-cide! That's what I'll have to write to my owners directly I get in."

"Unless you manage to recover him before to-morrow," I assented, dispassionately. . . . "I mean, alive."

He mumbled something which I really did not catch, and I turned my ear to him in a puzzled manner. He fairly bawled:

"The land—I say, the mainland is at least seven miles off my anchorage."

"About that."

My lack of excitement, of curiosity, of surprise, of any sort of pronounced interest, began to arouse his distrust. But except for the felicitous pretence of deafness I had not tried to pretend anything. I had felt utterly incapable of playing the part of ignorance properly, and therefore was afraid to try. It is also certain that he had brought some ready-made suspicions with him, and that he viewed my politeness as a strange and unnatural phenomenon. And yet how else could I have received him? Not heartily! That was impossible for psychological reasons, which I need not state here. My only object was to keep off his inquiries. Surlily? Yes, but surliness might have provoked a point-blank question. From its novelty to him and from its nature, punctilious courtesy was the manner best calculated to restrain the man. But there was the danger of his breaking through my defence bluntly. I could not, I think, have met him by a direct lie, also for psychological (not moral) reasons. If he had only known how afraid I was of his putting my feeling of identity with the other to the test! But, strangely enough—(I thought of it only afterwards)—I believe that he was not a little disconcerted by the reverse side of that weird situation, by something in me that reminded him of the man he was seeking—suggested a mysterious similitude to the young fellow he had distrusted and disliked from the first.

However that might have been, the silence was not very prolonged. He took another oblique step.

"I reckon I had no more than a two-mile pull to your ship. Not a bit more."

"And quite enough, too, in this awful heat," I said.

Another pause full of mistrust followed. Necessity, they say, is mother of invention, but fear, too, is not barren of ingenious suggestions. And I was afraid he would ask me point-blank for news of my other self.

"Nice little saloon, isn't it?" I remarked, as if noticing for the first time the way his eyes roamed from one closed door to the other. "And very well fitted out, too. Here, for instance," I continued, reaching over the back of my seat negligently and flinging the door open, "is my bath-room."

He made an eager movement, but hardly gave it a glance. I got up, shut the door of the bath-room, and invited him to have a look round, as if I were very proud of my accommodation. He had to rise and be shown round, but he went through the business without any raptures whatever.

"And now we'll have a look at my stateroom," I declared, in a voice as loud as I dared to make it, crossing the cabin to the starboard side with purposely heavy steps.

He followed me in and gazed around. My intelligent double had vanished. I played my part.

"Very convenient—isn't it?"

"Very nice. Very comf . . ." He didn't finish and went out brusquely as if to escape from some unrighteous wiles of mine. But it was not to be. I had been too frightened not to feel vengeful; I felt I had him on the run, and I meant to keep him on the run. My polite insistence must have had something menacing in it, because he gave in suddenly. And I did not let him off a single item; mate's room, pantry, storerooms, the very sail-locker which was also under the poop—he had to look into them all. When at last I showed him out on the quarter-deck he drew a long, spiritless sigh, and mumbled dismally that he must really be going back to his ship now. I desired my mate, who had joined us, to see to the captain's boat.

The man of whiskers gave a blast on the whistle which he used to wear hanging round his neck, and yelled, "Sephora's away!" My double down there in my cabin must have heard, and certainly could not feel more relieved than I. Four fellows came running out from somewhere forward and went over the side, while my own men, appearing on deck too, lined the rail. I escorted my visitor to the gangway ceremoniously, and nearly overdid it. He was a tenacious beast. On the very ladder he lingered, and in that unique, guiltily conscientious manner of sticking to the point:

"I say . . . you . . . you don't think that——"

I covered his voice loudly:

"Certainly not . . . I am delighted. Goodbye."

I had an idea of what he meant to say, and just saved myself by the privilege of defective hearing. He was too shaken generally to insist, but my mate, close witness of that parting, looked mystified and his face took on a thoughtful cast. As I did not want to appear as if I wished to avoid all communication with my officers, he had the opportunity to address me.

"Seems a very nice man. His boat's crew told our chaps a very extraordinary story, if what I am told by the steward is true. I suppose you had it from the captain, sir?"

"Yes. I had a story from the captain."

"A very horrible affair—isn't it, sir?"

"It is."

"Beats all these tales we hear about murders in Yankee ships."

"I don't think it beats them. I don't think it resembles them in the least."

"Bless my soul—you don't say so! But of course I've no acquaintance whatever with American ships, not I, so I couldn't go against your knowledge. It's horrible enough for me. . . . But the queerest part is that those fellows seemed to have some idea the man was hidden aboard here. They had really. Did you ever hear of such a thing?"

"Preposterous—isn't it?"

We were walking to and fro athwart the quarter-deck. No one of the crew forward could be seen (the day was Sunday), and the mate pursued:

"There was some little dispute about it. Our chaps took offence. 'As if we would harbour a thing like that,' they said. 'Wouldn't you like to look for him in our coal-hole?' Quite a tiff. But they made it up in the end. I suppose he did drown himself. Don't you, sir?"

"I don't suppose anything."

"You have no doubt in the matter, sir?"

"None whatever."

I left him suddenly. I felt I was producing a bad impression, but with my double there it was most trying to be on deck. And it was almost as trying to be below. Altogether a nerve-trying situation. But on the whole I felt less torn in two when I was with him. There was no one in the whole ship whom I dared take into my confidence. Since the hands had to know his story, it would have been impossible to pass him off for any one else, and an accidental discovery was to be dreaded now more than ever. . . .

The steward being engaged in laying the table for dinner, we could talk only with our eyes when I first went down. Later in the afternoon we had a cautious try at whispering. The Sunday quietness of the ship was against us; the stillness of air and water around her was against us; the elements, the men were against us—everything was against us in our secret partnership; time itself —for this could not go on forever. The very trust in Providence was, I suppose, denied to his guilt. Shall I confess that this thought cast me down very much? And as to the chapter of accidents which counts for so much in the book of success, I could only hope that it was closed. For what favourable accident could be expected?

"Did you hear everything?" were my first words as soon as we took up our position side by side, leaning over my bed-place.

He had. And the proof of it was his earnest whisper, "The man told you he hardly dared to give the order."

I understood the reference to be to that saving foresail.

"Yes. He was afraid of it being lost in the setting."

"I assure you he never gave the order. He may think he did, but he never gave it. He stood there with me on the break of the poop after the main-topsail blew away, and whimpered about our last hope—positively whimpered about it and nothing else—and the night coming on! To hear one's skipper go on like that in such weather was enough to drive any fellow out of his mind. It worked me up into a sort of desperation. I just took it into my own hands and went away from him, boiling, and—— But what's the use telling you? You know! . . . Do you think that if I had not been pretty fierce with them I should have got the men to do anything? Not it! The bo's'n perhaps? Perhaps! It wasn't a heavy sea—it was a sea gone mad! I suppose the end of the world will be something like that; and a man may have the heart to see it coming once and be done with it—but to have to face it day after day—— I don't blame anybody. I was precious little better than the rest. Only—I was an officer of that old coal-wagon, anyhow——"

"I quite understand," I conveyed that sincere assurance into his ear. He was out of breath with whispering; I could hear him pant slightly. It was all very simple. The same strung-up force which had given twenty-four men a chance, at least, for their lives, had, in a sort of recoil, crushed an unworthy mutinous existence.

But I had no leisure to weigh the merits of the matter—footsteps in the saloon, a heavy knock. "There's enough wind to get under way with, sir." Here was the call of a new claim upon my thoughts and even upon my feelings.

"Turn the hands up," I cried through the door. "I'll be on deck directly."

I was going out to make the acquaintance of my ship. Before I left the cabin our eyes met—the eyes of the only two strangers on board. I pointed to the recessed part where the little camp-stool awaited him and laid my finger on my lips. He made a gesture—somewhat vague—a little mysterious, accompanied by a faint smile, as if of regret.

This is not the place to enlarge upon the sensations of a man who feels for the first time a ship move under his feet to his own independent word. In my case they were not unalloyed. I was not wholly alone with my command; for there was that stranger in my cabin. Or rather, I was not completely and wholly with her. Part of me was absent. That mental feeling of being in two places at once affected me physically as if the mood of secrecy had penetrated my very soul. Before an hour had elapsed since the ship had begun to move, having occasion to ask the mate (he stood by my side) to take a compass bearing of the Pagoda, I caught myself reaching up to his ear in whispers. I say I caught myself, but enough had escaped to startle the man. I can't describe it otherwise than by saying that he shied. A grave, preoccupied manner, as though he were in possession of some perplexing intelligence, did not leave him henceforth. A little later I moved away from the rail to look at the compass with such a stealthy gait that the helmsman noticed it—and I could not help noticing the unusual roundness of his eyes. These are trifling instances, though it's to no commander's advantage to be suspected of ludicrous eccentricities. But I was also more seriously affected. There are to a seaman certain words, gestures, that should in given conditions come as naturally, as instinctively as the winking of a menaced eye. A certain order should spring on to his lips without thinking; a certain sign should get itself made, so to speak, without reflection. But all unconscious alertness had abandoned me. I had to make an effort of will to recall myself back (from the cabin) to the conditions of the moment. I felt that I was appearing an irresolute commander to those people who were watching me more or less critically.

And, besides, there were the scares. On the second day out, for instance, coming off the deck in the afternoon (I had straw slippers on my bare feet) I stopped at the open pantry door and spoke to the steward. He was doing something there with his back to me. At the sound of my voice he nearly jumped out of his skin,.as the saying is, and incidentally broke a cup.

"What on earth's the matter with you?" I asked, astonished.

He was extremely confused. "Beg your pardon, sir. I made sure you were in your cabin."

"You see I wasn't."

"No, sir. I could have sworn I had heard you moving in there not a moment ago. It's most extraordinary . . . very sorry, sir."

I passed on with an inward shudder. I was so identified with my secret double that I did not even mention the fact in those scanty, fearful whispers we exchanged. I suppose he had made some slight noise of some kind or other. It would have been miraculous if he hadn't at one time or another. And yet, haggard as he appeared, he looked always perfectly self-controlled, more than calm—almost invulnerable. On my suggestion he remained almost entirely in the bathroom, which, upon the whole, was the safest place. There could be really no shadow of an excuse for any one ever wanting to go in there, once the steward had done with it. It was a very tiny place. Sometimes he reclined on the floor, his legs bent, his head sustained on one elbow. At others I would find him on the camp-stool, sitting in his grey sleeping-suit and with his cropped dark hair like a patient, unmoved convict. At night I would smuggle him into my bed-place, and we would whisper together, with the regular footfalls of the officer of the watch passing and repassing over our heads. It was an infinitely miserable time. It was lucky that some tins of fine preserves were stowed in a locker in my stateroom; hard bread I could always get hold of; and so he lived on stewed chicken, paté de foie gras, asparagus, cooked oysters, sardines —on all sorts of abominable sham delicacies out of tins. My early morning coffee he always drank; and it was all I dared do for him in that respect.

Every day there was the horrible maneuvering to go through so that my room and then the bath-room should be done in the usual way. I came to hate the sight of the steward, to abhor the voice of that harmless man. I felt that it was he who would bring on the disaster of discovery. It hung like a sword over our heads.

The fourth day out, I think (we were then working down the east side of the Gulf of Siam, tack for tack, in light winds and smooth water)—the fourth day, I say, of this miserable juggling with the unavoidable, as we sat at our evening meal, that man, whose slightest movement I dreaded, after putting down the dishes ran up on deck busily. This could not be dangerous. Presently he came down again; and then it appeared that he had remembered a coat of mine which I had thrown over a rail to dry after having been wetted in a shower which had passed over the ship in the afternoon. Sitting stolidly at the head of the table I became terrified at the sight of the garment on his arm. Of course he made for my door. There was no time to lose.

"Steward," I thundered. My nerves were so shaken that I could not govern my voice and conceal my agitation. This was the sort of thing that made my terrifically whiskered mate tap his forehead with his forefinger. I had detected him using that gesture while talking on deck with a confidential air to the carpenter. It was too far to hear a word, but I had no doubt that this pantomine could only refer to the strange new captain.

"Yes, sir," the pale-faced steward turned resignedly to me. It was this maddening course of being shouted at, checked without rhyme or reason, arbitrarily chased out of my cabin, suddenly called into it, sent flying out of his pantry on incomprehensible errands, that accounted for the growing wretchedness of his expression.

"Where are you going with that coat?"

"To your room, sir."

"Is there another shower coming?"

"I'm sure I don't know, sir. Shall I go up again and see, sir?"

"No! never mind."

My object was attained, as of course my other self in there would have heard everything that passed. During this interlude my two officers never raised their eyes off their respective plates; but the lip of that confounded cub, the second mate, quivered visibly.

I expected the steward to hook my coat on and come out at once. He was very slow about it; but I dominated my nervousness sufficiently not to shout after him. Suddenly I became aware (it could be heard plainly enough) that the fellow for some reason or other was opening the door of the bath-room. It was the end. The place was literally not big enough to swing a cat in. My voice died in my throat and I went stony all over. I expected to hear a yell of surprise and terror, and made a movement, but had not the strength to get on my legs. Everything remained still. Had my second self taken the poor wretch by the throat? I don't know what I could have done next moment if I had not seen the steward come out of my room, close the door, and then stand quietly by the sideboard.

"Saved," I thought. "But, no! Lost! Gone! He was gone!"

I laid my knife and fork down and leaned back in my chair. My head swam. After a while, when sufficiently recovered to speak in a steady voice, I instructed my mate to put the ship round at eight o'clock himself.

"I won't come on deck," I went on. "I think I'll turn in, and unless the wind shifts I don't want to be disturbed before midnight. I feel a bit seedy."

"You did look middling bad a little while ago," the chief mate remarked without showing any great concern.

They both went out, and I stared at the steward clearing the table. There was nothing to be read on that wretched man's face. But why did he avoid my eyes I asked myself. Then I thought I should like to hear the sound of his voice.

"Steward!"

"Sir!" Startled as usual.

"Where did you hang up that coat?"

"In the bath-room, sir." The usual anxious tone. "It's not quite dry yet, sir."

For some time longer I sat in the cuddy. Had my double vanished as he had come? But of his coming there was an explanation, whereas his disappearance would be inexplicable. . . . I went slowly into my dark room, shut the door, lighted the lamp, and for a time dared not turn round. When at last I did I saw him standing bolt-upright in the narrow recessed part. It would not be true to say I had a shock, but an irresistible doubt of his bodily existence flitted through my mind. Can it be, I asked myself, that he is not visible to other eyes than mine? It was like being haunted. Motionless, with a grave face, he raised his hands slightly at me in a gesture which meant clearly, "Heavens! what a narrow escape!" Narrow indeed. I think I had come creeping quietly as near insanity as any man who has not actually gone over the border. That gesture restrained me, so to speak.

The mate with the terrific whiskers was now putting the ship on the other tack. In the moment of profound silence which follows upon the hands going to their stations I heard on the poop his raised voice: "Hard alee!" and the distant shout of the order repeated on the maindeck. The sails, in that light breeze, made but a faint fluttering noise. It ceased. The ship was coming round slowly; I held my breath in the renewed stillness of expectation; one wouldn't have thought that there was a single living soul on her decks. A sudden brisk shout, "Mainsail haul!" broke the spell, and in the noisy cries and rush overhead of the men running away with the main-brace we two, down in my cabin, came together in our usual position by the bed-place.

He did not wait for my question. "I heard him fumbling here and just managed to squat myself down in the bath," he whispered to me. "The fellow only opened the door and put his arm in to hang the coat up. All the same——"

"I never thought of that," I whispered back, even more appalled than before at the closeness of the shave, and marvelling at that something unyielding in his character which was carrying him through so finely. There was no agitation in his whisper. Whoever was being driven distracted, it was not he.

He was sane. And the proof of his sanity was continued when he took up the whispering again.

"It would never do for me to come to life again."

It was something that a ghost might have said. But what he was alluding to was his old captain's reluctant admission of the theory of suicide. It would obviously serve his turn—if I had understood at all the view which seemed to govern the unalterable purpose of his action.

"You must maroon me as soon as ever you can get amongst these islands off the Cambodge shore," he went on.

"Maroon you! We are not living in a boy's adventure tale," I protested. His scornful whispering took me up.

"We aren't indeed! There's nothing of a boy's tale in this. But there's nothing else for it. I want no more. You don't suppose I am afraid of what can be done to me? Prison or gallows or whatever they may please. But you don't see me coming back to explain such things to an old fellow in a wig and twelve respectable tradesmen, do you? What can they know whether I am guilty or not—or of *what* I am guilty, either? That's my affair. What does the Bible say? 'Driven off the face of the earth.' Very well. I am off the face of the earth now. As I came at night so I shall go."

"Impossible!" I murmured. "You can't."

"Can't? . . . Not naked like a soul on the Day of Judgment. I shall freeze on to this sleeping-suit. The Last Day is not yet—and . . . you have understood thoroughly. Didn't you?"

I felt suddenly ashamed of myself. I may say truly that I understood—and my hesitation in letting that man swim away from my ship's side had been a mere sham sentiment, a sort of cowardice.

"It can't be done now till next night," I breathed out. "The ship is on the off-shore tack and the wind may fail us."

"As long as I know that you understand," he whispered. "But of course you do. It's a great satisfaction to have got somebody to understand. You seem to have been there on purpose." And in the same whisper, as if we two whenever we talked had to say things to each other which were not fit for the world to hear, he added, "It's very wonderful."

We remained side by side talking in our secret way—but sometimes silent or just exchanging a whispered word or two at long intervals. And as usual he stared through the port. A breath of wind came now and again into our faces. The ship might have been moored in dock, so gently and on an even keel she slipped through the water, that did not murmur even at our passage, shadowy and silent like a phantom sea.

At midnight I went on deck, and to my mate's great surprise put the ship round on the other tack. His terrible whiskers flitted round me in silent criticism. I certainly should not have done it if it had been only a question of getting out of that sleepy gulf as quickly as possible. I believe he told the second mate, who relieved him, that it was a great want of judgment. The other only yawned. That intolerable cub shuffled about so sleepily and lolled against the rails in such a slack, improper fashion that I came down on him sharply.

"Aren't you properly awake yet?"

"Yes, sir! I am awake."

"Well, then, be good enough to hold yourself as if you were. And keep a look-out. If there's any current we'll be closing with some islands before daylight."

The east side of the gulf is fringed with islands, some solitary, others in groups. On the blue background of the high coast they seem to float on silvery patches of calm water, arid and grey, or dark green and rounded like clumps of evergreen bushes, with the larger ones, a mile or two long, showing the outlines of ridges, ribs of grey rock under the dank mantle of matted leafage. Unknown to trade, to travel, almost to geography, the manner of life they harbour is an unsolved secret. There must be villages—settlements of fishermen at least—on the largest of them, and some communication with the world is probably kept up by native craft. But all that forenoon, as we headed for them, fanned along by the faintest of breezes, I saw no sign of man or canoe in the field of the telescope I kept on pointing at the scattered group.

At noon I gave no orders for a change of course, and the mate's whiskers became much concerned and seemed to be offering themselves unduly to my notice. At last I said:

"I am going to stand right in. Quite in—as far as I can take her."

The stare of extreme surprise imparted an air of ferocity also to his eyes, and he looked truly terrific for a moment.

"We're not doing well in the middle of the gulf," I continued, casually. "I am going to look for the land breezes to-night."

"Bless my soul! Do you mean, sir, in the dark amongst the lot of all them islands and reefs and shoals?"

"Well—if there are any regular land breezes at all on this coast one must get close inshore to find them, mustn't one?"

"Bless my soul!" he exclaimed again under his breath. All that afternoon he wore a dreamy, contemplative appearance which in him was a mark of perplexity. After dinner I went into my stateroom as if I meant to take some rest. There we two bent our dark heads over a half-unrolled chart lying on my bed.

"There," I said. "It's got to be Koh-ring. I've been looking at it ever since sunrise. It has got two hills and a low point. It must be inhabited. And on the coast opposite there is what looks like the mouth of a biggish river—with some town, no doubt, not far up. It's the best chance for you that I can see."

"Anything. Koh-ring let it be."

He looked thoughtfully at the chart as if surveying chances and distances from a lofty height—and following with his eyes his own figure wandering on the blank land of Cochin-China, and then passing off that piece of paper clean out of sight into uncharted regions. And it was as if the ship had two captains to plan her course for her. I had been so worried and restless running up and down that I had not had the patience to dress that day. I had remained in my sleeping-suit, with straw slippers and a soft floppy hat. The closeness of the heat in the gulf had been most oppressive, and the crew were used to see me wandering in that airy attire.

"She will clear the south point as she heads now," I whispered into his ear. "Goodness only knows when, though, but certainly after dark. I'll edge her in to half a mile, as far as I may be able to judge in the dark——"

"Be careful," he murmured, warningly—and I realised suddenly that all my future, the only future for which I was fit, would perhaps go irretrievably to pieces in any mishap to my first command.

I could not stop a moment longer in the room. I motioned him to get out of sight and made my way on the poop. That unplayful cub had the watch. I walked up and down for a while thinking things out, then beckoned him over.

"Send a couple of hands to open the two quarter-deck ports," I said mildly.

He actually had the impudence, or else so forgot himself in his wonder at such an incomprehensible order, as to repeat:

"Open the quarter-deck ports! What for, sir?"

"The only reason you need concern yourself about is because I tell you to do so. Have them opened wide and fastened properly."

He reddened and went off, but I believe made some jeering remark to the carpenter as to the sensible practice of ventilating a ship's quarter-deck. I know he popped into the mate's cabin to impart the fact to him because the whiskers came on deck, as it were by chance, and stole glances at me from below—for signs of lunacy or drunkenness, I suppose.

A little before supper, feeling more restless than ever, I rejoined, for a moment, my second self. And to find him sitting so quietly was surprising, like something against nature, inhuman.

I developed my plan in a hurried whisper.

"I shall stand in as close as I dare and then put her round. I will presently find means to smuggle you out of here into the sail-locker, which communicates with the lobby. But there is an opening, a sort of square for hauling the sails out, which gives straight on the quarter-deck and which is never closed in fine weather, so as to give air to the sails. When the ship's way is deadened in stays and all the hands are aft at the main-braces you will have a clear road to slip out and get overboard through the open quarter-deck port. I've had them both fastened up. Use a rope's end to lower yourself into the water so as to avoid a splash—you know. It could be heard and cause some beastly complication."

He kept silent for a while, then whispered, "I understand."

"I won't be there to see you go," I began with an effort. "The rest . . . I only hope I have understood, too."

"You have. From first to last"—and for the first time there seemed to be a faltering, something strained in his whisper. He caught hold of my arm, but the ringing of the supper bell made me start. He didn't, though; he only released his grip.

After supper I didn't come below again till well past eight o'clock. The faint, steady breeze was loaded with dew; and the wet, darkened sails held all there was of propelling power in it. The night, clear and starry, sparkled darkly, and the opaque, lightless patches shifting slowly against the low stars were the drifting islets. On the port bow there was a big one more distant and shadowily imposing by the great space of sky it eclipsed.

On opening the door I had a back view of my very own self looking at a chart. He had come out of the recess and was standing near the table.

"Quite dark enough," I whispered.

He stepped back and leaned against my bed with a level, quiet glance. I sat on the couch. We had nothing to say to each other. Over our heads the officer of the watch moved here and there. Then I heard him move quickly. I knew what that meant. He was making for the companion; and presently his voice was outside my door.

"We are drawing in pretty fast, sir. Land looks rather close."

"Very well," I answered. "I am coming on deck directly."

I waited till he was gone out of the cuddy, then rose. My double moved too. The time had come to exchange our last whispers, for neither of us was ever to hear each other's natural voice.

"Look here!" I opened a drawer and took out three sovereigns. "Take this anyhow. I've got six and I'd give you the lot, only I must keep a little money to buy some fruit and vegetables for the crew from native boats as we go through Sunda Straights."

He shook his head.

"Take it," I urged him, whispering desperately. "No one can tell what ___"

He smiled and slapped meaningly the only pocket of the sleeping-jacket. It was not safe, certainly. But I produced a large old silk handkerchief of mine, and tying the three pieces of gold in a corner, pressed it on him. He was touched, I suppose, because he took it at last and tied it quickly round his waist under the jacket, on his bare skin.

Our eyes met; several seconds elapsed, till, our glances still mingled, I extended my hand and turned the lamp out. Then I passed through the cuddy, leaving the door of my room wide open. . . . "Steward!"

He was still lingering in the pantry in the greatness of his zeal, giving a rub-up to a plated cruet stand the last thing before going to bed. Being careful not to wake up the mate, whose room was opposite, I spoke in an undertone.

He looked round anxiously. "Sir!"

"Can you get me a little hot water from the galley?"

"I am afraid, sir, the galley fire's been out for some time now."

"Go and see."

He flew up the stairs.

"Now," I whispered, loudly, into the saloon—too loudly, perhaps, but I was afraid I couldn't make a sound. He was by my side in an instant—the double captain slipped past the stairs—through a tiny dark passage . . . a sliding door. We were in the sail-locker, scrambling on our knees over the sails. A sudden thought struck me. I saw myself wandering bareheaded, the sun beating on my dark poll. I snatched off my floppy hat and tried hurriedly in the dark to ram it on my other self. He dodged and fended off silently. I wonder what he thought had come to me before he understood and suddenly desisted. Our hands met gropingly, lingered united in a steady, motionless clasp for a second. . . . No word was breathed by either of us when they separated.

I was standing quietly by the pantry door when the steward returned.

"Sorry, sir. Kettle barely warm. Shall I light the spirit-lamp?"

"Never mind."

I came out on deck slowly. It was now a matter of conscience to shave the land as close as possible—for now he must go overboard whenever the ship was put in stays. Must! There could be no going back for him. After a moment I walked over to leeward and my heart flew into my mouth at the nearness of the land on the bow. Under any other circumstances I would not have held on a minute longer. The second mate had followed me anxiously.

I looked on till I felt I could command my voice.

"She will weather," I said then in a quiet tone.

"Are you going to try that, sir?" he stammered out incredulously.

I took no notice of him and raised my tone just enough to be heard by the helmsman.

"Keep her good full."

"Good full, sir."

The wind fanned my cheek, the sails slept, the world was silent. The strain of watching the dark loom of the land grow bigger and denser was too much for me. I had shut my eyes—because the ship must go closer. She must! The stillness was intolerable. Were we standing still?

When I opened my eyes the second view started my heart with a thump. The black southern hill of Koh-ring seemed to hang right over the ship like a towering fragment of the everlasting night. On that enormous mass of blackness there was not a gleam to be seen, not a sound to be heard. It was gliding irresistibly towards us and yet seemed already within reach of the hand. I saw the vague figures of the watch grouped in the waist, gazing in awed silence.

"Are you going on, sir?" inquired an unsteady voice at my elbow.

I ignored it. I had to go on.

"Keep her full. Don't check her way. That won't do now," I said, warningly.

"I can't see the sails very well," the helmsman answered me, in strange, quavering tones.

Was she close enough? Already she was, I won't say in the shadow of the land, but in the very blackness of it, already swallowed up as it were, gone too close to be recalled, gone from me altogether.

"Give the mate a call," I said to the young man who stood at my elbow as still as death. "And turn all hands up."

My tone had a borrowed loudness reverberated from the height of the land. Several voices cried out together; "We are all on deck, sir."

Then stillness again, with the great shadow gliding closer, towering higher, without a light, without a sound. Such a hush had fallen on the ship that she might have been a bark of the dead floating in slowly under the very gate of Erebus.

"My God! Where are we?"

It was the mate moaning at my elbow. He was thunderstruck, and as it were deprived of the moral support of his whiskers. He clapped his hands and absolutely cried out, "Lost!"

"Be quiet," I said, sternly.

He lowered his tone, but I saw the shadowy gesture of his despair. "What are we doing here?"

"Looking for the land wind."

He made as if to tear his hair, and addressed me recklessly.

"She will never get out. You have done it, sir. I knew it'd end in something like this. She will never weather, and you are too close now to stay. She'll drift ashore before she's round. O my God!"

I caught his arm as he was raising it to batter his poor devoted head, and shook it violently.

"She's ashore already," he wailed, trying to tear himself away.

"Is she? . . . Keep good full there!"

"Good full, sir," cried the helmsman in a frightened, thin, childlike voice.

I hadn't let go the mate's arm and went on shaking it. "Ready about, do you hear? You go forward"—shake—"and stop there"—shake—"and hold your noise"—shake—"and see these headsheets properly overhauled"—shake, shake—shake.

And all the time I dared not look towards the land lest my heart should fail me. I released my grip at last and he ran forward as if fleeing for dear life.

I wondered what my double there in the sail-locker thought of this commotion. He was able to hear everything—and perhaps he was able to understand why, on my conscience, it had to be thus close—no less. My first order "Hard alee!" re-echoed ominously under the towering shadow of Koh-ring as if I had shouted in a mountain gorge. And then I watched the land intently. In that smooth water and light wind it was impossible to feel the ship coming-to. No! I could not feel her. And my second self was making now ready to slip out and lower himself overboard. Perhaps he was gone already . . . ?

The great black mass brooding over our very mastheads began to pivot away from the ship's side silently. And now I forgot the secret stranger ready to depart, and remembered only that I was a total stranger to the ship. I did not know her. Would she do it? How was she to be handled?

I swung the mainyard and waited helplessly. She was perhaps stopped, and her very fate hung in the balance, with the black mass of Koh-ring like the gate of the everlasting night towering over her taffrail. What would she do now? Had she way on her yet? I stepped to the side swiftly, and on the shadowy water I could see nothing except a faint phosphorescent flash revealing the glassy smoothness of the sleeping surface. It was impossible to tell—and I had not learned yet the feel of my ship. Was she moving? What I needed was something easily seen, a piece of paper, which I could throw overboard and watch. I had nothing on me. To run down for it I didn't dare. There was no time. All at once my strained, yearning stare distinguished a white object floating within a yard of the ship's side. White on the black water. A phosphorescent flash passed under it. What was that thing? . . . I recognized my own floppy hat. It must have fallen off his head . . . and he didn't bother. Now I had what I wanted—the saving mark for my eyes. But I hardly thought of my other self, now gone from the ship, to be hidden for ever from all friendly faces, to be a fugitive and a vagabond on the earth, with no brand of the curse on his sane forehead to stay a slaying hand . . . too proud to explain.

And I watched the hat—the expression of my sudden pity for his mere flesh. It had been meant to save his homeless head from the dangers of the sun. And now—behold—it was saving the ship, by serving me for a mark to help out the ignorance of my strangeness. Ha! It was drifting forward, warning me just in time that the ship had gathered sternway.

"Shift the helm," I said in a low voice to the seaman standing still like a statue.

The man's eyes glistened wildly in the binnacle light as he jumped round to the other side and spun round the wheel.

I walked to the break of the poop. On the overshadowed deck all hands stood by the forebraces waiting for my order. The stars ahead seemed to be gliding from right to left. And all was so still in the world that I heard the quiet remark, "She's round," passed in a tone of intense relief between two seamen.

"Let go and haul."

The foreyards ran round with a great noise, amidst cheery cries. And now the frightful whiskers made themselves heard giving various orders. Already the ship was drawing ahead. And I was alone with her. Nothing! no one in the world should stand now between us, throwing a shadow on the way of silent knowledge and mute affection, the perfect communion of a seaman with his first command.

Walking to the taffrail, I was in time to make out, on the very edge of a darkness thrown by a towering black mass like the very gateway of Erebus —yes, I was in time to catch an evanescent glimpse of my white hat left behind to mark the spot where the secret sharer of my cabin and of my thoughts, as though he were my second self, had lowered himself into the water to take his punishment: a free man, a proud swimmer striking out for a new destiny.

STEPHEN CRANE

The Blue Hotel

I

The Palace Hotel at Fort Romper was painted a light blue, a shade that is on the legs of a kind of heron, causing the bird to declare its position against any background. The Palace Hotel, then, was always screaming and howling in a way that made the dazzling winter landscape of Nebraska seem only a gray swampish hush. It stood alone on the prairie, and when the snow was falling the town two hundred yards away was not visible. But when the traveler alighted at the railway station he was obliged to pass the Palace Hotel before he could come upon the company of low clapboard houses which composed Fort Romper, and it was not to be thought that any traveler could pass the Palace Hotel without looking at it. Pat Scully, the proprietor, had proved himself a master of strategy when he chose his paints. It is true that on clear days, when the great transcontinental expresses, long lines of swaying Pullmans, swept through Fort Romper, passengers were overcome at the sight, and the cult that knows the brown-reds and the subdivisions of the dark greens of the East expressed shame, pity, horror, in a laugh. But to the citizens of this prairie town and to the people who would naturally stop there, Pat Scully had performed a feat. With this opulence and splendor, these creeds, classes, egotisms, that streamed through Romper on the rails day after day, they had no color in common.

As if the displayed delights of such a blue hotel were not sufficiently enticing, it was Scully's habit to go every morning and evening to meet the leisurely trains that stopped at Romper and work his seductions upon any man that he might see wavering, gripsack in hand.

One morning, when a snow-crusted engine dragged its long string of freight cars and its one passenger coach to the station, Scully performed the marvel of catching three men. One was a shaky and quick-eyed Swede, with a great shining cheap valise; one was a tall bronzed cowboy, who was on his way to a ranch near the Dakota line; one was a little silent man from the East, who didn't look it, and didn't announce it. Scully practically made them prisoners. He was so nimble and merry and kindly that each probably felt it would be the height of brutality to try to escape. They trudged off over the creaking board sidewalks in the wake of the eager little Irishman. He wore a heavy fur cap squeezed tightly down on his head. It caused his two red ears to stick out stiffy, as if they were made of tin.

At last, Scully, elaborately, with boisterous hospitality, conducted them through the portals of the blue hotel. The room which they entered was small. It seemed to be merely a proper temple for an enormous stove, which, in the center, was humming with godlike violence. At various points on its surface the iron had become luminous and glowed yellow from the heat. Beside the stove Scully's son Johnnie was playing High-Five with an old farmer who had whiskers both gray and sandy. They were quarreling. Frequently the old farmer turned his face toward a box of sawdust—colored brown from tobacco juice—that was behind the stove, and spat with an air of great impatience and irritation. With a loud flourish of words Scully destroyed the game of cards, and bustled his son upstairs with part of the baggage of the new guests. He himself conducted them to three basins of the coldest water in the world. The cowboy and the Easterner burnished themselves fiery red with this water, until it seemed to be some kind of metal-polish. The Swede, however, merely dipped his fingers gingerly and with trepidation. It was notable that throughout this series of small ceremonies the three travelers were made to feel that Scully was very benevolent. He was conferring great favors upon them. He handed the towel from one to another with an air of philanthropic impulse.

Afterward they went to the first room, and, sitting about the stove, listened to Scully's officious clamor at his daughters, who were preparing the midday meal. They reflected in the silence of experienced men who tread carefully amid new people. Nevertheless, the old farmer, stationary, invincible in his chair near the warmest part of the stove, turned his face from the sawdust-box frequently and addressed a glowing common-place to the strangers. Usually he was answered in short but adequate sentences by either the cowboy or the Easterner. The Swede said nothing. He seemed to be occupied in making furtive estimates of each man in the room. One might have thought that he had the sense of silly suspicion which comes to guilt. He resembled a badly frightened man.

Later, at dinner, he spoke a little, addressing his conversation entirely to Scully. He volunteered that he had come from New York, where for ten years he had worked as a tailor. These facts seemed to strike Scully as fascinating, and afterward he volunteered that he had lived at Romper for fourteen years. The Swede asked about the crops and the price of labor. He seemed barely to listen to Scully's extended replies. His eyes continued to rove from man to man.

Finally, with a laugh and a wink, he said that some of these Western communities were very dangerous; and after this statement he straightened his legs under the table, tilted his head, and laughed again, loudly. It was plain that the demonstration had no meaning to the others. They looked at him wondering and in silence.

II

As the men trooped heavily back into the front room, the two little windows presented views of a turmoiling sea of snow. The huge arms of the wind were making attempts—mighty, circular, futile—to embrace the flakes as they sped. A gate-post like a still man with a blanched face stood aghast amid this profligate fury. In a hearty voice Scully announced the presence of a blizzard. The guests of the blue hotel, lighting their pipes, assented with grunts of lazy masculine contentment. No island of the sea could be exempt in the degree of this little room with its humming stove. Johnnie, son of Scully, in a tone which defined his opinion of his ability as a card-player, challenged the old farmer of both gray and sandy whiskers to a game of High-Five. The farmer agreed with a contemptuous and bitter scoff. They sat close to the stove, and squared their knees under a wide board. The cowboy and the Easterner watched the game with interest. The boy and the Easterner watched the game with interest. The Swede remained near the window, aloof, but with a countenance that showed signs of an inexplicable excitement.

The play of Johnnie and the gray-beard was suddenly ended by another quarrel. The old man arose while casting a look of heated scorn at his adversary. He slowly buttoned his coat, and then stalked with fabulous dignity from the room. In the discreet silence of all other men the Swede laughed. His laughter rang somehow childish. Men by this time had begun to look at him askance, as if they wished to inquire what ailed him.

A new game was formed jocosely. The cowboy volunteered to become the partner of Johnnie, and they all then turned to ask the Swede to throw in his lot with the little Easterner. He asked some questions about the game, and, learning that it wore many names, and that he had played it when it was under an alias, he accepted the invitation. He strode toward the men nervously, as if he expected to be assaulted. Finally, seated, he gazed from face to face and laughed shrilly. This laugh was so strange that the Easterner looked up quickly, the cowboy sat intent and with his mouth open, and Johnnie paused, holding the cards with still fingers.

Afterward there was a short silence. Then Johnnie said, "Well, let's get at it. Come on now!" They pulled their chairs forward until their knees were bunched under the board. They began to play, and their interest in the game caused the others to forget the manner of the Swede.

The cowboy was a board-whacker. Each time that he held superior cards he whanged them, one by one, with exceeding force, down upon the improvised table, and took the tricks with a glowing air of prowess and pride that sent thrills of indignation into the hearts of his opponents. A game with a board-whacker in it is sure to become intense. The countenances of the Easterner and the Swede were miserable whenever the cowboy thundered down his aces and kings, while Johnnie, his eyes gleaming with joy, chuckled and chuckled.

Because of the absorbing play none considered the strange ways of the Swede. They paid strict heed to the game. Finally, during a lull caused by a new deal, the Swede suddenly addressed Johnnie: "I suppose there have been a good many men killed in this room." The jaws of the others dropped and they looked at him.

"What in hell are you talking about?" said Johnnie.

The Swede laughed again his blatant laugh, full of a kind of false courage and defiance. "Oh, you know what I mean all right," he answered.

"I'm a liar if I do!" Johnnie protested. The card was halted, and the men stared at the Swede. Johnnie evidently felt that as the son of the proprietor he should make a direct inquiry. "Now, what might you be drivin' at, mister?" he asked. The Swede winked at him. It was a wink full of cunning. His fingers shook on the edge of the board. "Oh, maybe you think I have been to no-wheres. Maybe you think I'm a tenderfoot?"

"I don't know nothin' about you," answered Johnnie, "and I don't give a damn where you've been. All I got to say is that I don't know what you're driving at. There hain't never been nobody killed in this room."

The cowboy, who had been steadily gazing at the Swede, then spoke: "What's wrong with you, mister?"

Apparently it seemed to the Swede that he was formidably menaced. He shivered and turned white near the corners of his mouth. He sent an appealing glance in the direction of the little Easterner. During these moments he did not forget to wear his air of advanced pot-valor. "They say they don't know what I mean," he remarked mockingly to the Easterner.

The latter answered after prolonged and cautious reflection. "I don't understand you," he said, impassively.

The Swede made a movement then which announced that he thought he had encountered treachery from the only quarter where he had expected sympathy, if not help. "Oh, I see you are all against me, I see——"

The cowboy was in a state of deep stupefaction. "Say," he cried, as he tumbled the deck violently down upon the board, "say, what are you gittin' at, hey?"

The Swede sprang up with the celerity of a man escaping from a snake on the floor. "I don't want to fight!" he shouted. "I don't want to fight!"

The cowboy stretched his long legs indolently and deliberately. His hands were in his pockets. He spat into the sawdust-box. "Well, who the hell thought you did?" he inquired.

The Swede backed rapidly toward a corner of the room. His hands were out protectingly in front of his chest, but he was making an obvious struggle to control his fright. "Gentleman," he quavered, "I suppose I am going to be killed before I can leave this house! I suppose I am going to be killed before I can leave this house!" In his eyes was the dying-swan look. Through the windows could be seen the snow turning blue in the shadow of dusk. The wind tore at the house, and some loose thing beat regularly against the clapboards like a spirit tapping.

A door opened, and Scully himself entered! He paused in surprise as he noted the tragic attitude of the Swede. Then he said, "What's the matter here?"

The Swede answered him swiftly and eagerly: "These men are going to kill me."

"Kill you!" ejaculated Scully. "Kill you! What are you talkin'?"

The Swede made the gesture of a martyr.

Scully wheeled sternly upon his son. "What is this, Johnnie?"

The lad had grown sullen. "Damned if I know," he answered. "I can't make no sense to it." He began to shuffle the cards, fluttering them together with an angry snap. "He says a good many men have been killed in this room, or something like that. And he says he's goin' to be killed here too. I don't know what ails him. He's crazy, I shouldn't wonder."

Scully then looked for explanation to the cowboy, but the cowboy simply shrugged his shoulders.

"Kill you?" said Scully again to the Swede. "Kill you? Man, you're off your nut."

"Oh, I know," burst out the Swede. "I know what will happen. Yes, I'm crazy—yes. Yes, of course, I'm crazy—yes. But I know one thing——" There was a sort of sweat of misery and terror upon his face. "I know I won't get out of here alive."

The cowboy drew a deep breath, as if his mind was passing into the last stages of dissolution. "Well, I'm doggoned," he whispered to himself.

Scully wheeled suddenly and faced his son. "You've been troublin' this man!"

Johnnie's voice was loud with its burden of grievance. "Why, good Gawd, I ain't done nothin' to 'im."

The Swede broke in. "Gentlemen, do not disturb yourselves. I will leave this house. I will go away, because"—he accused them dramatically with his glance—"because I do not want to be killed."

Scully was furious with his son. "Will you tell me what is the matter, you young devil? What's the matter, anyhow? Speak out!"

"Blame it!" cried Johnnie in despair, "don't I tell you I don't know. I can't tell what ails him."

The Swede continued to repeat: "Never mind, Mr. Scully; never mind. I will leave this house. I will go away, because I do not wish to be killed. Yes, of course, I am crazy—yes. But I know one thing! I will go away. I will leave this house. Never mind, Mr. Scully; never mind. I will go away."

"You will not go 'way," said Scully. "You will not go 'way until I hear the reason of this business. If anybody has troubled you I will take care of him. This is my house. You are under my roof, and I will not allow any peaceable man to be troubled here." He cast a terrible eye upon Johnnie, the cowboy, and the Easterner.

"Never mind, Mr. Scully; never mind. I will go away. I do not wish to be killed." The Swede moved toward the door which opened upon the stairs. It was evidently his intention to go at once for his baggage.

"No, no," shouted Scully, peremptorily; but the white-faced man slid by him and disappeared. "Now," said Scully severely, "what does this mane?"

Johnnie and the cowboy cried together: "Why, we didn't do nothin' to 'im!"

Scully's eyes were cold. "No," he said, "you didn't?"

Johnnie swore a deep oath. "Why, this is the wildest loon I ever see. We didn't do nothin' at all. We were jest sittin' here playin' cards, and he——"

The father suddenly spoke to the Easterner, "Mr. Blanc," he said, "what has these boys been doin'?"

The Easterner reflected again. "I didn't see anything wrong at all," he said at last, slowly.

Scully began to howl. "But what does it mane?" He started ferociously at his son. "I have a mind to lather you for this, me boy."

Johnnie was frantic. "Well, what have I done?" he bawled at his father.

III

"I think you are tongue-tied," said Scully finally to his son, the cowboy, and the Easterner; and at the end of this scornful sentence he left the room.

Upstairs the Swede was swiftly fastening the straps of his great valise. Once his back happened to be half turned toward the door, and, hearing a noise there, he wheeled and sprang up, uttering a loud cry. Scully's wrinkled visage showed grimly in the light of the small lamp he carried. This yellow effulgence, streaming upward, colored only his prominent features, and left his eyes, for instance, in mysterious shadow. He resembled a murderer.

"Man! man!" he exclaimed, "have you gone daffy?"

"Oh, no! Oh, no!" rejoined the other. "There are people in this world who know pretty nearly as much as you do—understand?"

For a moment they stood gazing at each other. Upon the Swede's deathly pale cheeks were two spots brightly crimson and sharply edged, as if they had been carefully painted. Scully placed the light on the table and sat himself on the edge of the bed. He spoke ruminatively. "By cracky, I never heard of such a thing in my life. It's a complete muddle. I can't, for the soul of me, think how you ever got this idea into your head." Presently he lifted his eyes and asked: "And did you sure think they were going to kill you?"

The Swede scanned the old man as if he wished to see into his mind. "I did," he said at last. He obviously suspected that this answer might precipitate an outbreak. As he pulled on a strap his whole arm shook, the elbow wavering like a bit of paper.

Scully banged his hand impressively on the footboard of the bed. "Why, man, we're goin' to have a line of ilictric street-cars in this town next spring."

" 'A line of electric street-cars,' " repeated the Swede, stupidly.

"And," said Scully, "there's a new railroad goin' to be built down from Broken Arm to here. Not to mintion the four churches and the smashin' big brick school house. Then there's the big factory, too. Why, in two years Romper'll be a metro-pol-is."

Having finished the preparation of his baggage, the Swede straightened himself. "Mr. Scully," he said, with sudden hardihood, "how much do I owe you?"

"You don't owe me anythin'," said the old man, angrily.

"Yes, I do," retorted the Swede. He took seventy-five cents from his pocket and tendered it to Scully; but the latter snapped his fingers in disdainful refusal. However, it happened that they both stood gazing in a strange fashion at three silver pieces on the Swede's open palm.

"I'll not take your money," said Scully at last. "Not after what's been goin' on here." Then a plan seemed to strike him. "Here," he cried, picking up his lamp and moving toward the door. "Here! Come with me a minute."

"No," said the Swede, in overwhelming alarm.

"Yes," urged the old man. "Come on! I want you to come and see a picter—just across the hall—in my room."

The Swede must have concluded that his hour was come. His jaw dropped and his teeth showed like a dead man's. He ultimately followed Scully across the corridor, but he had the step of one hung in chains.

Scully flashed the light high on the wall of his own chamber. There was revealed a ridiculous photograph of a little girl. She was leaning against a balustrade of gorgeous decoration, and the formidable bang to her hair was prominent. The figure was as graceful as an upright sled-stake, and, withal, it was the hue of lead. "There," said Scully, tenderly, "that's the picter of my little girl that died. Her name was Carrie. She had the purtiest hair you ever saw! I was that fond of her, she——"

Turning then, he saw that the Swede was not contemplating the picture at all, but, instead, was keeping keen watch on the gloom in the rear.

"Look, man!" cried Scully, heartily. "That's the picter of my little gal that died. Her name was Carrie. And then here's the picter of my oldest boy, Michael. He's a lawyer in Lincoln, an' doin' well. I gave that boy a grand eddication, and I'm glad for it now. He's a fine boy. Look at 'im now. Ain't he bold as blazes, him there in Lincoln, an honored an' respicted gintleman! An honored and respicted gintleman," concluded Scully with a flourish. And, so saying, he smote the Swede jovially on the back.

The Swede faintly smiled.

"Now," said the old man, "there's only one more thing." He dropped suddenly to the floor and thrust his head beneath the bed. The Swede could hear his muffled voice. "I'd keep it under my piller if it wasn't for that boy Johnnie. Then there's the old woman—— Where is it now? I never put it twice in the same place. Ah, now come out with you!"

Presently he backed clumsily from under the bed, dragging with him an old coat rolled into a bundle. "I've fetched him," he muttered. Kneeling on the floor, he unrolled the coat and extracted from its heart a large yellow-brown whiskey-bottle.

His first maneuver was to hold the bottle up to the light. Reassured, apparently that nobody had been tampering with it, he thrust it with a generous movement toward the Swede.

The weak-kneed Swede was about to eagerly clutch this element of strength, but he suddenly jerked his hand away and cast a look of horror upon Scully.

"Drink," said the old man affectionately. He had risen to his feet, and now stood facing the Swede.

There was a silence. Then again Scully said: "Drink!"

The Swede laughed wildly. He grabbed the bottle, put it to his mouth; and as his lips curled absurdly around the opening and his throat worked, he kept his glance, burning with hatred, upon the old man's face.

IV

After the departure of Scully the three men, with the cardboard still upon their knees, preserved for a long time an astounded silence. Then Johnnie said: "That's the doddangedest Swede I ever see."

"He ain't no Swede," said the cowboy, scornfully.

"Well, what is he then?" cried Johnnie. "What is he then?"

"It's my opinion," replied the cowboy deliberately, "he's some kind of a Dutchman." It was a venerable custom of the country to entitle as Swedes all light-haired men who spoke with a heavy tongue. In consequence the idea of the cowboy was not without its daring. "Yes, sir," he repeated. "It's my opinion this feller is some kind of a Dutchman."

"Well, he says he's a Swede, anyhow," muttered Johnnie, sulkily. He turned to the Easterner: "What do you think, Mr. Blanc?"

"Oh, I don't know," replied the Easterner.

"Well, what do you think makes him act that way?" asked the cowboy.

"Why, he's frightened." The Easterner knocked his pipe against a rim of the stove. "He's clear frightened out of his boots."

"What at?" cried Johnnie and the cowboy together.

The Easterner reflected over his answer.

"Oh, I don't know, but it seems to me this man has been reading dime novels, and he thinks he's right out in the middle of it—the shootin' and stabbin' and all."

"But," said the cowboy, deeply scandalized, "this ain't Wyoming, ner none of them places. This is Nebrasker."

"Yes," added Johnnie, "an' why don't he wait till he gits *out* West?"

The traveled Easterner laughed. "It isn't different there even—not in these days. But he thinks he's right in the middle of hell."

Johnnie and the cowboy mused long.

"It's awful funny," remarked Johnnie at last.

"Yes," said the cowboy. "This is a queer game. I hope we don't git snowed in, because then we'd have to stand this here man bein' around with us all the time. That wouldn't be no good."

"I wish pop would throw him out," said Johnnie.

Presently they heard a loud stamping on the stairs, accompanied by ringing jokes in the voice of old Scully, and laughter, evidently from the Swede. The men around the stove stared vacantly at each other. "Gosh!" said the cowboy. The door flew open, and old Scully, flushed and anecdotal, came into the room. He was jabbering at the Swede, who followed him, laughing bravely. It was the entry of two roisterers from a banquet hall.

"Come now," said Scully sharply to the three seated men, "move up and give us a chance at the stove." The cowboy and the Easterner obediently sidled their chairs to make room for the new-comers. Johnnie, however, simply arranged himself in a more indolent attitude, and then remained motionless.

"Come! Git over, there," said Scully.

"Plenty of room on the other side of the stove," said Johnnie.

"Do you think we want to sit in the draught?" roared the father.

But the Swede here interposed with a grandeur of confidence. "No, no. Let the boy sit where he likes," he cried in a bullying voice to the father.

"All right! All right!" said Scully, deferentially. The cowboy and the Easterner exchanged glances of wonder.

The five chairs were formed in a crescent about one side of the stove. The Swede began to talk; he talked arrogantly, profanely, angrily. Johnnie, the cowboy, and the Easterner maintained a morose silence, while old Scully appeared to be receptive and eager, breaking in constantly with sympathetic ejaculations.

Finally the Swede announced that he was thirsty. He moved in his chair, and said that he would go for a drink of water.

"I'll git it for you," cried Scully at once.

"No," said the Swede, contemptuously. "I'll get it for myself." He arose and stalked with the air of an owner off into the executive parts of the hotel.

As soon as the Swede was out of hearing, Scully sprang to his feet and whispered intensely to the others: "Upstairs he thought I was tryin' to poison 'im."

"Say," said Johnnie, "this makes me sick. Why don't you throw 'im out in the snow?"

"Why, he's all right now," declared Scully. "It was only that he was from the East, and he thought this was a tough place. That's all. He's all right now."

The cowboy looked with admiration upon the Easterner. "You were straight," he said. "You were on to that there Dutchman."

"Well," said Johnnie to his father, "he may be all right now, but I don't see it. Other time he was scared, but now he's too fresh."

Scully's speech was always a combination of Irish brogue and idiom, Western twang and idiom, and scraps of curiously formal diction taken from the story-books and newspapers. He now hurled a strange mass of language at the head of his son. "What do I keep? What do I keep? What do I keep?" he demanded, in a voice of thunder. He slapped his knee impressively, to indicate that he himself was going to make reply, and that all should heed. "I keep a hotel," he shouted. "A hotel, do you mind? A guest under my roof has sacred privileges. He is to be intimidated by none. Not one word shall he hear that would prijudice him in favor of goin' away. I'll not have it. There's no place in this here town where they can say they iver took in a guest of mine because he was afraid to stay here." He wheeled suddenly upon the cowboy and the Easterner. "Am I right?"

"Yes, Mr. Scully," said the cowboy, "I think you're right."

"Yes, Mr. Scully," said the Easterner, "I think you're right."

V

At six-o'clock supper, the Swede fizzed like a firewheel. He sometimes seemed on the point of bursting into riotous song, and in all his madness he was encouraged by old Scully. The Easterner was encased in reserve; the cowboy sat in wide-mouthed amazement, forgetting to eat, while Johnnie wrathily demolished great plates of food. The daughters of the house, when they were obliged to replenish the biscuits, approached as warily as Indians, and, having succeeded in their purpose, fled with ill-concealed trepidation. The Swede domineered the whole feast, and he gave it the appearance of a cruel bacchanal. He seemed to have grown suddenly taller; he gazed, brutally disdainful, into every face. His voice rang through the room. Once when he jabbed out harpoon-fashion with his fork to pinion a biscuit, the weapon nearly impaled the hand of the Easterner, which had been stretched quietly out for the same biscuit.

After supper, as the men filed toward the other room, the Swede smote Scully ruthlessly on the shoulder. "Well, old boy, that was a good, square meal." Johnnie looked hopefully at his father; he knew that shoulder was tender from an old fall; and, indeed, it appeared for a moment as if Scully was going to flame out over the matter, but in the end he smiled a sickly smile and remained silent. The others understood from his manner that he was admitting his responsibility for the Swede's new viewpoint.

Johnnie, however, addressed his parent in an aside. "Why don't you license somebody to kick you downstairs?" Scully scowled darkly by way of reply.

When they were gathered about the stove, the Swede insisted on another game of High-Five. Scully gently deprecated the plan at first, but the Swede turned a wolfish glare upon him. The old man subsided, and the Swede canvassed the others. In his tone there was always a great threat. The cowboy and the Easterner both remarked indifferently that they would play. Scully said that he would presently have to go to meet the 6.58 train, and so the Swede turned menacingly upon Johnnie. For a moment their glances crossed like blades, and then Johnnie smiled and said, "Yes, I'll play."

They formed a square, with the little board on their knees. The Easterner and the Swede were again partners. As the play went on, it was noticeable that the cowboy was not boardwhacking as usual. Meanwhile, Scully, near the lamp, had put on his spectacles and, with an appearance curiously like an old priest, was reading a newspaper. In time he went out to meet the 6.58 train, and, despite his precautions, a gust of polar wind whirled into the room as he opened the door. Besides scattering the cards, it chilled the players to the marrow. The Swede cursed frightfully. When Scully returned, his entrance disturbed a cozy and friendly scene. The Swede again cursed. But presently they were once more intent, their heads bent forward and their hands moving swiftly. The Swede had adopted the fashion of board-whacking.

Scully took up his paper and for a long time remained immersed in matters which were extraordinarily remote from him. The lamp burned badly, and once he stopped to adjust the wick. The newspaper, as he turned from page to page, rustled with a slow and comfortable sound. Then suddenly he heard three terrible words: "You are cheatin'!"

Such scenes often prove that there can be little of dramatic import in environment. Any room can present a tragic front; any room can be comic. This little den was now hideous as a torture-chamber. The new faces of the men themselves had changed it upon the instant. The Swede held a huge fist in front of Johnnie's face, while the latter looked steadily over it into the blazing orbs of his accuser. The Easterner had grown pallid; the cowboy's jaw had dropped in that expression of bovine amazement which was one of his important mannerisms. After the three words, the first sound in the room was made by Scully's paper as it floated forgotten to his feet. His spectacles had also fallen from his nose, but by a clutch he had saved them in air. His hand, grasping the spectacles, now remained poised awkwardly and near his shoulder. He stared at the card-players.

Probably the silence was while a second elapsed. Then, if the floor had been suddenly twitched out from under the men they could not have moved quicker. The five had projected themselves headlong toward a common point. It happened that Johnnie, in rising to hurl himself upon the Swede, had stumbled slightly because of his curiously instinctive care for the cards and the board. The loss of the moment allowed time for the arrival of Scully, and also allowed the cowboy time to give the Swede a great push which sent him staggering back. The men found tongue together, and hoarse shouts of rage, appeal, or fear burst from every throat. The cowboy pushed and jostled feverishly at the Swede, and the Easterner and Scully clung wildly to Johnnie; but through the smoky air, above the swaying bodies of the peace-compellers, the eyes of the two warriors ever sought each other in glances of challenge that were at once hot and steely.

Of course the board had been overturned, and now the whole company of cards was scattered over the floor, where the boots of the men trampled the fat and painted kings and queens as they gazed with their silly eyes at the war that was waging above them.

Scully's voice was dominating the yells. "Stop now! Stop, I say! Stop, now——"

Johnnie, as he struggled to burst through the rank formed by Scully and the Easterner, was crying, "Well, he says I cheated! He says I cheated! I won't allow no man to say I cheated! If he says I cheated, he's a—— ——!"

The cowboy was telling the Swede, "Quit, now! Quit, d'ye hear——"

The screams of the Swede never ceased: "He did cheat! I saw him! I saw him——"

As for the Easterner, he was importuning in a voice that was not heeded: "Wait a moment, can't you? Oh, wait a moment. What's the good of a fight over a game of cards? Wait a moment——"

In this tumult no complete sentences were clear. "Cheat"—"Quit"—"He says"—these fragments pierced the uproar and rang out sharply. It was remarkable that, whereas Scully undoubtedly made the most noise, he was the least heard of any of the riotous band.

Then suddenly there was a great cessation. It was as if each man had paused for breath; and although the room was still lighted with the anger of men, it could be seen that there was no danger of immediate conflict, and at once Johnnie, shouldering his way forward, almost succeeded in confronting the Swede. "What did you say I cheated for? What did you say I cheated for? I don't cheat, and I won't let no man say I do!"

The Swede said, "I saw you! I saw you!"

"Well," cried Johnnie, "I'll fight any man what says I cheat!"

"No, you won't," said the cowboy. "Not here."

"Ah, be still, can't you?" said Scully, coming between them.

The quiet was sufficient to allow the Easterner's voice to be heard. He was repeating, "Oh, wait a moment, can't you? What's the good of a fight over a game of cards? Wait a moment!"

Johnnie, his red face appearing above his father's shoulders, hailed the Swede again. "Did you say I cheated?"

The Swede showed his teeth. "Yes."

"Then," said Johnnie, "we must fight."

"Yes, fight," roared the Swede. He was like a demoniac. "Yes, fight! I'll show you what kind of man I am! I'll show you who you want to fight! Maybe you think I can't fight! Maybe you think I can't! I'll show you, you skin, you cardsharp! Yes, you cheated! You cheated! You cheated!"

"Well, let's go at it, then, mister," said Johnnie, coolly.

The cowboy's brow was beaded with sweat from his efforts in intercepting all sorts of raids. He turned in despair to Scully. "What are you goin' to do now?"

A change had come over the Celtic visage of the old man. He now seemed all eagerness; his eyes glowed.

"We'll let them fight," he answered, stalwartly. "I can't put up with it any longer. I've stood this damned Swede till I'm sick. We'll let them fight."

VI

The men prepared to go out of doors. The Easterner was so nervous that he had great difficulty in getting his arms into the sleeves of his new leather coat. As the cowboy drew his fur cap down over his ears his hands trembled. In fact, Johnnie and old Scully were the only ones who displayed no agitation. These preliminaries were conducted without words.

Scully threw open the door. "Well, come on," he said. Instantly a terrific wind caused the flame of the lamp to struggle at its wick, while a puff of black smoke sprang from the chimney-top. The stove was in mid-current of the blast, and its voice swelled to equal the roar of the storm. Some of the scarred and bedabbled cards were caught up from the floor and dashed helplessly against the farther wall. The men lowered their heads and plunged into the tempest as into a sea.

No snow was falling, but great whirls and clouds of flakes, swept up from the ground by the frantic winds, were streaming southward with the speed of bullets. The covered land was blue with the sheen of an unearthly satin, and there was no other hue save where, at the low, black railway station —which seemed incredibly distant—one light gleamed like a tiny jewel. As the men floundered into a thigh-deep drift, it was known that the Swede was bawling out something. Scully went to him, put a hand on his shoulder, and projected an ear. "What's that you say?" he shouted.

"I say," bawled the Swede again, "I won't stand much show against this gang. I know you'll all pitch on me."

Scully smote him reproachfully on the arm.

"Tut, man!" he yelled. The wind tore the words from Scully's lips and scattered them far alee.

"You are all a gang of——" boomed the Swede, but the storm also seized the remainder of this sentence.

Immediately turning their backs upon the wind, the men had swung around a corner to the sheltered side of the hotel. It was the function of the little house to preserve here, amid this great devastation of snow, an irregular V-shape of heavily encrusted grass, which crackled beneath the feet. One could imagine the great drifts piled against the windward side. When the party reached the comparative peace of this spot, it was found that the Swede was still bellowing.

"Oh, I know what kind of a thing this is! I know you'll all pitch on me. I can't lick you all!"

Scully turned upon him panther-fashion. "You'll not have to whip all of us. You'll have to whip my son Johnnie. An' the man what troubles you durin' that time will have me to dale with."

The arrangements were swiftly made. The two men faced each other, obedient to the harsh commands of Scully, whose face, in the subtly luminous gloom, could be seen set in the austere impersonal lines that are pictured on the countenances of the Roman veterans. The Easterner's teeth were chattering, and he was hopping up and down like a mechanical toy. The cowboy stood rock-like.

The contestants had not stripped off any clothing. Each was in his ordinary attire. Their fists were up, and they eyed each other in a calm that had the elements of leonine cruelty in it.

During this pause, the Easterner's mind, like a film, took lasting impressions of three men—the iron-nerved master of the ceremony; the Swede, pale, motionless, terrible; and Johnnie, serene yet ferocious, brutish yet heroic. The entire prelude had in it a tragedy greater than the tragedy of action, and this aspect was accentuated by the long, mellow cry of the blizzard, as it sped the tumbling and wailing flakes into the black abyss of the south.

"Now!" said Scully.

The two combatants leaped forward and crashed together like bullocks. There was heard the cushioned sound of blows, and of a curse squeezing out from between the tight teeth of one.

As for the spectators, the Easterner's pent-up breath exploded from him with a pop of relief, absolute relief from the tension of the preliminaries. The cowboy bounded into the air with a yowl. Scully was immovable as from supreme amazement and fear at the fury of the fight which he himself had permitted and arranged.

For a time the encounter in the darkness was such a perplexity of flying arms that it presented no more detail than would a swiftly revolving wheel. Occasionally a face, as if illumined by a flash of light, would shine out, ghastly and marked with pink spots. A moment later, the men might have been known as shadows, if it were not for the involuntary utterance of oaths that came from them in whispers.

Suddenly a holocaust of warlike desire caught the cowboy, and he bolted forward with the speed of a broncho. "Go it, Johnnie! go it! Kill him! Kill him!"

Scully confronted him. "Kape back," he said; and by his glance the cowboy could tell that this man was Johnnie's father.

To the Easterner there was a monotony of unchangeable fighting that was an abomination. This confused mingling was eternal to his sense, which was concentrated in a longing for the end, the priceless end. Once the fighters lurched near him, and as he scrambled hastily backward he heard them breathe like men on the rack.

"Kill him, Johnnie! Kill him! Kill him! Kill him!" The cowboy's face was contorted like one of those agony masks in museums.

"Keep still," said Scully, icily.

Then there was a sudden loud grunt, incomplete, cut short, and Johnnie's body swung away from the Swede and fell with sickening heaviness to the grass. The cowboy was barely in time to prevent the mad Swede from flinging himself upon his prone adversary. "No, you don't," said the cowboy, interposing an arm. "Wait a second."

Scully was at his son's side. "Johnnie! Johnnie, me boy!" His voice had a quality of melancholy tenderness. "Johnnie! Can you go on with it?" He looked anxiously down into the bloody, pulpy face of his son.

There was a moment of silence, and then Johnnie answered in his ordinary voice, "Yes, I—it—yes."

Assisted by his father he struggled to his feet. "Wait a bit now till you git your wind," said the old man.

A few paces away the cowboy was lecturing the Swede. "No, you don't! Wait a second!"

The Easterner was plucking at Scully's sleeve. "Oh, this is enough," he pleaded. "This is enough! Let it go as it stands. This is enough!"

"Bill," said Scully, "git out of the road." The cowboy stepped aside.

"Now." The combatants were actuated by a new caution as they advanced toward collision. They glared at each other, and then the Swede aimed a lightning blow that carried with it his entire weight. Johnnie was evidently half stupid from weakness, but he miraculously dodged, and his fist sent the over-balanced Swede sprawling.

The cowboy, Scully, and the Easterner burst into a cheer that was like a chorus of triumphant soldiery, but before its conclusion the Swede had scuffed agilely to his feet and come in berserk abandon at his foe. There was another perplexity of flying arms, and Johnnie's body again swung away and fell, even as a bundle might fall from a roof. The Swede instantly staggered to a little wind-waved tree and leaned upon it, breathing like an engine, while his savage and flame-lit eyes roamed from face to face as the men bent over Johnnie. There was a splendor of isolation in his situation at this time which the Easterner felt once when, lifting his eyes from the man on the ground, he beheld that mysterious and lonely figure, waiting.

"Are you any good yet, Johnnie?" asked Scully in a broken voice.

The son gasped and opened his eyes languidly. After a moment he answered, "No—I ain't—any good—any—more." Then, from shame and bodily ill, he began to weep, the tears furrowing down through the bloodstain on his face. "He was too—too—too heavy for me."

Scully straightened and addressed the waiting figure. "Stranger," he said, evenly, "it's all up with our side." Then his voice changed into that vibrant huskiness which is commonly the tone of the most simple and deadly announcements. "Johnnie is whipped."

Without replying, the victor moved off on the route to the front door of the hotel.

The cowboy was formulating new and unspellable blasphemies. The Easterner was startled to find that they were out in a wind that seemed to come direct from the shadowed arctic floes. He heard again the wail of the snow as it was flung to its grave in the south. He knew now that all this time the cold had been sinking into him deeper and deeper, and he wondered that he had not perished. He felt indifferent to the condition of the vanquished man.

"Johnnie, can you walk?" asked Scully.

"Did I hurt—hurt him any?" asked the son.

"Can you walk, boy? Can you walk?"

Johnnie's voice was suddenly strong. There was a robust impatience in it. "I asked you whether I hurt him any!"

"Yes, yes, Johnnie," answered the cowboy, consolingly; "he's hurt a good deal."

They raised him from the ground, and as soon as he was on his feet he went tottering off, rebuffing all attempts at assistance. When the party rounded the corner they were fairly blinded by the pelting of the snow. It burned their faces like fire. The cowboy carried Johnnie through the drift to the door. As they entered, some cards again rose from the floor and beat against the wall.

The Easterner rushed to the stove. He was so profoundly chilled that he almost dared to embrace the glowing iron. The Swede was not in the room. Johnnie sank into a chair and, folding his arms on his knees, buried his face in them. Scully, warming one foot and then the other at a rim of the stove, muttered to himself with Celtic mournfulness. The cowboy had removed his fur cap, and with a dazed and rueful air he was running one hand through his tousled locks. From overhead they could hear the creaking of boards, as the Swede tramped here and there in his room.

The sad quiet was broken by the sudden flinging open of a door that led toward the kitchen. It was instantly followed by an inrush of women. They precipitated themselves upon Johnnie amid a chorus of lamentation. Before they carried their prey off to the kitchen, there to be bathed and harangued with that mixture of sympathy and abuse which is a feat of their sex, the mother straightened herself and fixed old Scully with an eye of stern reproach. "Shame be upon you, Patrick Scully!" she cried. "Your own son, too. Shame be upon you!"

"Shame be upon you, Patrick Scully!" The girls, rallying to this slogan, sniffed disdainfully in the direction of those trembling accomplices, the cowboy and the Easterner. Presently they bore Johnnie away, and left the three men to dismal reflection.

VII

"I'd like to fight this here Dutchman myself," said the cowboy, breaking a long silence.

Scully wagged his head sadly. "No, that wouldn't do. It wouldn't be right. It wouldn't be right."

"Well, why wouldn't it?" argued the cowboy. "I don't see no harm in it."

"No," answered Scully, with mournful heroism. "It wouldn't be right. It was Johnnie's fight, and now we mustn't whip the man just because he whipped Johnnie."

"Yes, that's true enough," said the cowboy; "but—he better not get fresh with me, because I couldn't stand no more of it."

"You'll not say a word to him," commanded Scully, and even then they heard the tread of the Swede on the stairs. His entrance was made theatric. He swept the door back with a bang and swaggered to the middle of the room. No one looked at him. "Well," he cried, insolently, at Scully, "I s'pose you'll tell me now how much I owe you?"

The old man remained stolid. "You don't owe me nothin'."

"Huh!" said the Swede, "huh! Don't owe 'im nothin'."

The cowboy addressed the Swede. "Stranger, I don't see how you come to be so gay around here."

Old Scully was instantly alert. "Stop!" he shouted, holding his hand forth, fingers upward. "Bill, you shut up!"

The cowboy spat carelessly into the sawdust-box. "I didn't say a word, did I?" he asked.

"Mr. Scully," called the Swede, "how much do I owe you?" It was seen that he was attired for departure, and that he had his valise in his hand.

"You don't owe me nothin'," repeated Scully in the same imperturbable way.

"Huh!" said the Swede. "I guess you're right. I guess if it was any way at all, you'd owe me somethin'. That's what I guess," He turned to the cowboy. "Kill him! Kill him! Kill him!' " he mimicked, and then guffawed victoriously. " 'Kill him!' " He was convulsed with ironical humor.

But he might have been jeering the dead. The three men were immovable and silent, staring with glassy eyes at the stove.

The Swede opened the door and passed into the storm, giving one derisive glance backward at the still group.

As soon as the door was closed, Scully and the cowboy leaped to their feet and began to curse. They trampled to and fro, waving their arms and smashing into the air with their fists. "Oh, but that was a hard minute!" wailed Scully. "That was a hard minute! Him there leerin' and scoffin'! One bang at his nose was worth forty dollars to me that minute! How did you stand it, Bill!"

"How did I stand it?" cried the cowboy in a quivering voice. "How did I stand it? Oh!"

The old man burst into sudden brogue. "I'd loike to take that Swede," he wailed, "and hould 'im down on a shtone flure and bate 'im to a jeelly wid a shtick!"

The cowboy groaned in sympathy. "I'd like to git him by the neck and ha-ammer him"—he brought his hand down on a chair with a noise like a pistol-shot—"hammer that there Dutchman until he couldn't tell himself from a dead coyote!"

"I'd bate 'im until he—"

"I'd show *him* some things—"

And then together they raised a yearning, fanatic cry—"Oh-o-oh! if we only could—"

"Yes!"

"Yes!"

"And then I'd—"

"O-o-oh!"

VIII

The Swede, tightly gripping his valise, tacked across the face of the storm as if he carried sails. He was following a line of little naked, gasping trees which, he knew, must mark the way of the road. His face, fresh from the pounding of Johnnie's fists, felt more pleasure than pain in the wind and the driving snow. A number of square shapes loomed upon him finally, and he knew them as the houses of the main body of the town. He found a street and made travel along it, leaning heavily upon the wind whenever, at a corner, a terrific blast caught him.

He might have been in a deserted village. We picture the world as thick with conquering and elate humanity, but here, with the bugles of the tempest pealing, it was hard to imagine a peopled earth. One viewed the existence of man then as a marvel, and conceded a glamour of wonder to these lice which were caused to cling to a whirling, fire-smitten, ice-locked, disease-stricken, space-lost bulb. The conceit of man was explained by this storm to be the very engine of life. One was a coxcomb not to die in it. However, the Swede found a saloon.

In front of it an indomitable red light was burning, and the snowflakes were made blood-color as they flew through the circumscribed territory of the lamp's shining. The Swede pushed open the door of the saloon and entered. A sanded expanse was before him, and at the end of it four men sat about a table drinking. Down one side of the room extended a radiant bar, and its guardian was leaning upon his elbows listening to the talk of the men at the table. The Swede dropped his valise upon the floor and, smiling fraternally upon the barkeeper, said, "Gimme some whisky, will you?" The man placed a bottle, a whisky-glass, and a glass of ice-thick water upon the bar. The Swede poured himself an abnormal portion of whisky and drank it in three gulps. "Pretty bad night," remarked the bartender, indifferently. He was making the pretension of blindness which is usually a distinction of his class; but it could have been seen that he was furtively studying the half-erased blood-stains on the face of the Swede. "Bad night," he said again.

"Oh, it's good enough for me," replied the Swede, hardily, as he poured himself some more whisky. The barkeeper took his coin and maneuvered it through its reception by the highly nickeled cash-machine. A bell rang; a card labeled "20 cts." had appeared.

"No," continued the Swede, "this isn't too bad weather. It's good enough for me."

"So?" murmured the barkeeper, languidly.

The copious drams made the Swede's eyes swim, and he breathed a trifle heavier. "Yes, I like this weather. I like it. It suits me." It was apparently his design to impart a deep significance to these words.

"So?" murmured the bartender again. He turned to gaze dreamily at the scroll-like birds and bird-like scrolls which had been drawn with soap upon the mirrors in back of the bar.

"Well, I guess I'll take another drink," said the Swede, presently. "Have something?"

"No, thanks! I'm not drinkin'," answered the bartender. Afterward he asked, "How did you hurt your face?"

The Swede immediately began to boast loudly. "Why, in a fight. I thumped the soul out of a man down here at Scully's hotel."

The interest of the four men at the table was at last aroused.

"Who was it?" said one.

"Johnnie Scully," blustered the Swede. "Son of the man what runs it. He will be pretty near dead for some weeks, I can tell you. I made a nice thing of him, I did. He couldn't get up. They carried him in the house. Have a drink?"

Instantly the men in some subtle way encased themselves in reserve. "No, thanks," said one. The group was of curious formation. Two were prominent local business men; one was the district attorney; and one was a professional gambler of the kind known as "square." But a scrutiny of the group would not have enabled an observer to pick the gambler from the men of more reputable pursuits. He was, in fact, a man so delicate in manner, when among people of fair class, and so judicious in his choice of victims, that in the strictly masculine part of the town's life he had come to be explicitly trusted and admired. People called him a thoroughbred. The fear and contempt with which his craft was regarded were undoubtedly the reason why his quiet dignity shone conspicuous above the quiet dignity of men who might be merely hatters, billiard-markers, or grocery clerks. Beyond an occasional unwary traveler who came by rail, this gambler was supposed to prey solely upon reckless and senile farmers, who, when flush with good crops, drove into town in all the pride and confidence of an absolutely invulnerable stupidity. Hearing at times in circuitous fashion of the despoilment of such a farmer, the important men of Romper invariably laughed in contempt of the victim, and if they thought of the wolf at all, it was with a kind of pride at the knowledge that he would never dare think of attacking their wisdom and courage. Besides, it was popular that this gambler had a real wife and two real children in a neat cottage in a suburb, where he led an exemplary home life; and when anyone even suggested a discrepancy in his character, the crowd immediately vociferated descriptions of this virtuous family circle. Then men who led exemplary home lives, and men who did not lead exemplary home lives, all subsided in a bunch, remarking that there was nothing more to be said.

However, when a restriction was placed upon him—as, for instance, when a strong clique of members of the new Pollywog Club refused to permit him, even as a spectator, to appear in the rooms of the organization—the candor and gentleness with which he accepted the judgment disarmed many of his foes and made his friends more desperately partisan. He invariably distinguished between himself and a respectable Romper man so quickly and frankly that his manner actually appeared to be a continual broadcast compliment.

And one must not forget to declare the fundamental fact of his entire position in Romper. It is irrefutable that in all affairs outside his business, in all matters that occur eternally and commonly between man, this thieving card-player was so generous, so just, so moral, that, in a contest, he could have put to flight the consciences of nine tenths of the citizens of Romper.

And so it happened that he was seated in this saloon with the two prominent local merchants and the district attorney.

The Swede continued to drink raw whisky, meanwhile babbling at the barkeeper and trying to induce him to indulge in potations. "Come on. Have a drink. Come on. What—no? Well, have a little one, then. By gawd, I've whipped a man tonight, and I want to celebrate. I whipped him good, too. Gentlemen," the Swede cried to the men at the table, "have a drink?"

"Ssh!" said the barkeeper.

The group at the table, although furtively attentive, had been pretending to be deep in talk, but now a man lifted his eyes toward the Swede and said, shortly, "Thanks. We don't want any more."

At this reply the Swede ruffled out his chest like a rooster. "Well," he exploded, "it seems I can't get anybody to drink with me in this town. Seems so, don't it? Well!"

"Ssh!" said the barkeeper.

"Say," snarled the Swede, "don't you try to shut me up. I won't have it. I'm a gentleman, and I want people to drink with me. And I want 'em to drink with me now. Now—do you understand?" He rapped the bar with his knuckles.

Years of experience had calloused the bartender. He merely grew sulky. "I hear you," he answered.

"Well," cried the Swede, "listen hard then. See those men over there? Well, they're going to drink with me and don't you forget it. Now you watch."

"Hi," yelled the barkeeper, "this won't do!"

"Why won't it?" demanded the Swede. He stalked over to the table, and by chance laid his hand upon the shoulder of the gambler. "How about this?" he asked wrathfully. "I asked you to drink with me."

The gambler simply twisted his head and spoke over his shoulder. "My friend, I don't know you."

"Oh, hell!" answered the Swede, "come and have a drink."

"Now, my boy," advised the gambler kindly, "take your hand off my shoulder and go 'way and mind your own business." He was a little, slim man, and it seemed strange to hear him use this tone of heroic patronage to the burly Swede. The other men at the table said nothing.

"What! You won't drink with me, you little dude? I'll make you, then! I'll make you!" The Swede had grasped the gambler frenziedly at the throat, and was dragging him from his chair. The other men sprang up. The barkeeper dashed around the corner of his bar. There was a great tumult, and then was seen a long blade in the hand of the gambler. It shot forward, and a human body, this citadel of virtue, wisdom, power, was pierced as easily as if it had been a melon. The Swede fell with a cry of supreme astonishment.

The prominent merchants and the district attorney must have at once tumbled out of the place backward. The bartender found himself hanging limply to the arm of a chair and gazing into the eyes of a murderer.

"Henry," said the latter, as he wiped his knife on one of the towels that hung beneath the bar rail, "you tell 'em where to find me. I'll be home, waiting for 'em." Then he vanished. A moment afterward the barkeeper was in the street dinning through the storm for help and, moreover, companionship.

The corpse of the Swede, alone in the saloon, had its eyes fixed upon a dreadful legend that dwelt atop of the cashmachine: "This registers the amount of your purchase."

IX

Months later, the cowboy was frying pork over the stove of a little ranch near the Dakota line, when there was a quick thud of hoofs outside, and presently the Easterner entered with the letters and the papers.

"Well," said the Easterner at once, "the chap that killed the Swede has got three years. Wasn't much, was it?"

"He has? Three years?" The cowboy poised his pan of pork, while he ruminated upon the news. "Three years. That ain't much."

"No. It was a light sentence," replied the Easterner as he unbuckled his spurs. "Seems there was a good deal of sympathy for him in Romper."

"If the bartender had been any good," observed the cowboy, thoughtfully, "he would have gone in and cracked that there Dutchman on the head with a bottle in the beginnin' of it and stopped all this here murderin'."

"Yes, a thousand things might have happened," said the Easterner, tartly.

The cowboy returned his pan of pork to the fire, but his philosophy continued. "It's funny, ain't it? If he hadn't said Johnnie was cheatin' he'd be alive this minute. He was an awful fool. Game played for fun, too. Not for money. I believe he was crazy."

"I feel sorry for that gambler," said the Easterner.

"Oh, so do I," said the cowboy. "He don't deserve none of it for killin' who he did."

"The Swede might not have been killed if everything had been square."

"Might not have been killed?" exclaimed the cowboy. "Everythin' square? Why, when he said that Johnnie was cheatin' and acted like such a jackass? And then in the saloon he fairly walked up to git hurt?" With these arguments the cowboy browbeat the Easterner and reduced him to rage.

"You're a fool!" cried the Easterner, viciously. "You're a bigger jackass than the Swede by a million majority. Now let me tell you one thing. Let me tell you something. Listen! Johnnie *was* cheating!"

" 'Johnnie' " said the cowboy, blankly. There was a minute of silence, and then he said, robustly, "Why, no. The game was only for fun."

"Fun or not," said the Easterner, "Johnnie was cheating. I saw him. I I know it. I saw him. And I refused to stand up and be a man. I let the Swede fight it out alone. And you—you were simply puffing around the place and wanting to fight. And then old Scully himself! We are all in it! This poor gambler isn't even a noun. He is kind of an adverb. Every sin is the result of a collaboration. We, five of us, have collaborated in the murder of this Swede. Usually there are from a dozen to forty women really involved in every murder, but in this case it seems to be only five men—you, I, Johnnie, old

Scully; and that fool of an unfortunate gambler came merely as a culmination, the apex of a human movement, and gets all the punishment."

The cowboy, injured and rebellious, cried out blindly into this fog of mysterious theory: "Well, I didn't do anythin', did I?"

JAMES JOYCE

Clay

The matron had given her leave to go out as soon as the women's tea was over and Maria looked forward to her evening out. The kitchen was spick and span: the cook said you could see yourself in the big copper boilers. The fire was nice and bright and on one of the side-tables were four very big barmbracks. These barmbracks seemed uncut; but if you went closer you would see that they had been cut into long thick even slices and were ready to be handed round at tea. Maria had cut them herself.

Maria was a very, very small person indeed but she had a very long nose and a very long chin. She talked a little through her nose, always soothingly: "Yes, my dear," and "No, my dear." She was always sent for when the women quarreled over their tubs and always succeeded in making peace. One day the matron had said to her:

"Maria, you are a veritable peace-maker!"

And the sub-matron and two of the Board ladies had heard the compliment. And Ginger Mooney was always saying what she wouldn't do to the dummy who had charge of the irons if it wasn't for Maria. Everyone was so fond of Maria.

The women would have their tea at six o'clock and she would be able to get away before seven. From Ballsbridge to the Pillar, twenty minutes; from the Pillar to Drumcondra, twenty minutes; and twenty minutes to buy the things. She would be there before eight. She took out her purse with the silver clasps and read again the words *A Present from Belfast*. She was very fond of that purse because Joe had brought it to her five years before when he and Alphy had gone to Belfast on a Whit-Monday trip. In the purse were two half-crowns and some coppers. She would have five shillings clear after paying tram fare. What a nice evening they would have, all the children singing! Only she hoped that Joe wouldn't come in drunk. He was so different when he took any drink.

Often he had wanted her to go and live with them; but she would have felt herself in the way (though Joe's wife was ever so nice with her) and she had become accustomed to the life of the laundry. Joe was a good fellow. She had nursed him and Alphy too; and Joe used often say:

"Mamma is mamma but Maria is my proper mother."

After the break-up at home the boys had got her that position in the *Dublin by Lamplight* laundry, and she liked it. She used to have such a bad opinion of Protestants but now she thought they were very nice people, a little quiet and serious, but still very nice people to live with. Then she had her plants in the conservatory and she liked looking after them. She had lovely ferns and wax-plants and, whenever anyone came to visit her, she always gave the visitor one or two slips from her conservatory. There was one thing she didn't like and that was the tracts on the walls; but the matron was such a nice person to deal with, so genteel.

When the cook told her everything was ready she went into the women's room and began to pull the big bell. In a few minutes the women began to come in by twos and threes, wiping their steaming hands in their petticoats and pulling down the sleeves of their blouses over their red steaming arms. They settled down before their huge mugs which the cook and the dummy filled up with hot tea, already mixed with milk and sugar in huge tin cans. Maria superintended the distribution of the barmbrack and saw that every woman got her four slices. There was a great deal of laughing and joking during the meal. Lizzie Fleming said Maria was sure to get the ring and, though Fleming had said that for so many Hallow Eves, Maria had to laugh and say she didn't want any ring or man either; and when she laughed her gray-green eyes sparkled with disappointed shyness and the tip of her nose nearly met the tip of her chin. Then Ginger Mooney lifted up her mug of tea and proposed Maria's health while all the other women clattered with their mugs on the table, and said she was sorry she hadn't a sup of porter to drink it in. And Maria laughed again till the tip of her nose nearly met the tip of her chin and till her minute body nearly shook itself asunder because she knew that Mooney meant well though, of course, she had the notions of a common woman.

But wasn't Maria glad when the women had finished their tea and the cook and the dummy had begun to clear away the tea-things! She went into her little bedroom and, remembering that the next morning was a mass morning, changed the hand of the alarm from seven to six. Then she took off her working shirt and her house-boots and laid her best skirt out on the bed and her tiny dress-boots beside the foot of the bed. She changed her blouse too and, as she stood before the mirror, she thought of how she used to dress for mass on Sunday morning when she was a young girl; and she looked with quaint affection at the diminutive body which she had so often adorned. In spite of its years she found it a nice tidy little body.

When she got outside the streets were shining with rain and she was glad of her old brown waterproof. The tram was full and she had to sit on the little stool at the end of the car, facing all the people, with her toes barely touching the floor. She arranged in her mind all she was going to do and thought how much better it was to be independent and to have your own money in your pocket. She hoped they would have a nice evening. She was sure they would but she could not help thinking what a pity it was Alphy and Joe were not speaking. They were always falling out now but when they were boys together they used to be the best of friends: but such was life.

She got out her tram at the Pillar and ferreted her way quickly among the crowds. She went into Downes's cake-shop but the shop was so full of people that it was a long time before she could get herself attended to. She bought a dozen of mixed penny cakes, and at last came out of the shop laden with a big bag. Then she thought what else would she buy: she wanted to buy something really nice. They would be sure to have plenty of apples and nuts. It was hard to know what to buy and all she could think of was cake. She decided to buy some plumcake but Downes's plumcake had not enough almond icing on top of it so she went over to a shop in Henry Street. Here she was a long time in suiting herself and the stylish young lady behind the counter, who was evidently a little annoyed by her, asked her was it wedding-cake she wanted to buy. That made Maria blush and smile at the young lady; but the young lady took it all very seriously and finally cut a thick slice of plumcake, parceled it up and said:

"Two-and-four, please."

She thought she would have to stand in the Drumcondra tram because none of the young men seemed to notice her but an elderly gentleman made room for her. He was a stout gentleman and he wore a brown hard hat; he had a square red face and a grayish mustache. Maria thought he was a colonel-looking gentleman and she reflected how much more polite he was than the young men who simply stared straight before them. The gentleman began to chat with her about Hallow Eve and the rainy weather. He supposed the bag was full of good things for the little ones and said it was only right that the youngsters should enjoy themselves while they were young. Maria agreed with him and favored him with demure nods and hems. He was very nice with her, and when she was getting out at the Canal Bridge she thanked him and bowed, and he bowed to her and raised his hat and smiled agreeably; and while she was going up along the terrace, bending her tiny head under the rain, she thought how easy it was to know a gentleman even when he has a drop taken.

Everybody said: "O, here's Maria!" when she came to Joe's house. Joe was there, having come home from business, and all the children had their Sunday dresses on. There were two big girls in from next door and games were going on. Maria gave the bag of cakes to the eldest boy, Alphy, to divide and Mrs. Donnelly said it was too good of her to bring such a big bag of cakes and made all the children say:

"Thanks, Maria."

But Maria said she had brought something special for papa and mamma, something they would be sure to like, and she began to look for her plumcake. She tried in Downes's bag and then in the pockets of her waterproof and then on the hallstand but nowhere could she find it. Then she asked all the children had any of them eaten it—by mistake, of course—but the children all said no and looked as if they did not like to eat cakes if they were to be accused of stealing. Everybody had a solution for the mystery and Mrs. Donnelly said it was plain that Maria had left it behind her in the tram. Maria, remembering how confused the gentleman with the grayish mustache had made her, colored with shame and vexation and disappointment. At the thought of the failure of her little surprise and of the two and four-pence she had thrown away for nothing she nearly cried outright.

But Joe said it didn't matter and made her sit down by the fire. He was very nice with her. He told her all that went on in his office, repeating for her a smart answer which he had made to the manager. Maria did not understand why Joe laughed so much over the answer he had made but she said that the manager must have been a very overbearing person to deal with. Joe said he wasn't so bad when you knew how to take him, that he was a decent sort so long as you didn't rub him the wrong way. Mrs. Donnelly played the piano for the children and they danced and sang. Then the two next-door girls handed round the nuts. Nobody could find the nutcrackers and Joe was nearly getting cross over it and asked how did they expect Maria to crack nuts without a nutcracker. But Maria said she didn't like nuts and that they weren't to bother about her. Then Joe asked would she take a bottle of stout and Mrs. Donnelly said there was port wine too in the house if she would prefer that. Maria said she would rather they didn't ask her to take anything: but Joe insisted.

So Maria let him have his way and they sat by the fire talking over old times and Maria thought she would put in a good word for Alphy. But Joe cried that God might strike him stone dead if ever he spoke a word to his brother again and Maria said she was sorry she had mentioned the matter. Mrs. Donnelly told her husband it was a great shame for him to speak that way of his own flesh and blood but Joe said Alphy was no brother of his and there was nearly being a row on the head of it. But Joe said he would not lose his temper on account of the night it was and asked his wife to open some more stout. The two next-door girls had arranged some Hallow Eve games and soon everything was merry again. Maria was delighted to see the children so merry and Joe and his wife in such good spirits. The next-door girls put some saucers on the table and then led the children up to the table, blindfold. One got the prayer-book and the other three got the water; and when one of the next-door girls got the ring Mrs. Donnelly shook her finger at the blushing girl as much as to say: O, I know all about it! They insisted on blindfolding Maria and leading her up to the table to see what she would get; and, while they were putting on the bandage, Maria laughed and laughed again till the tip of her nose nearly met the tip of her chin.

They led her up to the table amid laughing and joking and she put her hand out in the air as she was told to do. She moved her hand about here and there in the air and descended on one of the saucers. She felt a soft wet substance with her fingers and was surprised that nobody spoke or took off her bandage. There was a pause for a few seconds; and then a great deal of scuffling and whispering. Somebody said something about the garden, and at last Mrs. Donnelly said something very cross to one of the next-door girls and told her to throw it out at once: that was no play. Maria understood that it was wrong that time and so she had to do it over again: and this time she got the prayer-book.

After that Mrs. Donnelly played Miss McCloud's Reel for the children and Joe made Maria take a glass of wine. Soon they were all quite merry again and Mrs. Donnelly said Maria would enter a convent before the year was out because she had got the prayer-book. Maria had never seen Joe so nice to her as he was that night, so full of pleasant talk and reminiscences. She said they were all very good to her.

At last the children grew tired and sleepy and Joe asked Maria would she not sing some little song before she went, one of the old songs. Mrs. Donnelly said: "Do, please, Maria!" and so Maria had to get up and stand beside the piano. Mrs. Donnelly bade the children be quiet and listen to Maria's song. Then she played the prelude and said "Now, Maria!" and Maria, blushing very much, began to sing in a tiny quavering voice. She sang *I Dreamt that I Dwelt*, and when she came to the second verse she sang again:

> I dreamt that I dwelt in marble halls
>   With vassals and serfs at my side
> And of all who assembled within those walls
>   That I was the hope and the pride.
>
> I had riches too great to count, could boast
>   Of a high ancestral name,
> But I also dreamt, which pleased me most,
>   That you loved me still the same.

But no one tried to show her her mistake; and when she had ended her song Joe was very much moved. He said that there was no time like the long ago and no music for him like poor old Balfe, whatever other people might say; and his eyes filled up so much with tears that he could not find what he was looking for and in the end he had to ask his wife to tell him where the corkscrew was.

D. H. LAWRENCE

Tickets, Please

There is in the Midlands a single-line tramway system which boldly leaves the county town and plunges off into the black, industrial countryside, up hill and down dale, through the long ugly villages of workmen's houses, over canals and railways, past churches perched high and nobly over the smoke and shadows, through stark, grimy, cold little market-places, tilting away in a rush past cinemas and shops down to the hollow where the collieries are, then up again, past a little rural church, under the ash trees, on in a rush to the terminus, the last little ugly place of industry, the cold little town that shivers on the edge of the wild, gloomy country beyond. There the green and creamy coloured tram-car seems to pause and purr with curious satisfaction. But in a few minutes—the clock on the turret of the Co-operative Wholesale Society's Shops gives the time—away it starts once more on the adventure. Again there are the reckless swoops downhill, bouncing the loops: again the chilly wait in the hill-top market-place: again the breathless slithering round the precipitous drop under the church: again the patient halts at the loops, waiting for the outcoming car: so on and on, for two long hours, till at last the city looms beyond the fat gas-works, the narrow factories draw near, we are in the sordid streets of the great town, once more we sidle to a standstill at our terminus, abashed by the great crimson and cream-coloured city cars, but still perky, jaunty, somewhat dare-devil, green as a jaunty sprig of parsley out of a black colliery garden.

To ride on these cars is always an adventure. Since we are in war-time, the drivers are men unfit for active service: cripples and hunchbacks. So they have the spirit of the devil in them. The ride becomes a steeple-chase. Hurray! we have leapt in a clear jump over the canal bridges—now for the four-lane corner. With a shriek and a trail of sparks we are clear again. To be sure, a tram often leaps the rails—but what matter! It sits in a ditch till other trams come to haul it out. It is quite common for a car, packed with one solid mass of living people, to come to a dead halt in the midst of unbroken blackness, the heart of nowhere on a dark night, and for the driver and the girl conductor to call, "All get off—car's on fire!" Instead, however, of rushing out in a panic, the passengers stolidly reply: "Get on—get on! We're not coming out. We're stopping where we are. Push on, George." So till flames actually appear.

The reason for this reluctance to dismount is that the nights are howlingly cold, black, and windswept, and a car is a haven of refuge. From village to village the miners travel, for a change of cinema, of girl, of pub. The trams are desperately packed. Who is going to risk himself in the black gulf outside, to wait perhaps an hour for another tram, then to see the forlorn notice "Depot Only," because there is something wrong! Or to greet a unit of three bright cars all so tight with people that they sail past with a howl of derision. Trams that pass in the night.

This, the most dangerous tram-service in England, as the authorities themselves declare, with pride, is entirely conducted by girls, and driven by rash young men, a little crippled, or by delicate young men, who creep forward in terror. The girls are fearless young hussies. In their ugly blue uniform, skirts up to their knees, shapeless old peaked caps on their heads, they have all the *sang-froid* of an old non-commissioned officer. With a tram packed with howling colliers, roaring hymns downstairs and a sort of antiphony of obscenities upstairs, the lasses are perfectly at their ease. They pounce on the youths who try to evade their ticket-machine. They push off the men at the end of their distance. They are not going to be done in the eye—not they. They fear nobody—and everybody fears them.

"Hello, Annie!"

"Hello, Ted!"

"Oh, mind my corn, Miss Stone. It's my belief you've got a heart of stone, for you've trod on it again."

"You should keep it in your pocket," replies Miss Stone, and she goes sturdily upstairs in her high boots.

"Tickets, please."

She is peremptory, suspicious, and ready to hit first. She can hold her own against ten thousand. The step of that tram-car is her Thermopylae.

Therefore, there is a certain wild romance aboard these cars—and in the sturdy bosom of Annie herself. The time for soft romance is in the morning, between ten o'clock and one, when things are rather slack: that is, except market-day and Saturday. Thus Annie has time to look about her. Then she often hops off her car and into a shop where she has spied something, while the driver chats in the main road. There is very good feeling between the girls and the drivers. Are they not companions in peril, shipments aboard this careering vessel of a tram-car, for ever rocking on the waves of a stormy land.

Then, also, during the easy hours, the inspectors are most in evidence. For some reason, everybody employed in this tram-service is young: there are no grey heads. It would not do. Therefore the inspectors are of the right age, and one, the chief, is also good-looking. See him stand on a wet, gloomy morning, in his long oilskin, his peaked cap well down over his eyes, waiting to board a car. His face is ruddy, his small brown moustache is weathered, he has a faint impudent smile. Fairly tall and agile, even in his waterproof, he springs aboard a car and greets Annie.

"Hello, Annie! Keeping the wet out?"

"Trying to."

There are only two people in the car. Inspecting is soon over. Then for a long and impudent chat on the foot-board, a good, easy, twelve-mile chat.

The inspector's name is John Thomas Raynor—always called John Thomas, except sometimes, in malice, Coddy. His face sets in fury when he is addressed, from a distance, with this abbreviation. There is considerable scandal about John Thomas in half a dozen villages. He flirts with the girl conductors in the morning and walks out with them in the dark night, when they leave their tram-car at the depot. Of course, the girls quit the service frequently. Then he flirts and walks out with the newcomer: always providing she is sufficiently attractive, and that she will consent to walk. It is remarkable, however, that most of the girls are quite comely, they are all young, and this roving life aboard the car gives them a sailor's dash and recklessness. What matter how they behave when the ship is in port? To-morrow they will be aboard again.

Annie, however, was something of a Tartar, and her sharp tongue had kept John Thomas at arm's length for many months. Perhaps, therefore, she liked him all the more: for he always came up smiling, with impudence. She watched him vanquish one girl, then another. She could tell by the movement of his mouth and eyes, when he flirted with her in the morning, that he had been walking out with this lass, or the other, the night before. A fine cock-of-the-walk he was. She could sum him up pretty well.

In this subtle antagonism they knew each other like old friends, they were as shrewd with one another almost as man and wife. But Annie had always kept him sufficiently at arm's length. Besides, she had a boy of her own.

The Statutes fair, however, came in November, at Bestwood. It happened that Annie had the Monday night off. It was a drizzling ugly night, yet she dressed herself up and went to the fair ground. She was alone, but she expected soon to find a pal of some sort.

The roundabouts were veering round and grinding out their music, the side-shows were making as much commotion as possible. In the coconut shies there were no coconuts, but artificial war-time substitutes, which the lads declared were fastened into the irons. There was a sad decline in brilliance and luxury. None the less, the ground was muddy as ever, there was the same crush, the press of faces lighted up by the flares and the electric lights, the same smell of naphtha and a few fried potatoes, and of electricity.

Who should be the first to greet Miss Annie, on the show-ground but John Thomas. He had a black overcoat buttoned up to his chin, and a tweed cap pulled down over his brows, his face between was ruddy and smiling and handy as ever. She knew so well the way his mouth moved.

She was very glad to have a "boy." To be at the Statutes without a fellow was no fun. Instantly, like the gallant he was, he took her on the Dragons, grim-toothed, roundabout switchbacks. It was not nearly so exciting as a tram-car actually. But, then, to be seated in a shaking, green dragon, uplifted above the sea of bubble faces, careering in a rickety fashion in the lower heavens, whilst John Thomas leaned over her, his cigarette in his mouth, was after all the right style. She was a plump, quick, alive little creature. So she was quite excited and happy.

John Thomas made her stay on for the next round. And therefore she could hardly for shame repulse him when he put his arm round her and drew her a little nearer to him, in a very warm and cuddly manner. Besides, he was fairly discreet, he kept his movement as hidden as possible. She looked down and saw that his red, clean hand was out of sight of the crowd. And they knew each other so well. So they warmed up to the fair.

After the dragons they went on the horses. John Thomas paid each time, so she could but be complaisant. He, of course, sat astride on the outer horse—named "Black Bess"—and she sat sideways, towards him, on the inner horse—named "Wildfire." But of course John Thomas was not going to sit discreetly on "Black Bess," holding the brass bar. Round they spun and heaved, in the light. And round he swung on his wooden steed, flinging one leg across her mount, and perilously tipping up and down, across the space, half lying back, laughing at her. He was perfectly happy; she was afraid her hat was on one side, but she was excited.

He threw quoits on a table and won for her two large, pale blue hat-pins. And then, hearing the noise of the cinemas, announcing another performance, they climbed the boards and went in.

Of course, during these performances pitch darkness falls from time to time, when the machine goes wrong. Then there is a wild whooping, and a loud smacking of simulated kisses. In these moments John Thomas drew Annie towards him. After all, he had a wonderfully warm, cosy way of holding a girl with his arm, he seemed to make such a nice fit. And after all, it was pleasant to be so held: so very comforting and cosy and nice. He leaned over her and she felt his breath on her hair; she knew he wanted to kiss her on the lips. And after all, he was so warm and she fitted in to him so softly. After all, she wanted him to touch her lips.

But the light sprang up; she also started electrically, and put her hat straight. He left his arm lying nonchalantly behind her. Well, it was fun, it was exciting to be at the Statutes with John Thomas.

When the cinema was over they went for a walk across the dark, damp fields. He had all the arts of love-making. He was especially good at holding a girl, when he sat with her on a stile in the black drizzling darkness. He seemed to be holding her in space, against his own warmth and gratification. And his kisses were soft and slow and searching.

So Annie walked out with John Thomas, though she kept her own boy dangling in the distance. Some of the tram-girls chose to be huffy. But there, you must take things as you find them, in this life.

There was no mistake about it, Annie liked John Thomas a good deal. She felt so rich and warm in herself whenever he was near. And John Thomas really liked Annie, more than usual. The soft, melting way in which she could flow into a fellow, as if she melted into his very bones, was something rare and good. He fully appreciated this.

But with a developing acquaintance there began a developing intimacy. Annie wanted to consider him a person, a man; she wanted to take an intelligent interest in him, and to have an intelligent response. She did not want a mere nocturnal presence, which was what he was so far. And she prided herself that he could not leave her.

Here she made a mistake. John Thomas intended to remain a nocturnal presence; he had no idea of becoming an all-round individual to her. When she started to take an intelligent interest in him and his life and his character, he sheered off. He hated intelligent interest. And he knew that the only way to stop it was to avoid it. The possessive female was aroused in Annie. So he left her.

It is no use saying she was not surprised. She was at first startled, thrown out of her count. For she had been so very sure of holding him. For a while she was staggered, and everything became uncertain to her. Then she wept with fury, indignation, desolation, and misery. Then she had a spasm of despair. And then, when he came, still impudently, on to her car, still familiar, but letting her see by the movement of his head that he had gone away to somebody else for the time being and was enjoying pastures new, then she determined to have her own back.

She had a very shrewd idea what girls John Thomas had taken out. She went to Nora Purdy. Nora was a tall, rather pale, but well-built girl, with beautiful yellow hair. She was rather secretive.

"Hey!" said Annie, accosting her; then softly, "Who's John Thomas on with now?"

"I don't know," said Nora.

"Why tha does," said Annie, ironically lapsing into dialect. "Tha knows as well as I do."

"Well, I do, then," said Nora. "It isn't me, so don't bother."

"It's Cissy Meakin, isn't it?"

"It is, for all I know."

"Hasn't he got a face on him!" said Annie. "I don't half like his cheek. I could knock him off the foot-board when he comes round at me."

"He'll get dropped on one of these days," said Nora.

"Ay, he will when somebody makes up their mind to drop it on him. I should like to see him taken down a peg or two, shouldn't you?"

"I shouldn't mind," said Nora.

"You've got a quite as much cause to as I have," said Annie. "But we'll drop on him one of these days, my girl. What? Don't you want to?"

"I don't mind," said Nora.

But as a matter of fact, Nora was much more vindictive than Annie.

One by one Annie went the round of the old flames. It so happened that Cissy Meakin left the tramway service in quite a short time. Her mother made her leave. Then John Thomas was on the *qui vive*. He cast his eyes over his old flock. And his eyes lighted on Annie. He thought she would be safe now. Besides, he liked her.

She arranged to walk home with him on Sunday night. It so happened that her car would be in the depot at half-past nine: the last car would come in at 10:15. So John Thomas was to wait for her there.

At the depot the girls had a little waiting-room of their own. It was quite rough, but cosy, with a fire and an oven and a mirror, and table and wooden chairs. The half dozen girls who knew John Thomas only too well had arranged to take service this Sunday afternoon. So, as the cars began to come in, early, the girls dropped into the waiting-room. And instead of hurrying off home, they sat around the fire and had a cup of tea. Outside was the darkness and lawlessness of wartime.

John Thomas came on the car after Annie, at about a quarter to ten. He poked his head easily into the girls' waiting-room.

"Prayer-meeting?" he asked.

"Ay," said Laura Sharp. "Ladies only."

"That's me!" said John Thomas. It was one of his favourite exclamations.

"Shut the door, boy," said Muriel Baggaley.

"On which side of me?" said John Thomas.

"Which tha likes," said Polly Birkin.

He had come in and closed the door behind him. The girls moved in their circle, to make a place for him near the fire. He took off his great-coat and pushed back his hat.

"Who handles the teapot?" he said.

Nora Purdy silently poured him out a cup of tea.

"Want a bit o' my bread and drippin'?" said Muriel Baggaley to him.

"Ay, give us a bit."

And he began to eat his piece of bread.

"There's no place like home, girls," he said.

They all looked at him as he uttered this piece of impudence. He seemed to be sunning himself in the presence of so many damsels.

"Especially if you're not afraid to go home in the dark," said Laura Sharp.

"Me! By myself I am."

They sat till they heard the last tram come in. In a few minutes Emma Houselay entered.

"Come on, my old duck!" cried Polly Birkin.

"It *is* perishing," said Emma, holding her fingers to the fire.

"But—I'm afraid to, go home in, the dark," sang Laura Sharp, the tune having got into her mind.

"Who're you going with tonight, John Thomas?" asked Muriel Baggaley, coolly.

"Tonight?" said John Thomas. "Oh, I'm going home by myself tonight —all on my lonely-o."

"That's me!" said Nora Purdy, using his own ejaculation.

The girls laughed shrilly.

"Me as well, Nora," said John Thomas.

"Don't know what you mean," said Laura.

"Yes, I'm toddling," said he, rising and reaching for his overcoat.

"Nay," said Polly. "We're all here waiting for you."

"We've got to be up in good time in the morning," he said in the benevolent official manner.

They all laughed.

"Nay," said Muriel. "Don't leave us all lonely, John Thomas. Take one!"

"I'll take the lot, if you like," he responded gallantly.

"That you won't, either," said Muriel. "Two's company; seven's too much of a good thing."

"Nay—take one," said Laura. "Fair and square, all above board and say which."

"Ay," cried Annie, speaking for the first time. "Pick, John Thomas; let's hear thee."

"Nay," he said. "I'm going home quiet tonight. Feeling good, for once."

"Whereabouts?" said Annie. "Take a good un, then. But tha's got to take one of us!"

"Nay, how can I take one," he said, laughing uneasily. "I don't want to make enemies."

"You'd only make one," said Annie.

"The chosen one," added Laura.

"Oh, my! Who said girls!" exclaimed John Thomas, again turning, as if to escape. "Well—good-night."

"Nay, you've got to make your pick," said Muriel. "Turn your face to the wall and say which one touches you. Go on—we shall only just touch your back—one of us. Go on—turn your face to the wall, and don't look, and say which one touches you."

He was uneasy, mistrusting them. Yet he had not the courage to break away. They pushed him to a wall and stood him there with his face to it. Behind his back they all grimaced, tittering. He looked so comical. He looked around uneasily.

"Go on!" he cried.

"You're looking—you're looking!" they shouted.

He turned his head away. And suddenly, with a movement like a swift cat, Annie went forward and fetched him a box on the side of the head that set his cap flying, and himself staggering. He started round.

But at Annie's signal they all flew at him, slapping him, pinching him, pulling his hair, though more in fun than in spite or anger. He, however, saw red. His blue eyes flamed with strange fear as well as fury, and he butted through the girls to the door. It was locked. He wrenched at it. Roused, alert, the girls stood round and looked at him. He faced them, at bay. At that moment they were rather horrifying to him, as they stood in their short uniforms. He was distinctly afraid.

"Come on, John Thomas! Come on! Choose!" said Annie.

"What are you after? Open the door," he said.

"We sha'n't—not till you've chosen!" said Muriel.

"Chosen what?" he said.

"Chosen the one you're going to marry," she replied.

He hesitated a moment.

"Open the blasted door," he said, "and get back to your senses." He spoke with official authority.

"You've got to choose!" cried the girls.

"Come on!" cried Annie, looking him in the eye. "Come on! Come on!"

He went forward, rather vaguely. She had taken off her belt, and swinging it, she fetched him a sharp blow over the head with the buckle end. He sprang and seized her. But immediately the other girls rushed upon him, pulling and tearing and beating him. Their blood was now thoroughly up. He was their sport now. They were going to have their own back, out of him. Strange, wild creatures, they hung on him and rushed at him to bear him down. His tunic was torn right up the back, Nora had hold at the back of his collar, and was actually strangling him. Luckily the button burst. He struggled in a wild frenzy of fury and terror, almost mad terror. His tunic was simply torn off his back, his shirt-sleeves were torn away, his arms were naked. The girls rushed at him, clenched their hands on him and pulled at him: or they rushed at him and pushed him, butted him with all their might: or they struck him wild blows. He ducked and cringed and struck sideways. They became more intense.

At last he was down. They rushed on him, kneeling on him. He had neither breath nor strength to move. His face was bleeding with a long scratch, his brow was bruised.

Annie knelt on him, the other girls knelt and hung on to him. Their faces were flushed, their hair wild, their eyes were all glittering strangely. He lay at last quite still, with face averted, as an animal lies when it is defeated and at the mercy of the captor. Sometimes his eye glanced back at the wild faces of the girls. His breast rose heavily, his wrists were torn.

"Now, then, my fellow!" gasped Annie at length. "Now then—now——"

At the sound of her terrifying cold triumph, he suddenly started to struggle as an animal might, but the girls threw themselves upon him with unnatural strength and power, forcing him down.

"Yes—now, then!" gasped Annie at length.

And there was a dead silence, in which the thud of heart-beating was to be heard. It was a suspense of pure silence in every soul.

"Now you know where you are," said Annie.

The sight of his white, bare arm maddened the girls. He lay in a kind of trance of fear and antagonism. They felt themselves filled with supernatural strength.

Suddenly Polly started to laugh—to giggle wildly—helplessly—and Emma and Muriel joined in. But Annie and Nora and Laura remained the same, tense, watchful, with gleaming eyes. He winced away from these eyes.

"Yes," said Annie, in a curious low tone, secret and deadly. "Yes! You've got it now! You know what you've done, don't you? You know what you've done."

He made no sound or sign, but lay with bright, averted eyes, and averted, bleeding face.

"You ought to be *killed*, that's what you ought," said Annie tensely. "You ought to be *killed*." And there was a terrifying lust in her voice.

Polly was ceasing to laugh, and giving long-drawn Oh-h-hs and sighs as she came to herself.

"He's got to choose," she said vaguely.

"Oh, yes, he has," said Laura, with vindictive decision.

"Do you hear—do you hear?" said Annie. And with a sharp movement that made him wince, she turned his face to her.

"Do you hear?" she repeated, shaking him.

But he was quite dumb. She fetched him a sharp slap on the face. He started, and his eyes widened. Then his face darkened with defiance, after all.

"Do you hear?" she repeated.

He only looked at her with hostile eyes.

"Speak!" she said, putting her face devilishly near his.

"What?" he said, almost overcome.

"You've got to *choose*!" she cried, as if it were some terrible menace, and as if it hurt her that she could not exact more.

"What?" he said in fear.

"Choose your girl, Coddy. You've got to choose her now. And you'll get your neck broken if you play any more of your tricks, my boy. You're settled now."

There was a pause. Again he averted his face. He was cunning in his overthrow. He did not give in to them really—no, not if they tore him to bits.

"All right, then," he said, "I choose Annie." His voice was strange and full of malice. Annie let go of him as if he had been a hot coal.

"He's chosen Annie!" said the girls in chorus.

"Me!" cried Annie. She was still kneeling, but away from him. He was still prostrate, with averted face. The girls grouped uneasily around.

"Me!" repeated Annie, with a terrible bitter accent.

Then she got up, drawing away from him with strange disgust and bitterness.

"I wouldn't touch him," she said.

But her face quivered with a kind of agony, she seemed as if she would fall. The other girls turned aside. He remained lying on the floor, with his torn clothes and bleeding, averted face.

"Oh, if he's choosen—" said Polly.

"I don't want him—he can choose again," said Annie, with the same rather bitter hopelessness.

"Get up," said Polly, lifting his shoulder. "Get up."

He rose slowly, a strange, ragged, dazed creature. The girls eyed him from a distance, curiously, furtively, dangerously.

"Who wants him?" cried Laura roughly.

"Nobody," they answered with contempt. Yet each one of them waited for him to look at her, hoped he would look at her. All except Annie, and something was broken in her.

He, however, kept his face closed and averted from them all. There was a silence of the end. He picked up the torn pieces of his tunic, without knowing what to do with them. The girls stood about uneasily, flushed, panting, tidying their hair and their dress unconsciously, and watching him. He looked at none of them. He espied his cap in a corner and went and picked it up. He put it on his head, and one of the girls burst into a shrill, hysteric laugh at the sight he presented. He, however, took no heed but went straight to where his overcoat hung on a peg. The girls moved away from contact with him as if he had been an electric wire. He put on his coat and buttoned it down. Then he rolled his tunic-rags into a bundle, and stood before the locked door, dumbly.

"Open the door, somebody," said Laura.

"Annie's got the key," said one.

Annie silently offered the key to the girls. Nora unlocked the door.

"Tit for tat, old man," she said. "Show yourself a man, and don't bear a grudge."

But without a word or sign he had opened the door and gone, his face closed, his head dropped.

"That'll learn him," said Laura.

"Coddy!" said Nora.

"Shut up, for God's sake!" cried Annie fiercely, as if in torture.

"Well, I'm about ready to go, Polly. Look sharp!" said Muriel.

The girls were all anxious to be off. They were tidying themselves hurriedly, with mute, stupefied faces.

KATHERINE MANSFIELD

Her First Ball

Exactly when the ball began Leila would have found it hard to say. Perhaps her first real partner was the cab. It did not matter that she shared the cab with the Sheridan girls and their brother. She sat back in her own little corner of it, and the bolster on which her hand rested felt like the sleeve of an unknown young man's dress suit; and away they bowled, past waltzing lamp-posts and houses and fences and trees.

"Have you really never been to a ball before, Leila? But, my child, how too weird—" cried the Sheridan girls.

"Our nearest neighbour was fifteen miles," said Leila softly, gently opening and shutting her fan.

Oh, dear, how hard it was to be indifferent like the others! She tried not to smile too much; she tried not to care. But every single thing was so new and exciting . . . Meg's tuberoses, Jose's long loop of amber, Laura's little dark head, pushing above her white fur like a flower through snow. She would remember for ever. It even gave her a pang to see her cousin Laurie throw away the wisps of tissue paper he pulled from the fastenings of his new gloves. She would like to have kept those wisps as a keepsake, as a remembrance. Laurie leaned forward and put his hand on Laura's knee.

"Look here, darling," he said. "The third and the ninth as usual. Twig?"

Oh, how marvellous to have a brother! In her excitement Leila felt that if there had been time, if it hadn't been impossible, she couldn't have helped crying because she was an only child, and no brother had ever said "Twig?" to her; no sister would ever say, as Meg said to Jose that moment, "I've never known your hair go up more successfully than it has to-night!"

But, of course, there was no time. They were at the drill hall already; there were cabs in front of them and cabs behind. The road was bright on either side with moving fan-like lights, and on the pavement gay couples seemed to float through the air; little satin shoes chased each other like birds.

"Hold on to me, Leila; you'll get lost," said Laura.

"Come on, girls, let's make a dash for it," said Laurie.

Leila put two fingers on Laura's pink velvet cloak, and they were somehow lifted past the big golden lantern, carried along the passage, and pushed into the little room marked "Ladies." Here the crowd was so great there was hardly space to take off their things; the noise was deafening. Two benches on either side were stacked high with wraps. Two old women in white aprons ran up and down tossing fresh armfuls. And everybody was pressing forward trying to get at the little dressing-table and mirror at the far end.

A great quivering jet of gas lighted the ladies' room. It couldn't wait; it was dancing already. When the door opened again and there came a burst of tuning from the drill hall, it leaped almost to the ceiling.

Dark girls, fair girls were patting their hair, tying ribbons again, tucking handkerchiefs down the fronts of their bodices, smoothing marble-white gloves. And because they were all laughing it seemed to Leila that they were all lovely.

"Aren't there any invisible hair-pins?" cried a voice. "How most extraordinary! I can't see a single invisible hair-pin."

"Powder my back, there's a darling," cried someone else.

"But I must have a needle and cotton. I've torn simply miles and miles of the frill," wailed a third.

Then "Pass them along, pass them along!" The straw basket of programmes was tossed from arm to arm. Darling little pink-and-silver programmes, with pink pencils and fluffy tassels. Leila's fingers shook as she took one out of the basket. She wanted to ask someone, "Am I meant to have one too?" but she had just time to read: "Waltz 3. *Two, Two, in a Canoe.* Polka 4. *Making the Feathers Fly,*" when Meg cried, "Ready, Leila?" and they pressed their way through the crush in the passage towards the big double doors of the drill hall.

Dancing had not begun yet, but the band had stopped tuning, and the noise was so great it seemed that when it did begin to play it would never be heard. Leila, pressing close to Meg, looking over Meg's shoulder, felt that even the little quivering coloured flags strung across the ceiling were talking. She quite forgot to be shy; she forgot how in the middle of dressing she had sat down on the bed with one shoe off and one shoe on and begged her mother to ring up her cousins and say she couldn't go after all. And the rush of longing she had had to be sitting on the veranda of their forsaken up-country home, listening to the baby owls crying "More pork" in the moonlight, was changed to a rush of joy so sweet that it was hard to bear alone. She clutched her fan, and, gazing at the gleaming, golden floor, the azaleas, the lanterns, the stage at one end with its red carpet and gilt chairs and the band in a corner, she thought breathlessly, "How heavenly; how simply heavenly!"

All the girls stood grouped together at one side of the doors, the men at the other, and the chaperones in dark dresses, smiling rather foolishly, walked with little careful steps over the polished floor towards the stage.

"This is my little country cousin Leila. Be nice to her. Find her partners; she's under my wing," said Meg, going up to one girl after another.

Strange faces smiled at Leila—sweetly, vaguely. Strange voices answered, "Of course, my dear." But Leila felt the girls didn't really see her. They were looking towards the men. Why didn't the men begin? What were they waiting for? There they stood, smoothing their gloves, patting their glossy hair and smiling among themselves. Then, quite suddenly, as if they had only just made up their minds that that was what they had to do, the men came gliding over the parquet. There was a joyful flutter among the girls. A tall, fair man flew up to Meg, seized her programme, scribbled something; Meg passed him on to Leila. "May I have the pleasure?" He ducked and smiled. There came a dark man wearing an eyeglass, then cousin Laurie with a friend, and Laura with a little freckled fellow whose tie was crooked. Then quite an old man—fat, with a big bald patch on his head—took her programme and murmured, "Let me see, let me see!" And he was a long time comparing his programme, which looked black with names, with hers. It seemed to give him so much trouble that Leila was ashamed. "Oh, please don't bother," she said eagerly. But instead of replying the fat man wrote something, glanced at her again. "Do I remember this bright little face?" he said softly. "Is it known to me of yore?" At that moment the band began playing; the fat man disappeared. He was tossed away on a great wave of music that came flying over the gleaming floor, breaking the groups up into couples, scattering them, sending them spinning. . . .

Leila had learned to dance at boarding school. Every Saturday afternoon the boarders were hurried off to a little corrugated iron mission hall where Miss Eccles (of London) held her "select" classes. But the difference between that dusty-smelling hall—with calico texts on the walls, the poor terrified little woman in a brown velvet toque with rabbit's ears thumping the cold piano, Miss Eccles poking the girls' feet with her long white wand—and this was so tremendous that Leila was sure if her partner didn't come and she had to listen to that marvellous music and to watch the others sliding, gliding over the golden floor, she would die at least, or faint, or lift her arms and fly out of one of those dark windows that showed the stars.

"Ours, I think—"Someone bowed, smiled, and offered her his arm; she hadn't to die after all. Someone's hand pressed her waist, and she floated away like a flower that is tossed into a pool.

"Quite a good floor, isn't it?" drawled a faint voice close to her ear.

"I think it's most beautifully slippery," said Leila.

"Pardon!" The faint voice sounded surprised. Leila said it again. And there was a tiny pause before the voice echoed. "Oh, quite!" and she was swung round again.

He steered so beautifully. That was the great difference between dancing with girls and men, Leila decided. Girls banged into each other, and stamped on each other's feet; the girl who was gentleman always clutched you so.

The azaleas were separate flowers no longer; they were pink and white flags streaming by.

"Were you at the Bell's last week?" the voice came again. It sounded tired. Leila wondered whether she ought to ask him if he would like to stop.

"No, this is my first dance," said she.

Her partner gave a little gasping laugh. "Oh, I say," he protested.

"Yes, it is really the first dance I've ever been to." Leila was most fervent. It was such a relief to be able to tell somebody. "You see, I've lived in the country all my life up until now. . . ."

At that moment the music stopped, and they went to sit on two chairs against the wall. Leila tucked her pink satin feet under and fanned herself, while she blissfully watched the other couples passing and disappearing through the swing doors.

"Enjoying yourself, Leila?" asked Jose, nodding her golden head.

Laura passed and gave her the faintest little wink; it made Leila wonder for a moment whether she was quite grown up after all. Certainly her partner did not say very much. He coughed, tucked his handkerchief away, pulled down his waistcoat, took a minute thread off his sleeve. But it didn't matter. Almost immediately the band started, and her second partner seemed to spring from the ceiling.

"Floor's not bad," said the new voice. Did one always begin with the floor? And then, "Were you at the Neaves' on Tuesday?" And again Leila explained. Perhaps it was a little strange that her partners were not more interested. For it was thrilling. Her first ball! She was only at the beginning of everything. It seemed to her that she had never known what the night was like before. Up till now it had been dark, silent, beautiful very often—oh, yes— but mournful somehow. Solemn. And now it would never be like that again —it had opened dazzling bright.

"Care for an ice?" said her partner. And they went through the swing doors, down the passage, to the supper room. Her cheeks burned, she was fearfully thirsty. How sweet the ices looked on little glass plates, and how cold the frosted spoon was, iced too! And when they came back to the hall there was the fat man waiting for her by the door. It gave her quite a shock again to see how old he was; he ought to have been on the stage with the fathers and mothers. And when Leila compared him with her other partners he looked shabby. His waistcoat was creased, there was a button off his glove, his coat looked as if it was dusty with French chalk.

"Come along, little lady," said the fat man. He scarcely troubled to clasp her, and they moved away so gently, it was more like walking than dancing. But he said not a word about the floor. "Your first dance, isn't it?" he murmured.

"How *did* you know?"

"Ah," said the fat man, "that's what it is to be old!" He wheezed faintly as he steered her past an awkward couple. "You see, I've been doing this kind of thing for the last thirty years."

"Thirty years?" cried Leila. Twelve years before she was born!

"It hardly bears thinking about, does it?" said the fat man gloomily. Leila looked at his bald head, and she felt quite sorry for him.

"I think it's marvellous to be still going on," she said kindly.

"Kind little lady," said the fat man, and he pressed her a little closer, and hummed a bar of the waltz. "Of course," he said, "you can't hope to last anything like as long as that. No-o," said the fat man, "long before that you'll be sitting up there on the stage, looking on, in your nice black velvet. And these pretty arms will have turned into little short fat ones, and you'll beat time with such a different kind of fan—a black bony one." The fat man seemed to shudder. "And you'll smile away like the poor old dears up there, and point to your daughter, and tell the elderly lady next to you how some dreadful man tried to kiss her at the club ball. And your heart will ache, ache"—the fat man squeezed her closer still, as if he really was sorry for that poor heart—"because no one wants to kiss you now. And you'll say how unpleasant these polished floors are to walk on, how dangerous they are. Eh, Mademoiselle Twinkletoes?" said the fat man softly.

Leila gave a light little laugh, but she did not feel like laughing. Was it—could it all be true? It sounded terribly true. Was this first ball only the beginning of her last ball after all? At that the music seemed to change; it sounded sad, sad; it rose upon a great sigh. Oh. how quickly things changed! Why didn't happiness last for ever? For ever wasn't a bit too long.

"I want to stop," she said in a breathless voice. The fat man led her to the door.

"No," she said, "I won't go outside. I won't sit down. I'll just stand here, thank you." She leaned against the wall, tapping with her foot, pulling up her gloves and trying to smile. But deep inside her a little girl threw her pinafore over her head and sobbed. Why had he spoiled it all?

"I say, you know," said the fat man, "you mustn't take me seriously, little lady."

"As if I should!" said Leila, tossing her small dark head and sucking her underlip. . . .

Again the couples paraded. The swing doors opened and shut. Now new music was given out by the bandmaster. But Lelia didn't want to dance any more. She wanted to be home, or sitting on the veranda listening to those baby owls. When she looked through the dark windows at the stars, they had long beams like wings. . . .

But presently a soft, melting, ravishing tune began, and a young man with curly hair bowed before her. She would have to dance, out of politeness, until she could find Meg. Very stiffly she walked into the middle; very haughtily she put her hand on his sleeve. But in one minute, in one turn, her feet glided, glided. The lights, the azaleas, the dresses, the pink faces, the velvet chairs, all became one beautiful flying wheel. And when her next partner bumped into the fat man and he said, "Pardon," she smiled at him more radiantly than ever. She didn't even recognize him again.

KATHERINE ANNE PORTER

Flowering Judas

Braggioni sits heaped upon the edge of a straight-backed chair too small for him, and sings to Laura in a furry, mournful voice. Laura has begun to find reasons for avoiding her own house until the latest possible moment, for Braggioni is there almost every night. No matter how late she is, he will be sitting there with a surly, waiting expression, pulling at his kinky yellow hair, thumbing the strings of his guitar, snarling a tune under his breath. Lupe the Indian maid meets Laura at the door, and says with a flicker of a glance towards the upper room, "He waits."

Laura wishes to lie down, she is tired of her hairpins and the feel of her long tight sleeves, but she says to him, "Have you a new song for me this evening?" If he says yes, she asks him to sing it. If he says no, she remembers his favorite one, and asks him to sing it again. Lupe brings her a cup of chocolate and a plate of rice, and Laura eats at the small table under the lamp, first inviting Braggioni, whose answer is always the same: "I have eaten, and besides, chocolate thickens the voice."

Laura says, "Sing, then," and Braggioni heaves himself into song. He scratches the guitar familiarly as though it were a pet animal, and sings passionately off key, taking the high notes in a prolonged painful squeal. Laura, who haunts the markets listening to the ballad singers, and stops every day to hear the blind boy playing his reed-flute in Sixteenth of September Street, listens to Braggioni with pitiless courtesy, because she dares not smile at his miserable performance. Nobody dares to smile at him. Braggioni is cruel to everyone, with a kind of specialized insolence, but he is so vain of his talents, and so sensitive to slights, it would require a cruelty and vanity greater than his own to lay a finger on the vast cureless wound of his self-esteem. It would require courage, too, for it is dangerous to offend him, and nobody has this courage.

Braggioni loves himself with such tenderness and amplitude and eternal charity that his followers—for he is a leader of men, a skilled revolutionist, and his skin has been punctured in honorable warfare—warm themselves in the reflected glow, and say to each other: "He has a real nobility, a love of humanity raised above mere personal affections." The excess of this self-love has flowed out, inconveniently for her, over Laura, who, with so many others, owes her comfortable situation and her salary to him. When he is in a very good humor, he tells her, "I am tempted to forgive you for being a *gringa*. *Gringita!*" and Laura, burning, imagines herself leaning forward suddenly, and with a sound back-handed slap wiping the suety smile from his face. If he notices her eyes at these moments he gives no sign.

She knows what Braggioni would offer her, and she must resist tenaciously without appearing to resist, and if she could avoid it she would not admit even to herself the slow drift of his intention. During these long evenings which have spoiled a long month for her, she sits in her deep chair with an open book on her knees, resting her eyes on the consoling rigidity of the printed page when the sight and sound of Braggioni singing threaten to identify themselves with all her remembered afflictions and to add their weight to her uneasy premonitions of the future. The gluttonous bulk has become a symbol of her many disillusions, for a revolutionist should be lean, animated by heroic faith, a vessel of abstract virtues. This is nonsense, she knows it now and is ashamed of it. Revolution must have leaders, and leadership is a career for energetic men. She is, her comrades tell her, full of romantic error, for what she defines as cynicism in them is merely "a developed sense of reality." She is almost too willing to say, "I am wrong, I suppose I don't really understand the principles," and afterward she makes a secret truce with herself, determined not to surrender her will to such expedient logic. But she cannot help feeling that she has been betrayed irreparably by the disunion between her way of living and her feeling of what life should be, and at times she is almost contented to rest in this sense of grievance as a private store of consolation. Sometimes she wishes to run away, but she stays. Now she longs to fly out of this room, down the narrow stairs, and into the street where the houses lean together like conspirators under a single mottled lamp, and leave Braggioni singing to himself.

Instead she looks at Braggioni, frankly and clearly, like a good child who understands the rules of behavior. Her knees cling together under sound blue serge, and her round white collar is not purposely nun-like. She wears the uniform of an idea, and has renounced vanities. She was born Roman Catholic, and in spite of her fear of being seen by someone who might make a scandal of it, she slips now and again into some crumbling little church, kneels on the chilly stone, and says a Hail Mary on the gold rosary she bought in Tehuantepec. It is no good and she ends by examining the altar with its tinsel flowers and ragged brocades, and feels tender about the battered doll-shape of some male saint whose white, lace-trimmed drawers hang limply around his ankles below the hieratic dignity of his velvet robe. She has encased herself in a set of principles derived from her early training, leaving no detail of gesture or of personal taste untouched, and for this reason she will not wear lace made on machines. This is her private heresy, for in her special group the machine is sacred, and will be the salvation of the workers. She loves fine lace, and there is a tiny edge of fluted cobweb on this collar, which is one of twenty precisely alike, folded in blue tissue paper in the upper drawer of her clothes chest.

Braggioni catches her glance solidly as if he had been waiting for it, leans forward balancing his paunch between his spread knees, and sings with tremendous emphasis, weighing his words. He has, the song relates, no father and no mother, nor even a friend to console him; lonely as a wave of the sea he comes and goes, lonely as a wave. His mouth opens round and yearns sideways, his balloon checks grow oily with the labor of song. He bulges marvelously in his expensive garments. Over his lavender collar, crushed upon a purple necktie, held by a diamond hoop: over his ammunition belt of tooled leather worked in silver, buckled cruelly around his gasping middle: over the tops of his glossy yellow shoes Braggioni swells with ominous ripeness, his mauve silk hose stretched taut, his ankles bound with the stout leather thongs of his shoes.

When he stretches his eyelids at Laura she notes again that his eyes are the true tawny yellow cat's eyes. He is rich, not in money, he tells her, but in power, and this power brings with it the blameless ownership of things, and the right to indulge his love of small luxuries. "I have a taste for the elegant refinements," he said once, flourishing a yellow silk handerchief before her nose. "Smell that? It is Jockey Club, imported from New York." Nonetheless he is wounded by life. He will say so presently. "It is true everything turns to dust in the hand, to gall on the tongue." He sighs and his leather belt creaks like a saddle girth. "I am disappointed in everything as it comes. Everything." He shakes his head. "You, poor thing, you will be disappointed too. You are born for it. We are more alike than you realize in some things. Wait and see. Some day you will remember what I have told you, you will know that Braggioni was your friend."

Laura feels a slow chill, a purely physical sense of danger, a warning in her blood that violence, mutilation, a shocking death, wait for her with lessening patience. She has translated this fear into something homely, immediate, and sometimes hesitates before crossing the street. "My personal fate is nothing, except as the testimony of a mental attitude," she reminds herself, quoting from some forgotten philosophic primer, and is sensible enough to add, "Anyhow, I shall not be killed by an automobile if I can help it."

"It may be true I am as corrupt, in another way, as Braggioni," she thinks in spite of herself, "as callous, as incomplete," and if this is so, any kind of death seems preferable. Still she sits quietly, she does not run. Where could she go? Uninvited she has promised herself to this place; she can no longer imagine herself as living in another country, and there is no pleasure in remembering her life before she came here.

Precisely what is the nature of this devotion, its true motives, and what are its obligations? Laura cannot say. She spends part of her days in Xochimilco, near by, teaching the Indian children to say in English, "The cat is on the mat." When she appears in the classroom they crowd about her with smiles on their wise, innocent, clay-colored faces, crying, "Good morning, my titcher!" in immaculate voices, and they make of her desk a fresh garden of flowers every day.

During her leisure she goes to union meetings and listens to busy important voices quarreling over tactics, methods, internal politics. She visits the prisoners of her own political faith in their cells, where they entertain themselves with counting cockroaches, repenting of their indiscretions, composing their memoirs, writing out manifestos and plans for their comrades who are still walking about free, hands in pockets, sniffing fresh air. Laura brings them food and cigarettes and a little money, and she brings messages disguised in equivocal phrases from the men outside who dare not set foot in the prison for fear of disappearing into the cell kept empty for them. If the prisoners confuse night and day, and complain, "Dear little Laura, time doesn't pass in this infernal hole, and I won't know when it is time to sleep unless I have a reminder," she brings them their favorite narcotics, and says in a tone that does not wound them with pity, "Tonight will really be night for you," and though her Spanish amuses them, they find her comforting, useful. If they lose patience and all faith, and curse the slowness of their friends in coming to their rescue with money and influence, they trust her not to repeat everything, and if she inquires, "Where do you think we can find money, or influence?" they are certain to answer, "Well, there is Braggioni, why doesn't he do something?"

She smuggles letters from headquarters to men hiding from firing squads in back streets in mildewed houses, where they sit in tumbled beds and talk bitterly as if all Mexico were at their heels, when Laura knows positively they might appear at the band concert in the Alameda on Sunday morning, and no one would notice them. But Braggioni says, "Let them sweat a little. The next time they may be careful. It is very restful to have them out of the way for a while." She is not afraid to knock on any door in any street after midnight, and enter in the darkness, and say to one of these men who is really in danger: "They will be looking for you—seriously—tomorrow morning after six. Here is some money from Vicente. Go to Vera Cruz and wait."

She borrows money from the Roumanian agitator to give to his bitter enemy the Polish agitator. The favor of Braggioni is their disputed territory, and Braggioni holds the balance nicely, for he can use them both. The Polish agitator talks love to her over café tables, hoping to exploit what he believes is her secret sentimental preference for him, and he gives her misinformation which he begs her to repeat as the solemn truth to certain persons. The Roumanian is more adroit. He is generous with his money in all good causes, and lies to her with an air of ingenuous candor, as if he were her good friend and confidant. She never repeats anything they may say. Braggioni never asks questions. He has other ways to discover all that he wishes to know about them.

Nobody touches her, but all praise her gray eyes, and the soft, round under lip which promises gayety, yet is always grave, nearly always firmly closed: and they cannot understand why she is in Mexico. She walks back and forth on her errands, with puzzled eyebrows, carrying her little folder of drawings and music and school papers. No dancer dances more beautifully than Laura walks, and she inspires some amusing, unexpected ardors, which cause little gossip, because nothing comes of them. A young captain who had been in Zapata's army attempted, during a horseback ride near Cuernavaca, to express his desire for her with the noble simplicity befitting a rude folk-hero:

but gently, because he was gentle. This gentleness was his defeat, for when he alighted, and removed her foot from the stirrup, and essayed to draw her down into his arms, her horse, ordinarily a tame one, shied fiercely, reared and plunged away. The young hero's horse careered blindly after his stable-mate, and the hero did not return to the hotel until rather late that evening. At breakfast he came to her table in full charro dress, gray buckskin jacket and trousers with strings of silver buttons down the leg, and he was in a humorous, careless mood. "May I sit with you?" and "You are a wonderful rider. I was terrified that you might be thrown and dragged. I should never have forgiven myself. But I cannot admire you enough for your riding!"

"I learned to ride in Arizona," said Laura.

"If you ride with me again this morning, I promise you a horse that will not shy with you," he said. But Laura remembered that she must return to Mexico City at noon.

Next morning the children made a celebration and spent their playtime writing on the blackboard, "We lov ar ticher," and with tinted chalks they drew wreaths of flowers around the words. The young hero wrote her a letter: "I am a very foolish, wasteful, impulsive man. I should have first said I love you, and then you would not have run away. But you shall see me again." Laura thought, "I must send him a box of colored crayons," but she was trying to forgive herself for having spurred her horse at the wrong moment.

A brown, shock-haired youth came and stood in her patio one night and sang like a lost soul for two hours, but Laura could think of nothing to do about it. The moonlight spread a wash of gauzy silver over the clear spaces of the garden, and the shadows were cobalt blue. The scarlet blossoms of the Judas tree were dull purple, and the names of the colors repeated themselves automatically in her mind, while she watched not the boy, but his shadow, fallen like a dark garment across the fountain rim, trailing in the water. Lupe came silently and whispered expert counsel in her ear: "If you will throw him one little flower, he will sing another song or two and go away." Laura threw the flower, and he sang a last song and went away with the flower tucked in the band of his hat. Lupe said, "He is one of the organizers of the Typographers Union, and before that he sold corridos in the Merced market, and before that, he came from Guanajuato, where I was born. I would not trust any man, but I trust least those from Guanajuato."

She did not tell Laura that he would be back again the next night, and the next, nor that he would follow her at a certain fixed distance around the Merced market, through the Zócolo, up Francisco I. Madero Avenue, and so along the Paseo de la Reforma to Chapultepec Park, and into the Philosopher's Footpath, still with that flower withering in his hat, and an indivisible attention in his eyes.

Now Laura is accustomed to him, it means nothing except that he is nineteen years old and is observing a convention with all propriety, as though it were founded on a law of nature, which in the end it might well prove to be. He is beginning to write poems which he prints on a wooden press, and he leaves them stuck like handbills in her door. She is pleasantly disturbed by the abstract, unhurried watchfulness of his black eyes which will in time turn easily towards another object. She tells herself that throwing the flower was a mistake, for she is twenty-two years old and knows better; but she refuses to regret it, and persuades herself that her negation of all external events as they occur is a sign that she is gradually perfecting herself in the stoicism she strives to cultivate against that disaster she fears, though she cannot name it.

She is not at home in the world. Every day she teaches children who remain strangers to her, though she loves their tender round hands and their charming opportunist savagery. She knocks at unfamiliar doors not knowing whether a friend or a stranger shall answer, and even if a known face emerges from the sour gloom of that unknown interior, still it is the face of a stranger. No matter what this stranger says to her, nor what her message to him, the very cells of her flesh reject knowledge and kinship in one monotonous word. No. No. No. She draws her strength from this one holy talismanic word which does not suffer her to be led into evil. Denying everything, she may walk anywhere in safety, she looks at everything without amazement.

No, repeats this firm unchanging voice of her blood; and she looks at Braggioni without amazement. He is a great man, he wishes to impress this simple girl who covers her great round breasts with thick dark cloth, and who hides long, invaluably beautiful legs under a heavy skirt. She is almost thin except for the incomprehensible fullness of her breasts, like a nursing mother's, and Braggioni, who considers himself a judge of women, speculates again on the puzzle of her notorious virginity, and takes the liberty of speech which she permits without a sign of modesty, indeed, without any sort of sign, which is disconcerting.

"You think you are so cold, *gringita!* Wait and see. You will surprise yourself some day! May I be there to advise you!" He stretches his eyelids at her, and his ill-humored cat's eyes waver in a separate glance for the points of light marking the opposite ends of a smoothly drawn path between the swollen curve of her breasts. He is not put off by that blue serge, nor by her resolutely fixed gaze. There is all the time in the world. His cheeks are bellying with the wind of song. "O girl with the dark eyes," he sings, and reconsiders. "But yours are not dark. I can change all that. O girl with the green eyes, you have stolen my heart away!" then his mind wanders to the song, and Laura feels the weight of his attention being shifted elsewhere. Singing thus, he seems harmless, he is quite harmless, there is nothing to do but sit patiently and say "No," when the moment comes. She draws a full breath, and her mind wanders also, but not far. She dares not wander too far.

Not for nothing has Braggioni taken pains to be a good revolutionist and a professional lover of humanity. He will never die of it. He has the malice, the cleverness, the wickedness, the sharpness of wit, the hardness of heart, stipulated for loving the world profitably. *He will never die of it.* He will live to see himself kicked out from his feeding trough by other hungry world-saviors. Traditionally he must sing in spite of his life which drives him to bloodshed, he tells Laura, for his father was a Tuscany peasant who drifted to Yucatan and married a Maya woman: a woman of race, an aristocrat. They gave him the love and knowledge of music, thus: and under the rip of his thumbnail, the strings of the instrument complain like exposed nerves.

Once he was called Delgadito by all the girls and married women who ran after him; he was so scrawny all his bones showed under his thin cotton clothing, and he could squeeze his emptiness to the very backbone with his two hands. He was a poet and the revolution was only a dream then; too many women loved him and sapped away his youth, and he could never find enough to eat anywhere, anywhere! Now he is a leader of men, crafty men who whisper in his ear, hungry men who wait for hours outside his office for a word with him, emaciated men with wild faces who waylay him at the street gate with a timid, "Comrade, let me tell you . . ." and they blow the foul breath from their empty stomachs in his face.

He is always sympathetic. He gives them handfuls of small coins from his own pocket, he promises them work, there will be demonstrations, they must join the unions and attend the meetings, above all they must be on the watch for spies. They are closer to him than his own brothers, without them he can do nothing—until tomorrow, comrade!

Until tomorrow. "They are stupid, they are lazy, they are treacherous, they would cut my throat for nothing," he says to Laura. He has good food and abundant drink, he hires an automobile and drives in the Paseo on Sunday morning, and enjoys plenty of sleep in a soft bed beside a wife who dares not disturb him; and he sits pampering his bones in easy billows of fat, singing to Laura, who knows and thinks these things about him. When he was fifteen, he tried to drown himself because he loved a girl, his first love, and she laughed at him. "A thousand women have paid for that," and his tight little mouth turns down at the corners. Now he perfumes his hair with Jockey Club, and confides to Laura: "One woman is really as good as another for me, in the dark. I prefer them all."

His wife organizes unions among the girls in the cigarette factories, and walks in picket lines, and even speaks at meetings in the evening. But she cannot be brought to acknowledge the benefits of true liberty. "I tell her I must have my freedom, net. She does not understand my point of view." Laura has heard this many times. Braggioni scratches the guitar and meditates. "She is an instinctively virtuous woman, pure gold, no doubt of that. If she were not, I should lock her up, and she knows it."

His wife, who works so hard for the good of the factory girls, employs part of her leisure lying on the floor weeping because there are so many women in the world, and only one husband for her, and she never knows where nor when to look for him. He told her: "Unless you can learn to cry when I am not here, I must go away for good." That day he went away and took a room at the Hotel Madrid.

It is this month of separation for the sake of higher principles that has been spoiled not only for Mrs. Braggioni, whose sense of reality is beyond criticism, but for Laura, who feels herself bogged in a nightmare. Tonight Laura envies Mrs. Braggioni, who is alone, and free to weep as much as she pleases about a concrete wrong. Laura has just come from a visit to the prison, and she is waiting for tomorrow with a bitter anxiety as if tomorrow may not come, but time may be caught immovably in this hour, with herself transfixed, Braggioni singing on forever, and Eugenio's body not yet discovered by the guard.

Braggioni says: "Are you going to sleep?" Almost before she can shake her head, he begins telling her about the May-day disturbances coming on in Morelia, for the Catholics hold a festival in honor of the Blessed Virgin, and the Socialists celebrate their martyrs on that day. "There will be two independent processions, starting from either end of town, and they will march until they meet, and the rest depends . . ." He asks her to oil and load his pistols. Standing up, he unbuckles his ammunition belt, and spreads it laden across her knees. Laura sits with the shells slipping through the cleaning cloth dipped in oil, and he says again he cannot understand why she works so hard for the revolutionary idea unless she loves some man who is in it. "Are you not in love with someone?" "No," says Laura. "And no one is in love with you?" "No." "Then it is your own fault. No woman need go begging. Why, what is the matter with you? The legless beggar woman in the Alameda has a perfectly faithful lover. Did you know that?"

Laura peers down the pistol barrel and says nothing, but a long, slow faintness rises and subsides in her; Braggioni curves his swollen fingers around the throat of the guitar and softly smothers the music out of it, and when she hears him again he seems to have forgotten her, and is speaking in the hypnotic voice he uses when talking in small rooms to a listening, close-gathered crowd. Some day this world, now seemingly so composed and eternal, to the edges of every sea shall be merely a tangle of gaping trenches, of crashing walls and broken bodies. Everything must be torn from its accustomed place where it has rotted for centuries, hurled skyward and distributed, cast down again clean as rain, without separate identity. Nothing shall survive that the stiffened hands of poverty have created for the rich and no one shall be left alive except the elect spirits destined to procreate a new world cleansed of cruelty and injustice, ruled by benevolent anarchy: "Pistols are good, I love them, cannons are even better, but in the end I pin my faith to good dynamite," he concludes, and strokes the pistol lying in her hands. "Once I dreamed of destroying the city, in case it offered resistance to General Ortíz, but it fell into his hands like an overripe pear."

He is made restless by his own words, rises and stands waiting. Laura holds up the belt to him: "Put that on, and go kill somebody in Morelia, and you will be happier," she says softly. The presence of death in the room makes her bold. "Today, I found Eugenio going into a stupor. He refused to allow me to call the prison doctor. He had taken all the tablets I brought him yesterday. He said he took them because he was bored."

"He is a fool, and his death is his own business," says Braggioni, fastening his belt carefully.

"I told him if he had waited only a little while longer, you would have got him set free," says Laura. "He said he did not want to wait."

"He is a fool and we are well rid of him," says Braggioni, reaching for his hat.

He goes away. Laura knows his mood has changed, she will not see him any more for a while. He will send word when he needs her to go on errands into strange streets, to speak to the strange faces that will appear, like clay masks with the power of human speech, to mutter their thanks to Braggioni for his help. Now she is free, and she thinks, I must run while there is time. But she does not go.

Braggioni enters his own house where for a month his wife has spent many hours every night weeping and tangling her hair upon her pillow. She is weeping now, and she weeps more at the sight of him, the cause of all her sorrows. He looks about the room. Nothing is changed, the smells are good and familiar, he is well acquainted with the woman who comes toward him with no reproach except grief on her face. He says to her tenderly: "You are so good, please don't cry any more, you dear good creature." She says, "Are you tired, my angel? Sit here and I will wash your feet." She brings a bowl of water, and kneeling, unlaces his shoes, and when from her knees she raises her sad eyes under her blackened lids, he is sorry for everything, and bursts into tears. "Ah, yes, I am hungry, I am tired, let us eat something together," he says, between sobs. His wife leans her head on his arm and says, "Forgive me!" and this time he is refreshed by the solemn, endless rain of her tears.

Laura takes off her serge dress and puts on a white linen nightgown and goes to bed. She turns her head a little to one side, and lying still, reminds herself that it is time to sleep. Numbers tick in her brain like little clocks, soundless doors close of themselves around her. If you would sleep, you must not remember anything, the children will say tomorrow, good morning, my teacher, the poor prisoners who come every day bringing flowers to their jailor. 1-2-3-4-5—it is monstrous to confuse love with revolution, night with day, life with death—ah, Eugenio!

The tolling of the midnight bell is a signal, but what does it mean? Get up, Laura, and follow me: come out of your sleep, out of your bed, out of this strange house. What are you doing in this house? Without a word, without fear she rose and reached for Eugenio's hand, but he eluded her with a sharp, sly smile and drifted away. This is not all, you shall see—Murderer, he said, follow me, I will show you a new country, but it is far away and we must hurry. No, said Laura, not unless you take my hand, no; and she clung first to the stair rail, and then to the topmost branch of the Judas tree that bent down slowly and set her upon the earth, and then to the rocky ledge of a cliff, then to the jagged wave of a sea that was not water but a desert of crumbling stone. Where are you taking me, she asked in wonder but without fear. To death, and it is a long way off, and we must hurry, said Eugenio. No, said Laura, not unless you take my hand. Then eat these flowers, poor prisoner, said Eugenio in a voice of pity, take and eat: and from the Judas tree he stripped the warm bleeding flowers, and held them to her lips. She saw that his hand was fleshless, a cluster of small white petrified branches, and his eye sockets were without light, but she ate the flowers greedily for they satisfied both hunger and thirst. Murderer! said Eugenio, and Cannibal! This is my body and my blood. Laura cried No! and at the sound of her own voice, she awoke trembling, and was afraid to sleep again.

F. SCOTT FITZGERALD

Babylon Revisited

I

"And where's Mr. Campbell?" Charlie asked.

"Gone to Switzerland. Mr. Campbell's a pretty sick man, Mr. Wales."

"I'm sorry to hear that. And George Hardt?" Charlie inquired.

"Back in America, gone to work."

"And where is the Snow Bird?"

"He was in here last week. Anyway, his friend, Mr. Schaeffer, is in Paris."

Two familiar names from the long list of a year and a half ago. Charlie scribbled an address in his notebook and tore out the page.

"If you see Mr. Schaeffer, give him this," he said. "It's my brother-in-law's address. I haven't settled on a hotel yet."

He was not really disappointed to find Paris was so empty. But the stillness in the Ritz bar was strange and portentous. It was not an American bar any more—he felt polite in it, and not as if he owned it. It had gone back into France. He felt the stillness from the moment he got out of the taxi and saw the doorman, usually in a frenzy of activity at this hour, gossiping with a *chasseur* by the servant's entrance.

Passing through the corridor, he heard only a single, bored voice in the once-clamorous women's room. When he turned into the bar he traveled the twenty feet of green carpet with his eyes fixed straight ahead by old habit; and then, with his foot firmly on the rail, he turned and surveyed the room, encountering only a single pair of eyes that fluttered up from a newspaper in the corner. Charlie asked for the head barman, Paul, who in the latter days of the bull market had come to work in his own custom-built car—disembarking, however, with due nicety at the nearest corner. But Paul was at his country house today and Alix giving him information.

"No, no more," Charlie said, "I'm going slow these days."

Alix congratulated him: "You were going pretty strong a couple of years ago."

"I'll stick to it all right," Charlie assured him. "I've stuck to it for over a year and a half now."

"How do you find conditions in America?"

"I haven't been to America for months. I'm in business in Prague, representing a couple of concerns there. They don't know about me down there."

Alix smiled.

"Remember the night of George Hardt's bachelor dinner here?" said Charlie. "By the way, what's become of Claude Fessenden?"

Alix lowered his voice confidentially: "He's in Paris, but he doesn't come here any more. Paul doesn't allow it. He ran up a bill of thirty thousand francs, charging all his drinks and his lunches, and usually his dinner, for more than a year. And when Paul finally told him he had to pay, he gave him a bad check."

Alix shook his head sadly.

"I don't understand it, such a dandy fellow. Now he's all bloated up—" He made a plump apple of his hands.

Charlie watched a group of strident queens installing themselves in a corner.

"Nothing affects them," he thought. "Stocks rise and fall, people loaf or work, but they go on forever." The place oppressed him. He called for the dice and shook with Alix for the drink.

"Here for long, Mr. Wales?"

"I'm here for four or five days to see my little girl."

"Oh-h! You have a little girl?"

Outside, the fire-red, gas-blue, ghost-green signs shone smokily through the tranquil rain. It was late afternoon and the streets were in movement; the *bistros* gleamed. At the corner of the Boulevard des Capucines he took a taxi. The Place de la Concorde moved by in pink majesty; they crossed the logical Seine, and Charlie felt the sudden provincial quality of the left bank.

Charlie directed his taxi to the Avenue de l'Opera, which was out of his way. But he wanted to see the blue hour spread over the magnificent façade, and imagine that the cab horns, playing endlessly the first few bars of *Le Plus que Lent*, were the trumpets of the Second Empire. They were closing the iron grill in front of Brentano's Book-store, and people were already at dinner behind the trim little bourgeois hedge of Duval's. He had never eaten at a really cheap restaurant in Paris. Five-course dinner, four francs fifty, eighteen cents, wine included. For some odd reason he wished that he had.

As they rolled on to the Left Bank and he felt its sudden provincialism, he thought, "I spoiled this city for myself. I didn't realize it, but the days came along one after another, and then two years were gone, and everything was gone, and I was gone."

He was thirty-five, and good to look at. The Irish mobility of his face was sobered by a deep wrinkle between his eyes. As he rang his brother-in-law's bell in the Rue Palatine, the wrinkle deepened till it pulled down his brows; he felt a cramping sensation in his belly. From behind the maid who opened the door darted a lovely little girl of nine who shrieked "Daddy!" and flew up, struggling like a fish, into his arms. She pulled his head around by one ear and set her cheek against his.

"My old pie," he said.

"Oh, daddy, daddy, daddy, daddy, dads, dads, dads!"

She drew him into the salon, where the family waited, a boy and a girl his daughter's age, his sister-in-law and her husband. He greeted Marion with his voice pitched carefully to avoid feigned enthusiasm or dislike, but her response was more frankly tepid, though she minimized her expression of unalterable distrust by directing her regard toward his child. The two men clasped hands in a friendly way and Lincoln Peters rested his for a moment on Charlie's shoulder.

The room was warm and comfortably American. The three children moved intimately about, playing through the yellow oblongs that led to other rooms; the cheer of six o'clock spoke in the eager smacks of the fire and the sounds of French activity in the kitchen. But Charlie did not relax; his heart sat up rigidly in his body and he drew confidence from his daughter, who from time to time came close to him, holding in her arms the doll he had brought.

"Really extremely well," he declared in answer to Lincoln's question. "There's a lot of business there that isn't moving at all, but we're doing even better than ever. In fact, damn well. I'm bringing my sister over from America next month to keep house for me. My income last year was bigger than it was when I had money. You see, the Czechs——"

His boasting was for a specific purpose; but after a moment, seeing a faint restiveness in Lincoln's eye, he changed the subject:

"Those are fine children of yours, well brought up, good manners."

"We think Honoria's a great little girl too."

Marion Peters came back from the kitchen. She was a tall woman with worried eyes, who had once possessed a fresh American loveliness. Charlie had never been sensitive to it and was always surprised when people spoke of how pretty she had been. From the first there had been an instinctive antipathy between them.

"Well, how do you find Honoria?" she asked.

"Wonderful. I was astonished how much she's grown in ten months. All the children are looking well."

"We haven't had a doctor for a year. How do you like being back in Paris?"

"It seems very funny to see so few Americans around."

"I'm delighted," Marion said vehemently. "Now at least you can go into a store without their assuming you're a millionaire. We've suffered like everybody, but on the whole it's a good deal pleasanter."

"But it was nice while it lasted," Charlie said. "We were a sort of royalty, almost infallible, with a sort of magic around us. In the bar this afternoon"—he stumbled, seeing his mistake—"there wasn't a man I knew."

She looked at him keenly. "I should think you'd have had enough of bars."

"I only stayed a minute. I take one drink every afternoon, and no more."

"Don't you want a cocktail before dinner?" Lincoln asked.

"I take only one drink every afternoon, and I've had that."

"I hope you keep to it," said Marion.

Her dislike was evident in the coldness with which she spoke, but

Charlie only smiled; he had larger plans. Her very aggressiveness gave him an advantage, and he knew enough to wait. He wanted them to initiate the discussion of what they knew had brought him to Paris.

At dinner he couldn't decide whether Honoria was most like him or her mother. Fortunate if she didn't combine the traits of both that had brought them to disaster. A great wave of protectiveness went over him. He thought he knew what to do for her. He believed in character; he wanted to jump back a whole generation and trust in character again as the eternally valuable element. Everything else wore out.

He left soon after dinner, but not to go home. He was curious to see Paris by night with clearer and more judicious eyes than those of other days. He bought a *strapontin* for the Casino and watched Josephine Baker go through her chocolate arabesques.

After an hour he left and strolled toward Montmartre, up the Rue Pigalle into the Place Blanche. The rain had stopped and there were a few people in evening clothes disembarking from taxis in front of cabarets, and *cocottes* prowling singly or in pairs, and many Negroes. He passed a lighted door from which issued music, and stopped with the sense of familiarity; it was Bricktop's, where he had parted with so many hours and so much money. A few doors farther on he found another ancient rendezvous and incautiously put his head inside. Immediately an eager orchestra burst into sound, a pair of professional dancers leaped to their feet and a maître d'hôtel swooped toward him, crying, "Crowd just arriving, sir!" But he withdrew quickly.

"You have to be damn drunk," he thought.

Zelli's was closed, the bleak and sinister cheap hotels surrounding it were dark; up in the Rue Blanche there was more light and a local, colloquial French crowd. The Poet's Cave had disappeared, but the two great mouths of the Café of Heaven and the Café of Hell still yawned—even devoured, as he watched, the meager contents of a tourist bus—a German, a Japanese, and an American couple who glanced at him with frightened eyes.

So much for the effort and ingenuity of Montmartre. All the catering to vice and waste was on an utterly childish scale, and he suddenly realized the meaning of the word "dissipate"—to dissipate into thin air; to make nothing out of something. In the little hours of the night every move from place to place was an enormous human jump, an increase of paying for the privilege of slower and slower motion.

He remembered thousand-franc notes given to an orchestra for playing a single number, hundred-franc notes tossed to a doorman for calling a cab.

But it hadn't been given for nothing.

It had been given, even the most wildly squandered sum, as an offering to destiny that he might not remember the things most worth remembering, the things that now he would always remember—his child taken from his control, his wife escaped to a grave in Vermont.

In the glare of a *brasserie* a woman spoke to him. He bought her some eggs and coffee, and then, eluding her encouraging stare, gave her a twenty-franc note and took a taxi to his hotel.

II

He woke upon a fine fall day—football weather. The depression of yesterday was gone and he liked the people on the streets. At noon he sat opposite Honoria at Le Grand Vatel, the only restaurant he could think of not reminiscent of champagne dinners and long luncheons that began at two and ended in a blurred and vague twilight.

"Now, how about vegetables? Oughtn't you to have some vegetables?"

"Well, yes."

"Here's *épinards* and *chou-fleur* and carrots and *haricots*."

"I'd like *chou-fleur*."

"Wouldn't you like to have two vegetables?"

"I usually only have one at lunch."

The waiter was pretending to be inordinately fond of children. *"Qu'elle est mignonne la petite! Elle parle exactement comme une Française."*

"How about dessert? Shall we wait and see?"

The waiter disappeared. Honoria looked at her father expectantly.

"What are we going to do?"

"First, we're going to that toy store in the Rue Saint-Honoré and buy you anything you like. And then we're going to the vaudeville at the Empire."

She hesitated. "I like it about the vaudeville, but not the toy store."

"Why not?"

"Well, you brought me this doll." She had it with her. "And I've got lots of things. And we're not rich any more, are we?"

"We never were. But today you are to have anything you want."

"All right," she agreed resignedly.

When there had been her mother and a French nurse he had been inclined to be strict; now he extended himself, reached out for a new tolerance; he must be both parents to her and not shut any of her out of communication.

"I want to get to know you," he said gravely. "First let me introduce myself. My name is Charles J. Wales, of Prague."

"Oh, daddy!" her voice cracked with laughter.

"And who are you, please?" he persisted, and she accepted a rôle immediately: "Honoria Wales, Rue Palatine, Paris."

"Married or single?"

"No, not married. Single."

He indicated the doll. "But I see you have a child, madame."

Unwilling to disinherit it, she took it to her heart and thought quickly: "Yes, I've been married, but I'm not married now. My husband is dead."

He went on quickly, "And the child's name?"

"Simone. That's after my best friend at school."

"I'm very pleased that you're doing so well at school."

"I'm third this month," she boasted. "Elsie"—that was her cousin—"is only about eighteenth, and Richard is about at the bottom."

"You like Richard and Elsie, don't you?"

"Oh, yes, I like Richard quite well and I like her all right."

Cautiously and casually he asked: "And Aunt Marion and Uncle Lincoln —which do you like best?"

"Oh, Uncle Lincoln, I guess."

He was increasingly aware of her presence. As they came in, a murmur of ". . . adorable" followed them, and now the people at the next table bent all their silences upon her, staring as if she were something no more conscious than a flower.

"Why don't I live with you?" she asked suddenly. "Because mamma's dead?"

"You must stay here and learn more French. It would have been hard for daddy to take care of you so well."

"I don't really need much taking care of any more. I do everything for myself."

Going out of the restaurant, a man and a woman unexpectedly hailed him.

"Well, the old Wales!"

"Hello there, Lorraine. . . . Dunc."

Sudden ghosts out of the past: Duncan Schaeffer, a friend from college. Lorraine Quarrles, a lovely, pale blonde of thirty; one of a crowd who had helped them make months into days in the lavish times of three years ago.

"My husband couldn't come this year," she said, in answer to his question. "We're poor as hell. So he gave me two hundred a month and told me I could do my worst on that. . . . This your little girl?"

"What about coming back and sitting down?" Duncan asked.

"Can't do it." He was glad for an excuse. As always, he felt Lorraine's passionate, provocative attraction, but his own rhythm was different now.

"Well, how about dinner?" she asked.

"I'm not free. Give me your address and let me call you."

"Charlie, I believe you're sober," she said judicially. "I honestly believe he's sober, Dunc. Pinch him and see if he's sober."

Charlie indicated Honoria with his head. They both laughed.

"What's your address?" said Duncan skeptically.

He hesitated, unwilling to give the name of his hotel.

"I'm not settled yet. I'd better call you. We're going to see the vaudeville at the Empire."

"There! That's what I want to do," Lorraine said. "I want to see some clowns and acrobats and jugglers. That's just what we'll do, Dunc."

"We've got to do an errand first," said Charlie. "Perhaps we'll see you there."

"All right, you snob. . . . Good-by, beautiful little girl."

"Good-by."

Honoria bobbed politely.

Somehow, an unwelcome encounter. They liked him because he was functioning, because he was serious; they wanted to see him, because he was stronger than they were now, because they wanted to draw a certain sustenance from his strength.

At the Empire, Honoria proudly refused to sit upon her father's folded coat. She was already an individual with a code of her own, and Charlie was more and more absorbed by the desire of putting a little of himself into her before she crystallized utterly. It was hopeless to try to know her in so short a time.

Between the acts they came upon Duncan and Lorraine in the lobby where the band was playing.

"Have a drink?"

"All right, but not up at the bar. We'll take a table."

"The perfect father."

Listening abstractedly to Lorraine, Charlie watched Honoria's eyes leave their table, and he followed them wistfully about the room, wondering what they saw. He met her glance and she smiled.

"I liked that lemonade," she said.

What had she said? What had he expected? Going home in a taxi afterward, he pulled her over until her head rested against his chest.

"Darling, do you ever think about your mother?"

"Yes, sometimes," she answered vaguely.

"I don't want you to forget her. Have you got a picture of her?"

"Yes, I think so. Anyhow, Aunt Marion has. Why don't you want me to forget her?"

"She loved you very much."

"I loved her too."

They were silent for a moment.

"Daddy, I want to come and live with you," she said suddenly.

His heart leaped; he had wanted it to come like this.

"Aren't you perfectly happy?"

"Yes, but I love you better than anybody. And you love me better than anybody, don't you, now that mummy's dead?"

"Of course I do. But you won't always like me best, honey. You'll grow up and meet somebody your own age and go marry him and forget you ever had a daddy."

"Yes, that's true," she agreed tranquilly.

He didn't go in. He was coming back at nine o'clock and he wanted to keep himself fresh and new for the thing he must say then.

"When you're safe inside, just show yourself in that window."

"All right. Good-by, dads, dads, dads, dads."

He waited in the dark street until she appeared, all warm and glowing, in the window above and kissed her fingers out into the night.

III

They were waiting. Marion sat behind the coffee service in a dignified black dinner dress that just faintly suggested mourning. Lincoln was walking up and down with the animation of one who had already been talking. They were as anxious as he was to get into the question. He opened it almost immediately:

"I suppose you know what I want to see you about—why I really came to Paris."

Marion played with the black stars on her necklace and frowned.

"I'm awfully anxious to have a home," he continued. "And I'm awfully anxious to have Honoria in it. I appreciate your taking in Honoria for her mother's sake, but things have changed now"—he hesitated and then continued more forcibly—"changed radically with me, and I want to ask you to reconsider the matter. It would be silly for me to deny that about three years ago I was acting badly——"

Marion looked up at him with hard eyes.

"—but all that's over. As I told you, I haven't had more than a drink a day for over a year, and I take that drink deliberately, so that the idea of alcohol won't get too big in my imagination. You see the idea?"

"No," said Marion succinctly.

"It's a sort of stunt I set myself. It keeps the matter in proportion."

"I get you," said Lincoln. "You don't want to admit it's got any attraction for you."

"Something like that. Sometimes I forget and don't take it. But I try to take it. Anyhow, I couldn't afford to drink in my position. The people I represent are more than satisfied with what I've done, and I'm bringing my sister over from Burlington to keep house for me, and I want awfully to have Honoria too. You know that even when her mother and I weren't getting along well we never let anything that happened touch Honoria. I know she's fond of me and I know I'm able to take care of her and—well, there you are. How do you feel about it?"

He knew that now he would have to take a beating. It would last an hour or two hours, and it would be difficult, but if he modulated his inevitable resentment to the chastened attitude of the reformed sinner, he might win his point in the end.

Keep your temper, he told himself. You don't want to be justified. You want Honoria.

Lincoln spoke first: "We've been talking it over ever since we got your letter last month. We're happy to have Honoria here. She's a dear little thing, and we're glad to be able to help her, but of course that isn't the question——"

Marion interrupted suddenly. "How long are you going to stay sobe· Charlie?" she asked.

"Permanently, I hope."

"How can anybody count on that?"

"You know I never did drink heavily until I gave up business and came over here with nothing to do. Then Helen and I began to run around with——"

"Please leave Helen out of it. I can't bear to hear you talk about her like that."

He stared at her grimly; he had never been certain how fond of each other the sisters were in life.

"My drinking only lasted about a year and a half—from the time we came over until I—collapsed."

"It was time enough."

"It was time enough," he agreed.

"My duty is entirely to Helen," she said. "I try to think what she would have wanted me to do. Frankly, from the night you did that terrible thing you haven't really existed for me. I can't help that. She was my sister."

"Yes."

"When she was dying she asked me to look out for Honoria. If you hadn't been in a sanitarium then, it might have helped matters."

He had no answer.

"I'll never in my life be able to forget the morning when Helen knocked at my door, soaked to the skin and shivering and said you'd locked her out."

Charlie gripped the sides of the chair. This was more difficult than he expected; he wanted to launch out into a long expostulation and explanation, but he only said: "The night I locked her out—" and she interrupted, "I don't feel up to going over that again."

After a moment's silence Lincoln said: "We're getting off the subject. You want Marion to set aside her legal guardianship and give you Honoria. I think the main point for her is whether she has confidence in you or not."

"I don't blame Marion," Charlie said slowly, "but I think she can have entire confidence in me. I had a good record up to three years ago. Of course, it's within human possibilities I might go wrong any time. But if we wait much longer I'll lose Honoria's childhood and my chance for a home." He shook his head, "I'll simply lose her, don't you see?"

"Yes, I see," said Lincoln.

"Why didn't you think of all this before?" Marion asked.

"I suppose I did, from time to time, but Helen and I were getting along badly. When I consented to the guardianship, I was flat on my back in a sanitarium and the market had cleaned me out. I knew I'd acted badly, and I thought if it would bring any peace to Helen, I'd agree to anything. But now it's different. I'm functioning, I'm behaving damn well, so far as——"

"Please don't swear at me," Marion said.

He looked at her, startled. With each remark the force of her dislike became more and more apparent. She had built up all her fear of life into one wall and faced it toward him. This trivial reproof was possibly the result of some trouble with the cook several hours before. Charlie became increasingly alarmed at leaving Honoria in this atmosphere of hostility against himself; sooner or later it would come out, in a word here, a shake of the head there, and some of that distrust would be irrevocably implanted in Honoria. But he pulled his temper down out of his face and shut it up inside him; he had won a point, for Lincoln realized the absurdity of Marion's remark and asked her lightly since when she had objected to the word "damn."

"Another thing," Charlie said: "I'm able to give her certain advantages now. I'm going to take a French governess to Prague with me. I've got a lease on a new apartment——"

He stopped, realizing that he was blundering. They couldn't be expected to accept with equanimity the fact that his income was again twice as large as their own.

"I suppose you can give her more luxuries than we can," said Marion. "When you were throwing away money we were living along watching every ten francs. . . . I suppose you'll start doing it again."

"Oh, no," he said. "I've learned. I worked hard for ten years, you know—until I got lucky in the market, like so many people. Terribly lucky. It won't happen again."

There was a long silence. All of them felt their nerves straining, and for the first time in a year Charlie wanted a drink. He was sure now that Lincoln Peters wanted him to have his child.

Marion shuddered suddenly; part of her saw that Charlie's feet were planted on the earth now, and her own maternal feeling recognized the naturalness of his desire; but she had lived for a long time with a prejudice—a prejudice founded on a curious disbelief in her sister's happiness, and which, in the shock of one terrible night, had turned to hatred for him. It had all happened at a point in her life where the discouragement of ill health and adverse circumstances made it necessary for her to believe in tangible villainy and a tangible villain.

"I can't help what I think!" she cried out suddenly. "How much you were responsible for Helen's death, I don't know. It's something you'll have to square with your own conscience."

An electric current of agony surged through him; for a moment he was almost on his feet, an unuttered sound echoing in his throat. He hung on to himself for a moment, another moment.

"Hold on there," said Lincoln uncomfortably. "I never thought you were responsible for that."

"Helen died of heart trouble," Charlie said dully.

"Yes, heart trouble." Marion spoke as if the phrase had another meaning for her.

Then, in the flatness that followed her outburst, she saw him plainly and she knew he had somehow arrived at control over the situation. Glancing at her husband, she found no help from him, and as abruptly as if it were a matter of no importance, she threw up the sponge.

"Do what you like!" she cried, springing up from her chair. "She's your child. I'm not the person to stand in your way. I think if it were my child

I'd rather see her—" She managed to check herself. "You two decide it. I can't stand this. I'm sick. I'm going to bed."

She hurried from the room; after a moment Lincoln said:

"This has been a hard day for her. You know how strongly she feels—" His voice was almost apologetic: "When a woman gets an idea in her head."

"Of course."

"It's going to be all right. I think she sees now that you—can provide for the child, and we can't very well stand in your way or Honoria's way."

"Thank you, Lincoln."

"I'd better go along and see how she is."

"I'm going."

He was still trembling when he reached the street, but a walk down the Rue Bonaparte to the *quais* set him up, and as he crossed the Seine, fresh and new by the *quai* lamps, he felt exultant. But back in his room he couldn't sleep. The image of Helen haunted him. Helen whom he had loved so until they had senselessly begun to abuse each other's love, tear it into shreds. On that terrible February night that Marion remembered so vividly, a slow quarrel had gone on for hours. There was a scene at the Florida, and then he attempted to take her home, and then she kissed young Webb at a table; after that there was what she had hysterically said. When he arrived home alone he turned the key in the lock in wild anger. How could he know she would arrive an hour later alone, that there would be a snowstorm in which she wandered about in slippers, too confused to find a taxi? Then the aftermath, her escaping pneumonia by a miracle, and all the attendant horror. They were "reconciled," but that was the beginning of the end, as Marion, who had seen with her own eyes and who imagined it to be one of many scenes from her sister's martyrdom, never forgot.

Going over it again brought Helen nearer, and in the white, soft light that steals upon half sleep near morning he found himself talking to her again. She said that he was perfectly right about Honoria and that she wanted Honoria to be with him. She said she was glad he was being good and doing better. She said a lot of other things—very friendly things—but she was in a swing in a white dress, and swinging faster and faster all the time, so that at the end he could not hear clearly all that she said.

IV

He woke up feeling happy. The door of the world was open again. He made plans, vistas, futures for Honoria and himself, but suddenly he grew sad, remembering all the plans he and Helen had made. She had not planned to die. The present was the thing—work to do and someone to love. But not to love too much, for he knew the injury that a father can do to a daughter or a mother to a son by attaching them too closely: afterward, out in the world, the child would seek in the marriage partner the same blind tenderness and, failing probably to find it, turn against love and life.

It was another bright, crisp day. He called Lincoln Peters at the bank where he worked and asked if he could count on taking Honoria when he left for Prague. Lincoln agreed that there was no reason for delay. One thing—the legal guardianship. Marion wanted to retain that a while longer. She was upset by the whole matter, and it would oil things if she felt that the situation was still in her control for another year. Charlie agreed, wanting only the tangible, visible child.

Then the question of a governess. Charles sat in a gloomy agency and talked to a cross Béarnaise and to a buxom Breton peasant, neither of whom he could have endured. There were others whom he would see tomorrow.

He lunched with Lincoln Peters at Griffons, trying to keep down his exultation.

"There's nothing quite like your own child," Lincoln said. "But you understand how Marion feels too."

"She's forgotten how hard I worked for seven years there," Charlie said. "She just remembers one night."

"There's another thing." Lincoln hesitated. "While you and Helen were tearing around Europe throwing money away, we were just getting along. I didn't touch any of the prosperity because I never got ahead enough to carry anything but my insurance. I think Marion felt there was some kind of injustice in it—you not even working toward the end, and getting richer and richer."

"It went just as quick as it came," said Charlie.

"Yes, a lot of it stayed in the hands of *chasseurs* and saxophone players and maîtres d'hôtel—well, the big party's over now. I just said that to explain Marion's feeling about those crazy years. If you drop in about six o'clock tonight before Marion's too tired, we'll settle the details on the spot."

Back at his hotel, Charlie found a *pneumatique* that had been redirected from the Ritz bar where Charlie had left his address for the purpose of finding a certain man.

"DEAR CHARLIE: You were so strange when we saw you the other day that I wondered if I did something to offend you. If so, I'm not conscious of it. In fact, I have thought about you too much for the last year, and it's always been in the back of my mind that I might see you if I came over here. We *did* have such good times that crazy spring, like the night you and I stole the butcher's tricycle, and the time we tried to call on the president and you had the old derby rim and the wire cane. Everybody seems so old lately, but I don't feel old a bit. Couldn't we get together some time today for old time's sake? I've got a vile hang-over for the moment, but will be feeling better this afternoon and will look for you about five in the sweatshop at the Ritz.

"Always devotedly,
"LORRAINE."

His first feeling was one of awe that he had actually, in his mature years, stolen a tricycle and pedaled Lorraine all over the Étoile between the small hours and dawn. In retrospect it was a nightmare. Locking out Helen didn't fit in with any other act of his life, but the tricycle incident did—it was one of many. How many weeks or months of dissipation to arrive at that condition of utter irresponsibility?

He tried to picture how Lorraine had appeared to him then—very attractive; Helen was unhappy about it, though she said nothing. Yesterday, in the restaurant, Lorraine had seemed trite, blurred, worn away. He emphatically did not want to see her, and he was glad Alix had not given away his hotel address. It was a relief to think, instead, of Honoria, to think of Sundays spent with her and of saying good morning to her and of knowing she was there in his house at night, drawing her breath in the darkness.

At five he took a taxi and bought presents for all the Peters—a piquant cloth doll, a box of Roman soldiers, flowers for Marion, big linen handkerchiefs for Lincoln.

He saw, when he arrived in the apartment, that Marion had accepted the inevitable. She greeted him now as though he were a recalcitrant member of the family, rather than a menacing outsider. Honoria had been told she was going; Charlie was glad to see that her tact made her conceal her excessive happiness. Only on his lap did she whisper her delight and the question "When?" before she slipped away with the other children.

He and Marion were alone for a minute in the room, and on an impulse he spoke out boldly:

"Family quarrels are bitter things. They don't go according to any rules. They're not like aches or wounds; they're more like splits in the skin that won't heal because there's not enough material. I wish you and I could be on better terms."

"Some things are hard to forget," she answered. "It's a question of confidence." There was no answer to this and presently she asked, "When do you propose to take her?"

"As soon as I can get a governess. I hoped the day after tomorrow."

"That's impossible. I've got to get her things in shape. Not before Saturday."

He yielded. Coming back into the room, Lincoln offered him a drink.

"I'll take my daily whisky," he said.

It was warm here, it was a home, people together by a fire. The children felt very safe and important; the mother and father were serious, watchful. They had things to do for the children more important than his visit here. A spoonful of medicine was, after all, more important than the strained relations between Marion and himself. They were not dull people, but they were very much in the grip of life and circumstances. He wondered if he couldn't do something to get Lincoln out of his rut at the bank.

A long peal at the door-bell; the *bonne à tout faire* passed through and went down the corridor. The door opened upon another long ring, and then voices, and the three in the salon looked up expectantly; Richard moved to bring the corridor within his range of vision, and Marion rose. Then the maid came back along the corridor, closely followed by the voices, which developed under the light into Duncan Schaeffer and Lorraine Quarrles.

They were gay, they were hilarious, they were roaring with laughter. For a moment Charlie was astounded; unable to understand how they ferreted out the Peters' address.

"Ah-h-h!" Duncan wagged his finger roguishly at Charlie. "Ah-h-h!"

They both slid down another cascade of laughter. Anxious and at a loss, Charlie shook hands with them quickly and presented them to Lincoln and Marion. Marion nodded, scarcely speaking. She had drawn back a step toward the fire; her little girl stood beside her, and Marion put an arm about her shoulder.

With growing annoyance at the intrusion, Charlie waited for them to explain themselves. After some concentration Duncan said:

"We came to invite you out to dinner. Lorraine and I insist that all this shishi, cagy business 'bout your address got to stop."

Charlie came closer to them, as if to force them backward down the corridor.

"Sorry, but I can't. Tell me where you'll be and I'll phone you in half an hour."

This made no impression. Lorraine sat down suddenly on the side of a chair, and focusing her eyes on Richard, cried, "Oh, what a nice little boy! Come here, little boy." Richard glanced at his mother, but did not move. With a perceptible shrug of her shoulders, Lorraine turned back to Charlie:

"Come and dine. Sure your cousins won' mine. See you so sel'om. Or solemn."

"I can't," said Charlie sharply. "You two have dinner and I'll phone you."

Her voice became suddenly unpleasant. "All right, we'll go. But I remember once when you hammered on my door at four A.M. I was enough of a good sport to give you a drink. Come on, Dunc."

Still in slow motion, with blurred, angry faces, with uncertain feet, they retired along the corridor.

"Good night," Charlie said.

"Good night!" responded Lorraine emphatically.

When he went back into the salon Marion had not moved, only now her son was standing in the circle of her other arm. Lincoln was still swinging Honoria back and forth like a pendulum from side to side.

"What an outrage!" Charlie broke out. "What an absolute outrage!"

Neither of them answered. Charlie dropped into an armchair, picked up his drink, set it down again and said:

"People I haven't seen for two years having the colossal nerve——"

He broke off. Marion had made the sound "Oh!" in one swift, furious breath, turned her body from him with a jerk and left the room.

Lincoln set down Honoria carefully.

"You children go in and start your soup," he said, and when they obeyed, he said to Charlie:

"Marion's not well and she can't stand shocks. That kind of people make her really physically sick."

"I didn't tell them to come here. They wormed your name out of somebody. They deliberately——"

"Well, it's too bad. It doesn't help matters. Excuse me a minute."

Left alone, Charlie sat tense in his chair. In the next room he could hear the children eating, talking in monosyllables, already oblivious to the scene between their elders. He heard a murmur of conversation from a farther room and then the ticking bell of a telephone receiver picked up, and in a panic he moved to the other side of the room and out of earshot.

In a minute Lincoln came back. "Look here, Charlie. I think we'd better call off dinner for tonight. Marion's in bad shape."

"Is she angry with me?"

"Sort of," he said, almost roughly. "She's not strong and——"

"You mean she's changed her mind about Honoria?"

"She's pretty bitter right now. I don't know. You phone me at the bank tomorrow."

"I wish you'd explain to her I never dreamed these people would come here. I'm just as sore as you are."

"I couldn't explain anything to her now."

Charlie got up. He took his coat and hat and started down the corridor. Then he opened the door of the dining room and said in a strange voice, "Good night, children."

Honoria rose and ran around the table to hug him.

"Good night, sweetheart," he said vaguely, and then trying to make his voice more tender, trying to conciliate something, "Good night, dear children."

V

Charlie went directly to the Ritz bar with the furious idea of finding Lorraine and Duncan, but they were not there, and he realized that in any case there was nothing he could do. He had not touched his drink at the Peters, and now he ordered a whisky-and-soda. Paul came over to say hello.

"It's a great change," he said sadly. "We do about half the business we did. So many fellows I hear about back in the States lost everything, maybe not in the first crash, but then in the second. Your friend George Hardt lost every cent, I hear. Are you back in the States?"

"No, I'm in business in Prague."

"I heard that you lost a lot in the crash."

"I did," and he added grimly, "but I lost everything I wanted in the boom."

"Selling short."

"Something like that."

Again the memory of those days swept over him like a nightmare—the

237

people they had met travelling; then people who couldn't add a row of figures or speak a coherent sentence. The little man Helen had consented to dance with at the ship's party, who had insulted her ten feet from the table; the women and girls carried screaming with drinks or drugs out of public places——

—The men who locked their wives out in the snow, because the snow of twenty-nine wasn't real snow. If you didn't want it to be snow, you just paid some money.

He went to the phone and called the Peters' apartment; Lincoln answered.

"I called up because this thing is on my mind. Has Marion said anything definite?"

"Marion's sick," Lincoln answered shortly. "I know this thing isn't altogether your fault, but I can't have her go to pieces about it. I'm afraid we'll have to let it slide for six months; I can't take the chance of working her up to this state again."

"I see."

"I'm sorry, Charlie."

He went back to his table. His whisky glass was empty, but he shook his head when Alix looked at it questionably. There wasn't much he could do now except send Honoria some things; he would send her a lot of things tomorrow. He thought rather angrily that this was just money—he had given so many people money. . . .

"No, no more," he said to another waiter. "What do I owe you?"

He would come back some day; they couldn't make him pay forever. But he wanted his child, and nothing was much good now, beside that fact. He wasn't young any more, with a lot of nice things and dreams to have by himself. He was absolutely sure Helen wouldn't have wanted him to be so alone.

WILLIAM FAULKNER

A Rose for Emily

I

When Miss Emily Grierson died, our whole town went to her funeral: the men through a sort of respectful affection for a fallen monument, the women mostly out of curiosity to see the inside of her house, which no one save an old man-servant—a combined gardener and cook—had seen in at least ten years.

It was a big, squarish frame house that had once been white, decorated with cupolas and spires and scrolled balconies in the heavily lightsome style of the seventies, set on what had once been our most select street. But garages and cotton gins had encroached and obliterated even the august names of that neighborhood; only Miss Emily's house was left, lifting its stubborn and coquettish decay above the cotton wagons and the gasoline pumps—an eyesore among eyesores. And now Miss Emily had gone to join the representatives of those august names where they lay in the cedar-bemused cemetery among the ranked and anonymous graves of Union and Confederate soldiers who fell at the battle of Jefferson.

Alive, Miss Emily had been a tradition, a duty, and a care; a sort of hereditary obligation upon the town, dating from that day in 1894 when Colonel Sartoris, the mayor—he who fathered the edict that no Negro woman should appear on the streets without an apron—remitted her taxes, the dispensation dating from the death of her father on into perpetuity. Not that Miss Emily would have accepted charity. Colonel Sartoris invented an involved tale to the effect that Miss Emily's father had loaned money to the town, which the town, as a matter of business, preferred this way of repaying. Only a man of Colonel Sartoris' generation and thought could have invented it, and only a woman could have believed it.

When the next generation, with its more modern ideas, became mayors and aldermen, this arrangement created some little dissatisfaction. On the first of the year they mailed her a tax notice. February came, and there was no reply. They wrote her a formal letter, asking her to call at the sheriff's office at her convenience. A week later the mayor wrote her himself, offering to call or to send his car for her, and received in reply a note on paper of an archaic shape, in a thin, flowing calligraphy in faded ink, to the effect that she no longer went out at all. The tax notice was also enclosed, without comment.

They called a special meeting of the Board of Aldermen. A deputation waited upon her, knocked at the door through which no visitor had passed since she ceased giving china-painting lessons eight or ten years earlier. They were admitted by the old Negro into a dim hall from which a stairway mounted into still more shadow. It smelled of dust and disuse—a close, dank smell. The Negro led them into the parlor. It was furnished in heavy, leather-covered furniture. When the Negro opened the blinds of one window, they could see that the leather was cracked; and when they sat down, a faint dust rose sluggishly about their thighs, spinning with slow motes in the single sun-ray. On a tarnished gilt easel before the fireplace stood a crayon portrait of Miss Emily's father.

They rose when she entered—a small, fat woman in black, with a thin gold chain descending to her waist and vanishing into her belt, leaning on an ebony cane with a tarnished gold head. Her skeleton was small and spare; perhaps that was why what would have been merely plumpness in another was obesity in her. She looked bloated, like a body long submerged in motionless water, and of that pallid hue. Her eyes, lost in the fatty ridges of her face, looked like two small pieces of coal pressed into a lump of dough as they moved from one face to another while the visitors stated their errand.

She did not ask them to sit. She just stood in the door and listened quietly until the spokesman came to a stumbling halt. Then they could hear the invisible watch ticking at the end of the gold chain.

Her voice was dry and cold. "I have no taxes in Jefferson. Colonel Sartoris explained it to me. Perhaps one of you can gain access to the city records and satisfy yourselves."

"But we have. We are the city authorities, Miss Emily. Didn't you get a notice from the sheriff, signed by him?"

"I received a paper, yes," Miss Emily said. "Perhaps he considers himself the sheriff . . . I have no taxes in Jefferson."

"But there is nothing on the books to show that, you see. We must go by the—"

"See Colonel Sartoris. I have no taxes in Jefferson."

"But, Miss Emily—"

"See Colonel Sartoris." (Colonel Sartoris had been dead almost ten years.) "I have no taxes in Jefferson. Tobe!" The Negro appeared. "Show these gentlemen out."

II

So she vanquished them, horse and foot, just as she had vanquished their fathers thirty years before about the smell. That was two years after her father's death and a short time after her sweetheart—the one we believed would marry her—had deserted her. After her father's death she went out very little; after her sweetheart went away, people hardly saw her at all. A few of the ladies had the temerity to call, but were not received, and the only sign of life about the place was the Negro man—a young man then—going in and out with a market basket.

"Just as if a man—any man—could keep a kitchen properly," the ladies said; so they were not surprised when the smell developed. It was another link between the gross, teeming world and the high and mighty Griersons.

A neighbor, a woman, complained to the mayor, Judge Stevens, eighty years old.

"But what will you have me do about it, madam?" he said.

"Why, send her word to stop it," the woman said. "Isn't there a law?"

"I'm sure that won't be necessary," Judge Stevens said. "It's probably just a snake or a rat that nigger of hers killed in the yard. I'll speak to him about it."

The next day he received two more complaints, one from a man who came in diffident deprecation. "We really must do something about it, Judge. I'd be the last one in the world to bother Miss Emily, but we've got to do something." That night the Board of Aldermen met—three graybeards and one younger man, a member of the rising generation.

"It's simple enough," he said. "Send her word to have her place cleaned up. Give her a certain time do it in, and if she don't . . ."

"Dammit, sir," Judge Stevens said, "will you accuse a lady to her face of smelling bad?"

So the next night, after midnight, four men crossed Miss Emily's lawn and slunk about the house like burglars, sniffing along the base of the brickwork and at the cellar openings while one of them performed a regular sowing motion with his hand out of a sack slung from his shoulder. They broke open the cellar door and sprinkled lime there, and in all the outbuildings. As they recrossed the lawn, a window that had been dark was lighted and Miss Emily sat in it, the light behind her, and her upright torso motionless as that of an idol. They crept quietly across the lawn and into the shadow of the locusts that lined the street. After a week or two the smell went away.

That was when people had begun to feel really sorry for her. People in our town, remembering how old lady Wyatt, her great-aunt, had gone completely crazy at last, believed that the Griersons held themselves a little too high for what they really were. None of the young men were quite good enough for Miss Emily and such. We had long thought of them as a tableau, Miss Emily a slender figure in white in the background, her father a spraddled silhouette in the foreground, his back to her and clutching a horsewhip, the two of them framed by the backflung front door. So when she got to be thirty and was still single, we were not pleased exactly, but vindicated; even with insanity in the family she wouldn't have turned down all of her chances if they had really materialized.

When her father died, it got about that the house was all that was left to her; and in a way, people were glad. At last they could pity Miss Emily. Being left alone, and a pauper, she had become humanized. Now she too would know the old thrill and the old despair of a penny more or less.

The day after his death all the ladies prepared to call at the house and offer condolence and aid, as is our custom. Miss Emily met them at the door, dressed as usual and with no trace of grief on her face. She told them that her father was not dead. She did that for three days, with the ministers calling on her, and the doctors, trying to persuade her to let them dispose of the body. Just as they were about to resort to law and force, she broke down, and they buried her father quickly.

We did not say she was crazy then. We believed she had to do that. We remembered all the young men her father had driven away, and we knew that with nothing left, she would have to cling to that which had robbed her, as people will.

III

She was sick for a long time. When we saw her again, her hair was cut short, making her look like a girl, with a vague resemblance to those angels in colored church windows—sort of tragic and serene.

The town had just let the contracts for paving the sidewalks, and in the summer after her father's death they began the work. The construction company came with niggers and mules and machinery, and a foreman named Homer Barron, a Yankee—a big, dark, ready man, with a big voice and eyes lighter than his face. The little boys would follow in groups to hear him cuss the niggers, and the niggers singing in time to the rise and fall of picks. Pretty soon he knew everybody in town. Whenever you heard a lot of laughing anywhere about the square, Homer Barron would be in the center of the group. Presently we began to see him and Miss Emily on Sunday afternoons driving in the yellow-wheeled buggy and the matched team of bays from the livery stable.

At first we were glad that Miss Emily would have an interest, because the ladies all said, "Of course a Grierson would not think seriously of a Northerner, a day laborer." But there were still others, older people, who said that even grief could not cause a real lady to forget noblesse oblige—without calling it noblesse oblige. They just said, "Poor Emily. Her kinsfolk should come to her." She had some kin in Alabama; but years ago her father had fallen out with them over the estate of old lady Wyatt, the crazy woman, and there was no communication between the two families. They had not even been represented at the funeral.

And as soon as the old people said, "Poor Emily," the whispering began. "Do you suppose it's really so?" they said to one another. "Of course it is. What else could . . ." This behind their hands; rustling of craned silk and satin behind jalousies closed upon the sun of Sunday afternoon as the thin, swift clop-clop-clop of the matched team passed: "Poor Emily."

She carried her head high enough—even when we believed that she was fallen. It was as if she demanded more than ever the recognition of her dignity as the last Grierson; as if it had wanted that touch of earthiness to reaffirm her imperviousness. Like when she bought the rat poison, the arsenic. That was over a year after they had begun to say "Poor Emily," and while the two female cousins were visiting her.

"I want some poison," she said to the druggist. She was over thirty then, still a slight woman, though thinner than usual, with cold, haughty black eyes in a face the flesh of which was strained across the temples and about the eye-sockets as you imagine, a lighthouse-keeper's face ought to look. "I want some poison," she said.

"Yes, Miss Emily. What kind? For rats and such? I'd recom—"

"I want the best you have. I don't care what kind."

The druggist named several. "They'll kill anything up to an elephant. But what you want is—"

"Arsenic," Miss Emily said. "Is that a good one?"

"Is . . . arsenic? Yes, ma'am. But what you want—"

"I want arsenic."

The druggist looked down at her. She looked back at him, erect, her face like a strained flag. "Why, of course," the druggist said. "If that's what you want. But the law requires you to tell what you are going to use it for."

Miss Emily just stared at him, her head tilted back in order to look him eye for eye, until he looked away and went and got the arsenic and wrapped it up. The Negro delivery boy brought her the package; the druggist didn't come back. When she opened the package at home there was written on the box, under the skull and bones: "For rats."

IV

So the next day we all said, "She will kill herself"; and we said it would be the best thing. When she had first begun to be seen with Homer Barron, we had said, "She will marry him." Then we said, "She will persuade him yet," because Homer himself had remarked—he liked men, and it was known that he drank with the younger men in the Elks' Club—that he was not a marrying man. Later we said, "Poor Emily" behind the jalousies as they passed on Sunday afternoon in the glittering buggy, Miss Emily with her head high and Homer Barron with his hat cocked and a cigar in his teeth, reins and whip in a yellow glove.

Then some of the ladies began to say that it was a disgrace to the town and a bad example to the young people. The men did not want to interfere, but at last the ladies forced the Baptist minister—Miss Emily's people were Episcopal—to call upon her. He would never divulge what happened during that interview, but he refused to go back again. The next Sunday they again drove about the streets, and the following day the minister's wife wrote to Miss Emily's relations in Alabama.

So she had blood-kin under her roof again and we sat back to watch developments. At first nothing happened. Then we were sure that they were to be married. We learned that Miss Emily had been to the jeweler's and ordered a man's toilet set in silver, with the letters H. B. on each piece. Two days later we learned that she had bought a complete outfit of men's clothing, including a nightshirt, and we said, "They are married." We were really glad. We were glad because the two female cousins were even more Grierson than Miss Emily had ever been.

So we were not surprised when Homer Barron—the streets had been finished some time since—was gone. We were a little disappointed that there was not a public blowing-off, but we believed that he had gone on to prepare for Miss Emily's coming, or to give her a chance to get rid of the cousins. (By that time it was a cabal, and we were all Miss Emily's allies to help circumvent the cousins.) Sure enough, after another week they departed. And, as we had expected all along, within three days Homer Barron was back in town. A neighbor saw the Negro man admit him at the kitchen door at dusk one evening.

And that was the last we saw of Homer Barron. And of Miss Emily for some time. The Negro man went in and out with the market basket, but the front door remained closed. Now and then we would see her at a window for a moment, as the men did that night when they sprinkled the lime, but for almost six months she did not appear on the streets. Then we knew that this was to be expected too; as if that quality of her father which had thwarted her woman's life so many times had been too virulent and too furious to die.

When we next saw Miss Emily, she had grown fat and her hair was turning gray. During the next few years it grew grayer and grayer until it attained an even pepper-and salt iron-gray, when it ceased turning. Up to the day of her death at seventy-four it was still that vigorous iron-gray, like the hair of an active man.

From that time on her front door remained closed, save for a period of six or seven years, when she was about forty, during which she gave lessons in china-painting. She fitted up a studio in one of the downstairs rooms, where the daughters and granddaughters of Colonel Sartoris' contemporaries were sent to her with the same regularity and in the same spirit that they were sent to church on Sunday with a twenty-five-cent piece for the collection plate. Meanwhile her taxes had been remitted.

Then the newer generation became the backbone and the spirit of the town, and the painting pupils grew up and fell away and did not send their children to her with boxes of color and tedious brushes and pictures cut from the ladies' magazines. The front door closed upon the last one and remained closed for good. When the town got free postal delivery, Miss Emily alone refused to let them fasten the metal numbers above her door and attach a mailbox to it. She would not listen to them.

Daily, monthly, yearly we watched the Negro grow grayer and more stooped, going in and out with the market basket. Each December we sent her a tax notice, which would be returned by the post office a week later, unclaimed. Now and then we would see her in one of the downstairs windows—she had evidently shut up the top floor of the house—like the carven torso of an idol in a niche, looking or not looking at us, we could never tell which. Thus she passed from generation to generation—dear, inescapable, impervious, tranquil, and perverse.

And so she died. Fell ill in the house filled with dust and shadows, with only a doddering Negro man to wait on her. We did not even know she was sick; we had long since given up trying to get any information from the Negro. He talked to no one, probably not even to her, for his voice had grown harsh and rusty, as if from disuse.

She died in one of the downstairs rooms, in a heavy walnut bed with a curtain, her gray head propped on a pillow yellow and moldy with age and lack of sunlight.

V

The Negro met the first of the ladies at the front door and let them in, with their hushed, sibilant voices and their quick, curious glances, and then he disappeared. He walked right through the house and out the back and was not seen again.

The two female cousins came at once. They held the funeral on the second day, with the town coming to look at Miss Emily beneath a mass of bought flowers, with the crayon face of her father musing profoundly above the bier and the ladies sibilant and macabre; and the very old men—some in their brushed Confederate uniforms—on the porch and the lawn, talking of Miss Emily as if she had been a contemporary of theirs, believing that they had danced with her and courted her perhaps, confusing time with its mathematical progression, as the old do, to whom all the past is not a diminishing road but, instead, a huge meadow which no winter ever quite touches, divided from them now by the narrow bottle-neck of the most recent decade of years.

Already we knew that there was one room in that region above stairs which no one had seen in forty years, and which would have to be forced. They waited until Miss Emily was decently in the ground before they opened it.

The violence of breaking down the door seemed to fill this room with pervading dust. A thin, acrid pall as of the tomb seemed to lie everywhere upon this room decked and furnished as for a bridal: upon the valance curtains of faded rose color, upon the rose-shaded lights, upon the dressing table, upon the delicate array of crystal and the man's toilet things backed with tarnished silver, silver so tarnished that the monogram was obscured. Among them lay a collar and tie, as if they had just been removed, which, lifted, left upon the surface a pale crescent in the dust. Upon a chair hung the suit, carefully folded; beneath it the two mute shoes and the discarded socks.

The man himself lay in the bed.

For a long while we just stood there, looking down at the profound and fleshless grin. The body had apparently once lain in the attitude of an embrace, but now the long sleep that outlasts love, that conquers even the grimace of love, had cuckolded him. What was left of him, rotted beneath what was left of the nightshirt, had become inextricable from the bed in which he lay; and upon him and upon the pillow beside him lay that even coating of the patient and biding dust.

Then we noticed that in the second pillow was the indentation of a head. One of us lifted something from it, and leaning forward, that faint and invisible dust dry and acrid in the nostrils, we saw a long strand of iron-gray hair.

ERNEST HEMINGWAY

A Clean, Well-lighted Place

It was late and every one had left the café except an old man who sat in the shadow the leaves of the tree made against the electric light. In the daytime the street was dusty, but at night the dew settled the dust and the old man liked to sit late because he was deaf and now at night it was quiet and he felt the difference. The two waiters inside the café knew that the old man was a little drunk, and while he was a good client they knew that if he became too drunk he would leave without paying, so they kept watch on him.

"Last week he tried to commit suicide," one waiter said.

"Why?"

"He was in despair."

"What about?"

"Nothing."

"How do you know it was nothing?"

"He has plenty of money."

They sat together at a table that was close against the wall near the door of the café and looked at the terrace where the tables were all empty except where the old man sat in the shadow of the leaves of the tree that moved slightly in the wind. A girl and a soldier went by in the street. The street light shone on the brass number on his collar. The girl wore no head covering and hurried beside him.

"The guard will pick him up," one waiter said.

"What does it matter if he gets what he's after?"

"He had better get off the street now. The guard will get him. They went by five minutes ago."

The old man sitting in the shadow rapped on his saucer with his glass. The younger waiter went over to him.

"What do you want?"

The old man looked at him. "Another brandy," he said.

"You'll be drunk," the waiter said. The old man looked at him. The waiter went away.

"He'll stay all night," he said to his colleague. "I'm sleepy now. I never get into bed before three o'clock. He should have killed himself last week."

The waiter took the brandy bottle and another saucer from the counter inside the café and marched out to the old man's table. He put down the saucer and poured the glass full of brandy.

"You should have killed yourself last week," he said to the deaf man. The old man motioned with his finger. "A little more," he said. The waiter poured on into the glass so that the brandy slopped over and ran down the stem into the top saucer of the pile. "Thank you," the old man said. The waiter took the bottle back inside the café. He sat down at the table with his colleague again.

"He's drunk now," he said.

"He's drunk every night."

"What did he want to kill himself for?"

"How should I know?"

"How did he do it?"

"He hung himself with a rope."

"Who cut him down?"

"His niece."

"Why did they do it?"

"Fear for his soul."

"How much money has he got?"

"He's got plenty."

"He must be eighty years old."

"Anyway I should say he was eighty."

"I wish he would go home. I never get to bed before three o'clock. What kind of hour is that to go to bed?"

"He stays up because he likes it."

"He's lonely. I'm not lonely. I have a wife waiting in bed for me."

"He had a wife once too."

"A wife would be no good to him now."

"You can't tell. He might be better with a wife."

"His niece looks after him."

"I know. You said she cut him down."

"I wouldn't want to be that old. An old man is a nasty thing."

"Not always. This old man is clean. He drinks without spilling. Even now, drunk. Look at him."

"I don't want to look at him. I wish he would go home. He has no regard for those who must work."

The old man looked from his glass across the square, then over at the waiters.

"Another brandy," he said, pointing to his glass. The waiter who was in a hurry came over.

"Finished," he said, speaking with that omission of syntax stupid people employ when talking to drunken people or foreigners. "No more tonight. Close now."

"Another," said the old man.

"No. Finished." The waiter wiped the edge of the table with a towel and shook his head.

The old man stood up, slowly counted the saucers, took a leather coin purse from his pocket and paid for the drinks, leaving half a peseta tip.

The waiter watched him go down the street, a very old man walking unsteadily but with dignity.

"Why didn't you let him stay and drink?" the unhurried waiter asked. They were putting up the shutters. "It is not half-past two."

"I want to go home to bed."

"What is an hour?"

"More to me than to him."

"An hour is the same."

"You talk like an old man yourself. He can buy a bottle and drink at home."

"It's not the same."

"No, it is not," agreed the waiter with a wife. He did not wish to be unjust. He was only in a hurry.

"And you? You have no fear of going home before your usual hour?"

"Are you trying to insult me?"

"No, hombre, only to make a joke."

"No," the waiter who was in a hurry said, rising from pulling down the metal shutters. "I have confidence. I am all confidence."

"You have youth, confidence, and a job," the older waiter said. "You have everything."

"And what do you lack?"

"Everything but work."

"You have everything I have."

"No. I have never had confidence and I am not young."

"Come on. Stop talking nonsense and lock up."

"I am of those who like to stay late at the café," the older waiter said. "With all those who do not want to go to bed. With all those who need a light for the night."

"I want to go home and into bed."

"We are of two different kinds," the older waiter said. He was now dressed to go home. "It is not only a question of youth and confidence although those things are very beautiful. Each night I am reluctant to close up because there may be some one who needs the café."

"Hombre, there are bodegas open all night long."

"You do not understand. This is a clean and pleasant café. It is well-lighted. The light is very good and also, now, there are shadows of the leaves."

"Good night," said the younger waiter.

"Good night," the other said. Turning off the electric light he continued the conversation with himself. It is the light of course but it is necessary that the place be clean and pleasant. You do not want music. Certainly you do not want music. Nor can you stand before a bar with dignity although that is all that is provided for these hours. What did he fear? It was not fear or dread. It was a nothing that he knew too well. It was all a nothing and a man was nothing too. It was only that and light was all it needed and a certain cleanness and order. Some lived in it and never felt it but he knew it all was nada y pues nada y nada y pues nada. Our nada who art in nada, nada be thy name thy kingdom nada thy will be nada in nada as it is in nada. Give us this nada our daily nada and nada us our nada as we nada our nadas and nada us not into nada but deliver us from nada; pues nada. Hail nothing full of nothing, nothing is with thee. He smiled and stood before a bar with a shining steam pressure coffee machine.

"What's yours?" asked the barman.

"Nada."

"Otro loco mas," said the barman and turned away.

"A little cup," said the waiter.

The barman poured it for him.

"The light is very bright and pleasant but the bar is unpolished," the waiter said.

The barman looked at him but did not answer. It was too late at night for conversation.

"You want another copita?" the barman asked.

"No, thank you," said the waiter and went out. He disliked bars and bodegas. A clean, well-lighted café was a very different thing. Now, without thinking further, he would go home to his room. He would lie in the bed and finally, with daylight, he would go to sleep. After all, he said to himself, it is probably only insomnia. Many must have it.

FLANNERY O'CONNOR

Good Country People

Besides the neutral expression that she wore when she was alone, Mrs. Freeman had two others, forward and reverse, that she used for all her human dealings. Her forward expression was steady and driving like the advance of a heavy truck. Her eyes never swerved to left or right but turned as the story turned as if they followed a yellow line down the center of it. She seldom used the other expression because it was not often necessary for her to retract a statement, but when she did, her face came to a complete stop, there was an almost imperceptible movement of her black eyes, during which they seemed to be receding, and then the observer would see that Mrs. Freeman, though she might stand there as real as several grain sacks thrown on top of each other, was no longer there in spirit. As for getting anything across to her when this was the case, Mrs. Hopewell had given it up. She might talk her head off. Mrs. Freeman could never be brought to admit herself wrong on any point. She would stand there and if she could be brought to say anything, it was something like, "Well, I wouldn't of said it was and I wouldn't of said it wasn't," or letting her gaze range over the top kitchen shelf where there was an assortment of dusty bottles, she might remark, "I see you ain't ate many of them figs you put up last summer."

They carried on their most important business in the kitchen at breakfast. Every morning Mrs. Hopewell got up at seven o'clock and lit her gas heater and Joy's. Joy was her daughter, a large blonde girl who had an artificial leg. Mrs. Hopewell thought of her as a child though she was thirty-two years old and highly educated. Joy would get up while her mother was eating and lumber into the bathroom and slam the door, and before long, Mrs. Freeman would arrive at the back door. Joy would hear her mother call, "Come on in," and then they would talk for a while in low voices that were indistinguishable in the bathroom. By the time Joy came in, they had usually finished the weather report and were on one or the other of Mrs. Freeman's daughters, Glynese or Carramae. Joy called them Glycerin and Caramel. Glynese, a redhead, was eighteen and had many admirers; Carramae, a blonde, was only fifteen but already married and pregnant. She could not keep anything on her stomach. Every morning Mrs. Freeman told Mrs. Hopewell how many times she had vomited since the last report.

Mrs. Hopewell liked to tell people that Glynese and Carramae were two of the finest girls she knew and that Mrs. Freeman was a *lady* and that she was never ashamed to take her anywhere or introduce her to anybody they might meet. Then she would tell how she had happened to hire the

Freemans in the first place and how they were a godsend to her and how she had had them four years. The reason for her keeping them so long was that they were not trash. They were good country people. She had telephoned the man whose name they had given as a reference and he had told her that Mr. Freeman was a good farmer but that his wife was the nosiest woman ever to walk the earth. "She's got to be into everything," the man said. "If she don't get there before the dust settles, you can bet she's dead, that's all. She'll want to know all your business. I can stand him real good," he had said, "but me nor my wife neither could have stood that woman one more minute on this place." That had put Mrs. Hopewell off for a few days.

She had hired them in the end because there were no other applicants but she had made up her mind beforehand exactly how she would handle the woman. Since she was the type who had to be into everything, then, Mrs. Hopewell had decided, she would not only let her be into everything, she would *see to it* that she was into everything—she would give her the responsibility of everything, she would put her in charge. Mrs. Hopewell had no bad qualities of her own but she was able to use other people's in such a constructive way that she never felt the lack. She had hired the Freemans and she had kept them four years.

Nothing is perfect. This was one of Mrs. Hopewell's favorite sayings. Another was: that is life! And still another, the most important, was: well, other people have their opinions too. She would make these statements, usually at the table, in a tone of gentle insistence as if no one held them but her, and the large hulking Joy, whose constant outrage had obliterated every expression from her face, would stare just a little to the side of her, her eyes icy blue, with the look of someone who has achieved blindness by an act of will and means to keep it.

When Mrs. Hopewell said to Mrs. Freeman that life was like that, Mrs. Freeman would say, "I always said so myself." Nothing had been arrived at by anyone that had not first been arrived at by her. She was quicker than Mr. Freeman. When Mrs. Hopewell said to her after they had been on the place a while, "You know, you're the wheel behind the wheel," and winked, Mrs. Freeman had said, "I know it. I've always been quick. It's some that are quicker than others."

"Everybody is different," Mrs. Hopewell said.

"Yes, most people is," Mrs. Freeman said.

"It takes all kinds to make the world."

"I always said it did myself."

The girl was used to this kind of dialogue for breakfast and more of it for dinner; sometimes they had it for supper too. When they had no guests they ate in the kitchen because that was easier. Mrs. Freeman always managed to arrive at some point during the meal and to watch them finish it. She would stand in the doorway if it were summer but in the winter she would stand with one elbow on top of the refrigerator and look down on them, or she would stand by the gas heater, lifting the back of her skirt slightly. Occasionally she would stand against the wall and roll her head from side to side. At no time was she in any hurry to leave. All this was very trying on Mrs. Hopewell but she was a woman of great patience. She realized that nothing is perfect and that in the Freemans she had good country people and that if, in this day and age, you get good country people, you had better hang onto them.

She had had plenty of experience with trash. Before the Freemans she had averaged one tenant family a year. The wives of these farmers were not the kind you would want to be around you for very long. Mrs. Hopewell, who had divorced her husband long ago, needed someone to walk over the fields with her; and when Joy had to be impressed for these services, her remarks were usually so ugly and her face so glum that Mrs. Hopewell would say, "If you can't come pleasantly, I don't want you at all," to which the girl, standing square and rigid-shouldered with her neck thrust slightly forward, would reply, "If you want me, here I am—LIKE I AM."

Mrs. Hopewell excused this attitude because of the leg (which had been shot off in a hunting accident when Joy was ten). It was hard for Mrs. Hopewell to realize that her child was thirty-two now and that for more than twenty years she had had only one leg. She thought of her still as a child because it tore her heart to think instead of the poor stout girl in her thirties who had never danced a step or had any *normal* good times. Her name was really Joy but as soon as she was twenty-one and away from home, she had had it legally changed. Mrs. Hopewell was certain that she had thought and thought until she had hit upon the ugliest name in any language. Then she had gone and had the beautiful name, Joy, changed without telling her mother until after she had done it. Her legal name was Hulga.

When Mrs. Hopewell thought the name, Hulga, she thought of the broad blank hull of a battleship. She would not use it. She continued to call her Joy to which the girl responded but in a purely mechanical way.

Hulga had learned to tolerate Mrs. Freeman who saved her from taking walks with her mother. Even Glynese and Carramae were useful when they occupied attention that might otherwise have been directed at her. At first she had thought she could not stand Mrs. Freeman for she had found that it was not possible to be rude to her. Mrs. Freeman would take on strange resentments and for days together she would be sullen but the source of her displeasure was always obscure; a direct attack, a positive leer, blatant ugliness to her face—these never touched her. And without warning one day, she began calling her Hulga.

She did not call her that in front of Mrs. Hopewell who would have been incensed but when she and the girl happened to be out of the house together, she would say something and add the name Hulga to the end of it, and the big spectacled Joy-Hulga would scowl and redden as if her privacy had been intruded upon. She considered the name her personal affair. She had arrived at it first purely on the basis of its ugly sound and then the full genius of its fitness had struck her. She had a vision of the name working like the ugly sweating Vulcan who stayed in the furnace and to whom, presumably, the goddess had to come when called. She saw it as the name of her highest creative act. One of her major triumphs was that her mother had not been able to turn her dust into Joy, but the greater one was that she had been able to turn it herself into Hulga. However, Mrs. Freeman's relish for using the name only irritated her. It was as if Mrs. Freeman's beady steel-pointed eyes had penetrated far enough behind her face to reach some secret fact. Something about her seemed to fascinate Mrs. Freeman and then one day Hulga realized that it was the artificial leg. Mrs. Freeman had a special fondness for the details of secret infections, hidden deformities, assaults upon children. Of diseases, she preferred the lingering or incurable. Hulga had heard Mrs. Hopewell give her the details of the hunting accident, how the leg had been literally blasted off, how she had never lost consciousness. Mrs. Freeman could listen to it any time as if it had happened an hour ago.

When Hulga stumped into the kitchen in the morning (she could walk without making the awful noise but she made it—Mrs. Hopewell was certain—because it was ugly-sounding), she glanced at them and did not speak. Mrs. Hopewell would be in her red kimono with her hair tied around her head in rags. She would be sitting at the table, finishing her breakfast and Mrs. Freeman would be hanging by her elbow outward from the refrigerator, looking down at the table. Hulga always put her eggs on the stove to boil and then stood over them with her arms folded, and Mrs. Hopewell would look at her—a kind of indirect gaze divided between her and Mrs. Freeman—and would think that if she would only keep herself up a little, she wouldn't be so bad looking. There was nothing wrong with her face that a pleasant expression wouldn't help. Mrs. Hopewell said that people who looked on the bright side of things would be beautiful even if they were not.

Whenever she looked at Joy this way, she could not help but feel that it would have been better if the child had not taken the Ph.D. It had certainly not brought her out any and now that she had it, there was no more excuse for her to go to school again. Mrs. Hopewell thought it was nice for girls to go to school to have a good time but Joy had "gone through." Anyhow, she would not have been strong enough to go again. The doctors had told Mrs. Hopewell that with the best of care, Joy might see forty-five. She had a weak heart. Joy had made it plain that if it had not been for this condition, she would be far from these red hills and good country people. She would be in a university lecturing to people who knew what she was talking about. And Mrs. Hopewell could very well picture her there, looking like a scarecrow and lecturing to more of the same. Here she went about all day in a six-year-old skirt and a yellow sweat shirt with a faded cowboy on a horse embossed on it. She thought this was funny; Mrs. Hopewell thought it was idiotic and showed simply that she was still a child. She was brilliant but she didn't have a grain of sense. It seemed to Mrs. Hopewell that every year she grew less like other people and more like herself—bloated, rude, and squint-eyed. And she said such strange things! To her own mother she had said—without warning, without excuse, standing up in the middle of a meal with her face purple and her mouth half full—"Women! do you ever look inside? Do you ever look inside and see what you are *not*? God!" she had cried sinking down again and staring at her plate, "Malebranche was right: we are not our own light. We are not our own light!" Mrs. Hopewell had no idea to this day what brought that on. She had only made the remark, hoping Joy would take it in, that a smile never hurt anyone.

The girl had taken the Ph.D. in philosophy and this left Mrs. Hopewell at a complete loss. You could say, "My daughter is a nurse," or "My daughter is a school teacher," or even, "My daughter is a chemical engineer." You could not say, "My daughter is a philosopher." That was something that had ended with the Greeks and Romans. All day Joy sat on her neck in a deep chair, reading. Sometimes she went for walks but she didn't like dogs or cats or birds or flowers or nature or nice young men. She looked at nice young men as if she could smell their stupidity.

One day Mrs. Hopewell had picked up one of the books the girl had just put down and opening it at random, she read, "Science on the other hand, has to assert its soberness and seriousness afresh and declare that it is concerned solely with what-is. Nothing—how can it be for science anything but a horror and a phantasm? If science is right, then one thing stands firm: science wishes to know nothing of nothing. Such is after all the strictly scientific approach to Nothing. We know it by wishing to know nothing of Nothing." These words had been underlined with a blue pencil and they worked on Mrs. Hopewell like some evil incantation in gibberish. She shut the book quickly and went out of the room as if she were having a chill.

This morning when the girl came in, Mrs. Freeman was on Carramae. "She thrown up four times after supper," she said, "and was up twict in the night after three o'clock. Yesterday she didn't do nothing but ramble in the bureau drawer. All she did. Stand up there and see what she could run up on."

"She's got to eat," Mrs. Hopewell muttered, sipping her coffee, while she watched Joy's back at the stove. She was wondering what the child had said to the Bible salesman. She could not imagine what kind of a conversation she could possibly have had with him.

He was a tall gaunt hatless youth who had called yesterday to sell them a Bible. He had appeared at the door, carrying a large black suitcase that weighted him so heavily on one side that he had to brace himself against the door facing. He seemed on the point of collapse but he said in a cheerful voice, "Good morning, Mrs. Cedars!" and set the suitcase down on the mat. He was not a bad-looking young man though he had on a bright blue suit and yellow socks that were not pulled up far enough. He had prominent face bones and a streak of sticky-looking brown hair falling across his forehead.

"I'm Mrs. Hopewell," she said.

"Oh!" he said, pretending to look puzzled but with his eyes sparkling, "I saw it said 'The Cedars,' on the mailbox so I thought you was Mrs. Cedars!" and he burst out in a pleasant laugh. He picked up the satchel and under cover of a pant, he fell forward into her hall. It was rather as if the suitcase had moved first, jerking him after it. "Mrs. Hopewell!" he said and grabbed her hand. "I hope you are well!" and he laughed again and then all at once his face sobered completely. He paused and gave her a straight earnest look and said, "Lady, I've come to speak of serious things."

"Well, come in," she muttered, none too pleased because her dinner was almost ready. He came into the parlor and sat down on the edge of a straight chair and put the suitcase between his feet and glanced around the room as if he were sizing her up by it. Her silver gleamed on the two sideboards; she decided he had never been in a room as elegant as this.

"Mrs. Hopewell," he began, using her name in a way that sounded almost intimate, "I know you believe in Chrustian service."

"Well yes," she murmured.

"I know," he said and paused, looking very wise with his head cocked on one side, "that you're a good woman. Friends have told me."

Mrs. Hopewell never liked to be taken for a fool. "What are you selling?" she asked.

"Bibles," the young man said and his eye raced around the room before he added, "I see you have no family Bible in your parlor, I see that is the one lack you got!"

Mrs. Hopewell could not say, "My daughter is an atheist and won't let me keep the Bible in the parlor." She said, stiffening slightly, "I keep my Bible by my bedside." This was not the truth. It was in the attic somewhere.

"Lady," he said, "the word of God ought to be in the parlor."

"Well, I think that's a matter of taste," she began. "I think . . ."

"Lady," he said, "for a Chrustian, the word of God ought to be in every room in the house besides in his heart. I know you're a Chrustian because I can see it in every line of your face."

She stood up and said, "Well, young man, I don't want to buy a Bible and I smell my dinner burning."

He didn't get up. He began to twist his hands and looking down at them, he said softly, "Well lady, I'll tell you the truth—not many people want to buy one nowadays and besides, I know I'm real simple. I don't know how to say a thing but to say it. I'm just a country boy." He glanced up into her unfriendly face. "People like you don't like to fool with country people like me!"

"Why!" she cried, "good country people are the salt of the earth! Besides, we all have different ways of doing, it takes all kinds to make the world go 'round. That's life!"

"You said a mouthful," he said.

"Why, I think there aren't enough good country people in the world!" she said, stirred. "I think that's what's wrong with it!"

His face had brightened. "I didn't inraduce myself," he said. "I'm Manley Pointer from out in the country around Willohobie, not even from a place, just from near a place."

"You wait a minute," she said. "I have to see about my dinner." She went out to the kitchen and found Joy standing near the door where she had been listening.

"Get rid of the salt of the earth," she said, "and let's eat."

Mrs. Hopewell gave her a pained look and turned the heat down under the vegetables. "I can't be rude to anybody," she murmured and went back into the parlor.

He had opened the suitcase and was sitting with a Bible on each knee.

"You might as well put those up," she told him. "I don't want one."

"I appreciate your honesty," he said. "You don't see any more real honest people unless you go way out in the country."

"I know," she said, "real genuine folks!" Through the crack in the door she heard a groan.

"I guess a lot of boys come telling you they're working their way through college," he said, "but I'm not going to tell you that. Somehow," he said, "I don't want to go to college. I want to devote my life to Chrustian service. See," he said, lowering his voice, "I got this heart condition. I may not live long. When you know it's something wrong with you and you may not live long, well then, lady . . ." He paused, with his mouth open, and stared at her.

He and Joy had the same condition! She knew that her eyes were filling with tears but she collected herself quickly and murmured, "Won't you stay for dinner? We'd love to have you!" and was sorry the instant she heard herself say it.

"Yes mam," he said in an abashed voice, "I would sher love to do that!"

Joy had given him one look on being introduced to him and then throughout the meal had not glanced at him again. He had addressed several remarks to her, which she had pretended not to hear. Mrs. Hopewell could not understand deliberate rudeness, although she lived with it, and she felt she had always to overflow with hospitality to make up for Joy's lack of courtesy. She urged him to talk about himself and he did. He said he was the seventh child of twelve and that his father had been crushed under a tree when he himself was eight year old. He had been crushed very badly, in fact, almost cut in two and was practically not recognizable. His mother had got along the best she could by hard working and she had always seen that her children went to Sunday School and that they read the Bible every evening. He was now nineteen years old and he had been selling Bibles for four months. In that time he had sold seventy-seven Bibles and had the promise of two more sales. He wanted to become a missionary because he thought that was the way you could do most for people. "He who losest his life shall find it," he said simply and he was so sincere, so genuine and earnest that Mrs. Hopewell would not for the world have smiled. He prevented his peas from sliding onto the table by blocking them with a piece of bread which he later cleaned his plate with. She could see Joy observing sidewise how he handled his knife and fork and she saw too that every few minutes, the boy would dart a keen appraising glance at the girl as if he were trying to attract her attention.

After dinner Joy cleared the dishes off the table and disappeared and Mrs. Hopewell was left to talk with him. He told her again about his childhood and his father's accident and about various things that had happened to him. Every five minutes or so she would stifle a yawn. He sat for two hours until finally she told him she must go because she had an appointment in town. He packed his Bibles and thanked her and prepared to leave, but in the doorway he stopped and wrung her hand and said that not on any of his trips had he met a lady as nice as her and he asked her if he could come again. She had said she would always be happy to see him.

Joy had been standing in the road, apparently looking at something in the distance, when he came down the steps toward her, bent to the side with his heavy valise. He stopped where she was standing and confronted her directly. Mrs. Hopewell could not hear what he said but she trembled to think what Joy would say to him. She could see that after a minute Joy said something and that then the boy began to speak again, making an excited gesture with his free hand. After a minute Joy said something else at which the boy began to speak once more. Then to her amazement, Mrs. Hopewell saw the two of them walk off together, toward the gate. Joy had walked all the way to the gate with him and Mrs. Hopewell could not imagine what they had said to each other, and she had not yet dared to ask.

Mrs. Freeman was insisting upon her attention. She had moved from the refrigerator to the heater so that Mrs. Hopewell had to turn and face her in order to seem to be listening. "Glynese gone out with Harvey Hill again last night," she said. "She had this sty."

"Hill," Mrs. Hopewell said absently, "is that the one who works in the garage?"

"Nome, he's the one that goes to chiropracter school," Mrs. Freeman said. "She had this sty. Been had it two days. So she says when he brought her in the other night he says, 'Lemme get rid of that sty for you,' and she says, 'How?' and he says, 'You just lay yourself down acrost the seat of that car and I'll show you.' So she done it and he popped her neck. Kept on a-popping it several times until she made him quit. This morning," Mrs. Freeman said, "she ain't got no sty. She ain't got no traces of a sty."

"I never heard of that before," Mrs. Hopewell said.

"He ast her to marry him before the Ordinary," Mrs. Freeman went on, "and she told him she wasn't going to be married in no office."

"Well, Glynese is a fine girl," Mrs. Hopewell said. "Glynese and Carramae are both fine girls."

"Carramae said when her and Lyman was married Lyman said it sure felt sacred to him. She said he said he wouldn't take five hundred dollars for being married by a preacher."

"How much would he take?" the girl asked from the stove.

"He said he wouldn't take five hundred dollars," Mrs. Freeman repeated.

"Well we all have work to do," Mrs. Hopewell said.

"Lyman said it just felt sacred to him," Mrs. Freeman said. "The doctor wants Carramae to eat prunes. Says instead of medicine. Says them cramps is coming from pressure. You know where I think it is?"

"She'll be better in a few weeks," Mrs. Hopewell said.

"In the tube," Mrs. Freeman said. "Else she wouldn't be as sick as she is."

Hulga had cracked her two eggs into a saucer and was bringing them to the table along with a cup of coffee that she had filled too full. She sat down carefully and began to eat, meaning to keep Mrs. Freeman there by questions if for any reason she showed an inclination to leave. She could perceive her mother's eye on her. The first roundabout question would be about the Bible salesman and she did not wish to bring it on. "How did he pop her neck?" she asked.

Mrs. Freeman went into a description of how he had popped her neck. She said he owned a '55 Mercury but that Glynese said she would rather marry a man with only a '36 Plymouth who would be married by a preacher. The girl asked what if he had a '32 Plymouth and Mrs. Freeman said what Glynese had said was a '36 Plymouth.

Mrs. Hopewell said there were not many girls with Glynese's common sense. She said what she admired in those girls was their common sense. She said that reminded her that they had had a nice visitor yesterday, a young man selling Bibles. "Lord," she said, "he bored me to death but he was so sincere and genuine I couldn't be rude to him. He was just good country people, you know," she said, "—just the salt of the earth."

"I seen him walk up," Mrs. Freeman said, "and then later—I seen him walk off," and Hulga could feel the slight shift in her voice, the slight insinuation, that he had not walked off alone, had he? Her face remained expressionless but the color rose into her neck and she seemed to swallow it down with the next spoonful of egg. Mrs. Freeman was looking at her as if they had a secret together.

"Well, it takes all kinds of people to make the world go 'round," Mrs. Hopewell said. "It's very good we aren't all alike."

"Some people are more alike than others," Mrs. Freeman said.

Hulga got up and stumped, with about twice the noise that was necessary, into her room and locked the door. She was to meet the Bible salesman at ten o'clock at the gate. She had thought about it half the night. She had started thinking of it as a great joke and then she had begun to see profound implications in it. She had lain in bed imagining dialogues for them that were insane on the surface but that reached below to depths that no Bible salesman would be aware of. Their conversation yesterday had been of this kind.

He had stopped in front of her and had simply stood there. His face was bony and sweaty and bright, with a little pointed nose in the center of it, and his look was different from what it had been at the dinner table. He was gazing at her with open curiosity, with fascination, like a child watching a new fantastic animal at the zoo, and he was breathing as if he had run a great distance to reach her. His gaze seemed somehow familiar but she could not think where she had been regarded with it before. For almost a minute he didn't say anything. Then on what seemed an insuck of breath, he whispered, "You ever ate a chicken that was two days old?"

The girl looked at him stonily. He might have just put this question up for consideration at the meeting of a philosophical association. "Yes," she presently replied as if she had considered it from all angles.

"It must have been mighty small!" he said triumphantly and shook all over with little nervous giggles, getting very red in the face, and subsiding finally into his gaze of complete admiration, while the girl's expression remained exactly the same.

"How old are you?" he asked softly.

She waited some time before she answered. Then in a flat voice she said, "Seventeen."

His smiles came in succession like waves breaking on the surface of a little lake. "I see you got a wooden leg," he said. "I think you're real brave. I think you're real sweet."

The girl stood blank and solid and silent.

"Walk to the gate with me," he said. "You're a brave sweet little thing and I liked you the minute I seen you walk in the door."

Hulga began to move forward.

"What's your name?" he asked, smiling down on the top of her head.

"Hulga," she said.

"Hulga," he murmured, "Hulga. Hulga. I never heard of anybody name Hulga before. You're shy, aren't you, Hulga?" he asked.

She nodded, watching his large red hand on the handle of the giant valise.

"I like girls that wear glasses," he said. "I think a lot. I'm not like these people that a serious thought don't ever enter their heads. It's because I may die."

"I may die too," she said suddenly and looked up at him. His eyes were very small and brown, glittering feverishly.

"Listen," he said, "don't you think some people was meant to meet on account of what all they got in common and all? Like they both think serious thoughts and all?" He shifted the valise to his other hand so that the hand nearest her was free. He caught hold of her elbow and shook it a little. "I don't work on Saturday," he said. "I like to walk in the woods and see what Mother Nature is wearing. O'er the hills and far away. Pic-nics and things. Couldn't we go on a pic-nic tomorrow? Say yes, Hulga," he said and gave her a dying look as if he felt his insides about to drop out of him. He had even seemed to sway slightly toward her.

During the night she had imagined that she seduced him. She imagined that the two of them walked on the place until they came to the storage barn beyond the two back fields and there, she imagined, that things came to such a pass that she very easily seduced him and that then, of course, she had to reckon with his remorse. True genius can get an idea across even to an inferior mind. She imagined that she took his remorse in hand and changed it into a deeper understanding of life. She took all his shame away and turned it into something useful.

She set off for the gate at exactly ten o'clock, escaping without drawing Mrs. Hopewell's attention. She didn't take anything to eat, forgetting that food is usually taken on a picnic. She wore a pair of slacks and a dirty white shirt, and as an afterthought, she had put some Vapex on the collar of it since she did not own any perfume. When she reached the gate no one was there.

She looked up and down the empty highway and had the furious feeling that she had been tricked, that he had only meant to make her walk to the gate after the idea of him. Then suddenly he stood up, very tall, from behind a bush on the opposite embankment. Smiling, he lifted his hat which was new and wide-brimmed. He had not worn it yesterday and she wondered if he had bought it for the occasion. It was toast-colored with a red and white band around it and was slightly too large for him. He stepped from behind the bush still carrying the black valise. He had on the same suit and the same yellow socks sucked down in his shoes from walking. He crossed the highway and said, "I knew you'd come!"

The girl wondered acidly how he had known this. She pointed to the valise and asked, "Why did you bring your Bibles?"

He took her elbow, smiling down on her as if he could not stop. "You can never tell when you'll need the word of God, Hulga," he said. She had a moment in which she doubted that this was actually happening and then they began to climb the embankment. They went down into the pasture toward the words. The boy walked lightly by her side, bouncing on his toes. The valise did not seem to be heavy today; he even swung it. They crossed half the pasture without saying anything and then, putting his hand easily on the small of her back, he asked softly, "Where does your wooden leg join on?"

She turned an ugly red and glared at him and for an instant the boy looked abashed. "I didn't mean you no harm," he said. "I only meant you're so brave and all. I guess God takes care of you."

"No," she said, looking forward and walking fast, "I don't even believe in God."

At this he stopped and whistled. "No!" he exclaimed as if he were too astonished to say anything else.

She walked on and in a second he was bouncing at her side, fanning with his hat. "That's very unusual for a girl," he remarked, watching her out of the corner of his eye. When they reached the edge of the wood, he put his hand on her back again and drew her against him without a word and kissed her heavily.

The kiss, which had more pressure than feeling behind it, produced that extra surge of adrenalin in the girl that enables one to carry a packed trunk out of a burning house, but in her, the power went at once to the brain. Even before he released her, her mind, clear and detached and ironic anyway, was regarding him from a great distance, with amusement but with pity. She had never been kissed before and she was pleased to discover that it was an unexceptional experience and all a matter of the mind's control. Some people might enjoy drain water if they were told it was vodka. When the boy, looking expectant but uncertain, pushed her gently away, she turned and walked on, saying nothing as if such business, for her, were common enough.

He came along panting at her side, trying to help her when he saw a root that she might trip over. He caught and held back the long swaying blades of thorn vine until she had passed beyond them. She led the way and he came breathing heavily behind her. Then they came out on a sunlit hillside, sloping softly into another one a little smaller. Beyond, they could see the rusted top of the old barn where the extra hay was stored.

The hill was sprinkled with small pink weeds. "Then you ain't saved?" he asked suddenly, stopping.

The girl smiled. It was the first time she had smiled at him at all. "In my economy," she said, "I'm saved and you are damned but I told you I didn't believe in God."

Nothing seemed to destroy the boy's look of admiration. He gazed at her now as if the fantastic animal at the zoo had put its paw through the bars and given him a loving poke. She thought he looked as if he wanted to kiss her again and she walked on before he had the chance.

"Ain't there somewheres we can sit down sometime?" he murmured, his voice softening toward the end of the sentence.

"In that barn," she said.

They made for it rapidly as if it might slide away like a train. It was a large two-story barn, cool and dark inside. The boy pointed up the ladder that led into the loft and said, "It's too bad we can't go up there."

"Why can't we?" she asked.

"Yer leg," he said reverently.

The girl gave him a contemptuous look and putting both hands on the ladder, she climbed it while he stood below, apparently awestruck. She pulled herself expertly through the opening and then looked down at him and said, "Well, come on if you're coming," and he began to climb the ladder, awkwardly bringing the suitcase with him.

"We won't need the Bible," she observed.

"You never can tell," he said, panting. After he had got into the loft, he was a few seconds catching his breath. She had sat down in a pile of straw. A wide sheath of sunlight, filled with dust particles, slanted over her. She lay back against a bale, her face turned away, looking out the front opening of the barn where hay was thrown from a wagon into the loft. The two pink-speckled hillsides lay back against a dark ridge of woods. The sky was cloudless and cold blue. The boy dropped down by her side and put one arm under her and the other over her and began methodically kissing her face, making little noises like a fish. He did not remove his hat but it was pushed far enough back not to interfere. When her glasses got in his way, he took them off of her and slipped them into his pocket.

The girl at first did not return any of the kisses but presently she began to and after she had put several on his cheek, she reached his lips and remained there, kissing him again and again as if she were trying to draw all the breath out of him. His breath was clear and sweet like a child's and the kisses were sticky like a child's. He mumbled about loving her and about knowing when he first seen her that he loved her, but the mumbling was like the sleepy fretting of a child being put to sleep by his mother. Her mind, throughout this, never stopped or lost itself for a second to her feelings. "You ain't said you loved me none," he whispered finally, pulling back from her. "You got to say that."

She looked away from him off into the hollow sky and then down at a black ridge and then down farther into what appeared to be two green swelling lakes. She didn't realize he had taken her glasses but this landscape could not seem exceptional to her for she seldom paid close attention to her surroundings.

"You got to say it," he repeated. "You got to say you love me."

She was always careful how she committed herself. "In a sense," she began, "if you use the word loosely, you might say that. But it's not a word I use. I don't have illusions. I'm one of those people who see *through* to nothing."

The boy was frowning. "You got to say it. I said it and you got to say it," he said.

The girl looked at him almost tenderly. "You poor baby," she murmured. "It's just as well you don't understand," and she pulled him by the neck, face-down, against her. "We are all damned," she said, "but some of us have taken off our blindfolds and see that there's nothing to see. It's a kind of salvation."

The boy's astonished eyes looked blankly through the ends of her hair. "Okay," he almost whined, "but do you love me or don'tcher?"

"Yes," she said and added, "in a sense. But I must tell you something. There mustn't be anything dishonest between us." She lifted his head and looked him in the eye. "I am thirty years old," she said. "I have a number of degrees."

The boy's look was irritated but dogged. "I don't care," he said. "I don't care a thing about what all you done. I just want to know if you love me or don'tcher?" and he caught her to him and wildly planted her face with kisses until she said, "Yes, yes."

"Okay then," he said, letting her go. "Prove it."

She smiled, looking dreamily out on the shifty landscape. She had seduced him without even making up her mind to try. "How?" she asked, feeling that he should be delayed a little.

He leaned over and put his lips to her ear. "Show me where your wooden leg joins on," he whispered.

The girl uttered a sharp little cry and her face instantly drained of color. The obscenity of the suggestion was not what shocked her. As a child she had sometimes been subject to feelings of shame but education had removed the last traces of that as a good surgeon scrapes for cancer; she would no more have felt it over what he was asking than she would have believed in his Bible. But she was as sensitive about the artificial leg as a peacock about his tail. No one ever touched it but her. She took care of it as someone else would his soul, in private and almost with her own eyes turned away, "No," she said.

"I known it," he muttered, sitting up. "You're just playing me for a sucker."

"Oh no no!" she cried. "It joins on at the knee. Only at the knee. Why do you want to see it?"

The boy gave her a long penetrating look. "Because," he said, "it's what makes you different. You ain't like anybody else."

She sat staring at him. There was nothing about her face or her round freezing-blue eyes to indicate that this had moved her; but she felt as if her heart had stopped and left her mind to pump her blood. She decided that for the first time in her life she was face to face with real innocence. This boy, with an instinct that came from beyond wisdom, had touched the truth about her. When after a minute, she said in a hoarse high voice, "All right," it was like surrendering to him completely. It was like losing her own life and finding it again, miraculously, in his.

Very gently he began to roll the slack leg up. The artificial limb, in a white sock and brown flat shoe, was bound in a heavy material like canvas and ended in an ugly jointure where it was attached to the stump. The boy's face and his voice were entirely reverent as he uncovered it and said, "Now show me how to take it off and on."

She took it off for him and put it back on again and then he took it off himself, handling it as tenderly as if it were a real one. "See!" he said with a delighted child's face. "Now I can do it myself!"

"Put it back on," she said. She was thinking that she would run away with him and that every night he would take the leg off and every morning put it back on again. "Put it back on," she said.

"Not yet," he murmured, setting it on its foot out of her reach. "Leave it off for a while. You got me instead."

She gave a little cry of alarm but he pushed her down and began to kiss her again. Without the leg she felt entirely dependent on him. Her brain seemed to have stopped thinking altogether and to be about some other function that it was not very good at. Different expressions raced back and forth over her face. Every now and then the boy, his eyes like two steel spikes, would glance behind him where the leg stood. Finally she pushed him off and said, "Put it back on me now."

"Wait," he said. He leaned the other way and pulled the valise toward him and opened it. It had a pale blue spotted lining and there were only two Bibles in it. He took one of these out and opened the cover of it. It was hollow and contained a pocket flask of whiskey, a pack of cards, and a small blue box with printing on it. He laid these out in front of her one at a time in an evenly-spaced row, like one presenting offerings at the shrine of a goddess. He put the blue box in her hand. THIS PRODUCT TO BE USED ONLY FOR THE PREVENTION OF DISEASE, she read, and dropped it. The boy was unscrewing the top of the flask. He stopped and pointed, with a smile, to the deck of cards. It was not on ordinary deck but one with an obscene picture on the back of each card. "Take a swig," he said, offering her the bottle first. He held it in front of her, but like one mesmerized, she did not move.

Her voice when she spoke had an almost pleading sound. "Aren't you," she murmured, "aren't you just good country people?"

The boy cocked his head. He looked as if he were just beginning to understand that she might be trying to insult him. "Yeah," he said, curling his lip slightly, "but it ain't held me back none. I'm as good as you any day in the week."

"Give me my leg," she said.

He pushed it farther away with his foot. "Come on now, let's begin to have us a good time," he said coaxingly. "We ain't got to know one another good yet."

"Give me my leg!" she screamed and tried to lunge for it but he pushed her down easily.

"What's the matter with you all of a sudden?" he asked, frowning as he screwed the top on the flask and put it quickly back inside the Bible. "You just a while ago said you didn't believe in nothing. I thought you was some girl!"

Her face was almost purple. "You're a Christian!" she hissed. "You're a fine Christian! You're just like them all—say one thing and do another. You're a perfect Christian, you're . . ."

The boy's mouth was set angrily. "I hope you don't think," he said in a lofty indignant tone, "that I believe in that crap! I may sell Bibles but I know which end is up and I wasn't born yesterday and I know where I'm going!"

"Give me my leg!" she sceeched. He jumped up so quickly that she barely saw him sweep the cards and the blue box back into the Bible and throw the Bible into the valise. She saw him grab the leg and then she saw it for an instant slanted forlornly across the inside of the suitcase with a Bible at either side of its opposite ends. He slammed the lid shut and snatched up the valise and swung it down the hole and then stepped through himself.

When all of him had passed but his head, he turned and regarded her with a look that no longer had any admiration in it. "I've gotten a lot of interesting things," he said. "One time I got a woman's glass eye this way. And you needn't to think you'll catch me because Pointer ain't really my name. I use a different name at every house I call at and don't stay nowhere long. And I'll tell you another thing, Hulga," he said, using the name as if he didn't think much of it, "you ain't so smart. I been believing in nothing ever since I was born!" and then the toast-colored hat disappeared down the hole and the girl was left, sitting on the straw in the dusty sunlight. When she turned her churning face toward the opening, she saw his blue figure struggling successfully over the green speckled lake.

Mrs. Hopewell and Mrs. Freeman, who were in the back pasture, digging up onions, saw him emerge a little later from the woods and head across the meadow toward the highway. "Why, that looks like that nice dull young man that tried to sell me a Bible yesterday," Mrs. Hopewell said, squinting. "He must have been selling them to the Negroes back in there. He was so simple," she said, "but I guess the world would be better off if we were all that simple."

Mrs. Freeman's gaze drove forward and just touched him before he disappeared under the hill. Then she returned her attention to the evil-smelling onion shoot she was lifting from the ground, "Some can't be that simple," she said. "I know I never could."

DORIS LESSING

The Habit of Loving

In 1947 George wrote again to Myra, saying that now the war was well over she should come home and marry him. She wrote back from Australia, where she had gone with her two children in 1943 because there were relations there, saying she felt they had drifted apart; she was no longer sure she wanted to marry George. He did not allow himself to collapse. He cabled her the air fare and asked her to come over and see him. She came, for two weeks, being unable to leave the children for longer. She said she liked Australia; she liked the climate; she did not like the English climate any longer; she thought England was, very probably, played out; and she had become used to missing London. Also, presumably, to missing George Talbot.

For George this was a very painful fortnight. He believed it was painful for Myra, too. They had met in 1938, had lived together for five years, and had exchanged for four years the letters of lovers separated by fate. Myra was certainly the love of his life. He had believed he was of hers until now. Myra, an attractive woman made beautiful by the suns and beaches of Australia, waved goodbye at the airport, and her eyes were filled with tears.

George's eyes, as he drove away from the airport, were dry. If one person has loved another truly and wholly, then it is more than love that collapses when one side of the indissoluble partnership turns away with a tearful goodbye. George dismissed the taxi early and walked through St. James's Park. Then it seemed too small for him, and he went to the Green Park. Then he walked into Hyde Park and through to Kensington Gardens. When the dark came and they closed the great gates of the park he took a taxi home. He lived in a block of flats near the Marble Arch. For five years Myra had lived with him there, and it was here he had expected to live with her again. Now he moved into a new flat near Covent Garden. Soon after that he wrote Myra a very painful letter. It occurred to him that he had often received such letters, but had never written one before. It occurred to him that he had entirely underestimated the amount of suffering he must have caused in his life. But Myra wrote him a sensible letter back, and George Talbot told himself that now he must finally stop thinking about Myra.

Therefore he became rather less of a dilettante in his work than he had been recently, and he agreed to produce a new play written by a friend of his. George Talbot was a man of the theater. He had not acted in it for many years now; but he wrote articles, he sometimes produced a play, he made speeches on important occasions and was known by everyone. When he went into a restaurant people tried to catch his eye, and he often did not know who they were. During the four years since Myra had left, he had had a number of affairs with young women round and about the theater, for he had been lonely. He had written quite frankly to Myra about these affairs, but she had never mentioned them in her letters. Now he was very busy for some months and was seldom at home; he earned quite a lot of money, and he had a few more affairs with women who were pleased to be seen in public with him. He thought about Myra a great deal, but he did not write to her again, nor she to him, although they had agreed they would always be great friends.

One evening in the foyer of a theater he saw an old friend of his he had always admired, and he told the young woman he was with that that man had been the most irresistible man of his generation—no woman had been able to resist him. The young woman stared briefly across the foyer and said "Not really?"

When George Talbot got home that night he was alone, and he looked at himself with honesty in the mirror. He was sixty, but he did not look it. Whatever had attracted women to him in the past had never been his looks, and he was not much changed: a stoutish man, holding himself erect, gray-haired, carefully brushed, well-dressed. He had not paid much attention to his face since those many years ago when he had been an actor; but now he had an uncharacteristic fit of vanity and remembered that Myra had admired his mouth, while his wife had loved his eyes. He took to taking glances at himself in foyers and restaurants where there were mirrors, and he saw himself as unchanged. He was becoming conscious, though, of a discrepancy between that suave exterior and what he felt. Beneath his ribs his heart had become swollen and soft and painful, a monstrous area of sympathy playing enemy to what he had been. When people made jokes he was often unable to laugh; and his manner of talking, which was light and allusive and dry, must have changed, because more than once old friends asked him if he were depressed, and they no longer smiled appreciatively as he told his stories. He gathered he was not being good company. He understood he might be ill, and he went to the doctor. The doctor said there was nothing wrong with his heart, he had thirty years of life in him yet—luckily, he added respectfully, for the British theater.

George came to understand that the word "heartache" meant that a person could carry a heart that ached around with him day and night for, in his case, months, nearly a year now. He would wake in the night, because of the pressure of pain in his chest; in the morning he woke under a weight of grief. There seemed to be no end to it; and his thought jolted him into two actions. First, he wrote to Myra, a tender, carefully-phrased letter, recalling the years of their love. To this he got, in due course, a tender and careful reply. Then he went to see his wife. With her he was, and had been for many years, good friends. They saw each other often, but not so often now the children were grown-up; perhaps once or twice a year, and they never quarreled.

His wife had married again after they divorced, and now she was a widow. Her second husband had been a member of Parliament, and she worked for the Labor Party, and she was on a Hospital Advisory Committee and on the Board of Directors of a progressive school. She was fifty, but did not look it. On this afternoon she was wearing a slim gray suit and gray shoes, and her gray hair had a wave of white across the front which made her look distinguished. She was animated, and very happy to see George; and she talked about some deadhead on her hospital committee who did not see eye to eye with the progressive minority about some reform or other. They had always had their politics in common, a position somewhere left of center in the Labor Party. She had sympathized with his being a pacifist in the First World War—he had been for a time in prison because of it; he had sympathized with her militant feminism. Both had helped the strikers in 1926. In the thirties, after they were divorced, she had helped with money when he went on tour with a company acting Shakespeare to people on the dole, or hunger-marching.

Myra had not been at all interested in politics, only in her children. And in George, of course.

George asked his first wife to marry him again, and she was so startled that she let the sugar tongs drop and crack a saucer. She asked what had happened to Myra, and George said: "Well, dear, I think Myra forgot about me during those years in Australia. At any rate, she doesn't want me now." When he heard his voice saying this it sounded pathetic, and he was frightened, for he could not remember ever having to appeal to a woman. Except to Myra.

His wife examined him and said briskly: "You're lonely, George. Well, we're none of us getting any younger."

"You don't think you'd be less lonely if you had me around?"

She got up from her chair in order that she could attend to something with her back to him, and she said that she intended to marry again quite soon. She was marrying a man considerably younger than herself, a doctor who was in the progressive minority at her hospital. From her voice George understood that she was both proud and ashamed of this marriage, and that was why she was hiding her face from him. He congratulated her and asked her if there wasn't perhaps a chance for him yet? "After all, dear, we were happy together, weren't we? I've never really understood why that marriage ever broke up. It was you who wanted to break it up."

"I don't see any point in raking over that old business," she said, with finality, and returned to her seat opposite him. He envied her very much, looking young with her pink and scarcely lined face under that brave lock of deliberately whitened hair.

"But dear, I wish you'd tell me. It doesn't do any harm now, does it? And I always wondered. . . . I've often thought about it and wondered." He could hear the pathetic note in his voice again, but he did not know how to alter it.

"You wondered," she said, "when you weren't occupied with Myra."

"But I didn't know Myra when we got divorced."

268

"You knew Phillipa and Georgina and Janet and lord knows who else."

"But I didn't care about them."

She sat with her competent hands in her lap and on her face was a look he remembered seeing when she told him she would divorce him. It was bitter and full of hurt. "You didn't care about me either," she said.

"But we were happy. Well, I was happy . . ." he trailed off, being pathetic against all his knowledge of women. For, as he sat there, his old rake's heart was telling him that if only he could find them, there must be the right words, the right tone. But whatever he said came out in this hopeless, old dog's voice, and he knew that this voice could never defeat the gallant and crusading young doctor. "And I did care about you. Sometimes I think you were the only woman in my life."

At this she laughed. "Oh, George, don't get maudlin now, please."

"Well, dear, there was Myra. But when you threw me over there was bound to be Myra, wasn't there? There were two women, you and then Myra. And I've never never understood why you broke it all up when we seemed to be so happy."

"You didn't care for me," she said again. "If you had, you would never have come home from Phillipa, Georgina, Janet *et al* and said calmly, just as if it didn't matter to me in the least, that you had been with them in Brighton or wherever it was."

"But if I had cared about them I would never have told you."

She was regarding him incredulously, and her face was flushed. With What? Anger? George did not know.

"I remember being so proud," he said pathetically, "that we had solved this business of marriage and all that sort of thing. We had such a good marriage that it didn't matter, the little flirtations. And I always thought one should be able to tell the truth. I always told you the truth, didn't I?"

"Very romantic of you, dear George," she said drily; and soon he got up, kissed her fondly on the cheek, and went away.

He walked for a long time through the parks, hands behind his erect back, and he could feel his heart swollen and painful in his side. When the gates shut, he walked through the lighted streets he had lived in for fifty years of his life, and he was remembering Myra and Molly, as if they were one woman, merging into each other, a shape of warm easy intimacy, a shape of happiness walking beside him. He went into a little restaurant he knew well, and there was a girl sitting there who knew him because she had heard him lecture once on the state of the British theater. He tried hard to see Myra and Molly in her face, but he failed; and he paid for her coffee and his own and went home by himself. But his flat was unbearably empty, and he left it and walked down by the Embankment for a couple of hours to tire himself, and there must have been a colder wind blowing than he knew, for next day he woke with a pain in his chest which he could not mistake for heartache.

He had flu and a bad cough, and he stayed in bed by himself and did not ring up the doctor until the fourth day, when he was getting light-headed. The doctor said it must be the hospital at once. But he would not go to the hospital. So the doctor said he must have day and night nurses. This he submitted to until the cheerful friendliness of the nurses saddened him beyond bearing, and he asked the doctor to ring up his wife, who would find someone to look after him who would be sympathetic. He was hoping that Molly would come herself to nurse him, but when she arrived he did not like to mention it, for she was busy with preparations for her new marriage. She promised to find him someone who would not wear a uniform and make jokes. They naturally had many friends in common; and she rang up an old flame of his in the theater who said she knew of a girl who was looking for a secretary's job to tide her over a patch of not working, but who didn't really mind what she did for a few weeks.

So Bobby Tippett sent away the nurses and made up a bed for herself in his study. On the first day she sat by George's bed sewing. She wore a full dark skirt and a demure printed blouse with short frills at the wrist, and George watched her sewing and already felt much better. She was a small, thin, dark girl, probably Jewish, with sad black eyes. She had a way of letting her sewing lie loose in her lap, her hands limp over it; and her eyes fixed themselves, and a bloom of dark introspection came over them. She sat very still at these moments, like a small china figure of a girl sewing. When she was nursing George, or letting in his many visitors, she put on a manner of cool and even languid charm; it was the extreme good manners of heartlessness, and at first George was chilled; but then he saw through the pose; for whatever world Bobby Tippett had been born into he did not think it was the English class to which these manners belong. She replied with a "yes," or a "no," to questions about herself; he gathered that her parents were dead, but there was a married sister she saw sometimes; and for the rest she had lived around and about London, mostly by herself, for ten or more years. When he asked her if she had not been lonely, so much by herself, she drawled, "Why, not at all, I don't mind being alone." But he saw her as a small, brave child, a waif against London, and was moved.

He did not want to be the big man of the theater; he was afraid of evoking the impersonal admiration he was only too accustomed to; but soon he was asking her questions about her career, hoping that this might be the point of her enthusiasm. But she spoke lightly of small parts, odd jobs, scene painting and under-studying, in a jolly good-little-trouper's voice; and he could not see that he had come any closer to her at all. So at last he did what he had tried to avoid, and sitting up against his pillows like a judge or an impresario, he said: "Do something for me, dear. Let me see you." She went next door like an obedient child, and came back in tight black trousers, but still in her demure little blouse, and stood on the carpet before him, and went into a little song-and-dance act. It wasn't bad. He had seen a hundred worse. But he was very moved; he saw her now above all as the little urchin, the gamin, boy-girl and helpless. And utterly touching. "Actually," she said, "this is half of an act. I always have someone else."

There was a big mirror that nearly filled the end wall of the large, dark room. George saw himself in it, an elderly man sitting propped up on pillows watching the small doll-like figure standing before him on the carpet. He saw her turn her head toward her reflection in the darkened mirror, study it, and then she began to dance with her own reflection, dance against it, as it were. There were two small, light figures dancing in George's room; there was something uncanny in it. She began singing, a little broken song in stage cockney, and George felt that she was expecting the other figure in the mirror to sing with her; she was singing at the mirror as if she expected an answer.

"That's very good, dear," he broke in quickly, for he was upset, though he did not know why. "Very good indeed." He was relieved when she broke off and came away from the mirror, so that the uncanny shadow of her went away.

"Would you like me to speak to someone for you, dear? It might help. You know how things are in the theater," he suggested apologetically.

"I don't maind if I dew," she said in the stage cockney of her act; and for a moment her face flashed into a mocking, reckless, gamin-like charm. "Perhaps I'd better change back into my skirt?" she suggested. "More natural-like for a nurse, ain't it?"

But he said he liked her in her tight black trousers, and now she always wore them, and her neat little shirts; and she moved about the flat as a charming feminine boy, chattering to him about the plays she had had small parts in and about the big actors and actresses and producers she had spoken to, who were, of course, George's friends or, at least, equals. George sat up against his pillows and listened and watched, and his heart ached. He remained in bed longer than there was need, because he did not want her to go. When he transferred himself to a big chair, he said: "You mustn't think you're bound to stay here, dear, if there's somewhere else you'd rather go." To which she replied, with a wide flash of her black eyes, "But I'm resting, darling, resting. I've nothing better to do with myself." And then: "Oh aren't I awful, the things wot I sy?"

"But you do like being here? You don't mind being here with me, dear?" he insisted.

There was the briefest pause. She said: "Yes, oddly enough I do like it." The "oddly enough" was accompanied by a quick, half-laughing, almost flirtatious glance; and for the first time in many months the pressure of loneliness eased around George's heart.

Now it was a happiness to him because when the distinguished ladies and gentlemen of the theater or of letters came to see him, Bobby became a cool, silky little hostess; and the instant they had gone she relapsed into urchin charm. It was a proof of their intimacy. Sometimes he took her out to dinner or to the theater. When she dressed up she wore bold, fashionable clothes and moved with the insolence of a mannequin; and George moved beside her, smiling fondly, waiting for the moment when the black, restless, freebooting eyes would flash up out of the languid stare of the woman presenting herself for admiration, exchanging with him amusement at her posing, amusement at the world; promising him that soon, when they got back to the apartment, by themselves, she would again become the dear little girl or the gallant, charming waif.

Sometimes, sitting in the dim room at night, he would let his hand close over the thin point of her shoulder; sometimes, when they said good night, he bent to kiss her, and she lowered her head, so that his lips encountered her demure, willing forehead.

George told himself that she was unawakened. It was a phrase that had been the prelude to a dozen warm discoveries in the past. He told himself that she knew nothing of what she might be. She had been married, it seemed—she dropped this information once, in the course of an anecdote about the theater; but George had known women in plenty who after years of marriage had been unawakened. George asked her to marry him; and she lifted her small sleek head with an animal's startled turn and said: "Why do you want to marry me?"

"Because I like being with you, dear. I love being with you."

"Well, I like being with you." It had a questioning sound. She was questioning herself? "Strainge," she said in cockney, laughing. "Strainge but trew."

The wedding was to be a small one, but there was a lot about it in the papers. Recently several men of George's generation had married young women. One of them had fathered a son at the age of seventy. George was flattered by the newspapers, and told Bobby a good deal about his life that had not come up before. He remarked for instance that he thought his generation had been altogether more successful about this business of love and sex than the modern generation. He said, "Take my son, for instance. At his age I had had a lot of affairs and knew about women; but there he is, nearly thirty, and when he stayed here once with a girl he was thinking of marrying I know for a fact they shared the same bed for a week and nothing ever happened. She told me so. Very odd it all seems to me. But it didn't seem odd to her. And now he lives with another young man and listens to that long-playing record thing of his, and he's engaged to a girl he takes out twice a week, like a schoolboy. And there's my daughter, she came to me a year after she was married, and she was in an awful mess, really awful . . . it seems to me your generation are very frightened of it all. I don't know why."

"Why my generation?" she asked, turning her head with that quick listening movement. "It's not my generation."

"But you're nothing but a child," he said fondly.

He could not decipher what lay behind the black, full stare of her sad eyes as she looked at him now; she was sitting cross-legged in her black glossy trousers before the fire, like a small doll. But a spring of alarm had been touched in him and he didn't dare say any more.

"At thirty-five, I'm the youngest child alive," she sang, with a swift sardonic glance at him over her shoulder. But it sounded gay.

He did not talk to her again about the achievements of his generation.

After the wedding he took her to a village in Normandy where he had been once, many years ago, with a girl called Eve. He did not tell her he had been there before.

It was spring, and the cherry trees were in flower. The first evening he walked with her in the last sunlight under the white-flowering branches, his arm around her thin waist, and it seemed to him that he was about to walk back through the gates of a lost happiness.

They had a large comfortable room with windows which overlooked the cherry trees and there was a double bed. Madame Cruchot, the farmer's wife, showed them the room with shrewd, noncommenting eyes, said she was always happy to shelter honeymoon couples, and wished them a good night.

George made love to Bobby, and she shut her eyes, and he found she was not at all awkward. When they had finished, he gathered her in his arms, and it was then that he returned simply, with an incredulous awed easing of the heart, to a happiness which—and now it seemed to him fantastically ungrateful that he could have done—he had taken for granted for so many years of his life. It was not possible, he thought, holding her compliant body in his arms, that he could have been by himself, alone, for so long. It had been intolerable. He held her silent breathing body, and he stroked her back and thighs, and his hands remembered the emotions of nearly fifty years of loving. He could feel the memoried emotions of his life flooding through his body, and his heart swelled with a joy it seemed to him he had never known, for it was a compound of a dozen loves.

He was about to take final possession of his memories when she turned sharply away, sat up, and said: "I want a fag. How about yew?"

"Why, yes, dear, if you want."

They smoked. The cigarettes finished, she lay down on her back, arms folded across her chest, and said "I'm sleepy." She closed her eyes. When he was sure she was asleep, he lifted himself on his elbow and watched her. The light still burned, and the curve of her cheek was full and soft, like a child's. He touched it with the side of his palm, and she shrank away in her sleep, but clenched up, like a fist; and her hand, which was white and unformed, like a child's hand, was clenched in a fist on the pillow before her face.

George tried to gather her in his arms, and she turned away from him to the extreme edge of the bed. She was deeply asleep, and her sleep was unsharable. George could not endure it. He got out of bed and stood by the window in the cold spring night air, and saw the white cherry trees standing under the white moon, and thought of the cold girl asleep in her bed. He was there in the chill moonlight until the dawn came; in the morning he had a very bad cough and could not get up. Bobby was charming, devoted, and gay. "Just like old times, me nursing you," she commented, with a deliberate roll of her black eyes. She asked Madame Cruchot for another bed, which she placed in the corner of the room, and George thought it was quite reasonable she should not want to catch his cold; for he did not allow himself to remember the time in his past when quite serious illness had been no obstacle to the sharing of the dark; he decided to forget the sensualities of tiredness, or of fever, or of the extremes of sleeplessness. He was even beginning to feel ashamed.

For a fortnight the Frenchwoman brought up magnificent meals, twice a day, and George and Bobby drank a great deal of red wine and of calvados and made jokes with Madame Cruchot about getting ill on honeymoons. They returned from Normandy rather earlier than had been arranged. It would be better for George, Bobby said, at home, where his friends could drop in to see him. Besides, it was sad to be shut indoors in springtime, and they were both eating too much.

On the first night back in the flat, George waited to see if she would go into the study to sleep, but she came to the big bed in her pajamas, and for the second time, he held her in his arms for the space of the act, and then she smoked, sitting up in bed and looking rather tired and small and, George thought, terribly young and pathetic. He did not sleep that night. He did not dare move out of bed for fear of disturbing her, and he was afraid to drop off to sleep for fear his limbs remembered the habits of a lifetime and searched for hers. In the morning she woke smiling, and he put his arms around her, but she kissed him with small gentle kisses and jumped out of bed.

That day she said she must go and see her sister. She saw her sister often during the next few weeks and kept suggesting that George should have his friends around more than he did. George asked why didn't the sister come to see her here, in the flat? So one afternoon she came to tea. George had seen her briefly at the wedding and disliked her, but now for the first time he had a spell of revulsion against the marriage itself. The sister was awful—a commonplace, middle-aged female from some suburb. She had a sharp, dark face that poked itself inquisitively into the corners of the flat, pricing the furniture, and a thin acquisitive nose bent to one side. She sat, on her best behavior, for two hours over the teacups, in a mannish navy blue suit, a severe black hat, her brogued feet set firmly side by side before her; and her thin nose seemed to be carrying on a silent, satirical conversation with her sister about George. Bobby was being cool and well-mannered, as it were deliberately tired of life, as she always was when guests were there, but George was sure this was simply on his account. When the sister had gone, George was rather querulous about her; but Bobby said, laughing, that of course she had known George wouldn't like Rosa; she *was* rather ghastly; but then who had suggested inviting her? So Rosa came no more, and Bobby went out to meet her for a visit to the pictures, or for shopping. Meanwhile, George sat alone and thought uneasily about Bobby, or visited his old friends. A few months after they returned from Normandy, someone suggested to George that perhaps he was ill. This made George think about it, and he realized he was not far from being ill. It was because he could not sleep. Night after night he lay beside Bobby, after her cheerfully affectionate submission to him; and he saw the soft curve of her cheek on the pillow, the long dark lashes lying close and flat. Never had anything in his life moved him so deeply as that childish cheek, the shadow of those lashes. A small crease in one cheek seemed to him the signature of emotion; and the lock of black glossy hair falling across her forehead filled his throat with tears. His nights were long vigils of locked tenderness.

Then one night she woke and saw him watching her.

"What's the matter?" she asked, startled. "Can't you sleep?"

"I'm only watching you, dear," he said hopelessly.

She lay curled up beside him, her fist beside her on the pillow, between him and her. "Why aren't you happy?" she asked suddenly; and as George laughed with a sudden bitter irony, she sat up, arms around her knees, prepared to consider this problem practically.

"This isn't marriage; this isn't love," he announced. He sat up beside her. He did not know that he had never used that tone to her before. A portly man, his elderly face flushed with sorrow, he had forgotten her for the moment, and he was speaking across her from his past, resurrected in her, to his past. He was dignified with responsible experience and the warmth of a lifetime's responses. His eyes were heavy, satirical, and condemning. She rolled herself up against him and said with a small sad smile, "Then show me, George."

"Show you?" he said, almost stammering. "Show you?" But he held her, the obedient child, his cheek against hers, until she slept; then a too close pressure of his shoulder on hers caused her to shrink and recoil from him away to the edge of the bed.

In the morning she looked at him oddly, with an odd sad little respect, and said, "You know what, George? You've just got into the habit of loving."

"What do you mean, dear?"

She rolled out of bed and stood beside it, a waif in her white pajamas, her black hair ruffled. She slid her eyes at him and smiled. "You just want something in your arms, that's all. What do you do when you're alone? Wrap yourself around a pillow?"

He said nothing; he was cut to the heart.

"My husband was the same," she remarked gaily. "Funny thing is, he didn't care anything about me." She stood considering him, smiling mockingly. "Strainge, ain't it?" she commented and went off to the bathroom. That was the second time she had mentioned her husband.

That phrase, the habit of loving, made a revolution in George. It was true, he thought. He was shocked out of himself, out of the instinctive response to the movement of skin against his, the pressure of a breast. It seemed to him that he was seeing Bobby quite newly. He had not really known her before.

The delightful little girl had vanished, and he saw a young woman toughened and wary because of defeats and failures he had never stopped to think of. He saw that the sadness that lay behind the black eyes was not at all impersonal; he saw that the full curve of her cheek was the beginning of the softening into middle-age. He was appalled at his egotism. Now, he thought, he would really know her, and she would begin to love him in response to it.

Suddenly, George discovered in himself a boy whose existence he had totally forgotten. He had been returned to his adolescence. The accidental touch of her hand delighted him; the swing of her skirt could make him shut his eyes with happiness. He looked at her through the jealous eyes of a boy and began questioning her about her past, feeling that he was slowly taking possession of her. He waited for a hint of emotion in the drop of her voice, or a confession in the wrinkling of the skin by the full, dark, comradely eyes. At night, a boy again, reverence shut him into ineptitude. The body of George's sensuality had been killed stone dead. A month ago he had been a man vigorous with the skilled harboring of memory; the long use of his body. Now he lay awake beside this woman, longing—not for the past, for that past had dropped away from him, but dreaming of the future. And when he questioned her, like a jealous boy, and she evaded him, he could see it only as the locked virginity of the girl who would wake in answer to the worshiping boy he had become.

But still she slept in a citadel, one fist before her face.

Then one night she woke again, roused by some movement of his. "What's the matter now, George?" she asked, exasperated.

In the silence that followed, the resurrected boy in George died painfully.

"Nothing," he said. "Nothing at all." He turned away from her, defeated.

It was he who moved out of the big bed into the narrow bed in the study. She said with a sharp, sad smile, "Fed up with me, George? Well I can't help it, you know. I didn't ever like sleeping beside someone very much."

George, who had dropped out of his work lately, undertook to produce another play, and was very busy again; and he became drama critic for one of the big papers and was in the swim and at all the first nights. Sometimes Bobby was with him, in her startling, smart clothes, being amused with him at the whole business of being fashionable. Sometimes she stayed at home. She had the capacity for being by herself for hours, apparently doing nothing. George would come home from some crowd of people, some party, and find her sitting cross-legged before the fire in her tight trousers, chin in hand, gone off by herself into some place where he was now afraid to try and follow. He could not bear it again, putting himself in a position where he might hear the cold, sharp words that showed she had never had an inkling of what he felt, because it was not in her nature to feel it. He would come in late, and she would make them both some tea; and they would sit hand in hand before the fire, his flesh and memories quiet. Dead, he thought. But his heart ached.

He had become so used to the heavy load of loneliness in his chest that when, briefly, talking to an old friend, he became the George Talbot who had never known Bobby, and his heart lightened and his oppression went, he would look about him, startled, as if he had lost something. He felt almost light-headed without the pain of loneliness.

He asked Bobby if she weren't bored, with so little to do, month after month after month, while he was so busy. She said no, she was quite happy doing nothing. She wouldn't like to take up her old work again?

"I wasn't ever much good, was I?" she said.

"If you'd enjoy it, dear, I could speak to someone for you."

She frowned at the fire but said nothing. Later he suggested it again, and she sparked up with a grin and: "Well, I don't maind if I dew. . . ."

So he spoke to an old friend, and Bobby returned to the theater, to a small act in a little intimate review. She had found somebody, she said, to be the other half of her act. George was very busy with a production of *Romeo and Juliet,* and did not have time to see her at rehearsal, but he was there on the night *The Offbeat Revue* opened. He was rather late and stood at the back of the gimcrack little theater, packed tight with fragile little chairs. Everything was so small that the well-dressed audience looked too big, like over-size people crammed in a box. The tiny stage was left bare, with a few black and white posters stuck here and there, and there was one piano. The pianist was good, a young man with black hair falling limp over his face, playing as if he were bored with the whole thing. But he played very well. George, the man of the theater, listened to the first number, so as to catch the mood, and thought, Oh Lord, not again. It was one of the songs from the First World War, and he could not stand the flood of easy emotion it aroused. He refused to feel. Then he realized that the emotion was, in any case, blocked; the piano was mocking the song; "There's a Long, Long Trail" was being played like a five-finger exercise; and "Keep the Home Fires Burning" and "Tipperary" followed, in the same style, as if the piano were bored. People were beginning to chuckle, they had caught the mood. A young blond man with a moustache and wearing the uniform of 1914 came in and sang fragments of the songs, like a corpse singing; and then George understood he was supposed to be one of the dead of that war singing. George felt all his responses blocked, first because he could not allow himself to feel any emotion from that time at all—it was too painful; and then because of the five-finger exercise style, which contradicted everything, all pain or protest, leaving nothing, an emptiness. The show went on; through the twenties, with bits of popular songs from that time, a number about the General Strike, which reduced the whole thing to the scale of marionettes without passion, and then on to the thirties. George saw it was a sort of potted history, as it were—Noel Coward's falsely heroic view of his time parodied. But it wasn't even that. There was no emotion, nothing. George did not know what he was supposed to feel. He looked curiously at the faces of the people around him and saw that the older people looked puzzled, affronted, as if the show were an insult to them. But the younger people were in the mood of the thing. But what mood? It was the parody of a parody. When the Second World War was evoked by "Run Rabbit Run," played like *Lohengrin,* while the soldiers in the uniforms of the time mocked their own understated heroism from the other side of death, then George could not stand it. He did not look at the stage at all. He was waiting for Bobby to come on, so he could say that he had seen her. Meanwhile he smoked and watched the face of a very young man near him; it was a pale, heavy, flaccid face, but it was responding, it seemed from a habit of rancour, to everything that went on on the stage. Suddenly, the young face lit into sarcastic delight, and George looked at the stage. On it were two urchins, identical it seemed, in tight black glossy trousers, tight crisp white shirts. Both had short black hair, neat little feet placed side by side. They were standing together, hands crossed loosely before them at the waist, waiting for the music to start. The man at the piano, who had a cigarette in the corner of his mouth, began playing something very sentimental. He broke off and looked with sardonic inquiry at the urchins. They had not moved. They shrugged and rolled their eyes at him. He played a marching song, very loud and pompous. The urchins twitched a little and stayed still. Then the piano broke fast and sudden into a rage of jazz. The two puppets on the stage began a furious movement, their limbs clashing with each other and with the music, until they fell into poses of helpless despair while the music grew louder and more desperate. They tried again, whirling themselves into a frenzied attempt to keep up with the music. Then, two waifs, they turned their two small white sad faces at each other, and, with a formal nod, each took a phrase of music from the fast flood of sound that had already swept by them, held it, and began to sing. Bobby sang her bad stage-cockney phrases, meaningless, jumbled up, flat, hopeless; the other urchin sang drawling languid phrases from the upperclass jargon of the moment. They looked at each other, offering the phrases as it were, to see if they would be accepted. Meanwhile, the hard, cruel, hurtful music went on. Again the two went limp and helpless, unwanted, unaccepted. George, outraged and hurt, asked himself again: What am I feeling? What am I supposed to be feeling? For that insane nihilistic music demanded some opposition, some statement of affirmation, but the two urchins, half-boy, half-girl, as alike as twins (George had to watch Bobby carefully so as not to confuse her with "the other half of her act") were not even trying to resist the music. Then, after a long, sad immobility, they changed roles. Bobby took the languid jaw-writhing part of a limp young man, and the other waif sang false-cockney phrases in a cruel copy of a woman's voice. It was the parody of a parody of a parody. George stood tense, waiting for a resolution. His nature demanded that now, and quickly, for the limp sadness of the turn was unbearable, the two false urchins should flash out in some sort of rebellion. But there was nothing. The jazz went on like hammers; the whole room shook—stage, walls, ceiling—and it seemed the people in the room jigged lightly and helplessly. The two children on the stage twisted their limbs into the willful mockery of a stage convention, and finally stood side by side, hands hanging limp, heads lowered meekly, twitching a little while the music rose into a final crashing discord and the lights went out. George could not applaud. He saw that the damp-faced young man next to him was clapping wildly, while his lank hair fell all over his face. George saw that the older people were all, like himself, bewildered and insulted.

When the show was over, George went backstage to fetch Bobby. She was with "the other half of the act," a rather good-looking boy of about twenty, who was being deferential to the impressive husband of Bobby. George said to her: "You were very good, dear, very good indeed." She looked smilingly at him, half-mocking, but he did not know what it was she was mocking now. And she had been good. But he never wanted to see it again.

The revue was a success and ran for some months before it was moved to a bigger theater. George finished his production of *Romeo and Juliet* which, so the critics said, was the best London had seen for many years, and refused other offers of work. He did not need the money for the time being, and besides, he had not seen very much of Bobby lately.

But of course now she was working. She was at rehearsals several times a week, and away from the flat every evening. But George never went to her theater. He did not want to see the sad, unresisting children twitching to the cruel music.

It seemed Bobby was happy. The various little parts she had played with him—the urchin, the cool hostess, the dear child—had all been absorbed into the hard-working female who cooked him his meals, looked after him, and went out to her theater giving him a friendly kiss on the cheek. Their relationship was most pleasant and amiable. George lived beside this good friend, his wife Bobby, who was doing him so much credit in every way, and ached permanently with loneliness.

One day he was walking down the Charing Cross Road, looking into the windows of bookshops, when he saw Bobby strolling up the other side with Jackie, the other half of her act. She looked as he had never seen her: her dark face was alive with animation, and Jackie was looking into her face and laughing. George thought the boy very handsome. He had a warm gloss of youth on his hair and in his eyes; he had the lithe, quick look of a young animal.

He was not jealous at all. When Bobby came in at night, gay and vivacious, he knew he owed this to Jackie and did not mind. He was even grateful to him. The warmth Bobby had for "the other half of the act" overflowed toward him; and for some months Myra and his wife were present in his mind, he saw and felt them, two loving presences, young women who loved George, brought into being by the feeling between Jackie and Bobby. Whatever that feeling was.

The Offbeat Revue ran for nearly a year, and then it was coming off, and Bobby and Jackie were working out another act. George did not know what it was. He thought Bobby needed a rest, but he did not like to say so. She had been tired recently, and when she came in at night there was strain beneath her gaiety. Once, at night, he woke to see her beside his bed. "Hold me for a little, George," she asked. He opened his arms and she came into them. He lay holding her, quite still. He had opened his arms to the sad waif, but it was an unhappy woman lying in his arms. He could feel the movement of her lashes on his shoulder, and the wetness of tears.

He had not lain beside her for a long time, years, it seemed. She did not come to him again.

"You don't think you're working too hard, dear?" he asked once, looking at her strained face; but she said briskly, "No, I've got to have something to do, can't stand doing nothing."

One night it was raining hard, and Bobby had been feeling sick that day, and she did not come home at her usual time. George became worried and took a taxi to the theater and asked the doorman if she was still there. It seemed she had left some time before. "She didn't look too well to me, sir," volunteered the doorman, and George sat for a time in the taxi, trying not to worry. Then he gave the driver Jackie's address; he meant to ask him if he knew where Bobby was. He sat limp in the back of the taxi, feeling the heaviness of his limbs, thinking of Bobby ill.

The place was in a mews, and he left the taxi and walked over rough cobbles to a door which had been the door of stables. He rang, and a young man he didn't know let him in, saying yes, Jackie Dickson was in. George climbed narrow, steep, wooden stairs slowly, feeling the weight of his body, while his heart pounded. He stood at the top of the stairs to get his breath, in a dark which smelled of canvas and oil and turpentine. There was a streak of light under a door; he went toward it, knocked, heard no answer, and opened it. The scene was a high, bare, studio sort of place, badly lighted, full of pictures, frames, junk of various kinds. Jackie, the dark, glistening youth, was seated cross-legged before the fire, grinning as he lifted his face to say something to Bobby, who sat in a chair, looking down at him. She was wearing a formal dark dress and jewelry, and her arms and neck were bare and white. She looked beautiful, George thought, glancing once, briefly, at her face, and then away; for he could see on it an emotion he did not want to recognize. The scene held for a moment before they realized he was there and turned their heads with the same lithe movement of disturbed animals, to see him standing there in the doorway. Both faces froze. Bobby looked quickly at the young man, and it was in some kind of fear. Jackie looked sulky and angry.

"I've come to look for you, dear," said George to his wife. "It was raining and the doorman said you seemed ill."

"It's very sweet of you," she said and rose from the chair, giving her hand formally to Jackie, who nodded with bad grace at George.

The taxi stood in the dark, gleaming rain, and George and Bobby got into it and sat side by side, while it splashed off into the street.

"Was that the wrong thing to do, dear?" asked George, when she said nothing.

"No," she said.

"I really did think you might be ill."

She laughed, "Perhaps I am."

"What's the matter, my darling? What is it? He was angry, wasn't he? Because I came?"

"He thinks you're jealous," she said shortly.

"Well, perhaps I am rather," said George.

She did not speak.

"I'm sorry, dear, I really am. I didn't mean to spoil anything for you."

"Well, that's certainly *that*," she remarked, and she sounded impersonally angry.

"Why? But why should it be?"

"He doesn't like—having things asked of him," she said, and he remained silent while they drove home.

Up in the warmed, comfortable old flat, she stood before the fire, while he brought her a drink. She smoked fast and angrily, looking into the fire.

"Please forgive me, dear," he said at last. What is it? Do you love him? Do you want to leave me? If you do, of course you must. Young people should be together."

She turned and stared at him, a black strange stare he knew well.

"George," she said, "I'm nearly forty."

But darling, you're a child still. At least, to me."

"And he," she went on, "will be twenty-two next month. I'm old enough to be his mother." She laughed, painfully. "Very painful, maternal love . . . or so it seems . . . but then how should I know?" She held out her bare arm and looked at it. Then, with the fingers of one hand she creased down the skin of that bare arm toward the wrist, so that the aging skin lay in creases and folds. Then, setting down her glass, her cigarette held between tight, amused, angry lips, she wriggled her shoulders out of her dress, so that it slipped to her waist, and she looked down at her two small, limp, unused breasts. "Very painful, dear George," she said, and shrugged her dress up quickly, becoming again the formal woman dressed for the world. "He does not love me. He does not love me at all. Why should he?" She began singing:

> He does not love me
> With a love that is trew. . . .

Then she said in stage cockney, "Repeat; I could 'ave bin 'is muvver, see?" And with the old rolling derisive black flash of her eyes she smiled at George.

George was thinking only that this girl, his darling, was suffering now what he had suffered, and he could not stand it. She had been going through this for how long now? But she had been working with that boy for nearly two years. She had been living beside him, George, and he had had no idea at all of her unhappiness. He went over to her, put his old arms around her, and she stood with her head on his shoulder and wept. For the first time, George thought, they were together. They sat by the fire a long time that night, drinking, smoking and her head was on his knee and he stroked it, and thought that now, at last, she had been admitted into the world of emotion and they would learn to be really together. He could feel his strength stirring along his limbs for her. He was still a man, after all.

Next day she said she would not go on with the new show. She would tell Jackie he must get another partner. And besides, the new act wasn't really any good. "I've had one little act all my life," she said, laughing. "And sometimes it's fitted in, and sometimes it hasn't."

"What was the new act? What's it about?" he asked her.

She did not look at him. "Oh, nothing very much. It was Jackie's idea, really. . . ." Then she laughed. "It's quite good really, I suppose. . . ."

"But what is it?"

"Well, you see. . . ." Again he had the impression she did not want to look at him. "It's a pair of lovers. We make fun . . . it's hard to explain, without doing it."

"You make fun of love?" he asked.

"Well, you know, all the attitudes . . . the things people say. It's a man and a woman—with music of course. All the music you'd expect, played offbeat. We wear the same costume as for the other act. And then we go through all the motions. . . . It's rather funny, really . . ." she trailed off, breathless; seeing George's face. "Well," she said, suddenly very savage, "if it isn't all bloody funny, what is it?" She turned away to take a cigarette.

"Perhaps you'd like to go on with it after all?" he asked ironically.

"No. I can't. I really can't stand it. I can't stand it any longer, George," she said, and from her voice he understood she had nothing to learn from him of pain.

He suggested they both needed a holiday, so they went to Italy. They traveled from place to place, never stopping anywhere longer than a day, for George knew she was running away from any place around which emotion could gather. At night he made love to her, but she closed her eyes and thought of the other half of the act; and George knew it and did not care. But what he was feeling was too powerful for his old body; he could feel a lifetime's emotion beating through his limbs, making his brain throb.

Again they curtailed their holiday, to return to the comfortable old flat in London.

On the first morning after their return, she said: "George, you know you're getting too old for this sort of thing—it's not good for you; you look ghastly."

"But, darling, why? What else am I still alive for?"

"People'll say I'm killing you," she said, with a sharp, half angry, half amused, black glance.

"But, my darling, believe me. . . ."

He could see them both in the mirror; he, an old pursy man, head lowered in sullen obstinacy; she . . . but he could not read her face.

"And perhaps I'm getting too old?" she remarked suddenly.

For a few days she was gay, mocking, then suddenly tender. She was provocative, teasing him with her eyes; then she would deliberately yawn and say, "I'm going to sleep. Good night George."

"Well of course, my darling, if you're tired."

One morning she announced she was going to have a birthday party; it would be her fortieth birthday soon. The way she said it made George feel uneasy.

On the morning of her birthday she came into his study where he had been sleeping, carrying his breakfast tray. He raised himself on his elbow and gazed at her, appalled. For a moment he had imagined it must be another woman. She had put on a severe navy blue suit, cut like a man's; heavy black-laced shoes; and she had taken the wisps of black hair back off her face and pinned them into a sort of clumsy knot. She was suddenly, a middle-aged woman.

"But, my darling," he said, "my darling, what have you done to yourself?"

"I'm forty," she said. "Time to grow up."

"But, my darling, I do so love you in your nice clothes. I do so love you being beautiful in your lovely clothes."

She laughed, and left the breakfast tray beside his bed, and went clumping out on her heavy shoes.

That morning she stood in the kitchen beside a very large cake, on which she was carefully placing forty small pink candles. But it seemed only the sister had been asked to the party, for that afternoon the three of them sat around the cake and looked at one another. George looked at Rosa, the sister, in her ugly, straight, thick suit, and at his darling Bobby, all her grace and charm submerged into heavy tweed, her hair dragged back, without make-up. They were two middle-aged women, talking about food and buying.

George said nothing. His whole body throbbed with loss.

The dreadful Rosa was looking with her sharp eyes around the expensive flat, and then at George and then at her sister.

"You've let yourself go, haven't you, Bobby?" she commented at last. She sounded pleased about it.

Bobby glanced defiantly at George. "I haven't got time for all this nonsense any more," she said. "I simply haven't got time. We're all getting on now, aren't we?"

George saw the two women looking at him. He thought they had the same black, hard, inquisitive stare over sharp-bladed noses. He could not speak. His tongue was thick. The blood was beating through his body. His heart seemed to be swelling and filling his whole body, an enormous soft growth of pain. He could not hear for the tolling of the blood through his ears. The blood was beating up into his eyes, but he shut them so as not to see the two women.

STANLEY ELKIN

A Poetics for Bullies

I'm Push, the bully, and what I hate are new kids and sissies, dumb kids and smart, rich kids, poor kids, kids who wear glasses, talk funny, show off, patrol boys and wise guys and kids who pass pencils and water the plants —and cripples, *especially* cripples. Nobody loved I love.

One time I was pushing this red-haired kid (I'm a pusher, no hitter, no belter—an aggressor of marginal violence, I hate *real* force) and his mother stuck her head out of the window and shouted something I've never forgotten. *"Push,"* she yelled, *"you, Push.* You pick on him because you wish you had his red hair!" It's true. I did wish I had his red hair. I wish I were tall, or fat, or thin. I wish I had different eyes, different hands, a mother in the supermarket. I wish I were a man, a small boy, a girl in the choir. I'm a coveter, a Boston Blackie of the heart, casing the world. Endlessly I covet and case. (Do you know what makes me cry? The Declaration of Independence. "All men are created equal." That's beautiful.)

If you're a bully like me, you use your head. Toughness isn't enough. You beat them up, they report you. Then where are you? I'm not even particularly strong. (I used to be strong. I used to do exercise, work out, but strength implicates you, and often isn't an advantage anyway—read the judo ads. Besides, your big bullies aren't bullies at all—they're *athletes.* With them, beating guys up is a sport.) But what I lose in size and strength I make up for in courage. I'm very brave. That's a lie about bullies being cowards underneath. If you're a coward get out of the business.

I'm best at torment.

A kid has a toy bow, toy arrows. "Let Push look," I tell him.

They're suspicious, they know me. "Go way, Push," they say, these mama-warned, Push-doubters.

"Come on," I say, "come on."

"No, Push. I can't. My mother said I can't."

I raise my arms, spread them. I'm a bird—slow, powerful, easy, free. I move my head to public beak. I'm a thunderbird. "In the school where I go I have a teacher who teaches me magic," I say. "Arnold Salamancy, give Push your arrows. Give him one, he gives back two. Push is the God of the Neighborhood."

"Go way, Push," the kid says, uncertain.

"Right," Push says, himself again. "Right. I'll disappear. First the fingers." My fingers ball to fists. "My forearms next." They jackknife into my upper arms. "The arms." Quick as bird blink they snap behind my back, fit between the shoulder blades like a small knapsack. (I am double-jointed, Protean.) "My head," I say.

"No, Push," the kid says, terrified. I shudder and everything comes back, falls into place from the stem of self like a shaken puppet.

"The arrow, the arrow. Two where was one." He hands me an arrow. *"Trouble, trouble, double rubble!"* I snap it and give back the pieces.

Well, sure. There *is* no magic. If there were I would learn it. I would find out the words, the slow turns and strange passes, drain the bloods and get the herbs, do the fires like a vestal. I would look for the main chants. *Then* I'd change things. Push would!

But there's only casuistical trick. Sleight-of-mouth, the bully's poetics.

You know the formulas:

"Did you ever see a match burn twice?" you ask. Strike. Extinguish. Jab his flesh with the hot stub.

"Play Gestapo?"

"How do you play?"

"What's your name?"

"It's Morton."

I slap him. "You're lying."

"Adam and Eve and Pinch Me Hard went down to the lake for a swim. Adam and Eve fell in. Who was left?"

"Pinch Me Hard."

I do.

Physical puns, conundrums. Push the punisher, the conundrummer!

(I don't know what it is. Sometimes I think *I'm* the only new kid. In a room, the school, the playground, the neighborhood, I got the feeling I've just moved in, no one knows me. You know what I like? To stand in crowds. To wait with them at the airport to meet a plane. Someone asks what time it is. I'm the first to answer. Or at the ball park when the vendor comes. He passes the hot dog down the long row. I want *my* hands on it, too. On the dollar going up, the change coming down.)

I am ingenious, I am patient.

A kid is going downtown on the elevated train. He's got his little suit on, his shoes shined, he wears a cap. This is a kid going to the travel bureaus, the foreign tourist offices to get brochures, maps, pictures of the mountains for a unit at his school. This is a kid looking for extra credit. I follow him. He comes out of the Italian Tourist Information Center. His arms are full. I move from my place at the window. I follow for two blocks and bump into him as he steps from a curb. It is a *collision*. The pamphlets fall from his arms. Pretending confusion I walk on his paper Florence. I grind my heel in his Riviera. I climb Vesuvius and sack his Rome and dance on the Isle of Capri.

The Industrial Museum is a good place to find children. I cut some-body's five- or six-year-old kid brother out of the herd of eleven- and twelve-year-olds he's come with. *"Quick,"* I say. I pull him along the corridors, up the stairs, through the halls, down to a mezzanine landing. Breathless, I pause for a minute. "I've got some gum. Do you want a stick?" He nods. I stick him. I rush him into an auditorium and abandon him. He'll be lost for hours.

I sidled up to a kid at the movies. "You smacked my brother," I tell him. "After the show—I'll be outside."

I break up games. I hold the ball above my head. "You want it? Take it."

I go into barbershops. There's a kid waiting. "I'm next," I tell him, "understand?"

One day Eugene Kraftsman rang my bell. Eugene is afraid of me so he helps me. He's fifteen and there's something wrong with his saliva glands and he drools. His chin is always chapped. I tell him he has to drink a lot because he loses so much water.

"Push? Push," he says. He's wiping his chin with his tissues. "Push, there's this kid—"

"Better get a glass of water, Eugene."

"No, Push, no fooling, there's this new kid—he just moved in. You've got to see this kid."

"Eugene, get some water, please. You're drying up. I've never seen you so bad. There are deserts in you, Eugene."

"All right, Push, but then you've got to see—"

"Swallow, Eugene. You better swallow."

He gulps hard.

"Push, this is a kid and a half. Wait, you'll see."

"I'm very concerned about you, Eugene. You're dying of thirst, Eugene. Come into the kitchen with me."

I push him through the door. He's very excited. I've never seen him so excited. He talks at me over his shoulder, his mouth flooding, his teeth like the little stone pebbles at the bottom of a fishbowl. "He's got this sport coat, with a patch over the heart. Like a king, Push. No kidding."

"Be careful of the carpet, Eugene."

I turn on the taps in the sink. I mix in hot water. "Use your tissues, Eugene. Wipe your chin."

He wipes himself and puts the Kleenex in his pocket. All Eugene's pockets bulge. He looks with his bulging pockets, like a very clumsy smuggler.

"Wipe, Eugene. Swallow, you're drowning."

"He's got this funny accent—you could die." Excited, he tamps at his mouth like a diner, a tubercular.

"Drink some water, Eugene."

"No, Push. I'm not thirsty—really."

"Don't be foolish, kid. That's because your mouth's so wet. Inside where it counts you're drying up. It stands to reason. Drink some water."

"He has this crazy haircut."

"Drink," I command. I shake him. "Drink!"

"Push, I've got no glass. Give me a glass at least."

"I can't do that, Eugene. You've got a terrible sickness. How could I let you use our drinking glasses? Just lean under the tap and open your mouth."

He knows he'll have to do it, that I won't listen to him until he does. He bends into the sink.

"Push, it's *hot*," he complains. The water splashes into his nose, it gets on his glasses and for a moment his eyes are magnified, enormous. He pulls away and scrapes his forehead on the faucet.

"Eugene, you touched it. Watch out please. You're too close to the tap. Lean your head deeper into the sink."

"It's *hot*, Push."

"Warm water evaporates better. With your affliction you've got to evaporate fluids before they get into your glands."

He feeds again from the tap.

"Do you think that's enough?" I ask after a while.

"I do, Push, I really do," he says. He is breathless.

"Eugene," I say seriously, "I think you'd better get yourself a canteen."

"A canteen, Push?"

"That's right. Then you'll always have water when you need it. Get one of those Boy Scout models. The two-quart kind with a canvas strap."

"But you hate the Boy Scouts, Push."

"They make very good canteens, Eugene. *And wear it!* I never want to see you without it. Buy it today."

"All right, Push."

"Say it out."

He made the formal promise that I like to hear.

"Well then," I said, "let's go see this new kid of yours."

He took me to the school yard. "Wait," he said, "you'll see." He skipped ahead.

"Eugene," I said, calling him back. "Let's understand something. No matter what this new kid is like, nothing changes as far as you and I are concerned."

"Aw, Push," he said.

"Nothing, Eugene. I mean it. You don't get out from under me."

"Sure, Push, I know that."

There were just some kids in the far corner of the yard, sitting on the ground, leaning up against the wire fence. Bats and gloves and balls lay scattered around them. (It was where they told dirty jokes. Sometimes I'd come by during the little kids' recess and I'd get some of them and tell them all about what their daddies do to their mommies.)

"There. See? Do you see him?" Eugene, despite himself, seemed hoarse.

"Be quiet," I said, checking him, freezing as a hunter might. I stared.

He was a Prince, I tell you.

He was tall, tall even sitting down. His long legs comfortable in expensive wool, the trousers of a boy who had been on ships, jets; who owned a horse, perhaps; who knew Latin—what *didn't* he know?—somebody made up, like a kid in a play with a beautiful mother and a handsome father, who took his breakfast from a sideboard, and picked, even at fourteen and fifteen and

287

sixteen, his mail from a silver plate. He would have hobbies—stamps, stars, things lovely dead. He wore a sport coat, brown as wood, thick as heavy bark. The buttons were leather buds. His shoes seemed carved from horses' saddles, gunstocks. His clothes had grown once in nature. *What it must feel like inside these clothes*, I thought.

I looked at his face, his clear skin, and guessed at the bones, white as bleached wood. His eyes had skies in them. His yellow hair swirled on his head like a crayoned sun.

"Look, look at him," Eugene said. "The sissy. Get him, Push."

He was talking to them and I moved closer to hear his voice. It was clear, beautiful, but faintly foreign—like herb-seasoned meat.

When he saw me he paused, smiling. He waved. The others didn't look at me.

"Hello, there," he called. "Come over if you'd like. I've been telling the boys about tigers."

"Tigers," I said.

"Give him the 'match burn twice,' Push," Eugene whispered.

"Tigers, is it?" I said. "What do you know about tigers?" My voice was high.

"The 'match burn twice,' Push."

"Not so much as a Master Tugjah. I was telling the boys. In India there are men of high caste—Tugjahs, they're called. I was apprenticed to one once in the Southern Plains and might perhaps have earned my Mastership, but the Red Chinese attacked the northern frontier and—well—let's just say I had to leave. At any rate, these Tugjahs are as intimate with the tiger as you are with dogs. I don't mean they keep them as pets. The relationship goes deeper. Your dog is a service animal, as is your elephant."

"Did you ever see a match burn twice?" I asked suddenly.

"Why, no, can you do that? Is it a special match you use?"

"No," Eugene said. "it's an ordinary match. He uses an ordinary match."

"Can you do it with one of mine, do you think?"

He took a matchbook from his pocket and handed it to me. The cover was exactly the material of his jacket and in the center was a patch with a coat of arms identical to the one he wore over his heart.

I had the matchbook for a moment and then gave it back to him. "I don't feel like it," I said.

"Then some other time, perhaps," he said.

Eugene whispered to me. "His accent, Push, his funny *accent*."

"Some other time, perhaps," I said. (I am a good mimic. I can duplicate a particular kid's lisp, his stutter, a thickness in his throat. There were two or three here whom I had brought close to tears by holding up my mirror to their voices. I can parody their limps, their waddles, their girlish runs, their clumsy jumps. I can throw as they throw, catch as they catch.) I looked around. "Some other time, perhaps," I said again. No one would look at me.

"I'm so sorry," the new one said, "we don't know each other's names. You are?"

"I'm so sorry," I said. "You are?"

He seemed puzzled. Then he looked sad, disappointed. No one said anything.

"It don't sound the same," Eugene whispered.

It was true. I sounded nothing like him. I could imitate only defects, only flaws.

A kid giggled.

"Shh," the Prince said. He put one finger to his lips.

"Look at that," Eugene said under his breath. "He's a sissy."

He had begun to talk to them again. I squatted, a few feet away. I ran gravel through my loose fists, one bowl in an hourglass feeding another.

He spoke now of jungles, now of deserts. He told of ancient trade routes traveled by strange beasts. He described lost cities and a lake deeper at its shore than the deepest level of the sea. There was a story about a boy who had been captured by bandits. A woman in the story—it wasn't clear whether she was the boy's mother—had been tortured. His eyes clouded for a moment when he came to this part and he had to pause before continuing. Then he told how the boy escaped—it was cleverly done—and found help, mountain tribesmen riding elephants. The elephants charged the cave in which the moth—the woman—was still a prisoner. It might have collapsed and killed her but one old bull rushed in and, shielding her with his body, took the weight of the crashing rocks. Your elephant is a service animal.

I let a piece of gravel rest on my thumb and flicked it in a high arc above his head. Some of the others who had seen me stared, but the boy kept on talking. Gradually I reduced the range, allowing the chunks of gravel to come closer to his head.

"You see?" Eugene said quietly. "He's afraid. He pretends not to notice."

The arcs continued to diminish. The gravel went faster, straighter. No one was listening to him now, but he kept talking.

"—of magic," he said, "what Occidentals call 'a witch doctor.' There are spices that induce these effects. The Bogdovii was actually able to stimulate the growth of rocks with the powder. The Dutch traders were ready to go to war for the formula. Well, you can see what it could mean for the Low Countries. Without accessible quarries they've never been able to construct a permanent system of dikes. But with the Bogdovii's powder—" he reached out and casually caught the speeding chip as if it had been a ping-pong ball "—they could turn a grain of sand into a pebble, use the pebbles to grow stones, the stones to grow rocks. This little piece of gravel, for example, could be changed into a mountain." He dipped his thumb into his palm as I had and balanced the gravel on his nail. He flicked it. It rose from his nail like a missile and climbed an impossible arc. It disappeared. "The Bogdovii never revealed how it was done."

289

I stood up. Eugene tried to follow me.

"Listen," he said, "you'll get him."

"Swallow," I told him. "Swallow, you pig!"

I have lived my life in pursuit of the vulnerable—Push, the chink seeker, wheeler dealer in the flawed cement of the personality, a collapse maker. But what isn't vulnerable, *who* isn't? There is that which is unspeakable, so I speak it. "What will you do when you grow up, Push?" the Vocations Counselor at school once asked me. "Sir," I said, "I think I'd like to get into *quality control*." Me and the devil, we do God's dirty work after all.

I went home after I left him. I had turned once at the gate and there were the boys around him still. The useless Eugene had moved closer. *He* made room for him against the fence.

I ran into Frank the fat boy. He made a move to cross the street, but I had seen him and he went through a clumsy checking motion. I could tell he thought I would get him for that, but I moved by, indifferent to a grossness in which I had once delighted. As I passed he seemed puzzled, a little hurt, a little—this was astonishing—guilty. *Sure* guilty. Why *not* guilty? The forgiven tire of their exemption. Nothing could ever be forgiven and I forgave nothing. I held them to the mark. Who else cared about the fatties, about the dummies and slobs and clowns, about the gimps and squares and oafs and fools, the kids with a mouthful of mush, all those shut-ins of the mind and heart, all those losers? Frank the fat boy knew, and passed me shyly. His wide, fat body stiffened, forced jokishly martial when he saw me, had already become flaccid as he moved by, had already made one more forgiven surrender. Who cared?

The streets were full of failure. Let them be. There was a paragon, a paragon loose. What could he be doing here, why had he come, what did he want? It was unthinkable—so I thought it—that this hero from India and every- where had made his home here, lived, as Frank the fat boy did, as Eugene did, as *I* did, in an apartment, that he shared our lives.

In the afternoon I looked for Eugene. He was in the park, in a tree, a book in his lap. He leaned against the thick trunk.

"Eugene," I called up to him.

"Push, they're closed. It's Sunday, Push. The stores are closed. I looked for the canteen. The stores are closed."

"Where is he?"

"Who, Push? What do you want, Push?"

"*Him.* Your pal. The Prince. Where? Tell me, Eugene, or I'll shake you out of that tree. I'll burn you down. I swear it. Where is he?"

"No, Push. I was wrong about that guy. He's nice. He's really nice. Push, he told me about a doctor who could help me. Leave him alone, Push."

"Where, Eugene? *Where?* I count to three."

Eugene shrugged and came down the tree.

I found the name Eugene gave me—funny, foreign—over the bell in the outer hall. The buzzer sounded and I pushed open the door. I stood inside and looked up the carpeted stairs, the angled banisters.

"What is it?" The voice sounded old, worried.

"The new kid," I called, "the new kid."

"It's for you," I heard her say.

"Yes?" His voice, the one I couldn't mimic. I mounted the first stair. I leaned back against the wall and looked up through the high, boxy banister poles. It was like standing inside a pipe organ.

"Yes?"

From where I stood at the bottom of the stairs, I could see only—what was it?—a boot. He was wearing boots.

"Yes? What is it please?"

"You," I roared. "Glass of fashion, mold of form, it's me! It's Push the bully!"

I heard his soft, rapid footsteps coming down the stairs—a springy, spongy urgency. He jingled, the bastard! He had coins—I could see them: rough, golden, imperfectly round; raised massively gowned goddesses, their heads fingered smooth, their arms gone—and keys to strange boxes, thick doors. I saw his boots. I backed away.

"I brought you down," I said.

"Be quiet, please. There's a woman who's ill. A boy who must study. There's a man with bad bones. An old man needs sleep."

"He'll get it," I said.

"We'll go outside," he said.

"No. Do you live here? What do you do? Will you be in our school? Were you telling the truth?"

"Shh. Please. You're very excited."

"Tell me your name," I said. (It could be my campaign, I thought. His *name*. Scratched in new sidewalk, chalked onto walls, written on papers dropped in the street. To leave it behind like so many clues, to give him a fame, to take it away, to slash and cross out, to erase and to smear—my kid's witchcraft.) "Tell me your name."

"It's John," he said softly.

"What?"

"It's John."

"John what? Come on now. I'm Push the bully."

"John Williams," he said.

"John Williams? John Williams? Only that? Only John Williams?"

He smiled.

"Who's that on the bell? The name on the box?"

"She needs me," he said.

"Cut it out."

"I help her," he said.

"You stop that."

"There's a man that's in pain. A woman who's old. A husband that's worried. A wife that despairs."

"You're the bully," I said. "Your John Williams is a service animal," I yelled in the hall.

He turned and began to climb the stairs. His calves bloomed in their leather sheathing.

"Lover," I whispered to him.

He turned to me at the landing. "Hater," he said.

"We'll see," I said.

"We'll see what we'll see," he said.

That night, in enormous letters, I painted his name on the side of the gymnasium. In the morning it was still there, but it wasn't what I meant. There was nothing incantatory in the huge letters, no scream, no curse. I had never traveled with a gang, there had been no togetherness in my tearing, but this thing on the wall seemed the act of vandals, the low production of ruffians. When you looked at it you were surprised they had gotten the spelling right.

Astonishingly, it was allowed to remain. And each day there was something more celebrational in the giant name, something of increased hospitality, lavish welcome. John Williams might have been a football hero, or someone back from the kidnapers. Finally I had to take it off myself.

Something had changed.

Eugene was not wearing his canteen. Boys didn't break off their conversations when I came up to them. One afternoon a girl winked at me. (Push has never picked on girls. *Their* submissiveness is part of their nature. They are ornamental. I mean there is a way in which they function as part of the landscape, like flowers at a funeral. They have a strange cheerfulness. They are the organizers of pep rallies and dances. They put out the Year Book. They are a race of Gray Ladies. I can't bully them.)

John Williams was in the school, but except for brief glimpses in the hall I never saw him. Teachers would repeat the things he had said in their other classes. They read from his papers. In the gym the coach described plays he had made, set shots he had taken. Everyone talked about him, and girls made a reference to him a sort of love signal. If it was suggested that he had smiled at one of them the girl referred to would blush, or, what was worse, look aloofly mysterious. (*Then* I could have punished her, *then* I could.) Gradually his name began to appear on all their notebooks, in the margins of their texts. (It annoyed me to remember what *I* had done on the wall.) The big canvas books, with their careful, elaborate "J's" and "W's," took on the appearance of ancient, illuminated fables. It was the unconscious embroidery of love, hope's bright doodle. Even the administration was aware of him. In Assembly the principal announced that Williams had broken all existing records in the school's charity drives. She had never seen good citizenship like his before, she said.

It's one thing to live with a bully, another to live with a hero.

Everyone's hatred I understand, no one's love, everyone's grievance, no one's content.

I saw Mimmer. Mimmer should have graduated years ago. I saw Mimmer the dummy.

"Mimmer," I said, "you're in his class."

"He's very smart."

"Yes, but is it fair? You work harder. I've seen you study. You spend hours. Nothing comes. He was born knowing. You could have used just a little of what he's got so much of. It's not fair."

"He's very clever. It's wonderful," Mimmer says.

Sludz is crippled. He wears a shoe with a built-up heel to balance himself.

"Ah, Sludz," I say, "I've seen him run."

"He has beaten the horses in the park. It's very beautiful," Sludz says.

"He's handsome, isn't he, Clob?" Clob looks contagious, radio-active. He has severe acne. He is ugly *under* his acne.

"He gets the girls," Clob says.

He gets *everything*, I think. But I'm alone in my envy, awash in my own lust. It's as if I were a prophet to the deaf. Really. Schnooks, schnooks, I want to scream, dopes and settlers. What good does his smile do you, of what use is his good heart?

The other day I did something stupid. I went to the cafeteria and shoved a boy out of the way and took his place in the line. It was foolish, but their fear is almost all gone and I felt I had to show the flag. The boy only grinned and let me pass. Then someone called my name. It was *him*. I turned to face him. "Push," he said, "you forgot your silver." He handed it to a girl in front of him and she gave it to the boy in front of her and it came to me down the long line.

I plot, I scheme. Snares, I think, tricks and traps. I remember the old days when there were ways to snap fingers, crush toes, ways to pull noses, twist heads and punch arms—the oldtimey Flinch Law I used to impose, the gone bully magic of deceit. *But nothing works against him,* I think. (How does he know so much? He is bully prepared, that one. Not to be trusted.)

It is worse and worse.

In the cafeteria he eats with Frank. "You don't want those potatoes," he tells him. "Not the ice cream, Frank. One sandwich, remember. You lost three pounds last week." The fat boy smiles his fat love at him. John Williams puts his arm around him. He seems to squeeze him thin.

He's helping Mimmer to study. He goes over his lessons and teaches him tricks, shortcuts. "I want you up there with me on the Honor Roll, Mimmer."

I see him with Sludz. They go to the gym. I watch from the balcony. "Let's develop those arms, my friend." They work out with weights. Sludz's muscles grow, they bloom from his bones.

I lean over the rail. I shout down.

"He can bend iron bars. Can he peddle a bike? Can he walk on rough ground? Can he climb up a hill? Can he wait on a line? Can he dance with a girl? Can he go up a ladder or jump from a chair?"

Beneath me the rapt Sludz sits on a bench and raises a weight. He holds it arm's length, level with his chest. He moves it high, higher. It rises above his shoulders, his throat, his head. He bends back his neck to see what he's done. If the weight should fall now it would crush his throat. I stare down into his smile.

I see Eugene in the halls. I stop him. "Eugene, what's he done for you?" I ask. He smiles—he never did this—and I see his mouth's flood. "High tide," I say with satisfaction.

Williams has introduced Clob to a girl. They have double-dated.

A week ago John Williams came to my house to see me! I wouldn't let him in.

"Please open the door, Push. I'd like to chat with you. Will you open the door? Push? I think we ought to talk. I think I can help you to be happier."

I was furious. I didn't know *what* to say to him. "I don't want to be happy. Go way." It was what little kids used to say to me.

"*Please* let me help you."

"*Please* let me—" I began to echo. "Please let me alone."

"We ought to be friends, Push."

"No deals." I am choking, I am close to tears. What can I do? *What?* I want to kill him.

I double-lock the door and retreat into my room. He is still out there. I have tried to live my life so I could always keep the lamb from my door.

He has gone too far this time and, I think sadly, I will have to fight him. Push pushed. I think sadly of the pain. Push pushed. I will have to fight him. Not to preserve honor but its opposite. Each time I see him I will have to fight him. And then I think—*of course!* And *I* smile. He has done me a favor. I know it at once. If he fights me he fails. He fails if he fights me. *Push pushed pushes!* It's Physics! Natural Law! I know he'll beat me, but I won't prepare, I won't train, I won't use the tricks I know. It's strength against strength and my strength is as the strength of ten because my jaw is glass! *He doesn't know everything, not everything he doesn't.* And I think, I could go out now, he's still there, I could hit him in the hall, but I think, no, I want them to see, *I want them to see!*

The next day I am very excited. I look for Williams. He's not in the halls. I miss him in the cafeteria. Afterwards I look for him in the school yard where I first saw him. (He has them organized now. He teaches them games of Tibet, games of Japan, he gets them to play lost sports of the dead.) He does not disappoint me. He is there in the yard, a circle around him, a ring of the loyal.

I join the ring. I shove in between two kids I have known. They try to change places, they murmur and fret.

Williams sees me and waves. His smile could grow flowers. "Boys," he says, "boys, make room for Push. Join hands, boys." They welcome me to the circle. One takes my hand, then another. I give to each calmly.

I wait. *He doesn't know everything.*

"Boys," he begins, "today we're going to learn a game that the knights of the lords and kings of old France used to play in another century. Now you may not realize it, boys, because today when we think of a knight we think, too, of his fine charger, but the fact is that a horse was a rare animal, not a domestic European animal at all, but Asian. In Western Europe, for example, there was no such thing as a workhorse until the eighth century. Your horse was just too expensive to be put to heavy labor in the fields. This explains, incidentally, the prevalence of famine in Western Europe, whereas famine is unrecorded in Asia until the ninth century when Euro/Asian horse trading was at its height. It was not only expensive to purchase a horse, it was expensive to keep one. A cheap fodder wasn't developed in Europe until the tenth century. Then, of course, when you consider the terrific risks that the warrior horse of a knight naturally had to run, you begin to appreciate how expensive it would have been for the lord—unless he was extremely rich—to provide all his knights with horses. He'd want to make pretty certain that the knights who got them knew how to handle a horse. Only your knights errant—an elite, crack corps—ever had horses. We don't realize that most knights were *home* knights; *chevalier chez* they were called.

"This game, then, was devised to let the lord, or king, see which of his knights had the skill and strength in his hands to control a horse. Without moving your feet you must try to jerk the one next to you off-balance. Each man has two opponents so it's very difficult. If a man falls, or if his knee touches the ground, he's out. The circle is diminished but must close up again immediately. Now, once for practice only—"

"Just a minute," I interrupt.

"Yes, Push?"

I leave the circle and walk forward and hit him as hard as I can in the face.

He stumbles backward. The boys groan. He recovers. He rubs his jaw and smiles. I think he is going to let me hit him again. I am prepared for this. He knows what I'm up to and will use his passivity. Either way I win, but I am determined he shall hit me. I'm ready to kick him, but as my foot comes up he grabs my ankle and turns me forcefully. I spin in the air. He lets go and I fall heavily on my back. I am surprised at how easy it was but am content if they understand. I get up and am walking away, but there is an arm on my shoulder. He pulls me around roughly. He hits me.

"*Sic semper tyrannis!*" he exults.

"Where's your other cheek?" I ask, falling backward.

"One cheek for tyrants," he shouts. He pounces on me and raises his fist and I cringe. His anger is terrific. I do not want to be hit again.

"You see? You see?" I scream at the kids, but I have lost the train of my former reasoning. I have in no way beaten him. I can't remember what I had intended, but this I understand. I have in no way beaten him.

He lowers his fist and gets off my chest and they cheer. "Hurrah," they yell. "Hurrah, hurrah." The word seems funny to me.

He offers his hand when I try to rise. It is so difficult to know what to do. Oh God, it is so difficult to know which gesture is the right one. I don't even know this. He knows everything and I don't even know this. I am a fool on the ground, one hand behind me pushing up, the other not yet extended but itching in the palm where the need is. It is better to give than receive, surely. It is best not to need at all.

Appalled, guessing what I miss, I rise alone.

"Friends?" he asks. He offers to shake.

"Take it, Push." It's Eugene's voice.

"Go ahead, Push." Sludz limps forward.

"Push, hatred's so ugly," Clob says, his face shining.

"You'll feel better, Push," Frank, thinner, taller, urges softly.

"Push, don't be foolish," Mimmer says.

I shake my head. I may be wrong. I am probably wrong. All I know at last is what feels good. "Nothing doing," I growl. "No deals." I begin to talk, to spray my hatred at them. They are not an easy target even now. "Only your knights errant—your crack corps—ever have horses. Sludz may dance and Clob may kiss, but they'll never be good at it. *Push is no service animal*. No. No. Can you hear that, Williams? There isn't any magic, but your no is still stronger than your yes and distrust is where I put my faith." I turn to the boys. "What have you settled for? Only your knights errant ever have horses. What have you settled for? Will Mimmer do sums in his head? How do you like your lousy hunger, thin boy? Sludz, you can break me, but you can't catch me. And Clob will never shave without pain, and ugly, let me tell you, is *still* in the eye of the beholder!"

John Williams mourns for me. He grieves his gamy grief. No one has everything. Not even John Williams. He doesn't have *me*. He'll never have me, I think. If my life were only to deny him that it would almost be enough. I could do his voice now if I wanted. His corruption began when he lost me. "You," I shout, rubbing it in, "*indulger,* dispense me no dispensations. Push the bully hates your heart!"

"Shut him up, somebody," Eugene cries. His saliva spills from his mouth when he speaks.

"Swallow! *Pig, swallow!*"

He rushes toward me.

Suddenly I raise my arms and he stops. I feel a power in me. I am Push, Push the bully, God of the Neighborhood, its incarnation of envy and jealousy and need. I vie, strive, emulate, compete, a contender in every event there is. I didn't make myself. I probably can't save myself, but maybe that's the only need I haven't got. I taste my lack and that's how I win. By having nothing to lose. I want and I want and I will die wanting but first I will have something. This time I will have something. I say it aloud. "I will have something." I step toward them. The power makes me dizzy. It is enormous. They feel it. They back away. They crouch in the shadow of my outstretched wings. It isn't deceit this time but the real magic at last, the genuine thing—the cabala of my hate, of my irreconcilableness.

Logic is nothing. Desire is stronger.

I move toward Eugene. "*I will have something*," I roar.

"Stand back," he shrieks. "I'll spit in your eye."

"*I will have something*. I will have terror. I will have drought. I bring the dearth. Famine's contagious. And thirst. Privation, privation, barrenness, void. I dry up your glands, I poison your well."

He is choking, gasping, chewing furiously. He opens his mouth. It is dry. His throat is parched. There is sand on his tongue.

They moan. They are terrified, but they move up to see. We are thrown together. Sludz, Frank, Clob, Mimmer, the others, John Williams, myself. I can't stand them near me. I move against them. I shove them away. I force them off. I press them aside. I push through.

JOYCE CAROL OATES

Love and Death

In February 1963, a man named Marshall Hughes returned to his hometown to visit his father, a widower. This is not really the beginning of the story—that is, not the true beginning; but it would be his idea of the beginning.

His father lived alone with an older sister, who was his housekeeper and nurse. His name was also Marshall; he had been "big Marshall" at one time; now it was Marshall, Jr., who was big and his father who was small, though perhaps that was just a trick of the light. "No, keep that shut," his father kept saying, wagging his fingers toward the window, "it hurts my eyes." He sat up in bed, or in a big armchair near the bed, reading newspapers. He was a sharp, petulant old man who still had money, coming in from sources he was secretive about. Good for him, Marshall thought, as if his father's financial stability protected them both from something: good, let him stay that way, let him die happy.

The family house was large and drafty, Victorian in style. It struck Marshall as the prototype for houses in the cartoons of certain sophisticated magazines—cartoons meaningful only to a generation who have abandoned such houses, with nostalgia. His wife could look back at such a family home too. Marshall and his wife were well matched, both intelligent and pleasant and accustomed to certain delicacies that are the result of money—money kept invisible, of course. They had both belonged to the same kind of social group; they had gone to the same kind of schools, had the same kind of teachers. They were bound together before they had even met by the queer pleasing network of names that made up their world.

Marshall and Fran had been married for nine years in 1963, and they had three children. Marshall worked for a company that made electrical parts for other companies, an excellent business. And he needed to work, too, because the money that came to him and Fran from various sources was no more than seven or eight thousand a year, and he felt a strange satisfaction at the thought of "having to work," because there was a kind of settledness in that thought, a sense of safety. They went to a Presbyterian church mainly for their children's sakes. And they lived in an excellent suburb in the Midwest, several hundred miles from their families and, it would seem, centuries beyond the influence of the past.

So Marshall went back to visit. His conscience nudged him, his wife said, "Why don't you . . . ?", and he made up his mind to return, since his father wasn't well and it would be only a matter of time until the old man died. Marshall was worried that his father knew this. That was perhaps why his father kept saying sourly, "I'm going back to the office when the weather clears. This winter lasts too long."

"How is Dr. Fitzgerald?" Marshall said.

"Competent."

"Is his son doing well?"

"I wouldn't know about his son."

In such ways was Marshall's generation shouldered aside, squeezed out, ignored. Marshall, sensitive to his father's pride in himself and his power, never pursued any subjects that led to the forbidden subterranean world of time and mortality and death.

On the first evening of his visit he called Fran and was relieved to hear her voice—that cool, sane, immensely charming voice, which summoned up for him the elegant world of his home, his friends, his children, his wife. Whatever his father's people had achieved, there was none of the comfort of the new generation in it: its victories were grim, like its antique furniture. There was little joy in that generation. "How are the children?" Marshall asked over the telephone. Tears often stung his eyes when he called home from his business trips asking about the children. He thought of them mainly when he was away; when he was home they somehow eluded his concern.

"Oh, they all miss you. They love you," Fran said.

"Tell them to be good."

There were odd embarrassed moments when he and Fran could not think of the next thing to say. This was not in spite of their politeness with each other but because of it.

"Please take care of yourself," Marshall said.

"Take care of yourself," his wife answered.

The next morning he went out for a walk. He was prepared to see a decline in the neighborhood, but things weren't too bad. One or two of the old places were obviously vacant, another looked as if it must be a nursing home of some kind. It was a mild, sunny day, suggesting spring. Marshall went all the way down to the post office, which looked smaller than he remembered; there were four windows inside but only one was open, so he had to stand in line, and he noticed a woman near the front of the line who looked familiar. He stared at the back of her head. She wore a cloth coat of a cheap cut. A flimsy pink scarf was tied about her hair, which was in no particular style, though bleached blond. Marshall himself wore a topcoat of a good, dark material and gloves, and his expensive shoes were protected by rubbers. He was a tall, fairly handsome man of about forty. When the woman turned away from the window he caught his breath—yes, he did remember her.

She went over to one of the closed windows and set her purse down on the counter, so that she could put stamps on some envelopes. He watched her. She had a thin, frail, careless profile, not quite as he had remembered. He had remembered her as more solid. She licked the stamps and put them on the envelopes, oblivious of anyone around her. Marshall wondered whom she was writing to. He saw that her coat, which looked new, was too short for her skirt, which hung down an inch or so in an untidy way.

He kept watching her and thought surely she would notice him. He was almost at the window when she picked up her purse and turned to go, without seeing him. So there was nothing for him to do but follow her—he didn't want to call after her, and he didn't want her to get away. At the door he caught up with her and said, "Hello, it's Cynthia, isn't it? Cynthia?"

She turned and stared at him. He saw that she recognized him, and he saw also the sudden recoiling gesture, the half-demure protestation, as if he had caught her at a bad moment. "Oh, Marshall," she said flatly. Her eyes were a cold, critical gray. "Marshall Hughes."

He laughed in embarrassment, breathlessly. "I was sure it was you . . ."

"Are you back home again?"

"I'm visiting."

The corners of her mouth turned up, but not in a smile. Her lips were quite red. He was struck by the flat, blatant, tired look she was giving him, a look that must have been defensive. Her bleached hair, inside the scarf, had a festive and rather ludicrous appearance, framing so cold a face. Several strands of hair had been combed down onto her forehead in a style that was a little too girlish for her. Her nose was long, as he had remembered it, giving her a slightly hungry, impatient look, her nostrils were thin, nervous, her mouth sharply and ironically defined, with the shadows of lines at its corners. It was an intelligent look somehow imposed upon an ordinarily pretty woman's frail, conventional look; her plucked, arched eyebrows could have belonged to any unstylish woman, but that mouth looked as if it might have something to say.

"Well, it was a surprise, seeing you . . . I was sure it was you," Marshall said vaguely. The woman laughed in a short, humorless way, as if he had said something funny. "Do you still live around here? I mean—with your mother?"

"With my mother?" She laughed.

"Yes, I thought—I mean, weren't you living with her?" He was conscious of having said something stupid, having confused facts. She stared at him mockingly. "Well, where do you live? Nearby?"

"Yes, nearby," she said. Her irony was crude; he felt a pang of revulsion toward her.

"Well, how are you?" he said.

"All right."

"I live in Kansas City now myself. My wife and I have three children."

"That's nice."

"And you, are you married?"

"I was married."

He tried to smile, wanting her to smile. There was something cruel about her mouth. He resented her coldness and the proud, indifferent way in which she kept him there, asking her questions. The very look of his clothes embarrassed him; she looked so shabby, so sad, and there was no failure of his own that he could offer her.

"Where are you going now?" he said suddenly.

"Back."

"Back . . . ?"

"A few blocks away."

She moved toward the door. He followed, awkwardly. "Did you walk all the way down here, from your father's house?" she said.

"Yes. It's a fine day for a walk."

They descended the steps. He had the idea she wanted to get away, and he was anxious to keep her with him. He had to think of something to say. Years ago they had been involved with each other casually, and he had forgotten her, and yet now he did not want her to get away; her indifference made him uneasy.

"Could I buy you some coffee? Or lunch?"

"It's too early for lunch."

"It's after eleven."

"I didn't get up till ten."

Again he experienced a slight tug of revulsion. He himself always got up at seven, never slept later. "Some coffee then, down the street?"

"All right."

They went to a small restaurant which Marshall believed he could remember. The woman sat down and unbuttoned her coat and let it fall over the back of her chair as if she were quite accustomed to the place. She wore a deep pink sweater that was too tight for her, and with the coat off she looked younger, more gentle. The sweater was cheap, its neck stretched and a little soiled, but it cast up onto her face a soft pink that was flattering.

"How have you been all these years?" Marshall said.

"I've gotten along."

"It was quite an accident, running into you . . ."

"Yes," she said sarcastically. She was not yet smiling. Marshall was relieved when the waitress came to take their order. They were sitting across from each other at a small, wobbly table. The woman had not pulled her chair in, conscious of the smallness of the table, and so she sat back awkwardly. Marshall folded his coat neatly over a nearby chair, and with a deft movement that looked unplanned he pushed the table in toward her and drew his own chair up to it.

"Yes, it's quite a surprise," he said, rubbing his hands.

"Christ, do you have to keep saying that?"

"But I mean it." He flushed, as if embarrassed by her profanity. She had so much strength, mysterious strength, and he had none. Her eyes regarded him with an unsurprised, calculating look, a look he had never seen in any other woman, and he noticed with satisfaction that there were slight hollows beneath those eyes. She was about thirty-five now. In a few years she would age suddenly, and there would be no strength then, none of this sullen independence. He could not understand why he had followed her out of the post office.

"Did you say you were married now?" he said.

"Who wants to know?"

"I do. I want to know," he said weakly.

"Maybe I am, what difference does it make? Maybe I kicked him out. It's the same old story; anyway what difference does it make?"

"You certainly don't mean it makes no difference to you."

"No. I mean to you."

"But I care. I'm anxious to hear about you."

"Oh, Christ," she said. Her eyes moved about behind him with a remote, amused look, as if she were searching out someone to laugh with her over him. Marshall remembered that—he remembered this woman breaking off their conversation to gaze around in that stupid, indifferent, placid way, pretending she had better things to think about.

"How is your brother?" he said.

"Which one, Davey?" she said, more gently.

"Yes, what happened to him?"

"He's the same, he's married now. Working a night shift."

"And what about your mother?"

"Look, you know my mother died a long time ago. You know that."

Marshall frowned. He did not remember, and yet in a way he did remember. There was something sluggish about him. The woman leaned forward, crossing her arms at the wrists; her wrists were girlish and delicate. She said, "You certainly do remember. You're lying."

"What, lying?"

"You're lying." She smiled sourly. "Now tell me about your wife."

"But I want to talk about you."

She laughed. The waitress brought their coffee, and Marshall resented the distraction. The woman said, "You want to talk about me? Why the hell about me? Do you have a cigarette?"

He took out his package of cigarettes at once, anxious to please her. Unwrapping the package, jerking the red cellophane strip around, he was nervous, thinking that there was something vaguely obscene about what he was doing. He finally got a cigarette to stick out, and she took it. Lighting her cigarette was another awkward thing, but at last it was accomplished.

"So your brother is still in town?"

"Yes. You liked him, didn't you?" she said curiously.

"Why do you ask?"

"You liked him because he kept his nose out of our business. That was what you liked about him, and what you didn't like about my mother."

This stirred some memory in him; he nodded slowly. It would be better to agree.

"Your own mother, of course, was a bitch of another type. We won't mention her."

"You never saw my mother."

"I certainly did."

"When did you see her?"

"My God, you know very well—we saw her one day downtown, the two of us. We saw her with some other fat bitches, all dressed up, and you pointed her out to me. I remember that."

Marshall was a little shocked, but he made himself smile. "But if you only saw her . . . ?"

"I knew all about her. You told me. And is your father still alive?"

"Yes."

"You're here visiting him?"

"Yes."

"How long are you going to stay?" But then she tapped ashes from the cigarette onto the floor, nervously as if conscious of having said something wrong but not wanting to correct it.

"A few more days." He pushed the coffee cup aside, he had no desire for coffee. He watched her impatiently. "Well, never mind about that," he said. "What about you, are you married?"

"In a way."

"What does that mean?"

She shrugged her shoulders. With her thumb and two fingers she picked up the coffee cup, a precise little gesture of affectation that struck him. She was a pretty woman in spite of everything. Her hair was disheveled but clean, gleaming in the light from the window. He liked her hair. It was vulgar, that color, and showed that she wasn't so clever after all—what a phony color —but still he liked it on her.

He said, "Your hair looks good."

She lifted one shoulder in a lazy gesture of indifference.

"You used to wear it long. . . ?"

They sat for a while in silence. Then she said, "I have to leave now." She spoke stubbornly, as if arguing. Marshall said, hardly knowing what he would hear, "But where are you going?" Home, she told him. He asked what that meant; whom did she live with? By herself, she said, she lived by herself; but she worked in the evening, and she had some things to do, she had to wash things, go shopping. He asked her if he could come along. She swore in a gentle, weary, unsurprised way, staring at him; she shook her head. Marshall fumbled for the pack of cigarettes and put them away, nervously. The woman kept looking at him. He felt guilty suddenly and had to fight down an impulse to look over his shoulder, to see if anyone had heard.

They had met many years ago in a bar. She had been with one crowd, he with another. He had been introduced to her, asked her her name and telephone number, and a few days later had called her up. She had lived then in a big ugly house, a very old house. He remembered that house, and his shyness, and the girl's carefully made-up, mocking face, and the very high heels of the shoes that she wore.

"No, I have to leave," she said.

He helped her with her coat and put on his own, not bothering to button it.

"Where are you going now?"

"I told you, home."

"Where is that?"

"Close by." She looked sideways at him and smiled. "Do you want to walk me there?"

Her apartment was in a six-story building, an old building. For some reason Marshall was in a hurry, his heartbeat was choked and rapid. On the stairs his feet ached to carry him up fast, faster than he was going. The woman kept glancing sideways at him, ironically. On the banister her bare hand moved in jerks, a few inches at a time, and he watched this movement out of the corner of his eye.

At her door he watched as she put the key into the lock. This startled him, the way it went into the lock, forcing itself in and then turning easily. She said, "You should go back down," indicating with a jerk of her head the stairs behind them.

"Couldn't I stay awhile? Talk to you?"

"Oh, talk, what do you want to talk about? Talk!" she said in disgust.

"Could I see you later, then? Tonight?"

She had opened the door. She seemed impatient to get away, yet something made her linger; like him, she felt a peculiar tugging between them, an undefined force that would not release her. Marshall waited. He remembered her making him wait, in the old days, this sluttish girl who had nothing, really nothing, except what men like himself wanted to give her. Her profile, nearly overwhelmed by the bunch of blond hair that looked resilient and unreal as a dummy's wig, put him in mind of his wife's profile for an instant. But the two women were quite different. His wife had a healthy, wholesome, friendly face, she played golf with women like herself, she dressed with simple, excellent taste. What reminded him of her, in this woman, was no more than the fact that he was standing close to the woman. He had been close to few people in his life.

"Could I come in now? For a few minutes?"

He was perspiring, he was not himself. Her fingers, tapping impatiently on the doorknob, seemed to be tapping against his body, teasing him. He said, begging, "I won't stay long."

He had no impression of the room except that it was small. Windows at one end with their shades drawn; mingled odors of food. He felt as if he had broken through to something, liberated and floating in a way he could not control. It was a strange feeling. All his life he had said silently to others, Let me alone, don't touch me, talk to me but don't touch me, because I'm afraid of—afraid of what? He was afraid, that was enough. He and his wife said this to each other, silently, Let me alone, don't touch me—Cynthia took off her coat angrily and looked around at him. "I don't know why the hell you're here. Do you think it's fifteen years ago?"

This shocked him. "Fifteen years? Nothing ever happened—that long ago—" he said dizzily. He moved toward her. He put his arms around her, clumsy in his coat, and she stood there with a kind of contemptuous patience, a mockery of patience. "I don't think so much time went by—"

"All right."

"I've thought about you a great deal—"

"All right, sure."

"Could we go in there? Is that another room, could we go in there?"

"You'll have to give me some money."

"Yes."

"You used to give me money, right?"

"I don't know, yes, maybe—I don't remember. Did I give you money?" he asked, surprised.

"Certainly."

"I gave you money?"

"I was in love with you, sure, but I was never stupid," she said, in her flat amused voice. "What makes you think I'm stupid? Because I'm poor? Because I don't dress like your wife?"

"No, you're not stupid."

"Then give me some money, now."

He took out his wallet. He had the idea that she was degrading him in this manner, degrading herself, in order to block out the memory of their love together—that was all right, he understood her. She was protecting herself. He took out a number of bills, and smiling foolishly, handed them to her. She took them and began to smile too. "Yes, you gave me money," she said. "Otherwise why should I have bothered with you?"

They went into the other room. Marshall stopped thinking. When he began to think again, a while later, his mind was precise, and he looked around the room as if memorizing it. And when they went back out into the larger room, the woman yawning and indifferent at his side, he looked around that room too. He saw the cheap modern furniture, blond wood and green cushions, a table with a formica top, flowered drapes, a worn-out rug. He felt dislocated and quite empty. The room was so ugly that it saddened him.

"Let me see you again. I want to see you again," he said.

"You can take me to dinner tonight."

"Dinner? Really?"

"Yes, dinner. Good-bye."

He had to make excuses at home, saying he had met an old friend on his walk. When his aunt asked who this friend was, in her dry, suspicious spinster's voice, he really could not think of a name for several seconds. It was embarrassing. His father luckily paid no attention; he was reading newspapers. Marshall watched the old man, jealous of the attention he paid to all those papers when his son had traveled so far to see him. He noticed the way the old man pursed his lips, reading, working his lips as if mumbling secret words to himself, flexing his jaws. There was something outlandish and too intimate, almost indecent, in the way he worked his lips. Marshall looked away. Then he looked back, fascinated.

Marshall called his wife again that afternoon. He asked how the children were, how Fran was. Fine, fine. But one of the boys had cut his leg. Out playing. No, he hadn't been pushed, it was just an accident. Marshall tried to keep talking and listening. It was easier to talk than to listen. His wife's voice was very far away; the book-lined study in which he sat seemed somehow very far away too, its indistinct walls confining the air of another, older time, into which he had stepped accidentally. And he would step out of it again in a moment.

When he came to the woman's apartment that evening he was very nervous. She said, amused, "What's wrong with you? In the post office you were another person; now you're back to what you were fifteen years ago."

"But what was I, fifteen years ago?"

"What you are now."

"But what is that?"

"I can't tell you. How can I describe you to yourself?"

They had dinner in a dark, ordinary restaurant. A big air-conditioning unit was perched up above them on the wall, silent and ominous. As they ate their dinner, uninteresting food he barely tasted, he kept asking her about what she had meant, earlier. "Did I really give you money?"

"Yes, of course."

"And you took it?"

"Why wouldn't I take it?"

"Do you remember how we met? The first time?"

"You came in a certain bar to make a telephone call. Your friends were outside, waiting. You saw me and asked me something—asked me for change, for the telephone. You talked to me. Then you went out and told your friends to drive on without you, and you came back in, and the two of us went somewhere . . ." She paused, thinking. "Yes. We went to this place I sometimes stayed at, a flat a friend of mine rented."

"But it wasn't that way at all," Marshall said quickly.

"No? How was it then?"

"Didn't I call you up, later? Didn't I get your telephone number?"

"Yes. You asked me for my number, after we went back to that flat."

"Only after that?"

"Yes, don't you remember?"

He stared at her. Slowly, reluctantly, he began to remember. She had been a thin girl in a black dress, trying to look older than she was. She had been sitting at a table near the telephone booth, in a corner. "So we went back to a flat? A friend of yours had a flat?"

"Yes. We only went there once."

"It wasn't someone else?"

"You mean, instead of you? There were other men, yes, but it was you as well."

"But you say we only went there once?"

"I lived at home then. I was with my family."

"Yes. I remember that, of course."

"You remember my mother."

"Yes."

Her mother had screamed at him one day, a fat drunken woman who accused him of taking advantage of her daughter. Marshall had had to push her away, she had tried to strike him and scratch his face . . . Yes, he remembered that fat bitch of a woman; he was glad she was dead.

"You were glad when she died," Cynthia said.

"I wouldn't say that . . ."

"Yes, I would say it," Cynthia said flatly.

After dinner he said, "Why haven't you done more with yourself? Why are you still living in the same neighborhood, after so long?"

"I don't have any ambitions."

"You never got married?"

"I didn't say that."

"Or have children?"

"My real life isn't of any interest to you, it's nothing. What do you care if I did get married? All right, I did. Then it was ended, like that. No children. I'm not like people you know, I don't have any ambition. I don't care."

"It seems impossible . . ."

"But I wouldn't want to be your wife. I wouldn't want that."

"You wouldn't want to marry me?"

She laughed. "No, I wouldn't. I mean that I wouldn't want to be the woman who is your wife, now—I wouldn't want to be that woman."

Marshall had to think for a moment, recalling his wife. His heart fluttered as if he were in danger.

"You are two very different people," he said slowly.

They went back to her apartment. Near as he could come to her she always held him off, in a sense, observing him coldly. He could never get past the icy circle of her mind; she was always thinking about him, holding him apart from her. "What was your husband like?" he said. "Like anyone. An ordinary man," she said. "He didn't have money, did he?" he said. "Of course not," she said, "nobody has money except you."

He was reluctant to leave her; he wanted to stay all night, but his father would wonder about him; a vision of that ugly old mansion rose in his mind and made him stir guiltily. In the dark, it was difficult for him to know who he was. And yet it was a darkness that was not unfamiliar.

She snapped on the light. "I hope that from now on we can be friends, and forget each other."

"Why should we forget each other?"

"But you forgot me before. You never sent me any money."

"I didn't know you wanted money."

"You must have known. Everyone wants money," she said, without bothering to emphasize any of her words, just pronouncing them. He felt that she did not believe this, that it was nothing more than a means of holding him off. She had a strange face, this woman, an unhappy, brooding, and yet careless look, which her makeup seemed to parody. He was uncomfortable beneath her gaze. She might have been assessing any man, himself, or a stranger, making no distinction between them.

"I can send you money, when I get home."

She said nothing. Marshall went on, anxiously, "I want to ask you something before I leave. Why do you think I came over to you?"

"When, today? Or the first time?"

"Either time."

"Because you liked me, I suppose."

"But why—why do you think I like you?"

She shut her eyes wearily. "You mean, it seems crazy to you that you should be here? All right, yes, it is crazy. But I do know why you're here, as a matter of fact."

"Why?"

"Don't you know? Can't you guess?"

He felt a slight pang of terror, at the very softness of her voice. "What? What is it?"

"Do you remember what you said to me, the first time we met? I mean after we went back to that flat."

"No. What did I say?"

"You asked me my age, how long I had been doing that sort of thing. You asked me about the men I knew. You were very curious, very excited. Of course, you were a young man then—"

"And you were young too," he said nervously.

"Not in the same way. You were always pestering me then, back then— don't you remember?"

"I think you're mixing me up with someone else."

"Oh, hell," she laughed. "Go home, then."

"No, please. Couldn't you be mixing me up with someone else?"

"I don't forget things. There was a time when I loved you, and this time is closed off from what came before and what came after, and I can look back at it and remember it perfectly. What's strange is that you don't remember it."

"But I want to remember it."

"You asked me about the other men. You came to see me all the time, it was crazy. You wrote me letters though we lived in the same city, you gave me presents—jewelry and clothes—you were always bothering me. You liked to tease me about those other men, you'd sit on the edge of the bed and ask me questions, lots of questions. Don't you remember that?"

"No," Marshall said dully. But even as he spoke he knew it was true, and a sense of revulsion and anger stirred inside him.

"What do you remember, then?"

"I asked you your telephone number, and I called you up, a few days later," he said, as if reciting something. "I went to your house—your brother was working on his car, in the driveway. You introduced me to your mother. I think it was a Sunday, Sunday afternoon."

"But we met on Saturday night."

"This was the next day. You introduced me to your mother."

"Did you like that?"

"I thought that was nice."

"But you must have known I did it to make fun. My mother was always drunk, and I wanted to see how you'd act. Didn't you know that?"

Marshall was silent for a moment. Then he said, "But I don't remember any flat."

"Of course you remember."

"I think you're mixing me up with someone else."

"So you called me up, you met my mother, what else?"

"And then . . . we started seeing each other."

"What did we do?"

"We went to movies, out to dinner. We went dancing." He thought about this, watching her uneasily. Then his mind cleared, and he remembered that it was Fran he had done those things with.

"We went to rooms, to hotels," she said. "We drove around in your car."

"But you didn't seem to mind—"

"Why should I mind? You paid me."

"I remember that vaguely—"

"Vaguely, hell!"

She wanted him to leave, but he was reluctant. He clutched at something: "But you lied to me too. You said you had to work tonight."

"Did I?"

"I think you said that."

"Yes, I work some evenings. I have a real job; I'm a hostess in a restaurant. But I took tonight off."

"For me?"

She shrugged her shoulders. Of course, he had given her money—but he did not think that was significant.

She saw him to the door. He turned to leave, his face burning. It seemed to him that something was wrong, something was threatening. When he was out in the hall she said, in her low teasing voice, "Here's something else you won't remember either—how when we went out you talked to me about my life, how I was trapped, I had nowhere to go, no future—I'd get diseased or some maniac would kill me. You said you loved me, because I was just a tramp

309

and my mother was a drunk and so on—and you really did love me, but you don't remember any of it."

He made up his mind not to see her again, and the rest of his visit was spent in the old house. He sat with his father while the old man read his papers, the two of them quite oblivious of one another. Except from time to time Marshall glanced at his father and saw that queer silent smacking of his father's lips—again and again—and his very bowels seemed stirred by it, stirred to anger. He called Fran, as if in desperation. But her voice was distant, and what she spoke of seemed trivial. He wondered whether, if he put the receiver down gently, he might cut her out from his life altogether.

But of course this was nonsense. He was frightened at himself, at such thoughts. He had never in his life had such thoughts before. And he found himself recalling certain moments of his love-making with that woman when he thought of the possibility of her being diseased and of the great risk he was taking. It excited him, to think of this risk. Yet that was all nonsense, all disgusting. He was anxious to return home again.

A strange thing: he began seeing things that weren't there. Or rather, a foreign vision imposed itself upon them, distorting them violently. One day his aunt—a woman of over sixty, hefty, vague, sour, very religious—was cutting meat when he walked into the kitchen. He was eager to talk with someone. She was slicing pieces of raw meat off a large, fatty hunk, and something about her wet, blood-stained fingers and the tender pink meat and the flashing of the knife terrified him. He was almost sick. His aunt did not care to talk, and so he passed on through to the breakfast room and safely away . . . And another time at dinner he watched his father finish a glass of water, lifting it to his mouth and drinking in rather audible gasps until nothing was left, and Marshall thought: In just that way do people make love. It was not a thought that made sense. But it flashed clearly through his mind, as he watched his father empty the crystal goblet.

He was not going to call Cynthia, but on the last day he did. They talked vaguely as if they had nothing in common. "Now I'm leaving, I probably won't see you again," he said cautiously. She said, "Yes, good luck. I hope your father is well." The mention of his father startled him, for certainly she was thinking that he had to be back—didn't he?—when his father got worse, when his father died, he had to be back then, and he'd call her up, wouldn't he? He was trapped. So he said irritably, "Of course he's well. And now I'm going back. You'll see—a person can do one thing and then do the opposite thing, it doesn't matter. I won't be seeing you again."

He arrived back home in time for a dinner party. Everything was confused, gaily muddled. He had to tell his wife about the visit while they dressed, the two of them already late, a little giddy with the prospect of a familiar excellent evening before them. Marshall felt good; he felt quite safe. He kept chatting to his wife about all sorts of things, and she in her turn chatted about the latest news, which friends she had had lunch with, who was in town. He was amazed at how rich and complex and yet safe this life was, out here.

It was several hours before he even remembered that woman. At about ten o'clock they went in to dinner, into an elegant dining room, and their host opened a bottle of wine. He worked at the cork, making jokes, and seemed to be looking at Marshall as if Marshall were somehow the main point of the joke. Marshall felt sweat break out on his body. He couldn't quite make out the joke, but he did watch with a kind of terror the man's fingers working at the cork. Something was straining for release, something threatened to spurt out—Then the moment passed, it was over. Wine was poured into glasses in an ordinary way, and there was nothing behind it.

For more than a week he continued as his usual self, and then he had an overwhelming impulse to write to Cynthia. He was at his office, and he used business stationery, with the firm's Kansas City address on it. Let her see it. He wanted to give her proof of how successful he was. He wrote her a long, aimless, unplanned letter. It was chatty and superficial. Rereading it, he saw that the letter was quite obviously a disguise for something left unsaid—but he did not know what that was.

She did not reply to it.

Angered, he wrote again. This time he asked her specific questions, about her ex-husband, about her "present mode of living," about her plans for the future. This letter was five pages long, an inspired letter. Marshall had never been able to write to anyone and had always telephoned if he had anything to say, so he was both pleased and a little disturbed that he could write so much to that woman. She was so unimportant, after all.

He included in the letter a check for several hundred dollars, and this time she replied. She thanked him for the money and wrote a few more lines, just to be polite. He was enraged at this but did not know what he had expected. So he wrote again at once, ending his letter: "Write back. I want to hear anything you have to say. Tell me about your job, about your mother or anything."

As an afterthought he took some bills out of his wallet and slid them into the envelope. His fingers were shaking.

Her letter came a few weeks later. In ball-point ink she had written a few lines, mentioning the money. This was followed by a paragraph in pencil, evidently written at a later time, in which she did talk about her mother: "You both hated each other, and yet you were curious about each other. She knew you had money, and, who knows, she might end up with it herself—I'm sure that crossed her mind. And then, on the day she died, you had to hear everything about her and go right into her bedroom, though the poor woman had been in that bed a few hours before. And yet you two never really met except that one time and never talked to each other."

He read this and a fine dizzying film passed before his eyes. In such flat, blatant language, just as she spoke—what had she told him? Her mother's bedroom, what about that? Something seemed to be blocking his memory. So he wrote her again, careful to include a check this time (she had reproved him for sending money through the mail), and asked for more information. He waited eagerly for her to reply. But no reply came. He wondered if she had received the letter. When his wife mentioned that she had heard from a friend in Boston, Marshall turned to stare at her in amazement. Because it seemed to him that she was about to confront him with her knowledge of Cynthia, and he was excited not by the danger of his position but by the possibility of her having discovered a letter, having somehow intercepted it, and he would have allowed that if it meant he would at last hear from Cynthia . . . But no, the letter was truly from a friend, no irony was intended.

He wrote Cynthia again, begging and demanding that she answer. He sent her another check, this time for a thousand dollars. Angry, frustrated, he believed that she was blackmailing him and that she was a criminal; she ought to be arrested and punished. He hated her for her power over him and thought of revenge he might take upon her. He would do something, yes. He did hate her. And yet when her letter arrived his heart thudded as if he were indeed in love.

She wrote: "You asked me about her room, about that apartment. You remember the living room—the ugly furniture, the religious junk on the walls. All right. My mother died of some kind of seizure while she was in bed. I went in and found her. Her face was awful, it was not her face at all or any human face. Her eyes were bulging. I went up to her and saw how it was, and so I went out to call the police. That night you came over. You wanted to take care of me, you said I must be very upset. You looked around the living room and asked me if you could see the bedroom. So I took you in. You were very quiet, you seemed sad. In that room you asked me about her, whether she'd known about me, how she had died, and you were very interested in hearing about it—because you hated her, I think that was the reason. Then you comforted me and put your arms around me, and you insisted that we make love in that bed. You insisted upon that. You begged me. I didn't care because a person can do one thing, and then do the opposite, as you know. I didn't have a guilty conscience because I had been good to my mother, so I didn't care. And while we were making love you asked me about her, about her eyes in particular, which had especially frightened me. Like what? What did she look like? you kept asking. Doesn't this all make you laugh, now?"

He was sickened by that letter. "She's lying," he muttered, but at once he thought, "Yes, it was like that."

Feeling her power over him across the country he began to send her things, to buy her off. He sent her some clothes, having them mailed from expensive shops. That ought to please her. And notes with checks enclosed, now and then, anything to buy her off, shut her up. What was terrifying was that he had no way of knowing whether this would work, or whether his desperation would make her more bold. Suppose she wrote directly to his wife? Or went to see his father? He had given so much of himself to her, surrendered so much of his power, that she could destroy him if she wanted. And she never replied. What did her silence mean? He reread her letters again and again, lingering over the last one, sometimes lured into an erotic daze and unable to rouse himself—it was so vivid now, so real. Yes, he had certainly done that. He wanted very much to do it again. With Fran he was always too busy to talk, too tired to make love to her, and certainly this was a relief to her—she was not that kind of woman at all—yet his thoughts were preoccupied with his own body and its needs.

He thought, "When my father dies I'll have to go back." But his father did not die. His father never wrote either. He had to depend for news upon his own telephone calls, put through every Sunday evening. But he kept calling, faithfully. He had become quite a dutiful son now. And finally, Fran said again, "Would you like to visit your father?"

He had overheard her talking with a woman friend one evening, about how hard it was for men to take their father's deaths. Fran had been assured that, according to Freud, it was the single most traumatic event in a man's life; therefore, with Marshall, she had to be as sympathetic as possible. His father was not dying yet, Marshall thought, but that seemed almost irrelevant. The old man would die someday—perhaps. He pretended to think it over, knowing all along that he would give in and take the trip. It had been nearly a year since the last visit.

Planning for it, he was overcome with a strange lassitude. He would sit in his office, and daydreams forced themselves into his mind, as if he were being invaded by an alien, sordid force. He thought of that old flat—which he now remembered clearly—and its clutter, the dishes and underwear lying around, the stockings drying in the bathroom, he thought of Cynthia and what they had done together, which was not at all what he and Fran had ever done together, he thought of the money he had given that woman—it gave him pleasure to think of this—and, lingeringly, he thought of her mother's death, which seemed somehow to have taken place in the room with Cynthia and himself. He was tremendously excited by this. He did not understand it except to know that his body ached and seemed now to be the body of another man. It was hard to maneuver it, even to walk normally. He felt that at any moment he might take a false step, lunge off a sidewalk, bump someone. It was especially difficult to get through an evening with friends, because, where once he had been able to imagine himself as a certain person, a successful business executive named Marshall Hughes, now he felt that his internal self had become impatient, as if waking from a long sleep, and might demand recognition.

The more his wife chatted about her friends and her bridge circle, the more he felt that he loved her and could forget about her. When she talked about the children, she was his wife, she belonged to him. She could never disturb him. Their affection was the affection of friends or companions, there was nothing passionate or brutal about it. He loved her. He hated that woman who was blackmailing him, and his body stirred at the thought of her, excited and furious at the same time. Yes, he had to have his revenge on her! He could not spend the rest of his life being blackmailed by a prostitute. And yet, at this thought, he would fall off into another of his disturbing dreams, recalling her, shaking his head at the memory of her hair and her plucked eyebrows, she was so common, really, and he had to urge himself awake to get where he was going, to do his work, or to reply to his wife, who had begun to look at him a little strangely. So he decided to go back to visit his father.

He wanted to talk with her just once more, to say good-bye. He would ask for his letters. Why should she have anything against him? He was prepared to write out one more check, a sizable check, and all she would have to do would be to return his indiscreet letters and promise to forget him—it disturbed him to think that she might not forget him. On the plane he sat rigid, thinking. It was not quite thinking, perhaps, but planning, groping, inching along as if with his fingers. Of his father he hardly thought; the old man could take care of himself. What did that old man, or any other old man, know of the terrible dangers of life? Marshall nearly wept to think that he had so many years to go before he drifted into the sanctity of old age and death, the final safety, far safer than his suburban life and marriage. "Those old bastards don't let us through. They block things up. They don't move along," he thought in anguish.

At the airport he took a taxi at once to her neighborhood. But for some reason, he asked to be let out a few blocks away. Marshall's palms were damp with sweat, his entire body was damp, he seemed in a kind of vague, outraged daze. He was both lunging forward and holding himself back. He did not think at all, except to say to himself: "I'll talk her out of it." He walked the several blocks quickly and then stood for a while staring up at her lighted windows. Again he thought of nothing, not really. His body seemed to be thinking for him. It was protecting all the people who stood behind him, his father, his family, the people who worked for him, the people who were his friends. After a while he went inside and up the stairs to her door. He knocked on it. The knocking echoed jarringly in his brain, and he thought of all the letters he had written, so recklessly, and yet perhaps on purpose?—and he thought of the hours he had spent with that woman, losing himself in her, groveling in the darkness of her body and the mastery of her soiled, ugly life, and yet coming from her with no knowledge and no affection, nothing.

The door opened. A child of about twelve, a girl leaned out and looked at him. "Whatdaya want?" she said.

"Who lives here?" Marshall said. "What—what happened to—Where is—?"

"You want my father?" the girl said.

"But—when did you move in here?"

"Last summer." The girl looked at him, chewing gum. She seemed to see something interesting in his face. "You looking for somebody else?"

He turned away. He began to weep. His breath came in great gulps, as if he had just saved himself from a terrible danger. Descending the stairs, he grasped the banister and remembered the way she had held onto it, indifferently, lightly, and how, even then, he had wanted to reach over and snap her wrist. But it was better not to think of that. He would never think of it again, nor would he think of his having come to this apartment straight from the airport, drenched in sweat, his body stiffened and monstrous with desire; he would not think of that. When he felt better he called another taxi and went to his father's house.

The old man was about the same, perhaps getting senile. Not much change. He did not die for six years, and then his death was sudden. Marshall was nearly forty-seven at this time, and his own health was unsteady, so he had an excuse not to go to his father's funeral. But no one in the family believed him, even Fran did not really believe him, and they held it against him all his life: he was a man who hadn't even bothered with his father's death.

JAMES ALAN MC PHERSON

A Matter of Vocabulary

Thomas Brown stopped going to church at thirteen after one Sunday morning when he had been caught playing behind the minister's pulpit by several deacons who had come up into the room early to count the money they had collected in the Sunday School downstairs. Thomas had seen them putting some of the change in their pockets, and they had seen him trying to hide behind the big worn brown pulpit with the several black Bibles and the pitcher of iced water and the glass used by the minister in the more passionate parts of his sermons. It was a Southern Baptist Church.

"Come on down off that, little Brother Brown," one of the fat black-suited deacons had told him. "We see you tryin' to hide. Ain't no use tryin' to hide in God's House."

Thomas had stood up and looked at them; all three of them, big-bellied, severe, and religiously righteous. "I wasn't tryin' to hide," he said in a low voice.

"Then what was you doin' behind Reverend Stone's pulpit?"

"I was praying," Thomas had said.

After that he did not like to go to church. Still, his mother would make him go every Sunday morning; and being only thirteen and very obedient, he could find no excuse not to leave the house. But after leaving the house with his brother, Edward, he would not go all the way to church. He would make Edward, who was a year younger, leave him at a certain corner a few blocks away from the church where Saturday-night drunks were sleeping or waiting for the bars to open on Monday morning. His own father had been that way, and Thomas knew that the waiting was very hard. He felt good toward the men, being almost one of them, and liked to listen to them curse and threaten each other lazily in the hot Georgia sun. He liked to look into their faces and wonder what was in them that made them not care about anything except the bars opening on Monday morning. He liked to try to distinguish the different shades of black in their hands and arms and faces. And he liked the smell of them. But most of all he liked it when they talked to him and gave him an excuse for not walking down the street two blocks to the Baptist Church.

"Don't you ever get married, boy," Arthur, one of the meaner drunks with a missing eye, told him on several occasions.

The first time he had said it the boy had asked: "Why not?"

" 'Cause a bitch ain't shit, man. You mind you don' get married now, hear? A bitch'll take all yo money and then throw you out *in the street!*"

"Damn straight!" Leroy, another drunk much darker than Arthur and a longshoreman, said. "That's all they fit for, takin' a man's money and runnin' around."

Thomas would sit on the stoop of an old deserted house with the men lying on the ground below him, too lazy to brush away the flies that came at them from the urine-soaked dirt on the hot Sunday mornings, and he would look and listen and consider. And after a few weeks of this he found himself very afraid of girls.

Things about life had always come to him by listening and being quiet. He remembered how he had learned about being black, and about how some other people were not. And the difference it made. He felt at home sitting with the waiting drunks because they were black, and he knew that they liked him because for months before he had stopped going to church, he had spoken to them while passing, and they had returned his greeting. His mother had always taught him to speak to people in the streets because Southern blacks do not know how to live without neighbors who exchange greetings. He had noted, however, when he was seven or eight, that certain people did not return his greetings. At first he had thought that their silence was due to his own low voice: he had gone to a Catholic school for four years where the black-caped nuns put an academic premium on silence. He had learned that in complete silence lay his safety from being slapped or hit on the flat of the hand with a wooden ruler. And he had been a model student. But even when he raised his voice, intentionally, to certain people in the street they still did not respond. Then he had noticed that while they had different faces, like the nuns, whom he never thought of as real people, these nonspeakers were completely different in dress and color from the people he knew. But still, he wondered why they would not speak.

He never asked his mother or anyone else about it; ever since those four years with the nuns he did not like to talk much. And he began to consider certain things about his own person as possible reasons for these slights. He began to consider why it was necessary for one to go to the bathroom. He began to consider whether only people like him had to go to the toilet and whether or not this thing was the cause of his complexion; and whether the other people could know about the bathroom merely by looking at his skin and did not speak because they knew he did it. This bothered him a lot, but he never asked anyone about it. Not even his brother, Edward, with whom he shared a bed and with whom, in the night and dark closeness of the bed, there should have been no secret thoughts. Nor did he speak of it to Leroy, the most talkative drunk, who wet the dirt behind the old house where they sat with no shame in his face, and always shook himself in the direction of the Baptist Church, two blocks down the street.

"You better go to church," his mother told him when he was finally discovered. "If you don' go, you going to hell for sure."

"I don' think I wanna go back," he said.

"You'll be a Sinner if you don' go," she said, pointing her finger at him with great gravity. "You'll go to hell, sure enough."

Thomas felt doomed already. He had told the worst lie in the world in the worst place in the world, and he knew that going back to church would not save him now. He knew that there was a hell because the nuns had told him about it, and he knew that he would end up in one of the little rooms in that place. But he still hoped for some time in purgatory, with a chance to move into a better room later, if he could be very good for a while before he died. He wanted to be very good, and he tried very hard all the time not to have to go to the bathroom. But when his mother talked about hell, he thought again that perhaps he would have to spend all his time, after death, in that great fiery-hot burning room she talked about. She had been raised in the Southern Baptist Church, and had gone to church, to the same minister, all her life, up until the time she had to start working on Sundays. But she still maintained her faith and never talked, in her conception of hell and how it would be for Sinners, about the separate rooms for certain people. Listening to his mother in the kitchen talk about hell while she cooked supper and sweated, Thomas thought that perhaps she knew more than the nuns because there were so many people who believed like her, including the bald Reverend Stone in their church, in that one great burning room and the Judgment Day.

"The hour's gonna come when the Horn will blow," his mother told him while he cowered in the corner behind the stove, feeling the heat from it on his face. "The Horn's gonna blow all through the world on that Great Morning, and all them in the graves will hear it and be raised up," she would continue.

"Even Daddy?"

His mother paused, and let the spoon stand still in the pot on the stove. "Everybody," she said, "both the Quick and the Dead and everybody that's alive. Then the stars are gonna fall, and all the Sinners will be cryin' and tryin' to hide in the corners and under houses. But it won't do no good to hide. You can't hide from God. Then they gonna call the roll with everybody's name on it, and the sheeps are gonna be divided from the goats, the Good on the Right and the Bad on the Left. And then the ground's gonna open up, and all them on the Left are gonna fall right into a burnin' pool of fire and brimstone, and they're gonna be cryin' and screamin' for mercy, but there won't be none because it will be too late. Especially for those who don't repent and go to church."

Now his mother stood over him, her eyes almost red with emotion, her face wet from the stove and shining black, and very close to tears.

Thomas felt the heat from the stove where he sat in the corner next to the broom. He was scared. He thought about being on the Left with Leroy and Arthur, and all the men who sat on the corner two blocks away from the Baptist Church. He did not think it was at all fair.

"Won't there be rooms for different people?" he asked her.

"What kind of rooms?" his mother said.

"Rooms for people who ain't done too much wrong."

"There ain't gonna be no separate rooms for any Sinners on the *Left!*

Everybody on the Left is gonna fall right into the same fiery pit, and the ones on the Right will be raised up into glory. Where do you want to be, Tommy?"

He could think of nothing to say.

"You want to be on the Right or on the Left?"

"I don't know."

"What do you mean?" she said. "You still got time, son."

"I don't know if I can ever get over on the Right," Thomas said.

His mother looked down at him. She was a very warm person, and sometimes she hugged him or touched him on the face when he least expected it. But sometimes she was severe.

"You can still get on the Right side, Tommy, if you go to church."

"I don't see how I can," he said again.

"Go on back to church, son," his mother said.

"I'll go," Tommy said. But he was not sure whether he could ever go back again after what he had done right behind the pulpit. But to please her, and to make her know that he was really sorry and that he would really try to go back to church, and to make certain in her mind that he genuinely wanted to have a place on the Right on Judgment Day, he helped her cook dinner and then washed the dishes afterward.

They lived on the top floor of a gray wooden house next to a funeral parlor. Thomas and his brother could look out the kitchen window and down into the rear door of the funeral parlor, which was always open, and watch George Herbs, the mortician, working on the bodies. Sometimes George Herbs would come to the back door of the embalming room in his white coat and look up at them, and laugh, and wave for them to come down. They never went down. And after a few minutes of getting fresh air, George Herbs would look at them again and go back to his work.

Down the street, almost at the corner, was a police station. There were always fat, white-faced, red-nosed blue-suited policemen who never seemed to go anywhere sitting in the small room. Also, these two men had never spoken to Thomas except on one occasion when he had been doing some hard thinking about getting on the Right Side on Judgment Day.

He had been on his way home from school in the afternoon. It was fall, and he was kicking leaves. His eyes fell upon a green five-dollar bill on the black-sand sidewalk, just a few steps away from the station. At first he did not know what to do; he had never found money before. But finding money on the ground was a good feeling. He had picked up the bill and carried it home, to a house that needed it, to his mother. It was not a great amount of money to lose, but theirs was a very poor street; and his mother had directed him, without any hesitation, to turn in the lost five dollars at the police station. And he had done this, going to the station himself and telling the men, in a scared voice, how he had found the money, where he had found it, and how his mother had directed him to bring it to the station in case the loser should come in looking for it. The men had listened and then had spoken to him for the first time. They even eventually smiled at him and then at each other, and a man with a long red nose with gray spots on it had assured him, still smiling, that if the owner did not call for the five dollars in a week, they would bring the money to his house and it would be his. But the money never came to his house, and when he saw the red-nosed policeman coming out of the station much more than a week later, the man did not even look at him, and Thomas had known that he should not ask what had happened to the money. Instead, in his mind, he credited it against that Judgment Time when, perhaps, there would be some uncertainty about whether he should stand on the Right Side, or whether he should cry with Leroy and Arthur and the other sinners on the Left.

There was another interesting place on that street. It was across from his house, next to the Michelob Bar on the corner. It was an old brown house, and an old woman, Mrs. Quick, lived there. Every morning on his way to school, Thomas would see her washing her porch with potash and water in a steel tub and a little stiff broom. The boards on her porch were very white from so much washing, and he could see no reason why she should have to wash it every morning. She never had any visitors to track it except the Crab Lady, who, even though she stopped to talk with Mrs. Quick every morning on her route, never went up on the porch. Sometimes the Crab Lady's call would waken Thomas and his brother in the big bed they shared. "Crabs! Buy my crabs!" she would sing, like a big, loud bird because the words all ran together in her song, and it sounded to them like "Crabbonnieee crabs!" They both would race to the window in their underwear and watch her walking on the other side of the street, an old wicker basket balanced on her head and covered with a bright red cloth that moved up and down with the bouncing of the crabs under it as she walked. She was a big, dull-black woman and wore a checkered apron over her dress, and she always held one hand up to the basket on her head as she swayed down the black-dirt sidewalk. She did not sell many crabs on that street; they were too plentiful in the town. But still she came, every morning, with her song: "Crabbonniee crabs!"

"Wonder why she comes every morning," Thomas said to his brother once. "She oughta come at night when the guys are over at Michelob."

"Maybe she just comes by to talk to Mrs. Quick," Edward said.

And that was true enough. For every morning the Crab Lady would stop and talk to Mrs. Quick while Mrs. Quick washed down her porch. She would never set the basket on the ground while she talked, but stood all the time with one hand on her wide hip and the other balancing the basket on her head, talking. And Mrs. Quick would continue to scrub her porch. Both Thomas and his brother would watch them until their mother came in to make them wash and dress for school. Leaving the window, Thomas would try to get a last look at Mrs. Quick, her head covered by a white bandanna, her old back bent in scrubbing, still talking to the Crab Lady. He would wonder what they talked about every morning. Not knowing this bothered him, and he began to imagine their morning conversations. Mrs. Quick was West Indian and knew all about roots and voodoo, and Thomas was afraid of her. He suspected that they talked about voodoo and who in the neighborhood had been fixed. Roots were like voodoo, and knowing about them made Mrs. Quick something to be feared. Thomas thought that she must know everything about him and everyone in the world because once he and Edward and Luke, a fat boy who worked in the fish market around the corner, had put some salt and pepper and brown sand in a small tobacco pouch, and had thrown it on her white-wood porch, next to the screen door. They had done it as a joke and had run away afterward, into an alley between his house and the funeral parlor across the street, and waited for her to come out and discover the pouch. They had waited for almost fifteen minutes, and still she did not come out; and after all that time waiting it was not such a good joke anymore, and so they had gone off to the graveyard to gather green berries for their slingshots. But the next morning, on his way to school, Mrs. Quick had looked up from scrubbing her porch and called him over, across the dirt street. "You better watch yourself, boy," she had said. "You hear me?"

"Why?" Thomas had asked, frightened and eager to be running away to join his brother.

Mrs. Quick looked at him, very intensely. Her face was black and wrinkled, and her hair was white where it was not covered by the white bandanna. Her mouth was small and tight and deliberate, and her eyes were dark and red where they should have been white. "You left-handed, ain't you?"

"Yes ma'am."

"Then watch yourself. Watch yourself good, less you get fixed."

"I ain't done nothin'," he said. But he knew that she was aware that he was lying.

"You left-handed, ain't you?"

He nodded.

"Then you owe the Devil a day's work, and you better keep watch on yourself less you get fixed." Upon the last word in this pronouncement she had locked her eyes on his and seemed to look right into his soul. It was as if she knew that he was doomed to stand on the Left Side on That Day, no matter what good he still might do in life. He looked away, and far up the street he could see the Crab Lady swaying along in the dirt. Then he had run.

Late in the night there was another sound Thomas could hear in his bed, next to his brother. This sound did not come every night, but it was a steady sound, and it made him shiver when it did come. He would be lying close and warm against his brother's back, and the sound would bring him away from sleep.

"Mr. Jones! I love you, Mr. Jones!"

This was the horrible night sound of the Barefoot Lady, who came whenever she was drunk to rummage through the neighborhood garbage cans for scraps of food, and to stand before the locked door of the Herbert A. Jones Funeral Parlor and wake the neighborhood with her cry: "*Mr. Jones! I love you, Mr. Jones!*"

"Eddie, wake up!" He would push his brother's back. "It's the Barefoot Lady again."

Fully awake, they would listen to her pitiful moans, like a lonely dog at midnight or the faraway low whistle of a night train pushing along the edge of the town, heading north.

"She scares me," he would say to his brother.

"Yeah, Tommy," his brother would say.

There were certain creaking sounds about the old house that were only audible on the nights when she screamed.

"Why does she love Mr. Jones? He's a undertaker," he would ask his brother. But there would be no answer because his brother was younger than him and still knew how to be very quiet when he was afraid.

"Mr. Jones! I love you, Mr. Jones!"

"It's nighttime," Thomas would go on, talking to himself. "She ought to be scared by all the bodies he keeps in the back room. But maybe it ain't the bodies. Maybe Mr. Jones buried somebody for her a long time ago for free, and she likes him for it. Maybe she never gets no chance to see him in the daytime so she comes at night. I bet she remembers that person Mr. Jones buried for her for free and gets drunk and comes in the night to thank him."

"Shut up, Tommy, please," Eddie said in the dark. "I'm scared." Eddie moved closer to him in the bed and then lay very quiet. But he still made the covers move with his trembling.

"Mr. Jones! I love you, Mr. Jones!"

Thomas thought about the back room of the Herbert A. Jones Funeral Parlor and the blue-and-white neon sign above its door and the Barefoot Lady, with feet caked with dirt and layers of skin and long yellow-and-black toenails, standing under that neon light. He had only seen her once in the day, but that once had been enough. She wore rags and an old black hat, and her nose and lips were huge and pink, and her hair was long and thick and hanging far below her shoulders, and she had been drooling at the mouth. He had come across her one morning digging into their garbage can for scraps. He had felt sorry for her because he and his brother and his mother threw out very few scraps, and had gone back up the stairs to ask his mother for something to give her. His mother had sent down some fresh biscuits and fried bacon, and watching her eat with her dirty hands with their long black fingernails had made him sick. Now, in his bed, he could still see her eating the biscuits, flakes of the dough sticking to the bacon grease around her mouth. It was a bad picture to see above his bed in the shadows on the ceiling. And it did not help to close his eyes, because then he could see her more vividly, with all the horrible dirty colors of her rags and face and feet made sharper in his mind. He could see her the way he could see the bad men and monsters from *The Shadow* and *Suspense* and *Gangbusters* and *The Six Shooter* every night after his mother had made him turn off the big brown radio in the living room. He could see these figures, men with long faces and humps in their backs, and old women with streaming hair dressed all in black, and cats with yellow eyes, and huge rats, on the walls in the living room when it was dark there; and when he got into bed and closed his eyes, they really came alive and frightened him, the way the present picture in his mind of the Barefoot Lady, her long toenails scratching on the thirty-two stairs as she came up to make him give her more biscuits and bacon, was frightening him. He did not know what to do, and so he moved closer to his brother, who was asleep now. And downstairs, from below the blue-and-white neon sign above the locked door to the funeral parlor, he heard her scream again; a painful sound, lonely, desperate, threatening, impatient, angry, hungry, he had no word to place it.

"Mr. Jones! I love you, Mr. Jones!"

Both Thomas and his brother worked at the F & F Supermarket, owned by Milton and Sarah Feinburg. Between the two of them they made a good third of a man's salary. Thomas had worked himself up from carry-out boy and was now in the Produce Department, while his brother, who was still new, remained a carry-out boy. Thomas enjoyed the status he had over the other boys. He enjoyed not having to be put outside on the street like the boys up front whenever business was slow and Milton Feinburg wanted to save money. He enjoyed being able to work all week after school while the boys up front had to wait for weekends when there would be sales and a lot of shoppers. He especially liked becoming a regular boy because then he had to help mop and wax the floors of the store every Sunday morning and could not go to church. He knew that his mother was not pleased when he had been taken into the mopping crew because now he had an excuse not to attend church. But being on the crew meant making an extra three dollars, and he knew that she was pleased with the money. Still, she made him pray at night, and especially on Sunday.

His job was bagging potatoes. Every day after school and all day Saturday he would come into the air-conditioned produce room, put on a blue smock, take a fifty-pound sack of potatoes off a huge stack of sacks, slit open the sack and let the potatoes fall into a shopping cart next to a scale, and proceed to put them into five- and ten-pound plastic bags. It was very simple; he could do it in his sleep. Then he would spend the rest of the day bagging potatoes and looking out the big window, which separated the produce room from the rest of the store, at the customers. They were mostly white, and after almost a year of this type of work, he began to realize why they did not speak to him in the street. And then he did not mind going to the bathroom, knowing, when he did go, that all of them had to go, just as he did, in the secret places they called home. Some of them had been speaking to him for a long time now, on this business level, and he had formed some small friendships grounded in this.

He knew Richard Burke, the vet who had a war injury in his back and who walked funny. Richard Burke was the butcher's helper, who made hamburger from scraps of fat and useless meat cuttings and red powder in the back of the produce room, where the customers could not see. He liked to laugh when he mixed the red powder into the ground white substance, holding gobs of the soft stuff up over the big tub and letting it drip, and then dunking his hands down into the tub again. Sometimes he threw some of it at Thomas, in fun, and Thomas had to duck. But it was all in fun, and he did not mind it except when the red-and-white meat splattered the window and Thomas had to clean it off so that his view of the customers, as he bagged potatoes, would not be obstructed.

He thought of the window as a one-way mirror which allowed him to examine the people who frequented the store without being noticed himself. His line of vision covered the entire produce aisle, and he could see everyone who entered the store making their way down that aisle, pushing their carts and stopping, selectively, first at the produce racks, then at the meat counter, then off to the side, beyond his view, to the canned goods and frozen foods and toilet items to the unseen right of him. He began to invent names for certain of the regular customers, the ones who came at a special time each week. One man, a gross fat person with a huge belly and the rough red neck and face of a farmer, who wheeled one shopping cart before him while he pulled another behind, Thomas called Big Funk because, he thought, no one could be that fat and wear the same faded dungaree suit each week without smelling bad. Another face he called the Rich Old Lady, because she was old and pushed her cart along slowly, with a dignity shown by none of the other shoppers. She always bought parsley, and once, when Thomas was wheeling a big cart of bagged potatoes out to the racks, he passed her and for just an instant smelled a perfume that was light and very fine to smell. It did not linger in the air like most other perfumes he had smelled. And it seemed to him that she must have had it made just for her and that it was so expensive that it stayed with her body and would never linger behind her when she had passed a place. He liked that about her. Also, he had heard from the boys up front that she would never carry her own groceries to her house, no more than half a block from the store, and that no matter how small her purchases were, she would require a boy to carry them for her and would always tip a quarter. Thomas knew that there was always a general fight among the carry-out boys whenever she checked out. Such a fight seemed worthy of her. And after a while of watching her, he would make a special point of wheeling a cart of newly bagged potatoes out to the racks when he saw her come in the store, just to smell the perfume. But she never noticed him either.

"You make sure you don't go over on them scales now," Miss Hester, the produce manager, would remind him whenever she saw him looking for too long a time out the window. "Mr. Milton would git mad if you went over ten pounds."

Thomas always knew when she was watching him and just when she would speak. He had developed an instinct for this from being around her. He knew, even at that age, that he was brighter than she was; and he thought that she must know it too because he could sense her getting uncomfortable when she stood in back of him in her blue smock, watching him lift the potatoes to the plastic bag until it was almost full, and then the plastic bag up to the gray metal scale, and then watching the red arrow fly across to ten. Somehow it almost always stopped wavering at exactly ten pounds. Filling the bags was automatic with him, a conditioned reflex, and he could do it quite easily, without breaking his concentration on things beyond the window. And he knew that this bothered her a great deal; so much so, in fact, that she continually asked him questions, standing by the counter or the sink behind him, to make him aware that she was in the room. She was always nervous when he did not say anything for a long time, and he knew this too, and was sometimes silent, even when he had something to say, so that she could hear the thud and swish of the potatoes going into the bag, rhythmically, and the sound of the bags coming down on the scale, and after a second, the sound, sputtering and silken, of the tops of the bags being twisted and sealed in the tape machine. Thomas liked to produce these sounds for her because he knew she wanted something more.

Miss Hester had toes like the Barefoot Lady, except her nails were shorter and cleaner, and she was white. She always wore sandals, was hefty like a man, and had hair under her arms. Whenever she smiled he could not think of her face or smile as that of a woman. It was too tight. And her laugh was too loud and came from too far away inside her. And the huge crates of lettuce or cantaloupes or celery she could lift very easily made her even less a woman. She had short red-brown hair, and whenever he got very close to her it smelled funny, unlike the Rich Old Lady's smell.

"What you daydreamin' about so much all the time?" she asked him once.

"I was just thinking," he had said.

"What about?"

"School and things."

He could sense her standing behind him at the sink, letting her hands pause on the knife and the celery she was trimming.

"You gonna finish high school?"

"I guess so."

"You must be pretty smart, huh, Tommy?"

"No. I ain't so smart," he said.

"But you sure do think a lot."

"Maybe I just daydream," Thomas told her.

Her knife had started cutting into the celery branches again. He kept up his bagging.

"Well, anyway, you a good worker. You a good boy, Tommy."

Thomas did not say anything.

"Your brother, he's a good worker too. But he ain't like you though."

"I know," he said.

"He talks a lot up front. All the cashiers like him."

"Eddie likes to talk," Thomas said.

"Yeah," said Miss Hester. "Maybe he talks too much. Mr. Milton and Miss Sarah are watchin' him."

"What for?"

She stopped cutting the celery again. "I dunno," she said. "I reckon it's just that he talks a lot."

On Saturday nights Thomas and his brother would buy the family groceries in the F & F Supermarket. Checking the list made out by his mother gave Thomas a feeling of responsibility that he liked. He was free to buy things not even on the list, and he liked this too. They paid for the groceries out of their own money, and doing this, with some of the employees watching, made an especially good feeling for Thomas. Sometimes they bought ice cream or a pie or something special for their mother. This made them exceptional. The other black employees, the carry-out boys, the stock clerks, the bag boys, would have no immediate purpose in mind for their money beyond eating a big meal on Saturday nights or buying whiskey from a bootlegger because they were minors, or buying a new pair of brightly colored pants or pointed shoes to wear into the store on their days off, as if to make all the other employees see that they were above being, at least on this one day, what they were all the rest of the week.

Thomas and Edward did not have days off; they worked straight through the week, after school, and they worked all day on Saturdays. But Edward did not mop on Sunday mornings, and he still went to church. Thomas felt relieved that his brother was almost certain to be on the Right Side on That Day because he had stayed in the church and would never be exposed to all the stealing the mopping crew did when they were alone in the store on Sunday mornings with Lloyd Bailey, the manager, who looked the other way when they took packages of meat and soda and cartons of cigarettes. Thomas suspected that Mr. Bailey was stealing bigger things himself, and that Milton Feinburg, a big-boned Jew who wore custom-made shoes and smoked very expensive, bad-smelling green cigars, knew just what everyone was stealing and was only waiting for a convenient time to catch certain people. Thomas could see it in the way he smiled and rolled the cigar around in his mouth whenever he talked to certain of the bigger stealers; and seeing this, Thomas never stole. At first he thought it was because he was afraid of Milton Feinburg, who had green eyes that could look as deep as Mrs. Quick's; and then he thought that he could not do it because the opportunity only came on Sunday mornings when, if he had never told that first lie, he should have been in church.

Both Milton and Sarah Feinburg liked him. He could tell it by the way Sarah Feinburg always called him up to her office to clean. There were always rolls of coins on her desk, and scattered small change on the floor when he swept. But he never touched any of it. Instead, he would gather what was on the floor and stack the coins very neatly on her desk. And when she came back into the office after he had swept and mopped and waxed and dusted and emptied her wastebaskets, Miss Sarah Feinburg would smile at Thomas and say: "You're a good boy, Tommy."

He could tell that Milton Feinburg liked him because whenever he went to the bank for money he would always ask Thomas to come out to the car to help him bring the heavy white sacks into the store, and sometimes up to his office. On one occasion, he had picked Thomas up on the street, after school, when Thomas was running in order to get to work on time. Milton Feinburg had driven him to the store.

"I like you," Milton Feinburg told Thomas. "You're a good worker."

Thomas could think of nothing to say.

"When you quit school, there'll be a place in the store for you."

"I ain't gonna quit school," Thomas had said.

Milton Feinburg smiled and chewed on his green cigar. "Well, when you finish high school, you can come on to work full time. Miss Hester says you're a good worker."

"Bagging potatoes is easy," said Thomas.

Milton Feinburg smiled again as he drove the car. "Well, we can get you in the stock room, if you can handle it. Think you can handle it?"

"Sure," said Thomas. But he was not thinking of the stock room and unloading trucks and stacking cases of canned goods and soap in the big, musty, upstairs storeroom. He was thinking of how far away he was from finishing high school and how little that long time seemed to matter to Milton Feinburg.

Thomas was examining a very ugly man from behind his window one afternoon when Miss Hester came into the produce room from the front of the store. As usual, she stood behind him. And Thomas went on with his work and watching the very ugly man. This man was bald and had a long thin red nose that twisted down unnaturally, almost to the level of his lower lip. The man had no chin, only three layers of skin that lapped down onto his neck like a red-cloth necklace. Barney Benns, one of the stock clerks who occasionally passed through the produce room to steal an apple or a banana, had christened the very ugly man "Do-funny," just as he had christened Thomas "Little Brother" soon after he had come to the job. Looking at Do-funny made Thomas sad; he wondered how the man had lost his chin. Perhaps, he thought, Do had lost it in the war, or perhaps in a car accident. He was trying to picture just how Do-funny would look after the accident when he realized that his chin was gone forever, when Miss Hester spoke from behind him.

"Your brother's in a lotta trouble up front," she said.

Thomas turned to look at her. "What's the matter?"

Miss Hester smiled at him in that way she had, like a man. "He put a order in the wrong car."

"Did the people bring it back?"

"Yeah," she said. "But some folks is still missin' their groceries. They're out there now mad as hell."

"Was it Eddie lost them?"

"Yeah. Miss Sarah is mad as hell. Everybody's standin' round up there."

He looked through the glass window and up the produce aisle and saw his brother coming toward him from the front of the store. His brother was untying the knot in his blue smock when he came in the swinging door of the air-conditioned produce room. His brother did not speak to him but walked directly over to the sink next to Miss Hester and began to suck water from the black hose. He looked very hot, but only his nose was sweating. Thomas turned completely away from the window and stood facing his brother.

"What's the matter up front, Eddie?" he said.

"Nothing," his brother replied, his jaws tight.

"I heard you put a order in the wrong car and the folks cain't git it back," said Miss Hester.

"Yeah," said Eddie.

"Why you tryin' to hide back here?" she said.

"I ain't tryin' to hide," said Eddie.

Thomas watched them and said nothing.

"You best go on back up front there," Miss Hester said.

At that moment Miss Sarah Feinburg pushed through the door. She had her hands in the pockets of the blue sweater and she walked to the middle of the small, cool room and glared at Edward Brown. "Why are you back here?" Miss Sarah Feinburg asked Edward.

"I come back for some water."

"You know you lost twenty-seven dollars' worth of groceries up there?"

"It wasn't my fault," said Eddie.

"If you kept your mind on what you're supposed to do this wouldn't have happened. But no. You're always talking, always smiling around, always running your mouth with everybody."

"The people who got the wrong bags might bring them back," Eddie said. His nose was still sweating in the cool room. "Evidently somebody took my cart by mistake."

"*Evidently! Evidently!*" said Sarah Feinburg. "Miss Hester, you should please listen to *that! Evidently*. You let them go to school, and they think they know everything. *Evidently*, you say?"

"Yeah," said Eddie. Thomas saw that he was about to cry.

Miss Hester was still smiling like a man.

Sarah Feinburg stood with her hands in her sweater pockets and braced on her hips, looking Eddie in the face. Eddie did not hold his eyes down, and Thomas felt really good but sad that he did not.

"You get back up front," said Sarah Feinburg. And she shoved her way through the door again and out of the cool produce room.

"Evidently, evidently, that sure was funny," said Miss Hester when the fat woman was halfway down the produce aisle. "Lord, was she mad. I ain't never seen her git so mad."

Neither Thomas nor Eddie said anything.

Then Miss Hester stopped smiling. "You best git on back up front, Eddie."

"No," said Eddie. "I'm goin' home."

"You ain't quittin'?" said Miss Hester.

"Yeah."

"What for?"

"I dunno. I just gotta go home."

"But don't your folk need the money?"

"No," Eddie said.

He took off his blue smock and laid it on the big pile of fifty-pound potato sacks. "I'm goin' home," he said again. He did not look at his brother. He walked through the door, and slowly down the produce aisle and then out the front door, without looking at anything at all.

Then Thomas went over to the stack of unbagged potatoes and pushed the blue smock off the top sack and into a basket on the floor next to the stack. He picked up a fifty-pound sack and lugged it over to the cart and tore it open with his fingers, spilling its contents of big and small dirty brown potatoes into the cart. He could feel Miss Hester's eyes on him, on his arms and shoulders and hands as they moved. He worked very quickly and looked out the window into the store. Big Funk was supposed to come this afternoon. He had finished seven five-pound bags before Miss Hester moved from where she had been standing behind him, and he knew she was about to speak.

"You going to quit too, Tommy?"

"No," he said.

"I guess your folk do need the money now, huh?"

"No," he said. "We don't need the money."

She did not say anything else. Thomas was thinking about Big Funk and what could be done with the time if he did not come. He did not want to think about his brother or his mother or the money, or even the good feeling he got when Milton Feinburg saw them buying the Saturday-night groceries. If Big Funk did not come, then perhaps he could catch another glimpse of Do-funny before he left the store. The Rich Old Lady would not come again until next week. He decided that it would be necessary to record the faces and bodies of new people as they wandered, selectively, with their shopping carts beyond the big window glass. He liked it very much now that none of them ever looked up and saw him watching. That way he did not have to feel embarrassed or guilty. That way he would never have to feel compelled to nod his head or move his mouth or eyes, or make any indication of a greeting to them. That way he would never have to feel bad when they did not speak back.

In his bed that night, lying very close to his brother's back, Thomas thought again very seriously about the Judgment Day and the Left Side. Now, there were certain people he would like to have with him on the Left Side on That Day. He thought about church and how he could never go back because of the place where the deacons had made him tell his first great lie. He wondered whether it was because he did not want to have to go back to church on Sunday mornings that he had not quit. He wondered if it was because of the money or going to church or because of the window that he had not walked out of the store with his brother. That would have been good: the two of them walking out together. But he had not done it, and now he could not make himself know why. Suddenly, in the night, he heard the Barefoot Lady under the blue-and-white Herbert A. Jones neon light, screaming.

"Mr. Jones! I love you, Mr. Jones!"

But the sound did not frighten him now. He pushed against his brother's back.

"Eddie? *Eddie.*"

"Yeah?"

"Wonder why she does it?"

"I dunno."

"I wonder why," he said again.

Eddie did not answer. But after the sound of the woman came again, his brother turned over in the bed and said to Thomas:

"You gonna quit?"

"No."

"Why not? We could always carry papers."

"I dunno. I just ain't gonna quit. Not now."

"Well *I* ain't goin' back. I'll go back in there one day when I'm rich. I'm gonna go in and buy everything but hamburger."

"Yeah," said Thomas. But he was not listening to his brother.

"Mr. Jones! I love you, Mr. Jones!"

"And I'm gonna learn all the big words in the world too," his brother went on. "When I go back in there I'm gonna be talking so big that fat old Miss Sarah won't even be able to understand me."

"That'll be good," said Thomas. But he was thinking to himself now.

"You'll see," said Eddie. "I'll do it too."

But Thomas did not answer him. He was waiting for the sound to come again.

"Mr. Jones! I love you, Mr. Jones!"

And then he knew why the Barefoot Lady came to that place almost every night to cry when there was no one alive in the building to hear or care about her sound. He felt what she must feel. And he knew now why the causes of the sound had bothered him and would always bother him. There was a word in his mind now, a big word, that made good sense of her sound and the burning, feeling thing he felt inside himself. It was all very clear, and now he understood that the Barefoot Lady came in the night, not because she really loved Mr. Jones, or because he had once buried someone for her for free, or even because she liked the blue-and-white neon light. She came in the night to scream because she, like himself, was in misery, and did not know what else to do.

DIANE OLIVER

Neighbors

The bus turning the corner of Patterson and Talford Avenue was dull this time of evening. Of the four passengers standing in the rear, she did not recognize any of her friends. Most of the people tucked neatly in the double seats were women, maids and cooks on their way from work or secretaries who had worked late and were riding from the office building at the mill. The cotton mill was out from town, near the house where she worked. She noticed that a few men were riding too. They were obviously just working men, except for one gentleman dressed very neatly in a dark grey suit and carrying what she imagined was a push-button umbrella.

He looked to her as though he usually drove a car to work. She immediately decided that the car probably wouldn't start this morning so he had to catch the bus to and from work. She was standing in the rear of the bus, peering at the passengers, her arms barely reaching the over-head railing, trying not to wobble with every lurch. But every corner the bus turned pushed her head toward a window. And her hair was coming down too, wisps of black curls swung between her eyes. She looked at the people around her. Some of them were white, but most of them were her color. Looking at the passengers at least kept her from thinking of tomorrow. But really she would be glad when it came, then everything would be over.

She took a firmer grip on the green leather seat and wished she had on her glasses. The man with the umbrella was two people ahead of her on the other side of the bus, so she could see him between other people very clearly. She watched as he unfolded the evening newspaper, craning her neck to see what was on the front page. She stood impatiently trying to read the headlines, when she realized he was staring up at her rather curiously. Biting her lips she turned her head and stared out of the window until the downtown section was in sight.

She would have to wait until she was home to see if they were in the newspaper again. Sometimes she felt that if another person snapped a picture of them she would burst out screaming. Last Monday reporters were already inside the pre-school clinic when she took Tommy for his last polio shot. She didn't understand how anyone could be so heartless to a child. The flashbulb went off right when the needle went in and all the picture showed was Tommy's open mouth.

The bus pulling up to the curb jerked to a stop, startling her and confusing her thoughts. Clutching in her hand the paper bag that contained her uniform, she pushed her way toward the door. By standing in the back of the bus, she was one of the first people to step to the ground. Outside the bus, the evening air felt humid and uncomfortable and her dress kept sticking to her. She looked up and remembered that the weatherman had forecast rain. Just their luck—why, she wondered, would it have to rain on top of everything else?

As she walked along, the main street seemed unnaturally quiet but she decided her imagination was merely playing tricks. Besides, most of the stores had been closed since five o'clock.

She stopped to look at a reversible raincoat in Ivey's window, but although she had a full time job now, she couldn't keep her mind on clothes. She was about to continue walking when she heard a horn blowing. Looking around, half-scared but also curious, she saw a man beckoning to her in a grey car. He was nobody she knew but since a nicely dressed woman was with him in the front seat, she walked to the car.

"You're Jim Mitchell's girl, aren't you?" he questioned. "You Ellie or the other one?"

She nodded yes, wondering who he was and how much he had been drinking.

"Now honey," he said leaning over the woman, "you don't know me but your father does and you tell him that if anything happens to that boy of his tomorrow we're ready to set things straight." He looked her straight in the eye and she promised to take home the message.

Just as the man was about to step on the gas, the woman reached out and touched her arm. "You hurry up home, honey, it's about dark out here."

Before she could find out their names, the Chevrolet had disappeared around a corner. Ellie wished someone would magically appear and tell her everything that had happened since August. Then maybe she could figure out what was real and what she had been imagining for the past couple of days.

She walked past the main shopping district up to Tanner's where Saraline was standing in the window peeling oranges. Everything in the shop was painted orange and green and Ellie couldn't help thinking that poor Saraline looked out of place. She stopped to wave to her friend who pointed the knife to her watch and then to her boyfriend standing in the rear of the shop. Ellie nodded that she understood. She knew Sara wanted her to tell her grandfather that she had to work late again. Neither one of them could figure out why he didn't like Charlie. Saraline had finished high school three years ahead of her and it was time for her to be getting married. Ellie watched as her friend stopped peeling the orange long enough to cross her fingers. She nodded again but she was afraid all the crossed fingers in the world wouldn't stop the trouble tomorrow.

She stopped at the traffic light and spoke to a shrivelled woman hunched against the side of a building. Scuffing the bottom of her sneakers on the curb she waited for the woman to open her mouth and grin as she usually did. The kids used to bait her to talk, and since she didn't have but one tooth in her whole head they called her Doughnut Puncher. But the woman was still, the way everything else had been all week.

From where Ellie stood, across the street from the Sears and Roebuck parking lot, she could see their house, all of the houses on the single street white people called Welfare Row. Those newspaper men always made her angry. All of their articles showed how rough the people were on their street. And the reporters never said her family wasn't on welfare, the papers always said the family lived on that street. She paused to look across the street at a group of kids pouncing on one rubber ball. There were always white kids around their neighborhood mixed up in the games, but playing with them was almost an unwritten rule. When everybody started going to school nobody played together any more.

She crossed at the corner ignoring the cars at the stop light and the closer she got to her street the more she realized that the newspaper was right. The houses were ugly, there were not even any trees, just patches of scraggly bushes and grasses. As she cut across the sticky asphalt pavement covered with cars she was conscious of the parking lot floodlights casting a strange glow on her street. She stared from habit at the house on the end of the block and except for the way the paint was peeling they all looked alike to her. Now at twilight the flaking grey paint had a luminous glow and as she walked down the dirt sidewalk she noticed Mr. Paul's pipe smoke added to the hazy atmosphere. Mr. Paul would be sitting in that same spot waiting until Saraline came home. Ellie slowed her pace to speak to the elderly man sitting on the porch.

"Evening, Mr. Paul," she said. Her voice sounded clear and out of place on the vacant street.

"Eh, who's that?" Mr. Paul leaned over the rail. "What you say, girl?"

"How are you?" she hollered louder. "Sara said she'd be late tonight, she has to work." She waited for the words to sink in.

His head had dropped and his eyes were facing his lap. She could see that he was disappointed. "Couldn't help it," he said finally. "Reckon they needed her again." Then as if he suddenly remembered he turned toward her.

"You people be ready down there? Still gonna let him go tomorrow?"

She looked at Mr. Paul between the missing rails on his porch, seeing how his rolled up trousers seemed to fit exactly in the vacant banister space.

"Last I heard this morning we're still letting him go," she said.

Mr. Paul had shifted his weight back to the chair. "Don't reckon they'll hurt him," he mumbled, scratching the side of his face. "Hope he don't mind being spit on though. Spitting ain't like cutting. They can spit on him and nobody'll ever know who did it," he said, ending his words with a quiet chuckle.

Ellie stood on the sidewalk grinding her heel in the dirt waiting for the old man to finish talking. She was glad somebody found something funny to laugh at. Finally he shut up.

"Goodbye, Mr. Paul," she waved. Her voice sounded loud to her own ears. But she knew the way her head ached intensified noises. She walked home faster, hoping they had some aspirin in the house and that those men would leave earlier tonight.

From the front of her house she could tell that the men were still there. The living room light shone behind the yellow shades, coming through brighter in the patched places. She thought about moving the geranium pot from the porch to catch the rain but changed her mind. She kicked a beer can under a car parked in the street and stopped to look at her reflection on the car door. The tiny flowers of her printed dress made her look as if she had a strange tropical disease. She spotted another can and kicked it out of the way of the car, thinking that one of these days some kid was going to fall and hurt himself. What she wanted to do she knew was kick the car out of the way. Both the station wagon and the Ford had been parked in front of her house all week, waiting. Everybody was just sitting around waiting.

Suddenly she laughed aloud. Reverend Davis' car was big and black and shiny just like, but no, the smile disappeared from her face, her mother didn't like for them to say things about other people's color. She looked around to see who else came, and saw Mr. Moore's old beat up blue car. Somebody had torn away half of his NAACP sign. Sometimes she really felt sorry for the man. No matter how hard he glued on his stickers somebody always yanked them off again.

Ellie didn't recognize the third car but it had an Alabama license plate. She turned around and looked up and down the street, hating to go inside. There were no lights on their street, but in the distance she could see the bright lights of the parking lot. Slowly she did an about face and climbed the steps.

She wondered when her mama was going to remember to get a yellow bulb for the porch. Although the lights hadn't been turned on, usually June bugs and mosquitoes swarmed all around the porch. By the time she was inside the house she always felt like they were crawling in her hair. She pulled on the screen and saw that Mama finally had made Hezekiah patch up the holes. The globs of white adhesive tape scattered over the screen door looked just like misshapen butterflies.

She listened to her father's voice and could tell by the tone that the men were discussing something important again. She rattled the door once more but nobody came.

"Will somebody please let me in?" Her voice carried through the screen to the knot of men sitting in the corner.

"The door's open," her father yelled. "Come on in."

"The door is not open," she said evenly. "You know we stopped leaving it open." She was feeling tired again and her voice had fallen an octave lower.

"Yeah, I forgot, I forgot," he mumbled walking to the door.

She watched her father almost stumble across a chair to let her in. He was shorter than the light bulb and the light seemed to beam down on him, emphasizing the wrinkles around his eyes. She could tell from the way he pushed open the screen that he hadn't had much sleep either. She'd overheard him telling Mama that the people down at the shop seemed to be piling on the work harder just because of this thing. And he couldn't do anything or say anything to his boss because they probably wanted to fire him.

"Where's Mama?" she whispered. He nodded toward the back.

"Good evening, everybody," she said looking at the three men who had not looked up since she entered the room. One of the men half stood, but his attention was geared back to something another man was saying. They were sitting on the sofa in their shirt sleeves and there was a pitcher of ice water on the window sill.

"Your mother probably needs some help," her father said. She looked past him trying to figure out who the white man was sitting on the end. His face looked familiar and she tried to remember where she had seen him before. The men were paying no attention to her. She bent to see what they were studying and saw a large sheet of white drawing paper. She could see blocks and lines and the man sitting in the middle was marking a trail with the eraser edge of the pencil.

The quiet stillness of the room was making her head ache more. She pushed her way through the red embroidered curtains that led to the kitchen.

"I'm home, Mama," she said, standing in front of the back door facing the big yellow sun Hezekiah and Tommy had painted on the wall above the iron stove. Immediately she felt a warmth penetrating her skin. "Where is everybody?" she asked, sitting at the table where her mother was peeling potatoes.

"Mrs. McAllister is keeping Helen and Teenie," her mother said. "Your brother is staying over with Harry tonight." With each name she uttered, a slice of potato peeling tumbled to the newspaper on the table. "Tommy's in the bedroom reading that Uncle Wiggily book."

Ellie looked up at her mother but her eyes were straight ahead. She knew that Tommy only read the Uncle Wiggily book by himself when he was unhappy. She got up and walked to the kitchen cabinet.

"The other knives dirty?" she asked.

"No," her mother said, "look in the next drawer."

Ellie pulled open the drawer, flicking scraps of white paint with her fingernail. She reached for the knife and at the same time a pile of envelopes caught her eye.

"Any more come today?" she asked, pulling out the knife and slipping the envelopes under the dish towels.

"Yes, seven more came today," her mother accentuated each word carefully. "Your father has them with him in the other room."

"Same thing?" she asked picking up a potato and wishing she could think of some way to change the subject.

The white people had been threatening them for the past three weeks. Some of the letters were aimed at the family, but most of them were directed to Tommy himself. About once a week in the same handwriting somebody wrote that he'd better not eat lunch at school because they were going to poison him.

They had been getting those letters ever since the school board made Tommy's name public. She sliced the potato and dropped the pieces in the pan of cold water. Out of all those people he had been the only one the board had accepted for transfer to the elementary school. The other children, the members said, didn't live in the district. As she cut the eyes out of another potato she thought about the first letter they had received and how her father just set fire to it in the ashtray. But then Mr. Belk said they'd better save the rest, in case anything happened, they might need the evidence for court.

She peeped up again at her mother, "Who's that white man in there with Daddy?"

"One of Lawyer Belk's friends," she answered. "He's pastor of the church that's always on television Sunday morning. Mr. Belk seems to think that having him around will do some good." Ellie saw that her voice was shaking just like her hand as she reached for the last potato. Both of them could hear Tommy in the next room mumbling to himself. She was afraid to look at her mother.

Suddenly Ellie was aware that her mother's hands were trembling violently. "He's so little," she whispered and suddenly the knife slipped out of her hands and she was crying and breathing at the same time.

Ellie didn't know what to do but after a few seconds she cleared away the peelings and put the knives in the sink. "Why don't you lie down?" she suggested. "I'll clean up and get Tommy in bed." Without saying anything her mother rose and walked to her bedroom.

Ellie wiped off the table and draped the dishcloth over the sink. She stood back and looked at the rusting pipes powdered with a whitish film. One of these days they would have to paint the place. She tiptoed past her mother who looked as if she had fallen asleep from exhaustion.

"Tommy," she called softly, "come in and get ready for bed."

Tommy sitting in the middle of the floor did not answer. He was sitting the way she imagined he would be, cross-legged, pulling his ear lobe as he turned the ragged pages of *Uncle Wiggily at the Zoo*.

"What you doing, Tommy?" she said squatting on the floor beside him. He smiled and pointed at the picture of the ducks.

"School starts tomorrow," she said, turning a page with him. "Don't you think it's time to go to bed?"

"Oh Ellie, do I have to go now?" She looked down at the serious brown eyes and the closely cropped hair. For a minute she wondered if he questioned having to go to bed now or to school tomorrow.

"Well," she said, "aren't you about through with the book?" He shook his head. "Come on," she pulled him up, "you're a sleepy head." Still he shook his head.

"When Helen and Teenie coming home?"

"Tomorrow after you come home from school they'll be here."

She lifted him from the floor thinking how small he looked to be facing all those people tomorrow.

"Look," he said breaking away from her hand and pointing to a blue shirt and pair of cotton twill pants, "Mama got them for me to wear tomorrow."

While she ran water in the tub, she heard him crawl on top of the bed. He was quiet and she knew he was untying his sneakers.

"Put your shoes out," she called through the door, "and maybe Daddy will polish them."

"Is Daddy still in there with those men? Mama made me be quiet so I wouldn't bother them."

He padded into the bathroom with bare feet and crawled into the water. As she scrubbed him they played Ask Me A Question, their own version of Twenty Questions. She had just dried him and was about to have him step into his pajamas when he asked: "Are they gonna get me tomorrow?"

"Who's going to get you?" She looked into his eyes and began rubbing him furiously with the towel.

"I don't know," he answered. "Somebody I guess."

"Nobody's going to get you," she said, "who wants a little boy who gets bubblegum in his hair anyway—but us?" He grinned but as she hugged him she thought how much he looked like his father. They walked to the bed to say his prayers and while they were kneeling she heard the first drops of rain. By the time she covered him up and tucked the spread off the floor the rain had changed to a steady downpour.

When Tommy had gone to bed her mother got up again and began ironing clothes in the kitchen. Something, she said, to keep her thoughts busy. While her mother folded and sorted the clothes Ellie drew up a chair from the kitchen table. They sat in the kitchen for a while listening to the voices of the men in the next room. Her mother's quiet speech broke the stillness in the room.

"I'd rather," she said making sweeping motions with the iron, "that you stayed home from work tomorrow and went with your father to take Tommy. I don't think I'll be up to those people."

Ellie nodded. "I don't mind," she said, tracing circles on the oil cloth covered table.

"Your father's going," her mother continued. "Belk and Reverend Davis are too. I think that white man in there will probably go."

"They may not need me," Ellie answered.

"Tommy will," her mother said, folding the last dish towel and storing it in the cabinet.

"Mama, I think he's scared," the girl turned toward the woman. "He was so quiet while I was washing him."

"I know," she answered sitting down heavily. "He's been that way all day." Her brown wavy hair glowed in the dim lighting of the kitchen. "I told him he wasn't going to school with Jakie and Bob any more but I said he was going to meet some other children just as nice."

Ellie saw that her mother was twisting her wedding band around and around on her finger.

"I've already told Mrs. Ingraham that I wouldn't be able to come out tomorrow." Ellie paused. "She didn't say very much. She didn't even say anything about his pictures in the newspaper. Mr. Ingraham said we were getting right crazy but even he didn't say anything else."

She stopped to look at the clock sitting near the sink. "It's almost time for the cruise cars to begin," she said. Her mother followed Ellie's eyes to the sink. The policemen circling their block every twenty minutes was supposed to make them feel safe, but hearing the cars come so regularly and that light flashing through the shade above her bed only made her nervous.

She stopped talking to push a wrinkle out of the shiny red cloth, dragging her finger along the table edges. "How long before those men going to leave?" she asked her mother. Just as she spoke she heard one of the men say something about getting some sleep. "I didn't mean to run them away," she said smiling. Her mother half-smiled too. They listened for the sound of motors and tires and waited for her father to shut the front door.

In a few seconds her father's head pushed through the curtain. "Want me to turn down your bed now, Ellie?" She felt uncomfortable staring up at him, the whole family looked drained of all energy.

"That's all right," she answered. "I'll sleep in Helen and Teenie's bed tonight."

"How's Tommy?" he asked looking toward the bedroom. He came in and sat down at the table with them.

They were silent before he spoke. "I keep wondering if we should send him." He lit a match and watched the flame disappear into the ashtray, then he looked into his wife's eyes. "There's no telling what these fool white folks will do."

Her mother reached over and patted his hand. "We're doing what we have to do, I guess," she said. "Sometimes though I wish the others weren't so much older than him."

"But it seems so unfair," Ellie broke in, "sending him there all by himself like that. Everybody keeps asking me why the MacAdams didn't apply for their children."

"Eloise." Her father's voice sounded curt. "We aren't answering for the MacAdams, we're trying to do what's right for your brother. He's not old enough to have his own say so. You and the others could decide for yourselves, but we're the ones that have to do for him."

She didn't say anything but watched him pull a handful of envelopes out of his pocket and tuck them in the cabinet drawer. She knew that if anyone had told him in August that Tommy would be the only one going to Jefferson Davis they would not have let him go.

"Those the new ones?" she asked. "What they say?"

"Let's not talk about the letters," her father said. "Let's go to bed."

Outside they heard the rain become heavier. Since early evening she had become accustomed to the sound. Now it blended in with the rest of the noises that had accumulated in the back of her mind since the whole thing began.

As her mother folded the ironing board they heard the quiet wheels of the police car. Ellie noticed that the clock said twelve-ten and she wondered why they were early. Her mother pulled the iron cord from the switch and they stood silently waiting for the police car to turn around and pass the house again, as if the car's passing were a final blessing for the night.

Suddenly she was aware of a noise that sounded as if everything had broken loose in her head at once, a loudness that almost shook the foundation of the house. At the same time the lights went out and instinctively her father knocked them to the floor. They could hear the tinkling of glass near the front of the house and Tommy began screaming.

"Tommy, get down," her father yelled.

She hoped he would remember to roll under the bed the way they had practiced. She was aware of objects falling and breaking as she lay perfectly still. Her breath was coming in jerks and then there was a second noise, a smaller explosion but still drowning out Tommy's cries.

"Stay still," her father commanded. "I'm going to check on Tommy. They may throw another one."

She watched him crawl across the floor, pushing a broken flower vase and an iron skillet out of his way. All of the sounds, Tommy's crying, the breaking glass, everything was echoing in her ears. She felt as if they had been crouching on the floor for hours but when she heard the police car door slam, the luminous hands of the clock said only twelve-fifteen.

She heard other cars drive up and pairs of heavy feet trample on the porch. "You folks all right in there?"

She could visualize the hands pulling open the door, because she knew the voice. Sergeant Kearns had been responsible for patrolling the house during the past three weeks. She heard him click the light switch in the living room but the darkness remained intense.

Her father deposited Tommy in his wife's lap and went to what was left of the door. In the next fifteen minutes policemen were everywhere. While she rummaged around underneath the cabinet for a candle, her mother tried to hush up Tommy. His cheek was cut where he had scratched himself on the springs of the bed. Her mother motioned for her to dampen a cloth and put some petroleum jelly on it to keep him quiet. She tried to put him to bed again but he would not go, even when she promised to stay with him for the rest of the night. And so she sat in the kitchen rocking the little boy back and forth on her lap.

Ellie wandered around the kitchen but the light from the single candle put an eerie glow on the walls making her nervous. She began picking up pans, stepping over pieces of broken crockery and glassware. She did not want to go into the living room yet, but if she listened closely, snatches of the policemen's conversation came through the curtain.

She heard one man say that the bomb landed near the edge of the yard, that was why it had only gotten the front porch. She knew from their talk that the living room window was shattered completely. Suddenly Ellie sat down. The picture of the living room window kept flashing in her mind and a wave of feeling invaded her body making her shake as if she had lost all muscular control. She slept on the couch, right under that window.

She looked at her mother to see if she too had realized, but her mother was looking down at Tommy and trying to get him to close his eyes. Ellie stood up and crept toward the living room trying to prepare herself for what she would see. Even that minute of determination could not make her control the horror that she felt. There were jagged holes all along the front of the house and the sofa was covered with glass and paint. She started to pick up the picture that had toppled from the book shelf, then she just stepped over the broken frame.

Outside her father was talking and, curious to see who else was with him, she walked across the splinters to the yard. She could see pieces of the geranium pot and the red blossoms turned face down. There were no lights in the other houses on the street. Across from their house she could see forms standing in the door and shadows being pushed back and forth. "I guess the MacAdams are glad they just didn't get involved." No one heard her speak, and no one came over to see if they could help; she knew why and did not really blame them. They were afraid their house could be next.

Most of the policemen had gone now and only one car was left to flash the revolving red light in the rain. She heard the tall skinny man tell her father they would be parked outside for the rest of the night. As she watched the reflection of the police cars returning to the station, feeling sick on her stomach, she wondered now why they bothered.

Ellie went back inside the house and closed the curtain behind her. There was nothing anyone could do now, not even to the house. Everything was scattered all over the floor and poor Tommy still would not go to sleep. She wondered what would happen when the news spread through their section of town, and at once remembered the man in the grey Chevrolet. It would serve them right if her father's friends got one of them.

Ellie pulled up an overturned chair and sat down across from her mother who was crooning to Tommy. What Mr. Paul said was right, white people just couldn't be trusted. Her family had expected anything but even though they had practiced ducking, they didn't really expect anybody to try tearing down the house. But the funny thing was the house belonged to one of them. Maybe it was a good thing her family were just renters.

Exhausted, Ellie put her head down on the table. She didn't know what they were going to do about tomorrow, in the day time they didn't need electricity. She was too tired to think any more about Tommy, yet she could not go to sleep. So, she sat at the table trying to sit still, but every few minutes she would involuntarily twitch. She tried to steady her hands, all the time listening to her mother's sing-songy voice and waiting for her father to come back inside the house.

She didn't know how long she lay hunched against the kitchen table, but when she looked up, her wrists bore the imprints of her hair. She unfolded her arms gingerly, feeling the blood rush to her fingertips. Her father sat in the chair opposite her, staring at the vacant space between them. She heard her mother creep away from the table, taking Tommy to his room.

Ellie looked out the window. The darkness was turning to grey and the hurt feeling was disappearing. As she sat there she could begin to look at the kitchen matter-of-factly. Although the hands of the clock were just a little past five-thirty, she knew somebody was going to have to start clearing up and cook breakfast.

She stood and tiptoed across the kitchen to her parents' bedroom. "Mama," she whispered, standing near the door of Tommy's room. At the sound of her voice, Tommy made a funny throaty noise in his sleep. Her mother motioned for her to go out and be quiet. Ellie knew then that Tommy had just fallen asleep. She crept back to the kitchen and began picking up the dishes that could be salvaged, being careful not to go into the living room.

She walked around her father, leaving the broken glass underneath the kitchen table. "You want some coffee?" she asked.

He nodded silently, in strange contrast she thought to the water faucet that turned with a loud gurgling noise. While she let the water run to get hot she measured out the instant coffee in one of the plastic cups. Next door she could hear people moving around in the Williams' kitchen, but they too seemed much quieter than usual.

"You reckon everybody knows by now?" she asked, stirring the coffee and putting the saucer in front of him.

"Everybody will know by the time the city paper comes out," he said. "Somebody was here last night from the *Observer*. Guess it'll make front page."

She leaned against the cabinet for support watching him trace endless circles in the brown liquid with the spoon. "Sergeant Kearns says they'll have almost the whole force out there tomorrow," he said.

"Today," she whispered.

Her father looked at the clock and then turned his head.

"When's your mother coming back in here?" he asked, finally picking up the cup and drinking the coffee.

"Tommy's just off to sleep," she answered. "I guess she'll be in here when he's asleep for good."

She looked out the window of the back door at the row of tall hedges that had separated their neighborhood from the white people for as long as she remembered. While she stood there she heard her mother walk into the room. To her ears the steps seemed much slower than usual. She heard her mother stop in front of her father's chair.

"Jim," she said, sounding very timid, "what we going to do?" Yet as Ellie turned toward her she noticed her mother's face was strangely calm as she looked down on her husband.

Ellie continued standing by the door listening to them talk. Nobody asked the question to which they all wanted an answer.

"I keep thinking," her father said finally, "that the policemen will be with him all day. They couldn't hurt him inside the school building without getting some of their own kind."

"But he'll be in there all by himself," her mother said softly. "A hundred policemen can't be a little boy's only friends."

She watched her father wrap his calloused hands, still splotched with machine oil, around the salt shaker on the table.

"I keep trying," he said to her, "to tell myself that somebody's got to be the first one and then I just think how quiet he's been all week."

Ellie listened to the quiet voices that seemed to be a room apart from her. In the back of her mind she could hear phrases of a hymn her grandmother used to sing, something about trouble, her being born for trouble.

"Jim, I cannot let my baby go." Her mother's words, although quiet, were carefully pronounced.

"Maybe," her father answered, "it's not in our hands. Reverend Davis and I were talking day before yesterday how God tested the Israelites, maybe he's just trying us."

"God expects you to take care of your own," his wife interrupted. Ellie sensed a trace of bitterness in her mother's voice.

"Tommy's not going to understand why he can't go to school," her father replied. "He's going to wonder why, and how are we going to tell him we're afraid of them?" Her father's hand clutched the coffee cup. "He's going to be fighting them the rest of his life. He's got to start sometime."

"But he's not on their level. Tommy's too little to go around hating people. One of the others, they're bigger, they understand about things."

Ellie still leaning against the door saw that the sun covered part of the sky behind the hedges and the light slipping through the kitchen window seemed to reflect the shiny red of the table cloth.

"He's our child," she heard her mother say. "Whatever we do, we're going to be the cause." Her father had pushed the cup away from him and sat with his hands covering part of his face. Outside Ellie could hear a horn blowing.

"God knows we tried but I guess there's just no use." Her father's voice forced her attention back to the two people sitting in front of her. "Maybe when things come back to normal, we'll try again."

He covered his wife's chunky fingers with the palm of his hand and her mother seemed to be enveloped in silence. The three of them remained quiet, each involved in his own thoughts, but related, Ellie knew, to the same thing. She was the first to break the silence.

"Mama," she called after a long pause, "do you want me to start setting the table for breakfast?"

Her mother nodded.

Ellie turned the clock so she could see it from the sink while she washed the dishes that had been scattered over the floor.

"You going to wake up Tommy or you want me to?"

"No," her mother said, still holding her father's hand, "let him sleep. When you wash your face, you go up the street and call Hezekiah. Tell him to keep up with the children after school, I want to do something to this house before they come home."

She stopped talking and looked around the kitchen, finally turning to her husband. "He's probably kicked the spread off by now," she said. Ellie watched her father, who without saying anything walked toward the bedroom.

She watched her mother lift herself from the chair and automatically push in the stuffing underneath the cracked plastic cover. Her face looked set, as it always did when she was trying hard to keep her composure.

"He'll need something hot when he wakes up. Hand me the oatmeal," she commanded, reaching on top of the icebox for matches to light the kitchen stove.

poetry

Poetry is, for most of us, an everyday experience. We respond to song lyrics, to tone of voice, to words arranged so neatly and so well that we remember them for years thereafter. Poetry is basic—just as storytelling and performing—to any culture that uses language. The study of poetry operates principally from our own experience, from our exposure to language used well enough for its lines to become part of us. Knowledge about how poetry is written—what devices the poet chooses from, and how he uses them—permits us to see his world in an especially meaningful way. Poetry invites the reader to share in a complex intellectual task, and yet go beyond intellect and into feeling. We will all eventually form our own definition of what poetry is, and have sound reasons for our favorites.

The poetry in this section asks you to begin to define your poetic judgment. Which poems bring "sound and sense" together for you? Which give you the greatest insight about the meanings of human emotions? Of nature? How have the poet's voice, the choice and arrangement of his words, and his subject matter communicated to you?

GEOFFREY CHAUCER

Complaint to His Purse

To you, my purs, and to noon other wight,
Complaine I, for ye be my lady dere,
I am so sory, now that ye be light,
For certes, but if ye make me hevy cheere,
Me were as lief be laid upon my beere;[1]   5
For which unto youre mercy thus I crye:
Beeth hevy again, or elles moot[2] I die.

Now voucheth sauf this day er it be night
That I of you the blisful soun may heere,
Or see youre colour, lik the sonne bright,   10
That of yelownesse hadde nevere peere.
Ye be my life, ye be myn hertes steere,[3]
Queene of confort and of good compaignye:
Beeth hevy again, or elles moot I die.

Ye purs, that been to me my lives light   15
And saviour, as in this world down here,
Out of this tonne helpe me thurgh your might,
Sith that ye wol nat be my tresorere;[4]
For I am shave as neigh[5] as any frere.[6]
But yit I praye unto youre curteisye: 20
Beeth hevy again, or elles moot I die.

Envoy to Henry IV

O conquerour of Brutus Albioun,
Which that by line and free eleccioun
Been verray king, this song to you I sende:
And ye, that mowen[7] alle oure harmes amende,   25
Have minde upon my supplicacioun.

From *Chaucer's Poetry—An Anthology for the Modern Reader*, selected and edited by E. T. Donaldson. Copyright © 1958 by The Ronald Press Company, New York.

[1]bier [2]must [3]rudder, guide [4]disburser [5]close [6]friar [7]may

ANONYMOUS LYRIC (FIFTEENTH CENTURY)

God, That Madest All Things

God, that madest all things of nought
And with thy precious blood us bought,
   Mercy, help, and grace.
As thou art very god and man,
And of thy side thy blood ran,   5
   Forgive us our trespass.
The world, our flesh, the fiend our foe
Maketh us mis-think, mis-speak, mis-do—
   All thus we fall in blame.
Of all our sinnes, less and more,   10
Sweete Jesu, us rueth sore.
   Mercy, for thine holy name.

POPULAR BALLADS (FIFTEENTH CENTURY)

Lord Randal

1

"O where ha' you been, Lord Randal, my son?
And where ha' you been, my handsome young man?"
"I ha' been at the greenwood; mother, mak my bed soon,
For I'm wearied wi' huntin', and fain wad[1] lie down."

2

"And wha met ye there, Lord Randal, my son?   5
And wha met you there, my handsome young man?"
"O I met wi' my true-love; mother, mak my bed soon,
For I'm wearied wi' huntin', and fain wad lie down."

3

"And what did she give you, Lord Randal, my son?
And what did she give you, my handsome young man?"   10
"Eels fried in a pan; mother, mak my bed soon,
For I'm wearied wi' huntin', and fain wad lie down."

[1]would

4

"And wha gat your leavin's, Lord Randal, my son?
And wha gat your leavin's, my handsome young man?"
"My hawks and my hounds; mother, mak my bed soon,   15
For I'm wearied wi' huntin', and fain wad lie down."

5

"And what becam of them, Lord Randal, my son?
And what becam of them, my handsome young man?"
"They stretched their legs out and died; mother, mak my bed soon,
For I'm wearied wi' huntin', and fain wad lie down."   20

6

"O I fear you are poisoned, Lord Randal, my son!
I fear you are poisoned, my handsome young man!"
"O yes, I am poisoned; mother, mak my bed soon,
For I'm sick at the heart, and I fain wad lie down."

7

"What d' ye leave to your mother, Lord Randal, my son?   25
What d'ye leave to your mother, my handsome young man?"
"Four and twenty milk kye[2]; mother, mak my bed soon,
For I'm sick at the heart, and I fain wad lie down."

8

"What d' ye leave to your sister, Lord Randal, my son?
What d' ye leave to your sister, my handsome young man?"   30
"My gold and my silver; mother, mak my bed soon,
For I'm sick at the heart, and I fain wad lie down."

9

"What d' ye leave to your brother, Lord Randal, my son?
What d' ye leave to your brother, my handsome young man?"
"My houses and my lands; mother, mak my bed soon,   35
For I'm sick at the heart, and I fain wad lie down."

10

"What d' ye leave to your true-love, Lord Randal, my son?
What d' ye leave to your true-love, my handsome young man?"
"I leave her hell and fire; mother, mak my bed soon,
For I'm sick at the heart, and I fain wad lie down."   40

Child, No. 12.A.

From O. S. 155 *The Wheatley Manuscript.* Reprinted by permission of the Early English Text Society.

[2]kine, cattle

The Twa Corbies

1

As I was walking all alane,
I heard twa corbie making a mane;[1]
The tane[2] unto the t'other say,
"Where sall[3] we gang[4] and dine to-day?"

2

"In behint you auld fail[5] dike,
I wot there lies a new slain knight;
And naebody kens[6] that he lies there,
But his hawk, his hound, and lady fair.

3

"His hound is to the hunting gane,
His hawk to fetch the wild-fowl hame,
His lady's ta'en another mate,
So we may mak our dinner sweet.

4

"Ye'll sit on his white hause-bane,[7]
And I'll pike[8] out his bonny blue een;[9]
Wi' ae[10] lock o' his gowden[11] hair
We'll theek[12] our nest when it grows bare.

5

"Mony a one for him makes mane,
But nane sall ken where he is gane;
O'er his white banes, when they are bare,
The wind sall blaw for evermair."

Child, No. 26.

The Cherry-Tree Carol

1

Joseph was an old man,
    And an old man was he,
When he wedded Mary
    In the land of Galilee.

[1]moan   [2]one   [3]shall   [4]go   [5]turf   [6]knows   [7]neck-bone   [8]pick   [9]eyes   [10]one   [11]golden
[12]thatch

2

Joseph and Mary walked 5
   Through an orchard good,
Where was cherries and berries
   So red as any blood.

3

Joseph and Mary walked
   Through an orchard green, 10
Where was berries and cherries
   As thick as might be seen.

4

O then bespoke Mary,
   So meek and so mild:
"Pluck me one cherry, Joseph, 15
   For I am with child."

5

O then bespoke Joseph,
   With words most unkind:
"Let him pluck thee a cherry
   That brought thee with child." 20

6

O then bespoke the babe,
   Within his mother's womb:
"Bow down then the tallest tree
   For my mother to have some."

7

Then bowed down the highest tree 25
   Unto his mother's hand;
Then she cried, "See, Joseph,
   I have cherries at command."

8

O then bespake Joseph:
   "I have done Mary wrong; 30
But cheer up, my dearest,
   And be not cast down."

9

Then Mary plucked a cherry
  As red as the blood,
Then Mary went home   35
  With her heavy load.

10

Then Mary took her babe
  And sat him on her knee,
Saying, "My dear son, tell me
  What this world will be."   40

11

"O I shall be as dead, mother,
  As the stones in the wall;
O stones in the streets, mother,
  Shall mourn for me all.

12

"Upon Easter-day, mother,   45
  My uprising shall be;
O the sun and the moon, mother,
  Shall both rise with me."

Child, No. 54.A.

Bonny Barbara Allan

1

It was in and about the Martinmas time,
  When the green leaves were a falling,
That Sir John Graeme, in the West Country,
  Fell in love with Barbara Allan.

2

He sent his man down through the town,   5
  To the place where she was dwelling:
"O haste and come to my master dear,
  Gin[1] ye be Barbara Allan."

[1]if

3

O hooly,[2] hooly rose she up,
    To the place where he was lying,
And when she drew the curtain by:
    "Young man, I think you're dying."   10

4

"O it's I'm sick, and very, very sick,
    And 'tis a' for Barbara Allan."
"O the better for me ye s'[3] never be,   15
    Though your heart's blood were a-spilling."

5

"O dinna[4] ye mind, young man," said she,
    "When ye was in the tavern a drinking,
That ye made the healths gae[5] round and round,
    And slighted Barbara Allan?"   20

6

He turned his face unto the wall,
    And death was with him dealing:
"Adieu, adieu, my dear friends all,
    And be kind to Barbara Allan."

7

And slowly, slowly raise she up,   25
    And slowly, slowly left him,
And sighing said, she could not stay,
    Since death of life had reft him.

8

She had not gane a mile but twa,
    When she heard the dead-bell ringing,   30
And every jow[6] that the dead-bell geid,[7]
    It cried, "Woe to Barbara Allan!"

9

"O mother, mother, make my bed!
    O make it saft and narrow!
Since my love died for me to-day,   35
    I'll die for him to-morrow."

Child, No. 84.A.

[2]slowly, gently   [3]ye shall   [4]don't   [5]go   [6]stroke   [7]gave

Mary Hamilton

1

Word's gane to the kitchen,
    And word's gane to the ha',
That Marie Hamilton gangs[1] wi' bairn[2]
    To the hichest[3] Stewart of a'.

2

He's courted her in the kitchen,   5
    He's courted her in the ha',
He's courted her in the laigh cellar,
    And that was warst of a'.

3

She's tied it in her apron
    And she's thrown it in the sea;   10
Says, "Sink you, swim ye, bonny wee babe!
    You'll ne'er get mair o' me."

4

Down then cam the auld queen,
    Goud[4] tassels tying her hair:
"O Marie, where's the bonny wee babe   15
    That I heard greet sae sair?"

5

"There was never a babe intill[5] my room,
    As little designs to be;
It was but a touch o' my sair side,
    Come o'er my fair body."   20

6

"O Marie, put on your robes o' black,
    Or else your robes o' brown,
For ye maun[6] gang wi' me the night,
    To see fair Edinbro' town."

7

"I winna[7] put on my robes o' black,   25
    Nor yet my robes o' brown;
But I'll put on my robes o' white,
    To shine through Edinbro' town."

[1]goes [2]child [3]highest [4]gold [5]in [6]must [7]won't

8

When she gaed[8] up the Cannogate,
   She laughed loud laughters three;
But when she cam down the Cannogate
   The tear blinded her ee.[9]

30

9

When she gaed up the Parliament stair,
   The heel cam aff her shee;
And lang or[10] she cam down again
   She was condemned to dee.

35

10

When she cam down the Cannogate,
   The Cannogate sae free,
Many a lady looked o'er her window,
   Weeping for this lady.

40

11

"Ye need nae weep for me," she says,
   "Ye need nae weep for me;
For had I not slain mine own sweet babe,
   This death I wadna dee.

12

"Bring me a bottle of wine," she says,
   "The best that e'er ha'e,
That I may drink to my weil-wishers,
   And they may drink to me.

45

13

"Here's a health to the jolly sailors,
   That sail upon the main;
Let them never let on to my father and mother
   But what I'm coming hame.

50

14

"Here's a health to the jolly sailors,
   That sail upon the sea;
Let them never let on to my father and mother
   That I cam here to dee.

55

[8]went   [9]eye   [10]before

15

"O little did my mother think,
  The day she cradled me,
What lands I was to travel through,
  What death I was to dee.   60

16

"Oh little did my father think,
  The day he held up me,
What lands I was to travel through,
  What death I was to dee.

17

"Last night I washed the queen's feet,   65
  And gently laid her down;
And a' the thanks I've gotten the night
  To be hanged in Edinbro' town!

18

"Last night there was four Maries,
  The night there'll be but three;   70
There was Marie Seton, and Marie Beton,
  And Marie Carmichael, and me."

                                          Child, No. 173.A.

ANONYMOUS POEM (ELIZABETHAN)

The Silver Swan

The silver swan, who living had no note,
When death approached, unlocked her silent throat;
Leaning her breast against the reedy shore,
Thus sung her first and last, and sung no more:
"Farewell, all joys; Oh death, come close mine eyes;   5
More geese than swans now live, more fools than wise."

                                                      1612

SIR WALTER RALEIGH

Three Things There Be

Three things there be that prosper up apace
And flourish, whilst they grow asunder far,
But on a day, they meet all in one place,
And when they meet, they one another mar;
And they be these: the wood, the weed, the wag.   5
The wood is that which makes the gallow tree,
The weed is that which strings the hangman's bag,
The wag, my pretty knave, betokeneth thee.
Mark well, dear boy, whilst these assemble not,
Green springs the tree, hemp grows, the wag is wild;   10
But when they meet, it makes the timber rot,
It frets[1] the halter, and it chokes the child.
   Then bless thee, and beware, and let us pray
   We part not with thee at this meeting day.

ca. 1610

SIR PHILIP SIDNEY

Sonnet 5

It is most true that eyes are formed to serve
The inward light, and that the heavenly part
Ought to be king, from whose rules who do swerve,
Rebels to nature, strive for their own smart.
It is most true, what we call Cupid's dart   5
An image is, which for ourselves we carve,
And, fools, adore in temple of our heart,
Till that good god make church and churchman starve.
True, that true beauty virtue is indeed,
Whereof this beauty can be but a shade,   10
Which elements with mortal mixture breed.
True, that on earth, we are but pilgrims made,
And should in soul up to our country move.
True, and yet true that I must Stella love.

[1] frays

WILLIAM SHAKESPEARE

Sonnet 12

When I do count the clock that tells the time,
And see the brave day sunk in hideous night;
When I behold the violet past prime,
And sable curls, all silvered o'er with white;
When lofty trees I see barren of leaves,   5
Which erst[1] from heat did canopy the herd,
And summer's green all girded up in sheaves,
Borne on the bier with white and bristly beard,
Then of thy beauty do I question make,
That thou among the wastes of time must go,   10
Since sweets and beauties do themselves forsake
And die as fast as they see others grow;
And nothing 'gainst time's scythe can make defense
Save breed,[2] to brave him when he takes thee hence.

Sonnet 18

Shall I compare thee to a summer's day?
Thou art more lovely and more temperate:
Rough winds do shake the darling buds of May,
And summer's lease hath all too short a date:
Sometimes too hot the eye of heaven shines,   5
And often is his gold complexion dimmed;
And every fair from fair sometimes declines,
By chance or nature's changing course untrimmed;
But thy eternal summer shall not fade,
Nor lose possession of that fair thou ow'st;[1]   10
Nor shall death brag thou wander'st in his shade,
When in eternal lines to time thou grow'st:
So long as men can breathe, or eyes can see,
So long lives this, and this gives life to thee.

[1]formerly [2]progeny

[1]ownest

358

Sonnet 29

When, in disgrace with fortune and men's eyes,
I all alone beweep my outcast state,
And trouble deaf heaven with my bootless[1] cries,
And look upon myself, and curse my fate,
Wishing me like to one more rich in hope,   5
Featured like him, like him with friends possessed,
Desiring this man's art and that man's scope,
With what I most enjoy contented least;
Yet in these thoughts myself almost despising,
Haply I think on thee—and then my state,   10
Like to the lark at break of day arising
From sullen earth, sings hymns at heaven's gate;
For thy sweet love remembered such wealth brings
That then I scorn to change my state with kings.

Sonnet 30

When to the sessions of sweet silent thought
I summon up remembrance of things past,
I sigh the lack of many a thing I sought,
And with old woes new wail my dear time's waste:
Then can I drown an eye, unused to flow,   5
For precious friends hid in death's dateless[1] night,
And weep afresh love's long since canceled woe,
And moan the expense[2] of many a vanished sight:
Then can I grieve at grievances foregone,
And heavily from woe to woe tell o'er   10
The sad account of fore-bemoanéd moan,
Which I new pay as if not paid before.
But if the while I think on thee, dear friend,
All losses are restored and sorrows end.

[1]futile

[1]endless [2]loss

Sonnet 33

Full many a glorious morning have I seen
Flatter the mountain-tops with sovereign eye,
Kissing with golden face the meadows green,
Gilding pale streams with heavenly alchemy;
Anon permit the basest clouds to ride   5
With ugly rack on his celestial face,
And from the forlorn world his visage hide,
Stealing unseen to west with this disgrace:
Even so my sun one early morn did shine
With all-triumphant splendor on my brow;   10
But, out, alack! he was but one hour mine,
The region cloud hath masked him from me now.
Yet him for this my love no whit disdaineth;
Suns of the world may stain when heaven's sun staineth.

Sonnet 35

No more be grieved at that which thou hast done:
Roses have thorns, and silver fountains mud;
Clouds and eclipses stain both moon and sun,
And loathsome canker lives in sweetest bud.
All men make faults, and even I in this,   5
Authorizing thy trespass with compare,[1]
Myself corrupting, salving thy amiss,[2]
Excusing thy sins more than thy sins are;
For to thy sensual fault I bring in sense—
Thy adverse party is thy advocate—   10
And 'gainst myself a lawful plea commence.
Such civil war is in my love and hate
That I an áccessary needs must be
To that sweet thief which sourly robs from me.

Sonnet 55

Not marble, nor the gilded monuments
Of princes, shall outlive this powerful rhyme;
But you shall shine more bright in these conténts

[1]comparison [2]wrongdoing

Than unswept stone, besmeared with sluttish time.
When wasteful war shall statues overturn,   5
And broils root out the work of masonry,
Nor Mars his sword nor war's quick fire shall burn
The living record of your memory.
'Gainst death and all-oblivious enmity
Shall you pace forth; your praise shall still find room   10
Even in the eyes of all posterity
That wear this world out to the ending doom.[1]
So, till the judgment that yourself arise,
You live in this, and dwell in lovers' eyes.

Sonnet 64

When I have seen by time's fell[1] hand defaced
The rich-proud cost of outworn buried age;
When sometime[2] lofty towers I see down-razed,
And brass eternal slave to mortal rage;
When I have seen the hungry ocean gain   5
Advantage on the kingdom of the shore,
And the firm soil win of the watery main,
Increasing store with loss, and loss with store;
When I have seen such interchange of state,
Or state itself confounded to decay,   10
Ruin hath taught me thus to ruminate,
That time will come and take my love away.
This thought is as a death, which cannot choose
But weep to have that which it fears to lose.

Sonnet 65

Since brass, nor stone, nor earth, nor boundless sea
But sad mortality o'er-sways their power,
How with this rage shall beauty hold a plea,
Whose action is no stronger than a flower?

[1]Judgment Day

[1]destroying   [2]formerly

O, how shall summer's honey breath hold out   5
Against the wreckful siege of battering days,
When rocks impregnable are not so stout,
Nor gates of steel so strong, but Time decays?
O fearful meditation! where, alack,
Shall Time's best jewel from Time's chest lie hid?   10
Or what strong hand can hold his swift foot back?
Or who his spoil of beauty can forbid?
O, none, unless this miracle have might,
That in black ink my love may still shine bright.

Sonnet 73

That time of year thou mayst in me behold
When yellow leaves, or none, or few, do hang
Upon those boughs which shake against the cold,
Bare ruined choirs, where late the sweet birds sang.
In me thou see'st the twilight of such day   5
As after sunset fadeth in the west;
Which by and by black night doth take away,
Death's second self, that seals up all in rest.
In me thou see'st the glowing of such fire,
That on the ashes of his youth doth lie,   10
As the deathbed whereon it must expire,
Consumed with that which it was nourished by.
This thou perceiv'st, which makes thy love more strong,
To love that well which thou must leave ere long.

Sonnet 94

They that have power to hurt and will do none,
That do not do the thing they most do show,
Who, moving others, are themselves as stone,
Unmovéd, cold, and to temptation slow;
They rightly do inherit heaven's graces   5
And husband nature's riches from expense;[1]
They are the lords and owners of their faces,
Others but stewards of their excellence.
The summer's flower is to the summer sweet,
Though to itself it only live and die,   10

But if that flower with base infection meet,
The basest weed outbraves[2] his dignity:
For sweetest things turn sourest by their deeds;
Lilies that fester smell far worse than weeds.

Sonnet 97

How like a winter hath my absence been
From thee, the pleasure of the fleeting year!
What freezings have I felt, what dark days seen!
What old December's bareness eveywhere!
And yet this time removed was summer's time,   5
The teeming autumn, big with rich increase,
Bearing the wanton burthen of the prime,[1]
Like widowed wombs after their lords' decease;
Yet this abundant issue seemed to me
But hope of orphans and unfathered fruit;   10
For summer and his pleasures wait on thee,
And, thou away, the very birds are mute;
Or, if they sing, 'tis with so dull a cheer
That leaves look pale, dreading the winter's near.

Sonnet 98

From you have I been absent in the spring,
When proud-pied April, dressed in all his trim,
Hath put a spirit of youth in everything,
That heavy Saturn laughed and leaped with him.
Yet nor the lays of birds, nor the sweet smell   5
Of different flowers in odor and in hue,
Could make me any summer's story tell,
Or from their proud lap pluck them where they grew;
Nor did I wonder at the lily's white,
Nor praise the deep vermilion in the rose;   10
They were but sweet, but figures of delight,
Drawn after you, you pattern of all those.
Yet seemed it winter still, and, you away,
As with your shadow I with these did play.

[1]expenditure   [2]excels

[1]spring

Sonnet 116

Let me not to the marriage of true minds
Admit impediments. Love is not love
Which alters when it alteration finds,
Or bends with the remover to remove:
Oh, no! it is an ever-fixéd mark,   5
That looks on tempests and is never shaken;
It is the star to every wandering bark,
Whose worth's unknown, although his height be taken.
Love's not Time's fool, though rosy lips and cheeks
Within his bending sickle's compass come;   10
Love alters not with his brief hours and weeks,
But bears it out even to the edge of doom.
If this be error and upon me proved,
I never writ, nor no man ever loved.

Sonnet 130

My mistress' eyes are nothing like the sun;
Coral is far more red than her lips' red;
If snow be white, why then her breasts are dun;
If hairs be wires, black wires grow on her head.
I have seen roses damasked,[1] red and white,   5
But no such roses see I in her cheeks;
And in some perfumes is there more delight
Than in the breath that from my mistress reeks.
I love to hear her speak, yet well I know
That music hath a far more pleasing sound;   10
I grant I never saw a goddess go;[2]
My mistress, when she walks, treads on the ground.
And yet, by heaven, I think my love as rare
As any she belied with false compare.

Sonnet 138

When my love swears that she is made of truth,
I do believe her, though I know she lies,

[1]variegated [2]walk

That she might think me some untutored youth,
Unlearnéd in the world's false subtleties.
Thus vainly thinking that she thinks me young,   5
Although she knows my days are past the best,
Simply I credit her false-speaking tongue:
On both sides thus is simple truth suppressed.
But wherefore says she not she is unjust?
And wherefore say not I that I am old?   10
Oh, love's best habit is in seeming trust,
And age in love loves not to have years told.
Therefore I lie with her and she with me,
And in our faults by lies we flattered be.

Who Is Silvia?

Who is Silvia? What is she,
    That all our swains commend her?
Holy, fair, and wise is she;
    The heaven such grace did lend her,
That she might admiréd be.   5

Is she kind as she is fair?
    For beauty lives with kindness.
Love doth to her eyes repair
    To help him of his blindness,
And, being helped, inhabits there.   10

Then to Silvia let us sing
    That Silvia is excelling;
She excels each mortal thing
    Upon the dull earth dwelling.
To her let us garlands bring.   15

                                        1595?   1623

When Daffodils Begin to Peer

When daffodils begin to peer,
    With heigh! the doxy[1] over the dale,
Why, then comes in the sweet o' the year;
    For the red blood reigns in the winter's pale.

[1]trollop, mistress

365

The white sheet bleaching on the hedge,   5
   With heigh! the sweet birds, Oh, how they sing!
Doth set my pugging[2] tooth on edge;
   For a quart of ale is a dish for a king.

The lark, that tirra-lirra chants,
   With heigh! with heigh! the thrush and the jay,   10
Are summer songs for me and my aunts,[3]
   While we lie tumbling in the hay.

                            1611   1623

Where the Bee Sucks, There Suck I

Where the bee sucks, there suck I:
In a cowslip's bell I lie;
There I couch when owls do cry.
On the bat's back I do fly
After summer merrily.   5
Merrily, merrily shall I live now
Under the blossom that hangs on the bough.

                            1611   1623

JOHN DONNE

Song

Go and catch a falling star,
   Get with child a mandrake root,
Tell me where all past years are,
   Or who cleft the Devil's foot,
Teach me to hear mermaids singing   5
Or to keep off envy's stinging,
         And find
         What wind
Serves to advance an honest mind.

If thou beest born to strange sights,   10
   Things invisible to see,
Ride ten thousand days and nights,
   Till age snow white hairs on thee.

[2]thieving [3]sweethearts

Thou, when thou return'st, wilt tell me
All strange wonders that befell thee,_____ 15
       And swear
       Nowhere
Lives a woman true, and fair.

If thou find'st one, let me know,
    Such a pilgrimage were sweet; 20
Yet do not, I would not go,
    Though at next door we might meet;
Though she were true when you met her,
And last till you write your letter,
       Yet she 25
       Will be
False, ere I come, to two, or three.

Song

Sweetest love, I do not go
    For weariness of thee,
Nor in hope the world can show
    A fitter love for me;
       But since that I 5
Must die at last, tis best
To use myself in jest,
    Thus by feigned deaths to die.

Yesternight the sun went hence,
    And yet is here today; 10
He hath no desire nor sense,
    Nor half so short a way:
       Then fear not me,
But believe that I shall make
Speedier journeys, since I take 15
    More wings and spurs than he.

O how feeble is man's power,
    That if good fortune fall,
Cannot add another hour,
    Nor a lost hour recall! 20
       But come bad chance,
And we join to'it our strength,
And we teach it art and length,
    Itself o'er us to'advance.

When thou sigh'st, thou sigh'st not wind,   25
   But sigh'st my soul away;
When thou weep'st, unkindly kind,
   My life's blood doth decay.
     It cannot be
That thou lov'st me, as thou say'st,   30
If in thine my life thou waste;
   Thou art the best of me.

Let not thy divining heart
   Forethink me any ill;
Destiny may take thy part,   35
   And may thy fears fulfill;
     But think that we
Are but turned aside to sleep;
They who one another keep
   Alive, ne'er parted be.   40

The Anniversary

   All kings, and all their favorites,
   All glory, of honors, beauties, wits,
The sun itself, which makes times, as they pass,
Is elder by a year, now, than it was
When thou and I first one another saw: 5
All other things to their destruction draw,
   Only our love hath no decay;
This, no tomorrow hath, nor yesterday;
Running it never runs from us away,
But truly keeps his first, last, everlasting day.   10

   Two graves must hide thine and my corse;
If one might, death were no divorce:
Alas, as well as other princes, we
(Who prince enough in one another be)
Must leave at last in death, these eyes, and ears,   15
Oft fed with true oaths, and with sweet salt tears;
   But souls where nothing dwells but love
(All other thoughts being inmates[1]) then shall prove[2]
This, or a love increaséd there above,
When bodies to their graves, souls from their graves remove.   20

   And then we shall be throughly[3] blest,
   But we no more than all the rest;

[1]lodgers   [2]experience   [3]thoroughly

Here upon earth, were kings, and none but we
Can be such kings, nor of such subjects be;
Who is so safe as we, where none can do   25
Treason to us, except one of us two?
    True and false fears let us refrain,
Let us love nobly,'and live, and add again
Years and years unto years, till we attain
To write threescore, this is the second of our reign.   30

1633

Love's Alchemy

Some that have deeper digged love's mine than I,
Say where his centric happiness doth lie;
    I've loved, and got, and told,
But should I love, get, tell, till I were old,
I should not find that hidden mystery;   5
    O, 'tis imposture all:
And as no chemic yet th' elixir got,
    But glorifies his pregnant pot,
    If by the way to him befall
Some odoriferous thing, or médicinal;   10
    So lovers dream a rich and long delight,
    But get a winter-seeming summer's night.

Our ease, our thrift, our honor, and our day,
Shall we for this vain bubble's shadow pay?
    Ends love in this, that my man[1]   15
Can be as happy' as I can if he can
Endure the short scorn of a bridegroom's play?
    That loving wretch that swears,
'Tis not the bodies marry, but the minds,
    Which he in her angelic finds,   20
    Would swear as justly that he hears,
In that day's rude hoarse minstrelsy, the spheres.
    Hope not for mind in women; at their best
Sweetness and wit they're but mummy, possessed.

[1]servant   1633

369

A Valediction: Forbidding Mourning

As virtuous men pass mildly'away,
   And whisper to their souls to go,
Whilst some of their sad friends do say
   The breath goes now, and some say, No;

So let us melt, and make no noise,   5
   No tear-floods, nor sigh-tempests move,
'Twere profanation of our joys
   To tell the laity our love.

Moving of th' earth brings harms and fears,
   Men reckon what it did and meant;   10
But trepidation of the spheres,
   Though greater far, is innocent.

Dull sublunary lovers' love
   (Whose soul is sense) cannot admit
Absence, because it doth remove   15
   Those things which elemented it.

But we by'a love so much refined
   That our selves know not what it is,
Inter-assuréd of the mind,
   Care less, eyes, lips, and hands to miss.   20

Our two souls therefore, which are one,
   Though I must go, endure not yet
A breach, but an expansion,
   Like gold to airy thinness beat.

If they be two, they are two so   25
   As stiff twin compasses are two;
Thy soul, the fixed foot, makes no show
   To move, but doth, if th' other do.

And though it in the center sit,
   Yet when the other far doth roam,   30
It leans and hearkens after it,
   And grows erect, as that comes home.

Such wilt thou be to me, who must
   Like th' other foot, obliquely run;
Thy firmness makes my circle just,   35
   And makes me end where I begun.

1633

Elegy XIX. To His Mistress Going to Bed

Come, madam, come, all rest my powers defy,
Until I labor, I in labor lie.
The foe oft-times having the foe in sight,
Is tired with standing though he never fight.
Off with that girdle, like heaven's zone glistering,   5
But a far fairer world encompassing.
Unpin that spangled breastplate which you wear,
That th' eyes of busy fools may be stopped there.
Unlace yourself, for that harmonious chime
Tells me from you that now it is bed time.   10
Off with that happy busk,¹ which I envy,
That still can be, and still can stand so nigh.
Your gown, going off, such beauteous state reveals,
As when from flowry meads th' hill's shadow steals.
Off with that wiry coronet and show   15
The hairy diadem which on you doth grow:
Now off with those shoes, and then safely tread
In this love's hallowed temple, this soft bed.
In such white robes, heaven's angels used to be
Received by men; thou, Angel, bring'st with thee   20
A heaven like Mahomet's Paradise; and though
Ill spirits walk in white, we easily know
By this these angels from an evil sprite:
Those set our hairs, but these our flesh upright.
  License my roving hands, and let them go   25
Before, behind, between, above, below.
O my America! my new-found-land,
My kingdom, safeliest when with one man manned,
My mine of precious stones, my empery,²
How blest am I in this discovering thee!   30
To enter in these bonds is to be free;
Then where my hand is set, my seal shall be.
  Full nakedness!   All joys are due to thee,
As souls unbodied, bodies unclothed must be
To taste whole joys. Gems which you women use   35
Are like Atlanta's balls, cast in men's views,
That when a fool's eye lighteth on a gem,
His earthly soul may covet theirs, not them.
Like pictures, or like books' gay coverings made
For lay-men, are all women thus arrayed;   40
Themselves are mystic books, which only we
(Whom their imputed grace will dignify)

¹corset ²empire

Must see revealed.   Then, since that I may know,
As liberally as to a midwife, show
Thyself: cast all, yea, this white linen hence,   45
There is no penance due to innocence.
    To teach thee, I am naked first; why than,[3]
What needst thou have more covering than a man?

                                                                                                            1669

Holy Sonnet 1

Thou hast made me, and shall Thy work decay?
Repair me now, for now mine end doth haste;
I run to death, and death meets me as fast,
And all my pleasures are like yesterday.
I dare not move my dim eyes any way,   5
Despair behind, and death before doth cast
Such terror, and my feeble flesh doth waste
By sin in it, which it towards hell doth weigh.
Only Thou art above, and when towards Thee
By Thy leave I can look, I rise again;
But our old subtle foe so tempteth me   10
That nor one hour myself I can sustain.
Thy grave may wing me to prevent his art,
And Thou like adamant[1] draw mine iron heart.

                                                                                                            1635

Holy Sonnet 7

At the round earth's imagined corners, blow
Your trumpets, angels; and arise, arise
From death, you numberless infinities
Of souls, and to your scattered bodies go;
All whom the flood did, and fire shall, o'erthrow,
All whom war, dearth, age, agues, tyrannies,   5
Despair, law, chance hath slain, and you whose eyes
Shall behold God, and never taste death's woe.
But let them sleep, Lord, and me mourn a space;
For, if above all these, my sins abound,
'Tis late to ask abundance of Thy grace   10

[3]then

[1]loadstone

When we are there. Here on this lowly ground,
Teach me how to repent; for that's as good
As if Thou'hadst sealed my pardon with Thy blood.

1633

Holy Sonnet 8

If faithful souls be alike glorified
As angels, then my father's soul doth see,
And adds this even to full felicity,
That valiantly I hell's wide mouth o'erstride.
But if our minds to these souls be descried   5
By circumstances, and by signs that be
Apparent in us, not immediately,
How shall my mind's white truth by them be tried?
They see idolatrous lovers weep and mourn,
And vile blasphemous conjurers to call   10
On Jesus' name, and Pharisaical
Dissemblers feign devotion. Then turn,
O pensive soul, to God, for He knows best
Thy grief, for He put it into my breast.

1635

Holy Sonnet 10

Death, be not proud, though some have calléd thee
Mighty and dreadful, for thou are not so;
For those whom thou think'st thou dost overthrow
Die not, poor Death, nor yet canst thou kill me.
From rest and sleep, which but thy pictures be,   5
Much pleasure; then from thee much more must flow,
And soonest our best men with thee do go,
Rest of their bones, and soul's delivery.
Thou'art slave to fate, chance, kings, and desperate men,
And dost with poison, war, and sickness dwell,   10
And poppy'or charms can make us sleep as well
And better than thy stroke; why swell'st thou then?
One short sleep past, we wake eternally
And death shall be no more; Death, thou shalt die.

1633

Holy Sonnet 14

Batter my heart, three-personed God; for You
As yet but knock, breathe, shine, and seek to mend;
That I may rise and stand, o'erthrow me,'and bend
Your force to break, blow, burn, and make me new.
I, like an usurped town, to'another due,   5
Labor to'admit You, but O, to no end;
Reason, Your viceroy'in me, me should defend,
But is captíved, and proves weak or untrue.
Yet dearly'I love You,'and would be lovéd fain,
But am betrothed unto Your enemy.   10
Divorce me,'untie or break that knot again;
Take me to You, imprison me, for I,
Except You'enthrall me, never shall be free,
Nor ever chaste, except You ravish me.

1633

Holy Sonnet 18

Show me, dear Christ, Thy spouse so bright and clear.
What! is it she which on the other shore
Goes richly painted? or which, robbed and tore,
Laments and mourns in Germany and here?
Sleeps she a thousand, then peeps up one year?   5
Is she self-truth, and errs? now new, now'outwore?
Doth she,'and did she, and shall she evermore
On one, on seven, or on no hill appear?
Dwells she with us, or like adventuring knights
First travel we to seek, and then make love?   10
Betray,[1] kind husband, Thy spouse to our sights,
And let mine amorous soul court Thy mild dove,
Who is most true and pleasing to Thee then
When she's embraced and open to most men.

after 1615

[1] reveal

BEN JONSON

On My First Son

Farewell, thou child of my right hand, and joy;
My sin was too much hope of thee, loved boy:
Seven years thou'wert lent to me, and I thee pay,
Exacted by thy fate, on the just day.
O could I lose all father now! for why   5
Will man lament the state he should envý,
To have so soon 'scaped world's and flesh's rage,
And, if no other misery, yet age?
Rest in soft peace, and asked, say, "Here doth lie
Ben Jonson his best piece of poetry."   10
For whose sake henceforth all his vows be such
As what he loves may never like too much.

1616

Song: That Women Are But Men's Shadows

Follow a shadow, it still flies you;
Seem to fly it, it will pursue:
So court a mistress, she denies you;
Let her alone, she will court you.
Say, are not women truly, then,   5
Styled but the shadows of us men?
At morn and even shades are longest;
At noon they are or short or none:
So men at weakest, they are strongest,
But grant us perfect, they're not known.   10
Say, are not women truly, then,
Styled but the shadows of us men?

1616

Though I Am Young and Cannot Tell

Though I am young, and cannot tell
   Either what Death or Love is well,
Yet I have heard they both bear darts,
   And both do aim at human hearts.

And then again, I have been told   5
    Love wounds with heat, as Death with cold;
So that I fear they do but bring
    Extremes to touch, and mean one thing.

As in a ruin we it call
    One thing to be blown up, or fall;   10
Or to our end like way may have
    By a flash of lightning, or a wave;
So Love's inflaméd shaft or brand
    May kill as soon as Death's cold hand;
Except Love's fires the virtue have   15
    To fright the frost out of the grave.

                                                          1641

ROBERT HERRICK

Delight in Disorder

A sweet disorder in the dress
Kindles in clothes a wantonness
A lawn about the shoulders thrown
Into a fine distractiön;
An erring lace, which here and there   5
Enthralls the crimson stomacher;
A cuff neglectful, and thereby
Ribbons to flow confusedly;
A winning wave, deserving note,
In the tempestuous petticoat;   10
A careless shoestring, in whose tie
I see a wild civility;
Do more bewitch me than when art
Is too precise in every part.

                                                          1648

To the Virgins, to Make Much of Time

Gather ye rosebuds while ye may,
    Old time is still a-flying;
And this same flower that smiles today
    Tomorrow will be dying.

The glorious lamp of heaven, the sun,   5
    The higher he's a-getting,
The sooner will his race be run,
    And nearer he's to setting.

That age is best which is the first,
    When youth and blood are warmer;   10
But being spent, the worse, and worst
    Times still succeed the former.

Then be not coy, but use your time,
    And, while ye may, go marry;
For, having lost but once your prime,   15
    You may forever tarry.

                                                                1648

Upon a Child That Died

Here she lies, a pretty bud,
Lately made of flesh and blood,
Who as soon fell fast asleep
As her little eyes did peep.
Give her strewings, but not stir   5
The earth that lightly covers her.

                                                                1648

Upon Julia's Clothes

Whenas in silks my Julia goes,
Then, then, methinks, how sweetly flows
That liquefaction of her clothes.

Next, when I cast mine eyes, and see
That brave vibration, each way free,   5
O, how that glittering taketh me!

                                                                1648

JOHN MILTON

L'Allegro

Hence loathéd Melancholy
   Of Cerberus and blackest midnight born,
In Stygian cave forlorn
   'Mongst horrid shapes, and shrieks, and sights unholy,
Find out some uncouth[1] cell,   5
   Where brooding Darkness spreads his jealous wings,
And the night-raven sings;
   There under ebon shades, and low-browed rocks,
As ragged as thy locks,
   In dark Cimmerian desert ever dwell.   10
But come thou goddess fair and free,
In Heaven yclept[2] Euphrosyne,
And by men, heart-easing Mirth,
Whom lovely Venus at a birth
With two sister Graces more   15
To ivy-crownéd Bacchus bore;
Or whether (as some sager sing)
The frolic wind that breathes the spring,
Zephyr with Aurora playing,
As he met her once a-Maying,   20
There on beds of violets blue,
And fresh-blown[3] roses washed in dew,
Filled her with thee a daughter fair,
So buxom,[4] blithe, and debonair.[5]
Haste thee nymph, and bring with thee   25
Jest and youthful Jollity,
Quips and Cranks,[6] and wanton Wiles,
Nods, and Becks,[7] and wreathéd Smiles,
Such as hang on Hebe's cheek,
And love to live in dimple sleek;   30
Sport that wrinkled Care derides,
And Laughter, holding both his sides.
Come, and trip it as ye go
On the light fantastic toe,
And in thy right hand lead with thee,   35
The mountain nymph, sweet Liberty;
And if I give thee honor due,
Mirth, admit me of thy crew
To live with her and live with thee,

---

[1]unknown   [2]called   [3]newly bloomed   [4]merry   [5]pleasant   [6]jests   [7]curtseys

In unreprovéd pleasures free;   40
To hear the lark begin his flight,
And, singing, startle the dull night,
From his watch-tower in the skies,
Till the dappled dawn doth rise;
Then to come in spite[8] of sorrow,   45
And at my window bid good morrow,
Through the sweetbriar, or the vine,
Or the twisted eglantine.
While the cock with lively din,
Scatters the rear of darkness thin,   50
And to the stack, or the barn door,
Stoutly struts his dames before;
Oft listening how the hounds and horn
Cheerly rouse the slumbering morn,
From the side of some hoar hill,   55
Through the high wood echoing shrill.
Sometimes walking not unseen
By hedgerow elms, on hillocks green,
Right against the eastern gate,
Where the great sun begins his state,[9]   60
Robed in flames, and amber light,
The clouds in thousand liveries dight;[10]
While the plowman near at hand,
Whistles o'er the furrowed land,
And the milkmaid singeth blithe,   65
And the mower whets his scythe,
And every shepherd tells his tale,
Under the hawthorn in the dale.
Straight mine eye hath caught new pleasures
Whilst the landscape round it measures,   70
Russet lawns and fallows gray,
Where the nibbling flocks do stray,
Mountains on whose barren breast
The laboring clouds do often rest;
Meadows trim with daisies pied,[11]   75
Shallow brooks and rivers wide.
Towers and battlements it sees
Bosomed high in tufted trees,
Where perhaps some beauty lies,
The cynosure[12] of neighboring eyes.   80
Hard by, a cottage chimney smokes,
From betwixt two aged oaks,

[8]contempt [9]progress [10]dressed [11]variegated [12]North Star

Where Corydon and Thyrsis met,
Are at their savory dinner set
Of herbs, and other country messes,   85
Which the neat-handed Phyllis dresses;
And then in haste her bower she leaves,
With Thestylis to bind the sheaves;
Or if the earlier season lead
To the tanned haycock in the mead.   90
Sometimes with secure[13] delight
The upland hamlets will invite,
When the merry bells ring round
And the jocund rebecks sound
To many a youth and many a maid,   95
Dancing in the checkered shade;
And young and old come forth to play
On a sunshine holiday,
Till the livelong daylight fail;
Then to the spicy nut-brown ale,   100
With stories told of many a feat,
How fairy Mab the junkets eat;[14]
She was pinched and pulled, she said,
And he, by Friar's lantern[15] led,
Tells how the drudging goblin sweat   105
To earn his cream-bowl, duly set,
When in one night, ere glimpse of morn,
His shadowy flail hath threshed the corn
That ten day-laborers could not end;
Then lies him down the lubber[16] fiend,   110
And, stretched out all the chimney's[17] length,
Basks at the fire his hairy strength;
And crop-full out of doors he flings
Ere the first cock his matin rings.
Thus done the tales, to bed they creep,   115
By whispering winds soon lulled asleep.
Towered cities please us then,
And the busy hum of men,
Where throngs of knights and barons bold,
In weeds[18] of peace high triumphs hold,   120
With store of ladies, whose bright eyes
Rain influence, and judge the prize
Of wit, or arms, while both contend
To win her grace, whom all commend.
There let Hymen oft appear   125

---

[13]carefree   [14]ate   [15]will-o'-the-wisp   [16]loutish   [17]fireplace's   [18]garments

In saffron robe, with taper clear,
And pomp, and feast, and revelry,
With masque, and antique pageantry;
Such sights as youthful poets dream
On summer eves by haunted stream.   130
Then to the well-trod stage anon,
If Jonson's learned sock be on,
Or sweetest Shakespeare, fancy's child,
Warble his native wood-notes wild.
And ever against eating cares   135
Lap me in soft Lydian airs
Married to immortal verse
Such as the meeting soul may pierce
In notes, with many a winding bout[19]
Or linkéd sweetness long drawn out,   140
With wanton heed, and giddy cunning,
The melting voice through mazes running;
Untwisting all the chains that tie
The hidden soul of harmony;
That Orpheus' self may heave his head   145
From golden slumber on a bed
Of heaped Elysian flowers, and hear
Such strains as would have won the ear
Of Pluto, to have quite set free
His half-regained Eurydice.   150
These delights if thou canst give,
Mirth, with thee I mean to live.

ca. 1631   1645

Il Penseroso

Hence vain deluding Joys,
  The brood of Folly without father bred.
How little you bestead,[1]
  Or fill the fixéd mind with all your toys;[2]
Dwell in some idle brain,   5
  And fancies fond[3] with gaudy shapes possess,
As thick and numberless
  As the gay motes that people the sunbeams,
Or likest hovering dreams,

[19]turn

[1]profit   [2]trifles   [3]foolish

The fickle pensioners[4] of Morpheus' train.   10
But hail thou Goddess, sage and holy,
Hail, divinest Melancholy,
Whose saintly visage is too bright
To hit[5] the sense of human sight;
And therefore to our weaker view,   15
O'erlaid with black, staid Wisdom's hue.
Black, but such as in esteem,
Prince Memnon's sister might beseem,
Or that starred Ethiope queen that strove
To set her beauty's praise above   20
The sea nymphs, and their powers offended.
Yet thou art higher far descended;
Thee bright-haired Vesta long of yore
To solitary Saturn bore;
His daughter she (in Saturn's reign   25
Such mixture was not held a stain).
Oft in glimmering bowers and glades
He met her, and in secret shades
Of woody Ida's inmost grove,
While yet there was no fear of Jove.   30
Come pensive nun, devout and pure,
Sober, steadfast, and demure,
All in a robe of darkest grain,[6]
Flowing with majestic train,
And sable stole of cypress lawn   35
Over thy decent shoulders drawn.
Come, but keep thy wonted state,
With even step and musing gait,
And looks commercing with the skies,
Thy rapt soul sitting in thine eyes: 40
There held in holy passion still,
Forget thyself to marble, till
With a sad[7] leaden downward cast,
Thou fix them on the earth as fast.
And join with thee calm Peace and Quiet,   45
Spare Fast, that oft with gods doth diet,
And hears the Muses in a ring
Aye round about Jove's altar sing.
And add to these retired Leisure,
That in trim gardens takes his pleasure;   50
But first, and chiefest, with thee bring,
Him that yon soars on golden wing,

[4]retainers   [5]affect   [6]color   [7]serious

Guiding the fiery-wheeléd throne,
The cherub Contemplation;
And the mute Silence hist[8] along   55
'Less Philomel will deign a song,
In her sweetest, saddest plight,
Smoothing the rugged brow of night,
While Cynthia checks her dragon yoke
Gently o'er th' accustomed oak;   60
Sweet bird that shunn'st the noise of folly,
Most musical, most melancholy!
Thee chantress oft the woods among,
I woo to hear thy evensong;
And missing thee, I walk unseen   65
On the dry smooth-shaven green,
To behold the wandering moon,
Riding near her highest noon,
Like one that had been led astray
Through the Heaven's wide pathless way;   70
And oft as if her head she bowed,
Stooping through a fleecy cloud.
Oft on a plat[9] of rising ground,
I hear the far-off curfew sound,
Over some wide-watered shore,   75
Swing slow with sullen roar;
Or if the air will not permit,
Some still removéd place will fit,
Where glowing embers through the room
Teach light to counterfeit a gloom   80
Far from all resort of mirth,
Save the cricket on the hearth,
Or the bellman's[10] drowsy charm,
To bless the doors from nightly harm;
Or let my lamp at midnight hour   85
Be seen in some high lonely tower,
Where I may oft outwatch the Bear,
With thrice great Hermes, or unsphere
The spirit of Plato to unfold
What worlds, or what vast regions hold   90
The immortal mind that hath forsook
Her mansion in this fleshly nook;
And of those demons that are found
In fire, air, flood, or underground,
Whose power hath a true consent[11]   95

8beckon 9plot 10night-watchman's 11correspondence

With planet, or with element.
Some time let gorgeous Tragedy
In sceptered pall[12] come sweeping by,
Presenting Thebes, or Pelops' line,
Or the tale of Troy divine.   100
Or what (though rare) of later age
Ennobled hath the buskined stage.
But, O sad virgin, that thy power
Might raise Musaeus from his bower,
Or bid the soul of Orpheus sing   105
Such notes as, warbled to the string,
Drew iron tears down Pluto's cheek,
And made Hell grant what Love did seek.
Or call up him that left half told
The story of Cambuscan bold,   110
Of Camball, and of Algarsife,
And who had Canacee to wife,
That owned the virtuous[13] ring and glass,
And of the wondrous horse of brass,
On which the Tartar king did ride;   115
And if aught else great bards beside
In sage and solemn tunes have sung,
Of tourneys and of trophies hung,
Of forests and enchantments drear,
Where more is meant than meets the ear.   120
Thus, Night, oft see me in thy pale career,
Till civil-suited morn appear,
Not tricked and frounced[14] as she was wont,
With the Attic boy to hunt,
But kerchiefed in a comely cloud,   125
While rocking winds are piping loud,
Or ushered with a shower still,
When the gust hath blown his fill,
Ending on the rustling leaves,
With minute-drops from off the eaves.   130
And when the sun begins to fling
His flaring beams, me, Goddess, bring
To archéd walks of twilight groves,
And shadows brown that Sylvan loves
Of pine or monumental oak,   135
Where the rude ax with heavéd stroke,
Was never heard the nymphs to daunt,
Or fright them from their hallowed haunt.

[12]robe   [13]potent   [14]curled

There in close covert by some brook,
Where no profaner eye may look,   140
Hide me from day's garish eye,
While the bee with honeyed thigh,
That at her flowery work doth sing,
And the waters murmuring
With such consort[15] as they keep,   145
Entice the dewy-feathered sleep;
And let some strange mysterious dream,
Wave at his wings in airy stream,
Of lively portraiture displayed,
Softly on my eyelids laid.   150
And as I wake, sweet music breathe
Above, about, or underneath,
Sent by some spirit to mortals good,
Or th' unseen genius[16] of the wood.
But let my due feet never fail   155
To walk the studious cloister's pale,[17]
And love the high embowéd roof,
With antic pillars massy proof,
And storied windows richly dight,[18]
Casting a dim religious light.   160
There let the pealing organ blow,
To the full-voicéd choir below,
In service high, and anthems clear,
As may with sweetness, through mine ear,
Dissolve me into ecstasies,   165
And bring all heaven before mine eyes.
And may at last my weary age
Find out the peaceful hermitage,
The hairy gown and mossy cell,
Where I may sit and rightly spell[19]   170
Of every star that Heaven doth show,
And every herb that sips the dew
Till old experience do attain
To something like prophetic strain.
These pleasures, Melancholy, give,   175
And I with thee will choose to live.

                                                        ca. 1631   1645

---

[15]harmony   [16]indwelling spirit   [17]enclosure   [18]dressed   [19]speculate

When I Consider How My Light Is Spent

When I consider how my light is spent
  Ere half my days, in this dark world and wide,
  And that one talent which is death to hide
  Lodged with me useless, though my soul more bent
To serve therewith my Maker, and present   5
  My true account, lest he returning chide;
  "Doth God exact day-labor, light denied?"
  I fondly[1] ask; but Patience to prevent
That murmur, soon replies, "God doth not need
  Either man's work or his own gifts; who best   10
  Bear his mild yoke, they serve him best. His state
Is kingly. Thousands at his bidding speed
  And post o'er land and ocean without rest:
  They also serve who only stand and wait."

                    ca. 1652   1673

SIR JOHN DENHAM

Excerpts from Cooper's Hill

My eye, descending from the hill, surveys
Where Thames amongst the wanton valleys strays.
Thames, the most loved of all the ocean's sons,
By his old sire, to his embraces runs,
Hasting to pay his tribute to the sea,   5
Like mortal life to meet eternity.
Though with those streams he no resemblance hold,
Whose foam is amber and their gravel gold;
His genuine, and less guilty wealth to explore,
Search not his bottom, but survey his shore,   10
O'er which he kindly spreads his spacious wing,
And hatches plenty for the ensuing spring.
Not then destroys it with too fond a stay,
Like mothers which their infants overlay;
Nor with a sudden and impetuous wave,   15
Like profuse kings, resumes the wealth he gave.
No unexpected inundations spoil
The mower's hopes, nor mock the plowman's toil;

[1] foolishly

386

But God-like his unwearied bounty flows;
First loves to do, then loves the good he does.   20
Nor are his blessings to his banks confined,
But free and common as the sea or wind;
When he to boast, or to disperse his stores,
Full of the tributes of his grateful shores,
Visits the world, and in his flying towers   25
Brings home to us, and makes the Indies ours;
Finds wealth where 'tis, bestows it where it wants,
Cities in deserts, woods in cities plants,
So that to us no thing, no place is strange,
While his fair bosom is the world's exchange.   30
O could I flow like thee, and make they stream
My great example, as it is my theme!
Though deep, yet clear, though gentle, yet not dull,
Strong without rage, without o'er-flowing full.

RICHARD LOVELACE

To Lucasta, Going to the Wars

Tell me not, sweet, I am unkind
That from the nunnery
Of thy chaste breast and quiet mind,
To war and arms I fly.

True, a new mistress now I chase,   5
The first foe in the field;
And with a stronger faith embrace
A sword, a horse, a shield.

Yet this inconstancy is such
As you too shall adore;   10
I could not love thee, dear, so much,
Loved I not honor more.

1649

The Grasshopper

To my noble friend, Mr. Charles Cotton

O thou that swing'st upon the waving hair
   Of some well-filléd oaten beard,

Drunk every night with a delicious tear
  Dropped thee from heaven, where now th' art reared;

The joys of earth and air are thine entire,   5
  That with thy feet and wings dost hop and fly;
And, when thy poppy¹ works, thou dost retire
  To thy carved acorn-bed to lie.

Up with the day, the sun thou welcom'st then,
  Sport'st in the gilt plats² of his beams,   10
And all these merry days mak'st merry men,
  Thyself, and melancholy streams.

But ah, the sickle! Golden ears are cropped;
  Ceres and Bacchus bid good night;
Sharp, frosty fingers all your flowers have topped,   15
  And what scythes spared, winds shave off quite.

Poor verdant fool, and now green ice! thy joys,
  Large and as lasting as thy perch of grass,
Bid us lay in 'gainst winter rain, and poise³
  Their floods with an o'erflowing glass.   20

Thou best of men and friends! we will create
  A genuine summer in each other's breast,
And spite of this cold time and frozen fate,
  Thaw us a warm seat to our rest.

Our sacred hearths shall burn eternally,   25
  As vestal flames; the North Wind, he
Shall strike his frost-stretched wings, dissolve, and fly
  This Etna in epitome.

Dropping December shall come weeping in,
  Bewail th' usurping of his reign: 30
But when in showers of old Greek we begin,
  Shall cry he hath his crown again!

Night, as clear Hesper, shall our tapers whip
  From the light casements where we play,
And the dark hag from her black mantle strip,   35
  And stick there everlasting day.

Thus richer than untempted kings are we,
  That, asking nothing, nothing need:
Though lord of all what seas embrace, yet he
  That wants himself is poor indeed.   40

                                                                        1649

¹sleeping potion ²hair braids ³balance

388

ANDREW MARVELL

To His Coy Mistress

Had we but world enough, and time,
This coyness, lady, were no crime.
We would sit down, and think which way
To walk, and pass our long love's day.
Thou by the Indian Ganges' side   5
Should'st rubies find; I by the tide
Of Humber would complain. I would
Love you ten years before the flood,
And you should, if you please, refuse
Till the conversion of the Jews.   10
My vegetable love should grow
Vaster than empires and more slow;
An hundred years should go to praise
Thine eyes, and on thy forehead gaze;
Two hundred to adore each breast,   15
But thirty thousand to the rest;
An age at least to every part,
And the last age should show your heart.
For, lady, you deserve this state,[1]
Nor would I love at lower rate.   20
    But at my back I always hear
Time's wingéd chariot hurrying near;
And yonder all before us lie
Deserts of vast eternity.
Thy beauty shall no more be found;   25
Nor, in thy marble vault, shall sound
My echoing song; then worms shall try
That long-preserved virginity,
And your quaint[2] honor turn to dust,
And into ashes all my lust: 30
The grave's a fine and private place,
But none, I think, do there embrace.
    Now therefore, while the youthful hue
Sits on thy skin like morning glow,
And while thy willing soul transpires[3]   35
At every pore with instant fires,
Now let us sport us while we may,
And now, like amorous birds of prey,
Rather at once our time devour

[1]dignity   [2]over-subtle   [3]breathes out

Than languish in his slow-chapped[4] power. 40
Let us roll all our strength and all
Our sweetness up into one ball,
And tear our pleasures with rough strife
Thorough the iron gates of life:
Thus, though we cannot make our sun 45
Stand still, yet we will make him run.

1681

EDWARD TAYLOR

Meditation Six

Am I thy gold? Or purse, Lord, for thy wealth,
  Whether in mine or mint refined for thee?
I'm counted so, but count me o'er thyself,
  Lest gold washed face, and brass in heart I be.
  I fear my touchstone touches when I try 5
  Me and my counted gold too overly.

Am I new minted by thy stamp indeed?
  Mine eyes are dim; I cannot clearly see.
Be thou my spectacles that I may read
  Thine image and inscription stamped on me. 10
  If thy bright image do upon me stand,
  I am a golden angel in thy hand.

Lord, make my soul thy plate, thine image bright
  Within the circle of the same enfile.
And on its brims in golden letters write 15
  Thy supersciption in an holy style.
  Then I shall be thy money, thou my horde:
  Let me thy angel be, be thou my Lord.

From *The Poetical Works of Edward Taylor*, Thomas H. Johnson, ed., (Princeton Paperback, 1966). Copyright Rockland, 1939; Princeton University Press, 1943: "Meditation Six"; "Hus-wifery." Reprinted by permission of Princeton University Press.

[4]slow-jawed

Huswifery

Make me, O Lord, thy spinning wheel complete.
   Thy holy word my distaff make for me.
Make mine affections thy swift flyers neat,
   And make my soul thy holy spool to be.
    My conversation make to be thy reel,   5
    And reel the yarn thereon spun on thy wheel.

Make me thy loom then, knit therein this twine;
   And make thy holy spirit, Lord, wind quills.
Then weave the web thyself. The yarn is fine.
    Thine ordinances make my fulling mills.   10
    Then dye the same in heavenly colors choice,
    All pinked[1] with varnished[2] flowers of paradise.

Then clothe therewith mine understanding, will,
   Affections, judgment, conscience, memory,
My words, and actions, that their shine may fill   15
    My ways with glory and thee glorify.
    Then mine apparel shall display before ye
    That I am clothed in holy robes for glory.

JOSEPH ADDISON

Ode

The spacious firmament on high,
With all the blue ethereal sky,
And spangled heavens, a shining frame,
Their great Original proclaim.
The unwearied sun from day to day   5
Does his Creator's power display,
And publishes to every land
The work of an almighty hand.

Soon as the evening shades prevail,
The moon takes up the wondrous tale,   10
And nightly to the listening earth
Repeats the story of her birth;
Whilst all the stars that round her burn,
And all the planets in their turn,

[1]ornamented / [2]luminous

Confirm the tidings as they roll,   15
And spread the truth from pole to pole.
What though in solemn silence, all
Move round this dark terrestrial ball?   20
What though nor real voice nor sound
Amidst their radiant orbs be found?
In Reason's ear they all rejoice,
And utter forth a glorious voice,
Forever singing as they shine:
"The hand that made us is divine!"

                                                          1712

THOMAS GRAY

Elegy Written in a Country Churchyard

The curfew tolls the knell of parting day,
   The lowing herd wind slowly o'er the lea,
The plowman homeward plods his weary way,
   And leaves the world to darkness and to me.

Now fades the glimmering landscape on the sight,   5
   And all the air a solemn stillness holds,
Save where the beetle wheels his droning flight,
   And drowsy tinklings lull the distant folds;

Save that from yonder ivy-mantled tower
   The moping owl does to the moon complain   10
Of such, as wandering near her secret bower,
   Molest her ancient solitary reign.

Beneath those rugged elms, that yew tree's shade,
   Where heaves the turf in many a moldering heap,
Each in his narrow cell forever laid,   15
   The rude[1] forefathers of the hamlet sleep.

The breezy call of incense-breathing morn,
   The swallow twittering from the straw-built shed,
The cock's shrill clarion, or the echoing horn,[2]
   No more shall rouse them from their lowly bed.   20

For them no more the blazing hearth shall burn,
   Or busy housewife ply her evening care;
No children run to lisp their sire's return,
   Or climb his knees the envied kiss to share.

[1]rustic   [2]hunting horn

Oft did the harvest to their sickle yield,   25
    Their furrow oft the stubborn glebe[3] has broke;
How jocund did they drive their team afield!
    How bowed the woods beneath their sturdy stroke!

Let not Ambition mock their useful toil,
    Their homely joys, and destiny obscure;   30
Nor Grandeur hear with a disdainful smile
    The short and simple annals of the poor.

The boast of heraldry, the pomp of power,
    And all that beauty, all that wealth e'er gave,
Awaits alike the inevitable hour.   35
    The paths of glory lead but to the grave.

Nor you, ye proud, impute to these the fault,
    If Memory o'er their tomb no trophies raise,
Where through the long-drawn aisle and fretted[4] vault
    The pealing anthem swells the note of praise.   40

Can storied urn or animated[5] bust
    Back to its mansion call the fleeting breath?
Can Honor's voice provoke[6] the silent dust,
    Or Flattery soothe the dull cold ear of Death?

Perhaps in this neglected spot is laid   45
    Some heart once pregnant with celestial fire;
Hands that the rod of empire might have swayed,
    Or waked to ecstasy the living lyre.

But Knowledge to their eyes her ample page
    Rich with the spoils of time did ne'er unroll;   50
Chill Penury repressed their noble rage,
    And froze the genial current of the soul.

Full many a gem of purest ray serene,
    The dark unfathomed caves of ocean bear:
Full many a flower is born to blush unseen,   55
    And waste its sweetness on the desert air.

Some village Hampden, that with dauntless breast
    The little tyrant of his fields withstood;
Some mute inglorious Milton here may rest,
    Some Cromwell guiltless of his country's blood.   60

The applause of listening senates to command,
    The threats of pain and ruin to despise,
To scatter plenty o'er a smiling land,
    And read their history in a nation's eyes,

[3]soil [4]ornamented [5]lifelike [6]call forth

Their lot forbade: nor circumscribed alone 65
    Their growing virtues, but their crimes confined;
Forbade to wade through slaughter to a throne,
    And shut the gates of mercy on mankind,

The struggling pangs of conscious truth to hide,
    To quench the blushes of ingenuous shame, 70
Or heap the shrine of Luxury and Pride
    With incense kindled at the Muse's flame.

Far from the madding[7] crowd's ignoble strife,
    Their sober wishes never learned to stray;
Along the cool sequestered vale of life 75
    They kept the noiseless tenor of their way.

Yet even these bones from insult to protect
    Some frail memorial still erected nigh,
With uncouth rhymes and shapeless sculpture decked,
    Implores the passing tribute of a sigh. 80

Their name, their years, spelt by the unlettered Muse,
    The place of fame and elegy supply:
And many a holy text around she strews,
    That teach the rustic moralist to die.

For who to dumb Forgetfulness a prey, 85
    This pleasing anxious being e'er resigned,
Left the warm precincts of the cheerful day,
    Nor cast one longing lingering look behind?

On some fond breast the parting soul relies,
    Some pious drops the closing eye requires; 90
Even from the tomb the voice of Nature cries,
    Even in our ashes live their wonted fires.

For thee, who mindful of the unhonored dead
    Dost in these lines their artless tale relate;
If chance, by lonely contemplation led, 95
    Some kindred spirit shall inquire thy fate,

Haply some hoary-headed swain may say,
    "Oft have we seen him at the peep of dawn
Brushing with hasty steps the dews away
    To meet the sun upon the upland lawn. 100

"There at the foot of yonder nodding beech
    That wreathes its old fantastic roots so high,
His listless length at noontide would he stretch,
    And pore upon the brook that babbles by.

[7]milling

"Hard by yon wood, now smiling as in scorn,
    Muttering his wayward fancies he would rove,
Now dropping, woeful wan, like one forlorn,
    Or crazed with care, or crossed in hopeless love. 105

"One morn I missed him on the customed hill,
    Along the heath and near his favorite tree; 110
Another came; nor yet beside the rill,
    Nor up the lawn, nor at the wood was he;

"The next with dirges due in sad array
    Slow through the churchway path we saw him borne.
Approach and read (for thou canst read) the lay, 115
    Graved on the stone beneath yon aged thorn."

The Epitaph

Here rests his head upon the lap of Earth
    A youth to Fortune and to Fame unknown.
Fair Science[8] frowned not on his humble birth,
    And Melancholy marked him for her own. 120

Large was his bounty, and his soul sincere,
    Heaven did a recompense as largely send:
He gave to Misery all he had, a tear,
    He gained from Heaven ('twas all he wished) a friend.

No father seek his merits to disclose, 125
    Or draw his frailties from their dead abode
(There they alike in trembling hope repose),
    The bosom of his Father and his God.

                      ca. 1742–50   1751

OLIVER GOLDSMITH

When Lovely Woman Stoops to Folly

When lovely woman stoops to folly,
    And finds too late that men betray,
What charm can soothe her melancholy,
    What art can wash her guilt away?

The only art her guilt to cover, 5
    To hide her shame from every eye,
To give repentance to her lover,
    And wring his bosom—is to die.

                                  1766

[8]Learning

PHILIP FRENEAU

The Indian Burying Ground

In spite of all the learned have said,
    I still my opinion keep;
The posture, that we give the dead,
    Points out the soul's eternal sleep.

Not so the ancients of these lands—   5
    The Indian, when from life released,
Again is seated with his friends,
    And shares again the joyous feast.

His imaged birds, and painted bowl,
    And venison, for a journey dressed,   10
Bespeak the nature of the soul,
    Activity, that knows no rest.

His bow, for action ready bent,
    And arrows, with a head of stone,
Can only mean that life is spent,   15
    And not the old ideas gone.

Thou, stranger, that shalt come this way,
    No fraud upon the·dead commit—
Observe the swelling turf, and say
    They do not lie, but here they sit.   20

Here still a lofty rock remains,
    On which the curious eye may trace
(Now wasted, half, by wearing rains)
    The fancies of a ruder race.

Here still an aged elm spires,   25
    Beneath whose far-projecting shade
(And which the shepherd still admires)
    The children of the forest played!

There oft a restless Indian queen
    (Pale Shebah, with her braided hair)   30
And many a barbarous form is seen
    To chide the man that lingers there.

By midnight moons, o'er moistening dews;
    In habit for the chase arrayed,
The hunter still the deer pursues,   35
    The hunter and the deer, a shade!

And long shall timorous fancy see
   The painted chief, and pointed spear,
And Reason's self shall bow the knee
   To shadows and delusions here.   40

                  1787   1788

WILLIAM BLAKE

To the Evening Star

Thou fair-hair'd angel of the evening,
Now, while the sun rests on the mountains, light
Thy bright torch of love; thy radiant crown
Put on, and smile upon our evening bed!
Smile on our loves; and, while thou drawest the   5
Blue curtains of the sky, scatter thy silver dew
On every flower that shuts its sweet eyes
In timely sleep. Let thy west wind sleep on
The lake; speak silence with thy glimmering eyes,
And wash the dusk with silver. Soon, full soon,   10
Dost thou withdraw; then the wolf rages wide,
And the lion glares thro' the dun forest:
The fleeces of our flocks are cover'd with
Thy sacred dew: protect them with thin influence.

                  1783

Holy Thursday [I.]

'Twas on a Holy Thursday, their innocent faces clean,
The children walking two & two, in red & blue & green,
Grey headed beadles walkd before with wands as white as snow,
Till into the high dome of Paul's they like Thames' waters flow.

O what a multitude they seemd, these flowers of London town!   5
Seated in companies they sit with radiance all their own.
The hum of multitudes was there, but multitudes of lambs,
Thousands of little boys & girls raising their innocent hands.

From *The Prose and Poetry of William Blake* edited by David Erdman, with a commentary by Harold Bloom, copyright © 1965 by David V. Erdman and Harold Bloom. Reprinted by permission of Doubleday & Company, Inc.

Now like a mighty wind they raise to heaven the voice of song,
Or like harmonious thunderings the seats of heaven among.   10
Beneath them sit the aged men, wise guardians of the poor;
Then cherish pity, lest you drive an angel from your door.

                                                              1789

The Little Black Boy

My mother bore me in the southern wild,
And I am black, but O! my soul is white;
White as an angel is the English child:
But I am black as if bereav'd of light.

My mother taught me underneath a tree,   5
And sitting down before the heat of day,
She took me on her lap and kisséd me,
And pointing to the east, began to say:

"Look on the rising sun: there God does live,
And gives his light, and gives his heat away;   10
And flowers and trees and beasts and men receive
Comfort in morning, joy in the noon day.

"And we are put on earth a little space,
That we may learn to bear the beams of love,
And these black bodies and this sun-burnt face   15
Is but a cloud, and like a shady grove.

"For when our souls have learn'd the heat to bear,
The cloud will vanish; we shall hear his voice,
Saying: 'Come out from the grove, my love & care,
And round my golden tent like lambs rejoice.'"   20

Thus did my mother say, and kisséd me;
And thus I say to little English boy:
When I from black and he from white cloud free,
And round the tent of God like lambs we joy,

I'll shade him from the heat till he can bear   25
To lean in joy upon our father's knee;
And then I'll stand and stroke his silver hair,
And be like him, and he will then love me.

                                                              1789

WILLIAM WORDSWORTH

Lines

Composed A Few Miles Above Tintern Abbey On Revisiting The Banks Of
The Wye During A Tour. July 13, 1798

    Five years have passed; five summers, with the length
Of five long winters! and again I hear
These waters, rolling from their mountain-springs
With a soft inland murmur. Once again
Do I behold these steep and lofty cliffs,   5
That on a wild secluded scene impress
Thoughts of more deep seclusion; and connect
The landscape with the quiet of the sky.
The day is come when I again repose
Here, under this dark sycamore, and view   10
These plots of cottage ground, these orchard tufts,
Which at this season, with their unripe fruits,
Are clad in one green hue, and lose themselves
'Mid groves and copses. Once again I see
These hedgerows, hardly hedgerows, little lines   15
Of sportive wood run wild; these pastoral farms,
Green to the very door; and wreaths of smoke
Sent up, in silence, from among the trees!
With some uncertain notice, as might seem
Of vagrant dwellers in the houseless woods,   20
Or of some Hermit's cave, where by his fire
The Hermit sits alone.

              These beauteous forms,
Through a long absence, have not been to me
As is a landscape to a blind man's eye;
But oft, in lonely rooms, and 'mid the din   25
Of towns and cities, I have owed to them,
In hours of weariness, sensations sweet,
Felt in the blood, and felt along the heart;
And passing even into my purer mind,
With tranquil restoration—feelings too   30
Of unremembered pleasure; such, perhaps,
As have no slight or trivial influence
On that best portion of a good man's life,
His little, nameless, unremembered, acts
Of kindness and of love. Nor less, I trust,   35
To them I may have owed another gift,

Of aspect more sublime; that blessed mood,
In which the burthen of the mystery,
In which the heavy and the weary weight
Of all this unintelligible world,   40
Is lightened—that serene and blessed mood,
In which the affections gently lead us on—
Until, the breath of this corporeal frame
And even the motion of our human blood
Almost suspended, we are laid asleep   45
In body, and become a living soul;
While with an eye made quiet by the power
Of harmony, and the deep power of joy,
We see into the life of things.

                          If this
Be but a vain belief, yet, oh! how oft—   50
In darkness and amid the many shapes
Of joyless daylight; when the fretful stir
Unprofitable, and the fever of the world,
Have hung upon the beatings of my heart—
How oft, in spirit, have I turned to thee,   55
O sylvan Wye! thou wanderer through the woods,
How often has my spirit turned to thee!

   And now, with gleams of half-extinguished thought,
With many recognitions dim and faint,
And somewhat of a sad perplexity,   60
The picture of the mind revives again;
While here I stand, not only with the sense
Of present pleasure, but with pleasing thoughts
That in this moment there is life and food
For future years. And so I dare to hope,   65
Though changed, no doubt, from what I was when first
I came among these hills; when like a roe
I bounded o'er the mountains, by the sides
Of the deep rivers, and the lonely streams,
Wherever nature led—more like a man   70
Flying from something that he dreads than one
Who sought the thing he loved. For nature then
(The coarser pleasures of my boyish days,
And their glad animal movements all gone by)
To me was all in all.—I cannot paint   75
What then I was. The sounding cataract
Haunted me like a passion; the tall rock,
The mountain, and the deep and gloomy wood,
Their colors and their forms, were then to me

An appetite; a feeling and a love,   80
That had no need of a remoter charm,
By thought supplied, nor any interest
Unborrowed from the eye.—That time is past,
And all its aching joys are now no more,
And all its dizzy raptures. Not for this   85
Faint[1] I, nor mourn nor murmur; other gifts
Have followed; for such loss, I would believe,
Abundant recompense. For I have learned
To look on nature, not as in the hour
Of thoughtless youth; but hearing oftentimes   90
The still, sad music of humanity,
Nor harsh nor grating, though of ample power
To chasten and subdue. And I have felt
A presence that disturbs me with the joy
Of elevated thoughts; a sense sublime   95
Of something far more deeply interfused,
Whose dwelling is the light of setting suns,
And the round ocean and the living air,
And the blue sky, and in the mind of man:
A motion and a spirit, that impels   100
All thinking things, all objects of all thought,
And rolls through all things. Therefore am I still
A lover of the meadows and the woods,
And mountains; and of all that we behold
From this green earth; of all the mighty world   105
Of eye, and ear—both what they half create,
And what perceive; well pleased to recognize
In nature and the language of the sense
The anchor of my purest thoughts, the nurse,
The guide, the guardian of my heart, and soul   110
Of all my moral being.

             Nor perchance,
If I were not thus taught, should I the more
Suffer my genial spirits[2] to decay:
For thou art with me here upon the banks
Of this fair river; thou my dearest Friend,   115
My dear, dear Friend; and in thy voice I catch
The language of my former heart, and read
My former pleasures in the shooting lights
Of thy wild eyes. Oh! yet a little while
May I behold in thee what I was once,   120
My dear, dear Sister! and this prayer I make,

[1]become discouraged   [2]vital energies

Knowing that Nature never did betray
The heart that loved her; 'tis her privilege,
Through all the years of this our life, to lead
From joy to joy: for she can so inform 125
The mind that is within us, so impress
With quietness and beauty, and so feed
With lofty thoughts, that neither evil tongues,
Rash judgments, nor the sneers of selfish men,
Nor greetings where no kindness is, nor all 130
The dreary intercourse of daily life,
Shall e'er prevail against us, or disturb
Our cheerful faith, that all which we behold
Is full of blessings. Therefore let the moon
Shine on thee in thy solitary walk; 135
And let the misty mountain winds be free
To blow against thee: and, in after years,
When these wild ecstasies shall be matured
Into a sober pleasure; when thy mind
Shall be a mansion for all lovely forms, 140
Thy memory be as a dwelling place
For all sweet sounds and harmonies; oh! then,
If solitude, or fear, or pain, or grief
Should be thy portion, with what healing thoughts
Of tender joy wilt thou remember me, 145
And these my exhortations! Nor, perchance—
If I should be where I no more can hear
Thy voice, nor catch from thy wild eyes these gleams
Of past existence—wilt thou then forget
That on the banks of this delightful stream 150
We stood together; and that I, so long
A worshiper of Nature, hither came
Unwearied in that service; rather say
With warmer love—oh! with far deeper zeal
Of holier love. Nor wilt thou then forget, 155
That after many wanderings, many years
Of absence, these steep woods and lofty cliffs,
And this green pastoral landscape, were to me
More dear, both for themselves and for thy sake!

1798

She Dwelt Among the Untrodden Ways

She dwelt among the untrodden ways
  Beside the springs of Dove.

A Maid whom there were none to praise
  And very few to love;

A violet by a mossy stone   5
  Half hidden from the eye!
—Fair as a star, when only one
  Is shining in the sky.

She lived unknown, and few could know
  When Lucy ceased to be;   10
But she is in her grave, and, oh,
  The difference to me!

1800

London, 1802

Milton! thou shouldst be living at this hour:
England hath need of thee: she is a fen
Of stagnant waters: altar, sword, and pen,
Fireside, the heroic wealth of hall and bower,
Have forfeited their ancient English dower   5
Of inward happiness. We are selfish men;
Oh! raise us up, return to us again;
And give us manners, virtue, freedom, power.
Thy soul was like a Star, and dwelt apart;
Thou hadst a voice whose sound was like the sea: 10
Pure as the naked heavens, majestic, free,
So didst thou travel on life's common way,
In cheerful godliness; and yet thy heart
The lowliest duties on herself did lay.

1807

My Heart Leaps Up

My heart leaps up when I behold
  A rainbow in the sky:
So was it when my life began;
So is it now I am a man;
So be it when I shall grow old,   5
  Or let me die!
The Child is father of the Man;
And I could wish my days to be
Bound each to each by natural piety.

1807

Ode

Intimations Of Immortality From Recollections Of Early Childhood

The Child is father of the Man;
And I could wish my days to be
Bound each to each by natural piety.

1

There was a time when meadow, grove, and stream,
The earth, and every common sight,
    To me did seem
    Appareled in celestial light,
The glory and the freshness of a dream.   5
It is not now as it hath been of yore—
    Turn whereso'er I may,
      By night or day,
The things which I have seen I now can see no more.

2

    The Rainbow comes and goes,   10
    And lovely is the Rose,
    The Moon doth with delight
Look round her when the heavens are bare,
    Waters on a starry night
    Are beautiful and fair;   15
  The sunshine is a glorious birth;
  But yet I know, where'er I go,
That there hath passed away a glory from the earth.

3

Now, while the birds thus sing a joyous song,
  And while the young lambs bound   20
    As to the tabor's sound,
To me alone there came a thought of grief:
A timely utterance gave that thought relief,
    And I again am strong:
The cataracts blow their trumpets from the steep;   25
No more shall grief of mine the season wrong;
I hear the Echoes through the mountains throng,
The Winds come to me from the fields of sleep,
    And all the earth is gay;
      Land and sea   30
    Give themselves up to jollity,
    And with the heart of May

Doth every Beast keep holiday—
Thou Child of Joy,
Shout round me, let me hear thy shouts, thou happy   35
Shepherd-boy!

4

Ye blessèd Creatures, I have heard the call
Ye to each other make; I see
The heavens laugh with you in your jubilee;
My heart is at your festival,   40
My head hath its coronal,
The fullness of your bliss, I feel—I feel it all.
Oh, evil day! if I were sullen
While Earth herself is adorning,
This sweet May morning,   45
And the Children are culling
On every side,
In a thousand valleys far and wide,
Fresh flowers; while the sun shines warm,
And the Babe leaps up on his Mother's arm—   50
I hear, I hear, with joy I hear!
—But there's a Tree, of many, one,
A single Field which I have looked upon,
Both of them speak of something that is gone:
The Pansy at my feet   55
Doth the same tale repeat:
Whither is fled the visionary gleam?
Where is it now, the glory and the dream?

5

Our birth is but a sleep and a forgetting:
The Soul that rises with us, our life's Star,   60
Hath had elsewhere its setting,
And cometh from afar:
Not in entire forgetfulness,
And not in utter nakedness,
But trailing clouds of glory do we come   65
From God, who is our home:
Heaven lies about us in our infancy!
Shades of the prison-house begin to close
Upon the growing Boy
But he   70
Beholds the light, and whence it flows,
He sees it in his joy;
The Youth, who daily farther from the east

Must travel, still is Nature's Priest,
And by the vision splendid   75
Is on his way attended;
At length the Man perceives it die away,
And fade into the light of common day.

6

Earth fills her lap with pleasures of her own;
Yearnings she hath in her own natural kind,   80
And, even with something of a Mother's mind,
    And no unworthy aim,
    The homely[1] Nurse doth all she can
To make her foster child, her Inmate Man,
    Forget the glories he hath known,   85
And that imperial palace whence he came.

7

Behold the Child among his newborn blisses,
A six-years' Darling of a pygmy size!
See, where 'mid work of his own hand he lies,
Fretted[2] by sallies of his mother's kisses,   90
With light upon him from his father's eyes!
See, at his feet, some little plan or chart,
Some fragment from his dream of human life,
Shaped by himself with newly-learnéd art;
    A wedding or a festival,   95
    A mourning or a funeral;
      And this hath now his heart,
    And unto this he frames his song;
      Then will he fit his tongue
To dialogues of business, love, or strife;   100
    But it will not be long
    Ere this be thrown aside,
    And with new joy and pride
The little Actor cons another part;
Filling from time to time his "humorous stage"   105
With all the Persons, down to palsied Age,
That Life brings with her in her equipage;
    As if his whole vocation
    Were endless imitation.

8

Thou, whose exterior semblance doth belie   110
    Thy Soul's immensity;

[1]simple, kindly [2]vexed

Thou best Philosopher, who yet dost keep
Thy heritage, thou Eye among the blind,
That, deaf and silent, read'st the eternal deep,
Haunted forever by the eternal mind—   115
   Mighty Prophet! Seer blest!
   On whom those truths do rest,
Which we are toiling all our lives to find,
In darkness lost, the darkness of the grave;
Thou, over whom thy Immortality   120
Broods like the Day, a Master o'er a Slave,
A Presence which is not to be put by;
Thou little Child, yet glorious in the might
Of heaven-born freedom on thy being's height,
Why with such earnest pains dost thou provoke   125
The years to bring the inevitable yoke,
Thus blindly with thy blessedness at strife?
Full soon thy Soul shall have her earthly freight,
And custom lie upon thee with a weight,
Heavy as frost, and deep almost as life!   130

9

   O joy! that in our embers
   Is something that doth live,
   That nature yet remembers
   What was so fugitive!
The thought of our past years in me doth breed   135
Perpetual benediction: not indeed
For that which is most worthy to be blest;
Delight and liberty, the simple creed
Of Childhood, whether busy or at rest,
With new-fledged hope still fluttering in his breast—   140
   Not for these I raise
   The song of thanks and praise;
  But for those obstinate questionings
  Of sense and outward things,
   Fallings from us, vanishings;   145
  Blank misgivings of a Creature
Moving about in worlds not realized,
High instincts before which our mortal Nature
Did tremble like a guilty Thing surprised;
   But for those first affections,   150
   Those shadowy recollections,
  Which, be they what they may,
Are yet the fountain light of all our day,
Are yet a master light of all our seeing;

Uphold us, cherish, and have power to make   155
Our noisy years seem moments in the being
Of the eternal Silence: truths that wake,
      To perish never;
Which neither listlessness, nor mad endeavor,
      Nor Man nor Boy,   160
Nor all that is at enmity with joy,
Can utterly abolish or destroy!
      Hence in a season of calm weather
      Though inland far we be,
Our Souls have sight of that immortal sea   165
      Which brought us hither,
    Can in a moment travel thither,
And see the Children sport upon the shore,
And hear the mighty waters rolling evermore.

10

Then sing, ye Birds, sing, sing a joyous song!   170
      And let the young Lambs bound
      As to the tabor's sound!
We in thought will join your throng,
      Ye that pipe and ye that play,
      Yet that through your hearts today   175
      Feel the gladness of the May!
What though the radiance which was once so bright
Be now forever taken from my sight,
      Though nothing can bring back the hour
Of splendor in the grass, of glory in the flower;   180
      We will grieve not, rather find
      Strength in what remains behind;
      In the primal sympathy
      Which having been must ever be;
      In the soothing thoughts that spring   185
      Out of human suffering;
      In the faith that looks through death,
In years that bring the philosophic mind.

11

And O, ye Fountains, Meadows, Hills, and Groves,
Forebode not any severing of our loves!   190
Yet in my heart of hearts I feel your might;
I only have relinquished one delight
To live beneath your more habitual sway.
I love the Brooks which down their channels fret,
Even more than when I tripped lightly as they;   195

The innocent brightness of a newborn Day
　　Is lovely yet;
The clouds that gather round the setting sun
Do take a sober coloring from an eye
That hath kept watch o'er man's mortality;　　　　　　　200
Another race hath been, and other palms[3] are won.
Thanks to the human heart by which we live,
Thanks to its tenderness, its joys, and fears,
To me the meanest[4] flower that blows[5] can give
Thoughts that do often lie too deep for tears.　　　　　　205

　　　　　　　　　　　　　　　　　　　1802–4　　1807

I Wandered Lonely As a Cloud

I wandered lonely as a cloud
That floats on high o'er vales and hills,
When all at once I saw a crowd,
A host, of golden daffodils;
Beside the lake, beneath the trees,
Fluttering and dancing in the breeze.　　　　　　　　5

Continuous as the stars that shine
And twinkle on the milky way,
They stretched in never-ending line
Along the margin of a bay:
Ten thousand saw I at a glance,　　　　　　　　　10
Tossing their heads in sprightly dance.

The waves beside them danced; but they
Outdid the sparkling waves in glee;
A poet could not but be gay,
In such a jocund[1] company;　　　　　　　　　15
I gazed—and gazed—but little thought
What wealth the show to me had brought:

For oft, when on my couch I lie
In vacant or in pensive mood,
They flash upon that inward eye　　　　　　　　20
Which is the bliss of solitude;
And then my heart with pleasure fills,
And dances with the daffodils.

　　　　　　　　　　　　　　　　　　　　1807

[3]symbols of victory　　[4]most ordinary　　[5]blooms

[1]cheerful

She Was a Phantom of Delight

She was a Phantom[1] of delight
When first she gleamed upon my sight;
A lovely Apparition, sent
To be a moment's ornament;
Her eyes as stars of Twilight fair;   5
Like Twilight's, too, her dusky hair;
But all things else about her drawn
From May-time and the cheerful Dawn;
A dancing Shape, an Image gay,
To haunt, to startle, and way-lay.   10

I saw her upon nearer view,
A Spirit, yet a Woman too!
Her household motions light and free,
And steps of virgin-liberty;
A countenance in which did meet   15
Sweet records, promises as sweet;
A Creature not too bright or good
For human nature's daily food;
For transient sorrows, simple wiles,
Praise, blame, love, kisses, tears, and smiles.   20

And now I see with eye serene
The very pulse of the machine;
A Being breathing thoughtful breath,
A Traveler between life and death;
The reason firm, the temperate will,   25
Endurance, foresight, strength, and skill;
A perfect Woman, nobly planned,
To warn, to comfort, and command;
And yet a Spirit still, and bright
With something of angelic light.   30

1807

The World Is Too Much with Us

The world is too much with us; late and soon,
Getting and spending, we lay waste our powers;
Little we see in Nature that is ours;

[1] vivid image

410

We have given our hearts away, a sordid boon![1]
This Sea that bares her bosom to the moon,   5
The winds that will be howling at all hours,
And are up-gathered now like sleeping flowers,
For this, for everything, we are out of tune;
It moves us not.—Great God! I'd rather be   10
A Pagan suckled in a creed outworn;
So might I, standing on this pleasant lea,
Have glimpses that would make me less forlorn;
Have sight of Proteus rising from the sea;
Or hear old Triton blow his wreathéd horn.

                                                    1807

SAMUEL TAYLOR COLERIDGE

Kubla Khan

Or A Vision In A Dream. A Fragment

In Xanadu did Kubla Khan
A stately pleasure dome decree:
Where Alph, the sacred river, ran
Through caverns measureless to man
    Down to a sunless sea.   5
So twice five miles of fertile ground
With walls and towers were girdled round:
And there were gardens bright with sinuous rills,
Where blossomed many an incense-bearing tree;
And here were forests ancient as the hills,   10
Enfolding sunny spots of greenery.

But oh! that deep romantic chasm which slanted
Down the green hill athwart a cedarn cover!
A savage place! as holy and enchanted
As e'er beneath a waning moon was haunted   15
By woman wailing for her demon lover!
And from this chasm, with ceaseless turmoil seething,
As if this earth in fast thick pants were breathing,
A mighty fountain momently was forced:
Amid whose swift half-intermitted burst   20
Huge fragments vaulted like rebounding hail,
Or chaffy grain beneath the thresher's flail:
And 'mid these dancing rocks at once and ever

[1]gift

411

It flung up momently the sacred river.
Five miles meandering with a mazy motion   25
Through wood and dale the sacred river ran,
Then reached the caverns measureless to man,
And sank in tumult to a lifeless ocean:
And 'mid this tumult Kubla heard from far
Ancestral voices prophesying war!   30

    The shadow of the dome of pleasure
    Floated midway on the waves;
    Where was heard the mingled measure
    From the fountain and the caves.
It was a miracle of rare device,   35
A sunny pleasure dome with caves of ice!

    A damsel with a dulcimer
    In a vision once I saw:
    It was an Abyssinian maid,
    And on her dulcimer she played,   40
    Singing of Mount Abora.
    Could I revive within me
    Her symphony and song,
    To such a deep delight 'twould win me,
That with music loud and long,   45
I would build that dome in air,
That sunny dome! those caves of ice!
And all who heard should see them there,
And all should cry, Beware! Beware!
His flashing eyes, his floating hair!   50
Weave a circle round him thrice,
And close your eyes with holy dread,
For he on honey-dew hath fed,
And drunk the milk of Paradise.

                         1797–98   1816

Dejection: An Ode

Late, late yestreen I saw the new Moon,
With the old Moon in her arms;
And I fear, I fear, my master dear!
We shall have a deadly storm.
       Ballad of Sir Patrick Spence

1

    Well! If the bard was weather-wise, who made
      The grand old ballad of Sir Patrick Spence,

This night, so tranquil now, will not go hence
Unroused by winds, that ply a busier trade
Than those which mold yon cloud in lazy flakes, 5
Or the dull sobbing draft, that moans and rakes
Upon the strings of this Aeolian lute,
    Which better far were mute.
    For lo! the New-moon winter-bright!
    And overspread with phantom light, 10
      (With swimming phantom light o'erspread
      But rimmed and circled by a silver thread)
I see the old Moon in her lap, foretelling
    The coming-on of rain and squally blast.
And oh! that even now the gust were swelling, 15
    And the slant night shower driving loud and fast!
Those sounds which oft have raised me, whilst they awed,
    And sent my soul abroad,
Might now perhaps their wonted[1] impulse give,
Might startle this dull pain, and make it move and live! 20

2

A grief without a pang, void, dark, and drear,
    A stifled, drowsy, unimpassioned grief,
    Which finds no natural outlet, no relief,
      In word, or sigh, or tear—
O Lady! in this wan and heartless mood, 25
To other thoughts by yonder throstle wooed,
    All this long eve, so balmy and serene,
Have I been gazing on the western sky,
    And its peculiar tint of yellow green:
And still I gaze—and with how blank an eye! 30
And those thin clouds above, in flakes and bars,
That give away their motion to the stars;
Those stars, that glide behind them or between,
Now sparkling, now bedimmed, but always seen:
Yon crescent Moon, as fixed as if it grew 35
In its own cloudless, starless lake of blue;
I see them all so excellently fair,
I see, not feel, how beautiful they are!

3

    My genial spirits[2] fail;
    And what can these avail 40
To lift the smothering weight from off my breast?

[1]usual   [2]vital energies

It were a vain endeavor,
          Though I should gaze forever
On that green light that lingers in the west:
I may not hope from outward forms to win   45
The passion and the life, whose fountains are within.

4

O Lady! we receive but what we give,
And in our life alone does Nature live:
Ours is her wedding garment, ours her shroud!
     And would we aught behold, of higher worth,   50
Than that inanimate cold world allowed
To the poor loveless ever-anxious crowd,
     Ah! from the soul itself must issue forth
A light, a glory, a fair luminous cloud
          Enveloping the Earth—   55
And from the soul itself must there be sent
     A sweet and potent voice, of its own birth,
Of all sweet sounds the life and element!

5

O pure of heart! thou need'st not ask of me
What this strong music in the soul may be!   60
What, and wherein it doth exist,
This light, this glory, this fair luminous mist,
This beautiful and beauty-making power.
     Joy, virtuous Lady! Joy that ne'er was given,
Save to the pure, and in their purest hour,   65
Life, and Life's effluence, cloud at once and shower,
Joy, Lady! is the spirit and the power,
Which wedding Nature to us gives in dower
     A new Earth and new Heaven,
Undreamt of by the sensual and the proud—   70
Joy is the sweet voice, Joy the luminous cloud—
          We in ourselves rejoice!
And thence flows all that charms or ear or sight,
     All melodies the echoes of that voice,
All colors a suffusion from that light.   75

6

There was a time when, though my path was rough,
     This joy within me dallied with distress,
And all misfortunes were but as the stuff
     Whence Fancy made me dreams of happiness:
For hope grew round me, like the twining vine,   80

And fruits, and foliage, not my own, seemed mine.
But now afflictions bow me down to earth:
Nor care I that they rob me of my mirth;
    But oh! each visitation
Suspends what nature gave me at my birth,   85
    My shaping spirit of Imagination.
For not to think of what I needs must feel,
    But to be still and patient, all I can;
And haply by abstruse research to steal
    From my own nature all the natural man—   90
    This was my sole resource, my only plan:
Till that which suits a part infects the whole,
And now is almost grown the habit of my soul.

7

Hence, viper thoughts, that coil around my mind,
    Reality's dark dream!   95
I turn from you, and listen to the wind,
    Which long has raved unnoticed. What a scream
Of agony by torture lengthened out
That lute sent forth! Thou Wind, that rav'st without,
    Bare crag, or mountain tairn,[3] or blasted tree,   100
Or pine grove whither woodman never clomb,
Or lonely house, long held—the witches' home,
    Methinks were fitter instruments for thee,
Mad lutanist! who in this month of showers,
Of dark-brown gardens, and of peeping flowers,   105
Mak'st devils' yule, with worse than wintry song,
The blossoms, buds, and timorous leaves among.
    Thou actor, perfect in all tragic sounds!
Thou mighty poet, e'en to frenzy bold!
    What tell'st thou now about?   110
    'Tis of the rushing of an host in rout,
    With groans, of trampled men, with smarting wounds—
At once they groan with pain, and shudder with the cold!
But hush! there is a pause of deepest silence!
    And all that noise, as of a rushing crowd,   115
With groans, and tremulous shudderings—all is over—
    It tells another tale, with sounds less deep and loud!
    A tale of less affright,
    And tempered with delight,
As Otway's self had framed the tender lay—   120
    'Tis of a little child
    Upon a lonesome wild,

[3]pool

Not far from home, but she hath lost her way:
And now moans low in bitter grief and fear,
And now screams loud, and hopes to make her mother hear.   125

8

'Tis midnight, but small thoughts have I of sleep:
Full seldom may my friend such vigils keep!
Visit her, gentle Sleep! with wings of healing,
   And may this storm be but a mountain birth,
May all the stars hang bright above her dwelling,   130
   Silent as though they watched the sleeping Earth!
      With light heart may she rise,
      Gay fancy, cheerful eyes,
   Joy lift her spirit, joy attune her voice;
To her may all things live, from pole to pole,   135
Their life the eddying of her living soul!
   O simple spirit, guided from above,
Dear Lady! friend devoutest of my choice,
Thus mayest thou ever, evermore rejoice.

                                        1802   1817

GEORGE GORDON, LORD BYRON

So We'll Go No More A-Roving

1

So we'll go no more a-roving
   So late into the night,
Though the heart be still as loving,
   And the moon be still as bright.

2

For the sword outwears its sheath,   5
   And the soul wears out the breast,
And the heart must pause to breathe,
   And Love itself have rest.

3

Though the night was made for loving,
   And the day returns too soon,   10
Yet we'll go no more a-roving
   By the light of the moon.

                                        1817   1836

PERCY BYSSHE SHELLEY

Ozymandias

I met a traveler from an antique land
Who said: Two vast and trunkless legs of stone
Stand in the desert . . . Near them, on the sand,
Half sunk, a shattered visage lies, whose frown,
And wrinkled lip, and sneer of cold command,   5
Tell that its sculptor well those passions read
Which yet survive, stamped on these lifeless things,
The hand that mocked them, and the heart that fed:
And on the pedestal these words appear:
"My name is Ozymandias, king of kings: 10
Look on my works, ye Mighty, and despair!"
Nothing beside remains. Round the decay
Of that colossal wreck, boundless and bare
The lone and level sands stretch far away.

1818

Stanzas Written in Dejection, Near Naples

1

The sun is warm, the sky is clear,
    The waves are dancing fast and bright,
Blue isles and snowy mountains wear
    The purple noon's transparent might,
    The breath of the moist earth is light,   5
Around its unexpanded buds;
    Like many a voice of one delight,
The winds, the birds, the ocean floods,
The City's voice itself is soft like Solitude's.

2

I see the Deep's untrampled floor   10
    With green and purple seaweeds strown;
I see the waves upon the shore,
    Like light dissolved in star-showers, thrown:
    I sit upon the sands alone—
The lightning of the noontide ocean   15
    Is flashing round me, and a tone
Arises from its measured motion;
How sweet! did any heart now share in my emotion.

3

Alas! I have no hope nor health,
    Nor peace within nor calm around,   20
Nor that content surpassing wealth
    The sage in meditation found,
    And walked with inward glory crowned—
Nor fame, nor power, nor love, nor leisure.
    Others I see whom these surround—   25
Smiling they live, and call life pleasure;
To me that cup has been dealt in another measure.

4

Yet now despair itself is mild,
    Even as the winds and waters are;
I could lie down like a tired child,   30
    And weep away the life of care
    Which I have borne and yet must bear,
Till death like sleep might steal on me,
    And I might feel in the warm air
My cheek grow cold, and hear the sea   35
Breathe o'er my dying brain its last monotony.

5

Some might lament that I were cold,
    As I, when this sweet day is gone,
Which my lost heart, too soon grown old,
    Insults with this untimely moan;   40
    They might lament—for I am one
Whom men love not—and yet regret,
    Unlike this day, which, when the sun
    Shall on its stainless glory set,
Will linger, though enjoyed, like joy in memory yet.   45

                                     1818   1824

To a Skylark

Hail to thee, blithe Spirit!
    Bird thou never wert,
That from Heaven, or near it,
    Pourest thy full heart
In profuse strains of unpremeditated art.   5

    Higher still and higher

From the earth thou springest
  Like a cloud of fire;
    The blue deep thou wingest,
And singing still dost soar, and soaring ever singest.   10

  In the golden lightning
    Of the sunken sun,
  O'er which clouds are bright'ning,
    Thou dost float and run;
Like an unbodied joy whose race is just begun.   15

  The pale purple even
    Melts around thy flight;
  Like a star of Heaven,
    In the broad daylight
Thou art unseen, but yet I hear thy shrill delight,   20

  Keen as are the arrows
    Of that silver sphere,[1]
  Whose intense lamp narrows
    In the white dawn clear
Until we hardly see—we feel that it is there.   25

All the earth and air
  With thy voice is loud,
  As, when night is bare,
    From one lonely cloud
The moon rains out her beams, and Heaven is overflowed.   30

  What thou art we know not;
    What is most like thee?
  From rainbow clouds there flow not
    Drops so bright to see
As from thy presence showers a rain of melody.   35

  Like a Poet hidden
    In the light of thought,
  Singing hymns unbidden,
    Till the world is wrought
To sympathy with hopes and fears it heeded not: 40

  Like a high-born maiden
    In a palace tower,
  Soothing her love-laden
    Soul in secret hour
With music sweet as love, which overflows her bower: 45

[1]star

Like a glowworm golden
  In a dell of dew,
Scattering unbeholden
  Its aërial hue
Among the flowers and grass, which screen it from the view!   50

Like a rose embowered
  In its own green leaves,
By warm winds deflowered,
  Till the scent it gives
Makes faint with too much sweet those heavy-wingéd thieves: 55

Sound of vernal showers
  On the twinkling grass,
Rain-awakened flowers,
  All that ever was
Joyous, and clear, and fresh, thy music doth surpass: 60

Teach us, Sprite[2] or Bird,
  What sweet thoughts are thine:
I have never heard
  Praise of love or wine
That panted forth a flood of rapture so divine.   65

Chorus Hymeneal,
  Or triumphant chant,
Matched with thine would be all
  But an empty vaunt,
A thing wherein we feel there is some hidden want.   70

What objects are the fountains
  Of thy happy strain?
What fields, or waves, or mountains?
  What shapes of sky or plain?
What love of thine own kind? what ignorance of pain?   75

With thy clear keen joyance
  Languor cannot be:
Shadow of annoyance
  Never came near thee:
Thou lovest—but ne'er knew love's sad satiety.   80

Waking or asleep,
  Thou of death must deem
Things more true and deep
  Than we mortals dream,
Or how could thy notes flow in such a crystal stream?   85

[2]spirit

We look before and after,
    And pine for what is not:
Our sincerest laughter
    With some pain is fraught;
Our sweetest songs are those that tell of saddest thought.   90

Yet if we could scorn
    Hate, and pride, and fear;
If we were things born
    Not to shed a tear,
I know not how thy joy we ever should come near.   95

Better than all measures
    Of delightful sound,
Better than all treasures
    That in books are found,
Thy skill to poet were, thou scorner of the ground!   100

Teach me half the gladness
    That thy brain must know,
Such harmonious madness
    From my lips would flow
The world should listen then—as I am listening now.   105

1820

JOHN KEATS

On First Looking into Chapman's Homer

Much have I traveled in the realms of gold,
    And many goodly states and kingdoms seen;
    Round many western islands have I been
Which bards in fealty[1] to Apollo hold.
Oft of one wide expanse had I been told   5
    That deep-browed Homer ruled as his demesne;[2]
    Yet did I never breathe its pure serene[3]
Till I heard Chapman speak out loud and bold:
Then felt I like some watcher of the skies
    When a new planet swims into his ken;   10
Or like stout Cortez when with eagle eyes
    He stared at the Pacific—and all his men
Looked at each other with a wild surmise—
    Silent, upon a peak in Darien.

1816

[1]allegiance   [2]domain   [3]atmosphere

Ode on a Grecian Urn

1

Thou still unravished bride of quietness,
    Thou foster child of silence and slow time,
Sylvan historian, who canst thus express
    A flowery tale more sweetly than our rhyme:
What leaf-fringed legend haunts about thy shape   5
    Of deities or mortals, or of both,
        In Tempe or the dales of Arcady?
    What men or gods are these? What maidens loath?
What mad pursuit? What struggle to escape?
      What pipes and timbrels? What wild ecstasy?   10

2

Heard melodies are sweet, but those unheard
    Are sweeter; therefore, ye soft pipes, play on;
Not to the sensual ear, but, more endeared,
    Pipe to the spirit ditties of no tone:
Fair youth, beneath the trees, thou canst not leave   15
    Thy song, nor ever can those trees be bare;
      Bold Lover, never, never canst thou kiss,
Though winning near the goal—yet, do not grieve;
    She cannot fade, though thou hast not thy bliss,
    Forever wilt thou love, and she be fair!   20

3

Ah, happy, happy boughs! that cannot shed
    Your leaves, nor ever bid the Spring adieu;
And, happy melodist, unweariéd,
    Forever piping songs forever new;
More happy love! more happy, happy love!   25
    Forever warm and still to be enjoyed,
      Forever panting, and forever young;
All breathing human passion far above,
    That leaves a heart high-sorrowful and cloyed,
      A burning forehead, and a parching tongue.   30

4

Who are these coming to the sacrifice?
    To what green altar, O mysterious priest,
Lead'st thou that heifer lowing at the skies,
    And all her silken flanks with garlands dressed?
What little town by river or sea shore,   35
    Or mountain-built with peaceful citadel,

Is emptied of this folk, this pious morn?
And, little town, thy streets forevermore
    Will silent be; and not a soul to tell
    Why thou art desolate, can e'er return.   40

5

O Attic shape! Fair attitude! with brede[1]
    Of marble men and maidens overwrought,
With forest branches and the trodden weed;
    Thou, silent dorm, dost tease us out of thought
As doth eternity: Cold Pastoral!   45
    When old age shall this generation waste,
      Thou shalt remain, in midst of other woe
    Than ours, a friend to man, to whom thou say'st,
"Beauty is truth, truth beauty,"—that is all
    Ye know on earth, and all ye need to know.   50

                        May 1819   1820

To Autumn

1

Season of mists and mellow fruitfulness,
    Close bosom-friend of the maturing sun;
Conspiring with him how to load and bless
    With fruit the vines that round the thatch-eaves run;
To bend with apples the mossed cottage-trees,   5
    And fill all fruit with ripeness to the core;
      To swell the gourd, and plump the hazel shells
    With a sweet kernel; to set budding more,
And still more, later flowers for the bees,
Until they think warm days will never cease,   10
      For Summer has o'er-brimmed their clammy cells.

2

Who hath not seen thee oft amid thy store?
    Sometimes whoever seeks abroad may find
Thee sitting careless on a granary floor,
    Thy hair soft-lifted by the winnowing wind;   15
Or on a half-reaped furrow sound asleep,
    Drowsed with the fume of poppies, while thy hook
      Spares the next swath and all its twinéd flowers:
And sometimes like a gleaner thou dost keep

[1]woven pattern

Steady thy laden head across a brook;
Or by a cider-press, with patient look,
   Thou watchest the last oozings hours by hours.

3

Where are the songs of Spring? Aye, where are they?
   Think not of them, thou hast thy music too—
While barréd clouds bloom the soft-dying day,
   And touch the stubble-plains with rosy hue;
Then in a wailful choir the small gnats mourn
   Among the river sallows,[1] borne aloft
     Or sinking as the light wind lives or dies;
And full-grown lambs loud bleat from hilly bourn;[2]
   Hedge crickets sing; and now with treble soft
   The redbreast whistles from a garden-croft;
     And gathering swallows twitter in the skies.

September 19, 1819   1820

RALPH WALDO EMERSON

The Rhodora

On Being Asked, Whence Is The Flower?

In May, when sea-winds pierced our solitudes,
I found the fresh Rhodora in the woods,
Spreading its leafless blooms in a damp nook,
To please the desert and the sluggish brook.
The purple petals, fallen in the pool,
Made the black water with their beauty gay;
Here might the red-bird come his plumes to cool,
And court the flower that cheapens his array.
Rhodora! if the sages ask thee why
This charm is wasted on the earth and sky,
Tell them, dear, that if eyes were made for seeing,
Then Beauty is its own excuse for being:
Why thou wert there, O rival of the rose!
I never thought to ask, I never knew;
But, in my simple ignorance, suppose
The self-same Power that brought me there brought you.

1834   1839, 1847

[1] low-growing willows [2] field

Brahma

If the red slayer thinks he slays,
    Or if the slain think he is slain,
They know not well the subtle ways
    I keep, and pass, and turn again.

Far or forgot to me is near;
    Shadow and sunlight are the same;   5
The vanished gods to me appear;
    And one to me are shame and fame.

They reckon ill who leave me out;
    When me they fly, I am the wings;   10
I am the doubter and the doubt,
    And I the hymn the Brahmin sings.

The strong gods pine for my abode,
    And pine in vain the sacred Seven,   15
But thou, meek lover of the good!
    Find me, and turn thy back on heaven.

                    1856   1857, 1867

EDGAR ALLAN POE

Sonnet—To Science

Science! true daughter of Old Time thou art!
    Who alterest all things with thy peering eyes.
Why preyest thou thus upon the poet's heart,
    Vulture, whose wings are dull realities?
How should he love thee? or how deem thee wise?   5
    Who wouldst not leave him in his wandering
To seek for treasure in the jeweled skies,
    Albeit he soared with an undaunted wing?
Hast thou not dragged Diana from her car?
    And driven the Hamadryad from the wood   10
To seek a shelter in some happier star?
    Hast thou not torn the Naiad[1] from her flood,
The Elfin from the green grass, and from me
The summer dream beneath the tamarind tree?

                    1829   1829, 1845

[1] river nymph

425

To Helen

Helen, thy beauty is to me
  Like those Nicean barks of yore,
That gently, o'er a perfumed sea,
  The weary, way-worn wanderer bore
  To his own native shore.   5

On desperate seas long wont to roam,
  Thy hyacinth hair, thy classic face,
Thy Naiad airs have brought me home
  To the glory that was Greece
And the grandeur that was Rome.   10

Lo! in yon brilliant window-niche
  How statue-like I see thee stand!
  The agate lamp within thy hand,
Ah! Psyche, from the regions which
  Are Holy Land!   15

                      1823   1831, 1845

The City in the Sea

Lo! Death has reared himself a throne
In a strange city lying alone
Far down within the dim West,
Where the good and the bad and the worst and the best
Have gone to their eternal rest.   5
There shrines and palaces and towers
(Time-eaten towers that tremble not!)
Resemble nothing that is ours.
Around, by lifting winds forgot,
Resignedly beneath the sky   10
The melancholy waters lie.

No rays from the holy heaven come down
On the long night-time of that town;
But light from out the lurid sea
Streams up the turrets silently—   15
Gleams up the pinnacles far and free—
Up domes—up spires—up kingly halls—
Up fanes—up Babylon-like walls—
Up shadowy long-forgotten bowers

Of sculptured ivy and stone flowers—   20
Up many and many a marvelous shrine
Whose wreathéd friezes intertwine
The viol, the violet, and the vine.
Resignedly beneath the sky
The melancholy waters lie.   25
So blend the turrets and shadows there
That all seem pendulous in air,
While from a proud tower in the town
Death looks gigantically down.

There open fanes and gaping graves   30
Yawn level with the luminous waves;
But not the riches there that lie
In each idol's diamond eye—
Not the gaily-jeweled dead
Tempt the waters from their bed;   35
For no ripples curl, alas!
Along that wilderness of glass—
No swellings tell that winds may be
Upon some far-off happier sea—
No heavings hint that winds have been   40
On seas less hideously serene.

But lo, a stir is in the air!
The wave—there is a movement there!
As if the towers had thrust aside,
In slightly sinking, the dull tide—   45
As if their tops had feebly given
A void within the filmy Heaven.
The waves have now a redder glow—
The hours are breathing faint and low—
And when, amid no earthly moans,   50
Down, down that town shall settle hence,
Hell, rising from a thousand thrones,
Shall do it reverence.

                                            1831, 1845

Eldorado

Gaily bedight,
    A gallant knight,
In sunshine and in shadow,
    Had journeyed long,

Singing a song, 5
In search of Eldorado.

But he grew old—
This knight so bold—
And o'er his heart a shadow
Fell as he found 10
No spot of ground
That looked like Eldorado.

And, as his strength
Failed him at length,
He met a pilgrim shadow— 15
"Shadow," said he,
"Where can it be—
This land of Eldorado?"

"Over the Mountains
Of the Moon, 20
Down the Valley of the Shadow,
Ride, boldly ride,"
The shade replied,—
"If you seek for Eldorado!"

1849

Annabel Lee

It was many and many a year ago,
    In a kingdom by the sea,
That a maiden there lived whom you may know
    By the name of Annabel Lee;
And this maiden she lived with no other thought 5
    Than to love and be loved by me.

She was a child and *I* was a child,
    In this kingdom by the sea,
But we loved with a love that was more than love—
    I and my Annabel Lee— 10
With a love that the wingéd seraphs of Heaven
    Coveted her and me.

And this was the reason that, long ago,
    In this kingdom by the sea,
A wind blew out of a cloud by night 15
    Chilling my Annabel Lee;

So that her highborn kinsmen came
    And bore her away from me,
To shut her up in a sepulchre
    In this kingdom by the sea.   20

The angels, not half so happy in Heaven,
    Went envying her and me:
Yes! that was the reason (as all men know,
    In this kingdom by the sea)
That the wind came out of the cloud, chilling   25
    And killing my Annabel Lee.

But our love it was stronger by far than the love
    Of those who were older than we—
    Of many far wiser than we—
And neither the angels in Heaven above   30
    Nor the demons down under the sea,
Can ever dissever my soul from the soul
    Of the beautiful Annabel Lee:

For the moon never beams without bringing me dreams
    Of the beautiful Annabel Lee;   35
And the stars never rise but I see the bright eyes
    Of the beautiful Annabel Lee;
And so, all the night-tide, I lie down by the side
Of my darling, my darling, my life and my bride,
    In her sepulchre there by the sea—   40
    In her tomb by the side of the sea.

1849, 1850

ALFRED, LORD TENNYSON

The Lotos-Eaters

"Courage!" he said, and pointed toward the land,
"This mounting wave will roll us shoreward soon."
In the afternoon they came unto a land
In which it seeméd always afternoon.
All round the coast the languid air did swoon,   5
Breathing like one that hath a weary dream.
Full-faced above the valley stood the moon;
And, like a downward smoke, the slender stream
Along the cliff to fall and pause and fall did seem.

A land of streams! some, like a downward smoke, 10
Slow-dropping veils of thinnest lawn, did go;
And some through wavering lights and shadows broke,
Rolling a slumbrous sheet of foam below.
They saw the gleaming river seaward flow
From the inner land; far off, three mountain-tops, 15
Three silent pinnacles of aged snow,
Stood sunset-flushed; and, dewed with showery drops,
Up-clomb the shadowy pine above the woven copse.

The charméd sunset lingered low adown
In the red West; through mountain clefts the dale 20
Was seen far inland, and the yellow down
Bordered with palm, and many a winding vale
And meadow, set with slender galingale;
A land where all things always seemed the same!
And round about the keel with faces pale, 25
Dark faces pale against that rosy flame,
The mild-eyed melancholy Lotos-eaters came.

Branches they bore of that enchanted stem,
Laden with flower and fruit, whereof they gave
To each, but whoso did receive of them 30
And taste, to him the gushing of the wave
Far far away did seem to mourn and rave
On alien shores; and if his fellow spake,
His voice was thin, as voices from the grave;
And deep-asleep he seemed, yet all awake, 35
And music in his ears his beating heart did make.

They sat them down upon the yellow sand,
Between the sun and moon upon the shore;
And sweet it was to dream of fatherland,
Of child, and wife, and slave; but evermore 40
Most weary seemed the sea, weary the oar,
Weary the wandering fields of barren foam.
Then someone said, "We will return no more;"
And all at once they sang, "Our island home
Is far beyond the wave; we will no longer roam." 45

Choric Song

1

There is sweet music here that softer falls
Than petals from blown roses on the grass,
Or night-dews on still waters between walls
Of shadowy granite, in a gleaming pass;

Music that gentlier on the spirit lies, 50
Than tired eyelids upon tired eyes;
Music that brings sweet sleep down from the blissful skies.
Here are cool mosses deep,
And through the moss the ivies creep,
And in the stream the long-leaved flowers weep, 55
And from the craggy ledge the poppy hangs in sleep.

2

Why are we weighed upon with heaviness,
And utterly consumed with sharp distress,
While all things else have rest from weariness?
All things have rest: why should we toil alone, 60
We only toil, who are the first of things,
And make perpetual moan,
Still from one sorrow to another thrown;
Nor ever fold our wings,
And cease from wanderings, 65
Nor steep our brows in slumber's holy balm;
Nor harken what the inner spirit sings,
"There is no joy but calm!"—
Why should we only toil, the roof and crown of things?

3

Lo! in the middle of the wood, 70
The folded leaf is wooed from out the bud
With winds upon the branch, and there
Grows green and broad, and takes no care,
Sun-steeped at noon, and in the moon
Nightly dew-fed; and turning yellow 75
Falls, and floats adown the air.
Lo! sweetened with the summer light,
The full-juiced apple, waxing over-mellow,
Drops in a silent autumn night.
All its allotted length of days 80
The flower ripens in its place,
Ripens and fades, and falls, and hath no toil,
Fast-rooted in the fruitful soil.

4

Hateful is the dark-blue sky,
Vaulted o'er the dark-blue sea. 85
Death is the end of life; ah, why
Should life all labor be?
Let us alone. Time driveth onward fast

And in a little while our lips are dumb.
Let us alone. What is it that will last?   90
All things are taken from us, and become
Portions and parcels of the dreadful past.
Let us alone. What pleasure can we have
To war with evil? Is there any peace
In ever climbing up the climbing wave?   95
All things have rest, and ripen toward the grave
In silence—ripen, fall, and cease:
Give us long rest or death, dark death, or dreamful ease.

5

How sweet it were, hearing the downward stream,
With half-shut eyes ever to seem   100
Falling asleep in a half-dream!
To dream and dream, like yonder amber light,
Which will not leave the myrrh-bush on the height;
To hear each other's whispered speech;
Eating the Lotos day by day,   105
To watch the crisping ripples on the beach,
And tender curving lines of creamy spray;
To lend our hearts and spirits wholly
To the influence of mild-minded melancholy;
To muse and brood and live again in memory,   110
With those old faces of our infancy
Heaped over with a mound of grass,
Two handfuls of white dust, shut in an urn of brass!

6

Dear is the memory of our wedded lives,
And dear the last embraces of our wives   115
And their warm tears; but all hath suffered change;
For surely now our household hearths are cold,
Our sons inherit us, our looks are strange,
And we should come like ghosts to trouble joy.
Or else the island princes over-bold   120
Have eat our substance, and the minstrel sings
Before them of the ten years' war in Troy,
And our great deeds, as half-forgotten things.
Is there confusion in the little isle?
Let what is broken so remain.   125
The Gods are hard to reconcile;
'Tis hard to settle order once again.
There *is* confusion worse than death,
Trouble on trouble, pain on pain,

Long labor unto aged breath, 130
Sore tasks to hearts worn out by many wars
And eyes grown dim with gazing on the pilot-stars.

7

But, propt on beds of amaranth and moly,
How sweet—while warm airs lull us, blowing lowly—
With half-dropt eyelid still, 135
Beneath a heaven dark and holy,
To watch the long bright river drawing slowly
His waters from the purple hill—
To hear the dewy echoes calling
From cave to cave through the thick-twined vine— 140
To watch the emerald-colored water falling
Through many a woven acanthus-wreath divine!
Only to hear and see the far-off sparkling brine,
Only to hear were sweet, stretched out beneath the pine.

8

The Lotos blooms below the barren peak, 145
The Lotos blows by every winding creek;
All day the wind breathes low with mellower tone;
Through every hollow cave and alley lone
Round and round the spicy downs the yellow Lotos-dust is blown.
We have had enough of action, and of motion we, 150
Rolled to starboard, rolled to larboard, when the surge was seething free,
Where the wallowing monster spouted his foam-fountains in the sea.
Let us swear an oath, and keep it with an equal mind,
In the hollow Lotos-land to live and lie reclined
On the hills like Gods together, careless of mankind. 155
For they lie beside their nectar, and the bolts are hurled
Far below them in the valleys, and the clouds are lightly curled
Round their golden houses, girdled with the gleaming world;
Where they smile in secret, looking over wasted lands,
Blight and famine, plague and earthquake, roaring deeps and fiery sands, 160
Clanging fights, and flaming towns, and sinking ships, and praying hands.
But they smile, they find a music centered in a doleful song
Steaming up, a lamentation and an ancient tale of wrong,
Like a tale of little meaning though the words are strong;
Chanted from an ill-used race of men that cleave the soil, 165
Sow the seed, and reap the harvest with enduring toil,
Storing yearly little dues of wheat, and wine and oil;
Till they perish and they suffer—some, 'tis whispered—down in hell
Suffer endless anguish, others in Elysian valleys dwell,
Resting weary limbs at last on beds of asphodel. 170

Surely, surely, slumber is more sweet than toil, the shore
Than labor in the deep mid-ocean, wind and wave and oar;
O, rest ye, brother mariners, we will not wander more.

1832, 1842

Ulysses

It little profits that an idle king,
By this still hearth, among these barren crags,
Matched with an aged wife, I mete and dole
Unequal laws unto a savage race,
That hoard, and sleep, and feed, and know not me.   5
I cannot rest from travel; I will drink
Life to the lees. All times I have enjoyed
Greatly, have suffered greatly, both with those
That loved me, and alone; on shore, and when
Through scudding drifts the rainy Hyades   10
Vext the dim sea. I am become a name;
For always roaming with a hungry heart
Much have I seen and known—cities of men
And manners, climates, councils, governments,
Myself not least, but honored of them all,—   15
And drunk delight of battle with my peers,
Far on the ringing plains of windy Troy.
I am a part of all that I have met;
Yet all experience is an arch wherethrough
Gleams that untraveled world whose margin fades   20
For ever and for ever when I move.
How dull it is to pause, to make an end,
To rust unburnished, not to shine in use!
As though to breathe were life! Life piled on life
Were all too little, and of one to me   25
Little remains; but every hour is saved
From that eternal silence, something more,
A bringer of new things; and vile it were
For some three suns to store and hoard myself,
And this gray spirit yearning in desire   30
To follow knowledge like a sinking star,
Beyond the utmost bound of human thought.
    This is my son, mine own Telemachus,
To whom I leave the sceptor and the isle,
Well-loved of me, discerning to fulfill   35
This labor, by slow prudence to make mild

A rugged people, and through soft degrees
Subdue them to the useful and the good.
Most blameless is he, centered in the sphere
Of common duties, decent not to fail   40
In offices of tenderness, and pay
Meet adoration to my household gods,
When I am gone. He works his work, I mine.
    There lies the port; the vessel puffs her sail;
There gloom the dark, broad seas. My mariners,   45
Souls that have toiled, and wrought, and thought with me,
That ever with a frolic welcome took
The thunder and the sunshine, and opposed
Free hearts, free foreheads—you and I are old;
Old age hath yet his honor and his toil.   50
Death closes all; but something ere the end,
Some work of noble note, may yet be done,
Not unbecoming men that strove with gods.
The lights begin to twinkle from the rocks;
The long day wanes; the slow moon climbs; the deep   55
Moans round with many voices. Come, my friends,
'Tis not too late to seek a newer world.
Push off, and sitting well in order smite
The sounding furrows; for my purpose holds
To sail beyond the sunset, and the baths   60
Of all the western stars, until I die.
It may be that the gulfs will wash us down;
It may be we shall touch the Happy Isles,
And see the great Achilles, whom we knew.
Though much is taken, much abides; and though   65
We are not now that strength which in old days
Moved earth and heaven, that which we are, we are,
One equal temper of heroic hearts,
Made weak by time and fate, but strong in will
To strive, to seek, to find, and not to yield.   70

1833   1842

HENRY DAVID THOREAU

Love Equals Swift and Slow

> Love equals swift and slow,
>> And high and low,
> Racer and lame,
>> The hunter and his game.

1849

WALT WHITMAN

When I Heard the Learn'd Astronomer

When I heard the learn'd astronomer,
When the proofs, the figures, were ranged in columns before me,
When I was shown the charts and diagrams, to add, divide, and measure them,
When I sitting heard the astronomer where he lectured with much applause in
    the lecture-room,   5
How soon unaccountable I became tired and sick,
Till rising and gliding out I wander'd off by myself,
In the mystical moist night-air, and from time to time,
Look'd up in perfect silence at the stars.

1865, 1865

Out of the Cradle Endlessly Rocking

Out of the cradle endlessly rocking,
Out of the mocking-bird's throat, the musical shuttle,
Out of the Ninth-month midnight,
Over the sterile sands and the fields beyond, where the child leaving his bed
    wander'd alone, bareheaded, barefoot,
Down from the shower'd halo,   5
Up from the mystic play of shadows twining and twisting as if they were alive,
Out from the patches of briers and blackberries,
From the memories of the bird that chanted to me,
From your memories sad brother, from the fitful risings and fallings I heard,
From under that yellow half-moon late-risen swollen as if with tears,   10

From *Poems of Nature* by Henry David Thoreau (Boston: Houghton Mifflin Company).

From those beginning notes of yearning and love there in the mist,
From the thousand responses of my heart never to cease,
From the myriad thence-arous'd words,
From the word stronger and more delicious than any,
From such as now they start the scene revisiting,   15
As a flock, twittering, rising, or overhead passing,
Borne hither, ere all eludes me, hurriedly,
A man, yet by these tears a little boy again,
Throwing myself on the sand, confronting the waves,
I, chanter of pains and joys, uniter of here and hereafter,   20
Taking all hints to use them, but swiftly leaping beyond them,
A reminiscence sing.

Once Paumanok,
When the lilac-scent was in the air and Fifth-month grass was growing,
Up this seashore in some briers,   25
Two feather'd guests from Alabama, two together,
And their nest, and four light-green eggs spotted with brown,
And every day the he-bird to and fro near at hand,
And every day the she-bird crouch'd on her nest, silent, with bright eyes,
And every day I, a curious boy, never too close, never disturbing them,   30
Cautiously peering, absorbing, translating.

Shine! shine! shine!
Pour down your warmth, great sun!
While we bask, we two together.

Two together!   35
Winds blow south, or winds blow north,
Day come white, or night come black,
Home, or rivers and mountains from home,
Singing all time, minding no time,
While we two keep together.   40

Till of a sudden,
May-be kill'd, unknown to her mate,
One forenoon the she-bird crouch'd not on the nest,
Nor return'd that afternoon, nor the next,
Nor ever appear'd again.   45

And thenceforward all summer in the sound of the sea,
And at night under the full of the moon in calmer weather,
Over the hoarse surging of the sea,
Or flitting from brier to brier by day,
I saw, I heard at intervals the remaining one, the he-bird,   50
The solitary guest from Alabama.

Blow! blow! blow!

Blow up sea-winds along Paumanok's shore;
I wait and I wait till you blow my mate to me.

Yes, when the stars glisten'd,   55
All night long on the prong of a moss-scallop'd stake,
Down almost amid the slapping waves,
Sat the lone singer wonderful causing tears.

He call'd on his mate,
He pour'd forth the meanings which I of all men know.   60

Yes my brother I know,
The rest might not, but I have treasur'd every note,
For more than once dimly down to the beach gliding,
Silent, avoiding the moonbeams, blending myself with the shadows,
Recalling now the obscure shapes, the echoes, the sounds and sights after   65
    their sorts,
The white arms out in the breakers tirelessly tossing,
I, with bare feet, a child, the wind wafting my hair,
Listen'd long and long.

Listen'd to keep, to sing, now translating the notes,
Following you my brother.   70

Soothe! soothe! soothe!
Close on its wave soothes the wave behind,
And again another behind embracing and lapping, every one close,
But my love soothes not me, not me.

Low hangs the moon, it rose late,   75
It is lagging—O I think it is heavy with love, with love.

O madly the sea pushes upon the land,
With love, with love.

O night! do I not see my love fluttering out among the breakers?
What is that little black thing I see there in the white?   80

Loud! loud! loud!
Loud I call to you, my love!
High and clear I shoot my voice over the waves,
Surely you must know who is here, is here,
You must know who I am, my love.   85

Low-hanging moon!
What is that dusky spot in your brown yellow?
O it is the shape, the shape of my mate!
O moon do not keep her from me any longer.

Land! land! O land!   90

Whichever way I turn, O I think you could give me my mate back again if you
    only would,
For I am almost sure I see her dimly whichever way I look.

O rising stars!
Perhaps the one I want so much will rise, will rise with some of you.

O throat! O trembling throat!   95
Sound clearer through the atmosphere!
Pierce the woods, the earth,
Somewhere listening to catch you must be the one I want.

Shake out carols!
Solitary here, the night's carols!   100
Carols of lonesome love! death's carols!
Carols under that lagging, yellow, waning moon!
O under that moon where she droops almost down into the sea!
O reckless despairing carols.

But soft! sink low!   105
Soft! let me just murmur,
And do you wait a moment you husky-nois'd sea,
For somewhere I believe I heard my mate responding to me,
So faint, I must be still, be still to listen,
But not altogether still, for then she might not come immediately to me.   110

Hither my love!
Here I am! here!
With this just-sustain'd note I announce myself to you,
This gentle call is for you my love, for you.

Do not be decoy'd elsewhere,   115
That is the whistle of the wind, it is not my voice,
That is the fluttering, the fluttering of the spray,
Those are the shadows of leaves.

O darkness! O in vain!
O I am very sick and sorrowful.   120

O brown halo in the sky near the moon, drooping upon the sea!
O troubled reflection in the sea!
O throat! O throbbing heart!
And I singing uselessly, uselessly all the night.

O past! O happy life! O songs of joy!   125
In the air, in the woods, over fields,
Loved! loved! loved! loved! loved!
But my mate no more, no more with me!
We two together no more.

The aria sinking,   130
All else continuing, the stars shining,
The winds blowing, the notes of the bird continuous echoing,
With angry moans the fierce old mother incessantly moaning,
On the sands of Paumanok's shore gray and rustling,
The yellow half-moon enlarged, sagging down, drooping, the face of the sea   135
    almost touching,
The boy ecstatic, with his bare feet the waves, with his hair the atmosphere
    dallying,
The love in the heart long pent, now loose, now at last tumultuously bursting,
The aria's meaning, the ears, the soul, swiftly depositing,

The strange tears down the cheeks coursing,
The colloquy there, the trio, each uttering,   140
The undertone, the savage old mother incessantly crying,
To the boy's soul's questions sullenly timing, some drown'd secret hissing,
To the outsetting bard.

Demon or bird! (said the boy's soul,)
Is it indeed toward your mate you sing? or is it really to me?   145
For I, that was a child, my tongue's use sleeping, now I have heard you,
Now in a moment I know what I am for, I awake,
And already a thousand singers, a thousand songs, clearer, louder and more
    sorrowful than yours,
A thousand warbling echoes have started to life within me, never to die.

O you singer solitary, singing by yourself, projecting me,   150
O solitary me listening, never more shall I cease perpetuating you,
Never more shall I escape, never more the reverberations,
Never more the cries of unsatisfied love be absent from me,
Never again leave me to be the peaceful child I was before what there in the
    night,
By the sea under the yellow and sagging moon,   155
The messenger there arous'd, the fire, the sweet hell within,
The unknown want, the destiny of me.

O give me the clew! (it lurks in the night here somewhere,)
O if I am to have so much, let me have more!

A word then, (for I will conquer it,)   160
The word final, superior to all,
Subtle, sent up—what is it?—I listen;
Are you whispering it, and have been all the time, you sea-waves?
Is that it from your liquid rims and wet sands?

Whereto answering, the sea,   165
Delaying not, hurrying not,
Whisper'd me through the night, and very plainly before daybreak,

Lisp'd to me the low and delicious word death,
And again death, death, death, death,
Hissing melodious, neither like the bird nor like my arous'd child's heart,   170
But edging near as privately for me rustling at my feet,
Creeping thence steadily up to my ears and laving me softly all over,
Death, death, death, death, death.

Which I do not forget,
But fuse the song of my dusky demon and brother,   175
That he sang to me in the moonlight on Paumanok's gray beach,
With the thousand responsive songs at random,
My own songs awaked from that hour,
And with them the key, the word up from the waves,
The word of the sweetest song and all songs,   180
That strong and delicious word which, creeping to my feet,
(Or like some old crone rocking the cradle, swathed in sweet garments, bending
        aside,)
The sea whisper'd me.

1859   1881

When Lilacs Last in the Dooryard Bloom'd

1

When lilacs last in the dooryard bloom'd,
And the great star early droop'd in the western sky in the night,
I mourn'd, and yet shall mourn with ever-returning spring.

Ever-returning spring, trinity sure to me you bring,
Lilac blooming perennial and dropping star in the west,   5
And thought of him I love.

2

O powerful western fallen star!
O shades of night—O moody, tearful night!
O great star disappear'd—O the black murk that hides the star!
O cruel hands that hold me powerless—O helpless soul of me!   10
O harsh surrounding cloud that will not free my soul.

3

In the dooryard fronting an old farm-house near the white-wash'd palings,
Stands the lilac-bush tall-growing with heart-shaped leaves of rich green,
With many a pointed blossom rising delicate, with the perfume strong I love,
With every leaf a miracle—and from this bush in the dooryard,   15
With delicate-color'd blossoms and heart-shaped leaves of rich green,
A sprig with its flower I break.

4

In the swamp in secluded recesses,
A shy and hidden bird is warbling a song.

Solitary the thrush,   20
The hermit withdrawn to himself, avoiding the settlements,
Sings by himself a song.

Song of the bleeding throat,
Death's outlet song of life, (for well dear brother I know,
If thou wast not granted to sing thou would'st surely die.)   25

5

Over the breast of the spring, the land, amid cities,
Amid lanes and through old woods, where lately the violets peep'd from the
        ground, spotting the gray debris,
Amid the grass in the fields each side of the lanes, passing the endless grass,
Passing the yellow-spear'd wheat, every grain from its shroud in the dark-brown
        fields uprisen,
Passing the apple-tree blows of white and pink in the orchards,   30
Carrying a corpse to where it shall rest in the grave,
Night and day journeys a coffin.

6

Coffin that passes through lanes and streets,
Through day and night with the great cloud darkening the land,
With the pomp of the inloop'd flags with the cities draped in black,   35
With the show of the States themselves as of crape-veil'd women standing,
With processions long and winding and the flambeaus of the night,
With the countless torches lit, with the silent sea of faces and the unbared heads,
With the waiting depot, the arriving coffin, and the sombre faces,
With dirges through the night, with the thousand voices rising strong and   40
        solemn,
With all the mournful voices of the dirges pour'd around the coffin,
The dim-lit churches and the shuddering organs—where amid these you journey,
With the tolling tolling bells' perpetual clang,
Here, coffin that slowly passes,
I give you my sprig of lilac.   45

7

(Nor for you, for one alone,
Blossoms and branches green to coffins all I bring,
For fresh as the morning, thus would I chant a song for you O sane and sacred
        death.

All over bouquets of roses,

442

O death, I cover you over with roses and early lilies,   50
But mostly and now the lilac that blooms the first,
Copious I break, I break the sprigs from the bushes,
With loaded arms I come, pouring for you,
For you and the coffins all of you O death.)

8

O western orb sailing the heaven,   55
Now I know what you must have meant as a month since I walk'd,
As I walk'd in silence the transparent shadowy night,
As I saw you had something to tell as you bent to me night after night,
As you droop'd from the sky low down as if to my side, (while the other stars
    all look'd on,)
As we wander'd together the solemn night, (for something I know not what kept   60
    me from sleep,)
As the night advanced, and I saw on the rim of the west how full you were of
    woe,
As I stood on the rising ground in the breeze in the cool transparent night,
As I watch'd where you pass'd and was lost in the netherward black of the
    night,
As my soul in its trouble dissatisfied sank, as where you sad orb,
Concluded, dropt in the night, and was gone.   65

9

Sing on there in the swamp,
O singer bashful and tender, I hear your notes, I hear your call,
I hear, I come presently, I understand you,
But a moment I linger, for the lustrous star has detain'd me,
The star my departing comrade holds and detains me.   70

10

O how shall I warble myself for the dead one there I loved?
And how shall I deck my song for the large sweet soul that has gone?
And what shall my perfume be for the grave of him I love?

Sea-winds blown from east and west,
Blown from the Eastern sea and blown from the Western sea, till there on the   75
    prairies meeting,
These and with these and the breath of my chant,
I'll perfume the grave of him I love.

11

O what shall I hang on the chamber walls?
And what shall the pictures be that I hang on the walls,
To adorn the burial-house of him I love?   80

Pictures of growing spring and farms and homes,

With the Fourth-month eve at sundown, and the gray smoke lucid and bright,

With floods of the yellow gold of the gorgeous, indolent, sinking sun, burning, expanding the air,

With the fresh sweet herbage under foot, and the pale green leaves of the trees prolific,

In the distance the flowing glaze, the breast of the river, with a wind-dapple here and there,   85

With ranging hills on the banks, with many a line against the sky, and shadows,

And the city at hand with dwellings so dense, and stacks of chimneys,

And all the scenes of life and the workshops, and the workmen homeward returning.

12

Lo, body and soul—this land,

My own Manhattan with spires, and the sparkling and hurrying tides, and the ships,   90

The varied and ample land, the South and the North in the light, Ohio's shores and flashing Missouri,

And ever the far-spreading prairies cover'd with grass and corn.

Lo, the most excellent sun so calm and haughty,

The violet and purple morn with just-felt breezes,

The gentle soft-born measureless light,   95

The miracle spreading bathing all, the fulfill'd noon,

The coming eve delicious, the welcome night and the stars,

Over my cities shining all, enveloping man and land.

13

Sing on, sing on you gray-brown bird,

Sing from the swamps, the recesses, pour your chant from the bushes,   100

Limitless out of the dusk, out of the cedars and pines.

Sing on dearest brother, warble your reedy song,

Loud human song, with voice of uttermost woe.

O liquid and free and tender!

O wild and loose to my soul—O wondrous singer!   105

You only I hear—yet the star holds me, (but will soon depart,)

Yet the lilac with mastering odor holds me.

14

Now while I sat in the day and look'd forth,

In the close of the day with its light and the fields of spring, and the farmers preparing their crops,

In the large unconscious scenery of my land with its lakes and forests,   110

In the heavenly aerial beauty, (after the perturb'd winds and the storms,)
Under the arching heavens of the afternoon swift passing, and the voices of
    children and women.
The many-moving sea-tides, and I saw the ships how they sail'd,
And the summer approaching with richness, and the fields all busy with labor,
And the infinite separate houses, how they all went on, each with its meals and   115
    minutia of daily usages,
And the streets how their throbbings throbb'd, and the cities pent—lo, then and
    there,
Falling upon them all and among them all, enveloping me with the rest,
Appear'd the cloud, appear'd the long black trail,
And I knew death, its thought, and the sacred knowledge of death.

Then with the knowledge of death as walking one side of me,   120
And the thought of death close-walking the other side of me,
And I in the middle as with companions, and as holding the hands of com-
    panions,
I fled forth to the hiding receiving night that talks not,
Down to the shores of the water, the path by the swamp in the dimness,
To the solemn shadowy cedars and ghostly pines so still.   125

And the singer so shy to the rest receiv'd me,
The gray-brown bird I know receiv'd us comrades three,
And he sang the carol of death, and a verse for him I love.

From deep secluded recesses,
From the fragrant cedars and the ghostly pines so still,   130
Came the carol of the bird.

And the charm of the carol rapt me,
As I held as if by their hands my comrades in the night,
And the voice of my spirit tallied the song of the bird.

Come lovely and soothing death,   135
Undulate round the world, serenely arriving, arriving,
In the day, in the night, to all, to each,
Sooner or later delicate death.

Prais'd be the fathomless universe,
For life and joy, and for objects and knowledge curious,   140
And for love, sweet love—but praise! praise! praise!
For the sure-enwinding arms of cool-enfolding death.

Dark mother always gliding near with soft feet,
Have none chanted for thee a chant of fullest welcome?
Then I chant it for thee, I glorify thee above all,   145
I bring thee a song that when thou must indeed come, come unfalteringly.

Approach strong deliveress,

When it is so, when thou hast taken them I joyously sing the dead,
Lost in the loving floating ocean of thee,
Laved in the flood of thy bliss O death.   150

From me to thee glad serenades,
Dances for thee I propose saluting thee, adornments and feastings for thee,
And the sights of the open landscape and the high-spread sky are fitting,
And life and the fields, and the huge and thoughtful night.

The night in silence under many a star,   155
The ocean shore and the husky whispering wave whose voice I know,
And the soul turning to thee O vast and well-veil'd death,
And the body gratefully nestling close to thee.

Over the tree-tops I float thee a song,
Over the rising and sinking waves, over the myriad fields and the prairies wide,   160
Over the dense-pack'd cities all and the teeming wharves and ways,
I float this carol with joy, with joy to thee O death.

15

To the tally of my soul,
Loud and strong kept up the gray-brown bird,
With pure deliberate notes spreading filling the night.   165

Loud in the pines and cedars dim,
Clear in the freshness moist and the swamp-perfume,
And I with my comrades there in the night.

While my sight that was bound in my eyes unclosed,
As to long panoramas of visions.   170

And I saw askant the armies,
I saw as in noiseless dreams hundreds of battle-flags,
Borne through the smoke of the battles and pierc'd with missiles I saw them,
And carried hither and yon through the smoke, and torn and bloody,
And at last but a few shreds left on the staffs, (and all in silence,)   175
And the staffs all splinter'd and broken.

I saw battle-corpses, myriads of them,
And the white skeletons of young men, I saw them,
I saw the debris and debris of all the slain soldiers of the war,
But I saw they were not as was thought,   180
They themselves were fully at rest, they suffer'd not,
The living remain'd and suffer'd, the mother suffer'd,
And the wife and the child and the musing comrade suffer'd,
And the armies that remain'd suffer'd.

16

Passing the visions, passing the night,   185
Passing, unloosing the hold of my comrade's hands,

Passing the song of the hermit bird and the tallying song of my soul,
Victorious song, death's outlet song, yet varying ever-altering song,
As low and wailing, yet clear the notes, rising and falling, flooding the night,
Sadly sinking and fainting, as warning and warning, and yet again bursting   190
     with joy,
Covering the earth and filling the spread of the heaven,
As that powerful psalm in the night I heard from recesses,
Passing, I leave thee lilac with heart-shaped leaves,
I leave thee there in the door-yard, blooming, returning with spring.

I cease from my song for thee,   195
From my gaze on thee in the west, fronting the west, communing with thee,
O comrade lustrous with silver face in the night.

Yet each to keep and all, retrievements out of the night,
The song, the wondrous chant of the gray-brown bird,
And the tallying chant, the echo arous'd in my soul,   200
With the lustrous and drooping star with the countenance full of woe,
With the holders holding my hand nearing the call of the bird,
Comrades mine and I in the midst, and their memory ever to keep, for the dead
     I loved so well,
For the sweetest, wisest soul of all my days and lands—and this for his dear
     sake,
Lilac and star and bird twined with the chant of my soul,   205
There in the fragrant pines and the cedars dusk and dim.
                                                    1865–66   1881

A Noiseless Patient Spider

A noiseless patient spider,
I mark'd where on a little promontory it stood isolated,
Mark'd how to explore the vacant vast surrounding,
It launch'd forth filament, filament, filament, out of itself,
Ever unreeling them, ever tirelessly speeding them.   5

And you O my soul where you stand,
Surrounded, detached, in measureless oceans of space,
Ceaselessly musing, venturing, throwing, seeking the spheres to connect them,
Till the bridge you will need be form'd, till the ductile anchor hold,
Till the gossamer thread you fling catch somewhere, O my soul.   10
                                                    1868   1881

MATTHEW ARNOLD

Dover Beach

The sea is calm tonight.
The tide is full, the moon lies fair
Upon the straits; on the French coast the light
Gleams and is gone; the cliffs of England stand,
Glimmering and vast, out in the tranquil bay.   5
Come to the window, sweet is the night-air!
Only, from the long line of spray
Where the sea meets the moon-blanched land,
Listen! you hear the grating roar
Of pebbles which the waves draw back, and fling,   10
At their return, up the high strand,
Begin, and cease, and then again begin,
With tremulous cadence slow, and bring
The eternal note of sadness in.

Sophocles long ago   15
Heard it on the Aegean, and it brought
Into his mind the turbid ebb and flow
Of human misery; we
Find also in the sound a thought,
Hearing it by this distant northern sea.   20
The Sea of Faith
Was once, too, at the full, and round earth's shore
Lay like the folds of a bright girdle furled.
But now I only hear
Its melancholy, long, withdrawing roar,   25
Retreating, to the breath
Of the night-wind, down the vast edges drear
And naked shingles of the world.

Ah, love, let us be true
To one another! for the world, which seems   30
To lie before us like a land of dreams,
So various, so beautiful, so new,
Hath really neither joy, nor love, nor light,
Nor certitude, nor peace, nor help for pain;
And we are here as on a darkling plain   35
Swept with confused alarms of struggle and flight,
Where ignorant armies clash by night.

1867

EMILY DICKINSON

98

One dignity delays for all—
One mitred Afternoon—
None can avoid this purple—
None evade this Crown!

Coach, it insures, and footmen—   5
Chamber, and state, and throng—
Bells, also, in the village
As we ride grand along!

What dignified Attendants!
What service when we pause!   10
How loyally at parting
Their hundred hats they raise!

How pomp surpassing ermine
When simple You, and I,
Present our meek escutscheon   15
And claim the rank to die!

                                                    1859?   1890

165

A *Wounded* Deer—leaps highest—
I've heard the Hunter tell—
'Tis but the Extasy of *death*—
And then the Brake is still!

The *Smitten* Rock that gushes!   5
The *trampled* Steel that springs!
A Cheek is always redder
Just where the Hectic stings!

Mirth is the Mail of Anguish—
In which it Cautious Arm,   10
Lest anybody spy the blood
And "you're hurt" exclaim!

                                                    1860?   1890

214

I taste a liquor never brewed—
From Tankards scooped in Pearl—
Not all the Frankfort Berries
Yield such an Alcohol!

Inebriate of Air—am I—   5
And Debauchee of Dew—
Reeling—thro endless summer days—
From inns of Molten Blue—

When "Landlords" turn the drunken Bee
Out of the Foxglove's door—   10
When Butterflies—renounce their "dram"—
I shall but drink the more!

Till Seraphs swing their snowy Hats—
And Saints—to windows run—
To see the little Tippler   15
From Manzanilla come!

                                                    1860?

241

I like a look of Agony,
Because I know it's true—
Men do not sham Convulsion,
Nor simulate, a Throe—

The Eyes glaze once—and that is Death—   5
Impossible to feign
The Beads upon the Forehead
By homely Anguish strung.

                                          1861?   1890

258

There's a certain Slant of light,
Winter Afternoons—
That oppresses, like the Heft
Of Cathedral Tunes—

Heavenly Hurt, it gives us—   5
We can find no scar,
But internal difference,
Where the Meanings, are—

None may teach it—Any—
'Tis the Seal Despair—   10
An imperial affliction
Sent us of the Air—

When it comes, the Landscape listens—
Shadows—hold their breath—
When it goes, 'tis like the Distance   15
On the look of Death—

1861?   1890

287

A Clock stopped—
Not the Mantel's—
Geneva's farthest skill
Can't put the puppet bowing—
That just now dangled still—   5

An awe came on the Trinket!
The Figures hunched, with pain—
Then quivered out of Decimals—
Into Degreeless Noon—

It will not stir for Doctor's—   10
This Pendulum of snow—
The Shopman importunes it—
While cool—concernless No—

Nods from the Gilded pointers—
Nods from the Seconds slim—   15
Decades of Arrogance between
The Dial life—
And Him—

1861?   1896

303

The Soul selects her own Society—
Then—shuts the Door—

To her divine Majority—
Present no more—

Unmoved—she notes the Chariots—pausing—   5
At her low Gate—
Unmoved—an Emperor be kneeling
Upon her Mat—

I've known her—from an ample nation—
Choose One—   10
Then—close the Valves of her attention—
Like Stone—

                                    1862?   1890

305

The difference between Despair
And Fear—is like the One
Between the instant of a Wreck—
And when the Wreck has been—

The Mind is smooth—no Motion—   5
Contented as the Eye
Upon the Forehead of a Bust—
That knows—it cannot see—

                                    1862?   1914

328

A Bird came down the Walk—
He did not know I saw—
He bit an Angleworm in halves
And ate the fellow, raw,

And then he drank a Dew   5
From a convenient Grass—
And then hopped sidewise to the Wall
To let a Beetle pass—

He glanced with rapid eyes
That hurried all around—   10
They looked like frightened Beads, I thought—
He stirred his Velvet Head

Like one in danger, Cautious,
I offered him a Crumb
And he unrolled his feathers   15
And rowed him softer home—

Than Oars divide the Ocean,
Too silver for a seam—
Or Butterflies, off Banks of Noon
Leap, plashless as they swim.   20

                                              1862   1891

341

After great pain, a formal feeling comes—
The Nerves sit ceremonious, like Tombs—
The stiff Heart questions was it He, that bore,
And Yesterday, or Centuries before?

The Feet, mechanical, go round—   5
Of Ground, or Air, or Ought—[1]
A Wooden way
Regardless grown,
A Quartz contentment, like a stone—

This is the Hour of Lead—   10
Remembered, if outlived,
As Freezing persons, recollect the Snow—
First—Chill—then Stupor—then the letting go—

                                              1862?   1929

449

I died for Beauty—but was scarce
Adjusted in the Tomb
When One who died for Truth, was lain
In an adjoining Room—

[1]nothing, a void

                                                                 453

He questioned softly "Why I failed"?
"For Beauty", I replied—
"And I—for Truth—Themself are One—
We Brethren, are", He said—

And so, as Kinsmen, met a Night—
We talked between the Rooms—
Until the Moss had reached our lips—
And covered up—our names—

1862?   1890

465

I heard a Fly buzz—when I died—
The Stillness in the Room
Was like the Stillness in the Air—
Between the Heaves of Storm—

The Eyes around—had wrung them dry—
And Breaths were gathering firm
For that last Onset—when the King
Be witnessed—in the Room—

I willed my Keepsakes—Signed away
What portion of me be
Assignable—and then it was
There interposed a Fly—

With Blue—uncertain stumbling Buzz—
Between the light—and me—
And then the Windows failed—and then
I could not see to see—

1862?   1896

479

She dealt her pretty words like Blades—
How glittering they shone—
And every One unbared a Nerve
Or wantoned with a Bone—

She never deemed—she hurt—

That—is not Steel's Affair—
A vulgar grimace in the Flesh—
How ill the Creatures bear—

To Ache is human—not polite—
The Film upon the eye   10
Mortality's Old Custom—
Just locking up—to Die.

                                                    1862?   1929

585

I like to see it lap the Miles—
And lick the Valleys up—
And stop to feed itself at Tanks—
And then—prodigious step

Around a Pile of Mountains—   5
And supercilious peer
In Shanties—by the sides of Roads—
And then a Quarry pare

To fit its sides
And crawl between   10
Complaining all the while
In horrid—hooting stanza—
Then chase itself down Hill—

And neigh like Boanerges—
Then—prompter than a Star   15
Stop—docile and omnipotent
At its own stable door—

                                                    1862?   1891

640

I cannot live with You—
It would be Life—
And Life is over there—
Behind the Shelf

The Sexton keeps the Key to—
Putting up
Our Life—His Porcelain—
Like a Cup—

Discarded of the Housewife—
Quaint—or Broke—
A newer Sevres pleases—
Old Ones crack—

I could not die—with You—
For One must wait
To shut the Other's Gaze down—
You—could not—

And I—Could I stand by
And see You—freeze—
Without my Right of Frost—
Death's privilege?

Nor could I rise—with You—
Because Your Face
Would put out Jesus'—
That New Grace

Glow plain—and foreign
On my homesick Eye—
Except that You than He
Shone closer by—

They'd judge Us—How—
For You—served Heaven—You know,
Or sought to—
I could not—

Because You saturated Sight—
And I had no more Eyes
For sordid excellence
As Paradise

And were You lost, I would be—
Though My Name
Rang loudest
On the Heavenly fame—

And were You—saved—
And I—condemned to be
Where You were not—
That self—were Hell to Me—

5

10

15

20

25

30

35

40

So We must meet apart—   45
You there—I—here—
With just the Door ajar
That Oceans are—and Prayer—
And that White Sustenance—
Despair—   50

                                                        1862?   1890

712

Because I could not stop for Death—
He kindly stopped for me—
The Carriage held but just Ourselves—
And Immortality.

We slowly drove—He knew no haste   5
And I had put away
My labor and my leisure too,
For His Civility—

We passed the School, where Children strove
At Recess—in the Ring—   10
We passed the Fields of Gazing Grain—
We passed the Setting Sun—

Or rather—He passed Us—
The Dews drew quivering and chill—
For only Gossamer, my Gown—   15
My Tippet—only Tulle—

We paused before a House that seemed
A Swelling of the Ground—
The Roof was scarcely visible—
The Cornice—in the Ground—   20

Since then—'tis Centuries—and yet
Feels shorter than the Day
I first surmised the Horses Heads
Were toward Eternity—

                                                        1863?   1890

732

She rose to His Requirement—dropt
The Playthings of Her Life

To take the honorable Work
Of Woman, and of Wife—

If ought She missed in Her new Day,   5
Of Amplitude, or Awe—
Or first Prospective—Or the Gold
In using, wear away,

It lay unmentioned—as the Sea
Develop Pearl, and Weed,   10
But only to Himself—be known
The Fathoms they abide—

                                           1863?   1890

986

A narrow Fellow in the Grass
Occasionally rides—
You may have met Him—did you not
His notice sudden is—

The Grass divides as with a Comb—   5
A spotted shaft is seen—
And then it closes at your feet
And opens further on—

He likes a Boggy Acre
A Floor too cool for Corn—   10
Yet when a Boy, and Barefoot—
I more than once at Noon
Have passed, I thought, a Whip lash
Unbraiding in the Sun
When stooping to secure it   15
It wrinkled, and was gone—

Several of Nature's People
I know, and they know me—
I feel for them a transport
Of cordiality—   20

But never met this Fellow
Attended, or alone
Without a tighter breathing
And Zero at the Bone—

                                           1866, 1891

1078

The Bustle in a House
The Morning after Death
Is solemnest of industries
Enacted upon Earth—

The Sweeping up the Heart   5
And putting Love away
We shall not want to use again
Until Eternity.

1866   1890

1207

He preached upon "Breadth" till it argued him narrow—
The Broad are too broad to define
And of "Truth" until it proclaimed him a Liar—
The Truth never flaunted a Sign—

Simplicity fled from his counterfeit presence   5
As Gold the Pyrites would shun—
What confusion would cover the innocent Jesus
To meet so enabled a Man!

1872   1891

1540

As imperceptibly as Grief
The Summer lapsed away—
Too imperceptible at last
To seem like Perfidy—
A Quietness distilled   5
As Twilight long begun,
Or Nature spending with herself
Sequestered Afternoon—
The Dusk drew earlier in—
The Morning foreign shone—   10
A courteous, yet harrowing Grace,
As Guest, that would be gone—

And thus, without a Wing
Or service of a Keel
Our Summer made her light escape   15
Into the Beautiful.

                                              1865, 1882?   1891

1755

To make a prairie it takes a clover and one bee,
One clover, and a bee,
And revery.
The revery alone will do,
If bees are few.   5

                                                          1896

CHRISTINA ROSSETTI

Song

When I am dead, my dearest,
    Sing no sad songs for me;
Plant thou no roses at my head,
    Nor shady cypress tree:
Be the green grass above me   5
    With showers and dewdrops wet:
And if thou wilt, remember,
    And if thou wilt, forget.

I shall not see the shadows,
    I shall not feel the rain;   10
I shall not hear the nightingale
    Sing on as if in pain:
And dreaming through the twilight
    That doth not rise nor set,
Haply I may remember,   15
    And haply may forget.

                                              1848   1862

THOMAS HARDY

A Broken Appointment

You did not come,
And marching Time drew on, and wore me numb.
Yet less for loss of your dear presence there
Than that I thus found lacking in your make
That high compassion which can overbear   5
Reluctance for pure lovingkindness' sake
Grieved I, when, as the hope-hour stroked its sum,
You did not come.

You love not me,
And love alone can lend you loyalty;   10
—I know and knew it. But, unto the store
Of human deeds divine in all but name,
Was it not worth a little hour or more
To add yet this: Once you, a woman, came
To soothe a time-torn man; even though it be   15
You love not me?

1902

GERARD MANLEY HOPKINS

God's Grandeur

The world is charged with the grandeur of God.
    It will flame out, like shining from shook foil;
    It gathers to a greatness, like the ooze of oil
Crushed. Why do men then now not reck his rod?
Generations have trod, have trod, have trod;   5
    And all is seared with trade; bleared, smeared with toil;
    And wears man's smudge and shares man's smell: the soil
Is bare now, nor can foot feel, being shod.

And for all this, nature is never spent;
    There lives the dearest freshness deep down things; 10

And though the last lights off the black West went
  Oh, morning, at the brown brink eastward, springs—
Because the Holy Ghost over the bent
  World broods with warm breast and with ah! bright wings.

1877   1895

Felix Randal

Felix Randal the farrier,[1] O is he dead then? my duty all ended,
Who have watched his mould of man, big-boned and hardy-handsome
Pining, pining, till time when reason rambled in it and some
Fatal four disorders, fleshed there, all contended?

Sickness broke him. Impatient, he cursed at first, but mended   5
Being anointed and all; though a heavenlier heart began some
Months earlier, since I had our sweet reprieve and ransom
Tendered to him. Ah well, God rest him all road ever he offended!

This seeing the sick endears them to us, us too it endears.
My tongue had taught thee comfort, touch had quenched thy tears,   10
Thy tears that touched my heart, child, Felix, poor Felix Randal;
How far from then forethought of, all thy more boisterous years,
When thou at the random grim forge, powerful amidst peers,
Didst fettle for the great grey drayhorse his bright and battering sandal!

1880   1918

[As Kingfishers Catch Fire, Dragonflies Draw Flame]

As kingfishers catch fire, dragonflies draw flame;
  As tumbled over rim in roundy wells
  Stones ring; like each tucked[1] string tells, each hung bell's   5
Bow swung finds tongue to fling out broad its name;
Each mortal thing does one thing and the same:
  Deals out that being indoors each one dwells;
  Selves—goes itself; *myself* it speaks and spells,
Crying *What I do is me: for that I came.*

[1]blacksmith

[1]touched, plucked

462

I say more: the just man justices;
    Keeps gráce: thát keeps all his goings graces;   10
Acts in God's eye what in God's eye he is—
    Chríst. For Christ plays in ten thousand places,
Lovely in limbs, and lovely in eyes not his
    To the Father through the features of men's faces.

1882?   1918

[I Wake and Feel the Fell of Dark, Not Day]

I wake and feel the fell of dark, not day.
What hours, O what black hoürs we have spent
This night! what sights you, heart, saw; ways you went!
And more must, in yet longer light's delay.

With witness I speak this. But where I say   5
Hours I mean years, mean life. And my lament
Is cries countless, cries like dead letters sent
To dearest him that lives alas! away.

I am gall, I am heartburn. God's most deep decree
Bitter would have me taste: my taste was me;
Bones built in me, flesh filled, blood brimmed the curse.   10

Selfyeast of spirit a dull dough sours. I see
The lost are like this, and their scourge to be
As I am mine, their sweating selves, but worse.

1885   1918

[My Own Heart Let Me More Have Pity On]

My own heart let me more have pity on; let
Me live to my sad self hereafter kind,
Charitable; not live this tormented mind
With this tormented mind tormenting yet.

I cast for comfort I can no more get   5
By groping round my comfortless, than blind
Eyes in their dark can day or thirst can find
Thirst's all-in-all in all a world of wet.

Soul, self; come, poor Jackself, I do advise
You, jaded, let be; call off thoughts awhile   10
Elsewhere; leave comfort root-room; let joy size

At God knows when to God knows what; whose smile
's not wrung, see you; unforeseen times rather—as skies
Betweenpie mountains—lights a lovely mile.

1885   1918

[Thou Art Indeed Just, Lord . . .]

Justus quidem tu es, Domine, si disputem tecum: verumtamen justa loquar ad te: Quare via impiorum prosperatur? & c.[1]

Thou art indeed just, Lord, if I contend
With thee; but, sir, so what I plead is just.
Why do sinners' ways prosper? and why must
Disappointment all I endeavour end?
   Wert thou my enemy, O thou my friend,   5
How wouldst thou worse, I wonder, than thou dost
Defeat, thwart me? Oh, the sots and thralls of lust
Do in spare hours more thrive than I that spend,
Sir, life upon thy cause. See, banks and brakes
Now, leavèd how thick! lacèd they are again   10
With fretty chervil, look, and fresh wind shakes
Them; birds build—but not I build; no, but strain,
Time's eunuch, and not breed one work that wakes.
Mine, O thou lord of life, send my roots rain.

1889   1893

A. E. HOUSMAN

Loveliest of Trees, the Cherry Now

Loveliest of trees, the cherry now
Is hung with bloom along the bough,
And stands about the woodland ride
Wearing white for Eastertide.

[1]"Righteous art thou, O Lord, when I plead with thee: yet let me talk with thee of thy judgments: Wherefore doth the way of the wicked prosper? . . ." (Jeremiah xii, 1)

From "A Shropshire Lad"—Authorized Edition—from *The Collected Poems of A. E. Housman.* Copyright 1939, 1940, © 1959 by Holt, Rinehart and Winston, Inc. Copyright © 1967, 1968 by Robert E. Symons. Reprinted by permission of Holt, Rinehart and Winston, Inc.; The Society of Authors, literary representative of the Estate of A. E. Housman; and Jonathan Cape Ltd.

Now, of my threescore years and ten,
Twenty will not come again,
And take from seventy springs a score,
It only leaves me fifty more.

And since to look at things in bloom
Fifty springs are little room,
About the woodlands I will go
To see the cherry hung with snow.

5

10

1896

To an Athlete Dying Young

The time you won your town the race
We chaired you through the market-place;
Man and boy stood cheering by,
And home we brought you shoulder-high.

Today, the road all runners come,
Shoulder-high we bring you home,
And set you at your threshold down,
Townsman of a stiller town.

5

Smart lad, to slip betimes away
From fields where glory does not stay
And early though the laurel grows
It withers quicker than the rose.

10

Eyes the shady night has shut
Cannot see the record cut,
And silence sounds no worse than cheers
After earth has stopped the ears:

15

Now you will not swell the rout
Of lads that wore their honors out,
Runners whom renown outran
And the name died before the man.

20

So set, before its echoes fade,
The fleet foot on the sill of shade,
And hold to the low lintel up
The still-defended challenge-cup.

And round that early-laureled head   25
Will flock to gaze the strengthless dead,
And find unwithered on its curls
The garland briefer than a girl's.

                                                                      1896

With Rue My Heart Is Laden

With rue my heart is laden
    For golden friends I had,
For many a rose-lipt maiden
    And many a lightfoot lad.

By brooks too broad for leaping   5
    The lightfoot boys are laid;
The rose-lipt girls are sleeping
    In fields where roses fade.

                                                                      1896

Eight O'clock

He stood, and heard the steeple
    Sprinkle the quarters on the morning town.
One, two, three, four, to market-place and people
    It tossed them down.

Strapped, noosed, nighing his hour,   5
    He stood and counted them and cursed his luck;
And then the clock collected in the tower
    Its strength, and struck.

                                                                      1922

WILLIAM BUTLER YEATS

The Lake Isle of Innisfree

I will arise and go now, and go to Innisfree,
And a small cabin build there, of clay and wattles made:
Nine bean-rows will I have there, a hive for the honey-bee,
And live alone in the bee-loud glade.

And I shall have some peace there, for peace comes dropping slow,　　5
Dropping from the veils of the morning to where the cricket sings;
There midnight's all a glimmer, and noon a purple glow,
And evening full of the linnet's wings.

I will arise and go now, for always night and day
I hear lake water lapping with low sounds by the shore;　　10
While I stand on the roadway, or on the pavements gray,
I hear it in the deep heart's core.

                                                1892

The Wild Swans at Coole

The trees are in their autumn beauty,
The woodland paths are dry,
Under the October twilight the water
Mirrors a still sky;
Upon the brimming water among the stones　　5
Are nine-and-fifty swans.

The nineteenth autumn has come upon me
Since I first made my count;
I saw, before I had well finished,
All suddenly mount　　10
And scatter wheeling in great broken rings
Upon their clamorous wings.

I have looked upon those brilliant creatures,
And now my heart is sore.
All's changed since I, hearing at twilight,　　15
The first time on this shore,

The bell-beat of their wings above my head,
Trod with a lighter tread.

Unwearied still, lover by lover,
They paddle in the cold   20
Companionable streams or climb the air;
Their hearts have not grown old;
Passion or conquest, wander where they will,
Attend upon them still.

But now they drift on the still water,   25
Mysterious, beautiful;
Among what rushes will they build,
By what lake's edge or pool
Delight men's eyes when I awake some day
To find they have flown away?   30

                                                    1917

The Second Coming

Turning and turning in the widening gyre
The falcon cannot hear the falconer;
Things fall apart; the center cannot hold;
Mere anarchy is loosed upon the world,
The blood-dimmed tide is loosed, and everywhere   5
The ceremony of innocence is drowned;
The best lack all conviction, while the worst
Are full of passionate intensity.

Surely some revelation is at hand;
Surely the Second Coming is at hand;   10
The Second Coming! Hardly are those words out
When a vast image out of *Spiritus Mundi*
Troubles my sight: somewhere in sands of the desert
A shape with lion body and the head of a man,
A gaze blank and pitiless as the sun,   15
Is moving its slow thighs, while all about it
Reel shadows of the indignant desert birds.
The darkness drops again; but now I know
That twenty centuries of stony sleep

Were vexed to nightmare by a rocking cradle,   20
And what rough beast, its hour come round at last,
Slouches towards Bethlehem to be born?

1921

Leda and the Swan

A sudden blow: the great wings beating still
Above the staggering girl, her thighs caressed
By the dark webs, her nape caught in his bill,
He holds her helpless breast upon his breast.

How can those terrified vague fingers push   5
The feathered glory from her loosening thighs?
And how can body, laid in that white rush,
But feel the strange heart beating where it lies?

A shudder in the loins engenders there
The broken wall, the burning roof and tower   10
And Agamemnon dead.
                    Being so caught up,
So mastered by the brute blood of the air,
Did she put on his knowledge with his power
Before the indifferent beak could let her drop?   15

1923   1924

Sailing to Byzantium

1

That is no country for old men. The young
In one another's arms, birds in the trees
—Those dying generations—at their song,
The salmon-falls, the mackerel-crowded seas,
Fish, flesh, or fowl, commend all summer long   5
Whatever is begotten, born, and dies.
Caught in that sensual music all neglect
Monuments of unaging intellect.

2

An aged man is but a paltry thing,
A tattered coat upon a stick, unless　　　　　　　　10
Soul clap its hands and sing, and louder sing
For every tatter in its mortal dress,
Nor is there singing school but studying
Monuments of its own magnificence;
And therefore I have sailed the seas and come　　15
To the holy city of Byzantium.

3

O sages standing in God's holy fire
As in the gold mosaic of a wall,
Come from the holy fire, perne in a gyre,
And be the singing-masters of my soul.　　　　　20
Consume my heart away; sick with desire
And fastened to a dying animal
It knows not what it is; and gather me
Into the artifice of eternity.

4

Once out of nature I shall never take　　　　　　25
My bodily form from any natural thing,
But such a form as Grecian goldsmiths make
Of hammered gold and gold enameling
To keep a drowsy Emperor awake;
Or set upon a golden bough to sing　　　　　　30
To lords and ladies of Byzantium
Of what is past, or passing, or to come.

　　　　　　　　　　　　　　　　　　1927

EDWIN ARLINGTON ROBINSON

Miniver Cheevy

Miniver Cheevy, child of scorn,
　　Grew lean while he assailed the seasons;
He wept that he was ever born,
　　And he had reasons.

Miniver loved the days of old   5
    When swords were bright and steeds were prancing;
The vision of a warrior bold
    Would set him dancing.

Miniver sighed for what was not,
    And dreamed, and rested from his labors;   10
He dreamed of Thebes and Camelot,
    And Priam's neighbors.

Miniver mourned the ripe renown
    That made so many a name so fragrant;
He mourned Romance, now on the town,   15
    And Art, a vagrant.

Miniver loved the Medici,
    Albeit he had never seen one;
He would have sinned incessantly
    Could he have been one.   20

Miniver cursed the commonplace
    And eyed a khaki suit with loathing;
He missed the medieval grace
    Of iron clothing.

Miniver scorned the gold he sought,   25
    But sore annoyed was he without it;
Miniver thought, and thought, and thought,
    And thought about it.

Miniver Cheevy, born too late,
    Scratched his head and kept on thinking;   30
Miniver coughed, and called it fate,
    And kept on drinking.

                                                     1910

Uncle Ananias

His words were magic and his heart was true,
    And everywhere he wandered he was blessed.
Out of all ancient men my childhood knew
    I choose him and I mark him for the best.
Of all authoritative liars, too,   5
    I crown him loveliest.

How fondly I remember the delight
    That always glorified him in the spring;

The joyous courage and the benedight[1]
 Profusion of his faith in everything!
He was a good old man, and it was right
 That he should have his fling.   10

And often, underneath the apple-trees,
 When we surprised him in the summer time,
With what superb magnificence and ease   15
 He sinned enough to make the day sublime!
And if he liked us there about his knees,
 Truly it was no crime.

All summer long we loved him for the same
 Perennial inspiration of his lies;   20
And when the russet wealth of autumn came,
 There flew but fairer visions to our eyes—
Multiple, tropical, winged with a feathery flame,
 Like birds of paradise.

So to the sheltered end of many a year   25
 He charmed the seasons out with pageantry
Wearing upon his forehead, with no fear,
 The laurel of approved iniquity.
And every child who knew him, far or near,
 Did love him faithfully.   30

             1910

Mr. Flood's Party

Old Eben Flood, climbing alone one night
Over the hill between the town below
And the forsaken upland hermitage
That held as much as he should ever know
On earth again of home, paused warily.   5
The road was his with not a native near;
And Eben, having leisure, said aloud,
For no man else in Tilbury Town to hear:

"Well, Mr. Flood, we have the harvest moon
Again, and we may not have many more;   10

[1]blessed

The bird is on the wing, the poet says,
And you and I have said it here before.
Drink to the bird." He raised up to the light
The jug that he had gone so far to fill,
And answered huskily: "Well, Mr. Flood,   15
Since you propose it, I believe I will."

Alone, as if enduring to the end
A valiant armor of scarred hopes outworn,
He stood there in the middle of the road
Like Roland's ghost winding a silent horn.   20
Below him, in the town among the trees,
Where friends of other days had honored him,
A phantom salutation of the dead
Rang thinly till old Eben's eyes were dim.

Then, as a mother lays her sleeping child   25
Down tenderly, fearing it may awake,
He set the jug down slowly at his feet
With trembling care, knowing that most things break;
And only when assured that on firm earth
It stood, as the uncertain lives of men   30
Assuredly did not, he paced away,
And with his hand extended paused again:

"Well, Mr. Flood, we have not met like this
In a long time; and many a change has come
To both of us, I fear, since last it was   35
We had a drop together. Welcome home!"
Convivially returning with himself,
Again he raised the jug up to the light,
And with an acquiescent quaver said:
"Well, Mr. Flood, if you insist, I might.   40

"Only a very little, Mr. Flood—
For auld lang syne. No more, sir; that will do."
So, for the time, apparently it did,
And Eben evidently thought so too;
For soon amid the silver loneliness   45
Of night he lifted up his voice and sang,
Secure, with only two moons listening,
Until the whole harmonious landscape rang—

"For auld lang syne." The weary throat gave out,
The last word wavered; and the song being done,   50
He raised again the jug regretfully
And shook his head, and was again alone.

There was not much that was ahead of him,
And there was nothing in the town below—
Where strangers would have shut the many doors   55
That many friends had opened long ago.

                                                                    1920?

STEPHEN CRANE

There Was Crimson Clash of War

There was crimson clash of war.
Lands turned black and bare;
Women wept;
Babes ran, wondering.
There come one who understood not these things.   5
He said: "Why is this?"
Whereupon a million strove to answer him.
There was such intricate clamor of tongues,
That still the reason was not.

                                                                    1895

JAMES WELDON JOHNSON

O Black and Unknown Bards

O black and unknown bards of long ago,
How came your lips to touch the sacred fire?
How, in your darkness, did you come to know
The power and beauty of the ministrel's lyre?
Who first from midst his bonds lifted his eyes?   5
Who first from out the still watch, lone and long,
Feeling the ancient faith of prophets rise
Within his dark-kept soul, burst into song?

Heart of what slave poured out such melody
As "Steal away to Jesus"? On its strains   10
His spirit must have nightly floated free,
Though still about his hands he felt his chains.

Who heard great "Jordan roll"? Whose starward eye
Saw chariot "swing low"? And who was he
That breathed that comforting, melodic sigh,   15
"Nobody knows de trouble I see"?

What merely living clod, what captive thing,
Could up toward God through all its darkness grope,
And find within its deadened heart to sing
These songs of sorrow, love and faith, and hope?   20
How did it catch that subtle undertone,
That note in music heard not with the ears?
How sound the elusive reed so seldom blown,
Which stirs the souls or melts the heart to tears.

Not that great German master in his dream   25
Of harmonies that thundered amongst the stars
At the creation, ever heard a theme
Nobler than "Go down, Moses." Mark its bars
How like a mighty trumpet-call they stir
The blood. Such are the notes that men have sung   30
Going to valorous deeds; such tones that were
That helped make history when Time was young.

There is a wide, wide wonder in it all,
That from degraded rest and servile toil
The fiery spirit of the seer should call   35
These simple children of the sun and soil.
O black slave singers, gone, forgot, unfamed,
You—you alone, of all the long, long line
Of those who've sung untaught, unknown, unnamed,
Have stretched out upward, seeking the divine.   40

You sang not deeds of heroes or of kings;
No chant of bloody war, no exulting pean
Of arms-won triumphs; but your humble strings
You touched in chord with music empyrean.
You sang far better than you knew; the songs   45
That for your listeners' hungry hearts sufficed
Still live,—but more than this to you belongs:
You sang a race from wood and stone to Christ.

1930

PAUL LAURENCE DUNBAR

Little Brown Baby

Little brown baby wif spa'klin' eyes,
   Come to yo' pappy, an' set on his knee.
What you been doin', suh—makin' san' pies?
   Look at dat bib—you's ez du'ty ez me.
Look at dat mouf—dat's merlasses, I bet;   5
   Come hyeah, Maria, an' wipe off his han's.
Bees gwine to ketch you an' eat you up yit,
   Bein' so sticky an sweet—goodness lan's!

Little brown baby wif spa'klin' eyes,
   Who's pappy's darlin' an' who's pappy's chile?   10
Who is it all de day nevah once tries
   Fu' to be cross, er once loses dat smile?
Whah did you git dem teef? My, you's a scamp!
   Whah did dat dimple come f'om in yo' chin?
Pappy do' know you—I b'lieves you's a tramp;   15
   Mammy, dis hyeah's some ol' straggler got in!

Let's th'ow him outen de do' in de san',
   We do' want stragglers a-layin' 'roun' hyeah;
Let's gin him 'way to de big buggah-man;
   I know he's hidin' erroun' hyeah right neah.   20
Buggah-man, buggah-man, come in de do',
Hyeah's a bad boy you kin have fu' to eat.
Mammy an' pappy do' want him no mo',
   Swaller him down f'om his haid to his feet!

Dah, now, I t'ought dat you'd hug me up close.   25
   Go back, ol' buggah, you sha'n't have dis boy.
He ain't no tramp, ner no straggler, of co'se;
   He's pappy's pa'dner an' playmate an' joy.
Come to you' pallet now—go to yo' res';
   Wisht you could allus know ease an' cleah skies;   30
Wisht you could stay jes' a chile on my breas'—
   Little brown baby wif spa'klin' eyes!

1899?

Reprinted by permission of Dodd, Mead & Company, Inc. from *The Complete Poems of Paul Laurence Dunbar*.

The Debt

This is the debt I pay
Just for one riotous day,
Years of regret and grief,
Sorrow without relief.

Pay it I will to the end—   5
Until the grave, my friend,
Gives me a true release—
Gives me the clasp of peace.

Slight was the thing I bought,
Small was the debt I thought,   10
Poor was the loan at best—
God! but the interest!

                                                                   1903

ROBERT FROST

Mending Wall

Something there is that doesn't love a wall,
That sends the frozen-ground-swell under it
And spills the upper boulders in the sun,
And makes gaps even two can pass abreast.
The work of hunters is another thing: 5
I have come after them and made repair
Where they have left not one stone on a stone,
But they would have the rabbit out of hiding,
To please the yelping dogs. The gaps I mean,
No one has seen them made or heard them made,   10
But at spring mending-time we find them there.
I let my neighbor know beyond the hill;
And on a day we meet to walk the line
And set the wall between us once again.
We keep the wall between us as we go.   15
To each the boulders that have fallen to each.
And some are loaves and some so nearly balls
We have to use a spell to make them balance:
"Stay where you are until our backs are turned!"
We wear our fingers rough wtih handling them.   20

Oh, just another kind of outdoor game,
One on a side. It comes to little more:
There where it is we do not need the wall:
He is all pine and I am apple orchard.
My apple trees will never get across   25
And eat the cones under his pines, I tell him.
He only says, "Good fences make good neighbors."
Spring is the mischief in me, and I wonder
If I could put a notion in his head:
"Why do they make good neighbors? Isn't it   30
Where there are cows? But here there are no cows.
Before I built a wall I'd ask to know
What I was walling in or walling out,
And to whom I was like to give offense.
Something there is that doesn't love a wall,   35
That wants it down." I could say "Elves" to him,
But it's not elves exactly, and I'd rather
He said it for himself. I see him there,
Bringing a stone grasped firmly by the top
In each hand, like an old-stone savage armed.   40
He moves in darkness as it seems to me,
Not of woods only and the shade of trees.
He will not go behind his father's saying,
And he likes having thought of it so well
He says again, "Good fences make good neighbors."   45

                                                              1914

Birches

When I see birches bend to left and right
Across the lines of straighter darker trees,
I like to think some boy's been swinging them.
But swinging doesn't bend them down to stay
As ice storms do. Often you must have seen them   5
Loaded with ice a sunny winter morning
After a rain. They click upon themselves
As the breeze rises, and turn many-colored
As the stir cracks and crazes their enamel.

Soon the sun's warmth makes them shed crystal shells
Shattering and avalanching on the snow crust—
Such heaps of broken glass to sweep away
You'd think the inner dome of heaven had fallen.
They are dragged to the withered bracken by the load,
And they seem not to break; though once they are bowed
So low for long, they never right themselves:
You may see their trunks arching in the woods
Years afterwards, trailing their leaves on the ground
Like girls on hands and knees that throw their hair
Before them over their heads to dry in the sun.
But I was going to say when Truth broke in
With all her matter of fact about the ice-storm,
I should prefer to have some boy bend them
As he went out and in to fetch the cows—
Some boy too far from town to learn baseball,
Whose only play was what he found himself,
Summer or winter, and could play alone.
One by one he subdued his father's trees
By riding them down over and over again
Until he took the stiffness out of them,
And not one but hung limp, not one was left
For him to conquer. He learned all there was
To learn about not launching out too soon
And so not carrying the tree away
Clear to the ground. He always kept his poise
To the top branches, climbing carefully
With the same pains you use to fill a cup
Up to the brim, and even above the brim.
Then he flung outward, feet first, with a swish,
Kicking his way down through the air to the ground.
So was I once myself a swinger of birches.
And so I dream of going back to be.
It's when I'm weary of considerations,
And life is too much like a pathless wood
Where your face burns and tickles with the cobwebs
Broken across it, and one eye is weeping
From a twig's having lashed across it open.
I'd like to get away from earth awhile
And then come back to it and begin over.
May no fate willfully misundertsand me
And half grant what I wish and snatch me away
Not to return. Earth's the right place for love:
I don't know where it's likely to go better.
I'd like to go by climbing a birch tree,

And climb black branches up a snow-white trunk   55
Toward heaven, till the tree could bear no more,
But dipped its top and set me down again.
That would be good both going and coming back.
One could do worse than be a swinger of birches.

1916

Stopping by Woods on a Snowy Evening

Whose woods these are I think I know
His house is in the village though;
He will not see me stopping here
To watch his woods fill up with snow.

My little horse must think it queer   5
To stop without a farmhouse near
Between the woods and frozen lake
The darkest evening of the year.

He gives his harness bells a shake
To ask if there is some mistake.   10
The only other sound's the sweep
Of easy wind and downy flake.

The woods are lovely, dark and deep.
But I have promises to keep,
And miles to go before I sleep,   15
And miles to go before I sleep.

1923

The Gift Outright

The land was ours before we were the land's.
She was our land more than a hundred years
Before we were her people. She was ours
In Massachusetts, in Virginia,
But we were England's, still colonials,   5
Possessing what we still were unpossessed by,

Possessed by what we now no more possessed.
Something we were withholding made us weak
Until we found it was ourselves
We were withholding from our land of living,   10
And forthwith found salvation in surrender.
Such as we were we gave ourselves outright
(The deed of gift was many deeds of war)
To the land vaguely realizing westward,
But still unstoried, artless, unenhanced,   15
Such as she was, such as she would become.

1942

Fire and Ice

Some say the world will end in fire,
Some say in ice.
From what I've tasted of desire
I hold with those who favor fire.
But if it had to perish twice,   5
I think I know enough of hate
To say that for destruction ice
Is also great
And would suffice.

Nothing Gold Can Stay

Nature's first green is gold,
Her hardest hue to hold.
Her early leaf's a flower;
But only so an hour.
Then leaf subsides to leaf.   5
So Eden sank to grief,
So dawn goes down to day.
Nothing gold can stay.

CARL SANDBURG

Chicago

Hog Butcher for the World,
Tool Maker, Stacker of Wheat,
Player with Railroads and the Nation's Freight Handler;
Stormy, husky, brawling,
City of the Big Shoulders: 5

They tell me you are wicked and I believe them, for I have seen your painted
    women under the gas lamps luring the farm boys.
And they tell me you are crooked and I answer: Yes, it is true I have seen the
    gunman kill and go free to kill again.
And they tell me you are brutal and my reply is: On the faces of women and
    children I have seen the marks of wanton hunger.
And having answered so I turn once more to those who sneer at this my city
    and I give them back the sneer and say to them:
Come and show me another city with lifted head singing so proud to be alive   10
    and coarse and strong and cunning.
Flinging magnetic curses amid the toil of piling job on job, here is a tall bold
    slugger set vivid against the little soft cities;
Fierce as a dog with tongue lapping for action, cunning as a savage pitted
    against the wilderness,
      Bareheaded,
      Shoveling,
      Wrecking,   15
      Planning,
      Building, breaking, rebuilding,
Under the smoke, dust all over his mouth, laughing with white teeth,
Under the terrible burden of destiny laughing as a young man laughs,
Laughing even as an ignorant fighter laughs who has never lost a battle,   20
Bragging and laughing that under his wrist is the pulse, and under his ribs the
    heart of the people,
             Laughing!
Laughing the stormy, husky, brawling laughter of Youth, half-naked, sweating,
    proud to be Hog Butcher, Tool Maker, Stacker of Wheat, Player with Rail-
    Roads and Freight Handler to the Nation.

                                              1916

Grass

Pile the bodies high at Austerlitz and Waterloo.
Shovel them under and let me work—
>> I am the grass; I cover all.

And pile them high at Gettysburg
And pile them high at Ypres and Verdun.   5
Shovel them under and let me work.
Two years, ten years, and passengers ask the conductor:
>> What place is this?
>> Where are we now?

>> I am the grass.   10
>> Let me work.

>> 1918

Fish Crier

I know a Jew fish crier down on Maxwell Street with a voice like a north wind
    blowing over corn stubble in January.
He dangles herring before prospective customers evincing a joy identical with
    that of Pavlowa dancing.
His face is that of a man terribly glad to be selling fish, terribly glad that God
    made fish, and customers to whom he may call his wares from a pushcart.

Killers

I am singing to you
Soft as a man with a dead child speaks;
Hard as a man in handcuffs,
Held where he cannot move:

Under the sun   5
Are sixteen million men,
Chosen for shining teeth,
Sharp eyes, hard legs,
And a running of young warm blood in their wrists.

And a red juice runs on the green grass;   10
And a red juice soaks the dark soil.
And the sixteen million are killing . . . and killing and killing.

    I never forget them day or night:
They beat on my head for memory of them;
They pound on my heart and I cry back to them,   15
To their homes and women, dreams and games.

    I wake in the night and smell the trenches,
And hear the low stir of sleepers in lines—
Sixteen million sleepers and pickets in the dark:
Some of them long sleepers for always,   20
Some of them tumbling to sleep tomorrow for always,
Fixed in the drag of the world's heartbreak,
Eating and drinking, toiling . . . on a long job of killing.
    Sixteen million men.

WALLACE STEVENS

Sunday Morning

1

Complacencies of the peignoir, and late
Coffee and oranges in a sunny chair,
And the green freedom of a cockatoo
Upon a rug mingle to dissipate
The holy hush of ancient sacrifice.   5
She dreams a little, and she feels the dark
Encroachment of that old catastrophe,
As a calm darkens among water-lights.
The pungent oranges and bright, green wings
Seem things in some procession of the dead,   10
Winding across wide water, without sound.
The day is like wide water, without sound,
Stilled for the passing of her dreaming feet
Over the seas, to silent Palestine,
Dominion of the blood and sepulchre.   15

2

Why should she give her bounty to the dead?
What is divinity if it can come
Only in silent shadows and in dreams?
Shall she not find in comforts of the sun,

In pungent fruit and bright, green wings, or else   20
In any balm or beauty of the earth,
Things to be cherished like the thought of heaven?
Divinity must live within herself:
Passions of rain, or moods in falling snow;
Grievings in loneliness, or unsubdued   25
Elations when the forest blooms; gusty
Emotions on wet roads on autumn nights;
All pleasures and all pains, remembering
The bough of summer and the winter branch.
These are the measures destined for her soul.   30

3

Jove in the clouds had his inhuman birth.
No mother suckled him, no sweet land gave
Large-mannered motions to his mythy mind
He moved among us, as a muttering king,
Magnificent, would move among his hinds,[1]   35
Until our blood, commingling, virginal,
With heaven, brought such requital to desire
The very hinds discerned it, in a star.
Shall our blood fail? Or shall it come to be
The blood of paradise? And shall the earth   40
Seem all of paradise that we shall know?
The sky will be much friendlier then than now,
A part of labor and a part of pain,
And next in glory to enduring love,
Not this dividing and indifferent blue.   45

4

She says, "I am content when wakened birds,
Before they fly, test the reality
Of misty fields, by their sweet questionings;
But when the birds are gone, and their warm fields
Return no more, where, then, is paradise?"   50
There is not any haunt of prophecy,
Nor any old chimera of the grave,
Neither the golden underground, nor isle
Melodious, where spirits gat them home,
Nor visionary south, nor cloudy palm   55
Remote on heaven's hill, that has endured
As April's green endures; or will endure
Like her remembrance of awakened birds,
Or her desire for June and evening, tipped
By the consummation of the swallow's wings.   60

[1]shepherds

5

She says, "But in contentment I still feel
The need of some imperishable bliss."
Death is the mother of beauty; hence from her,
Alone, shall come fulfilment to our dreams
And our desires. Although she strews the leaves   65
Of sure obliteration on our paths,
The path sick sorrow took, the many paths
Where triumph rang its brassy phrase, or love
Whispered a little out of tenderness,
She makes the willow shiver in the sun   70
For maidens who were wont to sit and gaze
Upon the grass, relinquished to their feet.
She causes boys to pile new plums and pears
On disregarded plate. The maidens taste
And stray impassioned in the littering leaves.   75

6

Is there no change of death in paradise?
Does ripe fruit never fall? Or do the boughs
Hang always heavy in that perfect sky,
Unchanging, yet so like our perishing earth,
With rivers like our own that seek for seas   80
They never find, the same receding shores
That never touch with inarticulate pang?
Why set the pear upon those river-banks
Or spice the shores with odors of the plum?
Alas, that they should wear our colors there,   85
The silken weavings of our afternoons,
And pick the strings of our insipid lutes!
Death is the mother of beauty, mystical,
Within whose burning bosom we devise
Our earthly mothers waiting, sleeplessly.   90

7

Supple and turbulent, a ring of men
Shall chant in orgy on a summer morn
Their boisterous devotion to the sun,
Not as a god, but as a god might be,
Naked among them, like a savage source.   95
Their chant shall be a chant of paradise,
Out of their blood, returning to the sky;
And in their chant shall enter, voice by voice,

²celestial beings

The windy lake wherein their lord delights,
The trees, like serafin,[2] and echoing hills,   100
That choir among themselves long afterward.
They shall know well the heavenly fellowship
Of men that perish and of summer morn.
And whence they came and whither they shall go
The dew upon their feet shall manifest.   105

8

She hears, upon that water without sound,
A voice that cries, "The tomb in Palestine
Is not the porch of spirits lingering.
It is the grave of Jesus, where he lay."
We live in an old chaos of the sun,   110
Or old dependency of day and night,
Or island solitude, unsponsored, free,
Of that wide water, inescapable.
Deer walk upon our mountains, and the quail
Whistle about us their spontaneous cries;   115
Sweet berries ripen in the wilderness;
And, in the isolation of the sky,
At evening, casual flocks of pigeons make
Ambiguous undulations as they sink,
Downward to darkness, on extended wings.   120

                                            1915   1923

The Idea of Order at Key West

She sang beyond the genius of the sea.
The water never formed to mind or voice,
Like a body wholly body, fluttering
Its empty sleeves; and yet its mimic motion
Made constant cry, caused constantly a cry,   5
That was not ours although we understood,
Inhuman, of the veritable ocean.

The sea was not a mask. No more was she.
The song and water were not medleyed sound
Even if what she sang was what she heard,   10
Since what she sang was uttered word by word.
It may be that in all her phrases stirred

The grinding water and the gasping wind;
But it was she and not the sea we heard.
For she was the maker of the song she sang. 15
The ever-hooded, tragic-gestured sea
Was merely a place by which she walked to sing.
Whose spirit is this? we said, because we knew
It was the spirit that we sought and knew
That we should ask this often as she sang. 20

If it was only the dark voice of the sea
That rose, or even colored by many waves;
If it was only the outer voice of sky
And cloud, of the sunken coral water-walled,
However clear, it would have been deep air, 25
The heaving speech of air, a summer sound
Repeated in a summer without end
And sound alone. But it was more than that,
More even than her voice, and ours, among
The meaningless plungings of water and the wind, 30
Theatrical distances, bronze shadows heaped
On high horizons, mountainous atmospheres
Of sky and sea.
                    It was her voice that made
The sky acutest at its vanishing. 35
She measured to the hour its solitude.
She was the single artificer of the world
In which she sang. And when she sang, the sea,
Whatever self it had, became the self
That was her song, for she was the maker. Then we, 40
As we beheld her striding there alone,
Knew that there never was a world for her
Except the one she sang and, singing, made.

Ramon Fernandez, tell me, if you know,
Why, when the singing ended and we turned 45
Toward the town, tell why the glassy lights,
The lights in the fishing boats at anchor there,
As the night descended, tilting in the air,
Mastered the night and portioned out the sea,
Fixing emblazoned zones and fiery poles, 50
Arranging, deepening, enchanting night.

Oh! Blessed rage for order, pale Ramon,
The maker's rage to order words of the sea,
Words of the fragrant portals, dimly-starred,

And of ourselves and of our origins,
In ghostlier demarcations, keener sounds.

1935

WILLIAM CARLOS WILLIAMS

Portrait of a Lady

Your thighs are appletrees
whose blossoms touch the sky.
Which sky? The sky
where Watteau hung a lady's
slipper. Your knees   5
are a southern breeze—or
a gust of snow. Agh! what
sort of man was Fragonard?
—as if that answered
anything. Ah, yes—below   10
the knees, since the tune
drops that way, it is
one of those white summer days,
the tall grass of your ankles
flickers upon the shore—   15
Which shore?—
the sand clings to my lips—
Which shore?
Agh, petals maybe. How
should I know?   20
Which shore? Which shore?
I said petals from an appletree.

1915

The Young Housewife

At ten A.M. the young housewife
moves about in negligee behind

the wooden walls of her husband's house.
I pass solitary in my car.

Then again she comes to the curb   5
to call the ice-man, fish-man, and stands
shy, uncorseted, tucking in
stray ends of hair, and I compare her
to a fallen leaf.

The noiseless wheels of my car   10
rush with a crackling sound over
dried leaves as I bow and pass smiling.

                                                                    1917

The Red Wheelbarrow

so much depends
upon

a red wheel
barrow

glazed with rain   5
water

beside the white
chickens.

                                                                    1923

EZRA POUND

The Garden

En robe de parade.
    —Samain

Like a skein of loose silk blown against a wall
She walks by the railing of a path in Kensington Gardens,
And she is dying piecemeal
        of a sort of emotional anemia.

And round about there is a rabble   5
Of the filthy, sturdy, unkillable infants of the very poor.
They shall inherit the earth.

In her is the end of breeding.
Her boredom is exquisite and excessive.
She would like some one to speak to her,   10
And is almost afraid that I
            will commit that indiscretion.

1916

In a Station of the Metro

The apparition of these faces in the crowd;
Petals on a wet, black bough.

1916

ROBINSON JEFFERS

Boats in a Fog

Sports and gallantries, the stage, the arts, the antics of dancers,
The exuberant voices of music,
Have charm for children but lack nobility; it is bitter earnestness
That makes beauty; the mind
Knows, grown adult.   5
            A sudden fog-drift muffled the ocean,
A throbbing of engines moved in it,
At length, a stone's throw out, between the rocks and the vapor,
One by one moved shadows
Out of the mystery, shadows, fishing-boats, trailing each other,   10
Following the cliff for guidance,
Holding a difficult path between the peril of the sea-fog
And the foam on the shore granite.
One by one, trailing their leader, six crept by me,
Out of the vapor and into it,   15
The throb of their engines subdued by the fog, patient and cautious,
Coasting all round the peninsula
Back to the buoys in Monterey harbor. A flight of pelicans
Is nothing lovelier to look at;
The flight of the planets is nothing nobler; all the arts lose virtue   20

Against the essential reality
Of creatures going about their business among the equally
Earnest elements of nature.

1924

To the Stone-Cutters

Stone-cutters fighting time with marble, you foredefeated
Challengers of oblivion
Eat cynical earnings, knowing rock splits, records fall down,
The square-limbed Roman letters
Scale in the thaws, wear in the rain.   5
    The poet as well
Builds his monument mockingly;
For man will be blotted out, the blithe earth die, the brave sun
Die blind, his heart blackening:
Yet stones have stood for a thousand years, and pained thoughts found   10
The honey peace in old poems.

1925

Night

The ebb slips from the rock, the sunken
Tide-rocks lift streaming shoulders
Out of the slack, the slow west
Sombering its torch; a ship's light
Shows faintly, far out,   5
Over the weight of the prone ocean
On the low cloud.

Over the dark mountain, over the dark pinewood,
Down the long dark valley along the shrunken river,
Returns the splendor without rays, the shining of shadow,   10
Peace-bringer, the matrix of all shining and quieter of shining.
Where the shore widens on the bay she opens dark wings
And the ocean accepts her glory. O soul worshipful of her
You like the ocean have grave depths where she dwells always,
And the film of waves above that takes the sun takes also   15

Her, with more love. The sun-lovers have a blond favorite,
A father of lights and noises, wars, weeping and laughter,
Hot labor, lust and delight and the other blemishes. Quietness
Flows from her deeper fountain; and he will die; and she is immortal.

Far off from here the slender   20
Flocks of the mountain forest
Move among stems like towers
Of the old redwoods to the stream,
No twig crackling; dip shy
Wild muzzles into the mountain water   25
Among the dark ferns.

O passionately at peace you being secure will pardon
The blasphemies of glowworms, the lamp in my tower, the fretfulness
Of cities, the cressets of the planets, the pride of the stars.
This August night in a rift of cloud Antares reddens,   30
The great one, the ancient torch, a lord among lost children,
The earth's orbit doubled would not girdle his greatness, one fire
Globed, out of grasp of the mind enormous; but to you O Night
What? Not a spark? What flicker of a spark in the faint far glimmer
Of a lost fire dying in the desert, dim coals of a sand-pit the Bedouins   35
Wandered from at dawn . . . Ah singing prayer to what gulfs tempted
Suddenly are you more lost? To us the near-hand mountain
Be a measure of height, the tide-worn cliff at the sea-gate a measure
        of continuance.

The tide, moving the night's
Vastness with lonely voices,   40
Turns, the deep dark-shining
Pacific leans on the land,
Feeling his cold strength
To the outmost margins: you Night will resume
The stars in your time.   45

O passionately at peace when will that tide draw shoreward?
Truly the spouting fountains of light, Antares, Arcturus,
Tire of their flow, they sing one song but they think silence.
The striding winter giant Orion shines, and dreams darkness.
And life, the flicker of men and moths and the wolf on the hill, 50
Though furious for continuance, passionately feeding, passionately
Remaking itself upon its mates, remembers deep inward
The calm mother, the quietness of the womb and the egg,
The primal and the latter silences: dear Night it is memory
Prophesies, prophecy that remembers, the charm of the dark.   55
And I and my people, we are willing to love the four-score years
Heartily; but as a sailor loves the sea, when the helm is for harbor.

Have men's minds changed,
Or the rock hidden in the deep of the waters of the soul
Broken the surface? A few centuries 60
Gone by, was none dared not to people
The darkness beyond the stars with harps and habitations.
But now, dear is the truth. Life is grown sweeter and lonelier,
And death is no evil.

1925

Shine, Perishing Republic

While this America settles in the mold of its vulgarity, heavily thickening to
    empire,
And protest, only a bubble in the molten mass, pops and sighs out, and the
    mass hardens,

I sadly smiling remember that the flower fades to make fruit, the fruit rots to
    make earth.
Out of the mother; and through the spring exultances, ripeness and decadence;
    and home to the mother.

You making haste haste on decay: not blameworthy; life is good, be it stubbornly   5
    long or suddenly
A mortal splendor: meteors are not needed less than mountains: shine, perishing
    republic.

But for my children, I would have them keep their distance from the thickening
    center; corruption
Never has been compulsory, when the cities lie at the monster's feet there are
    left the mountains.

And boys, be in nothing so moderate as in love of man, a clever servant,
    insufferable master.
There is the trap that catches noblest spirits, that caught—they say—God, when   10
    he walked on earth.

1924

T. S. ELIOT

The Love Song of J. Alfred Prufrock

S'io credesse che mia risposta fosse
A persona che mai tornasse al mondo,
Questa fiamma staria senza piu scosse.
Ma perciocche giammai di questo fondo
Non torno vivo alcun, s'i'odo il vero,
Senza tema d'infamia ti rispondo.[1]

From Collected Poems 1909–1962 by T. S. Eliot. Reprinted by permission of Harcourt Brace Jovanovich, Inc. and Faber and Faber Ltd.

[1]"If I thought that my reply would be to one who would ever return to the world, this flame would stay without further movement; but since none has ever returned alive from this depth, if what I hear is true, I answer you without fear of infamy." Dante, Inferno (xxvii, 61–66).

Let us go then, you and I,
When the evening is spread out against the sky
Like a patient etherized upon a table;
Let us go, through certain half-deserted streets,
The muttering retreats   5
Of restless nights in one-night cheap hotels
And sawdust restaurants with oyster-shells:
Streets that follow like a tedious argument
Of insidious intent
To lead you to an overwhelming question. . .   10
Oh, do not ask, "What is it?"
Let us go and make our visit.

In the room the women come and go
Talking of Michelangelo.

The yellow fog that rubs its back upon the window-panes   15
The yellow smoke that rubs its muzzle on the window-panes
Licked its tongue into the corners of the evening,
Lingered upon the pools that stand in drains,
Let fall upon its back the soot that falls from chimneys,
Slipped by the terrace, made a sudden leap,   20
And seeing that it was a soft October night,
Curled once about the house, and fell asleep.

And indeed there will be time
For the yellow smoke that slides along the street,
Rubbing its back upon the window-panes;   25
There will be time, there will be time
To prepare a face to meet the faces that you meet;
There will be time to murder and create,
And time for all the works and days of hands
That lift and drop a question on your plate;   30
Time for you and time for me,
And time yet for a hundred indecisions,
And for a hundred visions and revisions,
Before the taking of a toast and tea.

In the room the women come and go   35
Talking of Michelangelo.

And indeed there will be time
To wonder, "Do I dare?" and, "Do I dare?"
Time to turn back and descend the stair,
With a bald spot in the middle of my hair—   40
[They will say: "How his hair is growing thin!"]
My morning coat, my collar mounting firmly to the chin,

My necktie rich and modest, but asserted by a simple pin—
[They will say: "But how his arms and legs are thin!"]
Do I dare   45
Disturb the universe?
In a minute there is time
For decisions and revisions which a minute will reverse.

For I have known them all already, known them all:
Have known the evenings, mornings, afternoons,   50
I have measured out my life with coffee spoons;
I know the voices dying with a dying fall
Beneath the music from a farther room.
    So how should I presume?

And I have known the eyes already, known them all—   55
The eyes that fix you in a formulated phrase,
And when I am formulated, sprawling on a pin,
When I am pinned and wriggling on the wall,
Then how should I begin
To spit out all the butt-ends of my days and ways?   60
    And how should I presume?

And I have known the arms already, known them all—
Arms that are braceleted and white and bare
[But in the lamplight, downed with light brown hair!]
Is it perfume from a dress   65
That makes me so digress?
Arms that lie along a table, or wrap about a shawl.
    And should I then presume?
    And how should I begin?

                 .   .   .   .   .

Shall I say, I have gone at dusk through narrow streets   70
And watched the smoke that rises from the pipes
Of lonely men in shirt-sleeves, leaning out of windows? . . .

I should have been a pair of ragged claws
Scuttling across the floors of silent seas.

                 .   .   .   .   .

And the afternoon, the evening, sleeps so peacefully!   75
Smoothed by long fingers,
Asleep . . . tired . . . or it malingers,
Stretched on the floor, here beside you and me.
Should I, after tea and cakes and ices,
Have the strength to force the moment to its crisis?   80
But though I have wept and fasted, wept and prayed.
Though I have seen my head [grown slightly bald] brought in upon a platter,

I am no prophet—and here's no great matter;
I have seen the moment of my greatness flicker,
And I have seen the eternal Footman hold my coat, and snicker,   85
And in short, I was afraid.

And would it have been worth it, after all,
After the cups, the marmalade, the tea,
Among the porcelain, among some talk of you and me,
Would it have been worth while,   90
To have bitten off the matter with a smile,
To have squeezed the universe into a ball
To roll it toward some overwhelming question,
To say: "I am Lazarus, come from the dead,
Come back to tell you all, I shall tell you all"—   95
If one, settling a pillow by her head,
    Should say: "That is not what I meant at all.
    That is not it, at all."

And would it have been worth it, after all,
Would it have been worth while,   100
After the sunsets and the dooryards and the sprinkled streets,
After the novels, after the teacups, after the skirts that trail along the floor—
And this, and so much more?—
It is impossible to say just what I mean!
But as if a magic lantern threw the nerves in patterns on a screen: 105
Would it have been worth while
If one, settling a pillow or throwing off a shawl,
And turning toward the window, should say:
    "That is not it at all."
    That is not what I meant, at all."   110

        .   .   .   .   .   .

No! I am not Prince Hamlet, nor was meant to be;
Am an attendant lord, one that will do
To swell a progress, start a scene or two,
Advise the prince; no doubt, an easy tool,
Deferential, glad to be of use,   115
Politic, cautious, and meticulous;
Full of high sentence,[2] but a bit obtuse;
At times, indeed, almost ridiculous—
Almost, at times, the Fool.
I grow old . . . I grow old . . .   120
I shall wear the bottoms of my trousers rolled.

Shall I part my hair behind? Do I dare to eat a peach?

[2]sententiousness

I shall wear white flannel trousers, and walk upon the beach.
I have heard the mermaids singing, each to each.
I do not think that they will sing to me.   125

I have seen them riding seaward on the waves
Combing the white hair of the waves blown back
When the wind blows the water white and black.

We have lingered in the chambers of the sea
By sea-girls wreathed with seaweed red and brown   130
Till human voices wake us, and we drown.

                                                    1917

The Hollow Men

Mistah Kurtz—he dead.

                                      A penny for the Old Guy

I

        We are the hollow men
        We are the stuffed men
        Leaning together
        Headpiece filled with straw. Alas!
        Our dried voices, when   5
        We whisper together
        Are quiet and meaningless
        As wind in dry grass
        Or rats' feet over broken glass
        In our dry cellar   10

            Shape without form, shade without colour,
        Paralysed force, gesture without motion;

            Those who have crossed
        With direct eyes, to death's other Kingdom
        Remember us—if at all—not as lost   15
        Violent souls, but only
        As the hollow men
        The stuffed men.

II

        Eyes I dare not meet in dreams
        In death's dream kingdom   20

These do not appear:
There, the eyes are
Sunlight on a broken column
There, is a tree swinging
And voices are   25
In the wind's singing
More distant and more solemn
Than a fading star.

   Let me be no nearer
In death's dream kingdom   30
Let me also wear
Such deliberate disguises
Rat's coat, crowskin, crossed staves
In a field
Behaving as the wind behaves   35
No nearer—

   Not that final meeting
In the twilight kingdom

III

This is the dead land
This is cactus land   40
Here the stone images
Are raised, here they receive
The supplication of a dead man's hand
Under the twinkle of a fading star.

   Is it like this   45
In death's other kingdom
Waking alone
At the hour when we are
Trembling with tenderness
Lips that would kiss   50
Form prayers to broken stone.

IV

The eyes are not here
There are no eyes here
In this valley of dying stars
In this hollow valley   55
This broken jaw of our lost kingdoms

   In this last of meeting places
We grope together
And avoid speech

Gathered on this beach of the tumid river   60

    Sightless, unless
The eyes reappear
As the perpetual star
Multifoliate rose
Of death's twilight kingdom   65
The hope only
Of empty men.

V

Here we go round the prickly pear
Prickly pear prickly pear
Here we go round the prickly pear   70
At five o'clock in the morning.

    Between the idea
And the reality
Between the motion
And the act   75
Falls the Shadow

                        For Thine is the Kingdom

    Between the conception
And the creation
Between the emotion
And the response   80
Falls the Shadow

                        Life is very long

    Between the desire
And the spasm
Between the potency
And the existence   85
Between the essence
And the descent
Falls the Shadow

                        For Thine is the Kingdom

    For Thine is
Life is   90
For Thine is the

    This is the way the world ends
This is the way the world ends
This is the way the world ends
Not with a bang but a whimper.   95

                      1925

Journey of the Magi

'A cold coming we had of it,
Just the worst time of the year
For a journey, and such a long journey:
The ways deep and the weather sharp,
The very dead of winter.'   5
And the camels galled, sore-footed, refractory,
Lying down in the melting snow.
There were times we regretted
The summer palaces on slopes, the terraces,
And the silken girls bringing sherbet.   10
Then the camel men cursing and grumbling
And running away, and wanting their liquor and women,
And the night-fires going out, and the lack of shelters,
And the cities hostile and the towns unfriendly
And the villages dirty and charging high prices: 15
A hard time we had of it.
At the end we preferred to travel all night,
Sleeping in snatches,
With the voices singing in our ears, saying
That this was all folly.   20

Then at dawn we came down to a temperate valley,
Wet, below the snow line, smelling of vegetation;
With a running stream and a water-mill beating the darkness,
And three trees on the low sky,
And an old white horse galloped away in the meadow.   25
Then we came to a tavern with vine-leaves over the lintel,
Six hands at an open door dicing for pieces of silver,
And feet kicking the empty wine-skins.
But there was no information, and so we continued
And arrived at evening, not a moment too soon   30
Finding the place; it was (you may say) satisfactory.

All this was a long time ago, I remember,
And I would do it again, but set down
This set down
This: were we led all that way for   35
Birth or Death? There was a Birth, certainly,
We had evidence and no doubt. I had seen birth and death,
But had thought they were different; this Birth was
Hard and bitter agony for us, like Death, our death.
We returned to our places, these Kingdoms,   40
But no longer at ease here, in the old dispensation,

With an alien people clutching their gods.
I should be glad of another death.

1927

ARCHIBALD MAC LEISH

You, Andrew Marvell

And here face down beneath the sun
And here upon earth's noonward height
To feel the always coming on
The always rising of the night

To feel creep up the curving east   5
The earthy chill of dusk and slow
Upon those under lands the vast
And ever climbing shadow grow

And strange at Ecbatan the trees
Take leaf by leaf the evening strange   10
The flooding dark about their knees
The mountains over Persia change

And now at Kermanshah the gate
Dark empty and the withered grass
And through the twilight now the late   15
Few travelers in the westward pass

And Baghdad darken and the bridge
Across the silent river gone
And through Arabia the edge
Of evening widen and steal on   20

And deepen on Palmyra's street
The wheel rut in the ruined stone
And Lebanon fade out and Crete
High through the clouds and overblown

And over Sicily the air   25
Still flashing with the landward gulls
And loom and slowly disappear
The sails above the shadowy hulls

And Spain go under and the shore
Of Africa the gilded sand   30
And evening vanish and no more
The low pale light across that land

Nor now the long light on the sea
And here face downward in the sun
To feel how swift how secretly   35
The shadow of the night comes on. . . .

                                                                                1930

Empire Builders

The Museum Attendant:

This is *The Making of America in Five Panels:*

This is Mister Harriman making America:
Mister-Harriman-is-buying-the-Union-Pacific-at-Seventy:
The Sante Fe is shining on his hair.

This is Commodore Vanderbilt making America: 5
Mister-Vanderbilt-is-eliminating-the-short-interest-in-Hudson:
Observe the carving on the rocking chair.

This is J. P. Morgan making America:
(The Tennessee Coal is behind to the left of the Steel Company.)
Those in mauve are braces he is wearing.   10

This is Mister Mellon making America:
Mister-Mellon-is-represented-as-a-symbolic-figure-in-aluminum-
Strewing-bank-stocks-on-a-burnished-stair.

This is the Bruce is the Barton making America:
Mister-Barton-is-selling-us-Doctor's-Deliciousest-Dentifrice.
This is he in biege with the canary.   15

You have just beheld the Makers making America:
This is The Making of America in Five Panels:
America lies to the west-southwest of the switch-tower:
There is nothing to see of America but land.   20

The Original Document under the Panel Paint:

"To Thos. Jefferson Esq. his obd't serv't
M. Lewis: captain: detached:
                              Sir:

Having in mind your repeated commands in this matter,
And the worst half of it done and the streams mapped,   25

And we here on the back of this beach beholding the
Other ocean—two years gone and the cold

Breaking with rain for the third spring since St. Louis,
The crows at the fishbones on the frozen dunes,

The first cranes going over from south north,   30
And the river down by a mark of the pole since the morning,

And time near to return, and a ship (Spanish)
Lying in for the salmon, and fearing chance or the

Drought or the Sioux should deprive you of these discoveries—
Therefore we send by sea in this writing.   35

                                 Above the
Platte there were long plains and a clay country:
Rim of the sky far off, grass under it,

Dung for the cook fires by the sulphur licks.
After that there were low hills and the sycamores,   40

And we poled up by the Great Bend in the skiffs:
The honey bees left us after the Osage River.

The wind was west in the evening, and no dew and the
Morning Star larger and whiter than usual—

The winter rattling in the brittle haws.   45
The second year there was sage and the quail calling.

All that valley is good land by the river:
Three thousand miles and the clay cliffs and

Rue and beargrass by the water banks
And many birds and the brant going over and tracks of   50

Bear, elk, wolves, marten: the buffalo
Numberless so that the cloud of their dust covers them:

The antelope fording the fall creeks, and the mountains and
Grazing lands and the meadow lands and the ground

Sweet and open and well-drained.   55
                            We advise you to
Settle troops at the forks and to issue licenses:

Many men will have living on these lands.
There is wealth in the earth for them all and the wood standing

And wild birds on the water where they sleep.   60
There is stone in the hills for the towns of a great people . . ."

You have just beheld the Makers Making America:

They screwed her scrawny and gaunt with their seven-year panics:
They bought her back on their mortgages old-whore-cheap:

They fattened their bonds at her breasts till the thin blood ran from them.   65

Men have forgotten how full clear and deep
The Yellowstone moved on the gravel and the grass grew
When the land lay waiting for her westward people!

                                                                          1933

Not Marble nor the Gilded Monuments

The praisers of women in their proud and beautiful poems
Naming the grave mouth and the hair and the eyes
Boasted those they loved should be forever remembered
These were lies

The words sound but the face in the Istrian sun is forgotten   5
The poet speaks but to her dead ears no more
The sleek throat is gone—and the breast that was troubled to listen
Shadow from door

Therefore I will not praise your knees nor your fine walking
Telling you men shall remember your name as long   10
As lips move or breath is spent or the iron of English
Rings from a tongue

I shall say you were young and your arms straight and your mouth scarlet
I shall say you will die and none will remember you
Your arms change and none remember the swish of your garments   15
Nor the click of your shoe

Not with my hand's strength not with difficult labor
Springing the obstinate words to the bones of your breast
And the stubborn line to your young stride and the breath to your breathing
And the beat to your haste   20
Shall I prevail on the hearts of unborn men to remember

(What is a dead girl but a shadowy ghost
Or a dead man's voice but a distant and vain affirmation
Like dream words most)
Therefore I will not speak of the undying glory of women   25
I will say you were young and straight and your skin fair
And you stood in the door and the sun was a shadow of leaves on your shoulders
And a leaf on your hair

I will not speak of the famous beauty of dead women
I will say the shape of a leaf lay once on your hair   30
Till the world ends and the eyes are out and the mouths broken
Look! It is there!

E. E. CUMMINGS

All in Green Went My Love Riding

All in green went my love riding
on a great horse of gold
into the silver dawn.

four lean hounds crouched low and smiling
the merry deer ran before.   5

Fleeter be they than dappled dreams
the swift sweet deer
the red rare deer.

Four red roebuck at a white water
the cruel bugle sang before.   10

Horn at hip went my love riding
riding the echo down
into the silver dawn.

four lean hounds crouched low and smiling
the level meadows ran before.   15

Softer be they than slippered sleep
the lean lithe deer
the fleet flown deer.

Four fleet does at a gold valley
the famished arrow sang before.   20

Bow at belt went my love riding
riding the mountain down
into the silver dawn.

four lean hounds crouched low and smiling
the sheer peaks ran before.   25

Paler be they than daunting death
the sleek slim deer
the tall tense deer.

Four tall stags at a green mountain
the lucky hunter sang before.   30

All in green went my love riding
on a great horse of gold
into the silver dawn.

four lean hounds crouched low and smiling
my heart fell dead before.   35

In Just-   spring

in Just-
spring   when the world is mud-
luscious the little
lame balloonman

whistles   far   and wee   5

and eddieandbill come
running from marbles and
piracies and it's
spring

when the world is puddle-wonderful   10

the queer
old balloonman whistles
far   and   wee
and bettyandisbel come dancing

from hop-scotch and jump-rope and   15

it's
spring
and
     the

          goat-footed   20
balloonMan   whistles
far
and
wee

1923

the Cambridge ladies who live in furnished souls

the Cambridge ladies who live in furnished souls
are unbeautiful and have comfortable minds
(also, with the church's protestant blessings
daughters, unscented shapeless spirited)
they believe in Christ and Longfellow, both dead,   5
are invariably interested in so many things—
at the present writing one still finds
delighted fingers knitting for the is it Poles?
perhaps. While permanent faces coyly bandy
scandal of Mrs. N and Professor D   10
. . . . the Cambridge ladies do not care, above
Cambridge if sometimes in its box of
sky lavender and cornerless, the
moon rattles like a fragment of angry candy

1923

"next to of course god america i

"next to of course god america i
love you land of the pilgrims' and so forth oh
say can you see by the dawn's early my
country 'tis of centuries come and go
and are no more what of it we should worry   5
in every language even deafanddumb
thy sons acclaim your glorious name by gorry
by jingo by gee by gosh by gum
why talk of beauty what could be more beautiful than these heroic happy dead   10
who rushed like lions to the roaring slaughter
they did not stop to think they died instead
then shall the voice of liberty be mute?"
He spoke. And drank rapidly a glass of water

1926

anyone lived in a pretty how town

anyone lived in a pretty how town
(with up so floating many bells down)

spring summer autumn winter
he sang his didn't he danced his did.

Women and men(both little and small)   5
cared for anyone not at all
they sowed their isn't they reaped their same
sun moon stars rain

children guessed(but only a few
and down they forgot as up they grew   10
autumn winter spring summer)
that noone loved him more by more

when by now and tree by leaf
she laughed his joy she cried his grief
bird by snow and stir by still   15
anyone's any was all to her

someones married their everyones
laughed their cryings and did their dance
(sleep wake hope and then)they
said their nevers they slept their dream   20

stars rain sun moon
(and only the snow can begin to explain
how children are apt to forget to remember
with up so floating many bells down)

one day anyone died i guess   25
(and noone stooped to kiss his face)
busy folk buried them side by side
little by little and was by was

all by all and deep by deep
and more by more they dream their sleep   30
noone and anyone earth by april
wish by spirit and if by yes.

Women and men(both dong and ding)
summer autumn winter spring
reaped their sowing and went their came   35
sun moon stars rain

                                              1940

i sing of Olaf glad and big

i sing of Olaf glad and big
whose warmest heart recoiled at war:
a conscientious object-or

his wellbelovéd colonel(trig
westpointer most succinctly bred)
took erring Olaf soon in hand;
but—though an host of overjoyed
noncoms(first knocking on the head
him)do through icy waters roll
that helplessness which others stroke
with brushes recently employed
anent this muddy toiletbowl,
while kindred intellects evoke
allegiance per blunt instruments—
Olaf (being to all intents
a corpse and wanting any rag
upon what God unto him gave)
responds,without getting annoyed
"I will not kiss your f.ing flag"

straightway the silver bird looked grave
(departing hurriedly to shave)

but—though all kinds of officers
(a yearning nation's blueeyed pride)
their passive prey did kick and curse
until for wear their clarion
voices and boots were much the worse,
and egged the firstclassprivates on
his rectum wickedly to tease
by means of skilfully applied
bayonets roasted hot with heat—
Olaf(upon what were once knees)
does almost ceaselessly repeat
"there is some s. I will not eat"

our president,being of which
assertions duly notified
threw the yellowsonofabitch
into a dungeon,where he died
Christ(of His mercy infinite)
i pray to see;and Olaf,too

preponderatingly because
unless statistics lie he was
more brave than me:more blond than you.

HART CRANE

Proem: To Brooklyn Bridge

How many dawns, chill from his rippling rest
The seagull's wings shall dip and pivot him,
Shedding white rings of tumult, building high
Over the chained bay waters Liberty—

Then, with inviolate curve, forsake our eyes   5
As apparitional as sails that cross
Some page of figures to be filed away;
—Till elevators drop us from our day . . .

I think of cinemas, panoramic sleights
With multitudes bent toward some flashing scene   10
Never disclosed, but hastened to again,
Foretold to other eyes on the same screen;

And Thee, across the harbor, silver-paced
As though the sun took steps of thee, yet left
Some motion ever unspent in thy stride,—   15
Implicitly thy freedom staying thee!

Out of some subway scuttle, cell or loft
A bedlamite speeds to thy parapets,
Tilting there momently, shrill shirt ballooning,
A jest falls from the speechless caravan.   20

Down Wall, from girder into street noon leaks,
A rip-tooth of the sky's acetylene;
All afternoon the cloud-flown derricks turn . . .
Thy cables breathe the North Atlantic still.

And obscure as that heaven of the Jews,   25
Thy guerdon . . . Accolade thou dost bestow
Of anonymity time cannot raise;
Vibrant reprieve and pardon thou dost show.

O harp and altar, of the fury fused,
(How could mere toil align thy choiring strings!)   30
Terrific threshold of the prophet's pledge,
Prayer of pariah, and the lover's cry,—

Again the traffic lights that skim thy swift
Unfractioned idiom, immaculate sigh of stars,
Beading thy path—condense eternity: 35
And we have seen night lifted in thine arms.

Under thy shadow by the piers I waited;
Only in darkness is thy shadow clear.
The City's fiery parcels all undone,
Already snow submerges an iron year . . .   40

O Sleepless as the river under thee,
Vaulting the sea, the prairies' dreaming sod,
Unto us lowliest sometime sweep, descend
And of the curveship lend a myth to God.

The River

[. . . and past the din and slogans of the year—]

Stick your patent name on a signboard
brother—all over—going west—young man
Tintex—Japalac—Certain-teed Overalls ads
and lands sakes! under the new playbill ripped
in the guaranteed corner—see Bert Williams what?   5
Minstrels when you steal a chicken just
save me the wing for if it isn't
Erie it ain't for miles around a
Mazda—and the telegraphic night coming on Thomas
a Ediford—and whistling down the tracks   10
a headlight rushing with the sound—can you
imagine—while an EXpress makes time like
SCIENCE—COMMERCE and the HOLYGHOST
RADIO ROARS IN EVERY HOME WE HAVE THE NORTHPOLE
WALLSTREET AND VIRGINBIRTH WITHOUT STONES OR   15
WIRES OR EVE RUNning brooks connecting ears
and no more sermons windows flashing roar
Breathtaking—as you like it . . . eh?

                    So the 20th Century—so
whizzed the Limited—roared by and left   20
three men, still hungry on the tracks, ploddingly
watching the tail lights wizen and converge, slipping gimleted and neatly out of sight.

                    *

[to those whose addresses are never near]

The last bear, shot drinking in the Dakotas

512

Loped under wires that span the mountain stream.   25
Keen instruments, strung to a vast precision
Bind town to town and dream to ticking dream.
But some men take their liquor slow—and count
—Though they'll confess no rosary nor clue—
The river's minute by the far brook's year.   30
Under a world of whistles, wires and steam
Caboose-like they go ruminating through
Ohio, Indiana—blind baggage—
To Cheyenne tagging . . . Maybe Kalamazoo.

Time's rendings, time's blendings they construe   35
As final reckonings of fire and snow;
Strange bird-wit, like the elemental gist
Of unwalled winds they offer, singing low
My Old Kentucky Home and *Casey Jones*,
Some Sunny Day. I heard a road-gang chanting so.   40
And afterwards, who had a colt's eyes—one said,
"Jesus! Oh I remember watermelon days!" And sped
High in a cloud of merriment, recalled
"—And when my Aunt Sally Simpson smiled," he
     drawled—   45
"It was almost Louisiana, long ago."
"There's no place like Booneville though, Buddy,"
One said, excising a last burr from his vest,
"—For early trouting." Then peering in the can,
"—But I kept on the tracks." Possessed, resigned,   50
He trod the fire down pensively and grinned,
Spreading dry shingles of a beard. . . .

                         Behind
My father's cannery works I used to see
Rail-squatters ranged in nomad raillery,
The ancient men—wifeless or runaway   55
Hobo-trekkers that forever search
An empire wilderness of freight and rails.
Each seemed a child, like me, on a loose perch,
Holding to childhood like some termless play.
John, Jake or Charley, hopping the slow freight   60
—Memphis to Tallahassee—riding the rods,
Blind fists of nothing, humpty-dumpty clods.

[but who have touched her, knowing her without name]

Yet they touch something like a key perhaps.
From pole to pole across the hills, the states
—They know a body under the wide rain;   65

Youngsters with eyes like fjords, old reprobates
With racetrack jargon,—dotting immensity
They lurk across her, knowing her yonder breast
Snow-silvered, sumac-stained or smoky blue—
Is past the valley-sleepers, south or west.   70
—As I have trod the rumorous midnights, too,
And past the circuit of the lamp's thin flame
(O Nights that brought me to her body bare!)
Have dreamed beyond the print that bound her name.
Trains sounding the long blizzards out—I heard   75
Wail into distances I knew were hers.
Papooses crying on the wind's long mane
Screamed redskin dynasties that fled the brain,
—Dead echoes! But I knew her body there,
Time like a serpent down her shoulder, dark,   80
And space, an eaglet's wing, laid on her hair.

[nor the myths of her fathers . . .]

Under the Ozarks, domed by Iron Mountain,
The old gods of the rain lie wrapped in pools
Where eyeless fish curvet a sunken fountain
And re-descend with corn from querulous crows.   85
Such pilferings make up their timeless eatage,
Propitiate them for their timber torn
By iron, iron—always the iron dealt cleavage!
They doze now, below axe and powder horn.

And Pullman breakfasters glide glistening steel   90
From tunnel into field—iron strides the dew—
Straddles the hill, a dance of wheel on wheel.
You have a half-hour's wait at Siskiyou,
Or stay the night and take the next train through.
Southward, near Cairo passing, you can see   95
The Ohio merging,—borne down Tennessee;
And if it's summer and the sun's in dusk
Maybe the breeze will lift the River's musk
—As though the waters breathed that you might know
Memphis Johnny, Steamboat Bill, Missouri Joe.   100
Oh, lean from the window, if the train slows down,
As though you touched hands with some ancient clown,
—A little while gaze absently below
And hum Deep River with them while they go.

Yes, turn again and sniff once more—look see,   105
O Sheriff, Brakeman and Authority—
Hitch up your pants and crunch another quid,

For you, too, fed the River timelessly.
And few evade full measure of their fate;
Always they smile out eerily what they seem.   110
I could believe he joked at heaven's gate—
Dan Midland—jolted from the cold brake-beam.

Down, down—born pioneers in time's despite,
Grimed tributaries to an ancient flow—
They win no frontier by their wayward plight,   115
But drift in stillness, as from Jordan's brow.

You will not hear it as the sea; even stone
Is not more hushed by gravity . . . But slow,
As loth to take more tribute—sliding prone
Like one whose eyes were buried long ago   120

The River, spreading, flows—and spends your dream.
What are you, lost within this tideless spell?
You are your father's father, and the stream—
A liquid theme that floating niggers swell.

Damp tonnage and alluvial march of days—   125
Nights turbid, vascular with silted shale
And roots surrendered down of moraine clays:
The Mississippi drinks the farthest dale.

O quarrying passion, undertowed sunlight!
The basalt surface drags a jungle grace   130
Ochreous and lynx-barred in lengthening might;
Patience; and you shall reach the biding place!

Over De Soto's bones the freighted floors
Throb past the City storied of three thrones.
Down two more turns the Mississippi pours   135
(Anon tall ironsides up from salt lagoons)

And flows within itself, heaps itself free.
All fades but one thin skyline 'round . . . Ahead
No embrace opens but the stinging sea;
The River lifts itself from its long bed,   140

Poised wholly on its dream, a mustard glow
Tortured with history, its one will—flow!
—The Passion spreads in wide tongues, choked and slow,
Meeting the Gulf, hosannas silently below.

National Winter Garden

Outspoken buttocks in pink beads
Invite the necessary cloudy clinch
Of bandy eyes. . . . No extra mufflings here:
The world's one flagrant, sweating cinch.

And while legs waken salads in the brain   5
You pick your blonde out neatly through the smoke.
Always you wait for someone else though, always—
(Then rush the nearest exit through the smoke).

Always and last, before the final ring
When all the fireworks blare, begins   10
A tom-tom scrimmage with a somewhere violin,
Some cheapest echo of them all—begins.

And shall we call her whiter than the snow?
Sprayed first with ruby, then with emerald sheen—
Least tearful and least glad (who knows her smile?)   15
A caught slide shows her sandstone grey between.

Her eyes exist in swivellings of her teats,
Pearls whip her hips, a drench of whirling strands.
Her silly snake rings begin to mount, surmount
Each other—turquoise fakes on tinselled hands.   20

We wait that writhing pool, her pearls collapsed,
—All but her belly buried in the floor;
And the lewd trounce of a final muted beat!
We flee her spasm through a fleshless door. . . .

Yet, to the empty trapeze of your flesh,   25
O Magdalene, each comes back to die alone.
Then you, the burlesque of our lust—and faith,
Lug us back lifeward—bone by infant bone.

ALLEN TATE

Ode to the Confederate Dead

Row after row with strict impunity
The headstones yield their names to the element,
The wind whirrs without recollection;
In the riven troughs the splayed leaves

"Ode to the Confederate Dead" is reprinted with the permission of Charles Scribner's Sons from *Poems* (1960) by Allen Tate.

Pile up, of nature the casual sacrament   5
To the seasonal eternity of death;
Then driven by the fierce scrutiny
Of heaven to their election in the vast breath,
They sough the rumor of mortality.

Autumn is desolation in the plot   10
Of a thousand acres where these memories grow
From the inexhaustible bodies that are not
Dead, but feed the grass row after rich row.
Think of the autumns that have come and gone!
Ambitious November with the humors of the year,   15
With a particular zeal for every slab,
Staining the uncomfortable angels that rot
On the slabs, a wing chipped here, an arm there:
The brute curiosity of an angel's stare
Turns you, like them, to stone,   20
Transforms the heaving air
Till plunged to a heavier world below
You shift your sea-space blindly
Heaving, turning like the blind crab.

    Dazed by the wind, only the wind   25
    The leaves flying, plunge

You know who have waited by the wall
The twilight certainty of an animal,
Those midnight restitutions of the blood
You know—the immitigable pines, the smoky frieze   30
Of the sky, the sudden call: you know the rage,
The cold pool left by the mounting flood,
Of muted Zeno and Parmenides.
You who have waited for the angry resolution
Of those desires that should be yours tomorrow,   35
You know the unimportant shrift of death
And praise the vision
And praise the arrogant circumstance
Of those who fall
Rank upon rank, hurried beyond decision—   40
Here by the sagging gate, stopped by the wall.

    Seeing, seeing only the leaves
    Flying, plunge and expire

Turn your eyes to the immoderate past,
Turn to the inscrutable infantry rising   45
Demons out of the earth—they will not last.

Stonewall, Stonewall, and the sunken fields of hemp,
Shiloh, Antietam, Malvern Hill, Bull Run.
Lost in that orient of the thick and fast
You will curse the setting sun.   50

   Cursing only the leaves crying
   Like an old man in a storm

You hear the shout, the crazy hemlocks point
With troubled fingers to the silence which
Smothers you, a mummy, in time.   55
    The hound bitch
Toothless and dying, in a musty cellar
Hears the wind only.

    Now that the salt of their blood
Stiffens the saltier oblivion of the sea,   60
Seals the malignant purity of the flood,
What shall we who count our days and bow
Our heads with a commemorial woe
In the ribboned coats of grim felicity,
What shall we say of the bones, unclean,   65
Whose verdurous anonymity will grow?

The ragged arms, the ragged heads and eyes
Lost in these acres of the insane green?
The gray lean spiders come, they come and go;
In a tangle of willows without light   70
The singular screech-owl's tight
Invisible lyric seeds the mind
With the furious murmur of their chivalry.

   We shall say only the leaves
   Flying, plunge and expire   75

We shall say only the leaves whispering
In the improbable mist of nightfall
That flies on multiple wing:
Night is the beginning and the end
And in between the ends of distraction   80
Waits mute speculation, the patient curse
That stones the eyes, or like the jaguar leaps
For his own image in a jungle pool, his victim.

What shall we say who have knowledge
Carried to the heart? Shall we take the act   85
To the grave? Shall we, more hopeful, set up the grave
In the house? The ravenous grave?

Leave now
The shut gate and the decomposing wall:
The gentle serpent, green in the mulberry bush,   90
Riots with his tongue through the hush—
Sentinel of the grave who counts us all!

1928

LANGSTON HUGHES

The Negro Speaks of Rivers

(To W. E. B. Dubois)

I've known rivers:
I've known rivers ancient as the world and older than the
    flow of human blood in human veins.

My soul has grown deep like the rivers.

I bathed in the Euphrates when dawns were young.   5
I built my hut near the Congo and it lulled me to sleep.
I looked upon the Nile and raised the pyramids above it.
I heard the singing of the Mississippi when Abe Lincoln
    went down to New Orleans, and I've seen its muddy
    bosom turn all golden in the sunset.   10

I've known rivers:
Ancient, dusky rivers.

My soul has grown deep like the rivers.

1926

COUNTEE CULLEN

Heritage

For Harold Jackman

What is Africa to me:
Copper sun or scarlet sea,

Jungle star or jungle track,
Strong bronzed men, or regal black
Women from whose loins I sprang   5
When the birds of Eden sang?
One three centuries removed
From the scenes his fathers loved,
Spicy grove, cinnamon tree,
What is Africa to me?   10

So I lie, who all day long
Want no sound except the song
Sung by wild barbaric birds
Goading massive jungle herds,
Juggernauts of flesh that pass   15
Trampling tall defiant grass
Where young forest lovers lie,
Plighting troth beneath the sky.
So I lie, who always hear,
Though I cram against my ear   20
Both my thumbs, and keep them there,
Great drums throbbing through the air.
So I lie, whose fount of pride,
Dear distress, and joy allied,
Is my somber flesh and skin,   25
With the dark blood dammed within
Like great pulsing tides of wine
That, I fear, must burst the fine
Channels of the chafing net
Where they surge and foam and fret.   30

Africa? A book one thumbs
Listlessly, till slumber comes.
Unremembered are her bats
Circling through the night, her cats
Crouching in the river reeds,   35
Stalking gentle flesh that feeds
By the river brink; no more
Does the bugle-throated roar
Cry that monarch claws have leapt
From the scabbards where they slept.   40
Silver snakes that once a year
Doff the lovely coats you wear,
Seek no covert in your fear
Lest a mortal eye should see;
What's your nakedness to me?   45
Here no leprous flowers rear

Fierce corollas in the air;
Here no bodies sleek and wet,
Dripping mingled rain and sweat,
Tread the savage measures of 50
Jungle boys and girls in love.
What is last year's snow to me,
Last year's anything? The tree
Budding yearly must forget
How its past arose or set— 55
Bough and blossom, flower, fruit,
Even what shy bird with mute
Wonder at her travail there,
Meekly labored in its hair.
One three centuries removed 60
From the scenes his fathers loved,
Spicy grove, cinnamon tree,
What is Africa to me?

So I lie, who find no peace
Night or day, no slight release 65
From the unremittent beat
Made by cruel padded feet
Walking through my body's street.
Up and down they go, and back,
Treading out a jungle track. 70
So I lie, who never quite
Safely sleep from rain at night—
I can never rest at all
When the rain begins to fall;
Like a soul gone mad with pain 75
I must match its weird refrain;
Ever must I twist and squirm,
Writhing like a baited worm,
While its primal measures drip
Through my body, crying, "Strip! 80
Doff this new exuberance.
Come and dance the Lover's Dance!"
In an old remembered way
Rain works on me night and day.
Quaint, outlandish heathen gods 85
Black men fashion out of rods,
Clay, and brittle bits of stone,
In a likeness like their own,
My conversion came high-priced;
I belong to Jesus Christ, 90

Preacher of Humility;
Heathen gods are naught to me.

Father, Son, and Holy Ghost,
So I make an idle boast;
Jesus of the twice-turned cheek,   95
Lamb of God, although I speak
With my mouth thus, in my heart
Do I play a double part.
Ever at Thy glowing altar
Must my heart grow sick and falter,   100
Wishing He I served were black,
Thinking then it would not lack
Precedent of pain to guide it,
Let who would or might deride it;

Surely then this flesh would know   105
Yours had borne a kindred woe.
Lord, I fashion dark gods, too,
Daring even to give You
Dark despairing features where,
Crowned with dark rebellious hair,   110
Patience wavers just so much as
Mortal grief compels, while touches
Quick and hot, of anger, rise
To smitten cheek and weary eyes.
Lord, forgive me if my need   115
Sometimes shapes a human creed.
All day long and all night through,
One thing only must I do:
Quench my pride and cool my blood,
Lest I perish in the flood,   120
Lest a hidden ember set
Timber that I thought was wet
Burning like the dryest flax,
Melting like the merest wax,
Lest the grave restore its dead.   125
Not yet has my heart or head
In the least way realized
They and I are civilized.

                                              1925

Yet Do I Marvel

I doubt not God is good, well-meaning, kind.
And did He stoop to quibble could tell why
The little buried mole continues blind,
Why flesh that mirrors Him must some day die,
Make plain the reason tortured Tantalus   5
Is baited by the fickle fruit, declare
If merely brute caprice dooms Sisyphus
To struggle up a never-ending stair.
Inscrutable His ways are, and immune
To catechism by a mind too strewn   10
With petty cares to slightly understand
What awful brain compels His awful hand.
Yet do I marvel at this curious thing:
To make a poet black, and bid him sing!

W. H. AUDEN

Musée des Beaux Arts

About suffering they were never wrong,
The Old Masters: how well they understood
Its human position; how it takes place
While someone else is eating or opening a window or just walking dully along;
How, when the aged are reverently, passionately waiting   5
For the miraculous birth, there always must be
Children who did not specially want it to happen, skating
On a pond at the edge of the wood:
They never forgot
That even the dreadful martyrdom must run its course   10
Anyhow in a corner, some untidy spot
Where the dogs go on with their doggy life and the torturer's horse
Scratches its innocent behind on a tree.

In Breughel's *Icarus*, for instance: how everything turns away
Quite leisurely from the disaster; the ploughman may   15
Have heard the splash, the forsaken cry,
But for him it was not an important failure; the sun shone

As it had to on the white legs disappearing into the green
Water; and the expensive delicate ship that must have seen
Something amazing, a boy falling out of the sky,   20
Had somewhere to get to and sailed calmly on.

1940

THEODORE ROETHKE

Root Cellar

Nothing would sleep in that cellar, dank as a ditch,
Bulbs broke out of boxes hunting for chinks in the dark,
Shoots dangled and drooped,
Lolling obscenely from mildewed crates,
Hung down long yellow evil necks, like tropical snakes.   5
And what a congress of stinks!
Roots ripe as old bait,
Pulpy stems, rank, silo-rich,
Leaf-mold, manure, lime, piled against slippery planks.
Nothing would give up life: 10
Even the dirt kept breathing a small breath.

1948

The Meadow Mouse

1

In a shoe box stuffed in an old nylon stocking
Sleeps the baby mouse I found in the meadow,
Where he trembled and shook beneath a stick
Till I caught him up by the tail and brought him in,
Cradled in my hand,   5
A little quaker, the whole body of him trembling,
His absurd whiskers sticking out like a cartoon-mouse,
His feet like small leaves,
Little lizard-feet,
Whitish and spread wide when he tried to struggle away,   10
Wriggling like a minuscule puppy.

Now he's eaten his three kinds of cheese and drunk from his bottle-cap watering-
    trough—
So much he just lies in one corner,
His tail curled under him, his belly big   15
As his head; his bat-like ears
Twitching, tilting toward the least sound.
Do I imagine he no longer trembles
When I come close to him?
He seems no longer to tremble.   20

2

But this morning the shoe-box house on the back porch is empty.
Where has he gone, my meadow mouse,
My thumb of a child that nuzzled in my palm?
To run under the hawk's wing,
Under the eye of the great owl watching from the elm-tree,   25
To live by courtesy of the shrike, the snake, the tom-cat.

I think of the nestling fallen into the deep grass,
The turtle gasping in the dusty rubble of the highway,
The paralytic stunned in the tub, and the water rising—
All things innocent, hapless, forsaken.   30

1964

STEPHEN SPENDER

The Cries of Evening

I hear the cries of evening, while the paw
Of dark, creeps up the turf:
Sheep bleating, swaying gull's cry, the rook's "Caw,"
The hammering surf.

I am inconstant, yet this constancy   5
Of natural rest, pulls at my heart;
Town-bred, I feel the roots of each earth-cry
Tear me apart.

These are the creaking of the dusty day
When the dog Night bites sharp,   10
These fingers grip my soul and tear away
And pluck me like a harp.

I feel the huge sphere turn, the great wheel sing
While beasts move to their ease:
Sheep's love, gull's peace—I feel my chattering   15
Uncared by these.

                                                                    1933

HENRY REED

Lessons of the War

To Alan Mitchell

Vixi duellis nuper idoneus
Et militavi non sine gloria

1. Naming of Parts

Today we have naming of parts. Yesterday,
We had daily cleaning. And tomorrow morning,
We shall have what to do after firing. But today,
Today we have naming of parts. Japonica
Glistens like coral in all of the neighboring gardens,   5
        And today we have naming of parts.

This is the lower sling swivel. And this
Is the upper sling swivel, whose use you will see,
When you are given your slings. And this is the piling swivel,
Which in your case you have not got. The branches   10
Hold in the gardens their silent, eloquent gestures,
    Which in our case we have not got.

This is the safety-catch, which is always released
With an easy flick of the thumb. And please do not let me
See anyone using his finger. You can do it quite easy   15
If you have any strength in your thumb. The blossoms
Are fragile and motionless, never letting anyone see
        Any of them using their finger.

And this you can see is the bolt. The purpose of this
Is to open the breech, as you see. We can slide it   20
Rapidly backwards and forwards: we call this
Easing the spring. And rapidly backwards and forwards
The early bees are assaulting and fumbling the flowers:
        They call it easing the Spring.

They call it easing the Spring: it is perfectly easy 25
If you have any strength in your thumb: like the bolt,
And the breech, and the cocking-piece, and the point of balance,
Which in our case we have not got; and the almond-blossom
Silent in all of the gardens and the bees going backwards and forwards,
      For today we have naming of parts. 30

2. Judging Distances

Not only how far away, but the way that you say it
Is very important. Perhaps you may never get
The knack of judging a distance, but at least you know
How to report on a landscape: the central sector,
The right of arc and that, which we had last Tuesday, 35
      And at least you know

That maps are of time, not place, so far as the army
Happens to be concerned—the reason being,
Is one which need not delay us. Again, you know
There are three kinds of tree, three only, the fir and the poplar, 40
And those which have bushy tops to; and lastly
      That things only seem to be things.

A barn is not called a barn, to put it more plainly,
Or a field in the distance, where sheep may be safely grazing.
You must never be over-sure. You must say, when reporting: 45
At five o'clock in the central sector is a dozen
Of what appear to be animals; whatever you do,
      Don't call the bleeders *sheep*.

I am sure that's quite clear; and suppose, for the sake of example,
The one at the end, asleep, endeavors to tell us 50
What he sees over there to the west, and how far away,
After first having come to attention. There to the west,
On the fields of summer the sun and the shadows bestow
      Vestments of purple and gold.

The still white dwellings are like a mirage in the heat, 55
And under the swaying elms a man and a woman
Lie gently together. Which is, perhaps, only to say
That there is a row of houses to the left of arc,
And that under some poplars a pair of what appear to be humans
      Appear to be loving. 60

Well that, for an answer, is what we might rightly call
Moderately satisfactory only, the reason being,
Is that two things have been omitted, and those are important.
The human beings, now: in what direction are they,

And how far away, would you say? And do not forget   65
    There may be dead ground in between.

There may be dead ground in between; and I may not have got
The knack of judging a distance; I will only venture
A guess that perhaps between me and the apparent lovers,
(Who, incidentally, appear by now to have finished,)   70
At seven o'clock from the houses, is roughly a distance
    Of about one year and a half.

3. Unarmed Combat

In due course of course you will all be issued with
Your proper issue; but until tomorrow,
You can hardly be said to need it; and until that time,   75
We shall have unarmed combat. I shall teach you
The various holds and rolls and throws and breakfalls
    Which you may sometimes meet.

And the various holds and rolls and throws and breakfalls
Do not depend on any sort of weapon,   80
But only on what I might coin a phrase and call
The ever-important question of human balance,
And the ever-important need to be in a strong
    Position at the start.

There are many kinds of weakness about the body   85
Where you would least expect, like the ball of the foot.
But the various holds and rolls and throws and breakfalls
Will always come in useful. And never be frightened
To tackle from behind: it may not be clean to do so,
    But this is global war.   90

So give them all you have, and always give them
As good as you get; it will always get you somewhere.
(You may not know it, but you can tie a Jerry
Up without rope; it is one of the things I shall teach you.)
Nothing will matter if only you are ready for him.   95
    The readiness is all.

The readiness is all. How can I help but feel
I have been here before? But somehow then,
I was the tied-up one. How to get out
Was always then my problem. And even if I had   100
A piece of rope I was always the sort of person
    Who threw the rope aside.

And in my time I have given them all I had,
Which was never as good as I got, and it got me nowhere.

And the various holds and rolls and throws and breakfalls   105
Somehow or other I always seemed to put
In the wrong place. And as for war, my wars
        Were global from the start.

Perhaps I was never in a strong position,
Or the ball of my foot got hurt, or I had some weakness   110
Where I had least expected. But I think I see your point.
While awaiting a proper issue, we must learn the lesson
Of the ever-important question of human balance.
        It is courage that counts.

Things may be the same again; and we must fight   115
Not in the hope of winning but rather of keeping
Something alive: so that when we meet our end,
It may be said that we tackled wherever we could,
That battle-fit we lived, and though defeated,
        Not without glory fought.   120

                                                                        1946

DYLAN THOMAS

The Force That Through the Green Fuse Drives the Flower

The force that through the green fuse drives the flower
Drives my green age; that blasts the roots of trees
Is my destroyer.
And I am dumb to tell the crooked rose
My youth is bent by the same wintry fever.   5

The force that drives the water through the rocks
Drives my red blood; that dries the mouthing streams
Turns mine to wax.
And I am dumb to mouth unto my veins
How at the mountain spring the same mouth sucks.   10

The hand that whirls the water in the pool
Stirs the quicksand; that ropes the blowing wind
Hauls my shroud sail.

And I am dumb to tell the hanging man
How of my clay is made the hangman's lime.   15

The lips of time leech to the fountain head;
Love drips and gathers, but the fallen blood
Shall calm her sores.
And I am dumb to tell a weather's wind
How time has ticked a heaven round the stars.   20

And I am dumb to tell the lover's tomb
How at my sheet goes the same crooked worm.

                                                                              1934

Fern Hill

Now as I was young and easy under the apple boughs
About the lilting house and happy as the grass was green,
    The night above the dingle starry,
        Time let me hail and climb
    Golden in the heydays of his eyes,   5
And honored among wagons I was prince of the apple towns
And once below a time I lordly had the trees and leaves
        Trail with daisies and barley
    Down the rivers of the windfall light.

And as I was green and carefree, famous among the barns   10
About the happy yard and singing as the farm was home,
    In the sun that is young once only,
        Time let me play and be
    Golden in the mercy of his means,
And green and golden I was huntsman and herdsman, the calves   15
Sang to my horn, the foxes on the hills barked clear and cold,
        And the sabbath rang slowly
    In the pebbles of the holy streams.

All the sun long it was running, it was lovely, the hay
Fields high as the house, the tunes from the chimneys, it was air   20
    And playing, lovely and watery
        And fire green as grass.
    And nightly under the simple stars
As I rode to sleep the owls were bearing the farm away,

All the moon long I heard, blessed among stables, the night-jars   25
    Flying with the ricks, and the horses
        Flashing into the dark.

And then to awake, and the farm, like a wanderer white
With the dew, come back, the cock on his shoulder: it was all
    Shining, it was Adam and maiden,   30
        The sky gathered again
    And the sun grew round that very day.
So it must have been after the birth of the simple light
In the first, spinning place, the spellbound horses walking warm
    Out of the whinnying green stable   35
        On to the fields of praise.

And honored among foxes and pheasants by the gay house
Under the new made clouds and happy as the heart was long,
    In the sun born over and over,
        I ran my heedless ways,   40
    My wishes raced through the house high hay
And nothing I cared, at my sky blue trades, that time allows
In all his tuneful turning so few and such morning songs
    Before the children green and golden
        Follow him out of grace,   45

Nothing I cared, in the lamb white days, that time would take me
Up to the swallow thronged loft by the shadow of my hand,
    In the moon that is always rising,
        Nor that riding to sleep
    I should hear him fly with the high fields   50
And wake to the farm forever fled from the childless land.
Oh as I was young and easy in the mercy of his means,
        Time held me green and dying
    Though I sang in my chains like the sea.

        1946

In My Craft or Sullen Art

In my craft or sullen art
Exercised in the still night
When only the moon rages
And the lovers lie abed
With all their griefs in their arms,   5
I labor by singing light
Not for ambition or bread

Or the strut and trade of charms
On the ivory stages
But for the common wages   10
Of their most secret heart.

Not for the proud man apart
From the raging moon I write
On these spindrift pages
Nor for the towering dead   15
With their nightingales and psalms
But for the lovers, their arms
Round the griefs of the ages,
Who pay no praise or wages
Nor heed my craft or art.   20

1946

GWENDOLYN BROOKS

kitchenette building

We are things of dry hours and the involuntary plan,
Grayed in, and gray. "Dream" makes a giddy sound, not strong
Like "rent," "feeding a wife," "satisfying a man."

But could a dream send up through onion fumes
Its white and violet, fight with fried potatoes   5
And yesterday's garbage ripening in the hall,
Flutter, or sing an aria down these rooms

Even if we were willing to let it in,
Had time to warm it, keep it very clean,
Anticipate a message, let it begin?   10

We wonder. But not well! not for a minute!
Since Number Five is out of the bathroom now,
We think of lukewarm water, hope to get in it.

1945

my dreams, my works, must wait till after hell

I hold my honey and I store my bread
In little jars and cabinets of my will.
I label clearly, and each latch and lid
I bid, Be firm till I return from hell.
I am very hungry. I am incomplete.   5
And none can tell when I may dine again.
No man can give me any word but Wait,
The puny light. I keep eyes pointed in;
Hoping that, when the devil days of my hurt
Drag out to their last dregs and I resume   10
On such legs as are left me, in such heart
As I can manage, remember to go home,
My taste will not have turned insensitive
To honey and bread old purity could love.

1945

Medgar Evers

For Charles Evers

The man whose height his fear improved he
arranged to fear no further. The raw
intoxicated time was time for better birth or
a final death.

Old styles, old tempos, all the engagement of   5
the day—the sedate, the regulated fray—
the antique light, the Moral rose, old gusts,
tight whistlings from the past, the mothballs
in the Love at last our man forswore.

Medgar Evers annoyed confetti and assorted   10
brands of businessmen's eyes.

The shows came down: to maxims and surprise.
And palsy.

Roaring no rapt arise-ye to the dead, he
leaned across tomorrow. People said that   15
he was holding clean globes in his hands.

1968

From *In the Mecca* by Gwendolyn Brooks. Copyright © 1964 by Gwendolyn Brooks Blakely. Reprinted by permission of Harper & Row, Publishers, Inc.

LAWRENCE FERLINGHETTI

The Pennycandystore Beyond the El

The pennycandystore beyond the El
is where I first
        fell in love
                with unreality
Jellybeans glowed in the semi-gloom   5
of that september afternoon
A cat upon the counter moved among
                the licorice sticks
        and tootsie rolls
        and Oh Boy Gum   10

Outside the leaves were falling as they died

A wind had blown away the sun

A girl ran in
Her hair was rainy
Her breasts were breathless in the little room   15

Outside the leaves were falling
        and they cried
              Too soon! too soon!

                              1958

Sweet and Various the Woodlark

        sweet and various the woodlark

           who sings at the unbought gate

    and yet how many

        wild beasts
           how many mad   5
    in the civil thickets

        Hölderlin
           in his stone tower
  or in that kind carpenter's house

at Tübingen

or then Rimbaud

his "nightmare and logic"

a sophism of madness

But we have our own more recent

who also fatally assumed   15

that some direct connection

does exist between

language and reality

word and world

which is a laugh   20

if you ask me

I too have drunk and seen

the spider

1958

RICHARD WILBUR

Objects

Meridians are a net
Which catches nothing; that sea-scampering bird
The gull, though shores lapse every side from sight, can yet
Sense him to land, but Hanno had not heard

Hesperidean song,   5
Had he not gone by watchful periploi:
Chalk rocks, and isles like beasts, and mountain stains along
The water-hem, calmed him at last nearby

The clear high hidden chant
Blown from the spellbound coast, where under drifts   10
Of sunlight, under plated leaves, they guard the plant
By praising it. Among the wedding gifts

Of Herë, were a set
Of golden McIntoshes, from the Greek
Imagination. Guard and gild what's common, and forget   15
Uses and prices and names; have objects speak.

There's classic and there's quaint,
And then there is that devout intransitive eye

From *Things of this World*, © 1956, by Richard Wilbur. Reprinted by permission of Harcourt Brace Jovanovich, Inc.

Of Pieter de Hooch: see feinting from his plot of paint
The trench of light on boards, the much-mended dry   20

Courtyard wall of brick,
And sun submerged in beer, and streaming in glasses,
The weave of a sleeve, the careful and undulant tile. A quick
Change of the eye and all this calmly passes

Into a day, into magic.   25
For is there any end to true textures, to true
Integuments; do they ever desist from tacit, tragic
Fading away? Oh maculate, cracked, askew,

Gay-pocked and potsherd world
I voyage, where in every tangible tree   30
I see afloat among the leaves, all calm and curled,
The Cheshire smile which sets me fearfully free.

                                                         1947

Beasts

            Beasts in their major freedom
          Slumber in peace tonight. The gull on his ledge
Dreams in the guts of himself the moon-plucked waves below,
          And the sunfish leans on a stone, slept
              By the lyric water;   5

              In which the spotless feet
          Of deer make dulcet splashes, and to which
The ripped mouse, safe in the owl's talon, cries
          Concordance. Here there is no such harm
              And no such darkness   10

          As the self-same moon observes
        Where, warped in window-glass, it sponsors now
The werewolf's painful change. Turning his head away
          On the sweaty bolster, he tries to remember
              The mood of manhood,   15

              But lies at last, as always,
          Letting it happen, the fierce fur soft to his face,
Hearing with sharper ears the wind's exciting minors,
          The leaves' panic, and the degradation
              Of the heavy streams.   20

Meantime, at high windows
Far from thicket and pad-fall, suitors of excellence
Sigh and turn from their work to construe again the painful
Beauty of heaven, the lucid moon
And the risen hunter,   25

Making such dreams for men
As told will break their hearts as always, bringing
Monsters into the city, crows on the public statues,
Navies fed to the fish in the dark
Unbridled waters.   30

THOM GUNN

On the Move

"Man, you gotta Go."

The blue jay scuffling in the bushes follows
Some hidden purpose, and the gust of birds
That spurts across the field, the wheeling swallows,
Have nested in the trees and undergrowth.
Seeking their instinct, or their poise, or both,   5
One moves with an uncertain violence
Under the dust thrown by a baffled sense
Or the dull thunder of approximate words.

On motorcycles, up the road, they come:
Small, black, as flies hanging in heat, the Boys,   10
Until the distance throws them forth, their hum
Bulges to thunder held by calf and thigh.
In goggles, donned impersonality,
In gleaming jackets trophied with the dust,
They strap in doubt—by hiding it, robust—   15
And almost hear a meaning in their noise.

Exact conclusion of their hardiness
Has no shape yet, but from known whereabouts
They ride, direction where the tires press.
They scare a flight of birds across the field: 20

From *The Sense of Movement* by Thom Gunn. Reprinted by permission of Faber and Faber Ltd.

Much that is natural, to the will must yield.
Men manufacture both machine and soul,
And use what they imperfectly control
To dare a future from the taken routes.

It is a part solution, after all.   25
One is not necessarily discord
On earth; or damned because, half animal,
One lacks direct instinct, because one wakes
Afloat on movement that divides and breaks.
One joins the movement in a valueless world,   30
Choosing it, till, both hurler and the hurled,
One moves as well, always toward, toward.

A minute holds them, who have come to go:
The self-defined, astride the created will
They burst away; the towns they travel through   35
Are home for neither bird nor holiness,
For birds and saints complete their purposes.
At worst, one is in motion; and at best,
Reaching no absolute, in which to rest,
One is always nearer by not keeping still.   40

Tamer and Hawk

I thought I was so tough,
But gentled at your hands
Cannot be quick enough
To fly for you and show
That when I go I go   5
At your commands.

Even in flight above
I am no longer free:
You seeled me with your love,
I am blind to other birds—   10
The habit of your words
Has hooded me.

As formerly, I wheel
I hover and I twist,
But only want the feel,   15
In my possessive thought,
Of catcher and of caught
Upon your wrist.

From *Fighting Terms* by Thom Gunn. Reprinted by permission of Faber and Faber Ltd.

You but half civilise,
Taming me in this way.
Through having only eyes
For you I fear to lose,
I lose to keep, and choose
Tamer as prey.

20

SYLVIA PLATH

The Rival

If the moon smiled, she would resemble you.
You leave the same impression
Of something beautiful, but annihilating.
Both of you are great light borrowers.
Her O-mouth grieves at the world; yours is unaffected,   5

And your first gift is making stone out of everything.
I wake to a mausoleum; you are here,
Ticking your fingers on the marble table, looking for cigarettes,
Spiteful as a woman, but not so nervous,
And dying to say something unanswerable.   10

The moon, too, abases her subjects,
But in the daytime she is ridiculous.
Your dissatisfactions, on the other hand,
Arrive through the mailslot with loving regularity,
White and blank, expansive as carbon monoxide.   15

No day is safe from news of you,
Walking about in Africa maybe, but thinking of me.

1966

Morning Song

Love set you going like a fat gold watch.
The midwife slapped your footsoles, and your bald cry
Took its place among the elements.

Our voices echo, magnifying your arrival. New statue.
In a drafty museum, your nakedness   5
Shadows our safety. We stand round blankly as walls.

LEROI JONES

In Memory of Radio

Who has ever stopped to think of the divinity of Lamont Cranston?
(Only Jack Kerouac, that I know of: & me.
The rest of you probably had on WCBS and Kate Smith,
Or something equally unattractive.)

What can I say?   5
It is better to have loved and lost
Than to put linoleum in your living rooms?

Am I a sage or something?
Mandrake's hypnotic gesture of the week?
(Remember, I do not have the healing powers of Oral Roberts . . .   10
I cannot, like F. J. Sheen, tell you how to get saved & rich!
I cannot even order you to gaschamber satori like Hitler or Goody Knight

& Love is an evil word.
Turn it backwards/see, what I mean?
An evol word. & besides   15
Who understands it?
I certainly wouldn't like to go out on that kind of limb.

Saturday mornings we listened to Red Lantern & his undersea folk.
At 11, Let's Pretend/& we did/& I, the poet, still do, Thank God!

What was it he used to say (after the transformation, when he was safe   20
& invisible & the unbelievers couldn't throw stones?) "Heh, heh, heh,
Who knows what evil lurks in the hearts of men? The Shadow knows."

O, yes he does
O, yes he does.
An evil word it is,   25
This Love.

                                                                    1961

The Turncoat

The steel fibrous slant & ribboned glint
of water. The Sea. Even my secret speech is moist
with it. When I am alone & brooding, locked in
with dull memories & self hate, & the terrible disorder
of a young man.   5

I move slowly. My cape spread stiff & pressing cautiously
in the first night wind off the Hudson. I glide down
onto my own roof, peering in at the pitiful shadow of myself.

How can it mean anything? The stop & spout, the
wind's dumb shift. Creak of the house & wet smells   10
coming in. Night forms on my left. The blind still
up to admit a sun that no longer exists. Sea move.

I dream long bays & towers . . . & soft steps on moist sand.
I become them, sometimes. Pure flight. Pure fantasy. Lean.

1961

JOHN LENNON AND PAUL MC CARTNEY

Let It Be

When I find myself in times of trouble, Mother Mary comes to me,
Speaking words of wisdom, let it be.
And in my hour of darkness, she is standing right in front of me,
Speaking words of wisdom, let it be.

Let it be, let it be, let it be, let it be,   5
Whisper words of wisdom, let it be.

But when the broken-hearted people living in the world agree,
There will be an answer, let it be.
But though they may be parted, there is still a chance that they may see,
There will be an answer, let it be.   10

Let it be, let it be, let it be, let it be,
Yeah there will be an answer, let it be.
Let it be, let it be, let it be, let it be,
Whisper words of wisdom, let it be.

"Let It Be" by John Lennon and Paul McCartney. Reprinted by permission of Maclen Music, Inc.

And when the night is cloudy, there is still a light that shines on me,
Shine until tomorrow, let it be.
I wake up to the sound of music, Mother Mary comes to me,
Speaking words of wisdom, let it be.

Let it be, let it be, let it be, yeah let it be,
There will be an answer, let it be,
Let it be, let it be, let it be, yeah let it be,
There will be an answer, let it be,
Let it be, let it be, let it be, yeah let it be,
Whisper words of wisdom, let it be.

drama

Drama asks that its audience play a double role: simultaneously we are expected to "suspend disbelief" and enter into the play as if it were a "real" happening, and yet we are also asked to be aware that the dramatic world portrayed for us is not our own—we are to watch it, to evaluate it, to learn from it, and, finally, to leave it. Even though most of our own experience with drama has come from films and television programs, drama originated in religious rituals, and only in recent centuries has moved into what we recognize as theaters or sound stages. But drama as ritual, either on stage or on television, takes us into the playwright's conception of the world. His subjects may range from war to water pollution, from race relations to personal integrity; the play may be set in ancient Greece, America's deep South, or a nineteenth-century drawing room. In any case, we will see humans in conflict—with their families, their communities, or, perhaps, even themselves. From these humans and their conflicts we have a good chance to learn more about ourselves.

The dramas in this section ask you to define what the dramatic experience is. How does the playwright draw us into his unique world? Why are we meant to admire some characters and dislike others? What does drama teach us about human aspirations, human emotions, and human capacity?

ARISTOPHANES

Lysistrata

Translated by
Dennis Roby

Characters

> LYSISTRATA
> KALONIKE
> MYRRINE
> LAMPITO
> CHORUS OF OLD MEN
> CHORUS OF OLD WOMEN
> ATHENIAN MAGISTRATE
> STRATYLLIS
> KINESIAS
> SPARTAN HERALD
> SPARTAN AMBASSADORS
> ATHENIAN AMBASSADORS
> DOOR-KEEPER
> GATE-CRASHERS

LYSISTRATA: If somebody'd invited them to a bacchanal for one of the gods, this
street would be so packed you couldn't get through. But now there's not
a woman in sight—except for my neighbor coming out over there. Good
morning, Kalonike.

KALONIKE: The same to you, Lysistrata. Why, what's wrong? You shouldn't look   5
so glum. That frown does very little for you.

LYSISTRATA: I'm afraid that women do even less for me. No wonder the men
think we're all sneaky wenches!

KALONIKE: Good heavens, aren't we?

LYSISTRATA: I *told* those girls we'd be meeting here today on important business,   10
but they haven't come. They're still home asleep.

KALONIKE: Oh, they'll show up. It's just hard to get out of the house. They've got
husbands and children to tend to—not to mention servants to wake up.

LYSISTRATA: But what we've got to do here is more important!

KALONIKE: Well, if it's so important, what is it? Is it big?   15

LYSISTRATA: Very big.

KALONIKE: Hmmm. And is it thick?

LYSISTRATA: Yes, quite thick.

KALONIKE: And the girls *still* aren't here??

LYSISTRATA: That isn't quite what I had in mind. If it were, they'd have been   20
here long ago. What I want to talk about is something I've come upon
while tossing and turning many sleepless nights.

KALONIKE: Well, it must be pretty small if you've been tossing and turning on it
so much.

LYSISTRATA: So small, in fact, that the safety of all Greece lies with us women.   25

KALONIKE: With the women? Then Greece's chances are pretty slim.

LYSISTRATA: It all depends on us whether the Peloponnesians are to be elimi-
nated. . .

KALONIKE: Things would be better if they weren't around, by god!

LYSISTRATA: . . . and the Boetians decimated.   30

KALONIKE: Kill all of them—except, of course, those tasty eels they catch up
there.

LYSISTRATA: I won't talk like this about Athens, but you can guess my meaning.
Oh, if those girls from Boetia and the Peloponnesus would only come.
Why, together we can save Greece!   35

KALONIKE: But what kind of clever, intelligent thing could women do? We just
sit around in our yellow dresses and gowns, all made-up and perfumed.

LYSISTRATA: Those are just the things I expect to save us: Yellow dresses, makeup, and perfume.

KALONIKE: You mean it?   40

LYSISTRATA: Not one man will raise his spear against another. . .

KALONIKE: Then I'll dye everything yellow!

LYSISTRATA: . . . nor take up a shield. . .

KALONIKE: I'll buy a new nightie.

LYSISTRATA: . . . or a dagger.   45

KALONIKE: And I'll get some new perfume too!

LYSISTRATA: Now do you see why the girls should have come?

KALONIKE: Do I? They should have flown here!

LYSISTRATA: I know it's very Athenian to be late for everything, but not even
the girls from the sea-coast or Salamis have arrived.   50

KALONIKE: Their husbands probably climbed on them before they climbed into
the boats.

LYSISTRATA: And none of the Acharnian women either.

KALONIKE: Theagenes' wife was consulting Hecate, so I think she'll be here. Oh
look, someone's coming! I wonder where they're from?   55

LYSISTRATA: Angyre.

KALONIKE: It sure smells like it.

MYRRINE: Are we late, Lysistrata? Well, aren't you going to say anything?

LYSISTRATA: I don't appreciate your being late for something this important,
Myrrine.   60

MYRRINE: Sorry, but I could hardly find my girdle in the dark. But if this is so urgent, you'd better tell us about it.

LYSISTRATA: Let's wait a few minutes until the Boetian and Peloponnesian girls get here.

MYRRINE: That's a good idea—but look, here comes Lampito! 65

LYSISTRATA: My favorite Spartan! Hello, Lampito. My, you look lovely. Your complexion's glowing and you're so healthy all over. Why I bet you could choke a bull.

LAMPITO: Whah Ah do believe Ah could. Ah exahcise mahself, y'know. Ah jump an kick mah bottom. 70

LYSISTRATA: And what nice tits you have too.

LAMPITO: Y'all ah pinchin' me like Ah was a cow at the sacrifice!

LYSISTRATA: Where is this girl from?

LAMPITO: She's the representative from Boetia.

LYSISTRATA: Yes, Boetia, where they have those beautiful plains. 75

KALONIKE: I'd say there wasn't much grass on her plain.

LYSISTRATA: And who is this maiden?

LAMPITO: A good one, by gawd, from Corinth.

KALONIKE: I didn't know anything good still lived in Corinth.

LAMPITO: Well, who-all called this bunch of women togethah? 80

LYSISTRATA: I did.

LAMPITO: What do you want from us?

MYRRINE: Good heavens, my dear, tell us what this is all about.

LYSISTRATA: I will, but first I have to ask one small question.

MYRRINE: Go ahead. 85

LYSISTRATA: Don't you miss your husbands, the fathers of your children, gone off with the army? I know that every one of your husbands is away from home on duty.

KALONIKE: My husband's been in Thrace for five months—guarding his own general. 90

MYRRINE: And mine's done seven months on Pylos.

LAMPITO: Mahn no soonah than gets home an he grabs up his shield and flies off again.

LYSISTRATA: You can't even have an affair, all the lovers are gone too. Why, since the Milesians betrayed us, I haven't even seen a good six-inch 95 leather substitute. Are you with me then, if I can find a way to end the war?

MYRRINE: Yes, by god, even if I had to hock my dress and drink down the profits!

KALONIKE: I'd be cut in half like a flounder and give half away! 100

LAMPITO: Ah'd climb Mt. Tagetos if Ah could see a peace.

LYSISTRATA: I'll tell you then. I won't keep it any longer. If we are going to compel the men to make peace, we must abstain. . . .

KALONIKE: Abstain from what? Come on, out with it!

LYSISTRATA: Will you do it then? 105
KALONIKE: We'll do it if it kills us.
LYSISTRATA: We must abstain from sex. Wait a minute! Why are you turning
away? Where are you going? You're turning pale and sticking out your
lower lip. Why the tears? Are you going to do it or not?
MYRRINE: I won't! Let the war go on. 110
KALONIKE: Hell no. Let the war go on!
LYSISTRATA: Really, Mrs. Flounder? You just said you'd be split in half.
KALONIKE: I'd do anything but this. If you want, I'll even walk through fire.
That would be better than sleeping alone. Why, there's nothing like it,
Lysistrata. 115
LYSISTRATA: How about you?
MYRRINE: I'd rather walk through fire too.
LYSISTRATA: How lewd can you get? It's no wonder they write tragedies about
women, we've got sex on the brain! But, my dear Spartan friend, if you
alone will stand by me, all will be saved. Will you vote with me? 120
LAMPITO: Mah gawd, it's tough foah women to sleep without theah men, but
theah's moah need of peace.
LYSISTRATA: Oh my dearest friend, you're the only true woman here!
KALONIKE: But if we—heaven forbid—hold off like you say, will it really bring
peace any sooner? 125
LYSISTRATA: Much sooner, I swear. If we sit at home all perfumed and sexy and
let the men see us naked, they'll get all excited. Then if we let them get
close but hold off at the end, they'll make peace quick enough. You'll
see!
LAMPITO: Ah recall that when Menelaus snuck a peek at Helen's melons, he 130
tossed away his sword.
KALONIKE: But what if our men simply leave us?
LYSISTRATA: Well, like Pherecrates said, help yourself.
KALONIKE: Those imitations don't do much for me. But what if they drag us into
bed by force? 135
LYSISTRATA: Hang onto the door.
KALONIKE: If they beat us, then what?
LYSISTRATA: Give in grudgingly. They won't enjoy forcing you. Harass them
other ways too, and I guarantee they'll quickly give up. No man likes
an unresponsive woman. 140
KALONIKE: Well, if this seems good to the two of you, it's all right with us.
LAMPITO: We'll puhsuade ouah men to keep an honest an' just peace, but Ah
don't know how anyone could puhsuade those crazy Athenians.
LYSISTRATA: Never you mind, we'll persuade them.
LAMPITO: Not while they've got theah boats an' all that money up in the 145
Acropolis.
LYSISTRATA: That's all been taken care of. While we were agreeing on this;
the old women were given orders to seize the Acropolis while pretending
to make sacrifices there.

LAMPITO: Whah, if that's the case, everything should be just fahn! 150

LYSISTRATA: Well then, why don't we all quickly take an oath to bind us together?

LAMPITO: You put it befoah us, an we'll sweah it!

LYSISTRATA: Good. Now, where is that policewoman? You there, what are you looking at? Put your shield face down in front of me and then go get me 155 something to sacrifice.

KALONIKE: Lysistrata, *what* are we swearing an oath on?

LYSISTRATA: What on? On a shield. We'll kill a sheep on a shield just like they did in Aeschylus once.

KALONIKE: Oh no, Lysistrata! You shouldn't swear for peace on a shield. 160

LYSISTRATA: Well what sort of an oath shall we have then?

KALONIKE: If we could get a white horse, we could sacrifice it.

LYSISTRATA: Where would you get a white horse?

KALONIKE: But how will we swear our oath?

LYSISTRATA: I've got it! Place a large cup bottom-down before me. We'll slay a 165 jug of wine from Thrace and swear over the cup an oath to add no water.

LAMPITO: Oh indeed! Theah's no sayin' how much Ah approve that oath.

LYSISTRATA: Fetch a cup and wine-jug from inside.

KALONIKE: Oh girls! What a big cup! Why it's fun just to hold it. 170

LYSISTRATA: Put that down here and bring me the jug—er, I mean, our sacrificial boar. Oh goddess Persuasion and oh loving-cup accept this sacrificial victim and be kind to us women!

KALONIKE: Nice healthy-looking blood, and it flows nicely.

LAMPITO: It shoah smells sweetly, bah Castor! 175

MYRRINE: Let me be the first to swear, girls.

KALONIKE: No, by Aphrodite, we'll draw lots for it!

LYSISTRATA: Lampito, put your hands on the cup. One of you girls repeat after me for the rest. Remember, all of you must swear and remain faithful to this: *I will have nothing to do with lover or husband* 180

KALONIKE: I will have nothing to do with lover or husband

LYSISTRATA: *or any other upstanding member of the male sex*

KALONIKE: or any other upstanding member of the male sex—Alas, my knees are shaking, Lysistrata!

LYSISTRATA: *and to live as a virgin at home* 185

KALONIKE: and to live as a virgin at home

LYSISTRATA: *nicely made-up and wearing my sexiest clothes*

KALONIKE: nicely made-up and wearing my sexiest clothes

LYSISTRATA: *so that my husband will lust for me.*

KALONIKE: so that my husband will lust for me. 190

LYSISTRATA: *But I'll never give in willingly to my husband,*

KALONIKE: But I'll never give in willingly to my husband,

LYSISTRATA: *and if he forces me,*

KALONIKE: and if he forces me,

LYSISTRATA: *I'll be grudging and unresponsive.*   195
KALONIKE: I'll be grudging and unresponsive.
LYSISTRATA: *I will not point my toes toward the ceiling,*
KALONIKE: I will not point my toes toward the ceiling,
LYSISTRATA: *nor will I crouch down on all fours.*
KALONIKE: nor will I crouch down on all fours.   200
LYSISTRATA: *If I abide my oath, may I afterwards drink of this wine-cup,*
KALONIKE: If I abide my oath, may I afterwards drink of this wine-cup,
LYSISTRATA: *and if I transgress, may I drink a cup of water.*
KALONIKE: and if I transgress, may I drink a cup of water.
LYSISTRATA: Will you all swear to these things?   205
MYRRINE: By god, yes!
LYSISTRATA: Well then, I'll consume the sacrifice.
KALONIKE: Share it, dear, so we can all be friends with one another.
LAMPITO: What's all that yellin'?
LYSISTRATA: It's what I told you about: the old women have seized the Acropolis.   210
You'd better get home to Sparta, Lampito, and get things going. You
can leave these girls as hostages with us. We'll go and join the others
in the Acropolis and help them bolt the doors.
KALONIKE: But don't you think the men will soon storm the Acropolis and throw
us out?   215
LYSISTRATA: I don't care about them. They haven't got enough fire and threats
to open those gates, unless they agree to our terms!
KALONIKE: By Aphrodite, they'll never take us! Otherwise we'd be called weak
and cowardly.

*(The women go off into the Acropolis, and the CHORUS OF OLD MEN comes on, carrying
large pieces of wood.)*

LEADER OF THE CHORUS OF OLD MEN: Come on, Drakes, let's go! That log must be   220
moved even if it hurts your shoulder!
CHORUS OF OLD MEN: So many unexpected things happen in a long life, Strymo-
dorus. Why who would have expected to hear that the women, whom
we thought were weak and kept at home, have taken over the Acropolis
and locked its gates?   225
LEADER: Hurry up to the Acropolis as fast as you can, Philurgus! We'll have to
lay those logs out in a circle and set them on fire to smoke those old
bags out—Lykon's wife first!
CHORUS: By Demeter, those broads won't laugh at me! Even Kleomenes, who
took the Acropolis once, didn't leave it scot-free. He had to give me his   230
armor and leave in his undershirt, all hairy and six years without a bath!
LEADER: Oh we fought that man savagely! Seventeen ranks of warriors slept
nightly at his gates. Shouldn't we do even better against these women—
whom both Euripedes and the gods hate? If we don't, I'll hide my war-
trophies!   235

CHORUS: But the rest of the way to the Acropolis is all up-hill! How can we haul such a load without a mule? Oh, this log is crushing my shoulder, but we'd better not stop. Our fire might blow out before we get to the top! Whew! Ugh! Oh what a horrible smoke! Lord Herakles! What terrible thing attacked me from the fire-pot? It bites my eyes like a mad dog! 240 Arrrg—a rabid succession of bites! But press on! We'll takes the Acropolis and succor the goddess! Hecch! Augh! Oh this smoke!

LEADER: The fire is breathing on account of the gods. Why don't we put down this firewood and light a grapevine from the pot? Then we could throw it inside and batter the door. Of course, if the women don't open up, 245 we could set the door on fire and suffocate them with the smoke. Put down the wood. Gasp. The smoke! Dear me! Is there no front-line general here to aid us with the wood? There, it's all down! Now you can go to work, fire-pot. Kindle your coals and light this torch, so I can be first to reach the Acropolis! Oh goddess of Victory, help us to overcome those 250 insolent women up there, and give us a trophy as a sign of victory!

(*The* CHORUS OF OLD WOMEN *enters, carrying water pitchers.*)

LEADER OF THE CHORUS OF OLD WOMEN: I think I see smoke and fire, girls. We'd better hurry!

CHORUS OF OLD WOMEN: Fly, fly, Nikodike, before those destructive old goats and their harsh laws thump poor Kritylle and set Kaluke to roast! But I'm 255 afraid we're too late! This morning while I was trying to fill the water pots for emergencies, in the midst of all that clamor and crashing of crockery, jostling with slaves and commoners, I heard those senile old men slowly lugging logs—as if for someone's bath—and threatening to burn those abominable women to a crisp. Oh goddess, protect our 260 women! Don't let them burn! They've taken your temple to protect all Greece from war and madness. When the fire comes from below, oh Athene, carry water with us!

WOMEN'S LEADER: Wait! What was that? Oh how debauched! Doing something like that in the temple—how impious! 265

MEN'S CHORUS: That's a surprise! There's a swarm of them guarding these doors too.

WOMEN'S CHORUS: Fart at us, will you? We may not be many, but we're only part of a hidden multitude.

MEN'S CHORUS: Oh Phaedrias, should we let them talk like that? Why don't we 270 break some firewood across their backs?

WOMEN'S CHORUS: Let's put our pitchers on the ground, so our hands are free for fighting.

MEN'S CHORUS: By god, all they need is a couple of belts in the jaw, and they'd shut up! 275

WOMEN'S CHORUS: Oh yeah? Hit me. I'm standing here waiting. You won't have to worry about some bitch grabbing your balls after I get through with you!

MEN'S CHORUS: You shut up or you'll never make it to old age!

WOMEN'S CHORUS: Just touch Stratyllis. Come on, try it! 280

MEN'S CHORUS: Suppose I thump that foul wench with my knuckles?

WOMEN'S CHORUS: We'll eat up your lungs and tear out your liver!

MEN'S CHORUS: Euripides the poet sure was smart. He knew how shameless women are!

WOMEN'S CHORUS: Come on, Rodippe, let's pick up our water pitchers. 285

MEN'S CHORUS: You god-hated creatures, why did you bring that water up here?

WOMEN'S CHORUS: And why did you bring fire, you decrepit thing—to incinerate yourself?

MEN'S CHORUS: No, we came to make a funeral pyre out of your friends. 290

WOMEN'S CHORUS: Well, then we came to put your fire out.

MEN'S CHORUS: You'll put *my* fire out?

WOMEN'S CHORUS: It won't take long to show you.

MEN'S CHORUS: Since I have this torch, I don't know why I shouldn't fricassee you right now! 295

WOMEN'S CHORUS: I hope you have some soap, because your bath water's ready.

MEN'S CHORUS: You'd give me a bath, you moldy hag?

WOMEN'S CHORUS: Just like we give all the brides.

MEN'S CHORUS: Did you hear that insolence?

WOMEN'S CHORUS: I'm a free-born citizen too. 300

MEN'S CHORUS: You'll stop that noise or else!

WOMEN'S CHORUS: Oh brother! You won't be sitting in court any more.

MEN'S CHORUS: Set her hair on fire!

WOMEN'S CHORUS: Do your stuff, water!

MEN'S CHORUS: Good grief! 305

WOMEN'S CHORUS: Wasn't it hot enough?

MEN'S CHORUS: Hot enough? Cut it out! Why did you do that?

WOMEN'S CHORUS: I watered you so you'd grow.

MEN'S CHORUS: But I'm withering already from trembling! Brrr!

WOMEN'S CHORUS: Well, since you've got a fire, warm yourself by it. 310

(An Athenian MAGISTRATE enters.)

MAGISTRATE: What, has female insolence erupted again, with tambourines and shouting for Bacchus and mourning for Adonis from the roof-tops, like I heard the other day in the Assembly? Then Demostratus—damn him— was urging we sail for Sicily, and his dancing wife yelled "Alas, Adonis!" Next he moved we draft Zacynthian soldiers. His tipsy wife screamed 315 from the roof "Mourn for Adonis," and he forced his motion through, that polluted abomination of the gods! These are the sort of excesses we can expect from women!

MEN'S CHORUS: Then wait 'til you hear about today's wantonness! They insulted us and then soaked us with so much water from their pitchers that we 320 had to wring our clothes as if we'd pissed in them!

552

MAGISTRATE: By Poseidon, we deserve this. For we teach them the insolence from which these actions spring. We say to a tradesman: "Oh Goldsmith, my wife was dancing the other night when the peg which fastens the clasp of that necklace you repaired fell out. I must now sail for 325 Salamis, but if you can manage it, please come over tonight and fix her up with another peg." Someone else says to a young shoemaker with a man-sized tool: "Oh shoemaker, the cross-strap of my wife's sandal pinches her little toe, which is quite delicate. Would you come by at noon and loosen things up for her?" Now, when I, as magistrate, wish 330 to buy some oars and need cash, I find the gates have been shut by women! But this isn't the way to open them. Bring in the crowbars! I'll fix their insolence. What are you gaping at, you profligate? Where are you looking? Can't you do anything but scout for a tavern? Don't look so innocent. Wedge those crowbars under the gates like this. I'll yank on 335 this one.

(LYSISTRATA enters.)

LYSISTRATA: You don't need to break in, I've come out of my own free will. You don't need crowbars—you need to use your heads.
MAGISTRATE: Oh really, you wretch? Where's that officer? Arrest her and tie her hands behind her back. 340
LYSISTRATA: If he so much as lays a finger on me, he'll regret being a public servant!
MAGISTRATE: What, are you afraid? Just grab her around the waist. And you help him and then tie her up.

(KALONIKE enters.)

KALONIKE: You lay one hand on her and I'll stomp you until your insides pour 345 out!
MAGISTRATE: From the looks of you, something's poured out already. Where's the other officer? Bind her first because of her big mouth.

(Enter MYRRINE.)

MYRRINE: If he lays a finger on her, by Phosphorus, he'll soon need a doctor!
MAGISTRATE: What is this? Where's the officer? Hold her! I'll put an end to this 350 commotion.

(Enter STRATYLLIS.)

STRATYLLIS: If he so much as touches her, by Artemis, he'll scream with every hair I yank out!
MAGISTRATE: How horrible! That soldier is hidden too. But we can't be beaten by women. Come on, Skythians, join ranks for battle! 355

LYSISTRATA: By the gods, you ought to be told that we have four completely armed companies of women in the Acropolis.

MAGISTRATE: Bind their hands, oh Skythians!

LYSISTRATA: Oh comrades-in-battle, or seed-greens-and-egg-market-ladies, oh garlic-bread-purveying-hostesses, come forth! Draw on them! Carp at them! Strike! Scream! Ward them off! Be sassy! Enough! Fall back! Don't take any spoils! 360

MAGISTRATE: Good grief, my officers have taken the worst of it!

LYSISTRATA: What did you expect? Did you suppose you'd come to fight slaves or that we weren't determined? 365

MAGISTRATE: By Apollo, I know you're determined if there's a bar nearby.

MEN'S CHORUS: You're a waster of words, Magistrate of Athens. Why engage in conversation with these beasts? Or didn't you hear about the bath they gave us—without any powder, too?

WOMEN'S CHORUS: But, my dear, it's wrong to attack your neighbors, and a 370 black eye is the necessary result. Why, I'd love to be a peaceful, idle maiden, bothering no one, not even moving a straw—that is until someone tries to take honey from my wasp's nest.

MEN'S CHORUS: Oh Zeus, how shall we deal with these monsters? This is unbearable! We'll have to figure out why they would want to seize our 375 greatest and most sacred temple, the Acropolis.

MEN'S LEADER: Question them, but don't be misled and embarrass all of us. It would be disgraceful if we could solve this and let the opportunity pass.

MAGISTRATE: I'd like to know first, by god, why you chose to lock up the Acropolis and bar its doors? 380

LYSISTRATA: In order to keep the money from you, so you couldn't use it for war.

MAGISTRATE: What, does money cause wars?

LYSISTRATA: And all our difficulties. Peisander and some other officials always stirred up some phoney issues in order to steal money. That's why we 385 wanted the Acropolis. You won't be able to take that money now.

MAGISTRATE: But what will you do with it?

LYSISTRATA: You ask me that? Why, we'll manage it ourselves.

MAGISTRATE: You'll manage the money?

LYSISTRATA: What's so strange about that? It's customary. Don't we normally 390 manage all of your money?

MAGISTRATE: But not this money!

LYSISTRATA: Why not?

MAGISTRATE: Well, we pay our war expenses from it.

LYSISTRATA: But it's not necessary for war to have first priority. 395

MAGISTRATE: But how can we be safe otherwise?

LYSISTRATA: We'll save you!

MAGISTRATE: You?

LYSISTRATA: Yes, us.

MAGISTRATE: How loathsome! 400

554

LYSISTRATA: All right, we'll save you without your permission.

MAGISTRATE: How nauseating!

LYSISTRATA: You may be angry, but we'll still do it.

MAGISTRATE: By Demeter, it's unjust!

LYSISTRATA: Sir, we have to save you. 405

MAGISTRATE: And what if I don't want you to?

LYSISTRATA: That will just make us more determined.

MAGISTRATE: But why do you care about war and peace?

LYSISTRATA: We'll be glad to tell you.

MAGISTRATE: Speak quickly or you'll be sorry. 410

LYSISTRATA: You'd better listen carefully—and keep your hands under control.

MAGISTRATE: I can't! I'm too angry!

STRATYLLIS: You'll be the sorrier for it!

MAGISTRATE: Croak to yourself, you old hag! You do the talking, Lysistrata.

LYSISTRATA: All right. Ever since the war began, we have discreetly endured 415
all that you men have done. You never allowed us to mumble about it,
of course, and we didn't like that. But we knew things weren't going
well, and we could often hear you at home, mangling some great issue.
Yet even if we cheerfully asked "What did you do on the peace treaty
in the Assembly today, dear?" we'd get "What business is it of yours? 420
Shut up!" for a reply.

STRATYLLIS: But I never shut up!

MAGISTRATE: You probably got belted too!

LYSISTRATA: Well, I shut up—at least until I saw that you men had done something even more foolish. Then I had to ask my husband how you men 425
could make such a senseless mistake. He looked at me in disbelief,
as if I should run back to my spinning or be knocked in the head, and
snarled "War is men's business!"

MAGISTRATE: He's right, by god!

LYSISTRATA: Right in what way, you no-good? All that attitude led to was poor 430
judgement. It wasn't long before you were out in the streets asking if
there were any men left in Athens and getting "No" for an answer. So
we joined together and gathered these women here to save all of
Greece. We had no reason to wait. Now we're going to speak, and
you'll have to be quiet while we correct you. 435

MAGISTRATE: You would correct us men?

LYSISTRATA: I said be quiet.

MAGISTRATE: You abomination! Me be quiet for you who wear veils around
your heads? I'd rather die!

LYSISTRATA: Well, if that bothers you, here, take my veil and wrap it around 440
your head—and then be quiet.

MYRRINE: Here, take this little wicker basket.

LYSISTRATA: Here's some wool to card and some beans to munch on. Oh, don't
forget your girdle. War, you know, is women's business!

WOMEN'S LEADER: Put down your pitchers, girls, so that we'll be ready to assist the others. 445

WOMEN'S CHORUS: I'll never grow tired of dancing; my knees won't grow weary or wear out. I will bear all sacrifices among these others who are so excellent in nature, in grace and courage, in wisdom, patriotism, and sensibility! Advance angrily, you women born of courageous grand- 450 mothers and mothers like stinging nettles, don't relent! For now the wind is right!

LYSISTRATA: Oh Love and Cyprus-born Aphrodite, breathe desirability down upon our breasts and thighs and make the men stand up smoothly for us, so that we may be called peacemakers in Greece. 455

MAGISTRATE: What are you going to do?

LYSISTRATA: First, we're going to keep all those raving, heavily-armed soldiers out of the market place.

STRATYLLIS: That's right, by god!

LYSISTRATA: Now they come down to the market all armored, looking like 460 Korybants in the vegetables and crockery.

MAGISTRATE: Good heavens, that's all part of being a man.

LYSISTRATA: But it's pretty laughable when you see someone with a Gorgon's head emblazoned on his shield haggling over a fish.

STRATYLLIS: That's nothing. I saw some long-haired cavalry commander sitting 465 on his horse, pouring the soup he'd just bought from a woman into his helmet. Then there was this crazy Thracian, shaking his shield and javelin like he was Tereus fresh out of Euripedes' play. He frightened away a woman selling figs and gobbled down her stock!

MAGISTRATE: And just how will you be able to put an end to Greece's many 470 problems?

LYSISTRATA: Very simply.

MAGISTRATE: How? Show me!

LYSISTRATA: Just as when our thread is tangled and we move our spindles back and forth to loosen it, so we would put an end to the war by sending 475 ambassadors back and forth.

MAGISTRATE: You fools! You think you can stop this war with wool and thread and spindles?

LYSISTRATA: If you had any brains, you men would handle the government the way we women handle our wool at home. 480

MAGISTRATE: Oh really? How's that?

LYSISTRATA: Start with a good bath to wash out all the filth. Then, after stretching it out to dry, beat out the bad parts with a stick and pick out all the burrs. Of course, if you should find a lump of conspirators, scheming for election, pluck them out and tear them to pieces. Next, 485 comb and card it all into one basket, mixing in together aliens, visitors, and friends—even those in debt to the city. And the colonies of Athens, don't leave them out like loose threads. Then take all of these, draw

them out, comb them, and gather them all into one great ball, from
which you then can weave a cloak for all the people.   490

MAGISTRATE: How about that! All these wild and wooly plans from women who
have practically nothing to do with the war.

LYSISTRATA: You wretch! This war is twice as hard on us! First, we bear the sons
who serve as soldiers. . . .

MAGISTRATE: Be quiet! Don't open old wounds!   495

LYSISTRATA: And then, when we ought to be rejoicing and enjoying our youth,
we have to sleep alone because of the army. You men aren't at home
while our lonely girls are growing old in their bedrooms.

MAGISTRATE: But don't men grow old too?

LYSISTRATA: Yes, but if a man comes home gray-headed from the army, he can   500
quickly marry a young woman. When a woman's time grows short, she
can't do this. She can only sit idly, without hope of marriage.

MAGISTRATE: But if an old man could get an erection. . .

LYSISTRATA: What's keeping you from dying anyway? We'll get you a coffin,
and I'll mix up a honey-cake with which you can bribe Cerberus, the   505
watch-dog of Hades. And, here, you can take these flowers for a crown.

KALONIKE: And here's some water for your flowers.

MYRRINE: And here's some from me too!

LYSISTRATA: Let's see, do you need anything else? Make way, Charon is calling
you for your trip across the Styx. Don't delay!   510

MAGISTRATE: Isn't this outrageous to do this to me? I'm going to show myself
to the other magistrates—just as I am!   (*The* MAGISTRATE *exits.*)

LYSISTRATA: What, are you mad because we didn't lay the body out? We'll
give you the proper ceremonies on the third day after your demise!

(LYSISTRATA, KALONIKE, *and* MYRRINE *all exit.*)   515

MEN'S LEADER: We can't lie in bed if we are to be free, men. Let's strip and get
to work on this matter!

MEN'S CHORUS: This matter seems to me to have more and more of an odor. In
fact, I strongly smell the prior tyranny of Hippias. I greatly fear that
Spartan men, meeting at Kleisthenes' house, have used deceit to stir up
those damned women to seize the money in the Acropolis—from which   520
I get my wages!

MEN'S LEADER: Because they do such things as criticize the government, chatter
about shields and armaments, and fraternize with the Spartans—Why I'd
trust a hungry wolf before I'd trust them!—I think they're contriving a
tyranny against us! But they won't tyrannize me. I'll keep alert and al-   525
ways conceal my sword in a branch of myrtle. I'll stand in my armor
in the market-place next to the statue of Aristegeiton, who helped kill
that last tyrant's brother, and from that very spot, I'll belt that grey-
haired old witch over there right on the jaw!

WOMEN'S LEADER: Do that and your own mother won't know you when you get   530
home! Put your pitchers down, girls.

WOMEN'S CHORUS: We must needs speak, fellow citizens, about our city. Naturally, it raised me in softness and splendor. When I was seven, I straightforward became one of those to carry Pallas' holy things. At ten, I ground corn for Athene, and later I portrayed a bear in my yellow robe for Artemis at Brauron. When I was a fair maiden, I wore a necklace of dried figs and carried the sacred basket in the procession. 535

WOMEN'S LEADER: With all this given to me, don't I owe the city what useful advice I can give? Don't bear a grudge against me because I'm a woman and seek to improve our present situation. By heaven, I have a 540 share in it too, for I contribute men! I can't say as much for you old goats: You've squandered the contributions your grandfathers gave in the Persian war, you don't pay the war tax now, and what's worse, you are risking destroying all of us as well! What do you matter? If I don't like what you say, I'll whack you in the face with this boot! 545

MEN'S CHORUS: Can you believe this insolence? If we've got any balls, we must attack them and finish this business! Come on, men, strip! A man needs to smell like a man. It isn't fitting to be wrapped up in these fig-leaves! Lead on, just like when we came from Leipsydrum to overthrow that tyrant! Shake off your old age, for we must fight again! 550

MEN'S LEADER: If we give them the slightest thing they'll take advantage of it—any handicraft! They will build ships and attempt to fight against us like the queen who sailed at Artemisia. And if they turn to horsemanship, we'd best forget our knights, for women are best in the saddle and don't slip away at a good clip. Look at the Amazons Mikon painted fighting 555 on horseback against the men! We must catch all of these women and restrain them with wooden collars.

WOMEN'S CHORUS: If you provoke me, I'll turn loose my animal nature and shear you until you scream for help from the others! But now we must strip off our dresses, so that we smell like women with our teeth clenched in 560 fury. Jut let some one come toward me! He'll never eat garlic or beans again. Come on! I'll fix you like Aesop's beetle broke the eagle's eggs!

WOMEN'S LEADER: You don't bother me as long as Lampito and Ismenia, that well-born girl from Thebes, are alive. You don't have enough power, not even if you decreed it seven times over. You bums! Not only do we hate 565 you—your neighbors do too! Yesterday at the feast of Hekate, I asked my children's neighbor to attend, a lovely, useful child—a little Boetian eel. But your decrees wouldn't allow it. And you won't stop voting them until someone yanks your leg and breaks your neck!

(LYSISTRATA enters.)

WOMEN'S LEADER: Oh leader of this resolute undertaking, why do you come 570 to us so angry-looking?

LYSISTRATA: It's the deeds of wicked women and the female mind—they've made me lose heart and set me pacing up and down!

WOMEN'S LEADER: What? What are you saying?

LYSISTRATA: It's true! It's true!   575

WOMEN'S LEADER: What's true? Tell us!

LYSISTRATA: It would be shameful to tell you, but even worse to pass over it in silence.

WOMEN'S LEADER: Don't conceal something that's important to me!

LYSISTRATA: Oh, all right. In a word, we want to get laid!   580

WOMEN'S LEADER: Oh Zeus!

LYSISTRATA: Why call on him? It's true. I can no longer hold them off from the men. They sneak away. The first one tried vainly to use an opening down by Pan's cave. The second tried to desert by wriggling down a rope. I caught a third by the hair as she was taking off on a sparrow   585 for the town's best brothel. They're all making excuses so they can go home. Why there's someone now! You! Where do you think you're going?

FIRST WOMAN: I want to go home. The moths are cutting my Milesian wools to pieces!   590

LYSISTRATA: Moths, schmoths—get back inside!

FIRST WOMAN: I'll be right back, by the two goddesses! I just want to open them up and spread them out on my bed.

LYSISTRATA: No opening, no spreading, no going home.

FIRST WOMAN: But am I to let my wool be ruined?   595

LYSISTRATA: If necessary.

SECOND WOMAN: Oh poor me! Oh my poor flax, which I left at home unhackled!

LYSISTRATA: Well, here's another, leaving for unhackled flax. Get back in there!

SECOND WOMAN: But, by Phosphor, I will strip my flax and be right back!

LYSISTRATA: No stripping, period. If you started this, the others would want to   600 do it too.

THIRD WOMAN: Oh divine Eileithyia, keep back this birth until I come to some more appropriate place than the temple!

LYSISTRATA: What is this nonsense?

THIRD WOMAN: I'm going to have a baby *right now!*   605

LYSISTRATA: But you weren't pregnant yesterday.

THIRD WOMAN: But I am today. Send me home quickly, Lysistrata, so I can find a midwife!

LYSISTRATA: What sort of story is this? What have you got here that's so hard anyway?   610

THIRD WOMAN: It's a male child.

LYSISTRATA: By Aphrodite, it's not! You've got something brass under your dress, and it's hollow too. Let me see it! You fool, using Athene's sacred helmet to pretend you're pregnant?

THIRD WOMAN: And so I am, by Zeus!   615

LYSISTRATA: Well, then what's this enormous helmet for?

THIRD WOMAN: It's so that if the birth overtakes me while I'm still in the Acropolis, I would go inside the helmet and give birth—just as doves do!

LYSISTRATA: Nonsense! Stop making excuses, it's all too clear what you're up to. Why don't you just wait here a week or two until we can think of a name for this helmet? 620

FOURTH WOMAN: But I can't get any sleep here ever since I saw the snake that guards the temple!

FIFTH WOMAN: I'll be destroyed by the owls! All night I'm kept awake by those abusive owls! 625

LYSISTRATA: You devils! Stop your quackery! You may desire your husbands, but do you think that they don't desire you? I *know* the nights they spend are hard. Bear up, my dears, and persevere just a little longer, for according to a recent oracle we will prevail—if we don't quarrel. Here is the oracle! 630

WOMEN'S CHORUS: Read us what it says!

LYSISTRATA: *When the swallows crouch together in one place, keeping away from the old coots and fleeing the lusty larks, there will be a rest from ills, and high-thundering Zeus will put the upper one below.*

WOMEN'S CHORUS: Does that mean we'll lie on top? 635

LYSISTRATA: *But if the swallows quarrel and take flight out of the holy temple, it will be apparent that there was never a more lecherous bird.*

WOMEN'S CHORUS: The oracle's clear enough, by heaven! Let us not renounce our hard efforts; let's go back inside. It would be disgraceful to betray the oracle! 640

MEN'S CHORUS: I'd like to tell you a story which I heard when I was still a child. Once upon a time there was a certain young man named Melanion, who fled marriage and went into the mountains of the wilderness. There he wove nets and hunted hares and had a dog, and he refused to return home because of his hate. Melanion loathed women, and we chaste 645 fellows feel the same way!

A MAN: How about a kiss, granny!

A WOMAN: Try it and you won't need an onion to shed real tears!

MAN: I meant by lifting my leg and kicking you!

WOMAN: You have a great hairy thicket, I see. 650

MAN: Myronides the warrior was rugged there. "Blackbottomed" all his enemies called him. And so was Phormio.

WOMEN'S CHORUS: I'd like to tell you something in response to your story about Melanion. Timon dwelt in untrodden land, surrounding his face with thorns, straight from the Furies, no doubt, and he was filled with hate, 655 uttering innumerable curses at evil men. But while he hated you men, he was as sweet as could be toward us women!

A WOMAN: How'd you like a lick in the chops?

A MAN: Sure, fatso, I'm not afraid!

WOMAN: How about a good, swift kick? 660

MAN: But then your hair would show!

WOMAN: I may be old, but I keep it well trimmed!

LYSISTRATA: Oh! Oh girls! Come quickly over here!

A WOMAN: What is it? Why did you shout?

LYSISTRATA: A man! I see a man coming, seized with Aphrodite's passion! 665

WOMAN: Oh lady, ruler over Cyprus, Cytheria, and Paphos, let us keep on as we have been! Where is he? Where's this man?

LYSISTRATA: Down there, beside Demeter's temple.

WOMAN: My god, he certainly is. But who is he?

LYSISTRATA: Everybody look! Does anyone know him? 670

MYRRINE: Good heaven, I do! It's my husband, Kinesias.

LYSISTRATA: Your job, Myrrine, will be to roast and turn him, to cheat him completely, to love him and not to love him, and to supply him everything except what we swore over the wine-cup.

MYRRINE: Don't worry. I'll do it. 675

LYSISTRATA: I'll join with you in tricking him—I'll roast him good! But, now, get back out of the way!

KINESIAS: Oh how agonizing! I'm stretched taut as a drum and have these spasms! I'm tortured on the wheel!

LYSISTRATA: Who is this inside the sentries? 680

KINESIAS: I.

LYSISTRATA: A man?

KINESIAS: A man, certainly.

LYSISTRATA: Then you may certainly get out of here!

KINESIAS: But who are you that throws me out? 685

LYSISTRATA: Today's look-out!

KINESIAS: By all the gods, call out Myrrine for me now!

LYSISTRATA: I should call Myrrine out for you? And who are you?

KINESIAS: This is her husband, Kinesias.

LYSISTRATA: Why, hello, you dear man! Your name and reputation are not un- 690
known among us. Your wife always mentions you. She doesn't take an egg or an apple that she doesn't say "This is for Kinesias!"

KINESIAS: Oh, by heaven!

LYSISTRATA: By Aphrodite. And if we're talking about men, your wife always interrupts and says immediately that all the rest are really not much 695 when compared with Kinesias.

KINESIAS: Come on now, call her!

LYSISTRATA: What then? What will you give me?

KINESIAS: Well, all I have is this you see before me. What I have, I'll give to you. 700

LYSISTRATA: Well, I'm going down to call her now.

KINESIAS: Be quick, please! I've had nothing enjoyable in life since she left the house. I'm so vexed; everything seems a wilderness to me. I have no desire for food—I'm consumed by fire! It's this erection I've got!

MYRRINE: I love him, oh I love Him, but he doesn't want to be loved by me! 705
Don't you call me to him!

KINESIAS: Oh sweetest little Myrrine, why are you doing this? Come on down here!

MYRRINE: By god, I'll not leave this very spot!

KINESIAS: I'm calling you. Won't you come down, Myrrine?   710

MYRRINE: You may be calling me, but you don't want me!

KINESIAS: I don't want you? Look again!

MYRRINE: Go away!

KINESIAS: Won't you even listen to your child? You, call to your mommy.

CHILD: Mommy, mommy, mommy!   715

KINESIAS: What's the matter with you? Don't you pity your poor child who's
been unwashed and unfed for six days?

MYRRINE: I certainly pity him because his father is so negligent toward him!

KINESIAS: Come down to your child, my darling!

MYRRINE: The trials of motherhood! I must go down, alas!   720

KINESIAS: Why she seems much younger, and she looks at me much more
gently than she did before. And as for her arrogance and being annoyed at me—it just makes me all the hotter!

MYRRINE: Oh you darling child with such a nasty father! Come here so mommy
can kiss you!   725

KINESIAS: Why have you done this to me, listening to those other women and
bringing both of us to grief?

MYRRINE: Keep your hands to yourself!

KINESIAS: But everything at home, mine and yours, is being ruined!

MYRRINE: I don't really care.   730

KINESIAS: You don't care if the hens are pecking your wool to shreds?

MYRRINE: Certainly not.

KINESIAS: It's been so long since you joined me in Aphrodite's sacred rites,
won't you come back home?

MYRRINE: No, by god, I won't until all of you men become friends and put an   735
end to this war!

KINESIAS: Well, if that's what we have to do, we'll do it!

MYRRINE: Fine, and when you *do* do it, I'll come home. For now, I'm sworn to
stay here.

KINESIAS: Well then, lie down with me here for a while.   740

MYRRINE: Nothing doing. But I can't say I don't love you.

KINESIAS: You love me? Then why won't you lie down, Myrrine?

MYRRINE: Are you kidding? In front of the child?

KINESIAS: Good grief, Manes, carry him home! There, he's out of the way. Now
will you lie down?   745

MYRRINE: And just where, you miserable specimen, are we going to lie down?

KINESIAS: Where? Down by Pan's cave would be good.

MYRRINE: How would I purify myself afterwards so I could come back into the
Acropolis?

KINESIAS: Easy, you could bathe at that pool below the cave.   750

MYRRINE: But I've taken an oath! You wretch, would you make me swear
falsely?

KINESIAS: Don't worry about it. I'll take responsibility for your oath.

562

MYRRINE: Well, I'd better go get a bed for the two of us.

KINESIAS: Don't bother, the ground will do. 755

MYRRINE: No, by Apollo! Even though you're a no-good, I won't let you lie on the ground. (MYRRINE *exits*.)

KINESIAS: Well, it's obvious that she loves me!

(MYRRINE *returns with a cot*.)

MYRRINNE: There. Now hurry up and lie down, and I'll take off my clothes. Wait a minute! I forgot the mattress. 760

KINESIAS: A mattress? But I don't need a mattress.

MYRRINE: No mattress? By Artemis, how disgraceful!

KINESIAS: Come on, give me a kiss!

MYRRINE: There.

KINESIAS: That's more like it! Get going and hurry back here! 765

(MYRRINE *exits and then returns*.)

MYRRINE: Here's the mattress. Lie down now, and I'll take off my clothes. But something's missing—we don't have a pillow!

KINESIAS: I don't want a pillow!

MYRRINE: By heaven, I do! (MYRRINE *exits*.)

KINESIAS: My equipment will atrophy if I have to wait much longer! 770

(MYRRINE *re-enters with a pillow*.)

MYRRINE: Lift up your head!

KINESIAS: I've already had enough!

MYRRINE: Enough already?

KINESIAS: Enough of that stuff, my little treasure!

MYRRINE: My girdle is already loosened. Now remember: Don't you try and 775 fool me about that peace treaty.

KINESIAS: May the gods destroy me immediately!

MYRRINE: Oh, but we don't have a blanket!

KINESIAS: By god, I don't want one! I want to screw!

MYRRINE: And you will. I'll be right back! (MYRRINE *exits*.) 780

KINESIAS: This woman and her bed-supplies are ruining me.

(MYRRINE *returns with a blanket*.)

MYRRINE: Now raise yourself up.

KINESIAS: But I've been up for hours!

MYRRINE: How'd you like some ointment?

KINESIAS: By Apollo, no! 785

MYRRINE: You'll get some, by Aphrodite, whether you want it or not!

(MYRRINE *exits*.)

KINESIAS: Oh Lord Zeus, let that ointment spill!

(MYRRINE *returns with the ointment.*)

MYRRINE: Hold out your hand. Take some and rub it in.

KINESIAS: This ointment isn't very sweet, by Apollo. In fact, it smells more of
wasting time than it does of marriage!   790

MYRRINE: Why, how silly of me? I brought that awful stuff from Rhodes by
mistake.

KINESIAS: It'll do just fine, dear.

MYRRINE: Don't be ridiculous.   (MYRRINE *exits with ointment.*)

KINESIAS: May heaven pulverize the first ointment-maker!   795

(MYRRINE *returns.*)

MYRRINE: Here, take this nice long vase.

KINESIAS: I've got one of my own, thanks. Now, don't provoke me any more.
Just lie down and don't bring me anything else!

MYRRINE: I'll do just that, by Artemis. See, I'm untying my shoes. But you realize,
dear, that I'll do this only if you vote for the treaty?   800

KINESIAS: I'll consider it—   (MYRRINE *runs back into the Acropolis.*)

KINESIAS: That woman has ruined me! I've been murdered! Demolished! Oh,
what's to become of me? Whom will I lay? After being cheated by the
most beautiful one of all, how will this little fellow standing in front of
me be cared for? Where's the brothel-keeper? I must hire a nursemaid!   805

MEN'S CHORUS: Oh how terribly the deceived soul suffers! I have pity on you,
oh yes I do! What soul could stand it? What kidneys or hips? What
testicles or rump? All straining in the morning and unable to screw!

KINESIAS: Oh Zeus, what terrible spasms!

MEN'S LEADER: She's certainly done you in, that despicable tart!   810

KINESIAS: No, by the gods, she is lovely and sweet!

MEN'S LEADER: Sweet? A foul and polluted sweetness if there ever was one!

MEN'S CHORUS: Oh Zeus, Zeus, send us a miracle, a great storm and hurricane
to whirl these women away! End over end, send them flying, then suddenly throw them back to earth—right onto our waiting uprights!   815

(*Enter the* MAGISTRATE *and a* SPARTAN HERALD, *from opposite parts of the stage.*)

HERALD: Wheah is the Senate an its Presidents? Ah wish to delivah some new
dispatches.

MAGISTRATE: What are you: A man or some god of the vineyard?

HERALD: By the gawds, Ah'm a herald, young fellah, an Ah've come from
Spahta about the peace treaty.   820

MAGISTRATE: Well then, why are hiding that spear beneath your armpit?

HERALD: My lawd! Not me! No!

MAGISTRATE: Why do you turn around like that, throwing your cloak in front
of you? Has your groin swollen from your trip?

564

HERALD: This man's senile, bah Castor! 825

MAGISTRATE: You lewd devil, you've got an erection!

HERALD: No, by heaven, Ah do not! Stop talkin' foolishness!

MAGISTRATE: Well, what is that you've got there?

HERALD: Uh, it's a Spahtan message-scroll.

MAGISTRATE: If it is, then I've got one of my own—and I'm no Spartan! But you 830
can tell me the truth, I know what's been going on. How are things
going with you Spartans?

HERALD: All us Spahtans ah erect, and ouah allies are upright too. We all need
milk-pails!

MAGISTRATE: Where did this evil fall upon you from? From Pan? 835

HERALD: No, Ah believe Lampito was first, but then all the women in Spahta,
jus' like at the staht of a race, all at once drove us men from between
theah legs!

MAGISTRATE: How are things now?

HERALD: We'ah in trouble. In the city we have to turn ouah backs to the wind 840
like we were carryin' a lamp. An the women won't let us touch 'em
unless we all agree to make a treaty with you-all.

MAGISTRATE: The women on all sides have conspired to do this. Now I understand exactly! Hurry home and tell them to send ambassadors with full
power to make peace here at once. I'll request our Assembly to elect 845
ambassadors, and if necessary, I'll display my erection for emphasis!

HERALD: Everything you say is excellent! Ah'll *fly* home!

(*Both* MAGISTRATE *and* HERALD *exit.*)

MEN'S CHORUS: There is no wild beast—even fire!—as unconquerable as a
woman! Even a leopard isn't that shameless! 850

WOMEN'S CHORUS: You sorry creature! You're always making war on me, when
you might have me for your steadfast friend!

MEN'S CHORUS: As far as I'm concerned, I'll never stop hating women!

WOMEN'S CHORUS: As you wish. For the present, I can no longer disregard your
nakedness. I'm afraid you look ridiculous. I'll put this shirt on you.

MEN'S CHORUS: This certainly isn't a hateful gesture, although I was in a hateful 855
temper when I pulled my shirt off.

WOMEN'S CHORUS: Now you look more like a man and are no longer ridiculous.
If it won't offend you, I'll take out that wild beast which is in your eye
right now.

MEN'S CHORUS: It's been bothering me. Here take my ring and rake it out. Then 860
let me see it. He's been biting my eye for a long time, by god!

WOMEN'S CHORUS: I'll be glad to, although you were born a foul-tempered sort.
Why what a huge great gnat! Don't you see it? It must be from the
Tricorysian marshes.

MEN'S CHORUS: By god, that's gratifying! He's been making holes in me for such 865
a long time that the tears pour out now that he's gone!

WOMEN'S CHORUS: Even though you were so terrible before, I'll wipe away your
tears and kiss you.

MEN'S CHORUS: Don't kiss me!

WOMEN'S CHORUS: I will if you want me to or not! 870

MEN'S CHORUS: Damnation! You're born flatterers all right! The proverb is certainly true: You can't live with these terrors, but you can't live without them either! So we'll make a treaty together. From here on I won't do anything to you, so long as you do nothing to me! Now, let's join together and begin our song: 875

TOTAL CHORUS: We are not preparing to say nasty things about any of our citizens. On the contrary, we have good things to say for all! We've had quite enough bad times—not very long ago. So tell every man and woman that if they need some money—say two or three minas—we have plenty in our purses inside. And there's no need to pay us back either— 880 if peace ever comes!

We're inviting some Karystian guests to dinner, handsome and noble men. We'll have soup inside and suckling-pig with beautiful, tender meat. Come along and join in! Bathe yourselves and your children early in the day and then come on over. Walk right in, there's no 885 need to knock. Act like it's your own house—although the door is locked!

MEN'S LEADER: Here come the Spartan ambassadors, dragging their beards. How curious! They seem to have some sort of fence wrapped around their thighs. Men of Sparta, let me welcome you, and then tell us how things are in your city. 890

SPARTAN: Ah don't need to say much about it, you can plainly see ouah situation!

MEN'S CHORUS: Dear me, things certainly do look tense.

SPARTAN: Unspeakably so, but what can we say? Let someone establish peace foah all of us on his own terms! 895

MEN'S CHORUS: I see some of the local boys lifting their cloaks away from their bellies, just like the wrestlers do. Perhaps this sickness rises from athletics.

(*Enter several* ATHENIANS.)

ATHENIAN: Who can tell me where Lysistrata is? We have some hard problems 900 we need to solve.

MEN'S CHORUS: It looks like the same ailment. Are you racked by spasms toward morning?

ATHENIAN: By the gods, we're destroyed by them! It's so bad that if we don't make peace soon we'll have to rape our girlish friend, Kleisthenes!

MEN'S CHORUS: Why don't you put your cloaks back on so those people who castrate the statues around here don't see you? 905

ATHENIAN: By heaven, that's a good idea!

SPARTAN: By the gods, that certainly is! Let's put ouah garments around us too!

ATHENIAN: That's better. Uh, greetings to you, men of Sparta! Things have been pretty miserable here in Athens.

SPARTAN (*in an aside to one of his comrades*): My deah boy, just think how 910 miserable we'd be if they'd seen us giving ouahselves a hand!

566

ATHENIAN: Well, then, **Spartans**, we have but one question to ask of you: Why are you here?

SPARTAN: We'ah ambassadors foah peace.

ATHENIAN: That's good to hear—we are too. I guess we'd better summon   915
Lysistrata; she's the only one who can reconcile us.

SPARTAN: By heaven, call her or anybody else who can do it!

ATHENIAN: It looks like we won't need to call her. It appears she's heard us already.

(LYSISTRATA *enters*.)

CHORUS: Welcome, you best of all women! You must now be noble and lenient,   920
august and difficult, gentle and experienced. Drawn together by desire,
the leaders of all Greece are calling out for everything to be entrusted
to you!

LYSISTRATA: This shouldn't be too difficult if I can keep them from lusting after
one another. Of course, if they start that, I'd know right away. Hmmm,   925
where's Miss Peace?

(*While* LYSISTRATA *is speaking,* MISS PEACE *enters—nude.*)

LYSISTRATA: Now, girls, bring the Spartan envoys to me. Don't be harsh or rude
—leave that foolishness to your husbands. Instead, be nice and ladylike,
and if some don't give you their hand, just fetch them by those long
handles under their shirts. The rest of you bring those Athenians over   930
here. If they're unfriendly, give them the same treatment. Now, you
Spartans stand next to me, and you Athenians on the other side, and
both of you listen to what I have to say. I am a woman, but I have a
brain in my head, and my judgement isn't bad, and I'm not poorly
educated since I've had ample opportunity to hear my father and other   935
elders speak at length. I want to begin here by criticizing both of you.
When it comes to religious rites at Olympia, Thermopoliae, or Delphi
—and I could name a lot more if I wanted to!—you all join together,
sprinkling water out of a common dish at the altar. Yet when the hated
barbarian is nearby, you destroy *Greek* men and cities! That's my first   940
criticism.

(*The men having been paying increasing attention to* MISS PEACE.)

ATHENIAN: This erection is ruining me!

LYSISTRATA: Next I'll turn to you Spartans. Don't you remember how Perikleidas
the Spartan came as a suppliant before the altars of Athens? He sat, his
face pale against the crimson of his robes, and begged for an army.   945
It was then when Messene threatened you and that earthquake ravaged
your city. Kimon came with 4000 soldiers and saved Sparta. And now

567

you're ravaging the land of the Athenians—who treated you so well before!

ATHENIAN: By god, they're wrong to do this, Lysistrata!   950

SPARTAN: We ah wrong, Ah agree, but that bottom ovah theah is jus' right!

LYSISTRATA: Do you Athenians think I'm going to let you off? Well, don't you forget that when you were exiles in the countryside, the Spartans came with spears and killed many of the Thessalians and the other allies of that tyrant, Hippias. They were the only ones who fought alongside you   955
that day, and because of them you now wear the mantle of democracy instead of the shirts of exiles!

SPARTAN: Ah have nevah seen a woman so fine!

ATHENIAN: That's the sweetest-looking Peace I've ever laid eyes on!

LYSISTRATA: You helped each other so much before, why are you fighting now?   960
Why not stop this wickedness? Why don't you make a peace? What's stopping you?

SPARTAN: Why nothing's stoppin' us. We'll do it if they'll just give us back that nice round piece.

ATHENIAN: What piece was that, Sir?   965

SPARTAN: Uh, Pylos. We've been feelin' the lack of it foah some time now.

ATHENIAN: By Poseidon, you won't get it!

LYSISTRATA: Let them have it, my friend.

ATHENIAN: But then where will we go for excitement?

LYSISTRATA: Demand another piece in return.   970

ATHENIAN: All right. In return for Pylos, we want wooded Echinus, then Melis, that valley behind it, and last of all those leg-like walls of Megaria.

SPARTAN: Not all that, bah gawd! Yo'ah raving!

LYSISTRATA: Talk about raving! Why argue over some legs?

ATHENIAN: I'm ready to strip naked and start plowing!   975

SPARTAN: An Ah'd like to staht mah fertilizing early in the morning!

LYSISTRATA: Once we've made peace, you can do all these things. But if that's to happen, you'll have to go consult with your allies about it.

ATHENIAN: Consult our allies? Why, *all* of us are erect! Don't you think our allies would like to join with us in wanting to screw?   980

SPARTAN: Ouah's would, bah Castor!

ATHENIAN: And the Karystian mercenaries too!

LYSISTRATA: Wonderful! Now then, as soon as you're properly purified, we women will entertain you in the Acropolis with the food we have stored up. Then everyone will take his wife and go home!   985

SPARTAN: Do lead on—wheahevah you wish!

ATHENIAN: But quickly, by god!

(*All exit except the* CHORUS.)

CHORUS: Cloaks, bedding, inlaid work, robes with sweeping trains—everything I own I will give cheerfully to the children or to anyone's daughter who must carry the sacred basket. Take everything from inside, I tell you!   990
Nothing is so tightly locked that you can't break the seals and carry off

whatever's inside! So help yourself—although it's all been carefully hidden!

       If you have no wheat for your servants or your many little children, come and take mine and some goodsized loaves as well! Let the poor come too with bags and sacks for grain—my boy Manes will pour it on! You're welcome at my door—but beware of the dog! 995

(CHORUS *exits. Several* GATE-CRASHERS *enter and attempt to join the celebration offstage, but are barred by the* DOOR-KEEPER.)

FIRST GATE-CRASHER: Open the door!

DOOR-KEEPER: Why don't you beat it?

FIRST GATE-CRASHER: You're just going to sit there? Why I should roast you with 1000 this torch! Good grief, that's vulgar! I won't do it. But then if that's what it takes to please you folks in the audience, we'll keep trying!

SECOND GATE-CRASHER: And the rest of us will suffer through it with you!

DOOR-KEEPER: If you don't get out of here, I'll yank your hair out! Come on, get! The Spartans inside have finished eating and would like to leave in 1005 peace.

(*The* GATE-CRASHERS *leave, and two* ATHENIANS *enter.*)

FIRST ATHENIAN: Wow! I've never seen a bash like this! Why those Spartans were quite agreeable, and we're pretty cheerful and clever ourselves when we've got some wine in our bellies!

SECOND ATHENIAN: That's true, because when we're sober, we're not of sound 1010 mind. If I could persuade us Athenians, we'd always send out our ambassadors drunk. As it is, if we go to Sparta sober, we're so busy looking for some way to cause mischief that we don't hear what they're saying. Instead we hear something they didn't say, and that's what goes into our report when we get home. But now everything's so pleasant that if 1015 someone sang the wrong words to a song, we'd all pretend not to notice and swear it was just grand!

(*The two* ATHENIANS *exit. One of the* GATE-CRASHERS *returns.*)

DOOR-KEEPER: Are you bums coming back again? Get out of here, you no-good!

GATE-CRASHER: By god, the party's already over!

(*The* GATE-CRASHER *leaves as* LYSISTRATA, *the Athenian and Spartan delegations, and the* CHORUS *all come back on stage.*)

SPARTAN: My deah, deah friend, take up youah flute an Ah'll dance and sing 1020 foah you Athenians and ouahselves!

ATHENIAN: My pleasure, by the gods. I'd love to see you dance!

SPARTAN: Oh Memory, you who know both us an' the Athenians, inspiah the young men with youah song! Tell how at Artemisium Athens swept godlike across the sea to rout the Persians, an' how Leonidas led us foath 1025 like wild boars whettin' theah teeth. Oh the sweat ran off ouah faces and down ouah legs, foah the Persians were as many as the sands of the sea! Huntress Aphrodite, slayuh of wild beasts, come hithah to ouah treaty-making, virgin goddess, to join us togethah foah a long time! Let love keep this treaty, and let wilyness and trickery cease. Heah, Oh virgin huntress, come heah! 1030

LYSISTRATA: Now that all has been made well, you may return home, Oh Spartans, and you Athenians too. Let each husband stand by his wife and each wife by her husband. Dance to the gods for our good fortune —but be careful not to make these same mistakes again! 1035

CHORUS: Bring on the Chorus, the Graces, and Artemis! Summon her twin brother, gracious Apollo, and call sparkling-eyed Bacchus from among the Maenades! Call Zeus, god of the lightning, his happy partner and queen, and all the goddesses as witnesses so that we do not forget this generous peace Aphrodite has made! Oh joy! Joy! Jump up! Hooray! 1040 Victory! Oh boy! Oh boy! Wheeeeeee! Oh Spartan, how about an even newer song?

SPARTAN: Oh deah Spahtan muse, quit ouah lovely Mount Tagetos and come with us to celebrate Apollo, Lord of Amyclae, and Athene housed in brass! Praise Tyndareus' twin sons who play beside the rivah Eurotas! 1045 Come on, join in, swirling youah skirts, as Spartans we sing, dancing and pounding ouah feet! Like colts, the maidens dance beside the Eurotas bearing the ivy-wrapped thyrsus, theah haih streaming like Baccantes— Leda's daughtah, chaste and faih, leads the chorus! Lead on! Hold youah haih with youah hand and leap on youah feet like a deah! Y'all 1050 clap to help the chorus! And all praise the goddess, the strongest and all-triumphant, brass-housed Athene!

(*All exit.*)

WILLIAM SHAKESPEARE

Othello

Characters

> DUKE OF VENICE
> BRABANTIO, *a Senator*
> SENATORS
> GRATIANO, *Brother to Brabantio*
> LODOVICO, *Kinsman to Brabantio*
> OTHELLO, *a noble Moor; in the service of the Venetian State*
> CASSIO, *his Lieutenant*
> IAGO, *his Ancient*
> RODERIGO, *a Venetian Gentleman*
> MONTANO, *Othello's predecessor in the Government of Cyprus*
> CLOWN, *Servant to Othello*
> DESDEMONA, *Daughter to Brabantio, and Wife to Othello*
> EMILIA, *Wife to Iago*
> BIANCA, *Mistress to Cassio*
> SAILOR, OFFICERS, GENTLEMEN, MESSENGERS, MUSICIANS, HERALDS, ATTENDANTS

SCENE: *For the first Act, in Venice; during the rest of the Play, at a Sea-port in Cyprus*

ACT I

Scene 1 [Venice. A street.]

(*Enter* RODERIGO *and* IAGO.)

RODERIGO: Tush! Never tell me; I take it much unkindly
    That thou, Iago, who hast had my purse
    As if the strings were thine, shouldst know of this.[1]
IAGO: 'Sblood,[2] but you will not hear me:
    If ever I did dream of such a matter,   5
    Abhor me.
RODERIGO: Thou told'st me thou didst hold him[3] in thy hate.
IAGO: Despite me if I do not. Three great ones of the city,
    In personal suit to make me his lieutenant,
    Off-capp'd[4] to him; and, by the faith of man,   10

---

[1]*i.e.*, Othello's successful courtship of Desdemona   [2]by God's blood   [3]*i.e.*, Othello   [4]took off their caps

I know my price, I am worth no worse a place;
But he, as loving his own pride and purposes,
Evades them, with a bombast circumstance[5]
Horribly stuff'd with epithets of war;
And, in conclusion,   15
Nonsuits[6] my mediators;[7] for, 'Certes,'[8] says he,
'I have already chose my officer.'
And what was he?
Forsooth, a great arithmetician,
One Michael Cassio, a Florentine,   20
A fellow almost damn'd in a fair wife;[9]
That never set a squadron in the field,
Nor the division of a battle knows
More than a spinster; unless[10] the bookish theoric,[11]
Wherein the toged consuls can propose   25
As masterly as he: mere prattle, without practice,
Is all his soldiership. But he, sir, had the election;
And I—of whom his eyes had seen the proof
At Rhodes, at Cyprus, and on other grounds
Christian and heathen—must be be-lee'd[12] and calm'd   30
By debitor and creditor; this counter-caster,[13]
He, in good time, must his lieutenant be,
And I—God bless the mark!—his Moorship's ancient.[14]

RODERIGO: By heaven, I rather would have been his hangman.

IAGO: Why, there's no remedy: 'tis the curse of the service, 35
Preferment goes by letter and affection,
Not by the old gradation,[15] where each second
Stood heir to the first. Now, sir, be judge yourself,
Whe'r[16] I in any just term am affin'd[17]
To love the Moor.   40

RODERIGO: I would not follow him then.

IAGO: O! sir, content you;
I follow him to serve my turn upon him;
We cannot all be masters, nor all masters
Cannot be truly follow'd. You shall mark
Many a duteous and knee-crooking knave,   45
That, doting on his own obsequious bondage,
Wears out his time, much like his master's ass,
For nought but provender, and when he's old, cashier'd;

[5]pompous wordiness, circumlocution [6]turns down [7]spokesmen [8]in truth [9]A much
debated phrase. In the Italian source the Captain (i.e., Cassio) was married, and it may be that
Shakespeare originally intended Bianca to be Cassio's wife but later changed his mind and
failed to alter the phrase here accordingly. Or perhaps Iago simply sneers at Cassio as a
notorious ladies' man. [10]except [11]theory [12]left without wind for my sails [13]bookkeeper
(cf. "arithmetician" above) [14]ensign (but Iago's position in the play seems to be that of
Othello's aide de camp) [15]seniority [16]whether [17]obliged

Whip me such honest knaves. Others there are
Who, trimm'd in forms and visages of duty,   50
Keep yet their hearts attending on themselves,
And, throwing but shows of service on their lords,
Do well thrive by them, and when they have lin'd their coats
Do themselves homage: these fellows have some soul;
And such a one do I profess myself. For, sir,   55
It is as such as you are Roderigo,
Were I the Moor, I would not be Iago:
In following him, I follow but myself;
Heaven is my judge, not I for love and duty,
But seeming so, for my peculiar end: 60
For when my outward action doth demonstrate
The native act and figure of my heart
In compliment extern,[18] 'tis not long after
But I will wear my heart upon my sleeve
For daws to peck at: I am not what I am.   65

RODERIGO: What a full fortune does the thick-lips owe,[19]
    If he can carry 't thus!

IAGO: Call up her father;
    Rouse him, make after him, poison his delight,
    Proclaim him in the streets, incense her kinsmen,
    And, though he in a fertile climate dwell,[20]   70
    Plague him with flies; though that his joy be joy,
    Yet throw such changes of vexation on 't
    As it may lose some colour.

RODERIGO: Here is her father's house; I'll call aloud.

IAGO: Do, with like timorous[21] accent and dire yell   75
    As when, by night and negligence, the fire
    Is spied in populous cities.

RODERIGO: What, ho! Brabantio! Signior Brabantio, ho!

IAGO: Awake! what, ho! Brabantio! thieves! thieves! thieves!
    Look to your house, your daughter, and your bags!   80
    Thieves! thieves!

(Enter BRABANTIO, above, at a window.)

BRABANTIO: What is the reason of this terrible summons?
    What is the matter there?

RODERIGO: Signior, is all your family within?

IAGO: Are your doors lock'd?   85

BRABANTIO: Why? wherefore ask you this?

IAGO: 'Zounds![22] sir, you're robb'd; for shame, put on your gown;

---

[18]external show [19]own [20]i.e., is fortunate [21]frightening [22]by God's wounds

Your heart is burst, you have lost half your soul;
Even now, now, very now, an old black ram
Is tupping[23] your white ewe. Arise, arise!
Awake the snorting[24] citizens with the bell,　　　　　　　　　90
Or else the devil will make a grandsire of you.
Arise, I say.

BRABANTIO:　What! have you lost your wits?

RODERIGO:　Most reverend signior, do you know my voice?

BRABANTIO:　Not I, what are you?　　　　　　　　　　　　　　95

RODERIGO:　My name is Roderigo.

BRABANTIO:　　　　　　　　　　　The worser welcome:
I have charg'd thee not to haunt about my doors:
In honest plainness thou hast heard me say
My daughter is not for thee; and now, in madness,
Being full of supper and distempering draughts,　　　　　100
Upon malicious knavery dost thou come
To start my quiet.

RODERIGO:　Sir, sir, sir!

BRABANTIO:　　　　　　　　But thou must needs be sure
My spirit and my place[25] have in them power
To make this bitter to thee.　　　　　　　　　　　　105

RODERIGO:　　　　　　　　　　Patience, good sir.

BRABANTIO:　What tell'st thou me of robbing? this is Venice;
My house is not a grange.[26]

RODERIGO:　　　　　　　　　　　Most grave Brabantio,
In simple and pure soul I come to you.

IAGO:　'Zounds! sir, you are one of those that will not serve God if the devil bid
you. Because we come to do you service and you think we are ruffians,　　110
you'll have your daughter covered with a Barbary horse; you'll have
your nephews neigh to you; you'll have coursers for cousins and gen-
nets[27] for germans.[28]

BRABANTIO:　What profane wretch art thou?

IAGO:　I am one, sir, that comes to tell you, your daughter and the Moor are　　115
now making the beast with two backs.

BRABANTIO:　Thou art a villain.

IAGO:　　　　　　　　　　You are—a senator.

BRABANTIO:　This thou shalt answer; I know thee, Roderigo.

RODERIGO:　Sir, I will answer any thing. But, I beseech you,
If't be your pleasure and most wise consent,—　　　　　　120
As partly, I find, it is,—that your fair daughter,
At this odd-even[29] and dull watch o' the night,
Transported with no worse nor better guard
But with a knave of common hire, a gondolier,

---

[23]copulating　　[24]snoring　　[25]position　　[26]isolated farm house
[27]Spanish horses　　[28]blood relations　　[29]between night and morning

To the gross clasps of a lascivious Moor,—
If this be known to you, and your allowance,[30]
We then have done you bold and saucy wrongs;
But if you know not this, my manners tell me
We have your wrong rebuke. Do not believe
That, from[31] the sense of all civility,
I thus would play and trifle with your reverence:
Your daughter, if you have not given her leave,
I say again, hath made a gross revolt;
Tying her duty, beauty, wit and fortunes
In[32] an extravagant[33] and wheeling stranger
Of here and every where. Straight satisfy yourself:
If she be in her chamber or your house,
Let loose on me the justice of the state
For thus deluding you.

BRABANTIO: Strike on the tinder, ho!
Give me a taper! call up all my people!
This accident[34] is not unlike my dream;
Belief of it oppresses me already.
Light, I say! light!   (Exit, from above.)

IAGO: Farewell, for I must leave you:
It seems not meet nor wholesome to my place
To be produc'd,[35] as, if I stay, I shall,
Against the Moor; for I do know the state,
However this may gall him with some check,[36]
Cannot with safety cast him; for he 's embark'd
With such loud reason to the Cyprus wars,—
Which even now stand in act,—that, for their souls,
Another of his fathom[37] they have none,
To lead their business; in which regard,
Though I do hate him as I do hell-pains,
Yet, for necessity of present life,
I must show out a flag and sign of love,
Which is indeed but sign. That you shall surely find him,
Lead to the Sagittary[38] the raised search;
And there will I be with him. So, farewell.   (Exit.)

(Enter below, BRABANTIO, and SERVANTS with torches.)

BRABANTIO: It is too true an evil: gone she is,
And what's to come of my despised time
Is nought but bitterness. Now, Roderigo,
Where didst thou see her? O, unhappy girl!

---

[30]by your approval   [31]away from   [32]to   [33]expatriate   [34]happening   [35]i.e., as a witness
[36]restraining adversity   [37]caliber, ability   [38]the name of an inn(?)

With the Moor, sayst thou? Who would be a father!
How didst thou know 'twas she? O, she deceives me
Past thought. What said she to you? Get more tapers!   165
Raise all my kindred! Are they married, think you?

RODERIGO: Truly, I think they are.

BRABANTIO: O heaven! How got she out? O treason of the blood:
Fathers, from hence trust not your daughters' minds
By what you see them act. Are there not charms   170
By which the property of youth and maidhood
May be abus'd? Have you not read, Roderigo,
Of some such thing?

RODERIGO: Yes sir, I have indeed.

BRABANTIO: Call up my brother. O! that you had had her.
Some one way, some another! Do you know   175
Where we may apprehend her and the Moor?

RODERIGO: I think I can discover him, if you please
To get good guard and go along with me.

BRABANTIO: Pray you, lead on. At every house I'll call;
I may command at most. Get weapons, ho!   180
And raise some special officers of night.
On, good Roderigo; I'll deserve[39] your pains.

                                                                    (*Exeunt.*)

Scene 2 [Another street.]

(*Enter* OTHELLO, IAGO, *and* ATTENDANTS, *with torches.*)

IAGO: Though in the trade of war I have slain men,
Yet do I hold it very stuff o' the conscience
To do no contriv'd murder: I lack iniquity   185
Sometimes to do me service. Nine or ten times
I had thought to have yerk'd[40] him here under the ribs.

OTHELLO: 'Tis better as it is.

IAGO: Nay, but he prated,
And spoke such scurvy and provoking terms
Against your honour   190
That, with the little godliness I have,
I did full hard forbear him. But, I pray, sir,
Are you fast married? Be assur'd of this,
That the magnifico[41] is much belov'd,
And hath in his effect a voice potential   195
As double[42] as the duke's; he will divorce you,

[39]i.e., reward   [40]stabbed   [41]one of the grandees, or rulers, of Venice; here, Brabantio
[42]Iago means that Brabantio's influence equals that of the Doge's, with his double vote.

Or put upon you what restaint and grievance
The law—with all his might to enforce it on—
Will give him cable.[43]

OTHELLO: Let him do his spite:
My services which I have done the signiory[44]   200
Shall out-tongue his complaints. 'Tis yet to know,[45]
Which when I know that boasting is an honour
I shall promulgate, I fetch my life and being
From men of royal siege, and my demerits[46]
May speak unbonneted[47] to as proud a fortune   205
As this[48] that I have reach'd; for know, Iago,
But that I love the gentle Desdemona,
I would not my unhoused[49] free condition
Put into circumscription and confine
For the sea's worth. But, look! what lights come yond?   210

IAGO: Those are the raised[50] father and his friends:
You were best[51] go in.

OTHELLO: Not I; I must be found:
My parts, my title, and my perfect[52] soul
Shall manifest me rightly. Is it they?

IAGO: By Janus,[53] I think no.   215

(*Enter* CASSIO *and certain* OFFICERS, *with torches.*)

OTHELLO: The servants of the duke, and my lieutenant.
The goodness of the night upon you, friends!
What is the news?

CASSIO: The duke does greet you, general,
And he requires your haste-post-haste appearance,
Even on the instant.   220

OTHELLO: What is the matter, think you?

CASSIO: Something from Cyprus, as I may divine.
It is a business of some heat;[54] the galleys
Have sent a dozen sequent[55] messengers
This very night at another's heels,
And many of the consuls,[56] rais'd and met,   225
Are at the duke's already. You have been hotly call'd for;
When, being not at your lodging to be found,
The senate hath sent about three several[57] quests
To search you out.

---

[43]i.e., scope   [44]the Venetian government   [45]i.e., the signiory does not as yet know   [46]merits   [47]i.e., as equals   [48]i.e., that of Desdemona's family   [49]unconfined   [50]aroused   [51]had better   [52]untroubled by a bad conscience   [53]the two-faced Roman god of portals and doors and (hence) of beginnings and ends   [54]urgency   [55]following one another   [56]i.e., senators   [57]separate

OTHELLO: 'Tis well I am found by you.
I will but spend a word here in the house,   230
And go with you.   *(Exit.)*
CASSIO: Ancient, what makes he here?
IAGO: Faith, he to-night hath boarded a land carrack;[58]
If it prove lawful prize, he's made for ever.
CASSIO: I do not understand.
IAGO: He 's married.
CASSIO: To who?

(Re-enter OTHELLO.)

IAGO: Marry,[59] to—Come, captain, will you go?   235
OTHELLO: Have with you.
CASSIO: Here comes another troop to seek for you.
IAGO: It is Brabantio. General, be advis'd;
He comes to bad intent.

(Enter BRABANTIO, RODERIGO, and OFFICERS, with torches and weapons.)

OTHELLO: Holla! stand there!
RODERIGO: Signior, it is the Moor.
BRABANTIO: Down with him, thief!

(They draw on both sides.)

IAGO: You, Roderigo! come, sir, I am for you.[60]   240
OTHELLO: Keep up your bright swords, for the dew will rust them.
Good signior, you shall more command with years
Than with your weapons.
BRABANTIO: O thou foul thief! where hast thou stow'd my daughter?
Damn'd as thou art, thou hast enchanted her;   245
For I'll refer me to all things of sense,
If she in chains of magic were not bound,
Whether a maid so tender, fair, and happy,
So opposite to marriage that she shunn'd
The wealthy curled darlings of our nation,   250
Would ever have, to incur a general mock,
Run from her guardage to the sooty bosom
Of such a thing as thou; to fear, not to delight.
Judge me the world, if 'tis not gross in sense[61]
That thou hast practis'd on her with foul charms,   255
Abus'd her delicate youth with drugs or minerals

---

[58]treasure ship   [59]by the Virgin Mary   [60]let you and me fight   [61]obvious

That weaken motion:[62] I'll have't disputed on;
'Tis probable, and palpable to thinking.
I therefore apprehend and do attach[63] thee
For an abuser of the world, a practiser   260
Of arts inhibited and out of warrant.[64]
Lay hold upon him: if he do resist,
Subdue him at his peril.

OTHELLO: Hold your hands,
Both you of my inclining,[65] and the rest:
Were it my cue to fight, I should have known it   265
Without a prompter. Where will you that I go
To answer this your charge?

BRABANTIO: To prison; till fit time
Of law and course of direct session[66]
Call thee to answer.

OTHELLO: What if I do obey?
How may the duke be therewith satisfied,   270
Whose messengers are here about my side,
Upon some present[67] business of the state
To bring me to him?

OFFICER: 'Tis true, most worthy signior;
The duke's in council, and your noble self,
I am sure, is sent for.   275

BRABANTIO: How! the duke in council!
In this time of the night! Bring him away.
Mine's not an idle cause: the duke himself,
Or any of my brothers of the state,[68]
Cannot but feel this wrong as 'twere their own;
For if such actions may have passage free,   280
Bond-slaves and pagans shall our statesmen be.   (*Exeunt.*)

Scene 3 [A Council Chamber.]

(*The* DUKE *and* SENATORS *sitting at a table.* OFFICERS *attending.*)

DUKE: There is no composition[69] in these news
      That gives them credit.

FIRST SENATOR: Indeed, they are disproportion'd;
      My letters say a hundred and seven galleys.

DUKE: And mine, a hundred and forty.   285

SECOND SENATOR: And mine, two hundred:

[62]normal reactions   [63]arrest   [64]prohibited and illegal   [65]party   [66]normal process of law
[67]immediate, pressing   [68]fellow senators   [69]consistency, agreement

But though they jump[70] not on a just[71] account,—
As in these cases, where the aim[72] reports,
'Tis oft with difference,—yet do they all confirm
A Turkish fleet, and bearing up to Cyprus.

DUKE: Nay, it is possible enough to judgment: 290
I do not so secure me in[73] the error,
But the main article[74] I do approve[75]
In fearful sense.

SAILOR (*within*): What, ho! what, ho! what, ho!

OFFICER: A messenger from the galleys.   295

(*Enter a* SAILOR.)

DUKE: Now, what 's the business?

SAILOR: The Turkish preparation makes for Rhodes;
So was I bid report here to the state
By Signior Angelo.

DUKE: How say you by this change?

FIRST SENATOR: This cannot be
By no[76] assay[77] of reason; 'tis a pageant[78]   300
To keep us in false gaze.[79] When we consider
The importancy of Cyprus to the Turk,
And let ourselves again but understand,
That as it more concerns the Turk than Rhodes,
So may he with more facile question bear[80] it,   305
For that it stands not in such warlike brace,[81]
But altogether lacks the abilities
That Rhodes is dress'd in: if we make thought of this,
We must not think the Turk is so unskilful
To leave that latest which concerns him first,   310
Neglecting an attempt of ease and gain,
To wake and wage a danger profitless.

DUKE: Nay, in all confidence, he's not for Rhodes

OFFICER: Here is more news.

(*Enter a* MESSENGER.)

MESSENGER: The Ottomites,[82] reverend and gracious,   315
Steering with due course toward the isle of Rhodes,
Have there injointed[83] them with an after fleet.[84]

FIRST SENATOR: Ay, so I thought. How many, as you guess?

---

[70]coincide   [71]exact   [72]conjecture   [73]draw comfort from   [74]substance   [75]believe   [76]any
[77]test   [78](deceptive) show   [79]looking in the wrong direction   [80]more easily capture
[81]state of defense   [82]Turks   [83]joined   [84]fleet that followed after

MESSENGER: Of thirty sail; and now they do re-stem[85]
     Their backward course, bearing with frank appearance   320
     Their purposes toward Cyprus. Signior Montano,
     Your trusty and most valiant servitor,
     With his free duty[86] recommends[87] you thus,
     And prays you to believe him.
DUKE: 'Tis certain then, for Cyprus.   325
     Marcus Luccicos, is not he in town?
FIRST SENATOR: He's now in Florence.
DUKE: Write from us to him; post-post-haste dispatch.
FIRST SENATOR: Here comes Brabantio and the valiant Moor.

(*Enter* BRABANTIO, OTHELLO, IAGO, RODERIGO, *and* OFFICERS.)

DUKE: Valiant Othello, we must straight employ you   330
     Against the general enemy Ottoman.
     (*To* BRABANTIO) I did not see you; welcome, gentle signior;
     We lack'd your counsel and your help to-night.
BRABANTIO: So did I yours. Good your Grace, pardon me;
     Neither my place nor aught I heard of business   335
     Hath rais'd me from my bed, nor doth the general care
     Take hold of me, for my particular grief
     Is of so flood-gate[88] and o'erbearing nature
     That it engluts and swallows other sorrows
     And it is still itself.   340
DUKE: Why, what 's the matter?
BRABANTIO: My daughter! O! my daughter.
DUKE: Dead?
SENATORS:
BRABANTIO: Ay, to me;
     She is abus'd, stol'n from me, and corrupted
     By spells and medicines bought of mountebanks;
     For nature so preposterously to err,
     Being not deficient, blind, or lame of sense,   345
     Sans[89] witchcraft could not.
DUKE: Whoe'er he be that in this foul proceeding
     Hath thus beguil'd your daughter of herself
     And you of her, the bloody book of law
     You shall yourself read in the bitter letter   350
     After your own sense; yea, though our proper[90] son
     Stood[91] in your action.[92]
BRABANTIO: Humbly I thank your Grace.
     Here is the man, this Moor; whom now, it seems,

---

[85]steer again [86]unqualified expressions of respect [87]informs [88]torrential [89]without [90]own
[91]were accused [92]suit

Your special mandate for the state affairs
Hath hither brought.   355

DUKE: ⎫
SENATORS: ⎬   We are very sorry for it.

DUKE (*to* OTHELLO):   What, in your own part, can you say to this?

BRABANTIO: Nothing, but this is so.

OTHELLO: Most potent, grave, and reverend signiors,
My very noble and approv'd[93] good masters,
That I have ta'en away this old man's daughter,   360
It is most true; true, I have married her:
The very head and front of my offending
Hath this extent, no more. Rude am I in my speech,
And little bless'd with the soft phrase of peace;
For since these arms of mine had seven years' pith,[94]   365
Till now some nine moons wasted,[95] they have us'd
Their dearest action in the tented field;
And little of this great world can I speak,
More than pertains to feats of broil and battle;
And therefore little shall I grace my cause   370
In speaking for myself. Yet, by your gracious patience,
I will a round[96] unvarnish'd tale deliver
Of my whole course of love; what drugs, what charms,
What conjuration, and what mighty magic,
For such proceeding I am charg'd withal,   375
I won his daughter.

BRABANTIO: A maiden never bold;
Of spirit so still and quiet, that her motion
Blush'd at herself;[97] and she, in spite of nature,
Of years, of country, credit, every thing,
To fall in love with what she fear'd to look on!   380
It is a judgment maim'd and most imperfect
That will confess[98] perfection so could err
Against all rules of nature, and must be driven
To find out practices of cunning hell,
Why this should be. I therefore vouch again   385
That with some mixtures powerful o'er the blood,
Or with some dram conjur'd to this effect,
He wrought upon her.

DUKE: To vouch this, is no proof,
Without more certain and more overt test
Than these thin habits[99] and poor likelihoods   390
Of modern[100] seeming do prefer against him.

---

[93]tested (by past experience)   [94]strength   [95]past   [96]blunt   [97]*i.e.*, (her modesty was such that)
she blushed at her own emotions or: could not move without blushing   [98]assert
[99]weak appearances   [100]commonplace

FIRST SENATOR: But, Othello, speak:
    Did you by indirect and forced courses
    Subdue and poison this young maid's affections;
    Or came it by request and such fair question[101]   395
    As soul to soul affordeth?
OTHELLO: I do beseech you;
    Send for the lady to the Sagittary,
    And let her speak of me before her father:
    If you do find me foul in her report,
    The trust, the office I do hold of you,   400
    Not only take away, but let your sentence
    Even fall upon my life.
DUKE: Fetch Desdemona hither.
OTHELLO: Ancient, conduct them; you best know the place.
                  (*Exeunt* IAGO *and* ATTENDANTS.)
    And, till she come, as truly as to heaven
    I do confess the vices of my blood,   405
    So justly to your grave ears I'll present
    How I did thrive in this fair lady's love,
    And she in mine.
DUKE: Say it, Othello.
OTHELLO: Her father lov'd me; oft invited me;   410
    Still[102] question'd me the story of my life
    From year to year, the battles, sieges, fortunes
    That I have pass'd.
    I ran it through, even from my boyish days
    To the very moment that he bade me tell it;   415
    Wherein I spake of most disastrous chances,
    Of moving accidents by flood and field,
    Of hair-breadth 'scapes i' the imminent deadly breach,
    Of being taken by the insolent foe
    And sold to slavery, of my redemption thence   420
    And portance[103] in my travel's history;
    Wherein of antres[104] vast and deserts idle,[105]
    Rough quarries, rocks, and hills whose heads touch heaven,
    It was my hint[106] to speak, such was the process;
    And of the Cannibals that each other eat,   425
    The Anthropophagi,[107] and men whose heads
    Do grow beneath their shoulders. This to hear
    Would Desdemona seriously incline;
    But still the house-affairs would draw her thence;
    Which ever as she could with haste dispatch,   430
    She'd come again, and with a greedy ear

[101]conversation   [102]always, regularly   [103]behavior   [104]caves   [105]empty, sterile
[106]opportunity   [107]man-eaters

Devour up my discourse. Which I observing,
Took once a pliant[108] hour, and found good means
To draw from her a prayer of earnest heart
That I would all my pilgrimage dilate,[109]   435
Whereof by parcels[110] she had something heard,
But not intentively:[111] I did consent;
And often did beguile her of her tears,
When I did speak of some distressful stroke
That my youth suffer'd. My story being done,   440
She gave me for my pains a world of sighs:
She swore, in faith, 'twas strange, 'twas passing[112] strange;
'Twas pitiful, 'twas wondrous pitiful:
She wish'd she had not heard it, yet she wish'd
That heaven had made her[113] such a man; she thank'd me,   445
And bade me, if I a friend that lov'd her,
I should but teach him how to tell my story,
And that would woo her. Upon this hint I spake.
She lov'd me for the dangers I had pass'd,
And I lov'd her that she did pity them.   450
This only is the witchcraft I have us'd:
Here comes the lady; let her witness it.

(*Enter* DESDEMONA, IAGO, *and* ATTENDANTS.)

DUKE: I think this tale would win my daughter too.
        Good Brabantio,
        Take up this mangled matter at the best;   455
        Men do their broken weapons rather use
        Than their bare hands.
BRABANTIO: I pray you, hear her speak:
        If she confess that she was half the wooer,
        Destruction on my head, if my bad blame
        Light on the man! Come hither, gentle mistress: 460
        Do you perceive in all this noble company
        Where most you owe obedience?
DESDEMONA: My noble father,
        I do perceive here a divided duty:
        To you I am bound for life and education;
        My life and education both do learn[114] me   465
        How to respect you; you are the lord of duty,
        I am hitherto your daughter: but here's my husband;
        And so much duty as my mother show'd
        To you, preferring you before her father,

[108]suitable [109]relate in full [110]piecemeal [111]in sequence [112]surpassing
[113]direct object; not "for her" [114]teach

So much I challenge[115] that I may profess   470
Due to the Moor my lord.

BRABANTIO: God be with you! I have done.
Please it your Grace, on to the state affairs:
I had rather to adopt a child than get it.
Come hither, Moor:
I here do give thee that with all my heart   475
Which, but thou hast[116] already, with all my heart
I would keep from thee. For your sake,[117] jewel,
I am glad at soul I have no other child;
For thy escape would teach me tyranny,
To hang clogs on them. I have done, my lord.   480

DUKE: Let me speak like yourself and lay a sentence,[118]
Which as a grize[119] or step, may help these lovers
Into your favour.
When remedies are past, the griefs are ended
By seeing the worst, which[120] late on hopes depended.   485
To mourn a mischief that is past and gone
Is the next way to draw new mischief on.
What cannot be preserv'd when Fortune takes,
Patience her injury a mockery makes.[121]
The robb'd that smiles steals something from the thief;   490
He robs himself that spends a bootless grief.

BRABANTIO: So let the Turk of Cyprus us beguile;
We lose it not so long as we can smile.
He bears the sentence[122] well that nothing bears
But the free comfort which from thence he hears;   495
But he bears both the sentence and the sorrow
That, to pay grief, must of poor patience borrow.
These sentences, to sugar, or to gall,
Being strong on both sides, are equivocal:[123]
But words are words; I never yet did hear   500
That the bruis'd heart was pierced[124] through the ear.
I humbly beseech you, proceed to the affairs of state.

DUKE: The Turk with a most mighty preparation makes for Cyprus. Othello, the
fortitude[125] of the place is best known to you; and though we have there
a substitute of most allowed sufficiency,[126] yet opinion, a sovereign mis-   505
tress of effects, throws a more safer voice on you:[127] you must therefore
be content to slubber[128] the gloss of your new fortunes with this more
stubborn[129] and boisterous expedition.

[115]claim as right   [116]didn't you have it   [117]because of you   [118]provide a maxim   [119]step
[120]the antecedent is "griefs"   [121]to suffer an irreparable loss patiently is to make light of
injury (i.e., to triumph over adversity)   [122](1) verdict, (2) maxim   [123]sententious comfort (like
the Duke's trite maxims) can hurt as well as soothe   [124](1)lanced (i.e., cured), (2) wounded
[125]strength   [126]admitted competence   [127]general opinion, which mainly determines action,
thinks Cyprus safer with you in command   [128]besmear   [129]rough

OTHELLO: The tyrant custom, most grave senators,
          Hath made the flinty and steel couch of war   510
          My thrice-driven[130] bed of down: I do agnize[131]
          A natural and prompt alacrity
          I find in hardness, and do undertake
          These present wars against the Ottomites.
          Most humbly therefore bending to your state,[132]   515
          I crave fit disposition[133] for my wife,
          Due reference of place and exhibition,[134]
          With such accommodation and besort[135]
          As levels with[136] her breeding.
DUKE: If you please,
          Be't at her father's.   520
BRABANTIO: I'll not have it so.
OTHELLO: Nor I.
DESDEMONA: Nor I; I would not there reside,
          To put my father in impatient thoughts
          By being in his eye. Most gracious duke,
          To my unfolding[137] lend your gracious ear;   525
          And let me find a charter[138] in your voice
          To assist my simpleness.
DUKE: What would you, Desdemona?
DESDEMONA: That I did love the Moor to live with him,
          My downright violence and storm of fortunes   530
          May trumpet to the world; my heart's subdu'd
          Even to the very quality of my lord;[139]
          I saw Othello's visage in his mind,
          And to his honours and his valiant parts
          Did I my soul and fortunes consecrate.   535
          So that, dear lords, if I be left behind,
          A moth of peace, and he go to the war,
          The rites[140] for which I love him are bereft me,
          And I a heavy interim shall support[141]
          By his dear[142] absence. Let me go with him.   540
OTHELLO: Let her have your voices.
          Vouch with me, heaven, I therefore beg it not
          To please the palate of my appetite,
          Nor to comply with heat,—the young affects[143]
          In me defunct,—and proper satisfaction,   545
          But to be free and bounteous to her mind;

---

[130]made as soft as possible   [131]recognize   [132]submitting to your authority   [133]disposal
[134]provision   [135]fitness   [136]is proper to   [137]explanation   [138]permission   [139]i.e., I have become
a soldier, like Othello   [140]i.e., of marriage, or of war, or of both   [141]endure   [142]closely concerning (*i.e.*, Desdemona)   [143]the passions of youth (hence, here, *immoderate* sexual passion)

And heaven defend[144] your good souls that you think
I will your serious and great business scant
For[145] she is with me. No, when light-wing'd toys
Of feather'd Cupid seel[146] with wanton dulness 550
My speculative and offic'd instruments,[147]
That[148] my disports corrupt and taint my business,
Let housewives make a skillet of my helm,
And all indign[149] and base adversities
Make head against my estimation![150] 555

DUKE: Be it as you shall privately determine,
Either for her stay or going. The affair cries haste,
And speed must answer it.

FIRST SENATOR: You must away to-night.

OTHELLO: With all my heart.

DUKE: At nine i' the morning here we'll meet again. 560
Othello, leave some officer behind,
And he shall our commission bring to you;
With such things else of quality and respect
As doth import you.[151]

OTHELLO: So please your Grace, my ancient;
A man he is of honesty and trust: 565
To his conveyance I assign my wife,
With what else needful your good grace shall think
To be sent after me.

DUKE: Let it be so.
Good-night to every one. (To BRABANTIO) And, noble signior,
If virtue no delighted[152] beauty lack, 570
Your son-in-law is far more fair than black.

FIRST SENATOR: Adieu, brave Moor! use Desdemona well.

BRABANTIO: Look to her, Moor, if thou hast eyes to see:
She has deceiv'd her father, and may thee.

                        (Exeunt DUKE, SENATORS, OFFICERS, &c.)

OTHELLO: My life upon her faith! Honest Iago, 575
My Desdemona must I leave to thee:
I prithee, let thy wife attend on her;
And bring them after in the best advantage.[153]
Come, Desdemona; I have but an hour
Of love, of worldly matters and direction, 580
To spend with thee: we must obey the time.

                        (Exeunt OTHELLO and DESDEMONA.)

RODERIGO: Iago!

IAGO: What sayst thou, noble heart?

144forbid   145because   146blind (v.) by sewing up the eyelids (a term from falconry)
147reflective and executive faculties and organs   148so that   149shameful   150reputation
151concern   152delightful   153opportunity

RODERIGO: What will I do, think'st thou?

IAGO: Why, go to bed, and sleep. 585

RODERIGO: I will incontinently[154] drown myself.

IAGO: Well, if thou dost, I shall never love thee after.
Why, thou silly gentleman!

RODERIGO: It is silliness to live when to live is torment; and then have we a
prescription to die when death is our physician. 590

IAGO: O! villanous; I have looked upon the world for four times seven years,
and since I could distinguish betwixt a benefit and an injury, I never
found man that knew how to love himself. Ere I would say, I would
drown myself for the love of a guinea-hen, I would change my humanity
with a baboon. 595

RODERIGO: What should I do? I confess it is my shame to be so fond;[155] but it
is not in my virtue[156] to amend it.

IAGO: Virtue! a fig! 'tis in ourselves that we are thus, or thus. Our bodies are
our gardens, to the which our wills are gardeners; so that if we will
plant nettles or sow lettuce, set hyssop and weed up thyme, supply it 600
with one gender[157] of herbs or distract it with many, either to have it
sterile with idleness or manured with industry, why, the power and cor-
rigible[158] authority of this lies in our wills. If the balance of our lives
had not one scale of reason to poise another of sensuality, the blood
and baseness of our natures would conduct us to most preposterous con- 605
clusions; but we have reason to cool our raging motions, our carnal
stings, our unbitted[159] lusts, whereof I take this that you call love to be a
sect or scion.[160]

RODERIGO: It cannot be.

IAGO: It is merely a lust of the blood and a permission of the will. Come, be 610
a man. Drown thyself! drown cats and blind puppies. I have professed
me thy friend, and I confess me knit to thy deserving with cables of
perdurable toughness; I could never better stead thee than now. Put
money in thy purse; follow these wars; defeat thy favour[161] with a
usurped[162] beard; I say, put money in thy purse. It cannot be that Des- 615
demona should long continue her love to the Moor,—put money in thy
purse,—nor he his to her. It was a violent commencement in her, and
thou shalt see an answerable sequestration;[163] put but money in thy
purse. These Moors are changeable in their wills;—fill thy purse with
money:—the food that to him now is as luscious as locusts,[164] shall be to 620
him shortly as bitter as coloquintida.[165] She must change for youth: when
she is sated with his body, she will find the error of her choice. She must
have change, she must: therefore put money in thy purse. If thou wilt
needs damn thyself, do it a more delicate way than drowning. Make all

[154]forthwith [155]infatuated [156]strength [157]kind [158]corrective [159]i.e., uncontrolled [160]off-
shoot [161]change thy appearance (for the worse?) [162]assumed [163]estrangement [164]sweet-
tasting fruits (perhaps the carob, the edible seed pod of an evergreen tree in the Mediterranean
area) [165]purgative derived from a bitter apple

the money thou canst. If sanctimony and a frail vow betwixt an erring[166]   625
barbarian and a super-subtle[167] Venetian be not too hard for my wits
and all the tribe of hell, thou shalt enjoy her; therefore make money.
A pox of drowning thyself! it is clean out of the way: seek thou rather
to be hanged in compassing thy joy than to be drowned and go without
her.   630

RODERIGO: Wilt thou be fast to my hopes, if I depend on the issue?[168]

IAGO: Thou art sure of me: go, make money. I have told thee often, and I
re-tell thee again and again, I hate the Moor; my cause is hearted;
thine hath no less reason. Let us be conjunctive[169] in our revenge against
him; if thou canst cuckold him, thou dost thyself a pleasure, me a sport.   635
There are many events in the womb of time which will be delivered.
Traverse;[170] go: provide thy money. We will have more of this to-
morrow. Adieu.

RODERIGO: Where shall we meet i' the morning?

IAGO: At my lodging.   640

RODERIGO: I'll be with thee betimes.

IAGO: Go to: farewell. Do you hear, Roderigo?

RODERIGO: What say you?

IAGO: No more of drowning, do you hear?

RODERIGO: I am changed. I'll sell all my land.   645

IAGO: Go to; farewell! put money enough in your purse.

(*Exit* RODERIGO.)

Thus do I ever make my fool my purse;
For I mine own gain'd knowledge should profane,
If I would time expend with such a snipe[171]
But for my sport and profit. I hate the Moor,   650
And it is thought abroad[172] that 'twixt my sheets
He has done my office: I know not if 't be true,
But I, for mere suspicion in that kind,
Will do as if for surety.[173] He holds me well;[174]
The better shall my purpose work on him.   655
Cassio's a proper[175] man; let me see now:
To get his place; and to plume up[176] my will
In double knavery; how, how? Let's see:
After some time to abuse Othello's ear
That he[177] is too familiar with his wife: 660
He hath a person and a smooth dispose[178]
To be suspected; framed[179] to make women false,
The Moor is of a free and open nature,
That thinks men honest that but seem to be so,
And will as tenderly be led by the nose   665

[166]vagabond   [167]exceedingly refined   [168]rely on the outcome   [169]allied   [170]march   [171]dupe
[172]people think   [173]as if it were certain   [174]in high regard   [175]handsome   [176]make ready
[177]i.e., Cassio   [178]bearing   [179]designed, apt

As asses are.
I have't; it is engender'd: hell and night
Must bring this monstrous birth to the world's light.

(*Exit.*)

ACT II

Scene 1 [A Sea-port Town in Cyprus. An open place near the Quay.]

(*Enter* MONTANO *and two* GENTLEMEN.)

MONTANO: What from the cape can you discern at sea?
FIRST GENTLEMAN: Nothing at all: it is a high-wrought flood;
     I cannot 'twixt the heaven and the main[180]
     Descry a sail.
MONTANO: Methinks the wind hath spoke aloud at land;   5
     A fuller blast ne'er shook our battlements;
     If it hath ruffian'd so upon the sea,
     What ribs of oak, when mountains melt on them,
     Can hold the mortise?[181] what shall we hear of this?
SECOND GENTLEMAN: A segregation[182] of the Turkish fleet;   10
     For do but stand upon the foaming shore,
     The chidden billow seems to pelt the clouds;
     The wind-shak'd surge, with high and monstrous mane,
     Seems to cast water on the burning bear[183]
     And quench the guards of the ever-fixed pole:[184]   15
     I never did like[185] molestation view
     On the enchafed[186] flood.
MONTANO: If that[187] the Turkish fleet
     Be not enshelter'd and embay'd, they are drown'd;
     It is impossible they bear it out.

(*Enter a* THIRD GENTLEMAN.)

THIRD GENTLEMAN: News, lad! our wars are done.   20
     The desperate tempest hath so bang'd the Turks
     That their designment halts;[188] a noble ship of Venice
     Hath seen a grievous wrack and suffrance[189]
     On most part of their fleet.
MONTANO: How! is this true?   25

---

[180]ocean [181]hold the joints together [182]scattering [183]Ursa Minor (the Little Dipper)
[184]Polaris, the North Star, almost directly above the Earth's axis, is part of the constellation
of the Little Bear, or Dipper. [185]similar [186]agitated [187]if [188]plan is stopped [189]damage

THIRD GENTLEMAN: The ship is here put in,
    A Veronesa;[190] Michael Cassio,
    Lieutenant to the warlike Moor Othello,
    Is come on shore: the Moor himself's at sea,
    And is in full commission here for Cyprus.
MONTANO: I am glad on 't; 'tis a worthy governor.   30
THIRD GENTLEMAN: But this same Cassio, though he speak of comfort
    Touching the Turkish loss, yet he looks sadly
    And prays the Moor be safe; for they were parted
    With foul and violent tempest.
MONTANO: Pray heaven he be;
    For I have serv'd him, and the man commands   35
    Like a full soldier. Let's to the sea-side, ho!
    As well to see the vessel that 's come in
    As to throw out our eyes for brave Othello,
    Even till we make the main and the aerial blue
    An indistinct regard.[191]   40
THIRD GENTLEMAN: Come, let's do so;
    For every minute is expectancy
    Of more arrivance.

(Enter CASSIO.)

CASSIO: Thanks, you the valiant of this warlike isle,
    That so approve the Moor. O! let the heavens   45
    Give him defence against the elements,
    For I have lost him on a dangerous sea.
MONTANO: Is he well shipp'd?
CASSIO: His bark is stoutly timber'd, and his pilot
    Of very expert and approv'd allowance;[192]   50
    Therefore my hopes, not surfeited to death,[193]
    Stand in bold cure.[194]

(Within, "A sail!—a sail!—a sail!" *Enter a* MESSENGER.)

CASSIO: What noise?
MESSENGER: The town is empty; on the brow o' the sea
    Stand ranks of people, and they cry "A sail!"   55
CASSIO: My hopes do shape him for the governor.

(Guns heard.)

[190]probably a *type* of ship, rather than a ship from Verona—not only because Verona is an inland city but also because of a "noble ship of Venice" above   [191]till our (straining) eyes can no longer distinguish sea and sky   [192]admitted and proven to be expert   [193]overindulged   [194]with good chance of being fulfilled

SECOND GENTLEMAN: They do discharge their shot of courtesy;
    Our friends at least.
CASSIO: I pray you, sir, go forth.
    And give us truth who 'tis that is arriv'd.
SECOND GENTLEMAN: I shall.   60

                                       (*Exit.*)

MONTANO: But, good lieutenant, is your general wiv'd?
CASSIO: Most fortunately: he hath achiev'd a maid
    That paragons[195] description and wild fame;
    One that excels the quirks[196] of blazoning pens,
    And in th' essential vesture of creation[197]   65
    Does tire the ingener.[198]

(*Re-enter* SECOND GENTLEMAN.)

                    How now! who has put in?
SECOND GENTLEMAN: 'Tis one Iago, ancient to the general.
CASSIO: He has had most favourable and happy speed:
    Tempests themselves, high seas, and howling winds,
    The gutter'd[199] rocks, and congregated sands,   70
    Traitors ensteep'd[200] to clog the guiltless keel,
    As having sense of beauty, do omit
    Their mortal[201] natures, letting so safely by
    The divine Desdemona.
MONTANO: What is she?
CASSIO: She that I spake of, our great captain's captain,   75
    Left in the conduct of the bold Iago,
    Whose footing[202] here anticipates our thoughts
    A se'nnight's[203] speed. Great Jove, Othello guard,
    And swell his sail with thine own powerful breath,
    That he may bless this bay with his tall[204] ship,   80
    Make love's quick pants in Desdemona's arms,
    Give renew'd fire to our extinated spirits,
    And bring all Cyprus comfort!

(*Enter* DESDEMONA, EMILIA, IAGO, RODERIGO, *and* ATTENDANTS.)

                  O! behold,
    The riches of the ship is come on shore.
    Ye men of Cyprus, let her have your knees.   85
    Hail to thee, lady! and the grace of heaven,
    Before, behind thee, and on every hand,

---

[195]exceeds, surpasses [196]ingenuities [197]i.e., just as God made her: or: (even in) the (mere) essence of human nature [198]inventor (i.e., of her praises?) [199]jagged, or: submerged [200]submerged [201]deadly [202]landing [203]week's [204]brave

Enwheel thee round!

DESDEMONA: I thank you, valiant Cassio.
    What tidings can you tell me of my lord?

CASSIO: He is not yet arriv'd; nor know I aught   90
    But that he's well, and will be shortly here.

DESDEMONA: O! but I fear—How lost you company?

CASSIO: The great contention of the sea and skies
    Parted our fellowship. But hark! a sail.

(Cry within, "A sail—a sail!" Guns heard.)

SECOND GENTLEMAN: They give their greeting to the citadel: 95
    This likewise is a friend.

CASSIO: See for the news!   *(Exit GENTLEMAN.)*
    Good ancient, you are welcome:—*(To* EMILIA*)* welcome, mistress.
    Let it not gall your patience, good Iago,
    That I extend my manners; 'tis my breeding
    That gives me this bold show of courtesy.   *(Kissing her.)*   100

IAGO: Sir, would she give you so much of her lips
    As of her tongue she oft bestows on me,
    You'd have enough.

DESDEMONA: Alas! she has no speech.

IAGO: In faith, too much;
    I find it still when I have list[205] to sleep: 105
    Marry, before your ladyship, I grant,
    She puts her tongue a little in her heart,
    And chides with thinking.[206]

EMILIA: You have little cause to say so.

IAGO: Come on, come on; you are pictures[207] out of doors,   110
    Bells[208] in your parlours, wild cats in your kitchens,
    Saints in your injuries, devils being offended,
    Players[209] in your housewifery,[210] and housewives[211] in your beds.

DESDEMONA: O! fie upon thee, slanderer.

IAGO: Nay, it is true, or else I am a Turk: 115
    You rise to play and go to bed to work.

EMILIA: You shall not write my praise.

IAGO: No, let me not.

DESDEMONA: What wouldst thou write of me, if thou shouldst praise me?

IAGO: O gentle lady, do not put me to 't,
    For I am nothing if not critical.   120

DESDEMONA: Come on; assay. There's one gone to the harbour?

IAGO: Ay, madam.

---

[205]wish [206]i.e., without words [207]i.e., made up, "painted" [208]i.e., jangly [209]triflers, wastrels [210]housekeeping [211](1) hussies, (2) (unduly) frugal with their sexual favors, (3) businesslike, serious

DESDEMONA: I am not merry, but I do beguile
              The thing I am by seeming otherwise.
              Come, how wouldst thou praise me?   125
IAGO: I am about it; but indeed my invention
         Comes from my pate[212] as birdlime does from frize;[213]
         It plucks out brains and all: but my muse labours
         And thus she is deliver'd.
         If she be fair and wise, fairness and wit,   130
         The one's for use, the other useth it.
DESDEMONA: Well prais'd! How if she be black and witty?
IAGO: If she be black,[214] and thereto have a wit,
         She'll find a white that shall her blackness fit.
DESDEMONA: Worse and worse.   135
EMILIA: How if fair and foolish?
IAGO: She never yet was foolish that was fair,
         For even her folly[215] help'd to an heir.
DESDEMONA: These are old fond[216] paradoxes to make fools laugh i' the
              alehouse. What miserable praise hast thou for her that's foul and   140
              foolish?
IAGO: There's none so foul and foolish thereunto.
         But does foul pranks which fair and wise ones do.
DESDEMONA: O heavy ignorance; thou praisest the worst best. But what praise
              couldst thou bestow on a deserving woman indeed, one that, in the   145
              authority of her merit, did justly put on the vouch[217] of very malice
              itself?
IAGO: She that was ever fair and never proud,
         Had tongue at will and yet was never loud,
         Never lack'd gold and yet went never gay,   150
         Fled from her wish and yet said "Now I may,"
         She that being anger'd, her revenge being nigh,
         Bade her wrong stay and her displeasure fly,
         She that in wisdom never was so frail
         To change the cod's head for the salmon's tail,[218]   155
         She that could think and ne'er disclose her mind,
         See suitors following and not look behind,
         She was a wight, if ever such wight were,—
DESDEMONA: To do what?
IAGO: To suckle fools and chronicle small beer.[219]   160
DESDEMONA: O most lame and impotent conclusion! Do not learn of him, Emilia,
              though he be thy husband. How say you, Cassio? Is he not a most pro-
              fane and liberal[220] counsellor?

[212]head   [213]coarse cloth   [214]brunette, dark-haired   [215]here also, wantonness   [216]foolish
[217]compel the approval   [218]to make a foolish exchange (a bawdy secondary meaning is
probable)   [219]i.e., keep petty household accounts   [220]free-spoken, licentious

594

CASSIO: He speaks home,[221] madam; you may relish him more in the soldier than in[222] the scholar.   165

IAGO (aside): He takes her by the palm: ay, well said, whisper; with as little a web as this will I ensnare as great a fly as Cassio. Ay, smile upon her, do; I will gyve[223] thee in thine own courtship. You say true, 'tis so, indeed. If such tricks as these strip you out of your lieutenantry, it had been better you had not kissed your three fingers so oft, which now   170 again you are most apt to play the sir[224] in. Very good; well kissed! an excellent courtesy! 'tis so, indeed. Yet again your fingers to your lips? would they were clyster-pipes[225] for your sake! (A trumpet heard.) The Moor! I know his trumpet.[226]

CASSIO: 'Tis truly so.   175

DESDEMONA: Let 's meet him and receive him.

CASSIO: Lo! where he comes.

(Enter OTHELLO and ATTENDANTS.)

OTHELLO: O my fair warrior!

DESDEMONA: My dear Othello!

OTHELLO: It gives me wonder great as my content
          To see you here before me. O my soul's joy!   180
          If after every tempest come such calms,
          May the winds blow till they have waken'd death!
          And let the labouring bark climb hills of seas
          Olympus-high, and duck again as low
          As hell's from heaven! If it were now to die,   185
          'Twere now to be most happy, for I fear
          My soul hath her content so absolute
          That not another comfort like to this
          Succeeds in unknown fate.

DESDEMONA: The heavens forbid
          But that our loves and comforts should increase   190
          Even as our days do grow!

OTHELLO: Amen to that, sweet powers!
          I cannot speak enough of this content;
          It stops me here! it is too much of joy;
          And this, and this, the greatest discords be   (Kissing her.)
          That e'er our hearts shall make!   195

IAGO (aside):   O! you are well tun'd now,
          But I'll set down[227] the pegs that make this music,
          As honest as I am.

OTHELLO: Come, let us to the castle.

[221]to the mark, aptly   [222]as . . . as   [223]entangle   [224]gentleman   [225]syringes, enema pipes
[226]i.e., Othello's distinctive trumpet call   [227]loosen

News, friends; our wars are done, the Turks are drown'd.
How does my old acquaintance of this isle?
Honey, you shall be well desir'd[228] in Cyprus;   200
I have found great love amongst them. O my sweet,
I prattle out of fashion, and I dote
In mine own comforts. I prithee, good Iago,
Go to the bay and disembark my coffers.
Bring thou the master to the citadel;   205
He is a good one, and his worthiness
Does challenge much respect. Come, Desdemona,
Once more well met at Cyprus.

(Exeunt all except IAGO *and* RODERIGO.)

IAGO: Do thou meet me presently at the harbour. Come hither. If thou be'st
valiant, as they say base men being in love have then a nobility in their   210
natures more than is native to them, list[229] me. The lieutenant to-night
watches on the court of guard:[230] first, I must tell thee this, Desdemona
is directly in love with him.

RODERIGO With him! Why, 'tis not possible.

IAGO: Lay thy finger thus, and let thy soul be instructed. Mark me with what   215
violence she first loved the Moor but for bragging and telling her fan-
tastical lies; and will she love him still for prating? let not thy discreet
heart think it. Her eye must be fed; and what delight shall she have to
look on the devil? When the blood is made dull with the act of sport,
there should be, again to inflame it, and to give satiety a fresh appetite,   220
loveliness in favour, sympathy in years, manners, and beauties; all which
the Moor is defective in. Now, for want of these required conveniences,
her delicate tenderness will find itself abused, begin to heave the
gorge,[231] disrelish and abhor the Moor; very nature will instruct her in
it, and compel her to some second choice. Now, sir, this granted, as it   225
is a most pregnant[232] and unforced position, who stands so eminently in
the degree of this fortune as Cassio does? a knave very voluble, no further conscionable[233] than in putting on the mere form of civil and hu-
mane seeming, for the better compassing of his salt[234] and most hidden
loose affection? why, none; why, none: a slipper[235] and subtle knave, a   230
finder-out of occasions, that has an eye can stamp and counterfeit advantages, though true advantage never present itself; a devilish knave!
Besides, the knave is handsome, young, and hath all those requisites in
him that folly and green minds look after; a pestilent complete knave!
and the woman hath found him already.   235

RODERIGO: I cannot believe that in her; she is full of most blessed condition.

IAGO: Blessed fig's end! the wine she drinks is made of grapes;[236] if she had
been blessed she would never have loved the Moor; blessed pudding!

[228]welcomed   [229]listen to   [230]guardhouse   [231]vomit   [232]obvious   [233]conscientious
[234]lecherous   [235]slippery   [236]i.e., she is only flesh and blood

Didst thou not see her paddle with the palm of his hand? didst not mark that? 240

RODERIGO: Yes, that I did; but that was but courtesy.

IAGO: Lechery, by this hand! an index[237] and obscure prologue to the history of lust and foul thoughts. They met so near with their lips, that their breaths embraced together. Villanous thoughts, Roderigo! when these mutualities so marshal the way, hard at hand comes the master and 245 main exercise, the incorporate[238] conclusion. Pish![239] But, sir, be you ruled by me: I have brought you from Venice. Watch you to-night; for the command, I'll lay't upon you: Cassio knows you not. I'll not be far from you: do you find some occasion to anger Cassio, either by speaking too loud, or tainting[240] his discipline; or from what other course you 250 please, which the time shall more favourably minister.

RODERIGO: Well.

IAGO: Sir, he is rash and very sudden in choler, and haply may strike at you: provoke him, that he may; for even out of that will I cause these of Cyprus to mutiny, whose qualification[241] shall come into no true taste 255 again but by the displanting of Cassio. So shall you have a shorter journey to your desires by the means I shall then have to prefer[242] them; and the impediment most profitably removed, without the which there were no expectation of our prosperity.

RODERIGO: I will do this, if I can bring it to any opportunity. 260

IAGO: I warrant thee. Meet me by and by at the citadel: I must fetch his necessaries ashore. Farewell.

RODERIGO: Adieu. (Exit.)

IAGO: That Cassio loves her, I do well believe it;
That she loves him, 'tis apt,[243] and of great credit:[244] 265
The Moor, howbeit that I endure him not,
Is of a constant, loving, noble nature;
And I dare think he'll prove to Desdemona
A most dear[245] husband. Now, I do love her too;
Not out of absolute lust,—though peradventure[246] 270
I stand accountant[247] for as great a sin,—
But partly led to diet my revenge,
For that I do suspect the lusty Moor
Hath leap'd into my seat; the thought whereof
Doth like a poisonous mineral gnaw my inwards; 275
And nothing can or shall content my soul
Till I am even'd with him, wife for wife;
Or failing so, yet that I put the Moor
At least into a jealousy so strong
That judgment cannot cure. Which thing to do, 280

[237]pointer [238]carnal [239]exclamation of disgust [240]disparaging [241]appeasement
[242]advance [243]natural, probable [244]easily believable [245]a pun on the word in the sense of: expensive [246]perchance, perhaps [247]accountable

If this poor trash[248] of Venice, whom I trash[249]
For his quick hunting, stand the putting-on,[250]
I'll have our Michael Cassio on the hip;
Abuse him to the Moor in the rank garb,[251]
For I fear Cassio with my night-cap too,   285
Make the Moor thank me, love me, and reward me
For making him egregiously an ass
And practising upon his peace and quiet
Even to madness. 'Tis here, but yet confus'd:
Knavery's plain face is never seen till us'd.   (*Exit.*)   290

Scene 2 [A Street.]

(*Enter a* HERALD *with a proclamation; people following.*)

HERALD: It is Othello's pleasure, our noble and valiant general, that, upon certain tidings now arrived, importing the mere[252] perdition of the Turkish fleet, every man put himself into triumph; some to dance, some to make bonfires, each man to what sport and revels his addiction leads him; for, besides these beneficial news, it is the celebration of his nuptial. So   295
much was his pleasure should be proclaimed. All offices[253] are open, and there is full liberty of feasting from this present hour of five till the bell has told eleven. Heaven bless the isle of Cyprus and our noble general Othello!   (*Exeunt.*)

Scene 3 [A Hall in the Castle.]

(*Enter* OTHELLO, DESDEMONA, CASSIO, *and* ATTENDANTS.)

OTHELLO: Good Michael, look you to the guard to-night: 300
        Let's teach ourselves that honourable stop,[254]
        Not to outsport discretion.
CASSIO: Iago hath direction what to do:
        But, notwithstanding, with my personal[255] eye
        Will I look to 't.   305
OTHELLO: Iago is most honest.
        Michael, good-night; to-morrow with your earliest
        Let me have speech with you. (*To* DESDEMONA.) Come, my dear love,
        The purchase made, the fruits are to ensue;
        That profit 's yet to come 'twixt me and you.
        Good-night.   310
                        (*Exeunt* OTHELLO, DESDEMONA, *and* ATTENDANTS.)

[248]i.e., Roderigo [249]check, control [250]inciting [251]gross manner [252]utter [253]kitchens and storehouses [254]discipline [255]own

(*Enter* IAGO.)

CASSIO: Welcome, Iago; we must to the watch.

IAGO: Not this hour, lieutenant; 'tis not yet ten o' the clock. Our general casts us thus early for the love of his Desdemona, who let us not therefore blame; he hath not yet made wanton the night with her, and she is sport for Jove.   315

CASSIO: She's a most exquisite lady.

IAGO: And, I'll warrant her, full of game.

CASSIO: Indeed, she is a most fresh and delicate creature.

IAGO: What an eye she has! methinks it sounds a parley[256] of provocation.

CASSIO: An inviting eye: and yet methinks right modest.   320

IAGO: And when she speaks, is it not an alarum[257] to love?

CASSIO: She is indeed perfection.

IAGO: Well, happiness to their sheets! Come, lieutenant, I have a stoup of wine, and here without are a brace[258] of Cyprus gallants that would fain have a measure to the health of black Othello.   325

CASSIO: Not to-night, good Iago: I have very poor and unhappy brains for drinking: I could well wish courtesy would invent some other custom of entertainment.

IAGO: O! they are our friends; but one cup: I'll drink for you.

CASSIO: I have drunk but one cup to-night, and that was craftily qualified[259]   330
too, and, behold, what innovation[260] it makes here: I am unfortunate in the infirmity, and dare not task my weakness with any more.

IAGO: What, man! 'tis a night of revels; the gallants desire it.

CASSIO: Where are they?

IAGO: Here at the door; I pray you, call them in.   (*Exit.*)   335

CASSIO: I'll do 't; but it dislikes me.

IAGO: If I can fasten but one cup upon him,
With that which he hath drunk to-night already,
He 'll be as full of quarrel and offence
As my young mistress' dog. Now, my sick fool Roderigo   340
Whom love has turn'd almost the wrong side out,
To Desdemona hath to-night carous'd
Potations pottle-deep;[261] and he's to watch.
Three lads of Cyprus, noble swelling spirits,
That hold their honours in a wary distance,[262]   345
The very elements[263] of this warlike isle,
Have I to-night fluster'd with flowing cups,
And they watch too. Now, 'mongst this flock of drunkards,
Am I to put our Cassio in some action
That may offend the isle. But here they come.   350

---

[256]conference   [257]call-to-arms   [258]pair   [259]diluted   [260]change, revolution   [261]bottoms-up
[262]take offense easily   [263]types

If consequence[264] do but approve my dream,
My boat sails freely, both with wind and stream.

(*Re-enter* CASSIO, *with him* MONTANO, *and* GENTLEMEN. SERVANT *following with wine.*)

CASSIO: 'Fore God, they have given me a rouse[265] already.
MONTANO: Good faith, a little one; not past a pint, as I am a soldier.
IAGO: Some wine, ho!   355

(*Sings*)

And let me the canakin[266] clink, clink;
And let me the canakin clink:
A soldier's a man;
A life's but a span;
Why then let a soldier drink.   360

    Some wine, boys!
CASSIO: 'Fore God, an excellent song.
IAGO: I learned it in England, where indeed they are most potent in potting; your Dane, your German, and your swag-bellied[267] Hollander,—drink, ho!—are nothing to your English.   365
CASSIO: Is your Englishman so expert in his drinking?
IAGO: Why, he drinks you[268] with facility your Dane dead drunk; he sweats not to overthrow your Almain;[269] he gives your Hollander a vomit ere the next pottle can be filled.
CASSIO: To the health of our general!   370
MONTANO: I am for it, lieutenant; and I'll do you justice.
IAGO: O sweet England!

(*Sings*)

King Stephen was a worthy peer,
  His breeches cost him but a crown;
He held them sixpence all too dear,
  With that he call'd the tailor lown.[270]   375
He was a wight of high renown,
  And thou art but of low degree:
'Tis pride that pulls the country down,
  Then take thine auld cloak about thee.   380

    Some wine, ho!
CASSIO: Why, this is a more exquisite song than the other.
IAGO: Will you hear't again?
CASSIO: No; for I hold him to be unworthy of his place that does those things.

---

[264]succeeding events   [265]drink   [266]small cup   [267]with a pendulous belly
[268]the "ethical" dative, *i.e.*, you'll see that he drinks   [269]German   [270]lout, rascal

Well, God's above all; and there be souls must be saved, and there be   385
souls must not be saved.

IAGO: It's true, good lieutenant.

CASSIO: For mine own part,—no offence to the general, nor any man of quality,
—I hope to be saved.

IAGO: And so do I too, lieutenant.   390

CASSIO: Ay; but by your leave, not before me; the lieutenant is to be saved
before the ancient. Let's have no more of this; let's to our affairs. God
forgive us our sins! Gentlemen, let's look to our business. Do not think,
gentlemen, I am drunk: this is my ancient; this is my right hand, and this
is my left hand. I am not drunk now; I can stand well enough, and speak   395
well enough.

ALL: Excellent well.

CASSIO: Why, very well, then; you must not think then that I am drunk.   (*Exit.*)

MONTANO: To the platform, masters; come, let's set the watch.

IAGO: You see this fellow that is gone before;   400
He is a soldier fit to stand by Caesar
And give direction; and do but see his vice;
'Tis to his virtue a just equinox,[271]
The one as long as the other; 'tis pity of him.
I fear the trust Othello puts him in,   405
On some odd time of his infirmity,
Will shake this island.

MONTANO: But is he often thus?

IAGO: 'Tis evermore the prologue to his sleep;
He'll watch the horologe a-double set,[272]
If drink rock not his cradle.   410

MONTANO: It were well
The general were put in mind of it.
Perhaps he sees it not; or his good nature
Prizes the virtue that appears in Cassio,
And looks not on his evils. Is not this true?

(*Enter* RODERIGO.)

IAGO (*aside to him*):   How now, Roderigo!   415
I pray you, after the lieutenant; go.   (*Exit* RODERIGO.)

MONTANO: And 'tis great pity that the noble Moor
Should hazard such a place as his own second
With one of an ingraft[273] infirmity;
It were an honest action to say   420
So to the Moor.

IAGO: Not I, for this fair island:

[271]equivalent   [272]stand watch twice twelve hours   [273]ingrained

I do love Cassio well, and would do much
To cure him of this evil. But hark; what noise?

(*Cry within, "Help! Help!" Re-enter* CASSIO, *driving in* RODERIGO.)

CASSIO: You rogue! your rascal!
MONTANO: What's the matter, lieutenant?
CASSIO: A knave teach me my duty!   425
        I 'll beat the knave into a twiggen[274] bottle.
RODERIGO: Beat me!
CASSIO: Dost thou prate, rogue?

(*Striking* RODERIGO.)

MONTANO (*staying him*):   Nay, good lieutenant;
        I pray you, sir, hold your hand.
CASSIO: Let me go, sir,
        Or I 'll knock you o'er the mazzard.[275]   430
MONTANO: Come, come; you're drunk.
CASSIO: Drunk!

(*They fight.*)

IAGO (*aside to* RODERIGO):   Away, I say! go out, and cry a mutiny.   (*Exit* RODERIGO.)
        Nay, good lieutenant! God's will, gentlemen!
        Help, ho! Lieutenant! sir! Montano! sir!
        Help, masters! Here 's a goodly watch indeed!   435

(*Bell rings.*)

        Who 's that that rings the bell? Diablo, ho!
        The town will rise: God's will! lieutenant, hold!
        You will be sham'd for ever.

(*Re-enter* OTHELLO *and* ATTENDANTS.)

OTHELLO: What is the matter here?
MONTANO: 'Zounds! I bleed still; I am hurt to the death.

(*He faints.*)

OTHELLO: Hold, for your lives!   440
IAGO: Hold, ho, lieutenant! Sir! Montano! gentlemen!
        Have you forgot all sense of place and duty?

[274]wicker   [275]head

602

Hold! the general speaks to you; hold for shame!

OTHELLO: Why, how now, ho! from whence ariseth this?
Are we turn'd Turks, and to ourselves do that   445
Which heaven hath forbid the Ottomites?
For Christian shame put by this barbarous brawl;
He that stirs next to carve for his own rage
Holds his soul light; he dies upon his motion.
Silence that dreadful bell! it frights the isle   450
From her propriety. What is the matter, masters?
Honest Iago, that look'st dead with grieving,
Speak, who began this? on thy love, I charge thee.

IAGO: I do not know; friends all but now, even now,
In quarter²⁷⁶ and in terms like bride and groom   455
Devesting²⁷⁷ them for bed; and then, but now,—
As if some planet had unwitted men,—
Swords out, and tilting one at other's breast,
In opposition bloody. I cannot speak
Any beginning to this peevish odds,²⁷⁸   460
And would in action glorious I had lost
Those legs that brought me to a part of it!

OTHELLO: How comes it, Michael, you are thus forgot?

CASSIO: I pray you, pardon me; I cannot speak.

OTHELLO: Worthy Montano, you were wont be civil;   465
The gravity and stillness of your youth
The world hath noted, and your name is great
In mouths of wisest censure:²⁷⁹ what's the matter,
That you unlace²⁸⁰ your reputation thus
And spend your rich opinion²⁸¹ for the name   470
Of a night-brawler? give me an answer to it.

MONTANO: Worthy Othello, I am hurt to danger;
Your officer, Iago, can inform you,
While I spare speech, which something now offends²⁸² me,
Of all that I do know; nor know I aught   475
By me that's said or done amiss this night,
Unless self-charity be sometimes a vice,
And to defend ourselves it be a sin
When violence assails us.

OTHELLO: Now, by heaven,
My blood begins my safer guides to rule,   480
And passion, having my best judgment collied,²⁸³
Assays to lead the way. If I once stir,
Or do but lift this arm, the best of you
Shall sink in my rebuke. Give me to know

---

²⁷⁶on duty ²⁷⁷undressing ²⁷⁸silly quarrel ²⁷⁹judgment ²⁸⁰undo ²⁸¹high reputation
²⁸²pains, harms ²⁸³clouded

How this foul rout began, who set it on;   485
And he that is approv'd[284] in this offence,
Though he had twinn'd with me—both at a birth—
Shall lose me. What! in a town of war,
Yet wild, the people's hearts brimful of fear,
To manage private and domestic quarrel,   490
In night, and on the court and guard of safety!
'Tis monstrous. Iago, who began 't?
MONTANO: If partially affin'd,[285] or leagu'd in office,
Thou dost deliver more or less than truth,
Thou art no soldier.   495
IAGO: Touch me not so near;
I had rather[286] have this tongue cut from my mouth
Than it should do offence to Michael Cassio;
Yet, I persuade myself, to speak the truth
Shall nothing wrong him. Thus it is, general.   500
Montano and myself being in speech,
There comes a fellow crying out for help,
And Cassio following with determin'd sword
To execute upon him. Sir, this gentleman
Steps in to Cassio, and entreats his pause;   505
Myself the crying fellow did pursue,
Lest by his clamour, as it so fell out,
The town might fall in fright; he, swift of foot,
Outran my purpose, and I return'd the rather
For that I heard the clink and fall of swords,   510
And Cassio high in oath, which till to-night
I ne'er might say before. When I came back,—
For this was brief,—I found them close together,
At blow and thrust, even as again they were
When you yourself did part them.   515
More of this matter can I not report:
But men are men; the best sometimes forget:
Though Cassio did some little wrong to him,
As men in rage strike those that wish them best,
Yet, surely Cassio, I believe, receiv'd   520
From him that fled some strange indignity,
Which patience could not pass.
OTHELLO: I know, Iago,
Thy honesty and love doth mince[287] this matter,
Making it light to Cassio. Cassio, I love thee;
But never more be officer of mine.
(Enter DESDEMONA, attended.)

[284]proved (i.e., guilty)   [285]favorably biased (by ties of friendship, or as Cassio's
fellow officer)   [286]more quickly   [287]moderate

Look! if my gentle love be not rais'd up: 525
(*To* CASSIO.) I'll make thee an example.

DESDEMONA: What's the matter?

OTHELLO: All's well now, sweeting; come away to bed.
Sir, for your hurts, myself will be your surgeon.
Lead him off.   (MONTANO *is led off.*)
Iago, look with care about the town,   530
And silence those whom this vile brawl distracted.
Come, Desdemona; 'tis the soldier's life,
To have their balmy slumbers wak'd with strife.

                                    (*Exeunt all but* IAGO *and* CASSIO.)

IAGO: What! are you hurt, lieutenant?

CASSIO: Ay; past all surgery.   535

IAGO: Marry, heaven forbid!

CASSIO: Reputation, reputation, reputation! O! I have lost my reputation. I
have lost the immortal part of myself, and what remains is bestial. My
reputation, Iago, my reputation!

IAGO: As I am an honest man, I thought you had received some bodily wound;   540
there is more offence in that than in reputation. Reputation is an idle and
most false imposition;[288] oft got without merit, and lost without deserving: you have lost no reputation at all, unless you repute yourself
such a loser. What! man; there are ways to recover the general again;
you are but now cast in his mood,[289] a punishment more in policy[290]   545
than in malice; even so as one would beat his offenceless dog to affright
an imperious lion. Sue to him again, and he is yours.

CASSIO: I will rather sue to be despised than to deceive so good a commander
with so slight, so drunken and so indiscreet an officer. Drunk! and speak
parrot![291] and squabble, swagger, swear, and discourse fustian[292] with   550
one's own shadow! O thou invisible spirit of wine! if thou hast no name
to be known by, let us call thee devil!

IAGO: What was he that you followed with your sword? What hath he done
to you?

CASSIO: I know not.   555

IAGO: Is't possible?

CASSIO: I remember a mass of things, but nothing distinctly; a quarrel, but
nothing wherefore. O God! that men should put an enemy in their
mouths to steal away their brains; that we should, with joy, pleasance,[293]
revel, and applause, transform ourselves into beasts.   560

IAGO: Why, but you are now well enough; how came you thus recovered?

CASSIO: It hath pleased the devil drunkenness to give place to the devil wrath;
one unperfectness shows me another, to make me frankly despise myself.

IAGO: Come, you are too severe a moraler. As the time, the place, and the

---

[288]something external   [289]dismissed because he is angry   [290]i.e., more for the sake of the example, or to show his fairness   [291]i.e., without thinking   [292]i.e., nonsense   [293]pleasure

condition of this country stands, I could heartily wish this had not be- 565
fallen, but since it is as it is, mend it for your own good.

CASSIO: I will ask him for my place again; he shall tell me I am a drunkard!
Had I as many mouths as Hydra,[294] such an answer would stop them
all. To be now a sensible man, by and by a fool, and presently a beast!
O strange! Every inordinate cup is unblessed and the ingredient[295] is a 570
devil.

IAGO: Come, come; good wine is a good familiar creature if it be well used;
exclaim no more against it. And, good lieutenant, I think you think I
love you.

CASSIO: I have well approved it, sir. I drunk! 575

IAGO: You or any man living may be drunk at some time, man. I'll tell you
what you shall do. Our general's wife is now the general: I may say so
in this respect, for that he hath devoted and given up himself to the
contemplation, mark, and denotement of her parts and graces: confess
yourself freely to her; importune her; she'll help to put you in your 580
place again. She is of so free, so kind, so apt, so blessed a disposition,
that she holds it a vice in her goodness not to do more than she is requested. This broken joint between you and her husband entreat her to
splinter;[296] and, my fortunes against any lay[297] worth naming, this crack
of your love shall grow stronger than it was before. 585

CASSIO: You advise me well.

IAGO: I protest, in the sincerity of love and honest kindness.

CASSIO: I think it freely; and betimes in the morning I will beseech the virtuous
Desdemona to undertake for me. I am desperate of my fortunes if they
check me here. 590

IAGO: You are in the right. Good-night, lieutenant; I must to the watch.

CASSIO: Good-night, honest Iago!   (Exit.)

IAGO: And what's he then that says I play the villain?
When this advice is free I give and honest,
Probal[298] to thinking and indeed the course 595
To win the Moor again? For 'tis most easy
The inclining Desdemona to subdue
In any honest suit! she's fram'd as fruitful[299]
As the free elements. And then for her
To win the Moor, were't to renounce his baptism, 600
All seals and symbols of redeemed sin,
His soul is so enfetter'd to her love,
That she may make, unmake, do what she list,
Even as her appetite shall play the god
With his weak function.[300] How am I then a villain 605
To counsel Cassio to this parallel[301] course,

---

[294]many-headed snake in Greek mythology   [295]contents   [296]bind up with splints
[297]wager   [298]provable   [299]generous   [300]faculties   [301]purposeful

Directly to his good? Divinity of hell!
When devils will the blackest sins put on,
They do suggest at first with heavenly shows,
As I do now; for while this honest fool   610
Plies Desdemona to repair his fortunes,
And she for him pleads strongly to the Moor,
I'll pour this pestilence into his ear
That she repeals[302] him for her body's lust;
And, by how much she strives to do him good,   615
She shall undo her credit with the Moor.
So will I turn her virtue into pitch,
And out of her own goodness make the net
That shall enmesh them all.

(Re-enter RODERIGO.)

                    How now, Roderigo!

RODERIGO: I do follow here in the chase, not like a hound that hunts, but one   620
that fills up the cry.[303] My money is almost spent; I have been to-night
exceedingly well cudgelled; and I think the issue will be, I shall have so
much experience for my pains; and so, with no money at all and a little
more wit, return again to Venice.

IAGO: How poor are they that have not patience!   625
How wound did ever heal but by degrees?
Thou know'st we work by wit and not by witchcraft,
And wit depends on dilatory time.
Does't not go well? Cassio hath beaten thee,
And thou by that small hurt hast cashiered Cassio.   630
Though other things grow fair against the sun,
Yet fruits that blossom first will first be ripe:
Content thyself awhile. By the mass, 'tis morning;
Pleasure and action make the hours seem short.
Retire thee; go where thou art billeted: 635
Away, I say; thou shalt know more hereafter:
Nay, get thee gone. (Exit RODERIGO.) Two things are to be done,
My wife must move for Cassio to her mistress;
I'll set her on;
Myself the while to draw the Moor apart,   640
And bring him jump[304] when he may Cassio find
Soliciting his wife: ay, that's the way:
Dull not device by coldness and delay.   (Exit.)

---

[302]i.e., seeks to recall   [303]pack (hunting term)   [304]at the exact moment

Scene 1 [Cyprus. Before the Castle.]

(*Enter* CASSIO, *and some* MUSICIANS.)

CASSIO: Masters, play here, I will content your pains;[305]
    Something that's brief; and bid "Good-morrow, general."   (*Music.*)

(*Enter* CLOWN.)

CLOWN: Why, masters, have your instruments been in Naples, that they speak
    i' the nose[306] thus?
FIRST MUSICIAN: How, sir, how?   5
CLOWN: Are these, I pray you, wind-instruments?
FIRST MUSICIAN: Ay, marry, are they, sir.
CLOWN: O! thereby hangs a tail.
FIRST MUSICIAN: Whereby hangs a tale, sir?
CLOWN: Marry, sir, by many a wind-instrument that I know. But, masters, here 's 10
    money for you; and the general so likes your music, that he desires you,
    for love's sake, to make no more noise with it.
FIRST MUSICIAN: Well, sir, we will not.
CLOWN: If you have any music that may not be heard, to 't again; but, as they
    say, to hear music the general does not greatly care.   15
FIRST MUSICIAN: We have none such, sir.
CLOWN: Then put up your pipes in your bag, for I'll away.
    Go; vanish into air; away!   (*Exeunt* MUSICIANS.)
CASSIO: Dost thou hear, mine honest friend?
CLOWN: No, I hear not your honest friend; I hear you.   20
CASSIO: Prithee, keep up thy quillets.[307] There's a poor piece of gold for thee.
    If the gentlewoman that attends the general's wife be stirring, tell her
    there's one Cassio entreats her a little favour of speech: wilt thou do
    this?
CLOWN: She is stirring, sir: if she will stir hither, I shall seem to notify unto her. 25
CASSIO: Do, good my friend.   (*Exit* CLOWN.)

(*Enter* IAGO.)

                In happy time, Iago.
IAGO: You have not been a-bed, then?
CASSIO: Why, no; the day had broke
    Before we parted. I have made bold, Iago,
    To send in to your wife; my suit to her   30

[305]reward your efforts [306]Naples was notorious for venereal disease, and syphilis was believed
to affect the nose. [307]quibbles

Is, that she will to virtuous Desdemona
Procure me some access.

IAGO: I'll send her to you presently;
And I'll devise a mean to draw the Moor
Out of the way, that your converse and business
May be more free.   35

CASSIO: I humbly thank you for 't.

                                      (Exit IAGO.)

                         I never knew
A Florentine more kind and honest.[308]

(Enter EMILIA.)

EMILIA: Good-morrow, good lieutenant: I am sorry
For your displeasure;[309] but all will soon be well.
The general and his wife are talking of it,   40
And she speaks for you stoutly: the Moor replies
That he you hurt is of great fame in Cyprus
And great affinity,[310] and that in wholesome wisdom
He might not but refuse you; but he protests he loves you,
And needs no other suitor but his likings   45
To take the safest occasion by the front[311]
To bring you in again.[312]

CASSIO: Yet, I beseech you,
If you think fit, or that it may be done,
Give me advantage of some brief discourse
With Desdemona alone.   50

EMILIA: Pray you, come in:
I will bestow you where you shall have time
To speak your bosom[313] freely.

CASSIO: I am much bound to you.   (Exeunt.)

Scene 2 [A Room in the Castle.]

(Enter OTHELLO, IAGO, and GENTLEMEN.)

OTHELLO: These letters give, Iago, to the pilot,
And by him do my duties to the senate;
That done, I will be walking on the works;   55
Repair there to me.

IAGO: Well, my good lord, I'll do 't.

OTHELLO: This fortification, gentlemen, shall we see 't?

GENTLEMEN: We 'll wait upon your lordship.   (Exeunt.)

---

[308]Cassio means that not even a fellow Florentine could behave to him in a friendlier fashion than does Iago. [309]disgrace [310]family connection [311]forelock [312]restore you (to Othello's favor) [313]heart, inmost thoughts

Scene 3 [Before the Castle.]

(*Enter* DESDEMONA, CASSIO, *and* EMILIA.)

DESDEMONA: Be thou assur'd, good Cassio, I will do
    All my abilities in thy behalf.   60
EMILIA: Good madam, do: I warrant it grieves my husband,
    As if the case were his.
DESDEMONA: O! that's an honest fellow. Do not doubt, Cassio,
    But I will have my lord and you again
    As friendly as you were.   65
CASSIO: Bounteous madam,
    Whatever shall become of Michael Cassio,
    He 's never any thing but your true servant.
DESDEMONA: I know't; I thank you. You do love my lord;
    You have known him long; and be you well assur'd
    He shall in strangeness[314] stand no further off   70
    Than in a politic[315] distance.
CASSIO: Ay, but, lady,
    That policy may either last so long,
    Or feed upon such nice[316] and waterish diet,
    Or breed itself so out of circumstance,
    That, I being absent and my place supplied,   75
    My general will forget my love and service.
DESDEMONA: Do not doubt[317] that; before Emilia here
    I give thee warrant of thy place. Assure thee,
    If I do vow a friendship, I'll perform it
    To the last article; my lord shall never rest;   80
    I'll watch him tame,[318] and talk him out of patience;
    His bed shall seem a school, his board a shrift;[319]
    I'll intermingle every thing he does
    With Cassio's suit. Therefore be merry, Cassio;
    For thy solicitor shall rather die   85
    Than give thy cause away.[320]

(*Enter* OTHELLO, *and* IAGO *at a distance.*)

EMILIA: Madam, here comes my lord.
CASSIO: Madam, I 'll take my leave.
DESDEMONA: Why, stay, and hear me speak.
CASSIO: Madam, not now; I am very ill at ease,   90
    Unfit for mine own purposes.
DESDEMONA: Well, do your discretion.   (*Exit* CASSIO.)

[314]aloofness   [315]i.e., dictated by policy   [316]slight, trivial   [317]fear   [318]outwatch him (*i.e.*, keep him awake) till he submits   [319]confessional   [320]abandon your cause

610

IAGO: Ha! I like not that.

OTHELLO: What dost thou say?

IAGO: Nothing, my lord: or if—I know not what.

OTHELLO: Was not that Cassio parted from my wife?   95

IAGO: Cassio, my lord? No, sure, I cannot think it,

That he would steal away so guilty-like,

Seeing you coming.

OTHELLO: I do believe 'twas he.

DESDEMONA: How now, my lord!

I have been talking with a suitor here,   100

A man that languishes in your displeasure.

OTHELLO: Who is 't you mean?

DESDEMONA: Why, your lieutenant, Cassio. Good my lord,

If I have any grace or power to move you,

His present[321] reconciliation take;   105

For if he be not one that truly loves you,

That errs in ignorance and not in cunning,

I have no judgment in an honest face.

I prithee[322] call him back.

OTHELLO: Went he hence now?

DESDEMONA: Ay, sooth; so humbled,   110

That he hath left part of his grief with me,

To suffer with him. Good love, call him back.

OTHELLO: Not now, sweet Desdemona; some other time.

DESDEMONA: But shall 't be shortly?

OTHELLO: The sooner, sweet, for you.

DESDEMONA: Shall 't be to-night at supper?   115

OTHELLO: No, not to-night.

DESDEMONA: To-morrow dinner, then?

OTHELLO: I shall not dine at home;

I meet the captains at the citadel.

DESDEMONA: Why, then, to-morrow night; or Tuesday morn;

Or Tuesday noon, or night; or Wednesday morn:

I prithee name the time, but let it not   120

Exceed three days: in faith, he's penitent;

And yet his trespass, in our common reason,—

Save that they say, the wars must make examples

Out of their best,—is not almost[323] a fault

To incur a private check.[324] When shall he come?   125

Tell me, Othello: I wonder in my soul,

What you could ask me, that I should deny,

Or stand so mammering[325] on. What! Michael Cassio,

That came a wooing with you, and so many a time,

---

[321]immediate   [322]pray thee   [323]hardly   [324](even) a private reprimand   [325]shilly-shallying

When I have spoke of you dispraisingly,   130
Hath ta'en your part; to have so much to do
To bring him in! Trust me, I could do much,—
OTHELLO: Prithee, no more; let him come when he will;
I will deny thee nothing.
DESDEMONA: Why, this is not a boon;   135
'Tis as I should entreat you wear your gloves,
Or feed on nourishing dishes, or keep you warm,
Or sue to you to do a peculiar profit
To your own person: nay, when I have a suit
Wherein I mean to touch your love indeed,
It shall be full of poise[326] and difficult weight,   140
And fearful to be granted.
OTHELLO: I will deny thee nothing:
Whereon, I do beseech thee, grant me this,
To leave me but a little to myself.
DESDEMONA: Shall I deny you? no: farewell, my lord.
OTHELLO: Farewell, my Desdemona: I'll come to thee straight.   145
DESDEMONA: Emilia, come. Be as your fancies teach you;
Whate'er you be, I am obedient.   (*Exit, with* EMILIA.)
OTHELLO: Excellent wretch![327] Perdition catch my soul,
But I do love thee! and when I love thee not,
Chaos is[328] come again.   150
IAGO: My noble lord,—
OTHELLO: What dost thou say, Iago?
IAGO: Did Michael Cassio, when you woo'd my lady,
Know of your love?
OTHELLO: He did, from first to last: why dost thou ask?
IAGO: But for a satisfaction of my thought;   155
No further harm.
OTHELLO: Why of thy thought, Iago?
IAGO: I did not think he had been acquainted with her.
OTHELLO: O! yes; and went between us very oft.
IAGO: Indeed!
OTHELLO: Indeed! ay, indeed; discern'st thou aught in that?   160
Is he not honest?
IAGO: Honest, my lord?
OTHELLO: Honest! ay, honest.
IAGO: My lord, for aught I know.
OTHELLO: What dost thou think?
IAGO: Think, my lord!
OTHELLO: Think, my lord!
By heaven, he echoes me,

---

[326]weight   [327]here, a term of endearment   [328]will have

As if there were some monster in his thought
Too hideous to be shown. Thou dost mean something:
I heard thee say but now, thou lik'dst not that,
When Cassio left my wife; what didst not like?
And when I told thee he was of my counsel
In my whole course of wooing, thou criedst, 'Indeed!'
And didst contract and purse thy brow together,
As if thou then hadst shut up in thy brain
Some horrible conceit.[329] If thou dost love me,
Show me thy thought.

IAGO: My lord, you know I love you.   175

OTHELLO: I think thou dost;
And, for[330] I know thou art full of love and honesty,
And weigh'st thy words before thou givest them breath,
Therefore these stops[331] of thine fright me the more;
For such things in a false disloyal knave
Are tricks of custom, but in a man that's just   180
They are close delations,[332] working from the heart
That passion cannot rule.

IAGO: For Michael Cassio,
I dare be sworn I think that he is honest.

OTHELLO: I think so too.

IAGO: Men should be what they seem;
Or those that be not, would they might seem none!   185

OTHELLO: Certain, men should be what they seem.

IAGO: Why then, I think Cassio's an honest man.

OTHELLO: Nay, yet there's more in this.
I pray thee, speak to me as to thy thinkings,
As thou dost ruminate, and give thy worst of thoughts   190
The worst of words.

IAGO: Good my lord, pardon me;
Though I am bound to every act of duty,
I am not bound to[333] that all slaves are free to.
Utter my thoughts? Why, say they are vile and false;
As where's that palace whereinto foul things   195
Sometimes intrude not? who has a breast so pure
But some uncleanly apprehensions[334]
Keep leets and law-days,[335] and in session sit
With meditations lawful?

OTHELLO: Thou dost conspire against thy friend, Iago,   200
If thou but think'st him wrong'd, and mak'st his ear
A stranger to thy thoughts.

---

[329]fancy [330]because [331]interruptions, hesitations [332]secret (i.e., involuntary, unconscious) revelations [333]bound with regard to [334]conceptions [335]sittings of the local courts

IAGO: I do beseech you,
Though I perchance am vicious in my guess,—
As, I confess, it is my nature's plague
To spy into abuses, and oft my jealousy[336]   205
Shapes faults that are not,—that your wisdom yet,
From one that so imperfectly conceits,
Would take no notice, nor build yourself a trouble
Out of his scattering and unsure observance.
It were not for your quiet nor your good,   210
Nor for my manhood, honesty, or wisdom,
To let you know my thoughts.
OTHELLO: What dost thou mean?
IAGO: Good name in man and woman, dear my lord,
Is the immediate jewel of[337] their souls:
Who steals my purse steals trash; 'tis something, nothing;   215
'Twas mine, 'tis his, and has been slave to thousands;
But he that filches from me my good name
Robs me of that which not enriches him,
And makes me poor indeed.
OTHELLO: By heaven, I'll know thy thoughts.   220
IAGO: You cannot, if my heart were in your hand;
Nor shall not, whilst 'tis in my custody.
OTHELLO: Ha!
IAGO: O! beware, my lord, of jealousy;
It is the green-ey'd monster which doth mock
The meat it feeds on; that cuckold[338] lives in bliss   225
Who, certain of his fate, loves not his wronger;
But, O! what damned minutes tells[339] he o'er
Who dotes, yet doubts; suspects, yet soundly loves!
OTHELLO: O misery!
IAGO: Poor and content is rich, and rich enough,   230
But riches fineless[340] is as poor as winter
To him that ever fears he shall be poor.
Good heaven, the souls of all my tribe defend
From jealousy!
OTHELLO: Why, why is this?
Think'st thou I'd make a life of jealousy,   235
To follow still the changes of the moon
With fresh suspicions? No; to be once in doubt
Is once to be resolved. Exchange me for a goat
When I shall turn the business of my soul
To such exsufflicate[341] and blown[342] surmises,   240

---

[336]suspicion   [337]jewel closest to   [338]husband of an adulterous woman   [339]counts
[340]boundless   [341]spat out (?)   [342]fly-blown

Matching thy inference. 'Tis not to make me jealous
To say my wife is fair, feeds well, loves company,
Is free of speech, sings, plays, and dances well;
Where virtue is, these are more virtuous:
Nor from mine own weak merits will I draw   245
The smallest fear, or doubt of her revolt;
For she had eyes, and chose me. No, Iago;
I'll see before I doubt; when I doubt, prove;
And, on the proof, there is no more but this,
Away at once with love or jealousy!   250
IAGO: I am glad of it; for now I shall have reason
To show the love and duty that I bear you
With franker spirit; therefore, as I am bound,
Receive it from me; I speak not yet of proof.
Look to your wife; observe her well with Cassio;   255
Wear your eye thus, not jealous nor secure:
I would not have your free and noble nature
Out of self-bounty[343] be abus'd; look to 't:
I know our country disposition[344] well;
In Venice they do let heaven see the pranks   260
They dare not show their husbands; their best conscience
Is not to leave 't undone, but keep 't unknown.
OTHELLO: Dost thou say so?
IAGO: She did deceive her father, marrying you;
And when she seem'd to shake and fear your looks,   265
She lov'd them most.
OTHELLO: And so she did.
IAGO: Why, go to,[345] then;
She that so young could give out such a seeming,
To seel her father's eyes up close as oak,
He thought 'twas witchcraft; but I am much to blame;
I humbly do beseech you of your pardon   270
For too much loving you.
OTHELLO: I am bound to thee for ever.
IAGO: I see, this hath a little dash'd your spirits.
OTHELLO: Not a jot, not a jot.
IAGO: I' faith, I fear it has.
I hope you will consider what is spoke
Comes from my love. But I do see you're mov'd;   275
I am to pray you not to strain my speech
To grosser issues nor to larger reach
Than to suspicion.
OTHELLO: I will not.

---

[343]innate generosity [344]i.e., that of Venice [345]colloquialism; here, something like "all right"

IAGO: Should you do so, my lord,
          My speech should fall into such vile success   280
          As my thoughts aim not at. Cassio's my worthy friend—
          My lord, I see you're mov'd.
OTHELLO: No, not much mov'd:
          I do not think but Desdemona's honest.[346]
IAGO: Long live she so! and long live you to think so!
OTHELLO: And yet, how nature erring from itself,—   285
IAGO: Ay, there's the point: as, to be bold with you,
          Not to affect many proposed matches
          Of her own clime,[347] complexion, and degree,[348]
          Whereto, we see, in all things nature tends;
          Foh! one may smell in such, a will most rank,   290
          Foul disproportion, thoughts unnatural.
          But pardon me; I do not in position[349]
          Distinctly[350] speak of her, though I may fear
          Her will, recoiling[351] to her better judgment,
          May fall to match you with her country forms   295
          And happily[352] repent.
OTHELLO: Farewell, farewell:
          If more thou dost perceive, let me know more;
          Set on thy wife to observe. Leave me, Iago.
IAGO: My lord, I take my leave.   (Going.)
OTHELLO: Why did I marry? This honest creature, doubtless,   300
          Sees and knows more, much more, than he unfolds.
IAGO (returning):   My lord, I would I might entreat your honour
          To scan this thing no further; leave it to time.
          Although 'tis fit that Cassio have his place,
          For, sure he fills it up with great ability,   305
          Yet, if you please to hold him off awhile,
          You shall by that perceive him and his means:
          Note if your lady strain his entertainment[353]
          With any strong or vehement importunity;
          Much will be seen in that. In the mean time,   310
          Let me be thought too busy[354] in my fears,
          As worthy cause I have to fear I am.
          And hold her free, I do beseech your honour.
OTHELLO: Fear not my government.
IAGO: I once more take my leave.   (Exit.)   315
OTHELLO: This fellow's of exceeding honesty,
          And knows all qualities, with a learned spirit,
          Of human dealings; if I do prove her haggard,[355]

[346]chaste   [347]country   [348]social rank   [349]in definite assertion   [350]specifically   [351]reverting
[352]perhaps   [353]urge his re-welcome (i.e., to Othello's trust and favor)   [354]meddlesome
[355]wild hawk

Though that her jesses[356] were my dear heart-strings,
I'd whistle her off and let her down the wind,[357]   320
To prey at fortune. Haply, for I am black,
And have not those soft parts of conversation
That chamberers[358] have, or, for I am declin'd
Into the vale of years—yet that's not much—
She's gone, I am abus'd;[359] and my relief   325
Must be to loathe her. O curse of marriage!
That we can call these delicate creatures ours,
And not their appetites. I had rather be a toad,
And live upon the vapour of a dungeon,
Than keep a corner in the thing I love   330
For others' uses. Yet, 'tis the plague of great ones;
Prerogativ'd[360] are they less than the base;
'Tis destiny unshunnable, like death:
Even then this forked plague[361] is fated to us
When we do quicken.[362]   335
Look! where she comes.
If she be false, O! then heaven mocks itself.
I'll not believe it.

(*Re-enter* DESDEMONA *and* EMILIA.)

DESDEMONA: How now, my dear Othello!
     Your dinner and the generous[363] islanders
     By you invited, do attend your presence.   340
OTHELLO: I am to blame.
DESDEMONA: Why do you speak so faintly?
     Are you not well?
OTHELLO: I have a pain upon my forehead here.[364]
DESDEMONA: Faith, that's with watching; 'twill away again:
     Let me but bind it hard, within this hour   345
     It will be well.
OTHELLO: Your napkin[365] is too little:

(*She drops her handkerchief.*)

     Let it alone. Come, I'll go in with you.
DESDEMONA: I am very sorry that you are not well.
                         (*Exeunt* OTHELLO *and* DESDEMONA.)
EMILIA: I am glad I have found this napkin;

356leather thongs by which the hawk's legs were strapped to the trainer's wrist
357I'd let her go and take care of herself   358courtiers; or (more specifically): gallants, frequen-
ters of bed chambers   359deceived   360privileged   361i.e., the cuckold's proverbial horns
362are conceived, come alive   363noble   364Othello again refers to his cuckoldom.
365handkerchief

This was her first remembrance from the Moor;   350
My wayward husband hath a hundred times
Woo'd me to steal it, but she so loves the token,
For he conjur'd her she should ever keep it,
That she reserves it evermore about her
To kiss and talk to. I'll have the work ta'en out,[366]   355
And give 't Iago:
What he will do with it heaven knows, not I;
I nothing but[367] to please his fantasy.[368]

(*Enter* IAGO.)

IAGO: How now! what do you here alone?
EMILIA: Do not you chide; I have a thing for you.   360
IAGO: A thing for me? It is a common thing—
EMILIA: Ha!
IAGO: To have a foolish wife.
EMILIA: O! is that all? What will you give me now
    For that same handkerchief?   365
IAGO: What handkerchief?
EMILIA: What handkerchief!
    Why, that the Moor first gave to Desdemona:
    That which so often you did bid me steal.
IAGO: Hath stol'n it from her?
EMILIA: No, faith; she let it drop by negligence,   370
    And, to the advantage, I, being there, took 't up.
    Look, here it is.
IAGO: A good wench; give it me.
EMILIA: What will you do with 't, that you have been so earnest
    To have me filch it?
IAGO: Why, what's that to you? (*Snatches it.*)   375
EMIILA: If it be not for some purpose of import
    Give 't me again; poor lady! she'll run mad
    When she shall lack it.
IAGO: Be not acknown on 't;[369] I have use for it.
    Go, leave me.   (*Exit* EMILIA.)   380
    I will in Cassio's lodging lose this napkin,
    And let him find it; trifles light as air
    Are to the jealous confirmations strong
    As proof of holy writ; this may do something.
    The Moor already changes with my poison: 385
    Dangerous conceits are in their natures poisons,
    Which at the first are scarce found to distaste,[370]

[366]pattern copied   [367]i.e., only want   [368]whim   [369]you know nothing about it
[370]scarce can be tasted

But with a little act upon the blood,
Burn like the mines of sulphur. I did say so:
Look! where he comes!   390

(*Enter* OTHELLO.)

                              Not poppy,[371] nor mandragora,[372]
          Nor all the drowsy syrups[373] of the world,
          Shall ever medicine thee to that sweet sleep
          Which thou owedst yesterday.
OTHELLO: Ha! ha! false to me?
IAGO: Why, how now, general! no more of that.
OTHELLO: Avaunt! be gone! thou hast set me on the rack;   395
          I swear 'tis better to be much abus'd
          Than but to know 't a little.
IAGO: How now, my lord!
OTHELLO: What sense had I of her stol'n hours of lust?
          I saw 't not, thought it not, it harm'd not me;
          I slept the next night well, was free and merry;   400
          I found not Cassio's kisses on her lips;
          He that is robb'd, not wanting what is stol'n,
          Let him not know 't, and he's not robb'd at all.
IAGO: I am sorry to hear this.
OTHELLO: I had been happy, if the general camp,[374]   405
          Pioners[375] and all, had tasted her sweet body,
          So[376] I had nothing known. O! now, for ever
          Farewell the tranquil mind; farewell content!
          Farewell the plumed troop and the big wars
          That make ambition virtue! O, farewell!   410
          Farewell the neighing steed, and the shrill trump,
          The spirit-stirring drum, the ear-piercing fife,
          The royal banner, and all quality,
          Pride, pomp, and circumstance[377] of glorious war!
          And, O you mortal engines,[378] whose rude throats   415
          The immortal Jove's dread clamours counterfeit,
          Farewell! Othello's occupation's gone!
IAGO: Is it possible, my lord?
OTHELLO: Villain, be sure thou prove my love a whore,
          Be sure of it; give me the ocular proof;   420
          Or, by the worth of mine eternal soul,
          Thou hadst been better have been born a dog
          Than answer my wak'd wrath.

[371]opium   [372]a soporific   [373]i.e., soporifies   [374]whole army
[375]lowest rank of manual laborers in the army   [376]as long as   [377]pageantry   [378]deadly artillery

IAGO: Is 't come to this?

OTHELLO: Make me to see 't; or, at the least, so prove it,
            That the probation[379] bear no hinge nor loop   425
            To hang a doubt on; or woe upon thy life!

IAGO: My noble lord,—

OTHELLO: If thou dost slander her and torture me,
            Never pray more; abandon all remorse;
            On horror's head horrors accumulate;   430
            Do deeds to make heaven weep, all earth amaz'd;
            For nothing canst thou to damnation add
            Greater than that.

IAGO: O grace! O heaven forgive me!
            Are you a man! have you a soul or sense?
            God be wi' you; take mine office. O wretched fool!   435
            That liv'st to make thine honesty a vice.
            O monstrous world! Take note, take note, O world!
            To be direct and honest is not safe.
            I thank you for this profit,[380] and, from hence
            I'll love no friend, sith[381] love breeds such offence.   440

OTHELLO: Nay, stay; thou shouldst be honest.

IAGO: I should be wise; for honesty's a fool,
            And loses that it works for.

OTHELLO: By the world,
            I think my wife be honest and think she is not;
            I think that thou art just and think thou art not.   445
            I'll have some proof. Her name, that was as fresh
            As Dian's[382] visage, is now begrim'd and black
            As mine own face. If there be cords or knives,
            Poison or fire or suffocating streams,
            I'll not endure it. Would I were satisfied!   450

IAGO: I see, sir, you are eaten up with passion.
            I do repent me that I put it to you.
            You would be satisfied?

OTHELLO: Would! nay, I will.

IAGO: And may; but how? how satisfied, my lord?
            Would you, the supervisor,[383] grossly gape on;   455
            Behold her tupp'd?

OTHELLO: Death and damnation! O!

IAGO: It were a tedious[384] difficulty, I think,
            To bring them to that prospect; damn them then,
            If ever mortal eyes do see them bolster[385]
            More[386] than their own! What then? how then?   460
            What shall I say? Where's satisfaction?

---

[379]proof   [380]lesson   [381]since   [382]Diana's, the goddess of the moon   [383]observer
[384]laborious   [385]lie together   [386]other

It is impossible you should see this,
Were they as prime[387] as goats, as hot as monkeys,
As salt as wolves in pride,[388] and fools as gross
As ignorance made drunk; but yet, I say,   465
If imputation, and strong circumstances,
Which lead directly to the door of truth,
Will give you satisfaction, you may have it.

OTHELLO: Give me a living reason she 's disloyal.

IAGO: I do not like the office;   470
But, sith I am enter'd in this cause so far,
Prick'd to 't by foolish honesty and love,
I will go on. I lay with Cassio lately;
And, being troubled with a raging tooth,
I could not sleep.   475
There are a kind of men so loose of soul
That in their sleeps will mutter their affairs;
One of this kind is Cassio.
In sleep I heard him say, "Sweet Desdemona,
Let us be wary, let us hide our loves!"   480
And then, sir, would he gripe[389] and wring my hand,
Cry, "O, sweet creature!" and then kiss me hard,
As if he pluck'd up kisses by the roots,
That grew upon my lips; then laid his leg
Over my thigh, and sigh'd, and kiss'd; and then   485
Cried, "Cursed fate, that gave thee to the Moor!"

OTHELLO: O monstrous! monstrous!

IAGO: Nay, this was but his dream.

OTHELLO: But this denoted a foregone conclusion:[390]
'Tis a shrewd doubt,[391] though it be but a dream.

IAGO: And this may help to thicken other proofs   490
That do demonstrate thinly.

OTHELLO: I'll tear her all to pieces.

IAGO: Nay, but be wise; yet we see nothing done;
She may be honest yet. Tell me but this:
Have you not sometimes seen a handkerchief
Spotted with strawberries in your wife's hand?   495

OTHELLO: I gave her such a one; 'twas my first gift.

IAGO: I know not that; but such a handkerchief—
I am sure it was your wife's—did I to-day
See Cassio wipe his beard with.

OTHELLO: If it be that,—

IAGO: If it be that, or any that was hers,   500
It speaks against her with the other proofs.

___

[387]lustful   [388]heat   [389]seize   [390]previous consummation   [391](1) cursed, (2) acute, suspicion

OTHELLO: O! that the slave had **forty thousand** lives;
        One is too poor, too weak for my revenge.
        Now do I see 'tis true. Look here, Iago;
        All my fond love thus do I blow to heaven: 505
        'Tis gone.
        Arise, black vengeance, from the hollow hell!
        Yield up, O love! thy crown and hearted throne
        To tyrannous hate. Swell, bosom, with thy fraught,[392]
        For 'tis of aspics'[393] tongues!   510
IAGO: Yet be content.[394]
OTHELLO: O! blood, blood, blood!
IAGO: Patience, I say; your mind, perhaps, may change.
OTHELLO: Never, Iago. Like to the Pontic sea,[395]
        Whose icy current and compulsive course
        Ne'er feels retiring ebb, but keeps due on   515
        To the Propontic and the Hellespont,[396]
        Even so my bloody thoughts, with violent pace,
        Shall ne'er look back, ne'er ebb to humble love,
        Till that a capable[397] and wide revenge
        Swallow them up.   (*Kneels.*) 520
                Now, by yond marble heaven,
        In the due reverence of a sacred vow
        I here engage my words.
IAGO: Do not rise yet.   (*Kneels.*)
        Witness, you ever-burning lights above!
        You elements that clip[398] us round about!
        Witness, that here Iago doth give up   525
        The execution of his wit, hands, heart,
        To wrong'd Othello's service! Let him command,
        And to obey shall be in me remorse,[399]
        What bloody business ever.[400]   (*They rise.*)
OTHELLO: I greet thy love,
        Not with vain thanks, but with acceptance bounteous,   530
        And will upon the instant put thee to 't:
        Within these three days let me hear thee say
        That Cassio's not alive.
IAGO: My friend is dead; 'tis done at your request:
        But let her live.   535
OTHELLO: Damn her, lewd minx! O, damn her!
        Come, go with me apart; I will withdraw.
        To furnish me with some swift means of death
        For the fair devil. Now art thou my lieutenant.

[392]burden   [393]poisonous snakes   [394]patient   [395]the Black Sea   [396]the Sea of Marmara, the Dardanelles   [397]comprehensive   [398]encompass   [399]probably a corrupt line; the meaning appears to be: "to obey shall be my solemn obligation"   [400]soever

IAGO: I am your own for ever.   (*Exeunt.*)

Scene 4 [Before the Castle.]

(*Enter* DESDEMONA, EMILIA, *and* CLOWN.)

DESDEMONA: Do you know, sirrah,[401] where Lieutenant Cassio lies?[402]   540
CLOWN: I dare not say he lies any where.
DESDEMONA: Why, man?
CLOWN: He is a soldier; and for one to say a soldier lies, is stabbing.[403]
DESDEMONA: Go to;[404] where lodges he?
CLOWN: To tell you where he lodges is to tell you where I lie.   545
DESDEMONA: Can anything be made of this?
CLOWN: I know not where he lodges, and for me to devise[405] a lodging, and
      say he lies here or he lies there, were to lie in mine own throat.
DESDEMONA: Can you inquire him out, and be edified by report?
CLOWN: I will catechize the world for him; that is, make questions, and by them 550
      answer.
DESDEMONA: Seek him, bid him come hither; tell him I have moved my lord in
      his behalf, and hope all will be well.
CLOWN: To do this is within the compass of man's wit, and therefore I will
      attempt the doing it.   (*Exit.*) 555
DESDEMONA: Where should I lose that handkerchief, Emilia?
EMILIA: I know not, madam.
DESDEMONA: Believe me, I had rather have lost my purse
      Full of cruzadoes;[406] and, but my noble Moor
      Is true of mind, and made of no such baseness   560
      As jealous creatures are, it were enough
      To put him to ill thinking.
EMILIA: Is he not jealous?
DESDEMONA: Who! he? I think the sun where he was born
      Drew all such humours from him.
EMILIA: Look! where he comes.
DESDEMONA: I will not leave him now till Cassio   565
      Be call'd to him.

(*Enter* OTHELLO.)

                    How is 't with you, my lord?
OTHELLO: Well, my good lady. (*Aside*) O! hardness to dissemble.
      How do you, Desdemona?
DESDEMONA: Well, my good lord.
OTHELLO: Give me your hand. This hand is moist,[407] my lady.

---

[401]common form of address to inferiors   [402]lives   [403]i.e., is cause for stabbing
[404]here apparently "Come on!"   [405]invent   [406]Portuguese gold coins
[407]a supposed symptom of a lustful nature

DESDEMONA: It yet has felt no age nor known no sorrow.   570
OTHELLO: This argues fruitfulness and liberal[408] heart;
          Hot, hot, and moist; this hand of yours requires
          A sequester[409] from liberty, fasting and prayer,
          Much castigation, exercise devout;
          For here's a young and sweating devil here,   575
          That commonly rebels. 'Tis a good hand,
          A frank one.
DESDEMONA: You may, indeed, say so;
          For 'twas that hand that gave away my heart.
OTHELLO: A liberal hand; the hearts of old gave hands,   580
          But our new heraldry[410] is hands not hearts.
DESDEMONA: I cannot speak of this. Come now, your promise.
OTHELLO: What promise, chuck?[411]
DESDEMONA: I have sent to bid Cassio come speak with you.
OTHELLO: I have a salt and sorry rheum offends me.   585
          Lend me thy handkerchief.
DESDEMONA: Here, my lord.
OTHELLO: That which I gave you.
DESDEMONA: I have it not about me.
OTHELLO: Not?
DESDEMONA: No, indeed, my lord.
OTHELLO: That is a fault.
          That handkerchief   590
          Did an Egyptian[412] to my mother give;
          She was a charmer,[413] and could almost read
          The thoughts of people; she told her, while she kept it,
          'Twould make her amiable[414] and subdue my father
          Entirely to her love, but if she lost it   595
          Or made a gift of it, my father's eye
          Should hold her loathed, and his spirits should hunt
          After new fancies.[415] She dying gave it me;
          And bid me, when my fate would have me wive,
          To give it her. I did so: and take heed on 't;   600
          Make it a darling like your precious eye;
          To lose 't or give 't away, were such perdition
          As nothing else could match.
DESDEMONA: Is 't possible?
OTHELLO: 'Tis true; there 's magic in the web of it;
          A sibyl,[416] that had number'd in the world   605
          The sun to course two hundred compasses,
          In her prophetic fury sew'd the work;

---

[408]with overtones of: too free, loose   [409]separation   [410]i.e., new heraldic symbolism (Othello means that the new way is not to give the heart together with the hand.)   [411]common term of endearment   [412]Gypsy   [413]sorceress   [414]lovable, desirable   [415]loves   [416]prophetess

The worms were hallow'd that did breed the silk,
And it was dy'd in mummy[417] which the skilful
Conserv'd of maidens' hearts.   610
DESDEMONA: Indeed! is 't true?
OTHELLO: Most veritable; therefore look to 't well.
DESDEMONA: Then would to heaven that I had never seen it!
OTHELLO: Ha! wherefore?
DESDEMONA: Why do you speak so startingly and rash?
OTHELLO: Is 't lost? is 't gone? speak, is it out o' the way?   615
DESDEMONA: Heaven bless us!
OTHELLO: Say you?
DESDEMONA: It is not lost: but what an if[418] it were?
OTHELLO: How!
DESDEMONA: I say, it is not lost.
OTHELLO: Fetch 't, let me see 't!
DESDEMONA: Why, so I can, sir, but I will not now.   620
        This is a trick to put me from my suit:
        Pray you let Cassio be receiv'd again.
OTHELLO: Fetch me the handkerchief; my mind misgives.
DESDEMONA: Come, come;
        You'll never meet a more sufficient[419] man.   625
OTHELLO: The handkerchief!
DESDEMONA: I pray, talk[420] me of Cassio.
OTHELLO: The handkerchief!
DESDEMONA: A man that all his time
        Hath founded his good fortunes on your love,
        Shar'd dangers with you,—
OTHELLO: The handkerchief!   630
DESDEMONA: In sooth, you are to blame.
OTHELLO: Away!   (Exit.)
EMILIA: Is not this man jealous?
DESDEMONA: I ne'er saw this before.
        Sure, there's some wonder in this handkerchief;
        I am most unhappy in the loss of it.   635
EMILIA: 'Tis not a year or two shows us a man;
        They are all but[421] stomachs, and we all but[421] food;
        They eat us hungerly, and when they are full
        They belch us. Look you! Cassio and my husband.

(Enter IAGO and CASSIO.)

IAGO: There is no other way; 'tis she must do 't: 640

---

[417]drug (medicinal or magic) derived from embalmed bodies   [418]if
[419]adequate   [420]talk to   [421]only . . . only

And, lo! the happiness:[422] go and importune her.

DESDEMONA: How now, good Cassio! what's the news with you?

CASSIO: Madam, my former suit: I do beseech you
That by your virtuous means I may again
Exist, and be a member of his love   645
Whom I with all the office[423] of my heart
Entirely honour; I would not be delay'd.
If my offence be of such mortal kind
That nor my service past, nor present sorrows,
Nor purpos'd merit in futurity,   650
Can ransom me into his love again,
But to know so must be my benefit;
So shall I clothe me in a forc'd content,
And shut myself up in some other course
To fortune's alms.   655

DESDEMONA: Alas! thrice-gentle Cassio!
My advocation is not now in tune;
My lord is not my lord; nor should I know him,
Were he in favour[424] as in humour alter'd.
So help me every spirit sanctified,
As I have spoken for you all my best   660
And stood within the blank of[425] his displeasure
For my free speech. You must awhile be patient;
What I can do I will, and more I will
Than for myself I dare: let that suffice you.

IAGO: Is my lord angry?   665

EMILIA: He went hence but now,
And certainly in strange unquietness.

IAGO: Can he be angry? I have seen the cannon,
When it hath blown his ranks[426] into the air,
And, like the devil, from his very arm
Puff'd his own brother; and can he be angry?   670
Something of moment[427] then; I will go meet him;
There's matter in 't indeed, if he be angry.

DESDEMONA: I prithee, do so. (*Exit* IAGO.) Something, sure, of state,[428]
Either from Venice, or some unhatch'd[429] practice
Made demonstrable here in Cyprus to him,   675
Hath puddled[430] his clear spirit; and, in such cases
Men's natures wrangle with inferior things,
Though great ones are their object. 'Tis even so;
For let our finger ache, and it indues[431]
Our other healthful members even to that sense   680
Of pain. Nay, we must think men are not gods,

---

[422]"what luck!" [423]duty [424]appearance [425]as the target for [426]i.e., his soldiers
[427]important [428]public affairs [429]abortive or budding plot [430]muddied [431]brings, leads

626

Nor of them look for such observancy[432]
As fits the bridal.[433] Beshrew me much, Emilia,
I was—unhandsome warrior as I am—
Arraigning his unkindness with[434] my soul;   685
But now I find I had suborn'd the witness,[435]
And he's indicted falsely.

EMILIA: Pray heaven it be state matters, as you think,
And no conception,[436] nor no jealous toy[437]
Concerning you.   690

DESDEMONA: Alas the day! I never gave him cause.

EMILIA: But jealous souls will not be answer'd so;
They are not ever jealous for the cause,
But jealous for they are jealous; 'tis a monster
Begot upon itself, born on itself.   695

DESDEMONA: Heaven keep that monster from Othello's mind!

EMILIA: Lady, amen.

DESDEMONA: I will go seek him. Cassio, walk hereabout;
If I do find him fit, I'll move your suit
And seek to effect it to my uttermost.   700

CASSIO: I humbly thank your ladyship.   (*Exeunt* DESDEMONA *and* EMILIA.)

(*Enter* BIANCA.)

BIANCA: Save you, friend Cassio!

CASSIO: What make you from home?
How is it with you, my most fair Bianca?
I' faith, sweet love, I was coming to your house.

BIANCA: And I was going to your lodging, Cassio.   705
What! keep a week away? seven days and nights?
Eight score eight hours? and lovers' absent hours.
More tedious than the dial eight score times?
O weary reckoning!

CASSIO: Pardon me, Bianca,
I have this while with leaden thoughts been press'd;   710
But I shall, in a more continuate[438] time,
Strike off[439] this score of absence. Sweet Bianca,

(*Giving her* DESDEMONA's *handkerchief.*)

Take me this work out.

BIANCA: O Cassio! whence came this?
This is some token from a newer friend;
To the felt absence now I feel a cause;   715

---

[432]attention   [433]wedding   [434]to   [435]i.e., caused my soul to bring in wrong charges
[436]fancy, supposition   [437]fancy   [438]uninterrupted   [439]cancel (*i.e.*, make up for)

        Is 't come to this? Well, well.

CASSIO: Go to, woman!
        Throw your vile guesses in the devil's teeth,
        From whence you have them. You are jealous now
        That this is from some mistress, some remembrance:
        No, in good troth, Bianca.   720

BIANCA: Why, whose is it?

CASSIO: I know not, sweet; I found it in my chamber.
        I like the work well; ere it be demanded,—[440]
        As like enough it will,—I'd have it copied;
        Take it and do 't; and leave me for this time.

BIANCA: Leave you! wherefore?   725

CASSIO: I do attend here on[441] the general,
        And think it no addition,[442] nor my wish,
        To have him see me woman'd.

BIANCA: Why, I pray you?

CASSIO: Not that I love you not.

BIANCA: But that you do not love me.
        I pray you, bring me on the way a little   730
        And say if I shall see you soon at night.

CASSIO: 'Tis but a little way that I can bring you,
        For I attend here; but I'll see you soon.

BIANCA: 'Tis very good; I must be circumstanc'd.[443]   (Exeunt.)

ACT IV

Scene 1 [Cyprus. Before the Castle.]

(Enter OTHELLO and IAGO.)

IAGO: Will you think so?

OTHELLO: Think so, Iago!

IAGO: What!
        To kiss in private?

OTHELLO: An unauthoriz'd kiss.

IAGO: Or to be naked with her friend a-bed
        An hour or more, not meaning any harm?

OTHELLO: Naked a-bed, Iago, and not mean harm?   5
        It is hypocrisy against the devil:[444]
        They that mean virtuously, and yet do so,
        The devil their virtue tempts, and they tempt heaven.

IAGO: If they do nothing, 'tis a venial slip;

---

[440]asked for   [441]wait for   [442]advantage, credit   [443]governed by circumstances
[444]i.e., by not committing the sin which the situation invites

But if I give my wife a handkerchief,— 10

OTHELLO: What then?

IAGO: Why, then, 'tis hers, my lord; and, being hers,
She may, I think, bestow 't on any man.

OTHELLO: She is protectress of her honour too;
May she give that? 15

IAGO: Her honour is an essence that's not seen;
They have it very oft that have it not:[445]
But for the handkerchief,—

OTHELLO: By heaven, I would most gladly have forgot it:—
Thou said'st,—O! it comes o'er my memory, 20
As doth the raven[446] o'er the infected house,
Boding to all,—he had my handkerchief.

IAGO: Ay, what of that?

OTHELLO: That 's not so good now.

IAGO: What,
If I had said I had seen him do you wrong?
Or heard him say, as knaves be such abroad,[447] 25
Who having, by their own importunate suit,
Or voluntary dotage[448] of some mistress,
Convinced or supplied them,[449] cannot choose
But they must blab.

OTHELLO: Hath he said any thing?

IAGO: He hath, my lord; but be you well assur'd, 30
No more than he'll unswear.

OTHELLO: What hath he said?

IAGO: Faith, that he did—I know not what he did.

OTHELLO: What? what?

IAGO: Lie—

OTHELLO: With her? 35

IAGO: With her, on her; what you will.

OTHELLO: Lie with her; lie on her! We say, lie on her, when they belie her. Lie
with her! that's fulsome. Handkerchief,—confessions,—handkerchief! To
confess, and be hanged for his labour. First, to be hanged, and then to
confess: I tremble at it. Nature would not invest herself in such shadowing
passion without some instruction.[450] It is not words that shake me thus. 40
Pish! Noses, ears, and lips. Is it possible?—Confess!—Handkerchief!—O
devil!

(Falls in a trance.)

IAGO: Work on,

---

[445]i.e., some unchaste women are thought chaste   [446](1)a bad omen, (2)a carrier of the plague
[447]as there are some such in the world   [448]foolish affection   [449]overcome (their reluctance) or
satisfied (their desires)   [450]I would not fall into such passion unless there were some real grounds
for it.

My medicine, work! Thus credulous fools are caught;
And many worthy and chaste dames even thus,   45
All guiltless, meet reproach. What, ho! my lord!
My lord, I say! Othello!

(*Enter* CASSIO.)

                    How now, Cassio!

CASSIO: What's the matter?

IAGO: My lord is fallen into an epilepsy;[451]
        This is his second fit; he had one yesterday.   50

CASSIO: Rub him about the temples.

IAGO: No, forbear;
        The lethargy[452] must have his quiet course,
        If not, he foams at mouth, and by and by
        Breaks out to savage madness. Look! he stirs;
        Do you withdraw yourself a little while,   55
        He will recover straight; when he is gone,
        I would on great occasion[453] speak with you.   (*Exit* CASSIO.)
        How is it, general? have you not hurt your head?

OTHELLO: Dost thou mock me?[454]

IAGO: I mock you! no, by heaven.
        Would you would bear your fortune like a man!   60

OTHELLO: A horned man's a monster and a beast.

IAGO: There's many a beast then, in a populous city,
        And many a civil[455] monster.

OTHELLO: Did he confess it?

IAGO: Good sir, be a man;
        Think every bearded fellow that's but yok'd   65
        May draw[456] with you; there 's millions now alive
        That nightly lie in those unproper[457] beds
        Which they dare swear peculiar;[458] your case is better.
        O! 'tis the spite of hell, the fiend's arch-mock,
        To lip[459] a wanton in a secure[460] couch,   70
        And to suppose her chaste. No, let me know;
        And knowing what I am, I know what she shall be.

OTHELLO: O! thou art wise; 'tis certain.

IAGO: Stand you awhile apart;
        Confine yourself but in a patient list.[461]
        Whilst you were here o'erwhelmed with your grief,—   75
        A passion most unsuiting such a man,—
        Cassio came hither; I shifted him away,

---

[451]seizure, fit   [452]coma   [453]important matter   [454]another allusion to the cuckold's horns
[455]citizen   [456]i.e., pull the burden of cuckolddom   [457]not exclusively their own   [458]exclusively
their own   [459]kiss   [460]i.e., without suspicion of having a rival   [461]bounds of patience

And laid good 'scuse upon your ecstasy;[462]
Bade him anon return and here speak with me;
The which he promis'd. Do but encave yourself, 80
And mark the fleers, the gibes, and notable scorns,
That dwell in every region of his face;
For I will make him tell the tale anew,
Where, how, how oft, how long ago, and when
He hath, and is again to cope[463] your wife: 85
I say, but mark his gesture. Marry, patience;
Or I shall say you are all in all in spleen,[464]
And nothing of a man.

OTHELLO: Dost thou hear, Iago?
I will be found most cunning in my patience;
But—does thou hear?—most bloody. 90

IAGO: That's not amiss;
But yet keep time[465] in all. Will you withdraw?   (OTHELLO goes apart.)
Now will I question Cassio of Bianca,
A housewife[466] that by selling her desires
Buys herself bread and clothes; it is a creature
That dotes on Cassio; as 'tis the strumpet's plague 95
To beguile many and be beguil'd by one.
He, when he hears of her, cannot refrain
From the excess of laughter. Here he comes:

(Re-enter CASSIO.)

As he shall smile, Othello shall go mad;
And his unbookish[467] jealousy must construe 100
Poor Cassio's smiles, gestures, and light behaviour
Quite in the wrong. How do you now, lieutenant?

CASSIO: The worser that you give me the addition[468]
Whose want[469] even kills me.

IAGO: Ply Desdemona well, and you are sure on 't. 105
(Speaking lower) Now, if this suit lay in Bianca's power,
How quickly should you speed!

CASSIO: Alas! poor caitiff![470]

OTHELLO: Look! how he laughs already!

IAGO: I never knew woman love man so.

CASSIO: Alas! poor rogue, I think, i' faith, she loves me. 110

OTHELLO: Now he denies it faintly, and laughs it out.

IAGO: Do you hear, Cassio?

OTHELLO: Now he importunes him

---

[462]derangement, trance   [463]close with   [464]completely overcome by passion   [465]maintain control
[466]hussy   [467]unpracticed, naïve   [468]title   [469]the want of which   [470]wretch

To tell it oe'r: go to; well said, well said.

IAGO: She gives it out that you shall marry her;
Do you intend it? 115

CASSIO: Ha, ha, ha!

OTHELLO: Do you triumph, Roman?[471] do you triumph?

CASSIO: I marry her! what? a customer?[472] I prithee, bear some charity to my
wit;[473] do not think it so unwholesome. Ha, ha, ha!

OTHELLO: So, so, so, so. They laugh that win.[474] 120

IAGO: Faith, the cry goes that you shall marry her.

CASSIO: Prithee, say true.

IAGO: I am a very villain else.

OTHELLO: Have you scored me?[475] Well.

CASSIO: This is the monkey's own giving out: she is persuaded I will marry her, 125
out of her own love and flattery, not out of my promise.

OTHELLO: Iago beckons me;[476] now he begins the story.

CASSIO: She was here even now; she haunts me in every place. I was the other
day talking on the sea-bank with certain Venetians, and thither comes
this bauble,[477] and, by this hand, she falls me thus about my neck;— 130

OTHELLO: Crying, 'O dear Cassio!' as it were; his gesture imports it.

CASSIO: So hangs and lolls and weeps upon me; so hales[478] and pulls me; ha,
ha, ha!

OTHELLO: Now he tells how she plucked him to my chamber. O! I see that nose
of yours, but not the dog I shall throw it to. 135

CASSIO: Well, I must leave her company.

IAGO: Before me![479] look, where she comes.

CASSIO: 'Tis such another fitchew![480] marry, a perfumed one.

(*Enter* BIANCA.)

What do you mean by this haunting of me?

BIANCA: Let the devil and his dam haunt you! What did you mean by that 140
same handkerchief you gave me even now? I was a fine fool to take it.
I must take out the work! A likely piece of work, that you should find it
in your chamber, and not know who left it there! This is some minx's
token, and I must take out the work! There, give it your hobby-horse;[481]
wheresoever you had it I'll take out no work on 't. 145

CASSIO: How now, my sweet Bianca! how now, how now!

OTHELLO: By heaven, that should be[482] my handkerchief!

BIANCA: An you'll come to supper to-night, you may; an you will not, come
when you are next prepared[483] for. (*Exit.*)

---

[471]i.e., one who triumphs (?) [472]courtesan, prostitute [473]give me credit for some sense
[474]"he who laughs last laughs longest" (?) [475]wounded, defaced (?); or: settled my account (?)
[476]signals [477]plaything [478]hauls [479]an exclamation of surprise [480]polecat,
noted both for its strong smell and for its lechery [481]harlot [482]i.e., I think it is
[483]expected (Bianca means that if he does not come that night, she will never want to see him
again.)

IAGO: After her, after her. 150

CASSIO: Faith, I must; she'll rail in the street else.

IAGO: Will you sup there?

CASSIO: Faith, I intend so.

IAGO: Well, I may chance to see you, for I would very fain[484] speak with you.

CASSIO: Prithee come; will you? 155

IAGO: Go to; say no more. (Exit CASSIO.)

OTHELLO (advancing): How shall I murder him, Iago?

IAGO: Did you perceive how he laughed at his vice?

OTHELLO: O! Iago!

IAGO: And did you see the handkerchief? 160

OTHELLO: Was that mine?

IAGO: Yours, by this hand; and to see how he prizes the foolish woman your wife! she gave it him, and he hath given it his whore.

OTHELLO: I would have him nine years a-killing. A fine woman! a fair woman! a sweet woman! 165

IAGO: Nay, you must forget that.

OTHELLO: Ay, let her rot, and perish, and be damned to-night; for she shall not live. No, my heart is turned to stone; I strike it, and it hurts my hand. O! the world hath not a sweeter creature; she might lie by an emperor's side and command him tasks. 170

IAGO: Nay, that's not your way.[485]

OTHELLO: Hang her! I do but say what she is. So delicate with her needle! An admirable musician! O, she will sing the savageness out of a bear. Of so high and plenteous wit and invention!

IAGO: She's the worse for all this. 175

OTHELLO: O! a thousand, a thousand times. And then, of so gentle a condition![486]

IAGO: Ay, too gentle.[487]

OTHELLO: Nay, that 's certain;—but yet the pity of it, Iago!
O! Iago, the pity of it, Iago! 180

IAGO: If you are so fond over her iniquity, give her patent to offend; for, if it touch not you, it comes near nobody.

OTHELLO: I will chop her into messes.[488] Cuckold me!

IAGO: O! 'tis foul in her.

OTHELLO: With mine officer! 185

IAGO: That 's fouler.

OTHELLO: Get me some poison, Iago; this night: I'll not expostulate with her, lest her body and beauty unprovide my mind again.[489] This night, Iago.

IAGO: Do it not with poison, strangle her in her bed, even the bed she hath contaminated. 190

OTHELLO: Good, good; the justice of it pleases; very good.

[484]gladly [485]proper course [486]so much the high-born lady [487]i.e., yielding [488]bits
[489]unsettle my intention

IAGO: And for Cassio, let me be his undertaker;[490] you shall hear more by mid-
        night.
OTHELLO: Excellent good. (*A trumpet within.*) What trumpet is that same?
IAGO: Something from Venice, sure. 'Tis Lodovico,   195
        Come from the duke; and see, your wife is with him.

(*Enter* LODOVICO, DESDEMONA, *and* ATTENDANTS.)

LODOVICO: God save you, worthy general!
OTHELLO: With all my heart, sir.
LODOVICO: The duke and senators of Venice greet you.

(*Gives him a packet.*)

OTHELLO: I kiss the instrument of their pleasures.

(*Opens the packet, and reads.*)

DESDEMONA: And what's the news, good cousin Lodovico?   200
IAGO: I am very glad to see you, signior;
        Welcome to Cyprus.
LODOVICO: I thank you. How does Lieutenant Cassio?
IAGO: Lives, sir.
DESDEMONA: Cousin, there 's fall'n between him and my lord   205
        An unkind[491] breach; but you shall make all well.
OTHELLO: Are you sure of that?
DESDEMONA: My lord?
OTHELLO (*reads*):   'This fail you not to do, as you will'—
LODOVICO: He did not call; he 's busy in the paper.   210
        Is there division[492] 'twixt my lord and Cassio?
DESDEMONA: A most unhappy one; I would do much
        To atone[493] them, for the love I bear to Cassio.
OTHELLO: Fire and brimstone!
DESDEMONA: My lord?
OTHELLO: Are you wise?
DESDEMONA: What! is he angry?   215
LODOVICO: May be the letter mov'd him;
        For, as I think, they do command him home,
        Deputing Cassio in his government.
DESDEMONA: Trust me, I am glad on 't.
OTHELLO: Indeed!
DESDEMONA: My lord?
OTHELLO: I am glad to see you mad.
DESDEMONA: Why, sweet Othello?

[490]dispatcher   [491]unnatural   [492]estrangement   [493]reconcile

OTHELLO: Devil!   *(Strikes her.)*   220

DESDEMONA: I have not deserved this.

LODOVICO: My lord, this would not be believ'd in Venice,
     Though I should swear I saw 't: 'tis very much;
     Make her amends, she weeps.

OTHELLO: O devil, devil!
     If that the earth could teem with woman's tears,   225
     Each drop she falls[494] would prove a crocodile.[495]
     Out of my sight!

DESDEMONA: I will not stay to offend you.   *(Going.)*

LODOVICO: Truly, an obedient lady;
     I do beseech your lordship, call her back.

OTHELLO: Mistress!   230

DESDEMONA: My lord?

OTHELLO: What would you with her, sir?

LODOVICO: Who, I, my lord?

OTHELLO: Ay; you did wish that I would make her turn:
     Sir, she can turn, and turn, and yet go on,
     And turn again; and she can weep, sir, weep;
     And she 's obedient, as you say, obedient,   235
     Very obedient. Proceed you in your tears.
     Concerning this, sir,—O well-painted passion!—
     I am commanded home. Get you away;
     I'll send for you anon. Sir, I obey the mandate,
     And will return to Venice. Hence! avaunt![496]   *(Exit* DESDEMONA.*)*   240
     Cassio shall have my place. And, sir, to-night,
     I do entreat that we may sup together;
     You are welcome, sir, to Cyprus. Goats and monkeys!   *(Exit.)*

LODOVICO: Is this the noble Moor whom our full senate
     Call all-in-all sufficient? is this the noble nature   245
     Whom passion could not shake? whose solid virtue
     The shot of accident nor dart of chance
     Could neither graze nor pierce?

IAGO: He is much chang'd.

LODOVICO: Are his wits safe? is he not light of brain?

IAGO: He's that he is; I may not breathe my censure.   250
     What he might be, if, what he might, he is not,
     I would to heaven he were![497]

LODOVICO: What! strike his wife!

IAGO: Faith, that was not so well; yet would I knew
     That stroke would prove the worst!

LODOVICO: Is it his use?

---

[494]lets fall   [495]the crocodile's tears were supposed to be hypocritical   [496]begone!
[497]another of Iagos gnomic speeches; perhaps approximately: "If now he is not himself, I wish
he would be what he could be!"

Or did the letters work upon his blood,
And new-create this fault?

IAGO: Alas, alas!
It is not honesty in me to speak
What I have seen and known. You shall observe him,
And his own courses[498] will denote him so
That I may save my speech. Do but go after   260
And mark how he continues.

LODOVICO: I am sorry that I am deceiv'd in him.   *(Exeunt.)*

Scene 2 [A Room in the Castle.]

(Enter OTHELLO *and* EMILIA.)

OTHELLO: You have seen nothing, then?
EMILIA: Nor ever heard, nor ever did suspect.
OTHELLO: Yes, you have seen Cassio and her together.   265
EMILIA: But then I saw no harm, and then I heard
        Each syllable that breath made up between them.
OTHELLO: What! did they never whisper?
EMILIA: Never, my lord.
OTHELLO: Nor send you out o' the way?
EMILIA: Never.
OTHELLO: To fetch her fan, her gloves, her mask, nor nothing?[499]   270
EMILIA: Never, my lord.
OTHELLO: That 's strange.
EMILIA: I durst, my lord, to wager she is honest,
        Lay down my soul at stake: if you think other,
        Remove your thought; it doth abuse your bosom.   275
        If any wretch have put this in your head,
        Let heaven requite it with the serpent's curse!
        For, if she be not honest, chaste, and true,
        There's no man happy; the purest of their wives
        Is foul as slander.   280
OTHELLO: Bid her come hither; go.   *(Exit* EMILIA.)
        She says enough; yet she 's a simple[500] bawd
        That cannot say as much. This is a subtle whore,
        A closet lock and key of villanous secrets;
        And yet she 'll kneel and pray; I have seen her do 't.

(Re-enter EMILIA *with* DESDEMONA.)

DESDEMONA: My lord, what is your will?   285
OTHELLO: Pray, chuck, come hither.

[498]actions   [499]anything   [500]simpleminded

636

DESDEMONA: What is your pleasure?

OTHELLO: Let me see your eyes;
Look in my face.

DESDEMONA: What horrible fancy's this?

OTHELLO (to EMILIA):   Some of your function,[501] mistress;
Leave procreants alone and shut the door;
Cough or cry 'hem' if any body come;   290
Your mystery,[502] your mystery, nay, dispatch.   (*Exit* EMILIA.)

DESDEMONA: Upon my knees, what doth your speech import?
I understand a fury in your words.
But not the words.

OTHELLO: Why, what art thou?   295

DESDEMONA: Your wife, my lord; your true
And loyal wife.

OTHELLO: Come, swear it, damn thyself;
Lest, being like one of heaven, the devils themselves
Should fear to seize thee; therefore be double-damn'd;
Swear thou art honest.

DESDEMONA: Heaven doth truly know it.

OTHELLO: Heaven truly knows that thou art false as hell.   300

DESDEMONA: To whom, my lord? with whom? how am I false?

OTHELLO: Ah! Desdemona; away, away, away!

DESDEMONA: Alas, the heavy day!—Why do you weep?
Am I the motive of these tears, my lord?
If haply you my father do suspect   305
An instrument of this your calling back,
Lay not your blame on me; if you have lost him,
Why, I have lost him too.

OTHELLO: Had it pleas'd heaven
To try me with affliction, had he rain'd
All kinds of sores and shames on my bare head,   310
Steep'd me in poverty to the very lips,
Given to captivity me and my utmost hopes,
I should have found in some part of my soul
A drop of patience; but, alas! to make me
The fixed figure for the time of scorn[503]   315
To point his slow and moving finger at;
Yet could I bear that too; well, very well:
But there, where I have garner'd[504] up my heart,
Where either I must live or bear no life,
The fountain from the which my current runs   320
Or else dries up; to be discarded thence!
Or keep it as a cistern for foul toads

---

[501]duty, business   [502]trade   [503]i.e., the scornful world   [504]stored

To knot and gender in!^{505} **Turn thy complexion there,**^{506}
Patience, thou young and rose-lipp'd cherubin;
Ay, there, look grim as hell!   325

DESDEMONA: I hope my noble lord esteems me honest.

OTHELLO: O! ay; as summer flies are in the shambles,^{507}
That quicken even with blowing. O thou weed!
Who art so lovely fair and smell'st so sweet
That the sense aches at thee, would thou hadst ne'er been born.   330

DESDEMONA: Alas! what ignorant sin have I committed?

OTHELLO: Was this fair paper, this most goodly book,
Made to write 'whore' upon? What committed!
Committed! O thou public commoner!^{508}
I should make very forges of my cheeks,   335
That would to cinders burn up modesty,
Did I but speak thy deeds. What committed!
Heaven stops the nose at it and the moon winks,^{509}
The bawdy wind that kisses all it meets
Is hush'd within the hollow mine of earth,   340
And will not hear it. What committed!
Impudent strumpet!

DESDEMONA: By heaven, you do me wrong.

OTHELLO: Are you not a strumpet?

DESDEMONA: No, as I am a Christian.
If to preserve this vessel for my lord
From any other foul unlawful touch   345
Be not to be a strumpet, I am none.

OTHELLO: What! not a whore?

DESDEMONA: No, as I shall be sav'd.

OTHELLO: Is it possible?

DESDEMONA: O! heaven forgive us.

OTHELLO: I cry you mercy,^{510} then;
I took you for that cunning whore of Venice   350
That married with Othello. You, mistress,
That have the office opposite to Saint Peter,
And keep the gate of hell!

(Re-enter EMILIA.)

                        You, you, ay, you!
We have done our course; there 's money for your pains.
I pray you, turn the key and keep our counsel.   *(Exit.)*   355

EMILIA: Alas! what does this gentleman conceive?^{511}
How do you, madam? how do you, my good lady?

---

^{505}bunch up and procreate ^{506}i.e., change your color to suit the "cistern for foul toads"
^{507}slaughterhouse ^{508}harlot ^{509}closes her eyes ^{510}beg your pardon ^{511}imagine

DESDEMONA: Faith, half asleep.

EMILIA: Good madam, what 's the matter with my lord?

DESDEMONA: With who?   360

EMILIA: Why, with my lord, madam.

DESDEMONA: Who is thy lord?

EMILIA: He that is yours, sweet lady.

DESDEMONA: I have none; do not talk to me, Emilia;
    I cannot weep, nor answer have I none,
    But what should go by water,[512] Prithee, to-night   365
    Lay on my bed my wedding sheets: remember:
    And call thy husband hither.

EMILIA: Here is a change indeed!   (*Exit.*)

DESDEMONA: 'Tis meet I should be us'd so, very meet.
    How have I been behav'd, that he might stick
    The small'st opinion on my least misuse?[513]   370

(*Re-enter* EMILIA, *with* IAGO.)

IAGO: What is your pleasure, madam? How is it with you?

DESDEMONA: I cannot tell. Those that do teach young babes
    Do it with gentle means and easy tasks;
    He might have chid me so; for, in good faith,
    I am a child to chiding.   375

IAGO: What's the matter, lady?

EMILIA: Alas; Iago, my lord hath so bewhor'd her,
    Thrown such despite[514] and heavy terms upon her,
    As true hearts cannot bear.

DESDEMONA: Am I that name, Iago?

IAGO: What name, fair lady?

DESDEMONA: Such as she says my lord did say I was.   380

EMILIA: He call'd her whore; a beggar in his drink
    Could not have laid such terms upon his callat.[515]

IAGO: Why did he so?

DESDEMONA: I do not know; I am sure I am none such.

IAGO: Do not weep, do not weep. Alas the day!   385

EMILIA: Has she forsook so many noble matches,
    Her father and her country and her friends,
    To be call'd whore? would it not make one weep?

DESDEMONA: It is my wretched fortune.

IAGO: Beshrew[516] him for it!
    How comes this trick upon him?   390

DESDEMONA: Nay, heaven doth know.

EMILIA: I will be hang'd, if some eternal villain,

---

[512]be conveyed by means of tears   [513]the least suspicion on my slightest misconduct
[514]abuse   [515]slut   [516]curse

                    Some busy and insinuating rogue,
                    Some cogging[517] cozening slave, to get some office,
                    Have not devis'd this slander; I 'll be hang'd else.
IAGO: Fie! there is no such man; it is impossible.   395
DESDEMONA: If any such there be, heaven pardon him!
EMILIA: A halter pardon him, and hell gnaw his bones!
                    Why should he call her whore? who keeps her company?
                    What place? what time? what form? what likelihood?
                    The Moor's abus'd by some most villanous knave,   400
                    Some base notorious knave, some scurvy fellow.
                    O heaven! that such companions[518] thou'dst unfold,
                    And put in every honest hand a whip
                    To lash the rascals naked through the world,
                    Even from the east to the west!   405
IAGO: Speak within door.
EMILIA: O! fie upon them. Some such squire he was
                    That turn'd your wit the seamy side without,[519]
                    And made you to suspect me with the Moor.
IAGO: You are a fool; go to.
DESDEMONA: O good Iago,
                    What shall I do to win my lord again?   410
                    Good friend, go to him; for, by this light of heaven,
                    I know not how I lost him. Here I kneel:
                    If e'er my will did trespass 'gainst his love,
                    Either in discourse of thought or actual deed,
                    Or that mine eyes, mine ears, or any sense,   415
                    Delighted them[520] in any other form;
                    Or that I do not yet,[521] and ever did,
                    And ever will, though he do shake me off
                    To beggarly divorcement, love him dearly,
                    Comfort forswear me! Unkindness may do much;   420
                    And his unkindness may defeat[522] my life,
                    But never taint my love. I cannot say 'whore':
                    It does abhor me now I speak the word;
                    To do the act that might the addition earn
                    Not the world's mass of vanity could make me.   425
IAGO: I pray you be content, 'tis but his humour;
                    The business of the state does him offence,
                    And he does chide with you.
DESDEMONA: If 'twere no other,—
IAGO: 'Tis but so, I warrant.   (Trumpets.)
                    Hark! how these instruments summon to supper;   430
                    The messengers of Venice stay the meat:

[517]cheating   [518]fellows (derogatory)   [519]outward   [520]found delight   [521]still   [522]destroy

Go in, and weep not; all things shall be well.

(*Exeunt* DESDEMONA *and* EMILIA.)

(*Enter* RODERIGO.)

How now, Roderigo!

RODERIGO: I do not find that thou dealest justly with me.

IAGO: What in the contrary?[523]   435

RODERIGO: Every day thou daffest me[524] with some device, Iago; and rather, as it seems to me now, keepest from me all conveniency,[525] than suppliest me with the least advantage of hope. I will indeed no longer endure it, nor am I yet persuaded to put up[526] in peace what already I have foolishly suffered.   440

IAGO: Will you hear me, Roderigo?

RODERIGO: Faith, I have heard too much, for your words and performances are no kin together.

IAGO: You charge me unjustly.

RODERIGO: With nought but truth. I have wasted myself out of my means. The   445
jewels you have had from me to deliver to Desdemona would half have corrupted a votarist;[527] you have told me she has received them, and returned me expectations and comforts of sudden respect[528] and acquaintance, but I find none.

IAGO: Well; go to; very well.   450

RODERIGO: Very well! go to! I cannot go to, man; nor 'tis not very well; by this hand, I say, it is very scurvy, and begin to find myself fobbed[529] in it.

IAGO: Very well.

RODERIGO: I tell you 'tis not very well. I will make myself known to Desdemona; if she will return me my jewels, I will give over my suit and repent my   455
solicitation; if not, assure yourself I will seek satisfaction of you.

IAGO: You have said now.[530]

RODERIGO: Ay, and said nothing, but what I protest intendment of doing.

IAGO: Why, now I see there's mettle in thee, and even from this instant do build on thee a better opinion than ever before. Give me thy hand,   460
Roderigo; thou hast taken against me a most just exception; but yet, I protest, I have dealt most directly in thy affair.

RODERIGO: It hath not appeared.

IAGO: I grant indeed it hath not appeared, and your suspicion is not without wit and judgment. But, Roderigo, if thou hast that in thee indeed, which   465
I have greater reason to believe now than ever, I mean purpose, courage, and valour, this night show it: if thou the next night following enjoy not Desdemona, take me from this world with treachery and devise engines for[531] my life.

---

[523]i.e., what reason do you have for saying that   [524]you put me off   [525]favorable circumstances
[526]put up with   [527]nun   [528]immediate consideration   [529]cheated   [530]i.e., "I suppose
you're through?" (?) or: "Now you're talking" (?)   [531]devices against

RODERIGO: Well, what is it? is it within reason and compass?   490

IAGO: Sir, there is especial commission come from Venice to depute Cassio in
Othello's place.

RODERIGO: Is that true? why, then Othello and Desdemona return again to
Venice.

IAGO: O, no! he goes into Mauritania, and takes away with him the fair Desde-   475
mona, unless his abode be lingered here by some accident; wherein
none can be so determinate[532] as the removing of Cassio.

RODERIGO: How do you mean, removing of him?

IAGO: Why, by making him uncapable of Othello's place; knocking out his
brains.   480

RODERIGO: And that you would have me do?

IAGO: Ay; if you dare do yourself a profit and a right. He sups to-night with
a harlotry,[533] and thither will I go to him; he knows not yet of his honourable fortune. If you will watch his going thence,—which I will fashion
to fall out between twelve and one,—you may take him at your plea-   485
sure; I will be near to second your attempt, and he shall fall between
us. Come, stand not amazed at it, but go along with me; I will show you
such as necessity in his death that you shall think yourself bound to put it
on him. It is now high supper-time, and the night grows to waste;
about it.   490

RODERIGO: I will hear further reason for this.

IAGO: And you shall be satisfied.   (Exeunt.)

Scene 3 [Another Room in the Castle.]

(*Enter* OTHELLO, LODOVICO, DESDEMONA, EMILIA, *and* ATTENDANTS.)

LODOVICO: I do beseech you, sir, trouble yourself no further.

OTHELLO: O! pardon me; 'twill do me good to walk.

LODOVICO: Madam, good-night; I humbly thank your ladyship.   495

DESDEMONA: Your honour is most welcome.

OTHELLO: Will you walk, sir?
O! Desdemona,—

DESDEMONA: My lord?

OTHELLO: Get you to bed on the instant; I will be returned forthwith; dismiss
your attendant there; look it be done.   500

DESDEMONA: I will, my lord.   (*Exeunt* OTHELLO, LODOVICO, *and* ATTENDANTS.)

EMILIA: How goes it now? He looks gentler than he did.

DESDEMONA: He says he will return incontinent;[534]
He hath commanded me to go to bed,
And bade me to dismiss you.   505

EMILIA: Dismiss me!

[532]effective   [533]harlot   [534]at once

642

DESDEMONA: It was his bidding; therefore, good Emilia,
Give me my nightly wearing, and adieu:
We must not now displease him.

EMILIA: I would you had never seen him.

DESDEMONA: So would not I; my love doth so approve him, 510
That even his stubbornness,[535] his cheeks[536] and frowns,—
Prithee, unpin me,—have grace and favour in them.

EMILIA: I have laid those sheets you bade me on the bed.

DESDEMONA: All 's one.[537] Good faith! how foolish are our minds!
If I do die before thee, prithee, shroud me 515
In one of those same sheets.

EMILIA: Come, come, you talk.

DESDEMONA: My mother had a maid call'd Barbara;
She was in love, and he she lov'd prov'd mad[538]
And did forsake her; she had a song of 'willow';
An old thing 'twas, but it express'd her fortune, 520
And she died singing it, that song to-night
Will not go from my mind: I have much to do
But to go hang my head all at one side,
And sing it like poor Barbara. Prithee, dispatch.

EMILIA: Shall I go fetch your night-gown? 525

DESDEMONA: No, unpin me here.
This Lodovico is a proper man.

EMILIA: A very handsome man.

DESDEMONA: He speaks well.

EMILIA: I know a lady in Venice would have walked barefoot to Palestine for
a touch of his nether lip. 530

DESDEMONA (*sings*):
The poor soul sat sighing by a sycamore tree,
Sing all a green willow;
Her hand on her bosom, her head on her knee,
Sing willow, willow, willow:
The fresh streams ran by her, and murmur'd her moans; 535
Sing willow, willow, willow:
Her salt tears fell from her, and soften'd the stones;—
Lay by these:—
Sing willow, willow, willow:
Prithee, hie thee;[539] he'll come anon.— 540
Sing all a green willow must be my garland.
Let nobody blame him, his scorn I approve,—

Nay, that's not next. Hark! who is it that knocks?

EMILIA: It is the wind.

---

[535]roughness [536]rebukes [537]i.e., doesn't matter [538]wild [539]hurry

DESDEMONA:

    I call'd my love false love; but what said he then?   545
      Sing willow, willow, willow:
    If I court moe[540] women, you'll couch with moe men.

    So, get thee gone; good-night. Mine eyes do itch;
    Doth that bode weeping?

EMILIA: 'Tis neither here nor there.

DESDEMONA: I have heard it said so. O! these men, these men!   550
    Dost thou in conscience think, tell me, Emilia,
    That there be women do abuse their husbands
    In such gross kind?

EMILIA: There be some such, no question.

DESDEMONA: Wouldst thou do such a deed for all the world?

EMILIA: Why, would not you?   555

DESDEMONA: No, by this heavenly light!

EMILIA: Nor I neither by this heavenly light;
    I might do 't as well i' the dark.

DESDEMONA: Wouldst thou do such a deed for all the world?

EMILIA: The world is a huge thing; 'tis a great price
    For a small vice.   560

DESDEMONA: In troth, I think thou wouldst not.

EMILIA: In troth, I think I should, and undo 't when I had done. Marry, I would
    not do such a thing for a joint-ring,[541] nor measures of lawn,[542] nor for
    gowns, petticoats, nor caps, nor any petty exhibition;[543] but for the
    whole world, who would not make her husband a cuckold to make him
    a monarch? I should venture purgatory for 't.   565

DESDEMONA: Beshrew me, if I would do such a wrong
    For the whole world.

EMILIA: Why, the wrong is but a wrong i' the world; and having the world for
    your labour, 'tis a wrong in your own world, and you might quickly
    make it right.   570

DESDEMONA: I do not think there is any such woman.

EMILIA: Yes, a dozen; and as many to the vantage,[544] as
    Would store[545] the world they played for.
    But I do think it is their husbands' faults
    If wives do fall. Say that they slack their duties,   575
    And pour our treasures into foreign laps,
    Or else break out in peevish jealousies,
    Throwing restraint upon us; or say they strike us,
    Or scant[546] our former having[547] in despite;
    Why, we have galls,[548] and though we have some grace,   580
    Yet have we some revenge. Let husbands know

---

[540]more [541]rings made in separable halves [542]fine linen [543]offer, gift [544]over and above
[545]populate [546]reduce [547]allowance [548]spirits, temper

Their wives have sense like them; they see and smell,
And have their palates both for sweet and sour,
As husbands have. What is it that they do
When they change us for others? Is it sport?[549]   585
I think it is; and doth affection breed it?
I think it doth; is 't frailty that thus errs?
It is so too; and have not we affections,
Desires for sport, and frailty, as men have?
Then, let them use us well; else let them know,   590
The ills we do, their ills instruct us so.
DESDEMONA: Good-night, good-night; heaven me such usage[550] send,
Not to pick bad from bad, but by bad mend!   *(Exeunt.)*

ACT V

Scene 1 [Cyprus. A Street.]

(Enter IAGO *and* RODERIGO.)

IAGO: Here, stand behind this bulk;[551] straight will he come:
Wear thy good rapier bare, and put it home.
Quick, quick; fear nothing; I'll be at thy elbow.
It makes us, or it mars us; think on that,
And fix most firm thy resolution.   5
RODERIGO: Be near at hand; I may miscarry in 't.
IAGO: Here, at thy hand: be bold, and take thy stand.   *(Retires.)*
RODERIGO: I have no great devotion to the deed;
And yet he has given me satisfying reasons:
'Tis but a man gone: forth, my sword; he dies.   10
IAGO: I have rubb'd this young quat[552] almost to the sense,[553]
And he grows angry. Now, whether he kill Cassio,
Or Cassio him, or each do kill the other,
Every way makes my gain: live Roderigo,
He calls me to a restitution large   15
Of gold and jewels that I bobb'd[554] from him,
As gifts to Desdemona;
It must not be: if Cassio do remain,
He hath a daily beauty in his life
That makes me ugly: and, besides, the Moor   20
May unfold me to him; there stand I in much peril.
No, he must die. But so;[555] I hear him coming.

(Enter CASSIO.)

[549]lust, sexual enjoyment   [550]habits (?), treatment (?)   [551]jutting part of a wall   [552]pimple
[553]to the quick   [554]swindled   [555]i.e., that's the only way

RODERIGO: I know his gait; 'tis he. Villain, thou diest!

(*Makes a pass at* CASSIO.)

CASSIO: That thrust had been mine enemy indeed
          But that my coat is better than thou know'st;   25
          I will make proof of thine.

(*Draws and wounds* RODERIGO.)

RODERIGO: O! I am slain.

(IAGO *from behind wounds* CASSIO *in the leg, and exit.*)

CASSIO: I am maim'd for ever. Help, ho! murder! murder! (*Falls.*)

(*Enter* OTHELLO, *at a distance.*)

OTHELLO: The voice of Cassio: Iago keeps his word.
RODERIGO: O! villain that I am!
OTHELLO: It is e'en so.
CASSIO: O, help, ho! light! a surgeon!   30
OTHELLO: 'Tis he: O brave Iago, honest and just!
          That hast such noble sense of thy friend's wrong;
          Thou teachest me. Minion,[556] your dear lies dead,
          And your unblest fate hies; strumpet, I come!
          Forth of my heart those charms, thine eyes, are blotted;   35
          Thy bed lust-stain'd shall with lust's blood be spotted.   (*Exit.*)

(*Enter* LODOVICO *and* GRATIANO, *at a distance.*)

CASSIO: What ho! no watch? no passage?[557] murder! murder!
GRATIANO: 'Tis some mischance; the cry is direful.
CASSIO: O, help!
LODOVICO: Hark!   40
RODERIGO: O wretched villain!
LODOVICO: Two or three groans: it is a heavy[558] night;
          These may be counterfeits; let's think 't unsafe
          To come in to the cry[559] without more help.
RODERIGO: Nobody come? then shall I bleed to death.   45
LODOVICO: Hark!

(*Re-enter* IAGO, *with a light.*)

[556](Cassio's) darling, *i.e.,* Desdemona   [557]passer-by   [558]dark   [559]where the cry comes from

GRATIANO: Here's one comes in his shirt, with light and weapons.

IAGO: Who's there? whose noise is this that cries on murder?

LODOVICO: We do not know.

IAGO: Did not you hear a cry?

CASSIO: Here, here! for heaven's sake, help me.   50

IAGO: What's the matter?

GRATIANO: This is Othello's ancient, as I take it.

LODOVICO: The same indeed; a very valiant fellow.

IAGO: What are you here that cry so grievously?

CASSIO: Iago? O! I am spoil'd, undone by villains!
    Give me some help.   55

IAGO: O me, lieutenant! what villains have done this?

CASSIO: I think that one of them is hereabout,
    And cannot make away.

IAGO: O treacherous villains!

(To LODOVICO and GRATIANO.) What are you there? come in, and give some
    help.   60

RODERIGO: O! help me here.

CASSIO: That's one of them.

IAGO: O murderous slave! O villain!

(Stabs RODERIGO.)

RODERIGO: O damn'd Iago! O inhuman dog!

IAGO: Kill me i' the dark! Where be these bloody thieves?
    How silent is this town! Ho! murder! murder!   65
    What may you be? are you of good or evil?

LODOVICO: As you shall prove us, praise us.

IAGO: Signior Lodovico?

LODOVICO: He, sir.

IAGO: I cry you mercy. Here 's Cassio hurt by villains.   70

GRATIANO: Cassio!

IAGO: How is it, brother?

CASSIO: My leg is cut in two.

IAGO: Marry, heaven forbid.
    Light, gentlemen; I'll bind it with my shirt.

(Enter BIANCA.)

BIANCA: What is the matter, ho? who is 't that cried?   75

IAGO: Who is 't that cried!

BIANCA: O my dear Cassio! my sweet Cassio!
    O Cassio, Cassio, Cassio!

IAGO: O notable strumpet! Cassio, may you suspect

Who they should be that have thus mangled you? 80

CASSIO: No.

GRATIANO: I am sorry to find you thus; I have been to seek you.

IAGO: Lend me a garter. So. O! for a chair,
To bear him easily hence!

BIANCA: Alas; he faints! O Cassio, Cassio, Cassio! 85

IAGO: Gentlemen all, I do suspect this trash[560]
To be a party in this injury.
Patience awhile, good Cassio. Come, come.
Lend me a light. Know we this face, or no?
Alas! my friend and my dear countryman, 90
Roderigo? no: yes, sure, O heaven! Roderigo.

GRATIANO: What! of Venice?

IAGO: Even he, sir: did you know him?

GRATIANO: Know him! ay.

IAGO: Signior Gratiano? I cry you gentle pardon;
These bloody accidents must excuse my manners, 95
That so neglected you.

GRATIANO: I am glad to see you.

IAGO: How do you, Cassio? O! a chair, a chair!

GRATIANO: Roderigo!

(*A chair brought in.*)

IAGO: He, he, 'tis he,—O! that's well said; the chair:
Some good men bear him carefully from hence; 100
I'll fetch the general's surgeon. (*To* BIANCA.) For you, mistress,
Save you your labour. He that lies slain here, Cassio,
Was my dear friend. What malice was between you?

CASSIO: None in the world; nor do I know that man.

IAGO (*to* BIANCA): What! look you pale? O! bear him out o' the air— 105

(CASSIO *and* RODERIGO *are borne off.*)

Stay you, good gentlemen. Look you pale, mistress?—
Do you perceive the gastness[561] of her eye?
Nay, if you stare, we shall hear more anon.
Behold her well; I pray you, look upon her.
Do you see, gentlemen? nay, guiltiness will speak 110
Though tongues were out of use.

(*Enter* EMILIA.)

EMILIA: 'Las! what's the matter? what's the matter, husband?

[560]i.e., Bianca   [561]terror

648

IAGO: Cassio hath here been set on in the dark
By Roderigo and fellows that are 'scaped:
He's almost slain, and Roderigo dead.   115
EMILIA: Alas! good gentleman; alas! good Cassio!
IAGO: This is the fruit of whoring. Prithee, Emilia,
Go know of Cassio where he supp'd to-night.
(To BIANCA.) What! do you shake at that?
BIANCA: He supp'd at my house; but I therefore shake not.   120
IAGO: O! did he so? I charge you, go with me.
EMILIA: Fie, fie upon thee, strumpet!
BIANCA: I am no strumpet, but of life as honest
As you that thus abuse me.
EMILIA: As I! foh! fie upon thee!
IAGO: Kind gentlemen, let 's go see poor Cassio dress'd.⁵⁶²   125
Come, mistress, you must tell 's another tale.
Emilia, run you to the citadel,
And tell my lord and lady what hath happ'd.
Will you go on afore? (Aside.) This is the night
That either makes me or fordoes⁵⁶³ me quite.   (Exeunt.)   130

Scene 2 [A Bedchamber in the Castle. DESDEMONA in bed asleep.
A light burning.]

(Enter OTHELLO.)

OTHELLO: It is the cause,⁵⁶⁴ it is the cause, my soul;
Let me not name it to you, you chaste stars!
It is the cause. Yet I'll not shed her blood,
Nor scar that whiter skin of hers than snow,   135
And smooth as monumental alabaster.
Yet she must die, else she'll betray more men.
Put out the light, and then put out the light:
If I quench thee, thou flaming minister,⁵⁶⁵
I can again thy former light restore,   140
Should I repent me; but once put out thy light,
Thou cunning'st⁵⁶⁶ pattern of excelling nature,
I know not where is that Promethean⁵⁶⁷ heat
That can thy light relume.⁵⁶⁸ When I have pluck'd the rose,
I cannot give it vital growth again,   145
It needs must wither: I'll smell it on the tree. (Kisses her.)

⁵⁶²bandaged   ⁵⁶³ruins   ⁵⁶⁴i.e., Desdemona's unchastity (Othello means that the severity of the
punishment is required by the nature of her sin.)   ⁵⁶⁵i.e., the candle   ⁵⁶⁶most intricately wrought
⁵⁶⁷in Greek mythology the demi-god Prometheus stole fire from the Gods and gave it to man
⁵⁶⁸relight

O balmy breath, that dost almost persuade
Justice to break her sword! One more, one more.
Be thus when thou art dead, and I will kill thee,
And love thee after. One more, and this the last:
So sweet was ne'er so fatal. I must weep,   150
But they are cruel tears; this sorrow 's heavenly,
It strikes where it doth love. She wakes.

DESDEMONA: Who's there? Othello?

OTHELLO: Ay, Desdemona.

DESDEMONA: Will you come to bed, my lord?

OTHELLO: Have you pray'd to-night, Desdemona?   155

DESDEMONA: Ay, my lord.

OTHELLO: If you bethink yourself of any crime
    Unreconcil'd as yet to heaven and grace,
    Solicit for it straight.

DESDEMONA: Alas! my lord, what may you mean by that?

OTHELLO: Well, do it, and be brief; I will walk by:[569]   160
    I would not kill thy unprepared spirit;
    No; heaven forfend;[570] I would not kill thy soul.

DESDEMONA: Talk you of killing?

OTHELLO: Ay, I do.

DESDEMONA: Then heaven
    Have mercy on me!

OTHELLO: Amen! with all my heart.

DESDEMONA: If you say so, I hope you will not kill me.   165

OTHELLO: Hum!

DESDEMONA: And yet I fear you; for you are fatal then
    When your eyes roll so. Why I should fear I know not,
    Since guiltiness I know not; but yet I feel I fear.

OTHELLO: Think on thy sins.   170

DESDEMONA: They are loves I bear to you.

OTHELLO: Ay, and for that thou diest.

DESDEMONA: That death's unnatural that kills for loving.
    Alas; why gnaw you so your nether lip?
    Some bloody passion shakes your very frame;
    These are portents,[571] but yet, I hope, I hope   175
    They do not point on me.

OTHELLO: Peace, and be still!

DESDEMONA: I will so. What 's the matter?

OTHELLO: That handkerchief which I so lov'd and gave thee
    Thou gav'st to Cassio.

DESDEMONA: No, by my life and soul!
    Send for the man and ask him.   180

[569]nearby   [570]forbid   [571]omens

OTHELLO: Sweet soul, take heed,
>   Take heed of perjury; thou 'rt on thy death-bed.
DESDEMONA: Ay, but not yet to die.
OTHELLO: Yes, presently;[572]
>   Therefore confess thee freely of thy sin;
>   For to deny each article with oath
>   Cannot remove nor choke the strong conception[573]   185
>   That I do groan withal. Thou art to die.
DESDEMONA: Then Lord have mercy on me!
OTHELLO: I say, amen.
DESDEMONA: And have you mercy too! I never did
>   Offend you in my life; never lov'd Cassio
>   But with such general warranty[574] of heaven   190
>   As I might love; I never gave him token.
OTHELLO: By heaven, I saw my handkerchief in 's hand.
>   O perjur'd woman! thou dost stone[575] my heart,
>   And mak'st me call what I intend to do
>   A murder, which I thought a sacrifice: 195
>   I saw the handkerchief.
DESDEMONA: He found it then;
>   I never gave it him. Send for him hither;
>   Let him confess a truth.
OTHELLO: He hath confessed.
DESDEMONA: What, my lord?
OTHELLO: That he hath us'd thee.   200
DESDEMONA: How? Unlawfully?
OTHELLO: Ay.
DESDEMONA: He will not say so.
OTHELLO: No; his mouth is stopp'd:
>   Honest Iago hath ta'en order for 't.[576]
DESDEMONA: O! my fear interprets. What! is he dead?
OTHELLO: Had all his hairs been lives, my great revenge   205
>   Had stomach[577] for them all.
DESDEMONA: Alas! he is betray'd and I undone.
OTHELLO: Out, strumpet! Weep'st thou for him to my face?
DESDEMONA: O! banish me, my lord, but kill me not!
OTHELLO: Down, strumpet!   210
DESDEMONA: Kill me to-morrow; let me live to-night!
OTHELLO: Nay, if you strive,—
DESDEMONA: But half an hour!
OTHELLO: Being done, there is no pause.
DESDEMONA: But while I say one prayer!
OTHELLO: It is too late.   (He smothers her.)

[572]at once   [573]belief   [574]permission   [575]turn to stone   [576]taken steps   [577]appetite

EMILIA (*within*): My lord, my lord! what, ho! my lord! my lord! 215
OTHELLO: What noise is this? Not dead? not yet quite dead?
      I that am cruel am yet merciful;
      I would not have thee linger in thy pain.
      So, so.
EMILIA (*within*): What, ho! my lord, my lord! 220
OTHELLO: Who's there?
EMILIA (*within*): O! good my lord, I would speak a word with you!
OTHELLO: Yes; 'tis Emilia: by and by.[578] She 's dead.
      'Tis like[579] she comes to speak of Cassio's death;
      The noise was high. Ha! no more moving?
      Still as the grave. Shall she come in? Were 't good?[580] 225
      I think she stirs again: no. What's best to do?
      If she come in she'll sure speak to my wife:
      My wife! my wife! what wife? I have no wife:
      O, insupportable! O heavy hour!
      Methinks it should be now a huge eclipse 230
      Of sun and moon, and that the affrighted globe
      Should yawn[581] at alteration.
EMILIA (*within*):   I do beseech you
      That I may speak with you, O! good my lord.
OTHELLO: I had forgot thee: O! come in, Emilia:
      Soft, by and by: let me the curtains draw. 235
      Where art thou?   (*Unlocks the door.*)

(*Enter* EMILIA.)

          What 's the matter with thee now?
EMILIA: O! my good lord, yonder's foul murder done.
OTHELLO: What! now?
EMILIA: But now, my lord.
OTHELLO: It is the very error[582] of the moon;
      She comes more near the earth than she was wont, 240
      And makes men mad.
EMILIA: Cassio, my lord, has kill'd a young Venetian
      Call'd Roderigo.
OTHELLO: Roderigo kill'd!
      And Cassio kill'd?
EMILIA: No, Cassio is not kill'd.
OTHELLO: Not Cassio kill'd! then murder's out of tune, 245
      And sweet revenge grows harsh.
DESDEMONA: O! falsely, falsely murder'd.
EMILIA: Alas! what cry is that?

[578]i.e., "just a moment" [579]likely [580]would that be wise [581]open up (as in an earthquake)
[582]straying

OTHELLO: That! what?

EMILIA: Out, and alas! that was my lady's voice:
    Help! Help, ho! help! O lady, speak again!   250
    Sweet Desdemona! O! sweet mistress, speak.

DESDEMONA: A guiltless death I die.

EMILIA: O! who hath done this deed?

DESDEMONA: Nobody; I myself; farewell:
    Commend me to my kind lord. O! farewell!   (Dies.) 255

OTHELLO: Why, how should she be murder'd?

EMILIA: Alas! who knows?

OTHELLO: You heard her say herself it was not I.

EMILIA: She said so; I must needs report the truth.

OTHELLO: She's like a liar gone to burning hell;
    'Twas I that kill'd her.   260

EMILIA: O! the more angel she,
    And you the blacker devil.

OTHELLO: She turn'd to folly, and she was a whore.

EMILIA: Thou dost belie her, and thou art a devil.

OTHELLO: She was false as water.

EMILIA: Thou art rash as fire to say
    That she was false: O! she was heavenly true.   265

OTHELLO: Cassio did tup her; ask thy husband else.
    O! I were damn'd beneath all depth in hell
    But that I did proceed[583] upon just grounds
    To this extremity. Thy husband knew it all.

EMILIA: My husband!   270

OTHELLO: Thy husband.

EMILIA: That she was false to wedlock?

OTHELLO: Ay, with Cassio. Nay, had she been true,
    If heaven would make me such another world
    Of one entire and perfect chrysolite,[584]   275
    I'd not have sold her for it.

EMILIA: My husband!

OTHELLO: Ay, 'twas he that told me first:
    An honest man he is, and hates the slime
    That sticks on filthy deeds.

EMILIA: My husband!

OTHELLO: What needs this iterance,[585] woman? I say thy husband.   280

EMILIA: O mistress! villany hath made mocks with love.
    My husband say that she was false!

OTHELLO: He, woman;
    I say, thy husband: dost understand the word?
    My friend, thy husband, honest, honest Iago.

---

[583]had I not proceeded   [584]topaz   [585]repetition

EMILIA: If he say so, may his pernicious soul 285
    Rot half a grain a day! he lies to the heart:
    She was too fond of her most filthy bargain.[586]
OTHELLO: Ha!
EMILIA: Do thy worst:
    This deed of thine is no more worthy heaven 290
    Than thou wast worthy her.
OTHELLO: Peace! you were best.[587]
EMILIA: Thou hast not half the power to do me harm
    As I have to be hurt. O gull! O dolt!
    As ignorant as dirt! thou hast done a deed,—
    I care not for thy sword; I'll make thee known, 295
    Though I lost twenty lives. Help! help, ho! help!
    The Moor has kill'd my mistress! murder! murder!

(Enter MONTANO, GRATIANO, IAGO, and others.)

MONTANO: What is the matter? How now, general!
EMILIA: O! are you come, Iago? you have done well,
    That men must lay their murders on your neck. 300
GRATIANO: What is the matter?
EMILIA: Disprove this villain if thou be'st a man:
    He says thou told'st him that his wife was false.
    I know thou didst not, thou 'rt not such a villain.
    Speak, for my heart is full. 305
IAGO: I told him what I thought, and told no more
    Than what he found himself was apt and true.
EMILIA: But did you ever tell him she was false?
IAGO: I did.
EMILIA: You told a lie, an odious damned lie; 310
    Upon my soul, a lie, a wicked lie;
    She false with Cassio! Did you say with Cassio?
IAGO: With Cassio, mistress. Go to, charm[588] your tongue.
EMILIA: I will not charm my tongue; I am bound to speak.
    My mistress here lies murder'd in her bed. 315
ALL: O heavens forfend!
EMILIA: And your reports have set the murder on.
OTHELLO: Nay, stare not, masters; it is true, indeed.
GRATIANO: 'Tis a strange truth.
MONTANO: O monstrous act! 320
EMILIA: Villany! villany! villany!
    I think upon 't, I think, I smell 't; O villany!
    I thought so then.[589] I'll kill myself for grief.

---

[586]i.e., Othello   [587]you'd better be quiet   [588]i.e., into silence   [589]cf. "I will be hang'd, if some

654

O! villany, villany!

IAGO: What! are you mad? I charge you, get you home.

EMILIA: Good gentlemen, let me have leave to speak: 325
'Tis proper I obey him, but not now.
Perchance, Iago, I will ne'er go home.

OTHELLO: O! O! O!   (*Falls on the bed.*)

EMILIA: Nay, lay thee down and roar,
For thou hast kill'd the sweetest innocent
That e'er did lift up eye.   330

OTHELLO: O! she was foul.   (*Rises.*)
I scarce did know you, uncle. There lies your niece,
Whose breath, indeed, these hands have newly stopp'd:
I know this act shows terrible and grim.

GRATIANO: Poor Desdemona! I am glad thy father's dead.
Thy match was mortal to him, and pure grief   335
Shore[590] his old thread in twain: did he live now,
This sight would make him do a desperate turn,
Yea, curse his better angel from his side,
And fall to reprobation.[591]

OTHELLO: 'Tis pitiful; but yet Iago knows   340
That she with Cassio hath the act of shame
A thousand times committed; Cassio confess'd it:
And she did gratify[592] his amorous works
With that recognizance and pledge of love
Which I first gave her. I saw it in his hand: 345
It was a handkerchief, an antique token
My father gave my mother.

EMILIA: O heaven! O heavenly powers!

IAGO: Come, hold your peace.

EMILIA: 'Twill out, 'twill out; I hold my peace, sir? no;
No, I will speak as liberal as the north;[593]   350
Let heaven and men and devils, let them all,
All, all, cry shame against me, yet I'll speak.

IAGO: Be wise, and get you home.

EMILIA: I will not.

(IAGO *threatens to stab* EMILIA.)

GRATIANO: Fie!
Your sword upon a woman!

EMILIA: O thou dull Moor! that handkerchief thou speak'st of   355

eternal villain, / Some busy and insinuating rogue, / Some cogging cozening slave, to get some
office, / Have not devis'd this slander; . . ." (IV, ii, pp. 639-40). Emilia means, not that she
guessed Iago's guilt, but that she rightly guessed the slanderer's motive.   [590]cut   [591]damnation
[592]reward   [593]i.e., the north wind (?), the supposedly free-spoken people of north England (?)

I found by fortune and did give my husband;
For often, with a solemn earnestness,
More than, indeed, belong'd to such a trifle,
He begg'd of me to steal it.

IAGO: Villainous whore!

EMILIA: She give it Cassio! no, alas! I found it,   360
And I did give 't my husband.

IAGO: Filth, thou liest!

EMILIA: By heaven, I do not, I do not, gentlemen.
O murderous coxcomb![594] what should such a fool
Do with so good a wife?

OTHELLO: Are there no stones[595] in heaven
But what serve for the thunder? Precious villain!   365

(He runs at IAGO. IAGO *stabs* EMILIA.*)*

GRATIANO: The woman falls: sure, he has kill'd his wife.   *(Exit* IAGO.*)*

EMILIA: Ay, ay; O! lay me by my mistress' side.

GRATIANO: He's gone; but his wife's kill'd.

MONTANO: 'Tis a notorious[596] villain. Take you this weapon,
Which I have here recover'd from the Moor.   370
Come, guard the door without; let him not pass,
But kill him rather. I'll after that same villain,
For 'tis a damned slave.   *(Exeunt* MONTANO *and* GRATIANO.*)*

OTHELLO: I am not valiant neither,
But every puny whipster[597] gets my sword.
But why should honour outlive honesty?   375
Let it go all.

EMILIA: What did thy song bode, lady?
Hark, canst thou hear me? I will play the swan,
And die in music:—

(Sings.) Willow, willow, willow.

Moor, she was chaste; she lov'd thee, cruel Moor;   380
So come my soul to bliss as I speak true;
So speaking as I think, I die, I die.   *(Dies.)*

OTHELLO: I have another weapon in this chamber;
It is a sword of Spain, the ice-brook's temper.[598]
O! here it is. Uncle, I must come forth.   385

GRATIANO *(within)*:   If thou attempt it, it will cost thee dear:
Thou hast no weapon, and perforce must suffer.

[594]idiot [595]i.e., thunderbolts (to strike Iago down) [596]notable [597]i.e., a small boy whipping a top
[598]tempered in icy water (or the reference may be to Innsbruck, famed for the quality of its steel,
but this hardly fits "a sword of Spain")

OTHELLO: Look in upon me then, and speak with me,
         Or, naked[599] as I am, I will assault thee.

(*Re-enter* GRATIANO.)

GRATIANO: What is the matter?   390
OTHELLO: Behold! I have a weapon;
         A better never did itself sustain
         Upon a soldier's thigh: I have seen the day,
         That with this little arm, and this good sword,
         I have made my way through more impediments
         Than twenty times your stop: but, O vain boast!   395
         Who can control his fate? 'tis not so now.
         Be not afraid, though you do see me weapon'd;
         Here is my journey's end, here is my butt,[600]
         And very sea-mark of my utmost sail.[601]
         Do you go back dismay'd? 'tis a lost fear;   400
         Man but a rush[602] against Othello's breast,
         And he retires. Where should Othello go?
         Now how dost thou look now? O ill-starr'd wench!
         Pale as thy smock! when we shall meet at compt,[603]
         This look of thine will hurl my soul from heaven,   405
         And fiends will snatch at it. Cold, cold, my girl!
         Even like thy chastity.
         O! cursed, cursed slave. Whip me, ye devils,
         From the possession of this heavenly sight!
         Blow me about in winds! roast me in sulphur!   410
         Wash me in steep-down gulfs of liquid fire!
         O Desdemona! Desdemona! dead!
         Oh! Oh! Oh!

(*Enter* LODOVICO, MONTANO, CASSIO *carried in a chair, and* OFFICERS *with* IAGO, *prisoner.*)

LODOVICO: Where is this rash and most unfortunate man?
OTHELLO: That's he that was Othello; here I am.   415
LODOVICO: Where is that viper? bring the villain forth.
OTHELLO: I look down towards his feet;[604] but that's a fable.
         If that thou be'st a devil, I cannot kill thee.   (*Wounds* IAGO.)
LODOVICO: Wrench his sword from him.   (OTHELLO *is disarmed.*)
IAGO: I bleed, sir; but not kill'd.
OTHELLO: I am not sorry neither; I'd have thee live;   420
         For, in my sense,[605] 'tis happiness to die.

---

[599]unarmed   [600]goal, end, limit   [601]destination of my farthest journey   [602]wield but a reed
[603]on the day of judgment   [604]i.e., for the Devil's cloven hoof   [605]the way I feel

LODOVICO: O thou Othello! that wert once so good,
　　　　Fall'n in the practice[606] of a damned slave,[607]
　　　　What shall be said to thee?
OTHELLO:　　　　　　　　　　Why, any thing:
　　　　An honourable murderer, if you will;　　　　　　　　　425
　　　　For nought did I in hate, but all in honour.
LODOVICO: This wretch hath part confess'd his villany:
　　　　Did you and he consent in Cassio's death?
OTHELLO: Ay.
CASSIO: Dear general, I never gave you cause.　　　　　　　　430
OTHELLO: I do believe it, and I ask your pardon.
　　　　Will you, I pray, demand that demi-devil
　　　　Why he hath thus ensnar'd my soul and body?
IAGO: Demand me nothing: what you know, you know:
　　　　From this time forth I never will speak word.　　　　　435
LODOVICO: What! not to pray?
GRATIANO:　　　　　　　　Torments will ope[608] your lips.
OTHELLO: Well, thou dost best.
LODOVICO: Sir, you shall understand what hath befall'n,
　　　　Which, as I think, you know not. Here is a letter
　　　　Found in the pocket of the slain Roderigo,　　　　　　440
　　　　And here another; the one of them imports
　　　　The death of Cassio to be undertook
　　　　By Roderigo.
OTHELLO: O villain!
CASSIO:　　　　　　Most heathenish and most gross!
LODOVICO: Now here's another discontented paper,　　　　　445
　　　　Found in his pocket too; and this, it seems,
　　　　Roderigo meant to have sent this damned villain,
　　　　But that, belike,[609] Iago in the interim[610]
　　　　Came in and satisfied him.
OTHELLO:　　　　　　　　O the pernicious caitiff!
　　　　How came you, Cassio, by that handkerchief　　　　　450
　　　　That was my wife's?
CASSIO:　　　　　　　I found it in my chamber;
　　　　And he himself confess'd but even now
　　　　That there he dropp'd it for a special purpose
　　　　Which wrought to his desire.
OTHELLO:　　　　　　　　O fool! fool! fool!
CASSIO: There is besides in Roderigo's letter　　　　　　　455
　　　　How he upbraids Iago that he made him
　　　　Brave me upon the watch; whereon it came
　　　　That I was cast:[611] and even but now he spake,

[606]plot, machination   [607]i.e., Iago   [608]open   [609]most likely   [610]in the meantime   [611]dismissed

After long seeming dead, Iago hurt him,
Iago set him on.   460
LODOVICO: You must forsake this room and go with us;
Your power and your command is taken off,
And Cassio rules in Cyprus. For this slave,
If there be any cunning cruelty
That can torment him much and hold him long,   465
It shall be his. You shall close prisoner rest,
Till that the nature of your fault be known
To the Venetian state. Come, bring him away.
OTHELLO: Soft you; a word or two before you go.
I have done the state some service, and they know 't;   470
No more of that. I pray you, in your letters,
When you shall these unlucky deeds relate,
Speak of me as I am; nothing extenuate,
Nor set down aught[612] in malice: then, must you speak
Of one that lov'd not wisely but too well;   475
Of one not easily jealous, but, being wrought,
Perplex'd[613] in the extreme; of one whose hand
Like the base Indian,[614] threw a pearl away
Richer than all his tribe; of one whose subdu'd[615] eyes
Albeit unused to the melting mood,   480
Drop tears as fast as the Arabian trees
Their med'cinable gum. Set you down this;
And say besides, that in Aleppo once,
Where a malignant and a turban'd Turk
Beat a Venetian and traduc'd the state,   485
I took by the throat the circumcised dog,
And smote him, thus.   (Stabs himself.)
LODOVICO: O bloody period![616]
GRATIANO: All that's spoke is marr'd.
OTHELLO: I kiss'd thee ere I killed thee; no way but this,   (Falling upon DESDEMONA.)
Killing myself to die upon a kiss.   (Dies.)   490
CASSIO: This did I fear, but thought he had no weapon;
For he was great of heart.
LODOVICO (to IAGO):   O Spartan dog!
More fell[617] than anguish, hunger, or the sea.
Look on the tragic loading of this bed;   495
This is thy work; the object poisons sight;
Let it be hid. Gratiano, keep the house,
And seize upon the fortunes of the Moor,
For they succeed on you. To you, lord governor,

612anything   613distracted   614The Folio reads "Iudean." Both readings denote the foolish infidel
who fails to appreciate the treasure he possesses.   615overcome (by grief)   616ending
617grim, cruel

Remains the censure of this hellish villain,
The time, the place, the torture; O! enforce it.
Myself will straight aboard, and to the state
This heavy act with heavy heart relate. *(Exeunt.)*

HENRIK IBSEN

An Enemy of the People

Characters

DOCTOR THOMAS STOCKMANN, *medical officer of the Baths.*
MRS. STOCKMANN, *his wife.*
PETRA, *their daughter, a teacher.*
EJLIF *and* MORTEN, *their sons, boys of thirteen.*
PETER STOCKMANN, *the doctor's elder brother, Burgomaster and Prefect of
Police, Chairman of the Board of Directors, etc.*
MORTEN KIIL, *master tanner, Mrs. Stockmann's foster-father.*
HOVSTAD, *editor of the "People's Messenger."*
BILLING, *on the staff.*
HORSTER, *a ship's captain.*
ASLAKSEN, *a printer.*
TOWNSFOLK *present at the meeting: all sorts and conditions of men, some women,
and a crowd of school-boys.*

SCENE: *A town on the south coast of Norway.*

ACT I

Evening. DR. STOCKMANN'S *sitting-room; with simple but cheerful furniture and decora-
tions. In the wall to the right are two doors, the first leading to the Doctor's
study, the second to an ante-room. In the opposite wall, facing the ante-room
door, a door leading to the other rooms. Near the middle of this wall stands the
stove, and further towards the foreground a sofa with looking-glass above it,
and in front of it an oval table with a cover. On the table a lighted lamp, with a
shade. In the back wall an open door leading to the dining-room. In the latter
is seen a dinner-table, with a lamp on it.* BILLING *is seated at the table, a ser-
viette under his chin.* MRS. STOCKMANN *stands by the table and hands him a
great plate of roast beef. The other seats round the table are empty; the table
is in some disorder, as at the end of a meal.*

MRS. STOCKMANN: Well, if you're an hour late, Mr. Billing, you must put up with
a cold supper.
BILLING (*eating*): That's excellent, delicious!
MRS. STOCKMANN: You know how Stockmann keeps to regular meal hours——
BILLING: It's all right. Indeed, I think it tastes better when I can sit down like this 5
and eat all by myself, and undisturbed.
MRS. STOCKMANN: Well, if you are satisfied I—— Surely there's Hovstad coming
too!

BILLING: Very likely.

(Enter BURGOMASTER STOCKMANN, *wearing an overcoat and an official gold-laced cap, and carrying a stick.)*

BURGOMASTER: Good evening, sister-in-law.   10

MRS. STOCKMANN *(coming into the sitting-room)*: What, you! Good evening. It is very nice of you to look in.

BURGOMASTER: I was just passing, and so—— *(Looks towards dining-room.)* Ah! I see you've still got company.

MRS. STOCKMANN *(rather awkwardly)*: Oh, no! Not at all; it is quite by chance.   15
(Hurriedly.) Won't you come in and have something?

BURGOMASTER: I? No, thanks. God forbid I should eat anything hot in the evening; that wouldn't suit *my* digestion.

MRS. STOCKMANN: Oh! just this once——

BURGOMASTER: No, no. Much obliged to you. I stick to tea and bread and butter.   20
That's more wholesome in the long run—and rather more economical, too.

MRS. STOCKMANN *(smiling)*: Now, you musn't think Thomas and I are mere spendthrifts.

BURGOMASTER: You're not, sister-in-law; far be it from me to say that. *(Pointing*   25
to doctor's study.) Perhaps he's not at home?

MRS. STOCKMANN: No, he's gone for a short stroll after supper—with the boys.

BURGOMASTER: Good gracious! Is that healthy? *(Listening.)* There he is.

MRS. STOCKMANN: No, that's not he. *(A knock.)* Come in! *(Enter* HOVSTAD, *the
editor, from the ante-room.)* Ah! it's Mr. Hovstad, who——   30

HOVSTAD: Yes, you must excuse me, but I was delayed at the printer's. Good evening, Burgomaster.

BURGOMASTER *(bowing rather stiffly)*: Mr. Hovstad! I suppose you've come on business?

HOVSTAD: Partly. About something for the paper.   35

BURGOMASTER: So I supposed. I hear my brother is an extremely prolific contributor to the *People's Messenger.*

HOVSTAD: Yes, he writes for the *Messenger* when he has some truths to speak upon one thing or another.

MRS. STOCKMANN *(to* HOVSTAD): But won't you——*(Points to dining-room.)*   40

BURGOMASTER: God forbid I should blame him for writing for the class of readers from whom he expects most appreciation. And, personally, I've no reason to bear your paper any ill-will, Mr. Hovstad.

HOVSTAD: No. I should think not.

BURGOMASTER: On the whole, there's a great deal of toleration in this town.   45
There's much public spirit here. And that's because we have one common interest which unites us all in one undertaking that equally concerns all right-thinking citizens.

HOVSTAD: Yes—the Baths.

BURGOMASTER: Just so. We have our magnificent new Baths. Yes! The Baths will be the center of life in this town, Mr. Hovstad, without doubt. 50

MRS. STOCKMANN: That's just what Thomas says.

BURGOMASTER: How extraordinary the development of our town has been even within the last few years. Money has circulated among the people, there is life and movement. Houses and ground-rents have risen in value. 55

HOVSTAD: And the difficulty of getting work is decreasing.

BURGOMASTER: And the poor-rates have been most satisfactorily lessened for the possessing class, and will be still further reduced if only we have a really fine summer this year—and plenty of visitors—lots of invalids, who'll give the Baths a reputation. 60

HOVSTAD: And I hear there's every prospect of that.

BURGOMASTER: Things look most promising. Every day inquiries about apartments and so forth come flowing in.

HOVSTAD: Then the doctor's essay is very opportune.

BURGOMASTER: Has he been writing something again? 65

HOVSTAD: It's something he wrote in the winter; recommending the Baths, and describing the advantageous sanitary conditions of our town. But at the time I didn't use it.

BURGOMASTER: Ha! I suppose there was some little hitch!

HOVSTAD: Not at all. But I thought it would be better to wait till the spring, for people are beginning to get ready now for their summer holidays. 70

BURGOMASTER: You're right, quite right, Mr. Hovstad.

MRS. STOCKMANN: Yes, Thomas is really indefatigable where the Baths are concerned.

BURGOMASTER: Why, of course, he's one of the staff. 75

HOVSTAD: Yes, he was really their creator.

BURGOMASTER: Was he? I occasionally hear that certain persons are of that opinion. But I should say I too have a modest share in that undertaking.

MRS. STOCKMANN: Yes, that's what Thomas is always saying.

HOVSTAD: Who wants to deny it, Burgomaster? You set the thing going, and put it on a practical footing. Everybody knows that I only meant that the idea originally was the doctor's. 80

BURGOMASTER: Yes, certainly my brother has had ideas in his time—worse luck! But when anything is to be set going, we want men of another stamp, Mr. Hovstad. And I should have expected that in this house at least. 85

MRS. STOCKMANN: But, my dear brother-in-law——

HOVSTAD: Burgomaster, how can you——

MRS. STOCKMANN: Do come in and take something, Mr. Hovstad; my husband is sure to be in directly.

HOVSTAD: Thanks; just a mouthful, perhaps. 90

(He goes into the dining-room.)

BURGOMASTER (speaking in a low voice): It's extraordinary that people who spring directly from the peasant-class never get rid of a want of tact.

MRS. STOCKMANN: But why should you care? Can't you and Thomas share the honor as brothers?

BURGOMASTER: Yes, one would suppose so; but it seems a share of the honor isn't enough for some persons. 95

MRS. STOCKMANN: How ridiculous! You and Thomas always get on so well together. There, I think I hear him.

(Goes to the door of the ante-room.)

DR. STOCKMANN *(laughing without)*: Here's a visitor for you, Katrine. Isn't it jolly here? Come in, Captain Horster. Hang your coat up there. Oh! you 100 don't even wear an overcoat? Fancy, Katrine, I caught him on the street, and I could hardly get him to come along. (CAPTAIN HORSTER *enters.*) In with you, boys. They're famished again! Come on, captain; you must have some of our beef.

(He forces HORSTER into the dining-room. EJLIF and MORTEN also join.)

MRS. STOCKMANN: But, Thomas, haven't you seen—— 105

DR. STOCKMANN *(turning round in the doorway)*: Oh! is that you, Peter? *(Goes up to him and holds out his hand.)* Now, this is splendid.

BURGOMASTER: Unfortunately, I must be off directly——

DR. STOCKMANN: Nonsense! We'll have some toddy in a minute. You haven't forgotten the toddy, Katrine? 110

MRS. STOCKMANN: Of course not; the water's boiling.

(She goes into the dining-room.)

BURGOMASTER: Toddy, too——!

DR. STOCKMANN: Yes; sit down, and you will see how cozy we shall be.

BURGOMASTER: Thanks; I never join in a drinking-bout.

DR. STOCKMANN: But this isn't a drinking-bout. 115

BURGOMASTER: It seems to me—— *(Looks towards the dining-room.)* It's wonderful how they can get through all that food.

DR. STOCKMANN: *(rubbing his hands)*: Yes, doesn't it do one good to see young people eat? Always hungry! They must eat! They need strength! It's they who have to stir up the ferment for the after-time, Peter. 120

BURGOMASTER: May I ask what there is to be "stirred up," as you call it?

DR. STOCKMANN: Well, you'll have to ask the young people that when the time comes. We shall not see it, of course. Two old fogies like us——

BURGOMASTER: There, there. Surely that's a very extraordinary expression to use—— 125

DR. STOCKMANN: Ah! you musn't mind what I say, Peter. For you must know I am so glad and content. I feel so unspeakably happy in the midst of all this growing, germinating life. After all, what a glorious time we do live in. It is as if a new world were springing up around us.

BURGOMASTER: Do you really think so? 130

DR. STOCKMANN: Well, of course, you can't see this as clearly as I do. You've spent all your life in this place, and so your perceptions have been dulled. But I, who had to live up there in that small hole in the north all those years, hardly ever seeing a soul to speak a stimulating word to me—all this affects me as if I were carried to the midst of a crowded city—— 135

BURGOMASTER: H'm! City——

DR. STOCKMANN: Oh! I know well enough that the conditions of life are small enough compared with many other towns. But here is life, growth, an infinity of things to work for and to strive for; and that is the main point. 140 (*Calling.*) Katrine, haven't there been any letters?

MRS. STOCKMANN (*in the dining-room*): No, none at all.

DR. STOCKMANN: And then, the comfortable income, Peter! That's something a man learns to appreciate when he has starved as we have——

BURGOMASTER: Good heavens!—— 145

DR. STOCKMANN: Oh yes! you can imagine that we were hard put to it up there. And now we can live like lords! To-day, for example, we had roast beef for dinner, and what's more, we've had some for supper, too. Won't you have some! Come along—just look at it, anyhow.

BURGOMASTER: No, no; certainly not. 150

DR. STOCKMANN: Well, then, look here. Do you see that fine tablecloth?

BURGOMASTER: Yes, I've noticed it already.

DR. STOCKMANN: And we've some nice lamps, too. Do you see? Katrine has bought them all out of her savings. And it all helps to make a house so homelike. Doesn't it? Come over here. No, no, no, not there! So—yes—do 155 you see how the light streams down—I do really think it looks very nice. Eh?

BURGOMASTER: Yes, when one can afford such luxuries.

DR. STOCKMANN: Oh! yes, I can afford it now. Katrine says I earn nearly as much as we spend. 160

BURGOMASTER: Yes—nearly!

DR. STOCKMANN: Besides, a man of science must live in some style. I'm certain a sheriff spends much more a year than I do.

BURGOMASTER: Yes, I dare say! A member of the superior magistracy!

DR. STOCKMANN: Yes, even a mere merchant! Such a fellow spends many times 165 as much.

BURGOMASTER: Well, that is unavoidable in his position.

DR. STOCKMANN: For the rest, I really don't spend anything unnecessarily, Peter. But I can't deny myself the delight of having people about me. I must have them. I, so long isolated, it is a necessity of life for me to see the 170 young, brave, determined, free-thinking, strenuous men gathered around me—and that they are, all of them, sitting there and eating so heartily. I should like you to know more of Hovstad——

BURGOMASTER: Ah, Hovstad! He was telling me that he is going to give another essay of yours. 175

DR. STOCKMANN: An essay of mine?

BURGOMASTER: Yes, about the Baths. An article written in the winter——

DR. STOCKMANN: Oh! that one—yes. But I don't want that to appear just now.

BURGOMASTER: Why not? This is the very time for it.

DR. STOCKMANN: Well, you may be right, under ordinary circumstances—— 180

(*Crosses the room.*)

BURGOMASTER: And what's unusual in the circumstances now?

DR. STOCKMANN (*standing still*): Peter, I can't tell you yet—not this evening, at all
events. This circumstances may turn out to be very unusual. On the other
hand, there may be nothing at all. Very likely it's only my fancy.

BURGOMASTER: Upon my word, you're very enigmatical. Is there anything in the 185
wind? Anything I'm to be kept in the dark about? I should think that I,
who am chairman——

DR. STOCKMANN: And I should think that I—— There! don't let's tear one another's hair, Peter.

BURGOMASTER: God forbid! I am not in the habit of "tearing hair," as you ex- 190
press it. But I must absolutely insist that everything concerning the Baths
shall be carried on in a business-like manner, and under proper authority. I can't consent to the following of devious and underhand ways.

DR. STOCKMANN: And am I in the habit of following devious and underhand
ways? 195

BURGOMASTER: Anyhow, you've an ingrained propensity for going your own
way. And that in a well-ordered community is almost as dangerous. The
individual must submit himself to the whole community, or, to speak
more correctly, bow to the authority that watches over the welfare of all.

DR. STOCKMANN: Maybe. But what the devil has that to do with me? 200

BURGOMASTER: Well, it's just this, my dear Thomas, that it seems you won't learn.
But take care; you'll have to pay for it one of these days. Now, I've
warned you. Good-by.

DR. STOCKMANN: Are you quite mad? You're altogether on the wrong tack.

BURGOMASTER: I'm not in the habit of being *that*. And I must beg that you 205
will—— (*Bowing towards the dining-room.*) Good-by, sister-in-law; good-
by gentlemen.

(*Exit.*)

MRS. STOCKMANN (*entering the room*): Is he gone?

DR. STOCKMANN: Yes, and in an awful rage, too.

MRS. STOCKMANN: But, dear Thomas, now what have you been up to again? 210

DR. STOCKMANN: Nothing at all. Surely he can't expect me to account for everything—beforehand.

MRS. STOCKMANN: And what are you to account to him for?

DR. STOCKMANN: H'm. Never mind about that, Katrine. It's very odd that there
are no letters. 215

(HOVSTAD, BILLING and HORSTER *have risen from table and come into the room.* EJLIF *and* MORTEN *enter soon after.*)

BILLING: Ah! God bless me! After a good meal one feels a new man.

HOVSTAD: The Burgomaster didn't seem in the best of tempers to-day.

DR. STOCKMANN: That's his stomach. He has a very poor digestion.

HOVSTAD: It's more especially us of the *Messenger* that he can't stomach.

MRS. STOCKMANN: I thought you got on with him well enough.   220

HOVSTAD: Oh, yes! But now we've only a truce.

BILLING: That's so. That word quite sums up the situation.

DR. STOCKMANN: We must bear in mind that Peter is a bachelor, poor devil! He
    has no home to be happy in, only business, business. And then that
    cursed weak tea, that's about all he takes. Now, then, put chairs round   225
    the table boys! Katrine, aren't we to have that punch soon?

MRS. STOCKMANN: I'm just getting it.

DR. STOCKMANN: And you, Captain Horster, sit down by me on the sofa. So rare
    a guest as you—— Be seated, gentlemen.

(*The men sit round the table,* MRS. STOCKMANN *brings in a tray with kettle, glasses,*
    water-bottles, etc.)

MRS. STOCKMANN: There you are! Here's arrak, and this is rum, and this is   230
    cognac. Now, help yourselves.

DR. STOCKMANN (*taking a glass*):   So we will! And now out with the cigars. Ejlif,
    you know where the box is. And you, Morten, may fetch my pipe. (*The
    boys go to the room right.*) I have a suspicion Ejlif cribs a cigar now and
    then, but I pretend not to notice it. (*Calls.*) And my skull-cap, Morten.   235
    Katrine, can't you tell him where I left it? Ah! he's got it. Now, friends,
    help yourselves. You know I stick to my pipe—this one has been on many
    a stormy journey with me up there in the north. (*They touch glasses.*)
    Your health! There's nothing like sitting here, warm and sheltered.

MRS. STOCKMANN (*who sits knitting*):   When do you sail, Captain Horster?   240

HORSTER: I hope I shall have everything straight by next week.

MRS. STOCKMANN: And you're going to America?

HORSTER: Yes, that's my intention.

BILLING: But then you won't be able to take part in the election of the new
    council.   245

HORSTER: Is there to be a new election here?

BILLING: Didn't you know?

HORSTER: No. I don't bother about things of that sort.

BILLING: But I suppose you take an interest in public affairs.

HORSTER: No, I don't understand anything about them.   250

BILLING: Still one ought to make use of one's vote.

HORSTER: Even those who don't understand anything about it?

BILLING: Understand? Now, what do you mean by that? Society is like a ship; every man must help in the steering.

HORSTER: That may be all right on shore, but at sea it would not do at all. 255

HOVSTAD: It is very remarkable how little most seafaring folk care about public matters.

BILLING: Most extraordinary.

DR. STOCKMANN: Seafaring folk are like birds of passage; they feel at home both in the south and in the north. So the rest of us have to be all the more 260 energetic, Mr. Hovstad. Will there be anything of public interest in the *People's Messenger* to-morrow?

HOVSTAD: Nothing of local interest. But the day after to-morrow I'm thinking of using your paper——

DR. STOCKMANN: Yes—damn it all, I say, you'll have to hold that over. 265

HOVSTAD: Really? And we'd just got room for it. I should say, too, that this was the very time for it——

DR. STOCKMANN: Yes, yes, you may be right, but you'll have to hold it over all the same. I'll explain to you by-and-by——

(PETRA enters with hat and cloak on, with a number of exercise books under her arm.)

PETRA: Good evening! 270

DR. STOCKMANN: Good evening, Petra! Is that you?

(They all bow. PETRA puts cloak on a chair by the door.)

PETRA: Here you all are, enjoying yourselves, while I've been out slaving!

DR. STOCKMANN: Well, then, you come and enjoy yourself too.

BILLING: May I mix you a little——

PETRA *(coming towards the table)*: Thanks, I'll help myself—you always make it 275 too strong. But, by-the-way, father, I've a letter for you.

(Goes to the chair where her things are lying.)

DR. STOCKMANN: A letter! From whom?

PETRA: I got it from the postman just as I was going out——

DR. STOCKMANN: And you only bring it me now?

PETRA: I really hadn't time to run up again. Forgive me, father—here it is. 280

DR. STOCKMANN *(taking letter)*: Let me see, let me see, child. Yes; all right!

MRS. STOCKMANN: It is *the* one you've been expecting so, Thomas.

DR. STOCKMANN: Yes, it is. Now, I must go to my room at once. Where shall I find a light, Katrine? Is there a lamp in the other room?

MRS. STOCKMANN: Yes—the lamp is lit. It's on the writing-table. 285

DR. STOCKMANN: Excuse me one moment.

(He goes to room R. and closes the door.)

668

PETRA: What can it be, mother?

MRS. STOCKMANN: I don't know. For the last few days he has been always on the look-out for the postman.

BILLING: Probably a country patient. 290

PETRA: Poor father! He really works too hard. (*Mixes her toddy.*) Ah! that'll be good.

HOVSTAD: Have you been teaching in the night-school as well to-day?

PETRA: Two hours.

BILLING: And in the morning four hours at the Institute—— 295

PETRA: Five hours.

MRS. STOCKMANN: And I see you've some exercises to correct this evening.

PETRA: Yes, quite a heap of them.

HORSTER: You've enough to do, it seems to me.

PETRA: Yes; but that's a good thing. One is so delightfully tired after it. 300

BILLING: Do you really think that?

PETRA: Yes, for then one sleeps so well.

MORTEN: I say, Petra, you must be a very great sinner.

PETRA: A sinner!

MORTEN: Yes, if you work so hard. Mr. Rörlund says work is a punishment for 305
our sins.

EJLIF: Bosh! You are a child to believe such stuff as that.

MRS. STOCKMANN: Come, come, Ejlif.

BILLING (*laughing*): No! that's too rich!

HOVSTAD: Would you like to work so hard, Morten? 310

MORTEN: No, I shouldn't.

HOVSTAD: Yes; but what will you turn out then?

MORTEN: I should like to be a Viking.

EJLIF: But then you'd have to be a heathen.

MORTEN: Then I'd be a heathen. 315

BILLING: There I agree with you, Morten. I say just the same.

MRS. STOCKMANN (*making a sign to him*): No, no, Mr. Billing, you don't.

BILLING: God bless me! I should. I'm a heathen, and I'm proud of it. You'll see
we shall all be heathens soon.

MORTEN: And shall we be able to do anything we like then? 320

BILLING: Well, you see, Morten——

MRS. STOCKMANN: Now, run away, boys; I'm sure you've some lessons to prepare
for to-morrow.

EJLIF: I may stay just a little longer.

MRS. STOCKMANN: No, not you either. Now be off; both of you. 325

(*The boys say good-night and go.*)

HOVSTAD: Do you think it does the boys any harm to hear these things?

MRS. STOCKMANN: Well, I don't know; but I don't like it.

PETRA: But, mother, I think that's ridiculous of you.

MRS. STOCKMANN: Maybe! But I don't like it—here, at home.

PETRA: There's so much falseness both at home and at school. At home you 330 mustn't speak, and at school you have to stand there and lie to the children.

HORSTER: You have to lie?

PETRA: Yes; don't you know that we have to teach many and many a thing we don't believe ourselves. 335

BILLING: Yes, we know that well enough.

PETRA: If only I could afford it I'd start a school myself, and things should be very different there.

BILLING: Ah! as to means——

HORSTER: If you are really thinking of doing that, Miss Stockmann, I shall be 340 delighted to let you have a room at my place. My big old house is nearly empty; there's a large dining-room on the ground floor——

PETRA (laughing): Yes, yes, thank you—but nothing will come of it.

HOVSTAD: Oh, no! Miss Petra will yet come over to the journalists, I fancy. By-the-way have you done anything at the English novel you promised to 345 translate for us?——

PETRA: Not yet. But you shall have it in good time.

DR. STOCKMANN (flourishing the letter): Here's some news, I think, will wake up the town!

BILLING: News? 350

MRS. STOCKMANN: What news?

DR. STOCKMANN: A great discovery, Katrine.

HOVSTAD: What?

MRS. STOCKMANN: Made by you?

DR. STOCKMANN: Yes—by me! (Walks up and down.) Now, let them come as 355 usual, and say these are fads and crack-brained fancies. But they'll not dare to. Ha! ha! I know they won't.

PETRA: Father, do tell us what it is.

DR. STOCKMANN: Well, well, give me time, and you shall hear all about it. If only Peter were here now! There, you see how we men can go about and 360 form judgments like blind moles——

HOVSTAD: What do you mean, doctor?

DR. STOCKMANN: Is it not the general opinion that the town is healthy?

HOVSTAD: Of course.

DR. STOCKMANN: Indeed, a quite exceptionally healthy place, worthy to be 365 recommended in the warmest manner to our fellowmen, both the sick and the whole——

MRS. STOCKMANN: My dear Thomas——

DR. STOCKMANN: And we've recommended and belauded it too. I have written again and again, both in the *Messenger* and in pamphlets—— 370

HOVSTAD: Yes, and what then?

DR. STOCKMANN: These Baths, that we have called the pulse of the town, the living nerves of the town—and the devil knows what else—

BILLING: "The town's palpitating heart"—it was thus that in one inspired moment I allowed myself to—— 375

DR. STOCKMANN: Ah, yes! that also! But do you know what in reality these mighty, magnificent, belauded Baths—that have cost so much money—do you know what they are?

HOVSTAD: No, what are they?

MRS. STOCKMANN: Why, what are they? 380

DR. STOCKMANN: The whole place is a pest-house.

PETRA: The Baths, father?

MRS. STOCKMANN (*at the same time*): Our Baths!

HOVSTAD (*also at the same time*): But, doctor——!

BILLING: Oh! it's incredible. 385

DR. STOCKMANN: The whole place, I tell you, is a whited sepulchre; noxious in the highest degree. All that filth up there in the mill dale, with its horrible stench, taints the water in the feed-pipes of the Baths; and the same damned muck oozes out on the shore——

HOVSTAD: Where the sea Baths are? 390

DR. STOCKMANN: There.

HOVSTAD: But how are you so certain of all this, doctor?

DR. STOCKMANN: I have investigated the conditions as conscientiously as possible. This long time I have had my doubts about it. Last year we had some extraordinary cases of illness—both typhoid and gastric attacks—— 395

MRS. STOCKMANN: Yes, I remember.

DR. STOCKMANN: At the time we thought the visitors had brought the infection with them; but since—last winter—I came to another conclusion. So I set about examining the water as well as I could.

MRS. STOCKMANN: It was this you were working so hard at! 400

DR. STOCKMANN: Yes, you may well say I've worked, Katrine. But here, you know, I hadn't the necessary scientific appliances, so I sent both our drinking and sea-water to the university for an exact analysis by a chemist.

HOVSTAD: And you have now received it? 405

DR. STOCKMANN (*showing letter*): Here it is. And it proves beyond dispute the presence of organic matter in the water—millions of infusoria. It is absolutely injurious to health, whether used internally or externally.

MRS. STOCKMANN: What a blessing you found it out in time.

DR. STOCKMANN: Yes, you may well say that. 410

HOVSTAD: And what do you intend to do now, doctor?

DR. STOCKMANN: Why, set things right, of course.

HOVSTAD: Do you think that can be done?

DR. STOCKMANN: It must be done. Else the whole Baths are useless, ruined. But there's no need for that. I'm quite clear as to what will have to be done. 415

MRS. STOCKMANN: But my dear Thomas, that you should have kept all this so secret!

DR. STOCKMANN: Would you have had me rush all over the town and chatter about it before I was quite certain. No thanks! I'm not so mad as that.

PETRA: But us at home—— 420

671

DR. STOCKMANN: Not one word to a living soul. But to-morrow you may run in to the Badger.

MRS. STOCKMANN: Oh! Thomas!

DR. STOCKMANN: Well, well, to your grandfather. He'll have something to won- der at now, the old fellow. He thinks I'm not all right in my head—yes, and there are plenty of others who think the same, I've noticed. But now the good folk will see—now they *will* see! (*Walks up and down rubbing his hands.*) What a stir there'll be in the town, Katrine. You can't imagine what it will be! All the water-pipes will have to be relaid.

HOVSTAD (*rising*): All the water-pipes?

DR. STOCKMANN: Why, of course. They're been laid too low down; they must be moved up to higher ground.

PETRA: So, after all you are right.

DR. STOCKMANN: Yes, do you remember, Petra? I wrote against it when they be- gan building them. But then no one would listen to me. Now, be sure, I'll speak straight out, for, of course, I have written a report to the directors. It has been lying there ready a whole week; I've only been waiting for this letter. But now they shall have it at once. See! Four closely written sheets. And the letter shall go too. A newspaper, Katrine! Get me some- thing to wrap them up in. There—that's it. Give it to——to—— (*Stamps.*) What the devil's her name? Well, give it to the girl, and tell her to take it at once to the Burgomaster.

(MRS. STOCKMANN *goes out with packet through the dining-room.*)

PETRA: What do you think Uncle Peter will say, father?

DR. STOCKMANN: What should he say? He'll be delighted that so important a fact has been discovered, I fancy.

HOVSTAD: I suppose you'll let me write a short notice about your discovery for the *Messenger.*

DR. STOCKMANN: Yes, I should be really obliged to you.

HOVSTAD: It is very desirable. The sooner the public know about it the better.

DR. STOCKMANN: Yes, so it is.

MRS. STOCKMANN (*returning*): She's gone with it.

BILLING: God bless me, doctor, you're the greatest man in the town.

DR. STOCKMANN: Oh, bosh! Why, after all, I've done no more than my duty. I've been lucky in digging for treasures; that's all; but all the same——

BILLING: Hovstad, don't you think the town ought to give Dr. Stockmann a torch-light procession?

HOVSTAD: I shall certainly see to it.

BILLING: And I'll talk it over with Aslaksen.

DR. STOCKMANN: No, dear friends. Let all such clap-trap alone. I won't hear of anything of the sort. And if the directors want to give me a higher salary, I won't take it. I tell you, Katrine, I will not take it.

MRS. STOCKMANN: And you will be right, Thomas.

PETRA (*raising her glass*): Your health, father.

HOVSTAD *and* BILLING: Your health, your health, doctor!

HORSTER: I wish you much joy of your discovery.

DR. STOCKMANN: Thanks, thanks, my good friends. I am so heartily glad—ah! it is in truth a blessing to know in one's own mind that one has deserved well of his native town and his fellow-citizens. Hurrah? Katrine!

(*He seizes her with both hands, and whirls her round with him.* MRS. STOCKMANN *screams and struggles. A burst of laughter, applause and cheers for the doctor. The boys thrust their heads in at the door.*)

ACT II

The same. The door of the dining-room is closed. Morning. MRS. STOCKMANN *enters from dining-room with a sealed letter in her hand, and goes to the room right first entrance, and peeps in.*

MRS. STOCKMANN: Are you there, Thomas?

DR. STOCKMANN (*within*):   Yes, I've just got back. (*Enters.*) What is it?

MRS. STOCKMANN: A letter from your brother.

DR. STOCKMANN: Ah! let's see. (*Opens envelope and reads.*) "The inclosed MS. remitted herewith—— (*Reads on, muttering.*) H'm——   5

MRS. STOCKMANN: Well, what does he say?

DR. STOCKMANN (*putting paper in his pocket*):   Nothing; he only writes that he'll come up himself about midday.

MRS. STOCKMANN: Then you must for once remember to stay at home.

DR. STOCKMANN: Oh! I can do that well enough, for I've finished my morning's   10
work.

MRS. STOCKMANN: I am very curious to know how he takes it.

DR. STOCKMANN: You'll see he won't be overpleased that I, and not he himself, have made the discovery.

MRS. STOCKMANN: Yes, aren't you afraid of that, too?   15

DR. STOCKMANN: No; at bottom you may be sure he'll be glad. But still—Peter is so damnably afraid that others besides himself should do anything for the good of the town.

MRS. STOCKMANN: Do you know, Thomas, you ought to be kind, and share the honors with him. Couldn't you say it was he that put you on the track——   20

DR. STOCKMANN: Yes, gladly, for aught I care, if only I can set matters straighter, I——

(*Old* MORTEN KIIL *peeps in through the further door, looks round inquiringly, and speaks slyly.*)

MORTEN KIIL: Is it—is it true?

MRS. STOCKMANN: Father, is that you?

DR. STOCKMANN: Hallo! Father-in-law, good morning, good morning.   25

MRS. STOCKMANN: But do come in.

MORTEN KIIL: Yes, if it's true; if not, I'm off again.

DR. STOCKMANN: If what is true?

MORTEN KIIL: That ridiculous story about the waterworks. Now, is it true?

DR. STOCKMANN: Why, of course it is. But how did you come to hear of *that*?   30

MORTEN KIIL (*coming in*):   Petra flew in on her way to school——

DR. STOCKMANN: No; did she though?

MORTEN KIIL: Ay, ay—and she told me—I thought she was only trying to make game of me; but that is not like Petra either.

DR. STOCKMANN: No, indeed; how could you think that?   35

MORTEN KIIL: Ah! one should never trust anybody. You can be made a fool of before you know it. So it is true after all?

DR. STOCKMANN: Most certainly it is. Now just sit down, father-in-law. And isn't it a real blessing for the town?

MORTEN KIIL (*suppressing his laughter*):   Blessing for the town?   40

DR. STOCKMANN: Yes, that I made the discovery at such a favorable time——

MORTEN KIIL (*as before*):   Yes, yes, yes; but I never would have believed you could have played your very own brother such a trick.

DR. STOCKMANN: Such a trick!

MRS. STOCKMANN: But really, dear father——   45

MORTEN KIIL (*resting his hands and chin on the top of his stick and winking slyly at the doctor*):   Now, what is it all about? Isn't it this way, that some animals has got into the water-pipes?

DR. STOCKMANN: Yes; infusorial animals.

MORTEN KIIL: And a good many of them have got in, Petra says; quite an enor-   50
mous number.

DR. STOCKMANN: Certainly. There may be hundreds of thousands.

MORTEN KIIL: But no one can see them. Isn't that so?

DR: STOCKMANN: True; no one can see them.

MORTEN KIIL: I'll be damned if that isn't the best thing I've heard from you.   55

DR. STOCKMANN: What do you mean?

MORTEN KIIL: But you'll never be able to make the Burgomaster believe anything of the sort.

DR. STOCKMANN: Well, that remains to be seen.

MORTEN KIIL: Do you really think he'll be so foolish?   60

DR. STOCKMANN: I hope the whole town will be so foolish.

MORTEN KIIL: The whole town. Well, that may be. But it serves them right; much good may it do them. They wanted to be so much cleverer than we old fellows. They chivvied me out of the chairmanship of the Board. Yes; I tell you they chivvied me out like a dog, that they did. But now it's their   65
turn. Only you keep the game up with them, Stockmann.

DR. STOCKMANN: Yes; but, father-in-law——

MORTEN KIIL: Keep it up, I say. If you can make the Burgomaster and his friends pay through the nose, I'll give a hundred crowns straight away for the poor.   70

674

DR. STOCKMANN: Now, that would be good of you.

MORTEN KIIL: Yes. I've not got much to throw away, as you know; but if you do that, I'll give the poor fifty crowns at Christmas.

(*Enter* HOVSTAD *from ante-room.*)

HOVSTAD: Good morning! Oh! I beg your pardon——

DR. STOCKMANN: Not at all. Come in, come in.   75

MORTEN KIIL: He! Is he in it, too?

HOVSTAD: What do you mean?

DR. STOCKMANN: Yes, of course, he's in it.

MORTEN KIIL: I might have known it! It must be put into the papers. Ah! you're the right sort, Stockmann. Let them have it. Now I'm off.   80

DR. STOCKMANN: Oh, no! Stop a little longer, father-in-law.

MORTEN KIIL: No. I'm off now. Play them as many tricks as you can; I'll see you don't lose by it.

                                        (*Exit.* MRS. STOCKMANN *goes off with him.*)

DR. STOCKMANN (*laughing*): Only think! That old fellow won't believe a word about that affair of the water-works.   85

HOVSTAD: Was that what he——?

DR. STOCKMANN: Yes; that was what we were talking about. And maybe you've come to do the same.

HOVSTAD: Yes. Have you a moment to spare, doctor?

DR. STOCKMANN: As many as you like, old man.   90

HOVSTAD: Have you heard anything from the Burgomaster?

DR. STOCKMANN: Not yet. He'll be here presently.

HOVSTAD: I've been thinking over the matter since last evening.

DR. STOCKMANN: Well——?

HOVSTAD: To you, as a doctor and a man of science, this business of the water-   95
works is an isolated affair. I fancy it hasn't occurred to you that a good many other things are connected with it.

DR. STOCKMANN: Yes—how? Let's sit down, old fellow. No—there, on the sofa.

(HOVSTAD *sits on sofa; the doctor on an easy chair on the other side of the table.*)

DR. STOCKMANN: Well, so you think——?

HOVSTAD: You said yesterday that the bad water is caused by impurities in the   100
soil——

DR. STOCKMANN: Yes, undoubtedly, it is caused by that poisonous swamp up in the mill dale.

HOVSTAD: Excuse me, doctor, but I think it is caused by quite another swamp.

DR. STOCKMANN: What sort of a swamp may that be?   105

HOVSTAD: The swamp our whole municipal life stands and rots in.

DR. STOCKMANN: Mr. Hovstad, whatever have you got hold of now?

HOVSTAD: All the affairs of the town have little by little come into the hands of a set of bureaucrats.

DR. STOCKMANN: Come, now, they're not all bureaucrats.   110

HOVSTAD: No; but those who are not are their friends and adherents. They are all wealthy men, the bearers of distinguished names in the town; it is they who control and govern us.

DR. STOCKMANN: But they are men of ability and shrewdness.

HOVSTAD: Did they show their ability and shrewdness when they laid down the   115
water-pipes where they are?

DR. STOCKMANN: No; that was, of course, very stupid of them. But that'll be set right now.

HOVSTAD: Do you think it will be done so smoothly?

DR. STOCKMANN: Well, smoothly or not smoothly, it'll have to be done.   120

HOVSTAD: Yes, if the press takes it up.

DR. STOCKMANN: Not at all necessary, my dear fellow; I'm sure my brother——

HOVSTAD: Excuse me, doctor, but I want you to know that I think of taking up the matter.

DR. STOCKMANN: In the paper?   125

HOVSTAD: Yes. When I took over the *People's Messenger,* I determined I would break up this ring of obstinate old blockheads who hold everything in their hands.

DR. STOCKMANN: But you yourself told me what it all ended in. You nearly ruined the paper.   130

HOVSTAD: Yes, we had to draw in our horns then, that's true enough. For there was the danger that the Baths wouldn't be started if these men were thrown out. But now matters are different, and now we can do without these gentry.

DR. STOCKMANN: Do without them, yes; but still we owe them much.   135

HOVSTAD: Which shall be paid to the full. But a journalist of such democratic opinions as mine can't let such an opportunity as this slip through his fingers. He must explode the fable of the infallibility of our rulers. Such stuff as this must be got rid of, like every other superstition.

DR. STOCKMANN: I agree with you there, Mr. Hovstad, with all my heart. If it is a   140
superstition, away with it.

HOVSTAD: Now, I should be sorry to deal too harshly with the Burgomaster, as he is your brother. But I know you think with me—the truth before all other considerations.

DR. STOCKMANN: Why, of course. But—but—   145

HOVSTAD: You mustn't think ill of me. I am neither more obstinate nor more ambitious than most men.

DR. STOCKMANN: But, my dear fellow, who says you are?

HOVSTAD: I come from humble folk, as you know, and I have had occasion to see what is wanted by the lower classes of society. And this is, that they   150
should have a share in the direction of public affairs, doctor. *This* develops power and knowledge and self-respect——

DR. STOCKMANN: I understand that perfectly.

HOVSTAD: Yes, and I think a journalist assumes an immense responsibility when he neglects an opportunity of aiding the masses, the poor, the oppressed. I know well enough that the upper classes will call this stirring up the people, and so forth, but they can do as they please, if only my conscience is clear, I—— 155

DR. STOCKMANN: Just so, just so, dear Mr. Hovstad. But still—deuce take it—(*a knock at the door*). Come in! 160

(*Enter* ASLAKSEN, *the printer, at the door of the ante-room. He is humbly but neatly dressed in black, wearing a white, slightly crumpled neckerchief, and carrying gloves and a felt hat.*)

ASLAKSEN: I beg your pardon, doctor, for making so bold——

DR. STOCKMANN: Hallo! if it isn't Printer Aslaksen!

ASLAKSEN: Yes, it is, doctor.

HOVSTAD (*getting up*): Do you want me, Aslaksen?

ASLAKSEN: No, I don't. I didn't know I should meet you here. No, it was for the doctor himself—— 165

DR. STOCKMANN: Well, what can I do for you?

ASLAKSEN: Is what I've heard from Mr. Billing true—that the doctor is thinking of getting us better water-works?

DR. STOCKMANN: Yes, for the Baths. 170

ASLAKSEN: Oh! yes, I know that. So I came to say that I'll back up the affair with all my might.

HOVSTAD (*to the doctor*): You see!

DR. STOCKMANN: I'm sure I thank you heartily, but——

ASLAKSEN: For it might do you no harm to have us middle-class men at your back. We now form a compact majority in the town—when we really make up our minds to. And it's always as well, doctor, to have the majority with you. 175

DR. STOCKMANN: That is undoubtedly true, but I can't conceive that any special preparation will be necessary. I think that in so clear and straightforward a matter—— 180

ASLAKSEN: Yes. But all the same, it can do no harm; for I know the local authorities so well. The people in power are not very much inclined to adopt suggestions coming from others. And so I think it wouldn't be amiss if we made some sort of a demonstration. 185

HOVSTAD: I think so too.

DR. STOCKMANN: Demonstrate, say you? But what do you want to demonstrate about?

ASLAKSEN: Of course with great moderation, doctor. I am always in favor of moderation; for moderation is a citizen's first virtue—at least those are my sentiments. 190

DR. STOCKMANN: We all know that about you, Aslaksen.

ASLAKSEN: Yes, I think I may claim that much. And this affair of the water-works is so very important for us small middle-class men. The Baths bid fair to become a kind of little gold-mine for the town. And it is through the Baths that the whole lot of us are going to get our living, especially we householders. And so we shall gladly support the Baths all we can. So, as I am chairman of the Householders' Association—— 195

DR. STOCKMANN: Well?

ASLAKSEN: And as I am agent for the Moderation Society—of course you know, doctor, that I work on behalf of moderation? 200

DR. STOCKMANN: To be sure, to be sure.

ASLAKSEN: So I naturally meet a great many people. And as I am known to be a temperate and lawabiding citizen, as the doctor himself well knows, I have a certain amount of influence in the town, a position of some au- 205 thority—though I say it that shouldn't.

DR. STOCKMANN: I know that very well, Mr. Aslaksen.

ASLAKSEN: Well, so you see it would be easy for me to get up an address, if it came to a pinch.

DR. STOCKMANN: An address? 210

ASLAKSEN: Yes, a kind of vote of thanks to you, from the citizens of the town, for bringing to light a matter of such importance to the whole community. It goes without staying that it will have to be drawn up with befitting moderation, so that the authorities and persons of position may not be set against it. And if only we are careful about that, no one can 215 take offense, I think.

HOVSTAD: Well, even if they didn't like it particularly——

ASLAKSEN: No, no, no; nothing to offend those in authority, Mr. Hovstad. No opposition to people who stand in such close relation to us; I've never gone in for that in my life; no good ever comes of it either. But no one 220 can object to the thoughtful, free expression of a citizen's opinion.

DR. STOCKMANN (*shaking his hand*): I can't tell you, dear Mr. Aslaksen, how heartily it delights me to find so much support among my fellow-citizens. I am so happy—so happy! Look here! Won't you take a drop of sherry? Eh? 225

ASLAKSEN: No, thank you; I never take any kind of spirituous drink.

DR. STOCKMANN: Well, then, a glass of beer—what say you to that?

ASLAKSEN: Thanks; not that either, doctor. I never take anything so early in the day. But now I'll be off to town, and talk with the householders, and prepare public opinion. 230

DR. STOCKMANN: Now, that is extremely good of you, Mr. Aslaksen; but I can't really get into my head that all these preparations are necessary; I think the matter will go of itself.

ASLAKSEN: Officials are always very slow, doctor—God forbid I should say this by way of accusation—— 235

HOVSTAD: To-morrow we'll stir them up in the paper, Aslaksen.

ASLAKSEN: But no violence, Mr. Hovstad. Proceed with moderation, or you'll do nothing with them. You take my advice, for I have gained experience in the school of life. And now I'll say good morning to the doctor. You know, now, that we small middle-class men, anyhow, stand behind you like a rock. You have the compact majority on your side, doctor.

DR. STOCKMANN: Many thanks, my dear Mr. Aslaksen. (*Holds out his hand.*) Good-by, good-by.

ASLAKSEN: Are you coming to the printing-office, Mr. Hovstad?

HOVSTAD: I'll come on presently. I've something to see to first.

ASLAKSEN: All right.

(Bows and goes. DR. STOCKMANN accompanies him into the ante-room.)

HOVSTAD (*as the doctor reënters*): Well, what do you say to that, doctor? Don't you think it is high time we weeded out and got rid of all this apathy and vacillation and cowardice?

DR. STOCKMANN: Are you speaking of Aslaksen?

HOVSTAD: Yes, I am. He is one of those who are in the swamp, though he's a good enough fellow in other things. And so are most of the people here; they're forever seesawing and oscillating from one side to the other, and what with scruples and doubts, they never dare to advance a step.

DR. STOCKMANN: Yes, but Aslaksen seems to me so thoroughly well-intentioned.

HOVSTAD: There is one thing I value more highly; that is to stand your ground as a trusty and self-reliant man.

DR. STOCKMANN: There I am quite with you.

HOVSTAD: That's why I am going to seize the opportunity now to see if I can't stir up the well-intentioned among them for once. The worship of authority must be rooted up in this town. This immense, inexcusable blunder of the water-works should be enough to open the eyes of every voter.

DR. STOCKMANN: Very well! If you think it is for the good of the community, so let it be; but not till I've spoken to my brother.

HOVSTAD: Anyhow, I'll be getting ready for a leader in the meanwhile. And if the Burgomaster won't go in for it——

DR. STOCKMANN: But how can you imagine such a thing?

HOVSTAD: It can be imagined well enough. And then——

DR. STOCKMANN: Well, then, I promise you; look here—then you may print my paper—put it in just as it is.

HOVSTAD: May I, really? Is that a promise?

DR. STOCKMANN (*handing him MS.*): There it is; take it with you. It can do no harm for you to read it; and then tell me what you think of it.

HOVSTAD: Thanks, thanks; I shall do so willingly. And now good-by doctor.

DR. STOCKMANN: Good-by, good-by. Yes, you'll see it will all go smoothly, Mr. Hovstad, so smoothly.

HOVSTAD: H'm! We shall see.

(Bows. Exits through ante-room.)

DR. STOCKMANN: Katrine! Hallo! you back, Petra?

PETRA (*entering*):   Yes, I've just got back from school.   280

MRS. STOCKMANN (*entering*):   Hasn't he been here yet?

DR. STOCKMANN: Peter? No; but I've been having a long talk with Hovstad. He
is quite overwhelmed at my discovery. For, you see, it is much further
reaching than I thought at first. And so he has placed his paper at my
disposal if occasion requires.   285

MRS. STOCKMANN: But do you think you will need it?

DR. STOCKMANN: Not I! But all the same, one is proud to think that the free,
independent press is on one's side. Just think! I've also had a visit from
the director of the Householders' Association.

MRS. STOCKMANN: Really! And what did he want?   290

DR. STOCKMANN: To offer me support, too. Every one of them will stand by me
if there should be any unpleasantness. Katrine, do you know what I
have behind me?

MRS. STOCKMANN: Behind you? No. What have you behind you?

DR. STOCKMANN: The compact majority!   295

MRS. STOCKMANN: Oh! Is that good for you, Thomas?

DR. STOCKMANN: Yes, indeed; I should think it was good! (*Rubbing his hands as
he walks up and down.*) Ah! by Jove! what a delight it is to be in such
fraternal union with one's fellow-citizens!

PETRA: And to do so much good, and be so helpful, father.   300

DR. STOCKMANN: And to do it, into the bargain, for one's native town!

MRS. STOCKMANN: There's the bell.

DR. STOCKMANN: That must be he. (*Knock at the door.*) Come in!

(*Enter* BURGOMASTER STOCKMANN *from the ante-room.*)

BURGOMASTER: Good morning.

DR. STOCKMANN: I'm glad to see you, Peter.   305

MRS. STOCKMANN: Good morning, brother-in-law. How are you?

BURGOMASTER: Oh, thanks, so, so. (*To the doctor.*) Yesterday evening, after
office hours, I received a dissertation from you concerning the condition
of the water connected with the Baths.

DR. STOCKMANN: Yes. Have you read it?   310

BURGOMASTER: I have.

DR. STOCKMANN: And what do you think of the affair?

BURGOMASTER: H'm——

MRS. STOCKMANN: Come, Petra.

(*She and* PETRA *go into the room, left.*)

BURGOMASTER (*after a pause*):   Was it really necessary to make all those investi-   315
gations behind my back?

DR. STOCKMANN: Yes, till I was absolutely certain I——

BURGOMASTER: And so you are certain now?

DR. STOCKMANN: Yes, and I suppose it has convinced you, too.

BURGOMASTER: Is it your intention to submit this statement to the board of di-   320
rectors as an official document?

DR. STOCKMANN: Of course. Why, something must be done in the matter, and
that promptly.

BURGOMASTER: After your wont, brother, you use very strong expressions in
your statement. Why, you actually say that what we offer our visitors is   325
a persistent poison!

DR. STOCKMANN: But, Peter, can it be called anything else? Only think—poisonous water both internally and externally! And that for poor sick
folk who come to us in good faith, and who pay us heavily to heal them.

BURGOMASTER: And from this you come to the conclusion that we must build a   330
sewer which will carry off all the supposed impurities from the Miller's
Dale, and re-lay all the water-pipes.

DR. STOCKMANN: Yes. Can you suggest any other alternative?—I know of none.

BURGOMASTER: I looked in at the town engineer's this morning, and so—half in
jest—I brought up the subject of these alterations as of a matter we   335
might, possibly, have to take into consideration at some future time.

DR. STOCKMANN: Possibly at some future time!

BURGOMASTER: He smiled at my apparent extravagance—naturally. Have you
taken the trouble to reflect upon what these proposed alterations would
cost? From the information I have received, these expenses would most   340
likely run up to several hundred thousand crowns!

DR. STOCKMANN: So much as that?

BURGOMASTER: Yes. But the worst is to come. The work would take at least two
years.

DR. STOCKMANN: Two years; do you mean to say two whole years?   345

BURGOMASTER: At least. And what are we to do in the meanwhile with the
Baths? Are we to close them? For that is what it would come to. Besides,
do you believe anyone would come here if the rumor got abroad that
the water is injurious to health?

DR. STOCKMANN: But, Peter, you know it is injurious.   350

BURGOMASTER: And all this now, just now, when the Baths are beginning to do
well. Neighboring towns, too, have some idea of establishing baths.
Don't you see that they would at once set to work to divert the full
stream of visitors to themselves? It's beyond a doubt! And we should be
left stranded! We should probably have to give up the whole costly   355
undertaking; and so you would have ruined your native town.

DR. STOCKMANN: I—ruined!

BURGOMASTER: It is only through the Baths that the town has any future worth
speaking of. You surely know that as well as I do.

DR. STOCKMANN: But what do you think should be done?   360

BURGOMASTER: Your statement has not succeeded in convincing me that the condition of the water at the Baths is as serious as you represent.

DR. STOCKMANN: I tell you it is, if anything, worse—or will be in the summer,
when the hot weather sets in.

BURGOMASTER: The existing supply of water for the Baths is once for all a fact, 365
and must naturally be treated as such. But probably the directors, at
some future time, will not be indisposed to take into their consideration
whether, by making certain pecuniary sacrifices, it may not be possible
to introduce some improvements.

DR. STOCKMANN: And do you imagine I could agree for a moment to such a 370
deception?

BURGOMASTER: Deception?

DR. STOCKMANN: Yes, it would be a deception—a fraud, a lie; an absolute crime
against the public, against all society.

BURGOMASTER: I have not, as I have already remarked, been able to attain the 375
conviction that there is really any such imminent danger.

DR. STOCKMANN: You have—you must have. My demonstration was so plainly
true and right. Of that I am sure! And you know that perfectly, Peter,
only you don't admit it. It was you who insisted that both the Baths and
the water-works should be laid out where they now are; and it is *that*, 380
it is that damned blunder which you won't confess. Pshaw! Do you think
I don't see through you?

BURGOMASTER: And even if that were so? If, perhaps, I do watch over my reputation with some anxiety, I do it for the good of the town. Without
moral authority I can not guide and direct affairs in such a manner as 385
I deem necessary for the welfare of the whole community. Therefore—
and on various other grounds—it is of great moment to me that your
statement should not be submitted to the board of directors. It must be
kept back for the good of all. Later on I will bring up the matter for
discussion, and we will do the best we can quietly; but nothing what- 390
ever, not a single word, of this unfortunate business must be made
public.

DR. STOCKMANN: But it can't be prevented now, my dear Peter.

BURGOMASTER: It must and shall be prevented.

DR. STOCKMANN: It can't be, I tell you; far too many people know about it 395
already.

BURGOMASTER: Know about it! Who? Surely not those fellows on the *People's
Messenger,* who——

DR. STOCKMANN: Oh, yes! They know, too. The liberal, independent press will
take good care you do your duty. 400

BURGOMASTER (*after a short pause*): You are an extremely reckless man, Thomas.
Haven't you reflected what the consequences of this may be to yourself?

DR. STOCKMANN: Consequences?—Consequences to me?

BURGOMASTER: Yes—to you and yours. 405

DR. STOCKMANN: What the devil do you mean?

BURGOMASTER: I believe I have at all times conducted myself towards you as a
useful and helpful brother.

DR. STOCKMANN: Yes, you have, and I thank you for it.

BURGOMASTER: I ask for nothing. To some extent I had to do this—for my own 410
    sake. I always hoped I should be able to keep you within certain bounds
    if I helped to improve your pecuniary position.

DR. STOCKMANN: What! So it was only for your own sake——?

BURGOMASTER: To some extent, I say. It is painful for a man in an official posi-
    tion when his nearest relative goes and compromises himself time after 415
    time.

DR. STOCKMANN: And you think I do that?

BURGOMASTER: Yes, unfortunately, you do, without yourself knowing it. Yours is
    a turbulent, pugnacious, rebellious spirit. And then you have an unhappy
    propensity for rushing into print upon every possible and impossible 420
    matter. You no sooner hit upon an idea than you must write at once
    some newspaper article or a whole pamphlet about it.

DR. STOCKMANN: Yes, but isn't it a citizen's duty, whenever he has a new idea,
    to communicate it to the public.

BURGOMASTER: Pshaw! The public doesn't need new ideas. The public is best 425
    served by the good old recognized ideas that they have already.

DR. STOCKMANN: And you say that thus bluntly——?

BURGOMASTER: Yes, I must speak to you frankly for once. Until now I have tried
    to avoid it, as I know how irritable you are; but now I am bound to
    speak certain truths to you, Thomas. You have no conception how much 430
    you injure yourself by your rashness. You complain of the authorities,
    aye, of the government itself—you even revile them and maintain you've
    been slighted, persecuted. But what else can you expect, firebrand that
    you are.

DR. STOCKMANN: What next! So I'm a firebrand, too, am I? 435

BURGOMASTER: Yes, Thomas, you are an extremely difficult man to work with.
    I know it from experience. You set yourself above all considerations;
    you seem quite to forget that it is I whom you have to thank for your
    position here as medical officer of the Baths.

DR. STOCKMANN: I had a right to it! I, and no one else! I was the first to discover 440
    that the town might become a flourishing water-place. I was the only
    one who saw it then. For years I stood alone struggling for this idea of
    mine, and I wrote and wrote——

BURGOMASTER: No doubt. But then the right time hadn't come. Of course, in
    that out-of-the-world hole of yours, you were not in a position to judge 445
    of that. As soon as the propitious moment came I—and others—took the
    matter in hand——

DR. STOCKMANN: Yes, and you bungled the whole of my splendid plan. Oh!
    we see now what shining lights you were.

BURGOMASTER: In my opinion we are now seeing that you again need some 450
    outlet for your pugnacity. You want to fly in the face of your superiors
    —and that's an old habit of yours. You can't endure any authority over
    you; you look jealously upon anyone who has a higher official post than
    yourself; you regard him as a personal enemy, and then it's all one to

you what kind of a weapon you use against him; one is as good as   455
another. But now I have called your attention to this, to the great interests at stake for the town, and consequently for me also. And therefore I tell you, Thomas, that I am inexorable in the demand I am about
to make of you!

DR. STOCKMANN: And what is this demand?   460

BURGOMASTER: As you have been so garrulous in talking about this unpleasant
business to outsiders, although it should have been kept an official
secret, of course it can't be hushed up. All sorts of rumors will be spread
everywhere, and the evil-disposed among us will swell these rumors with
all sorts of additions. It will, therefore, be necessary for you to meet   465
these rumors.

DR. STOCKMANN: I? How? I don't understand you.

BURGOMASTER: We venture to expect that after further investigation you will
come to the conclusion that the affair is not nearly so dangerous or
serious as you had, at the first moment, imagined.   470

DR. STOCKMANN: Ah! ha! So you expect that!

BURGOMASTER: Furthermore, we shall expect you to have confidence in the
Board of Directors, and to express your belief that they will thoroughly
and conscientiously carry out all measures for the removal of every
shortcoming.   475

DR. STOCKMANN: Yes; but you'll never be able to do that as long as you go on
tinkering and patching. I tell you that, Peter, and it is my deepest, most
sincere conviction.

BURGOMASTER: As an official you've no right to have any individual conviction.

DR. STOCKMANN (starting):   No right to any——   480

BURGOMASTER: As official, I say. In your private capacity, good gracious, that's
another matter. But as a subordinate servant of the Baths, you've no
right to express any conviction at issue with that of your superiors.

DR. STOCKMANN: That is going too far! I, a doctor, a man of science, have no
right to——   485

BURGOMASTER: The matter in question is not a purely scientific one; it is a complex affair; it is both a technical and an economic matter.

DR. STOCKMANN: Pshaw! What's that to me? What the devil do I care! I will
be free to speak out upon any subject on earth.

BURGOMASTER: As you please. But not a word about the Baths—we forbid that.   490

DR. STOCKMANN (shouting):   You forbid! you!—such fellows——

BURGOMASTER: I forbid you that—I, your chief; and when I forbid you anything,
you'll have to obey.

DR. STOCKMANN (controlling himself):   Peter, really, if you weren't my brother——

(PETRA throws open the door.)

PETRA: Father, you shall not submit to this!   495

(MRS. STOCKMANN *following her.*)

MRS. STOCKMANN: Petra, Petra!

BURGOMASTER: Ah! so we've been listening!

MRS. STOCKMANN: You spoke so loud; we couldn't help——

PETRA: Yes, I did stand there and listen.

BURGOMASTER: Well, on the whole, I'm glad——   500

DR. STOCKMANN: You spoke to me of forbidding and obeying——

BURGOMASTER: You forced me to speak to you in that tone.

DR. STOCKMANN: And have I, in a public declaration, to give myself the lie?

BURGOMASTER: We consider it absolutely necessary that you should issue a statement in the terms I have requested.   505

DR. STOCKMANN: And if I don't obey?

BURGOMASTER: Then we shall ourselves put forth a statement to reassure the
public.

DR. STOCKMANN: Well and good. Then I'll write against you. I hold to my opinion. I shall prove that *I* am right, and you wrong. And what will you say   510
to that?

BURGOMASTER: I shall then be unable to prevent your dismissal.

DR. STOCKMANN: What——

PETRA: Father! Dismissal!

MRS. STOCKMANN: Dismissal!   515

BURGOMASTER: Your dismissal from the Baths. I shall be obliged to urge that
notice be given you at once, in order to dissociate you from everything
concerning the Baths.

DR. STOCKMANN: And you would dare to do that!

BURGOMASTER: It is you yourself who play the daring game.   520

PETRA: Uncle, such treatment of a man like father is shameful.

MRS. STOCKMANN: Do be quiet, Petra.

BURGOMASTER: Ah, ah! We already allow ourselves to express an opinion. Of
course! (*To* MRS. STOCKMANN.) Sister-in-law, apparently you're the most
sensible person in the house. Use all your influence with your husband;   525
try to make him realize all this will bring with it, both for his family——

DR. STOCKMANN: My family concerns only myself.

BURGOMASTER: ——Both for his family, I say, and the town in which he lives.

DR. STOCKMANN: It is I who have the real good of the town at heart. I want to
lay bare the evils that, sooner or later, must come to light. Ah! You shall   530
yet see that I love my native town.

BURGOMASTER: You, who, in your blind obstinacy, want to cut off the town's
chief source of prosperity.

DR. STOCKMANN: The source is poisoned, man! Are you mad? We live by traf-
ficking in filth and garbage. The whole of our developing social life is   535
rooted in a lie!

BURGOMASTER: Idle fancies—or something worse. The man who makes such offensive insinuations against his own native place must be an enemy of the people.

DR. STOCKMANN (*going towards him*): And you dare to—— 540

MRS. STOCKMANN (*throwing herself between them*): Thomas!

PETRA (*seizing her father's arm*): Oh! hush, father.

BURGOMASTER: I will not expose myself to physical violence. You are warned now. Reflect upon what is due to yourself and to your family. Good-by.
(*Exit.*)

DR. STOCKMANN: And I must bear such treatment! In my own house. Katrine! 545 What do you think of it?

MRS. STOCKMANN: Indeed, it is a shame and an insult, Thomas——

PETRA: If only I could give it to uncle——

DR. STOCKMANN: It is my own fault. I ought to have rebelled against them long ago—have shown my teeth—and made them feel them! And so he called 550 me an enemy of the people. Me! I will not bear this; by heaven, I will not!

MRS. STOCKMANN: But, dear Thomas, after all, your brother has the power——

DR. STOCKMANN: Yes, but I have the right!

MRS. STOCKMANN: Ah, yes, right, right! What is the good of being right when 555 you haven't any might?

PETRA: Oh, mother! how can you talk so?

DR. STOCKMANN: What! No good in a free society to have right on your side? You are absurd, Katrine. And besides, haven't I the free and independent press with me? The compact majority behind me? That's might 560 enough, I should think!

MRS. STOCKMANN: But, good Heavens! Thomas, you're surely not thinking of——

DR. STOCKMANN: What am I not thinking of?

MRS. STOCKMANN: Of setting yourself up against your brother, I mean.

DR. STOCKMANN: What the devil would you have me do, if I didn't stick to what 565 is right and true?

PETRA: Yes, I too would like to know that?

MRS. STOCKMANN: But that will be of no earthly use. If they won't they won't.

DR. STOCKMANN: Ho, ho! Katrine, just wait awhile and you'll see I shall yet get the best of the battle. 570

MRS. STOCKMANN: Yes, you'll fight them—but you'll get your dismissal; that's what will happen.

DR. STOCKMANN: Well, then, I shall at any rate have done my duty towards the public, towards society. I to be called an enemy of the people.

MRS. STOCKMANN: But, towards your family, Thomas? To us here at home? Don't 575 you think your duty is to those for whom you should provide?

PETRA: Ah! mother, do not always think first and foremost of us.

MRS. STOCKMANN: Yes, it's all very well for you to talk; if need be you can stand alone. But think of the boys, Thomas, and think a little of yourself too, and of me—— 580

DR. STOCKMANN: But, really, you're quite mad, Katrine. Should I be such a miserable coward as to humble myself to Peter and his damned crew? Should I ever again in all my life have another happy hour?

MRS. STOCKMANN: That I can not say; but God preserve us from the happiness we shall all of us have if you remain obstinate. Then you would again 585 be without a livelihood, without any regular income. I think we had enough of that in the old days. Remember them, Thomas; think of what it all means.

DR. STOCKMANN (*struggling with himself and clenching his hands*): And such threats this officemonger dares utter to a free and honest man! Isn't it 590 horrible, Katrine?

MRS. STOCKMANN: Yes; that he is behaving badly to you is certainly true. But, good God! there is so much injustice to which we must submit here on earth! Here are the boys. Look at them! What is to become of them? Oh! no, no, you can not find it in your heart—— 595

(EJLIF *and* MORTEN *with school-books have entered meanwhile.*)

DR. STOCKMANN: The boys! (*Suddenly stands still firmly and decidedly.*) Never, though the whole earth should crumble, will I bend my neck beneath the yoke.

(*Goes towards his room.*)

MRS. STOCKMANN: Thomas, what are you going to do?
DR. STOCKMANN: I want to have the right to look into my boys' eyes when they 600 are grown men.
                                            (*Exit into room.*)
MRS. STOCKMANN (*bursts into tears*): Ah! God help and comfort us all!
PETRA: Father is brave! He will not give in!
        (*The boys ask wonderingly what it all means;* PETRA *signs to them to be quiet.*)

ACT III

The editor's room, People's Messenger. In the flat at the back a door left; to the right another door with glass panes, through which can be seen the printing-room. Another door right of the stage. In the middle of the room a large table covered with papers, newspapers and books. Lower down left, a window, and by it a writing desk and high chair. A few arm-chairs around the table; some others along the walls. The room is dingy and cheerless, the furniture shabby, the arm-chairs dirty and torn. Within the printing-room are seen a few compositors; farther within, a hand-press at work. HOVSTAD, the editor, is seated at the writing-desk. Presently BILLING enters from the right with the doctor's manuscript in his hand.

BILLING: Well, I must say!——

HOVSTAD (*writing*): Have you read it through?

BILLING: Yes, I should think I had.

HOVSTAD: Don't you think the doctor comes out strong?

BILLING: Strong! God bless me! he is crushing, that's what he is. Every word   5
falls like a lever—I mean like the blow of a sledge-hammer.

HOVSTAD: Yes, but these folk don't fall at the first blow.

BILLING: True enough, but we'll keep on hammering away, blow after blow,
till the whole lot of aristocrats come crashing down. As I sat in there
reading that, I seemed to hear the revolution thundering afar.   10

HOVSTAD: Sh! Don't let Aslaksen hear anything of that sort.

BILLING (*in a lower voice*): Aslaksen is a weak-kneed, cowardly fellow, who
hasn't any manhood about him. But this time surely you'll insist on having your own way. H'm? You'll print the doctor's paper?

HOVSTAD: Yes, if only the Burgomaster doesn't give way I——   15

BILLING: That would be damned unpleasant.

HOVSTAD: Well, whatever happens, fortunately we can turn the situation to our
account. If the Burgomaster won't agree to the doctor's proposal, he'll
have all the small middle-class against him—all the Householders' Association, and the rest of them. And if he does agree to it, he'll fall out   20
with the whole crew of big shareholders in the Baths, who, until now,
have been his main support——

BILLING: Ah! yes, yes; for it's certain they'll have to fork out a pretty heavy
sum——

HOVSTAD: You may take your oath of that. And then, don't you see, the ring   25
will be broken up, and we shall day by day show the public that the
Burgomaster is utterly unfit in all respects, and that all positions of trust
in the town, the whole municipal government, must be placed in the
hands of persons of liberal ideas.

BILLING: God bless me, but that's strikingly true. I see it, I see it. We are on the   30
eve of a revolution!

(*A knock at the door.*)

HOVSTAD: Sh—(*calls.*) Come in! (DR. STOCKMANN *enters from flat left,* HOVSTAD
going towards him). Ah! here's the doctor. Well?

DR. STOCKMANN: Print away, Mr. Hovstad.

HOVSTAD: Is it to go in just as it is?   35

BILLING: Hurrah!

DR. STOCKMANN: Print away, I tell you. Of course it is to go in as it is. Since
they will have it so, they shall! Now, there'll be war in the town, Mr.
Billing!

BILLING: War to the knife is what I want—to the knife, to the death, doctor!   40

DR. STOCKMANN: This article is only the beginning. My head's already full of
plans for four or five other articles. But where do you stow away
Aslaksen?

BILLING (*calling into the printing-room*): Aslaksen! just come here a moment.

HOVSTAD: Did you say four or five more articles? On the same subject? 45

DR. STOCKMANN: Heaven forbid, my dear fellow. No; they deal with quite different matters. But they all arise out of the water-works and the sewers. One thing leads to another, you know. It is like beginning to shake an old house, exactly the same.

BILLING: God bless me, that's true! And you can never do any good till you've 50 pulled down the whole rubbish.

ASLAKSEN (*enters from printing-room*): Pulled down! Surely the doctor is not thinking of pulling down the Baths?

HOVSTAD: Not at all! Don't be alarmed.

DR. STOCKMANN: No, we were talking of something quite different. Well, what 55 do you think of my article, Mr. Hovstad?

HOVSTAD: I think it is simply a masterpiece——

DR. STOCKMANN: Yes, isn't it? That does please me; that does please me.

HOVSTAD: It is so clear and to the point. One doesn't in the least need to be a specialist in order to understand the reasoning. I am sure every intelli- 60 gent, honest man will be on your side.

ASLAKSEN: And let us hope all the prudent ones, too.

BILLING: Both the prudent and imprudent—indeed, I think well-nigh the whole town.

ASLAKSEN: Well, then, we may venture to print it. 65

DR. STOCKMANN: I should think you could!

HOVSTAD: It shall go in to-morrow.

DR. STOCKMANN: Yes, plague take it, not one day must be lost. Look here, Aslaksen, this is what I wanted you for. You, personally, must take charge of the MS. 70

ASLAKSEN: Certainly, I will.

DR. STOCKMANN: Be as careful as if it were gold. No printers' errors, every word is important. I'll look in again, presently; then I can make any small corrections. Ah! I can't say how I long to see the thing in print— to hurl it forth—— 75

BILLING: To hurl it—yes, like a thunderbolt!

DR. STOCKMANN: And to submit it to the judgment of every intelligent fellow-citizen. Ah! you've no idea what I've had to put up with to-day. I've been threatened with all sorts of things. I was to be robbed of my most inalienable rights as a man. 80

BILLING: What! Your rights as a man!

DR. STOCKMANN: I was to be humbled, made a coward of, was to set my personal gain above my deepest, holiest convictions——

BILLING: God bless me! that is really too bad.

HOVSTAD: Well, just what was to be expected from that quarter. 85

DR. STOCKMANN: But they'll get the worst of it, I can promise them. Henceforth, every day I'll throw myself into the breach in the *Messenger;* bombard them with one article after another——

ASLAKSEN: Yes, but look here——

BILLING: Hurrah! There'll be war, there'll be war! 90

DR. STOCKMANN: I will smite them to the earth. I will crush them, level all their entrenchments to the ground before the eyes of all right-thinking men. I'll do it.

ASLAKSEN: But all the same be reasonable, doctor; proceed with moderation——

BILLING: Not at all, not at all; don't spare for dynamite. 95

DR. STOCKMANN (*going on imperturbably*): For, remember that henceforth it is not merely a question of water-works and sewers. No, the whole of society must be cleansed, disinfected——

BILLING: There sounded the word of salvation!

DR. STOCKMANN: All the old bunglers must be got rid of, you understand. And 100 that in every department! Such endless vistas have opened out before me to-day. It was not all clear to me until now, but now I will right everything. It is the young, vigorous banner-bearers we must seek, my friends; we must have new captains for all the outposts.

BILLING: Hear, hear! 105

DR. STOCKMANN: And if only we hold together all will go so smoothly, so smoothly. The whole revolution will be only like the launching of a ship. Don't you think so?

HOVSTAD: For my part, I believe we have now every prospect of placing our municipal affairs in the hands of those to whom they rightly belong. 110

ASLAKSEN: And if only we proceed with moderation, I really don't think there can be any danger.

DR. STOCKMANN: Who the devil cares whether there's danger or not? What I do I do in the name of truth and for conscience sake.

HOVSTAD: You are a man deserving of support, doctor. 115

ASLAKSEN: Yes, that's certain. The doctor is a true friend to the town; he is a sincere friend of society.

BILLING: God bless me! Dr. Stockmann is a friend of the people, Aslaksen.

ASLAKSEN: I think the Householders' Association will soon adopt that expression.

DR. STOCKMANN (*shaking their hands, deeply moved*): Thanks, thanks, my dear, 120 faithful friends, it does me good to hear you. My fine brother called me something very different just now. I'll pay him back with interest, though! But I must be off now to see a poor devil. I'll look in again, as I said. Be sure and take good care of the MS., Mr. Aslaksen, and on no account leave out any of my notes of exclamation! Rather put in a 125 few more. Well, good-by for the present; good-by, good-by.

(*Mutual salutations while they accompany him to the door.*)

(*Exit.*)

HOVSTAD: He'll be of invaluable service to us.

ASLAKSEN: Yes, so long as he confines himself to the Baths. But if he goes further it might not be advisable to go with him.

HOVSTAD: H'm! Well, that depends—— 130

BILLING: You are always so damned afraid, Aslaksen.

ASLAKSEN: Afraid? Yes, when it is a question of attacking local magnates, I am afraid, Mr. Billing; that, let me tell you, I have learnt in the school of experience. But go for higher politics, attack the government itself, and you'll see if I'm afraid. 135

BILLING: Oh! no; but that's where you contradict yourself.

ASLAKSEN: The fact is I am a conscientious man. If you attack governments you at least do society no harm, for the men attacked don't care a hang about it, you see; they stay where they are. But *local* authorities *can* be turned out, and thus a lot of know-nothings come to the front, and do 140 no end of harm both to the householders and others.

HOVSTAD: But the education of citizens by self-government—what do you think of *that?*

ASLAKSEN: When a man has anything to look after he can't think of every-thing, Mr. Hovstad. 145

HOVSTAD: Then I hope I may never have anything to look after.

BILLING: Hear, hear!

ASLAKSEN (*smiling*): H'm! (*Pointing to desk.*) Governor Stensgaard* sat in that editor's chair before you.

BILLING: Pooh! A turncoat like that! 150

HOVSTAD: I'm no weather-cock—and never will be.

ASLAKSEN: A politician must not swear to anything on earth, Mr. Hovstad. And as to you, Mr. Billing, you ought to take in a reef or two one of these days, since you're running for the post of secretary to the magistracy.

BILLING: I—— 155

HOVSTAD: Are you really, Billing?

BILLING: Well, yes—but, deuce take it, you know, I'm only doing so to annoy these wiseacres.

ASLAKSEN: Well, that doesn't concern me. But if I am called cowardly and in-consistent I should like to point out this: Printer Aslaksen's past is open 160 to everyone's inspection. I have not changed at all, except that I am perhaps more moderate. My heart still belongs to the people, but I do not deny that my reason inclines somewhat towards the authorities—at least to the local authorities.

(*Exit into printing-room.*)

BILLING: Don't you think we ought to get rid of him, Hovstad? 165

HOVSTAD: Do you know of anyone else that'll advance money for the paper and printing?

BILLING: It's a damned nuisance not having the necessary capital.

HOVSTAD (*sitting down by desk*): Yes, if we only had that——

BILLING: Suppose you applied to Dr. Stockmann? 170

*This is the only case in which Ibsen introduces persons who have appeared in earlier plays. Aslaksen figures in *De Unges Forbund* (The Young Men's League), of which play Stensgaard is the central character.

HOVSTAD: What would be the good? He has nothing himself.

BILLING: No; but he has a good man behind him—old Morten Kiil—the "badger," as they call him.

HOVSTAD (*writing*): Are you so sure he has anything?

BILLING: Yes; God bless me, I know it for certain. And part of it will certainly   175
go to Stockmann's family. He is sure to think of providing for them—anyhow, for the children.

HOVSTAD: Are you counting on *that*?

BILLING: Counting? Of course I don't count upon anything.

HOVSTAD: You're right there! And that post of secretary you shouldn't in the   180
least count upon; for I can assure you you won't get it.

BILLING: Do you think I don't know that as well as you? Indeed, I'm glad I
shall not get it. Such a rebuff fires one's courage—gives one a fresh
supply of gall, and one needs that in a god-forsaken place like this,
where any excitement is so rare.   185

HOVSTAD: Yes, yes.

BILLING: Well—they'll soon hear of me! Now I'll go and draw up the appeal
to the Householders' Association.

(*Exit into room R.*)

HOVSTAD (*sitting by desk, gnawing his pen, says slowly*): H'm! Yes, that'll do.
(*A knock at the door.*) Come in. (PETRA *enters from the door L. in flat.*   190
HOVSTAD *rising.*) What! Is it you? Here?

PETRA: Yes; please excuse me——

HOVSTAD: Won't you sit down?

PETRA: No, thanks; I must be off again directly.

HOVSTAD: I suppose it's something your father——   195

PETRA: No. I've come on my own account. (*Takes a book from the pocket of
her cloak.*) Here's that English story.

HOVSTAD: Why have you brought it back?

PETRA: I won't translate it.

HOVSTAD: But you promised so faithfully——   200

PETRA: Yes; but then I hadn't read it. And no doubt you've not read it either.

HOVSTAD: No; you know I can't read English, but——

PETRA: Exactly; and that's why I wanted to tell you that you must find something else. (*Putting book on table.*) This can't possibly go into the
Messenger.   205

HOVSTAD: Why not?

PETRA: Because it is in direct contradiction to your own opinions.

HOVSTAD: Well, but for the sake of the cause——

PETRA: You don't understand me yet. It is all about a super-natural power that
looks after the so-called good people here on earth, and turns all things   210
to their advantage at last, and all the bad people are punished.

HOVSTAD: Yes, but that's very fine. It's the very thing the public like.

PETRA: And would you supply the public with such stuff? Why, you don't believe

692

one word of it yourself. You know well enough that things don't really happen like that. 215

HOVSTAD: You're right there; but an editor can't always do as he likes. He often has to yield to public opinion in small matters. After all, politics is the chief thing in life—at any rate for a newspaper; and if I want the people to follow me along the path of emancipation and progress, I mustn't scare them away. If they find such a moral story down in the 220 cellar,* they're much more willing to stand what is printed above it—they feel themselves safer.

PETRA: For shame! You wouldn't be such a hypocrite, and weave a web to ensnare your readers. You are not a spider.

HOVSTAD: Thanks for your good opinion of me. No. That's Billing's idea, not 225 mine.

PETRA: Billing's!

HOVSTAD: Yes. At least he said so the other day. It was Billing who was so anxious to get the story into the paper; I don't even know the book.

PETRA: But how Billing, with his advanced views—— 230

HOVSTAD: Well, Billing is many-sided. He's running for the post of secretary to the magistracy, I hear.

PETRA: I don't believe that, Hovstad. How could he condescend to such a thing?

HOVSTAD: Well, that you must ask him.

PETRA: I could never have thought that of Billing. 235

HOVSTAD: No? Does that come as a revelation to you?

PETRA: Yes. And yet—perhaps not. Ah! I don't know.

HOVSTAD: We journalists aren't worth much, Miss Petra.

PETRA: Do you really think that?

HOVSTAD: I think so, sometimes. 240

PETRA: Yes, in the little everyday squabbles—that I can understand. But now that you have taken up a great cause——

HOVSTAD: You mean that affair of your father's.

PETRA: Exactly. But now I should think you must feel yourself worth more than the common herd. 245

HOVSTAD: Yes, to-day I do feel something of that sort.

PETRA: Yes, don't you feel that? Ah! it is a glorious career you have chosen. Thus to clear the way for despised truths and new ideas—to stand forth fearlessly on the side of a wronged man——

HOVSTAD: Especially when this wronged man is—h'm—I hardly know how to 250 put it.

PETRA: You mean when he is so true and honest.

HOVSTAD (*in a low voice*): I mean when he is your father——

PETRA (*as if she had received a blow*): *That?*

HOVSTAD: Yes, Petra—Miss Petra. 255

*The reference is to the continental plan; the feuilleton is separated from the main body of the page by a line.

PETRA: So *that* is what you think of first and foremost? Not the cause itself? Not the truth? Not father's big, warm heart?

HOVSTAD: Yes, of course, that as well.

PETRA: No, thank you; you've just let the cat out of the bag, Mr. Hovstad. Now I shall never trust you again in anything.   260

HOVSTAD: Can you reproach me because it is chiefly for your sake?

PETRA: What I am angry with you for is that you have not acted honestly towards my father. You told him it was only the truth and the good of the community you cared about. You have fooled both father and me. You are not the man you pretend to be. And I shall never forgive   265 you—never!

HOVSTAD: You should not say that so hardly, Miss Petra—not now.

PETRA: Why not now?

HOVSTAD: Because your father can't do without any help.   270

PETRA (*looking scornfully at him*): And that is what you are! Oh, shame!

HOVSTAD: No, no. I spoke thoughtlessly. You must not believe that.

PETRA: I know what to believe. Good-by.

(ASLAKSEN *enters from printing-room, hurriedly and mysteriously.*)

ASLAKSEN: Plague take it, Mr. Hovstad. (*Seeing* PETRA.) Sh! that's awkward.

PETRA: Well, there's the book. You must give it to someone else.

(*Going towards main door.*)

HOVSTAD (*following her*): But, Miss Petra——   275

PETRA: Good-by.

(*Exit.*)

ASLAKSEN: I say, Mr. Hovstad!

HOVSTAD: Well, what is it?

ASLAKSEN: The Burgomaster is out there, in the printing-office.

HOVSTAD: The Burgomaster?   280

ASLAKSEN: Yes. He wants to speak to you; he came in by the back door—he didn't want to be seen.

HOVSTAD: What's the meaning of this? Don't go. I will myself—— (*Goes towards printing-room, opens the door, and bows as the Burgomaster enters.*) Take care, Aslaksen, that——   285

ASLAKSEN: I understand.

(*Exit into printing-room.*)

BURGOMASTER: You didn't expect to see me here, Mr. Hovstad.

HOVSTAD: No, I can't say I did.

BURGOMASTER: Why, you've arranged everything most comfortably here; quite charming.   290

HOVSTAD: Oh!

BURGOMASTER: And I've come, without any sort of notice, to occupy your time.

HOVSTAD: You are very welcome; I am quite at your service. Let me take your cap and stick. (*He does so.*) And won't you sit down?

BURGOMASTER: Thanks. I have been much—very much annoyed to-day, Mr. Hovstad. 295

HOVSTAD: Indeed? Oh, yes! With all your various duties, Burgomaster——

BURGOMASTER: To-day I've been worried by the doctor.

HOVSTAD: You don't say so? The doctor?

BURGOMASTER: He's been writing a sort of statement to the directors concerning 300 certain supposed shortcomings of the Baths.

HOVSTAD: No, has he really?

BURGOMASTER: Yes; hasn't he told you? I thought he said——

HOVSTAD: Oh, yes, so he did. He said something about it.

ASLAKSEN (*from the office*): Wherever is the MS.——? 305

HOVSTAD: H'm? There it is on the desk.

ASLAKSEN: All right.

BURGOMASTER: Why, that is it——

ASLAKSEN: Yes, that's the doctor's paper, Burgomaster.

HOVSTAD: Oh! was *that* what you were speaking of? 310

BURGOMASTER: The very same. What do you think of it?

HOVSTAD: I'm not a professional man, and I've only glanced at it.

BURGOMASTER: And yet you are going to print it?

HOVSTAD: I can't very well refuse so distinguished a man——

ASLAKSEN: I have nothing to do with the editing of the paper, Burgomaster. 315

BURGOMASTER: Of course not.

ASLAKSEN: I merely print whatever comes into my hands.

BURGOMASTER: That's as it should be.

ASLAKSEN: So I must——

BURGOMASTER: No, stay one moment, Mr. Aslaksen. With your permission, Mr. 320 Hovstad——

HOVSTAD: By all means, Burgomaster.

BURGOMASTER: You are a discreet and thoughtful man, Mr. Aslaksen.

ASLAKSEN: I'm glad to hear you say so, Burgomaster.

BURGOMASTER: And a man of considerable influence. 325

ASLAKSEN: Chiefly among the small middle-class.

BURGOMASTER: The small taxpayers are the most numerous—here as everywhere.

ASLAKSEN: That's true enough.

BURGOMASTER: But I do not doubt that you know what the feeling of most of them is. Isn't that so? 330

ASLAKSEN: Yes, I think I may say that I do, Burgomaster.

BURGOMASTER: Well—if there is such a praiseworthy spirit of self-sacrifice among the less wealthy citizens of the town, I——

ASLAKSEN: How so?

HOVSTAD: Self-sacrifice? 335

BURGOMASTER: It is an excellent sign of public spirit—a most excellent sign. I was near saying I should not have expected it. But, of course, you know public feeling better than I do.

ASLAKSEN: Yes, but, Burgomaster——

BURGOMASTER: And assuredly it is no small sacrifice that the town is about to make. 340

HOVSTAD: The town?

ASLAKSEN: But I don't understand—it's about the Baths——

BURGOMASTER: According to a preliminary estimate, the alterations considered necessary by the doctor will come to several hundred thousand crowns. 345

ASLAKSEN: That's a large sum; but——

BURGOMASTER: Of course we shall be obliged to raise a municipal loan.

HOVSTAD (raising): You don't mean to say that the town——

ASLAKSEN: To be paid out of the rates? Out of the needy pockets of the small middle-class? 350

BURGOMASTER: Yes, my excellent Mr. Aslaksen, where should the funds come from?

ASLAKSEN: That's the business of the shareholders who own the Baths.

BURGOMASTER: The shareholders of the Baths are not in a position to go to further expense. 355

ASLAKSEN: Are you quite sure of that, Burgomaster?

BURGOMASTER: I have assured myself on the matter. So that if these extensive alterations are to be made, the town itself will have to bear the costs.

ASLAKSEN: Oh, damn it all!—I beg your pardon!—but this is quite another matter, Mr. Hovstad. 360

HOVSTAD: Yes, it certainly is.

BURGOMASTER: The worst of it is, that we shall be obliged to close the establishment for some two years.

HOVSTAD: To close it? To close it completely?

ASLAKSEN: For two years! 365

BURGOMASTER: Yes, the work will require that time at least.

ASLAKSEN: But damn it all! we can't stand that, Burgomaster. What are we householders to live on meanwhile?

BURGOMASTER: Unfortunately, that's extremely difficult to say, Mr. Aslaksen. But what would you have us do? Do you think a single visitor will come here 370 if we go about trying to persuade them into fancying the waters are poisoned, and that we are living on a pest ground, and the whole town——

ASLAKSEN: And it is all nothing but fancy?

BURGOMASTER: With the best intentions of the world, I've not been able to convince myself that it is anything else. 375

ASLAKSEN: But then it is quite inexcusable of Dr. Stockmann—I beg your pardon, Burgomaster, but——

BURGOMASTER: You are, unhappily, only speaking the truth, Mr. Aslaksen. Unfortunately, my brother has always been a headstrong man. 380

ASLAKSEN: And yet you are willing to support him in such a matter, Mr. Hovstad!

HOVSTAD: But who could possibly have imagined that——

BURGOMASTER: I have drawn up a short statement of the facts, as they appear from a sober-minded point of view. And in it I have hinted that various unavoidable drawbacks may be remedied by measures compatible with the finances of the Baths. 385

HOVSTAD (*pointing to the door L.*): Go in there for a moment.

BURGOMASTER: Yes; I brought it with me in case you——

ASLAKSEN (*quickly*): Damn it, there he is! 390

BURGOMASTER: Who? My brother?

HOVSTAD: Where, where?

ASLAKSEN: He's coming through the printing-room.

BURGOMASTER: What a nuisance! I should not like to meet him here, and yet there are several things I want to talk to you about. 395

HOVSTAD (*pointing to the door L.*): Go in there for a moment.

BURGOMASTER: But——?

HOVSTAD: You'll only find Billing there.

ASLAKSEN: Quick, quick, Burgomaster, he's just coming.

BURGOMASTER: Very well. But see that you get rid of him quickly. 400

(*Exit door L., which* ASLAKSEN *opens, bowing.*)

HOVSTAD: Be busy doing something, Aslaksen.

(*He sits down and writes.*)

DR. STOCKMANN (*entering from printing-room*): Here I am, back again!

HOVSTAD (*writing*): Already, doctor? Make haste, Aslaksen. We've no time to lose to-day.

DR. STOCKMANN (*to* ASLAKSEN): No proofs yet, I hear. 405

ASLAKSEN (*without turning round*): No; how could you think there would be?

DR. STOCKMANN: Of course not; but you surely understand that I am impatient. I can have no rest or peace until I see the thing in print.

HOVSTAD: H'm! It'll take a good hour yet. Don't you think so, Aslaksen?

ASLAKSEN: I am almost afraid it will. 410

DR. STOCKMANN: All right, all right, my good friends; then I'll look in again. I don't mind coming twice on such an errand. So great a cause—the welfare of the whole town; upon my word, this is no time to be idle. (*Just going, but stops and comes back.*) Oh! look here, there's one other thing I must talk to you about. 415

HOVSTAD: Excuse me. Wouldn't some other time——

DR. STOCKMANN: I can tell you in two words. You see it's only this. When people read my statement in the paper to-morrow, and find I've spent the whole winter silently working for the good of the town——

HOVSTAD: Yes; but doctor—— 420

DR. STOCKMANN: I know what you would say. You don't think it was a damned

697

bit more than my duty—my simple duty as a citizen. Of course I know that, just as well as you do. But you see, my fellow-citizens—good Lord! the kindly creatures think so much of me——

ASLAKSEN: Yes, your fellow-citizens did think very highly of you till to-day, doctor. 425

DR. STOCKMANN: And that's exactly what I'm afraid of, that—*this* is what I wanted to say: when all this comes to them—especially to the poorer class—as a summons to take the affairs of the town into their own hands for the future—— 430

HOVSTAD (*rising*): H'm doctor, I will not conceal from you——

DR. STOCKMANN: Aha! I thought there was something abrewing! But I won't hear of it. If they're going to get up anything——

HOVSTAD: How so?

DR. STOCKMANN: Well, anything of any sort, a procession with banners, or a banquet, or a subscription for a testimonial—or whatever it may be, you must give me your solemn promise to put a stop to it. And you too, Mr. Aslaksen; do you hear? 435

HOVSTAD: Excuse me, doctor; we might as well tell you the whole truth first, as last—— 440

(*Enter* MRS. STOCKMANN.)

MRS. STOCKMANN: Ah! just as I thought!

HOVSTAD: Hallo! Your wife, too?

DR. STOCKMANN: What the devil have you come here for, Katrine?

MRS. STOCKMANN: I should think you must know well enough what I've come for.

HOVSTAD: Won't you sit down? Or can——? 445

MRS. STOCKMANN: Thanks; please do not trouble. And you mustn't be vexed with me for coming here to fetch Stockmann, for you must bear in mind I'm the mother of three children.

DR. STOCKMANN: Stuff and nonsense! We all know that well enough!

MRS. STOCKMANN: It doesn't look as if you were thinking very much about your wife and children to-day, or you'd not be so ready to plunge us all into misfortune. 450

DR. STOCKMANN: Are you quite mad, Katrine? Mustn't a man with a wife and children proclaim the truth, do his utmost to be a useful and active citizen, do his duty by the town he lives in? 455

MRS. STOCKMANN: Everything in moderation, Thomas.

ASLAKSEN: That's just what I say. Moderation in all things.

MRS. STOCKMANN: And you are wronging us, Mr. Hovstad, when you entice my husband away from his house and home, and befool him with all this business. 460

HOVSTAD: I am not aware I have befooled any one in——

DR. STOCKMANN: Befool! Do you think I should let myself be made a fool of?

MRS. STOCKMANN: Yes, but you do. I know well that you are the cleverest man in the town, but you so easily allow yourself to be taken in, Thomas. (*To* HOVSTAD.) And only think, he will lose his post at the Baths if you print what he has written. 465

ASLAKSEN: What!

HOVSTAD: Yes, but you know, doctor——

DR. STOCKMANN (*laughing*): Ha, ha! just let them try! No, no, my dear, they daren't do it! I've the compact majority behind me, you see. 470

MRS. STOCKMANN: That's just the misfortune that you have such an awful thing behind you.

DR. STOCKMANN: Nonsense, Katrine; you get home and see after the house, and let me take care of society. How can you be so afraid when I am so confident and happy. (*Rubbing his hands and walking up and down.*) 475 Truth and the people must win the day; that you may be sure. Ah! I see the independent citizens gathering together as in triumphant host! (*Stopping by chair.*) Why, what the devil is that?

ASLAKSEN (*looking at it*): Oh. Lord!

HOVSTAD (*the same*): H'm! 480

DR. STOCKMANN: Why, here's the top-knot of authority!

(*He takes the Burgomaster's official cap carefully between the tips of his fingers and holds it up.*)

MRS. STOCKMANN: The Burgomaster's cap!

DR. STOCKMANN: And here's the staff of office, too! But how the deuce did they——

HOVSTAD: Well then—— 485

DR. STOCKMANN: Ah! I understand. He's been here to talk you over. Ha! ha! He brought his pigs to the wrong market! And when he caught sight of me in the printing-room (*bursts out laughing*) he took to his heels, Mr. Aslaksen?

ASLAKSEN (*hurriedly*): Exactly; he took to his heels, doctor. 490

DR. STOCKMANN: Took to his heels without his stick and—— Fiddle, faddle! Peter didn't make off without his belongings. But what the devil have you done with him? Ah!—in there, of course. Now you shall see, Katrine!

MRS. STOCKMANN: Thomas, I beg you——!

ASLAKSEN: Take care, doctor! 495

(DR. STOCKMANN *has put the* BURGOMASTER'S *cap on and taken his stick; then he goes up, throws open the door, and makes a military salute. The* BURGOMASTER *enters, red with anger. Behind him enters* BILLING.)

BURGOMASTER: What is the meaning of this folly?

DR. STOCKMANN: Be respectful, my good Peter. Now, it is I who am the highest authority in the town.

(*He struts up and down.*)

MRS. STOCKMANN (*almost crying*): But really, Thomas——!

BURGOMASTER: Give me my cap and stick! 500

DR. STOCKMANN: If you are the chief of police, I am the Burgomaster. I am master of the whole town, I tell you!

BURGOMASTER: Put down my cap, I say. Remember it is the official cap.

DR. STOCKMANN: Pish! Do you think the awakening leonine people will allow themselves to be scared by an official cap? For you will see, we are 505 going to have a revolution in the town tomorrow. You threatened to dismiss me, but now I dismiss you—dismiss you from all your offices of trust. You think I can not do it?—Oh, yes, I can! I have the irresistible force of society with me. Hovstad and Billing will thunder forth in the *People's Messenger*, and Printer Aslaksen will come forward at the 510 head of the whole Householders' Association——

ASLAKSEN: I shall not, doctor.

DR. STOCKMANN: Surely you will——

BURGOMASTER: Ah ha! Perhaps Mr. Hovstad is going to join the agitation?

HOVSTAD: No, Burgomaster. 515

ASLAKSEN: No, Mr. Hovstad isn't such a fool as to ruin both himself and the paper for the sake of a fancy.

DR. STOCKMANN (*looking about him*): What does all this mean?

HOVSTAD: You have represented your case in a false light, doctor; and therefore I am not able to give you my support. 520

BILLING: And after what the Burgomaster has been so kind as to tell me in there, I——

DR. STOCKMANN: In a false light! Charge me with that, if you will, only print my paper; I am man enough to stand by it.

HOVSTAD: I shall not print it. I can not, and will not, and dare not print it. 525

DR. STOCKMANN: You dare not? What nonsense! You're editor, and I suppose it is the editor that directs his paper.

ASLAKSEN: No, it's the readers, doctor.

BILLING: Luckily, it is.

ASLAKSEN: It is public opinion, the enlightened people, the householders, and 530 all the rest. It is they who direct a paper.

DR. STOCKMANN (*quietly*): And all these powers I have against me?

ASLAKSEN: Yes, you have. It would be absolute ruin for the townspeople if your paper were printed.

DR. STOCKMANN: So! 535

BURGOMASTER: My hat and stick. (DR. STOCKMANN *takes off the cap and lays it on the table. The* BURGOMASTER *takes them both.*) Your magisterial authority has come to an untimely end.

DR. STOCKMANN: The end is not yet. So it is quite impossible to print my paper in the *Messenger*. 540

HOVSTAD: Quite impossible; and for the sake of your family——

MRS. STOCKMANN: Oh! please leave his family out of the question, Mr. Hovstad.

BURGOMASTER (*takes a manuscript from his jacket*): This will be sufficient to enlighten the public, if you will print this: it is an authentic statement. Thanks. 545

HOVSTAD (*taking MS.*): Good! I'll see it is inserted at once.

DR. STOCKMANN: And not mine! You imagine you can silence me and the truth! But it won't be as easy as you think. Mr. Aslaksen, will you be good enough to print my MS. at once as a pamphlet—at my own cost—on my own responsibility. I'll take five hundred copies—no, I'll have six hundred. 550

ASLAKSEN: No. If you offered me its weight in gold I should not dare to lend my press to such a purpose, doctor. I must not, for the sake of public opinion. And you'll not get that printed anywhere in the whole town.

DR. STOCKMANN: Then give it me back.

HOVSTAD (*handing him MS.*): By all means. 555

DR. STOCKMANN: It shall be made public all the same. I'll read it at a mass meeting; all my fellow-citizens shall hear the voice of truth!

BURGOMASTER: There's not a society in the whole town that would let you their premises for such a purpose.

ASLAKSEN: Not a single one, I am certain. 560

BILLING: No, God bless me, I should think not!

MRS. STOCKMANN: That would be too shameful! But why are all these men against you?

DR. STOCKMANN (*angrily*): Ah! I'll tell you. It is because in this town all the men are old women—like you. They all think only of their families, and not 565 of the general good.

MRS. STOCKMANN: Then I will show them how an—an old woman can be a man, for once in a way. For *now* I will stand by you, Thomas.

DR. STOCKMANN: Bravely said, Katrine! For on my soul the truth will out. If I can't make them let any hall, I'll hire a drum, and I'll march through the 570 town with it; and I'll read my paper at every street corner.

BURGOMASTER: Surely you're not such an arrant fool as all that?

DR. STOCKMANN: I am.

ASLAKSEN: There's not a single man in the whole town who would go with you.

BILLING: No, God bless me, that there isn't. 575

MRS. STOCKMANN: Do not give in, Thomas. I will send the boys with you.

DR. STOCKMANN: That's a splendid idea!

MRS. STOCKMANN: Morten will be so pleased to go; Ejlif will go too—he too.

DR. STOCKMANN: Yes, and so will Petra. And you yourself, Katrine!

MRS. STOCKMANN: No, no, not I. But I'll stand at the window and watch you— 580 that I will do gladly.

DR. STOCKMANN (*throwing his arms about her and kissing her*): Thanks, thanks. Now, my good sirs, we are ready for the fight! Now, we'll see if cowardice can close the mouth of a patriot who labors only for the common- 585 weal.

(*He and his wife go out together through door L., in flat.*)

BURGOMASTER (*shaking his head doubtfully*): Now he's sent her mad too!

ACT IV

A large old-fashioned room in CAPTAIN HORSTER'S *house. An open folding-door in the background leads to an ante-room. Three windows, left. About the middle of the opposite wall is a small platform seat and on it a small table, two candles, a bottle of water, and a bell. The rest of the room is lighted by sconces placed between the windows. Left, near the front of the stage, is a table with a light on it, and by it a chair. In front to the right, a door, and near it a few chairs. Large meeting of all classes of townsfolk. In the crowd are a few women and school-boys. More and more people stream in, until the room is quite full.*

FIRST CITIZEN (*to another standing near him*):   So you're here, too, Lamstad?

SECOND CITIZEN: I always go to every meeting.

A BYSTANDER: I suppose you've brought your whistle?

SECOND CITIZEN: Of course I have; haven't you?

THIRD CITIZEN: Rather. And Skipper Evensen said he should bring a great big horn.   5

SECOND CITIZEN: What a fellow that Evensen is. (*Laughter among the groups of citizens.*)

FOURTH CITIZEN (*joining them*):   I say, what's it all about? What's going on here to-night?   10

SECOND CITIZEN: Why, it's Dr. Stockmann who is going to give a lecture against the Burgomaster.

FOURTH CITIZEN: But the Burgomaster's his brother.

FIRST CITIZEN: That doesn't matter. Dr. Stockmann isn't afraid, he isn't.

THIRD CITIZEN: But he's all wrong; they said so in the *People's Messenger*.   15

SECOND CITIZEN: Yes, he must be wrong this time, for neither the Householders' Association nor the Citizens' Club would let him have a hall.

FIRST CITIZEN: They wouldn't even let him have a hall at the Baths.

SECOND CITIZEN: No, you may be sure they wouldn't.

A MAN (*in another group*):   Now, whom are we to go with in this affair? H'm!   20

ANOTHER MAN: You just stick to Printer Aslaksen, and do what he does.

BILLING (*with a portfolio writing-case under his arm, makes his way through the crowd*):   Excuse me, gentlemen. Will you allow me to pass? I am going to report for the *Messenger*. A thousand thanks.

A WORKINGMAN: Who's he?   25

ANOTHER WORKINGMAN: Don't you know him? That's Billing, who writes for Aslaksen's paper.

(CAPTAIN HORSTER *enters, leading in* MRS. STOCKMANN *and* PETRA *by the right-hand door.* EJLIF *and* MORTEN *follow them.*)

HORSTER: I think you'll all be comfortable here. You can easily slip out if anything should happen.

MRS. STOCKMANN: Do you think there will be any trouble?   30

702

HORSTER: One can never tell—with such a crowd. But do sit down, and don't be
    anxious.
MRS. STOCKMANN: Ah! it was good of you to let Stockmann have this room.
HORSTER: Well, as no one else would, I——
PETRA: And it was brave too, Horster.   35
HORSTER: Shouldn't think it needed much courage.

(HOVSTAD and ASLAKSEN enter at the same moment, but make their way through the
    crowd separately.)

ASLAKSEN: Hasn't the doctor come yet?
HORSTER: He's waiting in there.

(Movement at the door in the background.)

HOVSTAD (to BILLING): There's the Burgomaster, look!
BILLING: Yes, God bless me, if he hasn't come to the fore after all.   40

(BURGOMASTER STOCKMANN makes his way blandly through the meeting, bows politely
    and stands by the wall L. Immediately after, DR. STOCKMANN enters from first
    R. Entrance. He is carefully dressed in frock-coat and white waist-coat. Faint ap-
    plause, met by a subdued hiss. Then silence.)

DR. STOCKMANN (in a low tone): Well, how do you feel, Katrine?
MRS. STOCKMANN: Oh! I'm all right. Now do, for once, keep your temper,
    Thomas.
DR. STOCKMANN: Oh! I can control myself well enough, dear. (Looks at his
    watch, ascends the raised platform, and bows.) It is a quarter past the   45
    time, so I will begin. (Takes out his MS.)
ASLAKSEN: But I suppose a chairman must be elected first.
DR. STOCKMANN: No; there's not the least necessity for that.
SEVERAL GENTLEMEN (shouting): Yes, yes.
BURGOMASTER: I am also of opinion that a chairman should be elected.   50
DR. STOCKMANN: But I have called this meeting to give a lecture, Peter!
BURGOMASTER: A lecture concerning the Baths may very possibly lead to diver-
    gence of opinion.
SEVERAL VOICES IN THE CROWD: A chairman! A chairman!
DR. STOCKMANN (controlling himself): Very well, then; let the meeting have it's 55
    will.
ASLAKSEN: Will not the Burgomaster take the chair?
THREE GENTLEMEN: Bravo! Bravo!
BURGOMASTER: For several reasons, which I am sure you will understand, I must
    decline. But, fortunately, we have here in our midst one whom I think we   60
    all can accept. I allude to the president of the Householders' Association,
    Mr. Aslaksen.
MANY VOICES: Yes, yes! Long live Aslaksen! Three cheers for Aslaksen.

(DR. STOCKMANN *takes his MS. and descends from platform.*)

ASLAKSEN: If I am called upon by the confidence of my fellow-citizens, I shall not be unwilling to—— 65

(*Applause and cheers.* ASLAKSEN *ascends the platform.*)

BILLING (*writing*): So—"Mr. Aslaksen was elected by acclamation——"

ASLAKSEN: And now, as I have been called to the chair, I take the liberty of saying a few brief words. I am a quiet, peace-loving man; I am in favor of discreet moderation and of—and of moderate discretion. That everyone who knows me, knows. 70

MANY VOICES: Yes, yes, Aslaksen!

ASLAKSEN: I have learnt in the school of life and of experience that moderation is the virtue which best becomes a citizen——

BURGOMASTER: Hear, hear!

ASLAKSEN: ——and it is discretion and moderation, too, that best serve the community. I will therefore beg our respected fellow-citizen who has called this meeting to reflect upon this and to keep within the bounds of moderation. 75

A MAN: Three cheers for the Moderation Society.

A VOICE: Go to the devil! 80

VOICES: Hush! hush!

ASLAKSEN: No interruptions, gentlemen! Does anyone wish to offer any observations?

BURGOMASTER: Mr. Chairman!

ASLAKSEN: Burgomaster Stockmann will address the meeting. 85

BURGOMASTER: In consideration of my close relationship—of which you are probably aware—to the gentleman who is at present medical officer to the Baths, I should very much have preferred not to speak here this evening. But the position I hold at the Baths, and my anxiety with regard to matters of the utmost importance to the town, force me to move a resolution. 90 I may, no doubt, assume that not a single citizen here present thinks it desirable that unreliable and exaggerated statements, as to the sanitary condition of the Baths and the town, should be disseminated over a wider area.

MANY VOICES: No, no, certainly not. We protest. 95

BURGOMASTER: I therefore beg to move, "That this meeting refuses to hear the medical officer of the Baths either lecture or speak upon the subject."

DR. STOCKMANN (*flaming up*): Refuses to hear—what nonsense!

MRS. STOCKMANN (*coughing*): H'm! h'm!

DR. STOCKMANN (*controlling himself*): Then I'm not to be heard. 100

BURGOMASTER: In my statement in the *People's Messenger* I have made the public acquainted with the most essential facts, so that all well-disposed citizens can easily draw their own conclusions. You will see from this that the medical officer's proposal—besides being a vote of censure against the leading men of the town—at bottom only means saddling the rate-paying inhabitants of the town with an unnecessary expense of at least a hundred thousand crowns. 105

(*Noise and some hissing*).

ASLAKSEN (*ringing the bell*): Order, gentlemen! I must take the liberty of supporting the Burgomaster's resolution. It is also *my* opinion there is something beneath the surface of the doctor's agitation. He speaks of the 110 Baths, but it is a revolution he is trying to bring about; he wants to place the municipal government of the town in other hands. No one doubts the intentions of Dr. Stockmann—God forbid! there can't be two opinions as to that. I, too, am in favor of self-government by the people, if only the cost do not fall too heavily upon the ratepayers. But in this case it 115 would do so, and for this reason I—damn it all—I beg your pardon—I can not go with Dr. Stockmann upon this occasion. You can buy even gold at too high a price; that's my opinion.

(*Loud applause on all sides.*)

HOVSTAD: I also feel bound to explain my attitude. In the beginning, Dr. Stockmann's agitation found favor in several quarters, and I supported it as 120 impartially as I could. But when we found we had allowed ourselves to be misled by a false statement——

DR. STOCKMANN: False!

HOVSTAD: Well, then, a somewhat unreliable statement. The Burgomaster's report has proved this. I trust no one here present doubts my liberal 125 principles; the attitude of the *Messenger* on all great political questions is well known to you all. But I have learned from experience and thoughtful men that in purely local matters a man must observe a certain amount of caution.

ASLAKSEN: I quite agree with the speaker. 130

HOVSTAD: And in the matter under discussion it is evident that Dr. Stockmann has public opinion against him. But, gentlemen, what is the first and foremost duty of an editor? Is it not to work in harmony with his readers? Has he not in some sort received a silent mandate to further assiduously and unweariedly the well-being of his constituents? or am I mistaken in 135 this?

MANY VOICES: No, no, no! Hovstad is right.

HOVSTAD: It has cost me a bitter struggle to break with a man in whose house I have of late been a frequent guest—with a man who up to this day has enjoyed the universal good-will of his fellow-citizens—with a man 140 whose only, or at any rate, whose chief fault is that he consults his heart rather than his head.

A FEW SCATTERED VOICES: That's true! Three cheers for Dr. Stockmann.

HOVSTAD: But my duty towards the community has forced me to break with him. Then, too, there is another consideration that compels me to oppose him, to stay him if possible from the fatal descent upon which he is entering: consideration for his family——

DR. STOCKMANN: Keep to the water-works and the sewers!

HOVSTAD: ——consideration for his wife and his unprovided-for children.

MORTEN: Is that us, mother?

MRS. STOCKMANN: Hush!

ASLAKSEN: I will now put the Burgomaster's resolution to the vote.

DR. STOCKMANN: It is not necessary. I haven't the slightest intention of speaking of all the filth at the Baths. No! you shall hear something quite different.

BURGOMASTER (*aside*): What nonsense has he got hold of now?

A DRUNKEN MAN: I'm a duly qualified ratepayer! And so I've a right to my opinion! My full, firm opinion is that——

SEVERAL VOICES: Silence, up there.

OTHERS: He's drunk! Turn him out!

(The drunken man is put out.)

DR. STOCKMANN: Can I speak?

ASLAKSEN (*ringing the bell*): Dr. Stockmann will address the meeting.

DR. STOCKMANN: I should have liked to see any one, but a few days ago, dare to make such an attempt to gag me as has been made here to-night! I would then have fought like a lion in defense of my holiest rights as a man. But now all this is quite indifferent to me, for now I have more important things to speak of. (*The people crowd closer round him.*) During the last few days I have thought, reflected much, have pondered upon so many things, till, at last, my head seemed to be in a whirl——

BURGOMASTER (*coughing*): H'm!

DR. STOCKMANN: ——but then I began to see things clearly; then I saw to the very bottom of the whole matter. And that is why I stand here this evening. I am about to make a great revelation to you, fellow-citizens! I am going to disclose that to you which is of infinitely more moment than the unimportant fact that our water-works are poisonous, and that our Hygienic Baths are built upon soil teeming with pestilence.

MANY VOICES (*shouting*): Don't listen to that! Shut up about that!

DR. STOCKMANN: I have said I should speak of the great discovery I have made within the last few days—the discovery that all our spiritual sources of life are poisoned, and that our whole bourgeois society rests upon a soil teeming with the pestilence of lies.

SEVERAL VOICES: What is he saying?

BURGOMASTER: Such an insinuation——

ASLAKSEN (*with hand on bell*): I must call upon the speaker to moderate his expressions.

DR. STOCKMANN: I have loved my native town as dearly as man could love the 185
home of his childhood. I was not old when I left our town, and distance,
privations, and memory threw, as it were, a strange glamor over the
town and its people. (*Some clapping and cheers of approval.*) Then for
years I found myself stranded in an out-of-the-way corner in the north.
Whenever I met any of the poor folk who lived there, hemmed in by 190
rocks, it seemed to me, many a time, that it would have been better for
those poor degraded creatures if they had had a cattle doctor to attend
them than a man like me. (*Murmurs in the room.*)

BILLING (*laying down his pen*): God bless me! But I've never heard——

HOVSTAD: It is an insult to an estimable peasantry. 195

DR. STOCKMANN: One moment! I do not think anyone can reproach me with
forgetting my native town up there. I brooded over my eggs like an
eider duck, and what I hatched—were plans for the Baths here. (*Applause
and interruptions.*) And when, at last, after a long time, fate arranged
all things so well and happily for me that I could come home again— 200
then, fellow-citizens, it seems to me that I hadn't another wish upon
earth. Yes; I had the one ardent, constant, burning desire to be useful
to the place of my birth, and to the people here.

BURGOMASTER: The method is rather extraordinary—h'm!

DR. STOCKMANN: And when I came here I rejoiced blindly in my happy illusions. 205
But yesterday morning—no, it was really two evenings ago—the eyes of
my mind were opened wide, and the first thing I saw was the extraordinary stupidity of the authorities.

(*Noise, cries and laughter. MRS. STOCKMANN coughs zealously.*)

BURGOMASTER: Mr. Chairman!

ASLAKSEN (*ringing bell*): In virtue of my office——! 210

DR. STOCKMANN: It is mean to catch me up on a word, Mr. Aslaksen. I only
meant that I became aware of the extraordinary muddling of which the
leading men have been guilty down there at the Baths. I detest leading
men—I've seen enough of these gentry in my time. They are like goats in
a young plantation; they do harm everywhere; they stand in the path 215
of a free man wherever he turns—and I should be glad if we could
exterminate them like other noxious animals——

(*Uproar in the room.*)

BURGOMASTER: Mr. Chairman, can such an expression be permitted?

ASLAKSEN: Doctor Stockmann——!

DR. STOCKMANN: I can't conceive how it is that I only now have seen through 220
these gentry; for haven't I had a magnificent example before my eyes
daily here in the town—my brother Peter—slow in grasping new ideas,
tenacious in prejudice——

(*Laughter, noise and whistling. MRS. STOCKMANN coughs. ASLAKSEN rings violently.*)

THE DRUNKEN MAN (*who has come in again*): Do you mean me? Sure enough, my name is Petersen, but damn me if—— 225

ANGRY VOICES: Out with that drunken man. Turn him out.

(*The man is again turned out.*)

BURGOMASTER: Who is that person?

A BYSTANDER: I don't know him, Burgomaster.

ANOTHER: He doesn't belong to this town.

A THIRD: Probably he's a loafer from——(*The rest is inaudible.*) 230

ASLAKSEN: The man was evidently intoxicated with Bavarian beer. Continue, Dr. Stockmann, but do strive to be moderate.

DR. STOCKMANN: Well, fellow-citizens, I will say no more about our leading men. If any one imagines, from what I have said here, that I want to exterminate these gentlemen to-night, he is mistaken—altogether mis- 235 taken. For I cherish the comforting belief that these laggards, these old remnants of a decaying world of thought, are doing this admirably for themselves. They need no doctor's help to hasten their end. Nor, indeed, is it this sort of people that are the most serious danger of society; it is not they who are the most effective in poisoning our spiritual life or 240 making pestilential the ground beneath our feet; it is not they who are the most dangerous enemies of truth and freedom in our society.

CRIES FROM ALL SIDES: Who, then? Who is it? Name, name.

DR. STOCKMANN: Yes, you may be sure I will name them. For *this* is the great discovery I made yesterday. (*In a louder tone.*) The most dangerous 245 enemies of truth and freedom in our midst are the compact majority. Yes, the damned, compact, liberal majority—they it is! Now you know it.

(*Immense noise in the room. Most are shouting, stamping and whistling. Several elderly gentlemen exchange stolen glances and seem amused. MRS. STOCKMANN rises nervously. EJLIF and MORTEN advance threateningly towards the school-boys, who are making a noise. ASLAKSEN rings the bell and calls for order. HOVSTAD and BILLING both speak, but nothing can be heard. At last quiet is restored.*)

ASLAKSEN: The chairman expects the speaker to withdraw his thoughtless remarks.

DR. STOCKMANN: Never, Mr. Aslaksen. For it is this great majority of our society 250 that robs me of my freedom, and wants to forbid me to speak the truth.

HOVSTAD: Right is always on the side of the majority.

BILLING: Yes, and the truth too, God bless me!

DR. STOCKMANN: The majority is never right. Never, I say. That is one of those conventional lies against which a free, thoughtful man must rebel. Who 255 are they that make up the majority of a country? Is it the wise men or the foolish? I think we must agree that the foolish folk are, at present, in a terribly overwhelming majority all around and about us the wide world over. But, devil take it, it can surely never be right that the foolish

should rule over the wise! (*Noise and shouts.*) Yes, yes, you can shout   260
me down, but you can not gainsay me. The majority has might—unhappily—but right it has not. I and a few others are right. The minority is
always right.

(*Much noise again.*)

HOVSTAD: Ha! ha! So Dr. Stockmann has turned aristocrat since the day before
yesterday!   265

DR. STOCKMANN: I have said that I will not waste a word on the little, narrow-
chested, short-winded crew that lie behind us. Pulsating life has nothing
more to do with them. But I do think of the few individuals among us who
have made all the new, germinating truths their own. These men stand,
as it were, at the outposts, so far in advance that the compact majority   270
has not yet reached them—and *there* they fight for truths that are too
lately borne into the world's consciousness to have won over the majority.

HOVSTAD: So the doctor is a revolutionist now.

DR. STOCKMANN: Yes, by Heaven, I am, Mr. Hovstad! For I am going to revolt
against the lie that truth resides in the majority. What sort of truths are   275
those that the majority is wont to take up? Truths so full of years that
they are decrepit. When a truth is as old as that, it is in a fair way to
become a lie, gentlemen. (*Laughter and interruption.*) Yes, yes, you may
believe me or not; but truths are by no means wiry Methuselahs, as some
people think. A normally-constituted truth lives—let me say—as a rule,   280
seventeen or eighteen years, at the outside twenty years, seldom longer.
But truths so stricken in years are always shockingly thin. And yet it
is only then that a majority takes them up and recommends them to
society as wholesome food. But I can assure you there is not much
nutritious matter in this sort of fare; and as a doctor I know something   285
about it. All these majority-truths are like last year's salt pork; they are
like rancid, moldy ham, producing all the moral scrofula that devastates
society.

ASLAKSEN: It seems to me that the honorable speaker is wandering very considerably from the subject.   290

BURGOMASTER: I quite agree with the chairman.

DR. STOCKMANN: I really think you quite mad, Peter! I am keeping as closely
to the subject as I possibly can, for what I am speaking of is only this—
that the masses, the majority, that damned compact majority—it is they,
I say, who are poisoning our spiritual life, and making pestilential the   295
ground beneath our feet.

HOVSTAD: And this the great, independent majority of the people do, just because they are sensible enough to reverence only assured and acknowledged truths?

DR. STOCKMANN: Ah! my dear Mr. Hovstad, don't talk so glibly about assured   300
truths! The truths acknowledged by the masses, the multitude, are truths

709

that the advanced guard thought assured in the days of our grandfathers. We, the fighters at the outposts now-a-days, we no longer
acknowledge them, and I don't believe that there is any other assured
truth but this—that society can not live, and live wholesomely, upon such   305
old, marrowless, lifeless truths as these.

HOVSTAD: But instead of all this vague talk, it would be more interesting to
learn what are these old, lifeless truths which we are living upon.

(*Approving applause generally.*)

DR. STOCKMANN: Ah! I couldn't go over the whole heap of abominations; but to
begin with, I'll just keep to one acknowledged truth, which at bottom is   310
a hideous lie, but which, all the same, Mr. Hovstad, and the *Messenger*,
and all adherents of the *Messenger* live upon.

HOVSTAD: And that is——?

DR. STOCKMANN: That is the doctrine that you have inherited from our forefathers, and that you heedlessly proclaim far and wide—the doctrine   315
that the multitude, the vulgar herd, the masses, are the pith of the
people—that, indeed, they are the people—that the common man, that
this ignorant, undeveloped member of society has the same right to
condemn or to sanction, to govern and to rule, as the few people of
intellectual power.   320

BILLING: Now really, God bless me——

HOVSTAD (*shouting at the same time*): Citizens, please note that!

ANGRY VOICES: Ho, ho! Aren't we the people? Is it only the grand folk who're
to govern?

A WORKINGMAN: Turn out the fellow who stands there talking such twaddle.   325

OTHERS: Turn him out!

A CITIZEN (*shouting*): Blow your horn, Evensen.

(*Loud hooting, whistling, and terrific noise in the room.*)

DR. STOCKMANN (*when the noise has somewhat subsided*): Now do be reasonable! Can't you bear to hear the voice of truth for once? Why, I don't
ask you all to agree with me straight away. But I did certainly expect   330
that Mr. Hovstad would be on my side, if he would but be true to himself. For Mr. Hovstad claims to be a free-thinker——

SEVERAL VOICES (*ask wondering, in a low voice*): Free-thinker, did he say. What?
Editor Hovstad a free-thinker?

HOVSTAD (*shouting*): Prove it, Dr. Stockmann! When have I said that in print?   335

DR. STOCKMANN (*reflecting*): No; by Heaven, you're right there. You've never
had the frankness to do that. Well, I won't get you into a scrape, Mr.
Hovstad. Let me be the free-thinker then. For now I'll prove, and on
scientific grounds, that the *Messenger* is leading you all by the nose
shamefully, when it tells you that you, that the masses, the vulgar herd,   340

are the true pith of the people. You see that is only a newspaper lie. The masses are nothing but the raw material that must be fashioned into the people. (*Murmurs, laughter, and noise in the room.*) Is it not so with all other living creatures on earth? How great the difference between a cultivated and an uncultivated breed of animals! Only look at a 345 common barn hen. What sort of meat do you get from such a skinny animal? Nothing to boast of! And what sort of eggs does it lay? A fairly decent crow or raven can lay eggs nearly as good. Then take a cultivated Spanish or Japanese hen, or take a finer pheasant or turkey—ah! then you see the difference. And then I take the dog, man's closest ally. 350 Think first of an ordinary common cur—I mean one of those loathsome, ragged, low mongrels, that haunt the streets, and are a nuisance to everybody. And place such a mongrel by the side of a poodle dog, who for many generations has been bred from a well-known strain, who has lived on delicate food, and has heard harmonious voices and music. 355 Don't you believe that the brain of a poodle has developed quite differently from that of a mongrel? Yes, you may depend upon that! It is educated poodles like this that jugglers train to perform the most extraordinary tricks. A common peasant-cur could never learn anything of the sort—not if he tried till Doomsday. 360

(*Laughing and chaffing are heard all around.*)

A CITIZEN (*shouting*): Do you want to make dogs of us now?

ANOTHER MAN: We are not animals, doctor.

DR. STOCKMANN: Yes, on my soul, but we are animals, old fellow! We're one and all of us as much animals as one could wish. But, truly, there aren't many distinguished animals among us. Ah! there is a terrible difference 365 between men-poodles and men-mongrels. And the ridiculous part of it is, that Editor Hovstad quite agrees with me so long as we speak of four-footed animals——

HOVSTAD: Oh! do drop them!

DR. STOCKMANN: All right! but so soon as I apply the law to the two-legged, 370 Mr. Hovstad is up in arms; then he no longer dares to stick to his own opinions, he does not dare to think out his own thoughts to their logical end; then he turns his whole doctrines upside down, and proclaims in the *People's Messenger* that barn-yard hens and gutter mongrels are precisely the finest specimens in the menagerie. But it is always thus 375 so long as you haven't work'd the vulgarity out of your system, and fought your way up to spiritual distinction.

HOVSTAD: I make no kind of pretensions to any sort of distinction. I come from simple peasants, and I am proud that my root lies deep among the masses, who are being jeered at now. 380

SEVERAL WORKMEN: Three cheers for Hovstad! Hurrah! hurrah!

DR. STOCKMANN: The sort of people I am speaking of you don't find only in the

711

lower classes; they crawl and swarm all around us—up to the very highest classes of society. Why, only look at your own smug, smart Burgomaster! Truly, my brother Peter is as much one of the vulgar herd as any man walking on two legs.   385

(*Laughter and hisses.*)

BURGOMASTER: I beg to protest against such personal allusions.

DR. STOCKMANN (*imperturbably*): ——and that not because he—like myself—is descended from a good-for-nothing old pirate of Pomerania, or somewhere thereabouts—yes, for that we are so——   390

BURGOMASTER: Absurd tradition! Has been refuted!

DR. STOCKMANN: ——but he is so because he thinks the thoughts of his forefathers, and holds the opinions of his forefathers. The people who do this, *they* belong to the unintellectual mob;—see—that's why my pretentious brother Peter is at bottom so utterly without refinement—and consequently so illiberal.   395

BURGOMASTER: Mr. Chairman——

HOVSTAD: So that the distinguished persons in this country are liberals? That's quite a new theory.

DR. STOCKMANN: Yes, that too is part of my new discovery. And you shall hear *this* also; that free thought is almost precisely the same thing as morality. And therefore I say that it is altogether unpardonable of the *Messenger* to proclaim day after day the false doctrine that it is the masses and the multitude, the compact majority, that monopolize free thought and morality, and that vice and depravity and all spiritual filth are only the oozings from education, as all the filth down there by the Baths oozes out from the Mill Dale Tan-works! (*Noise and interruptions.* DR. STOCKMANN *goes on imperturbably smiling in his eagerness.*) And yet this same *Messenger* can still preach about the masses and the many being raised to a higher level of life! But, in the devil's name—if the doctrine of the *Messenger* holds good, why, then, this raising up of the masses would be synonymous with hurling them into destruction! But, happily, it is only an old hereditary lie that education demoralizes. No, it is stupidity, poverty, the ugliness of life, that do this devil's work! In a house that isn't aired, and whose floors are not swept every day—my wife Katrine maintains that the floors ought to be scrubbed too, but we can't discuss that now;—well,—in such a house, I say, within two or three years, people lose the power of thinking or acting morally. A deficiency of oxygen enervates the conscience. And it would seem there's precious little oxygen in many and many a house here in the town, since the whole compact majority is unscrupulous enough to be willing to build up the prosperity of the town upon a quagmire of lies and fraud.   400 405 410 415 420

ASLAKSEN: I can not allow so gross an insult, leveled at all the citizens here present.

A GENTLEMAN: I move that the chairman order the speaker to sit down.   425

EAGER VOICES: Yes, yes, that's right! Sit down! Sit down!

DR. STOCKMANN (*flaring up*): Then I will proclaim the truth from the house-tops! I'll write to other newspapers outside the town! The whole land shall know how matters are ordered here.

HOVSTAD: It would almost seem as if the doctor wanted to ruin the town. 430

DR. STOCKMANN: Yes, I love my native town so well I would rather ruin it than see it flourishing upon a lie.

ASLAKSEN: That is speaking strongly.

(*Noise and whistling,* MRS. STOCKMANN *coughs in vain; the doctor no longer heeds her.*)

HOVSTAD (*shouting amid the tumult*): The man who would ruin a whole community must be an enemy of the people! 435

DR. STOCKMANN (*with growing excitement*): It doesn't matter if a lying community is ruined! It must be leveled to the ground, I say! All men who live upon lies must be exterminated like vermin! You'll poison the whole country in time; you'll bring it to such a pass that the whole country will deserve to perish. And should it come to this, I say, from the bottom of 440 my heart: Perish the country! Perish all its people!

A MAN (*in the crowd*): Why, he talks like a regular enemy of the people!

BILLING: There, God bless me! spoke the voice of the people!

MANY SHOUTING: Yes! yes! yes! He's an enemy of the people! He hates the country! He hates the people! 445

ASLAKSEN: Both as a citizen of this town and as a man, I am deeply shocked at what I have been obliged to listen to here. Dr. Stockmann has unmasked himself in a manner I should never have dreamt of. I am reluctantly forced to subscribe to the opinion just expressed by a worthy citizen, and I think we ought to give expression to this opinion. I there- 450 fore beg to propose, "That this meeting is of opinion that the medical officer of the Bath, Dr. Thomas Stockmann, is an enemy of the people."

(*Thunders of applause and cheers. Many form a circle round the doctor and hoot at him.* MRS. STOCKMANN *and* PETRA *have risen.* MORTEN *and* EJLIF *fight the other school-boys who have also been hooting. Some grown-up persons separate them.*)

DR. STOCKMANN (*to the people hooting*): Ah fools, that you are! I tell you that——

ASLAKSEN (*ringing*): The doctor is out of order in speaking. A regular vote must 455 be taken, and out of consideration for the feeling of those present the vote will be taken in writing and without names. Have you any blank paper, Mr. Billing?

BILLING: Here's both blue and white paper——

ASLAKSEN: That'll do. We shall manage more quickly this way. Tear it up. That's 460 it. (*To the meeting.*) Blue means no, white means yes. I will myself go round and collect the votes.

(The BURGOMASTER *leaves the room.* ASLASKEN *and a few citizens go round with pieces of paper in hats.)*

A GENTLEMAN (*to* HOVSTAD): Whatever is up with the doctor? What does it all mean?

HOVSTAD: Why, you know how irrepressible he is. 465

ANOTHER GENTLEMAN (*to* BILLING): I say, you're intimate with him. Have you ever noticed if he drinks?

BILLING: God bless me! I really don't know what to say. Toddy is always on the table whenever anyone calls.

THIRD GENTLEMAN: No, I rather think he's not always right in his head. 470

FIRST GENTLEMAN: Yes—I wonder if madness is hereditary in the family?

BILLING: I shouldn't wonder.

FOURTH GENTLEMAN: No, it's pure jealousy. He wants to be over the heads of the rest.

BILLING: A few days ago he certainly was talking about a rise in his salary, 475 but he did not get it.

ALL THE GENTLEMEN (*together*): Ah! that explains everything.

THE DRUNKEN MAN: I want a blue one, I do! And I'll have a white one too!

PEOPLE CALL OUT: There's the drunken man again! turn him out!

MORTEN KIIL: Well, Stockmann, do you see now what this tomfoolery leads to? 480

DR. STOCKMANN: I have done my duty.

MORTEN KIIL: What was that you said about the Mill Dale Tanneries?

DR. STOCKMANN: Why, you heard what I said; that all the filth comes from them.

MORTEN KIIL: From my tannery as well?

DR. STOCKMANN: Unfortunately, your tannery is the worst of all. 485

MORTEN KIIL: Will you put that in the papers too?

DR. STOCKMANN: I never keep anything back.

MORTEN KIIL: That may cost you dear, Stockmann!

(Exit.)

A FAT GENTLEMAN (*goes up to* HORSTER *without bowing to the ladies*): Well, Captain, so you lend your house to an enemy of the people. 490

HORSTER: I suppose I can do as I please with my own, sir.

THE MERCHANT: Then, of course, you can have no objection if I do the same with mine?

HORSTER: What do you mean, sir?

THE MERCHANT: You shall hear from me to-morrow. 495

(Turns away, and exits.)

PETRA: Wasn't that the shipowner?

HORSTER: Yes, that was Merchant Vik.

ASLASKEN (*with the voting papers in his hands, ascends the platform and rings*): Gentlemen! I have to acquaint you with the result of the vote. All, with one exception—— 500

A YOUNG GENTLEMAN: That's the drunken man?

ASLASKEN: With one exception—a tipsy man—this meeting of citizens declares the medical officer of the Baths, Dr. Thomas Stockmann, an enemy of the people. (*Cheers and applause.*) Three cheers for our honorable old community of citizens! (*Applause.*) Three cheers for our able and ener- 505 getic Burgomaster, who has so loyally put on one side the claims of kindred! (*Cheers.*) The meeting is dissolved.

BILLING: Three cheers for the chairman!

ALL: Hurrah for Printer Aslaksen!

DR. STOCKMANN: My hat and coat, Petra! Captain, have you room for pas- 510 sengers to the new world?

HORSTER: For you and yours, doctor, we'll make room.

DR. STOCKMANN: Good! Come Katrine! Come, boys!

(*He gives his wife his arm.*)

MRS. STOCKMANN (*in a low voice*): Dear Thomas, let us go out by the back way.

DR. STOCKMANN: No back ways, Katrine! (*In a louder voice.*) You shall hear of 515 the enemy of the people before he shakes the dust from his feet! I'm not so forgiving as a certain person: I don't say I forgive you, for you know not what you do.

ASLAKSEN (*shouting*): That is a blasphemous comparison, Dr. Stockmann.

BILLING: It is, God bl—— A serious man can't stand that! 520

A COARSE VOICE: And he threatens us into the bargain!

ANGRY CRIES: Let's smash the windows in his house! Let's give him a ducking!

A MAN (*in the crowd*): Blow your horn, Evensen! Ta-rata ra-ra!

(*Horn-blowing, whistling and wild shouting. The doctor, with his family, goes towards the door. HORSTER makes way for them.*)

ALL (*shouting after them as they go out*): Enemy of the people! Enemy of the people! Enemy of the people! 525

BILLING: Well, God bless me if I'd drink toddy at Dr. Stockmann's to-night!

(*The people throng towards the door; the noise is heard without from the street beyond; cries of "Enemy of the people! Enemy of the people!"*)

ACT V

DR. STOCKMANN'S *study. Bookcases and various preparations along the walls. In the background, a door leading to the ante-room; to the left first entrance, a door to the sitting-room. In wall right are two windows, all the panes of which are smashed. In the middle of the room is the doctor's writing-table, covered with books and papers. The room is in disorder. It is morning. DR. STOCKMANN in dressing-gown, slippers and skull-cap, is bending down and raking with an umbrella under one of the cabinets; at last he rakes out a stone.*

DR. STOCKMANN: Katrine, I've found another one.

MRS. STOCKMANN: Ah! you're sure to find lots more.

DR. STOCKMANN (*placing the stone on a pile of others on the table*): I shall keep these stones as sacred relics. Ejlif and Morten shall see them every day, and when they are grown men they shall inherit them from me. (*Poking under the bookcase.*) Hasn't——what the devil's her name?—the girl—hasn't she been for the glazier yet?

MRS. STOCKMANN: Yes, but he said he didn't know whether he'd be able to come to-day.

DR. STOCKMANN: You'll see he daren't come.

MRS. STOCKMANN: Well, Rudine also thought he didn't dare to come, because of the neighbors. What is it, Rudine?—All right. Here's a letter for you, Thomas.

DR. STOCKMANN: Let's see. (*Opens letter and reads.*) Ah,ha!

MRS. STOCKMANN: Whom is it from?

DR. STOCKMANN: From the landlord. He gives us notice.

MRS. STOCKMANN: Is it possible? Such a pleasantly-behaved man.

DR. STOCKMANN: He daren't do otherwise, he says. He is very loath to do it; but he daren't do otherwise on account of his fellow-citizens, out of respect for public opinion—is in a dependent position—does not dare to offend certain influential men——

MRS. STOCKMANN: There, you can see now, Thomas.

DR. STOCKMANN: Yes, yes, I see well enough; they are cowards, every one of them cowards in this town; no one dares do anything for fear of all the rest. But that's all the same to us, Katrine. Now we're journeying to the new world, and so——

MRS. STOCKMANN: Yes, but, Thomas, is that idea of the journey really well-advised?

DR. STOCKMANN: Perhaps you'd have me stay here where they have gibbeted me as an enemy of the people, branded me, and smashed my windows to atoms? And look here, Katrine, they have torn a hole in my black trousers.

MRS. STOCKMANN: Oh, dear, and they're the best you've got.

DR. STOCKMANN: One ought never to put on one's best trousers when one goes fighting for liberty and truth. Of course, you know I don't care so much about the trousers; you can always patch them up for me. But it is that the mob should dare to attack me as if they were my equals—*that's* what, for the life of me, I can't stomach.

MRS. STOCKMANN: Yes, they've been very insolent to you here, Thomas; but must we leave the country altogether on that account?

DR. STOCKMANN: Don't you think the plebeians are just as impertinent in other towns as here? Ah, yes, they are, my dear; they're pretty much of a muchness everywhere. Well, never mind, let the curs snap; *that* is not the worst; the worst is that all men are party slaves all the land over. Nor is it *that*—perhaps that's no better in the free west either; there, too, the compact majority thrives, and enlightened public opinion and all the other devil's trash flourishes. But you see the conditions are on a larger scale there than here; they may lynch you, but they don't torture you; they don't put the screw on a free soul there as they do at home here. And then, if need be, you can live apart. (*Walks up and down.*) If I only knew whether there were any primeval forest, any little South Sea island to be bought cheap——

MRS. STOCKMANN: Yes, but the boys, Thomas.

DR. STOCKMANN (*standing still*): What an extraordinary woman you are, Katrine! Would you prefer the boys to grow up amid such a society as ours? Why, you saw yourself yesterday evening that one-half of the population is quite mad, and if the other half hasn't lost its reason, that's because they're hounds who haven't any reason to lose.

MRS. STOCKMANN: But really, dear Thomas, you do say such imprudent things!

DR. STOCKMANN: Well! But isn't what I say the truth? Don't they turn all ideas upside down? Don't they stir up right and wrong in one mess of pottage? Don't they call lies what I know to be truth? But the maddest thing of all is that there are a whole mass of grown men, Liberals, who go about persuading themselves and others that they are free! Did you ever hear anything like it, Katrine?

MRS. STOCKMANN: Yes, yes it is certainly quite mad. But—— (PETRA *enters from sitting-room.*) Back from school already?

PETRA: Yes, I've been dismissed.

MRS. STOCKMANN: Dismissed?

DR. STOCKMANN: You, too!

PETRA: Mrs. Busk gave me notice, and so I thought it best to leave there and then.

DR. STOCKMANN: On my soul, you did right!

MRS. STOCKMANN: Who could have thought Mrs. Busk was such a bad woman?

PETRA: Oh! Mother, Mrs. Busk isn't really so bad; I saw clearly how much it pained her. But she didn't dare to do otherwise, she said; and so I'm dismissed.

DR. STOCKMANN (*laughing and rubbing his hands*): She dared not do otherwise, she too! Ah! that's delicious.

MRS. STOCKMANN: Ah! well! after the dreadful uproar last night——

PETRA: It wasn't only that. Now you shall hear, father!

DR. STOCKMANN: Well?

PETRA: Mrs. Busk showed me no less than three letters she had received this morning.

DR. STOCKMANN: Anonymous, of course?

PETRA: Yes.

DR. STOCKMANN: They didn't dare to give their names, Katrine——!

PETRA: And two of them wrote that a gentleman who frequently visits our house, said at the club last night that I had such extremely advanced opinions upon various matters.

DR. STOCKMANN: And, of course, you didn't deny that?

PETRA: Of course not. You know Mrs. Busk herself has pretty advanced opinions when we are alone together; but now this has come out about me she didn't dare keep me on.

MRS. STOCKMANN: And to think—it was one who came to our house! There, now, you see, Thomas, what comes of all your hospitality. 95

DR. STOCKMANN: We won't live any longer amid such foulness. Pack up as quickly as you can, Katrine; let us get away—the sooner the better.

MRS. STOCKMANN: Hush! I think there's some one outside in the passage. Just see, Petra. 100

PETRA (*opening door*): Ah! is it you, Captain Horster? Please come in.

HORSTER: Good morning. I thought I must just look in and see how you're getting on.

DR. STOCKMANN: Thanks; that's very beautiful of you.

MRS. STOCKMANN: And thanks for seeing us home, Captain Horster. 105

PETRA: But, however did you get back again?

HORSTER: Oh! that was all right. You know I'm pretty strong, and these folk's bark is worse than their bite.

DR. STOCKMANN: Isn't it marvelous, this piggish cowardice? Come here, I want to show you something! See, here are all the stones they threw in at us. 110 Only look at them! Upon my soul there aren't more than two decent big fighting stones in the whole lot; the rest are nothing but pebbles—mere nothings. And yet they stood down there, and yelled, and swore they'd slay me—the corrupt one;—but for deeds, for deeds—there's not much of that in this town! 115

HORSTER: Well, that was a good thing for you this time, anyhow, doctor.

DR. STOCKMANN: Of course it was. But it's vexatious all the same; for should it ever come to a serious, really important struggle, you'll see, Captain Horster, that public opinion will take to its heels, and the compact majority will make for the sea like a herd of swine. It is *this* that is so 120 sad to think of; it grieves me to the very heart. No, deuce take it—at the bottom all this is folly. They've said I am an enemy of the people; well, then, I'll be an enemy of the people.

MRS. STOCKMANN: You will never be that, Thomas.

DR. STOCKMANN: You'd better not take your oath of it, Katrine. A bad name 125 may work like a pin's prick in the lungs. And that damned word—I can't get rid of it; it has sunk into my diaphragm—there it lies and gnaws, and sucks like some acid. And magnesia is no good against that.

PETRA: Pshaw! You should only laugh at them, father.

HORSTER: The people will think differently yet, doctor. 130

MRS. STOCKMANN: Yes, Thomas, you may be as sure of that as you're standing here.

DR. STOCKMANN: Yes—perhaps when it is too late. Well, much good may it do them! Let them go on wallowing here in the mire, and repent that they have driven a patriot into exile. When do you sail, Captain Horster? 135

HORSTER: H'm!—it was really that I came to speak to you about——

DR. STOCKMANN: Has anything gone wrong with the ship?

HORSTER: No; but it's like this, I'm not going with it.

PETRA: Surely you have not been dismissed?

HORSTER (smiling): Yes, I have.   140

PETRA: You too!

MRS. STOCKMANN: There you see, Thomas.

DR. STOCKMANN: And for truth's sake! Ah! had I thought such a thing——

HORSTER: You mustn't take it to heart; I shall soon get a berth with some other
company.   145

DR. STOCKMANN: And this Merchant Vik! A wealthy man, independent of anyone! Good Heavens——

HORSTER: In other matters he is a thoroughly fair man, and he says himself he
would gladly have kept me on if only he dared.

DR. STOCKMANN: But he didn't dare—that goes without saying.   150

HORSTER: It wasn't easy, he said, when you belong to a party——

DR. STOCKMANN: That was a true saying of the honorable man's! A party is like
a sausage-machine; it grinds all the heads together in one mash; and
that's why there are so many blockheads and fatheads all seething
together!   155

MRS. STOCKMANN: Now really, Thomas!

PETRA (to HORSTER): If only you hadn't seen us home perhaps it would not have
come to this.

HORSTER: I don't regret it.

PETRA (holding out her hands): Thank you for that!   160

HORSTER (to DR. STOCKMANN): And so what I wanted to say to you was this: that
if you really want to leave I have thought of another way——

DR. STOCKMANN: That is good—only if we can get off——

MRS. STOCKMANN: Sh! Isn't that a knock?

PETRA: I'm sure that's uncle.   165

DR. STOCKMANN: Aha! (Calls.) Come in.

MRS. STOCKMANN: Dear Thomas, now do for once promise me——

(Enter Burgomaster from ante-room.)

BURGOMASTER: Oh! you're engaged. Then I'd better——

DR. STOCKMANN: No, no; come in.

BURGOMASTER: But I wanted to speak with you alone.   170

MRS. STOCKMANN: We'll go into the sitting-room.

HORSTER: And I'll look in again presently.

DR. STOCKMANN: No, no, go with them, Captain Horster, I must have further
information——

HORSTER: All right, then I'll wait.   175

(He follows MRS. STOCKMANN and PETRA into the sitting-room. The BURGOMASTER says
nothing, but casts glances at the windows.)

719

DR. STOCKMANN: Perhaps you find it rather drafty here to-day? Put your hat on.

BURGOMASTER: Thanks, if I may (*puts on hat*). I fancy I caught cold yesterday evening. I stood there shivering.

DR. STOCKMANN: Really? I should have said it was pretty warm.

BURGOMASTER: I regret that it was not in my power to prevent these nocturnal excesses.   180

DR. STOCKMANN: Have you nothing else to say to me?

BURGOMASTER (*producing a large letter*):   I've this document for you from the Directors of the Baths.

DR. STOCKMANN: I am dismissed?   185

BURGOMASTER: Yes, from to-day. (*Places letter on table.*) We are very sorry— but frankly, we dared not do otherwise on account of public opinion.

DR. STOCKMANN (*smiling*):   Dared not? I've heard that word already to-day.

BURGOMASTER: I beg of you to understand your position clearly. You must not, for the future, count upon any sort of practice in the town here.   190

DR. STOCKMANN: Deuce take the practice! But are you so sure of this?

BURGOMASTER: The Householders' Association is sending round a circular from house to house, in which all well-disposed citizens are called upon not to employ you, and I dare swear that not a single father of a family will venture to refuse his signature; he simply *dare* not.   195

DR. STOCKMANN: Well, well; I don't doubt that. But what then?

BURGOMASTER: If I might give you a piece of advice, it would be this—to go away for a time.

DR. STOCKMANN: Yes, I've had some thought of leaving this place.

BURGOMASTER: Good. When you've done so, and have had six months of re-   200
flection, then if, after mature consideration, you could make up your mind to acknowledge your error in a few words of regret——

DR. STOCKMANN: I might perhaps be reinstated, you think.

BURGOMASTER: Perhaps; it is not absolutely impossible.

DR. STOCKMANN: Yes, but how about public opinion? You daren't on account of   205
public opinion.

BURGOMASTER: Opinions are extremely variable things. And, to speak candidly, it is of the greatest importance for us to have such an admission from you.

DR. STOCKMANN: Then you may whistle for it! You remember well enough, damn   210
it, what I've said to you before about these foxes' tricks!

BURGOMASTER: At that time your position was infinitely more favorable; at that time you might have supposed you had the whole town at your back——

DR. STOCKMANN: Yes, and now I feel I've the whole town on my back. (*Flaring up.*) But no—not if I had the devil himself and his grandmother on my   215
back—never—never, I tell you!

BURGOMASTER: The father of a family must not act as you are doing; you must not, Thomas.

DR. STOCKMANN: Must not! There is but one thing on earth that a free man must not do, and do you know what that is?   220

BURGOMASTER: No.

DR. STOCKMANN: Of course not; but I will tell you. A free man must not behave like a blackguard; he must not so act that he would spit in his own face.

BURGOMASTER: That really sounds extremely plausible; and if there were not another explanation of your mulish obstinancy—but we know well enough there—— 225

DR. STOCKMANN: What do you mean by that?

BURGOMASTER: I'm sure you understand. But as your brother, and as a man of common sense, I give you this advice: don't build too confidently upon prospects and expectations that perhaps may fail you utterly. 230

DR. STOCKMANN: But what on earth are you driving at?

BURGOMASTER: Do you really want to make me believe that you are ignorant of the provisions Master Tanner Kiil has made in his will?

DR. STOCKMANN: I know that the little he has is to go to a home for old indigent workingmen. But what's that got to do with me? 235

BURGOMASTER: To begin with, it is not a "little" we're speaking of. Tanner Kiil is a fairly wealthy man.

DR. STOCKMANN: I've never had any idea of that!

BURGOMASTER: H'm! Really? Then you hadn't any idea either that a not inconsiderable portion of his fortune is to go to your children, and that you 240 and your wife are to enjoy the interest on it for life. Hasn't he told you that?

DR. STOCKMANN: No, on my soul! On the contrary, he was constantly grumbling because he was so preposterously over-taxed. But are you really so sure of this, Peter? 245

BURGOMASTER: I had it from a thoroughly reliable source.

DR. STOCKMANN: But, good Heavens! Why, then, Katrine is all right—and the children too! Oh! I must tell her—— (*Calls.*) Katrine, Katrine!

BURGOMASTER (*restraining him*): Hush! don't say anything about it yet.

MRS. STOCKMANN (*opening the door*): What is it? 250

DR. STOCKMANN: Nothing, my dear, go in again. (MRS. STOCKMANN *closes the door. He walks up and down.*) Provided for! Only think—all of them provided for! And that for life! After all it is a pleasant sensation to feel yourself secure!

BURGOMASTER: Yes, but it is not exactly so—you are not. Tanner Kiil can annul 255 his testament at any day or hour he chooses.

DR. STOCKMANN: But he won't do that, my good Peter. The badger is immensely delighted that I've attacked you and your wiseacre friends.

BURGOMASTER (*stops and looks searchingly at him*): Aha! that throws a new light upon a good many matters. 260

DR. STOCKMANN: What matters?

BURGOMASTER: So the whole affair has been a combined maneuvre. These violent, restless attacks which you, in the name of truth, have launched against the leading men of the town.

DR. STOCKMANN: What, what? 265

BURGOMASTER: So this was nothing but a preconcerted return for that vindictive old Morten Kiil's will.

DR. STOCKMANN (*almost speechless*): Peter—you're the most abominable plebeian I've ever known in my life.

BURGOMASTER: Everything is over between us. Your dismissal is irrevocable—for now we have a weapon against you. 270

(*Exit*).

DR. STOCKMANN: Shame! shame! shame! (*Calls.*) Katrine! The floor must be scrubbed after him! Tell her to come here with a pail—what's her name? —confound it—the girl with the sooty nose——

MRS. STOCKMANN (*in the sitting room*): Hush! hush! Thomas! 275

PETRA (*also in the doorway*): Father, here's grandfather, and he wants to know if he can speak to you alone.

DR. STOCKMANN: Yes, of course he can. Come in, father-in-law. (*Enters* MORTEN KIIL.) Well, what is it? Sit you down.

MORTEN KIIL: I'll not sit down. (*Looking about him.*) It looks cheerful here to-day, 280 Stockmann.

DR. STOCKMANN: Yes, doesn't it?

MORTEN KIIL: Sure enough it does; and you've plenty of fresh air, too; I should think you'd have enough of that oxygen you chattered about so much yesterday. You must have an awfully good conscience to-day, I should 285 think.

DR. STOCKMANN: Yes, I have.

MORTEN KIIL: So I should suppose. (*Striking himself upon the heart.*) But do you know what I've got here?

DR. STOCKMANN: Well, a good conscience, too, I hope. 290

MORTEN KIIL: Pshaw! No, something far better than that.

(*Takes out a large pocket-book, opens it and shows a mass of papers.*)

DR. STOCKMANN (*looking at him in astonishment*): Shares in the Baths.

MORTEN KIIL: They weren't difficult to get to-day.

DR. STOCKMANN: And you've been and bought these up——?

MORTEN KIIL: All I'd got the money to pay for. 295

DR. STOCKMANN: But, my dear father-in-law—just now, when the Baths are in such straits.

MORTEN KIIL: If you behave like a reasonable creature you can set the Baths going again.

DR. STOCKMANN: Aye, why you can see for yourself that I'm doing all I can. But 300 the people of this town are mad!

MORTEN KIIL: You said yesterday that the worst filth came from my tannery. Now, if that's really the truth, then my grandfather, and my father be- fore me, and I myself have all these years been littering the town like three destroying angels. Do you think I'll let such a stain remain upon me? 305

DR. STOCKMANN: Unfortunately, you can't help yourself now.

MORTEN KIIL: No, thanks. I stand for my good name and my rights. I have heard that the people call me "badger." Well, the badger is a swinish sort of animal, but they shall never be able to say that of me. I will live and die a clean man. 310

DR. STOCKMANN: And how will you manage *that*?

MORTEN KIIL: You shall make me clean, Stockmann.

DR. STOCKMANN: I!

MORTEN KIIL: Do you know with what money I've bought these shares? No, you can't know, but now I'll tell you. It's the money Katrine and Petra and 315 the little lads will have after me. Yes, for you see, I've invested my little all to the best advantage anyhow.

DR. STOCKMANN (*flaring up*): And you've thrown away Katrine's money like this!

MORTEN KIIL: O, yes; the whole of the money is entirely invested in the Baths 320 now. And now I shall really see if you're so possessed—demented—mad, Stockmann. Now, if you go on letting this dirt and filth result from my tannery, it'll be just the same as if you were to flay Katrine with a whip —and Petra, too, and the little lads. But no decent father of a family would ever do that—unless, indeed, he were a madman.

DR. STOCKMANN (*walking up and down*): Yes, but I *am* a madman; I *am* a mad- 325 man!

MORTEN KIIL: But I suppose you're not so stark mad where your wife and bairns are concerned.

DR. STOCKMANN: Why on earth didn't you speak to me before you went and bought all that rubbish? 330

MORTEN KIIL: What's done can't be undone.

DR. STOCKMANN (*walking about uneasily*): If only I weren't so certain about the affair! But I'm thoroughly convinced that I'm right!

MORTEN KIIL (*weighing the pocketbook in his hand*): If you stick to your madness these aren't worth much. 335

DR. STOCKMANN: But, deuce take it! surely science will be able to find some remedy, some antidote.

MORTEN KIIL: Do you mean something to kill the animals?

DR. STOCKMANN: Yes, or at least to make them innocuous.

MORTEN KIIL: Can't you try rat's-bane? 340

DR. STOCKMANN: Tush! Tush! But all the people say it is nothing but fancy! Let them have their own way, then! Haven't the ignorant, narrow-hearted curs reviled me for an enemy of the people; and did not they try to tear the clothes from off my back!

MORTEN KIIL: And they've smashed all the windows for you, too! 345

DR. STOCKMANN: Then, too, one's duty to one's family. I must talk it over with Katrine; she is such a stickler in matters of this sort.

MORTEN KIIL: That's right. You just follow the advice of a sensible woman.

DR. STOCKMANN (*going to him angrily*): How could you act so perversely! Staking Katrine's money and getting me into this horribly painful dilemma! I tell 350 you that when I look at you I seem to see the devil himself——

723

MORTEN KIIL: Then I'd better be off. But you must let me know your decision by 2 o'clock. If it's *no*, all the shares go to the charity—and that this very day.

DR. STOCKMANN: And what does Katrine get?

MORTEN KIIL: Not a brass farthing. (*The door of the ante-room opens.* MR. HOVSTAD *and* ASLAKSEN *are seen outside of it.*) Do you see these two there?   355

DR. STOCKMANN: What! And they actually dare to come to me here!

HOVSTAD: Why, of course we do.

ASLAKSEN: You see there is something we want to talk to you about.

MORTEN KIIL (*whispers*): Yes or no—by 2 o'clock.   360

ASLAKSEN (*with a glance at* HOVSTAD): Aha!

(Exit MORTEN KIIL.*)*

DR. STOCKMANN: Well, what is it you want with me? Be brief.

HOVSTAD: I can very well understand that you resent our conduct at the meeting yesterday——

DR. STOCKMANN: And that's what you call conduct! Yes, it was charming con-   365
duct! I call it misconduct—disgraceful. Shame upon you!

HOVSTAD: Call it what you will; but we *could* not do otherwise.

DR. STOCKMANN: You *dared* not, I suppose? Is not that so?

HOVSTAD: Yes, if you will have it.

ASLAKSEN: But why didn't you drop a word beforehand? Just the merest hint to   370
Mr. Hovstad or to me?

DR. STOCKMANN: A hint? What about?

ASLAKSEN: About what was at the bottom of it.

DR. STOCKMANN: I don't in the least understand you.

ASLAKSEN: Oh! yes, you do, Dr. Stockmann.   375

HOVSTAD: It's no good concealing it any longer now.

DR. STOCKMANN (*looking from one to the other*): Yes; but in the devil's own name——!

ASLAKSEN: May I ask—isn't your father-in-law going about the town and buying up all the shares in the Baths?   380

DR. STOCKMANN: Yes, he has bought shares in the Baths to-day, but——

ASLAKSEN: It would have been wiser if you'd set somebody else to do that—some one not so closely connected with you.

HOVSTAD: And then you ought not to have appeared under your own name. No one need have known that the attack on the Baths came from you.   385
You should have taken me into your counsels, Dr. Stockmann.

DR. STOCKMANN (*stares straight in front of him; a light seems to break upon him, and he looks thunder-stricken*): Are such things possible? Can such things be?

HOVSTAD (*smiling*): Well, we've seen they can. But you see it ought all to have   390
been managed with *finesse*. And then, too, you ought to have had several in it; for you know the responsibility is less for the individual when it is shared by others.

DR. STOCKMANN (*calmly*): In one word, gentlemen, what is it you want?

ASLAKSEN: Mr. Hovstad can best——   395

HOVSTAD: No, you explain, Aslaksen.

ASLAKSEN: Well, it's this; now that we know how the whole matter stands, we believe we shall be able to place the *People's Messenger* at your disposal.

DR. STOCKMANN: You dare do so, now? But how about public opinion? Aren't you afraid that a storm will burst out against us? 400

HOVSTAD: We must strive to ride out the storm.

ASLAKSEN: And the doctor try to manage his face-about with dexterity. As soon as your attack has produced its effect——

DR. STOCKMANN: As soon as my father-in-law and I have bought up the shares at a low price, you mean. 405

HOVSTAD: No doubt it is scientific reasons principally that have impelled you to take over the direction of the Baths.

DR. STOCKMANN: Of course; it was for scientific reasons that I made the old Badger go and buy up these shares. And then we'll tinker up the water-works a bit, and then dig about a bit by the shore down there, without it costing the town a half-crown. Don't you think that can be done? H'm? 410

HOVSTAD: I think so—if you have the *Messenger* to back you up.

ASLAKSEN: In a free society the press is a power, doctor.

DR. STOCKMANN: Yes, indeed, and so is public opinion; and you, Mr. Aslaksen —I suppose you'll be answerable for the Householders' Association? 415

ASLAKSEN: Both for the Association and the Moderation Society. You may rely upon that.

DR. STOCKMANN: But, gentlemen—really I am quite ashamed to mention such a thing—but—what return? 420

HOVSTAD: Of course, you know we should be best pleased to give you our support for nothing. But the *Messenger* is not very firmly established; it is not getting on as it ought; and just now, that there is so much to be done in general politics, I should be very sorry to have to stop the paper.

DR. STOCKMANN: Naturally; that would be very hard for a friend of the people like you. (*Flaring up.*) But I—I am an enemy of the people! (*Walking about the room.*) Wherever is my stick? Where the devil's my stick? 425

HOVSTAD: What do you mean?

ASLAKSEN: Surely you would not——

DR. STOCKMANN (*standing still*): And now, suppose I don't give you a single farthing out of all my shares? You must remember that we rich folk don't like parting with our money. 430

HOVSTAD: And *you* must remember that this business of the shares can be represented in two ways.

DR. STOCKMANN: Yes, you're the man for that; if I don't come to the rescue of the *Messenger*, you'll certainly see the affair in an evil light; you'll hunt me down, I suppose—bait me, try to strangle me as the dog does the hare. 435

HOVSTAD: That is a law of nature—every animal wishes to live.

ASLAKSEN: And must take its food where he can find it, you know.

DR. STOCKMANN: Then, go and see if you can't find some out there in the gutter 440 (*rushes about the room*); for now, by Heaven! we'll see which is the strongest animal of us three. (*Finds umbrella and swings it.*) Now, look here——

HOVSTAD: You surely don't mean to use violence to us!

ASLAKSEN: I say, take care of that umbrella!   445

DR. STOCKMANN: Out at the window with you, Mr. Hovstad!

HOVSTAD (*by the door of the ante-room*):   Are you quite mad?

DR. STOCKMANN: Out at the window, Mr. Aslaksen! Jump, I tell you! As well first as last.

ASLAKSEN (*running around the writing-table*):   Be moderate, doctor. I'm a deli-   450
cate man; I can stand so little. (*Screams.*) Help! help!

(MRS. STOCKMANN, PETRA *and* HORSTER *enter from sitting-room.*)

MRS. STOCKMANN: Good Heavens! Thomas, whatever is the matter?

DR. STOCKMANN (*brandishing the umbrella*):   Jump out, I tell you. Out into the gutter.

HOVSTAD: An assault upon a defenseless man! I call you to witness, Captain   455
Horster.

> (*Rushes off through the sitting-room.*)

ASLAKSEN (*at his wit's end*):   If only I knew the local conditions——

> (*He slinks out through the sitting-room door.*)

MRS. STOCKMANN (*holding back the doctor*):   Now, do restrain yourself, Thomas!

DR. STOCKMANN (*throwing down umbrella*):   On my soul, they've got off after all.

MRS. STOCKMANN: But what do they want with you?   460

DR. STOCKMANN: You shall hear that later; I've other matters to think of now. (*Goes to table and writes on a card.*) Look here, Katrine, what's written here?

MRS. STOCKMANN: Three big *Noes*; what is that?

DR. STOCKMANN: That, too, you shall learn later. (*Handing card.*) There, Petra;   465
let the girl run to the Badger's with this as fast as she can. Be quick!

> (PETRA *goes with the card.*)

DR. STOCKMANN: Well, if I haven't had visits to-day from all the emissaries of the devil, I don't know! But now I'll sharpen my pen against them till it is a dagger; I will dip it into venom and gall; I'll hurl my inkstand straight at their skulls.   470

MRS. STOCKMANN: Yes, but we're to go away, Thomas!

(PETRA *returns.*)

DR. STOCKMANN: Well!

PETRA: All right.

DR. STOCKMANN: Good. Go away, do you say? No, I'll be damned if we do; we stay where we are, Katrine.   475

PETRA: Stay!

MRS. STOCKMANN: Here in the town?

DR. STOCKMANN: Yes, here is the field of battle; here it shall be fought; here I will conquer! Now, as soon as my trousers are sewn up I'll go out into the town and look after a house, for we must have a roof over our heads for the winter. 480

HORSTER: That you can have with me.

DR. STOCKMANN: Can I?

HORSTER: Yes, indeed, you can. I've room enough, and, besides, I'm hardly ever at home. 485

MRS. STOCKMANN: Ah! How good it is of you, Horster.

PETRA: Thank you.

DR. STOCKMANN (holding out hand): Thanks, thanks! So that trouble, too, is over. And this very day I shall start on my work in earnest. Ah! there is so much to root out here, Katrine! But it's a good thing I've all my time at my disposal now; yes, for you know I've had notice from the Baths. 490

MRS. STOCKMANN (sighing): Ah, yes! I was expecting that.

DR. STOCKMANN: ——And now they want to take my practice in the bargain. But let them! The poor I shall keep anyhow—those who can't pay anything; and, good Lord! it's they who have the most need of me. But, by Heaven! I swear they shall hear me; I will preach to them in season and out of season, as it is written somewhere. 495

MRS. STOCKMANN: Dear Thomas, I fancy you've seen what good preaching does.

DR. STOCKMANN: You really are ridiculous, Katrine. Should I let myself be beaten off the field by public opinion, and the compact majority, and such deviltry? No, thanks. Besides, what I want is so simple, so clear and straightforward. I only want to drive into the heads of these curs that the Liberals are the worst foes of free men; that party-programmes wring the necks of all young living truths; that considerations of expediency turn morality and righteousness upside down, until life is simply hideous. Yes, Captain Horster, don't you think I shall be able to make the people understand that? 500 505

HORSTER: Maybe; I don't know much about such matters myself.

DR. STOCKMANN: Well, you see—now you shall hear! It is the party-leaders who must be got rid of. For you see, a party-leader is just like a wolf—like a starving wolf; if he is to exist at all he needs so many small beasts a year. Just look at Hovstad and Aslaksen! How many small beasts do not they devour; or else they mangle them and knock them about, so that they're fit for nothing else but householders and subscribers to the People's Messenger. (Sits on edge of table.) Now, Katrine, just come here; see how bravely the sun shines to-day. And the blessed fresh spring air, too, blowing in upon me. 510 515

MRS. STOCKMANN: Yes, if only we could live on sunshine and spring air, Thomas!

DR. STOCKMANN: Well, you'll have to pinch and save where you can—then it'll be all right. That's my least concern. Now what does trouble me is, that 520

I don't see any man free and brave enough to dare to take up my work after me.

PETRA: Ah! don't think of that, father. You have time before you. Why, see, there are the boys already.

(EJLIF and MORTEN enter from the sitting-room.)

MRS. STOCKMANN: Have you had a holiday to-day?   525

MORTEN: No; but we had a fight with the other fellows in the playtime——

EJLIF: That's not true; it was the other fellows who fought us.

MORTEN: Yes, and so Mr. Rörlund said it would be best if we stayed at home for a few days.

DR. STOCKMANN (snapping his fingers and springing down from the table): Now   530
I have it, now I have it, on my soul! Never shall you set foot in school again!

THE BOYS: Never go to school!

MRS. STOCKMANN: But really, Thomas——

DR. STOCKMANN: Never, I say. I'll teach you myself—that is to say, I'll not teach   535
you any blessed thing.

MORTEN: Hurrah!

DR. STOCKMANN: —— —— but I'll make free, noble-minded men of you. Look
here, you'll have to help me, Petra.

PETRA: Yes, father, you may be sure I will.   540

DR. STOCKMANN: And we'll have our school in the room where they reviled me
as an enemy of the people. But we must have more pupils. I must have
at least twelve boys to begin with.

MRS. STOCKMANN: You'll never get them here in this town.

DR. STOCKMANN: We shall see that. (To the boys.) Don't you know any street-   545
boys—some regular ragamuffins——?

MORTEN: Yes, father, I know lots!

DR. STOCKMANN: That's all right; bring me a few specimens of them. I want to
experiment with the good-for-nothings for once—there may be some
good heads amongst them.   550

MORTEN: But what are we to do when we've become free and noble-minded
men?

DR. STOCKMANN: Drive all the wolves out to the far west, boys.

(EJLIF looks rather doubtful; MORTEN jumps about, shouting hurrah!)

MRS. STOCKMANN: If only the wolves don't drive you out, Thomas.

DR. STOCKMANN: You are quite mad, Katrine! Drive me away! now that I'm the   555
strongest man in the town.

MRS. STOCKMANN: The strongest now?

DR. STOCKMANN: Yes, I dare to say so bold a word; that now I'm one of the
strongest men upon earth.

MORTEN: I say, father!

DR. STOCKMANN (*in a subdued voice*): Hush! you must not speak about it yet; but I have made a great discovery.

MRS. STOCKMANN: What, again?

DR. STOCKMANN: Assuredly. (*Gathers them about him, and speaks confidently.*) You see, the fact is that the strongest man upon earth is he who stands   565 most alone.

MRS. STOCKMANN (*shakes her head smiling*): Ah! Thomas——!

PETRA (*taking his hands trustfully*): Father!

ANTON CHEKHOV

Uncle Vanya

Characters

ALEXANDER SEREBRAKOFF, *a retired professor*
HELENA, *his wife, twenty-seven years old*
SONIA, *his daughter by a former marriage*
MME. VOITSKAYA, *widow of a privy councillor, and mother of Serebrakoff's first*
wife
IVAN (VANYA) VOITSKI, *her son*
MICHAEL ASTROFF, *a doctor*
ILIA (WAFFLES) TELEGIN, *an impoverished landowner*
MARINA, *an old nurse*
A WORKMAN

The scene is laid on SEREBRAKOFF'S *country place*

ACT I

A country house on a terrace. In front of it a garden. In an avenue of trees, under an
old poplar, stands a table set for tea, with a samovar, etc. Some benches and
chairs stand near the table. On one of them is lying a guitar. A hammock is
swung near the table. It is three o'clock in the afternoon of a cloudy day.
MARINA, *a quiet, grey-haired, little old woman, is sitting at the table knitting a stocking.*
ASTROFF *is walking up and down near her.*

MARINA: *(Pouring some tea into a glass)* Take a little tea, my son.
ASTROFF: *(Takes the glass from her unwillingly)* Somehow, I don't seem to want
    any.
MARINA: Then will you have a little vodka instead?
ASTROFF: No, I don't drink vodka every day, and besides, it is too hot now.   5
    (A pause) Tell me, nurse, how long have we known each other?
MARINA: *(Thoughtfully)* Let me see, how long is it? Lord—help me to remember.
    You first came here, into our parts—let me think—when was it? Sonia's
    mother was still alive—it was two winters before she died; that was
    eleven years ago—*(thoughtfully)* perhaps more.   10
ASTROFF: Have I changed much since then?
MARINA: Oh, yes. You were handsome and young then, and now you are an old
    man and not handsome any more. You drink, too.
ASTROFF: Yes, ten years have made me another man. And why? Because I am

overworked. Nurse, I am on my feet from dawn till dusk. I know no rest; 15
at night I tremble under my blankets for fear of being dragged out to
visit some one who is sick; I have toiled without repose or a day's freedom since I have known you; could I help growing old? And then,
existence is tedious, anyway; it is a senseless, dirty business, this life, and
goes heavily. Every one about here is silly, and after living with them 20
for two or three years one grows silly oneself. It is inevitable. (*Twisting
his moustache*) See what a long moustache I have grown. A foolish, long
moustache. Yes, I am as silly as the rest, nurse, but not as stupid; no,
I have not grown stupid. Thank God, my brain is not addled yet, though
my feelings have grown numb. I ask nothing, I need nothing, I love no 25
one, unless it is yourself alone. (*He kisses her head*) I had a nurse just
like you when I was a child.

MARINA: Don't you want a bite of something to eat?

ASTROFF: No. During the third week of Lent I went to the epidemic at Malitskoi.
It was eruptive typhoid. The peasants were all lying side by side in their 30
huts, and the calves and pigs were running about the floor among the
sick. Such dirt there was, and smoke! Unspeakable! I slaved among those
people all day, not a crumb passed my lips, but when I got home there
was still no rest for me; a switchman was carried in from the railroad; I
laid him on the operating table and he went and died in my arms under 35
chloroform, and then my feelings that should have been deadened
awoke again, my conscience tortured me as if I had killed the man. I sat
down and closed my eyes—like this—and thought: will our descendants
two hundred years from now, for whom we are breaking the road,
remember to give us a kind word? No, nurse, they will forget. 40

MARINA: Man is forgetful, but God remembers.

ASTROFF: Thank you for that. You have spoken the truth.

(*Enter* VOITSKI *from the house. He has been asleep after dinner and looks rather di-
shevelled. He sits down on the bench and straightens his collar.*)

VOITSKI: H'm. Yes. (*A pause*) Yes.

ASTROFF: Have you been asleep?

VOITSKI: Yes, very much so. (*He yawns*) Ever since the Professor and his wife 45
have come, our daily life seems to have jumped the track. I sleep at the
wrong time, drink wine, and eat all sorts of messes for luncheon and
dinner. It isn't wholesome. Sonia and I used to work together and never
had an idle moment, but now Sonia works alone and I only eat and
drink and sleep. Something is wrong. 50

MARINA: (*Shaking her head*) Such a confusion in the house! The Professor gets
up at twelve, the samovar is kept boiling all the morning, and everything has to wait for him. Before they came we used to have dinner at
one o'clock, like everybody else, but now we have it at seven. The
Professor sits up all night writing and reading, and suddenly, at two- 55

o'clock, there goes the bell! Heavens, what is that? The Professor wants some tea! Wake the servants, light the samovar! Lord, what disorder!

ASTROFF: Will they be here long?

VOITSKI: A hundred years! The Professor has decided to make his home here.

MARINA: Look at this now! The samovar has been on the table for two hours,   60
and they are all out walking!

VOITSKI: All right, don't get excited; here they come.

(Voices are heard approaching. SEREBRAKOFF, HELENA, SONIA, and TELEGIN come in from the depths of the garden, returning from their walk.)

SEREBRAKOFF: Superb! Superb! What beautiful views!

TELEGIN: They are wonderful, your Excellency.

SONIA: To-morrow we shall go into the woods, shall we, papa?   65

VOITSKI: Ladies and gentlemen, tea is ready.

SEREBRAKOFF: Won't you please be good enough to send my tea into the library? I still have some work to finish.

SONIA: I am sure you will love the woods.

(HELENA, SEREBRAKOFF, and SONIA go into the house. TELEGIN sits down at the table beside MARINA.)

VOITSKI: There goes our learned scholar on a hot, sultry day like this, in his   70
overcoat and goloshes and carrying an umbrella!

ASTROFF: He is trying to take good care of his health.

VOITSKI: How lovely she is! How lovely! I have never in my life seen a more beautiful woman.

TELEGIN: Do you know, Marina, that as I walk in the fields or in the shady   75
garden, as I look at this table here, my heart swells with unbounded happiness. The weather is enchanting, the birds are singing, we are all living in peace and contentment—what more could the soul desire?

(Takes a glass of tea.)

VOITSKI: (Dreaming) Such eyes—a glorious woman!

ASTROFF: Come, Ivan, tell us something.   80

VOITSKI: (Indolently) What shall I tell you?

ASTROFF: Haven't you any news for us?

VOITSKI: No, it is all stale. I am just the same as usual, or perhaps worse, because I have become lazy. I don't do anything now but croak like an old raven. My mother, the old magpie, is still chattering about the emancipation of   85
woman, with one eye on her grave and the other on her learned books, in which she is always looking for the dawn of a new life.

ASTROFF: And the Professor?

VOITSKI: The professor sits in his library from morning till night, as usual—

"Straining the mind, wrinkling the brow,   90
We write, write, write,

Without respite
Or hope of praise in the future or now."

Poor paper! He ought to write his autobiography; he would make a really splendid subject for a book! Imagine it, the life of a retired professor, as stale as a piece of hardtack, tortured by gout, headaches, and rheumatism, his liver bursting with jealousy and envy, living on the estate of his first wife, although he hates it, because he can't afford to live in town. He is everlastingly whining about his hard lot, though, as a matter of fact, he is extraordinarily lucky. He is the son of a common deacon and has attained the professor's chair, become the son-in-law of a senator, is called "your Excellency," and so on. But I'll tell you something; the man has been writing on art for twenty-five years, and he doesn't know the very first thing about it. For twenty-five years he has been chewing on other men's thoughts about realism, naturalism, and all such foolishness; for twenty-five years he has been reading and writing things that clever men have long known and stupid ones are not interested in; for twenty-five years he has been making his imaginary mountains out of molehills. And just think of the man's self-conceit and presumption all this time! For twenty-five years he has been masquerading in false clothes and has now retired, absolutely unknown to any living soul; and yet see him! stalking across the earth like a demi-god!

ASTROFF: I believe you envy him.

VOITSKI: Yes, I do. Look at the success he has had with women! Don Juan himself was not more favoured. His first wife, who was my sister, was a beautiful, gentle being, as pure as the blue heaven there above us, noble, greathearted, with more admirers than he has pupils, and she loved him as only beings of angelic purity can love those who are as pure and beautiful as themselves. His mother-in-law, my mother, adores him to this day, and he still inspires a sort of worshipful awe in her. His second wife is, as you see, a brilliant beauty; she married him in his old age and has surrendered all the glory of her beauty and freedom to him. Why? What for?

ASTROFF: Is she faithful to him?

VOITSKI: Yes, unfortunately she is.

ASTROFF: Why "unfortunately"?

VOITSKI: Because such fidelity is false and unnatural, root and branch. It sounds well, but there is no logic in it. It is thought immoral for a woman to deceive an old husband whom she hates, but quite moral for her to strangle her poor youth in her breast and banish every vital desire from her heart.

TELEGIN: (In a tearful voice) Vanya, I don't like to hear you talk so. Listen, Vanya; every one who betrays husband or wife is faithless, and could also betray his country.

VOITSKI: (Crossly) Turn off the tap, Waffles.

TELEGIN: No, allow me, Vanya. My wife ran away with a lover on the day after our wedding, because my exterior was unprepossessing. I have never failed in my duty since then. I love her and am true to her to this day. I help her all I can and have given my fortune to educate the daughter of herself and her lover. I have forfeited my happiness, but I have kept 140 my pride. And she? Her youth has fled, her beauty has faded according to the laws of nature, and her lover is dead. What has she kept?

(HELENA and SONIA *come in; after them comes* MME. VOITSKAYA *carrying a book. She sits down and begins to read. Some one hands her a glass of tea which she drinks without looking up.*)

SONIA: (*Hurriedly, to the nurse*) There are some peasants waiting out there. Go and see what they want. I shall pour the tea.
(*Pours out some glasses of tea.*)
(MARINA *goes out.* HELENA *takes a glass and sits drinking in the hammock.*)
ASTROFF: I have come to see your husband. You wrote me that he had rheuma- 145 tism and I know not what else, and that he was very ill, but he appears to be as lively as a cricket.
HELENA: He had a fit of the blues yesterday evening and complained of pains in his legs, but he seems all right again to-day.
ASTROFF: And I galloped over here twenty miles at breakneck speed! No matter, 150 though, it is not the first time. Once here, however, I am going to stay until to-morrow, and at any rate sleep *quantum satis.*
SONIA: Oh, splendid! You so seldom spend the night with us. Have you had dinner yet?
ASTROFF: No. 155
SONIA: Good. So you will have it with us. We dine at seven now. (*Drinks her tea*) This tea is cold!
TELEGIN: Yes, the samovar has grown cold.
HELENA: Don't mind, Monsieur Ivan, we will drink cold tea, then.
TELEGIN: I beg your pardon, my name is not Ivan, but Ilia, ma'am—Ilia Telegin, 160 or Waffles, as I am sometimes called on account of my pock-marked face. I am Sonia's godfather, and his Excellency, your husband, knows me very well. I now live with you, ma'am, on this estate, and perhaps you will be so good as to notice that I dine with you every day.
SONIA: He is our great help, our right-hand man. (*Tenderly*) Dear godfather, 165 let me pour you some tea.
MME. VOITSKAYA: Oh! Oh!
SONIA: What is it, grandmother?
MME. VOITSKAYA: I forgot to tell Alexander—I have lost my memory—I received a letter to-day from Paul Alexevitch in Kharkoff. He has sent me a new 170 pamphlet.
ASTROFF: Is it interesting?

MME. VOITSKAYA: Yes, but strange. He refutes the very theories which he defended seven years ago. It is appalling!

VOITSKI: There is nothing appalling about it. Drink your tea, mamma.   175

MME. VOITSKAYA: It seems you never want to listen to what I have to say. Pardon me, Jean, but you have changed so in the last year that I hardly know you. You used to be a man of settled convictions and had an illuminating personality——

VOITSKI: Oh, yes. I had an illuminating personality, which illuminated no one.   180 (*A pause*) I had an illuminating personality! You couldn't say anything more biting. I am forty-seven years old. Until last year I endeavoured, as you do now, to blind my eyes by your pedantry to the truths of life. But now— Oh, if you only knew! If you knew how I lie awake at night, heartsick and angry, to think how stupidly I have wasted my time when   185 I might have been winning from life everything which my old age now forbids.

SONIA: Uncle Vanya, how dreary!

MME. VOITSKAYA: (*To her son*) You speak as if your former convictions were somehow to blame, but you yourself, not they, were at fault. You have   190 forgotten that a conviction, in itself, is nothing but a dead letter. You should have done something.

VOITSKI: Done something! Not every man is capable of being a writer *perpetuum mobile* like your Herr Professor.

MME. VOITSKAYA: What do you mean by that?   195

SONIA: (*Imploringly*) Mother! Uncle Vanya! I entreat you!

VOITSKI: I am silent. I apologise and am silent.   (*A pause.*)

HELENA: What a fine day! Not too hot.   (*A pause.*)

VOITSKI: A fine day to hang oneself.

(TELEGIN *tunes the guitar.* MARINA *appears near the house, calling the chickens.*)

MARINA: Chick, chick, chick!   200

SONIA: What did the peasants want, nurse?

MARINA: The same old thing, the same old nonsense. Chick, chick, chick!

SONIA: Why are you calling the chickens?

MARINA: The speckled hen has disappeared with her chicks. I am afraid the crows have got her.   205

(TELEGIN *plays a polka. All listen in silence. Enter* WORKMAN.)

WORKMAN: Is the doctor here? (*To* ASTROFF) Excuse me, sir, but I have been sent to fetch you.

ASTROFF: Where are you from?

WORKMAN: The factory.

ASTROFF: (*Annoyed*) Thank you. There is nothing for it, then, but to go. (*Looking   210 around him for his cap*) Damn it, this is annoying!

SONIA: Yes, it is too bad, really. You must come back to dinner from the factory.

ASTROFF: No, I won't be able to do that. It will be too late. Now where, where —(To the WORKMAN) look here, my man, get me a glass of vodka, will 215 you? (The WORKMAN goes out) Where—where—(Finds his cap) One of the characters in Ostroff's plays is a man with a long moustache and short wits, like me. However, let me bid you good-bye, ladies and gentlemen. (To HELENA) I should be really delighted if you would come to see me some day with Miss Sonia. My estate is small, but if you are interested 220 in such things I should like to show you a nursery and seedbed whose like you will not find within a thousand miles of here. My place is surrounded by government forests. The forester is old and always ailing, so I superintend almost all the work myself.

HELENA: I have always heard that you were very fond of the woods. Of course 225 one can do a great deal of good by helping to preserve them, but does not that work interfere with your real calling?

ASTROFF: God alone knows what a man's real calling is.

HELENA: And do you find it interesting?

ASTROFF: Yes, very. 230

VOITSKI: (Sarcastically) Oh, extremely!

HELENA: You are still young, not over thirty-six or seven, I should say, and I suspect that the woods do not interest you as much as you say they do. I should think you would find them monotonous.

SONIA: No, the work is thrilling. Dr. Astroff watches over the old woods and 235 sets out new plantations every year, and he has already received a diploma and a bronze medal. If you will listen to what he can tell you, you will agree with him entirely. He says that forests are the ornaments of the earth, that they teach mankind to understand beauty and attune his mind to lofty sentiments. Forests temper a stern climate, and in 240 countries where the climate is milder, less strength is wasted in the battle with nature, and the people are kind and gentle. The inhabitants of such countries are handsome, tractable, sensitive, graceful in speech and gesture. Their philosophy is joyous, art and science blossom among them, their treatment of women is full of exquisite nobility—— 245

VOITSKI: (Laughing) Bravo! Bravo! All that is very pretty, but it is also unconvincing. So, my friend (To ASTROFF) you must let me go on burning firewood in my stoves and building my sheds of planks.

ASTROFF: You can burn peat in your stoves and build your sheds of stone. Oh, I don't object, of course, to cutting wood from necessity, but why destroy 250 the forests? The woods of Russia are trembling under the blows of the axe. Millions of trees have perished. The homes of the wild animals and birds have been desolated; the rivers are shrinking, and many beautiful landscapes are gone forever. And why? Because men are too lazy and stupid to stoop down and pick up their fuel from the ground. (To 255 HELENA) Am I not right, Madame? Who but a stupid barbarian could burn so much beauty in his stove and destroy that which he cannot make? Man is endowed with reason and the power to create, so that he may increase that which has been given him, but until now he has not created, but demolished. The forests are disappearing, the rivers are running dry, the game is exterminated, the climate is spoiled, and the earth becomes poorer and uglier every day. (*To* VOITSKI) I read irony in your eye; you do not take what I am saying seriously, and—and—after all, it may very well be nonsense. But when I pass peasant-forests that I have preserved from the axe, or hear the rustling of the young plantations set out with my own hands, I feel as if I had had some small share in improving the climate, and that if mankind is happy a thousand years from now I will have been a little bit responsible for their happiness. When I plant a little birch tree and then see it budding into young green and swaying in the wind, my heart swells with pride and I—(*Sees the* WORKMAN, *who is bringing him a glass of vodka on a tray*) however—(*He drinks*) I must be off. Probably it is all nonsense, anyway. Good-bye.

(*He goes toward the house. SONIA takes his arm and goes with him.*)

SONIA: When are you coming to see us again?

ASTROFF: I can't say.

SONIA: In a month?

(ASTROFF *and* SONIA *go into the house.* HELENA *and* VOITSKI *walk over to the terrace.*)

HELENA: You have behaved shockingly again. Ivan, what sense was there in teasing your mother and talking about *perpetuum mobile*? And at breakfast you quarreled with Alexander again. Really, your behaviour is too petty.

VOITSKI: But if I hate him?

HELENA: You hate Alexander without reason; he is like every one else, and no worse than you are.

VOITSKI: If you could only see your face, your gestures! Oh, how tedious your life must be.

HELENA: It is tedious, yes, and dreary! You all abuse my husband and look on me with compassion; you think, "Poor woman, she is married to an old man." How well I understand your compassion! As Astroff said just now, see how you thoughtlessly destroy the forests, so that there will soon be none left. So you also destroy mankind, and soon fidelity and purity and self-sacrifice will have vanished with the woods. Why cannot you look calmly at a woman unless she is yours? Because, the doctor was right, you are all possessed by a devil of destruction; you have no mercy on the woods or the birds or on women or on one another.

VOITSKI: I don't like your philosophy.

HELENA: That doctor has a sensitive, weary face—an interesting face. Sonia evidently likes him, and she is in love with him, and I can understand it. This is the third time he has been here since I have come, and I have not had a real talk with him yet or made much of him. He thinks I am disagreeable. Do you know, Ivan, the reason you and I are such friends? I think it is because we are both lonely and unfortunate. Yes, unfortunate. 300 Don't look at me in that way, I don't like it.

VOITSKI: How can I look at you otherwise when I love you? You are my joy, my life, and my youth. I know that my chances of being loved in return are infinitely small, do not exist, but I ask nothing of you. Only let me look at you, listen to your voice—— 305

HELENA: Hush, some one will overhear you.

(They go toward the house.)

VOITSKI: *(Following her)* Let me speak to you of my love, do not drive me away, and this alone will be my greatest happiness!

HELENA: Ah! This is agony!

(TELEGIN strikes the strings of his guitar and plays a polka. MME. VOITSKAYA writes something on the leaves of her pamphlet.)

The curtain falls.

ACT II

The dining-room of SEREBRAKOFF'S house. It is night. The tapping of the WATCHMAN'S rattle is heard in the garden. SEREBRAKOFF is dozing in an arm-chair by an open window and HELENA is sitting beside him, also half asleep.

SEREBRAKOFF: *(Rousing himself)* Who is here? Is it you, Sonia?

HELENA: It is I.

SEREBRAKOFF: Oh, it is you, Nelly. This pain is intolerable.

HELENA: Your shawl has slipped down. *(She wraps up his legs in the shawl)* Let me shut the window. 5

SEREBRAKOFF: No, leave it open; I am suffocating. I dreamt just now that my left leg belonged to some one else, and it hurt so that I woke. I don't believe this is gout, it is more like rheumatism. What time is it?

HELENA: Half past twelve. *(A pause.)*

SEREBRAKOFF: I want you to look for Batushka's works in the library to-morrow. 10 I think we have him.

HELENA: What is that?

SEREBRAKOFF: Look for Batushka to-morrow morning; we used to have him, I remember. Why do I find it so hard to breathe?

HELENA: You are tired; this is the second night you have had no sleep. 15

SEREBRAKOFF: They say that Turgenieff got angina of the heart from gout. I am afraid I am getting angina too. Oh, damn this horrible, accursed old age! Ever since I have been old I have been hateful to myself, and I am sure, hateful to you all as well.

HELENA: You speak as if we were to blame for your being old.   20

SEREBRAKOFF: I am more hateful to you than to any one.

(HELENA *gets up and walks away from him, sitting down at a distance.*)

SEREBRAKOFF: You are quite right, of course. I am not an idiot; I can understand you. You are young and healthy and beautiful, and longing for life, and I am an old dotard, almost a dead man already. Don't I know it? Of course I see that it is foolish for me to live so long, but wait! I shall   25
soon set you all free. My life cannot drag on much longer.

HELENA: You are overtaxing my powers of endurance. Be quiet, for God's sake!

SEREBRAKOFF: It appears that, thanks to me, everybody's power of endurance is being overtaxed; everybody is miserable, only I am blissfully triumphant. Oh, yes, of course!   30

HELENA: Be quiet! You are torturing me.

SEREBRAKOFF: I torture everybody. Of course.

HELENA: (*Weeping*) This is unbearable! Tell me, what is it you want me to do?

SEREBRAKOFF: Nothing.

HELENA: Then be quiet, please.   35

SEREBRAKOFF: It is funny that everybody listens to Ivan and his old idiot of a mother, but the moment I open my lips you all begin to feel ill-treated. You can't even stand the sound of my voice. Even if I am hateful, even if I am a selfish tyrant, haven't I the right to be one at my age? Haven't I deserved it? Haven't I, I ask you, the right to be respected, now that I am   40
old?

HELENA: No one is disputing your rights. (*The window slams in the wind*) The wind is rising, I must shut the window. (*She shuts it*) We shall have rain in a moment. Your rights have never been questioned by anybody.

(*The* WATCHMAN *in the garden sounds his rattle.*)

SEREBRAKOFF: I have spent my life working in the interests of learning. I am used   45
to my library and the lecture hall and to the esteem and admiration of my colleagues. Now I suddenly find myself plunged in this wilderness, condemned to see the same stupid people from morning till night and listen to their futile conversation. I want to live; I long for success and fame and the stir of the world, and here I am in exile! Oh, it is dreadful   50
to spend every moment grieving for the lost past, to see the success of others and sit here with nothing to do but to fear death. I cannot stand it! It is more than I can bear. And you will not even forgive me for being old!

HELENA: Wait, have patience; I shall be old myself in four or five years.

(SONIA *comes in.*)

SONIA: Father, you sent for Dr. Astroff, and now when he comes you refuse to see him. It is not nice to give a man so much trouble for nothing.

SEREBRAKOFF: What do I care about your Astroff? He understands medicine about as well as I understand astronomy.

SONIA: We can't send for the whole medical faculty, can we, to treat your   60
gout?

SEREBRAKOFF: I won't talk to that madman!

SONIA: Do as you please. It's all the same to me.

(*She sits down.*)

SEREBRAKOFF: What time is it?

HELENA: One o'clock.   65

SEREBRAKOFF: It is stifling in here. Sonia, hand me that bottle on the table.

SONIA: Here it is.   (*She hands him a bottle of medicine.*)

SEREBRAKOFF: (*Crossly*) No, not that one! Can't you understand me? Can't I ask you to do a thing?

SONIA: Please don't be captious with me. Some people may like it, but you   70
must spare me, if you please, because I don't. Besides, I haven't the time; we are cutting the hay to-morrow and I must get up early.

(VOITSKI *comes in dressed in a long gown and carrying a candle.*)

VOITSKI: A thunderstorm is coming up. (*The lightning flashes*) There it is! Go to bed, Helena and Sonia. I have come to take your place.

SEREBRAKOFF: (*Frightened*) No, no, no! Don't leave me alone with him! Oh,   75
don't. He will begin to lecture me.

VOITSKI: But you must give them a little rest. They have not slept for two nights.

SEREBRAKOFF: Then let them go to bed, but you go away too! Thank you. I implore you to go. For the sake of our former friendship do not protest against going. We will talk some other time——   80

VOITSKI: Our former friendship! Our former——

SONIA: Hush, Uncle Vanya!

SEREBRAKOFF: (*To his wife*) My darling, don't leave me alone with him. He will begin to lecture me.

VOITSKI: This is ridiculous.   85

(MARINA *comes in carrying a candle.*)

SONIA: You must go to bed, nurse, it is late.

MARINA: I haven't cleared away the tea things. Can't go to bed yet.

SEREBRAKOFF: No one can go to bed. They are all worn out, only I enjoy perfect happiness.

MARINA: (*Goes up to* SEREBRAKOFF *and speaks tenderly*) What's the matter, 90
master? Does it hurt? My own legs are aching too, oh, so badly. (*Arranges his shawl about his legs*) You have had this illness such a long time. Sonia's dead mother used to stay awake with you too, and wear herself out for you. She loved you dearly. (*A pause*) Old people want to be pitied as much as young ones, but nobody cares about them some- 95
how. (*She kisses* SEREBRAKOFF'S *shoulder*) Come, master, let me give you some linden-tea and warm your poor feet for you. I shall pray to God for you.

SEREBRAKOFF: (*Touched*) Let us go, Marina.

MARINA: My own feet are aching so badly, oh, so badly! (*She and* SONIA *lead* 100
SEREBRAKOFF *out*) Sonia's mother used to wear herself out with sorrow and weeping. You were still little and foolish then, Sonia. Come, come, master.

(SEREBRAKOFF, SONIA *and* MARINA *go out.*)

HELENA: I am absolutely exhausted by him, and can hardly stand.

VOITSKI: You are exhausted by him, and I am exhausted by my own self. I have 105
not slept for three nights.

HELENA: Something is wrong in this house. Your mother hates everything but her pamphlets and the professor; the professor is vexed, he won't trust me, and fears you; Sonia is angry with her father, and with me, and hasn't spoken to me for two weeks; I am at the end of my strength, and 110
have come near bursting into tears at least twenty times to-day. Something is wrong in this house.

VOITSKI: Leave speculating alone.

HELENA: You are cultured and intelligent, Ivan, and you surely understand that the world is not destroyed by villains and conflagrations, but by hate 115
and malice and all this spiteful tattling. It is your duty to make peace, and not to growl at everything.

VOITSKI: Help me first to make peace with myself. My darling! (*Seizes her hand.*)

HELENA: Let go! (*She drags her hand away*) Go away!

VOITSKI: Soon the rain will be over, and all nature will sigh and awake re- 120
freshed. Only I am not refreshed by the storm. Day and night the thought haunts me like a fiend, that my life is lost for ever. My past does not count, because I frittered it away on trifles, and the present has so terribly miscarried! What shall I do with my life and my love? What is to become of them? This wonderful feeling of mine will be 125
wasted and lost as a ray of sunlight is lost that falls into a dark chasm.

HELENA: I am as it were benumbed when you speak to me of your love, and I don't know how to answer you. Forgive me, I have nothing to say to you. (*She tries to go out*) Good-night!

VOITSKI: (*Barring the way*) If you only knew how I am tortured by the thought 130
that beside me in this house is another life that is being lost forever—it is yours! What are you waiting for? What accursed philosophy stands in your way? Oh, understand, understand——

741

HELENA: (*Looking at him intently*) Ivan, you are drunk!

VOITSKI: Perhaps. Perhaps.

HELENA: Where is the doctor?

VOITSKI: In there, spending the night with me. Perhaps I am drunk, perhaps I am; nothing is impossible.

HELENA: Have you just been drinking together? Why do you do that?

VOITSKI: Because in that way I get a taste of life. Let me do it, Helena!

HELENA: You never used to drink, and you never used to talk so much. Go to bed, I am tired of you.

VOITSKI: (*Falling on his knees before her*) My Sweetheart, my beautiful one——

HELENA: (*Angrily*) Leave me alone! Really, this has become too disagreeable.

(HELENA *goes out. A pause.*)

VOITSKI: (*Alone*) she is gone! I met her first ten years ago, at her sister's house, when she was seventeen and I was thirty-seven. Why did I not fall in love with her then and propose to her? It would have been so easy! And now she would have been my wife. Yes, we would both have been waked to-night by the thunderstorm, and she would have been frightened, but I would have held her in my arms and whispered: "Don't be afraid! I am here." Oh, enchanting dream, so sweet that I laugh to think of it. (*He laughs*) But my God! My head reels! Why am I so old? Why won't she understand me? I hate all that rhetoric of hers, that morality of indolence, that absurb talk about the destruction of the world—(*A pause*) Oh, how I have been deceived! For years I have worshipped that miserable gout-ridden professor. Sonia and I have squeezed this estate dry for his sake. We have bartered our butter and curds and peas like misers, and have never kept a morsel for ourselves, so that we could scrape enough pennies together to send to him. I was proud of him and of his learning; I received all his words and writings as inspired, and now? Now he has retired, and what is the total of his life? A blank! He is absolutely unknown, and his fame has burst like a soapbubble. I have been deceived; I see that now, basely deceived.

(ASTROFF *comes in. He has his coat on, but is without his waistcoat or collar, and is slightly drunk.* TELEGIN *follows him, carrying a guitar.*)

ASTROFF: Play!

TELEGIN: But every one is asleep.

ASTROFF: Play!

(TELEGIN *begins to play softly.*)

ASTROFF: Are you alone here? No woman about?

(*Sings with his arms akimbo.*)

"The hut is cold, the fire is dead;
Where shall the master lay his head?"

The thunderstorm woke me. It was a heavy shower. What time is it? 170

VOITSKI: The devil only knows.

ASTROFF: I thought I heard Helena's voice.

VOITSKI: She was here a moment ago.

ASTROFF: What a beautiful woman! (*Looking at the medicine bottles on the table*) Medicine, is it? What a variety we have; prescriptions from 175
Moscow, from Kharkoff, from Tula! Why, he has been pestering all the towns of Russia with his gout! Is he ill, or simply shamming?

VOITSKI: He is really ill.

ASTROFF: What is the matter with you to-night? You seem sad. Is it because you are sorry for the professor? 180

VOITSKI: Leave me alone.

ASTROFF: Or in love with the professor's wife?

VOITSKI: She is my friend.

ASTROFF: Already?

VOITSKI: What do you mean by "already"? 185

ASTROFF: A woman can only become a man's friend after having first been his acquaintance and then his beloved—then she becomes his friend.

VOITSKI: What vulgar philosophy!

ASTROFF: What do you mean? Yes, I must confess I am getting vulgar, but then, you see, I am drunk. I usually only drink like this once a month. 190
At such times my audacity and temerity know no bounds. I feel capable of anything. I attempt the most difficult operations and do them magnificently. The most brilliant plans for the future take shape in my head. I am on longer a poor fool of a doctor, but mankind's greatest benefactor. I evolve my own system of philosophy and all of you seem to crawl 195
at my feet like so many insects or microbes. (*To* TELEGIN) Play, Waffles!

TELEGIN: My dear boy, I would with all my heart, but do listen to reason; everybody in the house is asleep.

ASTROFF: Play!

(TELEGIN *plays softly.*)

ASTROFF: I want a drink. Come, we still have some brandy left. And then, as 200
soon as it is day, you will come home with me. (*He sees* SONIA, *who comes in at that moment.*)

ASTROFF: I beg your pardon, I have no collar on.

(*He goes out quickly, followed by* TELEGIN.)

SONIA: Uncle Vanya, you and the doctor have been drinking! The good fellows have been getting together! It is all very well for him, he has always 205
done it, but why do you follow his example? It looks dreadfully at your age.

VOITSKI: Age has nothing to do with it. When real life is wanting one must create an illusion. It is better than nothing.

SONIA: Our hay is all cut and rotting in these daily rains, and here you are 210
busy creating illusions! You have given up the farm altogether. I have
done all the work alone until I am at the end of my strength—(*Frightened*) Uncle! Your eyes are full of tears!

VOITSKI: Tears? Nonsense, there are no tears in my eyes. You looked at me
then just as your dead mother used to, my darling—(*He eagerly kisses* 215
her face and hands) My sister, my dearest sister, where are you now?
Ah, if you only knew, if you only knew!

SONIA: If she only knew what, Uncle?

VOITSKI: My heart is bursting. It is awful. No matter, though. I must go.

(*He goes out.*)

SONIA: (*Knocks at the door*) Dr. Astroff! Are you awake? Please come here for 220
a minute.

ASTROFF: (*Behind the door*) In a moment.

(*He appears in a few seconds. He has put on his collar and waistcoat.*)

ASTROFF: What do you want?

SONIA: Drink as much as you please yourself, if you don't find it revolting, but
I implore you not to let my uncle do it. It is bad for him. 225

ASTROFF: Very well; we won't drink any more. I am going home at once. That
is settled. It will be dawn by the time the horses are harnessed.

SONIA: It is still raining; wait till morning.

ASTROFF: The storm is blowing over. This is only the edge of it. I must go. And
please don't ask me to come and see your father any more. I tell him 230
he has gout, and he says it is rheumatism. I tell him to lie down, and he
sits up. To-day he refused to see me at all.

SONIA: He has been spoilt. (*She looks in the sideboard*) Won't you have a bite
to eat?

ASTROFF: Yes, please. I believe I will. 235

SONIA: I love to eat at night. I am sure we shall find something in here. They
say that he has made a great many conquests in his life, and that the
women have spoiled him. Here is some cheese for you.

(*They stand eating by the sideboard.*)

ASTROFF: I haven't eaten anything to-day. Your father has a very difficult
nature. (*He takes a bottle out of the sideboard*) May I? (*He pours him-* 240
self a glass of vodka) We are alone here, and I can speak frankly. Do
you know, I could not stand living in this house for even a month? This
atmosphere would stifle me. There is your father, entirely absorbed in his
books, and his gout; there is your Uncle Vanya with his hypochondria,
your grandmother, and finally, your step-mother—— 245

SONIA: What about her?

ASTROFF: A human being should be entirely beautiful: the face, the clothes, the
mind, the thoughts. Your step-mother is, of course, beautiful to look at,

but don't you see? She does nothing but sleep and eat and walk and bewitch us, and that is all. She has no responsibilities, everything is done for her—am I not right? And an idle life can never be a pure one. (*A pause*) However, I may be judging her too severely. Like your Uncle Vanya, I am discontented, and so we are both grumblers.

SONIA: Aren't you satisfied with life?

ASTROFF: I like life as life, but I hate and despise it in a little Russian country village, and as far as my own personal life goes, by heaven! there is absolutely no redeeming feature about it. Haven't you noticed if you are riding through a dark wood at night and see a little light shining ahead, how you forget your fatigue and the darkness and the sharp twigs that whip your face? I work, that you know—as no one else in the country works. Fate beats me on without rest; at times I suffer unendurably and I see no light ahead. I have no hope; I do not like people. It is long since I have loved any one.

SONIA: You love no one?

ASTROFF: Not a soul. I only feel a sort of tenderness for your old nurse for old-times' sake. The peasants are all alike; they are stupid and live in dirt, and the educated people are hard to get along with. One gets tired of them. All our good friends are petty and shallow and see no farther than their own noses; in one word, they are dull. Those that have brains are hysterical, devoured with a mania for self-analysis. They whine, they hate, they pick faults everywhere with unhealthy sharpness. They sneak up to me sideways, look at me out of a corner of the eye, and say: "That man is a lunatic," "That man is a wind-bag." Or, if they don't know what else to label me with, they say I am strange. I like the woods; that is strange. I don't eat meat; that is strange, too. Simple, natural relations between man and man or man and nature do not exist. (*He tries to go out;* SONIA *prevents him.*)

SONIA: I beg you, I implore you, not to drink any more!

ASTROFF: Why not?

SONIA: It is so unworthy of you. You are well-bred, your voice is sweet, you are even—more than any one I know—handsome. Why do you want to resemble the common people that drink and play cards? Oh, don't, I beg you! You always say that people do not create anything, but only destroy what heaven has given them. Why, oh, why, do you destroy yourself? Oh, don't, I implore you not to! I entreat you!

ASTROFF: (*Gives her his hand*) I won't drink any more.

SONIA: Promise me.

ASTROFF: I give you my word of honour.

SONIA: (*Squeezing his hand*) Thank you.

ASTROFF: I have done with it. You see, I am perfectly sober again, and so I shall stay till the end of my life. (*He looks at his watch*) But, as I was saying, life holds nothing for me; my race is run. I am old, I am tired,

I am trivial; my sensibilities are dead. I could never attach myself to any one again. I love no one, and—never shall! Beauty alone has the power to touch me still. I am deeply moved by it. Helena could turn my head in a day if she wanted to, but that is not love, that is not affection—— 295

(He shudders and covers his face with his hands.)

SONIA: What is it?

ASTROFF: Nothing. During Lent one of my patients died under chloroform.

SONIA: It is time to forget that. (A pause) Tell me, doctor, if I had a friend or a younger sister, and if you knew that she, well—loved you, what would 300 you do?

ASTROFF: (Shrugging his shoulders) I don't know. I don't think I should do anything. I should make her understand that I could not return her love—however, my mind is not bothered about those things now. I must start at once if I am ever to get off. Good-bye, my dear girl. At this rate we 305 shall stand here talking till morning. (He shakes hands with her) I shall go out through the sitting-room, because I am afraid your uncle might detain me. (He goes out.)

SONIA: (Alone) Not a word! His heart and soul are still locked from me, and yet for some reason I am strangely happy. I wonder why? (She laughs 310 with pleasure) I told him that he was well-bred and handsome and that his voice was sweet. Was that a mistake? I can still feel his voice vibrating in the air; it caresses me. (Wringing her hands) Oh! how terrible it is to be plain! I am plain, I know it. As I came out of church last Sunday I overheard a woman say, "She is a dear, noble girl, but what a pity 315 she is so ugly!" So ugly!

(HELENA comes in and throws open the window.)

HELENA: The storm is over. What delicious air! (A pause) Where is the doctor?

SONIA: He has gone.

(A pause.)

HELENA: Sonia!

SONIA: Yes? 320

HELENA: How much longer are you going to sulk at me? We have not hurt each other. Why not be friends? We have had enough of this.

SONIA: I myself— (She embraces HELENA) Let us make peace.

HELENA: With all my heart.

(They are both moved.)

SONIA: Has papa gone to bed? 325

HELENA: No, he is sitting up in the drawing-room. Heaven knows what reason you and I had for not speaking to each other for weeks. (Sees the open sideboard) Who left the sideboard open?

SONIA: Dr. Astroff has just had supper.

HELENA: There is some wine. Let us seal our friendship. 330

SONIA: Yes, let us.

HELENA: Out of one glass. (*She fills a wine-glass*) So, we are friends, are we?

SONIA: Yes. (*They drink and kiss each other*) I have long wanted to make friends, but somehow, I was ashamed to. (*She weeps.*)

HELENA: Why are you crying?   335

SONIA: I don't know. It is nothing.

HELENA: There, there, don't cry. (*She weeps*) Silly! Now I am crying too. (*A pause*) You are angry with me because I seem to have married your father for his money, but don't believe the gossip you hear. I swear to you I married him for love. I was fascinated by his fame and learning.   340 I know now that it was not real love, but it seemed real at the time. I am innocent, and yet your clever, suspicious eyes have been punishing me for an imaginary crime ever since my marriage.

SONIA: Peace, peace! Let us forget the past.

HELENA: You must not look so at people. It is not becoming to you. You must   345 trust people, or life becomes impossible.

SONIA: Tell me truly, as a friend, are you happy?

HELENA: Truly, no.

SONIA: I knew it. One more question: do you wish your husband were young?

HELENA: What a child you are! Of course I do. Go on, ask something else.   350

SONIA: Do you like the doctor?

HELENA: Yes, very much indeed.

SONIA: (*Laughing*) I have a stupid face, haven't I? He has just gone out, and his voice is still in my ears; I hear his step; I see his face in the dark window. Let me say all I have in my heart! But no, I cannot speak of it   355 so loudly. I am ashamed. Come to my room and let me tell you there. I seem foolish to you, don't I? Talk to me of him.

HELENA: What can I say?

SONIA: He is clever. He can do everything. He can cure the sick, and plant woods.   360

HELENA: It is not a question of medicine and woods, my dear, he is a man of genius. Do you know what that means? It means he is brave, profound, and of clear insight. He plants a tree and his mind travels a thousand years into the future, and he sees visions of the happiness of the human race. People like him are rare and should be loved. What if he does   365 drink and act roughly at times? A man of genius cannot be a saint in Russia. There he lives, cut off from the world by cold and storm and end- less roads of bottomless mud, surrounded by a rough people who are crushed by poverty and disease, his life one continuous struggle, with never a day's respite; how can a man live like that for forty years and   370 keep himself sober and unspotted? (*Kissing* SONIA) I wish you happiness with all my heart; you deserve it. (*She gets up*) As for me, I am a worth- less, futile woman. I have always been futile; in music, in love, in my husband's house—in a word, in everything. When you come to think of it, Sonia, I am really very, very unhappy. (*Walks excitedly up and down*)   375

Happiness can never exist for me in this world. Never. Why do you laugh?

SONIA: (*Laughing and covering her face with her hands*) I am so happy, so happy!

HELENA: I want to hear music. I might play a little.   380

SONIA: Oh, do, do! (*She embraces her*) I could not possibly go to sleep now. Do play!

HELENA: Yes, I will. Your father is still awake. Music irritates him when he is ill, but if he says I may, then I shall play a little. Go, Sonia, and ask him.

SONIA: Very well.   385

(*She goes out. The* WATCHMAN'S *rattle is heard in the garden.*)

HELENA: It is long since I have heard music. And now, I shall sit and play, and weep like a fool. (*Speaking out of the window*) Is that you rattling out there, Ephim?

VOICE OF THE WATCHMAN: It is I.

HELENA: Don't make such a noise. Your master is ill.   390

VOICE OF THE WATCHMAN: I am going away this minute. (*Whistles a tune.*)

SONIA: (*Comes back*) He says, no.

The curtain falls.

ACT III

The drawing-room of SEREBRAKOFF'S *house. There are three doors: one to the right, one to the left, and one in the centre of the room.* VOITSKI *and* SONIA *are sitting down.* HELENA *is walking up and down, absorbed in thought.*

VOITSKI: We were asked by the professor to be here at one o'clock. (*Looks at his watch*) It is now a quarter to one. It seems he has some communication to make to the world.

HELENA: Probably a matter of business.

VOITSKI: He never had any business. He writes twaddle, grumbles, and eats his   5
heart out with jealousy; that's all he does.

SONIA: (*Reproachfully*) Uncle!

VOITSKI: All right. I beg your pardon. (*He points to* HELENA) Look at her. Wandering up and down from sheer idleness. A sweet picture, really.

HELENA: I wonder you are not bored, droning on in the same key from morning   10
till night. (*Despairingly*) I am dying of this tedium. What shall I do?

SONIA: (*Shrugging her shoulders*) There is plenty to do if you would.

HELENA: For instance?

SONIA: You could help run this place, teach the children, care for the sick— isn't that enough? Before you and papa came, Uncle Vanya and I used   15
to go to market ourselves to deal in flour.

HELENA: I don't know anything about such things, and besides, they don't

748

interest me. It is only in novels that women go out and teach and heal the peasants; how can I suddenly begin to do it?

SONIA: How can you live here and not do it? Wait awhile, you will get used to it all. (*Embraces her*) Don't be sad, dearest. (*Laughing*) You feel miserable and restless, and can't seem to fit into this life, and your restlessness is catching. Look at Uncle Vanya, he does nothing now but haunt you like a shadow, and I have left my work to-day to come here and talk with you. I am getting lazy, and don't want to go on with it. Dr. Astroff hardly ever used to come here; it was all we could do to persuade him to visit us once a month, and now he has abandoned his forestry and his practice, and comes every day. You must be a witch.

VOITSKI: Why should you languish here? Come, my dearest, my beauty, be sensible! The blood of a Nixey runs in your veins. Oh, won't you let yourself be one? Give your nature the reins for once in your life; fall head over ears in love with some other water sprite and plunge down head first into a deep pool, so that the Herr Professor and all of us may have our hands free again.

HELENA: (*Angrily*) Leave me alone! How cruel you are! (*She tries to go out.*)

VOITSKI: (*Preventing her*) There, there, my beauty, I apologise. (*He kisses her hand*) Forgive me.

HELENA: Confess that you would try the patience of an angel.

VOITSKI: As a peace offering I am going to fetch some flowers which I picked for you this morning: some autumn roses, beautiful, sorrowful roses.

(*He goes out.*)

SONIA: Autumn roses, beautiful, sorrowful roses!

(*She and* HELENA *stand looking out of the window.*)

HELENA: September already! How shall we live through the long winter here? (*A pause*) Where is the doctor?

SONIA: He is writing in Uncle Vanya's room. I am glad Uncle Vanya has gone out, I want to talk to you about something.

HELENA: About what?

SONIA: About what?

(*She lays her head on* HELENA'S *breast.*)

HELENA: (*Stroking her hair*) There, there, that will do. Don't, Sonia.

SONIA: I am ugly!

HELENA: You have lovely hair.

SONIA: Don't say that! (*She turns to look at herself in the glass*) No, when a woman is ugly they always say she has beautiful hair or eyes. I have loved him now for six years; I have loved him more than one loves one's mother. I seem to hear him beside me every moment of the day. I feel the pressure of his hand on mine. If I look up, I seem to see him coming, and as you see, I run to you to talk of him. He is here every day now, but he never looks at me, he does not notice my presence. It is agony.

I have absolutely no hope, no, no hope. Oh, my God! Give me strength to endure. I prayed all last night. I often go up to him and speak to him and look into his eyes. My pride is gone. I am not mistress of myself. 60
Yesterday I told Uncle Vanya. I couldn't control myself, and all the servants know it. Every one knows that I love him.

HELENA: Does he?

SONIA: No, he never notices me.

HELENA: (*Thoughtfully*) He is a strange man. Listen, Sonia, will you allow me to 65
speak to him? I shall be careful, only hint. (*A pause*) Really, to be in uncertainty all these years! Let me do it!

(SONIA *nods an affirmative.*)

HELENA: Splendid! It will be easy to find out whether he loves you or not. Don't be ashamed, sweetheart, don't worry. I shall be careful; he will not notice a thing. We only want to find out whether it is yes or no, don't 70
we? (*A pause*) And if it is no, then he must keep away from here, is that so?

(SONIA *nods.*)

HELENA: It will be easier not to see him any more. We won't put off the examination an instant. He said he had a sketch to show me. Go and tell him at once that I want to see him. 75

SONIA: (*In great excitement*) Will you tell me the whole truth?

HELENA: Of course I will. I am sure that no matter what it is, it will be easier for you to bear than this uncertainty. Trust to me, dearest.

SONIA: Yes, yes. I shall say that you want to see his sketch. (*She starts out, but stops near the door and looks back*) No, it is better not to know—and 80
yet—there may be hope.

HELENA: What do you say?

SONIA: Nothing.

(*She goes out.*)

HELENA: (*Alone*) There is no greater sorrow than to know another's secret when you cannot help them. (*In deep thought*) He is obviously not in love with 85
her, but why shouldn't he marry her? She is not pretty, but she is so clever and pure and good, she would make a splendid wife for a country doctor of his years. (*A pause*) I can understand how the poor child feels. She lives here in this desperate loneliness with no one around her except these colourless shadows that go mooning about talking non- 90
sense and knowing nothing except that they eat, drink, and sleep. Among them appears from time to time this Dr. Astroff, so different, so handsome, so interesting, so charming. It is like seeing the moon rise on a dark night. Oh, to surrender oneself to his embrace! To lose oneself in his arms! I am a little in love with him myself! Yes, I am lonely without 95

him, and when I think of him I smile. That Uncle Vanya says I have the blood of a Nixey in my veins: "Give rein to your nature for once in your life!" Perhaps it is right that I should. Oh, to be free as a bird, to fly away from all your sleepy faces and your talk and forget that you have existed at all! But I am a coward, I am afraid; my conscience tor- 100 ments me. He comes here every day now. I can guess why, and feel guilty already; I should like to fall on my knees at Sonia's feet and beg her forgiveness, and weep.

(ASTROFF *comes in carrying a portfolio.*)

ASTROFF: How do you do? (*Shakes hands with her*) Do you want to see my sketch? 105
HELENA: Yes, you promised to show me what you had been doing. Have you time now?
ASTROFF: Of course I have!

(*He lays the portfolio on the table, takes out the sketch and fastens it to the table with thumb-tacks.*)

ASTROFF: Where were you born?
HELENA: (*Helping him*) In St. Petersburg. 110
ASTROFF: And educated?
HELENA: At the Conservatory there.
ASTROFF: You don't find this life very interesting, I dare say?
HELENA: Oh, why not? It is true I don't know the country very well, but I have read a great deal about it. 115
ASTROFF: I have my own desk there in Ivan's room. When I am absolutely too exhausted to go on I drop everything and rush over here to forget myself in this work for an hour or two. Ivan and Miss Sonia sit rattling at their counting-boards, the cricket chirps, and I sit beside them and paint, feeling warm and peaceful. But I don't permit myself this luxury 120 very often, only once a month. (*Pointing to the picture*) Look there! That is a map of our country as it was fifty years ago. The green tints, both dark and light, represent forests. Half the map, as you see, is covered with it. Where the green is striped with red the forests were inhabited by elk and wild goats. Here on this lake, lived great flocks of 125 swans and geese and ducks; as the old men say, there was a power of birds of every kind. Now they have vanished like a cloud. Beside the hamlets and villages, you see, I have dotted down here and there the various settlements, farms, hermit's caves, and water-mills. This country carried a great many cattle and horses, as you can see by the quantity 130 of blue paint. For instance, see how thickly it lies in this part; there were great herds of them here, an average of three horses to every house. (*A pause*) Now, look lower down. This is the country as it was twenty-

751

five years ago. Only a third of the map is green now with forests. There are no goats left and no elk. The blue paint is lighter, and so on, and so on. Now we come to the third part; our country as it appears to-day. We still see spots of green, but not much. The elk, the swans, the black-cock have disappeared. It is, on the whole, the picture of a regular and slow decline which it will evidently only take about ten or fifteen more years to complete. You may perhaps object that it is the march of progress, that the old order must give place to the new, and you might be right if roads had been run through these ruined woods, or if factories and schools had taken their place. The people then would have become better educated and healthier and richer, but as it is, we have nothing of the sort. We have the same swamps and mosquitoes; the same disease and want; the typhoid, the diphtheria, the burning villages. We are confronted by the degradation of our country, brought on by the fierce struggle for existence of the human race. It is the consequence of the ignorance and unconsciousness of starving, shivering, sick humanity that, to save its children, instinctively snatches at everything that can warm it and still its hunger. So it destroys everything it can lay its hands on, without a thought for the morrow. And almost everything has gone, and nothing has been created to take its place. (*Coldly*) But I see by your face that I am not interesting you.

HELENA: I know so little about such things!

ASTROFF: There is nothing to know. It simply isn't interesting, that's all.

HELENA: Frankly, my thoughts were elsewhere. Forgive me! I want to submit you to a little examination, but I am embarrassed and don't know how to begin.

ASTROFF: An examination?

HELENA: Yes, but quite an innocent one. Sit down. (*They sit down*) It is about a certain young girl I know. Let us discuss it like honest people, like friends, and then forget what has passed between us, shall we?

ASTROFF: Very well.

HELENA: It is about my step-daughter, Sonia. Do you like her?

ASTROFF: Yes, I respect her.

HELENA: Do you like her—as a woman?

ASTROFF: (*Slowly*) No.

HELENA: One more word, and that will be the last. You have not noticed anything?

ASTROFF: No, nothing.

HELENA: (*Taking his hand*) You do not love her. I see that in your eyes. She is suffering. You must realise that, and not come here any more.

ASTROFF: My sun has set, yes, and then I haven't the time. (*Shrugging his shoulders*) Where shall I find time for such things? (*He is embarrassed.*)

HELENA: Bah! What an unpleasant conversation! I am as out of breath as if I had been running three miles uphill. Thank heaven, that is over! Now let us forget everything as if nothing had been said. You are sensible. You understand. (*A pause*) I am actually blushing.

ASTROFF: If you had spoken a month ago I might perhaps have considered it, but now— (*He shrugs his shoulders*) Of course, if she is suffering—but I cannot understand why you had to put me through this examination. (*He searches her face with his eyes, and shakes his finger at her*) Oho, you are wily! 180

HELENA: What does this mean? 185

ASTROFF: (*Laughing*) You are a wily one! I admit that Sonia is suffering, but what does this examination of yours mean? (*He prevents her from retorting, and goes on quickly*) Please don't put on such a look of surprise; you know perfectly well why I come here every day. Yes, you know perfectly why and for whose sake I come! Oh, my sweet tigress! don't look at me in that way; I am an old bird! 190

HELENA: (*Perplexed*) A tigress? I don't understand you.

ASTROFF: Beautiful, sleek tigress, you must have your victims! For a whole month I have done nothing but seek you eagerly. I have thrown over everything for you, and you love to see it. Now then, I am sure you knew all this without putting me through your examination. (*Crossing his arms and bowing his head*) I surrender. Here you have me—now, eat me. 195

HELENA: You have gone mad!

ASTROFF: You are afraid!

HELENA: I am a better and stronger woman than you think me. Good-bye. 200
(*She tries to leave the room.*)

ASTROFF: Why good-bye? Don't say good-bye, don't waste words. Oh, how lovely you are—what hands! (*He kisses her hands.*)

HELENA: Enough of this! (*She frees her hands*) Leave the room! You have forgotten yourself.

ASTROFF: Tell me, tell me, where can we meet to-morrow? (*He puts his arm around her*) Don't you see that we must meet, that it is inevitable? 205

(*He kisses her.* VOITSKI *comes in carrying a bunch of roses, and stops in the doorway.*)

HELENA: (*Without seeing* VOITSKI) Have pity! Leave me! (*Lays her head on* ASTROFF's *shoulder*) Don't! (*She tries to break away from him.*)

ASTROFF: (*Holding her by the waist*) Be in the forest to-morrow at two o'clock. Will you? Will you? 210

HELENA: (*Sees* VOITSKI) Let me go! (*Goes to the window deeply embarrassed*) This is appalling!

VOITSKI: (*Throws the flowers on a chair, and speaks in great excitement, wiping his face with his handkerchief*) Nothing—yes, yes, nothing.

ASTROFF: The weather is fine to-day, my dear Ivan; the morning was overcast and looked like rain, but now the sun is shining again. Honestly, we have had a very fine autumn, and the wheat is looking fairly well. (*Puts his* 215 *map back into the portfolio*) But the days are growing short.

HELENA: (*Goes quickly up to* VOITSKI) You must do your best; you must use all your power to get my husband and myself away from here to-day! Do you hear? I say, this very day!   220

VOITSKI: (*Wiping his face*) Oh! Ah! Oh! All right! I—Helena, I saw everything!

HELENA: (*In great agitation*) Do you hear me? I must leave here this very day!

(SEREBRAKOFF, SONIA, MARINA, *and* TELEGIN *come in.*)

TELEGIN: I am not very well myself, your Excellency. I have been limping for two days, and my head——   225

SEREBRAKOFF: Where are the others? I hate this house. It is a regular labyrinth. Every one is always scattered through the twenty-six enormous rooms; one never can find a soul. (*Rings*) Ask my wife and Madame Voitskaya to come here!

HELENA: I am here already.   230

SEREBRAKOFF: Please, all of you, sit down.

SONIA: (*Goes up to* HELENA *and asks anxiously*) What did he say?

HELENA: I'll tell you later.

SONIA: You are moved. (*Looking quickly and inquiringly into her face*) I understand; he said he would not come here any more. (*A pause*) Tell me,   235
did he?

(HELENA *nods.*)

SEREBRAKOFF: (*To* TELEGIN) One can, after all, become reconciled to being an invalid, but not to this country life. The ways of it stick in my throat and I feel exactly as if I had been whirled off the earth and landed on a strange planet. Please be seated, ladies and gentlemen. Sonia! (SONIA   240
does not hear. She is standing with her head bowed sadly forward on her breast) Sonia! (*A pause*) She does not hear me. (*To* MARINA) Sit down too, nurse. (MARINA *sits down and begins to knit her stocking*) I crave your indulgence, ladies and gentlemen; hang your ears, if I may say so, on the peg of attention.   (*He laughs.*)   245

VOITSKI: (*Agitated*) Perhaps you do not need me—may I be excused?

SEREBRAKOFF: No, you are needed now more than any one.

VOITSKI: What is it you want of me?

SEREBRAKOFF: You—but what are you angry about? If it is anything I have done, I ask you to forgive me.   250

VOITSKI: Oh, drop that and come to business; what do you want?

(MME. VOITSKAYA *comes in.*)

SEREBRAKOFF: Here is mother. Ladies and gentlemen, I shall begin. I have asked you to assemble here, my friends, in order to discuss a very important matter. I want to ask you for your assistance and advice, and knowing your unfailing amiability I think I can count on both. I am a book-worm and a scholar, and am unfamiliar with practical affairs. I cannot, I find, dispense with the help of well-informed people such as you, Ivan, and you, Telegin, and you, mother. The truth is, *manet omnes una nox*, that is to say, our lives are in the hands of God, and as I am old and ill, I realise that the time has come for me to dispose of my property in regard to the interests of my family. My life is nearly over, and I am not thinking of myself, but I have a young wife and daughter. (*A pause*) I cannot continue to live in the country; we were not made for country life, and yet we cannot afford to live in town on the income derived from this estate. We might sell the woods, but that would be an expedient we could not resort to every year. We must find some means of guaranteeing to ourselves a certain more or less fixed yearly income. With this object in view, a plan has occurred to me which I now have the honour of presenting to you for your consideration. I shall only give you a rough outline, avoiding all details. Our estate does not pay on an average more than two per cent on the money invested in it. I propose to sell it. If we then invest our capital in bonds, it will earn us four to five per cent, and we should probably have a surplus over of several thousand roubles, with which we could buy a summer cottage in Finland——

VOITSKI: Hold on! Repeat what you just said; I don't think I heard you quite right.

SEREBRAKOFF: I said we would invest the money in bonds and buy a cottage in Finland with the surplus.

VOITSKI: No, not Finland—you said something else.

SEREBRAKOFF: I propose to sell this place.

VOITSKI: Aha! That was it! So you are going to sell the place? Splendid. The idea is a rich one. And what do you propose to do with my old mother and me and with Sonia here?

SEREBRAKOFF: That will be decided in due time. We can't do everything at once.

VOITSKI: Wait! It is clear that until this moment I have never had a grain of sense in my head. I have always been stupid enough to think that the estate belonged to Sonia. My father bought it as a wedding present for my sister, and I foolishly imagined that as our laws were made for Russians and not Turks, my sister's estate would come down to her child.

SEREBRAKOFF: Of course it is Sonia's. Has any one denied it? I don't want to sell it without Sonia's consent; on the contrary, what I am doing is for Sonia's good.

VOITSKI: This is absolutely incomprehensible. Either I have gone mad or—or——

MME. VOITSKAYA: Jean, don't contradict Alexander. Trust to him; he knows better than we do what is right and what is wrong.

VOITSKI: I shan't. Give me some water. (*He drinks*) Go ahead! Say anything you please—anything!

SEREBRAKOFF: I can't imagine why you are so upset. I don't pretend that my scheme is an ideal one, and if you all object to it I shall not insist. 300

(*A pause.*)

TELEGIN: (*With embarrassment*) I not only nourish feelings of respect toward learning, your Excellency, but I am also drawn to it by family ties. My brother Gregory's wife's brother, whom you may know; his name is Constantine Lakedemonoff, and he used to be a magistrate—

VOITSKI: Stop, Waffles. This is business; wait a bit, we will talk of that later. 305 (*To* SEREBRAKOFF) There now, ask him what he thinks; this estate was bought from his uncle.

SEREBRAKOFF: Ah! Why should I ask questions? What good would it do?

VOITSKI: The price was ninety-five thousand roubles. My father paid seventy and left a debt of twenty-five. Now listen! This place could never have 310 been bought had I not renounced my inheritance in favour of my sister, whom I deeply loved—and what is more, I worked for ten years like an ox, and paid off the debt.

SEREBRAKOFF: I regret ever having started this conversation.

VOITSKI: Thanks entirely to my own personal efforts, the place is entirely clear 315 of debts, and now, when I have grown old, you want to throw me out, neck and crop!

SEREBRAKOFF: I can't imagine what you are driving at.

VOITSKI: For twenty-five years I have managed this place, and have sent you the returns from it like the most honest of servants, and you have never 320 given me one single word of thanks for my work, not one—neither in my youth nor now. You allowed me a meagre salary of five hundred roubles a year, a beggar's pittance, and have never even thought of adding a rouble to it.

SEREBRAKOFF: What did I know about such things, Ivan? I am not a practical 325 man and don't understand them. You might have helped yourself to all you wanted.

VOITSKI: Yes, why did I not steal? Don't you all despise me for not stealing, when it would have been only justice? And I should not now have been a beggar! 330

MME. VOITSKAYA: (*Sternly*) Jean!

TELEGIN: (*Agitated*) Vanya, old man, don't talk in that way. Why spoil such pleasant relations? (*He embraces him*) Do stop!

VOITSKI: For twenty-five years I have been sitting here with my mother like a mole in a burrow. Our every thought and hope was yours and yours 335 only. By day we talked with pride of you and your work, and spoke your name with veneration; our nights we wasted reading the books and papers which my soul now loathes.

TELEGIN: Don't, Vanya, don't. I can't stand it.

SEREBRAKOFF: (*Wrathfully*) What under heaven do you want, anyway? 340

VOITSKI: We used to think of you as almost superhuman, but now the scales have fallen from my eyes and I see you as you are! You write on art without knowing anything about it. Those books of yours which I used to admire are not worth one copper kopeck. You are a hoax!

SEREBRAKOFF: Can't any one make him stop? I am going! 345

HELENA: Ivan, I command you to stop this instant! Do you hear me?

VOITSKI: I refuse! (SEREBRAKOFF *tries to get out of the room, but* VOITSKI *bars the door*) Wait! I have not done yet! You have wrecked my life. I have never lived. My best years have gone for nothing, have been ruined, thanks to you. You are my most bitter enemy! 350

TELEGIN: I can't stand it; I can't stand it. I am going.

(He goes out in great excitement.)

SEREBRAKOFF: But what do you want? What earthly right have you to use such language to me? Ruination! If this estate is yours, then take it, and let me be ruined!

HELENA: I am going away out of this hell this minute. *(Shrieks)* This is too much! 355

VOITSKI: My life has been a failure. I am clever and brave and strong. If I had lived a normal life I might have become another Schopenhauer or Dostoieffski. I am losing my head! I am going crazy! Mother, I am in despair! Oh, mother!

MME. VOITSKAYA: *(Sternly)* Listen, Alexander! 360

(SONIA falls on her knees beside the nurse and nestles against her.)

SONIA: Oh, nurse, nurse!

VOITSKI: Mother! What shall I do? But no, don't speak! I know what to do. *(To SEREBRAKOFF)* And you will understand me!

(He goes out through the door in the centre of the room and MME. VOITSKAYA follows him.)

SEREBRAKOFF: Tell me, what on earth is the matter? Take this lunatic out of my sight! I cannot possibly live under the same roof with him. His room *(He* 365 *points to the centre door)* is almost next door to mine. Let him take himself off into the village or into the wing of the house, or I shall leave here at once. I cannot stay in the same house with him.

HELENA: *(To her husband)* We are leaving to-day; we must get ready at once for our departure. 370

SEREBRAKOFF: What a perfectly dreadful man!

SONIA: *(On her knees beside the nurse and turning to her father. She speaks with emotion)* You must be kind to us, papa. Uncle Vanya and I are so unhappy! *(Controlling her despair)* Have pity on us. Remember how Uncle Vanya and Granny used to copy and translate your books for 375 you every night—every, every night. Uncle Vanya has toiled without rest; he would never spend a penny on us, we sent it all to you. We have not eaten the bread of idleness. I am not saying this as I should like to, but you must understand us, papa, you must be merciful to us.

HELENA: *(Very excited, to her husband)* For heaven's sake, Alexander, go and 380 have a talk with him—explain!

SEREBRAKOFF: Very well, I shall have a talk with him, but I won't apologise for a thing. I am not angry with him, but you must confess that his behaviour has been strange, to say the least. Excuse me, I shall go to him.

(He goes out through the centre door.)

HELENA: Be gentle with him; try to quiet him.   385

(She follows him out.)

SONIA: *(Nestling nearer to* MARINA*)* Nurse, oh, nurse!

MARINA: It's all right, my baby. When the geese have cackled they will be still again. First they cackle and then they stop.

SONIA: Nurse!

MARINA: You are trembling all over, as if you were freezing. There, there, little   390
orphan baby, God is merciful. A little linden-tea, and it will all pass away. Don't cry, my sweetest. *(Looking angrily at the door in the centre of the room)* See, the geese have all gone now. The devil take them!

(A shot is heard. HELENA *screams behind the scenes.* SONIA *shudders.)*

MARINA: Bang! What's that?

SEREBRAKOFF: *(Comes in reeling with terror)* Hold him! hold him! He has gone   395
mad!

*(*HELENA *and* VOITSKI *are seen struggling in the doorway.)*

HELENA: *(Trying to wrest the revolver from him)* Give it to me; give it to me, I tell you!

VOITSKI: Let me go, Helena, let me go! *(He frees himself and rushes in, looking everywhere for* SEREBRAKOFF*)* Where is he? Ah, there he is! *(He shoots at*   400
him. A pause) I didn't get him? I missed again? *(Furiously)* Damnation! Damnation! To hell with him!

(He flings the revolver on the floor, and drops helpless into a chair. SEREBRAKOFF *stands as if stupefied.* HELENA *leans against the wall, almost fainting.)*

HELENA: Take me away! Take me away! I can't stay here—I can't!

VOITSKI: *(In despair)* Oh, what shall I do? What shall I do?

SONIA: *(Softly)* Oh, nurse, nurse!   405

The curtain falls.

ACT IV

VOITSKI'S *bedroom, which is also his office. A table stands near the window; on it are ledgers, letter scales, and papers of every description. Near by stands a smaller table belonging to* ASTROFF, *with his paints and drawing materials. On the wall hangs a cage containing a starling. There is also a map of Africa on the wall, obviously of no use to anybody. There is a large sofa covered with buckram. A door to the left leads into an inner room; one to the right leads into the front hall, and before this door lies a mat for the peasants with their muddy boots to stand on. It is an autumn evening. The silence is profound.* TELEGIN *and* MARINA *sitting facing one another, winding wool.*

TELEGIN: Be quick, Marina, or we shall be called away to say good-bye before you have finished. The carriage has already been ordered.

MARINA: (*Trying to wind more quickly*) I am a little tired.

TELEGIN: They are going to Kharkoff to live.

MARINA: They do well to go. 5

TELEGIN: They have been frightened. The professor's wife won't stay here an hour longer. "If we are going at all, let's be off," says she, "we shall go to Kharkoff and look about us, and then we can send for our things." They are travelling light. It seems, Marina, that fate has decreed for them not to live here. 10

MARINA: And quite rightly. What a storm they have just raised! It was shameful!

TELEGIN: It was indeed. The scene was worthy of the brush of Aibazofski.

MARINA: I wish I'd never laid eyes on them. (*A pause*) Now we shall have things as they were again: tea at eight, dinner at one, and supper in the evening; everything in order as decent folks, as Christians like to have it. 15
(*Sighs*) It is a long time since I have eaten noodles.

TELEGIN: Yes, we haven't had noodles for ages. (*A pause*) Not for ages. As I was going through the village this morning, Marina, one of the shop-keepers called after me, "Hi! you hanger-on!" I felt it bitterly.

MARINA: Don't pay the least attention to them, master; we are all dependents 20
on God. You and Sonia and all of us. Every one must work, no one can sit idle. Where is Sonia?

TELEGIN: In the garden with the doctor, looking for Ivan. They fear he may lay violent hands on himself.

MARINA: Where is his pistol? 25

TELEGIN: (*Whispers*) I hid it in the cellar.

(VOITSKI *and* ASTROFF *come in.*)

VOITSKI: Leave me alone! (*To* MARINA *and* TELEGIN) Go away! Go away and leave me to myself, if but for an hour. I won't have you watching me like this!

TELEGIN: Yes, yes, Vanya. 30
(*He goes out on tiptoe.*)

MARINA: The gander cackles; ho! ho! ho!
(*She gathers up her wool and goes out.*)

VOITSKI: Leave me by myself!

ASTROFF: I would, with the greatest pleasure. I ought to have gone long ago, but I shan't leave you until you have returned what you took from me.

VOITSKI: I took nothing from you.   35

ASTROFF: I am not jesting, don't detain me, I really must go.

VOITSKI: I took nothing of yours.

ASTROFF: You didn't? Very well, I shall have to wait a little longer, and then you will have to forgive me if I resort to force. We shall have to bind you and search you. I mean what I say.   40

VOITSKI: Do as you please. (*A pause*) Oh, to make such a fool of myself! To shoot twice and miss him both times! I shall never forgive myself.

ASTROFF: When the impulse came to shoot, it would have been as well had you put a bullet through your own head.

VOITSKI: (*Shrugging his shoulders*) Strange! I attempted murder, and am not   45 going to be arrested or brought to trial. That means they think me mad. (*With a bitter laugh*) Me! I am mad, and those who hide their worthlessness, their dullness, their crying heartlessness behind a professor's mask, are sane! Those who marry old men and then deceive them under the noses of all, are sane! I saw you kiss her; I saw you in each other's   50 arms!

ASTROFF: Yes, sir, I did kiss her; so there.   (*He puts his thumb to his nose.*)

VOITSKI: (*His eyes on the door*) No, it is the earth that is mad, because she still bears us on her breast.

ASTROFF: That is nonsense.   55

VOITSKI: Well? Am I not a madman, and therefore irresponsible? Haven't I the right to talk nonsense?

ASTROFF: This is a farce! You are not mad; you are simply a ridiculous fool. I used to think every fool was out of his senses, but now I see that lack of sense is a man's normal state, and you are perfectly normal.   60

VOITSKI: (*Covers his face with his hands*) Oh! If you knew how ashamed I am! These piercing pangs of shame are like nothing on earth. (*In an agonised voice*) I can't endure them! (*He leans against the table*) What can I do? What can I do?

ASTROFF: Nothing.   65

VOITSKI: You must tell me something? Oh, my God! I am forty-seven years old. I may live to sixty; I still have thirteen years before me; an eternity! How shall I be able to endure life for thirteen years? What shall I do? How can I fill them? Oh, don't you see? (*He presses* ASTROFF's *hand convulsively*) Don't you see, if only I could live the rest of my life in some   70 new way! If I could only wake some still, bright morning and feel that life had begun again; that the past was forgotten and had vanished like smoke. (*He weeps*) Oh, to begin life anew! Tell me, tell me how to begin.

ASTROFF: (*Crossly*) What nonsense! What sort of a new life can you and I look   75 forward to? We can have no hope.

VOITSKI: None?

ASTROFF: None. Of that I am convinced.

760

VOITSKI: Tell me what to do. (*He puts his hand to his heart*) I feel such a burning
pain here. 80

ASTROFF: (*Shouts angrily*) Stop! (*Then, more gently*) It may be that posterity,
which will despise us for our blind and stupid lives, will find some road to
happiness; but we—you and I—have but one hope, the hope that we
may be visited by visions, perhaps by pleasant ones, as we lie resting in
our graves. (*Sighing*) Yes, brother, there were only two respectable, in- 85
telligent men in this county, you and I. Ten years or so of this life of
ours, this miserable life, have sucked us under, and we have become as
contemptible and petty as the rest. But don't try to talk me out of my
purpose! Give me what you took from me, will you?

VOITSKI: I took nothing from you. 90

ASTROFF: You took a little bottle of morphine out of my medicine-case. (*A pause*)
Listen! If you are positively determined to make an end to yourself, go
into the woods and shoot yourself there. Give up the morphine, or there
will be a lot of talk and guesswork; people will think I gave it to you.
I don't fancy having to perform a post-mortem on you. Do you think I 95
should find it interesting?

(SONIA *comes in.*)

VOITSKI: Leave me alone.

ASTROFF: (*To* SONIA) Sonia, your uncle has stolen a bottle of morphine out of
my medicine-case and won't give it up. Tell him that his behaviour is—
well, unwise. I haven't time, I must be going. 100

SONIA: Uncle Vanya, did you take the morphine?

ASTROFF: Yes, he took it. (*A pause*) I am absolutely sure.

SONIA: Give it up, Uncle Vanya! My misfortune is perhaps even greater than
yours, but I am not plunged in despair. I endure my sorrow, and shall
endure it until my life comes to a natural end. You must endure yours, 105
too. (*A pause*) Give it up! Dear, darling Uncle Vanya. Give it up! (*She
weeps*) You are so good, I am sure you will have pity on us and give it
up. You must endure your sorrow, Uncle Vanya; you must endure it.

(VOITSKI *takes a bottle from the drawer of the table and hands it to* ASTROFF.)

VOITSKI: There it is! (*To* SONIA) And now, we must get to work at once; we must
do something, or else I shall not be able to endure it. 110

SONIA: Yes, yes, to work! As soon as we have seen them off we shall go to
work. (*She nervously straightens out the papers on the table*) Everything
is in a muddle!

ASTROFF: (*Putting the bottle in his case, which he straps together*) Now I can
be off. 115

(HELENA *comes in.*)

HELENA: Are you here, Ivan? We are starting in a moment. Go to Alexander, he wants to speak to you.

SONIA: Go, Uncle Vanya. (*She takes* VOITSKI's *arm*) Come, you and papa must make peace; that is absolutely necessary.

(SONIA *and* VOITSKI *go out.*)

HELENA: I am going away. (*She gives* ASTROFF *her hand*) Good-bye.   120

ASTROFF: So soon?

HELENA: The carriage is waiting.

ASTROFF: Good-bye.

HELENA: You promised me you would go away yourself to-day.

ASTROFF: I have not forgotten. I am going at once. (*A pause*) Were you fright-   125
ened? Was it so terrible?

HELENA: Yes.

ASTROFF: Couldn't you stay? Couldn't you? To-morrow—in the forest——

HELENA: No. It is all settled, and that is why I can look you so bravely in the face. Our departure is fixed. One thing I must ask of you: don't think   130
too badly of me; I should like you to respect me.

ASTROFF: Ah! (*With an impatient gesture*) Stay, I implore you! Confess that there is nothing for you to do in this world. You have no object in life; there is nothing to occupy your attention, and sooner or later your feelings must master you. It is inevitable. It would be better if it hap-   135
pened not in Kharkoff or in Kursk, but here, in nature's lap. It would then at least be poetical, even beautiful. Here you have the forests, the houses half in ruins that Turgenieff writes of.

HELENA: How comical you are! I am angry with you and yet I shall always remember you with pleasure. You are interesting and original. You and   140
I will never meet again, and so I shall tell you—why should I conceal it? —that I am just a little in love with you. Come, one more last pressure of our hands, and then let us part good friends. Let us not bear each other any ill will.

ASTROFF: (*Pressing her hand*) Yes, go. (*Thoughtfully*) You seem to be sincere   145
and good, and yet there is something strangely disquieting about all your personality. No sooner did you arrive here with your husband than every one whom you found busy and actively creating something was forced to drop his work and give himself up for the whole summer to your husband's gout and yourself. You and he have infected us with   150
your idleness. I have been swept off my feet; I have not put my hand to a thing for weeks, during which sickness has been running its course unchecked among the people, and the peasants have been pasturing their cattle in my woods and young plantations. Go where you will, you and your husband will always carry destruction in your train. I am   155
joking of course, and yet I am strangely sure that had you stayed here we should have been overtaken by the most immense desolation. I would have gone to my ruin, and you—you would not have prospered. So go! E finita la comedia!

HELENA: (*Snatching a pencil off* ASTROFF's *table, and hiding it with a quick* 160
movement) I shall take this pencil for memory!

ASTROFF: How strange it is. We meet, and then suddenly it seems that we must
part forever. That is the way in this world. As long as we are alone,
before Uncle Vanya comes in with a bouquet—allow me—to kiss you
good-bye—may I? (*He kisses her on the cheek*) So! Splendid! 165

HELENA: I wish you every happiness. (*She glances about her*) For once in my
life, I shall! and scorn the consequences! (*She kisses him impetuously, and
they quickly part*) I must go.

ASTROFF: Yes, go. If the carriage is there, then start at once.

(*They stand listening.*)

ASTROFF: E finita! 170

(VOITSKI, SEREBRAKOFF, MME. VOITSKAYA *with her book*, TELEGIN, *and* SONIA *come in.*)

SEREBRAKOFF: (*To* VOITSKI) Shame on him who bears malice for the past. I have
gone through so much in the last few hours that I feel capable of writing
a whole treatise on the conduct of life for the instruction of posterity.
I gladly accept your apology, and myself ask your forgiveness. (*He
kisses* VOITSKI *three times.*) 175

(HELENA *embraces* SONIA.)

SEREBRAKOFF: (*Kissing* MME. VOITSKAYA's *hand*) Mother!

MME. VOITSKAYA: (*Kissing him*) Have your picture taken, Alexander, and send
me one. You know how dear you are to me.

TELEGIN: Good-bye, your Excellency. Don't forget us.

SEREBRAKOFF: (*Kissing his daughter*) Good-bye, good-bye all. (*Shaking hands* 180
with ASTROFF) Many thanks for your pleasant company. I have a deep
regard for your opinions and your enthusiasm, but let me, as an old man,
give one word of advice at parting: do something, my friend! Work! Do
something! (*They all bow*) Good luck to you all.

(*He goes out followed by* MME. VOITSKAYA *and* SONIA.)

VOITSKI: (*Kissing* HELENA's *hand fervently*) Good-bye—forgive me. I shall never 185
see you again!

HELENA: (*Touched*) Good-bye, dear boy.

(*She lightly kisses his head as he bends over her hand, and goes out.*)

ASTROFF: Tell them to bring my carriage around too, Waffles.

TELEGIN: All right, old man.

(ASTROFF *and* VOITSKI *are left behind alone.* ASTROFF *collects his paints and drawing
materials on the table and packs them away in a box.*)

ASTROFF: Why don't you go to see them off? 190

763

VOITSKI: Let them go! I—I can't go out there. I feel too sad. I must go to work on something at once. To work! To work!

(He rummages through his papers on the table. A pause. The tinkling of bells is heard as the horses trot away.)

ASTROFF: They have gone! The professor, I suppose, is glad to go. He couldn't be tempted back now by a fortune.

(MARINA comes in.)

MARINA: They have gone. 195
(She sits down in an arm-chair and knits her stocking.)

(SONIA comes in wiping her eyes.)

SONIA: They have gone. God be with them. *(To her uncle)* And now, Uncle Vanya, let us do something!
VOITSKI: To work! To work!
SONIA: It is long, long, since you and I have sat together at this table. *(She lights a lamp on the table)* No ink! *(She takes the inkstand to the cup-* 200 *board and fills it from an inkbottle)* How sad it is to see them go!

(MME. VOITSKAYA comes slowly in.)

MME. VOITSKAYA: They have gone.

(She sits down and at once becomes absorbed in her book. SONIA sits down at the table and looks through an account book.)

SONIA: First, Uncle Vanya, let us write up the accounts. They are in a dreadful state. Come, begin. You take one and I will take the other.
VOITSKI: In account with —— *(They sit silently writing.)* 205
MARINA: *(Yawning)* The sand-man has come.
ASTROFF: How still it is. Their pens scratch, the cricket sings; it is so warm and comfortable. I hate to go. *(The tinkling of bells is heard.)*
ASTROFF: My carriage has come. There now remains but to say good-bye to you, my friends, and to my table here, and then—away! 210
(He puts the map into the portfolio.)
MARINA: Don't hurry away; sit a little longer with us.
ASTROFF: Impossible.
VOITSKI: *(Writing)* And carry forward from the old debt two seventy-five——

(WORKMAN comes in.)

WORKMAN: Your carriage is waiting, sir.

ASTROFF: All right. (*He hands the* WORKMAN *his medicine-case, portfolio, and* 215
box) Look out, don't crush the portfolio!

WORKMAN: Very well, sir.

SONIA: When shall we see you again?

ASTROFF: Hardly before next summer. Probably not this winter, though, of
course, if anything should happen you will let me know. (*He shakes* 220
hands with them) Thank you for your kindness, for your hospitality, for
everything! (*He goes up to* MARINA *and kisses her head*) Good-bye, old
nurse!

MARINA: Are you going without your tea?

ASTROFF: I don't want any, nurse. 225

MARINA: Won't you have a drop of vodka?

ASTROFF: (*Hesitatingly*) Yes, I might.

(MARINA *goes out.*)

ASTROFF: (*After a pause*) My off-wheeler has gone lame for some reason. I noticed it yesterday when Peter was taking him to water.

VOITSKI: You should have him re-shod. 230

ASTROFF: I shall have to go around by the blacksmith's on my way home. It
can't be avoided. (*He stands looking up at the map of Africa hanging on
the wall*) I suppose it is roasting hot in Africa now.

VOITSKI: Yes, I suppose it is.

(MARINA *comes back carrying a tray on which are a glass of vodka and a piece of
bread.*)

MARINA: Help yourself. 235

(ASTROFF *drinks.*)

MARINA: To your good health! (*She bows deeply*) Eat your bread with it.

ASTROFF: No, I like it so. And now, good-bye. (*To* MARINA) You needn't come out
to see me off, nurse.

(*He goes out.* SONIA *follows him with a candle to light him to the carriage.* MARINA
sits down in her arm-chair.)

VOITSKI: (*Writing*) On the 2d of February, twenty pounds of butter; on the 16th,
twenty pounds of butter again. Buckwheat flour— 240

(*A pause. Bells are heard tinkling.*)

MARINA: He has gone. (*A pause.*)

(SONIA *comes in and sets the candle-stick on the table.*)

SONIA: He has gone.

VOITSKI: (*Adding and writing*) Total, fifteen—twenty-five—

(SONIA *sits down and begins to write.*)

MARINA: (*Yawning*) Oh, ho! The Lord have mercy.

(TELEGIN *comes in on tiptoe, sits down near the door, and begins to tune his guitar.*)

VOITSKI: (*To* SONIA, *stroking her hair*) Oh, my child, I am so miserable; if you   245
           only knew how miserable I am!

SONIA: What can we do? We must live our lives. (*A pause*) Yes, we shall live,
         Uncle Vanya. We shall live through the long procession of days before
         us, and through the long evenings; we shall patiently bear the trials that
         fate imposes on us; we shall work for others without rest, both now and   250
         when we are old; and when our last hour comes we shall meet it humbly,
         and there, beyond the grave, we shall say that we have suffered and
         wept, that our life was bitter, and God will have pity on us. Ah, then
         dear, dear Uncle, we shall see that bright and beautiful life; we shall
         rejoice and look back upon our sorrow here; a tender smile—and—we   255
         shall rest. I have faith, Uncle, fervent, passionate faith. (SONIA *kneels
         down before her uncle and lays her head on his hands. She speaks in a
         weary voice*) We shall rest. (TELEGIN *plays softly on the guitar*) We shall
         rest. We shall hear the angels. We shall see heaven shining like a jewel.
         We shall see all evil and all our pain sink away in the great compassion   260
         that shall enfold the world. Our life will be as peaceful and tender and
         sweet as a caress. I have faith; I have faith. (*She wipes away her tears*)
         My poor, poor Uncle Vanya, you are crying! (*Weeping*) You have never
         known what happiness was, but wait, Uncle Vanya, wait! We shall rest.
         (*She embraces him*) We shall rest. (*The* WATCHMAN's *rattle is heard in the*   265
         garden; TELEGIN *plays softly;* MME. VOITSKAYA *writes something on the
         margin of her pamphlet;* MARINA *knits her stocking*) We shall rest.

                        The curtain slowly falls.

TENNESSEE WILLIAMS

Suddenly Last Summer

Characters

MRS. VENABLE
DR. CUKROWICZ
MISS FOXHILL
MRS. HOLLY
GEORGE HOLLY
CATHARINE HOLLY
SISTER FELICITY

SCENE ONE

The set may be as unrealistic as the decor of a dramatic ballet. It represents part of a mansion of Victorian Gothic style in the Garden District of New Orleans on a late afternoon, between late summer and early fall. The interior is blended with a fantastic garden which is more like a tropical jungle, or forest, in the pre-historic age of giant fern-forests when living creatures had flippers turning to limbs and scales to skin. The colors of this jungle-garden are violent, especially since it is steaming with heat after rain. There are massive tree-flowers that suggest organs of a body, torn out, still glistening with undried blood; there are harsh cries and sibilant hissings and thrashing sounds in the garden as if it were inhabited by beasts, serpents and birds, all of savage nature. . . .

The jungle tumult continues a few moments after the curtain rises; then subsides into relative quiet, which is occasionally broken by a new outburst.

A lady enters with the assistance of a silver-knobbed cane. She has light orange or pink hair and wears a lavender lace dress, and over her withered bosom is pinned a starfish of diamonds.

She is followed by a young blond Doctor, all in white, glacially brilliant, very, very good-looking, and the old lady's manner and eloquence indicate her undeliberate response to his icy charm.

MRS. VENABLE: Yes, this was Sebastian's garden. The Latin names of the plants were printed on tags attached to them but the print's fading out. Those ones there—(*She draws a deep breath*)—are the oldest plants on earth, survivors from the age of the giant fern-forests. Of course in this semitropical climate—(*She takes another deep breath*)—some of the rarest   **5** plants, such as the Venus flytrap—you know what this is, Doctor? The Venus flytrap?

DOCTOR: An insectivorous plant?

MRS. VENABLE: Yes, it feeds on insects. It has to be kept under glass from early fall to late spring and when it went under glass, my son, Sebastian,   **10** had to provide it with fruit flies flown in at great expense from a Florida laboratory that used fruit flies for experiments in genetics. Well, I can't do that, Doctor. (*She takes a deep breath.*) I can't, I just can't do it! It's not the expense but the—

DOCTOR: Effort.   **15**

MRS. VENABLE: Yes. So goodbye, Venus flytrap!—like so much else . . . Whew! . . . (*She draws breath.*)—I don't know why, but—! I already feel I can lean on your shoulder, Doctor—Cu?—Cu?

DOCTOR: Cu-kro-wicz. It's a Polish word that means sugar, so let's make it simple and call me Doctor Sugar.   **20**

(*He returns her smile.*)

MRS. VENABLE: Well, now, Doctor Sugar, you've seen Sebastian's garden.

(*They are advancing slowly to the patio area.*)

DOCTOR: It's like a well-groomed jungle. . . .

MRS. VENABLE: That's how he meant it to be, nothing was accidental, everything was planned and designed in Sebastian's life and his—(*She dabs her forehead with her handkerchief which she had taken from her   **25** reticule*)—work!

DOCTOR: What was your son's work, Mrs. Venable?—besides this garden?

MRS. VENABLE: As many times as I've had to answer that question! D'you know it still shocks me a little?—to realize that Sebastian Venable the poet is still unknown outside of a small coterie of friends, including his mother.   **30**

DOCTOR: Oh.

MRS. VENABLE: You see, strictly speaking, his *life* was his occupation.

DOCTOR: I see.

MRS. VENABLE: No, you *don't* see, yet, but before I'm through, you will.— Sebastian was a poet! That's what I meant when I said his life was his   35
work because the work of a poet is the life of a poet and—vice versa, the life of a poet is the work of a poet, I mean you can't separate them, I mean—well, for instance, a salesman's work is one thing and his life is another—or can be. The same thing's true of—doctor, lawyer, merchant, *thief*!—But a poet's life is his work and his work is his life in a special   40
sense because—oh, I've already talked myself breathless and dizzy.

(The DOCTOR offers his arm.)

Thank you.

DOCTOR: Mrs. Venable, did your doctor okay this thing?

MRS. VENABLE *(breathless)*: What thing?

DOCTOR: Your meeting this girl that you think is responsible for your son's death?   45

MRS. VENABLE: I've waited months to face her because I couldn't get to St. Mary's to face her—I've had her brought here to my house. I won't collapse! She'll collapse! I mean her lies will collapse—not my truth—not the truth. . . . *Forward march, Doctor Sugar!*

(He conducts her slowly to the patio.)

Ah, we've *made* it, *ha ha*! I didn't know that I was so weak on my pins!   50
Sit down, Doctor. I'm not afraid of using every last ounce and inch of my little, left-over strength in doing just what I'm doing. I'm devoting all that's left of my life, Doctor, to the defense of a dead poet's reputation. Sebastian had no public name as a poet, he didn't want one, he refused to have one. He *dreaded, abhorred*!—false values that come from being   55
publicly known, from fame, from personal—exploitation. . . . Oh, he'd say to me: "Violet? Mother?—you're going to outlive me!!"

DOCTOR: What made him think that?

MRS. VENABLE: Poets are always clairvoyant!—And he had rheumatic fever when he was fifteen and it affected a heart-valve and he wouldn't stay   60
off horses and out of water and so forth. . . . "Violet? Mother? You're going to live longer than me, and then, when I'm gone, it will be yours, in your hands, to do whatever you please with!"—Meaning, of course, his future recognition!—That he *did* want, he wanted it after his death when it couldn't disturb him; then he did want to offer his work to the   65
world. All right. Have I made my point, Doctor? Well, here is my son's work, Doctor, here's his life going on!

(She lifts a thin gilt-edged volume from the patio table as if elevating the Host before

the altar. Its gold leaf and lettering catch the afternoon sun. It says Poem of
Summer. *Her face suddenly has a different look, the look of a visionary, an
exalted religieuse. At the same instant a bird sings clearly and purely in the
garden and the old lady seems to be almost young for a moment.*)

DOCTOR (*reading the title*):   Poem of Summer?
MRS. VENABLE: *Poem of Summer,* and the date of the summer, there are twenty-
five of them, he wrote one poem a year which he printed himself on an   70
eighteenth-century hand-press at his—atelier in the—French—Quarter—
so no one but he could see it. . . .

(*She seems dizzy for a moment.*)

DOCTOR: He wrote one poem a year?
MRS. VENABLE: One for each summer that we traveled together. The other nine
months of the year were really only a preparation.   75
DOCTOR: Nine months?
MRS. VENABLE: The length of a pregnancy, yes. . . .
DOCTOR: The poem was hard to deliver?
MRS. VENABLE: Yes, even with me! *Without* me, *impossible,* Doctor!—he wrote no
poem last summer.   80
DOCTOR: He died last summer?
MRS. VENABLE: Without me he died last summer, that was his last summer's poem.

(*She staggers; he assists her toward a chair. She catches her breath with difficulty.*)

One long-ago summer—now, why am I thinking of this?—my son, Sebastian, said, "Mother?—Listen to this!"—He read me Herman Melville's
description of the Encantadas, the Galapagos Islands. Quote—take five   85
and twenty heaps of cinders dumped here and there in an outside city
lot. Imagine some of them magnified into mountains, and the vacant lot,
the sea. And you'll have a fit idea of the general aspect of the
Encantadas, the Enchanted Isles—extinct volcanos, looking much as the
world at large might look—after a last conflagration—end quote. He   90
read me that description and said that we had to go there. And so we
did go there that summer on a chartered boat, a four-masted schooner,
as close as possible to the sort of a boat that Melville must have sailed
on. . . . We saw the Encantadas, but on the Encantadas we saw something Melville *hadn't* written about. We saw the great sea-turtles crawl   95
up out of the sea for their annual egg-laying. . . . Once a year the
female of the sea-turtle crawls up out of the equatorial sea onto the
blazing sand-beach of a volcanic island to dig a pit in the sand and
deposit her eggs there. It's a long and dreadful thing, the depositing of
the eggs in the sand-pits, and when it's finished the exhausted female   100
turtle crawls back to the sea half-dead. She never sees her offspring,

but we did. Sebastian knew exactly when the sea-turtle eggs would be hatched out and we returned in time for it. . . .

DOCTOR: You went back to the—?

MRS. VENABLE: Terrible Encantadas, those heaps of extinct volcanos, in time to   105
witness the hatching of the sea-turtles and their desperate flight to the sea!

(There is a sound of harsh bird-cries in the air. She looks up.)

—The narrow beach, the color of caviar, was all in motion! But the sky was in motion, too. . . .

DOCTOR: The sky was in motion, too?   110

MRS. VENABLE: —Full of flesh-eating birds and the noise of the birds, the horrible savage cries of the—

DOCTOR: Carnivorous birds?

MRS. VENABLE: Over the narrow black beach of the Encantadas as the just hatched sea-turtles scrambled out of the sand-pits and started their race   115
to the sea. . . .

DOCTOR: Race to the sea?

MRS. VENABLE: To escape the flesh-eating birds that made the sky almost as black as the beach!

(She gazes up again; we hear the wild, ravenous, harsh cries of the birds. The sound comes in rhythmic waves like a savage chant.)

And the sand all alive, all alive, as the hatched sea-turtles made their   120
dash for the sea, while the birds hovered and swooped to attack and hovered and—swooped to attack! They were diving down on the hatched sea-turtles, turning them over to expose their soft undersides, tearing the undersides open and rending and eating their flesh. Sebastian guessed that possibly only a hundredth of one per cent of their number would   125
escape to the sea. . . .

DOCTOR: What was it about this that fascinated your son?

MRS. VENABLE: My son was looking for—*(She stops short with a slight gasp.)*— Let's just say he was interested in sea-turtles!

DOCTOR: That isn't what you started to say.   130

MRS. VENABLE: I stopped myself just in time.

DOCTOR: Say what you started to say.

MRS. VENABLE: I started to say that my son was looking for God and I stopped myself because I thought you'd think "Oh, a pretentious young crackpot!"—which Sebastian was *not*!   135

DOCTOR: Mrs. Venable, doctors look for God, too.

MRS. VENABLE: Oh?

DOCTOR: I think they have to look harder for him than priests since they don't have the help of such well-known guidebooks and well-organized expositions as the priests have with their scriptures and—churches. . . . 140

MRS. VENABLE: You mean they go on a solitary safari like a poet?

DOCTOR: Yes. Some do. I do.

MRS. VENABLE: I believe, I *believe* you! (*She laughs, startled.*)

DOCTOR: Let me tell you something—the first operation I performed at Lion's
View.—You can imagine how anxious and nervous I was about the out- 145
come.

MRS. VENABLE: Yes.

DOCTOR: The patient was a young girl regarded as hopeless and put in the
Drum—

MRS. VENABLE: Yes. 150

DOCTOR: The name for the violent ward at Lion's View because it looks like the
inside of a drum with very bright lights burning all day and all night.—
So the attendants can see any change of expression or movement among
the inmates in time to grab them if they're about to attack. After the
operation I stayed with the girl, as if I'd delivered a child that might stop 155
breathing.—When they finally wheeled her out of surgery, I still stayed
with her. I walked along by the rolling table holding onto her hand—
with my heart in my throat. . . .

(*We hear faint music.*)

—It was a nice afternoon, as fair as this one. And the moment we
wheeled her outside, she whispered something, she whispered: "Oh, how 160
blue the sky is!"—And I felt proud, I felt proud and relieved, because
up till then her speech, everything that she'd babbled, was a torrent of
obscenities!

MRS. VENABLE: Yes, well, now, I can tell you without any hesitation that my son
was looking for God, I mean for a clear image of him. He spent that 165
whole blazing equatorial day in the crow's-nest of the schooner watching
this thing on the beach till it was too dark to see it, and when he came
down the rigging he said "Well, now I've seen Him!," and he meant
God.—And for several weeks after that he had a fever, he was delirious
with it.— 170

(*The Encantadas music then fades in again, briefly, at a lower level, a whisper.*)

DOCTOR: I can see how he *might* be, I think he *would* be disturbed if he thought
he'd seen God's image, an equation of God, in that spectacle you
watched in the Encantadas: creatures of the air hovering over and
swooping down to devour creatures of the sea that had had the bad
luck to be hatched on land and weren't able to scramble back into the 175
sea fast enough to escape that massacre you witnessed, yes, I can see
how such a spectacle could be equated with a good deal of—*experience,
existence!*—but not with *God!* Can *you?*

MRS. VENABLE: Dr. Sugar, I'm a reasonably loyal member of the Protestant
    Episcopal Church, but I understood what he meant.   180
DOCTOR: Did he mean we must rise above God?
MRS. VENABLE: He meant that God shows a savage face to people and shouts
    some fierce things at them, it's all we see or hear of Him. Isn't it all we
    ever really see and hear of Him, now?—Nobody seems to know why. . . .

(Music fades out again.)

      Shall I go on from there?   185
DOCTOR: Yes, do.
MRS. VENABLE: Well, next?—India—China—

(MISS FOXHILL appears with the medicine. MRS. VENABLE sees her.)

MISS FOXHILL: Mrs. Venable.
MRS. VENABLE: Oh, God—elixir of—. *(She takes the glass.)* Isn't it kind of the
    drugstore to keep me alive. Where was I, Doctor?   190
DOCTOR: In the Himalayas.
MRS. VENABLE: Oh yes, that long-ago summer. . . . In the Himalayas he almost
    entered a Buddhist monastery, had gone so far as to shave his head and
    eat just rice out of a wood bowl on a grass mat. He'd promised those
    sly Buddhist monks that he would give up the world and himself and all   195
    his worldly possessions to their mendicant order.—Well, I cabled his
    father, "For God's sake notify bank to freeze Sebastian's accounts!"—I
    got back this cable from my late husband's lawyer: "Mr. Venable
    critically ill Stop Wants you Stop Needs you Stop Immediate return
    advised most strongly. Stop. Cable time of arrival. . . ."   200
DOCTOR: Did you go back to your husband?
MRS. VENABLE: I made the hardest decision of my life. I stayed with my son. I got
    him through that crisis too. In less than a month he got up off the filthy
    grass mat and threw the rice bowl away—and booked us into Shep-
    heard's Hotel in Cairo and the Ritz in Paris—. And from then on, oh, we   205
    —still lived in a—world of light and shadow. . . .

(She turns vaguely with empty glass. He rises and takes it from her.)

      But the shadow was almost as luminous as the light.
DOCTOR: Don't you want to sit down now?
MRS. VENABLE: Yes, indeed I do, before I fall down.

(He assists her into wheelchair.)

      —Are your hind-legs still on you?   210
DOCTOR *(still concerned over her agitation)*:   —My what? Oh—hind legs!—Yes . . .

773

MRS. VENABLE: Well, then you're not a donkey, you're certainly not a donkey because I've been talking the hind-legs off a donkey—several donkeys. . . . But I had to make it clear to you that the world lost a great deal too when I lost my son last summer. . . . You would have liked my son, he would have been charmed by you. My son, Sebastian, was not a family snob or a money snob but he was a snob, all right. He was a snob about personal charm in people, he insisted upon good looks in people around him, and, oh, he had a perfect little court of young and beautiful people around him always, wherever he was, here in New *Orleans* or New York or on the Riviera or in Paris and Venice, he always had a little entourage of the beautiful and the talented and the young!

DOCTOR: Your son was young, Mrs. Venable?

MRS. VENABLE: Both of us were young, and stayed young, Doctor.

DOCTOR: Could I see a photograph of your son, Mrs. Venable?

MRS. VENABLE: Yes, indeed you could, Doctor. I'm glad that you asked to see one. I'm going to show you not one photograph but two. Here. Here is my son, Sebastian, in a Renaissance pageboy's costume at a masked ball in Cannes. Here is my son, Sebastian, in the same costume at a masked ball in Venice. These two pictures were taken twenty years apart. Now which is the older one, Doctor?

DOCTOR: This photograph looks older.

MRS. VENABLE: The photograph looks older but not the subject. It takes character to refuse to grow old, Doctor—successfully to refuse to. It calls for discipline, abstention. One cocktail before dinner, not two, four, six—a single lean chop and lime juice on a salad in restaurants famed for rich dishes.

(MISS FOXHILL *comes from the house.*)

MISS FOXHILL: Mrs. Venable, Miss Holly's mother and brother are—

(*Simultaneously* MRS. HOLLY *and* GEORGE *appear in the window.*)

GEORGE: Hi, Aunt Vi!

MRS. HOLLY: Violet dear, we're here.

MISS FOXHILL: They're here.

MRS. VENABLE: Wait upstairs in my upstairs living room for me.

(*To* MISS FOXHILL:)

Get them upstairs. I don't want them at that window during this talk.

(*To the* DOCTOR:)

Let's get away from the window.

(He wheels her to stage center.)

DOCTOR: Mrs. Venable? Did your son have a—well—what kind of a *personal,*   245
    well, *private* life did—
MRS. VENABLE: That's a question I wanted you to ask me.
DOCTOR: Why?
MRS. VENABLE: I haven't heard the girl's story except indirectly in a watered-
    down version, being too ill to go to hear it directly, but I've gathered   250
    enough to know that it's a hideous attack on my son's moral character
    which, being dead, he can't defend himself from. I have to be the
    defender. Now. Sit down. Listen to me . . .

(The DOCTOR sits.)

    . . . before you hear whatever you're going to hear from the girl when
    she gets here. My son, Sebastian, was chaste. Not c-h-a-s-e-d! Oh, he   255
    was chased in that way of spelling it, too, we had to be very fleet-
    footed I can tell you, with his looks and his charm, to keep ahead of
    pursuers, every kind of pursuer!—I mean he was c-h-a-s-t-e!—Chaste. . . .
DOCTOR: I understood what you meant, Mrs. Venable.
MRS. VENABLE: And you *believe* me, don't you?   260
DOCTOR: Yes, but—
MRS. VENABLE: But *what?*
DOCTOR: Chastity at—what age was your son last summer?
MRS. VENABLE: *Forty,* maybe. We really didn't count birthdays. . . .
DOCTOR: He lived a celibate life?   265
MRS. VENABLE: As strictly as if he'd vowed to! This sounds like vanity, Doctor,
    but really I was actually the only one in his life that satisfied the
    demands he made of people. Time after time my son would let people
    go, dismiss them!—because their, their, their!—*attitude* toward him was—
DOCTOR: Not as pure as—   270
MRS. VENABLE: My son, Sebastian, demanded! We were a famous couple.
    People didn't speak of Sebastian and his mother or Mrs. Venable and
    her son, they said "Sebastian and Violet, Violet and Sebastian are
    staying at the Lido, they're at the Ritz in Madrid. Sebastian and Violet,
    Violet and Sebastian have taken a house at Biarritz for the season,"   275
    and every appearance, every time we appeared, attention was centered
    on *us!—everyone else! Eclipsed!* Vanity? Ohhhh, no, Doctor, you can't
    call it that—
DOCTOR: I didn't call it that.
MRS. VENABLE: —It wasn't *folie de grandeur,* it was grandeur.   280
DOCTOR: I see.
MRS. VENABLE: An attitude toward life that's hardly been known in the world
    since the great Renaissance princes were crowded out of their palaces
    and gardens by successful shopkeepers!

DOCTOR: I see.

MRS. VENABLE: Most people's lives—what are they but trails of debris, each day more debris, more debris, long, long trails of debris with nothing to clean it all up but, finally, death. . . .

(We hear lyric music.)

My son, Sebastian, and I constructed our days, each day, we would—carve out each day of our lives like a piece of sculpture.—Yes, we left behind us a trail of days like a gallery of sculpture! But, last summer—

(Pause: the music continues.)

I can't forgive him for it, not even now that he's paid for it with his life!—he let in this—vandal! This—

DOCTOR: The girl that—?

MRS. VENABLE: That you're going to meet here this afternoon! Yes. He admitted this vandal and with her tongue for a hatchet she's gone about smashing our legend, the memory of—

DOCTOR: Mrs. Venable, what do you think is her reason?

MRS. VENABLE: Lunatics don't have reason!

DOCTOR: I mean what do you think is her—motive?

MRS. VENABLE: What a question!—We put the bread in her mouth and the clothes on her back. People that like you for that or even forgive you for it are, are—hen's teeth, Doctor. The role of the benefactor is worse than thankless, it's the role of a victim, Doctor, a sacrificial victim, yes, they want your blood, Doctor, they want your blood on the altar steps of their outraged, outrageous egos!

DOCTOR: Oh. You mean she resented the—

MRS. VENABLE: Loathed!—They can't shut her up at St. Mary's.

DOCTOR: I thought she'd been there for months.

MRS. VENABLE: I mean keep her still there. She babbles! They couldn't shut her up in Cabeza de Lobo or at the clinic in Paris—she babbled, babbled!—smashing my son's reputation.—On the Berengaria bringing her back to the States she broke out of the stateroom and babbled, babbled; even at the airport when she was flown down here, she babbled a bit of her story before they could whisk her into an ambulance to St. Mary's. This is a reticule, Doctor. (She raises a cloth bag.) A catch-all, carry-all bag for an elderly lady which I turned into last summer. . . . Will you open it for me, my hands are stiff, and fish out some cigarettes and a cigarette holder.

(He does.)

DOCTOR: I don't have matches.

MRS. VENABLE: I think there's a table-lighter on the table.

DOCTOR: Yes, there is.

(He lights it, it flames up high.)

My Lord, what a torch!

MRS. VENABLE *(with a sudden, sweet smile):*   "So shines a good deed in a naughty
world," Doctor—Sugar. . . .   325

(Pause. A bird sings sweetly in the garden.)

DOCTOR: Mrs. Venable?

MRS. VENABLE: Yes?

DOCTOR: In your letter last week you made some reference to a, to a—fund of
some kind, an endowment fund of—

MRS. VENABLE: I wrote you that my lawyers and bankers and certified public   330
accountants were setting up the Sebastian Venable Memorial Foundation
to subsidize the work of young people like you that are pushing out the
frontiers of art and science but have a financial problem. You have a
financial problem, don't you, Doctor?

DOCTOR: Yes, we do have that problem. My work is such a *new* and *radical*   335
thing that people in charge of state funds are naturally a little scared
of it and keep us on a small budget, so small that—. We need a separate
ward for my patients, I need trained assistants, I'd like to marry a girl I
can't afford to marry!—But there's also the problem of getting right
patients, not just—criminal psychopaths that the State turns over to us   340
for my operation!—because it's—well—risky. . . . I don't want to turn
you against my work at Lion's View but I have to be honest with you.
There is a good deal of risk in my operation. Whenever you enter the
brain with a foreign object . . .

MRS. VENABLE: Yes.   345

DOCTOR: —Even a needle-thin knife . . .

MRS. VENABLE: Yes.

DOCTOR: —In a skilled surgeon's fingers . . .

MRS. VENABLE: Yes.

DOCTOR: —There is a good deal of risk involved in—the operation. . . .   350

MRS. VENABLE: You said that it pacifies them, it quiets them down, it suddenly
makes them peaceful.

DOCTOR: Yes. It does that, that much we already know, but—

MRS. VENABLE: What?

DOCTOR: Well, it will be ten years before we can tell if the immediate benefits   355
of the operation will be lasting or—passing or even if there'd still be—
and this is what haunts me about it!—any possibility, afterwards, of
—reconstructing a—totally sound person, it may be that the person will

777

always be limited afterwards, relieved of acute disturbances but—
limited, Mrs. Venable. . . .   360

MRS. VENABLE: Oh, but what a blessing to them, Doctor, to be just peaceful,
to be just suddenly—peaceful. . . .

(*A bird sings sweetly in the garden.*)

After all that horror, after those nightmares; just to be able to lift up
their eyes and see—(*She looks up and raises a hand to indicate the sky*)
—a sky not as black with savage, devouring birds as the sky that we   365
saw in the Encantadas, Doctor.

DOCTOR: —Mrs. Venable? I can't guarantee that a lobotomy would stop her—
babbling!!

MRS. VENABLE: That may be, maybe not, but after the operation, who would
believe her, Doctor?   370

(*Pause: faint jungle music.*)

DOCTOR (*quietly*): My God. (*Pause.*)—Mrs. Venable, suppose after meeting the
girl and observing the girl and hearing this story she babbles—I still
shouldn't feel that her condition's—intractable enough! to justify the
risks of—suppose I shouldn't feel that non-surgical treatment such as
insulin shock and electric shock and—   375

MR. VENABLE: SHE'S HAD ALL THAT AT SAINT MARY'S!! Nothing else is left for
her.

DOCTOR: But if I disagreed with you? (*Pause.*)

MRS. VENABLE: That's just part of a question: finish the question, Doctor.

DOCTOR: Would you still be interested in my work at Lion's View? I mean would   380
the Sebastian Venable Memorial Foundation still be interested in it?

MRS. VENABLE: Aren't we always more interested in a thing that concerns us
personally, Doctor?

DOCTOR: Mrs. Venable!!

(CATHARINE HOLLY *appears between the lace window curtains.*)

You're such an innocent person that it doesn't occur to you, it obviously   385
hasn't even occurred to you that anybody less innocent than you are
could possibly interpret this offer of a subsidy as—well, as sort of a
bribe?

MRS. VENABLE (*laughs, throwing her head back*): Name it that—I don't care—.
There's just two things to remember. She's a destroyer. My son was a   390
creator!—Now if my honesty's shocked you—pick up your little black
bag without the subsidy in it, and run away from this garden!—Nobody's
heard our conversation but you and I, Doctor Sugar. . . .

(MISS FOXHILL *comes out of the house and calls.*)

MISS FOXHILL: Mrs. Venable?

MRS. VENABLE: What is it, what do you want, Miss Foxhill? 395

MISS FOXHILL: Mrs. Venable? Miss Holly is here, with—

(MRS. VENABLE *sees* CATHARINE *at the window.*)

MRS. VENABLE: Oh, my God. There she is, in the window!—I told you I didn't want her to enter my house again, I told you to meet them at the door and lead them around the side of the house to the garden and you didn't listen. I'm not ready to face her. I have to have my five o'clock 400 cocktail first, to fortify me. Take my chair inside. Doctor? Are you still here? I thought you'd run out of the garden. I'm going back through the garden to the other entrance. Doctor? Sugar? You may stay in the garden if you wish to or run out of the garden if you wish to or go in this way if you wish to or do anything that you wish to but I'm going 405 to have my five o'clock daiquiri, *frozen!*—before I face her. . . .

(All *during this she has been sailing very slowly off through the garden like a stately vessel at sea with a fair wind in her sails, a pirate's frigate or a treasure-laden galleon. The young* DOCTOR *stares at* CATHARINE *framed by the lace window curtains.* SISTER FELICITY *appears beside her and draws her away from the window. Music: an ominous fanfare.* SISTER FELICITY *holds the door for* CATHARINE *as the* DOCTOR *starts quickly forward. He starts to pick up his bag but doesn't.* CATHARINE *rushes out, they almost collide with each other.*)

CATHARINE: *Excuse me.*

DOCTOR: *I'm sorry. . . .*

(*She looks after him as he goes into the house.*)

SISTER FELICITY: Sit down and be still till your family come outside.

(*Dim Out*)

SCENE TWO

CATHARINE *removes a cigarette from a lacquered box on the table and lights it. The following quick, cadenced lines are accompanied by quick, dancelike movement, almost formal, as the* SISTER *in her sweeping white habit, which should be starched to make a crackling sound, pursues the girl about the white wicker patio table and among the wicker chairs: this can be accompanied by quick music.*

SISTER: What did you take out of that box on the table?

CATHERINE: Just a cigarette, Sister.

SISTER: Put it back in the box.

CATHERINE: Too late, it's already lighted.

SISTER: Give it here. 5

CATHARINE: Oh, please, let me smoke, Sister!

SISTER: Give it here.

CATHARINE: *Please*, Sister Felicity.

SISTER: Catharine, give it here. You know that you're not allowed to smoke at Saint Mary's. 10

CATHARINE: We're not at Saint Mary's, this is an afternoon out.

SISTER: You're still in my charge. I can't permit you to smoke because the last time you smoked you dropped a lighted cigarette on your dress and started a fire.

CATHARINE: Oh, I did not start a fire. I just burned a hole in my skirt because I 15 was half unconscious under medication. (*She is now back of a white wicker chair.*)

SISTER (*overlapping her*): Catharine, give it here.

CATHARINE: Don't be such a bully!

SISTER: Disobedience has to be paid for later. 20

CATHARINE: All right, I'll pay for it later.

SISTER (*overlapping*): Give me that cigarette or I'll make a report that'll put you right back on the violent ward, if you don't. (*She claps her hands twice and holds one hand out across the table.*)

CATHARINE (*overlapping*): I'm not being violent, Sister. 25

SISTER (*overlapping*): Give me that cigarette, I'm holding my hand out for it!

CATHARINE: All right, take it, here, take it!

(*She thrusts the lighted end of the cigarette into the palm of the SISTER'S hand. The SISTER cries out and sucks her burned hand.*)

SISTER: *You burned me with it!*

CATHARINE: I'm sorry, I didn't mean to.

SISTER (*shocked, hurt*): You deliberately burned me! 30

CATHARINE (*overlapping*): You said give it to you and so I gave it to you.

SISTER (*overlapping*): You stuck the lighted end of that cigarette in my hand!

CATHARINE (*overlapping*): I'm *sick*, I'm *sick*!—of being *bossed* and *bullied*!

SISTER (*commandingly*): *Sit down!*

(CATHARINE *sits down stiffly in a white wicker chair on forestage, facing the audience. The* SISTER *resumes sucking the burned palm of her hand. Ten beats. Then from inside the house the whirr of a mechanical mixer.*)

CATHARINE: There goes the Waring Mixer, Aunt Violet's about to have her five 35 o'clock frozen daiquiri, you could set a watch by it! (*She almost laughs.*

Then she draws a deep, shuddering breath and leans back in her chair, but her hands remain clenched on the white wicker arms.)—We're in Sebastian's garden. *My God, I can still cry!*

SISTER: Did you have any medication before you went out?   40

CATHARINE: No. I didn't have any. Will you give me some, Sister?

SISTER *(almost gently)*:   I can't. I wasn't told to. However, I think the doctor will give you something.

CATHARINE: The young blond man I bumped into?

SISTER: Yes. The young doctor's a specialist from another hospital.   45

CATHARINE: What hospital?

SISTER: A word to the wise is sufficient. . . .

(The DOCTOR *has appeared in the window.)*

CATHARINE *(rising abruptly)*:   I knew I was being watched, he's in the window, staring out at me!

SISTER: Sit down and be still. Your family's coming outside.   50

CATHARINE *(overlapping)*:   LION'S VIEW, IS IT! DOCTOR?

(She has advanced toward the bay window. The DOCTOR *draws back, letting the misty white gauze curtains down to obscure him.)*

SISTER *(rising with a restraining gesture which is almost pitying)*:   Sit down, dear.

CATHARINE: IS IT LION'S VIEW? DOCTOR?!

SISTER: Be still. . . .

CATHARINE: WHEN CAN I STOP RUNNING DOWN THAT STEEP WHITE STREET   55
IN CABEZA DE LOBO?

SISTER: Catharine, dear, sit down.

CATHARINE: I loved him, Sister! Why wouldn't he let me save him? I tried to hold onto his hand but he struck me away and ran, ran, ran in the wrong direction, Sister!   60

SISTER: Catharine, dear—be still.

(The SISTER *sneezes.)*

CATHARINE: Bless you, Sister. *(She says this absently, still watching the window.)*

SISTER: Thank you.

CATHARINE: The Doctor's still at the window but he's too blond to hide behind window curtains, he catches the light, he shines through them. *(She turns   65
from the window.)*—We were *going* to blonds, blonds were next on the menu.

SISTER: Be still now. Quiet, dear.

CATHARINE: Cousin Sebastian said he was famished for blonds, he was fed up with the dark ones and was famished for blonds. All the travel brochures   70
he picked up were advertisements of the blond northern countries. I think

781

he'd already booked us to—Copenhagen or—Stockholm.—Fed up with dark ones, famished for light ones: that's how he talked about people, as if they were—items on a menu.—"That one's delicious-looking, that one is appetizing," or "that one is *not* appetizing"—I think because he was really nearly half-starved from living on pills and salads. . . .   75

SISTER: *Stop it!*—Catharine, be still.

CATHARINE: He liked me and so I loved him. . . . (*She cries a little again.*) If he'd kept hold of my hand I could have saved him!—Sebastian suddenly said to me last summer: "Let's fly north, little bird—I want to walk under   80 those radiant, cold northern lights—I've never *seen* the aurora borealis!" —Somebody said once or wrote, once: "We're all of us children in a vast kindergarten trying to spell God's name with the wrong alphabet blocks!"

MRS. HOLLY (*offstage*): *Sister?*   85

(*The* SISTER *rises.*)

CATHARINE (*rising*): I think it's *me* they're calling, they call *me* "Sister," Sister!

SCENE THREE

The SISTER *resumes her seat impassively as the girl's mother and young brother appear from the garden. The mother,* MRS. HOLLY, *is a fatuous Southern lady who requires no other description. The brother,* GEORGE, *is typically good-looking, he has the best "looks" of the family, tall and elegant of figure. They enter.*

MRS. HOLLY: Catharine, dear! Catharine—

(*They embrace tentatively.*)

Well, well! Doesn't she look fine, George?

GEORGE: Uh huh.

CATHARINE: They send you to the beauty parlor whenever you're going to have a family visit. Other times you look awful, you can't have a compact or   5 lipstick or anything made out of metal because they're afraid you'll swallow it.

MRS. HOLLY (*giving a tinkly little laugh*): I think she looks just splendid, don't you, George?

GEORGE: Can't we talk to her without the nun for a minute?   10

MRS. HOLLY: Yes, I'm sure it's all right to. Sister?

CATHARINE: Excuse me, Sister Felicity, this is my mother, Mrs. Holly, and my bother, George.

SISTER: How do you do.

GEORGE: How d'ya do.   15

782

CATHARINE: This is Sister Felicity. . . .

MRS. HOLLY: We're so happy that Catharine's at Saint Mary's! So very grateful for all you're doing for her.

SISTER (*sadly, mechanically*): We do the best we can for her, Mrs. Holly.

MRS. HOLLY: I'm sure you do. Yes, well—I wonder if you would mind if we had a   20
little private chat with our Cathie?

SISTER: I'm not supposed to let her out of my sight.

MRS. HOLLY: It's just for a minute. You can sit in the hall or the garden and we'll call right back here the minute the private part of the little talk is over.

(SISTER FELICITY *withdraws with an uncertain nod and a swish of starched fabric.*)

GEORGE (*to Catherine*): Jesus! What are you up to? Huh? Sister? Are you trying   25
to RUIN us?!

MRS. HOLLY: GAWGE! WILL YOU BE QUIET. You're upsetting your sister!

(*He jumps up and stalks off a little, rapping his knee with his zipper-covered tennis racket.*)

CATHARINE: How elegant George looks.

MRS. HOLLY: George inherited Cousin Sebastian's wardrobe but everything else is in probate! Did you know that? That everything else is in probate and   30
Violet can keep it in probate just as long as she wants to?

CATHARINE: Where is Aunt Violet?

MRS. HOLLY: *George, come back here!*

(*He does, sulkily.*)

Violet's on her way down.

GEORGE: Yeah. Aunt Violet has an elevator now.   35

MRS. HOLLY: Yais, she has, she's had an elevator installed where the back stairs were, and, Sister, it's the cutest little thing you ever did see! It's paneled in Chinese lacquer, black an' gold Chinese lacquer, with lovely bird-pictures on it. But there's only room for two people at a time in it. George and I came down on foot.—I think she's havin' her frozen   40
daiquiri now, she still has a frozen daiquiri promptly at five o'clock ev'ry afternoon in the world . . . in warm weather. . . . Sister, the horrible death of Sebastian just about *killed* her!—She's now slightly better . . . but it's a question of time.—Dear, you know, I'm sure that you under-stand, why we haven't been out to see you at Saint Mary's. They said   45
you were too disturbed, and a family visit might disturb you more. But I want you to know that nobody, absolutely nobody in the city, knows a thing about what you've been through. Have they, George? Not a thing. Not a soul even knows that you've come back from Europe. When people enquire, when they question us about you, we just say that you've stayed   50

783

abroad to study something or other. (*She catches her breath.*) Now. Sister?—I want you to please be *very* careful what you say to your Aunt Violet about what happened to Sebastian in Cabeza de Lobo.

CATHARINE: What do you want me to say about what—?

MRS. HOLLY: Just don't repeat that same fantastic story! For my sake and George's sake, the sake of your brother and mother, don't repeat that horrible story again! Not to Violet! Will you? 55

CATHARINE: Then I am going to have to tell Aunt Violet what happened to her son in Cabeza de Lobo?

MRS. HOLLY: Honey, that's why you're here. She has *INSISTED* on hearing it straight from YOU! 60

GEORGE: You were the only witness to it, Cathie.

CATHARINE: No, there were others. That *ran.*

MRS. HOLLY: Oh, Sister, you've just had a little sort of a—*nightmare* about it! Now, listen to me, will you, Sister? Sebastian has left, has BEQUEATHED! —to you an' Gawge in his *will*— 65

GEORGE (*religiously*): *To each of us, fifty grand, each!—AFTER! TAXES!—GET IT?*

CATHARINE: Oh, yes, but if they give me an injection—I won't have any choice but to tell exactly what happened in Cabeza de Lobo last summer. Don't you see? I won't have any choice but to tell the truth. It makes you tell the truth because it shuts something off that might make you able not to and *everything* comes out, decent or *not* decent, you have no control, but always, always the truth! 70

MRS. HOLLY: Catharine, darling. I don't know the full story, but surely you're not too sick in your *head* to know in your *heart* that the story you've been telling is just—*too*— 75

GEORGE (*cutting in*): Cathie, Cathie, you got to forget that story! Can'tcha? For *your* fifty grand?

MRS. HOLLY: Because if Aunt Vi contests the will, and we know she'll contest it, she'll keep it in the courts forever!—We'll be— 80

GEORGE: It's in PROBATE NOW! And'll never get out of probate until you drop that story—we can't afford to hire lawyers good enough to contest it! So if you don't stop telling that crazy story, we won't have a pot to— —cook *greens* in! 85

(*He turns away with a fierce grimace and a sharp, abrupt wave of his hand, as if slapping down something. CATHARINE stares at his tall back for a moment and laughs wildly.*)

MRS. HOLLY: Catharine, don't laugh like that, it scares me, Catharine.

(*Jungle birds scream in the garden.*)

GEORGE (*turning his back on his sister*): Cathie, the money is all tied up.

(He stoops over the sofa, hands on flannel knees, speaking directly into CATHARINE'S face as if she were hard of hearing. She raises a hand to touch his cheek affectionately; he seizes the hand and removes it but holds it tight.)

If Aunt Vi decided to contest Sebastian's will that leaves us all of this cash?!—Am I coming through to you?

CATHARINE: Yes, little brother, you are.   90

GEORGE: You see, Mama, she's crazy like a coyote!

(He gives her a quick cold kiss.)

We won't get a single damn penny, honest t' God we won't! So you've just GOT to stop tellin' that story about what you say happened to Cousin Sebastian in Cabeza de Lobo, even if it's what it *couldn't* be, TRUE!—You got to drop it, Sister, you can't tell such a story to civilized   95
people in a civilized up-to-date-country!

MRS. HOLLY: Cathie, why, why, why!—did you invent such a tale?

CATHARINE: But, Mother, I DIDN'T invent it. I know it's a hideous story but it's a true story of our time and the world we live in and what did truly happen to Cousin Sebastian in Cabeza de Lobo. . . .   100

GEORGE: Oh, then you are going to tell it. Mama, she IS going to tell it! Right to Aunt Vi, and lose us a hundred thousand!—Cathie? You are a BITCH!

MRS. HOLLY: GAWGE!

GEORGE: I repeat it, a bitch! She isn't crazy, Mama, she's no more crazy than I am, she's just, just—PERVERSE! Was ALWAYS!—perverse. . . .   105

(CATHARINE turns away and breaks into quiet sobbing.)

MRS. HOLLY: Gawge, Gawge, apologize to Sister, this is no way for you to talk to your sister. You come right back over here and tell your sweet little sister you're sorry you spoke like that to her!

GEORGE (turning back to CATHARINE): I'm sorry, Cathie, but you know we NEED that money! Mama and me, we—Cathie? I got *ambitions*! And, Cathie,   110
I'm YOUNG!—I *want* things, I *need* them, Cathie! So will you please think about ME? Us?

MISS FOXHILL (offstage): Mrs. Holly? Mrs. Holly?

MRS. HOLLY: Somebody's callin' fo' me. Catharine, Gawge put it very badly but you know that it's TRUE! WE DO HAVE TO GET WHAT SEBASTIAN HAS   115
LEFT US IN HIS WILL, DEAREST! AND YOU WON'T LET US DOWN? PROMISE? YOU WON'T? LET US DOWN?

GEORGE (fiercely shouting): HERE COMES AUNT VI! Mama, Cathie, Aunt Violet's—here is Aunt Vi!

SCENE FOUR

MRS. VENABLE *enters downstage area. Entrance music.*

MRS. HOLLY: *Cathie! Here's Aunt Vi!*
MRS. VENABLE: She sees me and I see her. That's all that's necessary. Miss Foxhill, put my chair in this corner. Crank the back up a little.

(MISS FOXHILL *does this business.*)

> More. More. Not that much!—Let it back down a little. All right. Now, then, I'll have my frozen daiquiri, now. . . . Do any of you want coffee?   5
GEORGE: I'd like a chocolate malt.
MRS. HOLLY: Gawge!
MRS. VENABLE: This isn't a drugstore.
MRS. HOLLY: Oh, Gawge is just being Gawge.
MRS. VENABLE: That's what I *thought* he was being!   10

(*An uncomfortable silence falls.* MISS FOXHILL *creeps out like a burglar. She speaks in a breathless whisper, presenting a cardboard folder towards* MRS. VENABLE.)

MISS FOXHILL: Here's the portfolio marked Cabeza de Lobo. It has all your correspondence with the police there and the American consul.
MRS. VENABLE: I asked for the *English transcript*! It's in a separate—
MISS FOXHILL: Separate, yes, here it is!
MRS. VENABLE: Oh . . .   15
MISS FOXHILL: And here's the report of the private investigators and here's the report of—
MRS. VENABLE: Yes, yes, yes! Where's the doctor?
MISS FOXHILL: On the phone in the library!
MRS. VENABLE: Why does he choose such a moment to make a phone-call?   20
MISS FOXHILL: He didn't make a phone-call, he received a phone-call from—
MRS. VENABLE: Miss Foxhill, why are you talking to me like a burglar!?

(MISS FOXHILL *giggles a little desperately.*)

CATHARINE: Aunt Violet, she's frightened.—Can I move? Can I get up and move around till it starts?
MRS. HOLLY: Cathie, Cathie, dear, did Gawge tell you that he received bids   25
from every good fraternity on the Tulane campus and went Phi Delt because Paul Junior did?
MRS. VENABLE: I see that he had the natural tact and good taste to come here this afternoon outfitted from head to foot in clothes that belonged to my son!   30
GEORGE: You gave 'em to me, Aunt Vi.

MRS. VENABLE: I didn't know you'd parade them in front of me, George.

MRS. HOLLY (*quickly*): Gawge, tell Aunt Violet how grateful you are for—

GEORGE: I found a little Jew tailor on Britannia Street that makes alterations
so good you'd never guess that they weren't cut *out* for me to *begin* with!   35

MRS. HOLLY: *AND* so reasonable!—Luckily, since it seems that Sebastian's wonderful, wonderful bequest to Gawge an' Cathie is going to be tied up a
while!?

GEORGE: Aunt Vi? About the will?

(MRS. HOLLY *coughs.*)

I was just wondering if we can't figure out some way to, to—   40

MRS. HOLLY: Gawge means to EXPEDITE it! To get through the red tape quicker?

MRS. VENABLE: I understand his meaning. Foxhill, get the Doctor.

(*She has risen with her cane and hobbled to the door.*)

MISS FOXHILL (*exits calling*): Doctor!

MRS. HOLLY: Gawge, no more about money.

GEORGE: How do we know we'll ever see her again?   45

(CATHARINE *gasps and rises; she moves downstage, followed quickly by* SISTER FELICITY.)

SISTER (*mechanically*): What's wrong, dear?

CATHARINE: I think I'm just dreaming this, it doesn't seem real!

(MISS FOXHILL *comes back out, saying:*)

MISS FOXHILL: He had to answer an urgent call from Lion's View.

(*Slight, tense pause.*)

MRS. HOLLY: Violet! *Not* Lion's View!

(SISTER FELICITY *had started conducting* CATHARINE *back to the patio; she stops her,
now.*)

SISTER: Wait, dear.   50

CATHARINE: What for? I know what's coming.

MRS. VENABLE (*at same time*): Why? are you all prepared to put out a thousand
a month plus extra charges for treatments to keep the girl at St. Mary's?

MRS. HOLLY: Cathie? Cathie, dear?

(CATHARINE *has returned with the* SISTER.)

Tell Aunt Violet how grateful you are for her makin' it possible for you   55
to rest an' recuperate at such a sweet, sweet place as St. Mary's!

CATHARINE: No place for lunatics is a sweet, sweet place.

MRS. HOLLY: But the food's good there. Isn't the food good there?

CATHARINE: Just give me written permission not to eat fried grits. I had yard
privileges till I refused to eat fried grits.   60

SISTER: She lost yard privileges because she couldn't be trusted in the yard
without constant supervision or even with it because she'd run to the
fence and make signs to cars on the highway.

CATHARINE: Yes, I did, I did that because I've been trying for weeks to get a
message out of that "sweet, sweet place."   65

MRS. HOLLY: What message, dear?

CATHARINE: I got panicky, Mother.

MRS. HOLLY: Sister, I don't understand.

GEORGE: What're you scared of, Sister?

CATHARINE: What they might do to me now, after they've done all the rest!—   70
That man in the window's a specialist from Lion's View! We get newspapers. I know what they're . . .

(The DOCTOR comes out.)

MRS. VENABLE: Why, Doctor, I thought you'd left us with just that little black bag
to remember you by!

DOCTOR: Oh, no. Don't you remember our talk? I had to answer a call about   75
a patient that—

MRS. VENABLE: This is Dr. Cukrowicz. He says it means "sugar" and we can call
him "Sugar"—

(GEORGE laughs.)

He's a specialist from Lion's View.

CATHARINE *(cutting in)*:   WHAT DOES HE SPECIALIZE IN?   80

MRS. VENABLE: Something new. When other treatments have failed.

(Pause. The jungle clamor comes up and subsides again.)

CATHARINE: *Do you want to bore a hole in my skull and turn a knife in my
brain?* Everything else was done to me!

(MRS. HOLLY sobs. GEORGE raps his knee with the tennis racket.)

You'd have to have my mother's permission for that.

MRS. VENABLE: I'm paying to keep you in a private asylum.   85

CATHARINE: You're not my legal guardian.

MRS. VENABLE: Your mother's dependent on me. All of you are!—Financially. . . .

CATHARINE: I think the situation is—clear to me, now. . . .

MRS. VENABLE: Good! In that case. . . .

DOCTOR: I think a quiet atmosphere will get us the best results. 90

MRS. VENABLE: I don't know what you mean by a quiet atmosphere. She shouted, I didn't.

DOCTOR: Mrs. Venable, let's try to keep things on a quiet level, now. Your niece seems to be disturbed.

MRS. VENABLE: She has every reason to be. She took my son from me, and then 95 she—

CATHARINE: Aunt Violet, you're not being fair.

MRS. VENABLE: Oh, aren't I?

CATHARINE (to the others): She's not being fair.

(Then back to MRS. VENABLE:)

Aunt Violet, you know why Sebastian asked me to travel with him. 100

MRS. VENABLE: Yes, I do know why!

CATHARINE: You weren't able to travel. You'd had a—(She stops short.)

MRS. VENABLE: Go on! What had I had? Are you afraid to say it in front of the Doctor? She meant that I had a stroke.—I DID NOT HAVE A STROKE!— I had a slight aneurism. You know what that is, Doctor? A little vascular 105 convulsion! Not a hemorrhage, just a little convulsion of a blood-vessel. I had it when I discovered that she was trying to take my son away from me. Then I had it. It gave a little temporary—muscular—contraction.—To one side of my face. . . . (She crosses back into main acting area.) These people are not blood-relatives of mine, they're my dead husband's 110 relations. I always detested these people, my dead husband's sister and —her two worthless children. But I did more than my duty to keep their heads above water. To please my son, whose weakness was being excessively softhearted, I went to the expense and humiliation, yes, public humiliation, of giving this girl a debut which was a fiasco. Nobody liked 115 her when I brought her out. Oh, she had some kind of—notoriety! She had a sharp tongue that some people mistook for wit. A habit of laughing in the faces of decent people which would infuriate them, and also reflected adversely on me and Sebastian, too. But, he, Sebastian, was amused by this girl. While I was disgusted, sickened. And halfway 120 through the season, she was dropped off the party lists, yes, dropped off the lists in spite of my position. Why? Because she'd lost her head over a young married man, made a scandalous scene at a Mardi Gras ball, in the middle of the ballroom. Then everybody dropped her like a hot— rock, but—(She loses her breath.) My son, Sebastian, still felt sorry for 125 her and took her with him last summer instead of me. . . .

CATHARINE (springing up with a cry): I can't change truth, I'm not God! I'm not even sure that He could, I don't think God can change truth! How can I change the story of what happened to her son in Cabeza de Lobo?

MRS. VENABLE (*at the same time*): She was in love with my son!   130
CATHARINE (*overlapping*): Let me go back to Saint Mary's. Sister Felicity, let's go back to Saint—
MRS. VENABLE (*overlapping*): Oh, no! That's not where you'll go!
CATHARINE (*overlapping*): All right, *Lion's View* but don't ask me to—
MRS. VENABLE (*overlapping*): You *know* that you were!   135
CATHARINE (*overlapping*): That I was *what*, Aunt Violet?
MRS. VENABLE (*overlapping*): Don't call me "Aunt," you're the niece of my dead husband, not me!
MRS. HOLLY (*overlapping*): Catharine, Catharine, don't upset your—Doctor? Oh, Doctor!   140

(*But the* DOCTOR *is calmly observing the scene, with detachment. The jungle garden is loud with the sounds of its feathered and scaled inhabitants.*)

CATHARINE: I don't want to, I didn't want to come here! I know what she thinks, she thinks I murdered her son, she thinks that I was responsible for his death.
MRS. VENABLE: That's right. I told him when he told me that he was going with you in my place last summer that I'd never see him again and I never   145
did. And only you know why!
CATHARINE: Oh, my God, I—

(*She rushes out toward garden, followed immediately by the* SISTER.)

SISTER: Miss Catharine, Miss Catharine—
DOCTOR (*overlapping*): Mrs. Venable?
SISTER (*overlapping*): Miss Catharine?   150
DOCTOR (*overlapping*): Mrs. Venable?
MRS. VENABLE: What?
DOCTOR: I'd like to be left alone with Miss Catharine for a few minutes.
MRS. HOLLY: George, talk to her, George.

(GEORGE *crouches appealingly before the old lady's chair, peering close into her face, a hand on her knee.*)

GEORGE: Aunt Vi? Cathie can't go to Lion's View. Everyone in the Garden   155
District would know you'd put your niece in a state asylum, Aunt Vi.
MRS. VENABLE: Foxhill!
GEORGE: What do you want, Aunt Vi?
MRS. VENABLE: Let go of my chair. Foxhill? Get me away from these people!
GEORGE: Aunt Vi, listen, think of the talk it—   160
MRS. VENABLE: I can't get up! Push me, push me away!
GEORGE (*rising but holding chair*): I'll push her, Miss Foxhill.
MRS. VENABLE: Let go of my chair or—

MISS FOXHILL: Mr. Holly, I—
GEORGE: I got to talk to her.

(*He pushes her chair downstage.*)

MRS. VENABLE: Foxhill!
MISS FOXHILL: Mr. Holly, she doesn't want you to push her.
GEORGE: I know what I'm doing, leave me alone with Aunt Vi!
MRS. VENABLE: Let go me or I'll *strike* you!
GEORGE: Oh, Aunt Vi!

MRS. HOLLY: George—
MRS. VENABLE: Foxhill!
GEORGE: Aunt Vi?

(*She strikes at him with her cane. He releases the chair and* MISS FOXHILL *pushes her off. He trots after her a few steps, then he returns to* MRS. HOLLY, *who is sobbing into a handkerchief. He sighs, and sits down beside her, taking her hand. The scene fades as light is brought up on* CATHARINE *and the* SISTER *in the garden. The* DOCTOR *comes up to them.* MRS. HOLLY *stretches her arms out to* GEORGE, *sobbing, and he crouches before her chair and rests his head in her lap. She strokes his head. During this: the* SISTER *has stood beside* CATHARINE, *holding onto her arm.*)

CATHARINE: You don't have to hold onto me. I can't run away.
DOCTOR: Miss Catharine?

CATHARINE: What?
DOCTOR: Your aunt is a very sick woman. She had a stroke last spring?
CATHARINE: Yes, she did, but she'll never admit it. . . .
DOCTOR: You have to understand why.
CATHARINE: I do, I understand why. I didn't want to come here.

DOCTOR: Miss Catharine, do you hate her?
CATHARINE: I don't understand what hate is. How can you hate anybody and still be sane? You see, I still think I'm sane!
DOCTOR: You think she did have a stroke?
CATHARINE: She had a slight stroke in April. It just affected one side, the left side, of her face . . . but it was disfiguring, and after that, Sebastian couldn't use her.

DOCTOR: Use her? Did you say use her?

(*The sounds of the jungle garden are not loud but ominous*).

CATHARINE: Yes, we all use each other and that's what we think of as love, and not being able to use each other is what's—*hate*. . . .

DOCTOR: Do you hate her, Miss Catharine?
CATHARINE: Didn't you ask me that, once? And didn't I say that I didn't understand hate. A ship struck an iceberg at sea—everyone sinking—

DOCTOR: Go on, Miss Catharine!

CATHARINE: But that's no reason for everyone drowning for hating everyone   195
drowning! Is it, Doctor?

DOCTOR: Tell me: what was your feeling for your cousin Sebastian?

CATHARINE: He liked me and so I loved him.

DOCTOR: In what way did you love him?

CATHARINE: The only way he'd accept:—a sort of motherly way. I tried to save   200
him, Doctor.

DOCTOR: From what? Save him from what?

CATHARINE: Completing!—a sort of!—*image!*—he had of himself as a sort of!—
sacrifice to a!—*terrible* sort of a—

DOCTOR: —God?   205

CATHARINE: Yes, a—*cruel* one, Doctor!

DOCTOR: How did you feel about that?

CATHARINE: Doctor, my feelings are the sort of feelings that you have in a
dream. . . .

DOCTOR: Your life doesn't seem real to you?   210

CATHARINE: Suddenly last winter I began to write my journal in the third person.

(He grasps her elbow and leads her out upon forestage. At the same time MISS FOXHILL
    wheels MRS. VENABLE off, MRS. HOLLY weeps into a handkerchief and GEORGE
    rises and shrugs and turns his back to the audience.)

DOCTOR: Something happened last winter?

CATHARINE: At a Mardi Gras ball some—some boy that took me to it got too
drunk to stand up! (A short, mirthless note of laughter.) I wanted to go
home. My coat was in the cloakroom, they couldn't find the check for it   215
in his pockets. I said, "Oh, hell, let it go!"—I started out for a taxi.
Somebody took my arm and said, "I'll drive you home." He took off his
coat as we left the hotel and put it over my shoulders, and then I looked
at him and—I don't think I'd ever even seen him before then, really!—He
took me home in his car but took me another place first. We stopped   220
near the Duelling Oaks at the end of Esplanade Street. . . . Stopped!
—I said, "What for?"—He didn't answer, just struck a match in the car
to light a cigarette in the car and I looked at him in the car and I knew
"what for"!—I think I got out of the car before he got out of the car,
and we walked through the wet grass to the great misty oaks as if   225
somebody was calling us for help there!

(Pause. The subdued, toneless bird-cries in the garden turn to a single bird-song.)

DOCTOR: After that?

CATHARINE: I lost him.—He took me home and said an awful thing to me. "We'd
better forget it," he said, "my wife's expecting a child and—." —I just
entered the house and sat there thinking a little and then I suddenly   230

called a taxi and went right back to the Roosevelt Hotel ballroom. The ball was still going on. I thought I'd gone back to pick up my borrowed coat but that wasn't what I'd gone back for. I'd gone back to make a scene on the floor of the ballroom, yes, I didn't stop at the cloakroom to pick up Aunt Violet's old mink stole, no, I rushed right into the ballroom and spotted him on the floor and ran up to him and beat him as hard as I could in the face and chest with my fists till—Cousin Sebastian took me away.—After that, the next morning, I started writing my diary in the third person, singular, such as "She's still living this morning," meaning that *I* was. . . . —"WHAT'S NEXT FOR HER? GOD KNOWS!"—I couldn't go out any more.—However one morning my Cousin Sebastian came in my bedroom and said: "Get up!"—Well . . . if you're still alive after dying, well then, you're obedient, Doctor.—I got up. He took me downtown to a place for passport photos. Said: "Mother can't go abroad with me this summer. You're going to go with me this summer instead of Mother."—If you don't believe me, read my journal of Paris!—"She woke up at daybreak this morning, had her coffee and dressed and took a brief walk—"

DOCTOR: *Who* did?

CATHARINE: *She* did. *I* did—from the Hotel Plaza Athénée to the Place de l'Étoile as if pursued by a pack of Siberian wolves! (*She laughs her tired, helpless laugh.*)—Went right through all stop signs—couldn't wait for green signals.—"Where did she think she was going? Back to the Duelling Oaks?"—Everything chilly and dim but his hot, ravenous mouth! on—

DOCTOR: Miss Catharine, let me give you something.

(*The others go out, leaving* CATHARINE *and the* DOCTOR *onstage.*)

CATHARINE: Do I have to have the injection again, this time? What am I going to be stuck with this time, Doctor? I don't care. I've been stuck so often that if you connected me with a garden hose I'd make a good sprinkler.

DOCTOR (*preparing needle*): Please take off your jacket.

(*She does. The* DOCTOR *gives her an injection.*)

CATHARINE: I didn't feel it.

DOCTOR: That's good. Now sit down.

(*She sits down.*)

CATHARINE: Shall I start counting backwards from a hundred?

DOCTOR: Do you like counting backwards?

CATHARINE: Love it! Just love it! One hundred! Ninety-nine! Ninety-eight! Ninety-seven. Ninety-six. Ninety—five—. Oh!—I already feel it! How funny!

DOCTOR: That's right. Close your eyes for a minute.

(*He moves his chair closer to hers. Half a minute passes.*)

      Miss Catharine? I want you to give me something.

CATHARINE: Name it and it's yours, Doctor Sugar.

DOCTOR: Give me all your resistance.   270

CATHARINE: Resistance to what?

DOCTOR: The truth. Which you're going to tell me.

CATHARINE: The truth's the one thing I have never resisted!

DOCTOR: Sometimes people just think they don't resist it, but still do.

CATHARINE: They say it's at the bottom of a bottomless well, you know.   275

DOCTOR: Relax.

CATHARINE: Truth.

DOCTOR: Don't talk.

CATHARINE: Where was I, now? At ninety?

DOCTOR: You don't have to count backwards.   280

CATHARINE: At ninety something?

DOCTOR: You can open your eyes.

CATHARINE: Oh, I do feel funny!

(*Silence, pause.*)

      You know what I think you're doing? I think you're trying to hypnotize me. Aren't you? You're looking straight at me and doing something to   285 me with your eyes and your—eyes. . . . Is that what you're doing to me?

DOCTOR: Is that what you *feel* I'm doing?

CATHARINE: Yes! I feel so peculiar. And it's not just the drug.

DOCTOR: Give me all your resistance. See. I'm holding my hand out. I want you to put yours in mine and give me all your resistance. Pass all of   290 your resistance out of your hand to mine.

CATHARINE: Here's my hand. But there's no resistance in it.

DOCTOR: You are totally passive.

CATHARINE: Yes, I am.

DOCTOR: You will do what I ask.   295

CATHARINE: Yes, I will try.

DOCTOR: You will tell the true story.

CATHARINE: Yes, I will.

DOCTOR: The absolutely true story. No lies, nothing not spoken. Everything told, exactly.   300

CATHARINE: Everything. Exactly. Because I'll have to. Can I—can I stand up?

DOCTOR: Yes, but be careful. You might feel a little bit dizzy.

(*She struggles to rise, then falls back.*)

CATHARINE: I can't get up! Tell me to. Then I think I could do it.
DOCTOR: Stand up.

(*She rises unsteadily.*)

CATHARINE: How funny! Now I can! Oh, I do feel dizzy! Help me, I'm—   305

(*He rushes to support her.*)

   —about to fall over. . . .

(*He holds her. She looks out vaguely toward the brilliant, steaming garden. Looks back
   at him. Suddenly sways toward him, against him.*)

DOCTOR: You see, you lost your balance.
CATHARINE: No, I didn't. I did what I wanted to do without you telling me to.

(*She holds him tight against her.*)

   Let me! Let! Let! Let me! Let me, let me, oh, let me. . . .

(*She crushes her mouth to his violently. He tries to disengage himself. She presses her
   lips to his fiercely, clutching his body against her. Her brother GEORGE enters.*)

   Please hold me; I've been so lonely. It's lonelier than death, if I've gone   310
   mad, it's lonelier than death!
GEORGE (*shocked, disgusted*): Cathie!—you've got a hell of a nerve.

(*She falls back, panting, covers her face, runs a few paces and grabs the back of a
   chair. MRS. HOLLY enters.*)

MRS. HOLLY: What's the matter, George? Is Catharine ill?
GEORGE: No.
DOCTOR: Miss Catharine had an injection that made her a little unsteady.   315
MRS. HOLLY: What did he say about Catharine?

             (CATHARINE *has gone out into the dazzling jungle of the garden.*)

SISTER (*returning*): She's gone into the garden.
DOCTOR: That's all right, she'll come back when I call her.
SISTER: It may be all right for you. You're not responsible for her.

(MRS. VENABLE *has re-entered.*)

MRS. VENABLE: Call her now!   320

DOCTOR: Miss Catharine! Come back.

(*To the* SISTER:)

Bring her back, please, Sister!

(CATHARINE *enters quietly, a little unsteady.*)

Now, Miss Catharine, you're going to tell the true story.
CATHARINE: Where do I start the story?
DOCTOR: Wherever you think it started.   325
CATHARINE: I think it started the day he was born in this house.
MRS. VENABLE: Ha! You see!
GEORGE: Cathie.
DOCTOR: Let's start later than that. (*Pause.*) Shall we begin with last summer?
CATHARINE: Oh. Last summer.   330
DOCTOR: Yes. Last summer.

(*There is a long pause. The raucous sounds in the garden fade into a bird-song which is clear and sweet.* MRS. HOLLY *coughs.* MRS. VENABLE *stirs impatiently.* GEORGE *crosses downstage to catch* CATHARINE'S *eye as he lights a cigarette.*)

CATHARINE: Could I—?
MRS. VENABLE: Keep that boy away from her!
GEORGE: She wants to smoke, Aunt Vi.
CATHARINE: Something helps in the—hands. . . .   335
SISTER: Unh unh!
DOCTOR: It's all right, Sister. (*He lights her cigarette.*) About last summer: how did it begin?
CATHARINE: It began with his kindness and the six days at sea that took me so far away from the—Duelling Oaks that I forgot them, nearly. He was   340 affectionate with me, so sweet and attentive to me, that some people took us for a honeymoon couple until they noticed that we had— separate staterooms, and—then in Paris, he took me to Patou and Schiaparelli's—*this* is from Schiaparelli's! (*Like a child, she indicates her suit.*)—bought me so many new clothes that I gave away my old ones to   345 make room for my new ones in my new luggage to—travel. . . . I turned into a peacock! Of course, so was *he* one, too. . . .
GEORGE: *Ha Ha!*
MRS. VENABLE: Shh!
CATHARINE: But then I made the mistake of responding too much to his kindness,   350 of taking hold of his hand before he'd take hold of mine, of holding onto his arm and leaning on his shoulder, of appreciating his kindness more than he wanted me to, and, suddenly, last summer, he began to be restless, and—oh!

DOCTOR: Go on.

CATHARINE: The Blue Jay notebook!

DOCTOR: Did you say notebook?

MRS. VENABLE: I know what she means by that, she's talking about the school composition book with a Blue Jay trademark that Sebastian used for making notes and revisions on his "Poem of Summer." It went with him everywhere that he went, in his jacket pocket, even his dinner jacket. I have the one that he had with him last summer. *Foxhill! The Blue Jay notebook!*

(MISS FOXHILL *rushes in with a gasp.*)

It came with his personal effects shipped back from Cabeza de Lobo.

DOCTOR: I don't quite get the connection between new clothes and so forth and the Blue Jay notebook.

MRS. VENABLE: I HAVE IT!—Doctor, tell her I've found it.

(MISS FOXHILL *hears this as she comes back out of house: gasps with relief, retires.*)

DOCTOR: With all these interruptions it's going to be awfully hard to—

MRS. VENABLE: This is important. I don't know why she mentioned the Blue Jay notebook but I want you to see it. Here it is, here! (*She holds up a* *notebook and leafs swiftly through the pages.*) Title? "Poem of Summer," and the date of the summer—1935. After that: *what? Blank pages, blank pages,* nothing but *nothing!*—last summer. . . .

DOCTOR: What's that got to do with—?

MRS. VENABLE: His destruction? I'll tell you. A poet's vocation is something that rests on something as thin and fine as the web of a spider, Doctor. That's all that holds him *over!*—out of destruction. . . . Few, very few are able to do it alone! Great help is needed! I *did* give it! She *didn't.*

CATHARINE: She's right about that. I failed him. I wasn't able to keep the web from—breaking. . . . I saw it breaking but couldn't save or—repair it!

MRS. VENABLE: There now, the truth's coming out. We had an agreement between us, a sort of contract or covenant between us which he broke last summer when he broke away from me and took her with him, not me! When he was frightened and I knew when and what of, because his hands would shake and his eyes looked in, not out, I'd reach across a table and touch his hands and say not a word, just look, and touch his hands with my hand until his hands stopped shaking and his eyes looked out, not in, and in the morning, the poem would be continued. *Continued until it was finished!*

(*The following ten speeches are said very rapidly, overlapping.*)

CATHARINE: I couldn't!

MRS. VENABLE: *Naturally* not! He was *mine*! I *knew* how to help him, I *could*! You didn't, you couldn't!

DOCTOR: These interruptions—

MRS. VENABLE: I would say "You *will*" and he *would*, I—!

CATHARINE: Yes, you see, I failed him! And so, last summer, we went to Cabeza   395
de Lobo, we flew down there from where he gave up writing his poem
last summer. . . .

MRS. VENABLE: Because he'd broken our—

CATHARINE: Yes! Yes, something had broken, that string of pearls that old
mothers hold their sons by like a—sort of a—sort of—*umbilical* cord,   400
long—after . . .

MRS. VENABLE: She means that I held him back from—

DOCTOR: *Please!*

MRS. VENABLE: *Destruction!*

CATHARINE: All I know is that suddenly, last summer, he wasn't young any   405
more, and we went to Cabeza de Lobo, and he suddenly switched from
the evenings to the beach. . . .

DOCTOR: From evenings? To beach?

CATHARINE: I mean from the evenings to the afternoons and from the fa—fash—

(*Silence:* MRS. HOLLY *draws a long, long painful breath.* GEORGE *stirs impatiently.*)

DOCTOR: Fashionable! Is that the word you—?   410

CATHARINE: Yes. Suddenly, last summer Cousin Sebastian changed to the afternoons and the beach.

DOCTOR: What beach?

CATHARINE: In Cabeza de Lobo there is a beach that's named for Sebastian's
name saint, it's known as La Playa San Sebastian, and that's where he   415
started spending all afternoon, every day.

DOCTOR: What kind of beach was it?

CATHARINE: It was a big city beach near the harbor.

DOCTOR: It was a big public beach?

CATHARINE: Yes, public.   420

MRS. VENABLE: It's little statements like that that give her away.

(*The* DOCTOR *rises and crosses to* MRS. VENABLE *without breaking his concentration on*
CATHARINE.)

After all I've told you about his fastidiousness, can you accept such a
statement?

DOCTOR: You mustn't interrupt her.

MRS. VENABLE (*overlapping him*): That Sebastian would go every day to some   425
dirty free public beach near a harbor? A man that had to go out a mile
in a boat to find water fit to swim in?

DOCTOR: Mrs. Venable, no matter what she says you have to let her say it without any more interruptions or this interview will be useless.

MRS. VENABLE: I won't speak again. I'll keep still, if it kills me. 430

CATHARINE: I don't want to go on. . . .

DOCTOR: Go on with the story. Every afternoon last summer your Cousin Sebastian and you went out to this free public beach?

CATHARINE: No, it wasn't the free one, the free one was right next to it, there was a fence between the free beach and the one that we went to that 435 charged a small charge of admission.

DOCTOR: Yes, and what did you do there?

(He still stands beside MRS. VENABLE and the light gradually changes as the girl gets deeper into her story: the light concentrates on CATHARINE, the other figures sink into shadow.)

Did anything happen there that disturbed you about it?

CATHARINE: Yes!

DOCTOR: What? 440

CATHARINE: He bought me a swim-suit I didn't want to wear. I laughed. I said, "I can't wear that, it's a scandal to the jay-birds!"

DOCTOR: What did you mean by that? That the suit was immodest?

CATHARINE: My God, yes! It was a one-piece suit made of white lisle, the water made it transparent! *(She laughs sadly at the memory of it.)* —I didn't 445 want to swim in it, but he'd grab my hand and drag me into the water, all the way in, and I'd come out looking naked!

DOCTOR: Why did he do that? Did you understand why?

CATHARINE: —Yes! To attract!—Attention.

DOCTOR: He wanted you to attract attention, did he, because he felt you were 450 moody? Lonely? He wanted to shock you out of your depression last summer?

CATHARINE: Don't you understand? I was PROCURING for him!

(MRS. VENABLE'S gasp is like the sound that a great hooked fish might make.)

She used to do it, too.

(MRS. VENABLE cries out.)

Not consciously! She didn't *know* that she was procuring for him in the 455 smart, the fashionable places they used to go to before last summer! Sebastian was shy with people. She wasn't. Neither was I. We both did the same thing for him, made contacts for him, but she did it in nice places and in decent ways and I had to do it the way that I just told you!—Sebastian was lonely, Doctor, and the empty Blue Jay notebook 460 got bigger and bigger, so big it was big and empty as that big empty blue sea and sky. . . . I knew what I was doing. I came out in the French Quarter years before I came out in the Garden District. . . .

MRS. HOLLY: Oh, Cathie! Sister . . .

DOCTOR: Hush! 465

CATHARINE: And before long, when the weather got warmer and the beach so crowded, he didn't need me any more for that purpose. The ones on the free beach began to climb over the fence or swim around it, bands of homeless young people that lived on the free beach like scavenger dogs, hungry children. . . . So now he let me wear a decent dark suit. 470 I'd go to a faraway empty end of the beach, write postcards and letters and keep up my—third-person journal till it was—five o'clock and time to meet him outside the bathhouses, on the street. . . . He would come out, *followed.*

DOCTOR: Who would follow him out? 475

CATHARINE: The homeless, hungry young people that had climbed over the fence from the free beach that they lived on. He'd pass out tips among them as if they'd all—shined his shoes or called taxis for him. . . . Each day the crowd was bigger, noisier, greedier!—Sebastian began to be frightened.—At last we stopped going out there. . . . 480

DOCTOR: And then? After that? After you quit going out to the public beach?

CATHARINE: Then one day, a few days after we stopped going out to the beach —it was one of those white blazing days in Cabeza de Lobo, not a blazing hot *blue* one but a blazing hot *white* one.

DOCTOR: Yes? 485

CATHARINE: We had a late lunch at one of those open-air restaurants on the sea there.—Sebastian was white as the weather. He had on a spotless white silk Shantung suit and a white silk tie and a white panama and white shoes, white—white lizard skin—pumps! He—(*She throws back her head in a startled laugh at the recollection*)—kept touching his face and 490 his throat here and there with a white silk handkerchief and popping little white pills in his mouth, and I knew he was having a bad time with his heart and was frightened about it and that was the reason we hadn't gone out to the beach. . . .

(*During the monologue the lights have changed, the surrounding area has dimmed out and a hot white spot is focused on* CATHARINE.)

"I think we ought to go north," he kept saying, "I think we've done 495 Cabeza de Lobo, I think we've done it, don't you?" I thought we'd done it!—but I had learned it was better not to seem to have an opinion because if I did, well, Sebastian, well, you know Sebastian, he always preferred to do what no one else wanted to do, and I always tried to give the impression that I was agreeing reluctantly to his wishes . . . it 500 was a—game . . . .

SISTER: She's dropped her cigarette.

DOCTOR: I've got it, Sister.

(There are whispers, various movements in the penumbra. The DOCTOR fills a glass for her from the cocktail shaker.)

CATHARINE: Where was I? Oh, yes, that five o'clock lunch at one of those fish- 505
places along the harbor of Cabeza de Lobo, it was between the city and
the sea, and there were naked children along the beach which was
fenced off with barbed wire from the restaurant and we had our table
less than a yard from the barbed wire fence that held the beggars at
bay. . . . There were naked children along the beach, a band of fright- 510
fully thin and dark naked children that looked like a flock of plucked
birds, and they would come darting up to the barbed wire fence as if
blown there by the wind, the hot white wind from the sea, all crying out,
"Pan, pan, pan!"

DOCTOR (quietly): What's pan?

CATHARINE: The word for bread, and they made gobbling noises with their 515
little black mouths, stuffing their little black fists to their mouths and
making those gobbling noises, with frightful grins!—Of course we were
sorry that we had come to this place but it was too late to go. . . .

DOCTOR (quietly): Why was it "too late to go"?

CATHARINE: I told you Cousin Sebastian wasn't well. He was popping those 520
little white pills in his mouth. I think he had popped in so many of them
that they had made him feel weak. . . . His, his!—eyes looked—dazed,
but he said: "Don't look at those little monsters. Beggars are a social
disease in this country. If you look at them, you get sick of the country, it
spoils the whole country for you. . . ." 525

DOCTOR: Go on.

CATHARINE: I'm going on. I have to wait now and then till it gets clearer. Under
the drug it has to be a vision, or nothing comes. . . .

DOCTOR: All right?

CATHARINE: Always when I was with him I did what he told me. I didn't look 530
at the band of naked children, not even when the waiters drove them
away from the barbed wire fence with sticks!—Rushing out through a
wicket gate like an assault party in war!—and beating them screaming
away from the barbed wire fence with the sticks. . . . Then! (Pause.)

DOCTOR: Go on, Miss Catharine, what comes next in the vision? 535

CATHARINE: The, the, the!—band of children began to—serenade us. . . .

DOCTOR: Do what?

CATHARINE: Play for us! On instruments! Make music!—if you could call it
music. . . .

DOCTOR: Oh? 540

CATHARINE: Their, their—instruments were—instruments of percussion!—Do you
know what I mean?

DOCTOR (making a note): Yes. Instruments of percussion such as—drums?

CATHARINE: I stole glances at them when Cousin Sebastian wasn't looking, and
as well as I could make out in the white blaze of the sand-beach, the   545
instruments were tin cans strung together.

DOCTOR (*slowly, writing*): *Tin—cans—strung—together.*

CATHARINE: *And, and, and, and—and!—bits of metal, other bits of metal that
had been flattened out, made into—*

DOCTOR: What?   550

CATHARINE: *Cymbals! You know? Cymbals?*

DOCTOR: Yes. Brass plates hit together.

CATHARINE: That's right, Doctor.—Tin cans flattened out and clashed together!
—Cymbals. . . .

DOCTOR: Yes. I understand. What's after that, in the vision?   555

CATHARINE (*rapidly, panting a little*): And others had paper bags, bags made
out of—coarse paper!—with something on a string inside the bags which
they pulled up and down, back and forth, to make a sort of a—

DOCTOR: Sort of a—?

CATHARINE: Noise like—   560

DOCTOR: Noise like?

CATHARINE (*rising stiffly from chair*): Ooompa! Oompa! Oooooooompa!

DOCTOR: Ahhh . . . a sound like a *tuba?*

CATHARINE: That's right!—they made a sound like a tuba. . . .

DOCTOR: Oompa, oompa, oompa, like a tuba.   565

(*He is making a note of the description.*)

CATHARINE: Oompa, oompa, oompa, like a—

(*Short pause.*)

DOCTOR: —Tuba. . . .

CATHARINE: All during lunch they stayed at a—a fairly *close—distance.* . . .

DOCTOR: Go on with the vision, Miss Catharine.

CATHARINE (*striding about the table*): Oh, I'm going on, *nothing could stop it* 570
now!!

DOCTOR: Your Cousin Sebastian was *entertained* by this—*concert?*

CATHARINE: I think he was *terrified* of it!

DOCTOR: Why was he terrified of it?

CATHARINE: I think he recognized some of the musicians, some of the boys,   575
between childhood and—older. . . .

DOCTOR: What did he do? Did he do anything about it, Miss Catharine?—Did
he complain to the manager about it?

CATHARINE: *What* manager? God? Oh, *no!*—The manager of the fishplace on
the beach? Haha!—No!—You don't understand my cousin!   580

DOCTOR: What do you mean?

CATHARINE: *He!—accepted!—all!—as—how!—things!—are!—*And thought nobody

802

had any right to complain or interfere in any way whatsoever, and even though he knew that what was awful was awful, that what was wrong was wrong, and my Cousin Sebastian was certainly never sure that anything was wrong!—He thought it unfitting to ever take any action about anything whatsoever!—except to go on doing as something in him directed. . . . 585

DOCTOR: What did something in him direct him to do?—I mean on this occasion in Cabeza de Lobo. 590

CATHARINE: After the salad, before they brought the coffee, he suddenly pushed himself away from the table, and said, "They've got to stop that! Waiter, make them stop that. I'm not a well man, I have a heart condition, it's making me sick!"—This was the first time that Cousin Sebastian had ever attempted to correct a human situation!—I think perhaps that *that* was 595 his—fatal error. . . . It was then that the waiters, all eight or ten of them, charged out of the barbed wire wicket gate and beat the little musicians away with clubs and skillets and anything hard that they could snatch from the kitchen!—Cousin Sebastian left the table. He stalked out of the restaurant after throwing a handful of paper money on the table and he 600 fled from the place. I followed. It was all white outside. White hot, a blazing white hot, hot blazing white, at five o'clock in the afternoon in the city of—Cabeza de Lobo. It looked as if—

DOCTOR: It looked as if?

CATHARINE: As if a huge white bone had caught on fire in the sky and blazed 605 so bright it was white and turned the sky and everything under the sky white with it!

DOCTOR: —White . . .

CATHARINE: Yes—white . . .

DOCTOR: You followed your Cousin Sebastian out of the restaurant onto the hot 610 white street?

CATHARINE: Running up and down hill. . . .

DOCTOR: You ran up and down hill?

CATHARINE: No, no! *Didn't!*—move either way!—at first, we were—

(*During this recitation there are various sound effects. The percussive sounds described are very softly employed.*)

I rarely made any suggestion but *this* time I *did*. . . . 615

DOCTOR: What did you suggest?

CATHARINE: Cousin Sebastian seemed to be paralyzed near the entrance of the café, so I said, "Let's go." I remember that it was a very wide and steep white street, and I said, "Cousin Sebastian, down that way is the waterfront and we are more likely to find a taxi near there. . . . Or why don't 620 we go back in?—and have them *call* us a taxi! Oh, let's do! Let's do *that*, that's better!" And he said, "*Mad*, are you *mad*? Go back in that filthy place? Never! That gang of kids shouted vile things about me to the waiters!" "Oh," I said, "then let's go down toward the docks, down there at the bottom of the hill, let's not try to climb the hill in this dreadful heat." And Cousin Sebastian shouted, "Please shut up, let me handle this situation, will you? I want to handle this thing." And he started up the steep street with a hand stuck in his jacket where I knew he was having a pain in his chest from his palpitations. . . . But he walked faster and faster, in panic, but the faster he walked the louder and closer it got!

DOCTOR: What got louder?

CATHARINE: The music.

DOCTOR: The music again.

CATHARINE: The oompa-oompa of the—following band.—They'd somehow gotten through the barbed wire and out on the street, and they were following, following!—up the blazing white street. The band of naked children pursued us up the steep white street in the sun that was like a great white bone of a giant beast that had caught on fire in the sky!—Sebastian started to run and they all screamed at once and seemed to fly in the air, they outran him so quickly. I screamed. I heard Sebastian scream, he screamed just once before this flock of black plucked little birds that pursued him and overtook him halfway up the white hill.

DOCTOR: And you, Miss Catharine, what did *you* do, then?

CATHARINE: Ran!

DOCTOR: Ran where?

CATHARINE: Down! Oh, I ran down, the easier direction to run was down, down, down, down!—The hot, white, blazing street, screaming out "Help" all the way, till—

DOCTOR: What?

CATHARINE: —Waiters, police, and others—ran out of buildings and rushed back up the hill with me. When we got back to where my Cousin Sebastian had disappeared in the flock of featherless little black sparrows, he—he was lying naked as they had been naked against a white wall, and this you won't believe, nobody *has* believed it, nobody *could* believe it, nobody, nobody on earth could possibly believe it, and I don't *blame* them!—They had *devoured* parts of him.

(MRS. VENABLE *cries out softly.*)

Torn or cut parts of him away with their hands or knives or maybe those jagged tin cans they made music with, they had torn bits of him away and stuffed them into those gobbling fierce little empty black mouths of theirs. There wasn't a sound any more, there was nothing to see but Sebastian, what was left of him, that looked like a big white-paper-wrapped bunch of red roses had been *torn, thrown, crushed!*—against that blazing white wall. . . .

(MRS. VENABLE *springs with amazing power from her wheelchair, stumbles erratically but swiftly toward the girl and tries to strike her with her cane. The* DOCTOR

804

snatches it from her and catches her as she is about to fall. She gasps hoarsely several times as he leads her toward the exit.)

MRS. VENABLE (offstage): Lion's View! State asylum, cut this hideous story out of her brain!

(MRS. HOLLY sobs and crosses to GEORGE, who turns away from her saying:)

GEORGE— Mom, I'll quit school, I'll get a job, I'll—
MRS. HOLLY: Hush son! Doctor, can't you say something?

(Pause. The DOCTOR comes downstage. CATHARINE wanders out into the garden followed by the SISTER.)

DOCTOR (after a while, reflectively, into space): I think we ought at least to consider the possibility that the girl's story could be true. . . .

The End

BARRY BERMANGE

Scenes from Family Life

Cast

MARIE
ERIC, *her second husband*
WALTER, *her first husband*
THE CHILD

The action takes place on the evening of United Nations Day.

1. [Ext. Heath. Night.]

A very long shot of the trees, wind. After a time the camera moves very slowly to discover
  WALTER. *He is standing quite still.*

2. [Int. Living-room. Night.]

A dinner table set for four.
Pause.
The main light goes out.
A match is struck.
MARIE'S hand comes into view holding the match.
It lights three candles in a candlestick, then withdraws.
Pause.

3. [Int. The Bedroom. Night.]

ERIC *in front of a mirror, slowly knotting his tie.*
Pause.

4. [Int. Living-room. Night.]

MARIE'S *hands adjusting a knife, fork, spoon, flower, glass, then the candlestick, which*
  she moves a fraction of an inch.

5. [Int. Bedroom. Night.]

ERIC *studying his tie.*
Pause.
He pulls it off impatiently.

6. [Ext. Heath. Night.]

Trees, wind. It is beautiful, but desolate and oppressive.

7. [Int. Living-room. Night.]

The candlestick.
Pause.
MARIE'S *hand reappears to return it to its former position.*
We see her, elegantly dressed in white.
She studies the table thoughtfully, then the room, then looks at her watch, then the clock.
She listens to her watch, then winds it slowly.

8. [Int. Bedroom. Night.]

Row of ties.
ERIC'S *hand comes into view and selects one.*
Pause.
Slow panning shot round the bedroom, discovering ERIC *in front of the mirror knotting the new tie.*
Pause.

9. [Int. Living-room. Night.]

MARIE *looking quietly round the room.*
It is a tastefully-furnished room, a room on which much love and expense has been lavished, a room dramatically lit for a special occasion.
Divided by an arch it comprises a lounge area and a dining area.
The areas are lit: In the lounge by lamps, in the diner by candles.
Slow panning shot round the room, discovering MARIE *at the window.*

10. [Ext. Driving. Night.]

11. [Int. Bedroom. Night.]

ERIC *buttoning his jacket and standing back to look at himself.*

12. [Int. Hall. Night.]

Pause.
ERIC *comes out of the bedroom.*
He stops to adjust a picture.

13. [Int. Living-room. Night.]

MARIE.
ERIC *entering behind her.*
He turns and sees her.

ERIC: Any sign of them?
MARIE: Not as yet.
ERIC: They said 8.
MARIE: They'll be here soon.
ERIC: If they're coming that is.

14. [Ext. Street (2) Night.]

Shot of WALTER *turning a corner.*
Hold on the car as it drives away.

15. [Int. Living-room. Night.]

ERIC *pouring himself a drink.*
He looks round.
MARIE *has gone.*

16. [Int. The Bedroom. Night.]

MARIE *at the dressing table adjusting her makeup.*
ERIC *enters, glass in hand.*
She smiles at him in the mirror.
He drinks, and moves slowly round the room.

ERIC: I was wondering . . . I was shaving, it crossed my mind,
         perhaps it occurred to you.

Pause.

         That they've decided not to come.
MARIE: They will come.
ERIC: They may have realised what an ordeal it could be. Because an ordeal
         is what it will be.

Pause.

         If they come that is.
MARIE: They're coming, Eric. They said they would and they will.

He studies himself in the mirror.

ERIC: How do I look?
MARIE: Very nice.
ERIC: What about the tie . . . (*fingering it nervously*) . . . you think it'll do?
MARIE: It's a lovely tie.
ERIC: It matches the suit?

MARIE *smiles.*

> I thought I'd wear the blue one then I thought no . . . not the blue one.
> Then I saw this one. You're sure it's all right.

MARIE: I've told you.
ERIC: It matches the suit.
MARIE: You've got nothing to worry about.
ERIC: No. That's true, you're right. What have I got to worry about? Who's
coming to see us tonight, only Walter, who's Walter? Only your husband.
MARIE: He's not my husband now. You are my husband now.

She speaks to him as one would speak to a child. She is several years his elder.

ERIC: He's still your husband. (*Drinks*)

MARIE *rises and leaves the bedroom.*

ERIC: (*As she passes*) . . . In a manner of speaking.

17. [Int. Hall. Night.]

He follows her through the hall.

ERIC: Oh I know you're divorced, we can prove it. We've got documents, we
can prove you are married to me now.

18. [Int. Living-room. Night.]

MARIE *comes in.*
She sifts through some gramophone records.
ERIC *stays in the hall.*
He talks to her through the open doorway.

ERIC: But first you were married to him. (*Drinks*)
MARIE: That's all over now.
ERIC: Is it?
MARIE: You know it is.
ERIC: Then why is he coming tonight?
MARIE: To see us . . . to see how we are getting on . . . .

ERIC: Couldn't he have written?

MARIE: He could have.

ERIC: Why didn't he then? I would have. (*Sardonically*) "Dear Marie. How are you getting on? Keeping well are you? And how is little Antonia? Growing is she? Give her a kiss from Daddy. Say he sends his love." What could be easier?

MARIE: I would have to reply. It could lead to a regular correspondence. Would you like that? My writing to him regularly?

Pause.

ERIC'S *face peers slowly round the doorway.*

ERIC: I still think it's a mistake. (*Entering the room and looking round*) He used to live here, this was his home, you were his wife, it's a situation a man should avoid if he has his wits about him which, make no mistake, *he has.* (*Then pensively*) Unless he has other reasons for coming . . .

MARIE: What reasons?

ERIC: I don't know. (*Pause*) He may have other reasons.

Pause.

Of course . . .

MARIE: Yes?

ERIC: Oh what's the use.

He moves to the decanter and fills his glass.

I was only going to say that when this first came up . . . last Wednesday was it?

MARIE: Thursday.

ERIC: Thursday. The idea of his paying us a friendly little visit seemed reasonable . . . thoughtful . . . and rather touching in a way. Why shouldn't he? A divorce isn't the end of the world. Life continues. The two parties continue to live and breathe. They go their own separate ways, possibly marry again, as you have done, but fundamentally . . . and this is the point . . . (*Continuing softly, reflectively*) . . . when you get down and look at it closely . . . nothing . . . seems to have changed . . . not really . . . or if it has . . . hardly at all. The two parties . . .

MARIE *smiles.*

. . . in spite of all that's happened to them are somehow still united . . . by a bond that goes deeper than the Law.

MARIE: And so they should be. If they are rational human beings, which most of us are. The two parties spent a little time on earth together, a few golden moments. It's not something you can easily forget.

Pause.

ERIC: Golden moments? (*Pause*) With Walter?

Pause.

> I suppose you must have had some, you were married for quite some time, and of course there's Antonia, so at least you must have had one. Do you think about him?

MARIE: Sometimes.

ERIC: A lot?

MARIE: Not all that much.

ERIC: Occasionally.

MARIE: There are times . . .

ERIC: When you're with me?

MARIE: Sometimes . . .

ERIC: When I make love to you? Then?

MARIE: There have been times, I must confess . . .

ERIC: That proves it then, doesn't it?

MARIE: Proves what?

ERIC: That you . . . and him . . . you and Walter . . . you're still . . . (*Pauses*) Of course you are.

MARIE: What?

ERIC: Related.

Camera on MARIE.
Camera on ERIC.
Camera on WALTER in his car.
Pause.

19. [Ext. Street (3) Night.]

Traffic light at red.
It changes through to green.
The car, which has been stationary, moves quietly forward.
Hold on the car as it drives away.

20. [Int. Living-room. Night.]

ERIC watching MARIE.
Pause.

MARIE: You are imbuing this situation with a drama it doesn't possess. It's a little reunion, no more, no less, and completely accidental as you know. A chance meeting. It can happen to anyone.

She continues calmly, softly, as she has been since the beginning.

I ran into him in Baker Street. If I hadn't, nothing would have happened, nothing at all. He wouldn't have asked to come; we wouldn't be expecting him tonight. It was an accident. These things happen.

ERIC *watches her quietly.*

MARIE: Everything's going to be all right. He's very understanding, it will be just as bad for him and just as bad for her and just as bad for me, so we must try, all of us, to make the evening a success, which I'm sure it will be. They'll come. We'll have a bit to eat . . . a drink. A little chat. Then they'll go. And that will be that.

ERIC: Until the next time.

MARIE *turns and moves towards the diner.*

(*As she passes*) . . . There's bound to be a next time . . .

He follows her into the diner.

. . . once won't be enough for him. If he comes at all, he'll want to come again.

MARIE *stops at the window, and looks down.*
Pause.

MARIE: We shall see.

ERIC *comes out of the shadows behind her.*
He stops behind her.

ERIC: (*Softly*) Why today?

He looks at her quietly.

What made him choose today . . . Or was it you who chose it?

MARIE: I can't remember.

ERIC: Why today I wonder . . . Something special about it?

MARIE: No.

ERIC: You chose it just like that.

MARIE: Just like that.

ERIC: An anniversary?

MARIE: No.

ERIC: His birthday perhaps?

MARIE: That's in June.

ERIC: Why today then?

MARIE: They were free.

Camera on MARIE.
ERIC'S hand comes into view.
It glides slowly and gently towards her neck.

ERIC: (*Touching it*) I wonder what she's like . . . this girlfriend of his . . .

MARIE closes her eyes.

I wonder . . . if she's as beautiful . . . as you . . .

The hand strokes the neck.
MARIE smiles, in total submission.
Pause.

21. [Ext. Street (3A) Night.]

Shot of road as seen through WALTER'S windscreen.
Pan with the car as it turns off the road into a private drive and moves slowly and quietly towards an attractive block of flats.
View of the approaching car from the living room window.

22. [Int. Living-room. Night.]

MARIE and ERIC kissing.
The glare from the headlights illuminates their faces.
MARIE breaks away and looks down.
Pause.

MARIE: They're here.

ERIC appears behind her and looks down.

ERIC: Is that his car?

MARIE: His new one. He told me about it on Thursday.

23. [Ext. Drive way of block of flats. Night.]

Shot through WALTER'S windscreen as he brings the car to a standstill.
He pulls the handbrake, revs very gently, switches off the ignition.
He smiles and moves his hand towards the lightswitch.

24. [Int. Living-room. Night.]

MARIE *and* ERIC *watching.*
WALTER'S *headlights flash three times.*

ERIC: What's he doing?
MARIE: He remembered . . .
ERIC: Remembered what?
MARIE: The signal. What he always used to do when we were married . . .
when he came home at night . . . usually about this time. The car would
come up the drive. It would stop. And the lights would flash three times,
three times for Walter.
ERIC: What did it mean?

MARIE *smiles.*

MARIE: He was home.
ERIC: What did you do?
MARIE: (*Remembering*) . . . Come away from the window . . . leave the room
. . . go into the hall to welcome him . . .

She turns slowly.
ERIC *watches as she leaves the window and moves away from him towards the door.*
She goes out into the hall.
Camera on ERIC'S *face.*

25. [Int. Hall. Night.]

The front door.
Silence.

26. [Int. Living-room. Night.]

ERIC *gazing round, biting his lip.*

27. [Int. Hall. Night.]

MARIE *in the hall, watching the door.*

28. [Int. Landing on a lower floor. Night.]

Sound of ascending footsteps.

29. [Int. Hall. Night.]

MARIE.

30. [Int. Higher landing. Night.]

Silence, then ascending footsteps again.
They get louder.

31. [Int. Living-room. Night.]

ERIC *moving backwards, gazing round.*

32. [Int. Stairs and landing. Night.]

WALTER *climbing.*
We stay with him.
He comes to a landing and walks down a corridor.
He stops at a door, unbuttons his coat and puts his hand into his jacket pocket.

33. [Int. Hall. Night.]

MARIE.
The door she is watching.
Pause.
Sound of a key in the lock.
The door opens.
WALTER *enters and sees* MARIE.
He smiles.
MARIE *smiles.*
Pause.

WALTER: I'm home.

Pause.

34. [Int. Living-room. Night.]

ERIC *listening behind the main room door.*
He backs away.
The door opens.
MARIE *enters.*
She smiles at him.

MARIE: It's Walter, Eric.

WALTER *enters wearing a suit with a flower in the lapel.*
He moves towards ERIC *with one hand extended.*

WALTER: (*Warmly*) Eric . . .
ERIC: (*Smiling*) Walter . . .
MARIE: Celia couldn't come . . .

She closes the door.

WALTER: . . . perhaps another time. (*Reaching* ERIC) How nice to see you. (*Shaking his hand*) How are you?

ERIC: Not so bad.

WALTER: Keeping well?

ERIC: Mustn't complain.

WALTER: You're putting on weight.

ERIC: Am I?

WALTER: Aren't you?

MARIE: I'm to blame for that.

She joins them.
ERIC *moves to the drinks.*

WALTER: (*To* MARIE, *jokingly*) Still cooking exotica?

MARIE: He insists.

WALTER: Matelote Bonne Femme, Vinaigrette de Poisson, Brandade Parisienne . . .

MARIE: He eats twice as much as you.

WALTER: . . . I don't believe it.

MARIE: Don't you Eric.

ERIC: (*Pouring drinks*) What?

MARIE: Eat twice as much as Walter.

ERIC: (*Bringing the drinks over*) I wouldn't say that.

WALTER: It must be contentment then. (*Taking his drink with a smile*) I'm so glad.

His eyes meet ERIC'S.
Pause.
ERIC *smiles.*
WALTER *raises his glass.*

> To us.

MARIE *and* ERIC *raise their glasses.*
Pause.

> And Celia . . . (*smiling*) . . . Who will come another time.

They drink.
Moments later.
WALTER *moving quietly round the room.*
MARIE *and* ERIC *in the background.*
WALTER *stops.*
Pause.

> Home again, back in the dear old home. (*Gazes round sentimentally*) How time has flown . . .

MARIE: It has.

ERIC: Yes . . .

WALTER: . . . it seems like only yesterday that you introduced me to Eric. Remember?

MARIE: I remember.

WALTER: Quite a day. Yes . . . quite a day.

ERIC *shifts uncomfortably.*

(*Moving thoughtfully*) Let me see now, how were we situated, I remember, yes . . . I was standing exactly where Eric is standing now . . .

MARIE: So you were . . .

WALTER: And just as ill-at-ease.

ERIC *smiles.*

I was you know. Possibly more so. Like you I didn't know what to expect. (*Remembering*) I'd been waiting for what seemed hours . . . time stood still . . . I'd almost given you up . . . then in you came. You Eric. And you Marie. And we were formally introduced.

MARIE: Walter. Meet Eric. Eric. My husband Walter.

WALTER: Pleased to meet you Eric. Care for a drink?

MARIE *and* WALTER *smile.*

It seems an eternity ago.

MARIE: Yes . . .

WALTER: Time flies.

MARIE: It does . . .

WALTER: . . . doesn't it Eric. (*Going on quickly*) . . . It does indeed. And it seems to move in circles, retracing itself, picking up threads. (*Softly*) How many hours . . . nights . . . since last we three were together like this? Yet it seems like only yesterday . . . as though this were just another evening in my life . . . home from the office . . . car up the drive . . . three flashes on the lights . . . wife here to welcome me . . . a friend to dinner . . . (*Pause, then smiling*) Now I am the friend who has come.

MARIE: You are as welcome as Eric used to be.

Pause.

ERIC: That goes without saying.

Pause.

WALTER: Why shouldn't I be? (*Looking round*) Wasn't this once my home, my dear old happy home? . . . Oh the moments, the golden moments, I have spent in these rooms . . . how familiar they are to me, seeing them once again, how like old friends they are . . . these doors . . . these windows . . . of course I'm welcome, perhaps more so than Eric was, for all this once was mine, and what man wouldn't be welcome in the home that was once his own . . . eh Eric?

ERIC *stands quietly.*

Rather not talk about it?

Pause.

I understand. And you are perfectly within your rights . . . What is passed is passed . . . time has moved on . . . we are different people now . . . we must consider things as they are, as they are now, not as they were. (*Smiling*) Let's do that.

He puts one arm around MARIE, *the other round* ERIC, *and hugs them warmly.*

Let's make this a happy reunion. What do you say.
MARIE: (*Smiling*) Yes. Let's.

Camera on WALTER *smiling.*
Camera on ERIC.
Pause.
He smiles.
Pause.

35. [Int. Living-room. Night.]

Later.
The three of them at dinner.
WALTER *laughing.*
MARIE *laughing.*
ERIC *toying with his food.*

MARIE: But that's absurd . . . Tell him Eric . . .

ERIC *looks up enquiringly.*

. . . the idea . . . What put that into your mind?
WALTER: I know, I know, it seems silly now. But that's what I thought at the time.

MARIE *gives him a playfully reproachful glance.*

I did. I couldn't help it. Of course now . . . now I'm here . . . Well now

I see how wrong I was, but then . . . well naturally . . . meeting you in Baker Street like that, arranging this little get-together . . . when I got home naturally I thought about it deeply.

MARIE: About what?

WALTER: Coming here . . . Everything. It was only natural. (*Eats*)

MARIE: You mean you nearly didn't come?

Camera on ERIC *listening.*

WALTER: (*Noticing him*) All right, Eric?

ERIC: (*Embarrassed*) Yes . . .

WALTER *smiles at him warmly then turns back to* MARIE.

WALTER: Where was I . . . oh, yes . . .

ERIC *eats.*

WALTER: (*cont*) At one point, I must confess, it seemed better to decline.

MARIE: I would never have forgiven you. And Eric wouldn't have.

WALTER: I would never have forgiven myself. It's so nice here, so friendly . . .

He looks round at the candlelit diner.

MARIE: What made you change your mind?

WALTER *continues eating, then picks up his glass to drink.*
We see MARIE *looking at him.*

WALTER: Hmm?

MARIE: What made you change your mind?

WALTER: Oh I don't know . . . This and that . . . One thing then another . . . (*Drinks*)

MARIE: What specifically?

WALTER: A number of things . . . All sorts of things . . .

MARIE: Specifically.

WALTER: Well . . .

ERIC: Must we talk about this?

MARIE *and* WALTER *look at him.*
Pause.

ERIC: (*cont*) It seems a bit off.

WALTER: You'd rather not.

ERIC: It seems unnecessary.

WALTER: He's right.

ERIC: There must be other things to talk about.

WALTER: Of course there are.

ERIC: All kinds of things.

WALTER: Sure. We can talk about all kind of things, why bother ourselves with the past, why concern ourselves with things that are over and done with now that everything's sorted out neatly and to our mutual satisfaction. I'm here now. I've come. My thoughts about coming, the doubts, the hesitations . . . who cares about those? You are right. Let's change the subject. Let's talk about books. Or holidays. Let's talk about holidays . . .

MARIE: I want to know. (*Pause*) What made you change your mind?

WALTER: (*Continuing smoothly*) A number of things. You see basically dear Marie, dear Eric, when you get down and look at it closely one sees that we have very little in common now you and I . . . it is only the events of the past, you see, only those that bind us together. And the bond . . . it isn't even a bond really . . . is very frail, very tenuous . . . it defies description.

MARIE *and* ERIC *wait for him to continue.*
Pause.

> I thought about it deeply, at home, in my little room, at Gospel Oak . . . (*aside with a smile*) . . . that's where I'm living now . . . (*continuing*) . . . night after night after night, mulling it over in my mind, weighing the pros and cons of it, pondering what good, if any, or what possible bad might arise from it . . .

Pause.

> If I came that is.

He reaches for the wine bottle, fills first MARIE'S *then* ERIC'S *glass, then fills his own.*

> . . . well now, here's a pretty state of affairs . . . that's what I thought, at home there, in my squalid little room at Gospel Oak. (*Smiling*) You must come over and see it one day, I'd like you to, it would interest you.

MARIE: We would like to.

Pause.

ERIC: Yes . . .

Pause.

WALTER: We'll arrange something. I'll speak to Celia. We'll see what we can do to get you over. (*Pause*) Where was I . . .

MARIE: In your room.

WALTER: So I was. (*Pause*) Well, I thought, here's a pretty state of affairs, consider . . . you've been invited to dinner in the home that was once your own by the woman who was once your wife now married again to the man who was once your friend. And so I thought, well now . . . you've got to decide, you've been invited, you must accept or refuse. You can't leave it open, they are expecting you and who knows . . . while you are sitting here languishing in your chair they might be planning all sorts of exciting diversions on your behalf as once you and I used to do . . .

MARIE *smiles.*

. . . you and I, Marie, when we expected friends to dinner. Eric for instance. You came quite frequently didn't you.

ERIC *lowers his glass.*

(*Continuing*) And so I thought well now . . . a decision is called for either one way or the other but could I decide? You see one thought was uppermost in my mind, a thought which even now, even though I'm here, enjoying your kind hospitality, this lovely meal, these beautiful dumplings, your attentive company, this incredible Nuit St. George . . . One thought which seemed pertinent and worthy of reflection.

MARIE: What thought was that?

WALTER *smiles.*

WALTER: That surely it was a situation a man should avoid if he has his wits about him. (*Drinks*)

MARIE: Which you have.

WALTER: (*Sweetly*) I like to think so.

MARIE *smiles.*

(*Continuing*) Such a reunion . . . for a reunion is what it seemed to me it was . . . such a reunion . . . in spite of all the goodwill and bonhomie that lay behind it . . . I was sure it did . . such a reunion, to put it lightly, could I felt sure have led to a great deal of embarrassment for all concerned, for me for coming, for you Marie for inviting me, for Celia . . . poor Celia . . . for coming with me in what would surely have been a very compromising way to say the least . . . (*Pause*) and for you Eric for having to put up with us, especially me, surely the last person on earth you would wish to see sitting opposite you at a dinner table . . .

MARIE: Now that's not true . . . Tell him Eric . . .

WALTER *laughs.*

MARIE: Tell him you wanted him to come as much as I did.
WALTER: Go on Eric, tell me.
MARIE: He did.
WALTER: I can see.
MARIE: You've only got to look at him . . .

WALTER *does, and laughs.*

> . . . he's put on his nice new suit for you, haven't you darling . . . and his favourite tie.

WALTER: I should think so too. Didn't I for him?

MARIE *smiles.*
WALTER *quietens down.*
Pause.

> Remember . . . how nervous I was . . . the night you brought him home?

MARIE: I remember.
WALTER: It was the very first time you had done so.
MARIE: Yes.
WALTER: Quite a night.

He takes more wine.

> Up until then you had been seeing one another secretly . . . (*darkly*) clandestine meetings, trysts in the park after dark . . .

MARIE: . . . under the trees . . .
WALTER: . . . trips to Brighton . . .
MARIE: . . . even in Winter . . .
WALTER: . . . cryptic conversations over the telephone. It was a secret . . .
MARIE: . . . ours . . .
WALTER: . . . I wasn't supposed to know.

Pause.

MARIE: Did you?
WALTER: I had my doubts. What husband wouldn't have had.
MARIE: You didn't do anything.
WALTER: They lacked substance, they were shadows . . . nothing tangible . . . feelings . . . nothing positive . . . an idea at the back of my mind. Until you brought him home. There was something about him . . .

Studies ERIC *quietly.*
Pause.

822

And then I knew.

MARIE: How?

WALTER: I just did. A husband can detect these things sooner or later. (*Sighs*) Yes. Quite a day. Remember how nervous I was? (*Eats*)

MARIE: Just like you Eric, the same as you . . .

WALTER: . . . the business with the tie, remember? The times I went to that wardrobe, the times I changed that tie . . .

MARIE: (*To* ERIC) He kept walking round in circles, just like you, round and round and round . . .

WALTER: How do I look? I said . . .

MARIE: Very nice, I said . . .

WALTER: What about the tie? I said . . . you think it'll do? (*To* ERIC) You were due to arrive and I'd changed it three times and I still wasn't sure . . .

MARIE: It's a lovely tie . . .

WALTER: It matches the suit?

MARIE: I smiled . . .

WALTER: (*To* ERIC, *furtively*) . . . watching her . . . you know . . . out of the corner of my eye: I thought I'd wear the blue one then I thought no . . . not the blue one. Then I saw this one. You're sure it's all right.

MARIE: I've told you . . . (*To* ERIC) He was unbearable . . . worse than you . . .

WALTER: It matches the suit.

MARIE: You've got nothing to worry about.

WALTER: No. (*To* ERIC) This was me being sarcastic: No I said . . . (*To* ERIC) . . . quietly, it was more effective, she was being very difficult . . . no I said, that's true I said, you're right. What have I got to worry about? (*To* ERIC) Casually, you know . . . What have I got to worry about? (*To* ERIC) Very casually. Who's coming to see us tonight . . . (*To* ERIC) . . . Then very pointedly, underlining the name . . . only Eric. (*To* ERIC) See? Only Eric. (*To* ERIC) Like that. Then casually again, as though it was a friend who was coming, a very old, very dear old friend . . . Who's Eric? (*To* ERIC) Little pause. Tiny little pause.

Pause.

Only your lover.

WALTER: (*To* ERIC) Underlining lover . . . only your *lover* . . . (*To* ERIC) . . . spitting it out: Only your *lover*!

Pause.
He continues quietly.

Wasn't he?

MARIE *looks at* ERIC.

MARIE: Were you?

WALTER *looks at* ERIC.

WALTER: (*Playfully*) You were, weren't you?

Long pause.

MARIE: He'd rather not talk about it. He's perfectly within his rights . . . what is passed is passed . . . time has moved on . . . we are different people now . . . we must consider things as they are, as they are now, not as they were. (*Smiling*) Let's do that. Let's talk about books. Or holidays. Let's talk about holidays.

WALTER *raises his glass and drinks his wine while gazing at* ERIC *whose head is bowed.*
Pause.
MARIE *drinks her wine.*

36. [Ext. Heath. Night.]

Later.
Silence.
ERIC *comes into view walking slowly.*
We stay with him as he moves through some trees.
Shot of placard of St. Columbia's Hospital.
Pause.
ERIC *comes into view, pauses, reads the placard, looks round at the trees with a lost expression.*
Pause.

37. [Int. Living-room. Night.]

The lounge.
WALTER *pouring himself a drink.*
Pause.

38. [Int. The Bedroom. Night.]

MARIE *at the dressingtable adjusting her makeup.*
Pause.

39. [Int. Living-room. Night.]

WALTER *putting down the decanter, replacing the stopper, picking up his glass and drinking.*
Pause.

40. [Int. Bedroom. Night.]

MARIE *rising from the dressingtable, looking at herself in the mirror, smoothing her dress*
with her hands.
Pause.

41. [Int. Hall. Night.]

Pause.
MARIE *comes out of the bedroom.*
She stops to adjust the picture.

42. [Int. Living-room. Night.]

WALTER.
We pan slowly round the room and find him standing at the window.

43. [Ext. Driveway. Night.]

Shot of his car in the drive.
Pause.

44. [Int. Living-room. Night.]

Sound of a door opening.
WALTER *turns.*
MARIE *enters.*
Pause.

WALTER: Any sign of him?
MARIE: Not as yet.
WALTER: He said 10 minutes.
MARIE: He'll be here soon.
WALTER: If he comes back that is.

45. [Ext. Heath. Night.]

Slow panning shot of the empty heath.
Silence.

46. [Int. Living-room. Night.]

MARIE *on the settee in front of the fire.*
She sips her drink.
WALTER *emerges from the shadows of the diner and enters the lounge.*
He moves round it quietly, glass in hand.
He seems uneasy.

He looks at MARIE and approaches her slowly.
He stops behind her.
She turns.
They smile at one another.
WALTER moves round and joins her on the settee.
They sit in silence.
Pause.
WALTER drinks.
MARIE looks at him.
He smiles sadly.

WALTER: It's pretty obvious.
MARIE: What is?
WALTER: That I upset him.
MARIE: I suppose you did.
WALTER: I didn't mean to.
MARIE: No?
WALTER: It wasn't my intention to.

MARIE smiles.

       I thought it might be possible once I got here to overcome my feelings . . . somehow . . . I wasn't sure how but felt I might it seemed right to until I saw him . . . here . . . in such familiar surroundings . . . and saw myself as he must have seen me . . . as I used to see him. (*Pause*) I'm sorry if I did . . . I mean upset him. As I say, it wasn't my intention to.
MARIE: He'll be all right.
WALTER: (*Thoughtfully*) Yes . . . yes it would be a pity if I spoiled this happy reunion, this first I hope of many. Asking me here, inviting me back . . . it was very good of you, both of you, I mean that . . . I'm very touched. (*Pause*) If in my voice you detect a note of irony believe me it isn't intentional. I'm very happy to be here.
MARIE: We are very glad you came. Really we are.

They smile.

WALTER: I could have written of course. (*Drinks*)
MARIE: You could have.
WALTER: Perhaps I should have. (*Sardonically*) "Dear Marie. How are you getting on? Keeping well are you? And how is little Antonia?" . . . how is she by the way?
MARIE: She's fine.
WALTER: Growing is she?
MARIE: Yes. She's going to be tall.
WALTER: "Give her a kiss from Daddy. Say he sends his love." What could be easier?

MARIE: I would have to reply. It could lead to a regular correspondence. Would you like that? My writing to you regularly?

WALTER: Very much. Although I'm not sure that Eric would approve—did I approve when he wrote to you? Not that it matters; I'm here now. (*Frowning*) I think I chose for the best, it seemed much the better way . . . coming . . . rather than staying away . . . appearing in the flesh, appearing before you . . . in the flesh. (*Reflectively*) Much the better way. The effect I thought would be purgatorial meaning . . . not like Purgatory, not like that . . . *purging, cleansing,* it would clear the air!

MARIE: I thought so too.

WALTER: (*With sudden movement*) Everything happened so quickly!

MARIE: Yes.

WALTER: . . . at the time I mean, so fast! One moment you were there the next so quickly gone. I was alone. (*Pause*) We never met again, not properly: formal conversations in West End cafeterias . . . tortuous disquisitions over the telephone, letters, communiques, official intimations . . . arrangements . . . ordinances . . . dispensations . . . the setting up of strange legal rituals, the performance of these rituals in a building in the Strand: over

done with

finished.

(*Pause*) What about the flat?

MARIE: You have it.

WALTER: What about you?

MARIE: We'll manage.

WALTER: What about Antonia?

MARIE: We'll find a place, don't worry about us.

WALTER: I can't stay here without you . . . too many memories. It would be better I think if I left. You stay here with Eric, and the child. (*Pause*) We never met again, not properly, not as people. Even when I came to see Antonia . . . . . . Even then it wasn't the same . . . until I met you up in Town . . . quite by chance . . .

MARIE: Hello Walter.

WALTER: Marie! How nice to see you. Keeping well?

MARIE: Fine. You?

WALTER: Fine. How is Antonia?

MARIE: Fine.

WALTER: I've been meaning to come to see her. I've been awfully busy lately, what with one thing and another. I really must try to get across.

MARIE: Come to dinner. It would make a nice change for you.

WALTER: I'd like to.

MARIE: Next week some time?

WALTER: I'll bring a friend along. (*Pause*) Pity about Celia . . . she was so looking forward to coming. Perhaps another time.

MARIE: What's she like?

WALTER *smiles.*

WALTER: Eric would like her.
MARIE: Is she beautiful?
WALTER: Not as beautiful as you.

MARIE *smiles, rises, and moves towards the diner.*
She moves through the shadows to the window.
WALTER *rises slowly.*
MARIE *stops at the window and looks down.*
WALTER *comes out of the shadows.*
He stops behind her.
Pause.

        You think about me?
MARIE: Sometimes.
WALTER: A lot?
MARIE: Not all that much.
WALTER: Occasionally.
MARIE: There are times . . .
WALTER: When you're with Eric?

47. [Ext. Driveway. Night.]

Shot of ERIC *coming slowly up the drive.*

48. [Int. Living-room. Night.]

MARIE: Sometimes . . .
WALTER: When he makes love to you? Then?
MARIE: There have been times, I must confess . . .
WALTER: That proves it then, doesn't it?
MARIE: Proves what?
WALTER: That you . . . and I . . . we're still . . . (*Pause*) Of course we are.
MARIE: Related?
WALTER: Aren't we?
MARIE: Only by the events of the past.
WALTER: . . . by a bond that goes deeper than the Law.

49. [Ext. Driveway. Night.]

Shot of ERIC *pausing at* WALTER'S *car.*
We hear WALTER'S *voice.*

(WALTER: O.O.V.) There's no escaping it . . .
WALTER: . . . the past I mean.

ERIC *looks up.*

> You may run, you may flee from it, alter your whole way of life, change completely, become a different person . . . with a different name . . . it's still there, there's no escaping it . . . the past stays . . . influencing our present . . . hanging over our future like a cloud.

50. [Int. Living-room. Night.]

The candlestick.
MARIE *and* WALTER *watching the candles burning.*
Pause.

WALTER: I think about it often . . .
MARIE: So do I . . .
WALTER: The happy times we had together, the happy golden times. Naturally I get sentimental. What man wouldn't if he'd been through what I've been through . . . I try not to . . .
MARIE: I'm sure you must . . .
WALTER: . . . but however hard I try . . . reason always gives way to emotion.

Pause.

WALTER: Always . . . I think for hours on end about the old days. They are over now I say, don't dare deny they aren't, yet they are as near to me as yesterday.
MARIE: I know.

WALTER *smiles.*

WALTER: Remember Cornwall?

MARIE *smiles.*

> Redruth? Polperro? Marazion? . . .
MARIE: St. Columb? . . .
WALTER: St. Blazey? . . .
MARIE: Bude? . . .
WALTER: That other one . . . what was it called . . .
MARIE: Which one do you mean?
WALTER: Indian something . . . an Indian village . . .
MARIE: That one . . .
WALTER: Remember it?

Pause.

MARIE: The Village of Indian Queens . . .
WALTER: . . . as if I could forget. We wanted to live there . . .
MARIE: We liked the name . . .
WALTER: It wasn't much of a place but what a *name* . . . imagine it written on an envelope!
MARIE: Addressed to *you!*
WALTER: To *us!*

They laugh.

MARIE: I was expecting Antonia . . .
WALTER: Six months five days gone . . .
MARIE: It wasn't an official holiday . . .
WALTER: We just thought we'd get away . . .
MARIE: Let's get *away!*
WALTER: Let's go *somewhere!*
MARIE: We chose Cornwall . . . the sea . . . (*remembering*) It's so beautiful here . . .
WALTER: Would you like to live here? . . .
MARIE: If only we could . . .
WALTER: I'll build a house for you . . . we'll have a garden . . . our child will go to school here . . .
MARIE: If only we could . . . if only we could . . .

They gaze at the candles.

51.   [Int. Stairs and landing. Night.]

Shot of ERIC *coming up the stairs.*
He climbs slowly.
We hear WALTER'S *voice.*

WALTER: (O.O.V.) I often think about that.
MARIE: (O.O.V.) I too.
WALTER: (O.O.V.) It's silly I know, no good can come of it . . . of dwelling on the past so constantly with us. It makes for sentiment . . .

ERIC *comes slowly down the corridor.*

. . . and sentiment makes us tearful, and tearfulness . . . it gets us no-where, nowhere at all . . .

ERIC *stops at the door, unbuttons his coat and puts his hand into his jacket pocket.*

52. [Int. Hall. Night.]

The front door.
Silence.
Sound of a key in the lock.
The door opens.
ERIC enters.
He closes the door, takes off his coat and hangs it up next to WALTER'S.
He moves down the hall towards the main room.
He stops, listens, and returns to the nursery door.
He opens the door and looks in.

53. [Int. Nursery. Night.]

He enters the nursery leaving the door wide open.
We hold on the blackness of the room.
We hear WALTER'S voice.

WALTER: (O.O.V.) The past is over. What was . . . is no more. Face facts I tell myself time and time again, night after night, even when Celia is with me . . . more so when she is there . . . who *is* she? what am I doing with her? Poor Celia. She more than anything else . . . by virtue of her presence . . . brings home to me the full true measure of all that I am missing . . . all I pine for . . . all I wish to have again.

54. [Int. Living-room. Night.]

WALTER *looking at* MARIE.
Pause.

WALTER: You Marie.

She turns to him.
Pause.

      (*In a whisper*) I love you still . . .

Pause.

      I love you still.

Pause.
They slowly smile at one another.
The door opens.
They look up.
ERIC enters.

MARIE: Eric.

ERIC looks at them quietly then moves to the decanter and pours himself a drink.

      We were wondering where you'd got to . . . where have you been?
ERIC: With Antonia. You'd better go and see her. She's dreaming about the sea.
WALTER: May I go? I'd like to. She *is* the reason why I came.

He looks at ERIC who says nothing.
He smiles and leaves the room.
ERIC looks quietly at MARIE.
He sips his drink.
Pause.

55. [Int. Hall. Night.]

WALTER at the door of the nursery, opening it slowly.

56. [Int. Nursery. Night.]

Total darkness save for a bar of light which grows steadily wider as WALTER opens the door.
He stands silhouetted in the doorway looking in, then goes away.
We hold on the lighted doorway.
Pause.
He returns with a box of matches.
He strikes one and comes into the nursery.
Toys, dolls, drawings on the wall appear and fade from view as WALTER passes slowly with his match.
He stops.
He calls softly.

WALTER: Antonia?

The match goes out.
He fumbles with the box and lights another.
He gazes round the room.
Shot of ANTONIA sleeping soundly on a pillow of hair.
He moves quietly to her side.
He holds the match higher illuminating her face.
Pause.

WALTER: (cont) It's Daddy.

Pause.
The match goes out.

832

57. [Int. Living-room. Night.]

ERIC *refilling his glass.*
He carries it over to the fire and stares at the flames.
MARIE *emerges from the shadows of the diner and enters the lounge.*
She moves round it quietly.
She seems uneasy.
She looks at ERIC.
Pause.

MARIE: You didn't mind.
ERIC: Mind?
MARIE: His going to see Antonia.
ERIC: Why should I mind?
MARIE: I thought you might.
ERIC: He's her father isn't he?
MARIE: He doesn't see her often and it's the reason why he came.
ERIC: Then that's all right then isn't it.

He moves to the records and sifts through them slowly.
MARIE *watches him.*
Pause.

MARIE: Did you enjoy the dinner?
ERIC: No. No I can't say that I did. But I'm sure that as always it was very
          very good.
MARIE: Eric I'm sorry . . .
ERIC: I'm sure you are. (*Moves away*)
MARIE: I didn't think this would happen.
ERIC: (*Spinning round angrily*) I'll tell you something. You didn't *think*!
MARIE: It seemed such a good idea.
ERIC: For who, for *him*!

He moves restlessly.

MARIE: For all of us.
ERIC: Especially for *him*!
MARIE: No more for him than for you and me, for Celia too who was to have
          accompanied him. It seemed a good opportunity.
ERIC: For *revenge*?
MARIE: For clearing the air. It's been on our minds for so long now . . . the
          divorce . . . what we did to him . . . a shadow over our lives. I felt that
          if he came here . . . saw us together as a family . . . things would
          change.
ERIC: They've changed all right. Before we only suspected . . . now we have
          proof that as far as he's concerned the past four years count for

nothing! The divorce, our marriage, *nothing*! Everything that's happened to him, to us: the things he's done, the things we've done: our moments, his moments, *nothing*! They didn't *happen*! We only *dreamed* it! You heard him *say* so!

MARIE: When?

ERIC: Oh about two seconds after he got here . . . his little *homily* on *time*! Remember?

He smiles tipsily.

ERIC: (*cont*) . . . his poetic observations? . . . the way it moves in circles . . . retracing itself . . . picking up threads . . . the way it seemed like only yesterday that you were introducing me to him? . . .

MARIE: He was nervous . . .

ERIC *laughs.*

. . . he wanted to break the ice . . .

ERIC: . . . *stop*! You're breaking my heart. (*Then pausing thoughtfully*) He had other reasons, the same reasons that brought him here tonight—not your reasons . . . not to say hello how are you . . . other reasons . . . (*continuing quietly*) To appear in the flesh . . . to appear before us in the flesh . . . the reincarnation of our sins . . . to get his own back. That's why he came . . . to humiliate me! And by Christ he's succeeding. (*Drinks*)

MARIE: You honestly think that?

ERIC: I don't think anything. I *know*. I *saw*! I *heard* him!

He turns, as though lost, and gazes round the room.
Pause.

. . . what's he doing here? (*Then frowning*) Why did he come? . . .

MARIE: To see us . . . to see how we are getting on . . .

ERIC: What does he want from me?

Why come all that way just to humiliate me, all that way . . . just for that, why? . . . Revenge for what, because you loved me? Because you were the woman he married? That's all over now, history, you're divorced, we can prove it we've got documents we can prove . . . we've got proof . . . documents to prove you are married to me now, why should I stand . . . this is my . . . yours and my flat now, ours . . . he has no right, why should I stand for it! . . . I really ought to do something about getting him out of here, I must . . . I really should, before he starts to reminisce, go back further right back all the long long way to that holiday you had where was it Cornwall was it? That holiday by the sea you had . . . you told me about, I came . . . I came to dinner once . . .

you told me about the holiday by the sea where was it now . . . a place
. . .

Pause.

An Indian village what was it called . . . Queens . . . Indian Queens . . .

Pause.

. . . something about Indian Queens . . .

He becomes suddenly tearful.

. . . he'll go back there . . .

Pause.

ERIC: (*cont*) . . . he'll take you back there . . . .

Pause.

. . . he'll try to take you back there . . .

He stands quietly.
He gazes vacantly into space, his glass tilted forward pathetically.
Pause.

MARIE: Shall I tell him to go?

ERIC *frowns.*

Obviously you've had enough. As you say, this is our flat now; he has no
right to intrude. He'll understand.

She moves to the door.

ERIC: Wait! . . .

She stops, smiling.

. . . that wouldn't be nice, would it.
MARIE: He has come a long way . . .
ERIC: . . . turning him out into the night . . . sending him back to his little room
. . . (*considerately*) . . . not a nice thing to do . . . .
MARIE: He never did that to you when you came . . . . he was always very kind
to you . . . (*remembering*) . . . come on Eric, let's go for a ride . . . all
that time he gave you . . . fancy a drink Eric?

Let's go out and have one . . . drinks . . . rides . . . he treated you like a son . . . come to dinner Eric, we'd like you to, it would make a nice change for you . . . you came quite frequently didn't you . . . staying till the early hours of the morning . . . talking about books . . . and holidays . . .

Pause.

ERIC: It's possible . . .
MARIE: That you may be wrong about him? That his reasons for coming aren't the ones you suppose?

Pause.

ERIC: In any case . . . it's only the once . . . I mean it isn't going to happen again, he isn't going to make a habit of coming here . . . it's only the once. (*Pause*) Well. For one night and one night only I'll just have to grin and bear it won't I . . . like he used to do when I came to you, I'll grin and bear it like he did.

He grins sheepishly.

Now come and give your husband a great big kiss.

Camera on ERIC'S face.
Pause.
MARIE'S face comes into view.
They kiss.
The door opens suddenly.
WALTER enters.
He sees them kissing.
He frowns.

WALTER: Marie . . . what are you doing?

MARIE breaks away.
ERIC glares at him.

ERIC: Kissing her husband!

MARIE looks away, ashamed.

MARIE: Forgive me Walter . . . I don't know what came over me . . . it will never happen again.

ERIC looks at her unbelievingly.
Pause.

58. [Int. Living-room. Night.]

Later.
The candlestick.
ERIC *watching the candles burning.*
Silence.
WALTER *on the settee.*
MARIE *on the floor beside him.*
Pause.

WALTER: (*Quietly*) She is growing.
MARIE: Yes isn't she.
WALTER: She's going to be tall. A real beauty. Just like her mother. (MARIE *smiles*) And with a mind like her father's.
MARIE: Of limited intelligence.
WALTER: But with a great sense of humour! At least I hope so.
MARIE: You set great store by that.
WALTER: Don't you? I'm sure Eric does . . . do you Eric? (*Winks at* MARIE)
ERIC: What?
WALTER: Agree that a sense of humour is among the greatest things a man can possess.

Pause.
ERIC *emerges from the shadows of the diner.*
He moves to the decanter and pours a drink.

ERIC: It has it's advantages.

He takes the drink to WALTER.

ERIC: (*Handing it to him*) Scotch?
WALTER: How kind . . . but I don't think I ought . . .
ERIC: (*Firmly*) Drink it!

His eyes meet WALTER'S.
Pause.
WALTER *takes the glass.*
ERIC *turns to* MARIE.

ERIC: (*cont*) Would my wife care to join us?
MARIE: (*Turning*) Hmm?
ERIC: You are invited to partake of a little refreshment with us dear.
MARIE: Oh. Yes. A small one.
ERIC: Have a *big* one!

On the word 'big' he stretches out his arms and lowers them slowly.

　　　　It's a *reunion* isn't it?

He smiles, moves to the decanter, and pours a drink.
He takes it to MARIE.

ERIC:　There we are . . .

MARIE *takes it.*

　　　　. . . and now one for your husband. (*cont* . . .)

He returns to the decanter and pours his own.
He turns.
He raises his glass.

ERIC:　(*cont*) To us!

MARIE *and* WALTER *raise their glasses.*
Pause.

　　　　And Celia . . . (*smiling*) . . . who will come another time . . .

He drinks.
MARIE *and* WALTER *drink.*
ERIC *moves to the fire, deliberately passing* WALTER *to whom he murmurs*

　　　　. . . over my dead body.

He reaches the fire and smiles at the flames.
Pause.
He turns and looks at WALTER.
WALTER *smiles.*

WALTER:　If you insist.

MARIE *smiles.*
ERIC'S *face falls.*
WALTER *toasts him and drinks.*
ERIC *moves to a window and looks out.*
Rain is falling.
Pause.
WALTER *lowers his glass onto his chest.*

WALTER:　(*cont*) Yes. it has it's advantages and it's disadvantages as Eric says . . .
ERIC:　Objection! I didn't say disadvantages. I said advantages.

WALTER: . . . implying it has disadvantages too, how true. Well it's stood me in good stead over the years.

ERIC: Glad to hear it.

WALTER: Often is the time when I am forced to laugh at the face of adversity.

ERIC: Indeed? How terribly interesting. (*Drinks*)

WALTER: When the clouds of oppression begin to gather on the hilltops threatening to come down into the valley . . . what do I do?

ERIC: Raise your umbrella?

MARIE *laughs.*

WALTER: That's right Marie, I laugh!

He *laughs.*

MARIE: Does it stop them coming?

WALTER: It doesn't! But it stops me thinking about what will happen when they arrive!

MARIE *and* WALTER *laugh.*
ERIC *stands quietly.*
They *quieten down.*

> And so I go on . . . (*continuing quietly*) I suppose each of us has his own particular method of dealing with a given problem . . . right Eric? (*Drinks*)

ERIC: If you say so.

WALTER: Not that you have problems.

ERIC: Problems are relative.

WALTER: To what?

ERIC *doesn't reply.*

> You say they are relative. To what?

ERIC: The individual . . . the individual they confront.

WALTER: You think the problem confronts the man not the man the problem.

ERIC: I didn't say that.

WALTER: What did you say?

ERIC: (*After a pause*) Problems for one man need not necessarily be problems for another. Your problems differ from mine . . . different problems, seen from different points of view. We each have our own.

WALTER: (*Persisting*) My coming here tonight: would you call that a problem?

ERIC: Why should it be?

WALTER: It isn't?

ERIC *doesn't reply.*

Well is it or isn't it?

Pause.

ERIC: ... no problem.
WALTER: For you or for me?
ERIC: For me.
WALTER: What about me?
ERIC: That's for you to say. (*Turning*) Right Marie? It's for him to say, he must speak for himself, right?
WALTER: Antonia then. What about her?

ERIC *flinches.*

(*Probing*) Would you call her a problem? Another man's daughter? Nothing to do with you?
ERIC: Our learned friend is forgetting she is also the daughter of my wife. (*To* WALTER) That does make a difference you know.
WALTER: You think so?
ERIC: In so far as she is my responsibility now.
WALTER: She is also mine, which you seem to be forgetting. You forget too that the relationship between me and Antonia isn't what one might call circumstantial. It is a father-daughter relationship. A *blood* relationship. What's yours?
ERIC: Circumstantial. (*Smiling*) The same as one might call circumstantial the relationship that now exists between you and Marie ... I hope that answers your question.

WALTER *studies him quietly.*
MARIE *rises.*
Pause.

MARIE: How about some coffee.
ERIC: Good idea!
MARIE: Walter?
WALTER: (*Rising*) If it's not too much trouble ...
MARIE: ... not at all.

She moves to the door.
She pauses.

I shan't be long.

Pause.

Be nice to our guest won't you.

WALTER: Yes.

ERIC: (*Simultaneously*) Yes.

He looks sharply at WALTER.
WALTER *smiles and moves away.*
MARIE *smiles and leaves the room.*
Silence.
WALTER *moves round the room.*
ERIC *watches him closely.*
Pause.

WALTER: Such a comfortable . . . restful flat . . .

ERIC: You should know. You used to live here.

WALTER: Odd how I keep forgetting . . . that I am the guest visiting you . . .

ERIC: That's who you are.

WALTER: I keep lapsing . . . as though the past four years didn't happen, as though they were a dream . . . which of course they weren't, how could they have been? I would like them to have been. (*Gazing round*) Then all this would still be mine.

ERIC: Well it's mine now. And don't you forget it.

WALTER *nods wistfully.*
ERIC *goes to the records.*
Pause.

WALTER: You should see what I'm lumbered with now, at Gospel Oak. It's a pig-stye compared with this.

ERIC: Then you should feel at home there, shouldn't you.

WALTER *turns with a hurt expression.*
ERIC *takes a record to the gramophone and puts it on.*
Organ music filters quietly round the room.
ERIC *smiles.*

Too loud for you?

He reaches for the volume control.

ERIC: Little louder perhaps? (*cont . . .*)

He turns up the volume.
Organ music fills the room.
WALTER *stands helplessly.*
Pause.
ERIC *turns the volume down.*

ERIC: (*cont*) How's that?

He looks at WALTER.

Better?

WALTER *smiles confusedly.*
Camera on ERIC *grinning.*
Pause.
He turns the record off.
Silence.
He turns.
Pause.

I'll join you by the fire.

He moves to the settee.

I'll sit here, if I may . . .

He sits.
Pause.
He looks at WALTER.

Please sit down.

WALTER *doesn't move.*
Pause.

(*Firmly*) Sit!

Pause.
WALTER *sits.*

Now we are both sitting, host and guest alike, are you comfortable? It's not too warm for you? That's fine. (*Ultra-pleasantly*) You looked after me: I must look after you. You were good to me: I must be good to you. That's only fair. And we must be fair, mustn't we? Of course we must.

He sinks back comfortably with a curious smile.

How nice this is. Sitting here. You and I. Side by side. In the room that was once your own. A stranger would take us for friends, very old, very dear old friends who have shared a beautiful past . . . shot through with golden moments. (*Smiling*) As such a stranger would take us . . . you there, me here, side by side. In the room that was once your own . . . but which now belongs to me.

They sit quietly.
Pause.

842

WALTER: (Gently) Eric . . .

ERIC doesn't reply.

> Eric there is something I would like to say to you . . .

ERIC: Say it then.

Pause.

WALTER: I didn't mean to upset you.

ERIC: By sitting next to me?

WALTER: No before . . . at dinner . . . and when I arrived, about two seconds
after I got here . . . my little homily on time . . .

ERIC: That . . .

WALTER: Yes . . . And just now . . . in here . . . the things I said about your
relationship with Antonia, those cruel harsh things. How hurt you must
have been . . . what could I have been thinking of? What drove me to
such extremes?

Pause.

ERIC: It hasn't been an easy evening.

Pause.

> It's been a difficult evening.

WALTER: . . . because of me . . . my behaviour . . . how wrong of me. (Softly) It
can't be easy for you my boy, living with a child whose blood you do
not share, playing father to another father's child. I know how you must
feel.

ERIC: How do I feel?

WALTER: As sorry as I do. Less perhaps because my sorrow encompasses yours
because I am the cause of yours. But I am the cause of yours, you say.
That is over I say. Passed. Part of History. Time has moved on. We are
different people now . . . I am the visitor. (Heavily) My behaviour grieves
me.

ERIC: I am as much to blame as you are.

WALTER: For spoiling the reunion?

ERIC nods sadly.

> You only say that to lighten my heart.

ERIC: I mean it. We didn't give it a chance. Right from the start I had my doubts
about it.

WALTER: You did?

843

ERIC: . . . just like you. Doubts, hesitations, mulling it over in my mind, weighing the pros and cons of it, pondering what good, if any, or what possible bad might arise from it. An ordeal is what I knew it would be. And an ordeal is what it has been.

WALTER: It has. (*Pause*) Pity isn't it.

ERIC *nods.*

I ask because I would hate to think that our setting off on the wrong foot . . . as it were . . . might in some way preclude my coming here again . . .

ERIC *frowns.*

. . . I hope it won't.

He looks at ERIC.

ERIC: (*Guardedly*) . . . why no . . . Why should it?

He rises slowly.
WALTER *watches him.*

WALTER: (*Feeling his way*) I may come again?
ERIC: If you want to.
WALTER: Here . . . to the flat?
ERIC: Why not?
WALTER: I will in future find a welcome here?
ERIC: If you come . . . if you come.
WALTER: You will come to me? . . . to dinner? . . . you and Marie?
ERIC: We will try to.
WALTER: Then what are we so gloomy about? The reunion has succeeded, it has brought us together again, well hasn't it?
ERIC: (*Confusedly*) I suppose it has.
WALTER: (*Rising*) It has, it has, how pleased I am, you can see I am, you don't know what this means to me.

Camera on ERIC'S *face.*
Pause.
WALTER'S *face comes into view.*
Pause.

(*Softly*) Tell me again that I may come again.
ERIC: I said you could.
WALTER: Say it again.

ERIC. (*After a pause*) You may come again.

WALTER: You will come to me?

ERIC: We'll try.

WALTER: To dinner?

ERIC: If it can be arranged.

WALTER: Next week some time? Say you will.

ERIC: We'll do our best.

WALTER: You promise?

ERIC: Yes.

WALTER: Say it.

ERIC: I promise.

WALTER *smiles.*

WALTER: Let's drink to it.

He moves to the decanter and pours two drinks.
He returns with them.
He gives one to ERIC.
He raises his own.
He smiles.

WALTER: To us.

He drinks.
We hold on him as he does so.
He finishes.
We draw back.
ERIC has gone.
WALTER puts down his glass.
He looks towards the diner.
Pause.
The diner.
ERIC at the window watching the rain.
Pause.
WALTER comes out of the shadows.
He sees ERIC, pauses, then moves to the table.
He stares at the candles.
Pause.

WALTER: (*Gently*) Why shouldn't we?

ERIC *listens.*

> Be friends again . . . like before. You see I like you I'm . . . I'm genuinely fond of you.

Pause.

We have common interests.

Pause.

Given the chance . . . and the time . . . I'm sure we could learn a great deal from one another.

Pause.

ERIC: (*Distantly*) I'm not sure what you mean . . .
WALTER: By common interests?

ERIC *doesn't reply.*

I mean apart from Marie and Antonia . . . including them but not only them . . . I was speaking more in a universal sense . . . or am I being obscure? (*Brief pause*) All I am saying Eric is that I see no reason why we shouldn't see more of one another . . . as from tonight . . . or from next week rather when you come to dinner with me. It would do us good. (*Drinks*) We might even make a regular thing of it . . . now that a start's been made.

He moves slowly towards a chair.
He pauses thoughtfully.
ERIC *watches the rain trickling down the window.*
Silence.

Supposing I came once a month . . . or would that be too much of an imposition.
ERIC: Here?
WALTER: To the flat. Monthly. To begin with.

Pause.

ERIC: I'm not sure that Marie and I would always be free . . .
WALTER: It would depend of course on what you were doing . . . and I too of course . . . I'm not always free, neither is Celia, it would depend on what each of us was doing, although speaking for myself . . . I'm free most of the time . . .

Camera on WALTER.

. . . "free as nature first made man,
Ere the base laws of servitude began,
When wild in woods the noble savage ran" . . .

I never used to be, as you know, in the old days. There was always so much to do. Not any longer. Things have changed. Now . . .
I seem to spend my time . . . killing time . . .
devising ways and means of getting rid of it, through it, there's so much of it. But not always.
(Reflectively)
Occasionally the pattern changes,
the bubble of boredom bursts and I go out . . .
up West . . . losing myself in the colours, the gay bright colours,
the gay bright people,
the gay bright places . . . on my own of course.
It never used to be like that.
Once upon a time there were friends for all occasions;
I only have colleagues now, colleagues who
as soon as work is over scurry off home to gay bright garden cities . . .
families,
children, friends.

(Pause)

Sometimes I go into a pub.
I don't like pubs on the whole, they depress me, but the old City taverns so deeply steeped in history have a faded sort of charm especially of an evening when the gay bright people have gone.
It passes the time.
What else do I do . . . the cinema?
Occasionally.
A restaurant? Rarely. It's no fun eating on your own. Window-shopping? The West End is very gay at night, I go there often, I enjoy walking the streets on my own especially if it's raining especially round Baker Street, one gets this tremendous feeling of . . .
belonging, of having a place.

(Pause)

It passes the time.

It's better than being in my room . . . comparing life now with what it was.
(Then brightly)
Sometimes I go to a dance. I met Celia at a dance. (Smiles) Imagine me tripping the light fantastic!

(Pause)

It's difficult at dances though, for me I mean, having been married, difficult to speak to girls, pretty as they sometimes are—what can you say? And when you get them home, well, not to put too fine a point on it you probably know how mechanical the act of love can sometimes be, and afterwards when they go in my room there . . . this feeling of great desolation overcomes me so strong at times I have to go out again, over the Heath, to purify myself to expiate my shame. Once . . .

(*Remembering*) . . . quite some time ago . . .

in the Autumn I think it was . . . I think in September . . . I fell asleep on the Heath just like that.

A dance. A girl. Home.

A swift meeting of the flesh, then bang! . . . out I went . . . walking . . . resting near some trees behind a hospital . . . St. Columbia's . . . perhaps you know it.

(*Pause*) When I woke it was dawn. (*Laughs*) What must I have looked like! (*Shakes his head*) Amazing how you can let yourself go, you just go down and down, you wear the same shirt for weeks, the same old tie, forget to clean your shoes, forget to clean your teeth—now that's the beginning of the end, once you do that.

He smiles.
He continues quietly.

But tonight . . .

well tonight I made a special effort, as you can see . . .

clean shirt, clean tie, teeth, shoes, everything clean, I even pressed my suit, and look . . .

Looking at the flower in his lapel.

a little flower in my lapel. You see I had somewhere particular to go, someone particular to see,

this is what I miss most of all,

this is what I really need, would

once a month be too much for you?

ERIC *stands quietly.*

Discuss it with Marie, see what she says.

I think she'll agree, then later . . .

if things go well . . .

who knows, perhaps I could come once a fortnight, depending on what progress we made.

A visit every evening might also be arranged.

Like those you paid to me, but that would come later, it's a delicate
situation, it can't be rushed, we would have to get to know one another
again . . . gradually, over a period of years . . . the four of us
for the plan includes Celia whom you have yet to meet . . . you'll like
her.

Do you like my *plan?*

(Pause)

It seems quite a good plan as plans go, to me at least for this way
I'll see more of Antonia, my child, and that would be good for her. I *am*
her father. As young as she is she must often wonder about the old man
in the shabby raincoat who calls from time to time and gives her a kiss
and takes her down the River or to the Zoo, yes . . . it does seem a good
plan and I'm convinced it will appeal to Marie, does it to you?

Camera on ERIC.
WALTER'S *voice continues.*

WALTER: . . . my coming here every
          night like you did? . . . an
          habitual visitor like you were?

His voice becomes a whisper.

          Wouldn't work would it? How could
          you bear it?
          You'd suspect things, question my
          presence here
          like I questioned yours,
          you'd suspect Marie like I did
          and your suspicions, dear Eric,
          would be justified

          the same as mine were because

          sooner or later, dear Eric, she'd be
          unfaithful behind your back,
          dear Eric,
          the same as she was unfaithful to me . . .
          we'd see one another secretly . . .
          clandestine meetings,

```
                trysts in the park after dark . . .
                under the trees . . . trips to Brighton . . .
                even in Winter . . .
                cryptic conversations over the
                telephone . . . it would be a secret . . .
                ours . . .
                you wouldn't know a thing . . . would
                you? . . . would you? . . .
```

ERIC *frowns.*

```
WALTER:  Well would you?
ERIC:  I'd have my doubts about you . . .
WALTER:   . . . what husband wouldn't have . . .
         but you wouldn't do anything . . .
ERIC:   . . . they would lack substance . . .
WALTER:   . . . exactly . . .
ERIC:   . . . they would be shadows . . .
WALTER:   . . . precisely . . .
ERIC:   . . . nothing tangible . . .
WALTER:   . . . feelings . . .
ERIC:   . . . nothing positive . . .
WALTER:   . . . an idea at the back of your mind . . .
         so what would happen? . . .
ERIC:   . . . Marie would leave me . . . go with you . . .
```

He continues as though in a dream.

```
        . . . what about the flat?
WALTER:  She'd ask you to have it.
ERIC:  What about you?
WALTER:  We would manage.
ERIC:  What about Antonia?
WALTER:  We'll find a place, don't worry about us.
ERIC:  I can't stay here without you Marie . . . too many memories . . it would
       be better I think if I left . . . you stay here with Walter . . . and the
       child.
```

They stand quietly.
The rain runs down the window.
Pause.

```
WALTER:  (Gently) It wouldn't work, would it? Not that plan. It would take too
         long.
```

We need a quicker plan. Much better to get it over and done with.
There is no need for you to suffer as I did.
By leaving now
you will spare the feelings of us all.
You know that don't you.

Camera on ERIC.
He has a lost expression.
He nods slowly.
WALTER'S hand comes into view.
It rests gently on ERIC'S shoulder.
Pause.
ERIC turns.
He looks at WALTER with the expression of a worried little boy.

ERIC: *(Anxiously)* May I . . .

WALTER waits for him to continue.
Pause.

. . . may I stay for coffee?

Pause.

59. [Int. Living-room. Night.]

Later.
ERIC and WALTER sitting quietly.
MARIE pouring coffee.
Deep silence.
She hands a coffee to ERIC, a coffee to WALTER, then offers them sugar and cream.
ERIC takes sugar and cream.
WALTER takes sugar and cream.
MARIE takes sugar and cream.
They stir their coffee.
They drink it in silence.
Very long pause.
MARIE finishes.
She puts down her cup and saucer.
ERIC finishes.
He puts down his cup and saucer.
Pause.
WALTER finishes.
He puts down his cup and saucer.
Silence.

ERIC: It's been a lovely evening.

WALTER: Yes.
MARIE: Yes.

Silence.
ERIC rises.

ERIC: I ought to be going. It's getting late.

WALTER rises.

WALTER: I'll run you back in the car.

MARIE rises.

MARIE: I'll get your coats.

She goes out.
WALTER goes to a mirror and adjusts his tie.
ERIC stands quietly.
Pause.
MARIE re-enters with their coats.
They put them on in silence.
WALTER and MARIE give ERIC friendly smiles.

WALTER: Ready?

ERIC nods slowly.
Pause.

60. [Int. Hall. Night.]

MARIE comes out of the main room.
She moves to the front door and opens it.
Pause.
ERIC comes out of the main room.
He moves slowly towards the front door.
He pauses outside the nursery.
He frowns, as though unsure of what is happening.
WALTER comes out of the main room.
He pauses next to ERIC.
ERIC turns and looks at him.
WALTER smiles, puts his arm round him and helps him to the front door.
MARIE smiles at him.
He looks at her blankly then stares round the hall.
He sees WALTER'S cases in a corner.
He looks at them in a puzzled way then looks at WALTER.
WALTER smiles.

Pause.
He looks at MARIE.
She smiles and gives him her hand.

MARIE: Goodbye Eric.

ERIC *stands quietly holding her hand.*
Pause.

Come again. Come frequently.

Pause.
WALTER *helps him out into the hall.*
MARIE *watches them from the doorway.*
ERIC *turns.*
He looks at her helplessly.
She smiles as he is led away.
Pause.
MARIE *closes the door.*
Silence.
She looks down the hall towards the main room.
Pause.

61. [Int. Living-room. Night.]

Pause.
MARIE *enters.*
She looks towards the diner.
Pause.
The diner.
MARIE *comes out of the shadows, stops at the window, and looks down.*

62. [Ext. Driveway. Night]

View through wet glass of WALTER *and* ERIC *getting into the car.*
The car doors close.
The headlights come on.

63. [Int. Living-room. Night.]

MARIE, *the glare from the headlights illuminating her face.*
She watches dispassionately.
The light moves from her face as the car drives slowly away.
She stands quietly.
Pause.
She turns and looks round the diner.
Pause.
She looks towards the table.

Pause.
The candlestick, the almost burned down candles.
Pause.
MARIE'S face comes slowly into view.
She blows out the candles.
Pause.

64. [Int. Bedroom. Night.]

Later.
The bedroom.
Silence.
Slow panning shot discovering MARIE in bed reading a paper.
She turns a page.
Pause.

MARIE: It's United Nations Day.

Shot of WALTER at the dressing table.
He is wearing pyjamas.
He is combing his hair.

WALTER: Really?

He finishes combing his hair.
He rises, moves to the door and turns out the main light.
He moves to the bed, sits, and picks up the clock.

What time shall I set it for? The usual?

MARIE nods, lowers her paper to the floor and turns out her bedside lamp.
She settles down.
WALTER sets the clock and puts it on the bedside table.
He climbs into bed.
They lie quietly.
Pause.

WALTER: Nice evening.
MARIE: Yes.

Pause.

WALTER: Think I'll take the day off tomorrow. Go somewhere nice.
         The Zoo.
         Or down the River. We can take Antonia.
MARIE: That would be nice.

Pause.

WALTER: (*Sitting up*) Ready?
MARIE: Yes.

Pause.

WALTER: Goodnight.
MARIE: Goodnight.

WALTER *smiles.*
MARIE *smiles.*
WALTER *turns out the lights.*

Supose Cam   Closing
                        Credits
Fade Out

MICHAEL ROEMER AND ROBERT YOUNG

Nothing But a Man

(*Fade in.*)

Scene 1 [Ext. railroad tracks near Temple Hill, Alabama. Day.]

A section gang of 45 Negroes under the supervision of a white foreman is laying a section of track.

Scene 2 [Ext. bunk cars. Late afternoon]

A unit of weather-beaten box cars on a siding in the country. A radio blaring from one of the cars.
Several men; one hanging wash.

Scene 3 [Int. bunk car. Late afternoon]

Shots of FRANKIE and DUFF playing checkers with bottle tops. FRANKIE here (and later) chewing gum—his way of relieving tension.
DUFF'S queen takes most of FRANKIE'S pieces. Just before his last man is taken, FRANKIE sweeps his hand across the board in a resigning gesture, pushes back his chair, rises and exits frame.
DUFF grins, puts pieces into can.
JOCKO shaving in mirror, preening his face lovingly. Possibly with toothpick in mouth.
FRANKIE appears, studies him.
JOCKO gets restless, thinks FRANKIE is up to something.

JOCKO: Go to hell, Frankie.
FRANKIE: (grinning; but a note of aggression) Man—you sure one ugly nigger!

JOCKO leans down to basin to rinse face.
FRANKIE removes the cigarettes out of the sleeve of JOCKO'S T-shirt, where he keeps them rolled up Navy-style.

JOCKO: (drying his face; irritated; looking back after FRANKIE) Why don't you guys buy your own?!

FRANKIE has moved out of the shot.

FRANKIE: *(Looking into the pack of cigarettes)* Ought to give up smokin', Jocko.   5

He sails the cigarettes through the air. Camera pans with the pack across the car onto a bunk with a sleeping man.

FRANKIE: How much more we got on this stretch, Riddick?

RIDDICK—*writing letter on lower bunk.*

RIDDICK: *(looking up)* Five weeks, maybe six.
FRANKIE: Man—what a dump!

Camera pans with him. He stops in front of DUFF, who is sitting on a lower bunk and Clipping his fingernails. FRANKIE's back is turned to camera.

FRANKIE: What you gettin' all pretty for?

Close on DUFF.

DUFF: *(looking up with a grin)* Why don't you relax, Frankie?!   10

Scene 4 [Ext. landscape in outskirts of Temple Hill. Railroad tracks. Summer twilight]

Camera very close to track: a small track-car is moving toward the lens, carrying DUFF, FRANKIE, and JOCKO. As the car rushes past lens, cut to:
Shot on car: JOCKO listening to transistor radio. Woman's voice singing. JOCKO is silhouetted against sky.
Shot on car: FRANKIE, bent down, handling controls.
Shot on car: DUFF, against sky.
Shot on car: one or more of the men's faces seen against Negro shacks on the outskirts of town.
Shots from car: the approaches of town. Negro shacks along the right-of-way. A few people; children playing; voices of children.

Scene 5 [Int. pool hall. Night]

Close on metal ball rolling down interior of pinball machine. Lights, bells.
JOCKO, playing pinball machine, alone. A glass of beer resting on machine. He is chewing on a toothpick. When ball comes to rest, he shakes the machine and produces a tilt. Picks up beer glass while fishing for another nickel in his pocket.
Shots of other men, playing at tables. In groups.
Music from the juke box starts up.
The bar.
DUFF profiled in foreground, standing at bar with glass of beer. Shooting toward FRANKIE, who is standing at bar across the corner from DUFF. DORIS is seen at juke box in rear. She turns and moves into lens between DUFF and FRANKIE.

857

DORIS: Who's goin' to buy me a beer?

DORIS *has a woman's body, but the face of an innocent-depraved child. One cannot be sure she understands what is going on around her.*
DUFF *does not turn to her, remains profiled.*

FRANKIE: *(turning to her)* What's the matter, Doris? Business bad?
DORIS: *(putting her pocketbook on bar)* It sure is.
FRANKIE: *(with a grin)* Everybody givin' it away free, huh?
DORIS: You goin' to buy me a beer, Frankie?   5
FRANKIE: *(indicating Duff with a nod)* See Duff. He's a money man.
DORIS: *(turning to Duff)* What d'you say, Duff?
DUFF: *(to o.s. bartender; after glancing at Doris)* Give her a beer.
DORIS: Thanks, Duff. You a nice guy. Not like Frankie. *(this last with a pout)*

The bartender puts a beer down in front of DORIS.
FRANKIE *and* DORIS.
FRANKIE *has his right hand on* DORIS' *arm and is feeling it.*

FRANKIE: *(baiting her)* You know, Doris—you'd make some guy a swell wife.   10
DORIS: *(innocently)* You think so, Frankie?
FRANKIE: *(grinning)* Hell, you got steady work.

A mixture of confusion and hurt on DORIS' *face.*
Close on DUFF.

DUFF: *(turning in their direction)* Quit ridin' her, Frankie.

He drains his glass.

FRANKIE: I ain't ridin' her. Wouldn't ride her on a bet.

He snorts a short laugh, turns his back to bar and camera.
DUFF *has his wallet out and is putting a dollar bill on the bar.*

DORIS: Where you goin'?   15
DUFF: Out.
DORIS: Want me to come?
DUFF: No thanks.
DORIS: *(putting a hand on him)* Come on, honey—

He frees himself, picks up the dollar bill from the bar and moves past her around the corner of the bar. She looks after him. Camera pans over with him, past FRANKIE'S *back. He stops on the other side of* FRANKIE, *again putting the dollar bill onto the bar.*
FRANKIE *turns to* DUFF.

FRANKIE: Where you goin'?

DUFF: (*with a shrug*) 'Round town.

FRANKIE: What's so hot 'round town?

DUFF: (*with a grin, turning to go*) See you, Frankie.

FRANKIE: Don't want to fish you outa no jailhouse.

The bartender comes into the shot from right of frame to take the money.

Scene 6 [Ext. Baptist Church. Night]

Cars parked in open space beside building. The windows are lit up and a gospel hymn is heard from inside.
Camera pans into a close-up of DUFF.

Scene 7 [Int. church. Night]

Shots of choir singing. All in their Sunday best.
Shots of congregation singing. All in their Sunday best.
DUFF among others, at the door.
The pulpit. As the hymn comes to an end, the minister rises.

REV. DAWSON: I'm glad to see this meeting off to a good start. Now we'll take a break and then come back to hear from our distinguished guest— Reverend Butler of the Morgan Street Baptist Church in Birmingham.

High angle. The congregation is on its feet, with everyone shaking hands and exchanging greetings.

Scene 8 [Ext. church. Night]

Shots of the picnic in progress among the parked cars. People eating, talking, laughing. The buffet, close on the edge of a wooded area. Kids.
High angle. DUFF is standing somewhat isolated in the foreground when he is approached by a middle-aged woman, large and imposing. She obviously welcomes him warmly, although their dialogue is inaudible in the general noise.
The buffet—on the edge of a wooded area. Shooting past JOSIE. Most people have been served and the table is deserted except for a single man, whom JOSIE is serving.
The large middle-aged woman approaches, holding DUFF by the arm and steering him. He looks amused.
The man whom JOSIE was serving leaves.

MRS. MARSHALL: (*to* JOSIE) Josie—this is Brother Anderson. Now you give him some of that good food. He's a fine young man.

JOSIE, amused, picks up a plate and starts filling it. She looks down to hide her smile.

MRS. MARSHALL: (*to* DUFF) Well, I'll run along. Ain't it a wonderful meeting!

She turns to go.
DUFF.   *He turns from the woman to JOSIE.*

DUFF: That's fine, Miss. I'll take me some of that punch, too.
JOSIE: *(handing him plate)* You must be new in town.   5
DUFF: Thanks. Looks good.
JOSIE: *(filling cup with punch)* Haven't seen you around, have I?!
DUFF: *(chewing)* That's right. *(With a grin)* I'm new in town.

She smiles, hands him cup.

JOSIE: You working?
DUFF: Yeah. On the section gang.   10

He watches for her reaction across the top of the cup as he tastes the punch.
He drains the cup, puts it down.

DUFF: You work in town?
JOSIE: I teach school.
DUFF: *(eating)* Went to college, huh?
JOSIE: *(nodding, as she refills his cup)* In Birmingham.
DUFF: Oh yeah? That's *my* home town.   15
JOSIE: Your folks live there?
DUFF: *(shaking head)* No. My mother's dead.

The service inside the church has started again. We hear the preacher's voice and a loud
        response from the congregation.

JOSIE: *(piling dishes; clearing up)* Are you coming back in?
DUFF: Naw. Never had much use for hell-howlers.—You goin'?
JOSIE: *(with a smile; still clearing up)* My father's the preacher.   20
DUFF: *(grinning)* Oh yeah?—Well I guess you got no choice.
JOSIE: *(smiling)* That's right.

She goes down below the level of the table to pick up her pocketbook.
DUFF *puts down his plate.*

DUFF: *(grinning)* Look, I don't know what you been told 'bout section gangs,
        but how 'bout seein' me sometime?
JOSIE: *(coming around the table)* Maybe.   25

Scene 9 [Int. church. Night]

The Birmingham minister is in the middle of a dramatic revival sermon. He is a small
        dapper man, and a brilliant performer.
Shots of the congregation.

860

DUFF *near the door. While the minister's voice continues o.s., he turns and leaves.*

Scene 10 [Int. bunk car. Late afternoon]

Shots of RIDDICK, JOCKO, FRANKIE, *and* POP *playing poker at table.* JOCKO *catches fly, throws it on floor and steps on it while game continues. He is chewing on tooth-pick.*
FRANKIE *and* JOCKO. FRANKIE *stretches, raising his hands high.*

JOCKO: *(glancing up at Frankie's cards)* You got a lousy hand, Frankie.
FRANKIE: Yeah. I quit.

He leans forward, bringing his chair—which has been back on its rear legs—down with a bang, throws his cards onto the table and sweeps his few remaining nickels into the kitty. Then he gets up, picks up an old Flit-gun from the table, and exits frame. JOCKO *picks up* FRANKIE'S *cards and studies them.*
Pick up FRANKIE *in motion. Pan with him as he moves through car, spraying for flies with Flit-gun.*
Pan DUFF *into frame. He is polishing his shoes—one foot on table.* FRANKIE *sprays him as if the Flit-gun were a perfume atomizer.*

DUFF: *(grinning)* You got nothin' on your mind but your hair, Frankie. *(In the direction of the card game)* How 'bout your car, Riddick?

Over this last line, FRANKIE *attempts to spray under one of* DUFF'S *arms.*
RIDDICK *and* JOCKO.

RIDDICK: *(looking up from his cards)* Yeah, you can have it.   5
JOCKO: *(grinning)* Man—you won't like that back seat.

DUFF *is putting on his jacket.* FRANKIE *is revealed behind him as he slips into sleeve.*

FRANKIE: *(skeptical and concerned)* Why you messin' 'round with a gal like that?—You won't get no place!

DUFF *grins.*
RIDDICK, JOCKO, *and* POP *playing cards.*

JOCKO: *(in direction of* DUFF*)* Hell, they're all after the same thing.

POP *has been drinking out of a pint flask of corn whiskey.*

POP: *(putting bottle down)* Yeah. All a colored woman wants is your money.   10
JOCKO: *(deprecating grin)* What d'you know 'bout women, Pop?!
POP: Well, I got married to one of them.

RIDDICK *looks up. He didn't know.*

JOCKO: (*surprised*) I didn't know you was married.

POP: Sure. Got a sixteen-year-old girl.

JOCKO: That right?   15

He turns back to his cards.
Slight pause. JOCKO plays his hand.
DUFF comes up to table beside RIDDICK. RIDDICK is playing his hand.

JOCKO: (*looking up at* DUFF) Think you're goin' to make it with her?

JOCKO: (*still chewing toothpick*) Bet she's easy jam. Just get her drunk.

DUFF: (*to* RIDDICK; *who has put down his card*) How 'bout the keys?

Scene 11 [Int. Dawson dining room. Night]

Fairly comfortably furnished, Negro middle class. Clock? JOSIE, REV. DAWSON, and MRS.
DAWSON are finishing supper with coffee and pie.
On JOSIE. She is pouring a cup of coffee.
Formal shot of table, showing all three. Somewhat high angle. JOSIE pours coffee, passes
cup to her father. Silence.

MRS. DAWSON: (*in* REV. DAWSON'S *direction*) D'you think you ought to have more coffee, Frank? You won't be able to sleep.

REV. DAWSON: (*pushing cup away slightly*) I guess you're right.

MRS. DAWSON finishes her own cup.

MRS. DAWSON: What d'you know about this young man, Josie?

JOSIE. She is eating pie.

JOSIE: He works on the section gang.   5

She is not unaware of the effect this is going to have on REV. DAWSON and MRS. DAW-
SON, of course. In fact, she rather enjoys startling them, although her manner
does not show it.

MRS. DAWSON: (*quietly*) I know you pay no mind to my feelings, but d'you think it's right for you to go out with him?

JOSIE. She is finishing pie.

JOSIE: (*quietly; but a challenge*) I do.

MRS. DAWSON: (*turning to* REV. DAWSON) Perhaps *you* ought to tell her, Frank.

REV. DAWSON: (*he does believe what he says, but he is saying it largely for*   10
MRS. DAWSON) Well, Josie—we have a position in town. You have to remember that.—There're lots of other young men.

MRS. DAWSON: I don't think your mother would have approved.

JOSIE: *(quietly; now almost grave)* I do.

REV. DAWSON: *(all this is very painful to him)* Well, we don't want you going out with him.   15

JOSIE *says nothing.*

REV. DAWSON *drinks more of his coffee.*

MRS. DAWSON: *(to* REV. DAWSON; *L-R)* Is that all you're going to say, Frank?

REV. DAWSON: What else can I say?

MRS. DAWSON: *(coldly)* I see. *(turning to* JOSIE, *facing R-L)* Well, there's just one thing you can be looking for in a man like that.   20

JOSIE: *(with a flash of anger, but controlled)* I know that's what you think.

REV. DAWSON: *(tired; duty-bound)* Hush your mouth, child.

MRS. DAWSON *leaves in background, carrying dishes.*

REV. DAWSON *opens newspaper.* JOSIE *finishes her coffee.*

> The doorbell rings.

JOSIE: *(rising; quietly)* Good-bye, Dad.

REV. DAWSON *looks up, says nothing, and goes back to his paper.*

JOSIE *exits.*

Scene 12 [Int. road house. Night]

Shots of DUFF *and* JOSIE *dancing. From his p.o.v., perhaps slightly from above. Some shots past* DUFF. *She is surprisingly good, charmingly abandoned.*

Shots of other couples. The band.

> *The music comes to an end. The floor clears.*

A booth. Slightly from above. Beer on the table.

DUFF *and* JOSIE *come up.* JOSIE *tucks her blouse into her skirt.*

DUFF: *(grinning; still up)* Pretty good for a preacher's daughter.

She has sat down, smiling.

He sits down opposite her.

> *Slight pause. Both are sipping beer.*

DUFF: You know, I can't figure you out.

JOSIE: What d'you mean?

DUFF: *(with a quizzical look; rubbing his chin)* Why d'you come out with me? You slummin' or something?   5

JOSIE: No.

DUFF: *(grinning)* So what you doin' with a cat like me in a joint like this?

JOSIE: (*with a smile*) You don't think much of yourself, do you?

DUFF: (*put off*) Huh?! That's a funny thing to say!

JOSIE: (*amused by his strong reaction*) Well, you keep asking me why I'm here.   10

DUFF: (*relaxing into a grin*) Yeah. And you keep not answerin'.

JOSIE: (*more seriously*) Well, I like a place with lots of life. Nobody ever takes me here.

She picks up her glass.

DUFF: (*shaking his head*) Man—you're full of surprises.—How 'bout some more beer?   15

He looks around for a waiter.
Suddenly his expression changes.

DUFF: Hell—

Shooting past DUFF: FRANKIE and JOCKO are heading toward the booth.

FRANKIE: (*big grin*) Well, if it ain't Duff!

JOCKO: (*grinning too*) How you doin', baby? (*to JOSIE, appreciating her*) Hi, there.

JOSIE: (*looking up at them, amused*) Hi.   20

JOCKO: (*to DUFF*) Mind if we sit down?

DUFF: (*looking at them; quietly but pointedly*) We're just leavin', fellows.

FRANKIE: (*to JOCKO; with a good-natured grin*) Let's go, Jocko. The man's got homework. (*he winks at JOCKO, turns to DUFF*) See you, Duff.

DUFF: Yeah. See you in hell.   25

The two men move on.

JOSIE: Do they work on the section gang?

DUFF: (*grimace; still a bit disconcerted*) Yeah.

JOSIE: (*kidding him*) Well, they seem just like everyone else.

DUFF: (*with a grin*) Hell, I bet *you* think they got tails.

JOSIE smiles.
FRANKIE'S deep voice in the booth behind DUFF says: "We do!"
JOSIE grins.
DUFF turns.
Shot across top of booth behind DUFF.
FRANKIE in close foreground—seated with back to camera but face turned into lens, grinning. JOCKO is on the other side of the booth. He sticks his cigarette into his ear and blows the smoke out of his mouth.

DUFF: (*rising; to JOSIE*) Let's get out of here!   30

864

Pan with him as he moves over to JOSIE.
On FRANKIE, with JOCKO in background.

FRANKIE: *(quietly)* School teacher—my nappy head!

Scene 13 [Int. car. Night]

Good-luck charm bobbing under mirror. In the distance, a train is passing and the Diesel hoots mournfully.

JOSIE: *(looking at him)* I guess it's hard working on the road like that.
DUFF: *(head against seat; relaxed; looking forward rather than at her)* It's okay. Damn few places you can make eighty bucks a week.
JOSIE: I mean, you're kind of cut off, aren't you?
DUFF: That's fine with me. Keeps me out of trouble. 5
JOSIE: How d'you mean?
DUFF: *(quietly; relaxed)* Well, I don't get along so good most places, 'way things are.

She looks at him, an almost grave but sympathetic expression. Then she leans her head against the back of the seat (top of it). The rustle of silk as she crosses her legs.

JOSIE: *(a smile; not turned to him)* The beer made me dizzy.

A car drives up, its radio blaring and its headlights briefly lighting up the interior of the car.
JOSIE turns over her shoulder and glances out window.
The car has stopped and its lights dim down. The music is turned down.
JOSIE turns back, so that her face is straight up again. Her head is still against the back (top) of the seat.
JOSIE turns back from window, so that her face is straight up again. DUFF has been looking at her.

DUFF: *(quietly)* You got a lovely face, kid. *(A slight grimace)* Don't often get to 10
meet a girl like you.

She turns her head to him without raising it from the back of the seat, and smiles.

DUFF: Hell—

He leans forward and kisses her. We see the back of his head; her face is hidden.

DUFF: *(sitting up; with a grin; the back of his finger rubbing his chin)* How often you been kissed, baby?

JOSIE looks at him, a quizzical-amused expression appearing on her face. She isn't at all thrown by the question.—Her head is still against the seat.

JOSIE: Well, let's see—not counting tonight . . . (*turning her face up and away* 15
from him, pretending to add up the occasions) . . . must be about
twenty-eight times.

DUFF: (*grinning*) What's the matter with the local cats?

JOSIE: (*smiling*) Oh you know—preacher's daughter.

DUFF: (*seeing an opening*) You got a problem all right. 20

He moves in to kiss her again.
Something moves outside the open window, in back of her. She turns and looks up. The
camera tilts up.
A white boy in his late teens stands in the window. He is a little high, relaxed, chewing
gum.

BOY: (*not unfriendly*) Hi—

DUFF *and* JOSIE, *from* BOY'S *p.o.v.*
They are silent. JOSIE *is looking up at him.* DUFF *turns and sees him.* JOSIE *averts her*
eyes—either down or to DUFF. *Pause.*

VOICE OF SECOND BOY: (*calling from o.s.*) They doin' anything?

FIRST BOY: (*turning his back to camera and car; calling back*) Naw. Nothin'!

DUFF: (*quietly*) Get out of here, man!

JOSIE: (*frightened; quietly*) Don't, Duff. 25

FIRST BOY: (*relaxed*) Relax, man.

The SECOND BOY *appears in the window. He too is high. He is holding a flashlight.*

SECOND BOY: What's goin' on?

He passes the flashlight over DUFF'S *face, who looks at him with narrowing eyes, and*
across JOSIE—*who instinctively raises her arm over her breast.*
Pan with flashlight over DUFF'S *face,* JOSIE'S *face—and down over the upper part of her*
body.

DUFF: (*tension and suppressed rage*) Cut it out!

FIRST BOY: (*still relaxed, but the note of a threat*) Don't start no trouble, boy.

SECOND BOY: (*to* FIRST BOY) Let's go. (*pointing flashlight at* JOSIE) That's the 30
preacher's girl. Mess with him and you got old man Johnson on your
back.—Come on.

He turns and leaves.
The FIRST BOY *winks at* DUFF, *clicks his tongue, and follows the* SECOND BOY.
JOSIE *turns to* DUFF, *who is looking after him.*

JOSIE: (*still frightened*) Let's go, Duff.

DUFF: (*relaxing his muscles; but his face still shows tension*) Take it easy.

There is a metallic click. JOSIE looks down.

Pan down from DUFF'S face to his lap. He has closed his knife and is putting it into his pocket.

She looks at him. He looks at her, then reaches over to turn on the ignition.

O.S. the white boys have started their car and drive away.

JOSIE turns over her shoulder to look out of window.

Shot out of window. The car of the white boys is pulling away. The FIRST BOY is leaning out of the window, looking back at DUFF and JOSIE, and producing a loud rebel yell.

DUFF: *(turning to JOSIE; with a shake of his head and a half-grin)* Don't sound   35
human, do they?!

He starts the car.

Scene 14 [Ext. shots from moving car. Night]

Stately residential homes in the white section of town.

Scene 15 [Int. moving car. Night]

DUFF: How come you stay 'round this place?

JOSIE: *(quietly)* Well, my mother was the only good teacher the colored school ever had. Nobody bothers with those kids. They don't have a chance.

DUFF: You got more guts than me, baby. It's a no-good town.

JOSIE: *(gravely)* It's better than it used to be. Eight years ago they still had a lynching here. They tied a man to a car and dragged him to death.

Scene 16 [Ext. shots from moving car. Night]

The business district. Court House Square. The stores are still open.

JOSIE: *(quietly; this is very hard on her)* My father knew who did it, but he didn't say anything.

DUFF: Scared, huh?

JOSIE: *(gravely)* All of the colored folks are 'round here. They can't help it. They've been scared too long.

Scene 17 [Ext. shots from moving car. Night]

The colored section. A church clock strikes the hour.

JOSIE: How old were you when your mother died?

DUFF: 'Round nine.

JOSIE: What was she like?

DUFF: Nothin' but a husk. They crushed the life right out of her. *(With a faint grin)* Of course my Grandma blamed it on my father.   5

JOSIE: Did your Grandma raise you?

DUFF: *(with a grin)* Yeah.—When she wasn't workin' or prayin'.

JOSIE: Is she still living?

DUFF: *(shaking his head)* No. *(A smile that approaches tenderness)* Just hope white folks ain't runnin' heaven, or she'll catch hell up there just like   10 she done down here.

He steers the car to the curb.

DUFF: Here we are—

Scene 18 [Ext. shot from moving car. Night]

Approaching the Dawson home. The car slows down and stops.

Scene 19 [Int. stationary car. Night]

The car is still moving very slightly, comes to a stop.
DUFF *turns off the ignition. Then he turns to* JOSIE—*a slightly quizzical expression on his face.*

DUFF: Well, good night, baby—

He reaches for her.

JOSIE: *(a little nervous)* Not here, Duff.

DUFF: *(with a grin and a glance through the windshield)* I get it.

JOSIE: *(candidly)* But I'd like to see you again.

DUFF: You would, huh? *(Grinning)* If I was you, baby—I wouldn't go 'round   5 stickin' out my jugular vein.

JOSIE: What d'you mean?

DUFF: You almost got in trouble out there.

JOSIE: *(innocently)* You mean those boys?

DUFF: *(shaking his head; with a grin—grimace)* Guess I'll have to draw you a   10 picture.—Know why I took you out there in the first place?

JOSIE: *(a bit sheepishly)* I wouldn't have let you.

DUFF: *(amused)* Man—I'm not in the third grade. *(Pausing slightly)* Look, baby —you're a great girl, but you and I just don't mix.

JOSIE: *(casually)* I see.   15

She opens her pocketbook and takes out her lipstick.

DUFF: *(trying to explain himself)* Hell, I don't fit in with your type.

JOSIE: *(putting on lipstick in car mirror)* What type is that?

DUFF: Look, baby—what're we goin' to do *next* time? Have a long chat in the livin' room?!

JOSIE: (*turning to him with a smile; closing her lipstick*) On the porch.   20

DUFF: Yeah, and then?!

JOSIE: (*raised eyebrows*) What?

DUFF: Then we'd either hit the hay or get married. (*Looking at her and shaking his head*) Now *you* don't want to hit the hay, and *I* don't want to get married.   25

JOSIE: (*putting the lipstick into her pocketbook*) What makes you so sure *I* want to get married? (*Closing her pocketbook, turning to him*) You've got a very primitive idea of human relationships.

DUFF: (*defensive; a touch of anger*) Okay, I'm primitive! So what d'you want from me?   30

JOSIE: (*turning to him; grave—a sudden breakthrough of deep feeling*) Look, Duff—most of the men I know have had their back broken. You can just feel sorry for them.—When I met you the other day, I had a feeling that you're different. That's why I went out with you. (*Angry at herself for having shown her feelings*) Well, maybe you're a man, but I guess we   35
don't have much to say to each other.

DUFF: (*definitely taken aback; half-confused, half-pleased; not in command of situation*) Hell, baby, I don't know what to say.

JOSIE: (*opening car door*) Good night.

She leaves.
Slight pause. DUFF *is rubbing his chin with his hand.*
Then he starts the ignition.

Scene 20 [Ext. from moving car. Night]

JOSIE *is walking to the Dawson home, which is up ahead of car.*
Start shot from stationary car. Then car begins to move, and passes her.

Scene 21. [Int. bunk car. Night]

Pan across sleeping man to DUFF, *who is taking off his jacket.*

Scene 22. [Ext. field near railroad track. Day]

Some fifteen men hunting rabbits with home-made clubs. They encircle a patch of prairie grass and move in, yelling and stomping to flush out the animals. As soon as one jumps into view, the clubs are hurled with deadly accuracy.
Close shots of FRANKIE *and* JOCKO, *participating in the rabbit hunt.*

Scene 23. [Ext. River bank. Day]

POP *in the foreground, frying rabbit over fire.* JOCKO *in the rear, fishing.* POP *takes swig from corn-whiskey bottle.*
DUFF, *whittling on stick in foreground.* RIDDICK *reading magazine in background.*

Scene 24. [Int. Classroom. Day]

JOSIE *is writing arithmetic problems onto the blackboard.*
Shots of the children. They are busy copying the problems.
Reverse on classroom, with kids in foreground—backs turned to camera—and JOSIE *at the blackboard.*
The bell rings. Several of the kids close their books. One or two jump up. JOSIE *turns.*
On JOSIE. *She turns.*

JOSIE: Have you finished, Jackie?

On JACKIE. *He is standing. Other kids in close foreground.*

JACKIE: Yes, Ma'am.
JOSIE: (*with a stern touch*) Well, sit down and wait till class is dismissed.

He sits down again.
JOSIE *steps away from blackboard (in direction of windows).*
MLS of classroom.
JACKIE *sits down (seen from back).* JOSIE *leaves the blackboard for the nearest window. She begins closing it.*
Shot through window, as it comes down. Beyond it we see the schoolyard. Children playing in foreground. In the rear, DUFF *is sitting on one of the children's swings, moving idly.*
On JOSIE. *She smiles, turns to class.*

JOSIE: All right. Class dismissed.

Sound of class rising, scraping chairs, chattering voices, laughter.
JOSIE *turns to next window.*
LS Class, perhaps from door. JOSIE *closing second window at rear.*
The class rises, chattering, laughing; kids moving toward lens—leaving JOSIE *isolated at rear.*

Scene 25. [Ext. Schoolyard. Day]

High angle. The yard is empty. DUFF *and* JOSIE *on swings.* JOSIE *is swinging back and forth lightly.* DUFF *has twisted his swing sideways, so that he faces* JOSIE. *His feet are firmly planted on the ground and he is not moving.*

DUFF: (*with a smile*) At first it was real strange. Hell, I'd never been out of the

South, and Japan is a long way from Alabama. (*quietly; thoughtful*) Really got under my skin, though—the rice paddies and the mountains and those people. Like I was breathin' deep for the first time. (*with a grin*) Almost didn't come back.

JOSIE: Why did you?

DUFF: (*a shrug*) I don't know. Guess I belong here more than there.

JOSIE: Have you been up North?

DUFF: Yeah. I kicked around for a couple of months after the Army.—You been there?

JOSIE: No.

DUFF: Kind of strange, coming back here—ain't it? Well, maybe there ain't no other place. Like if you can't make it here, you can't make it no place. —Of course I ain't really makin' it now.

He jumps off the swing.

DUFF: At least they can't get to you if you keep on movin'.

He gives JOSIE'S swing a shove—sending her up into the air.

Scene 26. [Ext. Dawson house. Day. Rain]

DUFF and JOSIE are running up the porch steps. JOSIE opens the door.

Scene 27. [Int. Dawson living room. Day]

JOSIE comes through the doorway, with DUFF close behind her.

JOSIE: (*stopping*) Oh—I'm sorry.

Reverse angle: MR. JOHNSON, a white man in his middle years, is standing by the window. REV. DAWSON is standing by the mantel.

JOHNSON: (*lighting a cigar*) Come on in, Josie. We're all through.

JOSIE: Daddy, I'd like you to meet Duff Anderson.

DUFF: (*shaking hands*) How you been?

REV. DAWSON: All right, son.

JOSIE: This is Mr. Johnson, our school superintendent.

JOHNSON: (*nodding with friendly condescension*) 'lo.

JOSIE: (*taking her schoolbooks*) I'll be right back.

She leaves the room.

JOHNSON: (*picking up his coat; to DUFF*) So you're courtin' the preacher's girl,

huh? (*with a wink*) Well, just watch your step, boy—or he'll preach you 10
right into hell.

REV. DAWSON *helps him into his coat.*

JOHNSON: (*to* REV. DAWSON) Now I'm counting on you, Reverend.
REV. DAWSON: I know.
JOHNSON: Wouldn't do for one of your people to sue at a time like this.—And
I'll talk to the mayor. 15
REV. DAWSON: That'll make the folks very happy.
JOHNSON: Be seein' you, Reverend. (*to* DUFF, *with a grin*) Good luck, boy.
REV. DAWSON: (*seeing* JOHNSON *to the door*) Good-bye.

He closes the door.
There is a slight, embarrassed pause. REV. DAWSON *feels at a disadvantage, since* DUFF
has witnessed his relationship to JOHNSON.

REV. DAWSON: (*tentatively*) It's hard to know how to talk to the white folks these
days. 20
DUFF: (*quietly*) Guess it's never been easy.
REV. DAWSON: (*sitting down; ill-at-ease*) It's a changing time. (*leaning back; a
false note of relaxation*) Well, looks like we'll be getting a new school.
DUFF: (*quietly; not aggressively*) How come you ain't tryin' to send them to the
same school? 25
REV. DAWSON: Well, you've got to go easy on this integration. (*adding quickly*)
Mind you, I *know* it's going to come. But we haven't had any trouble in
town for eight years and we don't want any now.
DUFF: You can't live without trouble, can you?

DAWSON *says nothing, glances at* DUFF, *then looks away.*
DUFF *looks around the room. Then he changes the subject to avoid any further conflict.*

DUFF: Nice place you've got. 30
REV. DAWSON: Yes, the Lord's been pretty good to us.—I guess *you're* a church-
man.
DUFF: (*quietly*) Well—guess I'm not.
REV. DAWSON: Why? Don't you believe in the Lord?
DUFF: I do. (*with a faint grin*) But seems to me us colored do a whole lot of 35
church-goin'. It's the whites that need it real bad.
REV. DAWSON: A little humility never hurt anyone.
DUFF: (*a grin-grimace*) That's what the white folks keep tellin' us. (*he is not
deliberately trying to antagonize* REV. DAWSON. *But the antagonism exists,
of course*) 40
REV. DAWSON: It sounds to me like you've got all the answers.
DUFF: (*quickly*) I didn't say that.

REV. DAWSON: I think if you tried living in a town like this, instead of running free and easy, you'd soon change your tune.

DUFF: (*quietly*) I doubt it.

REV. DAWSON: I see. (*rising*) Well, I guess we don't have much to say to each other—do we?

DUFF: (*rising also; quietly, but with tension*) I guess not.

REV. DAWSON: And since we're talking, my wife and I don't want you hanging around our daughter.

DUFF: (*curbing his anger as well as he can*) That figures.—Kind of fits in with everything else.

Scene 28. [Ext. Dawson house. Rain. Day]

DUFF *comes out onto the porch. He stops and looks out into the rain. A moment later,* JOSIE *appears.*

JOSIE: I'm sorry.

DUFF: Ain't your fault.

JOSIE: (*sadly but without rancor*) That's the way he is.

DUFF: Yeah. Just like I figured.

JOSIE: What d'you mean?

DUFF: (*a sudden burst of anger*) Hell, I got no business here. I don't know what I been thinkin'!

Slight pause. Close on JOSIE. *This is the first indication she has had that* DUFF *has been thinking about her very seriously.*

JOSIE: (*quietly*) Look, Duff, I'm not working tomorrow.

DUFF: (*cutting her off*) Sorry, baby. I'm goin 'to Birmingham.

JOSIE: Just for the day?

DUFF: (*nodding*) Goin' to see my kid.

JOSIE: (*quietly, but very surprised*) I didn't know you had one.

DUFF: I do.

JOSIE: Are you married?

DUFF: (*abruptly*) No. (*putting up his collar*) Well, got to be goin'. See you.

He turns and heads down the steps into the rain.

Scene 29. [Int. Greyhound bus. Morning]

DUFF *enters. He has been running and is out of breath. He comes down the aisle, looking for a seat. Walks into CU, stops short, his attention caught by something o.s.*

DUFF: (*a grin spreading over his face*) What-do-you-know!

Pan to JOSIE. *She is sitting at a window seat, smiling up at him with an amused-quizzical* expression—*as if she were playing some kind of joke on him. She is wearing white gloves and a trim tailored suit.*

JOSIE: Surprised?

DUFF: Hell, no! Women're always followin' me 'round.

JOSIE: (*with a smile*) I'm going in to do my shopping.

DUFF: (*nodding; amused*) Yeah! It's real coincidence.

JOSIE: (*perfectly aware how obvious it all is*) That's right.

DUFF: (*grinning*) Okay. (*making believe he is about to go*) See you, baby—

JOSIE: Sit down, Duff. No point running away from coincidence.

DUFF: (*sitting down beside her*) Shoot, baby—you must be crazy.

The bus starts.
JOSIE, the smile still on her face, looks out of the window.

Scene 30. [Ext. Shot from moving bus. Day]

The main street of town.
(*Dissolve.*)

Scene 31. [Ext. Shot from moving bus. Day]

A vast industrial wasteland in Birmingham. In the foreground, rubble from a slum-clearing project.

Scene 32. [Int. Bus. Day]

JOSIE: (*turning to him*) How old is your little boy?

DUFF: Three.

JOSIE: What does he look like?

DUFF: (*shaking his head*) Haven't seen him in a couple of years.

He looks out of the window again.

Scene 33 [Ext. shot from moving bus. Day]

A run-down colored section of Birmingham.

Scene 34 [Ext. montage. Day]

Impressions of a poor Negro neighborhood.

Scene 35 [Ext. small dilapidated house. Day]

DUFF *is ringing the doorbell. He is carrying a large paper bag.*

The house door is open but the screen door is closed. The sound of a TV set from inside the house. A gospel music broadcast from a window somewhere.
No one has answered the bell.

DUFF: *(looking through the screen)* Anybody home?

Scene 36 [Int. shot through screen into Simms living room. Day]

In the far corner of the dimly-lit room, a woman is sitting holding a baby. She is chewing gum, looking straight at us.

WOMAN: *(without moving; in a flat, dead voice)* I'm listenin'.

DUFF: You Effie Simms?
WOMAN: What d'you want?
DUFF: Guess you're lookin' after my boy. I'm Duff Anderson.
WOMAN: 'Bout time you showed.—Door's open.   5

Scene 37 [Int. Simms living room. Day]

It is poorly-furnished and neglected-looking. The TV set is blaring from the next room, which is separated from the living room by a curtain.
As DUFF *enters,* EFFIE *leans back and pulls open the curtain. She is pregnant. Her movements, like her voice, are dulled and without vigor.*

EFFIE: *(calling into the other room)* James Lee—come in here and meet your daddy.

She lets the curtain fall to again.

DUFF: Where's Wilma?
EFFIE: She done moved to Detroit.
DUFF: Ain't she goin' to take the boy?   5
EFFIE: *(dressing the baby)* She got herself a husband now. They don't want him 'round. *(looking up at* DUFF*)* And I tell you, man, I got no use for him neither. Got two my own.
DUFF: I've been sendin' her money.
EFFIE: *(looking up at him)* She never gave me none.—You better find him a   10
place pretty quick.
DUFF: Like where?

EFFIE *gets up to rock the baby.*

EFFIE: I don't know. He's *your* boy.
DUFF: *(quietly; there's a deep hurt here which he tries to cover up)* I ain't so   15
sure. If I was, maybe I'd feel different.

EFFIE: (*opening the curtain into the other room and calling*) James Lee—I said for you to come in here.

DUFF *approaches the doorway.*

Scene 38 [Int. Simms bedroom. Day]

A small child is sitting on a newspaper spread out in front of the TV set, which is blaring away even though the image is badly scrambled. The child is half-dressed and there is a plate of food next to it.

Standing over at the bed, playing with a white kitten and a piece of string, is a three-year old boy, JAMES LEE. He looks up and approaches, stops and look at DUFF. His thumb is in his mouth.

DUFF: How you been, boy?

The boy stares.

EFFIE: Go on! Tell him.

The baby cries off-screen and she exits frame.

JAMES LEE: I been all right.
DUFF: (*holding out the paper bag*) Got you something.

JAMES LEE *takes the bag without saying anything and goes back to the bed.*

Scene 39 [Int. Simms living room. Day]

DUFF *lets the curtain fall shut.*

EFFIE: (*attending the baby; looking up*) Doctor says he could use some shots.
DUFF: Yeah. (*taking money out of his wallet*) I'll be sendin' the money to you from now on.

He puts the bills on the table.

EFFIE: Okay—
DUFF: Make sure he gets those shots—

5

He draws the curtain aside again and looks into the bedroom.

Scene 40 [Int. Simms bedroom. Day]

JAMES LEE *has unpacked a large stuffed animal and is setting it up on the bed. The kitten is watching.*

Scene 41 [Int. Simms living room. Day]

EFFIE: They say your dad's 'round town.
DUFF: (*letting the curtain go; turning*) That right? Thought he was North.
EFFIE: He come back. People seen him 'round.

Close on DUFF.

DUFF: (*rubbing his chin; a quizzical look*) Where's he at?

Scene 42 [Ext. moving shot. Day]

A street of bars, cheap hotels, storefront churches.
DUFF *is walking along the sidewalk, glancing at the house numbers. He stops in front of a sleazy-looking rooming house.*

Scene 43 [Int. stairs in rooming house. Day]

Swing music from somewhere in the building: a woman singing.
DUFF *is climbing the steps. The camera pans ahead of him to an open door at the head of the stairs. Inside, we can make out a man (WILL ANDERSON) lying, fully dressed, on a bed.*

Scene 44 [Int. Will Anderson's room. Day]

It is poorly furnished: a hot-plate with a perking coffee pot in one corner; clothes—including dresses—on pegs along the wall.
Shot across WILL ANDERSON toward the door. He is lying on a double bed, his eyes closed, chewing on a toothpick. He is in his forties, a huge, powerfully built man with a weather-beaten face.
DUFF *has appeared in the doorway.*

DUFF: You Will Anderson?
WILL: (*opening his eyes and turning to door*) Who're you?
DUFF: I'm Duff.

WILL *sits up on the bed and looks at him.*

WILL: (*matter-of-fact*) Wouldn't have known you.
DUFF: (*with a faint grin*) Wouldn't have known *you.*   5

Silence. WILL *lights a cigarette, using his right hand only.*

WILL: (*suspiciously*) What's on your mind?
DUFF: (*with a shrug*) Heard you were in town.
WILL: Just wanted a look at your old man, huh?

He rises. DUFF notices that one of his sleeves is hanging limp and empty. The arm has been amputated.

DUFF: *(with a grin)* That's right.

WILL: *(relaxing)* Nothin' much to see. *(walking around the room)* How 'bout a 10 drink?

DUFF: Okay.

WILL walks over to the sink.
DUFF joins him.

DUFF: *(indicating WILL's arm)* What happened?

WILL is opening a bottle of whiskey by sticking it under his good arm and uncorking it with his hand.

WILL: Workin' a saw-mill.

He puts the bottle down and picks up the empty sleeve.
He hands DUFF a generous shot of whiskey.

WILL: Here's how— 15

He empties his glass in two swallows. DUFF takes his more slowly.

DUFF: You been back long?

WILL: Coupla years. Couldn't take the cold no more. Funny thing—after twenty years up there, suddenly it got to me.

He pours himself another shot.
A woman appears in the doorway and enters the room without knocking. This is LEE. She is in her thirties and there is something distinctly attractive about her even though one can see in her face that she has been knocked around and deeply hurt.
Without paying any attention to the men, she puts down a shopping bag, takes the coffee pot off the hot-plate and sets it on the table.

WILL: Baby—want you to met Duff.

LEE: *(glancing at DUFF and nodding)* Hi. 20

WILL: *(with a trace of pride; he knows she is going to be surprised)* He's my son.

She looks at him again, with greater interest.

LEE: *(with a shade of irony in which she hides her feelings about everything)* What-do-you-know!—Come and have some coffee.

The men approach the table. LEE is pouring.

LEE: *(looking up at* DUFF*)* Sit down. I'm Lee.

They sit down.

WILL: *(to* LEE*)* You mad at me?   25
LEE: No. Why?
WILL: Nothin'.

He puts his hand briefly, in a bear-like gesture of tenderness, onto her hand.

WILL: *(to* DUFF*)* She's all right. Wouldn't have made it without her. Christ—I
      haven't worked in eight months. *(more confidently; patting his empty
      sleeve)* Waitin' for some insurance money. Oughta be worth a coupla   30
      thousand. And man, once I get it, I got plans to make me some more.
DUFF: *(interested)* How?
WILL: *(looking at him)* What do you care?
DUFF: *(with a shrug)* Just wondered.
WILL: Don't think I can do it, huh?!   35
LEE: *(quietly)* He didn't say that.
DUFF: *(matter-of-fact)* I didn't.
WILL: Yeah?

He looks at DUFF *a moment longer. Then he pushes his chair back and gets up.*

WILL: Well, let's get outa here. *(to* LEE*)* You got some money?

She looks at him dubiously.

WILL: I got that cooped-up feelin' again. This place gives me the willies.—   40
      Let's go.

DUFF *finishes his coffee and gets up.* LEE *is still sitting.*

WILL: *(to* LEE; *aggressively)* What's the matter? It's a celebration!

She gets up, the skeptical-tired expression still on her face.

Scene 45 [Int. bar. Day]

Dance music from the juke box.
DUFF, LEE, *and* WILL *are sitting at one of the tables.* WILL *has had several beers. The
      empty bottles stand in front of him.*

WILL: So what's this 'bout a woman? You got woman trouble?
DUFF: *(quietly)* I said I came in town with a girl.
WILL: Plannin' to get married?

DUFF: No.

WILL: You don't sound so sure.   5

LEE: (*with a smile*) Go ahead and get married.

WILL: (*turning on her aggressively*) Who asked you?! (*to* DUFF) What d'you have
        to get married for?

DUFF: (*with a grin*) Matter of fact, I done a lot of bangin' 'round.

WILL *looks at his son.*

WILL: (*nodding*) Yeah! (*with a faint grin*) That's how your mother 'n me got   10
        started. (*scratching his chin*) But man, you ain't got a chance without
        money. They take it all 'way from you.

He holds his glass out to LEE *for her to refill it from her bottle, since his own is empty.*

LEE: (*pushing the bottle over to him*) Pour your own trouble.

WILL: (*pouring*) Your mother used to lay for her boss, boy—did you know that?!

LEE: Shut up, Will.   15

WILL: (*giving the impression that none of this ever hurt him*) Okay—so what's
        a girl supposed to do? Me not workin' and her makin' a coupla bucks
        cleanin' house for a white man. (*to* DUFF; *vehemently*) I'm tellin' you, boy
        —keep away from marriage. Got to stay light on your feet or you won't
        make it.   20

DUFF *says nothing. He is trying to hide his feelings by covering the lower part of his face
     behind his hand.*

WILL: (*with a faint grin*) She good in the hay?

DUFF *looks at him, cold rage in his eyes.*

WILL: No point marryin' her just to find out. (*putting his hand on* LEE's *bare arm*)
        Is there, baby?!

LEE *tears herself loose.*

WILL: (*grinning; with a mean edge*) What's the matter? You got a complaint?!

LEE *looks at him, angry and disgusted. She has obviously gone through this kind of
    session before.*

WILL: Huh?!   25

LEE: (*quietly*) If you don't quit it, Will, I'm leaving.

WILL: You're breakin' my heart!

He sticks his thumb into his suspenders and snaps it at her.

WILL: (*a mean edge to his voice*) Well, what you waitin' for? Get the hell out! (*to* DUFF) One thing gets me is people sayin' they're goin' to do something, and then they don't.

30

He pushes the table back abruptly and rises.

WILL: (*placing his hand on* LEE's *shoulder*) Got to see the man 'bout a dog.

He leaves.

LEE *looks at* DUFF. *His eyes are hard.*

LEE: (*rising; quietly*) Let's dance, huh?

She takes his hand.
DUFF *gets up slowly.*

Scene 46 [Int. dance floor. Day]

Two or three couples are dancing. A slow number.
DUFF *and* LEE *walk out onto the floor.* LEE *is a good dancer.* DUFF *is still tense and grim.*

LEE: (*looking at him from the side*) Don't let him get you, Duff.
DUFF: (*shaking his head*) How often does he get like this?
LEE: Whenever he's got an edge on.
DUFF: How often is that?
LEE: He's been hitting it pretty hard.—He's got high blood pressure, too. (*Slight*   5 *pause; more softly*) Guess it's hard on him, having you around.

Slight pause.

DUFF: How you ever get tied up with a guy like that?
LEE: (*her hard ironic smile again*) Got myself in trouble and he treated me decent. That's how. (*she pauses*) (*quietly*) I won't be around once he gets on his feet.

10

The number comes to an end and they stop. LEE *looks at him, smiling her strange smile. They start back to the table.*

Scene 47 [Int. bar. The table. Day]

WILL *has come back and the waiter has just placed a new bottle of beer in front of him.* DUFF *and* LEE *return from the dance floor.*

WILL: (*looking up at them, with a mean grin*) Well, what d'you think of her?

DUFF *helps* LEE *into her chair. He hesitates before deciding to sit down again.*

WILL: (*a defensive threat in his voice*) I asked you somethin', boy!
DUFF: I heard you.
WILL: (*the twisted grin*) Pretty good for a one-armed nigger huh?!
DUFF: Great.   5

WILL *notices the tension in* DUFF'S *voice and immediately turns aggressive.*

WILL: What d'you want, anyway? Why you come and bother me for?!

LEE *puts a restraining hand on his arm.*

WILL: (*pushing her hand away*) What's that for? (*turning back to* DUFF) Okay,
         boy—beat it!
DUFF: (*looking at him and nodding*) Yeah—I guess so.
LEE: (*quietly*) He's your son, Will.   10
WILL: (*with a strange grin*) My son?—All I remember is a kid, never opened his
         mouth, lookin' at me with those big eyes like his mother. (*turning to*
         DUFF) Didn't I tell you to beat it?!
DUFF: (*rising*) I got the point.

WILL *refills his glass. He does not look at* DUFF *anymore.*

LEE: (*to* DUFF; *quietly*) Come back some other time, will you?   15
DUFF: (*with a sarcastic nod*) Sure.—Good luck . . .

Scene 48 [Int. luncheon counter in bus terminal. Day]

DUFF *is sitting at the counter, drinking coffee.* JOSIE *comes toward him, carrying some
         packages and smiling.*

JOSIE: Hi.
DUFF: I thought you weren't comin'.
JOSIE: (*putting her bundles down on the counter*) How did it go?
DUFF: What?
JOSIE: Your boy.   5
DUFF: (*with a shrug*) Okay, I guess.

He picks up his coffee cup.
JOSIE *sits down on the stool beside him. The counterman (white) approaches.*

JOSIE: (*to counterman*) I'd like some coffee, please.
DUFF: (*putting down his cup*) You know, I been thinkin' . . .

He stops, turns to her.

DUFF: How 'bout us gettin' married?

JOSIE is taking off her gloves. She stops, looks at him. This is the last thing she expected.

JOSIE: What? 10
DUFF: *(with a grin)* Don't look so scared!
JOSIE: *(quietly)* Are you serious?
DUFF: *(nodding; quietly)* Yeah.

JOSIE shakes her head in disbelief.
The counterman places a cup of coffee in front of her.

JOSIE: *(to the counterman)* Thank you.
DUFF: *(passing her the sugar)* Well, how 'bout it? 15
JOSIE: *(quietly)* What happened, Duff?
DUFF: Look, baby—I don't know 'bout you, but it's the right thing for me. I just know it is!

JOSIE turns away, puts sugar in her coffee.

DUFF: What-do-you-say?
JOSIE: *(a note of tension)* Don't push me, Duff. *(a little frantic)* It's too sudden. 20

She picks up her coffee cup and starts drinking.

DUFF: *(quietly)* Sure. Wouldn't be no picnic for you. *(a faint grin)* I ain't exactly house-broken.
JOSIE: What about that girl?
DUFF: She's nothin' to me, baby. That's all over.
JOSIE: *(her inability to cope with her feelings expressing itself in a sudden 25 outburst of anger)* I don't even know how you *feel* about me.
DUFF: *(frustrated)* Hell, baby—I'm askin' you to *marry* me.—What d'you want— a big scene?!

JOSIE can't help smiling.

JOSIE: No. *(turning to him, looking at him across the top of her coffee cup)* But a small one. 30

DUFF looks at her and notices that there are tears in her eyes.

DUFF: *(with a tender, happy grin)* It's Yes, huh?

JOSIE turns away, dabs at her eyes with the back of her hand.

Scene 49 [Int. bunk car. Early morning]

The men are getting dressed for work.
Open close on FRANKIE.

FRANKIE: I'll be a monkey's kid sister! What-do-you-want-to-do a thing like that for?

JOCKO: (*catching a fly, smashing it to the floor and stepping on it*) Musta knocked her up.

FRANKIE: What're you gonna get out of it.   5

DUFF: A lot, Frankie.

FRANKIE: (*aggressively*) Like what?

DUFF: A home, for one thing.

FRANKIE: You gonna sit at home the rest of your life?

DUFF: Better than wind up like a bum.   10

FRANKIE: (*looking at him*) What you signifyin'?!

DUFF: I weren't thinkin' of you, Frankie.

Slight pause.

FRANKIE: (*seriously concerned*) How you gonna class up to them?

DUFF: Ain't goin' to try. (*turning to* RIDDICK *who is putting on his shoes*) Fact, Riddick, I'll buy your jalopy.   15

RIDDICK: Okay with me.

JOCKO: (*with a grin*) Ole Doris sure goin' to miss you.

DUFF *grins, shakes his head.*

FRANKIE: (*grinning, but with a trace of aggression*) Just give him a couple of months. She's good-lookin' all right, but a girl like that, she don't know any tricks.   20

JOCKO: (*a twisted grin*) You know what Doris told me? She say: that Duff's a nice guy; wouldn't even charge him nothin'. (*shaking his head*) An' he has to get married!

FRANKIE: (*to* DUFF) Guess you'll be quittin' the railroad.

DUFF: That's right.   25

FRANKIE: (*shaking his head*) Man, you must be plumb outa your mind.—You'll be makin' twenty bucks a week, if you lucky.

He turns away.

RIDDICK: (*rising*) Goin' to work for white folk?

DUFF: I guess so.

RIDDICK: You'll be livin' on *their* terms.   30

DUFF: (*quietly*) We'll see.

RIDDICK: Just so you know what you're doin'.

He exits. DUFF *sits down to lace up his boots.*

DUFF: *(to the others)* I'm askin' you guys to the wedding.
FRANKIE: You disreligious bastard!
DUFF: *(with a grin)* But if one of you gets out of line, I'll bust his head off.   35
FRANKIE: *(on his way out; he has given up)* Well, ain't no skin off *my* back—

Scene 50 [Ext. shot from moving car. Day]

Shots of the Negro section in town. Shacks near the railroad track. The road is very bad.

Scene 51 [Int. car. Day]

Shots of DUFF *and* JOSIE *(Intercuts for 50).*

Scene 52 [Ext. shot from moving car. Day]

The car slows up and stops in front of a very modest old bungalow.

Scene 53 [Int. their future living room. Day]

It has not been lived in for quite a while. The shades are drawn. Old, worn-looking furnishings.
The door opens, and DUFF *and* JOSIE *enter.*

JOSIE: *(as she comes in)* I used to know the people. They've gone North.

DUFF *moves around the room. He kicks a rickety chair.*

DUFF: *(grinning)* I can see why.
JOSIE: What d'you think?
DUFF: Hell, it's great with me, baby. But how *you* goin' to like it?!
JOSIE: *(moving around room)* It'll be fine when I get done with it.
DUFF: *(raising window shade; with a grin)* Ain't exactly your dad's place.

Scene 54 [Ext. shot through window. Day]

Pan across the dirt road: lower middle class houses and shacks. End on porch of neighboring house.—A worn-looking man sitting on a rocker; a pregnant woman putting clothes into the old-fashioned washing machine by the front door. One of three small children is tugging at her skirt. She slaps him.
Recorded gospel music from an open window.

DUFF'S VOICE: Who're they?

Scene 55 [Int. living room. Day]

JOSIE *has joined him at the window.*

JOSIE: That's Bessie Hall. Barney works at the mill.
DUFF: *(turning to her; with a grin)* Guess you'll want a houseful of pickaninnies, huh?
JOSIE: *(with a smile)* Don't call them that.
DUFF: *(with a shrug; leaving window)* It's okay with me. Always liked kids.   5

JOSIE *moves toward* DUFF, *into a close-up:*

JOSIE: What about *your* boy?
DUFF: *(looking up at her)* What about him?
JOSIE: He could live with us.
DUFF: *(not at all at ease with the idea)* What for?
JOSIE: I think 't be nice.   10
DUFF: *(turning away)* Let's see how the two of us make out, huh?

He goes into the bedroom. JOSIE *follows.*

Scene 56 [Int. church. Day]

Organ music. The bride's side of the church is crowded, but on the groom's side only the two front rows are filled. These are occupied by members of the section gang, all of whom are dressed in their Sunday best. They look a little sheepish and uncomfortable. One is fussing with his tie. POP *passes his finger under his tight collar. (Pan across the men.)*

Cut to: DUFF *standing in front of the flower-decorated altar.* FRANKIE, *acting as best man, is standing beside him. He is nervously passing his hands over the many pockets in his suit: breast, jacket and pants—both front and rear. He locates what he is looking for in his right rear pocket and produces the ring box.* DUFF *grins at him and shakes his head.*

REV. DAWSON *appears in the pulpit and the music changes to a traditional wedding march. The congregation rises and everyone turns to the rear of the church.* DUFF *too has turned.*

The camera is on the aisle, slightly forward of the railroad men: JOSIE, *dressed in white, enters by herself and comes up the aisle. She looks very composed.*

As she approaches camera, we pan her past the railroad men. She smiles at them. Several of them look embarrassed. After she has passed, JOCKO *passes his index finger across his throat in a "Finished" gesture. Then he touches his fingertips together and raises his eyes heavenward in a mock-prayerful attitude.*

The camera pans forward to JOSIE, *who has stopped beside* DUFF. *They clasp hands and step forward toward the altar.*

As REV. DAWSON *begins the ceremony, the camera pulls back slowly in the center of the aisle until we see most of the church—with the young couple way back in the center.*

Scene 57 [Int. their bedroom. Early morning]

JOSIE *is curled up in bed, with closed eyes.* DUFF, *dressed and wearing his work-cap, is putting on his heavy boots. He moves as quietly as he can.*
A car horn honks outside. JOSIE *opens her eyes.*
DUFF *stands up, moves to the bed and looks down at her. Both are smiling now.*

JOSIE: *(quietly)* Good luck, baby—

DUFF *looks at her a moment longer. He shakes his head—*

DUFF: *(overcome by tenderness) (quietly)* Jesus—

He drops down beside her. The car horn honks again—prolonged this time.

Scene 58 [Ext. their house. Early morning]

A car is waiting at the curb, its motor running. The horn is still honking.
DUFF *comes out of the house (from back of camera), jumps down the steps and gets into the rear-seat. The car starts off.*

Scene 59 [Int. moving car. Early morning]

Barney *(the man who lives in the house next to* DUFF'S*) is sitting beside* DUFF *in the rear, smoking a cigarette. He is a sad, worn-looking man.—There are two men in front, beside the driver.*
One of them (JOE) *turns to* DUFF, *with a grin.*

JOE: Hard to get up in the mornin', huh?
DUFF: *(grinning)* Yeah.

JOE *nods, turns back to the front.*

DUFF: *(to* BARNEY*)* How you doin', Barney?
BARNEY: *(a listless shrug)* Okay.

The car comes to a halt again, and the horn honks.
DUFF *glances out.*

Scene 60 [Ext. shot from car window. Early morning]

A young man (WILLIE) *is sitting in a rocker on the porch of his house, smoking a cigar.*

DRIVER: *(opening the rear door; calling)* Come on, Willie! We're late.

WILLIE *has gotten out of his chair. He comes down the walk toward the car in an exaggerated imitation of Stepin Fetchit's shuffle.* WILLIE *is a clown, or part of him is.*

WILLIE: (*his voice as exaggerated as his walk*) Yazzuh, boss.—Ah's comin' as
          fast as ah cans.
DRIVER: (*shaking his head*) Not now, Willie! Let's go!
WILLIE: (*approaching the car*) You knows us niggers, boss. We jus' can't move   5
          like you white folks does. (*Climbing into the car; as if all his limbs were
          aching painfully*) Yazzuh—

Scene 61 [Int. car. Early morning]

WILLIE *has settled into the rear seat next to* DUFF. *He leans back—holding his cigar up
high—and proceeds to go into his white-boss act.*

WILLIE: (*flicking the ashes out through the window*) All right, Jethroe—takes me
          to the plant. And hurry—boy! Ah's got a heavy day.

DUFF *laughs, scratches his head.*
The car starts very fast, throwing WILLIE, BARNEY *and* DUFF *back violently.*

WILLIE: (*as soon as he recovers; to* DUFF) Ah tells you, man—you gives these
          niggers a machine, an' they go stark-ravin' wild.

DUFF *grins.*

Scene 62 [Int. entrance to plant. Day]

*The same men we saw in the car—*DUFF, BARNEY, JOE, WILLIE, *the* DRIVER *and a sixth
     man—are standing in line to punch their cards at the time clock. They are silent
     and their faces expressionless.*
A white supervisor watches each man as he punches in.

SUPERVISOR: (*as* DUFF *punches in*) You new?

DUFF *nods, moves on. The supervisor looks after him briefly.*

Scene 63 [Ext. millyard. Day]

Montage: the men at work, moving huge logs, etc. Among others, shots of DUFF, BARNEY,
     WILLIE, JOE.
A white foreman stops near DUFF, *watches him for a moment.*

FOREMAN: (*calling*) Hey, Jack!

DUFF *either has not heard or does not want to hear. He goes on working.*

FOREMAN: (*approaching; louder*) Hey, boy—I'm talkin' to you.
DUFF: (*turning; matter-of-fact*) Name's Duff.

FOREMAN: (with a good-natured grin)—How you doin'?   5

DUFF: (stopping his work) Okay.

FOREMAN: (checking DUFF's work) You doin' a good job.

DUFF: Thanks.

FOREMAN: (looking at him with a quizzical but not unfriendly expression) Don't say much—do you?

DUFF: (quietly; looking back at him) Guess not.   10

FOREMAN: (turning to go) Well, just so you do your work.

He leaves. DUFF goes back to work.

One or two of the other men (BARNEY among them) have been listening to the conversation. They too turn back to their jobs.

Scene 64 [Ext. millyard. Day]

Six Negro workers—DUFF, BARNEY, WILLIE, JOE, and two others—are sitting in a loose group on the logs, eating their lunches. Seated beside BARNEY is a white workman, who is drinking a bottle of pop. A second white is seen in the rear—not really part of the group.

Open close on the white workman:

WHITE: (putting down bottle; to DUFF—with a grin) Hell, I bet those black girls really go for you, huh?

DUFF is chewing. He looks at the white man and says nothing.

WHITE: (grinning) Must do. That's the best-lookin' colored girl in town.

DUFF still says nothing, continues eating.

WHITE: What's the matter?! (A grin) Still on your honeymoon, huh? (Turning to BARNEY) Jus' like you, Barney.—Been on your honeymoon twenty years,   5 huh?

BARNEY: (eating; without expression) Yessir.

The white man breaks a piece off BARNEY'S pie—It must be understood that he is in no sense aggressive at this point. On the contrary, this is his way of being friendly with Negroes.

WHITE: How many kids you got now, Barney?

BARNEY: Four.

The white man has put the piece of pie into his mouth.

WHITE: (chewing) Hmm—she can cook, too. (With a mock-leer) Man, it's no   10 wonder you been draggin' your tail on the job. Doin' your best work at home.

He laughs, punches BARNEY *on the arm.* BARNEY *manages a painful grin.*
The white man turns back to DUFF, *who has been watching with a set face.*

WHITE: (*his mood darkening somewhat*) What's the matter, boy? Never smile?

DUFF *looks at him but says nothing.*

WHITE: How come?
DUFF: (*quietly; trying to stay matter-of-fact*) I'll smile when it's funny.   15
WHITE: So it wasn't funny, huh? *I* thought it was! (*turning to* BARNEY) What d'you
          say, Barney? Was it funny?
BARNEY: (*trying to oblige with a grin*) Yeah. It was funny.
WHITE: Sure. (*to the others*) What d'you say, boys? Wasn't it funny?!

Answers of "Yeah!", "Sure!", etc.—none of them enthusiastic, but forthcoming nonethe-
less.

WHITE: (*with a shrug*) Sure! (*turning to* DUFF) Trouble with you, boy, is you ain't   20
          got no sense of humor. (*With the trace of something nasty*) Ought to
          smile more!
DUFF: (*quietly*) Yeah. I know.

He is putting away his lunch things.

WHITE: (*rising*) You new here, man. (*To the others*) See you fellows.

He leaves.
Slight pause. The other men feel awkward, exposed in front of DUFF.

JOE: (*trying to explain their behavior*) You know, man—that guy was tryin' to   25
          be friendly.
DUFF: Ain't my idea of friendliness.
BARNEY: Got to watch yourself pretty close.
WILLIE: (*with a short, angry laugh*) Yeah—if you want to get along, act the
          nigger.   30

He closes his lunch pail.

DUFF: Like hell!
FOURTH NEGRO: Man, you in Alabama!
DUFF: (*looking at them; quietly*) If you guys stuck together 'stead of laughin'
          when they walk all over you, maybe they wouldn't try it.
JOE: (*getting up*) Like hell they wouldn't.   35
WILLIE: (*rising also; with a short laugh*) They been doin' it all my life.
DUFF: Maybe it's time you stopped lettin' them.

890

FOURTH NEGRO: (*who has been silent until now; rising*) Man—you sound like a trouble man.

Medium-long shot: the group separating. DUFF *rises.*

Scene 65 [Int. kitchen. Evening]

DUFF, *still wearing his work-cap, is sitting at the table, finishing his dinner. He is drinking a Coke out of the bottle.* JOSIE, *in shorts, is drying dishes at the sink.*

JOSIE: Use the glass, honey. That's what it's for.

He pours the remaining drops elaborately into a glass. Then he sniffs the pie on his plate.

JOSIE: What's wrong?
DUFF: (*a mock-frown*) Smells like something crawled in there and died.
JOSIE: (*coming over with her towel; concerned*) Really?—I thought it was good.

DUFF *has put a large bite into his mouth.*

DUFF: (*eating; with a grin*) Baby—everything you cook is good.   5

He pulls her down onto his lap, still chewing.
JOSIE *moistens her lip with her tongue.*

JOSIE: (*with a grin*) You know, those women you used to know—
DUFF: (*putting a forkful of pie into her mouth*) What about them?
JOSIE: (*her mouth full; quizzically*) Am I as good as they?
DUFF: (*sipping the coffee; with a grin*) Very good coffee.
JOSIE: (*swallowing*) You didn't answer my question.   10
DUFF: (*eating again*) Honey—you're the best thing ever happened to me.
JOSIE: (*smiling*) You *still* didn't answer my question.

She kisses him quickly on mouth, nose and eyes. Then she scratches her nose on his shoulder.
DUFF *yawns. She covers his gaping mouth with her hand.*
He stretches luxuriously. JOSIE *gets up from his lap and pokes him in the belly.*

DUFF: (*collapsing*) Hey!

Scene 66 [Ext. the backyard. Day]

The house casts bright squares of light through the windows. Cha-cha-cha music blares from a radio somewhere; a crying baby; voices of playing children.
DUFF *and* JOSIE *appear around the side of the house and head for the laundry line. She is sitting high on his shoulder and carrying a basket on top of her head. She*

holds it in place with one hand while holding onto DUFF's head with the other. When they reach the lines, he lifts her down and they begin taking in the wash.

JOSIE: D'you know how to box?
DUFF: Why?
JOSIE: My kids want me to teach them.
DUFF: (dropping laundry into basket) Okay—put up your hands.

JOSIE puts up her fists in what she believes to be the correct boxing stance. He adjusts their level.

DUFF: Like so.—Now try and hit me.   5
JOSIE: (kidding him) I don't want to hurt you.
DUFF: (grinning) Don't worry, baby.

A high-angle shot: they spar around, with JOSIE throwing punches at him which he wards off easily.

DUFF: Harder! Come on!

JOSIE throws a series of windmill blows at his head. DUFF dances away—gradually taking on more and more of the Cha-cha-cha rhythm that is blaring over the radio— until he is actually dancing. JOSIE joins him, ruffling her hand over his head as she starts.
They dance among the laundry lines, with JOSIE taking down some of the wash. Off- screen, we hear the sound of a woman yelling angrily. JOSIE stops dancing.
A shot of BARNEY HALL's house: BARNEY is sitting out on the porch steps—vaguely seen. His wife BESSIE is on her way back into the house. The screen door slams shut behind her.

Scene 67 [Int. their bedroom. Night]

The light is out. DUFF and JOSIE are in bed.

DUFF: (lying on his back) It sure scares you, a guy like that—settin' out on the porch, doin' nothin'.—I seen hundreds of them, all my life.
JOSIE: (quietly) My father's never done a thing for them.

DUFF looks at her tenderly, touched by the pain she feels.
A Diesel hoots in the distance.

JOSIE: (looking at him; with a grave smile) I'm very happy, Duff.
DUFF: (grinning) Hell, you ought to be.   5
JOSIE: (with a smile) How about you?

DUFF laughs.
JOSIE slips out of her nightgown—but as a result disappears entirely into the dark.

892

Scene 68 [Int. their living room. Night]

JOSIE, DUFF *and four men of the section gang—who are the guests of the evening—are finishing supper with coffee and pie. JOSIE and DUFF are at opposite ends of the table. RIDDICK is next to JOSIE and FRANKIE next to DUFF, with JOCKO and POP on the other side.*

RIDDICK: (*putting down his cup; sincerely*) You sure done a great job, Mrs. Anderson.

There is general agreement.

JOSIE: (*smiling*) Thank you. But you haven't eaten much.

DUFF *has been watching the scene with a grin.*

RIDDICK: (*to* DUFF) How's that job comin'?
DUFF: Well, it ain't the railroad.—Man, those guys are scared.—Guess they've   5
    never known nothin' else but takin' it.
RIDDICK: They've all got families to support.
DUFF: (*nodding*) Yeah. (*with a faint grin; he gets some pleasure out of this*)
    And those white guys sure shoot up at you like a yeast cake if you just
    cock an eye at them.   10

Slight pause.

JOSIE: (*to the men*) I guess you'll all keep working together.
FRANKIE: Hell no. They're shippin' us all over the map.
DUFF: That's too bad.

Slight pause.

RIDDICK: (*to* JOSIE) There's some expert dishwashers here.

Ad-lib confirmations from the other men.

JOSIE: (*smiling*) I'll do them tomorrow. The kitchen's too small.   15
RIDDICK: (*rising*) Okay, fellows—give these folks some privacy.

The men rise. JOCKO *stretches. They file toward the door, picking up their caps on the
    way.* JOSIE *opens the door for them.*

FRANKIE: (*to* DUFF; *at the open door*) This is a swell place, man.
POP: (*next in line*) Lots better than the bunk car.
JOCKO: (*next*) Yeah. But you'll be sorry.
DUFF: (*grinning*) See you guys before you take off.   20

RIDDICK: (*shaking hands with* DUFF) Good to see you.
DUFF: Thanks.

RIDDICK *follows the others out—tipping his cap to* JOSIE, *who is standing just outside the door.*

RIDDICK: Good night, Ma'am.

Scene 69 [Ext. street. Night]

*The men are strung out along the street—*FRANKIE *ahead by himself,* JOCKO *and* POP *together, and* RIDDICK *bringing up the rear.*

Scene 70 [Ext. doorway. Night]

DUFF *has joined* JOSIE *outside the open door. They are silhouetted against the light from the living room. He puts his arm around* JOSIE's *shoulder and presses her against himself. She puts her head on his shoulder.*

Scene 71 [Int. their bathroom. Night]

Shot toward mirror above sink: DUFF *is washing his face. He is in his T-shirt and pajama pants. The steam rises and clouds the mirror. In the glass we can vaguely make out* JOSIE's *reflection. She is in the adjoining bedroom getting into her nightgown.*
DUFF *comes up from the sink. He wipes a section of the mirror.* JOSIE *is approaching.*

JOSIE: Something's itching me.

She stops and turns her back to him, presenting it to be scratched.
He scratches it.

JOSIE: A little higher.

He obliges.
Close on JOSIE.

JOSIE: (*with a sly smile*) How would you like to have a baby, Duff?

He turns her around so that she faces him, and looks at her with a quizzical expression.

DUFF: Huh?
JOSIE: Don't look so scared!   5
DUFF: You jivin' me?
JOSIE: Well, I haven't come around.
DUFF: (*shaking his head; with a happy grin*) Man—ain't that just like a nigger!
         (*holding her out at arm's length to inspect her belly; kidding*) Let's see—

JOSIE: Don't stare! There's nothing to see.

She moves past him to sink, starts washing her hands.
DUFF sits down on the bathtub.

DUFF: (*with a pleased grin*) Man—we sure hit the jackpot fast 'round here.
JOSIE: (*looking at him via the mirror; quietly*) How about your boy?
DUFF: (*his mood darkening somewhat*) Why d'you keep askin'?
JOSIE: I keep thinking about him.
DUFF: Well, he ain't mine.—So skip it, huh?

JOSIE looks at him a split-second longer. Then she brushes her teeth, gargles briefly.
Watching her, DUFF brightens into a grin. He gets up (while she is gargling) and embraces
her from the back.

DUFF: (*with a grin*) Baby—we're goin' to put a lot of little niggers into this
world.—Hell, we'll swamp 'em!

Scene 72 [Int. locker room, mill. Day]

Morning. DUFF is changing into his work clothes. Other men in the rear.

MAN'S VOICE: You Duff Anderson?
DUFF: (*looking up*) That's right.

A white plant supervisor—not dressed in work clothes—is standing above him. Through-
out the following scene his attitude is without personal vindictiveness. But he
is very much the man with rank.

SUPERVISOR: Want to talk to you.
DUFF: (*standing up*) Okay.
SUPERVISOR: I hear you tryin' to organize this place.
DUFF: (*calmly*) I don't know what you're talkin' 'bout.
SUPERVISOR: (*shaking his head*) That's no way to talk, boy. (*Returning to his*
original subject) Now we had one of them union men 'round here coupla
years ago. Stirred up a lot of trouble. They're always after you colored
boys.
DUFF: (*quietly*) I still don't know what you talkin' 'bout.
SUPERVISOR: You a union man?
DUFF: Used to be—on the railroad.
SUPERVISOR: (*nodding*) Uh-huh.—Well, this ain't the railroad. Now what's all
this talk 'bout *stickin'* together?
DUFF: (*a light dawning*) Well—what-do-you-know?!

He turns to the Negroes nearest him, who have been listening discreetly while getting
dressed for work. BARNEY is among them.—They avoid his look.

DUFF: (coldly; suppressing his rage) The boys been talkin'—huh?!

SUPERVISOR: (professionally) Look, boy—we got a smooth operation here, and I aim to keep it that way. Now I got an idea you're plannin' trouble.

DUFF: (still very tense and enraged, but aware that his job is at stake) That ain't so. 20

SUPERVISOR: Then what's all this talk about? Sounds like union talk to me.

DUFF: You got the wrong idea.

SUPERVISOR: (raising his voice slightly so that it can be heard by the other men) All right, then. I just want you to tell these boys here you didn't mean 25 what you said 'bout stickin' together 'n all.

DUFF stares at the men, cold anger in his eyes. They avoid his look. He says nothing.

SUPERVISOR: Want to keep your job, boy?

DUFF: (quietly; tensely) What d'you think?!

SUPERVISOR: Then do like I said. (to the others) Men—this here boy's got something to tell you-all. 30

Close on DUFF: he says nothing, his eyes stony, his jaw muscles moving.

SUPERVISOR: How 'bout it?

DUFF draws a deep breath. He says nothing.

SUPERVISOR: (no vindictiveness) Boy—you actin' like a nigger with no sense.—All right! Go down the office and get your pay. Tell them you're through.

DUFF turns to go. He walks through the other men as if they did not exist. When he has gone, they begin to move.

Scene 73 [Ext. shot from moving car. Day]

Court House Square: busy, mid-morning crowds.

Scene 74 [Int. car. Day]

Close on DUFF. His face is grim, set.

Scene 75 [Ext. shot from moving car. Day]

Passing the Negro grade school, the car slows down. Classes are in progress. A small group of children are doing gym in the yard.—The car speeds up again.

Scene 76 [Int. their bedroom. Night]

Close on cat, sitting on dresser. DUFF's hand comes into frame and, with a quick motion, places a small cardboard box over the cat's head.

Wider shot: DUFF, sitting at the dresser, watches the cat as it walks backward, trying to rid itself of the encumbrance. It succeeds.

Shot of JOSIE: she is on the bed in her pajamas, correcting school work.

JOSIE: *(looking up)* Don't, Duff.

DUFF *has put the box back over the cat's head, but very firmly this time. The cat becomes frantic and uses his claws in a violent attack on the box. He succeeds in pulling it off and jumps off the dresser. DUFF makes a lunge for him but fails to catch him.*

JOSIE: Stop it!

She gets up, moves toward him.

JOSIE: *(with a faint smile; as if he were a boy)* What is it?
DUFF: *(getting up)* I'm jumpy, that's all.

He drops down into an armchair. She sits down on the armrest and runs her hand over his hair.

DUFF: *(removing her hand)* I don't like bein' mothered. *(Getting up again)* Jesus,   5
baby—just leave me alone.

He moves toward the bed. JOSIE follows him, her face serious now.

DUFF *is lying down on the bed, his hands folded under his head. A train is passing through town and the diesel hoots. JOSIE sits down beside him.*

JOSIE: *(putting her hand on him)* Don't deny me, Duff.—What's troubling you?
DUFF: *(sardonically)* Hell, baby—I met this beautiful chick and she just dyin' for me.—Okay?
JOSIE: *(shaking her head; with a faint smile)* I can't reach you when you get   10
like that.
DUFF: *(looking at her)* Yeah. I'm sorry. *(softening)* But just how we goin' to make out, honey? I got to find a job.
JOSIE: You will.
DUFF: Pay is so damn low.—I don't want the kids to grow up like Barney's.   15
JOSIE: The important thing is for them to have a father and mother.
DUFF: *(impatiently)* Hell—that's just college talk! They got to eat and wear clothes, too. *(angrily)* Anyway, what kind of father you think I'll make if I don't have a decent job?!—I tell you, baby, maybe we ought to get out of here.   20

897

JOSIE: (*quietly*) We can always do *that*, Duff.
DUFF: (*after a slight pause; nodding; quietly*) Yeah. I know. I know.—I'm not really thinkin' 'bout it. (*with a grin*) Anyway, don't want those white guys smilin' to themselves when they see me pull out!—Hell!

JOSIE *smiles, pleased. She moistens her lips with her tongue.*

Scene 77 [Int. employment office, saw mill. Day]

Open close on white employment director.

DIRECTOR: Yeah. We can use you. Ever work a saw mill?

DUFF *is standing in front of his desk.*

DUFF: Yeah.
DIRECTOR: Where was that?
DUFF: (*after a slight pause*) Walker and Williams.
DIRECTOR: (*looking up at him*) What did you say your name is?
DUFF: (*quietly; a note of tension*) Anderson.

The director glances at a sheet of paper on his desk.

DIRECTOR: (*shaking his head; matter-of-fact*) Sorry, boy. There ain't nothin' here.

Scene 78 [Int. Negro pool hall. Morning]

The pool tables are fairly crowded.
DUFF *is standing at the bar drinking beer. The bartender is washing glasses.*

BARTENDER: Well, if you tried the mills, there ain't no other 'ndustry 'round here.
DUFF: How 'bout the furniture plant?
BARTENDER: (*with a grin*) Darkest thing they got in there is Coca-Cola.

DUFF *sips his beer.*

BARTENDER: If you want to work like a real nigger, you can always go out and chop cotton. Pay you three bucks a day, 'n all the cotton you can eat.
DUFF: (*his face set; quietly*) They done that too long in my family.

Scene 79 [Int. hotel lobby. Day]

DUFF *is standing at the desk, talking to the white manager.*

MANAGER: Yeah, I might have something for you, if you want to put on a uniform.

898

He nods in off-screen direction and the camera pans over: an elderly Negro, dressed in a bell-boy's uniform and cap, is standing by the elevator.

MANAGER: Pay's ten bucks a week, plus tips and lunch.
DUFF: *(with a faint nod)* I see. Ain't for me. Thanks.

He turns to go.

Scene 80 [Ext. shot from moving car. Day]

Negro men lounging around Court House steps.
Negro men idling on street corner.
Negro men in front of general store.

Scene 81 [Int. Negro eating place. Day]

Shot through window: WILLIE, the man who put on the 'Nigger' act in the car, is looking in. Pan with him as he approaches the door.
DUFF is sitting at the counter, finishing his lunch. WILLIE enters and sits down beside him.

WILLIE: *(quietly)* How you doin', man?
DUFF: *(a note of sarcasm)* Great.
WILLIE: Been meanin' to talk with you.

The counterman approaches.

WILLIE: *(to counterman)* Cupa' coffee.

Slight pause.

WILLIE: *(a little awkwardly)* You know, over at the mill there's just one guy that   5
talked.
DUFF: *(with an effort at indifference)* Oh yeah?
WILLIE: It's kinda late to say it, but we ought to've acted different.

The counterman brings the coffee.

WILLIE: Been to the other mill?
DUFF: I been there.   10

Slight pause.

WILLIE: It's just that we ain't used to seein' anyone stand up 'round here. Kinda
took us by surprise.

DUFF turns to him.

899

DUFF: (with a faint grin; he is pleased) Oh yeah? Well, that's good.

WILLIE grins.

Scene 82 [Int. general store. Day]

The PROPRIETOR is filling the grocery list of an elderly Negro country woman, obviously in town on her weekly shopping trip. He is placing the items in a cardboard box on the counter.—DUFF is waiting over at one side.

PROPRIETOR: (placing an item in the box) Now I want you to take a box of this, Mary. It'll come in handy.—How about soap?
MARY: I still got some.
PROPRIETOR: You sure now? Got a good buy on soap. (Indicating a display table) Take a look over there.   5

The old lady turns and walks to the table.

PROPRIETOR: (turning to DUFF; assuming he is a customer) Yes?
DUFF: ·I'm lookin' for work.
PROPRIETOR: (shaking his head) I got a boy, thanks.

DUFF nods and is about to leave.

PROPRIETOR: (with a grin; by way of a joke) You know, the way you dress, boy— (indicating DUFF's shirt and sweater)—you ought to be hirin' me!   10

DUFF turns and leaves.

Scene 83 [Int. beauty parlor, private home. Day]

DUFF comes in through the door.
JOSIE is having her hair done by a middle-aged woman. Gospel music from a radio in the next room. (Through an open door we see two children playing on the bed.)

JOSIE: (quietly) Hi—
DUFF: (sitting down) Don't ask me, baby—huh?

She looks at him.

DUFF: How much money you got with you?
JOSIE: About ten dollars.
DUFF: The water pump's busted. Cost forty bucks. I don't know if it's worth fixin'— (tension in his voice)—but Jesus, I need that car.
JOSIE: You can take what I've got. It's right there.

900

The beautician has been glancing up at DUFF while working on JOSIE's hair.
DUFF picks up her pocketbook from the chair next to his, opens the wallet and takes out
    some of the bills.

Scene 84 [Ext. open truck, moving. Day]

DUFF and a group of men are standing on the bed of the truck; rattling along the country
    road through the cotton landscape.

Scene 85 [Ext. shot from moving truck. Day]

Fields, shacks.

Scene 86 [Ext. cotton gin. Day]

A shape-up is in progress. A crowd of men, women, a few children.

FOREMAN: (on platform) Startin' tomorrow mornin' we got work for fifteen
    hands. All we're goin' to pay is two-fifty a day.—Can't pay you the
    three 'cause there ain't goin' to be much of a crop this year. Now those
    of you who want to work, step up and we'll take your names.

Most of the people step forward.
DUFF turns and walks away.

Scene 87 [Ext. their porch. Night]

A child is crying next-door.
Close on JOSIE:

JOSIE: It's not as hard on a girl. They're not afraid of us.

Wider shot: JOSIE is sitting on the steps. DUFF is using the back of a hatchet to repair a
    rickety chair.

JOSIE: You know, Duff—we do have enough money. Specially now.
DUFF: Sure, baby. 'Fact, I don't ever have to work no more. When that baby
    comes, I'll just stay home and send you back to school.
JOSIE: (angry herself) I'm trying to help, Duff. (She pauses) I could work even   5
    after the baby comes.
DUFF: (derisively) What the hell could you do?!
JOSIE: Day work.
DUFF: (furiously) Are you kiddin'?!—You're not goin' in no white home. (the
    matter is concluded for him; he turns back to hammering; slight pause)   10
    If one of them ever touched you, I'd kill him.
JOSIE: They wouldn't.

DUFF: (looking at her; tensely) Wouldn't they just?!—I seen them lookin' after you on the street.

He kicks the chair down the steps.

JOSIE: Don't, Duff.   15
DUFF: (moving down the steps) No point fixin' it. (Raising the axe high) No damn use.

The axe comes down onto the chair in a well-aimed blow.

JOSIE: (jumping up) Don't do that!

She moves down the steps.

DUFF: (swinging again) Watch out!

The axe falls and she jumps back, frightened.
Fury possesses DUFF now and he smashes the chair into splinters with a fast series of blows. Then he stands up, catches his breath and surveys the pile of wood.

DUFF: (with a kind of satisfaction; some of the rage has left him) Good kindlin'.   20

JOSIE, her face grave, turns to the house.

DUFF: (calling after her) What's bitin' you now?

She doesn't answer or turn, but continues up the steps toward the door.
He bounds up the steps after her and swings her around by the arm.

DUFF: (harshly; a tone of voice he has never used before) Didn't you hear me?!

JOSIE touches the place on her arm where he has held her.

JOSIE: (quietly) I can't bear to see you destructive like that. (looking at him; softly) I know you can't help it.
DUFF: (that was the wrong thing to say) Stop bein' so damn understandin', will   25 you?!

She turns and goes into the house.
DUFF alone.

Scene 88 [Int. their living room. Day]

Open close on REV. DAWSON. He is standing.

REV. DAWSON: (quietly) I know just how you feel. But believe me, you're going about it the wrong way.

DUFF *is sitting in the armchair. This is hard on him.*

DUFF: Don't look like there's a right way.

REV. DAWSON: Well, you have to be smart about it. Now they say you're a
trouble-maker. That's no good. Use a little psychology. Make them think   5
you're going along—and get what you want.

DUFF: (*controlled*) Ain't in me.

REV. DAWSON: I'm telling you: it's the only way. Learn how to handle yourself.

DUFF: (*with growing tension*) I told you, it ain't in me.

REV. DAWSON: You'll be in trouble, son.   10

DUFF: There's nothin' I can do 'bout that.

REV. DAWSON: (*turning unfriendly*) Well, just how are you going to support your
family?

DUFF: (*sliding way down into the chair*) I'm goin' to rob the bank.

REV. DAWSON: (*angrily*) Don't you get smart with me, boy—(*pacing a few steps;*   15
making an effort to calm himself) Maybe you ought to move. (*turning to*
DUFF) You'd be a lot better off in the North.

DUFF: (*with a sarcastic grin*) So I been told.

REV. DAWSON: It's for your own good.

DUFF: Oh yeah? (*rising*) I got a feelin', Reverend, you concerned 'bout your   20
good. (*almost gleefully; despite the tension*) Guess it looks bad, havin'
me for a son-in-law, huh?

REV. DAWSON: (*the anger rising again, uncontrolled*) You can be cocky now,
boy. But you won't last. You won't make it! I'm just sorry for Josie.—I
knew it wouldn't work out.   25

DUFF: (*in a cold quiet fury*) Well, at least she ain't married to no white man's
nigger. You been stoopin' so long, Reverend, you don't know how to
stand straight no more.—You just half a man!

The sound of a falling dish from the kitchen.

Scene 89 [Int. kitchen. Day]

Shooting down at JOSIE: *she is kneeling on the floor, picking up a broken glass. Her face*
is turned away from camera.
She cuts herself and puts the injured finger to her lips, turning her face to camera. Tears
are running down her cheeks.

Scene 90 [Int. living room. Day]

REV. DAWSON *has been crushed by* DUFF's *attack. He is very vulnerable. His voice is*
slightly hoarse and strained now, subdued.

REV. DAWSON: (*picking up his hat*) Well, I'll be seeing you.

DUFF: (*rising*) Yeah.

REV. DAWSON: *(stopping at the door)* Maybe I could talk to Bud Ellis. He might have a job for you at his filling station.

DUFF: *(non-committal)* Oh yeah?

REV. DAWSON: *(opening the door)* I'll do what I can.

JOSIE *has appeared in the kitchen doorway.*

JOSIE: 'Bye, Dad—

REV. DAWSON *nods to her, turns quickly and leaves.*

Scene 91 [Int. bedroom. Night]

Close on DUFF: *he is lying on the bed.*

DUFF: The *one* thing they can't stand is for you to be a man. Makes their whole crummy world fall apart.—But you just let them know you ain't a man, and you got no more trouble . . . *(looking in* JOSIE'S *direction)* How come you don't hate their guts?!

JOSIE *has been at the dresser. She comes over to the bed.*

JOSIE: I'm not afraid of them. 5

DUFF: *(tense sarcasm)* You were plenty scared that night in the car.

JOSIE: *(doing something; quietly)* Just of getting hurt.—But they can't touch me inside.

DUFF: Like hell they can't. They can reach right in with their damn white hands and turn you off and on. 10

JOSIE: *(sitting down beside him)* Not if you see them for what they are, Duff.

DUFF: *(jumping up; a cold rage)* Jesus, you're so full of talk, baby.—Well, you never really been a nigger—have you?!—livin' like that in your father's house! So just get out of my way!

JOSIE *is terribly hurt. She says nothing.*

Scene 92 [Ext. gas station. Night. It has been raining]

Rock-and-roll music from the office radio.
DUFF *is servicing a very old car. He slams the hood down hard.*

WILLIE: *(leaning out of open window; with a grin)* Don't do that, man, less you insured—'cause Joe sure as hell ain't.

JOE *is sitting next to him in the driver's seat.*
DUFF *moves over to him, grinning.*

904

DUFF: That'll be one-sixty.

JOE: (getting out his wallet) Why don't you come over for a beer when you get through?   5

DUFF: (glancing at Joe, as he takes the money) Okay—

MAN'S VOICE: (calling off-screen) Hey, Duff.

Cut to BUD ELLIS, the gas station owner. He is standing in front of the office door.

ELLIS: (calling) Run the truck down Holly Road when you get a chance. There's a guy in the ditch.

He returns to the phone in the office.

DUFF: (to JOE and WILLIE) See you fellows—   10

Scene 93 [Ext. country road. Night. Recent rain effect]

Shot from inside moving truck: a car has gone off the road and into a tree. The driver is standing by the roadside, waving a flashlight. Duff drives by, a grin on his face (it is a funny sight)—and pulls up just ahead.

The white owner of the car steps up to the cab. He is short, middle-aged and slightly drunk.—The radio in his car is playing pop music.

OWNER: (a worried look) Sure glad to see you, boy.

DUFF backs the truck up to the front of the wrecked car. The white man calls instructions to him ("little left!", " 'Nother foot!", "Hold it!"), getting in the way of the truck more often than helping.

DUFF jumps out of the cab to inspect the car. The front is badly damaged.

OWNER: (sheepishly) Guess I was lucky, huh? (trying to hide his nervousness under an attempt at humor) Little harder, and I'd never make that poker game.

DUFF starts lowering the chain on the hoist.

OWNER: (somewhat compulsive in his speech) Shouldn't have had that last drink.   5
My wife's going to give me hell.—See it's her car—

DUFF appears to pay no attention and says nothing. He drops down to the ground to attach the chain to the chassis.

OWNER: (squatting down with the light) Want me to hold the light, boy?

DUFF: (from under the car) No thanks.

OWNER: (standing up) Just tryin' to be helpful. (Just talking again) Lota folks

905

'round here got no use for nigrahs. (*shaking his head*) Just got to under- 10
stand 'em, that's all. (*bending down*) How you doin', boy?

DUFF: (*emerging from under the car*) Okay.

OWNER: (*testing the chains with his foot*) Looks a little loose.

DUFF: (*turning to the winch*) She'll do.

He starts winding the winch.

OWNER: (*watching anxiously*) She ain't comin' up even! 15

The chain slips and the car comes down with a crash.

OWNER: (*jumping back*) Jesus—I told you to watch it!

DUFF: (*coming back*) I'm sorry.

He inspects the car.

OWNER: (*angrily*) That's the trouble with you boys! Don't listen when a man
tells you something.

DUFF: (*with a glance at the white man*) She don't look no worse. 20

OWNER: (*inspecting the front end*) Don't do her no good to get banged like that.

DUFF *has dropped down to re-attach the chain.*

DUFF: (*under the car; with a grin*) Don't do her no good to go in a tree.

OWNER: (*bending down*) What did you say, boy?!

DUFF: (*at work; the radiator is leaking on him*) I said, she's in a great shape.

OWNER: (*flaring up*) I heard you! Now 'stead of bein' smart, just get that car 25
out of here! (*standing up*) Lucky it's me you're talkin' to.

Scene 94 [Int. garage at gas station. Night]

The doors are open and we can see the service area outside.
DUFF *is greasing a car which is up on the hydraulic lift.*
A car drives up outside, honking its horn loudly.

Scene 95 [Ext. gas station. Night]

*The car stops by the gas pump, still honking its horn. The man at the wheel is heavy-set
and in his forties.*
BUD ELLIS *and* DUFF *both approach*—BUD *from the office,* DUFF (*somewhat behind him*)
from the garage.

ELLIS: (*to the driver*) Yes?

DRIVER: Like some service from that boy there. (*He indicates* DUFF) Like the way
he takes care of us.

DUFF *has come up, wiping his hands on a grease rag.*

ELLIS: *(to* DUFF*)* Okay—

DUFF *nods and* ELLIS *returns to his office.*
DUFF *glances into the car and notices the owner of the wrecked car in the rear. A third
man is sitting beside him, and a fourth up front beside the driver.*

DUFF: *(on his guard, but matter-of-fact)* Fill her up?   5
DRIVER: No, boy. Thirty-eight cents worth of gas. And watch you don't make it
    thirty-nine!

All of the men are watching DUFF.
DUFF *starts the pump.*

DRIVER: We got business with you, boy.

DUFF *glances up from the pump.*

DRIVER: You gonna 'pologize to our friend here?

DUFF *says nothing, watches the pump.*

DRIVER: Didn't hear you say Yessir!   10

DUFF *turns off the pump.*

DRIVER: *(the threat becomes explicit)* Boy—you hear me?!
DUFF: *(quietly)* I heard you.
DRIVER: Don't they say Yessir! where you come from?
DUFF: *(coming to the window; quietly)* That'll be thirty-eight cents.
DRIVER: *(enraged)* Goddamnit, nigger—you must think you're white! Who d'you   15
    think you are—the king of Harlem?!

The others grin.

SECOND MAN: *(to* DUFF*)* How 'bout this windshield, boy? Like a little service.

DUFF *starts cleaning the windshield. His jaw muscles are working.*

THIRD MAN: Hell they're gettin' too big for their britches.
SECOND MAN: *(to* DUFF*)* That windshield ain't clean, boy! *(pointing to spot)*
    Look here!   20
DRIVER: *(reinforcing the second man)* Over here, nigger!

DUFF *cleans the indicated spot on the windshield.*

THIRD MAN: What's itchin' all these niggers these days?!

SECOND MAN: Yeah—his wife's the same way, struttin' through town like she owns the place—(*with a grin*)—shakin' that little rear-end.

THIRD MAN: It's all that education they're gettin'.   25

DRIVER: (*watching* DUFF; *tensely*) Real cool, ain't he! Like we ain't here.

DUFF: (*at the window again*) That'll be thirty-eight cents, please.

DRIVER: You in a big hurry, boy.

SECOND MAN: (*with a grin*) Yeah—he's trying to get home!

DRIVER: (*to* DUFF) Bet she's pretty hot, huh?!   30

DUFF: (*still quietly, but on the point of losing control*) Watch what you say, man!

The DRIVER *knows now that he has* DUFF *close to breaking. He continues with a grin.*

DRIVER: Bet she's a sly little nigger, that girl. Wouldn't mind a piece of her myself!

DUFF: (*breaking out*) Get out of here, man!

DRIVER: (*turning livid*) Who're you tellin' to get?!—You watch it, boy—or there'll   35
be some dyin' done 'round here.

DUFF: (*the fury dammed up into cold tense anger*) That dyin'll be done two ways.

OWNER: (*speaking for the first time*) Let's go, Al. He ain't worth it.

DRIVER: (*turning on him*) Now *you* stay out of it!   40

BUD ELLIS *has appeared in back of* DUFF.

ELLIS: (*quietly*) What's goin' on?

DRIVER: (*turning to* BUD) Better get rid of this white-eyed nigger!

ELLIS: (*quietly*) What happened?

DRIVER: Never mind! Just get rid of him. (*starting the car*) You keep him workin' here and this place won't be around. And I ain't kiddin'!   45

He drives off.

DUFF *has crossed over to the water tap. He bends down and runs the water over his face.*
ELLIS *approaches him.*

ELLIS: (*this is very painful for him*) Guess we got trouble.

DUFF: (*looking up through the water; this is just another white man to him*) You ain't got none, mister!

ELLIS: (*he means it*) I'm sorry, Duff.

DUFF: (*standing up; grimly*) Don't tell me! I know.   50

He turns and walks away.

Scene 96 [Int. their living room. Night]

The room is dark. A church clock is striking in town.
The door opens and DUFF *enters. He is drunk.*

DUFF: How you doin', baby?

JOSIE *has appeared in the doorway of the bedroom. She is in her nightgown.*

JOSIE: It's after three.
DUFF: (*aggressively*) How come you ain't sleepin'!?
JOSIE: (*quietly*) I called the gas station.
DUFF: (*dropping into the armchair*) Hell—if they don't blow up his place, they'll   5
    get him some other way.—Don't make no difference no-how . . . (*looking
    up at her; with the hostility of his father*) Any complaints?!

She looks at him, shakes her head.

DUFF: (*unable to bear her sympathy*) Don't look at me like that!

He gets up.

JOSIE: (*quietly*) I can't help it, Duff. I love you.

She tries to approach him.

DUFF: (*flinging her aside*) That don't do me one bit of good!—Shouldn't have   10
    married you in the first place!

Close-up on JOSIE.

DUFF: (*sarcastically*) Well, ain't you goin' to *say* something?
JOSIE: (*tonelessly*) There's nothing I can say.
DUFF: (*sharp sarcasm*) That'll be the first time!

He turns and heads into the bedroom.
JOSIE *starts to follow him, then stops and turns back into the living room.*

Scene 97 [Int. bedroom. Night]

A train is passing. The diesel hoots.
Close on JOSIE: *she is lying in bed on her side; her eyes are open. She hears* DUFF *stir
    and turns to him.*
He is sitting up and putting on his shoes.

JOSIE: (*quietly*) Where're you going?

Slight pause.—In the following dialogue, there is little anger left in DUFF. *He is cold,
    decided now. As far as he is concerned, it's all over.*

DUFF: (*getting up*) Soon as I get set I'll send for you.

JOSIE: (*quietly*) I don't think that'll happen.

DUFF: (*moving around the room*) You're better off without me.

JOSIE: You know that isn't true.   5

DUFF: (*putting on his jacket*) Hell, I can't even support you.

JOSIE: You still don't see it, do you?

DUFF: See what?

JOSIE: You're not a man because of a job.

DUFF: You don't know nothin' 'bout it, baby. Nothin'! (*Moving around the room,*   10
more to himself than to her) Hell—it's just like a lynchin'. Maybe they
don't castrate you with a knife, but they got other ways. (*Turning to her,
lashing out*) And don't kid yourself, baby—you did *your* bit all right!

On JOSIE.
DUFF *is gathering his things.*
He turns and leaves.

Scene 98 [Ext. street. Seen through window. Night]

DUFF'S car starts up outside and the headlights go on, shining directly into lens.

Scene 99 [Ext. window. Night]

JOSIE *is standing in the glare of the headlights. As the car begins to move away, her
face is plunged into darkness.*

Scene 100 [Int. stairway outside Will Anderson's room. Day]

DUFF *comes up the stairs and knocks at* WILL'S *door.*
There is a faint commotion outside. Then LEE opens up.

LEE: (*quietly*) 'Lo, Duff.

DUFF: Hi.

She looks completely worn out. There are deep circles under her eyes.

WILL'S VOICE: (*from inside the room*) Who is it?

LEE: (*turning abruptly*) Your son.

Scene 101 [Int. Will Anderson's room. Day]

WILL *is sitting at the table, his head leaning on his hand, ashen-faced, unshaved and
drunk to the point of collapse. There is an empty and a half-full bottle in front
of him. His clothes are disheveled.*

WILL: (*looking up*) I ain't got no son.

DUFF *says nothing.*
WILL *has raised himself with some difficulty and approaches* DUFF.

WILL: You Duff?

He lurches forward. DUFF *supports him.*

WILL: *(freeing himself with a jerk)* Beat it!

He comes very close to DUFF, *peering into his face.* DUFF *moves back slightly—almost involuntarily.*

WILL: *(with a short laugh)* Don't smell so good, huh? *(turning away)* Must have broken some records.   5

He reaches the table and leans on it for support. Then he uncorks the bottle that is still half-full.

DUFF: *(moving toward him)* Pop—

LEE *puts a restraining arm on him.*

LEE: Nothing you can do. Been like this for days.

WILL *is pouring himself a glass. His hand trembles violently.*

WILL: Got no use for nobody.

Suddenly the glass drops to the floor and he touches the back of his head as if it were hurting. He begins to weave unsteadily and LEE *and* DUFF *rush forward to support him. They help him to the bed. He is mumbling incoherently. He sits down on the bed, staring ahead.*

LEE: *(looking down at him; at the end of her strength)* Lie down and get some sleep.   10

Close on WILL: *he looks as if he were trying to say something but cannot find the words. He opens his mouth several times but doesn't produce a sound.*
LEE *turns away.* WILL *grasps her with his hand.*

LEE: *(freeing herself; impatiently)* Let go!

She walks toward DUFF, *indicating with a motion of her head that they should leave the room. But in the background* WILL *has risen again. He starts after* LEE, *then collapses into a chair.* LEE *turns back to him.*

LEE: (sharply) You stay put!
WILL: (looking up at her) I ain't drunk, honey.

He shakes his head as if to clear it. His eyes don't seem to focus properly.

LEE: Like hell you aren't.
WILL: (touching the back of his head) Got a thick feelin' here. Better now.   15

He closes his eyes.
DUFF has wetted a towel and hands it to LEE.

WILL: (starting up as if frightened) Where you at?

LEE begins to wipe the perspiration off his face.

LEE: Right here.
WILL: (nodding in direction of bed) I couldn't talk before—couldn't get the
      words out.
DUFF: (to LEE; quietly) Better get him to a hospital.   20
WILL: (rising suddenly; the old violence) Didn't I tell you to beat it?!
LEE: (taking his arm) Let's go, Will.
WILL: (closing his eyes; strangely meek) Anything you say, baby.

They start toward the door.

Scene 102 [Int. Duff's car. Day]

It is parked in front of the building.
DUFF is helping WILL into the back seat. LEE enters from the other side.
His head slumps onto her shoulder. His hand seeks and finds her breast.

Scene 103 [Int. Duff's car. Moving]

LEE is in back-seat, with WILL ANDERSON'S head in her lap.
LEE: Duff—he stopped breathin'.
DUFF stops the car, turns.

Scene 104 [Int. funeral parlor. Day]

A threadbare reception room with a loudly ticking clock on the mantel. Soft organ
      music piped in over a speaker.
Open close on UNDERTAKER.

UNDERTAKER: We thought you might want these—

Tilt down to desk: on it are some objects that the undertaker has evidently removed from

WILL ANDERSON'S *pockets; a metal watch, a ball point pen, some loose change, a worn-looking wallet and the cancelled bankbook.*
A shot including DUFF *and* LEE: *they are standing in front of the undertaker's desk.* DUFF *pockets the objects on the desk.*

UNDERTAKER: Would you like me to say a few words tomorrow?

DUFF *glances at* LEE.

DUFF: (*nodding*) Guess so.
UNDERTAKER: Have anything in mind?
DUFF: (*quietly*) I don't know. What you usually say.   5
UNDERTAKER: (*reassuringly*) I'll take care of it. (*Picking up pencil and pad from his desk*) Where was your father born?
DUFF: I don't know.

He glances at LEE, *but she indicates with a faint shake of her head that she doesn't know either.*

UNDERTAKER: His profession?
DUFF: (*with a faint shrug*) He worked around.   10
UNDERTAKER: (*jotting on pad*) And his age?
DUFF: (*hesitating slightly*) Forty-six.
UNDERTAKER: Any other family?
DUFF: Just me. (*Glancing at* LEE) Me 'n her.
UNDERTAKER: I guess that'll be all 'til tomorrow.   15

DUFF *nods. He and* LEE *turn to go.*

DUFF: (*quietly*) Thanks a lot.

Scene 105 [Ext. large cemetery. Day]

It is located on the edge of the city. Heavy traffic moves in the rear.
WILL ANDERSON'S *grave is open. The coffin rests on the edge.* DUFF *and* LEE *stand on opposite sides of it.* LEE *is wearing a hat and holding a small bunch of flowers. —Traffic sounds.*
The men raise the coffin on straps and lower it into the ground. Silently they begin filling in the grave. The thud of the earth on the hollow box.
LEE *quickly lays down the flowers and walks away.* DUFF *stays a moment longer, lost in his own thoughts. Then he notices that she has left and follows her to the path.*
LEE *is waiting for him a short distance away. They start down the path together.*
Dolly-shot:

LEE: What're you going to do?

DUFF *says nothing.*

913

LEE: (*without looking at him*) Want to come up the house!

DUFF *glances at her, but doesn't answer.*

LEE: You can stay there till you get on your feet. No point paying a hotel.
DUFF: (*quietly*) No thanks, Lee.
LEE: (*defensively; but quietly*) Just that I hate empty rooms.   5
DUFF: Sure.

Slight pause.

LEE: What're you going to do?
DUFF: I'm going back.
LEE: (*Looking at him*) Whatever for?
DUFF: (*with a faint smile*) Goin' to make me some trouble in that town, an'   10
     some changes.
LEE: They'll run you out.
DUFF: Like hell they will. (*With a faint smile; quietly*) They won't even get to me
     no more.
LEE: How're you going to live?   15
DUFF: (*the faint smile still*) Always chop cotton. Won't bother me none.
LEE: Good luck!

They have come to the cemetery gate, and stop. Heavy traffic outside.

DUFF: I'll drive you in.
LEE: I'll take the bus—

Suddenly close to tears, she looks through her pocketbook rapidly for a handkerchief.

LEE: Jesus—   20

She blows her nose. DUFF, *moved, takes her arm.*

LEE: (*looking up at him*) Don't be too hard on him.
DUFF: (*softly; with the faint suggestion of a smile*) Hell—I'm just like him.
LEE: (*putting her handkerchief away; she wasn't really listening*) I know he
     wasn't much of a father—
DUFF: Who is?!   25
LEE: Goodbye, Duff.

For a brief moment, she comes into his arms. A very lonely girl.

DUFF: (*moved*) Good luck, kid.

914

Long shot: DUFF and LEE at the cemetery gate. Heavy traffic in the foreground.—They separate and she walks away from him.

Scene 106 [Int. Duff's car. Day. Rain]

Shot through window: the car is parked outside the Simms house, where DUFF'S son has been staying. It is raining.
We see DUFF come down the stairs of the house. He is carrying JAMES LEE, a small suitcase, and the stuffed animal. He opens the door and deposits the boy on the front seat.
Then he walks around the front of the car and gets into the driver's seat from the other side.

DUFF: (to JAMES LEE with a grin) You get any further 'way, boy—you'll fall out the other side.

JAMES LEE is crowded as close to the door as he can get, holding the stuffed animal tightly in one arm and sucking his thumb.
DUFF starts the car.

Scene 107 [Ext. shot from moving car. Dawn]

The landscape just before sunrise.

Scene 108 [Int. car. Dawn]

DUFF is driving through the countryside. He glances at the boy, who is sleeping on the seat beside him. Then he accelerates the car rapidly, a smile on his face.

Scene 109 [Int. their living room. Dawn]

DUFF opens the door from outside and carries in JAMES LEE, still asleep. He puts him down in the armchair and exits again, leaving the front door open.
JOSIE enters from the bedroom. She is in her nightgown. She sees the sleeping boy and walks up to the chair.
Close on Josie: she is very moved.
She covers him with a blanket. There is a sound at the door, and she turns.
DUFF enters, carrying the boy's and his own things. JOSIE moves toward him and they embrace in the open doorway.

JOSIE: Duff—
DUFF: (quietly) Hi—

Slight pause.

DUFF: (quietly) Ain't goin' to be easy, honey. (He pauses) But baby, I feel so free inside—

JOSIE begins to cry—as if something had broken loose deep inside her.

1 2 3 4 5 6 7 8 9 10